Government Support Index HANDBOOK 2019

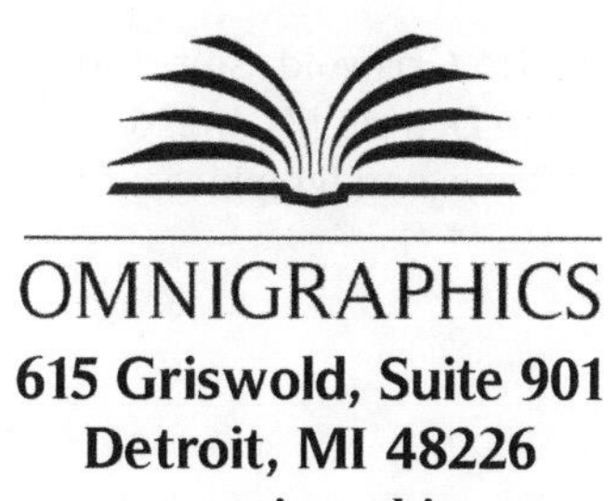

OMNIGRAPHICS
615 Griswold, Suite 901
Detroit, MI 48226
www.omnigraphics.com

Omnigraphics

Connie Harrison
Editor

ISBN 978-0-7808-1674-9

The information in this publication was compiled from the Catalog of Federal Domestic Assistance (CFDA), Federal Assistance Listings maintained by the General Services Administration, and other government funding data made available from USAspending.gov. While these sources are considered reliable and every effort has been made to ensure its reliability, the publisher will not assume liability for damages caused by inaccuracies, and makes no warranty, express or implied, on the accuracy of the information contained herein.

This book is printed on acid-free paper meeting the ANSI Z39.48 Standard. The infinity symbol that appears above indicates that the paper in this book meets that standard.

Printed in the United States of America

615 Griswold, Suite 901
Detroit, MI 48226
www.omnigraphics.com

Table of Contents

Forward

"In ordinary political discourse, the "common good" refers to those facilities—whether material, cultural or institutional—that the members of a community provide to all members in order to fulfill a relational obligation they all have to care for certain interests that they have in common."

—Hussain, Waheed, "The Common Good", The Stanford Encyclopedia of Philosophy (Spring 2018 Edition)

Disclaimer

We have endeavored to compile and present information in this book simply and accurately. The programs described intend to provide basic understanding of programs' benefits intended by their federal agencies.

Federal agency offices, contact details, and programs are subject to change over time. As a result, there may be unintended errors, inaccuracies, or omissions even whilst effort was made to avoid such mistakes.

The information in this publication was compiled from the Catalog of Federal Domestic Assistance (CFDA), Federal Assistance Listings maintained by the General Services Administration (GSA), and other government funding data made available from USAspending.gov. While these sources are considered reliable and every effort has been made to ensure its reliability, the publisher will not assume liability for damages caused by inaccuracies, and makes no warranty, express or implied, on the accuracy of the information contained herein.

The *GOVERNMENT SUPPORT INDEX HANDBOOK* users may share their comments about the book to the editor. Suggestions are welcome in order to improve upon any aspect of the book and are appreciated.

Editor
Omnigraphics
615 Griswold, Suite 901
Detroit, MI 48226
www.omnigraphics.com
editorial@omnigraphics.com

Introduction

Government Support Index Handbook provides a basic description of all domestic programs that offer financial and nonfinancial assistance from federal agencies, and helps readers distinguish which programs are administered to the public via local offices, from those administered from the federal agency headquarters.

This book includes 1,892 federal programs that are summarized from data contained in the Catalog of Federal Domestic Assistance (CFDA), maintained by the General Services Administration. It provides a basic profile of each program that condenses over 3,000 pages in the CFDA to just the essential details.

This book includes new programs that are created through federal authorization, including USC, ACT, Statute, Public Law and Executive Order, to meet new needs for the American public. While it's rare that programs are terminated, it is more common for programs to be replaced. Over time, the number of programs has grown from 989 in 1984 to 1,892 today.

When available, the following information is given for each program:

- Agency abbreviation and program number (shown graphically)
- Program name and Popular name, when applicable
- Award type(s)
- Purpose and objectives
- Applicant and Beneficiary eligibility rules
- Award range and average values awarded applicable to financial awards
- Funding values of recent awards by fiscal year
- Headquarters office address and contact

Each program is given an identifying graphic block. It shows each program by its agency abbreviation such as: HHS which refers to HEALTH AND HUMAN SERVICES, given in the Agency Index. It also identifies its Program number of five digits. The first two digits identify and coordinate to the administrative entity responsible for the program. The last three digits identify the program.

The arrangement of programs is organized into two sections. The first is programs administered by federal headquarters where contacts, pre-qualifications, application, and administration are handled from the federal agency directly. In this section, the sequence of programs is alphabetical by Program name. The second section contains programs administered by regional, state, and local offices which are first points of contact when both headquarters and regional offices are applicable. This section of programs is arranged by the administering agency and the programs are sequenced by Program number numerically. The program office locations and contact details appear before the program entries to which they apply.

Timeliness of Information

Currently, there are 54 federal agencies, departments, independent offices, and commissions that manage programs through their headquarter office, or through their 174 sub-agencies, or through regional, state, and local offices. Agencies may update programs, contacts, office, email, and website addresses. At the time of printing, the information provided in this book is accurate and has 90% likelihood of remaining so over the course of one year based on sampling of similar published directories.

However, in order to provide more timely updates, a companion website, *GOVERNMENT SUPPORT INDEX*, is made available with this book. This website provides updates or corrections to data with ongoing and regular frequency. The website includes annual updates to existing programs, and adds new programs as a result of agency updates and annual government fiscal year funding. Likewise, programs without annual updates for Fiscal Year 2019 are given in the website, but do not appear in the book. It is recommended to contact the agency for questions about the program's status. The government fiscal year runs from October 1 to September 30 of the current year. For example, Fiscal Year 2018 covers October 1, 2017 through September 30, 2018. Annual program updates appear in the website after the government's fiscal year end.

Federal Award Types

Programs are identified by 15 award types of federal domestic assistance which are either financial or nonfinancial.

The financial award types are:

1. Direct loans—loan of federal funds for a specific term, with or without interest, with repayment expected.

2. Direct payments/specified use—funds for a specified purpose, with no repayment expected.

3. Direct payments/unrestricted use—funds for use at will by the recipient, with no repayment expected.

4. Formula grants—funds are distributed to states or other recipients according to a formula (often population-based) for continuing activities not restricted to a specific project. No repayment is expected.

5. Guaranteed/insured loans—guarantee or insurance against loan defaults for private or public lending institutions, covering all or a portion of the amount borrowed.

6. Insurance—coverage for reimbursement of losses under specified conditions such as coverage from a federal agency directly or through a private company subject to program specifics.

7. Project grants—federal funds awarded for specific projects or services such as construction, research, planning and technical assistance. Funds may cover whole or part of project cost. Some project grants include cooperative agreements with local or state governments or organizations with federal granting agency to fulfill project's performance. No repayment is expected.

The nonfinancial award types are:

8. Advisory services/counseling—federal subject matter experts offering conferences, workshops, personal contact or publications for advice or consultation.

9. Federal employment—federal government jobs offered through OPM recruiting and hiring of civilian personnel. Ongoing federal agency employment activities are not considered a domestic assistance program.

10. Investigation of complaints—federal agencies examine or investigate claims of violations of federal law, policy or regulation. Claims must originate outside the federal government.

11. Sale, exchange or donation of property and goods—transfer of federally-owned real estate or personal property, commodities and goods such as equipment, supplies, food or drugs.

12. Specialized services—federal personnel that provide expertise as specific services for communities or individuals.

13. Technical information—prepared, published and distributed technical information made available through libraries and community centers.

14. Training—federal subject matter expertise to general public who are not employed by the federal government.

15. Use of property, facilities and equipment—temporary access and use of federally-owned resources with or without cost to the recipient.

Block grants are excluded from the list of award types as they typically act as formula grants or project grants. Also excluded from this list of award types is cooperative agreement that is an arrangement used in the administration of programs where mentioned.

Other forms of government assistance are part of ongoing government operations and not considered domestic programs. These are: procurement contracts, government foreign activities, federal employee recruitment programs, programs to benefit federal employees or military personnel, ongoing agency information services, and basic government functions.

Many programs offer more than a single award type. In these programs, a combination of financial and nonfinancial benefits are granted such as a program that includes project grant, specialized service, advisory services/counseling, and technical information.

Who May Obtain Government Support

The program Purpose is given to describe the objective, intent and use of the awarded fund or service. Assistance programs benefit the American public in various sectors of society such as public organizations, like libraries, that offer publications and technical information through their facilities and community outreach. Based on the program, because of laws or regulations governing its administration, assistance is awarded based on certain categories of applicants—e.g., farmers, states, small businesses, Native Americans, etc. Moreover, only specified categories of prospective recipients may apply.

Other programs may directly benefit only certain industries—e.g., shipbuilding or agriculture, or certain demographic groups such as the elderly, or teenagers, or immigrants from specific countries.

Yet under other federal programs, both eligible applicants and beneficiaries are the same; such as certain veterans, small businesses, and student programs.

The distinction between programs offering assistance specifically to eligible applicants, eligible beneficiaries, and eligible applicants/beneficiaries is identified by descriptions of Applicant Eligibility and Beneficiary Eligibility.

This distinction between eligible applicants and eligible beneficiaries is important to those seeking assistance and being awarded assistance or not. And members of the public may be ineligible to apply to certain programs, but may still be able to benefit from those programs.

Finding More Information

GOVERNMENT SUPPORT INDEX website provides a searchable menu of programs. It is recommended that readers of this book augment program search using the website. Users can discover programs and agency contacts by federal agency, award types, applicant/beneficiary eligibility and subject of need. It also includes a keyword-driven search box that complements this book. Additional program details are given for each program and organized in a thoughtful and procedural way as to guide the user through the search and evaluation of programs, eligibility, and application procedures. More informational resources will be added to continually improve access to and discovery of appropriate programs.

PROGRAMS ADMINISTERED BY FEDERAL HEADQUARTERS

Programs Administered by Federal Headquarters

HHS 93.423 1332 STATE INNOVATION WAIVERS "1332 Waiver Program"

Award: Cooperative Agreements

Purpose: To receive approval, the state must demonstrate that a proposed waiver will provide access to quality healthcare that is at least as comprehensive and affordable as would be provided without the waiver, will provide coverage to at least a comparable number of residents of the state as would be provided coverage without a waiver, and will not increase the federal deficit.

Applicant Eligibility: This funding opportunity is only open to US States, Territories and Possessions.

Beneficiary Eligibility: N/A

Award Range/Average: TBD

Funding: FY 17 $428,864; FY 18 est $244,719,917; FY 19 N/A FY 16 $0.

HQ: 7500 Security Boulevard
Baltimore, MD 21244
Phone: 301-492-4225
Email: michelle.koltov@cms.hhs.gov
http://www.cms.gov

1890 FACILITIES GRANTS PROGRAM "1890 FGP"

Award: Project Grants

Purpose: To assist in improving agricultural and food sciences institutions with equipment and other essential requirements.

Applicant Eligibility: Eligible applicants under this Program are the 1890 land-grant institutions, including Central State University, Tuskegee University, and West Virginia State University.

Beneficiary Eligibility: Extension Programs at the State and county level are available to the general public.

Award Range/Average: If minimum or maximum amounts of funding per competitive and/or capacity project grant, or cooperative agreement are established, these amounts will be announced in the annual Competitive Request for Application (RFA).

Funding: Project Grants (with Formula Distribution) FY 17 $0; FY 18 est $0; FY 19 est $18,904,653; FY 16 $0; Previously included in CFDA # 10.500, for the Cooperative Extension Service (CES). This represents a newly created CFDA number, which was part of an initiative to break out the separate programs contained in CFDA # 10.500 (CES).

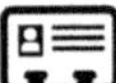

HQ: 1400 Independence Avenue SW, P.O. Box 2250
Washington, DC 20250-2250
Phone: 202-720-5305
Email: elewis@nifa.usda.gov
http://nifa.usda.gov/program/1890-land-grant-institutions-programs

USDA 10.216 1890 INSTITUTION CAPACITY BUILDING GRANTS "1890 Capacity (CBG)"

Award: Project Grants

Purpose: Conducting cooperative programs with Federal and nonfederal entities and build the research and teaching capacities of the 1890 land-grant institutions and Tuskegee University.

Applicant Eligibility: The 1890 land-grant institutions and Tuskegee University.

Beneficiary Eligibility: The seventeen 1890 land-grant institutions and Tuskegee University, non-1890 academic institutions, private industry, and the Department of Agriculture.

Award Range/Average: If minimum or maximum amounts of funding per competitive and/or capacity project grant, or cooperative agreement are established, these amounts will be announced in the annual Competitive Request for Application (RFA).

Funding: (Project Grants) FY 17 $18,260,989; FY 18 est $18,229,184; FY 19 est $18,225,848; FY 16 $18,293,606.

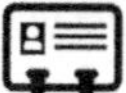

HQ: 1400 Independence Avenue SW, P.O. Box 2250
Washington, DC 20250-2250
Phone: 202-720-2324
Email: elewis@nifa.usda.gov
http://nifa.usda.gov/program/1890-land-grant-institutions-programs

1994 INSTITUTIONS RESEARCH PROGRAM "Tribal Colleges Research Grants Program (TCRGP)"

Award: Project Grants

Purpose: To provide support for agricultural research projects and investigative studies on food and agriscience.

Applicant Eligibility: N/A

Beneficiary Eligibility: 1994 Land-Grant Institutions (aka Tribal Colleges): Aaniiih Nakoda College; Bay Mills Community College; Blackfeet Community College; Cankdeska Cikana Community College; Chief Dull Knife College; College of Menominee Nation; College of the Muscogee Nation; Dine' College; Fond du Lac Tribal and Community College; Fort Peck Community College; Haskell Indian Nations University; Ilisagvik College; Institute of American Indian Arts; Keweenaw Bay Ojibwa Community College; Lac Courte Oreilles Ojibwa Community College; Leech Lake Tribal College; Little Big Horn College; Little Priest Tribal College; Navajo Technical University; Nebraska Indian Community College; Nueta, Hidatsa and Sahnish College; Northwest Indian College; Oglala Lakota College; Saginaw Chippewa Tribal College; Salish Kootenai College; Sinte Gleska University; Sisseton Wahpeton College; Sitting Bull College; Southwestern Indian Polytechnic Institute; Stone Child College; Tohono O'odham Community College; Turtle Mountain Community College; United Tribes Technical College; and White Earth Tribal and Community College.

Award Range/Average: If minimum or maximum amounts of funding per competitive and/or capacity project grant, or cooperative agreement are established, these amounts will be announced in the annual Competitive Request for Application (RFA). The most current RFA is available via: https://nifa.usda.gov/funding-opportunity/tribal-colleges-research-grants-program-tcrgp

Funding: Project Grants (Cooperative Agreements) FY 17 $1,670,933; FY 18 est $3,513,893; FY 19 est $1,665,845; FY 16 $1,674,391; - The difference between the appropriation and obligation numbers reflects legislative authorized set-asides deducted as appropriate, and in some cases the availability of obligational authority from prior years.

HQ: 1400 Independence Avenue SW, P.O. Box 2250
Washington, DC 20250-2250
Phone: 202-720-2324
Email: erin.riley@nifa.usda.gov
http://nifa.usda.gov/program/tribal-college-research-grant-program

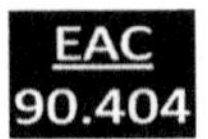

2018 HAVA ELECTION SECURITY GRANTS "HAVA Election Security Grants"

Award: Formula Grants

Purpose: To improve the administration of elections for Federal office, including to enhance election technology and make election security improvements.

Applicant Eligibility: Assistance is to be used to improve the administration of elections for federal office, including enhancing election technology and making election security improvements.

Beneficiary Eligibility: States, the District of Columbia, Puerto Rico, the Virgin Islands, Guam and American Samoa.

Award Range/Average: $600,000 - $34,560,000

Funding: FY 19 N/A FY 17 $0; FY 18 est $380,000,000.

HQ: 1315 E W Highway, Suite 4300
Silver Spring, MD 20910
Phone: 202-566-2166
Email: mabbott@eac.gov
http://www.eac.gov

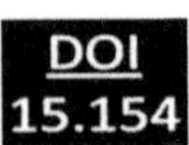

21ST CENTURY CONSERVATION SERVICE CORPS

Award: Cooperative Agreements

Purpose: Through this program, work and training opportunities are offered to young people and veterans in order to help the next generation of lifelong conservation stewards and protect, restore and enhance America's Great Outdoors.

Applicant Eligibility: N/A

Beneficiary Eligibility: N/A

Award Range/Average: Smallest: $25,000 Largest: $1,800,000.

Funding: N/A

HQ: 1849 C Street NW, Room 4257
Washington, DC 20240
Phone: 202-513-0692

Email: megan_olsen@ios.doi.gov
http://21csc.org

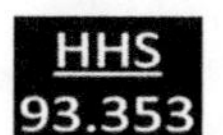

HHS 93.353 21ST CENTURY CURES ACT – BEAU BIDEN CANCER MOONSHOT

Award: Project Grants

Purpose: To provide support for initiatives funded under the 21st Century Cures Act to support cancer research, such as the development of cancer vaccines, the development of more sensitive diagnostic tests for cancer, immunotherapy and the development of combination therapies, and research that has the potential to transform the scientific field.

Applicant Eligibility: The awardee will be a university, college, hospital, public agency, nonprofit research institution or for-profit organization that applies and receives a grant for support of research by a named principal investigator. To be eligible for funding, a grant application must be approved for scientific merit and program relevance by a scientific review group and a national advisory council.

Beneficiary Eligibility: Any nonprofit or for-profit organization, company, or institution engaged in biomedical research.

Award Range/Average: Range: $202,275 to $4,695,150 Average $1,461

Funding: (Salaries and Expenses) FY 17 FY 18 FY 19 FY 16 N/A - (Cooperative Agreements) FY 17 $58,437,000; FY 18 est $112,656,000; FY 19 est $192,000,000; - Updated numbers for 2017, 2018, and 2019.

HQ: 9609 Medical Center Drive, Suite 7W532
Rockville, MD 20850
Phone: 240-276-6443
Email: battistc@mail.nih.gov
http://www.cancer.gov/research/key-initiatives/moonshot-cancer-initiative

HHS 93.368 21ST CENTURY CURES ACT – PRECISION MEDICINE INITIATIVE "All of Us Research Program"

Award: Cooperative Agreements

Purpose: To provide support for initiatives funded under the 21st Century Cures Act, the All of U.S. Research Program will gather data from one million or more diverse people living in the United States to accelerate research and improve health.

Applicant Eligibility: The awardee will be a university, college, hospital, public agency, nonprofit research institution or for-profit organization that applies and receives an award for support of research by a named principal investigator. To be eligible for funding, a grant application must be approved for scientific merit and program relevance by a scientific review group and a national advisory council.

Beneficiary Eligibility: Any nonprofit or for-profit organization, company, or institution engaged in biomedical research.

Award Range/Average: No Data Available.

Funding: Project Grants (Cooperative Agreements) FY 17 $40,000,000; FY 18 est $100,000,000; FY 19 est $186,000,000; FY 16 $0.

HQ: 6011 Executive Boulevard, Suite 214
Rockville, MD 20852
Phone: 301-594-0651
Email: justin.hentges@nih.gov
http://allofus.nih.gov

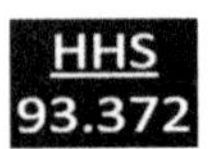

21ST CENTURY CURES ACT - BRAIN RESEARCH THROUGH ADVANCING INNOVATIVE NEUROTECHNOLOGIES "The BRAIN Initiative"

Award: Project Grants

Purpose: To provide support for initiatives funded under the 21st Century Cures Act.

Applicant Eligibility: The awardee will be a university, college, hospital, public agency, nonprofit research institution or for-profit organization that applies and receives a grant for support of research by a named principal investigator. To be eligible for funding, a grant application must be approved for scientific merit and program relevance by a scientific review group and a national advisory council.

Beneficiary Eligibility: Any nonprofit or for-profit organization, company, or institution engaged in biomedical research.

Award Range/Average: No Data Available.

Funding: Project Grants (Cooperative Agreements) FY 17 $10,000,000; FY 18 est $86,000,000; FY 19 est $115,000,000; FY 16 $0.

HQ: 31 Center Drive, Room 8A52
Rockville, MD 20892
Phone: 301-496-3167
Email: koroshetzw@nih.gov
http://www.braininitiative.nih.gov

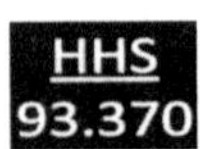

21ST CENTURY CURES ACT: REGENERATIVE MEDICINE INITIATIVE "Regenerative Medicine Initiative"

Award: Project Grants

Purpose: To provide support for initiatives funded under the 21st Century Cures Act to support the BRAIN Initiative's aim of revolutionizing our understanding of the human brain.

Applicant Eligibility: The awardee will be a university, college, hospital, public agency, nonprofit research institution or for-profit organization that applies and receives a grant for support of research by a named principal investigator. To be eligible for funding, a grant application must be approved for scientific merit and program relevance by a scientific review group and a national advisory council.

Beneficiary Eligibility: Any nonprofit or for-profit organization, company, or institution engaged in biomedical research.

Award Range/Average: No Data Available.

Funding: Project Grants (Cooperative Agreements) FY 17 $2,000,000; FY 18 est $10,000,000; FY 19 est $10,000,000; FY 16 $0.

HQ: 6701 Rockledge Drive, Room 7176
Bethesda, MD 20832
Phone: 301-827-7968
Email: pharesda@nhlbi.nih.gov

504 CERTIFIED DEVELOPMENT LOANS "504 Loans"

Award: Guaranteed/Insured Loans

Purpose: To assist small business concerns by providing long-term, fixed-rate financing for fixed assets.

Applicant Eligibility: Certified Development Companies (CDCs) package, close, and service these SBA-guaranteed loans to small businesses. A CDC must be incorporated under general State corporation statute, on a nonprofit basis, for the purpose of promoting economic growth in a particular area.

Beneficiary Eligibility: Small businesses must be independently owned and operated for profit. The small business applicant and its affiliates (affiliation defined at 13 CFR §121.

Award Range/Average: No Data Available.

Funding: FY 17 $271,000,000; FY 18 est $7,500,000,000; FY 19 est $1,000,000,000; FY 16 $41,000,000.

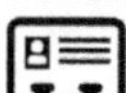

HQ: 409 3rd Street SW, 6th Floor
Washington, DC 20416
Phone: 202-205-9949
Email: linda.reilly@sba.gov
http://www.sba.gov

7(A) LOAN GUARANTEES "Regular Business Loans 7(a) Loans)"

Award: Guaranteed/Insured Loans

Purpose: To provide guaranteed loans from lenders to small businesses which are unable to obtain financing in the private credit marketplace, but can demonstrate an ability to repay loans if granted, in a timely manner.

Applicant Eligibility: N/A

Beneficiary Eligibility: Small businesses that meet the size and eligibility standards.

Award Range/Average: Additional information is available on SBA's website at www.sba.gov

Funding: FY 17 $24,012,000,000; FY 18 est $27,500,000,000; FY 19 est $30,000,000,000; FY 16 $22,734,000,000.

HQ: 409 3rd Street SW, 6th Floor
Washington, DC 20416
Phone: 202-205-7654
Email: robert.carpenter@sba.gov
http://www.sba.gov/partners/lenders/7a-loan-program

Programs Administered by Federal Headquarters

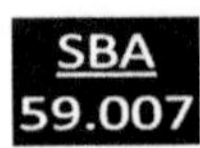

7(J) TECHNICAL ASSISTANCE

Award: Project Grants

Purpose: The purpose of the program is to provide Business Development Assistance for Small Disadvantaged Businesses.

Applicant Eligibility: Educational institutions, public or private organizations and businesses, individuals, State and local governments, Indian tribes and lending and financial institutions and sureties that have the capability to provide the required business development assistance.

Beneficiary Eligibility: 8(a) program certified firms, small disadvantaged businesses, businesses operating in areas of low-income or high-unemployment, and firms owned by low-income individuals like Economically Disadvantaged Women Owned Businesses.

Award Range/Average: No Data Available.

Funding: FY 17 $1,796,000; FY 18 est $2,800,000; FY 19 est $2,800,000; FY 16 $1,407,000.

HQ: 409 3rd Street SW, 6th Floor
Washington, DC 20416
Phone: 202-205-1904
Email: ajoy.sinha@sba.gov
http://www.sba.gov

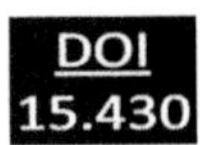

8(G) STATE COASTAL ZONE

Award: Direct Payments with Unrestricted Use

Purpose: Shares 27 percent of mineral leasing revenue derived from any lease issued after September 18, 1978, of any Federal tract which lies wholly or partially within 3 nautical miles of the Seaward boundary of any coastal state.

Applicant Eligibility: Revenue from qualified leasing will trigger automatic payment distribution computed in accordance with the law.

Beneficiary Eligibility: Leased Outer Continental Shelf Lands must be located within the 8(g) zone of a coastal state.

Award Range/Average: N/A

Funding: FY 17 $10,322,000; FY 19 est $12,908,000; FY 18 est $12,717,000.

HQ: 1849 C Street NW, P.O. Box 4211
Washington, DC 20240
Phone: 202-513-0600
http://www.onrr.gov

A COMPREHENSIVE APPROACH TO GOOD HEALTH & WELLNESS IN INDIAN COUNTY – FINANCED SOLELY BY PREVENTION & PUBLIC HEALTH "Tribal Wellness"

Award: Cooperative Agreements

Purpose: The five-year funding opportunity offers support to prevent heart disease, diabetes and associated risk factors in American Indian and Alaska Native communities through a holistic approach to population health and wellness.

Applicant Eligibility: Eligibility: Federally recognized American Indian Tribes and Alaska Native Villages and Corporations which meet the definition set forth in 25 U.S.C. Section 1603.

Beneficiary Eligibility: Federally recognized Indian Tribal Government, Individual/Family, Native American Organization, Pre-school, infant, Child, Youth, Senior Citizen, unemployed, welfare recipient, pension recipient, moderate income, low income, rural

Award Range/Average: Anticipated amounts are: FY 2014: $13-15 million; $14-15m per year with $65075 million over the five years; average annual award $500,000, range $300,000- $800,000

Funding: FY 17 $21,749,962; FY 18 est $21,674,906; FY 19 est $21,674,906; FY 16 $13,245,445.

HQ: 4770 Buford Highway, P.O. Box –F80
Atlanta, GA 30341
Phone: 770-488-6045
http://www.cdc.gov/chronicdisease/tribal/factsheet.htm

ABANDONED INFANTS

Award: Project Grants

Purpose: To prevent the abandonment of infants and young children, including the provision of services to members of the family for any condition that increases the probability of abandonment of an infant or young child.

Applicant Eligibility: State or local governments; federally- recognized Indian tribal governments; U.S. territories and possessions; and nonprofit organizations and universities.

Beneficiary Eligibility: Infants and young children impacted by HIV/AIDS and or substance abuse, their parents, families, and other caretakers.

Award Range/Average: In FY 2017 there were no new awards.

Funding: Project Grants (Discretionary) FY 17 $411,402; FY 18 est $0; FY 19 est $0; FY 16 $0; - No new funding has been provided for this program after FY 2015.

HQ: 330 C Street SW, Room 3519C
Washington, DC 20201
Phone: 202-401-5073
Email: jan.rothstein@acf.hhs.gov
http://www.acf.hhs.gov/cb

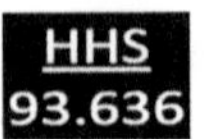

ACA – REINVESTMENT OF CIVIL MONEY PENALTIES TO BENEFIT NURSING HOME RESIDENTS

Award: Project Grants

Purpose: The purpose of this funding is to solicit applications to participate in a national federal grant program using Civil Money Penalty funds from nursing homes to support and otherwise benefit nursing home residents.

Applicant Eligibility: CMS seeks to fund activities that protect or improve the quality of care for residents. Funding under this opportunity is available to organizations/associations that are authorized by law to administer grants and contracts in support of national and regional programs.

Beneficiary Eligibility: General public.

Award Range/Average: N/A

Funding: FY 17 $261,185; FY 18 est $0; FY 19 est $0; FY 16 $0.

HQ: 7500 Security Boulevard
Baltimore, MD 21244
Phone: 410-786-1968
Email: sandra.phelps@cms.hhs.gov
http://www.cms.gov/medicare/provider-enrollment-and-certification/surveycertificationgeninfo/ltc-cmp-reinvestment.html

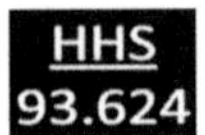

ACA – STATE INNOVATION MODELS: FUNDING FOR MODEL DESIGN & MODEL TESTING ASSISTANCE
"State Innovation Models (SIM)"

Award: Cooperative Agreements

Purpose: The State Innovation Models program is based on the premise that state innovation with broad stakeholder input and engagement, including multi-payer models, will accelerate delivery system transformation to provide better care at lower costs.

Applicant Eligibility: CMS invites the 50 state Governor's Offices, United States Territories Governors' Offices (American Samoa, Guam, Northern Mariana Islands, Puerto Rico, and the Virgin islands), and the Mayor's Office of the District of Columbia to apply. Only one application from a Governor per state is permitted for either a Model Design or a Model Test award (assuming the state applied and was not selected for funding under the first round of Model Test awards).

Beneficiary Eligibility: The emphasis is on targeting Medicare, Medicaid, and CHIP populations. Proposals will describe the target populations, geographic areas, or communities that will be the focus of service delivery and payment model testing, the current quality and beneficiary experience outcomes including current health population status, and the specific improvement targets expected from the model.

Award Range/Average: N/A

Funding: N/A

HQ: 7500 Security Boulevard
Baltimore, MD 21244
Phone: 410-786-9726
Email: karen.murphy@cms.hhs.gov
http://www.cms.gov

ACA – TESTING A MODEL OF DATA AGGREGATION UNDER THE COMPREHENSIVE PRIMARY CARE INITIATIVE

Award: Cooperative Agreements

Purpose: The Comprehensive Primary Care initiative is a multi-payer initiative fostering collaboration between public and private health insurance companies to strengthen primary care.

Applicant Eligibility: This project will ultimately benefit the primary care health professionals who participate in CPC and their patients. The aggregated data will be used by the primary care health professionals to improve care coordination and population health management, and to decrease costs.

Beneficiary Eligibility: Same as Applicant Eligibility.

Award Range/Average: The anticipated total funding per award, per budget period is $200,000 - $450,000.

Funding: FY 17 est $0; FY 15 $1,038,709; FY 18 est $0; FY 16 $0.

HQ: 7205 Windsor Boulevard

Windsor Mill, MD 21244

Phone: 410-786-7397

Email: leah.hendrick@cms.hhs.gov

http://innovation.cms.gov/initiatives/comprehensive-primary-care-initiative

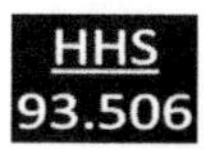

ACA NATIONWIDE PROGRAM FOR NATIONAL & STATE BACKGROUND CHECKS FOR DIRECT PATIENT ACCESS EMPLOYEES OF LONG TERM CARE FACILITIES & PROVIDERS

Award: Project Grants

Purpose: To establish a nationwide program to identify efficient, effective, and economical procedures for long term care facilities and providers to conduct background checks on a statewide basis on all prospective direct patient access employees.

Applicant Eligibility: CMS is inviting proposals from all States and U.S. territories to be considered for inclusion in this National Background Check Program. Federal matching funds are available to all States and U.S. territories.

Beneficiary Eligibility: These facilities and providers include skilled nursing facilities, nursing facilities, home health agencies, hospice care providers, long-term care hospitals, personal care service providers, adult day care providers, residential care providers, assisted living facilities, intermediate care facilities for the mentally retarded (ICFs/MR) and other entities that provide long-term care services, as specified by each participating State.

Award Range/Average: $1.5 million to $3 million

Funding: FY 17 $0; FY 18 est $5,368,848; FY 19 est $0; FY 16 $1,200,000.

HQ: 7500 Security Boulevard

Baltimore, MD 21244

Phone: 410-786-3270

Email: melissa.rice@cms.hhs.gov

http://www.cms.gov/medicare/provider-enrollment-and-certification/surveycertificationgeninfo/backgroundcheck.html

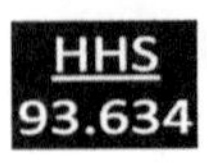

ACA SUPPORT FOR OMBUDSMAN & BENEFICIARY COUNSELING PROGRAMS FOR STATES PARTICIPATING IN THE MEDICARE-MEDICAID FINANCIAL ALIGNMENT INITIATIVE

Award: Cooperative Agreements

Purpose: Support for Demonstration Ombudsman Programs Serving Beneficiaries of State Demonstrations to Integrate Care for Medicare-Medicaid. CMS is presenting this Funding Opportunity Announcement to ensure that the beneficiaries of the Financial Alignment Demonstration models—as well as their caregivers and authorized representatives--have access to person-centered assistance in resolving problems and selecting appropriate healthcare coverage related to the Plans and providers.

Applicant Eligibility: States which have signed an MOU with CMS to implement one of the financial alignment demonstration models.

Beneficiary Eligibility: Same as Applicant Eligibility.

Award Range/Average: Awards range from $149,000- $ $1,494,476 per year.

Funding: FY 17 $6,136,831; FY 18 est $7,449,731; FY 19 est $5,910,921.

HQ: 7500 Security Boulevard
Baltimore, MD 21207
Phone: 410-786-8200
Email: kemuel.johnson@cms.hhs.gov
http://www.cms.gov/medicare-medicaid-coordination/medicare-and-medicaid-coordination/medicare-medicaid-coordination-office/alignmentinitiative/alignmentinitiative.html

ACADEMIC EXCHANGE PROGRAMS – EDUCATIONAL ADVISING & STUDENT SERVICES

Award: Cooperative Agreements

Purpose: The Department of State's Bureau of International Information Programs awards grants to cooperating organizations with experience in international exchanges for the administration of projects that enable U.S. experts to present lectures, serve as consultants, or conduct workshops and seminars for professional audiences worldwide.

Applicant Eligibility: Pursuant to the Mutual Educational and Cultural Exchange Act of 1961, as amended (Fulbright-Hays Act) the Bureau of Educational and Cultural Affairs of the U.S. Department of State awards grants and cooperative agreements to educational and cultural public or private nonprofit foundations or institutions. Applications may be submitted by public and private non-profit organizations meeting the provisions described in Internal Revenue Code section 26 USC 501(c)(3).

Beneficiary Eligibility: Beneficiaries include recipient organizations, educational institutions, other non-government organizations (NGOs) that meet the provisions described in Internal Revenue Code section 26 USC 501(c)(3), as well as sponsored participants, and the American people and the people of participating countries who interact with the international participants.

Award Range/Average: $500,000 to $5,499,999.

Funding: FY 17 $7,734,949; FY 18 est $7,734,949; FY 19 est $7,734,949; FY 16 $7,600,356.

HQ: (ECA/A/S/A) 2200 C Street NW SA-05, Room 04W12
Washington, DC 20037

Phone: 202-632-6353

Email: bollam@state.gov

http://eca.state.gov/about-bureau-0/organizational-structure/office-academic-exchanges

ACADEMIC EXCHANGE PROGRAMS – ENGLISH LANGUAGE PROGRAMS

Award: Cooperative Agreements

Purpose: The Bureau of Educational and Cultural Affairs (ECA) seeks to increase mutual understanding between the people of the United States and the people of other countries by means of educational and cultural exchange programs. ECA programs foster engagement and encourage dialogue with citizens around the world.

Applicant Eligibility: Pursuant to the Mutual Educational and Cultural Exchange Act of 1961, as amended (Fulbright-Hays Act) the Bureau of Educational and Cultural Affairs of the U.S. Department of State awards grants and cooperative agreements to educational and cultural public or private nonprofit foundations or institutions. Applications may be submitted by public and private non-profit organizations meeting the provisions described in Internal Revenue Code section 26 USC 501(c)(3).

Beneficiary Eligibility: Beneficiaries include recipient organizations, educational institutions, other non-government organizations (NGOs) that meet the provisions described in Internal Revenue Code section 26 USC 501(c)(3), as well as sponsored participants, and the American people and the people of participating countries who interact with the international participants.

Award Range/Average: $4,250,000 to $27,100,000.

Funding: FY 17 $37,950,000; FY 18 est $37,950,000; FY 19 est $37,950,000; FY 16 $38,871,273.

HQ: Office of English Language Programs English Language Fellow Program, 2200 C Street NW SA-05 Room 4B14

Washington, DC 20037

Phone: 202-632-9412

Email: danzcb@state.gov

http://americanenglish.state.gov/ae-programs

ACADEMIC EXCHANGE PROGRAMS – GRADUATE STUDENTS "The Fulbright Student Program"

Award: Project Grants

Purpose: Seeks to increase mutual understanding between the people of the United States and the people of other countries by means of educational and cultural exchange programs, including the exchange of scholars, researchers, professionals, students, and educators.

Applicant Eligibility: Pursuant to the Mutual Educational and Cultural Exchange Act of 1961, as amended (Fulbright-Hays Act) the Bureau of Educational and Cultural Affairs of the U.S. Department of State awards grants and cooperative agreements to educational and cultural public or private nonprofit foundations or institutions. Applications may be submitted by public and private non-profit organizations meeting the provisions described in Internal Revenue Code section 26 USC 501(c)(3).

Beneficiary Eligibility: Beneficiaries include recipient organizations, educational institutions, other non-government organizations (NGOs) that meet the provisions described in Internal Revenue Code section 26

USC 501(c)(3), as well as sponsored participants, and the American people and the people of participating countries who interact with the international participants.

Award Range/Average: $7,991,733 to $81,216,212.

Funding: Project Grants (Cooperative Agreements) FY 17 $89,207,945; FY 18 est $89,207,945; FY 19 est $89,207,945; FY 16 $96,004,350.

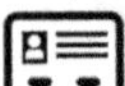

HQ: 2200 C Street NW SA-5 Fourth Floor, Room 4B07
Washington, DC 20037
Phone: 202-632-3238
http://exchanges.state.gov

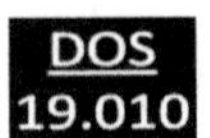

ACADEMIC EXCHANGE PROGRAMS – HUBERT H. HUMPHREY FELLOWSHIP PROGRAM
"Hubert H. Humphrey Fellowship Program"

Award: Cooperative Agreements

Purpose: Seeks to increase mutual understanding between the people of the United States and the people of other countries by means of educational and cultural exchange programs. The Humphrey Program brings young and mid-career professionals from developing countries to the United States for a year of non-degree graduate-level study, leadership development, and professional collaboration with U.S. counterparts.

Applicant Eligibility: N/A

Beneficiary Eligibility: N/A

Award Range/Average: N/A

Funding: FY 17 $11,438,615; FY 18 est $11,438,615; FY 19 est $11,438,615; FY 16 $11,982,116.

HQ: Department of Scholar and Professional Programs Hubert H Humphrey Fellowship Program 1400 K Street NW, Suite 700
Washington, DC 20005
Phone: 202-686-8664
Email: sedlinsjz@state.gov
http://exchanges.state.gov/non-us/program/hubert-h-humphrey-fellowship-program

ACADEMIC EXCHANGE PROGRAMS – SCHOLARS
"The Fulbright Scholar program"

Award: Project Grants; Cooperative Agreement

Purpose: Seeks to increase mutual understanding between the people of the United States and the people of other countries by means of educational and cultural exchange programs, including the exchange of scholars, researchers, professionals, students, and educators.

Applicant Eligibility: Pursuant to the Mutual Educational and Cultural Exchange Act of 1961, as amended (Fulbright-Hays Act) the Bureau of Educational and Cultural Affairs of the U.S. Department of State awards grants and cooperative agreements to educational and cultural public or private nonprofit foundations or institutions. Applications may be submitted by public and private non-profit organizations meeting the provisions described in Internal Revenue Code section 26 USC 501(c)(3).

Beneficiary Eligibility: Beneficiaries include recipient organizations, educational institutions, other non-government organizations (NGOs) that meet the provisions described in Internal Revenue Code section 26 USC 501(c)(3), as well as sponsored participants, and the American people and the people of participating countries who interact with the international participants.

Award Range/Average: $239,990 to $32,331,958.

Funding: (Cooperative Agreements) FY 17 $38,629,738; FY 18 est $38,629,738; FY 19 est $38,629,738; FY 16 $36,328,501.

HQ: 2200 C Street NW SA-5 Fourth Floor, Room 4B07
Washington, DC 20037
Phone: 202-632-3238
http://eca.state.gov/about-bureau-0/organizational-structure/office-academic-exchanges

ACADEMIC EXCHANGE PROGRAMS – SPECIAL ACADEMIC EXCHANGE PROGRAMS

Award: Cooperative Agreements; Project Grants

Purpose: Seeks to increase mutual understanding between the people of the United States and the people of other countries by means of educational and cultural exchange programs. The purpose of Special Academic Exchange Programs is to provide targeted support for U.S. and foreign students and others who may not otherwise have the resources to pursue international exchange opportunities or who are in fields directly relevant to identified needs in their countries.

Applicant Eligibility: Pursuant to the Mutual Educational and Cultural Exchange Act of 1961, as amended (Fulbright-Hays Act) the Bureau of Educational and Cultural Affairs of the U.S. Department of State awards grants and cooperative agreements to educational and cultural public or private nonprofit foundations or institutions. Applications may be submitted by public and private non-profit organizations meeting the provisions described in Internal Revenue Code section 26 USC 501(c)(3).

Beneficiary Eligibility: Beneficiaries include recipient organizations, educational institutions, other non-government organizations (NGOs) that meet the provisions described in Internal Revenue Code section 26 USC 501(c)(3), as well as sponsored participants, and the American people and the people of participating countries who interact with the international participants.

Award Range/Average: $350,000 to $14,090,000.

Funding: (Cooperative Agreements) FY 17 $19,925,000; FY 18 est $19,925,000; FY 19 est $19,925,000; FY 16 $18,150,000.

HQ: 2200 C Street NW SA-5 Fourth Floor, Room 4B07
Washington, DC 20037
Phone: 202-632-3238
http://eca.state.gov/about-bureau-0/organizational-structure/office-academic-exchanges

ACADEMIC EXCHANGE PROGRAMS – TEACHERS

Award: Cooperative Agreements

Purpose: Seeks to increase mutual understanding between the people of the United States and the people of other countries by means of educational and cultural exchange programs, including the exchange of scholars, researchers, professionals, students, and educators.

Applicant Eligibility: Pursuant to the Mutual Educational and Cultural Exchange Act of 1961, as amended (Fulbright-Hays Act) the Bureau of Educational and Cultural Affairs of the U.S. Department of State awards grants and cooperative agreements to educational and cultural public or private nonprofit foundations or institutions. Applications may be submitted by public and private non-profit organizations meeting the provisions described in Internal Revenue Code section 26 USC 501(c)(3).

Beneficiary Eligibility: Beneficiaries include recipient organizations, educational institutions, other non-government organizations (NGOs) that meet the provisions described in Internal Revenue Code section 26 USC 501(c)(3), as well as sponsored participants, and the American people and the people of participating countries who interact with the international participants.

Award Range/Average: $1,250,000 to $6,900,000.

Funding: FY 17 $12,731,249; FY 18 est $12,731,249; FY 19 est $12,731,249; FY 16 $12,279,999.

HQ: Teacher Exchange Branch 2200 C Street NW SA-05, Room 4S17
Washington, DC 20037
Phone: 202-632-6346
Email: kubanmm@state.gov
http://eca.state.gov/about-bureau/organizational-structure/office-global-educational-programs

ACADEMIC EXCHANGE PROGRAMS – UNDERGRADUATE PROGRAMS

Award: Cooperative Agreements

Purpose: Undergraduate programs include the Global Undergraduate Exchange Program (UGRAD); Study of the U.S. Institutes for Student Leaders; Community College Initiative Program (CCIP); and the Critical Language Scholarship (CLS) Program and Capacity-Building Program for U.S. Undergraduate Study Abroad. Seeks to increase mutual understanding between the people of the United States and the people of other countries by means of educational and cultural exchange programs. The main objective of the Undergraduate Programs is to provide targeted support for American students to pursue intensive language study abroad and for foreign students.

Applicant Eligibility: Pursuant to the Mutual Educational and Cultural Exchange Act of 1961, as amended (Fulbright-Hays Act) the Bureau of Educational and Cultural Affairs of the U.S. Department of State awards grants and cooperative agreements to educational and cultural public or private nonprofit foundations or institutions. Applications may be submitted by public and private non-profit organizations meeting the provisions described in Internal Revenue Code section 26 USC 501(c)(3).

Beneficiary Eligibility: Beneficiaries include recipient organizations, educational institutions, other non-government organizations (NGOs) that meet the provisions described in Internal Revenue Code section 26 USC 501(c)(3), as well as sponsored participants, and the American people and the people of participating countries who interact with the international participants.

Award Range/Average: $238,857 to $12,200000.

Funding: FY 17 $52,288,777; FY 18 est $52,288,777; FY 19 est $52,288,777.

HQ: 2200 C Street NW SA-5 Fourth Floor, Room 4CC16
Washington, DC 20037
Phone: 202-632-9265
http://exchanges.state.gov

ACA-TRANSFORMING CLINICAL PRACTICE INITIATIVE: PRACTICE TRANSFORMATION NETWORKS (PTNS) "TCPI"

Award: Cooperative Agreements

Purpose: The Transforming Clinical Practice Initiative model will test whether a three-pronged approach to national technical assistance will enable large scale transformation of thousands of clinician practices to deliver better care and result in better health outcomes at lower costs.

Applicant Eligibility: Interstate, Intrastate, Local, Sponsored Organizations, Federally Recognized Indian Tribal Government, Private Nonprofit Institution/Organization, Quasi-public Nonprofit Institution/ Organization, Other private Institution/Organization, Native American Organization, Specialty group, Small Business, Profit Organization, Other public Institution/Organization, Public Nonprofit Institution/ Organization, Other public Institution/Organization.

Beneficiary Eligibility: The Beneficiary eligibility includes the Applicant Eligibility above with the exception of Federal, Interstate, Student/Trainee and Graduate Students, Artist/Humanist, Engineer/ Architect, Builder/Contractor/Developer/Farmer/Rancher/Agriculture Producer/Industrialist/Business Person Small Business Person/Homeowner property Owner/Anyone/General Public.

Award Range/Average: This will be a new service delivery model. Therefore, no funds have been requested for past or current fiscal years.

Funding: FY 17 $134,572,992; FY 18 est $120,567,781; FY 19 est $0; FY 16 $136,555,218.

HQ: LT 7500 Security Boulevard
Baltimore, MD 21244
Phone: 410-786-5239
Email: fred.butler@cms.hhs.gov
http://www.innovation.cms.gov

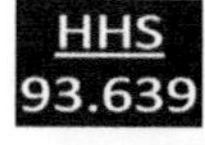

ACA-TRANSFORMING CLINICAL PRACTICE INITIATIVE: SUPPORT & ALIGNMENT NETWORKS (SANS) "TCPI"

Award: Cooperative Agreements

Purpose: The Transforming Clinical Practice Initiative model will test whether a three-pronged approach to national technical assistance will enable large scale transformation of thousands of clinician practices to deliver better care and result in better health outcomes at lower costs. Support Alignment Networks formed by group practices, healthcare systems, and others that join together to serve as trusted partners to provide clinician practices with quality improvement expertise, best practices, coaching and help as they prepare and begin clinical and operational practice transformation.

Applicant Eligibility: CMS anticipates that SANs will include but not be limited to organizations like Public Nonprofit Institution/Organization, Specialized group, Profit Organization, Private Nonprofit Institution/ Organization, Quasi-public Nonprofit Institution/Organization, Other private institution/organization.

Beneficiary Eligibility: The Beneficiary eligibility includes the list as noted above with the exception of Federal, Intrastate, Student/Trainee and Graduate Students, Artist/Humanist, Engineer/Architect, Builder/ Contractor/Developer, Farmer/Rancher/Agriculture Producer Industrialist/Business Person, Small Business Person, Homeowner, Property Owner, Anyone/General Public.

Award Range/Average: This will be a new service delivery model. Therefore, no funds have been requested for past or current fiscal years.

Funding: FY 17 $7,162,654; FY 18 est $7,104,814; FY 19 est $0; FY 16 $8,702,926.

HQ: LT 7500 Security Boulevard
Baltimore, MD 21244
Phone: 410-786-5239
Email: fred.butler@cms.hhs.gov
http://www.innovation.cms.gov

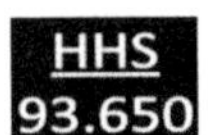

ACCOUNTABLE HEALTH COMMUNITIES "AHC"

Award: Formula Grants

Purpose: Assesses whether systematically identifying the health-related social needs of community- dwelling Medicare and Medicaid beneficiaries, including those who are dually eligible, and addressing their identified needs impacts those beneficiaries' total healthcare costs and their inpatient and outpatient utilization.

Applicant Eligibility: Community based organizations, Individual and group provider practices, Hospitals and health systems, Institutions of Higher Education, Local government entities and tribal organization from all 50 states, United States territories.

Beneficiary Eligibility: Potential applicants are limited to the eligible entities described in the sections above. Successful applicants will provide intervention services to community-dwelling Medicare and Medicaid beneficiaries, including dually eligible beneficiaries.

Award Range/Average: The anticipated total funding per award, per budget period is $500,000 - $900,000. The total amount of federal funds available is up to $30.84 million to 12 award recipients to implement the Assistance Track Intervention and $90.20 million to 20 award recipients to implement the Alignment Track Intervention.

Funding: FY 17 $20,820,582; FY 18 est $24,851,501; FY 19 est $24,724,633; FY 16 $0.

HQ: 7500 Security Boulevard
Baltimore, MD 21244
Phone: 410-786-8033
Email: alexander.billioux@cms.hhs.gov
http://www.innovation.cms.gov

ACL ASSISTIVE TECHNOLOGY STATE GRANTS FOR PROTECTION & ADVOCACY

Award: Formula Grants

Purpose: To provide protection and advocacy services under the Developmental Disabilities Assistance and Bill of Rights Act for the purpose of assisting in the acquisition, utilization, or maintenance of assistive technology for individuals with disabilities.

Applicant Eligibility: Designated protection and advocacy agencies in States and outlying areas only.

Beneficiary Eligibility: Persons with disabilities who may benefit from assistive technology services and devices.

Award Range/Average: N/A

Funding: FY 17 $4,450,000; FY 18 est $4,800,000; FY 19 FY 16 $4,450,000.

HQ: 330 C Street SW, Suite 1139-A
Washington, DC 20201
Phone: 202-795-7360
Email: ladeva.harris@acl.hhs.gov
http://www.acl.gov/programs/aging-and-disability-networks/state-protection-advocacy-systems

ACL ASSISTIVE TECHNOLOGY "State AT Grants"

Award: Project Grants

Purpose: To improve the provision of assistive technology to individuals with disabilities through comprehensive statewide programs of technology-related assistance, for individuals with disabilities of all ages.

Applicant Eligibility: States, including the District of Columbia, Puerto Rico, and outlying areas may apply. Applicants are designated by Governors.

Beneficiary Eligibility: Individuals with disabilities, States, and community-based organizations providing services to individuals with disabilities will benefit.

Award Range/Average: To Be Determined

Funding: (Formula Grants) FY 17 $26,470,517; FY 18 est $28,165,621; FY 19 est $28,170,000; FY 16 $26,554,000.

HQ: 330 C Street SW, Room 1317B
Washington, DC 20201
Phone: 202-795-7356
Email: robert.groenendaal@acl.hhs.gov
http://www.acl.gov/programs/assistive-technology/assistive-technology

ACL CENTERS FOR INDEPENDENT LIVING "CILs"

Award: Project Grants

Purpose: To support a Statewide network of centers for independent living (centers or CILs) and provide financial assistance to centers that comply with the standards and assurances in section 725(b) and (c) of the Rehabilitation Act of 1973, as amended (Rehabilitation Act) consistent with the design included in the State Plan for Independent Living for establishing a statewide network of centers.

Applicant Eligibility: Private non-profit organizations. An eligible agency under the CIL program is a consumer-controlled, community-based, cross-disability, nonresidential, private nonprofit agency or a state agency in states in which no eligible private non-profit organization applies for a grant.

Beneficiary Eligibility: Individuals with significant disabilities as defined in section 7(21)(B) of the Rehabilitation Act. This refers to an individual with a severe physical or mental impairment whose ability to function independently in the family or community or whose ability to obtain, maintain, or advance in employment is substantially limited and for whom the delivery of independent living services will improve the ability to function, continue functioning, or move toward functioning independently in the family or community or to continue in employment, respectively.

Award Range/Average: No Data Available.

Funding: Project Grants (Discretionary) FY 17 $78,305,000; FY 18 est $88,305,000; FY 19 N/A FY 16 $78,125,432.

HQ: 330 C Street SW
Washington, DC 20201
Phone: 202-795-7446
Email: corinna.stiles@acl.hhs.gov
http://www.acl.gov/programs/aging-and-disability-networks/centers-independent-living

HHS 93.844 ACL CENTERS FOR INDEPENDENT LIVING, RECOVERY ACT

Award: Project Grants

Purpose: To provide independent living services to individuals with significant disabilities to assist them to function more independently in family and community settings, by developing and supporting a statewide network of centers for independent living.

Applicant Eligibility: N/A

Beneficiary Eligibility: N/A

Award Range/Average: No Data Available.

Funding: (Project Grants) FY 17 $0; FY 18 est $0; FY 19 est $0; FY 16 $0.

HQ: 330 C Street SW
Washington, DC 20201
Phone: 202-495-7453
Email: roslyn.thompson@acl.hhs.gov

HHS 93.369 ACL INDEPENDENT LIVING STATE GRANTS "Independent Living Services"

Award: Formula Grants

Purpose: To provide financial assistance to States for expanding and improving the provision of independent living (IL) services to individuals with significant disabilities.

Applicant Eligibility: Any designated State Entity (DSE) in a State with an approved State Plan for Independent Living (SPIL) may apply for assistance under this program. The DSE is the State entity of such State as the agency that, on behalf of the State, receives, accounts for and disburses funds received under this chapter based on the SPIL.

Beneficiary Eligibility: Individuals with significant disabilities as defined in section 7(21)(B) of the Rehabilitation Act, as amended. This refers to an individual with a severe physical or mental impairment whose ability to function independently in the family or community or whose ability to obtain, maintain, or advance in employment is substantially limited and for whom the delivery of independent living services will improve the ability to function, continue functioning, or move toward functioning independently in the family or community or to continue in employment, respectively.

Award Range/Average: N/A

Funding: FY 17 $22,878,000; FY 18 est $24,878,000; FY 19 N/A FY 16 $22,878,000.

HQ: 330 C Street SW
Washington, DC 20201
Phone: 202-795-7446
Email: corinna.stiles@acl.hhs.gov
http://www.acl.gov

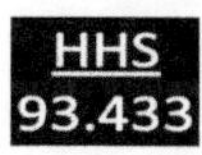

ACL NATIONAL INSTITUTE ON DISABILITY, INDEPENDENT LIVING, AND REHABILITATION RESEARCH "NIDILRR"

Award: Cooperative Agreements

Purpose: To support and coordinate research and its utilization in order to improve the lives of people of all ages with physical and mental disabilities, especially persons with severe disabilities, through identifying and eliminating causes and consequences of disability.

Applicant Eligibility: States, public, private, or nonprofit agencies and organizations, institutions of higher education, and Indian tribes and tribal organizations are eligible for research projects and specialized research activities related to the rehabilitation of individuals with disabilities; fellowships may be awarded to individuals.

Beneficiary Eligibility: Individuals with disabilities may benefit directly or indirectly from research and other activities conducted by grantees, such as technical assistance and dissemination.

Award Range/Average: The range and average vary greatly according to the competition.

Funding: FY 17 $103,970,000; FY 18 est $105,320,800; FY 19 FY 16 $103,970,000.

HQ: 330 C Street SW
Washington, DC 20201
Phone: 202-795-7305
Email: phillip.beatty@acl.hhs.gov
http://www.acl.gov/about-acl/about-national-institute-disability-independent-living-and-rehabilitation-research

ACQUIRED IMMUNODEFICIENCY SYNDROME (AIDS) ACTIVITY

Award: Cooperative Agreements

Purpose: Develops and implements HIV prevention programs of public information and education.

Applicant Eligibility: Public and private organizations, both nonprofit and for-profit (universities, colleges, research institutions and other public and private organizations); State and local governments, U.S. Territories and possessions; including American Indian/Alaska Native tribal governments or tribal organizations located wholly or in part within their boundaries, small and minority businesses, and businesses owned by women.

Beneficiary Eligibility: Official health and education agencies, as well as individuals subject to AIDS.

Award Range/Average: N/A

Funding: FY 17 $3,327,453; FY 18 est $3,327,453; FY 19 est $0; FY 16 $2,911,638; - PS14-1409; PS15-1505. Note: For FY 2018, HIV prevention activities and HIV surveillance will be combined into a new project, "Integrated HIV Surveillance and Prevention Programs"

HQ: 1600 Clifton Road, P.O. Box E-07
Atlanta, GA 30333
Phone: 404-639-1877
http://www.cdc.gov/hiv

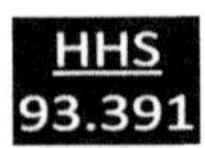

ACTIVITIES TO SUPPORT STATE, TRIBAL, LOCAL & TERRITORIAL (STLT) HEALTH DEPARTMENT RESPONSE TO PUBLIC HEALTH OR HEALTHCARE CRISES
"CDC Partner Crisis Response NOFO"

Award: Cooperative Agreements

Purpose: To establish a pool of organizations capable of rapidly providing essential expertise to governmental public health entities involved in a response.

Applicant Eligibility: Eligible applicants are limited to the following: 1. Nonprofits having a 501(c)(3) or 501(c)(6) status with the IRS, other than institutions of higher education.

Beneficiary Eligibility: Direct awards will be made to the non-governmental organizations described in the eligible applicant section. Beneficiaries of the support provided by those non-governmental organizations will include state health departments; tribal health organizations; local health departments; the District of Columbia; U.S. Territories; and other components of the public health system.

Award Range/Average: Due to the nature of the issues that would trigger CDC to activate this NOFO as designed, it is difficult to project the total funding amount that would be made available. When and if CDC activates this NOFO, it is expected to be only for the time necessary to respond to the emergency at hand, and that long-term recovery needs (and/or emergencies that shift from an epidemic to an endemic nature) would be addressed by other NOFOs as appropriate.

Funding: FY 17 FY 18 FY 19 est $0; FY 16 $0.

HQ: 1600 Clifton Road NE, P.O. Box K90
Atlanta, GA 30329-1602
Phone: 770-488-1602
http://www.cdc.gov/stltpublichealth/about-cstlts/index.html

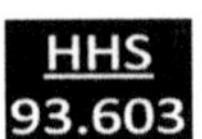

ADOPTION & LEGAL GUARDIANSHIP INCENTIVE PAYMENTS
"Adoption and Legal Guardianship Incentive Payments."

Award: Formula Grants

Purpose: Provides incentive to States and eligible Tribes to increase the number of children in foster care who find permanent homes through adoption or legal guardianship.

Applicant Eligibility: Applications are not required. States (including the District of Columbia, Puerto Rico, the U.S. Virgin Islands, Guam and American Samoa) and tribes that have an approved title IV-E plan and that submit data to the Adoption and Foster Care Analysis and Reporting System (AFCARS) are eligible to receive payments.

Beneficiary Eligibility: Beneficiaries are those children and families eligible under Title IV-B and Title IV-E of the Social Security Act, as amended.

Award Range/Average: FY 2017 earning year, 52 States earned incentive payments that ranged from $11,850 to $4,076,960, with an average award amount of $727,403.

Funding: FY 17 $37,824,982; FY 18 est $75,000,000; FY 19 est $75,000,000; FY 16 $37,943,000.

HQ: 330 C Street SW, Room 3512
Washington, DC 20201
Phone: 202-205-8552
Email: gail.collins@acf.hhs.gov
http://www.acf.hhs.gov/cb/focus-areas/adoption

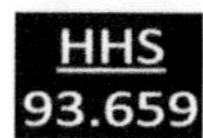

ADOPTION ASSISTANCE

Award: Formula Grants

Purpose: Provides Federal Financial Participation to states, Indian tribes, tribal organizations and tribal consortia in adoption subsidy costs for the adoption of children with special needs who cannot be reunited with their families and who meet certain eligibility tests. This assistance is intended to prevent inappropriately long stays in foster care and to promote the healthy development of children through increased safety, permanency and well-being.

Applicant Eligibility: Funds are available to states (including the District of Columbia, Puerto Rico, the U.S. Virgin Islands, Guam and American Samoa) and to tribes with approved title IV-E plans.

Beneficiary Eligibility: Eligible beneficiaries include certain children who are legally freed for adoption where an adoption assistance agreement has been entered into prior to the finalization of an adoption. These children must: (1) have been determined by the state or tribe to be special needs.

Award Range/Average: FY 2017 Grants to states ranged from: $788,754 to $575,653,089 with an average of $53,451,923.

Funding: FY 17 $2,780,000,000; FY 18 est $2,867,000,000; FY 19 est $2,800,000,000; FY 16 $2,539,323,468.

HQ: 330 C Street SW, Room 3509B
Washington, DC 20201
Phone: 202-205-8438
Email: eileen.west@acf.hhs.gov
http://www.acf.hhs.gov/cb/focus-areas/adoption

ADOPTION OPPORTUNITIES

Award: Project Grants

Purpose: To eliminate barriers, to adoption and to provide permanent, loving home environments for children who would benefit from adoption, particularly children with special needs.

Applicant Eligibility: Grants or Contracts: State, local government entities, public or private licensed child welfare or adoption agencies or community based organizations.

Beneficiary Eligibility: Children who are in foster care with the goal of adoption, especially children with special needs, that is, children who are older, minority children and infants and toddlers with disabilities who have a life-threatening condition.

Award Range/Average: FY 2017: $300,000 to $5,170,000 with an average of $1,053,919

Funding: Project Grants (Discretionary) FY 17 $22,132,311; FY 18 est $26,449,290; FY 19 est $19,470,000; FY 16 $28,479,778.

HQ: 330 C Street SW, Room 3503
Washington, DC 20201
Phone: 202-205-8172
Email: jan.shafer@acf.hhs.gov
http://www.acf.hhs.gov/cb/focus-areas/adoption

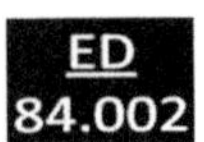

ADULT EDUCATION – BASIC GRANTS TO STATES

Award: Formula Grants

Purpose: To fund local programs like adult education and literacy services, including workplace literacy services, family literacy services, and English literacy and integrated English literacy-civics education programs.

Applicant Eligibility: Formula grants are made to designated eligible State agencies that under State law are responsible for administering or supervising statewide policy for adult education and literacy, including such entities as State educational agencies (SEAs), postsecondary agencies, or workforce agencies. State agencies must provide direct and equitable access to: local educational agencies; public or private nonprofit agencies; community-based organizations of demonstrated effectiveness; institutions of higher education; volunteer literacy organizations of demonstrated effectiveness; libraries; public housing authorities; nonprofit institutions not described above that have the ability to provide literacy services to adults and families; and consortia of the entities described above.

Beneficiary Eligibility: Adults and out-of-school youths who are 16 years of age and older, who are not enrolled or required to be enrolled in secondary school under State law, and who lack sufficient mastery of basic educational skills to enable them to function effectively in society or do not have a secondary school diploma or its recognized equivalent, and have not achieved an equivalent level of education, or are unable to speak, read, or write the English language.

Award Range/Average: FY 17: $13,509- $93,808,504; $10,033,707 average. FY 18: $12,158- $100,012,921; $10,458,559 average. FY 19: $10,942- $78,746,188; $8,376,707 average.

Funding: FY 17 $581,955,000; FY 18 est $16,955,000; FY 19 est $485,849,000; FY 16 $581,955,000.

HQ: 400 Maryland Avenue
Washington, DC 20202
Phone: 202-245-6836
Email: cheryl.keenan@ed.gov
http://www2.ed.gov/about/offices/list/ovae/pi/adulted/index.html

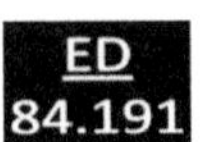

ADULT EDUCATION NATIONAL LEADERSHIP ACTIVITIES

Award: Cooperative Agreements; Project Grants; Direct Payments for Specified Use

Purpose: To support applied research, development, demonstration, dissemination, evaluation, and related activities that contribute towards the improvement of adult education and literacy activities nationally.

Applicant Eligibility: Postsecondary education institutions, public or private agencies or organizations, or consortia of these institutions, agencies, or organizations are eligible.

Beneficiary Eligibility: Basic education and literacy programs for adults seeking to obtain an education at the primary or secondary levels will benefit through national evaluation, research, leadership, and/or technical assistance efforts.

Award Range/Average: For Fiscal Year 2017: Range: $400,000 - $2,272,086; Average: $1,131,079.

Funding: Project Grants (Contracts) FY 17 $13,712,000; FY 18 est $13,712,000; FY 19 est $13,712,000; FY 16 $13,712,000.

HQ: OVAE Division of Adult Education and Literacy 400 Maryland Avenue SW
Washington, DC 20202
Phone: 202-245-7717
Email: christopher.coro@ed.gov
http://www2.ed.gov/programs/aenla/index.html

HHS 93.644 ADULT MEDICAID QUALITY: IMPROVING MATERNAL & INFANT HEALTH OUTCOMES IN MEDICAID & CHIP

Award: Cooperative Agreements

Purpose: Supports State Medicaid agencies in testing, collecting, and reporting to CMS a new developmental quality measure as part of the Center for Medicaid and CHIP Services Maternal and Infant Health Initiative. Additionally, the grant funding will support States' efforts to use these data to increase the rate of pregnancies that are intended through increased use of effective contraception.

Applicant Eligibility: Grant applicants are limited to the 51 State Medicaid Agencies and the Medicaid Agencies in the US Territories.

Beneficiary Eligibility: State Medicaid Agencies and the Medicaid Agencies in the US Territories.

Award Range/Average: A total of up to 25 grants could be awarded to States, the District of Columbia, and the US Territories. Grant awardees may receive up to $400,000 over the performance period assuming the grantee is found eligible for all payments.

Funding: FY 17 $1,332,223; FY 18 est $0; FY 19 est $0; FY 16 $1,248,605.

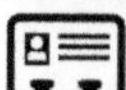

HQ: Bethesda 5600 Fishers Lane, P.O. Box 7700
Rockville, MD 20857
Phone: 301-492-4879
Email: kevin.hornbeak@cms.hhs.gov
http://www.cms.gov

ADVANCE INTEROPERABLE HEALTH INFORMATION TECHNOLOGY SERVICES TO SUPPORT HEALTH INFORMATION EXCHANGE

Award: Cooperative Agreements

Purpose: The Advance Interoperable Health IT Services to Support Health Information Exchange Cooperative Agreement Program will leverage investments and lessons learned from the previous State Health Information Exchange Cooperative Agreement Program to rapidly build capacity for the interoperable exchange of health information across the entire care continuum both within and across states while moving toward nationwide interoperability.

Applicant Eligibility: Either a State, Territory, or State Designated Entity was eligible to apply.

Beneficiary Eligibility: N/A

Award Range/Average: Average of each award is estimated at $2.47M.

Funding: Cooperative Agreements (Discretionary Grants) FY 18 FY 17 est $0; FY 16 est $0.

HQ: 330 C Street SW, Suite 7033A
Washington, DC 20201
Phone: 202-720-2861
Email: larry.jessup@hhs.gov
http://www.healthit.gov

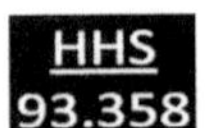

ADVANCED EDUCATION NURSING TRAINEESHIPS "AENT"

Award: Project Grants

Purpose: To increase the number of advanced practice nurses serving as primary care nurse practitioners or nurse midwives, with an emphasis on funding applicants who are prepared to meet the primary care needs of rural and underserved communities.

Applicant Eligibility: Eligible applicants are education programs that provide registered nurses with nurse practitioner and nurse-midwife education. Such programs may include schools of nursing, nursing centers, academic health centers, State or local governments, and other public or private nonprofit entities authorized by the Secretary to confer degrees to registered nurses for nurse practitioner nurse-midwife education.

Beneficiary Eligibility: The participating institutions select traineeship recipients. A recipient (student) must be enrolled in an advanced education nursing program in the recipient institution for preparation as a primary care nurse practitioner or nurse-midwife.

Award Range/Average: N/A

Funding: FY 17 $0; FY 18 est $0; FY 19 est $0; FY 16 $22,860,155.

HQ: Bureau of Health Workforce Division of Nursing and Public Health 5600 Fishers Lane, Room 11N94C
Rockville, MD 20857
Phone: 301-443-0856
Email: mmccalla@hrsa.gov
http://www.hrsa.gov

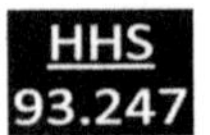

ADVANCED NURSING EDUCATION WORKFORCE GRANT PROGRAM "Advanced Nursing Education Workforce (ANEW), Advanced Nurse Education-Sexual Assault Nurse Examiner (ANE-SANE)"

Award: Project Grants

Purpose: To support innovative academic-practice partnerships to prepare advanced practice registered nursing students to practice in rural and underserved settings through academic and clinical training.

Applicant Eligibility: ANEW: Eligible applicants are collegiate schools of nursing, nursing centers, academic health centers, State or local governments, and other public or private nonprofit entities accredited by a national nurse education accrediting agency recognized by the Secretary of the U.S. Department of Education. In addition to the 50 states, only the District of Columbia, Guam, the Commonwealth of Puerto Rico, the Northern Mariana Islands, American Samoa, the U.S. Virgin Islands, the Federated States of Micronesia, the Republic of the Marshall Islands, and the Republic of Palau are eligible to apply.

Beneficiary Eligibility: Accredited schools of nursing, nursing centers, academic health centers, state or local governments, and other public or private nonprofit entities determined appropriate by the Secretary. ANE SANE: An eligible participant must be a citizen of the United States, a non-citizen national, or a foreign national who possesses a visa permitting permanent residence in the United States.

Award Range/Average: No Data Available.

Funding: FY 17 $34,472,917; FY 18 est $56,753,263; FY 19 est $0; FY 16 $29,134,346; - ANEW FY 17 $0; FY 18 est $8,000,000; FY 19 est $0; - ANEW SANE.

HQ: 5600 Fishers Lane, Room 11N74A
Rockville, MD 20857
Phone: 301-443-6739
Email: jyoung@hrsa.gov
http://www.hrsa.gov

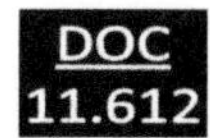

ADVANCED TECHNOLOGY PROGRAM "ATP"

Award: Project Grants

Purpose: To promote partnership for the development of technologies that offer significant economic benefits.

Applicant Eligibility: U.S. businesses and U.S. joint research and development ventures. Foreign-owned businesses are eligible for funding, provided they meet the requirements of Public Law 102-245, Sec.

Beneficiary Eligibility: Same as Applicant Eligibility

Award Range/Average: No Data Available.

Funding: (Formula Grants) FY 17 $0; FY 18 est $0; FY 19 est $0; FY 16 $21,000; - This program has been discontinued.

HQ: 100 Bureau Drive
Gaithersburg, MD 20899
Phone: 301-975-2684
Email: kimball.carpentier@nist.gov
http://www.nist.gov

ADVANCING SYSTEM IMPROVEMENTS FOR KEY ISSUES IN WOMEN'S HEALTH "Improving Health of Women and Girls"

Award: Cooperative Agreements

Purpose: To promote program and systems innovation, policy and performance management and strategic communications that will advance improvement for key issues in women's health.

Applicant Eligibility: Nonprofit organizations must provide evidence of tax-exempt status. When projects involve the collaborative efforts of more than one organization or require the use of services or facilities not under the direct control of the applicant, written assurances of specific support or agreements must be submitted by the affected parties.

Beneficiary Eligibility: All women and girls, adults and children, including those underserved and minority populations, usually residing in the U.S., including Bone Fide territories, cities and islands.

Award Range/Average: $500,000 - $2,200,000 for 1 - 3 grants; $200,000 - $300,000 for up to 5 grants

Funding: FY 17 est $9,534,078; FY 18 est $5,859,960; FY 16 $5,926,431.

HQ: 1101 Wootton Parkway Tower Building, Suite 550
Rockville, MD 20852
Phone: 240-453-8822
Email: eric.west@hhs.gov
http://www.womenshealth.gov

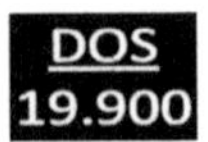

AEECA/ESF PD PROGRAMS
"Assistance for Europe, Eurasia, and Central Asia (AEECA) & Economic Support Fund (ESF) Public Diplomacy Programs (EUR/PD and SCA/PPD)"

Award: Project Grants

Purpose: To provide civil society and democracy building public diplomacy programs within Europe, Eurasia and Central Asia.

Applicant Eligibility: See individual federal assistance announcements on U.S. Embassy web sites in: Albania, Armenia, Azerbaijan, Belarus, Bosnia & Herzegovina, Georgia, Kazakhstan, Kosovo, Kyrgyzstan, Macedonia, Moldova, Montenegro, Russia, Serbia, Tajikistan, Turkmenistan, Ukraine, or Uzbekistan for details.

Beneficiary Eligibility: Only applicants NGO's from Albania, Armenia, Azerbaijan, Belarus, Bosnia & Herzegovina, Georgia, Kazakhstan, Kosovo, Kyrgyzstan, Macedonia, Moldova, Montenegro, Russia, Serbia, Tajikistan, Turkmenistan, Ukraine, or Uzbekistan are eligible for this program.

Award Range/Average: No Data Available.

Funding: FY 16 N/A FY 18 N/A FY 17 est $23,000,000.

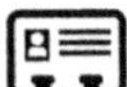
HQ: 2201 C Street NW, Room 3249
Washington, DC 20520
Phone: 202-647-8519
Email: langem2@state.gov
http://www.state.gov/p/eur/ace

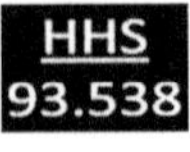

AFFORDABLE CARE ACT – NATIONAL ENVIRONMENTAL PUBLIC HEALTH TRACKING PROGRAM-NETWORK IMPLEMENTATION

Award: Cooperative Agreements

Purpose: National Center for Environmental Health, Division of Environmental Hazards and Health Effects, Environmental Health Tracking Branch is to establish and maintain a nationwide tracking network to obtain integrated health and environmental data and use it to provide information in support of actions that improve the health of communities.

Applicant Eligibility: Consistent with appropriation legislative history which began the Tracking initiative in FY 2002, states and local government health departments or their Bona Fide Agents.

Beneficiary Eligibility: The general public will benefit from the objectives of this program.

Award Range/Average: Approximate Average Award is $700,000. This amount is for the first 12-month budget period, and includes both direct and indirect costs. Floor of Individual Award Range is $ 500,000. Ceiling of Individual Award Range is $1,100,000.

Funding: FY 17 $0; FY 18 est $0; FY 19 est $0; FY 16 $0; Program was funded fully by Affordable Care Act (ACA)/Preventive and Public Health Fund (PPHF) for FY2012, FY2013 and FY2014.

HQ: 4770 Buford Highway
Atlanta, GA 30341-3717
Phone: 770-488-0711
http://ephtracking.cdc.gov

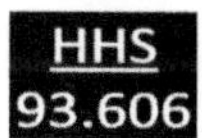

HHS 93.606 AFFORDABLE CARE ACT – PREPAREDNESS & EMERGENCY RESPONSE LEARNING CENTERS

"Preparedness and Emergency Response Learning Centers (PERLC)"

Award: Cooperative Agreements

Purpose: The program addresses legislative requirements, as stated in section 319F(d) of the Public Health Service, as part of a plan to improve the nation's public health and medical preparedness and response capabilities for emergencies, whether deliberate, accidental, or natural.

Applicant Eligibility: Eligible applicants for this project are accredited Schools of Public Health, as required by section 319F-2(d) of the Public Health Service Act. Only schools accredited by the Council on Education for Public Health are eligible.

Beneficiary Eligibility: The general public, and federal state, local, and tribal public health preparedness programs that protect the public from all-hazards will benefit from the objectives of this program.

Award Range/Average: FY 2011 Actual: $714,286 to $714,286 Avg - $714,286

Funding: N/A

HQ: OPHPR N1600 Clifton Road, P.O. Box D-29
Atlanta, GA 30029-4018
Phone: 404-639-5276
http://www.cdc.gov

HHS 93.519 AFFORDABLE CARE ACT (ACA) – CONSUMER ASSISTANCE PROGRAM GRANTS

Award: Project Grants

Purpose: To assist consumers with filing complaints and appeals, assist consumers with enrollment into health coverage, and educate consumers on their rights and responsibilities.

Applicant Eligibility: Consumer Assistance program grants are grants to States

Beneficiary Eligibility: Projects will benefit (1) Consumer Assistance Program

Award Range/Average: Available funds per applicant are based on State populations and requested funding amount. The award minimum is $200,000 unless applicant requests less than the minimum award amount.

Funding: N/A

HQ: 200 Independence Avenue SW
Washington, DC 20201
Phone: 202-260-6121
Email: michelle.feagins@hhs.gov
http://www.cms.gov/about-cms/aca/affordable-care-act-in-action-at-cms.html

AFFORDABLE CARE ACT (ACA) CHILDHOOD OBESITY RESEARCH DEMONSTRATION
"Childhood Obesity Research Demonstration"

Award: Cooperative Agreements

Purpose: To determine whether an integrated model of primary care and public health approaches in the community, such as policy, systems, and environmental supports for nutrition and physical activity, can improve underserved children's risk factors for obesity.

Applicant Eligibility: Initial applicants are identified above. FY14 is the final year of the 5 year agreement, as such only grantees already awarded under FOA DP11-1107 are currently eligible.

Beneficiary Eligibility: The general public will benefit from the objectives of this program, with a specific focus on low income children eligible for services under titles XIX and XXI of the Social Security Act; children and their families living at least 150% or higher federal poverty level; or catchment areas where 50% of students are in schools eligible for the National School Lunch Program.

Award Range/Average: Awards range was $1,750,000 for the initial 12 month period and $2,500,000 for the 16 month period - 2 awards total.

Funding: FY 17 $3,899,652; FY 18 est $0; FY 19 est $0; FY 16 $3,192,469; - The total estimated amount for the 28 month period is $8.5 Million.

HQ: Extramural Research Program Office 1600 Clifton Road
Atlanta, GA 30333
Phone: 770-488-8390
http://www.cdc.gov/obesity/strategies/healthcare/cord2.html

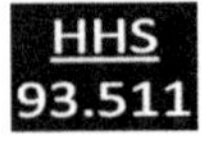

AFFORDABLE CARE ACT (ACA) GRANTS TO STATES FOR HEALTH INSURANCE PREMIUM REVIEW
"Premium Review Grants"

Award: Project Grants

Purpose: To assist States in reviewing and, if appropriate under State law, approving premium increases for health insurance coverage; providing information and certain data requirements to the HHS Secretary on premium increase patterns, and establishing and enhancing data centers that will compile and publish fee schedule information.

Applicant Eligibility: Grants to States (including the District of Columbia) and Territories for premium review. and Data Centers enhancing pricing transparency.

Beneficiary Eligibility: Same as Applicant Eligibility.

Award Range/Average: Grantees receive between $1,000,000 and $4,999,999 per grant year.

Funding: N/A

HQ: 200 Independence Avenue SW Hubert H Humphrey Building
Washington, DC 20201
Phone: 301-492-4182
Email: james.taing@cms.hhs.gov
http://www.cms.gov/cciio/index.html

HHS 93.093 AFFORDABLE CARE ACT (ACA) HEALTH PROFESSION OPPORTUNITY GRANTS "HPOG"

Award: Cooperative Agreements

Purpose: To provide education and training to Temporary Assistance for Needy Families (TANF) recipients and other low-income individuals for occupations in the healthcare field.

Applicant Eligibility: An eligible applicant is a State, an Indian tribe or tribal organization, an institution of higher education, a local workforce investment board established under section 117 of the Workforce Investment Act of 1998, a sponsor of an apprenticeship program registered under the National Apprenticeship Act or a community-based organization.

Beneficiary Eligibility: Eligible individual beneficiaries are individuals receiving assistance under the State TANF program; or other low-income individuals described by the eligible entity in its application for a grant under this section.

Award Range/Average: The range is $889,896 - $3,000,000. The average is 2,247,500.

Funding: Cooperative Agreements (Discretionary Grants) FY 17 $63,554,995; FY 18 est $71,920,000; FY 19 est $71,920,000; FY 16 $71,920,000; - (Training) FY 17 $1,135,781; FY 18 est $1,498,000; FY 19 est $1,498,000; - (Salaries and Expenses) FY 17 $923,591.

HQ: 330 C Street SW, Suite 3026
Washington, DC 20201
Phone: 816-426-2225
Email: kim.stupica-dobbs@acf.hhs.gov
http://www.acf.hhs.gov/ofa/programs/hpog

HHS 93.505 AFFORDABLE CARE ACT (ACA) MATERNAL, INFANT, AND EARLY CHILDHOOD HOME VISITING PROGRAM "MIECHV Program"

Award: Formula Grants

Purpose: To strengthen and improve the programs and activities carried out under Title V.

Applicant Eligibility: Eligibility for funding is limited to a single application from each State, the District of Columbia, Puerto Rico, Guam, the Virgin Islands, the Northern Mariana Islands, and American Samoa. The Governor has the responsibility and authority to designate which entity or group of entities will apply for and administer home visiting program funds on behalf of the State or US Territory.

Beneficiary Eligibility: Eligible families residing in communities in need of such services, as identified in a State needs assessment; Low-income eligible families; Eligible families who are pregnant women under age 21; Eligible families with a history of child abuse or neglect or have had interactions with child welfare services; Eligible families with a history of substance abuse or need substance abuse treatment; Eligible families that have users of tobacco products in the home; Eligible families that are or have children with low student achievement; Eligible families with children with developmental delays or disabilities; Eligible families who, or that include individuals serving or formerly serving in the Armed Forces, including those with members who have had multiple deployments outside the US Eligible family: A woman who is pregnant, and the father of the child if available, or o A parent or primary caregiver of the child, including grandparents or other relatives and foster parents serving as the child's primary caregiver from birth until kindergarten entry, including a noncustodial parent with an ongoing relationship with, and at times provides physical care for the child

Award Range/Average: Formula (2013): $1,000,000 – $11,234,549 Formula (2014): $1,000,000 - $11,923,154 Formula (2015) actual: $1,000,000 - $13,201,834 Competitive (2013): A Expansion – $1,428,900 - $8,949,070. B. Nonprofit - $589,685 - $5,479,908. Competitive (2014): A Expansion - $961,615 - $8,751,850 B Nonprofit - $1,000,000 - $5,801,252 Competitive (2015) actual: A Expansion - $2,344,479- $9,400,000 B Nonprofit - $1,000,000 - $6,402,965

Funding: (Formula Grants) FY 17 $37,028,190; FY 18 est $0; FY 19 est $0; FY 16 $0.

HQ: Division of Home Visiting and Early 5600 Fishers Lane, Room 18N-150
Rockville, MD 20857
Phone: 301-594-4149
Email: mbezuneh@hrsa.gov
http://mchb.hrsa.gov/programs/homevisiting

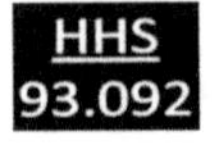

AFFORDABLE CARE ACT (ACA) PERSONAL RESPONSIBILITY EDUCATION PROGRAM "PREP"

Award: Formula Grants; Project Grants

Purpose: To educate adolescents and young adults on both abstinence and contraception for the prevention of pregnancy and sexually transmitted infections, including HIV/AIDS.

Applicant Eligibility: There is $55,250,000 appropriated annually to fund 59 States and Territories to enable them to carry out Personal Responsibility Education Programs (PREP). Eligible applicants include the 50 United States, the District of Columbia, Puerto Rico, Virgin Islands, Guam, American Samoa, Northern Mariana Islands, Federated States of Micronesia, the Republic of the Marshall Islands, and the Republic of Palau.

Beneficiary Eligibility: PREP shall provide services to adolescents and young adults. Applicants are encouraged to serve youth populations that are the most high-risk or vulnerable for pregnancies or otherwise have special circumstances, including youth in and aging of out foster care, homeless youth, youth with HIV/AIDS, victims of human trafficking, pregnant youth who are under 21 years of age, mothers who are under 21 years of age, and youth residing in areas with high birth rates for youth.

Award Range/Average: Each State or Territory shall be allotted at least $250,000 or an amount determined by a formula, using the number of individuals who have attained age 10 but not attained age 19 in the State or Territory to the total number of such individuals in the entire U.S. based on the most recent Census data, whichever is greater. Applicants for which Census data are N/A will be eligible for the minimum allocation of $250,000. The range for State PREP awards to 51 states and territories is $250,000 to $5,860,140.The range for the awards to 13 PREP Innovative Strategies grantees is $478,919 to $852,022. The range for the awards to 8 Tribal PREP grantees is $316,782 to $598,227. The range for the awards to the 21 Competitive PREP grantees is $250,000 to $794,240.

Funding: (Formula Grants) FY 17 $40,793,510; FY 18 est $43,726,481; FY 19 est $43,726,481; FY 16 $43,398,751; - Project Grants (Discretionary) FY 17 $23,200,127; FY 18 est $23,611,032; FY 19 est $23,611,032; FY 16 $25,404,896.

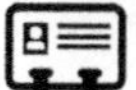

HQ: 330 C Street SW
Washington, DC 20021
Phone: 202-205-9605
Email: lebretia.white@acf.hhs.gov

AFFORDABLE CARE ACT (ACA) PRIMARY CARE RESIDENCY EXPANSION PROGRAM

"Primary Care Residency Expansion (PCRE); ACA PCRE"

Award: Project Grants

Purpose: To increase the number of physicians trained in family medicine, general internal medicine, and general pediatrics residency programs.

Applicant Eligibility: Eligible applicants include public or nonprofit private hospitals, schools of medicine or osteopathic medicine or a public or private nonprofit entity of which the Secretary has determined is capable of carrying out such grants. Applicants may request support for only one residency program (discipline).

Beneficiary Eligibility: Accredited primary care residency training programs in family medicine, general internal medicine, and general pediatrics. Project participants (residents) must be U.S. Citizens, non-citizen nationals, or foreign nationals who possess visas permitting permanent residence in the United States.

Award Range/Average: Total award amounts ranged from $960,000 to $3,840,000 per grantee during the period of funding. The average total award for the five year project period was $1,440,000.

Funding: FY 17 $0; FY 18 est $0; FY 19 est $0; FY 16 $0; - This program was fully funded with Public Health and Prevention Fund (PHPF) money – initial budget and project periods were 9/30/2010-9/29/2015.

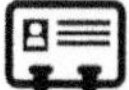

HQ: 5600 Fishers Lane, Room 15N190B
Rockville, MD 20857
Phone: 301-443-8437
Email: aanyanwu@hrsa.gov
http://www.hrsa.gov

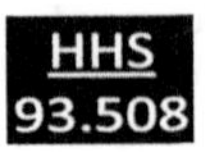

AFFORDABLE CARE ACT (ACA) TRIBAL MATERNAL, INFANT, AND EARLY CHILDHOOD HOME VISITING PROGRAM "Tribal Home Visiting (HV) Program and Tribal Research Center for Early Childhood (TRCEC)."

Award: Project Grants

Purpose: To offer assistance to eligible Tribes (or consortia of Tribes), Tribal Organizations, and Urban Indian Organizations, to strengthen and improve maternal and child health programs, improve service coordination for at-risk communities, and identify and provide comprehensive evidence-based home visiting services to families who reside in at-risk communities.

Applicant Eligibility: Only Tribes (or a consortium of Indian Tribes), Tribal Organizations, or Urban Indian Organizations, as defined by Section 4 of the Indian Health Care Improvement Act, Public Law 94-437, are eligible applicants for the Tribal HV Grant Program. For the TRCEC, only the following are eligible applicants: a) public and State controlled institutions of higher education; b) nonprofits having a 501(3)(3) status with the IRS, other than institutions of higher education; c) nonprofits without 501(c)(3) status with the IRS, other than institutions of higher education; (d) private institutions of higher education; e) for profit organizations other than small businesses; and f) small businesses.

Beneficiary Eligibility: For the Tribal HV program: Eligible families residing in at-risk American Indian/Alaskan Native communities in need of such services, as identified in a needs assessment; Low-income eligible families; Eligible families who are pregnant women under age 21; Eligible families with a history of child abuse or neglect or have had interactions with child welfare services; Eligible families with a history of substance abuse or need substance abuse treatment; Eligible families that have users of tobacco products in the home; Eligible families that are or have children with low student achievement; Eligible families with children with developmental delays or disabilities; and Eligible families who, or that include individuals serving or formerly serving in the Armed Forces, including those with members who have had multiple deployments outside the US. Eligible family: A woman who is pregnant, and the father of the child if available, or A parent or primary caregiver of the child, including grandparents or other relatives and foster parents serving as the child's primary caregiver from birth until kindergarten entry, including a noncustodial parent with an ongoing relationship with, and at times provides physical care for the child.

Award Range/Average: For the Tribal HV, the range of funding is $265,000- $775,000 per budget period. For the TRCEC, the range of funding is up to $600,000 per budget period and the average is $300,000.

Funding: (Cooperative Agreements) FY 17 $3,130,000; FY 18 est $0; FY 19 est $0.

HQ: Mary E Switzer Building 330 C Street SW, Suite 3014F
Washington, DC 20201
Phone: 202-260-8515
Email: anne.bergan@acf.hhs.gov
http://www.acf.hhs.gov/ecd/home-visiting/tribal-home-visiting

AFFORDABLE CARE ACT IMPLEMENTATION SUPPORT FOR STATE DEMONSTRATIONS TO INTEGRATE CARE FOR MEDICARE-MEDICAID ENROLLEES
"ACA Implementation Support for State Demonstrations (ISSD)"

Award: Cooperative Agreements

Purpose: The Funding Opportunity seeks to fund activities necessary to implement the demonstrations to integrate care for Medicare-Medicaid enrollees, especially those that promote beneficiary engagement and protection of beneficiary rights.

Applicant Eligibility: Funding under this opportunity is only available to states that were previously awarded a State Demonstration to Integrate Care for Dual Eligible Individuals - Design Contract in 2011 and associated state designated entities (i.e.

Beneficiary Eligibility: Under this funding opportunity, interventions shall primarily target individuals enrolled in both Medicare and Medicaid.

Award Range/Average: CMS expects to make awards ranging from $1,000,000 to $15,000,000 to each grantee to cover a two-year cooperative agreement period of performance, and CMS reserves the right to award less or more depending on the scope and nature of the individual applications received. Awardees may not receive the total award amount requested but may be asked to revise the work plan and reflect the funding that CMS will award.

Funding: Formula Grants (Cooperative Agreements) FY 17 $0; FY 18 est $0; FY 19 est $0; FY 16 $2,100,000.

HQ: 7500 Security Boulevard
Baltimore, MD 21244
Phone: 410-786-2237
Email: penny.williams@cms.hhs.gov

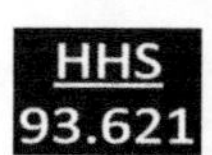

AFFORDABLE CARE ACT INITIATIVE TO REDUCE AVOIDABLE HOSPITALIZATIONS AMONG NURSING FACILITY RESIDENTS
"Nursing Facility Initiative"

Award: Project Grants

Purpose: The Centers for Medicare & Medicaid Services selected eligible organizations to test a series of evidence-based clinical interventions. Eligible organizations will partner with long-term care facilities and practitioners to implement and test a new payment model with the goal of improving the health and healthcare among LTC facility residents and ultimately reducing avoidable hospital admissions.

Applicant Eligibility: Applicants eligible to be enhanced care & coordination providers included, but were not limited to: Organizations that provide care coordination, case management, or related services; Medical care providers, such as physician practices; Health plans (although this initiative will not be capitated managed care); Public or not-for-profit organizations, such as Aging and Disability Resource Centers, Area Agencies on Aging, Behavioral Health Organizations, Centers for Independent Living, universities, or others; Integrated delivery networks, if they will extend their networks to include unaffiliated nursing facilities.

Nursing facilities, entities controlled by nursing facilities, or entities for which the primary line of business is the delivery of nursing facility/skilled nursing facility services were excluded from serving as enhanced care & coordination providers under this cooperative agreement.

Beneficiary Eligibility: The primary target population for the clinical interventions is fee-for-service Medicare-Medicaid enrollees in nursing facilities, but fee-for-service long-stay residents who are not yet Medicare-Medicaid enrollees will also benefit.

Award Range/Average: The seven (6) organizations which received funding are: Alabama Quality Assurance Foundation – Alabama, HealthInsight of Nevada – Nevada, Indiana University – Indiana, The Curators of the University of Missouri – Missouri, The Greater New York Hospital Foundation, Inc. – New York City, and UPMC Community Provider Services - Pennsylvania. The awards ranged from: $5 million to $25 million to cover a four-year period of performance.

Funding: (Cooperative Agreements) FY 17 $28,152,584; FY 18 est $28,367,101; FY 19 est $0; FY 16 $5,799,630.

HQ: 7500 Security Boulevard
Baltimore, MD 21214
Phone: 410-786-8786
Email: nicole.perry@cms.hhs.gov
http://www.cms.gov/medicare-medicaid-coordination/medicare-and-medicaid-coordination/medicare-medicaid-coordination-office/initiativetoreduceavoidablehospitalizations/avoidablehospitalizationsamongnursingfacilityresidents.html

HHS 93.537 AFFORDABLE CARE ACT MEDICAID EMERGENCY PSYCHIATRIC DEMONSTRATION

Award: Direct Payments for Specified Use

Purpose: To establish a demonstration project under which an eligible State (as described in subsection (c)) shall provide payment under the State Medicaid plan under title XIX of the Social Security Act to an institution for mental diseases (IMDs).

Applicant Eligibility: State Medicaid Agencies

Beneficiary Eligibility: Medicaid eligible (who are retroactively enrolled) and enrolled Medicaid beneficiaries who are the ages of 21 through 64, and who are in need of medical assistance to stabilize a psychiatric emergency medical condition.

Award Range/Average: Funds shall be allocated to eligible States on the basis of criteria, including a State's application and the availability of funds, as determined by the Secretary

Funding: FY 17 $0; FY 18 est $0; FY 19 est $0; FY 16 $486,637.

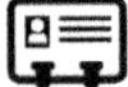

HQ: 7500 Security Boulevard
Baltimore, MD 21244
Phone: 410-786-4631
Email: debra.gillespie@cms.hhs.gov
http://innovation.cms.gov/initiatives/medicaid-emergency-psychiatric-demo

AFFORDABLE CARE ACT STATE HEALTH INSURANCE ASSISTANCE PROGRAM (SHIP) & AGING & DISABILITY RESOURCE CENTER (ADRC) OPTIONS COUNSELING FOR MEDICARE-MEDICAID INDIVIDUALS IN STATES WITH APPROVED FINANCIAL ALIGNMENT MODELS "SHIP and ADRC Options Counseling for Medicare-Medicaid Individuals in States with Approved Financial Alignment Models"

Award: Project Grants

Purpose: Provides funding over a three year period to states that have signed a Memorandum of Understanding with CMS to implement a CMS-approved State Financial Alignment Initiative.

Applicant Eligibility: Eligible applicants from the CMS-approved Financial Alignment States include any one of the State agencies that administers the ADRC and/or SHIP programs(s) within the State (e.g.

Beneficiary Eligibility: State Medicaid Agencies and the Medicaid Agencies in the Federal Territories – This cooperative agreement only serves beneficiaries that are dually eligible for Medicare and Medicaid coverage.

Award Range/Average: The total estimated amount of Federal funds available is $5,000,000. Individual awards will range from $250,000 to $1,000,000. States with a signed Memorandum of Understanding (MOU) that receive awards under this funding opportunity will, per that MOU, be required to support options counseling. Following the initial deadline, based on available funding, applications will be accepted for review and approval throughout fiscal year 2013 according to the due dates outlined in the funding opportunity announcement.

Funding: N/A

HQ: 200 Independence Avenue SW, Room 733H-02
Washington, DC 20201
Phone: 301-492-4319
Email: christopher.clark@cms.hhs.gov

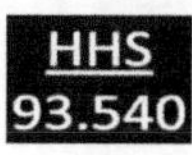

AFFORDABLE CARE ACT STREAMLINED SURVEILLANCE FOR VENTILATOR-ASSOCIATED PNEUMONIA: REDUCING BURDEN & DEMONSTRATING PREVENTABILITY; & PREVENTION & PUBLIC HEALTH FUND

Award: Cooperative Agreements

Purpose: To facilitate a study to demonstrate the utility and relevance of sVAP and promote acceptance of sVAP within the critical care community.

Applicant Eligibility: Eligible applicants include recipients funded under the CDC Prevention Epicenters Program (CI11-001): a. Chicago Prevention Epicenter b.

Beneficiary Eligibility: State and local health departments, U.S. Territories, and the general public.

Award Range/Average: Approximately $1,544,309 in FY 2011 was awarded fund 1 application. The award period was 24 months. An applicant may request a project period up to 24 months for a total of $1,544,309 including direct and indirect costs.

Funding: FY 17 $0; FY 18 est $0; FY 19 est $0; FY 16 $0; - Program added $30,000 (non-ACA funds) in FY 12 to reinstate a research aim from the initial proposal. The project period is the same and the total funding provided for this project was $1,574,309. This project is complete and no additional funding will be provided.

HQ: 1600 Clifton Road, P.O. Box A16
Atlanta, GA 30329
Phone: 404-639-7093

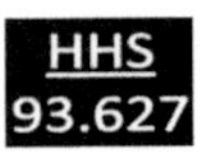

AFFORDABLE CARE ACT: TESTING EXPERIENCE & FUNCTIONAL ASSESSMENT TOOLS "TEFT"

Award: Project Grants

Purpose: Supports State Medicaid agencies in testing, collecting, and reporting the Initial Core Set of healthcare Quality Measures for Adults Enrolled in Medicaid to CMS. Additionally, the grant funding will also support States' efforts to use these data for improving the quality of care for adults covered by Medicaid.

Applicant Eligibility: Grant applicants are limited to the 51 State Medicaid Agencies and the Medicaid Agencies in the US Territories.

Beneficiary Eligibility: N/A

Award Range/Average: Grant awards up to $1 million for each 12-month budget period, with an estimated total of up to $2 million per Grantee over the two-year project period.

Funding: (Salaries and Expenses) FY 17 $9,534,339; FY 18 est $0; FY 19 est $0; FY 16 $827,670.

HQ: 200 Independence Avenue SW, Room 733H-02
Washington, DC 21201
Phone: 301-492-4312
Email: michelle.feagins@cms.hhs.gov
http://www.medicaid.gov/medicaid/ltss/teft-program/index.html

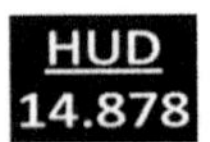

AFFORDABLE HOUSING DEVELOPMENT IN MAIN STREET REJUVENATION PROJECTS "Main Street"

Award: Project Grants

Purpose: To redevelop main street areas, preserve historic or traditional architecture in main street areas, enhance economic development efforts in main street areas, and to provide affordable housing in main street areas.

Applicant Eligibility: Eligible applicants include, and are limited to, Units of Local Government ("Local Government") that are subdivisions of State governments, and other governments listed in Section 102 of the Housing and Community Development Act of 1974. The jurisdiction of the Local Government must contain a population of no more than 50,000.

Beneficiary Eligibility: The beneficiaries are low-income families that occupy the newly developed affordable housing, and the local community that is benefiting from the Main Street rejuvenation project.

Award Range/Average: The grant amount was $500,000

Funding: FY 17 est $0; FY 16 est $0; FY 15 $0.

HQ: 451 7th Street SW, Room 4130
Washington, DC 20410
Phone: 202-401-8812
Email: lawrence.gnessin@hud.gov
http://www.hud.gov/mainstreet

HHS 93.866 AGING RESEARCH "Aging"

Award: Project Grants

Purpose: To encourage biomedical, social, and behavioral research and research training directed toward greater understanding of the aging process and the diseases, special problems, and needs of people as they age. The National Institute on Aging has established programs to pursue these goals.

Applicant Eligibility: Grants: Universities, colleges, medical, dental and nursing schools, schools of public health, laboratories, hospitals, State and local health departments, other public or private institutions (both for-profit and nonprofit), and individuals. National Research Service Award: Individual NRSAs may be made for postdoctoral training to applicants who hold a professional or scientific degree (M.

Beneficiary Eligibility: Any nonprofit or for-profit organization, company, or institution engaged in biomedical research. Students pursuing doctoral research training.

Award Range/Average: Awards vary in range depending on the particular activity codes. Individual fellowships range from $23,376 to $57,504 and average about $46,000. Research grants have much larger ranges - from $75,000 to several million dollars. Average costs of research grants are around $400,000. All costs are shown on a single year basis. Awards may be for up to five years.

Funding: FY 17 $1,995,000,000; FY 18 est $2,253,600,000; FY 19 est $1,995,000,000; FY 16 $1,596,005,000; - Amounts shown are actual/estimated amounts available for research grants including SBIR/STTR, centers, research career awards, research project grants, and cooperative agreements. (Project Grants (Capacity Building and Complaint Processing, Training) FY 17 $65,575,000; FY 18 est $76,000,000; FY 19 est $60,000,000.

HQ: National Institute on Aging 7201 Wisconsin Avenue, Room 2C218
Bethesda, MD 20892
Phone: 301-402-7715
http://www.nia.nih.gov

USDA 10.291 AGRICULTURAL & FOOD POLICY RESEARCH CENTERS

Award: Cooperative Agreements

Purpose: To conduct research on public policies and trade agreements such as farm and agricultural sectors, environment, rural economies, food and nutrition.

Applicant Eligibility: Applicants must have substantial experience in the field of research for which they are applying, including a history of providing (1) unbiased, nonpartisan economic analysis to Congress on the farm and agricultural sectors (including commodities, livestock, dairy, and specialty crops), the environment, rural families, households, and economies, and consumers, food, and nutrition; or (2) objective, scientific information to Federal agencies and the public to support and enhance efficient, accurate implementation of Federal drought preparedness and drought response programs, including inter agency thresholds used to determine eligibility for mitigation or emergency assistance.

Beneficiary Eligibility: Funds are awarded directly to the ultimate beneficiary. This is not a pass-through program.

Award Range/Average: 2016 range: $3,800,000 - $3,800,000 2016 average: $3,800,000 2017 range: $3,800,000 - $3,800,000 2017 average: $3,800,000 2018 range: $3,800,000 - $3,800,000 2018 average: $3,800,000

Funding: FY 17 $3,800,000; FY 18 est $3,800,000; FY 19 est $0; FY 16 $3,800,000.

HQ: 1400 Independence Avenue SW, Room 4434-S
Washington, DC 20250-3812
Phone: 202-690-2477
Email: hcolby@oce.usda.gov
http://www.usda.gov/oce

AGRICULTURAL & RURAL ECONOMIC RESEARCH, COOPERATIVE AGREEMENTS & COLLABORATIONS

Award: Cooperative Agreements; Project Grants; Dissemination of Technical Information

Purpose: ERS provides help for development, administration, and evaluation of agricultural and rural policies.

Applicant Eligibility: Any individual or organization in the U.S. and U.S. Territories is eligible to receive the popular or technical research publications that convey the research results, although there may be a fee.

Beneficiary Eligibility: See Applicant Eligibility.

Award Range/Average: N/A

Funding: (Project Grants) FY 17 $200,000; FY 18 est $400,000; FY 19 est $0; FY 16 $874,710; - (Cooperative Agreements) FY 17 $1,500,000; FY 18 est $1,500,000; FY 19 est $0; FY 16 $1,415,313.

HQ:
Washington, DC 20024-3231
Phone: 202-694-5008
http://www.ers.usda.gov

AGRICULTURAL MARKET & ECONOMIC RESEARCH

Award: Cooperative Agreements

Purpose: To conduct research on public policies and trade agreements such as farm and agricultural sectors, environment, rural economies, food and nutrition.

Applicant Eligibility: Applicants must have substantial experience in the field of research for which they are applying.

Beneficiary Eligibility: Funds are awarded directly to the ultimate beneficiary. This is not a pass-through program.

Award Range/Average: For FY 17, the range of Financial Assistance was $15,000 to $365,000, with an average award of $124,713.

Funding: FY 17 $1,572,000; FY 18 est $2,776,000; FY 19 est $400,000; FY 16 $1,476,093.

HQ: 1400 Independence Avenue SW, Room 4434-S
Washington, DC 20250-3812
Phone: 202-690-2477
Email: hcolby@oce.usda.gov
http://www.usda.gov/oce

AGRICULTURAL TRADE PROMOTION PROGRAM "ATP"

Award: Formula grants.

Purpose: The Agricultural Trade Promotion Program assists the U.S. agricultural industries to promote U.S. agricultural commodities in foreign markets.

Applicant Eligibility: To be approved, applicants must be: (1) A nonprofit U.S. agricultural trade organization; (2) a nonprofit state regional trade group; (3) a U.S. agricultural cooperative; or (4) a state agency.

Beneficiary Eligibility: CCC will enter into ATP agreements only where the eligible agricultural commodity is comprised of at least 50 percent U.S. origin content by weight, exclusive of added water.

Award Range/Average: From $22,000 to $9,611,000; $1,375,000.

Funding: Formula Grants (Cooperative Agreements) FY 17 FY 18 FY 19 est $200,000,000.

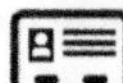

HQ: 1400 Independence Avenue SW
Washington, DC 20250
Phone: 202-720-4327
Email: curt.alt@fas.usda.gov
http://www.fsa.usda.gov

AGRICULTURE & FOOD RESEARCH INITIATIVE (AFRI) "AFRI"

Award: Project Grants

Purpose: To provide standard funds for research and education.

Applicant Eligibility: This initiative supports integrated and non-integrated programs. Please refer to Part III, A of the current Agriculture and Food Research Initiative (AFRI) Request for Applications for the complete eligibility requirements.

Beneficiary Eligibility: This initiative supports integrated and non-integrated programs. Please refer to Part III, A of the current Agriculture and Food Research Initiative (AFRI) Request for Applications (RFA) for the complete eligibility requirements.

Award Range/Average: If minimum or maximum amounts of funding per competitive and/or capacity project grant, or cooperative agreement are established, these amounts will be announced in the annual Competitive Request for Application (RFA).

Funding: FY 17 $342,971,061; FY 18 est $363,145,135; FY 19 est $319,205,682; FY 16 $320,740,856;

HQ: Institute of Bioenergy Climate and Environment 1400 Independence Avenue SW, P.O. Box 2210 Washington, DC 20250-2240

Phone: 202-401-4926

Email: ncavallaro@nifa.usda.gov

http://nifa.usda.gov/grants

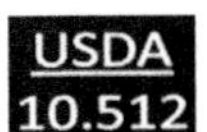

AGRICULTURE EXTENSION AT 1890 LAND-GRANT INSTITUTIONS "1890 LGIs – Section 1444 Extension"

Award: Formula Grants

Purpose: To support forest and agricultural extension activities.

Applicant Eligibility: Applications may only be submitted by 1890 Land-Grant Universities that conduct agricultural extension activities in accordance with NARETPA section 1444(a)(1): Alabama A&M University; Tuskegee University; University of Arkansas - Pine Bluff; Delaware State University; Florida A&M University; Fort Valley State University; Kentucky State University; Southern University; University of Maryland – Eastern Shore; Alcorn State University; Lincoln University; North Carolina A & T State University; Central State University, Langston University; South Carolina State University; Tennessee State University; Prairie View A&M University; Virginia State University; and West Virginia State University.

Beneficiary Eligibility: Same as Applicant Eligibility.

Award Range/Average: If minimum or maximum amounts of funding per competitive and/or capacity project grant, or cooperative agreement are established, these amounts will be announced in the annual Capacity Request for Application (RFA).

Funding: (Formula Grants) FY 17 $0; FY 18 est $0; FY 19 est $45,533,000; FY 16 $0; Previously included in CFDA # 10.500, for the Cooperative Extension Service (CES). This represents a newly created CFDA number, which was part of an initiative to break out the separate programs contained in CFDA # 10.500 (CES).

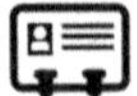

HQ: National Program Leader Institute of Youth Family and Community Division of Community and Education 1400 Independence Avenue SW, P.O. Box 2250

Washington, DC 20250-2250

Phone: 202-720-5305

Email: wesley.dean@nifa.usda.gov

http://nifa.usda.gov/program/1890-land-grant-institutions-programs

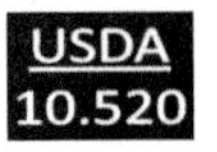

AGRICULTURE RISK MANAGEMENT EDUCATION PARTNERSHIPS COMPETITIVE GRANTS PROGRAM "ARME"

Award: Project Grants

Purpose: This grants program provides education for agricultural producers on risk management activities such as agricultural trade options, crop insurance, cash forward contracting, debt reduction, etc. Further, NIFA also provides risk management strategies for farmers and ranchers on various purposes and disciplines.

Applicant Eligibility: Qualified public and private entities (including land grant colleges, cooperative extension services, and colleges or universities) may use funds for the purpose of educating agricultural producers about the full range of risk management activities, including futures, options, agricultural trade options, crop insurance, cash forward contracting, debt reduction, production diversification, farm resources risk reduction, and other risk management strategies.

Beneficiary Eligibility: Applications may be submitted by qualified public and private entities. This includes all colleges and universities, Federal, State, and local agencies, nonprofit and for-profit private organizations or corporations, and other entities.

Award Range/Average: If minimum or maximum amounts of funding per competitive and/or capacity project grant, or cooperative agreement are established, these amounts will be announced in the annual Competitive Request for Application (RFA).

Funding: Project Grants (Discretionary) FY 17 $0; FY 18 est $0; FY 19 est $4,800,000; FY 16 $0. Previously included in CFDA # 10.500, for the Cooperative Extension Service (CES). This represents a newly created CFDA number, which was part of an initiative to break out the separate programs contained in CFDA # 10.500 (CES).

HQ: 1400 Independence Avenue SW, Room 4434
Washington, DC 20250
Phone: 202-690-3468
Email: toija.riggins@nifa.usda.gov
http://nifa.usda.gov/funding-opportunity/agriculture-risk-management-education-partnerships-arme-competitive-grants

USDA 10.616 AGRICULTURE WOOL APPAREL MANUFACTURERS TRUST FUND

"Agriculture Wool Apparel Manufacturers Trust Fund"

Award: Direct Payments with Unrestricted Use

Purpose: The Agriculture Wool Apparel Manufacturers Trust compensates for accidents to the domestic manufacturers resulting from tariffs on wool fabric.

Applicant Eligibility: Payments to reduce the injury to domestic manufacturers resulting from tariffs on wool fabric that are higher than tariffs on certain apparel articles made of wool fabric.

Beneficiary Eligibility: Beneficiaries limited to: each eligible manufacturer under paragraph (3) of section 4002(c) of the Wool Suit and Textile Trade Extension Act of 2004 (Public Law 108–429; 118 Stat. 2600), as amended by section 1633(c) of the Miscellaneous Trade and Technical Corrections Act of 2006 (Public Law 109–280; 120 Stat.

Award Range/Average: Benefits Range from approximately $14,000 to $5 million.

Funding: FY 17 $30,000,000; FY 18 est $30,000,000; FY 19 est $30,000,000; FY 16 $30,000,000.

HQ: 1400 Independence Avenue SW
Washington, DC 20250
Phone: 202-720-3538
http://www.fas.usda.gov

DOI 15.421 ALASKA COASTAL MARINE INSTITUTE "ALASKA CMI"

Award: Cooperative Agreements

Purpose: The Bureau of Ocean Energy Management oversees the exploration and development of oil, natural gas and other minerals and renewable energy alternatives on the Nations outer continental shelf. The purpose of the Alaska Coastal Marine Institute is to use highly qualified scientific expertise at local levels to collect and disseminate environmental information needed for OCS oil and gas and marine minerals decisions; address local and regional OCS-related environmental and resource issues of mutual interest; and strengthen the BOEM-State partnership in addressing OCS oil and gas and marine minerals information needs.

Applicant Eligibility: University of Alaska may make application for support by a named principal investigator. Non-UA scientists may participate in collaboration with a UA principal investigator.

Beneficiary Eligibility: Research scientists, Federal, State and local decision-makers, Native American Organizations, and the general public will ultimately benefit from the program.

Award Range/Average: Range is $12,000 to $360,000; Average $170,000.

Funding: FY 17 $684,800; FY 18 N/A FY 19 N/A FY 16 $1,059,000.

HQ: 381 Elden Street HM 3115
Herndon, VA 20170
Phone: 703-787-1087
Email: rodney.cluck@boem.gov
http://www.boem.gov

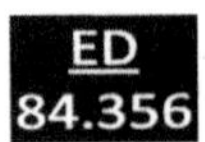

ALASKA NATIVE EDUCATIONAL PROGRAMS

Award: Project Grants

Purpose: To support projects that recognize and address the unique educational needs of Alaska Native students.

Applicant Eligibility: Alaska Native organizations with experience operating Alaska Native education programs; Alaska Native organizations that do not have experience operating Alaska Native education programs, but that apply in partnership with: a State educational agency (SEA) or an Alaska Native organization that operates an Alaska Native education program; or an entity located in Alaska and predominantly governed by Alaska Natives that has experience operating Alaska Native programs and is granted an official charter or sanction from at least one Alaska Native tribe or Alaska Native organization to carry out such programs.

Beneficiary Eligibility: Alaska Natives as defined in the Alaska Native Claims Settlement Act.

Award Range/Average: Range of new awards: $200,000- $1,000,000; Average new award: $550,000

Funding: FY 17 $32,453,000; FY 18 est $35,453,000; FY 19 est $0; FY 16 $32,453,000.

HQ: Department of Education OESE School Improvement Programs 400 Maryland Avenue SW
Washington, DC 20202
Phone: 202-260-1979
Email: almita.reed@ed.gov
http://www.ed.gov/programs/alaskanative/index.html

DOI 15.442

ALASKA NATIVE SCIENCE & ENGINEERING "ANSEP"

Award: Cooperative Agreements

Purpose: Alaska Native Science and Engineering Program (ANSEP) provides an opportunity to further engage Alaska's Native professionals, and develop the future scientific and engineering employment pool required to support the BSEE mission. The overall objective is to expand the professional science employment preparedness of ANSEP students and to develop a more diversified pool of highly educated professionals with the BSEE workforce to reflect the rich diversity of the Nation.

Applicant Eligibility: N/A

Beneficiary Eligibility: Research scientists, Federal, State and local decision-makers, the youth participants, BSEE, and the general public will ultimately benefit from the program.

Award Range/Average: Range is $50,000 to $250,000; Average $300,000

Funding: FY 17 $50,000; FY 18 est $50,000; FY 19 N/A FY 16 $50,000.

HQ: 45600 Woodlawn Road HE 2126
Sterling, VA 20166
Phone: 703-787-1630
Email: eric.turner@bsee.gov
http://www.bsee.gov

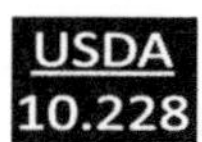

ALASKA NATIVE SERVING & NATIVE HAWAIIAN SERVING INSTITUTIONS EDUCATION GRANTS "ANNH Grants Program"

Award: Project Grants

Purpose: To promote education, research, agricultural sciences, and community development.

Applicant Eligibility: Individual public or private, non-profit Alaska Native-Serving and Native Hawaiian-Serving Institutions of higher education that meet the definitions of Alaska Native-Serving Institution or Native Hawaiian Serving Institution established in Title III, Part A of the Higher Education Act of 1965, as amended (20 U.S.C. 1059d.) are eligible institutions under this program.

Beneficiary Eligibility: Alaska Native Serving Institutions and Native Hawaiian Serving Institutions.

Award Range/Average: If minimum or maximum amounts of funding per competitive and/or capacity project grant, or cooperative agreement are established, these amounts will be announced in the annual Competitive Request for Application (RFA). The most current RFA is available via: https://nifa.usda.gov/funding-opportunity/alaska-native-serving-and-native-hawaiian-serving-institutions-education

Funding: FY 17 $3,065,340; FY 18 est $3,065,340; FY 19 est $3,058,455; FY 16 $3,065,565.

HQ: National Program Leader Institute of Youth Family and Community Division of Community and Education 1400 Independence Avenue SW, P.O. Box 2250
Washington, DC 20250-2250
Phone: 202-720-2324
Email: joyce.parker@nifa.usda.gov
http://nifa.usda.gov/program/alaska-native-serving-and-native-hawaiian-serving-institutions-education-competitive-grants

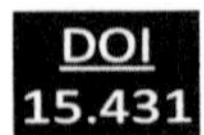

ALASKA SETTLEMENT AGREEMENT

Award: Direct Payments with Unrestricted Use

Purpose: Shares 100 percent with the State of Alaska to be paid monthly subject to late disbursement interest for contracts, leases, permits, rights-of-way, or easements under Section 6(h) of the Alaska Statehood Act.

Applicant Eligibility: Revenue from effected leases will trigger automatic payment distribution computed in accordance with the law.

Beneficiary Eligibility: Limited to Leases A-028056, A-028063, A-028135, A-028143, A-028103, A-028140, A-19230, A028055, and A-028047.

Award Range/Average: N/A

Funding: FY 19 est $31,000; FY 18 est $28,000; FY 17 $23,000.

HQ: Office of Natural Resources Revenue 1849 C Street NW, P.O. Box 4211
Washington, DC 20240
Phone: 202-513-0600
http://www.onrr.gov

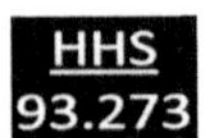

ALCOHOL RESEARCH PROGRAMS

Award: Project Grants

Purpose: To develop a sound fundamental knowledge base which can be applied to the development of improved methods of treatment and more effective strategies for preventing alcoholism and alcohol-related problems.

Applicant Eligibility: Public or private profit and nonprofit agencies, including State, local, or regional government agencies, universities, colleges, hospitals, academic or research institutions may apply for research grants. SBIR grants can be awarded only to domestic small businesses (entities that are independently owned and operated for profit, are not dominant in the field in which research is proposed, and have no more than 500 employees).

Beneficiary Eligibility: Public, profit and nonprofit private organizations.

Award Range/Average: No Data Available.

Funding: FY 17 $358,311,000; FY 18 est $384,657,000; FY 19 est $345,537,000; - Values reported include funds reported for PROJECT GRANTS including Project Grants and Fellowships. Values for Fellowship had been reported separately under Obligation#2 before, which has now been deleted.

HQ: National Institute on Alcohol Abuse and Alcoholism 5635 Fishers Lane, Room 2085
Rockville, MD 20852
Phone: 301-451-2067
Email: srinivar@mail.nih.gov
http://www.nih.gov

USDA 10.330

ALFALFA & FORAGE RESEARCH PROGRAM "AFRP"

Award: Project Grants

Purpose: To protect crops, reduce pest, improve seed production, and increase harvest production.

Applicant Eligibility: (1) State agricultural experiment stations; (2) colleges and universities; (3) university research foundations; (4) other research institutions and organizations; (5) Federal agencies, (6) national laboratories; (7) private organizations or corporations; (8) individuals who are U.S. citizens or permanent residents; and (9) any group consisting of 2 or more entities identified in (1) through (8).

Beneficiary Eligibility: Same as Applicant Eligibility.

Award Range/Average: If minimum or maximum amounts of funding per competitive and/or capacity project grant, or cooperative agreement are established, these amounts will be announced in the annual Competitive Request for Application (RFA).

Funding: FY 17 $2,083,825; FY 18 est $2,084,967; FY 19 est $0; FY 16 $1,853,634.

HQ: Institute of Food Production and Sustainability (IFPS) Division of Plant Systems - Production
1400 Independence Avenue SW, P.O. Box 2250
Washington, DC 20250-2250
Phone: 202-401-5024
Email: parag.chitnis@nifa.usda.gov
http://nifa.usda.gov/program/agronomic-forage-crops-program

ALLERGY & INFECTIOUS DISEASES RESEARCH "Allergy and Infectious Diseases Research"

Award: Project Grants

Purpose: To assist public and private nonprofit institutions and individuals to establish, expand and improve biomedical research and research training in infectious diseases and related areas; to conduct developmental research, to produce and test research materials.

Applicant Eligibility: Universities, colleges, hospitals, laboratories, and other public or private nonprofit domestic institutions, including State and local units of government, and individuals are eligible to make application for grant support of research by a named principal investigator or a research career development candidate. For-profit organizations are also eligible, with the exception of NRSA.

Beneficiary Eligibility: Any nonprofit or for-profit organization, company, or institution engaged in biomedical research.

Award Range/Average: from $2,500 to $6,395,901 and the average $426,165.

Funding: FY 17 $3,066,918,000; FY 18 est $3,307,663,000; FY 19 est $2,993,435,000; FY 16 $2,959,397,000.

HQ: 5601 Fishers Lane, Suite 5E39
Rockville, MD 20852
Phone: 301-761-7870
Email: kevin.richardson@nih.gov
http://www.niaid.nih.gov

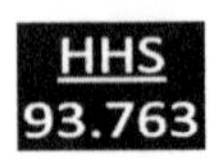

ALZHEIMER'S DISEASE INITIATIVE: SPECIALIZED SUPPORTIVE SERVICES PROJECT (ADI-SSS) THRU PREVENTION & PUBLIC HEALTH FUNDS (PPHF) "Alzheimer's Initiative"

Award: Project Grants

Purpose: Purpose of Alzheimer's Disease Initiative: Specialized Supportive Services project is to fill gaps in long term services and supports for persons living with Alzheimer's disease and related dementias and their caregivers by expanding the availability of specialized services and supports.

Applicant Eligibility: Funding eligibility is limited to public and/or private entities that are able to 1) demonstrate the existence of a dementia capable system dedicated to the population that they serve, and 2) articulate opportunities and additional services that would enhance and strengthen the existing system. Organizations that have not received previous awards through this program, individuals, foreign entities and sole proprietorship organizations are not eligible to compete for, or receive awards under this announcement.

Beneficiary Eligibility: Public and/or private entities that are able to 1) demonstrate the existence of a dementia capable system dedicated to the population that they serve, and 2) articulate opportunities and additional services that would enhance and strengthen the existing system. Eligible consumers of eligible applicants are the beneficiaries of this program.

Award Range/Average: As many as 10 grants forward funded for a period of 36 months with an award ceiling of $1,000,000 and a floor of $800,000.

Funding: FY 17 $10,500,000; FY 18 est $10,500,000; FY 19 FY 16 $10,500,000.

HQ: US Department of Health and Human Services 330 C Street SW
Washington, DC 20201
Phone: 202-795-7389
Email: erin.long@acl.hhs.gov
http://www.acl.gov

ALZHEIMER'S DISEASE PROGRAM INITIATIVE (ADPI) "Alzheimer's Disease Program Initiative (ADPI)"

Award: Cooperative Agreements

Purpose: To work at state and community levels to develop and expand the availability of dementia-capable supports and services for persons with Alzheimer's disease and related dementias (ADRD), their families, and their caregivers.

Applicant Eligibility: Funding eligibility is limited to public and/or private entities that are able to 1) demonstrate the existence of and their operation within a dementia-capable home and community-based system dedicated to the population that they serve, and 2) articulate opportunities and additional services that would enhance and strengthen the existing system. Community program applicants are not eligible to apply for or receive more than one grant through the ADPI program.

Beneficiary Eligibility: Eligible consumers of eligible applicants are the beneficiaries of this program, including (1) Individuals with Alzheimer's disease and related disorders; (2) families of those individuals; and (3) care providers of those individuals.

Award Range/Average: As many as 20 grants forward funded for a period of 36 months with an award ceiling of $1,200,000 and a floor of $800,000.

Funding: Cooperative Agreements (Discretionary Grants) FY 17 N/A FY 18 est $23,500,000; FY 19 est $19,490,000.

HQ: 330 C Street SW
Washington, DC 20201
Phone: 202-795-7389
Email: erin.long@acl.hhs.gov
http://www.acl.gov

ALZHEIMER'S DISEASE DEMONSTRATION GRANTS TO STATES

"Alzheimer's Disease Supportive Services Program"

Award: Cooperative Agreements

Purpose: To expand the availability of diagnostic and support services for persons with Alzheimer's Disease and Related Dementias (ADRD), their families, and their caregivers.

Applicant Eligibility: State government agencies are eligible for grant awards; the applicant agency is encouraged to have the support and active involvement of the Single State Agency on Aging. Only one application per State will be funded, however, multiple state and local agencies are encouraged to collaborate in planning and carrying out the project.

Beneficiary Eligibility: (1) Individuals with Alzheimer's disease and related disorders; (2) families of those individuals; and (3) care providers of those individuals.

Award Range/Average: 5 grants were awarded for a total of $2,294,892 in FY 15. The average was $458,978 per award.

Funding: FY 17 $4,800,000; FY 18 est $4,799,998; FY 19 FY 16 $4,800,000.

HQ: 330 C Street SW
Washington, DC 20201
Phone: 202-795-7389
Email: erin.long@acl.hhs.gov
http://www.acl.gov

AMERICAN OVERSEAS RESEARCH CENTERS

Award: Project Grants

Purpose: To enable American overseas research centers to promote postgraduate research, exchanges, and area studies.

Applicant Eligibility: The Secretary shall only award grants to centers that: (1) receive more than 50 percent of their funding from public or private United States sources; (2) have a permanent presence in the country in which the center is located; and (3) are organizations described in Section 501(c)(3) of the Internal Revenue Code of 1986 which are exempt from taxation under Section 501(a) of the Code.

Beneficiary Eligibility: Consortia of institutions of higher education that (1) receive more than 50 percent of their funding from public or private United States sources; (2) have a permanent presence in the country in which the center is located; and (3) are organizations described in Section 501(c)(3) of the Internal Revenue Code of 1986 which are exempt from taxation under Section 501(a) of the Code will benefit.

Award Range/Average: No Data Available.

Funding: FY 17 $540,000; FY 18 est $650,000; FY 19 est $0; FY 16 $756,732.

HQ: International and Foreign Language Education Department of Education 400 Maryland Avenue SW

Washington, DC 20202

Phone: 202-453-5690

Email: cheryl.gibbs@ed.gov

http://www.ed.gov/programs/iegpsaorc

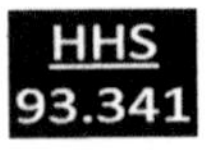

ANALYSES, RESEARCH & STUDIES TO ADDRESS THE IMPACT OF CMS' PROGRAMS ON AMERICAN INDIAN/ALASKA NATIVE (AI/AN) BENEFICIARIES & THE HEALTH CARE SYSTEM SERVING THESE BENEFICIARIES

Award: Cooperative Agreements

Purpose: To providing high quality healthcare to the American Indian/Alaska Native (AI/AN) community by providing research and analysis to increase the understanding of, access to, and impact of CMS' programs in Indian Country.

Applicant Eligibility: Eligibility is limited to the National Indian Health Board, and this single source award was approved by the Chief Grants Management Officer. NIHB meets the definition of "tribal organization "under the Indian Health Care Improvement Act (IHCIA) 25 USC Section 1603(26), with significant historical experience in providing outreach and education and the provision of health care information for Indian Tribes and Tribal Organizations.

Beneficiary Eligibility: The primary beneficiaries of this effort are American Indians and Alaska Natives who are eligible for CMS' programs to get them educated about and enrolled in CMS' programs, as appropriate, ensure that Indian health care providers can participate and are enrolled in CMS programs, and to reduce health disparities in tribal communities. By enrolling in CMS' programs, AI/ANs benefit by having greater access to services that may not be provided by their local Indian health care providers, and tribal communities benefit through increased resources to their Indian health care programs.

Award Range/Average: FY 2014 - $635,000 FY 2015 - $635,000 FY 2016 - $860,000 Approximate average award -- $800,000.

Funding: Cooperative Agreements (Discretionary Grants) FY 17 $800,000; FY 18 est $800,000; FY 19 est $800,000; FY 15 $885,000; FY 16 $860,000.

HQ: 7501 Security Boulevard, P.O. Box B3-30-03

Baltimore, MD 21244

Phone: 410-786-9954

Email: linda.gmeiner@cms.hhs.gov

http://www.nihb.org

USDA 10.207 ANIMAL HEALTH & DISEASE RESEARCH "AHDR"

Award: Formula Grants

Purpose: To provide funds for safeguard of domestic animal health and prevention of diseases.

Applicant Eligibility: Eligibility is restricted to the following public nonprofit institutions having demonstrable capacity in animal disease research: (1) Schools and Colleges of Veterinary Medicine; and (2) State Agricultural Experiment Stations. Funds are appropriated by Congress for distribution to States and eligible State institutions according to the statutory formula stated in the Act.

Beneficiary Eligibility: Same as Applicant Eligibility.

Award Range/Average: If minimum or maximum amounts of funding per Capacity, Competitive, and/or Non-Competitive project grant, or cooperative agreement are established, these amounts will be announced in the annual Capacity, Competitive, and/or Non-Competitive Request for Application (RFA). The most current RFA is available via: https://nifa.usda.gov/program/animal-health-and-disease-research-program

Funding: Formula Grants (Apportionments) FY 17 $3,696,260; FY 18 est $2,717,120; FY 19 est $0; FY 16 $3,706,320. NOTE: For FY 2019, a Budget was not requested to fund this program.

HQ: Institute of Food Production and Sustainability Division of Animal System 1400 Independence Avenue SW, P.O. Box 2240

Washington, DC 20250-2240

Phone: 202-401-4952

Email: dabrams@nifa.usda.gov

http://nifa.usda.gov/program/animal-health-research-and-disease-program

ANTI-DOPING ACTIVITIES

Award: Project Grants

Purpose: The program provides support to anti-doping efforts of the Office of National Drug Control Policy to educate athletes on the dangers and thereby eliminate the use of drugs in athletic competitions. It also provides support for legal efforts to adjudicate athletes appeals involving doping.

Applicant Eligibility: Anti-doping activities

Beneficiary Eligibility: Same as Applicant Eligibility.

Award Range/Average: No Data Available.

Funding: FY 17 $9,500,000; FY 18 est $9,500,000; FY 19 est $9,500,000; FY 16 $9,500,000.

HQ: 750 17th Street NW

Washington, DC 20503

Phone: 202-395-6739

Email: phuong_desear@ondcp.eop.gov

http://www.whitehouse.gov/ondcp/grants-programs

ANTITERRORISM EMERGENCY RESERVE

Award: Project Grants

Purpose: To support eligible victims of criminal mass violence and terrorism with appropriate services and/or reimburse eligible victims for expenses related to their victimization, encompassing two programs for victims of terrorism and/or mass violence. The Antiterrorism and Emergency Assistance Program (AEAP) provides assistance and compensation services for victims of domestic terrorism and intentional mass criminal violence and assistance for victims of international terrorism. The International Terrorism Victim Expense Reimbursement Program (ITVERP) provides reimbursement for victims of acts of international terrorism that occur outside the United States for expenses associated with that victimization.

Applicant Eligibility: AEAP: Criteria will vary depending on the grant. For terrorism or mass violence occurring within or outside the U.S., eligible applicants for funding under VOCA, Title II, 42 U.S.C.

Beneficiary Eligibility: AEAP: Public and private nonprofit victim assistance agencies; victims of domestic and international terrorism. Eligibility depends on the nature of the grant.

Award Range/Average: Varies depending on terrorism/mass violence event and specific need(s).

Funding: Project Grants (Contracts) FY 17 $36,570,775; FY 18 est $50,000,000; FY 19 est $50,000,000; FY 16 $0.

HQ: Department of Justice 810 Seventh Street NW
Washington, DC 20531
Phone: 202-305-2117
Email: allison.turkel@ojp.usdoj.gov
http://www.ovc.gov

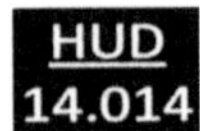

APPALACHIA ECONOMIC DEVELOPMENT INITIATIVE "CFDA Number: 14.270"

Award: N/A

Purpose: To increase access to capital for low-cost housing, business lending, and community facilities in the acutely under-served and under-capitalized Appalachia region.

Applicant Eligibility: N/A

Beneficiary Eligibility: N/A

Award Range/Average: 200,000 -350,000

Funding: FY 17 $183,000; FY 18 est $0; FY 19 est $0; - No additional funding for this program is anticipated for the upcoming fiscal year.

HQ: 451 7th Street SW, Room 7240
Washington, DC 20410
Phone: 202-402-4464
Email: thann.young@hud.gov
http://www.hudexchange.info

APPALACHIA ECONOMIC DEVELOPMENT INITIATIVE

Award: Project Grants

Purpose: To increase access to capital for business lending and development in the chronically under-served and -capitalized Appalachian region. It will also provide direct investment and technical assistance to community development lending and investing institutions that suffer from a lack of capacity to support business development.

Applicant Eligibility: Applicants that are eligible to participate in this initiative are State community and/or economic development agencies that apply on behalf of local rural nonprofit organizations in the Appalachia Region. Applicants may serve markets other than Appalachia residents and communities, using other sources of financing.

Beneficiary Eligibility: Eligible target markets for use of AEDI funds include geographic areas and/or populations, as described below. Geographic areas include the 420 counties in 13 states that make up the Appalachia Region, as defined by the Appalachian Regional Commission.

Award Range/Average: Up to $1,000,000

Funding: N/A

HQ: Office of Rural Housing and Economic Development US Department of Housing and Urban Development, 451 7th Street SW Room 7137

Washington, DC 20410

Phone: 877-787-2526

Email: thann.young@hud.gov

APPROPRIATE TECHNOLOGY TRANSFER FOR RURAL AREAS

Award: Cooperative Agreements

Purpose: To provide educational resources on sustainable agriculture to farmers, agriculture-related businesses, and community food organizations across the U.S.

Applicant Eligibility: Applicants are not eligible if they have been debarred or suspended or otherwise excluded from participation in Federal assistance programs under Executive Order 12549, "Debarment and Suspension." Applicants are not eligible if they have an outstanding judgement obtained by the U.S. in a Federal Court (other than U.S. Tax Court), are delinquent on the payment of Federal income taxes, or are delinquent on a Federal debt.

Beneficiary Eligibility: N/A

Award Range/Average: Average = 1,500,000 Range = 611,000 to 2,500,000

Funding: FY 17 $2,500,000; FY 18 est $2,750,000; FY 19 N/A FY 16 $2,500,000; - President budget not approved as of today.

HQ: Cooperative Programs Grants Division 1400 Independence Avenue SW Room 4208-S, P.O. Box 3253

Washington, DC 20250

Phone: 202-690-1374

http://www.atra.ncat.org

HHS 93.107 AREA HEALTH EDUCATION CENTERS "AHEC"

Award: Project Grants

Purpose: To enhance access to high quality, culturally competent healthcare through academic-community partnerships.

Applicant Eligibility: Entities eligible to apply for AHEC Infrastructure Development awards under 751(a)(1) are public or nonprofit private accredited schools of allopathic medicine and osteopathic medicine and incorporated consortia made up of such schools, or the parent institutions of such schools. In states and territories in which no AHEC program is in operation, an accredited school of nursing is an eligible applicant.

Beneficiary Eligibility: Beneficiaries include a full range of trainees: high school students from underrepresented minority populations or from disadvantaged or rural backgrounds, health professions students, faculty, and practitioners.

Award Range/Average: FY 2016 actual $105,438- $1,265,256 ; Average Award: $542,928. FY 2017 actual $206,000- $1,411,968; Average Award: $587,474. FY 2018 Est. $206,000- $1,662,000; Average Award: $596,323

Funding: (Cooperative Agreements) FY 17 $28,465,186; FY 18 est $36,121,238; FY 19 est $0; FY 16 $28,338,943.

HQ: Department of Health and Human Services 5600 Fishers Lane Parklawn Building
Rockville, MD 20857
Phone: 301-945-9383
Email: lbrayboy@hrsa.gov
http://bhw.hrsa.gov/grants/healthcareers

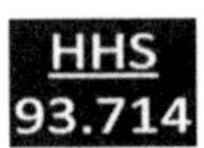

ARRA – EMERGENCY CONTINGENCY FUND FOR TEMPORARY ASSISTANCE FOR NEEDY FAMILIES (TANF) STATE PROGRAM "TANF Emergency Fund, Recovery Act"

Award: Formula Grants

Purpose: Provides economic stimulus to the nation while furthering the ACF mission to promote the economic and social well-being of children, youth, families, and communities. This Emergency Fund was in addition to the TANF Contingency Fund in section 403(b) of the Act that gives money to qualifying States during an economic downturn.

Applicant Eligibility: N/A

Beneficiary Eligibility: N/A

Award Range/Average: The range for ARRA actual allocations for FY 2014 was $608,842 to $3,328,006 with an average of $1,857,757.

Funding: FY 17 $0; FY 18 est $0; FY 19 FY 16 $0; - Up to $5 billion was available in FY 2009 and 2010. Funding is no longer provided for this program.

HQ: Department of Health and Human Services 330 C Street SW
Washington, DC 20201
Phone: 202-401-4731

Email: susan.golonka@acf.hhs.gov
http://www.acf.hhs.gov/programs/ofa

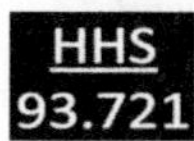

ARRA – HEALTH INFORMATION TECHNOLOGY PROFESSIONALS IN HEALTH CARE "Health Information Technology Education (HITE)"

Award: Cooperative Agreements; Project Grants

Purpose: PHSA 3016, as added by the Recovery Act, directs the Secretary to provide assistance to institutions of higher education to establish or expand health informatics education programs, including certification, undergraduate, and masters degree programs, for both healthcare and information technology students and incumbent healthcare workers to ensure the rapid and effective utilization and development of health information technologies.

Applicant Eligibility: Financial assistance to institutions of higher education, or consortia thereof, to rapidly develop and sustain a health information technology workforce.

Beneficiary Eligibility: Same as Applicant Eligibility.

Award Range/Average: Awards made to 7 organizations in the amount of $966,436 each.

Funding: Project Grants (Discretionary) FY 17 est $0; FY 18 FY 16 est $0.

HQ: Office of the National Coordinator for Health Information Technology 330 C Street SW
Washington, DC 20201
Phone: 202-720-2919
Email: carmel.halloun@hhs.gov
http://healthit.gov

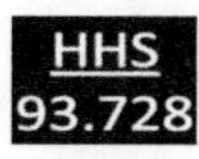

ARRA – STRATEGIC HEALTH IT ADVANCED RESEARCH PROJECTS (SHARP) "SHARP"

Award: Cooperative Agreements

Purpose: To competitively-award cooperative agreements to establish Strategic Health IT Advanced Research Projects, wherein the awardees will conduct research focusing on where breakthrough advances are needed to address well-documented problems that have impeded adoption of health IT and to accelerate progress towards achieving nationwide meaningful use of health IT in support of a high-performing, learning healthcare system.

Applicant Eligibility: Any entity submitting an application for this award must be a U.S.-based: public or private institution of higher education; or other public or private institution or organization with a research mission.

Beneficiary Eligibility: This Funding Opportunity Announcement (FOA) will result in new competitively-awarded cooperative agreements to establish Strategic Health IT Advanced Research Projects (SHARP). The awardees will conduct research focusing on where breakthrough advances are needed to address well-documented problems that have impeded adoption of health IT and to accelerate progress towards achieving nationwide meaningful use of health IT in support of a high-performing, learning health care system.

Award Range/Average: Awards may range from $10,000,000 - $18,000,000. Four awards each $15,000,000 were awarded in FY 2010.

Funding: Cooperative Agreements (Discretionary Grants) FY 18 est $0; FY 16 $0; FY 17 est $0; - Awards will be in the form of a cooperative agreement with a 4-year project period. Under this type of award, ONC will work collaboratively with each site to accomplish the goals of the award. Each cooperative agreement will anticipate a total budget of between $10 million and $18 million over the full 4-year project period.

HQ: 200 Independence SW
Washington, DC 22209
Phone: 202-690-7151
Email: avinash.shanbhag@hhs.gov
http://healthit.gov/policy-researchers-implementers/strategic-health-it-advanced-research-projects-sharp

DOC 11.619 ARRANGEMENTS FOR INTERDISCIPLINARY RESEARCH INFRASTRUCTURE

Award: Cooperative Agreements

Purpose: To establish interdisciplinary research infrastructure for federal researchers for innovations in measurement science, standards, and technology.

Applicant Eligibility: Public and private institutions of higher education, public and private hospitals, and other quasi-public and private non-profit organizations such as, but not limited to, community action agencies, research institutes, educational associations, and health centers. The term may include commercial organizations, foreign or international organizations (such as agencies of the United Nations) which are recipients, subrecipients, or contractors or subcontractors of recipients or subrecipients at the discretion of the DoC.

Beneficiary Eligibility: Same as Applicant Eligibility.

Award Range/Average: Dependent upon nature and type of grant

Funding: FY 17 $54,239,943; FY 18 est $22,229,000; FY 19 est $22,052,000; FY 16 $20,794,433.

HQ: 100 Bureau Drive
Gaithersburg, MD 20899
Phone: 301-975-4350
Email: margaret.phillips@nist.gov
http://www.nist.gov

HHS 93.846 ARTHRITIS, MUSCULOSKELETAL & SKIN DISEASES RESEARCH

Award: Project Grants

Purpose: To support research relevant to arthritis, musculoskeletal and skin diseases, the National Institute of Arthritis and Musculoskeletal and Skin Diseases supports research training and basic and clinical investigations including epidemiology and clinical trials in the areas of skin and rheumatic diseases and musculoskeletal diseases. The Division of Extramural Research promotes and supports basic, epidemiological, and clinical studies of skin and rheumatic and related diseases.

Applicant Eligibility: Research Grants: Individuals and public and private institutions, both nonprofit and for-profit, who propose to establish, expand, and improve research activities in health sciences and related fields. National Research Service Awards: Individuals must be nominated and sponsored by a public or private, for-profit or nonprofit institution having staff and facilities appropriate to the proposed research training program.

Beneficiary Eligibility: Same as Applicant Eligibility.

Award Range/Average: Research Grants: $632 to $2,646,510; $300,930. National Research Service Awards: $49,209 to $606,558; $239,254. SBIR: Phase 1 awards -- approximately $211,685; Phase II awards --approximately $584,849. STTR: Phase 1 awards -- approximately $123,874; Phase II awards --approximately $774,350.

Funding: (Project Grants) FY 17 $435,212,710; FY 18 est $461,326,710; FY 19 est $425,469,000; FY 16 $439,614,513; - This is the total for NIAMS Project Grants, including NRSA.

HQ: Office of Extramural Operations 6701 Democracy Boulevard, Suite 800
Bethesda, MD 20892
Phone: 301-435-5278
Email: melinda.nelson@nih.gov
http://www.niams.nih.gov

ARTS & ARTIFACTS INDEMNITY

Award: Insurance

Purpose: To provide for indemnification against loss or damage for eligible art works, artifacts, and objects.

Applicant Eligibility: Federal, State, and local government entities, and nonprofit agencies and institutions may apply.

Beneficiary Eligibility: Federal, State, and local government entities, and nonprofit agencies and institutions will benefit. Audiences of indemnified exhibitions will also benefit.

Award Range/Average: N/A

Funding: FY 18 FY 17 FY 19 - The figures in this section relate to claim payments, not obligations.

HQ: National Endowment for the Arts 400 7th Street SW
Washington, DC 20506
Phone: 202-682-5541
Email: loikop@arts.gov
http://www.arts.gov

ASPR SCIENCE PREPAREDNESS & RESPONSE GRANTS

Award: Cooperative Agreements; Project Grants

Purpose: Conducts preparedness and response research that will inform the ongoing response to, and recovery from disasters.

Applicant Eligibility: Research on environmental exposure: such as health risk from mold, toxic exposure, flooding of hospitals. Research on resilience factors Surveys regarding decision making during response and recovery.

Beneficiary Eligibility: Domestic, foreign and international public or private non-profit entities including state and local governments, Indian tribal governments and organizations (American Indian/Alaskan Native/Native American), faith-based organizations, community-based organizations, hospitals, and institutions of higher education.

Award Range/Average: No Data Available.

Funding: (Cooperative Agreements) FY 17 $0; FY 18 est $105,000; FY 19 est $105,000; FY 16 est $105,000.

HQ: HHS Headquarters 200 C Street SW
Washington, DC 20024
Phone: 202-260-0400
Email: virginia.simmons@hhs.gov
http://www.phe.gov

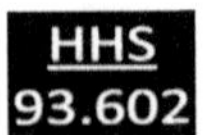

ASSETS FOR INDEPENDENCE DEMONSTRATION PROGRAM "AFI Program"

Award: Project Grants

Purpose: The program is to demonstrate and evaluate the effectiveness of asset-building projects that assist low-income people in becoming economically self-sufficient by teaching them about economic and consumer issues and enabling them to establish matched savings accounts called individual development accounts.

Applicant Eligibility: This program supports innovative projects administered by national, State-wide, regional and community-based organizations. Eligible applicants are: (1) Private nonprofit organizations that are tax exempt under Section 501(c)(3) of the Internal Revenue Code; (2) State or local governments or agencies or Tribal governments submitting applications jointly with; (3) credit unions designated as low-income credit unions by the National Credit Union Administration; or an organization designated as a Community Development Financial Institution by the Secretary of the Treasury.

Beneficiary Eligibility: The Assets for Independence Act limits eligibility for participation in AFI-funded projects to individuals and families with the following characteristics: 1) Individuals who are members of households that are eligible to receive support under the Federal Temporary Assistance for Needy Families program; 2) Individuals whose adjusted gross household income is less than twice the Federal poverty line, taking into consideration the number of household members, and whose household net worth as of the end of the prior calendar year was less than $10,000; and 3) Individuals whose adjusted gross household income enables them to qualify for the Federal Earned Income Tax Credit, taking into consideration the number of household members, and whose household net worth as of the end of the prior calendar year was less than $10,000. When determining the net worth of the household, a household's assets shall not be considered to include the primary dwelling unit and one motor vehicle owned by a member of the household.

Award Range/Average: The Office of Community Services (OCS) awards grants for this program ranging up to $1,000,000. The average grant is approximately $350,000. Eligible entities may apply for new grants up to the statutory limit of $1,000,000 for 5-year project periods.

Funding: Project Grants (Discretionary) FY 17 $0; FY 18 est $0; FY 19 est $0; FY 16 $13,655,768; - (Training) FY 17 $0; FY 18 est $0; FY 19 est $0; FY 16 $2,717,457.

HQ: 330 C Street SW, 5th Floor W
Washington, DC 20201
Phone: 202-401-9365
Email: lynda.perez@acf.hhs.gov
http://www.acf.hhs.gov/programs/ocs/afi

ASSISTANCE FOR ORAL DISEASE PREVENTION & CONTROL

Award: Cooperative Agreements

Purpose: To strengthen state oral health programs and public health core capacity to reduce inequalities in the oral health of targeted populations by establishing oral health leadership and program guidance and implementing science-based programs (including dental sealants and community water fluoridation) to improve oral and physical health.

Applicant Eligibility: Eligible applicants are the official State and territorial health agencies of the United States, the District of Columbia, tribal organizations, the Commonwealth of Puerto Rico, the Virgin Islands, Guam, the Northern Mariana Islands, the Federated States of Micronesia, the Republic of the Marshall Islands, the Republic of Palau, and American Samoa, or their Bona Fide Agents. For specific funding announcements, eligible applicants may be more limited, for example, State governments, including the District of Columbia, or their Bona Fide Agents.

Beneficiary Eligibility: States, political subdivisions of States, local health authorities, and individuals or organizations with specialized health interests will benefit.

Award Range/Average: No Data Available.

Funding: Project Grants (Cooperative Agreements) FY 17 $1,499,447; FY 18 est $0; FY 19 FY 16 $1,499,447; - The CFDA to support this program ended in FY 18. No funding for FY 18 and FY 19. A new program was announced using a different number.

HQ: 4770 Buford Highway, P.O. Box F80
Atlanta, GA 30341
Phone: 770-488-6075
http://www.cdc.gov

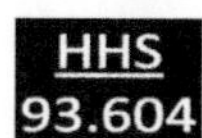

ASSISTANCE FOR TORTURE VICTIMS
"Services for Survivors of Torture"

Award: Project Grants; Direct Payments for Specified Use

Purpose: The Office of Refugee Resettlement provides funding and technical support to domestic survivors of torture programs. The Services for Survivors of Torture program assists persons who have suffered torture in a foreign country to regain their health and independence and build productive lives in the U.S.

Applicant Eligibility: Eligible applicants are public or private non-profit agencies.

Beneficiary Eligibility: The Services for Survivors of Torture program serves individuals and families, regardless of immigration status, who have suffered torture in a foreign country and are currently residing in the U.S.

Award Range/Average: Grant awards range from $172,900 to $444,600. The average award was $297,800.

Funding: (Salaries and Expenses) FY 17 $291,098; FY 18 est $335,000; FY 19 est $335,000; FY 16 $312,000; - Salaries and Administrative Costs(Project Grants) FY 17 $10,423,000; FY 18 est $10,400,000; FY 19 est $10,400,000; FY 16 $10,423,000.

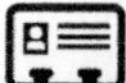

HQ: Division of Refugee Health Mary E Switzer Building 330 C Street SW
Washington, DC 20201
Phone: 202-401-5585
Email: curi.kim@acf.hhs.gov
http://www.acf.hhs.gov/programs/orr

HHS 93.945 ASSISTANCE PROGRAMS FOR CHRONIC DISEASE PREVENTION & CONTROL

Award: Cooperative Agreements

Purpose: The purpose of the program is to engage American Indian and Alaska Native communities in identifying and sharing healthy traditional ways of eating, being active, and communicating health information and support for diabetes prevention and wellness. (State Cardiovascular Health Programs (CVH); and Racial and Ethnic Approaches to Community Health (REACH));State Public Health Approaches to Improving Arthritis Outcomes, State Nutrition, Physical Activity and Obesity Programs. State Public Health, Actions to Prevent and Control Diabetes, Heart Disease Obesity and Associated Risk Factors and Promote School Health. Using Traditional Foods and Sustainable Ecological Approaches for Health Promotion and Diabetes Prevention in American Indian/Alaska Native Communities.

Applicant Eligibility: Eligible applicants are the official State and territorial health agencies of the United States, the District of Columbia, tribal organizations, the Commonwealth of Puerto Rico, the Virgin Islands, Guam, the Northern Mariana Islands, the Federated States of Micronesia, the Republic of the Marshall Islands, the Republic of Palau, and American Samoa. Other public and private nonprofit community based organizations are also eligible (see REACH).

Beneficiary Eligibility: State health agencies and community based organizations will benefit.

Award Range/Average: No Data Available.

Funding: (Cooperative Agreements) FY 17 $43,831,855; FY 18 est $2,998,160; FY 19 est $0; FY 16 $20,733,249; - This support non-PPHF funding for DP13-1305(This program ended in 2018) This CFDA reflects FY 18 funds that supports DP14-1406 (year 5) funding. The DP13-1305 ended in 2018.

HQ: DPH 4770 Buford Highway
Atlanta, GA 30341
Phone: 770-488-5269
http://www.cdc.gov

DHS 97.044 ASSISTANCE TO FIREFIGHTERS GRANT "Fire Grants"

Award: Project Grants

Purpose: AFG program provides financial assistance to fire departments, fire training academies and other EMS organizations to equip and train emergency personnel in fire and fire-related hazards.

Applicant Eligibility: Eligible applicants for AFG are limited to fire departments, nonaffiliated EMS organizations, and State Fire Training Academies. These organizations operating in any of the 50 States plus the District of Columbia, the Commonwealth of the Northern Mariana Islands, the Virgin Islands, Guam, American Samoa, and Puerto Rico are eligible for funding.

Beneficiary Eligibility: The ultimate beneficiaries of this program are the local or tribal communities serviced by the applicants, including, but not limited to, local businesses, homeowners and property owners. Additionally, children under 16 years of age, senior citizens, and firefighters would be the beneficiaries since these groups are the targeted "risk groups" for the fire prevention program.

Award Range/Average: Refer to program guidance.

Funding: FY 17 $310,499,998; FY 18 est $310,500,000; FY 19 est $0; FY 16 $345,000,000.

HQ: DHS/FEMA/Grant Programs Directorate Assistance to Firefighters Grant Program 400 C Street SW 3N
Washington, DC 20472-3635
Phone: 866-274-0960
http://www.fema.gov

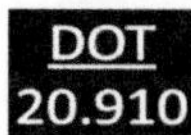

ASSISTANCE TO SMALL & DISADVANTAGED BUSINESSES

Award: Cooperative Agreements

Purpose: To enter into successful partnerships between OSDBU and chambers of commerce, community-based organizations, colleges and universities, community colleges, or trade associations, to establish regional Small Business Transportation Resource Centers (SBTRCs) to provide business assessment, technical assistance, technical assistance referrals, business training, and the dissemination of information regarding DOT and DOT funded contracting opportunities.

Applicant Eligibility: Established 501 C(6) tax-exempt Chambers of Commerce, Trade Associations and 501 C(3) nonprofit organization, community colleges, minority educational institutions, tribal colleges and universities that have the documented experience and capacity necessary to successfully operate and administer a coordinated, Small Business Transportation Resource Center (SBTRC) within their regions.

Beneficiary Eligibility: For the purpose of this program, the term small businesses refers to: 8 (a), small disadvantaged business (SDB), disadvantaged business enterprises (DBE), women-owned small business (WOB), HubZone, service- disabled veteran-owned business, and veteran owned small business.

Award Range/Average: Average of $150,000

Funding: (Salaries and Expenses) FY 17 $1,900,000; FY 18 est $1,900,000; FY 19 est $1,600,000; FY 16 $1,900,000.

HQ: Office of Small and Disadvantaged Business Utilization S-40 1200 New Jersey Avenue SE
Washington, DC 20590
Phone: 202-366-2253
Email: michelle.harris@dot.gov
http://www.transportation.gov/osdbu

ASSISTED LIVING CONVERSION FOR ELIGIBLE MULTIFAMILY HOUSING PROJECTS "ALCP"

Award: Project Grants

Purpose: To promote aging in place and prevent premature institutionalization of the target people.

Applicant Eligibility: Only private nonprofit owners of eligible multifamily assisted housing developments specified in Section 683(2)(B), (C), (D), (E), and (F) (Section 202 projects for the elderly, Rural Housing Section 515 projects receiving Section 8 rental assistance, projects receiving project-based rental assistance under Section 8, projects financed by a below-market interest rate loan or mortgage insured under Section 221(d)(3) of the Housing Act, or housing financed under Section 236 of the National Housing Act) that have been in occupancy for at least five years are eligible for funding. To be eligible, owners must meet the following criteria: (1) Must be in compliance with Loan Agreement, Capital Advance Agreement, Regulatory Agreement, Housing Assistance Payment Contract, Project Rental Assistance Contract, Rent Supplement or LMSA Contract, or any other HUD grant or contract document; (2) Must be in compliance with all fair housing and civil rights laws, statutes, regulations, and executive orders as enumerated in 24 CFR 5.

Beneficiary Eligibility: Eligible residents who meet the admissions/discharge requirements as established for assisted living by State and local licensing, or HUD frailty requirements under 24 CFR 891.205 if more stringent.

Award Range/Average: $2-6 million; average $4 million

Funding: FY 15 $16,000,000; FY 17 est $0; FY 16 est $0; - Reported under program 14.157 for FY 10, FY 11, and FY 12.

HQ: 451 7th Street SW, Room 6152
Washington, DC 20410
Phone: 202-708-3000
Email: katina.x.washington@hud.gov
http://hud.gov/program_offices/housing/mfh/alcp/alcphome

ASSISTED OUTPATIENT TREATMENT
"Assisted Outpatient Treatment Grant Program for Individuals with Serious Mental Illness (Short title: Assisted Outpatient Treatment [AOT])"

Award: Project Grants

Purpose: The Assisted Outpatient Treatment program which was passed as a pilot project under the Protecting Access to Medicare Act of 2014 provides grants for patient volunteers with serious medical illnesses. The program helps to improve the patient's health outcomes and reduce homelessness by providing referrals to medical and social service provides based on the volunteer's needs.

Applicant Eligibility: states, counties, cities mental health systems (including state mental health authorities), mental health courts, or any other entity with authority under the law of the state in which the applicant grantee is located to implement, monitor, and oversee AOT programs.

Beneficiary Eligibility: Same as Applicant Eligibility.

Award Range/Average: Up to $1,000,000.

Funding: Project Grants (Discretionary) FY 17 $13,315,079; FY 18 est $13,304,829; FY 19 est $13,311,112; FY 16 $12,429,662.

HQ: 5600 Fishers Lane
Rockville, MD 20857
Phone: 240-276-1418
Email: roger.george@samhsa.hhs.gov
http://www.samhsa.gov

HHS 93.469

ASSISTIVE TECHNOLOGY ALTERNATIVE FINANCING PROGRAM "AT AFP"

Award: Project Grants

Purpose: To support programs that provide for the purchase of AT devices and services, such as low-interest loan fund, an interest buy-down program, a revolving loan fund, and a loan guarantee program.

Applicant Eligibility: State agencies and community-based disability organizations that are directed by and operated for individuals with disabilities shall be eligible to compete.

Beneficiary Eligibility: The purpose of the Assistive Technology (AT) Alternative Financing Program (AFP) is to support programs that provide for the purchase of AT devices and services, such as low-interest loan fund, an interest buy-down program, a revolving loan fund, and a loan guarantee program. Successful applicants must emphasize consumer choice and control and build programs that will provide financing for the full array of AT devices and services and ensure that all people with disabilities, regardless of type of disability or health condition, age, level of income and residence have access tot the program.

Award Range/Average: The average award amount for three grants issued in FY 2017 is $664,670 for a total of $1,994,009. The estimate average award amount for three grants issued in FY 2018 is $661,512 for a total of $1,984,537.

Funding: Project Grants (Discretionary) FY 17 $1,994,009; FY 18 est $1,894,932; FY 19 est $1,990,000.

HQ: 330 C Street SW, Room 1317B
Washington, DC 20201
Phone: 202-795-7356
Email: robert.groenendaal@acl.hhs.gov
http://www.acl.gov/programs/assistive-technology/alternative-financing-program-awards

ASSISTIVE TECHNOLOGY NATIONAL ACTIVITIES "AT National Activities"

Award: Cooperative Agreement.

Purpose: To support activities to improve the administration of the AT Act in the following areas: national public awareness; state training and technical assistance; data collection and reporting; and research and development of assistive technology.

Applicant Eligibility: N/A

Beneficiary Eligibility: N/A

Award Range/Average: FY 2017 Range for Grants is $309,983 - $573,681 FY 2018 Range for Grants is $320,194 - $575,000

Funding: Cooperative Agreements (Discretionary Grants) FY 17 $883,664; FY 18 est $895,194; FY 19 est $895,194.

HQ: 330 C Street SW, Room 1317B
Washington, DC 20201
Phone: 202-795-7356
Email: robert.groenendaal@acl.hhs.gov
http://www.acl.hhs.gov

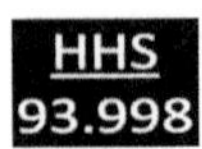

AUTISM & OTHER DEVELOPMENTAL DISABILITIES, SURVEILLANCE, RESEARCH, AND PREVENTION
"Autism and Other Developmental Disabilities"

Award: Cooperative Agreements

Purpose: The program funds the health agencies that work on planning, implementing and evaluating programs related to infant and child health, especially to autism and its developmental outcomes.

Applicant Eligibility: N/A

Beneficiary Eligibility: State; Consumer; Local; Public nonprofit institution/organization; Federally Recognized Indian Tribal Governments; Private nonprofit institution/organizations and others.

Award Range/Average: FY 17/18 range is depended upon funding availability. Award amount range is $75,000- $800,000.

Funding: FY 17 $5,099,939; FY 18 est $5,099,939; FY 19 est $4,200,000; FY 16 $5,624,841.

HQ: 4770 Buford Highway, P.O. Box E-86
Atlanta, GA 30341
Phone: 404-639-1938

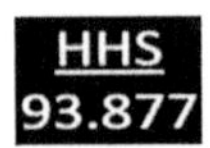

AUTISM COLLABORATION, ACCOUNTABILITY, RESEARCH, EDUCATION, AND SUPPORT
"Autism CARES"

Award: Project Grants

Purpose: The Program supports activities to provide information and education on autism spectrum disorder and other developmental disabilities to increase public awareness; and promote research into the development and validation of reliable screening tools and interventions for autism spectrum disorder and other developmental disabilities.

Applicant Eligibility: For training grants: eligible applicants include public or nonprofit agencies, including institutions of higher education. For research grants: eligible applicants include any public or private nonprofit entity, including research centers or networks.

Beneficiary Eligibility: For training grants: (1) Trainees in the health professions related to MCH; and (2) mothers and children who receive services through training programs. For research grants: public or private nonprofit entities, including research centers or networks.

Award Range/Average: Range of grant amounts: $100,000- $3,000,000.

Funding: FY 17 $1,598,704; FY 18 est $1,600,000; FY 19 est $2,000,000; FY 16 $44,217,073.

HQ: 5600 Fishers Lane
Rockville, MD 20857
Phone: 301-443-2170
Email: lkavanagh@hrsa.gov
http://hrsa.gov

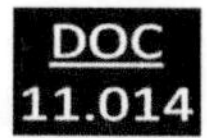

BAND 14 INCUMBENT SPECTRUM RELOCATION

Award: Project Grants

Purpose: The First Responder Network Authority holds a single, nationwide FCC license to utilize Band 14 spectrum frequencies for operating the Nationwide Public Safety Broadband Network. Incumbents around the nation who continue to operate narrowband systems on the FirstNet-licensed Band 14 frequencies must relocate their communications operations from Band 14 to ensure unencumbered spectrum for successful NPSBN development and operations.

Applicant Eligibility: State, county and municipal government public safety entities (and agencies thereof) that are currently FCC-licensed and operating on Band 14 for the express purposes of public safety communications as of the posting date of the federal funding opportunity for this grant program.

Beneficiary Eligibility: Only state, county and municipal government public safety entities who were Band 14 incumbents who were in need of financial assistance in relocating communications operations to other FCC-allocated spectrum assignments received funding through this program. Applicants submitted documentation showing current, active use of Band 14 frequencies.

Award Range/Average: Grant awards ranged from $13,470 to $10,783,799.92.

Funding: Project Grants (Discretionary) FY 17 $0; FY 18 est $0; FY 19 est $0; FY 15 est $0; FY 16 $23,786,713.80.

HQ: 12201 Sunrise Valley Drive, P.O. Box 243
Reston, VA 22201
Phone: 571-665-6147
Email: loren.southard@firstnet.gov
http://www.firstnet.gov

BANK ENTERPRISE AWARD PROGRAM "BEA Program"

Award: Project Grants

Purpose: To encourage insured depository institutions to increase their level of community development activities in the form of loans, investments, services, and technical assistance.

Applicant Eligibility: For Profit Organizations and Other Private Institution/Organizations in the form of FDIC-insured depository institutions.

Beneficiary Eligibility: Distressed communities as defined in 12 C.F.

Award Range/Average: FY 2015 Range of awards $7,500 to $265,496; Average Award $182,599; FY 2016 Range of awards $12,500 to 227,282; Average Award $182,599; FY 2017 Range of awards $15,000 to $233,387; Average Award $201,657

Funding: FY 17 $22,787,205; FY 18 est $25,000,000; FY 19 est $25,000,000; FY 16 $18,625,141.

HQ: 1500 Pennsylvania Avenue NW
Washington, DC 20036
Phone: 202-653-0300
http://www.cdfifund.gov

HHS 93.623 BASIC CENTER GRANT "Basic Center Program (BCP)"

Award: Project Grants

Purpose: Establishes or strengthens locally controlled community-based programs that address the immediate needs of runaway and homeless youth and their families.

Applicant Eligibility: States, localities, private entities, and coordinated networks of such entities are eligible to apply for a Basic Center Program grant unless they are part of the law enforcement structure or the juvenile justice system. Federally recognized Indian organizations are also eligible to apply for grants as private, non-profit agencies.

Beneficiary Eligibility: Runaway and homeless youth and their families are the beneficiaries. Services can be provided to youth up to the age of 18.

Award Range/Average: $100,000 to $200,000 per budget period. Average $168,535

Funding: FY 17 $53,744,000; FY 18 est $54,439,000; FY 19 est $54,439,000; FY 16 $51,310,582.

HQ: 330 C Street SW
Washington, DC 20201
Phone: 202-205-9560
Email: christopher.holloway@acf.hhs.gov
http://www.acf.hhs.gov/programs/fysb

HHS 93.640 BASIC HEALTH PROGRAM (AFFORDABLE CARE ACT) "BHP"

Award: Insurance

Purpose: Section 1331 of the Affordable Care Act gives states the option of creating a Basic Health Program, a health benefits coverage program for low-income residents who would otherwise be eligible to purchase coverage through the Health Insurance Marketplace.

Applicant Eligibility: Any State that submits a BHP Blueprint may be considered for certification by the Secretary of HHS.

Beneficiary Eligibility: The program is for specified individuals who do not qualify for Medicaid but whose income does not exceed 200 percent of the federal poverty level (FPL).

Award Range/Average: N/A – based on formula of state-specific data.

Funding: (Formula Grants) FY 17 $4,329,752,585; FY 18 est $5,270,000,000; FY 19 est $5,390,000,000; FY 16 $2,823,560,855.

HQ: 7500 Security Boulevard
Baltimore, MD 21244
Phone: 410-786-0719
Email: kelly.whitener@cms.hhs.gov
http://www.medicaid.gov/basic-health-program/index.html

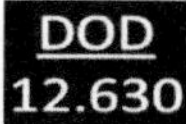

BASIC, APPLIED, AND ADVANCED RESEARCH IN SCIENCE & ENGINEERING

Award: Cooperative Agreements; Project Grants

Purpose: To support basic, applied, or advanced research in mathematical, physical, engineering, environmental, and life sciences, and other fields with good, long-term potential for contributing to technology for Department of Defense missions.

Applicant Eligibility: The eligibility for applicants will be in accordance with the individual program announcements, BAAs, or other notices of funding opportunity. Generally, competitions are open to private and public educational institutions that carry out science and engineering research and/or related science and engineering education; however, competition may be limited to a class of such institutions, such as Historically Black Colleges and Universities or other minority institutions (HBCUs/MIs).

Beneficiary Eligibility: Beneficiaries may include individual graduate and undergraduate students.

Award Range/Average: See individual BAAs for expected range of award accounts (generally vary from $50,000 to $3,000,000 over 1 to 5 year periods of performance).

Funding: (Project Grants) FY 17 $170,000,000; FY 18 est $229,440,324; FY 19 N/A FY 16 $212,730,088.

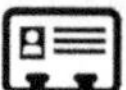

HQ: 4800 Mark Center Drive
Alexandria, VA 22350-1700
Phone: 571-372-6413
Email: barbara.j.orlando.civ@mail.mil

BEACON COMMUNITIES – COMMUNITY HEALTH PEER LEARNING PROGRAM

Award: Cooperative Agreements

Purpose: The Community Health Peer Learning Program will provide funding to an awardee to leverage and build upon healthcare delivery and practice transformation programs introduced through the Beacon Community Program and engage 15 communities addressing health challenges at the population level through a community-based collaborative approach.

Applicant Eligibility: The lead applicant must be a US-based non-profit organization or state, local, tribal or territorial government entity. Private providers and insurers will be encouraged to participate in the consortia.

Beneficiary Eligibility: The identification and dissemination of best practices and lessons learned will directly benefit organizations and communities advancing health information technology and exchange. The knowledge attained by these awarded communities will, in turn, benefit the nation's communities as a whole.

Award Range/Average: Award in the amount of $2,226,818 to a single Community Health Peer Learning Program awardee granted in Fiscal Year 2015.

Funding: (Salaries and Expenses) FY 16 est $0; FY 18 FY 17 est $0.

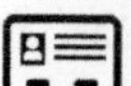

HQ: 330 C Street SW
Washington, DC 20201
Phone: 202-720-2919
Email: carmel.halloun@hhs.gov

USDA 10.311 BEGINNING FARMER & RANCHER DEVELOPMENT PROGRAM "BFRDP"

Award: Project Grants

Purpose: To assist beginning farmers by providing regional training and technical assistance to address their needs.

Applicant Eligibility: The recipient must be a collaborative, State, tribal, local, or regionally-based network or partnership of public or private entities, which may include: state cooperative extension service; community-based and nongovernmental organization; college or university (including institutions awarding associate degrees); or any other appropriate partner. Others may be eligible to apply.

Beneficiary Eligibility: Same as Applicant Eligibility.

Award Range/Average: If minimum or maximum amounts of funding per competitive and/or capacity project grant, or cooperative agreement are established, these amounts will be announced in the annual Competitive Request for Application (RFA).

Funding: (Cooperative Agreements) FY 17 $17,758,724; FY 18 est $17,792,373; FY 19 est $19,083,524; FY 16 $17,777,572.

HQ: Institute of Food Production and Sustainability Division of Agricultural Systems 1400 Independence Avenue SW, P.O. Box 2240

Washington, DC 20250-2240

Phone: 202-401-0151

Email: desiree.rucker@nifa.usda.gov

http://nifa.usda.gov/funding-opportunity/beginning-farmer-and-rancher-development-program-bfrdp

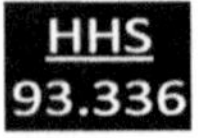

BEHAVIORAL RISK FACTOR SURVEILLANCE SYSTEM "Department of Health and Human Services (DHHS), Centers for Disease Control and Prevention (CDC), Center for Chronic Diseases and Health Promotion, Division of Population Health (DPH), Population Health Surveillance Branch (PHSB)."

Award: Cooperative Agreements

Purpose: To provide assistance to State and Territorial Health Departments to maintain and expand specific health surveillance on the behaviors of the general adult population that contribute to the occurrences and prevention of chronic diseases, injuries, and other public health threats through the Behavioral Risk Factor Surveillance System (BRFSS).

Applicant Eligibility: Eligible applicants are US State Health Departments and US Territories that have been funded under SO11-1101 and SO11-1102

Beneficiary Eligibility: BRFSS data is published on the CDC website and all of the above entities can access it.

Award Range/Average: N/A

Funding: (Cooperative Agreements) FY 17 $16,330,015; FY 18 est $15,297,786; FY 19 est $15,297,786; FY 16 $6,696,911; - FY 17 funding includes supplemental expansion.

HQ: 4770 Buford Highway
Atlanta, GA 30341
Phone: 404-498-0514
http://www.cdc.gov

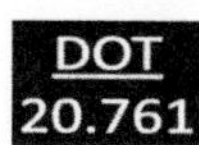

BIOBASED TRANSPORTATION RESEARCH "Biobased R&D"

Award: Project Grants

Purpose: Carries out bio based research of national importance at the National Biodiesel Board and at research centers identified in section 9011 of the Farm Security and Rural Investment Act of 2002 (7 U.S.C. 8109).

Applicant Eligibility: Earmark recipients as designated in SAFTEA- LU, Public Law 109-59, August 10, 2005 119 Stat. 1781, Subtitle B Title V Section 5101 (m).

Beneficiary Eligibility: Public and private nonprofit institutions of higher learning and industry trade groups.

Award Range/Average: The range was between $9,000,000 - $13,000,000.

Funding: FY 17 $0; FY 18 est $0; FY 19 est $0; FY 16 $0; - The program will be closing and each center will be required to submit their final reports except for South Dakota State University. The first Center to complete the research was Cornell University. University of Tennessee, Oregon State University, and Oklahoma State University are preparing to close in 2017. The program was not authorized for additional funding after 2010.

HQ: 1200 New Jersey Avenue SE E33-470
Washington, DC 20590
Email: shawn.johnson@dot.gov
http://ag.tennessee.edu/sungrantinitiative/pages/default.aspx

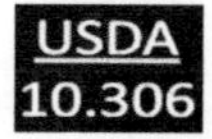

BIODIESEL "Biodiesel Fuel Education Program"

Award: Project Grants

Purpose: To promote biodiesel conservation and educate on the advantages of biodiesel and fuel safety.

Applicant Eligibility: Eligibility is restricted to nonprofit organizations or institution of higher education (as defined in section 101 of the Higher Education Act of 1965 (20 U.S.C. 1001)).

Beneficiary Eligibility: Nonprofit organizations or institutions of higher education (as defined in section 101 of the Higher Education Act of 1965 (20 U.S.C. 1001)).

Award Range/Average: If minimum or maximum amounts of funding per competitive and/or capacity project grant, or cooperative agreement are established, these amounts will be announced in the annual Competitive Request for Application (RFA). The most current RFA is available via: https://nifa.usda.gov/funding-opportunity/biodiesel-fuel-education

Funding: FY 17 $893,760; FY 18 est $896,640; FY 19 est $960,000; FY 16 $894,720.

HQ: Institute of Bioenergy Climate and Environment Division of Bioenergy 1400 Independence Avenue SW, P.O. Box 2210
Washington, DC 20250-2210

Phone: 202-401-5244
Email: wgoldner@nifa.usda.gov
http://nifa.usda.gov/funding-opportunity/biodiesel-fuel-education

BIOENERGY PROGRAM FOR ADVANCED BIOFUELS "Advanced Biofuel Payments Program"

Award: Direct Payments with Unrestricted Use

Purpose: To support and expand production of advanced biofuels by providing payments to eligible advanced biofuel producers.

Applicant Eligibility: Advance Biofuel Producer - an individual, corporation, company, foundation, association, labor organization, firm, partnership, society, joint stock company, group of organizations, or non-profit entity that produces and sells an advanced biofuel. An individual, corporation, company, foundation, association, labor company, group of organizations, or non-profit entity that blends or otherwise combines advanced biofuels into a blended biofuel is not considered an advanced biofuel producer under this Program.

Beneficiary Eligibility: The Advanced Biofuel Producer must produce a biofuel that meets the definition of advanced biofuel, be a solid, liquid, or gaseous advanced biofuel, be a final product. Fuel must be derived from renewable biomass other than corn kernel starch.

Award Range/Average: Awards are based on requests received and production for each producer. Budget has not been approved as of the update of this information, contact the office listed below for more information.

Funding: (Salaries and Expenses) FY 17 $15,000,000; FY 18 N/A FY 19 N/A FY 16 $15,000,000.

HQ: US Department of Agriculture Rural Development Energy Division 511 W 7th Street
Atlantic, IA 50022
Phone: 712-243-2107
Email: lisa.noty@wdc.usda.gov

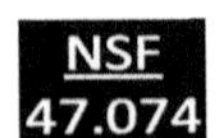

BIOLOGICAL SCIENCES "BIO"

Award: Project Grants

Purpose: To promote the progress of the biological sciences and thereby strengthen the Nation's scientific enterprise; to increase scientific knowledge and enhance understanding of major problems confronting the Nation.

Applicant Eligibility: Except where a program solicitation establishes more restrictive eligibility criteria, individuals and organizations in the following categories may submit proposals: Universities and colleges; Non-profit, non-academic organizations; For-profit organizations; State and local governments; and unaffiliated individuals. See the NSF Grant Proposal Guide, Chapter I.

Beneficiary Eligibility: N/A

Award Range/Average: Range Low $4,115 Range High $5,076,622 Average $181,871.

Funding: (Project Grants) FY 16 $723,780,000; FY 17 est $741,582,000; FY 18 est $672,110,000.

HQ: 2415 Eisenhower Avenue
Alexandria, VA 22314
Phone: 703-292-7162
Email: mfutrell@nsf.gov
http://nsf.gov/dir/index.jsp?org=bio

BIOMASS RESEARCH & DEVELOPMENT INITIATIVE COMPETITIVE GRANTS PROGRAM (BRDI) "BRDI"

Award: Project Grants

Purpose: To promote research, methods, and technologies for the production of biofuels and biobased products.

Applicant Eligibility: Eligible entities include: (A) an institution of higher education; (B) a National Laboratory; (C) a Federal research agency; (D) a State research agency; (E) a private sector entity; (F) a nonprofit organization; or (G) a consortium of 2 or more entities described in subparagraphs (A) through (F)

Beneficiary Eligibility: Same as Applicant Eligibility.

Award Range/Average: If minimum or maximum amounts of funding per competitive and/or capacity project grant, or cooperative agreement are established, these amounts will be announced in the annual Competitive Request for Application (RFA).

Funding: (Project Grants) FY 17 $2,506,479; FY 18 est $0; FY 19 est $0; FY 16 $2,572,807; Section 9008 "Biomass Research and Development" amounts for FYs 2014 and 2015 reflect the 2014 Farm Bill under Title IX - energy, which provides $3,000,000 for each of the Fiscal Years 2014 through 2017. Funding for this Farm Bill mandatory program is authorized for FYs 2014 through FY 2017.

HQ: Institute of Bioenergy Climate and Environment Division of Bioenergy 1400 Independence Avenue SW, P.O. Box 2210
Washington, DC 20250-2210
Phone: 202-401-5244
Email: wgoldner@nifa.usda.gov
http://nifa.usda.gov/program/biobased-products-processing-programs

BIOMEDICAL ADVANCED RESEARCH & DEVELOPMENT AUTHORITY (BARDA), BIODEFENSE MEDICAL COUNTERMEASURE DEVELOPMENT

Award: Cooperative Agreements; Project Grants

Purpose: To coordinate the acceleration of countermeasure and product advanced research and development by—(A) facilitating collaboration between the Department of Health and Human Services and other Federal agencies, relevant industries, academia, and other persons.

Applicant Eligibility: All types of entities are eligible, including highly qualified foreign nationals outside the United States either alone or in collaboration with American participants when such transactions may inure to the benefit of the American people. Applicants should review the individual funding opportunity announcements issued under this CFDA program.

Beneficiary Eligibility: All individuals including at-risk individuals such as children, pregnant women, elderly, and others at-risk who may be given special priority.

Award Range/Average: $30,000,000 to $55,000,000

Funding: Project Grants (Cooperative Agreements) FY 17 $55,000,000; FY 18 est $55,000,000; FY 19 est $55,000,000; FY 16 $30,000,000.

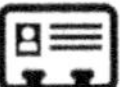

HQ: 330 Independence Avenue SW, Room G-640
Washington, DC 20201
Phone: 202-260-8535
Email: rick.bright@hhs.gov
http://www.medicalcountermeasures.gov

BIOMEDICAL RESEARCH & RESEARCH TRAINING

Award: Project Grants

Purpose: The National Institute of General Medical Sciences supports basic research that increases our understanding of biological processes and lays the foundation for advances in disease diagnosis, treatment, and prevention. It also provides leadership in training the next generation of scientists, in enhancing the diversity of the scientific workforce, and in developing research capacity throughout the country.

Applicant Eligibility: NIGMS trainees must be U.S. citizens, non-citizen nationals or permanent residents.

Beneficiary Eligibility: Any nonprofit or for-profit organization, company or institution engaged in biomedical research.

Award Range/Average: $20,000 to $10,000,000.

Funding: FY 17 $2,541,941,161; FY 18 est $2,679,402,000; FY 19 est $2,476,641,000; FY 16 $2,411,311,000.

HQ: 45 Center Drive, P.O. Box C6200
Bethesda, MD 20892
Phone: 301-496-7301
Email: atheys@nigms.nih.gov
http://www.nigms.nih.gov

BIOMONITORING PROGRAMS FOR STATE PUBLIC HEALTH LABORATORIES

Award: Cooperative Agreements

Purpose: To support the development or expansion of state-based biomonitoring programs, including necessary infrastructure, that will increase the capability and capacity of state public health laboratories.

Applicant Eligibility: N/A

Beneficiary Eligibility: N/A

Award Range/Average: No Data Available.

Funding: FY 17 $0; FY 18 est $0; FY 19 est $0; FY 16 $0; - This activity can now be found under CFDA 93.070.

HQ: 4770 Buford Highway, P.O. Box F45
Atlanta, GA 30341
Phone: 770-488-0563
http://www.cdc.gov

BIO-PREPAREDNESS COLLABORATORY

Award: Cooperative Agreements

Purpose: The program helps to identity and respond to biological and other health hazardous threats and helps create a safer environment for better health protection.

Applicant Eligibility: Specific information on applicant eligibility is identified in the funding opportunity announcement and program guidance.

Beneficiary Eligibility: Refer to the program guidance for further information.

Award Range/Average: Refer to program guidance.

Funding: (Salaries and Expenses) FY 17 $1,500,000; FY 18 est $850,000; FY 19 FY 16 $3,400,000.

HQ: Bio-Preparedness Collaboratory Office of Health Affairs 1120 Vermont Avenue NW Office 6-180
Washington, DC 20528
Phone: 202-254-2433
Email: reajul.mojumder@hq.dhs.gov
http://www.dhs.gov

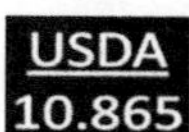

BIOREFINERY ASSISTANCE
"Section 9003- Biorefinery, Renewable Chemical, and Biobased Manufacturing Assistance Program"

Award: Guaranteed/Insured Loans

Purpose: To provide guarantees for the development, construction, and bio based product manufacturing facilities.

Applicant Eligibility: Eligible entities under the program include: individuals, entities, Indian tribes, or units of State or local government, corporations, farm cooperatives, farmer cooperative organizations, associations of agricultural producers, National Laboratories, institutions of higher education, rural electric cooperatives, public power entities, or consortia of any of those entities.

Beneficiary Eligibility: N/A

Award Range/Average: Maximum loan guarantee cannot exceed $250 million.

Funding: (Direct Payments for Specified Use) FY 17 N/A FY 18 est $180,004,000; FY 19 FY 16 est $124,000,000; - This program is mandatory, however, funds are given on a project by project bases.

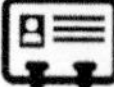

HQ: US Department of Agriculture Rural Development Business Programs Energy Branch, 1400 Independence Avenue SW
Washington, DC 20250

Phone: 202-690-2516

Email: aaron.morris@wdc.usda.gov

http://www.rd.usda.gov/programs-services/biorefinery-renewable-chemical-and-biobased-product-manufacturing-assistance

USDA 10.219 BIOTECHNOLOGY RISK ASSESSMENT RESEARCH "BRAG"

Award: Project Grants

Purpose: To assist Federal regulatory agencies in making science-based decisions about the effects of introducing into the environment genetically engineered organisms. The BRAG program provides Federal regulatory agencies with scientific information relevant to regulatory considerations derived from the risk assessment research that the program funds.

Applicant Eligibility: Any public or private research or educational institution or organization.

Beneficiary Eligibility: Same as Applicant Eligibility.

Award Range/Average: If minimum or maximum amounts of funding per competitive and/or capacity project grant, or cooperative agreement are established, these amounts will be announced in the annual Competitive Request for Application (RFA).

Funding: (Project Grants) FY 17 $3,926,101; FY 18 est $4,213,797; FY 19 est $3,833,002; FY 16 $2,433,375.

HQ: Institute of Food Production and Sustainability Division of Plant Systems-Production 1400 Independence Avenue SW, P.O. Box 2240

Washington, DC 20250-2240

Phone: 202-401-4202

Email: skwok@nifa.usda.gov

http://nifa.usda.gov/program/biotechnology-risk-assessment-research-grants-program

HHS 93.073 BIRTH DEFECTS & DEVELOPMENTAL DISABILITIES – PREVENTION & SURVEILLANCE

Award: Cooperative Agreements

Purpose: To work with State health agencies, universities, and public and private nonprofit organizations in planning, implementing coordinating or evaluating programs, research or surveillance activities related to improved birth outcomes, prevention of birth defects, and the improvement of infant and child health and developmental outcomes.

Applicant Eligibility: N/A

Beneficiary Eligibility: State; Consumer; Local; Public nonprofit institution/organization; Federally Recognized Indian Tribal Governments; Individual/Family; Private nonprofit institution/organizations and others.

Award Range/Average: FY 18/19 range is dependent upon funding availability. Award Amounts range from $5,000 to $1,500,000.

Funding: FY 17 $28,508,860; FY 18 est $27,387,577; FY 19 est $26,000,000; FY 16 $21,294,038.

 **HQ:** 1600 Clifton Road NE, P.O. Box E86
Atlanta, GA 30333
Phone: 404-498-2416
http://www.cdc.gov/ncbddd

BLOCK GRANTS FOR COMMUNITY MENTAL HEALTH SERVICES
"Mental Health Block Grant (MHBG)"

Award: Formula Grants

Purpose: Provides financial assistance to States and Territories to enable them to carry out the State's plan for providing comprehensive community mental health services to children and adults with a serious emotional disturbance or mental illness and monitor the progress in implementing a comprehensive community based mental health system.

Applicant Eligibility: State and U.S. Territory Governments

Beneficiary Eligibility: Recipients of State and U.S. Territory Governments

Award Range/Average: $50,000 to $69,180,482; Avg. $9,035,503

Funding: FY 18 est $533,094,735; FY 16 $504,664,421; FY 17 est $533,094,735.

HQ: Formula Grants Branch 5600 Fishers Lane
Rockville, MD 20857
Phone: 240-276-1078
Email: odessa.crocker@samhsa.hhs.gov
http://www.samhsa.gov

BLOCK GRANTS FOR PREVENTION & TREATMENT OF SUBSTANCE ABUSE
"Substance Abuse Block Grant (SABG)"

Award: Formula Grants

Purpose: To provide financial assistance to States and Territories to support projects to prevent, treat and rehabilitate activities directed to the diseases of alcohol and drug abuse.

Applicant Eligibility: State and U.S. Territory Governments; or Tribal Organizations. NOTE: Only the Red Lake Band of Chippewa Indians is eligible for direct award of Block Grants for Prevention and Treatment of Substance Abuse Funds, per the PHS Act.

Beneficiary Eligibility: Recipients of State and U.S. Territory Governments; or Tribal Organizations. NOTE: Only the Red Lake Band of Chippewa Indians is eligible for direct award of Block Grants for Prevention and Treatment of Substance Abuse Funds, per the PHS Act.

Award Range/Average: $133,476 to $254,417,734; Avg. $29,330,272

Funding: FY 17 $1,759,816,360; FY 18 est $1,760,353,800; FY 19 est $1,760,656,143; FY 16 $1,759,749,115.

HQ: Formula Grants Branch 5600 Fishers Lane
Rockville, MD 20857
Phone: 240-276-1078
Email: odessa.crocker@samhsa.hhs.gov
http://www.samhsa.gov

BLOOD DISEASES & RESOURCES RESEARCH "Division of Blood Diseases and Resources (DBDR)"

Award: Project Grants

Purpose: The Division of Blood Diseases and Resources supports research and research training on the pathophysiology, diagnosis, treatment, and prevention of non-malignant blood diseases, including anemias, sickle cell disease, thalassemia; leukocyte biology, pre-malignant processes such as myelodysplasia and myeloproliferative disorders; hemophilia and other abnormalities of hemostasis and thrombosis; and immune dysfunction.

Applicant Eligibility: Any nonprofit organization engaged in biomedical research and institutions or companies organized for profit may apply for almost any kind of grant. Only domestic, non-profit, private or public institutions may apply for NRSA Institutional Research Training Grants.

Beneficiary Eligibility: Any nonprofit or for-profit organization, company or institution engaged in biomedical research. Only domestic for-profit small business firms may apply for SBIR and STTR programs.

Award Range/Average: Grants: $8,557 to $4,697,455; $443,566. SBIR Phase I-- $150,000, Phase II- $1,000,000; STTR Phase I- $150,000, Phase II- $1,000,000.

Funding: (Project Grants) FY 17 $369,399,679; FY 18 est $398,048,443; FY 19 est $398,048,443.

HQ: 6701 Rockledge Drive, Room 7176
Bethesda, MD 20892
Phone: 301-827-7968
Email: pharesda@nhlbi.nih.gov
http://www.nhlbi.nih.gov/about/scientific-divisions/division-blood-diseases-and-resources

BLOOD DISORDER PROGRAM: PREVENTION, SURVEILLANCE, AND RESEARCH "Division of Blood Disorders - Prevention, Surveillance and Research"

Award: Cooperative Agreements

Purpose: To work with State health agencies and other public, private, and nonprofit organizations in planning, development, implementation, coordination, or evaluation of programs or other activities related to improved blood disorders.

Applicant Eligibility: N/A

Beneficiary Eligibility: N/A

Award Range/Average: FY 19 Financial Assistance is dependent upon funding availability. Award amounts range from $5,000 to $4,300,000.

Funding: (Cooperative Agreements) FY 17 $6,960,136; FY 18 est $7,033,048; FY 19 est $7,033,048; FY 16 $5,958,045.

HQ: 1600 Clifton Road NE, P.O. Box E64
Atlanta, GA 30333
Phone: 404-498-3950
Email: kra0@cdc.gov
http://www.cdc.gov/ncbddd

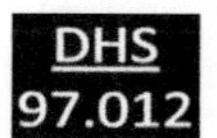

DHS 97.012

BOATING SAFETY FINANCIAL ASSISTANCE "RBS Program"

Award: Formula Grants; Project Grants

Purpose: The U.S. Coast Guard funds grant programs that encourage participation in boating safety and thereby reducing the number of accidents and injuries on waterways. It also assists local and State governments in developing and carrying out recreational boating safety programs.

Applicant Eligibility: States & Territories: States and Territories must have a Coast Guard-approved boating safety program as described by 46 U.S.C. 131: Recreational Boating Safety.

Beneficiary Eligibility: N/A

Award Range/Average: State and Territory grants are determined by a three-part formula mandated by statute. The 2018 nonprofit grants range from $50,000 to $550,000. The average award amount is approximately $160,000.

Funding: (Project Grants) FY 17 $113,048,728; FY 18 est $113,872,970; FY 19 est $114,681,835; FY 16 $114,325,732.

HQ: 2703 Martin Luther King Jr Avenue SE
Washington, DC 20593
Phone: 202-372-1055
Email: pavlo.oborski@uscg.mil
http://www.uscgboating.org

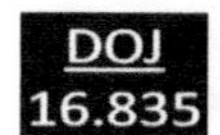

DOJ 16.835

BODY WORN CAMERA POLICY & IMPLEMENTATION "BWCPIP"

Award: Formula Grants; Cooperative Agreements; Project Grants; Use of Property, Facilities, and Equipment; Provision of Specialized Services; Advisory Services and Counseling; Dissemination of Technical Information; Training; Investigation of Complaints

Purpose: BJA helps law enforcement agencies in identifying effective methods for deploying technology and provides reliable digital media evidence for internal law enforcement.

Applicant Eligibility: Eligible applicants to be funded to deploy BWC programs are limited to public agencies of state government, units of local government, and federally recognized Indian tribal governments that perform law enforcement functions (as determined by the Secretary of the Interior);

or any department, agency, or instrumentality of the foregoing that performs criminal justice functions (including combinations of the preceding, one of which is designated as the primary applicant). Additionally, training and technical assistance services require applicants be national or regional public and private entities, including for-profit (commercial) and nonprofit organizations (including tribal nonprofit or for-profit organizations), faith-based and community organizations, and institutions of higher education (including tribal institutions of higher education) that support initiatives to improve the functioning of the criminal justice system.

Beneficiary Eligibility: Beneficiaries are the criminal justice agencies involved in a BWC program deployment and the communities involved.

Award Range/Average: N/A

Funding: (Project Grants) FY 17 $17,984,097; FY 18 est $22,500,000; FY 19 est $22,500,000; FY 16 $19,811,203.

HQ: US Department of Justice Bureau of Justice Assistance 810 7th Street NW
Washington, DC 20531
Phone: 202-616-3785
Email: john.markovic2@usdoj.gov
http://www.bja.gov

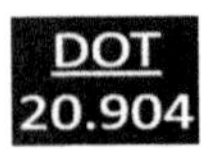

BONDING ASSISTANCE PROGRAM

Award: Training

Purpose: To encourage, promote, and assist minority entrepreneurs and businesses in getting transportation-related contracts, subcontracts, and projects.

Applicant Eligibility: The participant in bonding assistance program must be a construction contractor whom is or in the process of becoming certified as small and disadvantaged business to perform work on transportation-related project. Hereafter, the term small and disadvantaged business will refer to: 8(a), small disadvantaged business (SDB), disadvantaged business enterprises (DBE), women owned small business (WOB), HUBZone, service disabled veteran owned business (SDVOB), and veteran owned small business (VOSB).

Beneficiary Eligibility: The recipient of bonding assistance must be a small and disadvantaged business. Bonding Assistance provided under the American Recovery and Reinvestment Act of 2009 (ARRA) is only available to Disadvantaged Business Enterprises (DBE) certified under 49 Code of Federal Regulations Part 26.

Award Range/Average: N/A

Funding: (Training) FY 17 $0; FY 18 est $0; FY 19 est $0; FY 16 $494,709; - 2016-BEP $494,709.50 There were no budget request made because this program is fully funded.

HQ: 1200 New Jersey Avenue SE
Washington, DC 20590
Phone: 202-366-2253
Email: michelle.harris@dot.gov
http://www.transportation.gov/osdbu

BORDER COMMUNITY CAPITAL INITIATIVE "CFDA Number 14.266"

Award: N/A

Purpose: To increase access to capital for low-cost housing, business lending, and community facilities in the acutely under-served and under-capitalized U.S./Mexico border region.

Applicant Eligibility: Applicants that are eligible to participate in this initiative are community development lenders and investors, which may be local rural non-profit organizations or federally recognized tribes. Applicants do not need to be certified as Community Development Financial Institutions by the CDFI Fund.

Beneficiary Eligibility: Beneficiaries may include: • Current low income residents of colonias •Businesses owned by or serving low income residents of colonias; •Community facilities serving colonias communities or low income colonias residents; and •Owners of rental housing serving residents of colonias.

Award Range/Average: 200,000-1,000,000

Funding: N/A

HQ: 451 7th Street SW, Room 7240
Washington, DC 20410
Phone: 202-402-4464
Email: thann.young@hud.gov
http://www.hudexchange.info

BORDER COMMUNITY CAPITAL INITIATIVE

Award: Project Grants

Purpose: To increase community facilities in the acutely under-served and -capitalized U.S./Mexico border region. It will also provide direct investment and technical assistance to focus on affordable housing, small business and community facilities to benefit the residents of colonias.

Applicant Eligibility: Applicants that are eligible to participate in this initiative are community development lenders and investors, which may be local rural non-profit organizations or federally recognized tribes. Applicants do not need to be certified as Community Development Financial Institutions by the CDFI Fund at the time of application.

Beneficiary Eligibility: Eligible target markets for use of Border Initiative funds include geographic areas defined as colonias by The Cranston-Gonzalez National Afford Housing Act of 1990 (Pub. L.

Award Range/Average: Up to $2,000,000

Funding: (Project Grants) FY 17 est $0; FY 18 est $0; FY 16 $0; - This is a one time program using recaptured money from the RHED program.

HQ: Office of Rural Housing and Economic Development US Department of Housing and Urban Development, 451 7th Street SW Room 7137
Washington, DC 20410
Phone: 202-402-4464
Email: thann.young@hud.gov

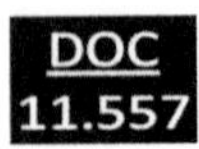

BROADBAND TECHNOLOGY OPPORTUNITIES PROGRAM (BTOP)

"Broadband Technology Opportunities Program (BTOP) - INACTIVE Funding for this program has ended."

Award: Project Grants

Purpose: The Broadband Technology Opportunities Program accelerates broadband deployment in unserved and underserved areas to ensure they have broadband connections.

Applicant Eligibility: INACTIVE - Funding for the BTOP program has ended.

Beneficiary Eligibility: Same as Applicant Eligibility.

Award Range/Average: No Data Available.

Funding: N/A

HQ: Office of Telecommunications and Inform US Department of Commerce NTIA Broadband USA, 1401 Constitution Avenue NW Room 4887

Washington, DC 20230

Phone: 202-482-4186

Email: dkinkoph@ntia.doc.gov

http://www.ntia.doc.gov/broadbandgrants

BUFFER ZONE PROTECTION PROGRAM (BZPP)

"BZPP"

Award: Project Grants

Purpose: The program provides funds to improve the safety and security preparedness in communities of high-priority and critical infrastructure assets.

Applicant Eligibility: States, as defined in the Homeland Security Act of 2002, means "any State of the United States, the District of Columbia, the Commonwealth of Puerto Rico, the Virgin Islands, Guam, American Samoa, the Commonwealth of the Northern Mariana Islands, and any possession of the United States." The State's SAA is the only agency eligible to apply for BZPP grant funds and is responsible for obligating BZPP grant awards to the responsible jurisdiction(s) that have authority over the identified CIKR sites.

Beneficiary Eligibility: State and local governmental jurisdiction(s) responsible for the CI/KR sites.

Award Range/Average: Depending upon the assessment by DHS of the needs of identified CIKR facility; $200,000 to $5,200,000.

Funding: FY 18 est $0; FY 16 $0; FY 17 est $0; - Program was last funded in FY 2010. This program will remain open due to open awards.

HQ: Department of Homeland Security/FEMA DHS/FEMA 400 C Street SW

Washington, DC 20472-3625

Phone: 800-368-6498

http://www.fema.gov

BUILDING CAPACITY OF THE PUBLIC HEALTH SYSTEM TO ADDRESS EBOLA THROUGH NATIONAL NONPROFIT ORGANIZATIONS
"Strengthening the Public Health System in US-affiliated Pacific Islands"

Award: Cooperative Agreements

Purpose: To ensure provision of capacity building assistance (CBA) to address Ebola-related needs.

Applicant Eligibility: N/A

Beneficiary Eligibility: N/A

Award Range/Average: 1 award at approximate average award of $2,000,000

Funding: N/A

HQ: 2920 Brandywine Road, P.O. Box K-98
Atlanta, GA 30341
Phone: 770-488-2756
Email: lbrowning@cdc.gov
http://www.cdc.gov

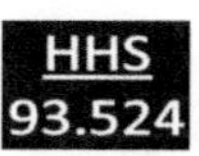

BUILDING CAPACITY OF THE PUBLIC HEALTH SYSTEM TO IMPROVE POPULATION HEALTH THROUGH NATIONAL, NON-PROFIT ORGANIZATIONS- FINANCED IN PART BY PREVENTION & PUBLIC HEALTH FUNDS (PPHF)
"CBA to Strengthen Public Health Infrastructure and Performance"

Award: Cooperative Agreements

Purpose: Cover projects under two funding initiatives specific capacity building activities (CBA) under PPHF; and CBA activities under an umbrella cooperative agreement for unique target populations.

Applicant Eligibility: 1. Eligible Applicants: Organizations with nonprofit 501(c)(3) or nonprofit 501(c)(6) IRS status (other than institutions of higher education).

Beneficiary Eligibility: Beneficiaries include state health departments; tribal health organizations; local health departments; the District of Columbia; U.S. Territories; and other components of the public health system. The general public will also serve as beneficiaries.

Award Range/Average: The floor of individual award range is $4 million for Category A, $1 million for Category B and $100,000 for Category C. The approximate average award ranges for the 12-month budget period are up to $9 million for Category A, up to $2.5 million for Category B and up to $1 million for Category C.

Funding: FY 17 $13,948,483; FY 18 est $0; FY 19 est $0; FY 16 $11,356,472; - This CFDA program represents the PPHF-funded portion of cooperative agreement CDC-RFA-OT13-1302. CFDA number 93.424 reflects the Non-PPHF portion of funding awarded to this vehicle. The sum of funding for these two CFDAs equals the total actual or estimated funding for this vehicle in a given FY.

HQ: 4770 Buford Highway NE, P.O. Box K-90
Atlanta, GA 30345
Phone: 770-488-1523
http://www.cdc.gov/stltpublichealth/funding/rfaot13.html

BULLETPROOF VEST PARTNERSHIP PROGRAM "BVP"

Award: Direct Payments for Specified Use

Purpose: To provide up to 50% of the cost of armored vests for state, local, and tribal jurisdictions.

Applicant Eligibility: Only chief executives of jurisdictions (or their designees) may apply for funds. Jurisdictions are defined as general purpose units of local government (e.

Beneficiary Eligibility: Only law enforcement officers may receive vests through this program. According to the Act, "law enforcement officer" means any officer, agent, or employee of a State, unit of local government, or an Indian tribe authorized by law or by a government agency to engage in or supervise the prevention, detection, or investigation of any violation of criminal law, or authorized by law to supervise sentenced criminal offenders.

Award Range/Average: N/A

Funding: FY 17 $17,394,757; FY 18 est $22,500,000; FY 19 est $22,500,000.

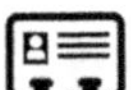
HQ: US Department of Justice Bureau of Justice Assistance 810 7th Street NW
Washington, DC 20531
Phone: 877-758-3787
http://ojp.gov/bvpbasi/home.html

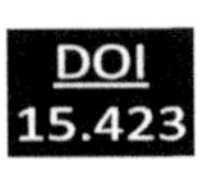

BUREAU OF OCEAN ENERGY MANAGEMENT (BOEM) ENVIRONMENTAL STUDIES (ES) "ESP"

Award: Cooperative Agreements

Purpose: The Bureau of Ocean Energy Management provides major economic and energy benefits and also oversees the exploration and development of oil, natural gas and other minerals and renewable energy alternatives on the nations outer continental shelf. The purpose of the Environmental Studies Program is to obtain the information needed for the assessment and the management of environmental impacts; to predict impacts on marine biota; and to monitor the human, marine, and coastal environments to provide time series and data trend information.

Applicant Eligibility: State agencies, public universities, and non-profits in affected states may apply. More than one institution may collaborate in the preparation of an application for assistance.

Beneficiary Eligibility: Research scientists, Federal, State and local decision-makers, Native American Organizations, and the general public will ultimately benefit from the program.

Award Range/Average: Range is $150,000 to $1,200,000; Average $350,000.

Funding: FY 17 $7,600,000; FY 18 N/A FY 19 N/A FY 16 $4,952,461.

HQ: 45600 Woodland Road
Sterling, VA 20166
Phone: 703-787-1087
Email: rodney.cluck@boem.gov
http://www.boem.gov

BUREAU OF OCEAN ENERGY MANAGEMENT RENEWABLE ENERGY
"Renewable Energy Program"

Award: Cooperative Agreements

Purpose: Oversees the leasing of areas on the outer continental shelf for development of renewable energy facilities. The program not only supports decisions made within the Department of the Interior, but also provides coastal states and local governments with the information necessary to ensure that all stages of offshore renewable energy projects are conducted in a manner to protect both the human and natural environments.

Applicant Eligibility: State agencies and public universities may apply. More than one institution may collaborate in the preparation of an application for assistance.

Beneficiary Eligibility: Research scientists, Federal, state and local decision makers, Native American Organizations, and the general public will ultimately benefit from the program.

Award Range/Average: Range is $100,000 to $1,000,000; Average $500,000.

Funding: FY 17 $700,000; FY 18 N/A FY 19 N/A.

HQ: 381 Elden Street HM 3115
Herndon, VA 20170
Phone: 703-787-1662
Email: mary.boatman@boem.gov
http://www.boem.gov

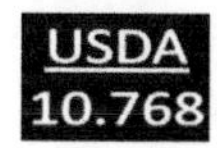

BUSINESS & INDUSTRY LOANS
"B&I Guaranteed Loan Program"

Award: Guaranteed/Insured Loans

Purpose: The B&I Guaranteed Loan Program is to develop business, industry, and employment to improve the economic condition in rural communities.

Applicant Eligibility: A borrower may be a cooperative organization, corporation, partnership, or other legal entity organized and operated on a profit or nonprofit basis; an Indian tribe on a Federal or State reservation or other Federally recognized tribal group; a public body; or an individual.

Beneficiary Eligibility: N/A

Award Range/Average: N/A

Funding: (Guaranteed/Insured Loans) FY 17 $892,244,000; FY 18 est $1,200,000,000; FY 19 N/A FY 16 $920,000,000; - no approved President budget as of today.

Programs Administered by Federal Headquarters

HQ: B and I Processing Branch US Department of Agriculture 1400 Independence Avenue SW, P.O. Box 3224
Washington, DC 20250-3224
Phone: 202-690-4103
Email: brenda.griffin@wdc.usda.gov
http://www.rd.usda.gov/programs-services/business-industry-loan-guarantees

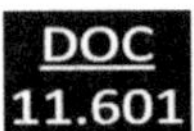

CALIBRATION PROGRAM

Award: Provision of Specialized Services

Purpose: To assist with a system of physical measurement in the U.S.

Applicant Eligibility: Calibrations and tests are provided on a fee basis to state and local governments, academic institutions, scientific laboratories, industrial firms, corporations, and individuals.

Beneficiary Eligibility: N/A

Award Range/Average: No Data Available.

Funding: (Sale, Exchange, or Donation of Property and Goods) FY 17 $7,798,732; FY 18 est $7,632,000; FY 19 est $7,582,000; FY 16 $7,481,000.

HQ: 100 Bureau Drive Building 221, Room B-266
Gaithersburg, MD 20899
Phone: 301-975-2356
Email: martin.wilson@nist.gov
http://www.nist.gov/calibrations

CALIFORNIA REFUGE ACCOUNT

Award: Direct Payments with Unrestricted Use

Purpose: Shares 40.87 percent with the State of California.

Applicant Eligibility: Revenue from effected land leasing will trigger automatic payment distribution computed in accordance with the Authorization.

Beneficiary Eligibility: The State shares 38 percent of well production attributable to the portion of the well within 500 feet of the State/Federal boundary, 62 percent outside the 500 feet. Consequently, the total State share of the revenue equals 40.

Award Range/Average: N/A

Funding: (Direct Payments for Specified Use) FY 17 $1,000; FY 18 est $1,000; FY 19 est $1,000.

HQ: Office of Natural Resources Revenue 1849 C Street NW, P.O. Box 4211
Washington, DC 20240
Phone: 202-513-0600
http://www.onrr.gov

CANCER BIOLOGY RESEARCH

Award: Cooperative Agreements; Project Grants

Purpose: To provide fundamental information on the cause and nature of cancer in people, with the expectation that this will result in better methods of prevention, detection and diagnosis, and treatment of neoplastic diseases.

Applicant Eligibility: The awardee will be a university, college, hospital, public agency, nonprofit research institution or for-profit organization that submits an application and receives a grant for support of research by a named principal investigator. To be eligible for funding, a grant application must be approved for scientific merit and program relevance by a scientific review group and a national advisory council.

Beneficiary Eligibility: Any nonprofit or for-profit organization, company, or institution engaged in biomedical research.

Award Range/Average: Range: $75,582 to $2,917,422 Average: $401,838

Funding: (Salaries and Expenses) FY 17 $569,576,000; FY 18 est $475,693,000; FY 19 FY 16 $523,277,000; - Cancer Biology Research Grants FY 2016 act. $510,555,000- SBIR/STTR $3,905,000 - Other Research $8,839,000 FY 2017 est. $539,414,000 - SBIR/STTR $4,260,000.

HQ: ORRPC DEA NCI 9609 Medical Center Drive Seventh Floor W Tower 7W530, P.O. Box 9750 Rockville, MD 20850

Phone: 240-276-6442

Email: shamala@mail.nih.gov

http://dcb.nci.nih.gov

CANCER CAUSE & PREVENTION RESEARCH
"Cancer Cause and Prevention Research"

Award: Cooperative Agreements; Project Grants

Purpose: To identify cancer risks and risk reduction strategies, to identify factors that cause cancer in man, and to discover and develop mechanisms for cancer prevention in man.

Applicant Eligibility: The awardee will be a university, college, hospital, public agency, nonprofit research institution or for-profit organization that submits an application and receives a grant or cooperative agreement for support of research by a named principal investigator. SBIR grants can be awarded only to domestic small businesses (entities that are independently owned and operated for profit, are not dominant in the field in which research is proposed, and have no more than 500 employees).

Beneficiary Eligibility: Any nonprofit or for-profit organization, company, or institution engaged in biomedical research on cancer.

Award Range/Average: Range: $60,790 to $3,500,336 Average: $499,481

Funding: Project Grants (Cooperative Agreements) FY 17 $625,494,250; FY 18 est $659,584,600; FY 19 N/A FY 16 $643,076,000; (Cooperative Agreements) FY 17 $622,353,000; FY 18 est $640,658,077; FY 19 est $429,228,103.

HQ: ORRPC DEA NCI 9609 Medical Center Drive Seventh Floor W Tower 7W530, P.O. Box 9750 Rockville, MD 20850

Phone: 240-276-6442

Email: shamala@mail.nih.gov
http://dcb.nci.nih.govf

HHS 93.397 CANCER CENTERS SUPPORT GRANTS "Cancer Centers"

Award: Cooperative Agreements; Project Grants

Purpose: To provide an organizational focus and stimulus for the highest quality cancer research that effectively promotes interdisciplinary cancer research aimed toward the ultimate goal of reducing cancer incidence, mortality and morbidity.

Applicant Eligibility: Any nonprofit institution within the United States with a peer-reviewed cancer research base of 4.0 million dollars in direct costs may apply for a Cancer Center Support Grant.

Beneficiary Eligibility: University, college, public agency or research institution in the U.S.

Award Range/Average: Range: $144,556 to $12,352,942 Average: $2,285,090

Funding: (Project Grants) FY 17 $544,194,000; FY 18 est $504,000,000; FY 19 FY 16 $545,296,000; - Cancer Centers Support Grants. FY 2016 act. $545,296,000 FY 2017 est. $544,194,000 FY 2018 est. $504,000,000(Project Grants) FY 17 $534; FY 18 est $511; FY 19 est $347.

HQ: ORRPC DEA NCI 9609 Medical Center Drive Seventh Floor W Tower 7W530, P.O. Box 9750
Rockville, MD 20850
Phone: 240-276-6442
Email: shamala@mail.nih.gov
http://cancercenters.cancer.gov

HHS 93.399 CANCER CONTROL "Cancer Control Grants"

Award: Project Grants

Purpose: To reduce cancer risk, incidence, morbidity, and mortality and enhance quality of life in cancer survivors through an orderly sequence from research on interventions and their impact in defined populations to the broad, systematic application of the research results through dissemination and diffusion strategies.

Applicant Eligibility: The awardee will be a university, college, hospital, public agency, nonprofit research institution or for-profit organization that submits an application and receives a grant or cooperative agreement for support of research by a named principal investigator. SBIR grants can be awarded only to domestic small businesses (entities that are independently owned and operated for profit, are not dominant in the field in which research is proposed, and have no more than 500 employees).

Beneficiary Eligibility: University, college, hospital, public agency, nonprofit research institutions or for-profit organizations will benefit.

Award Range/Average: N/A

Funding:N/A

HQ: 9609 Medical Center Drive Seventh Floor W Tower 7W532, P.O. Box 9750
Rockville, MD 20850
Phone: 240-276-6442

Email: battistc@mail.nih.gov
http://cancercontrol.cancer.gov

CANCER DETECTION & DIAGNOSIS RESEARCH

Award: Cooperative Agreements; Project Grants

Purpose: To improve screening and early detection strategies and to develop accurate diagnostic techniques and methods for predicting the course of disease in cancer patients.

Applicant Eligibility: The awardee will be a university, college, hospital, public agency, nonprofit research institution or organization, unit of tribal government, or a for-profit organization that submits an application and receives a grant or cooperative agreement for support of research by a named principal investigator. SBIR grants can be awarded only to domestic small businesses (entities that are independently owned and operated for profit, are not dominant in the field in which research is proposed, and have no more than 500 employees).

Beneficiary Eligibility: Any nonprofit or for-profit organization, company, or institution engaged in biomedical research.

Award Range/Average: Range: $76,750 to 2,339,503 Average: 481,800

Funding: (Cooperative Agreements) FY 17 $351; FY 18 est $361; FY 19 est $235.

HQ: ORRPC DEA NCI 9609 Medical Center Drive Seventh Floor W Tower 7W530, P.O. Box 9750
Rockville, MD 20850
Phone: 240-276-6442
Email: shamala@mail.nih.gov
http://prevention.cancer.gov

CANCER PREVENTION & CONTROL PROGRAMS FOR STATE, TERRITORIAL & TRIBAL ORGANIZATIONS FINANCED IN PART BY PREVENTION & PUBLIC HEALTH FUNDS
"National Breast and Cervical Cancer Early Detection Program (NBCCEDP) - PPHF"

Award: Cooperative Agreements

Purpose: Works with official State and territorial health agencies or their designees, in developing comprehensive breast and cervical cancer early detection programs.

Applicant Eligibility: Eligible applicants are the official State health agencies of the United States

Beneficiary Eligibility: Eligible applicants are the official State health agencies of the United States, the District of Columbia, the Commonwealth of Puerto Rico, the Virgin Islands, Guam, the Northern Mariana Islands, the Federated States of Micronesia, the Republic of the Marshall Islands, American Samoa, American Indian and Alaska Native tribes and tribal organizations as defined in Section 4 of the Indian Self-Determination and Education Assistance Act.

Award Range/Average: No PPHF Funds used in FY 16. This co-op ended 6/29/2017.

Funding: (Cooperative Agreements) FY 17 $0; FY 18 est $0; FY 19 FY 16 $0; - No PPHF Funds used in FY 16. This co-op ended 6/29/2017. No PPHF funds used for this NOFO.

HQ: 4770 Buford Highway NE, P.O. Box F76
Atlanta, GA 30341
Phone: 770-488-1074
http://www.cdc.gov

CANCER PREVENTION & CONTROL PROGRAMS FOR STATE, TERRITORIAL & TRIBAL ORGANIZATIONS
"Cancer Prevention and Control Programs for State, Territorial and Tribal Organizations"

Award: Cooperative Agreements

Purpose: FOA's purpose is to transition a highly-functional public health infrastructure for cancer prevention and control into new roles and functions to anticipate the nation's needs over the next decade by developing organized screening programs and offer evidence-based, scalable interventions that already exist and can be broadly implemented.

Applicant Eligibility: Program 1; State governments or their bona fide agents (includes the District of Columbia); Territorial governments or their bona fide agents in the Commonwealth of Puerto Rico, the Virgin Islands, the Commonwealth of the Northern Marianna Islands, American Samoa, Guam, the Federated States of Micronesia, the Republic of the Marshall Islands, and the Republic of Palau; American Indian or Alaska Native tribal governments (federally recognized or state-recognized); Native American tribal governments (Federally recognized); Native American tribal organizations (other than Federally recognized tribal governments); American Indian or Alaska native tribally designated organizations; Program 2 – Limited Competition Justification has been submitted Program 3; State governments or their bona fide agents (includes the District of Columbia); Territorial governments or their bona fide agents in the Commonwealth of Puerto Rico, the Virgin Islands, the Commonwealth of the Northern Marianna Islands, American Samoa, Guam, the Federated States of Micronesia,

Beneficiary Eligibility: Same as Applicant Eligibility.

Award Range/Average: 250K - 750K

Funding: FY 17 $213,282,386; FY 18 est $214,043,345; FY 19 est $214,043,345; FY 16 $0; - FY 17 DP17-1701 Total $213,282,518 Program 1 NBCCEDP - $153,100,000 Program 2 NCCCP - $21358130 Program 3 NPCR - $39,285,256.

HQ: 4770 Buford Highway NE, P.O. Box F-76
Atlanta, GA 30341
Phone: 770-488-4378
http://www.cdc.gov

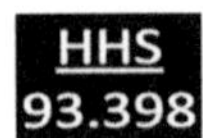

CANCER RESEARCH MANPOWER
"Cancer Manpower Grants"

Award: Project Grants

Purpose: To make available support to nonprofit and for-profit institutions interested in providing biomedical training opportunities for individuals interested in careers in basic, clinical, and prevention research.

Applicant Eligibility: University, college, hospital, public agency, or nonprofit research institution for institutional grants and individuals for fellowships. The applicant institution must be able to provide the staff and facilities and be responsible for the selection of trainees and overall direction of the training.

Beneficiary Eligibility: University, college, hospital, public agency, nonprofit research institution or for-profit institution.

Award Range/Average: Range: $4,200 to $1,097,811 Average: $144,391

Funding: FY 17 $172,980,000; FY 18 est $171,566,000; FY 19 est $167,220,000; FY 16 $167,877,000; - Cancer Research Manpower Grants FY 2016 act. $167,877,000 FY 2017 act. $172,980,000 FY 2018 est. $171,566,000 FY2019 est. $167,220,000.

HQ: ORRPC DEA NCI 9609 Medical Center Drive Seventh Floor W Tower 7W530, P.O. Box 9750
Rockville, MD 20850
Phone: 240-276-6442
Email: shamala@mail.nih.gov
http://www.cancer.gov/researchandfunding/training

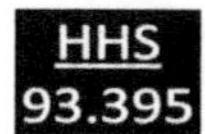

CANCER TREATMENT RESEARCH
"Cancer Treatment Research"

Award: Cooperative Agreements; Project Grants

Purpose: To develop the means to cure as many cancer patients as possible and to control the disease in those patients who are not cured.

Applicant Eligibility: The awardee will be a university, college, hospital, public agency, nonprofit research institution, or for-profit organization that submits an application and receives a grant or cooperative agreement for support of research by a named principal investigator. SBIR grants can be awarded only to domestic small businesses (entities that are independently owned, and operated for profit, are not dominant in the field in which research is proposed and have no more than 500 employees).

Beneficiary Eligibility: Any nonprofit or for-profit organization, company, or institution engaged in biomedical research.

Award Range/Average: Range: $68,748 to $22,965,613 Average: $465,625

Funding: (Cooperative Agreements) FY 17 $503; FY 18 est $518; FY 19 est $350.

HQ: ORRPC DEA NCI 9609 Medical Center Drive Seventh Floor W Tower 7W530, P.O. Box 9750
Rockville, MD 20850
Phone: 240-276-6442
Email: shamala@mail.nih.gov
http://www.cancer.gov/cancertopics/treatment

CAPACITY BUILDING ASSISTANCE (CBA) FOR HIGH-IMPACT HIV PREVENTION
"CBA for High-Impact HIV Prevention"

Award: Cooperative Agreements

Purpose: To reduce morbidity and mortality by preventing cases and complications of HIV and other sexually transmitted diseases by building the capacity of healthcare organizations, community based organizations, and State and local health departments. The grants and cooperative agreements may be for training, technical assistance, or information dissemination; HIV testing and diagnosis; interventions and strategies that support targeted HIV prevention and the HIV care continuum; and use of data for program quality improvement.

Applicant Eligibility: Any State, and, in consultation with the appropriate State Health Authority, any political subdivision of a State, including American Indian/Alaska Native tribal governments or tribal organizations located wholly or in part within their boundaries

Beneficiary Eligibility: Official public health agencies of State and local governments, including the District of Columbia, the Commonwealth of Puerto Rico, the Virgin Islands, Guam, the Northern Mariana Islands, the Federated States of Micronesia, the Republic of the Marshall Islands, the Republic of Palau, and American Samoa.

Award Range/Average: No Data Available.

Funding: (Cooperative Agreements) FY 17 $0; FY 18 est $0; FY 19 est $5,000,000; FY 16 est $0; FY 15 $0.

HQ: NCHHSTP/OD 3300 Clifton Road, P.O. Box E-07
Atlanta, GA 30333
Phone: 404-639-8531
http://www.cdc.gov

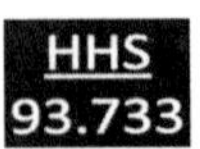

CAPACITY BUILDING ASSISTANCE TO STRENGTHEN PUBLIC HEALTH IMMUNIZATION INFRASTRUCTURE & PERFORMANCE – FINANCED IN PART BY THE PREVENTION & PUBLIC HEALTH FUND (PPHF)
"Immunization Program – 2012 Prevention and Public Health Fund and Other Capacity-Building Activities"

Award: Cooperative Agreements

Purpose: The program improves the efficiency, effectiveness, and/or quality of immunization practices by strengthening the immunization information technology infrastructure, building capacity for public health department insurance billing, and expanding immunization delivery partnerships so that more children, adolescents, and adults are protected against vaccine-preventable diseases.

Applicant Eligibility: Eligibility is limited to the current 64 CDC Immunization Program grantees and some program areas have more specific criteria. Private individuals; private, nonprofit agencies; and Indian tribes are not eligible.

Beneficiary Eligibility: Any U.S. state, political subdivision and U.S. territories (as described above), and other public entities will benefit.

Award Range/Average: Awards will range from approximately $25,000 to $900,000 with an average of approximately $300,000.

Funding: FY 17 $238,718,050; FY 18 est $1,336,505; FY 19 est $0; FY 16 $197,663,255; - Future year funding is unknown and subject to the availability of funds.

HQ: 1600 Clifton Road, P.O. Box 19
Atlanta, GA 30333
Phone: 404-639-7824
http://www.cdc.gov

USDA 10.326 CAPACITY BUILDING FOR NON-LAND GRANT COLLEGES OF AGRICULTURE (NLGCA)

Award: Project Grants

Purpose: To encourage the NLGCA institutions to instruct on education, research, agriculture, and renewable resources.

Applicant Eligibility: Same as Beneficiary Eligibility.

Beneficiary Eligibility: A non-land-grant public college or university offering a baccalaureate or higher degree in the study of agriculture or forestry, faculty of NLGCA, students engaged in the study of agriculture or forestry, the public, interested members of the agriculture, renewable resources, and other relevant and interested communities.

Award Range/Average: If minimum or maximum amounts of funding per competitive and/or capacity project grant, or cooperative agreement are established, these amounts will be announced in the annual Competitive Request for Application (RFA).

Funding: Project Grants (Cooperative Agreements) FY 17 $4,790,100; FY 18 est $4,736,100; FY 19 est $0; FY 16 $4,789,875.

HQ: Institute of Youth Family and Community 1400 Independence Avenue SW, P.O. Box 2250
Washington, DC 20250-2250

Phone: 202-720-1973

Email: elewis@nifa.usda.gov

http://nifa.usda.gov/program/capacity-building-grants-non-land-grant-colleges-agriculture-program

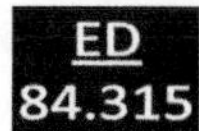

CAPACITY BUILDING FOR TRADITIONALLY UNDERSERVED POPULATIONS
"Capacity Building"

Award: Project Grants

Purpose: To enhance the capacity and increase the participation of historically Black colleges and universities, Hispanic serving institutions of higher education, and other institutions of higher education where minority enrollment is at least 50 percent.

Applicant Eligibility: States and public and nonprofit agencies and organizations may apply.

Beneficiary Eligibility: Historically Black colleges and universities; (2) Hispanics serving institutions of higher education; (3) Indian tribal colleges and universities (4) other institutions of higher education whose minority student enrollment is at least 50 percent; and (5) Indian Tribes.

Award Range/Average: N/A

Funding: FY 17 $960,490; FY 18 est $910,490; FY 19 est $910,490; FY 16 $968,490.

HQ: Department of Education OSERS Rehabilitation Services Administration 400 Maryland Avenue SW
Washington, DC 20202-2649

Phone: 202-245-7423

Email: mary.lovley@ed.gov

http://www.ed.gov/about/offices/list/osers/rsa/index.html

DOJ 16.746 CAPITAL CASE LITIGATION INITIATIVE "CCLI"

Award: Project Grants

Purpose: The Capital Case Litigation Initiative provides assistance to prosecutors in litigation capital cases. The Wrongful Conviction Review Program prevents wrongful convictions.

Applicant Eligibility: Capital Case Litigation Initiative: Applicants are limited to state agencies in states that authorize capital punishment and that conduct, or will conduct prosecutions in which capital punishment is sought. For the state agency to be eligible, its state must have an "effective system" for providing competent legal representation for indigent defendants in capital cases.

Beneficiary Eligibility: Same as Applicant Eligibility.

Award Range/Average: See the current fiscal year's solicitation available at www.bja.gov.

Funding: FY 17 $2,258,304; FY 18 est $2,684,411; FY 19 FY 16 $2,212,804.

HQ: US Department of Justice Bureau of Justice Assistance 810 7th Street NW
Washington, DC 20531
Phone: 202-616-6500
http://www.bja.gov/programdetails.aspx?program_id=52

TREAS 21.011 CAPITAL MAGNET FUND "CMF"

Award: Project Grants

Purpose: To attract financing for and increase investment in affordable housing for low-income, very low-income, and extremely low-income people.

Applicant Eligibility: Applicants must be (1) a Treasury certified CDFI; or (2) a nonprofit organization having as one of its principal purposes the development or management of affordable housing.

Beneficiary Eligibility: Low income, very low-income, and extremely low-income people as set forth in 12 C.F.

Award Range/Average: FY 2017 Range of CMF Awards was from $500,000 to $7,500,000. The average FY 2017 Award was $3,000,000. The maximum allowable award by statute is 15% of the annual available funding.

Funding: (Project Grants) FY 17 $120,043,656; FY 18 est $142,900,000; FY 19 est $145,000,000; FY 16 $91,500,000.

HQ: Capital Magnet Fund 1500 Pennsylvania Avenue NW
Washington, DC 20036
Phone: 202-653-0300
http://www.cdfifund.gov/programs-training/programs/cmf/pages/default.aspx

HHS 93.799

CARA ACT – COMPREHENSIVE ADDICTION & RECOVERY ACT OF 2016

"CARA - Comprehensive Addiction and Recovery Act Enhancement Grant"

Award: Project Grants

Purpose: Prevents and reduces the abuse of opioids or methamphetamines and the abuse of prescription medications among youth ages 12-18 in communities throughout the United States. Grants awarded through the CARA Act are intended as an enhancement to current or formerly funded Drug-Free Communities Support Program grant award recipients as established community-based youth substance use prevention coalitions capable of effecting community-level change.

Applicant Eligibility: The statutory authority for this program, 42 USC 1536 of the Comprehensive Addiction and Recovery Act, limits eligibility to domestic public and private nonprofit entities that are current or former Drug-Free Communities (DFC) Support Program recipients. Eligible applicants are community-based coalitions addressing local youth opioid, methamphetamine, and/or prescription medication abuse.

Beneficiary Eligibility: The purpose of this program is to prevent and reduce the abuse of opioids or methamphetamines and the abuse of prescription medications among youth ages 12-18 in communities throughout the United States *For the purposes of this FOA, "youth" is defined as individuals 18 years of age and younger.

Award Range/Average: Total Available Funding: $2,750,000 Estimated Award Up to $50,000.

Funding: (Salaries and Expenses) FY 17 $0; FY 18 est $2,744,145; FY 19 est $2,750,000; FY 16 $0.

HQ: Formula Grants Branch 5600 Fishers Lane
Rockville, MD 20857
Phone: 240-276-1078
Email: odessa.crocker@samhsa.hhs.gov
http://www.samhsa.gov

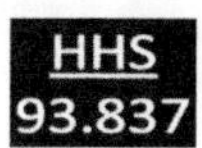

CARDIOVASCULAR DISEASES RESEARCH

Award: Project Grants

Purpose: To foster heart and vascular research in the basic, translational, clinical and population sciences, and to foster training to build talented young investigators in these areas.

Applicant Eligibility: Any nonprofit organization engaged in biomedical research and institutions or companies organized for profit may apply for almost any kind of grant. Only domestic, non-profit, private or public institutions may apply for NRSA Institutional Research Training Grants.

Beneficiary Eligibility: Any nonprofit or for-profit organization, company or institution engaged in biomedical research. Only domestic for-profit small business firms may apply for SBIR and STTR programs.

Award Range/Average: Grants: $2,710 to $18,967,704; $448,135. SBIR Phase I - $150,000; Phase II - up to $1,000,000; STTR Phase I - $100,000, Phase II - $750,000.

Funding: FY 17 $1,370,064,859; FY 18 est $1,476,320,136; FY 19 est $1,476,320,136.

Programs Administered by Federal Headquarters

HQ: 6701 Rockledge Drive, Room 7176
Bethesda, MD 20892
Phone: 301-827-7968
Email: pharesda@nhlbi.nih.gov
http://www.nhlbi.nih.gov/about/scientific-divisions/division-cardiovascular-sciences

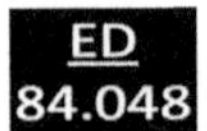

CAREER & TECHNICAL EDUCATION – BASIC GRANTS TO STATES

Award: Formula Grants

Purpose: To develop academic, career, and technical skills for secondary and postsecondary students who enroll in career and technical education programs.

Applicant Eligibility: The Department of Education makes formula grants to State boards for career and technical education or the agency responsible for overseeing career and technical education in States. Eligible recipients for subgrants include local educational agencies and postsecondary institutions.

Beneficiary Eligibility: A wide range of individuals pursuing career and technical education will benefit.

Award Range/Average: The range or awards in FY 2018 was $4,693,077 to $120,196,084.

Funding: FY 17 $1,099,381,153; FY 18 est $1,173,158,653; FY 19 est $1,099,381,153; FY 16 $1,099,381,153.

HQ: Department of Education OCTAE Division of High School Postsecondary and Career Education, 400 Maryland Avenue SW
Washington, DC 20202
Phone: 202-245-7846
Email: sharon.miller@ed.gov
http://cte.ed.gov

CAREER & TECHNICAL EDUCATION – GRANTS TO NATIVE AMERICANS & ALASKA NATIVES

Award: Project Grants

Purpose: To make grants, cooperative agreements, or enter into contracts with Indian tribes, tribal organizations, Alaska Native entities, plan, conduct, and administer programs or authorized programs by and consistent with the Carl D. Perkins Career and Technical Education Act of 2006.

Applicant Eligibility: Federally recognized Indian tribes, tribal organizations, Alaska Native entities, and consortia of any of these entities may apply. Additionally, Bureau-funded schools proposing to use their award to assist secondary schools operated and supported by the U.S. Department of the Interior to carry out career and technical education programs may apply.

Beneficiary Eligibility: Federally recognized Indian tribes, tribal organizations, and Alaska Natives, and Bureau-funded schools except for Bureau-funded schools proposing to use their grants to support secondary school CTE programs.

Award Range/Average: Range: $300,000- $600,000 Average award: $450,000

Funding: FY 17 $13,969,975; FY 18 est $14,907,475; FY 19 est $13,969,975; FY 16 $13,969,975.

HQ: Department of Education OCTAE Division of Academic and Technical Education 400 Maryland Avenue SW
Washington, DC 20202-7241
Phone: 202-245-7792
Email: linda.mayo@ed.gov
http://cte.ed.gov/grants/discretionary-grants

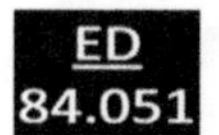

CAREER & TECHNICAL EDUCATION – NATIONAL PROGRAMS

Award: Project Grants

Purpose: To support directly or through grants, contracts, or cooperative agreements, for research, development, demonstration, dissemination, evaluation, assessment, capacity-building, and technical assistance activities to improve the quality and effectiveness of career and technical education (CTE) programs authorized under the Perkins Act IV.

Applicant Eligibility: Depending on the activity to be funded, eligible applicants may include institutions of higher education or consortia of institutions of higher education, public or private nonprofit organizations, or consortia thereof, and State boards designated as the sole State agencies for the administration of State career and technical education, or consortia thereof.

Beneficiary Eligibility: CTE sole State agencies; local educational agencies; CTE providers, and CTE students.

Award Range/Average: Varies by program competition.

Funding: FY 17 $7,421,000; FY 18 est $7,421,000; FY 19 est $20,000,000; FY 16 $7,421,000.

HQ: Department of Education OCTAE Division of Academic and Technical Education 400 Maryland Avenue SW
Washington, DC 20202
Phone: 202-245-7767
Email: robin.utz@ed.gov
http://www2.ed.gov/programs/venp/index.html

CDC UNDERGRADUATE PUBLIC HEALTH SCHOLARS PROGRAM (CUPS): A PUBLIC HEALTH EXPERIENCE TO EXPOSE UNDERGRADUATES INTERESTED IN MINORITY HEALTH TO PUBLIC HEALTH & THE PUBLIC HEALTH PROFESSIONS

Award: Cooperative Agreements

Purpose: To implement a national summer training program to introduce undergraduate and graduate students, including but not limited to those from under-represented and underserved racial and ethnic minority populations, to public health and biomedical sciences.

Applicant Eligibility: Funds are to be used for recruitment, orientation, placement, mentorship and follow-up tracking of undergraduate and graduate students.

Beneficiary Eligibility: OMHHE will collaborate with educational institutions, including those serving minority populations, to increase the knowledge, diversity, and skills of students in public health through internship and fellowship programs.

Award Range/Average: $2,745,067 to $3,000,000.

Funding: FY 17 $3,550,107; FY 18 est $3,432,944; FY 19 est $3,500,000; FY 16 $2,745,067.

HQ: 2900 Woodcock Boulevard
Atlanta, GA 30013
Phone: 770-488-1387
Email: gld1@cdc.gov
http://www.cdc.gov

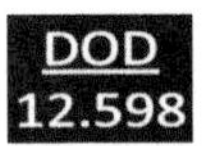

CENTERS FOR ACADEMIC EXCELLENCE
"Intelligence Community Centers for Academic Excellence"

Award: Project Grants

Purpose: To enhance the recruitment and retention of an ethnically and culturally diverse intelligence community workforce with capabilities critical to the national security interests.

Applicant Eligibility: N/A

Beneficiary Eligibility: N/A

Award Range/Average: $300,000 - $400,000 per year

Funding: (Salaries and Expenses) FY 17 $3,916,608; FY 18 est $1,198,528; FY 19 N/A FY 16 $3,250,911; - FY 18 estimate is to renew optional years for existing grants.

HQ: ADI4A 200 MacDill Boulevard Joint Base Bolling Anacostia
Washington, DC 20340
Phone: 202-231-4195
Email: tonia.smith@dodiis.mil
http://www.dia.mil/training/ic-centers-for-academic-excellence/become-an-ic-cae

CENTERS FOR DISEASE CONTROL & PREVENTION – RESIDENT POSTDOCTORAL PROGRAM IN MICROBIOLOGY
"CDC Resident Postdoctoral Program in Microbiology"

Award: Cooperative Agreements

Purpose: To conduct a resident postdoctoral fellowship program in microbiology in infectious diseases laboratories at the Centers for Disease Control and Prevention (CDC).

Applicant Eligibility: Eligible applicants must have experience and demonstrated success in administering training programs in public health laboratory/microbiology research or other life sciences.

Beneficiary Eligibility: This program contributes to developing a public health laboratory workforce for the diagnosis, prevention and control of infectious diseases in the United States and abroad. The nation's public is the ultimate recipient of benefits from this program.

Award Range/Average: Awards have ranged from ~ $500k - $1.3M for FY 2012-FY 2018.

Funding: FY 17 $486,126; FY 18 est $0; FY 19 est $1,000,000; FY 16 $1,258,661; - No new funds awarded in FY 18. FY 18 award was funded with carryover funds.

HQ: 1600 Clifton Road, P.O. Box C18
Atlanta, GA 30329
Phone: 404-639-7722
Email: aslaughter@cdc.gov
http://www.cdc.gov

CENTERS FOR DISEASE CONTROL & PREVENTION INVESTIGATIONS & TECHNICAL ASSISTANCE
"CDC, Technical Assistance, Vital Statistics"

Award: Cooperative Agreements

Purpose: To assist State and local health authorities and other health related organizations in controlling communicable diseases, chronic diseases and disorders, and other preventable health conditions.

Applicant Eligibility: States, political subdivisions of States, local health authorities, Federally recognized or state recognized American Indian/Alaska Native tribal governments and organizations with specialized health interests may apply. Colleges, universities, private nonprofit and public nonprofit domestic organizations, research institutions, faith-based organizations, and managed care organizations for some specific programs such as Diabetes.

Beneficiary Eligibility: Same as Applicant Eligibility.

Award Range/Average: No Data Available.

Funding: FY 17 $6,242,247; FY 18 est $6,564,572; FY 19 FY 16 $6,564,573; - Because this is a CDC-wide CFDA# this is to identify the HHS/CDC CSELS/DHIS portion/update for: FY 14 ($6,695,957), FY 15 ($6,565,572) and FY 16 ($6564572) and FY 17 (6564572) above NCCDPHP funding for this NOFO FY 16($5,455,639), FY 17($5,782,651), FY 18($5,481,262) these programs will end FY 19.

HQ: 4770 Buford Highway
Atlanta, GA 30341
Phone: 770-488-5314
Email: ehill@cdc.gov
http://www.cdc.gov

CENTERS FOR HOMELAND SECURITY
"COE"

Award: Cooperative Agreements; Project Grants

Purpose: The program funds homeland-security led research and education work at U.S. colleges and universities.

Applicant Eligibility: Eligible applicants are accredited U.S. institutions of higher education.

Beneficiary Eligibility: Public and private colleges and universities.

Award Range/Average: No Data Available.

Funding: (Salaries and Expenses) FY 17 $33,133,563; FY 18 est $24,972,999; FY 19 est $14,250,000; FY 16 $33,592,811.

HQ: Department of Homeland Security University Programs S and T 245 Murray Lane Building 410, P.O. Box 0205
Washington, DC 20523
Phone: 202-254-8680
Email: matthew.coats@hq.dhs.gov
http://www.hsuniversityprograms.org

CENTERS FOR INTERNATIONAL BUSINESS EDUCATION

Award: Project Grants

Purpose: To provide a comprehensive university approach to improve the teaching of international business and to engage in research to promote the international competitiveness of U.S. business.

Applicant Eligibility: Accredited public and nonprofit private institutions of higher education, or consortia of such institutions, that establish a center advisory council before the date Federal assistance is received may apply. This council will conduct extensive planning concerning the scope of the center's activities and the design of its program prior to establishing the center.

Beneficiary Eligibility: Students and faculty of accredited institutions of higher education will benefit.

Award Range/Average: To be determined.

Funding: FY 17 $4,571,000; FY 18 est $4,571,000; FY 19 est $0; FY 16 $4,571,000.

HQ: International and Foreign Language Education Department of Education 400 Maryland Avenue SW
Washington, DC 20202
Phone: 202-453-7521
Email: timothy.duvall@ed.gov
http://www.ed.gov/programs/iegpscibe

CENTERS FOR MEDICARE & MEDICAID SERVICES (CMS) RESEARCH, DEMONSTRATIONS & EVALUATIONS "CMS Research"

Award: Project Grants

Purpose: The Centers for Medicare & Medicaid Services conducts research, demonstrations, and evaluations in support of CMS' key role as a beneficiary-centered purchaser of high-quality healthcare at a reasonable cost.

Applicant Eligibility: Grants or cooperative agreements may be made to private, or public agencies or organizations, including State agencies that administer the Medicaid program. Private profit organizations may apply.

Beneficiary Eligibility: All Medicare and Medicaid beneficiaries are eligible.

Award Range/Average: N/A

Funding: (Cooperative Agreements) FY 17 $650,000; FY 18 est $500,000; FY 19 est $500,000; FY 16 $650,000.

HQ: Office of Research Center for Strategic Planning 7500 Security Boulevard
Baltimore, MD 21244
Phone: 800-633-4277

CENTERS FOR RESEARCH & DEMONSTRATION FOR HEALTH PROMOTION & DISEASE PREVENTION
"Prevention Research Centers"

Award: Cooperative Agreements

Purpose: To establish, maintain, and operate multi-disciplinary academic-based centers that conduct high-quality applied health promotion and disease prevention research.

Applicant Eligibility: Eligible applicants are accredited schools of medicine, schools of osteopathy, and schools of public health as defined in Section 701 (4) of Public Health Service Act.

Beneficiary Eligibility: Academic health centers, scientist/researchers, operational public health programs, targeted high risk groups, selected demonstration areas, and the general public.

Award Range/Average: No Data Available.

Funding: FY 16 $19,084,000; FY 18 est $19,084,000; FY 17 est $19,083,950.

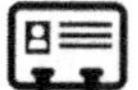

HQ:
Atlanta, GA 30341
Phone: 770-488-6384
http://www.cdc.gov/prc

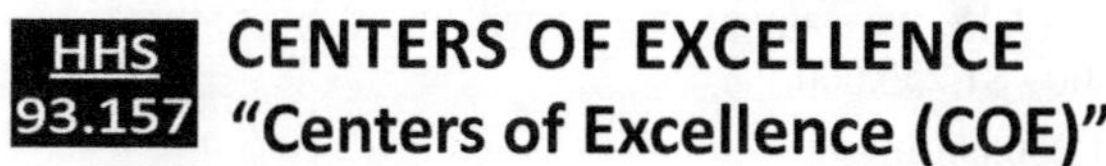

HHS 93.157

CENTERS OF EXCELLENCE
"Centers of Excellence (COE)"

Award: Project Grants

Purpose: To assist eligible schools in supporting programs of excellence in health professions education for underrepresented minority (URM) individuals.

Applicant Eligibility: Eligible applicants include designated Historically Black Colleges and Universities (HBCUs) and health professions schools that are accredited schools of allopathic medicine; osteopathic medicine; dentistry; pharmacy; or a graduate program in behavioral or mental health; or other public and nonprofit health or educational entities that meet the required conditions regarding: underrepresented minorities as described in Section 736 of the Public Health Service Act. Native American Centers of Excellence are eligible, as specified in statute.

Beneficiary Eligibility: Designated HBCUs and eligible health professions schools must recruit and train a significant number of underrepresented minority students in medicine, dentistry, and pharmacy; recruit, train, and retain underrepresented minority faculty recruitment; and facilitate faculty and student research activities.

Award Range/Average: HBCUs: FY 2016 actual: $2,339,598 to $3,498,237; Average: $3,000,000 FY 2017actual: $2,502,475 to $3,499,317; Average: $3,000,000 FY 2018 est.: $2,753,488 to $3,177,641; Average: $3,000,000 Non-HBCUs: FY 2016 actual: $620,509 to $700,000: Average: $676,427 FY 2017 est.: $ 606,099 to $693,000: Average: $660,250 FY 2018 est.: $ 666,526 to $700,000; Average: $692,192

Funding: FY 17 $20,464,265; FY 18 est $22,444,523; FY 19 est $0; FY 16 $20,552,091.

HQ: Department of Health and Human Services 5600 Fishers Lane, Room 15N-62C
Rockville, MD 20857
Phone: 301-443-0550
Email: dsellers-mccarthy@hrsa.gov
http://bhw.hrsa.gov/grants/healthcareers

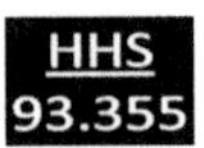

CERTIFIED HEALTH IT SURVEILLANCE CAPACITY & INFRASTRUCTURE IMPROVEMENT COOPERATIVE AGREEMENT PROGRAM
"Surveillance Capacity Cooperative Agreement"

Award: Cooperative Agreements

Purpose: To implement and use the most advanced health information technology (health IT) and the electronic exchange of health information.

Applicant Eligibility: The purpose of these cooperative agreements is to support ONC's mission to improving the surveillance capacity and infrastructure that exists for health IT certified under the ONC Health IT Certification Program, with a particular focus on capabilities that are directly related to interoperability.

Beneficiary Eligibility: The purpose of this cooperative agreement is to advance the market's ability to electronically exchange health information through the use of certified health IT and to ensure that the products function in the production environment in the form and manner they are certified to. While the beneficiaries are ultimately the broader public at-large, the direct beneficiaries include those who work directly with certified health IT products.

Award Range/Average: $1,250,000 allocated for FY 17-18. We estimate that we will award one to three awards total; amounts will range between $400,000 - $1,250,000.

Funding: FY 16 $0; N/A FY 18 est $0; FY 17 est $1,250,000.

HQ: 330 C Street SW
Washington, DC 20201
Phone: 202-720-2919
Email: carmel.halloun@hhs.gov
http://www.healthit.gov/certification

HHS 93.599

CHAFEE EDUCATION & TRAINING VOUCHERS PROGRAM (ETV)

Award: Formula Grants

Purpose: Provides resources to states and eligible Indian tribes to make available vouchers for postsecondary training and education to youth who have experienced foster care at age 14 or older, who have aged of foster care, or who have been adopted or left for kinship guardianship from the public foster care system after age 16.

Applicant Eligibility: State governments, including the 50 states, the District of Columbia, Puerto Rico, and U.S. Virgin Islands (hereafter "states"), Guam and American Samoa, and eligible Indian tribes, Indian tribal organizations, or Indian tribal consortia (hereafter "tribes") with an approved plan.

Beneficiary Eligibility: Youth and young adults who have experienced foster care at age 14 or older, youth who exited foster care or kinship guardianship at age 16 or older, and youth who aged out of foster care.

Award Range/Average: FY 2017 States: $69,550 to $5,556,457 with an average of $816,208 per state FY 2017 Tribes: $4,012 to $14,043 with an average of $7,083 per tribe

Funding: (Formula Grants) FY 17 $42,471,176; FY 18 est $42,608,115; FY 19 est $42,500,000; FY 16 $42,608,145.

HQ: 330 C Street SW, Room 3509A
Washington, DC 20201
Phone: 202-690-7888
Email: catherine.heath@acf.hhs.gov
http://www.acf.hhs.gov/programs/cb

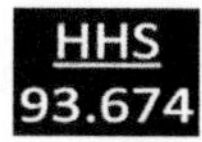

CHAFEE FOSTER CARE INDEPENDENCE PROGRAM "The Chafee Program"

Award: Formula Grants

Purpose: Assists states and eligible Indian tribes in establishing and carrying out programs designed to assist youth who experienced foster care at age 14 or older, youth who leave foster care for adoption or kinship guardianship after attaining age 16, and former foster care recipients between 18 and 21 years, to make a successful transition to adulthood and self-sufficiency.

Applicant Eligibility: State governments, including the 50 states, the District of Columbia, Puerto Rico, and the U.S. Virgin Islands (hereafter "states"), and eligible Indian tribes, Indian tribal organizations or Indian tribal consortia (hereafter "tribes").

Beneficiary Eligibility: Youth who experienced foster care at 14 or older, youth who left foster care for adoption or kinship guardianship after attaining age 16, and former foster care recipients between 18 and 21 years may receive services under the Chafee program. States or tribes that operate an extended foster care program for youth up to age 21 have the option to extend services under the Chafee program to youth up to their 23rd birthday.

Award Range/Average: FY 2017 Grants for states range from $500,000 to $17,011,836 with an average of $2,651,756. FY 2017 Grants for tribes range from $12,284 to $42,994 with an average of $21,685.

Funding: FY 17 $137,900,000; FY 18 est $137,900,000; FY 19 est $137,900,000; FY 16 $137,900,000.

HQ: 330 C Street SW, Room 3509A
Washington, DC 20201
Phone: 202-690-7888
Email: catherine.heath@acf.hhs.gov
http://www.acf.dhhs.gov/programs/cb

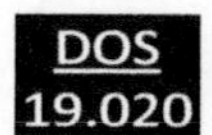

CHARLES B. RANGEL INTERNATIONAL AFFAIRS PROGRAM "Rangel Program"

Award: Cooperative Agreements; Cooperative Agreements; Project Grants

Purpose: Program develops a source of trained men and women, from academic fields representing the skill needs of the Department who are dedicated to representing America's interests abroad. It encourages the application of members of minority groups historically underrepresented in the Foreign Service, women, and those with financial need. It develops a source of trained men and women, from academic fields representing the skill needs of the Department who are dedicated to representing America's interests abroad.

Applicant Eligibility: Assistance supports activities and financial obligations such as tuition costs, student travel, program administration costs and other costs as they relate to the administration of the Charles B. Rangel international Affairs Program.

Beneficiary Eligibility: Applications may be submitted by public and private non-profit organizations. Please refer to Grant.

Award Range/Average: Please see obligations

Funding: N/A

HQ: HR/REE, Room H-518 SA-1 2401 E Street NW
Washington, DC 20522
Phone: 202-261-8892
Email: georgecm@state.gov

DHS 97.040 CHEMICAL STOCKPILE EMERGENCY PREPAREDNESS PROGRAM "CSEPP"

Award: Cooperative Agreements

Purpose: The program assists local and State communities to plan ahead and respond to accidents that involve chemical weaponry.

Applicant Eligibility: Applications are accepted only from the State of Colorado and the Commonwealth of Kentucky. These eligible States house the U.S. Army stockpiles unitary chemical warfare agent as bulk chemicals and munitions.

Beneficiary Eligibility: State, local and tribal governments, and general public.

Award Range/Average: Refer to program guidance.

Funding: (Project Grants) FY 17 $34,674,089; FY 18 est $40,786,923; FY 19 est $21,153,456; FY 16 $20,300,000.

HQ: Department of Homeland Security National Preparedness Directorate Technological Hazards Division, 400 C Street SW 16825 S Seton Avenue
Washington, DC 20472-3025
Phone: 202-212-7961
Email: thomas.warnock@fema.dhs.gov
http://www.fema.gov/technological-hazards-division-contacts

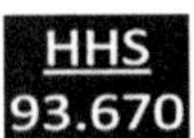

HHS 93.670 CHILD ABUSE & NEGLECT DISCRETIONARY ACTIVITIES

Award: Project Grants

Purpose: Improves the national, state, and community activities for the prevention, assessment, identification, and treatment of child abuse and neglect through research, demonstration, evaluation of best practices, dissemination of information, and technical assistance.

Applicant Eligibility: Grants: States, local governments, tribes, public agencies or private agencies or organizations (or combinations of such agencies or organizations)engaged in activities related to the prevention, identification, and treatment of child abuse and neglect. Contracts: Public and private agencies.

Beneficiary Eligibility: Children that have been abused or neglected, or that are at-risk for abuse or neglect, and their families.

Award Range/Average: FY 2017 grants ranged between $103,663 to $3,000,000 with an average award of $779,313.

Funding: Project Grants (Discretionary) FY 17 $16,365,591; FY 18 est $18,476,082; FY 19 est $14,564,732; FY 16 $19,188,802.

HQ: 330 C Street SW, Room 3503
Washington, DC 20201
Phone: 202-205-8172
Email: jan.shafer@acf.hhs.gov
http://www.acf.hhs.gov/programs/cb

HHS 93.669 CHILD ABUSE & NEGLECT STATE GRANTS "CAPTA state grants"

Award: Formula Grants

Purpose: Assists States in the support and improvement of their child protective services systems.

Applicant Eligibility: This includes States, the District of Columbia, Puerto Rico, Guam, the U.S. Virgin Islands, American Samoa, and the Commonwealth of the Northern Mariana Islands.

Beneficiary Eligibility: There are no eligibility requirements associated with the beneficiaries of these funds (abused and neglected children and their families).

Award Range/Average: In FY 2017 grants ranged from $55,163 to $2,795,812 with an average award of $450,511.

Funding: FY 17 $25,228,638; FY 18 est $85,285,000; FY 19 est $85,000,000; FY 16 $25,310,000.

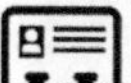

HQ: 330 C Street SW, Room 3512
Washington, DC 20201
Phone: 202-205-8552
Email: gail.collins@acf.hhs.gov
http://www.acf.dhhs.gov/programs/cb

HHS 93.575 CHILD CARE & DEVELOPMENT BLOCK GRANT "Child Care and Development Fund (CCDF)"

Award: Formula Grants

Purpose: Funds to help certain low-income families access child care and to improve the quality of child care for all children.

Applicant Eligibility: Eligibility: All 50 States, the District of Columbia, the Virgin Islands, Puerto Rico, Guam, American Samoa, the Commonwealth of the Northern Mariana Islands, and Federally recognized Tribal Governments and consortia.

Beneficiary Eligibility: Children under age 13 (or, at the option of the grantee, up to age 19, if physically or mentally incapable of self-care or under court supervision), who (1) reside with a family whose income does not exceed 85 percent of the State median income for a family of the same size, and (2) who reside with a parent (or parents) who is working or attending job training or educational program, or who are in need of, or are receiving, protective services. A Lead Agency shall re-determine a child's eligibility for child care services no sooner than 12 months following the initial determination or most recent re-determination.

Award Range/Average: For States, including DC and Puerto Rico, the range of grants in FY 2017 is: $3,544,566 to $305,025,145. The average grant is $52,642,308. For 260 Tribal grantees, the range of grants in FY 2017 is: $34,878 to $7,595,340; the average grant is $302,077. For the four Territories, the range of grants in FY 2017 is $2,336,771 to $5,382,561; the average grant is $ 3,570,000.

Funding: FY 17 $2,856,000,000; FY 18 est $5,226,000,000; FY 19 est $3,006,000,000; FY 16 $2,761,000,000.

HQ: OCC/ACF/HHS 330 C Street SW
Washington, DC 20201
Phone: 202-401-2113
Email: abdihakin.abdi@acf.hhs.gov
http://www.acf.hhs.gov/programs/occ

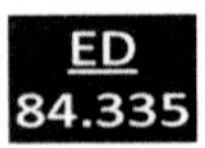

CHILD CARE ACCESS MEANS PARENTS IN SCHOOL

Award: Project Grants

Purpose: Supports the participation of low-income parents in postsecondary education through the provision of campus-based child care services.

Applicant Eligibility: An institution of higher education is eligible to apply if the total amount of all Federal Pell Grant funds awarded to students enrolled at the institution of higher education for the preceding fiscal year equals or exceeds $350,000.

Beneficiary Eligibility: Low-income student parents enrolled in postsecondary programs will benefit.

Award Range/Average: $10,000 - $300,000

Funding: FY 17 $15,134,000; FY 18 est $50,000,000; FY 19 est $0; FY 16 $15,134,000.

HQ: Department of Education Higher Education Programs 400 Maryland Avenue SW
Washington, DC 20202
Phone: 202-453-5649
Email: antionette.edwards@ed.gov
http://www.ed.gov/programs/campisp

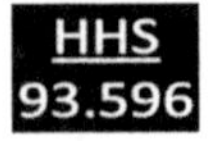

CHILD CARE MANDATORY & MATCHING FUNDS OF THE CHILD CARE & DEVELOPMENT FUND
"Child Care and Development Fund (CCDF)"

Award: Formula Grants

Purpose: The Child Care and Development Fund is the primary federal funding source to help certain low-income families access child care and to improve the quality of child care for all children.

Applicant Eligibility: Eligibility: All 50 States, the District of Columbia, and Federally recognized Tribal Governments, including Alaskan Native Corporations.

Beneficiary Eligibility: Children under age 13 (or, at the option of the grantee, up to age 19, if physically or mentally incapable of self-care or under court supervision), who (1) reside with a family whose income does not exceed 85 percent of the State median income for a family of the same size, and (2) who reside with a parent (or parents) who is working or attending job training or educational program, who or are in need of, or are receiving protective services. A Lead Agency shall re-determine a child's eligibility for child care services no sooner than 12 months following the initial determination or most recent re-determination.

Award Range/Average: For States, including DC, the range of grants in FY 2017 is: $9,299,533 to $ 507,475,945; the average grant is $ 89,344,311. For 242 Tribal grantees, the range of grants in FY 2017 is: $4,445 to $6,892,618; the average grant is $225,251. The Territories do not receive Mandatory funding.

Funding: FY 17 $2,917,000,000; FY 18 est $2,917,000,000; FY 19 est $2,917,000,000; FY 16 $2,916,771,935.

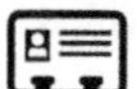

HQ: 330 C Street SW
Washington, DC 20201
Phone: 202-401-2113
Email: abdihakin.abdi@acf.hhs.gov
http://www.acf.hhs.gov/programs/occ

HHS 93.312 CHILD DEVELOPMENT AND, SURVEILLANCE, RESEARCH & PREVENTION

Award: Cooperative Agreements

Purpose: Supports State health agencies, universities, and public and private nonprofit organizations in planning, implementing, coordinating, or evaluating programs related to promoting optimal child health.

Applicant Eligibility: N/A

Beneficiary Eligibility: In addition to the eligible applicants, other groups who will receive benefits from the program include persons with or at-risk for developmental delays, developmental disabilities, mental disorders, or neurobehavioral disorders such as Attention-Deficit/Hyperactivity Disorder, Tourette syndrome and the conditions that co-occur with them; family members of persons with or at-risk for developmental delays, developmental disabilities, mental disorders, or neurobehavioral disorders such as Attention-Deficit/Hyperactivity Disorder, Tourette syndrome and the conditions that co-occur with them; minority populations, including Spanish speaking populations, infants, children, youth, adults; Federally Recognized Indian Tribal Governments; individual and families; educators, health care professionals, Private nonprofit institution/organizations and others.

Award Range/Average: The FY 18/19 range is dependent upon funding availability. Awards amounts may range from $300,000 to $1,000,000.

Funding: FY 17 $1,750,000; FY 18 est $1,750,000; FY 19 est $1,750,000; FY 16 $1,750,000.

HQ: 1600 Clifton Road NE, P.O. Box 88
Atlanta, GA 30033
Phone: 404-498-4159

HHS 93.865

CHILD HEALTH & HUMAN DEVELOPMENT EXTRAMURAL RESEARCH
"Child Health and Human Development"

Award: Project Grants

Purpose: To conduct and support laboratory research, clinical trials, and studies with people that explore health processes by examining the impact of disabilities, diseases, and defects on the lives of individuals. With this information, the NICHD hopes to restore, increase, and maximize the capabilities of people affected by disease and injury.

Applicant Eligibility: Universities, colleges, medical, dental and nursing schools, schools of public health, laboratories, hospitals, State and local health departments, other public or private institutions, both nonprofit and for-profit, and individuals. National Research Service Award: Support is provided for academic and research training only, in health and health-related areas that are periodically specified by the National Institutes of Health.

Beneficiary Eligibility: Any nonprofit or for-profit organization, company, or institution engaged in biomedical or biobehavioral research.

Award Range/Average: For research project grants, fiscal year 2018, range is $50,000 to $5,000,000; average is $458,488. Individual research fellowship awards: Basic stipend (first year beyond the doctoral degree) of approximately $45,000. The sponsoring institution will be provided, on application, with an allowance of up to approximately $8,000 per year to help defray the cost of training. No dependency allowances. SBIR: Average Phase I awards are for approximately $225,000 (grant activity R43 - for up to six months); Phase II awards may be made for amounts up to $1,500,000 (grant activity R44 - for up to two years).

Funding: FY 17 $979,273,038; FY 18 est $1,043,607,000; FY 19 est $949,511,000; FY 16 $945,498,160.

HQ: 6710-B Rockledge Drive, Room 2216
Bethesda, MD 20892-7510
Phone: 301-435-6856
Email: ehayunga@mail.nih.gov
http://www.nichd.nih.gov/pages/index.aspx

CHILD SUPPORT ENFORCEMENT DEMONSTRATIONS & SPECIAL PROJECTS
"Special Improvement Projects"

Award: Project Grants

Purpose: Provides federal funds for information dissemination and technical assistance to states, training of federal and state staff to improve state child support programs, and research, demonstration, and special projects of regional or national significance relating to the operation of child support programs.

Applicant Eligibility: This funding is available to all organizations that meet the program eligibility requirement.

Beneficiary Eligibility: Beneficiaries vary depending on funding topics, which change to meet agency policy and research goals.

Award Range/Average: N/A

Funding: (Project Grants) This program was not funded in FY 2017, no funding is anticipated for FY 2018 and 2019.

HQ: 330 C Street SW
Washington, DC 20201
Phone: 202-401-4578
Email: michelle.jadczak@acf.hhs.gov
http://www.acf.dhhs.gov/programs/cse/grants

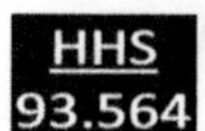

CHILD SUPPORT ENFORCEMENT RESEARCH

Award: Project Grants

Purpose: To provide federal funds for experimental, pilot, or demonstration projects that are likely to assist in promoting the objectives of Part D of Title IV.

Applicant Eligibility: Section 1115 grants may be made only to State or Tribal Child Support Enforcement agencies or their umbrella agencies.

Beneficiary Eligibility: Only Title IV-D Child Support Agencies or Tribal Child Support Program operating a comprehensive program.

Award Range/Average: $150,000 to $800,000. Average changes each fiscal year.

Funding: FY 17 $4,000,000; FY 18 est $4,000,000; FY 19 est $4,000,000; FY 16 $4,000,000.

HQ: 330 C Street SW
Washington, DC 20201
Phone: 202-401-4578
Email: michelle.jadczak@acf.hhs.gov
http://www.acf.hhs.gov/programs/cse

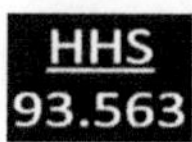

CHILD SUPPORT ENFORCEMENT

Award: Formula Grants

Purpose: To enforce the support obligations owed by absent parents to their children.

Applicant Eligibility: All States, the District of Columbia, Puerto Rico, Virgin Islands, and Guam. Each of these jurisdictions is required to establish or designate a single and separate State Child Support Enforcement Agency.

Beneficiary Eligibility: The State must provide support enforcement services to: (1) All applicants for, or recipients of TANF, Foster Care Maintenance Payments, and Medicaid, for whom an assignment to the State of support rights has been made and who are in need of such services; (2) all individuals who cease to receive TANF; (3) individuals who provide authorization to the IV-D agency to continue support enforcement services; and (4) any other individual who is in need of such services and who has applied for them.

Award Range/Average: FY 2017, from $3,796,650 to $500,224,386; Average Award Amount $65,291,622, and FY 2018, from $3,893,572 to $512,994,207; Average Award Amount 66,958,399, and FY 2019, from $3,903,852 to $514,348,645; Average Award Amount $67,135,187.

Funding: FY 17 $3,569,501,998; FY 18 est $3,660,624,909; FY 19 est $3,670,289,909; FY 16 $3,399,123,428.

HQ: 330 C Street SW, 5th Floor
Washington, DC 20201
Phone: 202-401-5101
Email: rjackson@acf.hhs.gov
http://www.acf.dhhs.gov/programs/cse

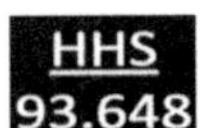

CHILD WELFARE RESEARCH TRAINING OR DEMONSTRATION

Award: Project Grants

Purpose: Supports research and demonstration projects which are of national or regional significance and special projects for the demonstration of new methods which show promise of substantial contribution to the advancement of child welfare.

Applicant Eligibility: Eligible applicants include public or other nonprofit institutions of higher learning, public or other nonprofit agencies or organizations engaged in research on child welfare activities; and state or local public agencies responsible for administering, or supervising the administration of the title IV-B plan.

Beneficiary Eligibility: Grants are made to accredited public or other nonprofit institutions of higher learning, public or other nonprofit agencies and/or organizations and to state or local child welfare agencies for specific projects for training prospective and current personnel for work in the field of child welfare, including trainee-ships with stipends; child welfare demonstration projects of national or regional significance; and for utilization of child welfare research to encourage experimental and special types of welfare services.

Award Range/Average: $432,742 to $4,240,690 with average of $1,061,856.

Funding: Project Grants (Discretionary) FY 17 $9,611,141; FY 18 est $9,970,284; FY 19 est $10,648,000; FY 16 $8,539,355.

HQ: 330 C Street SW, Room 3504
Washington, DC 20201
Phone: 202-205-8807
Email: jane.morgan@acf.hhs.gov
http://www.acf.hhs.gov/programs/cb

CHILDHOOD LEAD POISONING PREVENTION PROJECTS, STATE & LOCAL CHILDHOOD LEAD POISONING PREVENTION & SURVEILLANCE OF BLOOD LEAD LEVELS IN CHILDREN "Childhood Lead Poisoning Prevention Program (CLPPP))"

Award: Project Grants

Purpose: To develop and/or enhance a surveillance system that monitors all blood lead levels.

Applicant Eligibility: Assistance will be provided to State health departments or their bonafide agents and the health departments of the following five local jurisdictions (or their bonafide agents)that have the highest estimated number of children with elevated blood lead levels : New York, NY; Chicago, IL; Detroit, MI; Los Angeles County, CA, and Philadelphia, PA, or their bona fide agents. Also eligible are health departments or other official organizational authorities of the District of Columbia, the Commonwealth of Puerto Rico, the Virgin Islands, the Commonwealth of the Northern Mariana Islands, American Samoa, Guam, the Federated States of Micronesia, the Republic of the Marshall Islands, the Republic of Palau, and federally recognized Indian tribal governments.

Beneficiary Eligibility: In addition to the eligible applicants, others who receive benefits from the program include infants and children from six months to six years of age who are screened for lead poisoning and family members who care for lead-poisoned children. Lead poisoning potentially affects all children, but disproportionately affects minority children and children of low-income families.

Award Range/Average: No Data Available.

Funding: (Cooperative Agreements) FY 17 $3,222,179; FY 18 est $3,222,179; FY 19 est $3,222,179; FY 16 $0.

HQ: 4772 Buford Highway, P.O. Box F47
Atlanta, GA 30341
Phone: 770-488-0563
http://www.cdc.gov

CHILDREN EXPOSED TO VIOLENCE
"Defending Childhood"

Award: Project Grants

Purpose: Children Exposed to Violence Program reduces the frequency and severity of violence in homes and schools, assists children exposed to violence, and promotes safety and well-being of children.

Applicant Eligibility: N/A

Beneficiary Eligibility: N/A

Award Range/Average: Awards may range up to $2.5 million.

Funding: Project Grants (Discretionary) FY 17 FY 18 FY 19 est $8,000,000.

HQ: 810 Seventh Street NW 2136
Washington, DC 20531
Phone: 202-307-9963
Email: robin.delany-shabazz@usdoj.gov
http://ojjdp.ncjrs.org

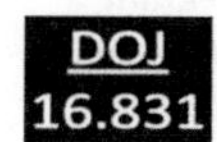

CHILDREN OF INCARCERATED PARENTS
"Children of Incarcerated Parents Demonstration"

Award: Project Grants

Purpose: To develop strategies to strengthen the relationships between parents and children and provisions that will enhance youth development and innovative approaches to communication.

Applicant Eligibility: The target population for this program is incarcerated parents who have minor children younger than 18.

Beneficiary Eligibility: N/A

Award Range/Average: award amounts vary according to solicitation

Funding: (Salaries and Expenses) FY 17 $4,176,332; FY 18 est $5,000,000; FY 19 est $5,000,000; FY 16 $2,989,296.

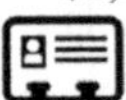

HQ: Office of Juvenile Justice and Delinquency Prevention
Washington, DC 20531
Phone: 202-616-5176
Email: kathy.mitchell@usdoj.gov
http://www.ojjdp.gov

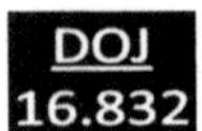

CHILDREN OF INCARCERATED PARENTS WEB PORTAL "COIP Web Portal"

Award: Project Grants

Purpose: To promote government initiatives to support children of incarcerated parents and their caregivers.

Applicant Eligibility: Funds may be used for an array of activities designed to develop a new or enhance and existing web site that would accomplish the goals of the program

Beneficiary Eligibility: The beneficiaries of this program are youth, families, and specialized service providers who can provide services to youth, incarcerated parents, and the communities

Award Range/Average: Award amounts vary according to the appropriation amount

Funding: (Salaries and Expenses) FY 17 $416,661; FY 18 est $500,000; FY 19 est $500,000.

HQ: Office of Juvenile Justice and Delinquency Prevention 810 7th Street NW
Washington, DC 20531
Phone: 202-307-5911
http://www.ojjdp.gov

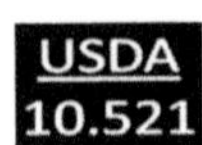

CHILDREN, YOUTH & FAMILIES AT-RISK "CYFAR, CYFAR-SCP and CYFAR-PDTA"

Award: Project Grants

Purpose: The Land-grant Institutions and Cooperative Extension Systems in collaboration provide education for youth, professional development, and military skills to contribute for lives. The CYFAR program provides educational resources and technological skills for youth.

Applicant Eligibility: Applications may only be submitted by Cooperative Extension at 1890 Land-grant Institutions, including Tuskegee University, Central State University, and West Virginia State University; 1862 Land-grant Colleges and Universities; and the University of the District of Columbia.

Beneficiary Eligibility: Same as Applicant Eligibility.

Award Range/Average: If minimum or maximum amounts of funding per competitive and/or capacity project grant, or cooperative agreement are established, these amounts will be announced in the annual Competitive Request for Application (RFA).

Funding: FY 17 $0; FY 18 est $0; FY 19 est $8,037,990; FY 16 $0. Previously included in CFDA # 10.500. This represents a newly created CFDA number, which was part of an initiative to break out the separate programs contained in CFDA # 10.500.

HQ: Institute of Youth Family and Community (IYFC) Division of Youth and 4-H 1400 Independence Avenue SW, P.O. Box 2250
Washington, DC 20250-2250
Phone: 202-720-5305
Email: elewis@nifa.usda.gov
http://nifa.usda.gov/program/children-youth-and-families-risk-cyfar

CHILDREN'S HEALTH INSURANCE PROGRAM "CHIP"

Award: Formula Grants

Purpose: Provides funds to States to enable them to maintain and expand child health assistance to uninsured, low-income children, low-income pregnant women and legal immigrants.

Applicant Eligibility: States with an approved child health plan under this title [42 U.S.C. Section1397aa et seq].

Beneficiary Eligibility: Targeted low-income children will benefit. These children are defined (for the purposes of Title XXI) as children who have been determined eligible by the State for child health assistance under their State plan; are low-income children as defined by each state and are not found to be covered under a group health plan or under other health insurance coverage.

Award Range/Average: For the Connecting Kids to Coverage Cooperative Agreements, the projected awards will range from ($250,000 up to $1,000,000). FY 2018, the range is from $3,072,998 (American Samoa) to $2,825,935,404 (California).

Funding: Formula Grants (Apportionments) FY 17 $15,952,148,232; FY 18 est $16,927,943,818; FY 19 est $18,293,238,755; FY 16 $13,958,271,478.

HQ: 7500 Security Boulevard
Baltimore, MD 21244
Phone: 410-786-5780
Email: grace.ponte@cms.hhs.gov
http://www.cms.gov

CHILDREN'S HOSPITALS GRADUATE MEDICAL EDUCATION PAYMENT PROGRAM "CHGME Payment Program"

Award: Direct Payments for Specified Use

Purpose: To provide funds to freestanding children's teaching hospitals to support the training of pediatric and other residents in graduate medical education (GME) programs.

Applicant Eligibility: Applicants (children's teaching hospitals) must meet the following eligibility requirements in accordance with the Federal Register Notice, Vol. 66, No. 41 published on March 1, 2001.

Beneficiary Eligibility: Any public or private nonprofit and profit freestanding children's teaching hospital with an accredited residency training program which meets all eligibility requirements may apply.

Award Range/Average: FY 17 Range: $31,808- $21,117,097; Average $4,876,268 in combined DME and IME payments. FY 18 Range est: $32,000- $22,000,000; Average $5,000,000 in combined DME and IME payments.

Funding: FY 17 $282,823,526; FY 18 est $295,000,000; FY 19 est $295,000,000; FY 16 $279,033,446.

HQ: Bureau of Health Workforce
Rockville, MD 20857
Phone: 301-443-8681
Email: mlee1@hrsa.gov
http://bhw.hrsa.gov/grants/medicine/chgme

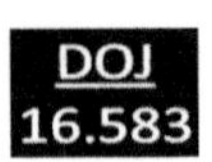

CHILDREN'S JUSTICE ACT PARTNERSHIPS FOR INDIAN COMMUNITIES "CJA"

Award: Project Grants; Direct Payments for Specified Use

Purpose: To provide funding, technical assistance, and training to help American Indian and Alaska Native communities develop, establish, and operate programs designed to improve the investigation, prosecution, and handling of cases of child abuse and neglect.

Applicant Eligibility: Federally recognized Indian tribal governments and nonprofit Indian organizations that provide services to American Indians and Alaska Natives. Specific criteria will vary depending on the grant.

Beneficiary Eligibility: American Indian and Alaskan Native youth who are victims of child abuse and/or child sexual abuse.

Award Range/Average: No Data Available.

Funding: (Project Grants) FY 17 $2,946,093; FY 18 est $3,000,000; FY 19 est $3,000,000; FY 16 N/A.

HQ: Office of Victims of Crime Department of Justice 810 Seventh Street NW
Washington, DC 20531
Phone: 202-307-5983
Email: yolanda.gibson@usdoj.gov
http://www.justice.gov

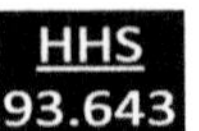

CHILDREN'S JUSTICE GRANTS TO STATES

Award: Formula Grants

Purpose: Encourages states to enact reforms which are designed to improve the assessment and investigation of suspected child abuse and neglect cases, including cases of suspected child sexual abuse and exploitation, in a manner that limits additional trauma to the child and the child's family.

Applicant Eligibility: States (including Puerto Rico and the District of Columbia), Virgin Islands, Guam, American Samoa, and the Commonwealth of the Northern Marianas.

Beneficiary Eligibility: Beneficiaries include state governments and victims of child abuse and neglect, particularly child sexual abuse and exploitation.

Award Range/Average: FY 2017: $53,269 to $1,788,425 with an average grant of $303,571.

Funding: (Formula Grants) FY 17 $17,000,000; FY 18 est $15,974,483; FY 19 est $17,000,000; FY 16 $17,000,000.

HQ: Office on Child Abuse and Neglect 330 C Street SW, Room 3419B
Washington, DC 20201
Phone: 202-205-4539
Email: lauren.fischman@acf.hhs.gov
http://www.acf.dhhs.gov/programs/cb

CHOICE NEIGHBORHOODS IMPLEMENTATION GRANTS

Award: Project Grants

Purpose: To transform neighborhoods of poverty into feasible mixed-income neighborhoods with access to economic activities.

Applicant Eligibility: For Choice Neighborhoods Implementation Grants, Public Housing Agencies (PHAs), local governments, non-profits, and for-profit developers that apply jointly with a public entity.

Beneficiary Eligibility: Same as Applicant Eligibility.

Award Range/Average: Range is $24,214,284 to $30,000,000. Average is $29,035,714

Funding: FY 17 $132,280,927; FY 18 est $145,000,000; FY 19 est $0; FY 16 $500,000.

HQ: 451 7th Street SW, Room 4130
Washington, DC 20410
Phone: 202-402-5461
http://www.hud.gov/cn

CHOICE NEIGHBORHOODS PLANNING GRANTS

Award: Project Grants

Purpose: To support the development of comprehensive neighborhood Transformation Plans that integrate effective strategies to implement public and/or assisted housing revitalization, coordination, and design of supportive services.

Applicant Eligibility: Choice Neighborhoods Planning Grants will support the development of comprehensive neighborhood Transformation Plans. The Transformation Plan should integrate effective strategies to implement public and/or assisted housing revitalization, the coordination and design of supportive services, including educational opportunities for children, and neighborhood-level planning to improve a range of neighborhood assets.

Beneficiary Eligibility: For Choice Neighborhoods Planning Grants, the ultimate beneficiaries are residents of the severely distressed public and/or assisted housing unit and residents of the surrounding community these grants aim to engage in the creation of the community drafted Transformation Plan.

Award Range/Average: Grants ranged from $350,000 to $1,300,000; Average: $825,000 (FY 17) and $808,333 (FY 18)

Funding: FY 17 $2,155,727; FY 18 est $5,000,000; FY 19 est $0; FY 16 $2,155,727.

HQ: 451 7th Street SW, Room 4130
Washington, DC 20410
Phone: 202-402-5461
http://www.hud.gov/cn

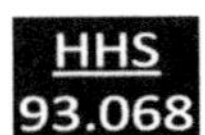

CHRONIC DISEASES: RESEARCH, CONTROL, AND PREVENTION
"Research, Control, and Prevention"

Award: Cooperative Agreements

Purpose: To assist State and local health agencies, health related organizations, and other public and private organizations in their efforts to prevent and control chronic diseases and disorders through research, development, capacity building, and intervention.

Applicant Eligibility: Applications may be submitted by State or local governments or their Bona Fide Agents (this includes the District of Columbia, the Commonwealth of Puerto Rico, the Virgin Islands, the Commonwealth of the Northern Marianna Islands, American Samoa, Guam, the Federated States of Micronesia, the Republic of the Marshall Islands, and the Republic of Palau). Eligible applicants also include public and private nonprofit organizations, for profit organizations, small, minority, women-owned businesses, universities, colleges, research institutions, hospitals, community-based organizations, faith-based organizations, Federally recognized Indian tribal governments, Indian tribes, and Indian tribal organizations.

Beneficiary Eligibility: The general public will benefit from the objectives of this program.

Award Range/Average: N/A

Funding: (Cooperative Agreements) FY 17 $0; FY 18 est $0; FY 19 est $0; FY 16 est $0; - Project is closed.

HQ: 1600 Clifton Road
Atlanta, GA 30333
Phone: 770-488-8390
http://www.cdc.gov

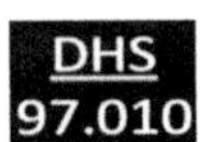

CITIZENSHIP EDUCATION & TRAINING

Award: Cooperative Agreements; Project Grants

Purpose: The Citizenship and Integration Grant Program ensures the availability of high-quality citizenship preparation services for low-income and underserved permanent residents in communities across the nation.

Applicant Eligibility: Community-and faith-based organizations, public libraries, as well other nonprofit institutions/organizations that conduct citizenship education classes for permanent residents, are eligible. Restrictions on the type of organization eligible to apply for a specific funding opportunity will be identified in the announcement.

Beneficiary Eligibility: Immigrant Service Providers; Refugee/Alien.

Award Range/Average: Not applicable for dissemination of technical information projects.

Funding: Project Grants (Contracts) FY 17 $10,000,000; FY 18 est $10,000,000; FY 19 est $10,000,000; FY 16 $10,000,000.

HQ: USCIS 245 Murray Lane SW Building 410, P.O. Box 0115
Washington, DC 20528
Phone: 202-357-7927
Email: stephen.t.mchale@uscis.dhs.gov
http://www.uscis.gov/grants

CIVIL RIGHTS TRAINING & ADVISORY SERVICES (EQUITY ASSISTANCE CENTERS)

Award: Project Grants

Purpose: To provide technical assistance and training services to school districts and governmental agencies to cope with educational problems occasioned by race, sex, religion, and national origin desegregation.

Applicant Eligibility: Any private, nonprofit organization or any public agency (other than a State educational agency or school board) may apply.

Beneficiary Eligibility: Educational personnel and elementary and secondary students in local school districts benefit.

Award Range/Average: In FY 17, $1,636,261 average. In FY 18, $1,634,250 average. In FY 19, $1,634,250 average.

Funding: FY 17 $6,575,000; FY 18 est $6,575,000; FY 19 est $6,575,000; FY 16 $6,575,000.

HQ: Department of Education 400 Maryland Avenue SW LBJ Building, Room 3E206
Washington, DC 20202
Phone: 202-453-5990
Email: david.cantrell@ed.gov
http://www.ed.gov/programs/equitycenters/index.html

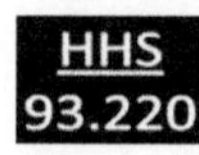

CLINICAL RESEARCH LOAN REPAYMENT PROGRAM FOR INDIVIDUALS FROM DISADVANTAGED BACKGROUNDS "NIH Clinical Research Loan Repayment Program; CR LRP"

Award: Direct Payments for Specified Use

Purpose: To recruit and retain health professionals from disadvantaged backgrounds to conduct clinical research at the National Institutes of Health (NIH) by providing for the repayment of educational loans.

Applicant Eligibility: Eligible applicants must: (1) Be a citizen, national, or permanent resident of the United States; (2) possess a M.D.

Beneficiary Eligibility: Clinical researchers from disadvantaged backgrounds who have unpaid educational loans will benefit from this program.

Award Range/Average: For initial 2-year contracts, loan repayments range from $4,000 to $70,000, Tax reimbursements range from $1,977 to $34,598. The average contract cost which includes loan and tax reimbursement is $68,454.

Funding: (Project Grants) FY 17 $0; FY 18 est $31,882; FY 19 est $102,550; FY 16 $0; - During Fiscal Year 2016, there were no new or renewal applications submitted to the Clinical Research Loan Repayment Program for Individuals from Disadvantaged Backgrounds. However, it is projected that there will be three submissions in 2017.

HQ: US Department of Health and Human Services Building 2, Room 2E18 2 Center Drive
Bethesda, MD 20892-0230
Phone: 301-402-1283
Email: colep@mail.nih.gov
http://www.lrp.nih.gov

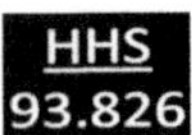

CLOSING THE GAP BETWEEN STANDARDS DEVELOPMENT & IMPLEMENTATION

Award: Cooperative Agreements

Purpose: To establish a mechanism for ongoing long-term collaborative engagement with Health Level 7 International in order to support advancements in the technical standards necessary to achieve interoperability among health IT systems.

Applicant Eligibility: Sole source award to Health Level 7 International

Beneficiary Eligibility: The beneficiaries will include all health care organizations and patients using electronic health records.

Award Range/Average: No Data Available.

Funding: FY 17 $850,000; FY 18 est $1,360,000; FY 19 FY 16 est $0.

HQ: 330 C Street SW, Suite 726-G
Washington, DC 20201
Phone: 202-691-2132
Email: matthew.rahn@hhs.gov
http://www.healthit.gov

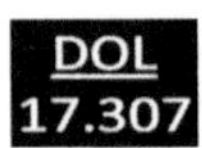

COAL MINE WORKERS' COMPENSATION "Black Lung"

Award: Direct Payments with Unrestricted Use

Purpose: Provides benefits to coal miners who have become totally disabled due to coal workers' pneumoconiosis (CWP), and to widows and other surviving dependents of miners who have died of this disease.

Applicant Eligibility: The miner (including some workers involved in coal transportation in and around mines and coal mine construction workers) must have worked in the Nation's coal mines or a coal preparation facility and become "totally disabled" (as defined in the Act) from pneumoconiosis. The applicant may be able to work in areas other than coal mines and still be eligible for benefits.

Beneficiary Eligibility: Disabled coal miners, widows and other surviving dependents of the deceased.

Award Range/Average: On January 1, 2018 new monthly rates went into effect for Black Lung. The rates are as follows: PART B MONTHLY BENEFITS RATES (claims approved by the Social Security Administration - payments received around the 3rd of each month): Primary beneficiary: $660, Primary beneficiary and one dependent: $990, Primary beneficiary and two dependents: $1,155, Primary beneficiary and three or more dependents: $1,320. PART C BLACK LUNG MONTHLY BENEFIT RATES (claims approved by the Department of Labor - payments received around the 15th of each month): Primary beneficiary: $660.10, Primary beneficiary and one dependent: $990.10, Primary beneficiary and two dependents: $1,155.10, Primary beneficiary and three or more dependents: $1,320.10.

Funding: (Direct Payments with Unrestricted Use) FY 17 $270,444,012; FY 18 est $244,480,000; FY 19 est $236,592,000; FY 16 $275,988,029; - These are benefits for both Parts B & C of the program.

HQ: Division of Coal Mine Workers Compensation 200 Constitution Avenue NW
Washington, DC 20210
Phone: 202-693-0046
http://www.dol.gov/owcp/dcmwc

COAL MINERS RESPIRATORY IMPAIRMENT TREATMENT CLINICS & SERVICES
"Black Lung Clinics Program (BLCP) and the Black Lung Center of Excellence (BLCE)"

Award: Cooperative Agreements

Purpose: The Black Lung Clinics Program aims to reduce the morbidity and mortality associated with occupationally-related coal mine dust lung disease through the provision of medical, outreach, educational, and benefits counseling services to coal miners and their families.

Applicant Eligibility: The BLCP is open to any state or public or private entity that meets the requirements of the program. This includes faith-based and community-based organizations as well as federally-recognized Tribes and Tribal organizations.

Beneficiary Eligibility: Per 42 CFR Part55a, a "coal miner" is defined as: Any individual who works or has worked in or around a coal mine or coal preparation facility in the extraction or preparation of coal. The term also includes an individual who works or has worked in coal mine construction or transportation in and around a coal mine, to the extent that the individual was exposed to coal dust as a result of employment.

Award Range/Average: BLCP (FY 2017): Range of awards (est.): $187,740 - 658,427. Average award (est.): $466,072 BLCE (FY 2017): Range of award (est.): $150,000. Average award (est.): $150,000 BLCP & BLCE combined (FY 2017): Range of awards (est.): $150,000 - 658,427 Average award (est.): $446,318.

Funding: (Cooperative Agreements) FY 17 $150,000; FY 18 est $125,000; FY 19 est $125,000; FY 16 $150,000; - BLCE(Project Grants) FY 17 $6,991,084; FY 18 est $6,991,084; FY 19 est $9,875,000; FY 16 $6,537,443; - BLCP.

HQ: 5600 Fishers Lane
Rockville, MD 20857
Phone: 301-945-9819
Email: ahutchings@hrsa.gov
http://www.hrsa.gov/ruralhealth

COCHRAN FELLOWSHIP PROGRAM-INTERNATIONAL TRAINING-FOREIGN PARTICIPANT
"Cochran Fellowship Program"

Award: Project Grants; Direct Payments for Specified Use

Purpose: To deliver quality training in meeting the food security needs and strengthen agricultural businesses in the United States.

Applicant Eligibility: The Cochran Program solicits proposals for training from U.S. institutions of higher education, nonprofit organizations, U.S. agricultural trade and market development associations, and private agribusinesses.

Beneficiary Eligibility: Technical assistance provided through these agreements benefits foreign governments and agricultural institutions in their countries.

Award Range/Average: Training activities last approximately two weeks. Average cost of each project is $60,000.

Funding: (Direct Payments for Specified Use) FY 17 $3,231,412; FY 18 est $3,100,000; FY 19 est $4,200,000; FY 16 $4,078,009.

HQ: 1400 Independence Avenue SW
Washington, DC 20250-1031
Phone: 202-690-0947
Email: desiree.thomas@fas.usda.gov
http://www.fas.usda.gov/programs/cochran-fellowship-program

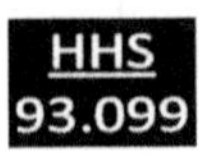

COLLABORATION WITH THE WORLD HEALTH ORGANIZATION & ITS REGIONAL OFFICES FOR GLOBAL HEALTH SECURITY & THE INTERNATIONAL HEALTH REGULATIONS (IHR 2005)

Award: Cooperative Agreements

Purpose: To help WHO Member States strengthen their capabilities to support the International Health Regulations (IHR), an international agreement that requires Member States to prevent and respond to acute public health risks that have the potential to cross borders.

Applicant Eligibility: Only the World Health Organization and its regional offices are eligible to apply. For purposes of this document, the term "WHO" includes its regional offices (e.

Beneficiary Eligibility: The World Health Organization and its regional offices work will benefit individuals worldwide, including in the U.S., through collaboration with National Ministries of Health and other organizations/institutions. The purpose is to support WHO to reduce the global disease burden through improved international capacity to detect and respond to emerging infectious diseases and other threats.

Award Range/Average: Awards ranged and averaged between $600K (PAHO) and $18M (WHO)

Funding: FY 17 N/A FY 18 est $0; FY 19 est $0; FY 16 $4,288,312; - This program includes awards made under two cooperative agreements (PAHO & WHO).

HQ: 1600 Clifton Road, P.O. Box E29
Atlanta, GA 30329
Phone: 404-639-4276
http://www.cdc.gov

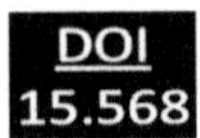

COLORADO RIVER PILOT SYSTEM CONSERVATION "Pilot System Conservation Program (PSCP)"

Award: Cooperative Agreements

Purpose: Conservation projects that creates "system water" through voluntary compensated reductions in water use. All water conserved as a result of the SCPP becomes system water with the sole purpose of increasing storage levels in Lakes Powell and Mead and does not accrue to the benefit of any individual user.

Applicant Eligibility: Eligibility of the Upper Colorado River Commission established through PL 113-235.

Beneficiary Eligibility: Pursuant to PL 113-235, participation in the Pilot Program is limited to Entitlement Holders in the Lower Colorado Division States and Colorado River Water Users in the Upper Colorado River Basin.

Award Range/Average: Range: $1,065,000 Average: $1,065,000

Funding: (Cooperative Agreements) FY 19 est $1,065,000; FY 17 $1,065,000; FY 18 est $1,065,000.

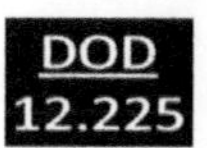

COMMERCIAL TECHNOLOGIES FOR MAINTENANCE ACTIVITIES PROGRAM "CTMA"

Award: Cooperative Agreements

Purpose: To advance the development, integration, and use of commercial sustainment technologies and processes.

Applicant Eligibility: N/A

Beneficiary Eligibility: N/A

Award Range/Average: The projected range of financial assistance to be applied to CTMA annually is historically in the range of $10M- $25M. The average expected financial assistance is $15M annually.

Funding: FY 17 $27,503,485; FY 18 est $42,801,277; FY 19 est $42,801,277; FY 16 $17,848,393.

HQ: 1225 S Clark Street, Suite 910
Arlington, VA 22202
Phone: 703-545-3559
Email: debral@ncms.org
http://www.ncms.org/ctma

COMMUNITY ASSISTANCE PROGRAM STATE SUPPORT SERVICES ELEMENT (CAP-SSSE) "CAP-SSSE"

Award: Cooperative Agreements

Purpose: The program provides technical assistance to the flood insurance program to evaluate the National Flood Insurance Program and build the State and community floodplain management expertise and capacity.

Applicant Eligibility: The Cooperative Agreement is only available to the state or territorial agency so designated by the Governor, as the state or territorial National Flood Insurance Program State Coordinating Agency. The CAP-SSSE is administered through the Mitigation Division of each FEMA Regional Office.

Beneficiary Eligibility: The direct beneficiary of the CAP-SSSE is the individual State receiving financial assistance. In addition, participating NFIP communities and local governments which receive flood plain management and flood loss reduction assistance provided by the State are also (indirect) beneficiaries as a consequence of the services they receive.

Award Range/Average: $10,400,000 Total Funding for all 50 states and US Territories.

Funding: FY 17 $10,400,000; FY 18 est $10,400,000; FY 19 est $10,400,000; FY 16 $10,400,000.

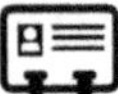

HQ: Community Assistance Program - State Support Services FEMA 400 C Street SW
Washington, DC 20472
Phone: 202-212-3460
Email: julie.grauer@fema.dhs.gov
http://www.fema.gov/community-assistance-program-state-support-services-element

COMMUNITY COMPASS TECHNICAL ASSISTANCE & CAPACITY BUILDING "Community Compass TA"

Award: Cooperative Agreements

Purpose: To help HUD's customers navigate complex housing and community development challenges by equipping them with the knowledge, skills, tools, capacity, and systems to implement HUD programs and policies successfully and be more effective stewards of HUD funding. The goal is to empower communities by providing effective technical assistance and capacity building so that successful program implementation is sustained over the long term.

Applicant Eligibility: Awardees tasked to provide technical assistance to PHAs must have at least one staff, subcontractor, or consultant that has at least five years of demonstrated Public Housing programs experience, including agency operations, voucher programs, property management operations, and capital investment programs including capital improvements and various methods of housing development. In addition, awardees tasked to provide technical assistance to PHAs must have at least one staff, subcontractor, or consultant that has at least two years of demonstrated finance and underwriting experience related to RAD conversions.

Beneficiary Eligibility: Selected providers will be deployed as HUD deems most necessary across the country to assist organizations receiving HUD funds to improve performance and management of HUD funds.

Award Range/Average: The Range is between $250,000 and $20,000,000.

Funding: FY 17 $57,423,608; FY 18 est $72,500,000; FY 19 N/A FY 16 $58,000,000.

HQ: Seventh Street SW Room 7218, P.O. Box 451
Washington, DC 20147
Phone: 202-708-3176
Email: stephanie.v.stone@hud.gov
http://portal.hud.gov/hudportal/hud?src=/program_offices/comm_planning/about/cpdta

COMMUNITY CONNECT GRANT PROGRAM "Community Connect"

Award: Project Grants

Purpose: To provide grants to eligible rural communities to provide facilities such as schools, education centers, hospitals, law enforcement agencies, public safety organizations, etc.

Applicant Eligibility: To be eligible for a grant, the applicant must: (a) be legally organized as an incorporated organization, an Indian tribe or tribal organization, a state or local unit of government, or other legal entity, including cooperatives or private corporations or limited liability companies organized on a for profit or not-for profit basis, and (b) have the legal capacity and authority to own and operate the broadband facilities as proposed in its application, to enter into contracts and to otherwise comply with applicable federal statutes and regulations.

Beneficiary Eligibility: The people living in rural areas and to improve rural opportunities through the availability of access to high speed broadband networks.

Award Range/Average: The Agency will publish, annually in the Federal Register, a Notice of Funds Availability that sets forth the maximum and minimum funding for each grant. In FY 2016, grants ranged from $481,000 to $3,000,000 and averaged $1,733,872. In FY 2017, grants can range from $500,000 to $3,000,000 and the average will not be known until selections are made.

Funding: FY 17 $34,500,000; FY 18 est $20,000,000; FY 19 est $0; FY 16 $15,604,851.

HQ: 1400 Independence Avenue SW, P.O. Box 1590
Washington, DC 20250
Phone: 202-720-0800
Email: chad.parker@wdc.usda.gov
http://www.rd.usda.gov/programs-services/community-connect-grants

COMMUNITY DEVELOPMENT BLOCK GRANTS/ENTITLEMENT GRANTS

"Community Development Block Grant program for Entitlement Communities"

Award: Formula Grants

Purpose: To provide decent housing, suitable living environment, and expanding economic opportunities, principally for persons of low and moderate income.

Applicant Eligibility: Recipients are states; cities in Metropolitan Areas designated by OMB as a central city of the Metropolitan Area; other cities over 50,000 in Metropolitan Areas; and qualified urban counties of at least 200,000 (excluding the population in entitlement cities located within the boundaries of such counties) are eligible to receive CDBG entitlement grants determined by a statutory formula.

Beneficiary Eligibility: The principal beneficiaries of CDBG funds are low- and moderate-income persons (generally defined as a member of a family having an income equal to or less than the Section 8 low income limit established by HUD). The recipient must certify that at least 70 percent of the grant funds received during a 1, 2, or 3-year period, that it designates, are expended for activities that will principally benefit low- and moderate-income persons.

Award Range/Average: From low of $72,231 to a high of $178,008,585 for New York City; average grant $2,956,494.

Funding: FY 17 $3,060,000; FY 18 est $3,365,000; FY 19 est $3,365,000; FY 16 $3,060,000.

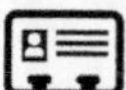

HQ: 451 7th Street SW, Room 7282
Washington, DC 20410
Phone: 202-402-3416
Email: otis.d.collins@hud.gov
http://www.hud.gov/offices/cpd/index.cfm

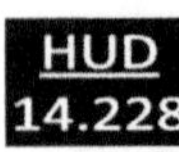

COMMUNITY DEVELOPMENT BLOCK GRANTS/STATE'S PROGRAM & NON-ENTITLEMENT GRANTS IN HAWAII "State CDBG"

Award: Formula Grants

Purpose: To provide decent housing, a suitable living environment, and expanding economic opportunities, principally for persons of low- and moderate-income.

Applicant Eligibility: Forty-nine State governments and the Commonwealth of Puerto Rico receive funds from HUD under this program. The state of Hawaii does not participate and HUD allocates the state's share of funds to the three Hawaii non-entitled counties.

Beneficiary Eligibility: The principal beneficiaries of CDBG funds are low- and moderate- income persons. For non-metropolitan areas, low- and moderate- income is generally defined as 80 percent of the median income for non-metropolitan areas of the State or of the county, whichever is higher, adjusted for family size.

Award Range/Average: State grant amounts are determined by formula. Of the 50 grants allocated to states under the State CDBG program in FY 2016, the average (mean) grant amount is $17,860,874. Grant amounts range from $2,037,326 to $60,199,998. These totals do not include Hawaii's allocation awarded to its 3 non-entitled counties. Hawaii's share of the 2016 allocation is $4,919194.

Funding: FY 17 est $897,900; FY 16 $897,900; FY 18 N/A.

HQ: 451 7th Street SW, Room 7184
Washington, DC 20410
Phone: 202-402-5716
Email: james.e.hoemann@hud.gov
http://www.hudexchange.info/cdbg-state

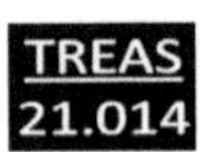

COMMUNITY DEVELOPMENT FINANCIAL INSTITUTIONS BOND GUARANTEE PROGRAM "BGP"

Award: Guaranteed/Insured Loans

Purpose: To support community development lending and investment by providing a new source of long-term capital to certified Community Development Financial Institutions (CDFIs).

Applicant Eligibility: The Act defines Eligible CDFIs and authorizes the CDFI Fund to determine which entities may serve as Qualified Issuers.

Beneficiary Eligibility: Eligible CDFIs must use the Bond Proceeds for Eligible Community and Economic Development Purposes. This may include, but is not limited to, lending activities in low-income communities and underserved rural areas such as: owner-occupied home mortgages, charter schools, and municipal and community entity lending, among others.

Award Range/Average: No Data Available.

Funding: FY 17 $245,000,000; FY 18 est $150,000,000; FY 19 est $500,000,000; FY 14 $500,000,000; FY 16 $500,000,000.

HQ: 1500 Pennsylvania Avenue NW
Washington, DC 20036

Phone: 202-653-0421

http://www.cdfifund.gov/programs-training/programs/cdfi-bond/pages/default.aspx

TREAS 21.020 COMMUNITY DEVELOPMENT FINANCIAL INSTITUTIONS PROGRAM "CDFI Program"

Award: Project Grants

Purpose: To promote economic revitalization and community development through investment and assistance to Community Development Financial Institutions (CDFIs).

Applicant Eligibility: Only certified CDFIs are eligible to apply for Financial Assistance awards. Certified CDFIs and entities seeking to become certified CDFIs may apply for Technical Assistance awards.

Beneficiary Eligibility: Investment Areas and Targeted Populations, as defined in 12 C.F.

Award Range/Average: FY 2017 Range of Financial Assistance Awards were $150,000 to $1,096,905; FY 2017 Small and/or Emerging CDFI Assistance (SECA) Average Financial Assistance Awards were $478,000 capped at $700,000; FY 2017 Core Average Financial Assistance Award was $810,000 and capped at $2,000,000. FY 2017 Range of Technical Assistance Awards were $45,000 - $125,000; FY 2017 Average Technical Assistance Awards were $116,000.

Funding: FY 17 $192,934,431; FY 18 est $185,000,000; FY 19 est $182,000,000; FY 15 $160,296,627; FY 16 $148,157,493; FY 14 $160,831,795.

HQ: 1500 Pennsylvania Avenue NW
Washington, DC 20036
Phone: 202-653-0421
http://www.cdfifund.gov/programs-training/programs/cdfi-program/pages/default.aspx

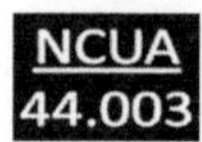

NCUA 44.003 COMMUNITY DEVELOPMENT REVOLVING LOAN FUND ACCESS FOR CREDIT UNIONS "CDRLF Program"

Award: N/A

Purpose: To assist low-income designated credit unions (LICUs) in providing basic financial services to their members to stimulate economic activities in their communities.

Applicant Eligibility: Federal and state chartered credit unions that have a low-income designation from the NCUA and/or appropriate state regulator pursuant to NCUA Rules and Regulation at §701.34(a)(1) or §741.

Beneficiary Eligibility: A credit union wishing to participate must serve a field of membership which is comprised primarily of low-income individuals. To participate in the CDRLF Program, a federally chartered credit union must be currently designated as a "low-income" credit union as set forth in NCUA's Rules and Regulations.

Award Range/Average: Smallest FY 16 grant award - $200 Largest FY 16 grant award - $15,000 Average FY 16 grant award - $8,085 Smallest FY 17 grant award - $1,500 Largest FY 17 grant award - $25,000 Average FY 17 grant award - $8,719

Funding: Project Grants (Special) FY 17 $2,389,085; FY 18 est $2,000,000; FY 19 est $2,000,000; - (Direct Loans) FY 17 $500,000; FY 18 est $2,000,000; FY 19 N/A - This portion reflects the loans issued as part of the CDRLF Program. Loan amounts range from $10,000 to $500,000.

COMMUNITY DISASTER LOANS

Award: Direct Loans

Purpose: The program provides loans to a local government that has suffered a substantial loss of revenues in a disaster-designated area to help communities to recover effectively in accordance with PPD-8.

Applicant Eligibility: Applicants must be in a designated major disaster area and must demonstrate that they meet the specific conditions of FEMA Disaster Assistance Regulations 44 CFR Part 206, Subpart K, Community Disaster Loans. To be eligible the applicant must demonstrate: 1) a substantial loss of revenues as a result of a major disaster; 2) a need for financial assistance to perform its governmental functions.

Beneficiary Eligibility: Local governments in a designated disaster area.

Award Range/Average: N/A

Funding: FY 17 $13,553,600; FY 18 est $590,152,423; FY 19 est $385,000,000; FY 16 $707,002.

HQ: 500 C Street SW, P.O. Box 3163
Washington, DC 20472
Phone: 202-646-5761
Email: martha.polanco.2@fema.dhs.gov
http://www.dhs.gov

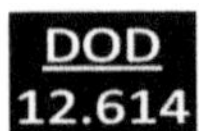

COMMUNITY ECONOMIC ADJUSTMENT ASSISTANCE FOR ADVANCE PLANNING & ECONOMIC DIVERSIFICATION

Award: Project Grants

Purpose: To assist State and local governments to lessen an area's dependence on defense expenditures by preparing economic diversification strategies, and contingency strategies and schematic land use plans for the potential redevelopment of a military installation prior to closure or realignment decisions.

Applicant Eligibility: Applicants for this assistance are to contact the Office of Economic Adjustment and a Project Manager will be assigned to work with the applicant to determine eligibility for assistance under this program. States, counties, municipalities, other political subdivisions of a State, special purpose units of a State or local government, and tribal nations are eligible for this assistance if a substantial portion of the economic activity or population of the applicant's geographic area is dependent on defense expenditures.

Beneficiary Eligibility: States and communities, including workers, businesses, and other community interests, that could be affected by Defense budget reductions and base closures/realignments.

Award Range/Average: $1,000,000 - $4,000,000; $2,000,000

Funding: FY 16 est $3,744,937; FY 15 est $8,230,150; FY 17 N/A.

HQ: 2231 Crystal Drive, Suite 520
Arlington, VA 22202-3711
Phone: 703-697-2130
http://www.oea.gov

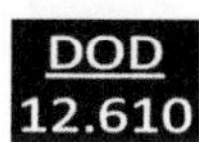

COMMUNITY ECONOMIC ADJUSTMENT ASSISTANCE FOR COMPATIBLE USE & JOINT LAND USE STUDIES

Award: Project Grants

Purpose: To assist State and local governments to mitigate or prevent incompatible civilian land use/activity that is likely to impair the continued operational utility of a Department of Defense (DoD) military installation.

Applicant Eligibility: Applicants for this assistance are to contact the Office of Economic Adjustment and a Project Manager will be assigned to work with the applicant to determine eligibility for assistance under this program. States, counties, municipalities, other political subdivisions of a State, and special purpose units of a State or local government are eligible for this assistance if the Director, Office of Economic Adjustment determines that the encroachment of the civilian community is likely to impair the continued operational utility of the military installation.

Beneficiary Eligibility: States and communities, including local property owners, as well as the local military installation.

Award Range/Average: $50,000 - $750,000; $250,000

Funding: (Project Grants) FY 17 est $11,770,000; FY 15 $5,667,021; FY 16 est $6,445,937.

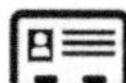

HQ: 2231 Crystal Drive, Suite 520
Arlington, VA 22202-3711
Phone: 703-697-2130
http://www.oea.gov

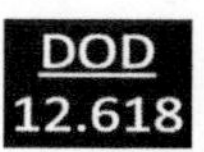

COMMUNITY ECONOMIC ADJUSTMENT ASSISTANCE FOR ESTABLISHMENT OR EXPANSION OF A MILITARY INSTALLATION

Award: Cooperative Agreements; Project Grants

Purpose: To plan and carry out local adjustments in local public services and facilities, workforce training programs, and other community economic development activities in response to the proposed or actual expansion, establishment, or growth of a military installation by the Department of Defense (DoD).

Applicant Eligibility: Applicants for this assistance are to contact the Office of Economic Adjustment and a Project Manager will be assigned to work with the applicant to determine eligibility for assistance under this program. U.S. States and Territories, counties, municipalities, other political subdivisions of a State, special purpose units of a State or local government, and tribal nations are eligible for this assistance if: 1) community impact assistance is not otherwise available; 2) the expansion, establishment, or growth involves the assignment to the installation of (i) more than 2,000 military, civilian, and contractor Department of Defense personnel, or (ii) more military, civilian, and contractor DoD personnel than the number equal to ten percent of the number of persons employed in counties or municipalities within fifteen miles of the installation, whichever is lesser; and, 3) The Secretary, through the Office of Economic

Adjustment, determines the action is likely to have a direct and significant adverse consequence on the affected community.

Beneficiary Eligibility: States, Territories and communities, including workers, businesses and other community interests that are affected by Department of Defense installation establishment or expansion actions.

Award Range/Average: The range of assistance is projected to be from $300,000 to $1 million.

Funding: (Salaries and Expenses) FY 16 $0; FY 18 est $1,100,000; FY 19 N/A FY 17 $0.

HQ: 2231 Crystal Drive, Suite 520
Arlington, VA 22202-3711
Phone: 703-697-2130
http://www.oea.gov

DOD 12.607 COMMUNITY ECONOMIC ADJUSTMENT ASSISTANCE FOR REALIGNMENT OR CLOSURE OF A MILITARY INSTALLATION

Award: Project Grants

Purpose: To plan and carry out adjustment strategies; engage the private sector in order to plan and undertake community economic development and base redevelopment; and, partner with the Military Departments in response to the proposed or actual expansion, establishment, realignment or closure of a military installation by the Department of Defense (DoD).

Applicant Eligibility: Applicants for this assistance are to contact the Office of Economic Adjustment and a Project Manager will be assigned to work with the applicant to determine eligibility for assistance under this program. States, counties, municipalities, other political subdivisions of a State, special purpose units of a State or local government, and tribal nations are eligible for this assistance if there is a proposed or actual realignment or closure of a military installation that is likely to have a direct and significant adverse consequence on the affected community.

Beneficiary Eligibility: States and communities, including workers, businesses, and other community interests that are affected by Department of Defense base closures and realignments.

Award Range/Average: Range: $79,560 - $2,331,240 Average grant: $648,093

Funding: (Project Grants) FY 16 est $11,665,667; FY 15 est $11,300,000; FY 17 N/A.

HQ: 2231 Crystal Drive, Suite 520
Arlington, VA 22202-3711
Phone: 703-697-2130
http://www.oea.gov

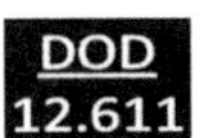

DOD 12.611 COMMUNITY ECONOMIC ADJUSTMENT ASSISTANCE FOR REDUCTIONS IN DEFENSE INDUSTRY EMPLOYMENT

Award: Project Grants

Purpose: To assist States and local governments to plan and carry out community adjustment and economic diversification activities in response to reductions in defense industry employment.

Applicant Eligibility: Applicants for this assistance are to contact the Office of Economic Adjustment and a Project Manager will be assigned to work with the applicant to determine eligibility for assistance under this program. States, counties, municipalities, other political subdivisions of a State, special purpose units of a State or local government, and tribal nations are eligible for this assistance if there is: a publicly announced planned major reduction in Department of Defense (DoD) spending; the closure or significantly reduced operations of a defense facility as the result of the merger, acquisition, or consolidation of the defense contractor operating the defense facility; the cancellation or termination of a DoD contract; or the failure to proceed with an approved major weapon system program if these actions will have a direct and significant adverse impact on a community or its residents.

Beneficiary Eligibility: States and communities, including workers, businesses, and other community interests, that may be affected by Defense actions.

Award Range/Average: $250,000 - $1,500,000; $500,000

Funding: (Project Grants) FY 16 est $10,028,299; FY 17 N/A FY 15 est $10,000,000.

HQ: 2231 Crystal Drive, Suite 520
Arlington, VA 22202-3711
Phone: 703-697-2130
http://www.oea.gov

DOD 12.604 COMMUNITY ECONOMIC ADJUSTMENT ASSISTANCE FOR REDUCTIONS IN DEFENSE SPENDING

Award: Cooperative Agreements; Project Grants; Dissemination of Technical Information

Purpose: Provides assistance to State and local governments affected by qualifying Department of Defense actions.

Applicant Eligibility: Applicants for this assistance are to contact the Office of Economic Adjustment and a Project Manager will be assigned to work with the applicant to determine eligibility for assistance under this program. States, counties, municipalities, other political subdivisions of a State, special purpose units of a State or local government, and tribal nations are eligible for this assistance if there are reductions in Defense spending resulting in a proposed or actual military and/or civilian personnel reduction resulting from a reduction in spending.

Beneficiary Eligibility: States and communities, including workers, businesses, and other community interests that are affected by a qualifying Department of Defense action.

Award Range/Average: $300,000 - $400,000

Funding: (Project Grants) FY 16 est $669,563; FY 17 N/A FY 15 est $1,500,000.

HQ: 2231 Crystal Drive, Suite 520
Arlington, VA 22202-3711
Phone: 703-697-2130
http://www.oea.gov

USDA 10.766 COMMUNITY FACILITIES LOANS & GRANTS

Award: Project Grants; Direct Loans; Guaranteed/Insured Loans

Purpose: To maximize community facilities by providing essential services to rural residents.

Applicant Eligibility: City, county, and State agencies; political and quasi-political subdivisions of States and associations, including corporations, Indian tribes on Federal and State reservations and other federally recognized Indian tribes; and existing private corporations which: (1) are operated on a not-for-profit basis; (2) have or will have the legal authority necessary for constructing, operating, and maintaining the proposed facility or service and for obtaining, giving security for, and repaying the loan; and (3) are unable to finance the proposed project from its own resources or through commercial credit at reasonable rates and terms. Assistance is authorized for eligible applicants in rural areas of the States, Puerto Rico, the Virgin Islands, Guam, American Samoa, the commonwealth of the Northern Mariana Islands, the Marshall Islands, the Republic of Palaw, and the Federated States of Micronesia.

Beneficiary Eligibility: Loans for essential community facilities are made to eligible entities who provide essential community services to the population living within the service area of the facility or being served by the facility. Beneficiaries include farmers, ranchers, rural residents, rural businesses, and other users of such public facilities in eligible applicant areas as set out above.

Award Range/Average: 2017 Direct Loan ranged from $1,800 to $113,000,000. Average: $3,677,066. Guaranteed Loan ranged from $500,000 to $16,500,000. Average: $4,417,853. Grants ranged from $1,200-$238,000. Average $31,043.

Funding: (Project Grants) FY 17 $23,600,000; FY 18 est $24,700,000; FY 19 est $25,000,000; FY 16 $25,000,000; - (Direct Loans) FY 17 $2,366,000,000; FY 18 est $2,520,000,000; FY 19 est $2,500,000,000; FY 16 $2,200,000,000; - (Guaranteed/Insured Loans) FY 17 $141,300

HQ: 1400 Independence Avenue SW
Washington, DC 20250
Phone: 202-720-1498
http://www.rd.usda.gov

Award: Project Grants

Purpose: To support and develop food projects designed to meet the food needs of low-income people; increase the self-reliance of communities; and promote comprehensive responses to local food, farm, and nutrition issues.

Applicant Eligibility: Proposals may be submitted by private nonprofit entities. Because projects must promote comprehensive responses to local food, farm, and nutrition issues, applicants are encouraged to seek and create partnership among public, private nonprofit and private for-profit organizations or firms.

Beneficiary Eligibility: Low income people.

Award Range/Average: If minimum or maximum amounts of funding per competitive and/or capacity project grant, or cooperative agreement are established, these amounts will be announced in the annual Competitive Request for Application (RFA).

Funding: FY 17 $8,640,000; FY 18 est $8,640,000; FY 19 est $8,640,000; FY 16 $8,640,000.

HQ: Division of Nutrition 1400 Independence Avenue SW, P.O. Box 2225
Washington, DC 20250-2225
Phone: 202-401-2138
Email: max.teplitski@nifa.usda.gov
http://nifa.usda.gov/program/community-food-projects-competitive-grant-program-cfpcgp

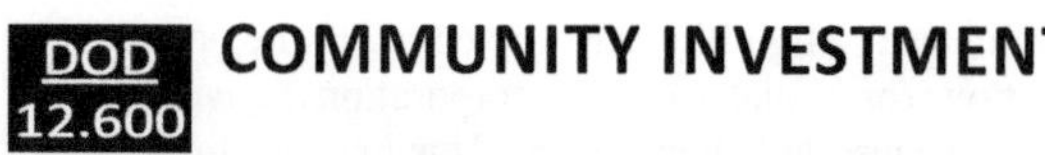

DOD 12.600 COMMUNITY INVESTMENT

Award: Cooperative Agreements; Project Grants; Dissemination of Technical Information

Purpose: Provides assistance authorized by statute.

Applicant Eligibility: Applicant eligibility for this program may be directed or restricted by statute and Department of Defense policy. Applicants for this assistance are to contact the Office of Economic Adjustment and a Project Manager will be assigned to work with the applicant to determine eligibility for assistance under this program.

Beneficiary Eligibility: Beneficiaries under this program may be directed or restricted by statute and/or Department of Defense policy.

Award Range/Average: Average: $20,260,000

Funding: (Direct Payments for Specified Use) FY 15 est $58,000,000; FY 17 N/A FY 16 est $126,658,173.

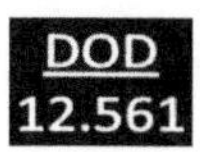

HQ: 2231 Crystal Drive, Suite 520
Arlington, VA 22202-3711
Phone: 703-697-2130
http://www.oea.gov

DOD 12.561 COMMUNITY PARTNERS IN SUICIDE PREVENTION
"Community Partners in Suicide Prevention Outreach and Education"

Award: Project Grants

Purpose: To conduct outreach and education efforts around mental health, substance use disorders, traumatic brain injury, and suicide prevention.

Applicant Eligibility: N/A

Beneficiary Eligibility: N/A

Award Range/Average: Grants range from $500,000 to $2,500,000.

Funding: (Salaries and Expenses) FY 17 $0; FY 18 est $0; FY 19 N/A FY 16 $0; - This program was last funded in FY 15. No further awards or obligations are expected under this program.

HQ: 4800 Mark Center Drive, Suite 05J25
Arlington, VA 22350
Email: malcolm.k.hawkins.civ@mail.mil
http://www.dspo.mil/aboutdspo

HHS 93.570 COMMUNITY SERVICES BLOCK GRANT DISCRETIONARY AWARDS
"Community Economic Development & Rural Community Facilities Programs"

Award: Project Grants

Purpose: To assist businesses in creating jobs for low-income individuals, i.e., develop employment and business development opportunities for low-income individuals.

Applicant Eligibility: For Community Economic Development, eligibility is restricted to private, locally initiated, nonprofit community development corporations (or affiliates of such corporations) governed by a board consisting of residents of the community and business and civic leaders. This includes faith based community development corporations.

Beneficiary Eligibility: A project must be targeted to address the needs of a specific segment of low-income individuals or families. The official poverty line established by the Director of the Office of Management and Budget, published annually by the Department of Health and Human Services is used as a criterion of eligibility in the Community Economic Development Discretionary Grant program.

Award Range/Average: Up to $800,000 for Community Economic Development and $798,000 Rural Community Development Activities.

Funding: (Training) FY 17 $101,650; FY 18 est $111,540; FY 19 est $0; FY 16 $35,000; - This funding is for the RCD program.Project Grants (Discretionary) FY 17 $17,358,014; FY 18 est $17,344,742; FY 19 est $0; FY 16 $27,410,948; - This funding is for the CED program.Project Grants (Discretionary) FY 17 $7,236,906; FY 18 est $7,753,041; FY 19 est $0; FY 16 $6,391,349; - This funding is for the RCD program.(Training) FY 17 $262,981; FY 18 est $2,263,595; FY 19 est $0; FY 16 $298,830; - This funding is for the CED program.

HQ: OCS Grants Operation Center 1401 Mercantile Lane, Suite 401
Largo, MD 20774
Phone: 855-792-6551
Email: gerald.shanklin@acf.hhs.gov
http://www.acf.hhs.gov/programs/ocs/csbg

COMMUNITY SERVICES BLOCK GRANT "CSBG"

Award: Formula Grants

Purpose: To provide services and activities having a measurable and potential major impact on causes of poverty in the community or those areas of the community where poverty is a particularly acute problem.

Applicant Eligibility: The Secretary is authorized to make grants to States. This includes each of the 50 States, the District of Columbia, the Commonwealth of Puerto Rico, Guam, the Virgin Islands, American Samoa, and the Commonwealth of the Northern Mariana Islands.

Beneficiary Eligibility: States make grants to qualified locally-based nonprofit community antipoverty agencies and other eligible entities which provide services to low-income individuals and families. The official poverty line, as established by the Secretary of Health and Human Services, is used as a criterion of eligibility in the Community Services Block Grant program.

Award Range/Average: $1,019 to $55,942,793; average $5,242,585

Funding: (Formula Grants) FY 17 $696,825,612; FY 18 est $703,856,755; FY 19 est $0; FY 16 $703,729,255; - (Training) FY 17 $1,536,812; FY 18 est $1,134,068; FY 19 est $0; FY 16 $1,105,612; - (Formula Grants) FY 17 $1,394,136; FY 18 est $1,542,000; FY 19 est $0; FY 1

HQ: 330 C Street SW 5th Floor W, P.O. Box 5425
Washington, DC 20201
Phone: 202-401-4666
Email: seth.hassett@acf.hhs.gov
http://www.acf.hhs.gov/programs/ocs/csbg

COMMUNITY-BASED CHILD ABUSE PREVENTION GRANTS

Award: Formula Grants

Purpose: Supports community-based efforts to develop, operate, expand, and enhance, and coordinate initiatives, programs, and activities to prevent child abuse and neglect and to support the coordination of resources and activities to better strengthen and support families to reduce the likelihood of child abuse and neglect.

Applicant Eligibility: States, the District of Columbia, Puerto Rico, the U.S. Virgin Islands, Guam, American Samoa, the Commonwealth of the Northern Mariana Islands are eligible. Before a state can apply, the Governor must designate a lead entity to administer the funds for the implementation of community-based child abuse and neglect prevention programs and activities.

Beneficiary Eligibility: There are no eligibility requirements. Beneficiaries, which include children and their families, organizations providing community-based, prevention focused programs and activities designed to prevent child abuse and neglect.

Award Range/Average: $200,000 to $3,279,098 with an average of $671,334. In FY 2017 for tribes the range of financial assistance was from $128,392 to $132,546 with an average of $131,140.

Funding: (Formula Grants) FY 17 $37,594,753; FY 18 est $37,722,708; FY 19 est $38,000,000; FY 16 $39,467,605; - Project Grants (Discretionary) FY 17 $1,793,420; FY 18 est $1,793,292; FY 19 est $1,790,000.

HQ: Office on Child Abuse and Neglect 330 C Street SW, Room 3403
Washington, DC 20201
Phone: 202-205-8879
Email: julie.fliss@acf.hhs.gov
http://www.acf.hhs.gov/cb/resource/cbcap-state-grants

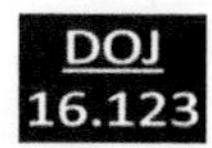

COMMUNITY-BASED VIOLENCE PREVENTION PROGRAM

Award: Project Grants

Purpose: To support a coordinated and multidisciplinary approach to community youth gun and gang violence through prevention, intervention, suppression, and reentry in targeted communities. This Program will work with community-based organizations to develop and implement strategies to reduce and prevent violence, particularly shootings, and killings.

Applicant Eligibility: Eligible applicants are limited to states (including territories), units of local government, federally recognized tribal governments as determined by the Secretary of the Interior, nonprofit organizations, and for-profit organizations (including tribal nonprofit and for-profit organizations), as well as institutions of higher education (including tribal institutions of higher education). For-profit organizations (as well as other recipients) must agree to forgo any profit or management fee.

Beneficiary Eligibility: N/A

Award Range/Average: N/A

Funding: (Project Grants) FY 17 $6,666,574; FY 18 est $8,000,000; FY 19.

HQ: Office of Juvenile Justice and Delinquency Prevention
Washington, DC 20531

Phone: 202-514-1289
Email: james.antal@usdoj.gov
http://ojjdp.gov

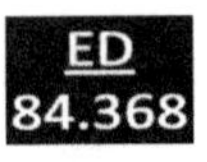

COMPETITIVE GRANTS FOR STATE ASSESSMENTS (FORMERLY, GRANTS FOR ENHANCED ASSESSMENT INSTRUMENTS)

Award: Project Grants

Purpose: To improve the quality, validity, and reliability of State academic assessments; and to measure student academic achievement through the use of multiple measures from multiple sources.

Applicant Eligibility: State educational agencies (SEAs) and/or consortia of SEAs are eligible to receive grants.

Beneficiary Eligibility: Same as Applicant Eligibility.

Award Range/Average: The average award is $7,500,000

Funding: FY 17 $0; FY 18 est $8,948,000; FY 19 est $0; FY 16 $0.

HQ: Department of Education 400 Maryland Avenue SW
Washington, DC 20202
Phone: 202-260-9737
Email: james.butler@ed.gov
http://www.2.ed.gov/programs/eag/index.html

COMPETITIVE GRANTS: PROMOTING K-12 STUDENT ACHIEVEMENT AT MILITARY-CONNECTED SCHOOLS "The Department of Defense Education Activity (DoDEA) Educational Partnership Grant Program."

Award: Project Grants

Purpose: The DoDEA Educational Partnership Grant Program provide resources for local education agencies [LEAs] to meet the academic, social and emotional needs of the highly mobile military-connected students in their community.

Applicant Eligibility: Awards will be made to local educational agencies (LEAs) on behalf of their eligible school(s). To qualify all participating schools must have a 15 percent or greater military dependent student enrollment.

Beneficiary Eligibility: K-12 students are the primary beneficiaries, although the grants may also fund teacher professional development.

Award Range/Average: In FY 16, DoDEA awarded 56 grants that ranged from $250,000 to $1,500,000. These awards are implemented over a 5 year cycle.

Funding: Project Grants (Discretionary) FY 17 N/A FY 18 est $16,350,000; FY 19 N/A FY 12 $52,394,021; FY 14 $43,680,473; FY 13 $58,255,681; FY 16 $66,540,827.

HQ: 4800 Mark Center Drive
Alexandria, VA 22350
Phone: 571-372-6026
http://www.dodea.edu/partnership/grants.cfm

COMPLEX HUMANITARIAN EMERGENCY & WAR-RELATED INJURY PUBLIC HEALTH ACTIVITIES

Award: Project Grants

Purpose: To bring public health and epidemiologic principles to the aid of populations affected by complex humanitarian emergencies.

Applicant Eligibility: The general public will benefit from the objectives of this program.

Beneficiary Eligibility: Same as Applicant Eligibility.

Award Range/Average: n/a

Funding: Project Grants (Cooperative Agreements) FY 17 N/A FY 18 N/A FY 19 est $10,940,076; FY 16 $15,096,832.

HQ: 1600 Clifton Road, P.O. Box E29
Atlanta, GA 30329
Phone: 404-639-4276
http://www.cdc.gov

COMPREHENSIVE CENTERS

Award: Project Grants

Purpose: To support comprehensive centers that provide training, professional development, and technical assistance to State educational agencies, local educational agencies, regional educational agencies, and schools in the region where the center is located.

Applicant Eligibility: Research organizations, institutions, agencies, institutions of higher education (IHEs), or partnerships among such entities, or individuals with the demonstrated ability or capacity to carry out the required activities, including providing training to States, school districts, and schools, may apply.

Beneficiary Eligibility: Agencies supporting or providing elementary and secondary education will benefit, including State and local educational agencies, regional educational agencies, the Bureau of Indian Education, Indian tribes, community-based organizations, and other recipients of funds under the ESEA.

Award Range/Average: The Department made 22 new awards in FY 2012, 15 for regional centers and 7 for content centers. The range of awards over the entire 5 year grant period was $4.0 to $23.5 million for the regional centers (median award of $14.2 million) and $6.3 to $12.1 million for the content centers (median award of $6.9 million).

Funding: FY 17 $50,000,000; FY 18 est $52,000,000; FY 19 est $0; FY 16 $51,445,000.

HQ: School Support and Rural Programs Department of Education, 400 Maryland Avenue SW LBJ Building Room 3E206

Washington, DC 20202
Phone: 202-453-6930
Email: kim.okahara@ed.gov
http://www.ed.gov/programs/newccp/index.html

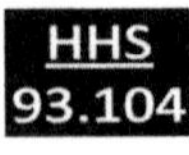

COMPREHENSIVE COMMUNITY MENTAL HEALTH SERVICES FOR CHILDREN WITH SERIOUS EMOTIONAL DISTURBANCES (SED) "CMHS Child Mental Health Service Initiative"

Award: Project Grants

Purpose: To provide community-based systems of care for children and adolescents with a serious emotional disturbance and their families.

Applicant Eligibility: States, political subdivisions of a State, such as county or local governments, and Federally Recognized Indian Tribal governments.

Beneficiary Eligibility: Children under age 22 with a diagnosed serious emotional disturbance, serious behavioral disorder, or serious mental disorder.

Award Range/Average: $376,096 to $2,000,000; $1,329,454

Funding: Project Grants (Discretionary) FY 17 $97,618,856; FY 18 est $75,404,791; FY 19 est $53,233,985; FY 16 $86,224,702.

HQ: 5600 Fishers Lane
Rockville, MD 20857
Phone: 240-276-1418
Email: roger.george@samhsa.hhs.gov
http://www.samhsa.gov

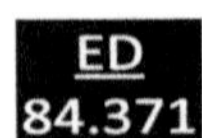

COMPREHENSIVE LITERACY DEVELOPMENT

Award: Project Grants

Purpose: To advance literacy skills, including pre-literacy skills, reading and writing for students from birth through grade 12, including English learner and students with disabilities.

Applicant Eligibility: State educational agencies are eligible applicants.

Beneficiary Eligibility: The Comprehensive Literacy Development program benefits children and youth from birth through 12th grade.

Award Range/Average: No Current Data Available.

Funding: (Project Grants) FY 17 $190,000,000; FY 18 est $190,000,000; FY 19 est $0; FY 16 $190,000,000.

HQ: 400 Maryland Avenue SW
Washington, DC 20202
Phone: 202-260-2551
Email: sylvia.lyes@ed.gov
http://www.ed.gov/programs/strivingreaders/index.html

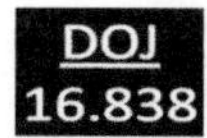

COMPREHENSIVE OPIOID ABUSE SITE-BASED PROGRAM "COAP"

Award: Cooperative Agreements; Project Grants

Purpose: The Comprehensive Opioid Abuse Site-based Program reduces opioid misuse fatalities. It also supports the clinical decision-making and prevents the misuse.

Applicant Eligibility: For TTA - eligible applicants are limited to for-profit (commercial) organizations, nonprofit organizations (including tribal nonprofit and for-profit organizations), and institutions of higher education (including tribal institutions of higher education) that have experience delivering training and technical assistance nationwide. For-profit organizations must agree to forgo any profit or management fee.

Beneficiary Eligibility: Program aims to plan and implement comprehensive strategies in response to the growing national opioid epidemic.

Award Range/Average: N/A

Funding: (Cooperative Agreements) FY 17 $11,743,182; FY 18 est $145,000,000; FY 19 est $20,000,000.

HQ: US Department of Justice Bureau of Justice Assistance 810 7th Street NW
Washington, DC 20531
Phone: 202-616-6500
http://www.ojp.gov

COMPUTER & INFORMATION SCIENCE & ENGINEERING "CISE"

Award: Project Grants

Purpose: To support investigator-initiated research and education in all areas of computer and information science and engineering; advance the development and use of cyberinfrastructure across the science and engineering enterprise; and contribute to the education and training.

Applicant Eligibility: Except where a program solicitation establishes more restrictive eligibility criteria, individuals and organizations in the following categories may submit proposals: Universities and colleges; Non-profit, non-academic organizations; For-profit organizations; State and local governments; and unaffiliated individuals. See the NSF Grant Proposal Guide, Chapter I.

Beneficiary Eligibility: N/A

Award Range/Average: Range Low $4,110 Range High $11,538,069 Average $168,526

Funding: (Project Grants) FY 17 est $935,403,000; FY 18 est $838,920,000; FY 16 $935,203,000; - 1) FY 2016 Obligation projections are the FY 2016 NSF Current Plan 2) FY 2016 Obligations are the FY 2016 NSF Appropriations Actual.

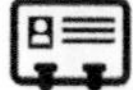

HQ: 2415 Eisenhower Avenue, Suite C10000
Alexandria, VA 22314
Phone: 703-292-8900
Email: cwhitson@nsf.gov
http://nsf.gov/dir/index.jsp?org=cise

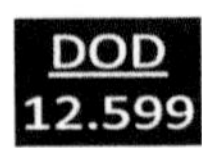

CONGRESSIONALLY DIRECTED ASSISTANCE "Annual Congressionally Directed Assistance"

Award: Cooperative Agreements; Project Grants

Purpose: To implement Congressionally directed assistance for the purposes identified in the Department of Defense ("DoD") annual appropriations act.

Applicant Eligibility: Types of organizations that may apply vary with the statutory requirements and appropriate sources of supporting information. Examples of organizations that have received assistance include nonprofit organizations, educational institutions, memorial organizations, local governments and cultural organizations.

Beneficiary Eligibility: Eligible beneficiaries are determined in accordance with the applicable statutory authorization.

Award Range/Average: Dependent on the language and direction found in the annual Defense Appropriations Act.

Funding: (Project Grants) FY 17 FY 18 FY 19 est $44,000,000; FY 13 $82,615,407; FY 14 est $46,797,902; FY 15 est $50,000,000.

HQ: 1155 Defense Pentagon
Washington, DC 20301
Phone: 703-545-1046
Email: karen.rooney@whs.mil
http://cdmrp.army.mil

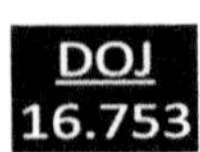

CONGRESSIONALLY RECOMMENDED AWARDS "Congressionally Recommended"

Award: Project Grants

Purpose: To improve the functioning of the criminal justice system by assisting victims of crime.

Applicant Eligibility: State and local government agencies as well as public and private nonprofit organizations and federally recognized Indian Tribal governments are eligible to receive funds including faith-based and community organizations, under this program.

Beneficiary Eligibility: State and local governments, public and private organizations, and tribal governments.

Award Range/Average: Varies.

Funding: (Project Grants) FY 17 $0; FY 18 est $0; FY 19 est $0; FY 16 $686,527.

HQ: US Department of Justice Bureau of Justice Assistance 810 7th Street NW
Washington, DC 20531
Phone: 202-616-6500
http://ojp.gov/grants101/typesoffunding.htm#directedawards

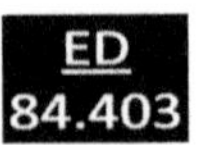

CONSOLIDATED GRANT TO THE OUTLYING AREAS

Award: Formula Grants

Purpose: To make an annual consolidated grant to assist an Insular Area in carrying out one or more State-administered formula grant programs of the Department.

Applicant Eligibility: Virgin Islands, Guam, American Samoa and the Commonwealth of the Northern Mariana Islands.

Beneficiary Eligibility: Same as Applicant Eligibility.

Award Range/Average: Estimated FY 2018 awards range from approximately $15.2 million to $31.2 million.

Funding: (Formula Grants) FY 17 $84,021,706; FY 18 est $90,085,800; FY 19 est $0; FY 16 $73,109,915; - Information for FY 2019 is not yet available.

HQ: School Support and Rural Programs Department of Education, 400 Maryland Avenue SW LBJ Building Room 3E206

Washington, DC 20202

Phone: 202-453-5990

Email: david.cantrell@ed.gov

http://www.ed.gov/about/offices/list/oese/sst/index.html

CONSORTIUM FOR TOBACCO USE CESSATION TECHNICAL ASSISTANCE FINANCED SOLELY BY PREVENTION & PUBLIC HEALTH FUNDS

"Consortium for Tobacco Use Cessation Technical Assistance"

Award: Cooperative Agreements

Purpose: Provide technical assistance to state tobacco control programs and national and state partners.

Applicant Eligibility: A Bona Fide Agent is an agency/organization identified by the state as eligible to submit an application under the state eligibility in lieu of a state application. If applying as a bona fide agent of a state or local government, a legal, binding agreement from the state or local government as documentation of the status is required.

Beneficiary Eligibility: The general public will benefit from the objectives of this program.

Award Range/Average: No Data Available.

Funding: FY 17 $450,000; FY 18 est $450,000; FY 19 est $0; FY 16 $450,000; - This program received a 12-month extension to the Period of Performance. It will end 2019.

HQ: NCCDPHP 4770 Buford Highway NE MSK50

Atlanta, GA 30341

Phone: 770-488-1172

Email: sbabb@cdc.gov

http://www.cdc.gov/tobacco/about/coop-agreements/consortium/index.htm

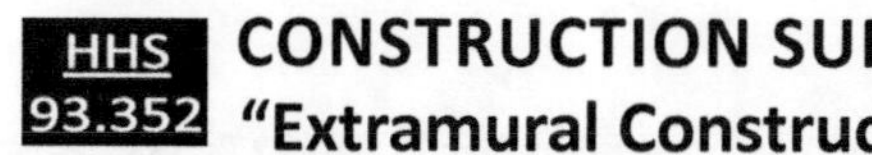

CONSTRUCTION SUPPORT

"Extramural Construction"

Award: Project Grants

Purpose: To renovate existing research facilities and build new research facilities to meet basic and clinical space requirements, laboratory safety, biohazard containment, and animal care standards.

Applicant Eligibility: Construction

Beneficiary Eligibility: Public nonprofit institution/organization

Award Range/Average: No Data Available.

Funding: (Project Grants) FY 18 est $0; FY 16 $0; FY 17 est $0.

HQ: 6701 Democracy Boulevard Room 957, P.O. Box 4874
Bethesda, MD 20892-4874
Phone: 301-435-0864
Email: pnewman@mail.nih.gov
http://dpcpsi.nih.gov/orip/index

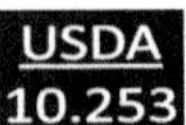

CONSUMER DATA & NUTRITION RESEARCH

Award: Cooperative Agreements; Project Grants; Dissemination of Technical Information

Purpose: ERS provides help for development, administration, and evaluation of agricultural and rural policies.

Applicant Eligibility: Any individual or organization in the U.S. and U.S. Territories is eligible to receive the popular or technical research publications that convey the research results, although there may be a fee.

Beneficiary Eligibility: Same as Applicant Eligibility.

Award Range/Average: No Data Available.

Funding: (Cooperative Agreements) FY 17 $1,100,000; FY 18 est $1,100,000; FY 19 est $0; FY 16 $1,074,282; - (Project Grants) FY 17 $2,700,000; FY 18 est $2,700,000; FY 19 est $0; FY 16 $2,691,366.

HQ: 355 E Street SW, Room 5-254
Washington, DC 20024-3231
Phone: 202-694-5008
Email: nthomas@ers.usda.gov
http://www.ers.usda.gov

CONSUMER OPERATED & ORIENTED PLAN [CO-OP] PROGRAM

Award: Direct Loans

Purpose: To provide assistance to applicants for activities related to establishing and maintaining a Consumer Operated and Oriented (CO-OP), nonprofit health insurance issuer.

Applicant Eligibility: To be eligible to apply for a loan under the CO-OP program, an applicant must intend to become a CO-OP.

Beneficiary Eligibility: N/A

Award Range/Average: Loan Range: $56,656,900 to $265,133,000 Average Loan Size: $ $106,278,338.

Funding: (Direct Loans) FY 17 $0; FY 18 est $0; FY 19 est $0; FY 16 $0.

HQ: 200 Independence Avenue SW, Room 739H
Washington, DC 20201

Phone: 301-492-4127
Email: reed.cleary@cms.hhs.gov
http://www.cms.gov

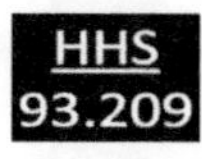

CONTRACEPTION & INFERTILITY RESEARCH LOAN REPAYMENT PROGRAM "CIR LRP"

Award: Direct Payments for Specified Use

Purpose: To provide an incentive for health professionals to work in areas of reproductive extramural contraception and/or infertility research.

Applicant Eligibility: Applicants must be a U.S. citizen (or U.S. national or permanent resident) and a physician, Ph.D.-level scientist, nurse, physician's assistant, graduate student, or postgraduate research fellow training in the health professions. You must commit to conduct contraception and infertility research for 50% of your time (at least 20 hours weekly based on a 40 hour week) for two years and it must be funded by a domestic nonprofit or U.S. Government (Federal, state or local) entity. Also, the research must not be prohibited by Federal law or NIH policy.

Beneficiary Eligibility: Assistance in the form of loan repayments will be made to qualified health professionals (including graduate students) who are participants in the CIR-LRP.

Award Range/Average: In fiscal year 2017 the range of financial assistance was between $10,622 and $97,300. The average contract cost was $57,385.

Funding: (Direct Payments for Specified Use) FY 17 $1,090,000; FY 18 est $1,149,000; FY 19 est $1,061,000; FY 16 $995,110.

HQ: 6710B Rockledge Drive, Room 2421C
Bethesda, MD 20817
Phone: 301-435-6989
Email: kaufmans@mail.nih.gov
http://www.lrp.nih.gov

CONTRIBUTIONS TO INTERNATIONAL ORGANIZATIONS FOR OVERSEAS ASSISTANCE "Contributions to International Organizations for Overseas Assistance"

Award: Project Grants; Direct Payments for Specified Use

Purpose: Provides voluntary and assessed contributions to Public International Organizations to carry out humanitarian assistance activities overseas benefitting refugees, victims of conflict, and other persons of concern.

Applicant Eligibility: Voluntary and assessed contributions to Public International Organizations to provide assistance to refugees and victims of conflict overseas.

Beneficiary Eligibility: Refugees, victims of conflict, and other persons of concern requiring protection and assistance.

Award Range/Average: No Data Available.

Funding: (Direct Payments for Specified Use) FY 13 $1,780,736,111; FY 18 est $2,600,000,000; FY 12 $1,313,962,613; FY 14 $2,275,509,158; FY 16 $2,585,558,782; FY 17 est $2,600,000,000.

HQ: 2025 E Street NW
Washington, DC 20522-0908
Phone: 202-453-9239
Email: hembreeel@state.gov
http://www.state.gov/j/prm/index.htm

COOPERATING TECHNICAL PARTNERS "CTP"

Award: Cooperative Agreements

Purpose: The CTP program's objective is to deliver data for creating public awareness on flood hazards and steps to take that can reduce risk to life and property.

Applicant Eligibility: Only qualified CTPs are eligible for federal assistance awards through this program. Eligible recipients generally include entities who already perform certain functions in flood risk analysis, flood hazard identification, flood risk communication and mitigation processes in States and local communities to reduce flood losses and protect life and property from the risk of future flood damage.

Beneficiary Eligibility: State, local, specialized group, small business, general public.

Award Range/Average: Range: $20,000 to $2,480,600 Average: approximately $400,000

Funding: FY 17 $66,000,000; FY 18 est $114,000,000; FY 19 est $25,000,000; FY 16 $73,921,944.

HQ: Federal Insurance and Mitigation Administration (FIMA) 400 C Street SW
Washington, DC 20024
Phone: 202-212-1054
Email: laura.alego@fema.dhs.gov
http://fema.gov

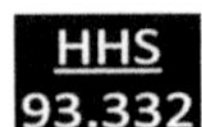

COOPERATIVE AGREEMENT TO SUPPORT NAVIGATORS IN FEDERALLY-FACILITATED EXCHANGES "Navigator Grants"

Award: Cooperative Agreements

Purpose: To develop and implement a Navigator grant program. Navigators will serve consumers in States with a FFM, including State Partnership Marketplaces.

Applicant Eligibility: Funding through the cooperative agreement is open to individuals and private and public entities including community and consumer-focused nonprofit groups; trade, industry and professional associations; commercial fishing industry organizations; ranching and farming organizations; chambers of commerce; unions; resource partners of the Small Business Administration; licensed insurance agents and brokers; and other public or private entities. Other entities may include but are not limited to Indian Tribes, tribal organizations, urban Indian organizations, and State or local human services.

Beneficiary Eligibility: The PPACA, HHS Notice of Benefit and Payment Parameters for 2019 Final Rule, effective 6/18/2018, changed the following: 1) The elimination of the previous regulatory requirements that each Exchange must have at least two Navigator entities and that one of these entities must be a community and consumer-focused non-profit (CCFN); and 2) The elimination of the requirement to maintain a physical presence in the Exchange service area Navigators were proposing to serve.

Award Range/Average: Current Fiscal Year: 2018 Projection: up to $10,000,000

Funding: FY 17 $36,108,220; FY 18 est $36,800,000; FY 19 est $36,800,000; FY 16 $643,000,000.

HQ: 7501 Wisconsin Avenue
Bethesda, MD 20814
Phone: 301-492-4319
http://www.cms.gov/cciio/programs-and-initiatives/health-insurance-marketplaces/assistance.html

COOPERATIVE AGREEMENTS FOR STATE-BASED COMPREHENSIVE BREAST & CERVICAL CANCER EARLY DETECTION PROGRAMS

"National Breast and Cervical Cancer Early Detection Program (NBCCEDP)"

Award: Cooperative Agreements

Purpose: To work with State and territorial health agencies or their designees, and tribal health agencies in developing comprehensive breast and cervical cancer early detection programs.

Applicant Eligibility: Eligible applicants are the official State health agencies of the United States, the District of Columbia, the Commonwealth of Puerto Rico, the Virgin Islands, Guam, the Northern Mariana Islands, the Federated States of Micronesia, the Republic of the Marshall Islands, American Samoa, American Indian and Alaska Native tribes and tribal organizations as defined in Section 4 of the Indian Self-Determination and Education Assistance Act.

Beneficiary Eligibility: Official State and Territorial health agencies, women especially low-income women.

Award Range/Average: 96,735 to 9,692,758; $2,234,163

Funding: (Cooperative Agreements) FY 17 $0; FY 18 est $0; FY 19 est $0; FY 16 $213,282,518; - In FY 17, this project was re-competed under DP17-1701.

HQ: 4770 Buford Highway, P.O. Box F76
Atlanta, GA 30341
Phone: 770-488-4880
Email: fwong@cdc.gov
http://www.cdc.gov/cancer

COOPERATIVE AGREEMENTS FOR STATE-BASED DIABETES CONTROL PROGRAMS & EVALUATION OF SURVEILLANCE SYSTEMS (DPCPS)
""Behavioral Risk Factor Surveillance System (BRFSS)"

Award: Cooperative Agreements

Purpose: The Diabetes Prevention and Control Programs are funded to prevent diabetes, reduce or prevent the complications associated with the disease and eliminate health disparities related to diabetes. The program achieves its goals by partnering with state-wide diabetes communities.

Applicant Eligibility: Eligible applicants are the official State and territorial health agencies of the United States, the District of Columbia, the Commonwealth of Puerto Rico, the Virgin Islands, Guam, the Northern Mariana Islands, the Federated States of Micronesia, the Republic of the Marshall Islands, the Republic of Palau, and American Samoa.

Beneficiary Eligibility: State health agencies will benefit.

Award Range/Average: No Data Available.

Funding: FY 17 $0; FY 18 est $0; FY 19 est $0; FY 16 $0.

HQ: 2877 Brandywine Road Williams Building
Atlanta, GA 30341
Phone: 770-488-1094
Email: bpark@cdc.gov
http://www.cdc.gov

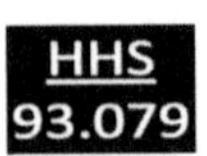

COOPERATIVE AGREEMENTS TO PROMOTE ADOLESCENT HEALTH THROUGH SCHOOL-BASED HIV/STD PREVENTION & SCHOOL-BASED SURVEILLANCE

Award: Cooperative Agreements

Purpose: To improve the health and well-being of our nation's youth by working with education and health agencies, and other organizations to reduce HIV, STD, teen pregnancy, and related risk behaviors among middle and high school students.

Applicant Eligibility: Component 1 eligible applicants are limited to: State Governments or their Bona Fide Agents (includes the District of Columbia); Local Governments or their Bona Fide Agents; Territorial Governments or their Bona Fide Agents in the Commonwealth of Puerto Rico, the Virgin Islands, the Commonwealth of the Northern Mariana Islands, American Samoa, Guam, the Federated States of Micronesia, the Republic of the Marshall Islands, and the Republic of Palau Governments; American Indian or Alaska Native tribal governments (federally recognized or state-recognized); and American Indian or Alaska native tribally designated organizations.

Beneficiary Eligibility: Official state education agencies in states and territories in the United States (including the District of Columbia, the Commonwealth of Puerto Rico, American Samoa, Commonwealth of the Northern Mariana Islands, Federated States of Micronesia, Guam, the Republic of the Marshall Islands, the Republic of Palau, and the U.S. Virgin Islands); local education agencies; public and private non-profit organizations that serve education organizations; school-aged youth; and school personnel including, but not limited to, teachers, school nurses, paraprofessionals, and school administrators.

Award Range/Average: Awards will range from approximately $20,000 to $450,000 with an average of approximately $200,000.

Funding: FY 17 $18,428,564; FY 18 est $17,000,000; FY 19 est $17,000,000.

HQ: CDC NCHHSTP DASH 1600 Clifton Road NE, P.O. Box E-75
Atlanta, GA 30333
Phone: 404-718-8333
http://www.cdc.gov/healthyyouth

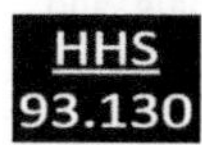

HHS 93.130 COOPERATIVE AGREEMENTS TO STATES/TERRITORIES FOR THE COORDINATION & DEVELOPMENT OF PRIMARY CARE OFFICES
"State Primary Care Offices (PCO)"

Award: Cooperative Agreements

Purpose: To coordinate local, State, and Federal resources contributing to primary care service delivery and workforce issues in the State.

Applicant Eligibility: States or territories, political subdivisions of States, agencies of States, or other public entities that operate solely within one State or represent multiple territories where appropriate. These entities must provide statewide coverage for primary health care issues and represent or have relationships with the broad range of primary health care delivery systems and programs in the State.

Beneficiary Eligibility: Health Professional Shortage Areas and Medically Underserved Areas/Populations within States and Territories will benefit from this program. Primary Care Offices (PCO) submit applications for designation status, which are reviewed and processed by the Division of Policy and Shortage Designation.

Award Range/Average: For FY 2017, awards ranged from $152,056 to $444,379; Average award per recipient $203,509. For FY 2018, est awards ranged from $152,056 to $444,379; Average award per recipient $203,509.

Funding: FY 17 $10,899,000; FY 18 est $10,899,000; FY 19 est $10,899,000.

HQ: Shortage Designation Branch Division of Policy and Shortage Designation Bureau of Health Workforce, 5600 Fishers Lane Room 11W16
Rockville, MD 20852
Phone: 301-594-4454
http://www.hrsa.gov

HHS 93.938 COOPERATIVE AGREEMENTS TO SUPPORT COMPREHENSIVE SCHOOL HEALTH PROGRAMS TO PREVENT THE SPREAD OF HIV & OTHER IMPORTANT HEALTH PROBLEMS
"SHEPSA"

Award: Project Grants

Purpose: To improve a youth's well-being and prepare them for a healthy future.

Applicant Eligibility: Eligible applicants are official States (including the District of Columbia, the Commonwealth of Puerto Rico, American Samoa, Commonwealth of the Northern Marina Islands, Federated States of Micronesia, Guam, the Republic of the Marshall Islands, the Republic of Palau, and the U.S. Virgin Islands), Tribal Governments, large urban school districts (with the highest number of reported AIDS cases, high levels of poverty, and student enrollment greater than 75,000 students), and national non-governmental organizations.

Beneficiary Eligibility: Official State education agencies in states and territories in the United States, local education agencies; national private sector organizations and their constituents; universities and colleges; school-age youth, including minority youth, youth in high-risk situations, and youth with special education needs; college-age youth; and school personnel, including teachers, school nurses, paraprofessionals, and school administrators.

Award Range/Average: $1,000 to $678,000; $283,600

Funding: (Cooperative Agreements) FY 13 was the last year of funding for this program. Funding provided a cost extension only.

HQ: 1600 Clifton Road NE, P.O. Box E-75
Atlanta, GA 30333
Phone: 404-718-8333
http://www.cdc.gov/healthyyouth

HHS 93.946 COOPERATIVE AGREEMENTS TO SUPPORT STATE-BASED SAFE MOTHERHOOD & INFANT HEALTH INITIATIVE PROGRAMS
"Safe Motherhood and Infant Health (Reproductive Health)"

Award: Cooperative Agreements

Purpose: To promote optimal and equitable health in women and infants and to identify and address male and female reproductive issues and infant health issues by providing technical assistance, consultation and training.

Applicant Eligibility: Official State and Territorial public health agencies. City of New York public health agency and District of Columbia.

Beneficiary Eligibility: Same as Applicant Eligibility.

Award Range/Average: No Data Available.

Funding: (Cooperative Agreements) FY 17 $5,674,659; FY 18 est $5,610,606; FY 19 est $5,610,606; FY 16 $15,747,560; - This CFDA support three programs DP17-1702; DP15-1508; DP15-1507.

HQ: DRH 4770 Buford Highway
Atlanta, GA 30341
Phone: 770-488-6245
http://www.cdc.gov

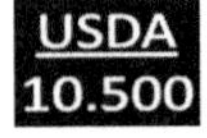

USDA 10.500 COOPERATIVE EXTENSION SERVICE
"CES"

Award: Formula Grants; Project Grants

Purpose: The program deals with funds and other requirements to develop agriculture, extension works, and awareness on various disciplines such as; (a) Formula funds to conduct agriculture and other extension works. (b) Funds for special needs is provided to maximize agricultural and other extension works. (c) The extension special needs program is to strengthen families and communities to self-sustain during disasters. (d) The cooperative extension program creates awareness for disaster preparedness, response, and remediation. (e) To provide awareness, education, and other technical information for various purposes. (d) The CSRS and FERS provide information on retirement contribution and other assistance. (e) To expand food and nutrition, developing agriculture through modern ways, and education on farming. (f) To provide funds for conserving renewable resources. (g) To assist youth with various development programs and much more.

Applicant Eligibility: SPECIAL NOTE: Please refer to the Competitive, Non-Competitive and/or Capacity Requests for Applications (RFAs) for further specific and pertinent details. RFAs are generally released annually.

Beneficiary Eligibility: Extension Programs at the State and county level are available to the general public.

Award Range/Average: If minimum or maximum amounts of funding per the Capacity, Competitive, and/or Non-Competitive project grant, or cooperative agreement are established, these amounts will be announced in the annual Capacity, Competitive, and/or Non-Competitive Request for Application (RFA).

Funding: (Project Grants) FY 17 $455,489,177; FY 18 est $458,054,144; FY 19 est $0.

COOPERATIVE FORESTRY RESEARCH "McIntire-Stennis Cooperative Forestry Research Act (M/S) Program"

Award: Formula Grants

Purpose: To compensate for the protection of forestland, forestry research, advancement of technological, and ecosystems.

Applicant Eligibility: Funds are appropriated by Congress for distribution to State institutions certified as eligible by a State representative designated by the Governor of each State. Funds are apportioned among States by the Secretary of Agriculture after consultation with a National Advisory Council representing the State- certified forestry schools and other groups concerned with forestry research.

Beneficiary Eligibility: Same as Applicant Eligibility.

Award Range/Average: If minimum or maximum amounts of funding per the Capacity, Competitive, and/or Non-Competitive project grant, or cooperative agreement are established, these amounts will be announced in the annual Capacity, Competitive, and/or Non-Competitive Request for Application (RFA).

Funding: Formula Grants (Apportionments) FY 17 $31,849,841; FY 18 est $31,888,021; FY 19 est $27,066,778; FY 16 $31,920,685.

HQ: 1400 Independence Avenue SW, P.O. Box 2210
Washington, DC 20250-2210
Email: wgoldner@nifa.usda.gov
http://nifa.usda.gov/program/mcintire-stennis-capacity-grant

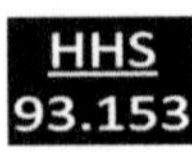

COORDINATED SERVICES & ACCESS TO RESEARCH FOR WOMEN, INFANTS, CHILDREN, AND YOUTH "Ryan White HIV/AIDS Program (RWHAP) Part D Women, Infants, Children and Youth (WICY) Program"

Award: Project Grants

Purpose: To provide family-centered care in the outpatient or ambulatory care setting (directly or through contracts or MOU) to low income, uninsured, and medically underserved women (25 years and older) living with HIV, infants (up to two years of age) exposed to or living with HIV, children (ages two to 12) living with HIV, and youth (ages 13 to 24) living with HIV and additional support services to affected family members.

Applicant Eligibility: Public and nonprofit private entities (including a health facility operated by or pursuant to a contract with the Indian Health Service, and faith-based and Tribes/Tribal organizations) that provide family-centered care involving outpatient or ambulatory care (directly or through contracts or memoranda of understanding (MOUs)) for WICY living with HIV/AIDS.

Beneficiary Eligibility: Women, infants, children, and youth living with HIV and their affected family members.

Award Range/Average: $113,823 - $2,185,691 ; Average $583,894. Supplemental grants are limited to $150,000.

Funding: (Project Grants) FY 17 $67,287,901; FY 18 est $67,147,778; FY 19 est $67,147,778; FY 16 $63,903,447; - WICY(Project Grants) FY 17 $3,343,871; FY 18 est $2,250,000; FY 19 est $2,250,000; FY 16 $2,717,295; - Supplemental.

HQ: 5600 Fishers Lane, Room 9N18
Rockville, MD 20857
Phone: 301-443-3944
Email: mhitch@hrsa.gov
http://www.hrsa.gov

COURT APPOINTED SPECIAL ADVOCATES "CASA"

Award: Cooperative Agreements

Purpose: The CASA program fosters care system for children and provides advocacy for abused and neglected children.

Applicant Eligibility: As set forth in the authorizing language in 42 U.S.C. Section 13013, the successful applicant shall be: (1) a national organization that has broad membership among court-appointed special advocate programs (OJJDP defines as having a network of volunteers representing the interests of abused and neglected children operating in a minimum of 40 of the nation's 56 states and territories) and in providing training and technical assistance to court-appointed special advocate programs; or (2) a local public or not-for-profit agency that has demonstrated the willingness to initiate, sustain, and expand a court-appointed special advocate program.

Beneficiary Eligibility: N/A

Award Range/Average: N/A

Funding: FY 17 $7,504,895; FY 18 est $12,000,000; FY 19 est $9,000,000.

HQ: Office of Juvenile Justice and Delinquency Prevention US Department of Justice 810 7th Street NW
Washington, DC 20735
Phone: 202-305-1270
Email: darian.hanrahan@usdoj.gov
http://www.ojjdp.gov

CRIME VICTIM ASSISTANCE/DISCRETIONARY GRANTS

Award: Project Grants; Direct Payments for Specified Use

Purpose: To improve the overall quality of services delivered to crime victims through the provision of training and technical assistance to providers.

Applicant Eligibility: Criteria will vary depending on the grant or grant program. Generally, eligible applicants may include American Indian/Alaska Native Tribes and tribal organizations, States, United States Attorneys' offices, universities and colleges, eligible public agencies that provide victim services and private nonprofit agencies.

Beneficiary Eligibility: Eligible victim assistance agencies. Eligibility depends on the nature of the grant but may include a wide variety of public and private nonprofit agencies.

Award Range/Average: OVC anticipates awarding grants ranging from $35,000 to $2.4 million, with an average award amount of $250,000.

Funding: (Project Grants) FY 17 $103,802,946; FY 18 est $0; FY 19 FY 16 N/A.

HQ: Office for Victims of Crime 810 Seventh Street NW
Washington, DC 20531
Phone: 202-307-5983
Email: zoe.french@usdoj.gov
http://www.ovc.gov

CRIME VICTIM ASSISTANCE

Award: Formula Grants

Purpose: Providing an annual grant from the Crime Victims Fund to each State and eligible territory for the financial support of services to crime victims by eligible crime victim assistance programs.

Applicant Eligibility: All states, the District of Columbia, the Puerto Rico, the U.S. Virgin Islands, American Samoa, Guam, and the Northern Mariana Islands are eligible to receive an annual VOCA victim assistance formula grant. Eligible agencies that receive VOCA victim assistance formula grant funds must meet the eligibility requirements specified in the Victims of Crime Act (VOCA), 34 U.S.C.

Beneficiary Eligibility: Eligible crime victim assistance programs.

Award Range/Average: Base of $500,000 to each State, Commonwealth, and the District of Columbia. Territories of Northern Mariana Islands, Guam, and American Samoa receive a base of $200,000. Remaining dollars will be divided based on population.

Funding: FY 17 $1,846,507,314; FY 18 est $3,328,058,065; FY 19 est $1,305,958,825; FY 16 est $1,000,000,000.

HQ: Domestic and International Victim Assistance Division Office for Victims of Crime Department of Justice
Washington, DC 20531
Phone: 202-307-5983
Email: toni.thomas@usdoj.gov
http://www.ojp.usdoj.gov/ovc

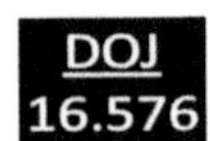

CRIME VICTIM COMPENSATION

Award: Formula Grants

Purpose: Awarding grants to each state, the District of Columbia, the U.S. Virgin Islands, and the Commonwealth of Puerto Rico to support state crime victim compensation programs.

Applicant Eligibility: States, the District of Columbia, the Commonwealth of Puerto Rico, the U.S. Virgin Islands, Guam, and any other possession or territory of the United States who have an established eligible crime victim compensation program, and who meet the eligibility requirements discussed above.

Beneficiary Eligibility: Victims of crime that results in death or physical or personal injury and are determined eligible under the State victim compensation statute. State compensation statutes either declare that coverage extends generally to any crime resulting in physical or personal injury, or they list all specific crimes that can be covered.

Award Range/Average: Each State receives 60 percent of its prior year payout of State compensation funds

Funding: (Formula Grants) FY 17 $133,032,000; FY 18 est $128,685,000; FY 19 est $128,685,000; FY 16 $2,217,900,941.

HQ: US Department of Justice Office for Victims of Crime State Compensation and Assistance Division, 810 7th Street NW
Washington, DC 20531
Phone: 202-307-5983
Email: toni.thomas@usdoj.gov
http://www.ovc.gov

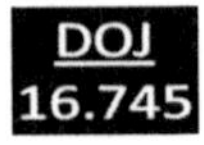

CRIMINAL & JUVENILE JUSTICE & MENTAL HEALTH COLLABORATION PROGRAM "JMHCP"

Award: Project Grants

Purpose: To increase public safety through collaboration for individuals with mental illness, to maintain jail capacity for violent offenders, to increase public safety and reduce recidivism, and to support law enforcement.

Applicant Eligibility: Applicants are limited to States, units of local government, Indian tribes, and tribal organizations. BJA will only accept joint applications; each application must include a mental health agency as well as a unit of government with responsibility for criminal justice activities.

Beneficiary Eligibility: General Public.

Award Range/Average: In amounts consistent with the applicant's proposed project and the BJA's plans, priorities and levels of financing.

Funding: FY 17 $10,963,114; FY 18 est $30,000,000; FY 19 est $10,000,000; FY 16 $8,476,120.

HQ: US Department of Justice Office for Victims of Crime State Compensation and Assistance Division, 810 7th Street NW
Washington, DC 20531
Phone: 202-616-6500
Email: maria.fryer@usdoj.gov
http://www.bja.gov/programdetails.aspx?program_id=66

CRIMINAL JUSTICE RESEARCH & DEVELOPMENT GRADUATE RESEARCH FELLOWSHIPS
"Graduate Research Fellowship Program"

Award: Project Grants

Purpose: Providing awards to accredited universities for the support of doctoral students engaged in research relevant to ensuring public safety, preventing and controlling crime, and ensuring the fair and impartial administration of criminal justice in the United States.

Applicant Eligibility: Degree-granting academic institutions in the United States. The institution must be fully accredited by one of the regional institutional accreditation agencies recognized by the U.S. Secretary of Education.

Beneficiary Eligibility: The ultimate beneficiaries of this program are graduate students engaged in research relevant to criminal justice, forensic science, and public safety.

Award Range/Average: Maximum award amounts: $32,000 for GRF-SBS; $50,000/yr. for GRF-STEM.

Funding: N/A

HQ: National Institute of Justice 810 7th Street NW
Washington, DC 20531
Phone: 202-307-2942
Email: eric.d.martin@ojp.usdoj.gov
http://www.nij.gov

CRISIS COUNSELING
"CCP"

Award: Project Grants

Purpose: The Crisis Counseling Assistance and Training Program provides support to individuals and communities in recovering from the challenging effects of natural and human-caused disasters through the provision of community-based outreach and psycho-educational services.

Applicant Eligibility: States are eligible for grants. If the Governor determines, during an assessment of the need for crisis counseling services, that because of unusual circumstances or serious conditions within the State or local mental health network, the State cannot carry out the crisis counseling program, he/she may identify a public or private mental health agency or organization to carry out the program or request the Department of Homeland Security's Federal Emergency Management Agency (FEMA) Regional Director to identify, with assistance of the Secretary of the Department of Health and Human Services (DHHS), such an agency or organization.

Beneficiary Eligibility: In order to be eligible for services under this program, an individual must be a resident of the designated disaster area or must have been in the designated area at the time the disaster occurred.

Award Range/Average: N/A

Funding: FY 18 est $26,996,637; FY 17 est $24,542,397; FY 16 $22,311,270.

HQ: Individual Assistance Department of Homeland Security 500 C Street SW, 6th Floor
Washington, DC 20472-3100
Phone: 202-212-1117
http://www.fema.gov/media-library/assets/documents/24411

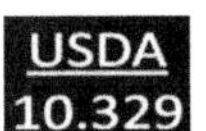

CROP PROTECTION & PEST MANAGEMENT COMPETITIVE GRANTS PROGRAM
"Crop Protection and Pest Management (CPPM)"

Award: Project Grants

Purpose: The CPPM compensates for the regional and national pest management. It supports national research efforts on food security and other implementations.

Applicant Eligibility: Colleges and universities are eligible to submit applications for the CPPM program.

Beneficiary Eligibility: Same as Applicant Eligibility.

Award Range/Average: If minimum or maximum amounts of funding per competitive and/or capacity project grant, or cooperative agreement are established, these amounts will be announced in the annual Competitive Request for Application (RFA).

Funding: Project Grants (Discretionary) FY 17 $18,862,054; FY 18 est $19,021,619; FY 19 est $0; FY 16 $16,290,485.

HQ: 1400 Independence Avenue SW, P.O. Box 2240
Washington, DC 20024
Phone: 202-401-1761
Email: larry.jacobson@nifa.usda.gov
http://nifa.usda.gov/program/crop-protection-and-pest-management-competitive-grants-program

CSELS PARTNERSHIP: STRENGTHENING PUBLIC HEALTH LABORATORIES
"Laboratory Leadership, Workforce Training and Management Development"

Award: Cooperative Agreements

Purpose: To enhance and strengthen the work and functionality of public health laboratories both domestically and abroad.

Applicant Eligibility: Applicants must have experience with enhancing and strengthening the work and functionality of public health laboratories both domestically and abroad. The overarching goal is to improve several aspects of public health laboratories.

Beneficiary Eligibility: Same as Applicant Eligibility.

Award Range/Average: Subject to avail funds.

Approximate Average Award: $27 M Floor Award Amount: $7M Ceiling Award Amount: $30 Anticipated Award Date: July 1, 2015 Budget Period Length: 12 months Project Period Length: 5 years

Funding: FY 17 $24,626,569; FY 18 est $27,552,526; FY 19 est $32,000,000; FY 16 $27,856,840.

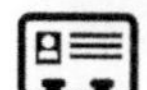

HQ: 2400 Century Center Boulevard
Atlanta, GA 30345
Phone: 404-498-6757
http://www.cdc.gov

CUBAN/HAITIAN ENTRANT PROGRAM
"Cuban/Haitian Entrant Program"

Award: Cooperative Agreements

Purpose: The program offers resettlement services to people especially Cubans and Haitians, who have been paroled into the country by the Department of Homeland Security.

Applicant Eligibility: Public or Private, nonprofit organizations or agencies, and under certain conditions for-profit organizations, agencies, or institutions.

Beneficiary Eligibility: Cuban and Haitian nationals who meet the definition of entrant set forth in Title V, Section 501(e) of Public Law 96-422.

Award Range/Average: Refer to program guidance.

Funding: FY 17 $19,343,607; FY 18 est $4,886,000; FY 19 est $0; FY 16 $18,132,120.

HQ: DHS/USCIS/IO/HAB 20 Massachusetts Avenue NW, 3rd Floor
Washington, DC 20530
Phone: 800-375-5283
Email: john.w.bird@uscis.dhs.gov
http://www.uscis.gov/humanitarian/humanitarian-parole/cuban-haitian-entrant-program-chep

CULTURAL, TECHNICAL & EDUCATIONAL CENTERS

Award: Cooperative Agreements

Purpose: Assists various organizations identified by Congress to achieve objectives specified by Congress. The Bureau of Educational and Cultural Affairs (ECA) seeks to increase mutual understanding between the people of the United States and the people of other countries by means of educational and cultural exchange programs. It is premised on the knowledge that mutual understanding, the development of future leaders, and the benefits of education programs.

Applicant Eligibility: Organizations specifically identified by Congress in agency appropriations legislation.

Beneficiary Eligibility: Beneficiaries are those served by the organizations receiving awards.

Award Range/Average: $774,683 to $16,700,000.

Funding: FY 17 $17,474,863; FY 18 est $17,474,863; FY 19 est $17,474,863; FY 16 $17,475,007.

HQ: Office of Academic Exchanges 2200 C Street NW SA-05, Room 4N6
Washington, DC 20037

Phone: 202-632-6067
Email: meieraw2@state.gov
http://exchanges.state.gov

DOS 19.035 CYBER CAPACITY BUILDING "Cyber Capacity Building"

Award: Cooperative Agreements; Project Grants
Purpose: Enhances global cybersecurity.
Applicant Eligibility: N/A
Beneficiary Eligibility: N/A
Award Range/Average: N/A
Funding: N/A

HQ: 2201 C street NW
Washington, DC 20520
Phone: 202-647-3918
Email: lahaiejmc@state.gov

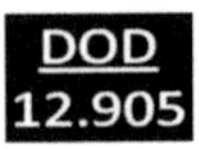

CYBERSECURITY CORE CURRICULUM "CyberSecurity Core Curriculum"

Award: Project Grants
Purpose: To develop Cybersecurity Core Curriculum that will ensure cybersecurity graduates who wish to join the Federal Government have the requisite knowledge and skills.
Applicant Eligibility: Must be a U.S. college or University, a public or private school or school system, or a not-for-profit educational institution. The principal investigator and program staff must be U.S. citizens or permanent residents of the United States.
Beneficiary Eligibility: Same as Applicant Eligibility.
Award Range/Average: Estimated range is $40,000 to $1,000,000. This is the first year so no average is available
Funding: (Salaries and Expenses) FY 17 $6,396,954; FY 18 est $6,396,954; FY 19 N/A FY 16 $0.

HQ: 9800 Savage Road
Fort George G. Meade, DC 20755
Phone: 443-479-4327
Email: dlberr1@nsa.gov
http://www.nsa.gov

CYBERSECURITY EDUCATION & TRAINING ASSISTANCE PROGRAM (CETAP) "CETAP"

Award: Project Grants

Purpose: The program helps the Department of Homeland Security to secure civilian government computer systems to analyze and reduce cyber threats.

Applicant Eligibility: Specific information on applicant eligibility is identified in the funding opportunity announcements.

Beneficiary Eligibility: Refer to program guidance.

Award Range/Average: Refer to the funding opportunity announcements.

Funding: (Salaries and Expenses) FY 17 $4,000,000; FY 18 est $4,300,000; FY 19 est $4,300,000; FY 16 $4,000,000.

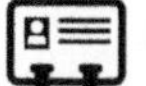

HQ: DHS 245 Murray Lane SW Building 410, P.O. Box 0640
Washington, DC 20528
Phone: 703-705-6672
Email: latasha.mccord@hd.dhs.gov
http://www.dhs.gov

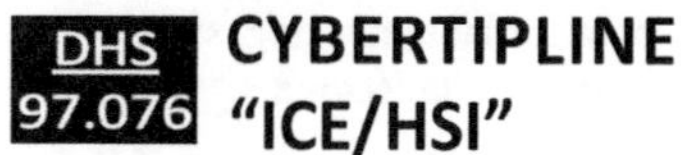

DHS 97.076 CYBERTIPLINE "ICE/HSI"

Award: Project Grants

Purpose: The funding program creates an awareness on using CyberTipline® to report abductions, abuse and/or sexual exploitation of children and thereby assist the global law enforcement in their recovery.

Applicant Eligibility: Non-profits with 501©(3) IRS status, other than institution of higher education Non-profits without 501(3) IRS status, other than institution of higher education For-profit organizations other than small businesses Small Businesses

Beneficiary Eligibility: General public.

Award Range/Average: Amount may vary.

Funding: FY 17 $305,000; FY 18 est $305,000; FY 19 est $305,000; FY 16 $305,000.

HQ: DHS/ICE Homeland Security Investigations 11320 Random Hills Rd, Suite 400
Fairfax, VA 22030
Phone: 703-293-9207
Email: margie.m.jones@ice.dhs.gov
http://www.dhs.gov

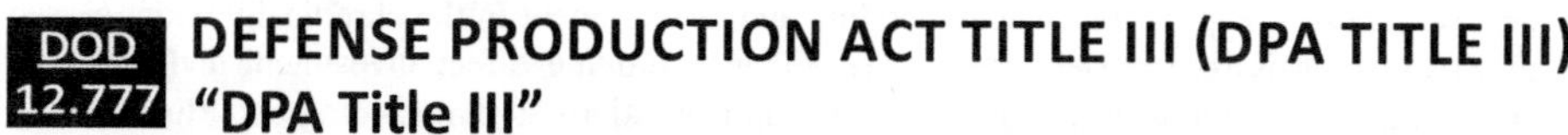

DOD 12.777 DEFENSE PRODUCTION ACT TITLE III (DPA TITLE III) "DPA Title III"

Award: Cooperative Agreements; Project Grants; Direct Loans

Purpose: Creates, maintains, protects, expands, or restores domestic industrial base capabilities essential for the national defense.

Applicant Eligibility: The Title III Office makes the determination of applicant eligibility and assistance types based on the criticality of the national defense need and availability of funds.

Beneficiary Eligibility: Same as Applicant Eligibility.

Award Range/Average: No Data Available.

Funding: (Cooperative Agreements) FY 19 N/A FY 17 est $44,000,000; FY 16 FY 18 est $0.

HQ: ACC-NJ-ET 1 Buffington Street Building 40Benet Laboratories
Watervliet, NY 12189
Phone: 518-266-5100
Email: travis.t.clemons.civ@mail.mil
http://www.businessdefense.gov/programs/dpa-title-iii

DELTA COMMUNITY CAPITAL INITIATIVE (DCCI) "CFDA Number: 14.271"

Award: N/A

Purpose: To increase access to capital for low-cost housing, business lending, and community facilities in the acutely under-served and under-capitalized Lower Mississippi Delta region.

Applicant Eligibility: Organizations and businesses that provide direct investment and technical assistance to community development lending and investing institutions that focus on affordable housing, small business and community facilities to benefit the residents of Lower Mississippi Delta Region.

Beneficiary Eligibility: small business owners, low income persons seeking jobs, job training.

Award Range/Average: $200,000 - $1,000,000. Average award was approximately $480,000.

Funding: (Project Grants) FY 17 $0; FY 18 est $0; FY 19 est $0; - DDCI was funded by recaptured Rural Housing and Economic Development program on a one time only basis. No future funding has been identified for this program.

HQ: 451 7th Street SW, Room 7240
Washington, DC 20410
Phone: 202-402-4464
Email: jackie.williams@hud.gov
http://www.hudexchange.info

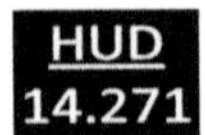

DELTA COMMUNITY CAPITAL INITIATIVE "DCCI"

Award: Project Grants

Purpose: To increase access to capital for business lending and development in the chronically under-served and -capitalized Lower Mississippi Delta region. It will also provide direct investment and technical assistance to community development lending and investing institutions so that funding opportunities will be more effective to the under-served residents of Lower Mississippi Delta Region.

Applicant Eligibility: Applicants that are eligible to participate in this initiative are community development lenders and investors, which may be local rural non-profit organizations or federally recognized tribes. Applicants do not need to be certified as Community Development Financial Institutions by the CDFI Fund at the time of application.

Beneficiary Eligibility: Eligible target markets for use of DCCI funds include businesses owned by or serving low income residents of the Lower Mississippi Delta Region. The Delta region includes the 252 counties and parishes in eight states that make up the Lower Mississippi Delta Region, as defined by the Delta Regional Authority.

Award Range/Average: Actual amount was $1,478,040.

Funding: (Project Grants) FY 17 est $0; FY 16 $0; FY 18 est $0; - This is a one time program using recaptured money from the RHED program.

HQ: Office of Rural Housing and Economic Development US Department of Housing and Urban Development, 451 7th Street SW Room 7137

Washington, DC 20410

Phone: 877-787-2526

http://www.hudexchange.info/programs/dcci

DELTA HEALTH CARE SERVICES GRANT PROGRAM

Award: Project Grants

Purpose: To assist the Delta Region through cooperation among healthcare professionals, institutions of higher education, research institutions, and other organizations in the Delta Region.

Applicant Eligibility: Eligible applicants are consortiums of the following: regional institutions of higher education, academic health and research institutes, and/or economic development entities located within the Delta Region. Applicants are not eligible if they have been debarred or suspended.

Beneficiary Eligibility: Ultimate beneficiaries must be located in rural areas in the Delta Region.

Award Range/Average: Range = $50,000 to $500,000.

Funding: Project Grants (Discretionary) FY 17 $3,000,000; FY 18 est $3,000,000; FY 19 N/A FY 16 est $3,000,000.

HQ: Cooperative Programs Grants Division 1400 Independence Avenue SW Room 4208-S, P.O. Box 3253

Washington, DC 20250-1550

Phone: 202-690-1374

Email: melinda.c.martin@wdc.usda.gov

http://www.rd.usda.gov/programs-services/delta-health-care-services-grants

DEMOLITION & REVITALIZATION OF SEVERELY DISTRESSED PUBLIC HOUSING "HOPE VI"

Award: Project Grants

Purpose: To improve the living environment for public housing residents of severely distressed public housing projects; revitalize the sites on which gravely distressed public housing projects are located; lessen alienation and reduce the denseness of low-income families; build sustainable mixed-income communities; and provide well-coordinated.

Applicant Eligibility: For HOPE VI Revitalization Grants, Public Housing Agencies (PHAs) operating public housing units are eligible to apply. Indian Housing Authorities and PHAs that only administer the Section 8 Program are not eligible to apply.

Beneficiary Eligibility: Same as Applicant Eligibility.

Award Range/Average: N/A

Funding: This program is no longer active and has $0 funding.

HQ: 451 7th Street SW, Room 4130
Washington, DC 20410
Phone: 202-402-5788
Email: leigh.e.vanrij@hud.gov
http://www.hud.gov/offices/pih/programs/ph/hope6

HHS 93.327 DEMONSTRATION GRANTS FOR DOMESTIC VICTIMS OF HUMAN TRAFFICKING

"Domestic Victims of Human Trafficking Program"

Award: Cooperative Agreements; Project Grants

Purpose: To conduct community assessments with the goal to build capacity, create partnerships, and deliver comprehensive, quality services to domestic victims.

Applicant Eligibility: Eligible organizations includes: state governments, tribes, units of local government, and non-profit, non-governmental victim service organizations. Victim service organizations include those who by nature of their current operations serve victims of sexual assault, sexual violence, domestic violence, human trafficking, and youth homelessness.

Beneficiary Eligibility: Eligible recipients for DVHT program services include United States citizens and lawful permanent residents.

Award Range/Average: $150,000 to $300,000 per grant for the three-year project period. The average grant award is $263,000.

Funding: (Project Grants) FY 17 $3,423,912; FY 18 est $3,423,912; FY 19 est $3,423,912; FY 16 $3,423,912.

HQ: 330 C Street SW, 4th Floor
Washington, DC 20201
Phone: 202-401-9372
Email: katherine.chon@acf.hhs.gov
http://www.acf.hhs.gov/programs/otip

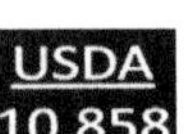

USDA 10.858 DENALI COMMISSION GRANTS & LOANS

"RUS – Denali Commission Grants"

Award: Project Grants

Purpose: To provide loans to the Denali Commission for the benefit of rural communities in Alaska.

Applicant Eligibility: The Denali Commission, a Federal Agency, is the only eligible applicant.

Beneficiary Eligibility: Beneficiaries are residents of rural communities in Alaska with extremely high energy costs. Eligible beneficiary communities must apply for assistance directly to the Denali Commission and eligible projects must be on Denali Commission Annual Approved Work Plan.

Award Range/Average: Grant awards have ranged from $2,310,686 to $18,500,000.

Funding: FY 17 $2,500,000; FY 18 est $1,000,000; FY 19 est $0; FY 16 $2,500,000.

HQ: 1400 Independence Avenue, P.O. Box 1560
Washington, DC 20250

Phone: 202-720-9545
Email: christopher.mclean@wdc.usda.gov
http://www.denali.gov

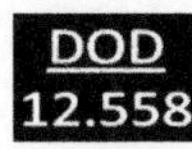
DOD
12.558

DEPARTMENT OF DEFENSE IMPACT AID (SUPPLEMENT, CWSD, BRAC)
"DoD Impact Aid"

Award: Direct Payments with Unrestricted Use

Purpose: To reimburse local educational agencies (LEAs) for education related costs for military dependent children enrolled in the LEA during the specified school year.

Applicant Eligibility: Only LEAs eligible for Federal Impact Aid pursuant to Section 7703 of Title 20, U.S.C. may be eligible for one or more of the three independent DoD Impact Aid Programs.

Beneficiary Eligibility: Please see the DoD Impact Aid web site for detailed eligibility information: http://www.dodea.

Award Range/Average: N/A

Funding: FY 17 $35,000,000; FY 18 N/A FY 19 est $35,000,000; FY 16 $35,000,000.

HQ: 4800 Mark Center Drive
Alexandria, VA 22350-1400
Phone: 571-372-5870
Email: marilyn.hall@ed.gov
http://www2.ed.gov/about/offices/list/oese/impactaid/index.html

DOL
17.791

DEPARTMENT OF LABOR CHIEF EVALUATION OFFICE
"Department of Labor Evaluation Grants"

Award: Project Grants

Purpose: Examines the impact of the agencies' programs and policies is by conducting rigorous research and evaluation studies that allow DOL to learn systematically about and improve the effectiveness of programs and services.

Applicant Eligibility: The following organizations are eligible to apply: Public/State Controlled Institution of Higher Education; Alaska Native and Native Hawaiian Serving Institutions; Asian American and Native American Pacific Islander-Serving Institutions; Indian/Native American Tribal Government (Federally Recognized); Indian/Native American Tribal Government (Other than Federally Recognized); Indian/ Native American Tribally Designated Organization; Private Institution of Higher Education; Hispanic-serving Institution; Historically Black Colleges and Universities (HBCUs); Tribally Controlled Colleges and Universities (TCCUs)

Beneficiary Eligibility: N/A

Award Range/Average: No Data Available.

Funding: Project Grants (Discretionary) FY 17 $1,968,946; FY 18 est $0; FY 19 est $0; FY 16 $0.

HQ: US Department of Labor Frances Perkins Building 200 Constitution Avenue NW, Room S2312
Washington, DC 20210

Phone: 202-693-5087
http://www.dol.gov/asp/evaluation

DEVELOPMENT & COORDINATION OF RURAL HEALTH SERVICES
"Rural Assistance Center Program"

Award: Cooperative Agreements

Purpose: For the development and coordination of rural health services.

Applicant Eligibility: Public or private entities with a service commitment to and experience with rural issues at a national level. Applicant must directly employ a project director with a professional record in national rural health and/or social services policy issues, and directly employ staff for the Information Center, with exceptions only through written agreement with ORHP.

Beneficiary Eligibility: The rural health information clearinghouse is a gateway to information on rural health and social services for residents in rural areas of the United States and for all others interested in these issues.

Award Range/Average: Average award is $2,100,000.

Funding: (Project Grants) FY 17 $2,100,000; FY 18 est $2,100,000; FY 19 N/A FY 16 $2,100,000.

HQ: 5600 Fishers Lane, Room 17W41D
Rockville, MD 20857
Phone: 301-443-0835
Email: shirsch@hrsa.gov
http://www.hrsa.gov/ruralhealth

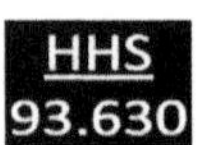

DEVELOPMENTAL DISABILITIES BASIC SUPPORT & ADVOCACY GRANTS
"State Councils on Developmental Disabilities and Protection and Advocacy Systems"

Award: Formula Grants

Purpose: The Developmental Disabilities Basic Support and Advocacy Grants to enable individuals with developmental disabilities to become independent, productive, integrated and included into their communities. Funding under these programs is to assist States in the development of a plan for a comprehensive and coordinated system of services and other activities to enhance the lives of individuals with developmental disabilities and their families to their maximum potential.

Applicant Eligibility: State grant agencies are the designated State agencies of the respective States, the District of Columbia, Puerto Rico, Virgin Islands, Guam, Northern Mariana Islands, American Samoa. Under the basic developmental disabilities program, the designated State agency must not provide or pay for services to individuals with developmental disabilities, unless it has held such designation on the date of the enactment of the Developmental Disabilities Assistance and Bill of Rights Act Amendments of 1994, and the Governor of the State (or the legislature, where appropriate and in accordance with State law) determines prior to June 30, 1994, not to change the designation of such agency.

Beneficiary Eligibility: To be eligible for a grant, an agency must be designated to administer the program on behalf of the State. The Basic Program benefits individuals with developmental disabilities through systems change.

Award Range/Average: Basic Support: $450,000; Protection and Advocacy: $200,000.

Funding: FY 17 $110,939,608; FY 18 est $116,734,000; FY 19 FY 16 $110,916,393.

HQ: 330 C Street SW, Suite 1122
Washington, DC 20201
Phone: 202-795-7401
Email: ophelia.mclain@acl.hhs.gov

DEVELOPMENTAL DISABILITIES PROJECTS OF NATIONAL SIGNIFICANCE
"Developmental Disabilities Projects of National Significance"

Award: Project Grants

Purpose: Provides for grants, contracts and cooperative agreements for projects of national significance that create opportunities for individuals with intellectual and developmental disabilities to directly and fully contribute to, and participate in, all facets of community life; and support the development of national and State policies that reinforce, promote the self-determination, independence, productivity, and integration and inclusion of individuals with intellectual and developmental disabilities in all facets of community life.

Applicant Eligibility: In general, any State, local, public or private nonprofit organization or agency may apply.

Beneficiary Eligibility: Same as Applicant Eligibility.

Award Range/Average: The range is $50,000 to $500,000.

Funding: Cooperative Agreements (Discretionary Grants) FY 17 $10,000,000; FY 18 est $12,000,000; FY 19 N/A FY 16 $10,000,000.

HQ: 330 C Street SW
Washington, DC 20201
Phone: 202-795-7334
Email: allison.cruz@acl.hhs.gov

DIABETES, DIGESTIVE, AND KIDNEY DISEASES EXTRAMURAL RESEARCH

Award: Project Grants

Purpose: To promote extramural basic and clinical biomedical research that improves the understanding of the mechanisms underlying disease and leads to improved preventions, diagnosis, and treatment of diabetes, digestive, and kidney diseases.

Applicant Eligibility: Project Grants: Universities, colleges, medical, dental and nursing schools, schools of public health, laboratories, hospitals, State and local health departments, other public or private institutions, both non-profit and for-profit, and individuals who propose to establish, expand, and improve research activities in health sciences and related fields. NRSAs: Support is provided for academic and research training only, in health and health-related areas that are periodically specified by the National Institutes of Health.

Beneficiary Eligibility: Health professionals, graduate students, health professional students, scientists, and researchers, any nonprofit or for-profit organization, company, or institution engaged in biomedical research. Project Grants: Although no degree of education is either specified or required, nearly all successful applicants have doctoral degrees in one of the sciences or professions.

Award Range/Average: Project Grants: Range of $1,200 to $30,000,000; $442,000 average NRSAs: Range of $358 to $735,000; $125,000 average SBIR: Range of $30,000 to $1,803,000; $522,000 average

Funding: FY 17 $1,649,244,000; FY 18 est $1,734,068,000; FY 19 est $1,613,162,000; FY 16 $1,606,588,000.

HQ: 31 Center Drive, Room 9A34
Bethesda, MD 20892
Phone: 301-594-8842
Email: shorterm@mail.nih.gov
http://www2.niddk.nih.gov

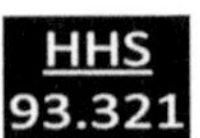

DIETARY SUPPLEMENT RESEARCH PROGRAM

Award: Cooperative Agreements; Project Grants

Purpose: To identify projects that should be conducted or supported by national research institutes; identify multi-disciplinary research related to dietary supplements that should be conducted or supported; and promote coordination and collaboration among entities conduction research.

Applicant Eligibility: Awards can be made to domestic, public or private, non-profit or profit organization, institution of higher learning, university, hospital, laboratory, or other institution including state and local units of government and tribal entities. Some initiatives will accept applications from foreign organizations.

Beneficiary Eligibility: Institutions as described above.

Award Range/Average: The maximum funding under future program announcements is $100,000 for any single award per year.

Funding: (Project Grants) FY 17 $10,944,349; FY 18 est $10,312,690; FY 19 est $10,312,690; FY 16 $1,871,822.

HQ: 6100 Executive Boulevard, Suite 3B01
Rockville, MD 20852
Phone: 301-496-0168
Email: davisci@mail.nih.gov
http://ods.od.nih.gov

DISABILITIES PREVENTION "Disability and Health"

Award: Cooperative Agreements

Purpose: To support National Centers on Disability to develop, implement, evaluate, and disseminate non-research activities aimed at reducing health disparities and improving the health of people with mobility limitations and/or intellectual disabilities (ID) across their lifespans.

Applicant Eligibility: Based on available funding for fiscal year 2016, CDC issued competitive awards to two National Centers on Disability and 19 State-based Disability and Health Programs. Eligibility for the National Centers on Disability included: Public and State controlled institutions of higher education; Native American tribal organizations (other than Federally recognized tribal governments); Nonprofits having a 501(c)(3) status with the IRS, other than institutions of higher education; Nonprofits without 501(c)(3) status with the IRS, other than institutions of higher education; and Private colleges and universities.

Beneficiary Eligibility: In addition to the eligible applicants, other groups who will receive benefits from the program include persons with disabilities and their family members of persons with disabilities, persons with limb loss, minority populations, refugees, infants, children, youth, adults, senior citizens, women, all educational levels, all income levels, urban, suburban, and rural populations, health/ rehabilitation professionals, scientists, educators, and researchers.

Award Range/Average: National Centers on Disability: FY 16 range is $1,500,000 to $4,500,000; FY 17 range is $1,500,000 to $6,700,000. State-based Disability and Health Programs: FY 16/17 range is $150,000 to $450,000.

Funding: FY 17 $13,390,900; FY 18 est $16,478,400; FY 19 est $16,478,400; FY 16 $11,399,995.

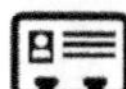 **HQ:** 1600 Clifton Road, P.O. Box 88
Atlanta, GA 30333
Phone: 404-498-6730
Email: jxt4@cdc.gov
http://www.cdc.gov/ncbddd/disabilityandhealth/index.html

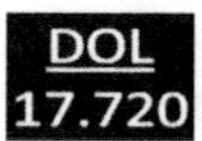

DOL 17.720 DISABILITY EMPLOYMENT POLICY DEVELOPMENT "Office of Disability Employment Policy (ODEP)"

Award: Cooperative Agreements

Purpose: Provides national leadership on disability employment policy to the Department of Labor and other Federal agencies.

Applicant Eligibility: Nonprofit and for-profit organizations, State and local government agencies, academic institutions, and other entities are typically eligible. Eligibility requirements are detailed in each solicitation for cooperative agreements or grant applications.

Beneficiary Eligibility: Detailed in each solicitation for cooperative agreements or grant applications.

Award Range/Average: Recent awards for cooperative agreements and grants have ranged from approximately $300,000 to $1,800,000 per year, depending on the project needs as detailed in the solicitation for cooperative agreement or grant applications and availability of funds. Awards have been to non-profit and for-profit organizations, State and local government agencies, academic institutions, and other entities.

Funding: (Salaries and Expenses) FY 17 N/A FY 18 est $11,000,000; FY 19 N/A FY 16 N/A.

 **HQ:** 200 Constitution Ave. NW, Room S-1303
Washington, DC 20210
Phone: 202-693-7880, 81
http://www.dol.gov/odep

DOT 20.905 DISADVANTAGED BUSINESS ENTERPRISES SHORT TERM LENDING PROGRAM

"Short Term Lending Program"

Award: Guaranteed/Insured Loans

Purpose: To obtain accounts receivable financing for the performance of eligible transportation-related contracts originating from the Department of Transportation (DOT), its grantees, recipients, their contractors and subcontractors.

Applicant Eligibility: The recipient of a line of credit must be a certified DBE, or certified small business, including; 8(a); Small Disadvantaged Business (SDB): HUBZONE; Women-Owned Small Business (WOSB); and Service-Disabled Veteran-Owned Business (SDVOB).

Beneficiary Eligibility: Small Business/Small Business Person.

Award Range/Average: The maximum line of credit is $750,000. There is no minimum line of credit amount.

Funding: FY 17 $8,158,000; FY 18 est $0; FY 19 est $0; FY 16 $250,000; - Funds are used to for S&E as well as subsidies, and bank administrative fees.

HQ: Department of Transportation 1200 New Jersey Avenue SE
Washington, DC 20590
Phone: 202-366-2253
http://www.transportation.gov/osdbu

HHS 93.923 DISADVANTAGED HEALTH PROFESSIONS FACULTY LOAN REPAYMENT PROGRAM (FLRP)

"FLRP"

Award: Direct Payments for Specified Use

Purpose: The Faculty Loan Repayment Program provides loan repayment assistance to faculty members from economically and environmentally disadvantaged backgrounds with eligible health professions degree or certificates to serve at eligible academic institutions.

Applicant Eligibility: Eligible applicants must: (1) be U.S. citizens (either U.S. born or naturalized), U.S. nationals or lawful permanent residents; (2) be from an economically or environmentally disadvantaged background; (3) have a degree or certificate in one of the following health profession disciplines: allopathic, osteopathic, podiatric or veterinary medicine; dentistry, pharmacy, optometry, nursing (RN or APRN), physician assistants, allied health, or graduate programs in public health or behavioral and mental health; or are enrolled in an approved graduate training program in one of the health professions listed above, or are enrolled as full-time students (in the disciplines listed above) at an accredited health professions institution and are in the final course of study or program leading to a degree from that institution; (4) have an employment commitment from an eligible health professions school for a full-time or part-time (as defined by the school) faculty position for a minimum of 2 years; and (5) have a written agreement with an eligible health professions school that has agreed to pay full or partial match toward the principal and interest for the applicant's education loans in equivalent loan repayment amounts made by HHS under FLRP. For institutions that are unable to provide matching loan repayments, applicants must provide an official letter from the employer requesting a full or partial waiver with supporting documentation justifying the undue financial hardship necessary for a waiver to be granted.

Beneficiary Eligibility: Same as Applicant Eligibility.

Award Range/Average: FY 17 Range - $45,911 to $59,853; FY 17 Average: $49,709 FY 18 est Range - $10,000 to $59,853 FY 18 est Average: $56,667

Funding: (Project Grants) FY 17 $1,093,597; FY 18 est $1,190,000; FY 19 est $0; FY 16 $1,190,054.

HQ: Division of Health Careers and Financial Support Bureau of Health Workforce (BHW)
Rockville, MD 20857
Phone: 301-594-4130
http://bhw.hrsa.gov/loansscholarships/flrp

DISASTER ASSISTANCE LOANS "7(b) Loans (DL))"

Award: Direct Loans

Purpose: Provides loans to the survivors of declared disasters for uninsured or otherwise uncompensated physical damage and economic injury.

Applicant Eligibility: Eligible applicants must have suffered physical property loss or economic injury as a result of a disaster which occurred in an area declared by the President or SBA. They must also demonstrate an ability and willingness to repay the loan.

Beneficiary Eligibility: Business concerns, charitable and nonprofit organizations, and individuals. Agricultural enterprises are ineligible.

Award Range/Average: Additional information provided on SBA's website at www.sba.gov/Disaster.

Funding: FY 17 $12,970,000,000; FY 18 est $1,600,000,000; FY 19 est $1,100,000,000; FY 16 $1,181,000,000.

HQ: Office of Disaster Assistance 409 3rd Street, 6th Floor
Washington, DC 20416
Phone: 202-205-6734
Email: alan.escobar@sba.gov
http://www.sba.gov/disaster

DISASTER ASSISTANCE PROJECTS "Earmarked Projects or Limited Scope Disaster Projects. Restricted to entities designated by DHS or congressional statute."

Award: Cooperative Agreements

Purpose: The program provides funding for disaster assistance projects that help in disaster response and recovery.

Applicant Eligibility: Funds are restricted to nonfederal entities, e.g. State, local government, private, public, profit or nonprofit organization, Indian Tribal government or individual specified by DHS or U.S. Appropriation Statute.

Beneficiary Eligibility: State, local government, private, public, profit or nonprofit organization, Indian Tribal government or individual specified by U.S. Appropriation Statute.

Award Range/Average: Each "earmark" or project funding is designated by the appropriation statute or identified by the program office.

Funding: (Project Grants) FY 17 $2,767,367,674; FY 18 est $221,791,574; FY 19 est $221,791,574.

HQ: Community Services Branch/Individual Assistance Division/Recovery Directorate 500 C Street SW
Washington, DC 20472
Phone: 202-646-2500
http://www.fema.gov

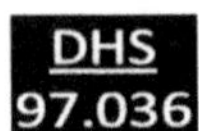

DISASTER GRANTS – PUBLIC ASSISTANCE (PRESIDENTIALLY DECLARED DISASTERS)

Award: Project Grants

Purpose: The program offers assistance to State and local governments and other non-profits in repairing and restoring or replacing public properties damaged during disasters and calamities.

Applicant Eligibility: State and local governments, other political subdivisions such as a special districts, federally recognized Indian tribal governments, Alaska Native villages or organizations, but not Alaska Native Corporations, and certain Private Non-Profit organizations in designated emergency or major disaster areas.

Beneficiary Eligibility: Eligible work must be required as a result of the disasters; be located in a designated emergency or major disaster area; and be the legal responsibility of the applicant.

Award Range/Average: N/A.

Funding: FY 17 $3,738,941,530; FY 18 est $6,000,000,000; FY 19 est $6,000,000,000; FY 16 $5,858,591,041.

HQ: 500 C Street SW
Washington, DC 20472
Phone: 202-646-4136
http://www.fema.gov

DISASTER LEGAL SERVICES "DLS"

Award: Direct Payments for Specified Use

Purpose: The Disaster Legal Services Program provides legal assistance to low-income individuals who are unable to secure legal services adequate to meet their disaster-related needs.

Applicant Eligibility: FEMA enters into a contract with the American Bar Association Young Lawyers Division to cover the administrative costs of implementing and managing the Disaster Legal Services program.

Beneficiary Eligibility: Service provision is geared toward low-income individuals who, prior to or because of the disaster, are unable to secure legal services adequate to meet their disaster-related needs.

Award Range/Average: N/A.

Funding: (Provision of Specialized Services) FY 17 $43,795; FY 18 est.

HQ: Disaster Assistance Directorate Department of Homeland Security 500 C Street SW, 6th Floor
Washington, DC 20472-3100
Phone: 202-646-2500
http://www.fema.gov/media-library/assets/documents/24413

DHS 97.034 DISASTER UNEMPLOYMENT ASSISTANCE "DUA"

Award: Project Grants

Purpose: The program provides benefits for individuals who lose their employment status due to a disaster and are not eligible for regular unemployment insurance.

Applicant Eligibility: The State Workforce Agency (SWA) applies for Disaster Unemployment Assistance funds to provide to eligible beneficiaries.

Beneficiary Eligibility: Refer to program guidance.

Award Range/Average: No Data Available.

Funding: (Direct Payments for Specified Use) FY 17 $113,197,875; FY 18 est $50,040,000; FY 19 est $50,040,000; FY 16 $3,013,865.

HQ: Department of Homeland Security 500 C Street SW, 6th Floor
Washington, DC 20472-3100
Phone: 202-646-2500
http://www.fema.gov/media-library/assets/documents/24418

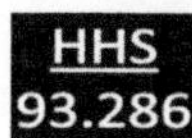

HHS 93.286 DISCOVERY & APPLIED RESEARCH FOR TECHNOLOGICAL INNOVATIONS TO IMPROVE HUMAN HEALTH

Award: Project Grants

Purpose: To support hypothesis, design, technology, or device-driven research related to the discovery, design, development, validation, and application of technologies for biomedical imaging and bioengineering.

Applicant Eligibility: Any corporation, public or private institution or agency, or other legal entity, either nonprofit or for-profit, may apply for a research grant. An applicant for an individual NRSA must be a citizen of the United States or lawfully admitted for permanent residence.

Beneficiary Eligibility: Any nonprofit or for-profit organization, company, or institution engaged in biomedical research.

Award Range/Average: FY 17 Actual Range: $3,000 - $2,241,498; Avg.: $397,299 FY 18 estimate Range: $3,000- $2,082,080; Avg.: $405,002 FY 19 estimate Range: $3,000 - $1,899,165; Avg.: $351,324

Funding: Project Grants (Discretionary) FY 17 $293,604,000; FY 18 est $309,421,000; FY 19 est $196,390,000; FY 16 $27,998,000.

HQ: 6707 Democracy Boulevard
Bethesda, MD 20892
Phone: 301-496-9474
Email: georged@nih.gov
http://www.nibib.nih.gov

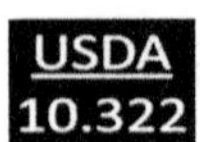

DISTANCE EDUCATION GRANTS FOR INSTITUTIONS OF HIGHER EDUCATION IN INSULAR AREAS

"Grants for Insular Areas - Distance Education Grants for Insular Areas (DEG)"

Award: Project Grants

Purpose: To promote distance education technology, higher education in insular areas, and other teaching programs.

Applicant Eligibility: Individual land-grant colleges and universities, and other institutions that have secured land-grant status through Federal legislation, and which are located in Insular Areas are automatically eligible for awards under the DEG grants program, either as direct applicants or as parties to a consortium agreement.

Beneficiary Eligibility: Same as Applicant Eligibility.

Award Range/Average: If minimum or maximum amounts of funding per competitive and/or capacity project grant, or cooperative agreement are established, these amounts will be announced in the annual Competitive Request for Application (RFA).

Funding: (Project Grants) FY 17 $768,000; FY 18 est $800,000; FY 19 est $1,916,160; FY 16 $768,000.

HQ: Institute of Youth Family and Community Division of Community and Education 1400 Independence Avenue SW, P.O. Box 2250
Washington, DC 20250-2250
Phone: 202-720-2324
Email: elewis@nifa.usda.gov
http://nifa.usda.gov/program/resident-instruction-grants-riia-and-distance-education-grants-deg-institutions-highe

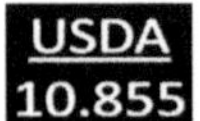

DISTANCE LEARNING & TELEMEDICINE LOANS & GRANTS

"DLT - Distance Learning and Telemedicine"

Award: Project Grants; Direct Loans

Purpose: To promote telemedicine, telecommunications, computer networks, related advanced technologies, educational and medical benefits for those living in rural areas.

Applicant Eligibility: To be eligible to receive a grant, loan and grant combination, or loan, the applicant must be legally organized as an incorporated organization or partnership, an Indian tribe or tribal organization, a state or local unit of government, a consortium, or other legal entity. The applicant must have legal capacity to contract with RUS.

Beneficiary Eligibility: The people living in rural areas are beneficiaries, particularly in the areas of medical and health-related services, education, training and medical services.

Award Range/Average: $50,000 to $500,000 with an average of $322,334

Funding: (Project Grants) FY 17 $27,700,000; FY 18 est $20,000,000; FY 19 est $20,000,000.

HQ: 1400 Independence Avenue SW, P.O. Box 1590
Washington, DC 20250
Phone: 202-720-9564
Email: chad.parker@wdc.usda.gov
http://www.rd.usda.gov/programs-services/distance-learning-telemedicine-grants

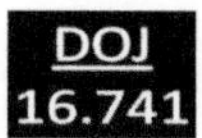

DNA BACKLOG REDUCTION PROGRAM

Award: Cooperative Agreements

Purpose: To assist in analyzing forensic DNA and providing laboratories to process more DNA samples and other forensic technologies to track sexual assault.

Applicant Eligibility: N/A

Beneficiary Eligibility: N/A

Award Range/Average: N/A

Funding: (Formula Grants) FY 17 $97,122,118; FY 18 est $130,000,000; FY 19 est $105,000,000; FY 16 $100,649,672.

HQ: US Department of Justice National Institute of Justice 810 7th Street NW
Washington, DC 20531
Phone: 202-616-9264
Email: charles.heurich@usdoj.gov
http://nij.gov

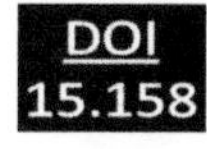

DOI NATIONAL FIRE PLAN

Award: Cooperative Agreements

Purpose: The objective of this program is to provide Cooperative Agreements to aid the Office of the Secretary, Office of Wildland Fire (OWF) in facilitating communication, cooperation and coordination between Federal, State, and local partners in support of the National Fire Plan. Funds shall be used by the recipient to assist the Office of Wildland Fire in preparation of training curriculum related to a variety of issues, such as safety and leadership.

Applicant Eligibility: Public or private nonprofit institution/organizations.

Beneficiary Eligibility: Anyone within the Fire Use/Protection community.

Award Range/Average: No Data Available.

Funding: Cooperative Agreements (Discretionary Grants) FY 17 $10,000; FY 18 est $10,000; FY 19 N/A FY 16 $25,000; - This was a new program in 2016 which was never awarded. We are planning to go forward with both the 2016 intended and then we will work on 2017 estimated.

HQ: Office of Wildland Fire 300 E Mallard Drive, Suite 170
Boise, ID 83706
Phone: 208-334-6195
Email: amy_kishpaugh@ios.doi.gov

DOLLAR HOME SALES

Award: Sale, Exchange, or Donation of Property and Goods

Purpose: Fostering housing opportunities for low-to-moderate income families and address specific community needs.

Applicant Eligibility: Local government legally authorized by local law to make the purchase.

Beneficiary Eligibility: Low- to moderate-income families and communities.

Award Range/Average: No Data Available.

Funding: (Sale, Exchange, or Donation of Property and Goods) FY 15 FY 17 FY 16 - Reported Under 14.311.

HQ: 451 7th Street SW
Washington, DC 20410
Phone: 800-225-5342
http://www.hud.gov/offices/hsg/sfh/reo/goodn/dhmabout.cfm

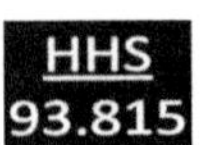

DOMESTIC EBOLA SUPPLEMENT TO THE EPIDEMIOLOGY & LABORATORY CAPACITY FOR INFECTIOUS DISEASES (ELC) "ELC"

Award: Cooperative Agreements

Purpose: The ELC Competing Supplement addresses priority domestic capacity building around Ebola and other emerging and highly-infectious diseases. The Competing Supplement provides additional resources to accelerate ELC activities around infection control assessment and response, laboratory safety, and global migration, border interventions, and migrant health.

Applicant Eligibility: Eligible applicants consist of state, local, and U.S. territory/possession governments.

Beneficiary Eligibility: Direct beneficiaries include all 50 states, Washington, D.C.

Award Range/Average: No Data Available.

Funding: (Cooperative Agreements) FY 17 $554,500; FY 18 est $0; FY 19 est $0; FY 16 $3,933,196.

HQ: 1600 Clifton Road NE, P.O. Box C18
Atlanta, GA 30333
Phone: 404-639-7379
Email: amoconnor@cdc.gov
http://www.cdc.gov

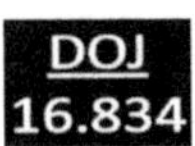

DOMESTIC TRAFFICKING VICTIM PROGRAM "Domestic Trafficking Victim Program"

Award: Project Grants

Purpose: The Domestic Trafficking Victim Program improves the outcomes for children and youth who are victims of human trafficking. It enhances multidisciplinary and jurisdiction approach to human trafficking and responds to victims of child pornography.

Applicant Eligibility: N/A

Beneficiary Eligibility: N/A

Award Range/Average: N/A

Funding: (Project Grants) FY 17 $4,586,000; FY 18 est $5,000,000; FY 19 est $5,000,000; FY 16 $4,609,723; - $2,000,000 per year automatically transferred to OJJDP.

HQ: 810 Seventh Street NW
Washington, DC 20531
Phone: 202-353-7223
http://www.ovc.gov

DRIVER'S LICENSE SECURITY GRANT PROGRAM
"Driver's License Security Grant Program"

Award: Project Grants

Purpose: The program funds to help reduce and prevent terrorism and fraud by improving the accuracy and reliability of personal identification documents like the driver's license and identification cards.

Applicant Eligibility: The issuing authority for motor vehicle licenses in each State or territory, as identified by the DHS, is the only agency eligible to apply for the Driver's License Security Grant Program.

Beneficiary Eligibility: State, U.S. Territory and local governments, intrastate, interstate, small business, general public, other public institution/organizations.

Award Range/Average: Will be identified in the solicitation/program guidance.

Funding: (Project Grants); Program was last funded in FY2011. This program will remain open due to open awards.

HQ:
Washington, DC 20472-3615
Phone: 800-368-6498
http://www.fema.gov/government/grant/index.shtm

DRUG ABUSE & ADDICTION RESEARCH PROGRAMS

Award: Project Grants; Training

Purpose: To support basic and clinical neuroscience, biomedical, behavioral and social science, epidemiologic, health services and health disparity research.

Applicant Eligibility: For research grants the following organizations/institutions are eligible to apply: Public/State Controlled Institutions of Higher Education; Private Institutions of Higher Education: Hispanic-serving Institutions, Historically Black Colleges and Universities (HBCUs), Tribally Controlled Colleges and Universities (TCCUs), and Alaska Native and Native Hawaiian Serving Institutions; Nonprofits with 501(c)(3) IRS Status (Other than Institutions of Higher Education); Nonprofits without 501(c)(3) IRS Status (Other than Institutions of Higher Education); Small Businesses; For-Profit Organizations (Other than Small Businesses); State Governments; Indian/Native American Tribal Governments (Federally Recognized); Indian/Native American Tribally Designated Organizations; County Governments; City or Township Governments; Special District Governments; Independent School Districts; Public Housing Authorities/Indian Housing Authorities; and Other(s): Eligible Agencies of the Federal Government, Faith-based or Community-based Organizations, U.S. Territory or Possession, Indian/Native American Tribal Governments (Other than Federally Recognized), Regional Organizations, and Non-domestic (non-U.S.) Entities (Foreign Organizations). Eligible Individuals: Any individual, or individuals (multiple PDs/PIs), with the skills, knowledge, and resources necessary to carry out the proposed research as the PD/PI is invited to work with his/her organization to develop an application for support.

Beneficiary Eligibility: Public or private profit and nonprofit sponsored organizations and individuals, minority groups, small businesses, health professionals, students, trainees, scientists and general public.

Award Range/Average: Range- $3,000 to $5,146,000; Average- $527,100

Funding: (Project Grants) FY 17 $844,906,000; FY 18 est $884,445,000; FY 19 est $898,474,000; FY 16 $821,038,000.

HQ: NIDA 6001 Executive Boulevard, Room 4241
Bethesda, MD 20892
Phone: 301-827-5705
Email: chollan1@nida.nih.gov
http://www.drugabuse.gov

DOJ 16.585

DRUG COURT DISCRETIONARY GRANT PROGRAM "Drug Court Program (DCP)"

Award: Project Grants

Purpose: To equip courts and community supervision systems with the necessary tools and resources, utilizing the most current evidence-based practices and principles, to intervene with participants who abuse substances while preparing them for success in the community.

Applicant Eligibility: Grants can be awarded to states, state courts, local courts, units of local government and Indian tribal governments, acting directly or through agreements with other public or private entities. Applicants may choose to submit joint applications with other eligible jurisdictions for statewide, regional, and multijurisdictional drug court programs.

Beneficiary Eligibility: States, local governments, Indian tribal governments, public or private entities.

Award Range/Average: Varies based upon appropriation.

Funding: (Project Grants) FY 17 $38,944,583; FY 18 est $75,000,000; FY 19 est $43,000,000.

HQ: Department of Justice 810 Seventh Street NW
Washington, DC 20531
Phone: 202-616-6500
http://www.bja.gov

EOP 95.005

DRUG COURT TRAINING & TECHNICAL ASSISTANCE

Award: Project Grants

Purpose: The grant that is awarded by the Office of National Drug Control Policy helps to establish training and technical assistance to advance criminal justice reforms that include drug courts handling justice-involved cases of individuals with substance use disorders.

Applicant Eligibility: Organizations with expert knowledge of drug courts and extensive experience in brokering and developing training and technical assistance for drug court professionals are eligible. The trainings and technical assistance will require organizations with relevant subject matter expertise and extensive experience in developing and providing training and technical assistance for a variety of disciplines.

Beneficiary Eligibility: N/A

Award Range/Average: varies by appropriated amount

Funding: (Project Grants) FY 17 $3,400,000; FY 18 est $4,000,000; FY 19 est $2,000,000.

HQ: 750 17th Street NW
Washington, DC 20503
Phone: 202-395-6739
Email: phuong_desear@ondcp.eop.gov
http://www.whitehouse.gov/ondcp

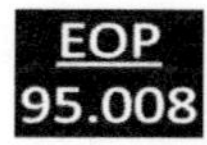

DRUG-FREE COMMUNITIES SUPPORT PROGRAM – NATIONAL YOUTH LEADERSHIP INITIATIVE

Award: Cooperative Agreements

Purpose: The program helps to implement the National Youth Leadership Initiative which helps to diversify youth population and provides technical assistance to prevent substance use and make their community a drug-free one.

Applicant Eligibility: Applicants must be a non-profit entity (501(c)3) with expert knowledge and extensive experience in community mobilizing using the Seven Strategies for Community Change. Applicants must have served as an essential partner in assisting the Drug-Free Communities (DFC) Support Program with technical assistance to community coalitions in their substance use prevention efforts.

Beneficiary Eligibility: Supports NYLI training program, where there is strong participation by DFC-funded communities.

Award Range/Average: No Data Available.

Funding: (Cooperative Agreements) FY 17 $0; FY 18 est $250,000; FY 19 est $0; FY 16 $200,000.

HQ: 750 17th Street NW
Washington, DC 20503
Phone: 202-395-6739
Email: phuong_desear@ondcp.eop.gov
http://www.whitehouse.gov/ondcp

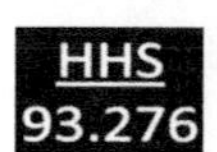

DRUG-FREE COMMUNITIES SUPPORT PROGRAM GRANTS "Drug Free Community Grants (DFC). Drug-Free Communities Mentoring Program (DFC-M)"

Award: Project Grants

Purpose: To increase the capacity of community coalitions to reduce substance abuse, and over time, to reduce substance abuse among adults through strengthening collaboration among communities, public, and private entities.

Applicant Eligibility: Community coalitions must demonstrate that the community coalition has worked together for a period of not less than 6 months on substance abuse reduction initiatives. The coalition must: meet the composition requirements; ensure that there is substantial community volunteer effort; ensure that the coalition is a nonprofit, charitable, educational organization, or unit of local government, or is affiliated with an eligible organization or entity; possess a strategy to be self-sustaining; provide a 100-150 percent cash or in-kind match; and agree to participate in an evaluation of the coalition's program.

Beneficiary Eligibility: Community coalitions, children, youth, and adults, those at-risk of substance abuse, and private nonprofit, and public community agencies.

Award Range/Average: $75,000 to $125,000; Avg. $124.510

Funding: Project Grants (Discretionary) FY 17 $89,383,587; FY 18 est $71,408,103; FY 19 est $47,325,981; FY 16 $85,749,165.

HQ: 5600 Fishers Lane
Rockville, MD 20857
Phone: 240-276-1078
Email: odessa.crocker@samhsa.hhs.gov
http://www.samhsa.gov

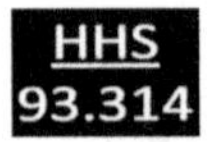

EARLY HEARING DETECTION & INTERVENTION INFORMATION SYSTEM (EHDI-IS) SURVEILLANCE PROGRAM "EHDI Information System"

Award: Cooperative Agreements

Purpose: To assist EHDI programs in developing and maintaining a sustainable, centralized newborn hearing screening tracking and surveillance system capable of accurately identifying, matching, collecting, and reporting data on all occurrent births that is unduplicated and individually identifiable.

Applicant Eligibility: N/A

Beneficiary Eligibility: State and local governments or their Bona Fide Agents (this includes the District of Columbia, the Commonwealth of Puerto Rico, the Virgin Islands, the Commonwealth of the Northern Marianna Islands, American Samoa, Guam, the Federated States of Micronesia, the Republic of the Marshall Islands, and the Republic of Palau

Award Range/Average: Award Amounts range is $150,000.

Funding: (Cooperative Agreements) FY 17 $7,204,926; FY 18 est $7,008,952; FY 19 est $7,008,952; FY 16 $7,023,971.

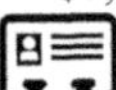

HQ: 1600 Clifton Road NE, P.O. Box E87
Atlanta, GA 30333
Phone: 404-498-3034
Email: deg4@cdc.gov
http://www.cdc.gov/ncbddd

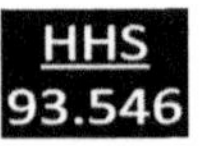

EARLY RETIREE REINSURANCE PROGRAM

Award: Direct Payments for Specified Use

Purpose: To provide reimbursement to sponsors of participating employment-based plans for a portion of the cost of health benefits for early retirees and their spouses, surviving spouses, and dependents.

Applicant Eligibility: In order to have been eligible for the ERRP, a plan sponsor must have completed and submitted an ERRP application to the ERRP Center on or before May 5, 2011. In summary, the plan sponsor must be an organization that provides health benefits to Early Retirees, have programs and procedures in place that generate cost savings with respect to participants with chronic and high-cost conditions, use reimbursements appropriately, ensure that policies and procedures are in place to protect against fraud, waste and abuse under ERRP, and agree to the Plan Sponsor Agreement included in the ERRP application.

Beneficiary Eligibility: If approved, both the sponsor, and early retirees and their spouses, surviving spouses and their dependents are direct or indirect beneficiaries of the program.

Award Range/Average: Smallest: $50.96; Largest: $387,187,079.81; Average: $1,745,808.92.

Funding: (Direct Payments for Specified Use) FY 17 $0; FY 18 est $0; FY 19 est $0; FY 16 $0; - There is appropriated to the Secretary, $5,000,000,000 to carry out the program under this section. Such funds shall be available without fiscal year limitation. Program ends January 1, 2014.

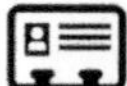

HQ: 200 Independence Avenue SW
Washington, DC 20201
Phone: 301-492-4312
Email: michelle.feagins@hhs.gov
http://www.cms.gov

EARTHQUAKE CONSORTIUM
"Earthquake Consortium and State Support (ECSS)"

Award: Cooperative Agreements

Purpose: The program acts as an approach to reduce the loss of lives and property to earthquakes by implementing earthquake risk-reduction activities at a local level.

Applicant Eligibility: The purpose of this funding is to support the earthquake mitigation efforts of States and Territories with Moderate to Very High seismic risk as determined by the Program Office, and the earthquake mitigation efforts of earthquake Consortia and Partners including CUSEC, NESEC, WSSPC, CREW, EERI, FLASH, SCEC, and ATC. These efforts include 1) delivering and increasing awareness and education; 2) developing policies, tools, and products; and 3) implementing programs or projects to support risk reduction and resilience activities from earthquake and other hazards.

Beneficiary Eligibility: Eligible States and Territories with Moderate to Very High seismic risks as determined by the Program Office, and earthquake Consortia and Partners including CUSEC, NESEC, WSSPC, CREW, EERI, FLASH, SCEC, and ATC.

Award Range/Average: Refer to the official Notice of Funding Opportunity on Grants.gov by year for actual target allocations by program by eligible applicant.

Funding: Project Grants (Cooperative Agreements) FY 17 $3,460,501; FY 18 est $3; FY 19 est $3; FY 16 $3,278,500.

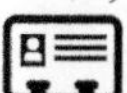

HQ: Federal Insurance and Mitigation Administration (FIMA) 400 C Street SW
Washington, DC 20009
Phone: 202-646-4037
Email: gabriele.javier@fema.dhs.gov
http://www.fema.gov/building-science

EAST ASIA & PACIFIC GRANTS PROGRAM "U.S. Department of State, Bureau of East Asian and Pacific Affairs, Grant Awards"

Award: Cooperative Agreements; Project Grants

Purpose: To support the foreign assistance goals and objectives of the Department of State, Bureau of East Asian Affairs, as delineated in the FY Bureau Strategic and Resource Plan.

Applicant Eligibility: Department of State, EAP Bureau does not issue domestic grants. Any and all grants will go to entities that operate overseas in support of our international foreign assistance goals and objectives.

Beneficiary Eligibility: Same as Applicant Eligibility.

Award Range/Average: Depends on specific grant award. See www.grants.gov for specific announcement.

Funding: Project Grants (Discretionary) - The above includes the annual grant for The Asia Foundation.

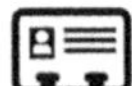

HQ: 2201 C Street NW, Room 5313
Washington, DC 20520
Phone: 202-647-9446
Email: wyckoffar@state.gov
http://www.state.gov/j/drl/p/c22947.htm

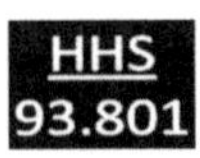

EBOLA HEALTHCARE PREPAREDNESS & RESPONSE FOR SELECT CITIES WITH ENHANCED AIRPORT ENTRANCE SCREENINGS FROM AFFECTED COUNTRIES IN WEST AFRICA

Award: Project Grants

Purpose: To enable public health departments serving regions where enhanced airport screenings are occurring to procure personal protective equipment and supplies, train staff, retrofit facilities, and carry out other necessary Ebola-specific preparedness, response, and recovery activities.

Applicant Eligibility: Eligible applicants are state or city departments of public health serving the five major airports wherein the Department of Homeland Security (DHS) is conducting enhanced airport entrance screenings for Ebola.

Beneficiary Eligibility: State or city departments of public health listed above, hospitals and supporting health care systems

Award Range/Average: Est. Average Amount: $142,857

Funding: (Project Grants) FY 17 N/A FY 18 N/A FY 19 FY 16 est $1,000,000.

HQ: 200 C Street SW, Room C4K12
Washington, DC 20020
Phone: 202-245-0740
Email: stephen.tise@hhs.gov
http://www.phe.gov

EBOLA SUPPORT: TRANSMISSION & PREVENTION CONTROL, PUBLIC HEALTH PREPAREDNESS, VACCINE DEVELOPMENT

Award: Cooperative Agreements

Purpose: Support infection control programs throughout hospitals and other healthcare facilities to control transmission of Ebola, pathogens similar to Ebola, and those transmitted similarly to Ebola. Identify and implement healthcare worker requirements, policies and programs for training and competency of infection control practices.

Applicant Eligibility: Eligibility requirements will be delineated in the funding opportunity announcement.

Beneficiary Eligibility: All eligibility requirements will be delineated in the NOFO.

Award Range/Average: No Data Available.

Funding: N/A

HQ: 1600 Clifton Road NE
Atlanta, GA 30052
Phone: 404-718-8832
Email: bsg2@cdc.gov

ECA INDIVIDUAL GRANTS
"Individual Grants, U.S. academics and professionals, Bureau of Educational and Cultural Affairs (ECA)"

Award: Project Grants

Purpose: Provides individual assistance awards by the Bureau of Educational and Cultural Affairs to experts and other influential or distinguished persons in the United States, including academics and professionals, athletes and coaches and creative and performing artists, with funds appropriated to and authorized by the Bureau of Educational and Cultural Affairs.

Applicant Eligibility: Individuals in fields of specialized knowledge or skill, and other influential or distinguished persons.

Beneficiary Eligibility: Beneficiaries include selected participants and the people of participating countries.

Award Range/Average: $769.93 to $820.18.

Funding: (Project Grants (including individual awards) FY 17 $3,986; FY 18 est $3,986; FY 19 est $3,986; FY 16 $97,564.

HQ: US Department of State Executive Office Grants Division
Washington, DC 20037
Phone: 202-632-6365
Email: thompsondl1@state.gov
http://eca.state.gov

DOD 12.617 ECONOMIC ADJUSTMENT ASSISTANCE FOR STATE GOVERNMENTS

Award: Project Grants

Purpose: Provides technical and financial assistance to a State, or an entity of State government, to enhance its capacities to assist communities, businesses, and workers affected by Defense program activity to plan and carry out community adjustment and economic diversification activities; support local adjustment and diversification efforts; and stimulate cooperation between statewide and local adjustment and diversification efforts.

Applicant Eligibility: States, entities of States, Indian Tribal Governments, the District of Columbia, U.S. Territories and possessions. Applicants are to contact the Office of Economic Adjustment and a Project Manager will be assigned to work with the applicant to determine eligibility.

Beneficiary Eligibility: States, Indian Tribal Governments, and communities, including workers, businesses, and other community interests affected by Defense budget reductions, base closures/realignments, and/or civilian encroachment that is likely to impair the continued operational utility of a military installation.

Award Range/Average: $1,000,000 – $7,200,000, $1,900,000

Funding: (Project Grants) FY 16 est $43,242,528; FY 15 est $38,953,711; FY 17 N/A.

HQ: 2231 Crystal Drive, Suite 520
Arlington, VA 22202-3711
Phone: 703-697-2130
http://www.oea.gov

ECONOMIC STATECRAFT

Award: Project Grants

Purpose: Places economics and market forces at the center of U.S. foreign policy by both harnessing global economic forces to advance America's foreign policy and employing the tools of foreign policy to shore up our economic strength.

Applicant Eligibility: N/A

Beneficiary Eligibility: N/A

Award Range/Average: N/A

Funding: (Project Grants)

HQ: 2201 C Street, Room 3741
Washington, DC 20520
Phone: 202-647-4032
Email: hetrickc@state.gov
http://www.state.gov/e/eb/econstatecraft/index.htm

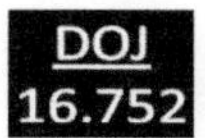

ECONOMIC, HIGH-TECH, AND CYBER CRIME PREVENTION

Award: Project Grants

Purpose: The Economic, High-Technology, White Collar, and Internet Crime Prevention National TTA Program prevents and investigates economic, high-tech, white collar, and internet crimes. It increases the knowledge of criminal justice practitioners and updates criminal justice agencies.

Applicant Eligibility: Eligible applicants include national, regional, State, or local public and private entities, including for-profit (commercial) and nonprofit organizations, faith-based and community organizations, institutions of higher education, tribal jurisdictions, and units of local government.

Beneficiary Eligibility: State, local, tribal, and local territorial law enforcement agencies, prosecutor, and other criminal justice agencies.

Award Range/Average: Varies.

Funding: (Cooperative Agreements) FY 17 $10,833,183; FY 18 est $14,000,000; FY 19 est $11,000,000.

HQ: US Department of Justice Bureau of Justice Assistance 810 7th Street NW
Washington, DC 20531
Phone: 202-616-6500
Email: david.p.lewis@usdoj.gov
http://www.nw3c.org

ECONOMIC, SOCIAL, AND POLITICAL DEVELOPMENT OF THE TERRITORIES

Award: Formula Grants; Project Grants; Direct Payments With Unrestricted Use

Purpose: To pursue the Department's mission of Fulfilling Our Trust and Insular Responsibilities by executing activities that reinforce healthcare capacity, strengthen island economies, and fulfill U.S. Compact obligations.

Applicant Eligibility: Eligible applicants are the U.S. territories of Guam, American Samoa, the U.S. Virgin Islands, and the Commonwealth of the Northern Mariana Islands, the state of Hawaii; the Freely Associated States of the Federated States of Micronesia, the Republic of the Marshall Islands, and the Republic of Palau; and any non-profit institutions/organizations whose missions directly benefit the seven insular areas.

Beneficiary Eligibility: Beneficiaries are the U.S. territories of Guam, American Samoa, the U.S. Virgin Islands, and the Commonwealth of the Northern Mariana Islands; the state of Hawaii; and the Freely Associated States of the Federated States of Micronesia, the Republic of the Marshall Islands, and the Republic of Palau.

Award Range/Average: Range from a few thousand dollars to tens of millions annually. The average award amount varies annually.

Funding: (Direct Payments with Unrestricted Use) FY 19 N/A FY 17 $288,000,000; FY 18 est $288,000,000;(Project Grants) FY 17 $319,867,000; FY 18 est $427,773,000; FY 19 N/A.

HQ: Department of Interior 1849 C Street NW, P.O. Box 2429
Washington, DC 20240

Phone: 202-208-3913
Email: aimee_munzi@ios.doi.gov
http://www.doi.gov/oia

HHS 93.827 EDUCATING STATE-LEVEL STAKEHOLDERS ON STRATEGIES TO ADDRESS WINNABLE BATTLES IN PUBLIC HEALTH

Award: Cooperative Agreements

Purpose: The purpose of the project is to reduce the burden of leading causes of death and disability by providing capacity building assistance to states to address priority health issues.

Applicant Eligibility: Applicants should be sufficiently connected to state executive branch and/or legislative branch members across the United States in order to accomplish the goal of working with a geographically diverse set of states from all regions of the U.S. Further, the applicant must be well versed both in public health issues such as CDC Winnable Battles and in how states approach and implement policies and practices that impact public health.

Beneficiary Eligibility: N/A

Award Range/Average: Fiscal Year: 2015 Estimated Total Funding: $1,000,000. Approximate Total Fiscal Year Funding: $200,000 Approximate Project Period Funding: $1,000,000. Total Project Period Length: 5 year(s) Expected Number of Awards: 1 Approximate Average Award: $200,000 Per Budget Period.

Funding: (Cooperative Agreements) FY 17 $15,000; FY 18 est $200,000; FY 19 est $58,750; FY 16 $150,000.

HQ: CLFT Building 21 Room 10005, P.O. Box D37
Atlanta, GA 30331
Phone: 404-639-7413

NSF 47.076 EDUCATION & HUMAN RESOURCES "EHR"

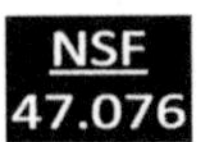

Award: Project Grants

Purpose: To provide leadership and ensure the vitality of the Nation's science, technology, engineering and mathematics (STEM) education enterprise.

Applicant Eligibility: Except where a program solicitation establishes more restrictive eligibility criteria, individuals and organizations in the following categories may submit proposals: Universities and colleges; Non-profit, non-academic organizations; For-profit organizations; State and local governments; and unaffiliated individuals. See the NSF Grant Proposal Guide Chapter I.

Beneficiary Eligibility: N/A

Award Range/Average: Range Low $10,000 Range High $33,416,922 Average $294,186.

Funding: (Project Grants) FY 16 est $878,970,000; FY 17 est $898,870,000.

HQ: 4201 Wilson Boulevard Stafford I, Suite 805
Arlington, VA 22230
Phone: 703-292-7306
Email: aedelman@nsf.gov
http://www.nsf.gov/dir/index.jsp?org=ehr

HUD 14.416 EDUCATION & OUTREACH INITIATIVES "FHIP EOI"

Award: Cooperative Agreements

Purpose: To develop, implement, carry out, or coordinate programs and/or activities to educate the public about their rights under, the Fair Housing Act (42 U.S.C. 3601-3619) or about State or local laws that provide substantially equivalent rights and remedies for alleged discriminatory housing practices.

Applicant Eligibility: Qualified Fair Housing Enforcement Organizations, other Fair Housing Enforcement Organizations, other non-profit organizations representing groups of persons protected under Title VIII of the Civil Rights Act of 1968, State and local agencies certified by the Secretary under Section 810(f) of the Fair Housing Act, or other public or private entities that are formulating or carrying out programs to prevent or eliminate discriminatory housing practices.

Beneficiary Eligibility: N/A

Award Range/Average: $125,000 to 1,000,000

Funding: (Cooperative Agreements) FY 17 $7,049,935; FY 18 est $7,450,000; FY 19 est $4,450,000; FY 16 $7,049,935.

HQ: 451 7th Street SW, Room 5222
Washington, DC 20410
Phone: 202-402-7054
Email: paula.stone@hud.gov
http://www.hud.gov/offices/fheo/partners.fhip/fhip.cfm

EDUCATION & PREVENTION GRANTS TO REDUCE SEXUAL ABUSE OF RUNAWAY, HOMELESS & STREET YOUTH "Street Outreach Program (SOP)"

Award: Project Grants

Purpose: Provides grants available to nonprofit agencies for the purpose of providing street-based services to runaway, homeless and street youth who have been subjected to, or are at risk of being subjected to sexual abuse, prostitution, human trafficking, sexual exploitation, or other forms of victimization.

Applicant Eligibility: Private, nonprofit agencies are eligible to apply for Street Outreach Program grants. Federally recognized Indian organizations are also eligible to apply for grants as private, non-profit agencies.

Beneficiary Eligibility: Runaway and homeless street youth are the beneficiaries of SOPs.

Award Range/Average: $100,000 to $150,000 per budget period; average award is $134,458

Funding: Project Grants (Discretionary) FY 17 $15,967,750; FY 18 est $15,426,900; FY 19 est $15,426,900.

HQ: 330 C Street SW
Washington, DC 20024
Phone: 202-205-9560
Email: christopher.holloway@acf.hhs.gov
http://www.acf.hhs.gov/programs/fysb

EDUCATION FOR HOMELESS CHILDREN & YOUTH

Award: Formula Grants

Purpose: To establish an Office of Coordinator for Education of Homeless Children and Youths; to develop a State plan for the education of homeless children; and to make subgrants to local educational agencies (LEAs) to support the education of those children.

Applicant Eligibility: State educational agencies in the 50 States, the District of Columbia, and Puerto Rico may apply. Funds are also reserved for the Outlying Areas and the Department of Interior/Bureau of Indian Education.

Beneficiary Eligibility: Homeless children and youth in elementary and secondary schools (and homeless preschool children and their parents benefit.

Award Range/Average: FY 17 range of awards: $192,500- $9,004,642FY 2017 average State award: $1,439,769. FY 18 range of awards: $212,500- $10,563,703 FY 2018 average State award: $1,587,885. FY 19 range of awards: $192,500- $9,585,594 FY 2019 average State award: $1,439,577.

Funding: FY 17 $77,000,000; FY 18 est $85,000,000; FY 19 est $77,000,000.

HQ: Department of Education 400 Maryland Avenue SW
Washington, DC 20202
Phone: 202-401-0962
Email: john.mclaughlin@ed.gov
http://www.ed.gov/programs/homeless/index.html

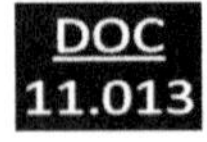

EDUCATION QUALITY AWARD AMBASSADORSHIP

Award: Cooperative Agreements

Purpose: To support Malcolm Baldrige National Quality Award Program encourages other organizations to strive for performance.

Applicant Eligibility: Applicants must have recently received the Malcolm Baldrige National Quality Award.

Beneficiary Eligibility: Public from 18 sponsored organizations.

Award Range/Average: Not to exceed $100,000 over the life of the grant.

Funding: (Cooperative Agreements) FY 17 $0; FY 18 est $0; FY 19 est $0; FY 16 $206,067.

HQ: 100 Bureau Drive, P.O. Box A-600
Gaithersburg, MD 20899-1020
Phone: 301-975-8942
Email: barbara.fischer@nist.gov
http://www.nist.gov/baldrige

EDUCATION RESEARCH, DEVELOPMENT & DISSEMINATION

Award: Project Grants

Purpose: To support research activities that improve the quality of education, reduce the achievement gap between high-performing and low-performing students, and increase the completion of postsecondary education.

Applicant Eligibility: Applicants that have the ability and capacity to conduct scientifically valid research are eligible to apply. Eligible applicants include, but are not limited to, non-profit and for-profit organizations and public and private agencies and institutions, such as colleges and universities.

Beneficiary Eligibility: Institutions and individuals involved with education will benefit.

Award Range/Average: The 2017 grant awards ranged in size from $200,000 to $10 million. The 2017 SBIR awards ranged from $148,573 to $150,000 for Phase I awards and $897,953 to $900,000 for Phase II awards. Applicants for 2018 and 2019 grant awards could request funding of $100,000 to $5,000,000 for projects lasting from 1 to 5 years, depending on the competition. The 2018 SBIR Phase I contract awards will be in amounts up to $200,000 for awards up to 6-months in length; the SBIR Phase II contract awards will be in amounts up to $900,000 for up to 2 years.

Funding: Project Grants (Contracts) FY 17 $22,684,505; FY 18 est $27,394,618; FY 19 est $29,725,000; FY 16 $27,745,518; - (Project Grants) FY 17 $164,815,495; FY 18 est $165,300,382; FY 19 est $157,775,000; FY 16 $154,292,737.

HQ: Department of Education 550 12th Street SW, Room 4118
Washington, DC 20202
Phone: 202-245-7833
Email: emily.doolittle@ed.gov
http://ies.ed.gov/ncer

EDUCATIONAL & CULTURAL EXCHANGE PROGRAMS APPROPRIATION OVERSEAS GRANTS

Award: Cooperative Agreements; Project Grants

Purpose: Provides assistance awards by U.S. diplomatic missions abroad made directly to eligible organizations in the United States using funds appropriated to and authorized by the Bureau of Educational and Cultural Affairs for the purpose of supporting international exchanges that addresses the issues of mutual interest to the United States and other countries, consistent with the program criteria established in the Department's annual appropriation.

Applicant Eligibility: Projects must support the development of mutual understanding between the United States and other countries in any area of importance to U.S. interests in those countries.

Beneficiary Eligibility: Beneficiaries include individuals selected for participation in the project, educational institutions, and Americans and people of other countries who interact with international participants.

Award Range/Average: $3,500 up to approximately $84,328. A typical award may total $50,000 or less.

Funding: (Project Grants) FY 17 $3,444,574; FY 18 est $3,444,574; FY 19 est $3,444,574; FY 16 $1,403,343.

HQ: US Department of State Executive Office Budget and Financial Management Division, 2200 C Street SA-5 Room 04-P04
Washington, DC 20522-0504
Phone: 202-632-3358
Email: robinsonyj@state.gov
http://exchanges.state.gov

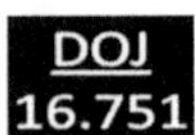

EDWARD BYRNE MEMORIAL COMPETITIVE GRANT PROGRAM
"Byrne Competitive Program"

Award: Project Grants

Purpose: To improve the criminal justice system by preventing crimes and enforcement of criminal law and assist in the rehabilitation, supervision, and care of criminal offenders.

Applicant Eligibility: Eligible applicants include national, regional, State, or local public and private entities, including for-profit (commercial) and nonprofit organizations, faith-based and community organizations, institutions of higher education, tribal jurisdictions, and units of local government.

Beneficiary Eligibility: State and local governments, public and private organizations, individuals and tribal governments.

Award Range/Average: Varies.

Funding: FY 17 $4,577,858; FY 18 est $1,000,000; FY 19 FY 16 $7,200,000.

HQ: US Department of Justice Bureau of Justice Assistance 810 7th Street NW
Washington, DC 20531
Phone: 202-616-6500
http://www.bja.gov

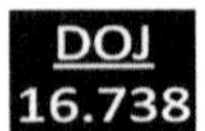

EDWARD BYRNE MEMORIAL JUSTICE ASSISTANCE GRANT PROGRAM
"Byrne JAG Program"

Award: Formula Grants; Project Grants

Purpose: Providing states, tribes, and local governments with critical funding necessary to support a range of program areas including law enforcement, prosecution and court, prevention and education, corrections and community corrections, drug treatment and enforcement, planning, evaluation, and technology improvement, crime victim and witness initiatives and mental health programs, and related law enforcement and corrections programs.

Applicant Eligibility: JAG: All States, the District of Columbia, Guam, America Samoa, the Commonwealths of Puerto Rico, the Virgin Islands, and the Northern Mariana Islands. Units of local government are eligible consistent with established guidelines.

Beneficiary Eligibility: JAG grants are awarded to States, including the District of Columbia, the Commonwealth of Puerto Rico, the Northern Mariana Islands, the Virgin Islands, Guam, and American Samoa, as well as eligible units of local government (including tribes).

Award Range/Average: $10,000 to $37,000,000.

Funding: (Formula Grants) FY 17 $303,543,145; FY 18 est $415,500,000; FY 19 est $402,000,000; FY 16 $434,522,436.

HQ: US Department of Justice Bureau of Justice Assistance 810 7th Street NW
Washington, DC 20531
Phone: 202-616-6500
http://www.bja.gov/programdetails.aspx?program_id=59

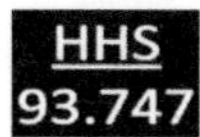

ELDER ABUSE PREVENTION INTERVENTIONS PROGRAM "Elder Abuse Prevention Intervention Projects"

Award: Cooperative Agreements

Purpose: To develop, implement, and evaluate successful or promising interventions, practices, and programs to prevent elder abuse, neglect, and exploitation, including adult protective services programs.

Applicant Eligibility: Eligible entities for grants authorized under Section 411 of the Older Americans Act are: domestic public or private non-profit entities including state and local governments, Indian tribal governments and organizations (American Indian/Alaskan Native/Native American), faith-based organizations, community-based organizations, hospitals, and institutions of higher education, are eligible. For grants authorized under Section 2042 of the Patient Protection and Affordable Care Act, state government entities are eligible to apply.

Beneficiary Eligibility: N/A

Award Range/Average: FY 2017: 5 New Awards (Range $176,850 - $492,500); 20 Continuation Awards (Range $100,000 - $488,550) FY 2018: 22 New Awards (Range $75,000 - $500,000); 5 Continuation Awards (Range $186,021 - $581,780) FY 2019: 5 New Awards (Range $150,000 - $500,000); 22 Continuation Awards (Range $75,000 - $500,000)

Funding: Cooperative Agreements (Discretionary Grants) FY 17 $7,748,535; FY 18 est $8,317,646; FY 19 est $6,500,000.

HQ: Administration on Aging
Washington, DC 20201
Phone: 202-795-7467
Email: stephanie.whittiereliason@acl.hhs.gov
http://www.acl.gov

EMERGENCY COMMUNITY WATER ASSISTANCE GRANTS

Award: Project Grants

Purpose: To assist rural residents to have an adequate quantity of water that meets the standards of the Safe Drinking Water Act.

Applicant Eligibility: Eligible beneficiaries include (1) Public bodies or governmental entities such as municipalities, counties, districts, authorities, and other political subdivisions of a State, (2) nonprofit organizations such as associations, cooperatives, and private nonprofit corporations, (3) Native American Indian tribes on Federal and State reservations and other federally recognized Indian tribes. Projects must serve rural areas, excluding any city or town having a population greater than 10,000.

Beneficiary Eligibility: Users of the applicant systems, which are previously described as public bodies, private nonprofit corporations, and federally-recognized Indian tribes.

Award Range/Average: $21,500 to $500,000. Average: $267,276

Funding: (Project Grants) FY 18 est $22,000,000; FY 16 $13,498,782; FY 17 est $22,000,000.

HQ: 1400 Independence Avenue SW
Washington, DC 20250
Phone: 202-720-0986
Email: edna.primrose@wdc.usda.gov
http://www.rd.usda.gov/programs-services/all-programs/water-environmental-programs

EMERGENCY FOOD & SHELTER NATIONAL BOARD PROGRAM "EFSP"

Award: Project Grants

Purpose: The EFSP program provides economic assistance to the poor during a disaster situation to help them recover from potential burdens.

Applicant Eligibility: Since funds are initially distributed to jurisdictions based on either a National Board formula or recommendations from State Set-Aside Committees, there is no application process for jurisdictions. All jurisdictions are considered within the National Board formula and all jurisdictions in an individual State may be considered by the State Set-Aside Committee for either initial or additional (if the jurisdiction had previously been selected by the National Board) funding.

Beneficiary Eligibility: The law directs that the Local Boards, which manage the program at the local level, shall "determine which private nonprofit organizations or public organizations of the local government in the individual locality shall receive grants to act as service providers." The range of participant groups on the Local Boards include the affiliates of the National Board membership which consists of American Red Cross, Catholic Charities USA, The Jewish Federations of North America, National Council of Churches of Christ in the USA, The Salvation Army, and United Way Worldwide, with a local government representative replacing FEMA.

Award Range/Average: Refer to program guidance.

Funding: FY 17 $120,000,000; FY 18 est $120,000,000; FY 19 est $120,000,000; FY 16 $120,000,000.

HQ: Community Services Branch/Individual Assistance Division/Recovery Directorate DHS, 500 C Street SW Room 614
Washington, DC 20472
Phone: 202-646-2500
http://www.fema.gov/media-library/assets/documents/24422

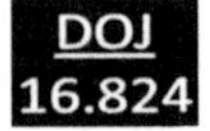

EMERGENCY LAW ENFORCEMENT ASSISTANCE GRANT "EFLEA"

Award: Project Grants

Purpose: To provide necessary law enforcement assistance to State government in response to threats to lives and property of citizens.

Applicant Eligibility: N/A

Beneficiary Eligibility: N/A

Award Range/Average: Awards may be made up to the amount available under this program.

Funding: (Project Grants) FY 17 $13,849,826; FY 18 est $16,000,000; FY 19 est $0; FY 16 $0.

HQ: US Department of Justice Bureau of Justice Assistance 810 7th Street NW
Washington, DC 20531
Phone: 202-616-6500
Email: tracey.trautman@usdoj.gov
http://www.bja.gov

EMERGENCY MANAGEMENT BASELINE ASSESSMENTS GRANT (EMBAG) "EMBAG"

Award: Direct Payments for Specified Use

Purpose: The EMBAG Program supervises the ANSI-certified standards for emergency preparedness and response. It assesses and evaluates the State and local level emergency management organizations and also ensures that the 32 core capabilities identified in the National Preparedness Goal are delivered.

Applicant Eligibility: Any non-profit organization that can sufficiently demonstrate through their application significant experience in providing assessments of state emergency management organizations using peer review and nationally recognized emergency management standards and that can meet the objectives of this program is eligible to apply.

Beneficiary Eligibility: State and territory emergency management programs.

Award Range/Average: No Data Available.

Funding: (Direct Payments for Specified Use) FY 17 $444,379; FY 18 est $569,379; FY 19 est $569,379; FY 16 $660,000.

HQ: FEMA 400 C Street NW
Washington, DC 20472-3630
Phone: 202-786-9451
Email: sharon.kushnir@fema.dhs.gov
http://www.fema.gov

EMERGENCY MANAGEMENT INSTITUTE (EMI) INDEPENDENT STUDY PROGRAM "ISP"

Award: Training

Purpose: The program provides over 195 courses on emergency management to government officials to help them prepare for threats against the national security that includes natural disasters, pandemics and acts of terrorism.

Applicant Eligibility: Unlimited Application. Anyone/general public - Any person(s), without regard to specified eligibility criteria.

Beneficiary Eligibility: Anyone/General Public.

Award Range/Average: N/A

Funding: (Training) FY 17 $753,235; FY 18 est $585,926; FY 19 est $676,319; FY 16 $753,235.

HQ: Department of Homeland Security Protection and National Preparedness National Preparedness Directorate, National Training and Education Division Emergency Management Institute
Emmitsburg, MD 21727
Phone: 301-447-1057
http://www.training.fema.gov/is

DHS 97.028 EMERGENCY MANAGEMENT INSTITUTE (EMI) RESIDENT EDUCATIONAL PROGRAM

Award: Training

Purpose: The program helps to improve the emergency management practices in local and State level through systematic preparation against threats such as natural disasters and other acts of terrorism.

Applicant Eligibility: Individuals assigned to an emergency management position in State, local, tribal, or Territorial government are eligible. Restrictions apply, however; refer to program guidance document or contact administering program office for additional information.

Beneficiary Eligibility: General Public.

Award Range/Average: N/A

Funding: (Training) FY 17 $1,770,453; FY 18 est $1,400,000; FY 19 est $1,900,000; FY 16 $1,770,453.

HQ: Protection and National Preparedness National Preparedness Directorate National Training and Education Division, 16825 S Seton Avenue
Emmitsburg, MD 21727
Phone: 301-447-1507
http://www.training.fema.gov

DHS 97.026 EMERGENCY MANAGEMENT INSTITUTE TRAINING ASSISTANCE
"Student Stipend Reimbursement Program (SEP)"

Award: Direct Payments for Specified Use

Purpose: To pay for the travel expenses of state, local and tribal officials who attend training courses on emergency management for systematic preparation on terrorism, cyber attacks and other natural disasters.

Applicant Eligibility: Individuals who are assigned to an emergency management position in State, local or tribal government are eligible. Some restrictions apply, refer to program guidance document or contact administering program office for additional information.

Beneficiary Eligibility: Specialized Group.

Award Range/Average: N/A

Funding: FY 17 $1,646,952; FY 18 est $1,500,000; FY 19 est $1,500,000; FY 16 $1,527,227.

HQ: Protection and National Preparedness National Preparedness Directorate National Training and Education Division, 16825 S Seton Avenue
Emmitsburg, MD 21727

Phone: 301-447-1286

http://www.training.fema.gov

EMERGENCY MANAGEMENT PERFORMANCE GRANTS "EMPG"

Award: Formula Grants

Purpose: The Emergency Management Performance Grant Program assists local and State governments in emergency preparedness for natural disasters and other hazards.

Applicant Eligibility: State (includes District of Columbia, public institutions of higher education and hospitals), U.S. Territories and possessions (includes institutions of higher education and hospitals) All 56 States and territories, as well as the Republic of the Marshall Islands and the Federated States of Micronesia, are eligible to apply for FY 2018 EMPG funds. Either the SAA or the State's EMA is eligible to apply for EMPG funds.

Beneficiary Eligibility: Funding under this program is ultimately used by emergency management organizations and programs of States, the District of Columbia, territories and possessions of the Unites States, local, and Indian Tribal governments.

Award Range/Average: No Data Available.

Funding: (Formula Grants) FY 17 $350,100,000; FY 18 est $350,099,998; FY 19 est $350,099,998; FY 16 $350,100,100.

HQ: Department of Homeland Security 400 C Street SW

Washington, DC 20523

Phone: 800-368-6498

http://www.iaem.com/documents/empg-roi-report-iaem-nema-06mar2018.pdf

EMERGENCY MEDICAL SERVICES FOR CHILDREN "EMS for Children"

Award: Cooperative Agreements; Project Grants

Purpose: To support demonstration projects for the expansion and improvement of emergency medical services for children.

Applicant Eligibility: State Governments and Accredited Schools of Medicine

Beneficiary Eligibility: All children will benefit from the project grants administered by this program, including children from minority groups.

Award Range/Average: $130,000 to $3,000,000; $232.668

Funding: (Project Grants) FY 17 $17,393,910; FY 18 est $19,311,470; FY 19 est $18,088,783; FY 16 $17,016,778.

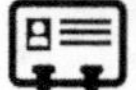

HQ: Maternal and Child Health Bureau 5600 Fishers Lane, Room 18N-54

Rockville, MD 20857

Phone: 301-443-1527

Email: tmorrison-quinata@hrsa.gov

http://www.hrsa.gov

DHS 97.052 EMERGENCY OPERATIONS CENTER "EOC"

Award: Project Grants

Purpose: The grant program provides funds for construction or renovation of a State or local emergency operations center.

Applicant Eligibility: Specific information on applicant eligibility is identified in the funding opportunity announcement and in the EOC Grant Program Guidance and Application Kit

Beneficiary Eligibility: Funding under this program is ultimately to benefit State and local governments.

Award Range/Average: Refer to in the EOC Grant Program Guidance and Application Kit.

Funding: (Project Grants) Program was last funded in FY2010. This program will remain open due to open awards.

HQ: Grant Programs Directorate Department of Homeland Security FEMA 400 C Street SW

Washington, DC 20472-3615

Phone: 800-368-6498

http://www.fema.gov

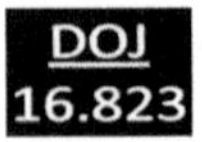

EMERGENCY PLANNING FOR JUVENILE JUSTICE FACILITIES

Award: Project Grants

Purpose: To provide funds to States to address the needs of children, youth, and families involved in the justice system during an emergency.

Applicant Eligibility: 1) US Territories; state; The only eligible applicant for these funds is the designated state agency that receives Title II Formula Grant funds from OJJDP 2) law, justice, and legal services; youth development; planning

Beneficiary Eligibility: Local; state; child; youth.

Award Range/Average: $70,000- $91,000

Funding: Project Grants (Discretionary) FY 17 $416,661; FY 18 est $500,000; FY 19 est $500,000.

HQ: US Department of Justice Office of Juvenile Justice and Delinquency Prevention 810 7th Street NW

Washington, DC 20531

Phone: 202-514-4817

Email: kellie.dressler@usdoj.gov

http://www.ojjdp.gov

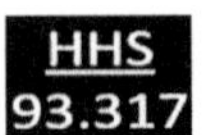

EMERGING INFECTIONS PROGRAMS

Award: Cooperative Agreements

Purpose: To assist in local, state, and national efforts to prevent, control, and monitor the public health impact of infectious diseases.

Applicant Eligibility: Eligibility is limited to State governments (specifically, state health departments) or their Bona Fide Agents (this includes the District of Columbia, the Commonwealth of Puerto Rico, the Virgin Islands, the Commonwealth of the Northern Marianna Islands, American Samoa, Guam, the Federated States of Micronesia, the Republic of the Marshall Islands, and the Republic of Palau).

The EIP infrastructure depends on a direct relationship with public health agencies that have sufficient legal authority and responsibility to perform public health surveillance and response activities.

Beneficiary Eligibility: Beneficiaries of this program include State and local health departments, the District of Columbia, U.S. Territories, and the general public.

Award Range/Average: $1.5M to 4M annually, with an average of $2.6M.

Funding: (Cooperative Agreements) FY 17 $20,362,615; FY 18 est $26,055,351; FY 19 est $26,000,000; FY 16 $65,697.

HQ: 1600 Clifton Road NE, P.O. Box C18
Atlanta, GA 30329
Phone: 404-639-6146
Email: roa3@cdc.gov
http://www.cdc.gov

HHS 93.860 EMERGING INFECTIONS SENTINEL NETWORKS

Award: Cooperative Agreements

Purpose: The Emerging Infections Sentinel Networks monitors and evaluates conditions that are not covered by health department surveillance and are likely to be seen by specific kinds of health providers. They contribute to surveillance for emerging infectious diseases, including drug resistant, foodborne and waterborne, and vaccine-preventable or potentially vaccine-preventable diseases, and enhance information exchange leading to early identification of and response to trends and outbreaks.

Applicant Eligibility: Eligibility for this program is open, however, only institutions/organizations that meet and can demonstrate the necessary qualifications described in the published NOFOs for this program should apply. Additional eligibility information is also described below: There are both research and non-research funding opportunities under this program.

Beneficiary Eligibility: Health Professionals - Anyone/general public

Award Range/Average: Award Range: $250k– $930k Average Award: $530k

Funding: FY 17 $1,730,000; FY 18 est $1,591,000; FY 19 est $1,600,000.

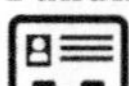

HQ: 1600 Clifton Road, P.O. Box C18
Atlanta, GA 30329
Phone: 404-639-7722
Email: aslaughter@cdc.gov
http://www.cdc.gov

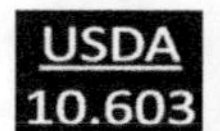

USDA 10.603 EMERGING MARKETS PROGRAM "EMP"

Award: Direct Payments for Specified Use

Purpose: The Emerging Markets Program maximizes exporting of U.S. agricultural commodities to markets of eligible organizations. It promotes food and rural businesses for emerging markets.

Applicant Eligibility: Applicants must be U. S. Citizen.

Beneficiary Eligibility: There are 4 types of eligible activities: (1) Assistance to U.S. individual experts in assessing the food and rural business systems of other countries. This type of EMP project must include all three of the following: Conduct an assessment of the food and rural business system needs of an emerging market. Make recommendations on measures necessary to enhance the effectiveness of these systems. Identify opportunities and projects to enhance the effectiveness of the emerging market's food and rural business systems.

Award Range/Average: Generally grants are for small, focused projects ranging from $7,000 up to $500,000.

Funding: (Project Grants) FY 17 $7,700,000; FY 18 est $7,000,000; FY 19 est $7,000,000; FY 16 est $7,007,580.

HQ: 1400 Independence Avenue SW
Washington, DC 20050
Phone: 202-720-8557
Email: lona.powell@fas.usda.gov
http://www.fas.usda.gov/programs/emerging-markets-program-emp

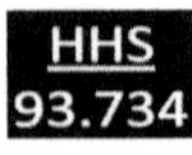

EMPOWERING OLDER ADULTS & ADULTS WITH DISABILITIES THROUGH CHRONIC DISEASE SELF-MANAGEMENT EDUCATION PROGRAMS – FINANCED BY PREVENTION & PUBLIC HEALTH FUNDS (PPHF)

"Chronic Disease Self-Management Education Programs"

Award: Cooperative Agreements; Project Grants

Purpose: The agreements are intended to increase the number of chronic disease self-management education program participants, while concurrently increasing the sustainability of these proven programs in the aging and disability networks.

Applicant Eligibility: Eligible applicants are domestic public or private non-profit entities including state and local governments, Indian tribal governments and organizations (American Indian/Alaskan Native/ Native American), faith-based organizations, community-based organizations, hospitals, and institutions of higher education.

Beneficiary Eligibility: The ultimate beneficiaries of this funding opportunity are older and disabled adults with chronic conditions residing in States, Tribes and Territories.

Award Range/Average: FY 2018 Range: $145,255 - $850,000

Funding: (Salaries and Expenses) FY 17 $8,000,000; FY 18 est $8,000,000; FY 19 N/A FY 16 $8,000,000.

HQ: US Department of Health and Human Services 330 C Street SW
Washington, DC 20201
Phone: 202-795-7379
Email: kristie.kulinski@acl.hhs.gov
http://www.acl.gov

DOL 17.310 ENERGY EMPLOYEES OCCUPATIONAL ILLNESS COMPENSATION

Award: Direct Payments with Unrestricted Use

Purpose: Provides lump-sum monetary payments and medical benefits to covered employees and, where applicable, to survivors of such employees, of the Department of Energy (DOE), its predecessor agencies and certain of its vendors, contractors and subcontractors.

Applicant Eligibility: Employees and, where applicable, to survivors of such employees, of the Department of Energy (DOE), its predecessor agencies, certain of its vendors, contractors and subcontractors, and uranium miners, millers and ore transporters covered by section 5 of RECA, who are or were engaged in covered employment related to the testing or production of nuclear weapons.

Beneficiary Eligibility: Same as Applicant Eligibility.

Award Range/Average: Maximum monetary lump-sum payment under Part B is $150,000 per covered employee; maximum monetary lump-sum payment under Part E is $250,000 per covered employee. No limitation on payment of medical expenses.

Funding: (Direct Payments with Unrestricted Use) FY 17 $1,245,989,269; FY 18 est $1,295,310,000; FY 19 est $1,301,594,000; FY 16 $1,110,137,484.

HQ: Division of Energy Employees Occupational Illness Compensation 200 Constitution Avenue NW
Washington, DC 20210
Phone: 202-693-0081
http://www.dol.gov/owcp/energy

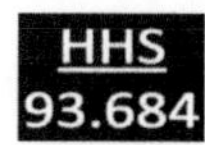

ENGAGING STATE & LOCAL EMERGENCY MANAGEMENT AGENCIES TO IMPROVE ABILITY TO PREPARE FOR & RESPOND TO ALL – HAZARDS EVENTS

Award: Cooperative Agreements

Purpose: The program prepare the nation's public health systems to minimize the consequences associated with all-hazards events.

Applicant Eligibility: Applicant must have experience as a professional association of and for emergency management directors from all 50 states, eight U.S. territories, and the District of Columbia, the applicant's unique ability in representing state emergency management directors will greatly assist with emergency preparedness planning and coordination efforts between public health and emergency management sectors nationally.

Beneficiary Eligibility: Same as Applicant Eligibility.

Award Range/Average: Approximate Average Award: $150K. Budget Period Length: 12 months Project Period Length: 5 years

Funding: (Salaries and Expenses) FY 17 $0; FY 18 est $0; FY 19 est $150,000.

HQ: 1600 Clifton Road, P.O. Box D29
Atlanta, GA 30029-4018
Phone: 404-639-5276
Email: vbk5@cdc.gov
http://www.cdc.gov

NSF 47.041 ENGINEERING GRANTS "ENG"

Award: Project Grants

Purpose: To improve the quality of life and the economic strength of the Nation by fostering innovation, creativity, and excellence in engineering education and research.

Applicant Eligibility: Except where a program solicitation establishes more restrictive eligibility criteria, individuals and organizations in the following categories may submit proposals: Universities and colleges; Non-profit, non-academic organizations; for-profit organizations; State and local governments; and unaffiliated individuals. See the NSF Grant Proposal Guide, Chapter I.

Beneficiary Eligibility: N/A

Award Range/Average: Range Low $4,000 Range High $15,899,312 Average $151,256

Funding: (Project Grants) FY 17 $930,920,000; FY 18 est $972,160,000; FY 19 est $921,430,000; FY 16 $923,530,000; - 1) FY 2017 Obligations are the FY 2017 Appropriations Actuals 2) FY 2018 Obligations estimates are the FY 2018 NSF Current Plan 3) FY 2019 Obligatio

HQ: 2415 Eisenhower Avenue
Alexandria, VA 22314
Phone: 703-292-4494
Email: dduttere@nsf.gov
http://nsf.gov/dir/index.jsp?org=eng

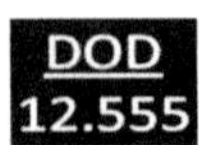

DOD 12.555 ENGLISH FOR HERITAGE LANGUAGE SPEAKERS SCHOLARSHIPS "EHLS Program"

Award: Project Grants

Purpose: The English for Heritage Language Speakers (EHLS) program is designed to provide intensive English language instruction for U. S. citizens who are native speakers of critical languages.

Applicant Eligibility: Currently, the program is administered at Georgetown University in Washington, DC through a contract.

Beneficiary Eligibility: (1) Must be a U.S. citizen at the time of application; (2) Must have a minimum proficiency in English of advanced low (as defined by ACTFL) or level 2 (as defined by ILR); (3) must also possess excellent skills in your heritage/native language (ILR level 3/ACTFL superior language proficiency or higher in all modalities of English; (4) Must have received at least an undergraduate degree by the time of application; and (5) may not be a current U.S. government employee. Eligible native languages of interest are updated annually, a list of which is available on the program website.

Award Range/Average: Awards are for $30,000 in 2010. There is no range or average.

Funding: (Project Grants (including individual awards) FY 17 $790,000; FY 18 est $790,000; FY 19 N/A FY 16 $790,000.

HQ: 4800 Mark Center Drive, Suite 08 G 08
Alexandria, VA 22350
Phone: 571-256-0753
Email: kevin.j.gormley.civ@mail.mil
http://www.cal.org/ehls

ENGLISH LANGUAGE ACQUISITION STATE GRANTS

Award: Formula Grants

Purpose: To ensure that English learners (ELs), including immigrant children and youth, attain English proficiency and meet the same challenging State academic standards that all children are expected to meet.

Applicant Eligibility: States with approved State plans and outlying areas are eligible to receive funds.

Beneficiary Eligibility: English learners and immigrant children and youth benefit.

Award Range/Average: FY 18 $92,598 - $150,624,531; $12,713,793 average.

Funding: FY 17 $684,469,000; FY 18 est $681,011,655; FY 19 est $681,021,655.

HQ: 400 Maryland Avenue SW
Washington, DC 20202
Phone: 202-453-6886
Email: katherine.cox@ed.gov
http://www2.ed.gov/programs/sfgp/index.html

ENHANCE SAFETY OF CHILDREN AFFECTED BY SUBSTANCE ABUSE
"Regional Partnership Grants or RPGs"

Award: Project Grants

Purpose: To provide, an integration of program activities and services that are designed to increase well-being, improve permanency outcomes, and enhance the safety of children who are in an out-of-home placement or are at risk of being placed in out-of-home care as a result of a parent's or caretaker's substance abuse.

Applicant Eligibility: State governments, county governments, local governments, city or township governments, regional organizations, U.S. territory or possession, independent school districts, public and state-controlled institutions of higher education, Indian/Native American tribal governments (federally recognized), Indian/Native American tribal organizations (other than federally recognized), Indian/Native American tribally designated organizations, public/Indian housing authorities, non-profits with 501(c)(3) IRS status (other than institutions of higher education), non-profits without 501(c)(3) IRS status (other than institutions of higher education), private institutions of higher education, for-profit organizations (other than small businesses), small businesses, Hispanic-serving institutions, historically Black colleges and universities (HBCUs), tribally controlled colleges and universities (TCCUs), Alaska Native and Native Hawaiian serving institutions, and special district governments. Foreign entities are not eligible under this announcement.

Beneficiary Eligibility: Agencies or organizations serving children and families who have experienced or are at risk of experiencing an out of home placement as a result of a parent's or caregiver's substance abuse.

Award Range/Average: $532,000 to $600,000 with an average of $595,743.

Funding: Project Grants (Discretionary) FY 17 $12,510,611; FY 18 est $30,979,514; FY 19 est $30,000,000; FY 16 $14,148,747.

HQ: Office on Child Abuse and Neglect Childrens Bureau 330 C Street SW, Room 3419C
Washington, DC 20201
Phone: 202-401-2887

Email: jean.blankenship@acf.hhs.gov

http://www.acf.hhs.gov/programs/cb

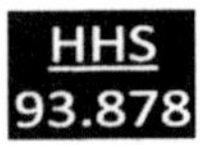

ENHANCE THE ABILITY OF EMERGENCY MEDICAL SERVICES (EMS) TO TRANSPORT PATIENTS WITH HIGHLY INFECTIOUS DISEASES (HID)

Award: Cooperative Agreements

Purpose: Enhance state and local level emergency medical services operational plans for the management of confirmed or suspected high consequence infection diseases.

Applicant Eligibility: The applicant must be a nonprofit organization representing all of the 50 state emergency medical services officials.

Beneficiary Eligibility: EMS officials and operators at the state and local levels

Award Range/Average: $250,000- $350,000

Funding: (Salaries and Expenses) FY 17 $350,000; FY 18 est $350,000; FY 19 est $350,000; FY 16 $349,999.

HQ: Division of Health System Policy 200 C Street SW

Washington, DC 20201

Phone: 202-690-3830

Email: gregg.margolis@hhs.gov

http://www.phe.gov

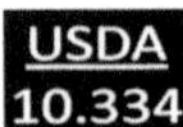

ENHANCING AGRICULTURAL OPPORTUNITIES FOR MILITARY VETERANS COMPETITIVE GRANTS PROGRAM

Award: Project Grants

Purpose: Enhancing Agricultural Opportunities for Military Veterans provides grants for military veterans and crates farming and ranching opportunities.

Applicant Eligibility: Funds may be used to provide grants to nonprofit organizations for programs and services to establish and enhance farming and ranching opportunities for military veterans.

Beneficiary Eligibility: Same as Applicant Eligibility.

Award Range/Average: If minimum or maximum amounts of funding per competitive and/or capacity project grant, or cooperative agreement are established, these amounts will be announced in the annual Competitive Request for Application (RFA).

Funding: Project Grants (Discretionary) FY 17 $4,979,500; FY 18 est $4,757,600; FY 19 est $0.

HQ: 1400 Independence Avenue SW, Room 4434

Washington, DC 20250

Phone: 202-690-3468

Email: belrod@nifa.usda.gov

http://nifa.usda.gov/funding-opportunity/enhancing-agricultural-opportunities-military-veterans-competitive-grants

ENHANCING THE LOGICAL OBSERVATION IDENTIFIERS NAMES & CODES (LOINC®) STANDARD TO MEET U.S. INTEROPERABILITY NEEDS "LOINC"

Award: N/A

Purpose: To expedite improvements and bridge gaps between Health Level 7 International's (HL7®) Fast Healthcare Interoperability Resources (FHIR®).

Applicant Eligibility: The Regenstrief Institute is the only entity to apply for this award.

Beneficiary Eligibility: N/A

Award Range/Average: $625,000 allocated for FY 18. One award will be made to the Regenstrief Institute.

Funding: (Cooperative Agreements) FY 17 FY 18 est $625,000.

HQ: 330 C Street SW
Washington, DC 20201
Phone: 202-720-2919
Email: carmel.halloun@hhs.gov
http://www.healthit.gov

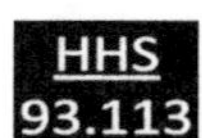

ENVIRONMENTAL HEALTH "National Institute of Environmental Health Sciences"

Award: Project Grants

Purpose: To identify of agents that pose a hazard and threat of disease, disorders and defects in humans; the development of effective public health or disease prevention strategies.

Applicant Eligibility: Research Grants, Cooperative Agreements, Science Education Grants, SBIR Grants, Independent Scientist Awards, Mentored Research Scientist Development Award, Mentored Clinical Scientist Development Award, and the Academic Career Awards: A university, college, hospital, State, local or tribal governments, nonprofit research institution, or for-profit organization may submit an application and receive a grant for support of research by a named principal investigator. Candidates for Academic Career Awards and Midcareer Investigator Awards in Patient Oriented Research must have a doctoral degree and peer-reviewed, independent, research support at the time the award is made.

Beneficiary Eligibility: For Research Grants: Any nonprofit or for-profit organization, company, or institution engaged in biomedical research. For Centers and Training Grants: University-based nonprofit institutions; for-profit organizations conducting research; and individuals nominated by a private institution conducting research.

Award Range/Average: Range: $2,000 to $1,749,000 Average: $342,223

Funding: FY 17 $334,076,000; FY 18 est $354,076,000; FY 19 est $326,777,000.

HQ: 111 TW Alexander Drive
Research Triangle Park, NC 27709
Phone: 984-287-3784
Email: encarna1@niehs.nih.gov
http://www.niehs.nih.gov

HHS 93.070 ENVIRONMENTAL PUBLIC HEALTH & EMERGENCY RESPONSE

Award: Cooperative Agreements

Purpose: To bring public health and epidemiologic principles together to identify, clarify, and reduce the impact of complex environmental threats, including terrorist threats and natural disasters, on populations, domestic and foreign.

Applicant Eligibility: N/A

Beneficiary Eligibility: N/A

Award Range/Average: $10,000 to $1,500,000

Funding: (Cooperative Agreements) FY 17 $50,695,987; FY 18 est $45,960,170; FY 19 est $50,695,987; FY 16 $54,079,771.

HQ: 4770 Buford Highway, P.O. Box F45
Atlanta, GA 30341
Phone: 770-488-0563
Email: vio9@cdc.gov
http://www.cdc.gov

HHS 93.943 EPIDEMIOLOGIC RESEARCH STUDIES OF ACQUIRED IMMUNODEFICIENCY SYNDROME (AIDS) & HUMAN IMMUNODEFICIENCY VIRUS (HIV) INFECTION IN SELECTED POPULATION GROUPS

"Epidemiologic Research Studies of AIDS and HIV"

Award: Cooperative Agreements

Purpose: To support research of HIV-related epidemiologic issues concerning risks of transmission, the natural history and transmission of the disease in certain populations.

Applicant Eligibility: Eligible applicants include States, political subdivisions of States or their agents or instrumentalities, private research organizations, including American Indian/Alaska Native tribal governments or tribal organizations located wholly or in part within their boundaries, other public and private nonprofit organizations, and for-profit organizations.

Beneficiary Eligibility: State and local health agencies; private research organizations, public and private nonprofit organizations, for profit organizations; minority groups, including American Indian/Alaska Native tribal governments or tribal organizations located wholly or in part within their boundaries, and persons physically afflicted with AIDS/HIV infection.

Award Range/Average: No Data Available.

Funding: FY 17 $1,936,620; FY 18 est $600,000; FY 19 est $0; FY 16 $2,500,000.

HQ: 1600 Clifton Road NE, P.O. Box E-07
Atlanta, GA 30333
Phone: 404-639-1877
Email: lrw3@cdc.gov
http://www.cdc.gov

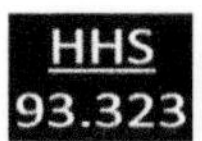

EPIDEMIOLOGY & LABORATORY CAPACITY FOR INFECTIOUS DISEASES (ELC)
"ELC"

Award: Cooperative Agreements

Purpose: To protect the public health and safety of the American people by enhancing the capacity of public health agencies to effectively detect, respond, prevent and control known and emerging (or re-emerging) infectious diseases.

Applicant Eligibility: Eligible applicants consist of state, local, and U.S. territory/possession governments currently funded under CDC-RFA-CI10-1012 or CDC-RFA-CK12-1201. Specifically, these include: all 50 states, Washington, D.

Beneficiary Eligibility: Direct beneficiaries include all 50 states, Washington, D.C.

Award Range/Average: Subject to availability of Funds

Funding: (Cooperative Agreements) FY 17 $259,572,511; FY 18 est $208,775,519; FY 19 FY 16 $197,654,769.

HQ: 1600 Clifton Road NE, P.O. Box C18

Atlanta, GA 30333

Phone: 404-639-7379

Email: amoconnor@cdc.gov

http://www.cdc.gov/ncezid/dpei/epidemiology-laboratory-capacity.html

EQUAL OPPORTUNITY IN HOUSING
"Fair Housing"

Award: Investigation of Complaints

Purpose: To provide fair housing throughout the country and an administrative enforcement system that is subject to judicial review.

Applicant Eligibility: Any aggrieved person, or the Assistant Secretary, may file a complaint based on an alleged discriminatory housing practice because of race, color, religion, sex, national origin, familial status or disability status. The complaint may be filed with the Department of Housing and Urban Development or a State or local fair housing agency whose law has been determined to be substantially equivalent to the Federal Fair Housing Act.

Beneficiary Eligibility: Anyone alleging to have been discriminated against in violation of the Fair Housing Act.

Award Range/Average: No Data Available.

Funding: Project Grants (Cooperative Agreements or Contracts) FY 17 N/A FY 18 N/A FY 19 FY 16 N/A - Fund 0333 is no longer active. (Salaries and Expenses) FY 17 $71,227,000; FY 18 est $69,808,000; FY 19 est $71,312,000; FY 16 $64,180,000.

HQ: 451 7th Street SW, Room 5208

Washington, DC 20410

Phone: 202-402-3264

Email: gordon.f.patterson@hud.gov

http://www.hud.gov/complaints/housediscrim.cfm

DOS 19.123 EUR/ACE HUMANITARIAN ASSISTANCE PROGRAM
"EUR/ACE Humanitarian Assistance Program"

Award: Project Grants

Purpose: Provides vital humanitarian assistance to vulnerable populations in countries of the former Soviet Union.

Applicant Eligibility: Since 1992, the EUR/ACE HA program has been assisting those in need with food, clothing and medicine. Small Reconstruction Projects fund structural repairs such as bathrooms and kitchens of recipient institutions in a cost-effective way.

Beneficiary Eligibility: All grantees under this program are U.S. based non-profit organizations

Award Range/Average: between $ 100,000 and $,600,00

Funding: (Salaries and Expenses)

HQ: 2201 C Street NW
Washington, DC 20003
Phone: 202-647-7272
Email: shankn@state.gov

EUR/ACE NATIONAL ENDOWMENT FOR DEMOCRACY SMALL GRANTS
"National Endowment for Democracy (NED) Small Grants Program in Europe, Eurasia and Central Asia"

Award: Project Grants

Purpose: Advances democracy in Europe, Eurasia and Central Asia by providing support to indigenous civil society organizations.

Applicant Eligibility: This program is awarded on a non-competitive basis.

Beneficiary Eligibility: N/A

Award Range/Average: No Data Available.

Funding: N/A

HQ: 2201 C Street NW
Washington, DC 20520
Phone: 202-647-7703
Email: krystelnb@state.gov

DOS 19.878 EUR-OTHER

Award: Project Grants

Purpose: To promote democratic and free market transitions in the former communist countries of Central and Eastern Europe and Eurasia, enabling them to overcome their past and become reliable, productive members of the Euro-Atlantic community of Western democracies.

Applicant Eligibility: This program is awarded on a non-competitive basis.

Beneficiary Eligibility: N/A

Award Range/Average: No Data Available.

Funding: (Project Grants)

HQ: 2201 C Street NW
Washington, DC 20052
Phone: 202-647-8002
Email: gupmanam@state.gov

EVERY STUDENT SUCCEEDS ACT/PRESCHOOL DEVELOPMENT GRANTS
"ESSA/Preschool Development Grants Birth-5"

Award: Project Grants

Purpose: Seeks to assist States in helping low-income and disadvantaged children enter Kindergarten prepared and ready to succeed in school and to help improve the transitions from the early care and education setting to elementary school.

Applicant Eligibility: In addition to the 50 States eligible to apply for these grants in FY2018, the District of Columbia and Puerto Rico are also eligible. In the first year of ESSA PDG implementation (Initial Planning Grants), priority will be given to States not previously awarded under the previous PDG of 2014.

Beneficiary Eligibility: In addition to the 50 States, DC, Puerto Rico, and local communities, beneficiaries include children birth through 5 and their families.

Award Range/Average: $5-10M per Grant Award

Funding: (Project Grants) FY 19 N/A FY 16 $0; FY 17 $0; N/A FY 18 est $243,500,000.

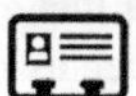

HQ: Switzer Building 330 C Street SW, Room 4010A
Washington, DC 20201
Phone: 202-401-5138
Email: richard.gonzales@acf.hhs.gov
http://www.acf.hhs.gov/occ

EVIDENCE-BASED FALLS PREVENTION PROGRAMS FINANCED SOLELY BY PREVENTION & PUBLIC HEALTH FUNDS (PPHF)
"Falls Prevention"

Award: Cooperative Agreements

Purpose: The cooperative agreements are intended to increase the number of evidence-based falls prevention programs available to older adults, while concurrently increasing the sustainability of these proven programs in the aging and disability networks.

Applicant Eligibility: Eligible applicants for grants are domestic public or private non-profit entities including state and local governments, Indian tribal governments and organizations (American Indian/ Alaskan Native/Native American), faith-based organizations, community-based organizations, hospitals, and institutions of higher education. Any additional restrictions/guidance will be provided in the funding opportunity announcement(s).

Beneficiary Eligibility: The ultimate beneficiaries of this funding opportunity are older and disabled adults at risk for falls residing in states, tribes, and territories.

Award Range/Average: Range: $107,477 - $515,590

Funding: Cooperative Agreements (Discretionary Grants) FY 17 $5,000,000; FY 18 est $5,000,000; FY 19 est $5,000,000; FY 16 $5,000,000.

HQ: US Department of Health and Human Services One Massachusetts Avenue NW
Washington, DC 20201
Phone: 202-357-3508
Email: casey.dicocco@acl.hhs.gov
http://www.acl.gov

USDA 10.514 EXPANDED FOOD & NUTRITION EDUCATION PROGRAM "EFNEP"

Award: Formula Grants; Project Grants

Purpose: The purpose of this funding is to assist socially disadvantaged families. The EFNEP assists by providing awareness of diet quality and physical activity, food resource management, food safety, and food security.

Applicant Eligibility: Only Auburn University; Alabama A & M University; Tuskegee University; University of Alaska; American Samoa Community College; University of Arizona; University of Arkansas; University of Arkansas – Pine Bluff; University of California; Central State University, Colorado State University; University of Connecticut; University of Delaware; Delaware State University; University of the District of Columbia; University of Florida; Florida A & M University; University of Georgia; Fort Valley State University; University of Guam; University of Hawaii; University of Idaho; University of Illinois; Purdue University; Iowa State University; Kansas State University; University of Kentucky; Kentucky State University; Louisiana State University; Southern University; University of Maine; University of Maryland (College Park); University of Maryland (Eastern Shore); University of Massachusetts; Michigan State University; College of Micronesia; University of Minnesota; Mississippi State University; Alcorn State University; University of Missouri; Lincoln University; Montana State University; University of Nebraska; University of Nevada; University of New Hampshire; Rutgers University; New Mexico State University; Cornell University; North Carolina State University; North Carolina A & T University; North Dakota State University; Northern Marianas College; Ohio State University; Central State University; Oklahoma State University; Langston University; Oregon State University; Pennsylvania State University; University of Puerto Rico; University of Rhode Island; Clemson University; South Carolina State University; South Dakota State University; University of Tennessee; Tennessee State University; Texas A&M University; Prairie View A & M University; Utah State University; University of Vermont; University of the Virgin Islands; Virginia Polytechnic Institute and State University; Virginia State University; Washington State 7 University; West Virginia University; West Virginia State University; University of Wisconsin; and University of Wyoming may submit applications.

Beneficiary Eligibility: Same as Applicant Eligibility.

Award Range/Average: If minimum or maximum amounts of funding per competitive and/or capacity project grant, or cooperative agreement are established, these amounts will be announced in the annual Request for Application (RFA).

Funding: (Formula Grants) FY 17 $0; FY 18 est $0; FY 19 est $67,293,480; FY 16 $0.

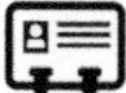

HQ: 1400 Independence Avenue SW, P.O. Box 2225
Washington, DC 20250-2225
Phone: 202-720-5004
Email: hchipman@nifa.usda.gov
http://nifa.usda.gov/program/expanded-food-and-nutrition-education-program-efnep

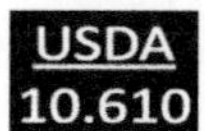

EXPORT GUARANTEE PROGRAM "The GSM-102 Program"

Award: Guaranteed/Insured Loans

Purpose: The U.S. Department of Agriculture's Export Credit Guarantee Program encourages financing for commercial exports of U.S. agricultural products. It reduces financial risk. USDA's Foreign Agricultural Service administers the credit guarantees.

Applicant Eligibility: Export Credit guarantee Program (GSM-102) provides credit guarantees to encourage financing of commercial exports of U.S. agricultural products, while providing competitive credit terms to buyers. By reducing financial risk to lenders, credit guarantees encourage exports to buyers in countries, mainly developing countries, that have sufficient financial strength to have foreign exchange available for scheduled payments.

Beneficiary Eligibility: Exporters or the exporters assignee are the direct beneficiaries and must meet the applicant eligibility requirements. Interested parties, including U.S. exporters, foreign buyers, banks, may request that the CCC establish a GSM-102 program for a country or region.

Award Range/Average: No Data Available.

Funding: (Guaranteed/Insured Loans) FY 17 $1,578,800,312; FY 18 est $1,900,000,000; FY 19 est $5,500,000,000; FY 16 $6,748,000,000.

HQ: 1400 independence Avenue SW, P.O. Box 1025
Washington, DC 20250
Phone: 202-720-9389
Email: brad.hoppe@fas.usda.gov
http://www.fas.usda.gov/programs/export-credit-guarantee-program-gsm-102

EXTRAMURAL RESEARCH FACILITIES RESTORATION PROGRAM: HURRICANES HARVEY, MARIA, AND IRMA – CONSTRUCTION

Award: Project Grants

Purpose: The program will fund disaster response and recovery, and other expenses directly related to Hurricane Harvey, Hurricane Irma, or Hurricane Maria, which are in the FEMA-declared major disaster states, relevant to supporting the recovery of losses at non-Federal biomedical or behavioral research facilities.

Applicant Eligibility: Applicants will be required to attest (at time of application) that funds requested will not be used for costs that are reimbursed by the Federal Emergency Management Agency, under a contract for insurance, or by self-insurance. Terms and Conditions of the award will stipulate that the grantee must reimburse HHS for any costs that are subsequently covered by the Federal Emergency Management Agency, under a contract for insurance, or by self-insurance.

Beneficiary Eligibility: N/A

Award Range/Average: N/A

Funding: (Project Grants) FY 18 est $25,000,000; FY 17 N/A FY 19 est $0.

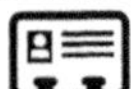

HQ:
Bethesda, MD 20892
http://www.nih.gov

HHS 93.853 EXTRAMURAL RESEARCH PROGRAMS IN THE NEUROSCIENCES & NEUROLOGICAL DISORDERS

Award: Project Grants

Purpose: To support extramural research funded by the National Institute of Neurological Disorders and Stroke (NINDS) including basic research that explores the fundamental structure and function of the brain and the nervous system; research to understand the causes and origins of pathological conditions of the nervous system with the goal of preventing these disorders.

Applicant Eligibility: Research Grants: Any public, private, nonprofit, or for-profit institution is eligible to apply. For-profit institutions are not eligible for Institutional National Research Service Awards but are eligible for Individual NRSAs.

Beneficiary Eligibility: Health professionals, graduate students, health professional students, scientists, and researchers.

Award Range/Average: Research grants: $9,219 to $6,297,501; $401,755. National Research Service Awards: Institutional $46,245 to $470,547; $209,407. Individual: $5,467 to $66,354; $42,241. SBIR/STTR: Phase 1 not to exceed $150,000; Phase II not to exceed $1,000,000; however with appropriate justification, budget caps for Phase I and Phase II are $225,000 and $1,500,00 respectively

Funding: Project Grants (Contracts) FY 17 $77,040,446; FY 18 est $84,100,762; FY 19 est $83,259,754; FY 16 $80,749,958; - (Project Grants) FY 17 $1,287,637,739; FY 18 est $1,384,919,691; FY 19 est $1,268,462,215; FY 16 $1,216,538,446.

HQ: 6001 Executive Boulevard, Suite 3309
Rockville, MD 20892
Phone: 301-496-9248
Email: finkelsr@nih.gov
http://www.ninds.nih.gov

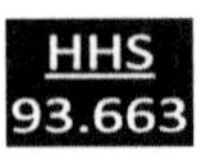

HHS 93.663 EXTRAMURAL RESEARCH RESTORATION PROGRAM: HURRICANES HARVEY, MARIA, AND IRMA – NON-CONSTRUCTION

Award: Project Grants

Purpose: The program will fund disaster response and recovery, and other expenses directly related to Hurricane Harvey, Hurricane Irma, or Hurricane Maria, which are in the FEMA-declared major disaster states, relevant to supporting the recovery of losses at non-Federal biomedical or behavioral research facilities.

Applicant Eligibility: Applicants will be required to attest (at time of application) that funds requested will not be used for costs that are reimbursed by the Federal Emergency Management Agency, under a contract for insurance, or by self-insurance. Terms and Conditions of the award will stipulate that the grantee must reimburse HHS for any costs that are subsequently covered by the Federal Emergency Management Agency, under a contract for insurance, or by self-insurance.

Beneficiary Eligibility: Same as Applicant Eligibility.

Award Range/Average: N/A

Funding: (Project Grants) FY 18 est $25,000,000; FY 19 est $0; FY 17 N/A.

HQ:
Bethesda, MD 20892

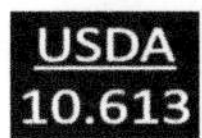

FACULTY EXCHANGE PROGRAM
"Faculty Exchange Program"

Award: Project Grants; Direct Payments for Specified Use

Purpose: The Faculty Exchange Program promotes agricultural education and research in developing countries by providing training programs.

Applicant Eligibility: The Faculty Exchange Program solicits proposals from public universities and state cooperative institutions in the United States.

Beneficiary Eligibility: Technical assistance and training provided through these agreements benefit foreign universities and related agricultural institutions in their countries.

Award Range/Average: Approximately $30000 - $45000 per participant.

Funding: (Direct Payments for Specified Use) FY 17 $714,881; FY 18 est $915,000; FY 19 est $600,000; FY 16 $714,881.

HQ: 1400 Independence Avenue SW #3226, P.O. Box 1030
Washington, DC 20250
Phone: 202-690-1940
Email: tim.sheehan@fas.usda.gov
http://www.fas.usda.gov/programs/faculty-exchange-program

FAIR HOUSING ASSISTANCE PROGRAM STATE & LOCAL
"FHAP"

Award: Project Grants

Purpose: To assist State and local fair housing enforcement agencies for complaint processing, training, technical assistance, education and outreach, data and information systems, and other activities.

Applicant Eligibility: Eligible applicants include State and local government fair housing enforcement agencies administering fair housing laws that have been certified by HUD as providing substantially equivalent rights and remedies as those provided by the Fair Housing Act and which have executed formal written Agreements with HUD to process housing discrimination complaints. In determining eligibility, HUD may also take into consideration whether a jurisdiction is already served by a FHAP agency.

Beneficiary Eligibility: Any person or group of persons aggrieved by a discriminatory housing practice because of race, color, religion, sex, disability, familial status or national origin.

Award Range/Average: Funding is provided for capacity building, complaint processing, training, and administrative costs. Funding may also be available for partnership efforts and special enforcement efforts.

Funding: (Formula Grants) FY 18 est $24,300,000; FY 16 $19,735,652; FY 17 est $24,300,000.

HQ: 451 7th Street SW
Washington, DC 20410
Phone: 202-402-2126
Email: joseph.a.pelletier@hud.gov
http://www.hud.gov/offices/fheo/partners/fhap/index.cfm

FAIR HOUSING INITIATIVES PROGRAM "FHIP"

Award: Cooperative Agreements

Purpose: To educate the public about fair housing rights under the Fair Housing Act; 42 U.S.C. 3601-3619 or State or local laws.

Applicant Eligibility: State and local government agencies, public or private nonprofit organizations or institutions- and other public or private entities that are formulating or carrying out programs to prevent or eliminate discriminatory housing practices. Applicants for funding of testing activities must have at least one year of experience in complaint intake, complaint investigation, testing for fair housing violations, and enforcement of meritorious claims.

Beneficiary Eligibility: Individual/Family, Minority group, Specialized group.

Award Range/Average: $125,000- $1,000,000

Funding: (Project Grants) FY 17 $16,013,813; FY 18 est $62,480,816; FY 19 est $35,300,000; FY 16 $38,300,000.

HQ: 451 7th Street SW, Room 5222
Washington, DC 20410
Phone: 202-402-7054
Email: paula.stone@hud.gov
http://www.hud.gov/offices/fheo/partners/fhip/fhip.cfm

FAIR HOUSING ORGANIZATION INITIATIVES "FHIP FHOI"

Award: Project Grants

Purpose: To develop, implement, carry out, or coordinate programs and/or activities that provide enforcement of fair housing rights under the Fair Housing Act; (42 U.S.C. 3601-3619) or State or local laws that provide substantially equivalent rights and remedies for alleged discriminatory housing practices.

Applicant Eligibility: Qualified Fair Housing Enforcement Organizations or Fair Housing Enforcement Organizations and nonprofit groups organizing to build their capacity to provide fair housing enforcement.

Beneficiary Eligibility: Any person or group of persons aggrieved by discriminatory housing practices because of race, color, religion, sex disability familial status or national origin. Also, any person or group of persons, including landlords or real estate agents, to prevent discriminatory housing practices because of race, color, religion, sex, disability, familial status or national origin.

Award Range/Average: $125,000- $1,000,000

Funding: (Project Grants) FY 17 $900,000; FY 18 est $500,000; FY 19 est $500,000; FY 16 $900,000.

HQ: 451 7th Street SW, Room 5222
Washington, DC 20410
Phone: 202-402-7054
Email: paula.stone@hud.gov
http://www.hud.gov/office/fheo/partners.fhip/fhip.cfm

FAMILY & COMMUNITY VIOLENCE PREVENTION PROGRAM

Award: Cooperative Agreements

Purpose: Provides support interventions to employ violence prevention and crime reduction models and a public health approach to provide critical life skills development, academic skills, career advisement, and mentoring.

Applicant Eligibility: State and local governments or their Bona Fide Agents (this includes the District of Columbia, the Commonwealth of Puerto Rico, the Virgin Islands, the Commonwealth of the Northern Mariana Islands, American Samoa, Guam, the Federated States of Micronesia, the Republic of the Marshall Islands, and the Republic of Palau), Nonprofit with 501(c)(3) IRS status (other than institution of higher education), Nonprofit without 501(c)(3) IRS status (other than institution of higher education), For-profit organizations (other than small business); for profit organizations must agree to forgo any profit or management fee, Small, minority, and women-owned business, Universities, Colleges, Research institutions, Hospitals, Community-based organizations, Faith-based organizations, Federally recognized or state-recognized American Indian/Alaska Native Tribal governments, American Indian/Alaska Native tribally designated organizations, Alaska Native health organizations, Urban Indian health organizations, Tribal epidemiology centers, Political subdivisions of states (in consultation with states)

Beneficiary Eligibility: Target populations: Alaskan Natives; American Indians; Asians; Blacks/African Americans; Hispanics/Latinos; Native Hawaiians and other Pacific Islanders; or subgroups of these populations; economically or environmentally disadvantaged populations; limited English populations. However, services may not be denied to otherwise eligible individuals based on race or ethnicity.

Award Range/Average: FY2019 Proposed Awards range from $370,000 to $425,000

Funding: (Cooperative Agreements) FY 16 $4,746,036; FY 17 est $4,103,509; FY 18 est $4,103,509.

HQ: 1101 Wootton Parkway Tower Building, Suite 550
Rockville, MD 20852
Phone: 240-453-8822
Email: eric.west@hhs.gov
http://www.minorityhealth.hhs.gov

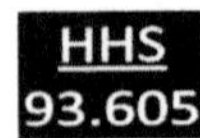

FAMILY CONNECTION GRANTS

Award: Project Grants

Purpose: Provides matching grants to state, local or tribal child welfare agencies, institutions of higher education, and private nonprofit organizations that have experience in working with foster children or children in kinship care arrangements for the purpose of helping children who are in, or at risk of entering, foster care to reconnect with family members.

Applicant Eligibility: State, local or tribal child welfare agencies, institutions of higher education, and private nonprofit organizations that have experience in working with foster children or children in kinship care arrangements.

Beneficiary Eligibility: Public or private nonprofit agencies or organizations or tribal child welfare agencies, or institutions of higher education working with foster children, children in kinship care arrangements or children at risk of entering foster care, that help the children reconnect with family members.

Award Range/Average: $446,667 to $608,329 with an average of $525,028.

Funding: Project Grants (Discretionary) FY 17 $1,575,084; FY 18 est $476,858; FY 19 est $1,800,000; FY 16 $2,751,449; - Program authorization expired in FY 2014 but grants continue to be funded from previous years' appropriation.

HQ: 330 C Street SW, Room 3504
Washington, DC 20201
Phone: 202-205-8172
Email: jan.shafer@acf.hhs.gov
http://www.acf.hhs.gov/programs/cb

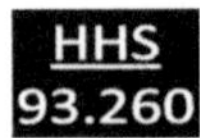

FAMILY PLANNING PERSONNEL TRAINING
"Family Planning Training"

Award: Project Grants

Purpose: Provides job specific training for personnel to improve the delivery of family planning services.

Applicant Eligibility: Any public entity (including city, county, local, regional, or State government) or nonprofit private entity located in a State (including the District of Columbia, Puerto Rico, the Commonwealth of the Northern Mariana Islands, Guam, American Samoa, the Virgin Islands, the Federated States of Micronesia, the Republic of the Marshall Islands and the Republic of Palau) is eligible to apply for a grant under this program. Faith based organizations are eligible to apply.

Beneficiary Eligibility: Personnel delivering family planning services in Title X projects.

Award Range/Average: FY 17 $800,000- $4,000,000 FY 18 $895,000- $3,500,000 FY 19 $900,000- $4,000,000

Funding: (Project Grants) FY 17 $4,800,000; FY 18 N/A FY 19 FY 16 $4,750,000; - (Project Grants) FY 17 $5,882,950; FY 18 est $4,392,000; FY 19 N/A - Past Fiscal Year (2017) 2 awards, totaling $4,800,000 Current Fiscal Year (2018) 2 awards, totaling $4,395,000

HQ: Office of Grants Management 1101 Wootton Parkway Tower Building, Suite 550
Rockville, MD 20852
Phone: 240-453-8822

Email: eric.west@hhs.gov
http://www.hhs.gov/opa

FAMILY PLANNING SERVICE DELIVERY IMPROVEMENT RESEARCH GRANTS
"Family Planning Service Delivery Improvement"

Award: Project Grants

Purpose: The grants help develop research studies of projects under family planning service delivery improvement that falls under Title X of Section 1001 of the Public Health Service Act.

Applicant Eligibility: Any public entity (city, county, local, regional, or State government) or private nonprofit entity located in a State (including the District of Columbia, Puerto Rico, the Commonwealth of the Northern Marianas Islands, Guam, American Samoa, the Virgin Islands, the Federated States of Micronesia, the Republic of Marshall Islands and the Republic of Palau) is eligible to apply for a grant under this program. Faith based organizations are eligible to apply.

Beneficiary Eligibility: All levels of government and nonprofit entities responsible for the efficient and effective delivery of family planning services; providers and recipients of family planning services; and the general public.

Award Range/Average: FY 19 $250,000 - $750,000

Funding: (Project Grants) FY 18 N/A FY 16 $1,461,000; FY 17 est $1,300,000.

HQ: 1101 Wootton Parkway Tower Building, Suite 550
Rockville, MD 20852
Phone: 240-453-8822
Email: eric.west@hhs.gov
http://www.hhs.gov/opa

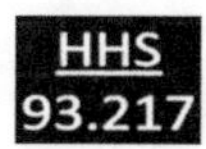

FAMILY PLANNING SERVICES
"Family Planning Services"

Award: Project Grants

Purpose: To establish and operate voluntary family planning services projects, which shall provide family planning services to all persons desiring such services, with priority for services to persons from low-income families.

Applicant Eligibility: Any public (including city, county, local, regional, or State government) entity or nonprofit private entity located in a State (including the District of Columbia, Puerto Rico, Guam, the Commonwealth of the Northern Mariana Islands, American Samoa, the Virgin Islands, the Federated States of Micronesia, the Republic of Marshall Islands and the Republic of Palau) is eligible to apply for a grant. Faith based organizations are eligible to apply.

Beneficiary Eligibility: Persons who desire family planning services and who would not otherwise have access to them. Priority to be given to persons from low-income families.

Award Range/Average: $150,000- $20,000,000

Funding: (Project Grants) FY 17 $255,627,000; FY 18 est $257,002,000; FY 19 N/A FY 16 $254,667,500.

HQ: 1101 Wootton Parkway Tower Building, Suite 550
Rockville, MD 20852

Phone: 240-453-8822
Email: eric.west@hhs.gov
http://www.hhs.gov/opa

FAMILY SELF-SUFFICIENCY PROGRAM "FSS"

Award: Project Grants

Purpose: To promote the development of local strategies to enable participating families to increase earned income and financial literacy, reduce or eliminate the need for welfare assistance, and make progress toward economic independence and self-sufficiency.

Applicant Eligibility: Eligible applicants are public housing agencies (PHAs) and tribes/Tribally Designated Housing Entities (TDHEs).

Beneficiary Eligibility: Individuals and families who are participants in the Housing Choice Voucher program or Public Housing program are eligible to receive benefits from the FSS program.

Award Range/Average: $13,000 - $1,300,000; Average $40,000- $69,000

Funding: (Project Grants) FY 17 $149,921,000; FY 18 est $75,000,000; FY 19 est $75,000,000; FY 16 $149,921,000.

HQ: 451 7th Street SW
Washington, DC 20410
Phone: 202-402-2341
Email: anice.s.chenault@hud.gov
http://portal.hud.gov/hudportal/hud?src=/program_offices/public_indian_housing/programs/hcv/fss

FAMILY SMOKING PREVENTION & TOBACCO CONTROL ACT REGULATORY RESEARCH "NIH-FDA Tobacco Control Regulatory Research"

Award: Cooperative Agreements; Project Grants; Training

Purpose: To provide the authority to regulate tobacco product manufacturing, distribution and marketing.

Applicant Eligibility: Applicants should review the eligibility information in the individual funding opportunity announcements issued under this CFDA.

Beneficiary Eligibility: This Tobacco Control Regulatory Research Program will support research aimed at providing guidance and evidence to develop regulation for tobacco product manufacturing, distribution and marketing. The general public will ultimately benefit.

Award Range/Average: No Data Available.

Funding: (Project Grants) FY 17 $89,111,387; FY 18 est $83,249,000; FY 19 est $73,894,000; FY 16 $95,272,556; - Funds provided by the FDA CTP through an IDDA to NIH for the support of Family Smoking Prevention and Tobacco Control Act.

HQ: 6100 Executive Boulevard Room 3B01, P.O. Box 7530
Bethesda, MD 20892-7530
Phone: 301-451-8681

http://prevention.nih.gov/tobacco-regulatory-science-program

FAMILY SUPPORT PAYMENTS TO STATES ASSISTANCE PAYMENTS
"Adult Programs in the Territories"

Award: Formula Grants

Purpose: Provides aid to the aged, blind, and the permanently and totally disabled in Guam, Puerto Rico, and the Virgin Islands.

Applicant Eligibility: Agencies must operate under Department of Health and Human Services (HHS) approved plans and agreements, which must comply with all Federal statutory and regulatory requirements governing these programs.

Beneficiary Eligibility: The beneficiary must be needy.

Award Range/Average: This funding range is $716,830 to $31,046,869 with an average of $10,998,552.

Funding: (Formula Grants) FY 17 $32,995,657; FY 18 est $33,000,000; FY 19 est $33,000,000; FY 16 $32,969,628.

HQ: Office of Family Assistance Department of Health and Human Services 330 C Street SW
Washington, DC 20201
Phone: 202-401-4731
Email: susan.golonka@acf.hhs.gov
http://www.acf.hhs.gov/programs/ofa

FAMILY TO FAMILY HEALTH INFORMATION CENTERS
"F2F HICs"

Award: Project Grants

Purpose: To develop and support Family to Family Health Information Centers.

Applicant Eligibility: Eligible applicants include public and private entities, including an Indian tribe or tribal organization (as those terms are defined at 25 U.S.C. 450b), faith-based organizations, and community-based organizations.

Beneficiary Eligibility: Projects will benefit (1) public or private agencies, organizations and institutions engaged in activities for CYSHCN; (2) family members and children who receive services through the program; and (3) professionals and trainees who provide services to CYSHCN.

Award Range/Average: Awards range from roughly $35,864 to $96, 750.

Funding: (Project Grants) FY 17 $4,482,153; FY 18 est $5,708,250; FY 19 est $5,708,250; FY 16 $4,769,968.

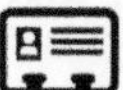

HQ: Maternal and Child Health Bureau US Department of Health and Human Services, Room 18W09-A 5600 Fishers Lane
Rockville, MD 20857
Phone: 301-443-7220
Email: tzerislassie@hrsa.gov
http://www.mchb.hrsa.gov

FAMILY UNIFICATION PROGRAM (FUP)

Award: Direct Payments for Specified Use

Purpose: To aid families without adequate housing and youths ages 18-21 years old who left foster care at age 16 or older and lack adequate housing.

Applicant Eligibility: Applicants are limited to public housing agencies. A public housing agency (PHA) is defined as any State, county, municipality or other governmental entity or public body (or agency or instrumentality thereof) which is authorized to engage in or assist in the development or operation of housing for very low income families; and, a consortium of PHAs; any other nonprofit entity that was administering a Section 8 tenant-based program on October 21, 1998; or, for an area outside the jurisdiction of a PHA administering a voucher program, a private nonprofit entity or a governmental entity or public body that would otherwise lack jurisdiction to administer the program in such area.

Beneficiary Eligibility: Families and youths that are income eligible under the HCV program regulations at 24 CFR 982.201 may receive a voucher awarded under the FUP.

Award Range/Average: Serving 39 PHA's

Funding: (Direct Payments for Specified Use) FY 17 $3,450,499,867; FY 18 est $10,000,000; FY 19 est $3,910,174,977.

HQ: 451 7th Street SW, Room 4210
Washington, DC 20410
Phone: 202-708-0477
Email: laure.rawson@hud.gov
http://www.hud.gov/program_offices/public_indian_housing

FAMILY VIOLENCE PREVENTION & SERVICES/ DISCRETIONARY

"Family Violence Prevention and Services Act Discretionary Grants"

Award: Cooperative Agreements

Purpose: Funds a wide range of discretionary activities for the purpose of providing resource information, training and technical assistance to improve the capacity of individuals, organizations, government entities, and communities to prevent family violence, domestic violence, and dating violence and to provide effective intervention services.

Applicant Eligibility: Depending on the purpose of the project and the statutory requirements, an applicant may be a nonprofit private organization, tribal organization, federally-recognized Indian tribe, Native Hawaiian organization, local public agency, institution of higher education, private organization, Alaska Native Village, or nonprofit Alaska Native Regional Corporation.

Beneficiary Eligibility: These discretionary grants and contracts will benefit victims of family violence, domestic violence, dating violence, and their dependents, families, other interested persons, the general public, and communities and government entities.

Award Range/Average: FY 2016 National Hotline: $8,250,000 Discretionary National Resource Centers and Training and Technical Assistance Centers: $450,000 - $1,400,000 Discretionary Service and Demonstration Grants: $133,333 - $133,334 Specialized Services for Abused Parents and Their Children:

$375,000 FY 2017 National Hotline: $8,223,479 Discretionary National Resource Centers and Training and Technical Assistance Centers: $450,000 - $1,400,000 Specialized Services for Abused Parents and Their Children: $385,785 - $385,786

Funding: Cooperative Agreements (Discretionary Grants) FY 17 $8,223,479; FY 18 est $9,250,000; FY 19 est $9,250,000. Cooperative Agreements (Discretionary Grants) FY 17 $11,865,000; FY 18 est $11,860,000; FY 19 est $11,860,000. Cooperative Agreements (Discretionary Grants) FY 17 $4,629,426; FY 18 est $5,750,000; FY 19 est $5,750,000.

HQ: 330 C Street SW, Suite 3622C
Washington, DC 20024
Phone: 202-690-6898
Email: kenya.fairley@acf.hhs.gov
http://www.acf.hhs.gov/programs/fysb/programs/family-violence-prevention-services

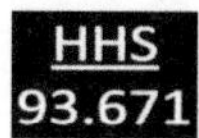

HHS 93.671 FAMILY VIOLENCE PREVENTION & SERVICES/DOMESTIC VIOLENCE SHELTER & SUPPORTIVE SERVICES "Formula Grants for States and Native American Tribes (including Alaska Native Villages) and Tribal Organizations"

Award: Formula Grants

Purpose: Assists States and Native American Tribes and Tribal Organizations in efforts to increase public awareness about, and primary and secondary prevention of family violence, domestic violence, and dating violence; and assist States and Tribes in efforts to provide immediate shelter and supportive services for victims of family violence, domestic violence, or dating violence, and their dependents.

Applicant Eligibility: Eligible applicants for the State Grants are the 50 States, the District of Columbia, the Commonwealth of Puerto Rico, and the U.S. territories of Guam, American Samoa, the United States Virgin Islands, and the Commonwealth of the Northern Mariana Islands. Eligible applicants for the Tribal Grants are the federally recognized Indian Tribes (including Alaska Native Villages), or a tribal organization or nonprofit private organization authorized by an Indian Tribe.

Beneficiary Eligibility: This program will benefit victims of family violence, domestic violence, and dating violence, and their dependents.

Award Range/Average: FY 2017 States: $727,674 - $8,999,499 Territories: $127,215 Indian Tribes: $17,600 - $1,590,000

Funding: (Formula Grants) FY 17 $101,771,794; FY 18 est $104,125,000; FY 19 est $104,125,000; (Formula Grants) FY 17 $14,538,828; FY 18 est $19,875,000; FY 19 est $19,875,000.

HQ: 330 C Street SW, Suite 3620C
Washington, DC 20201
Phone: 202-205-7746
Email: rebecca.odor@acf.hhs.gov
http://www.acf.hhs.gov/programs/fysb/programs/family-violence-prevention-services

FAMILY VIOLENCE PREVENTION & SERVICES/STATE DOMESTIC VIOLENCE COALITIONS
"Family Violence Prevention and Services Act Grants to State Domestic Violence Coalitions"

Award: Formula Grants

Purpose: Provides funding for State Domestic Violence Coalitions to confirm the federal commitment to reducing domestic violence.

Applicant Eligibility: To be eligible for a grant under Section 10411, an entity shall be a statewide nongovernmental nonprofit private domestic violence organization that has a membership that includes a majority of the primary-purpose domestic violence service providers in the State; has board membership that is representative of primary-purpose domestic violence service providers, and which may include representatives of the communities in which the services are being provided in the State; has as its purpose to provide education, support, and technical assistance to such service providers to enable the providers to establish and maintain shelter and supportive services for victims of domestic violence and their dependents; and serves as an information clearinghouse, primary point of contact, and resource center on domestic violence for the State and supports the development of policies, protocols, and procedures to enhance domestic violence intervention and prevention in the State.

Beneficiary Eligibility: This program will benefit youth and adult victims of family violence, domestic violence, dating violence, their children and other dependents, their families, other persons affected by such violence including friends, relatives, and the general public. The program will also benefit communities, including the State and business and nonprofit sectors.

Award Range/Average: The estimated award amount is $265,625.

Funding: FY 17 $0; FY 18 est $14,875,000; FY 19 est $14,875,000; FY 16 $14,500,000.

HQ: 330 C Street SW, Suite 3620C
Washington, DC 20201
Phone: 202-205-7746
Email: rebecca.odor@acf.hhs.gov
http://www.acf.hhs.gov/programs/fysb/programs/family-violence-prevention-services

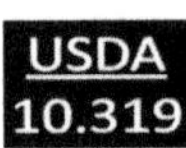

FARM BUSINESS MANAGEMENT & BENCHMARKING COMPETITIVE GRANTS PROGRAM
"FBMB"

Award: Project Grants

Purpose: To initiate a research program and compensate for improving farm management and farm financial management.

Applicant Eligibility: Applications may be submitted by qualified public and private entities. Pursuant to 7 U.S.C.

Beneficiary Eligibility: Same as Applicant Eligibility.

Award Range/Average: If minimum or maximum amounts of funding per competitive and/or capacity project grant, or cooperative agreement are established, these amounts will be announced in the annual Competitive Request for Application (RFA).

Funding: Project Grants (Cooperative Agreements) FY 17 $1,346,556; FY 18 est $1,918,875; FY 19 est $0; FY 16 $1,349,565.

HQ: Institute of Youth Family and Community Division of Family and Consumer Sciences 1400 Independence Avenue SW, P.O. Box 2250

Washington, DC 20250-2250

Phone: 202-720-4795

Email: abalsano@nifa.usda.gov

http://nifa.usda.gov/funding-opportunity/farm-business-management-and-benchmarking-fbmb-competitive-grants-program

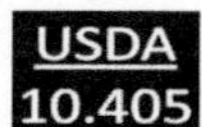

FARM LABOR HOUSING LOANS & GRANTS "Labor Housing"

Award: Project Grants; Guaranteed/Insured Loans

Purpose: To provide low-rent housing facilities and essential requirements for farm laborers.

Applicant Eligibility: Loans are available to farmers, family farm partnership, family farm corporations, or an association of farmers. Loans and grants are available to States, Puerto Rico, the U.S. Virgin Islands, political subdivisions of States, broad-based public or private nonprofit organizations, federally recognized Indian Tribes and non- profit corporations of farm workers.

Beneficiary Eligibility: A domestic farm laborer is any person who receives a substantial portion of his/her income as a laborer on a farm in the United States and is either (1) a citizen of the United States, or (2) has been legally admitted for permanent residency.

Award Range/Average: No Data Available.

Funding: (Direct Loans) FY 17 $34,900,000; FY 18 est $8,000,000; FY 19 est $8,000,000; FY 16 $27,000,000.

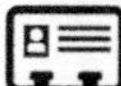

HQ: 1400 Independence Avenue SW

Washington, DC 20250

Phone: 202-720-1604

Email: cb.alonso@wdc.usda.gov

http://www.rd.usda.gov/programs-services/farm-labor-housing-direct-loans-grants

FEDERAL & STATE TECHNOLOGY PARTNERSHIP PROGRAM "Federal and State Technology (FAST) Partnership Program"

Award: Cooperative Agreements

Purpose: To strengthen the technological competitiveness of small business concerns in the U.S.

Applicant Eligibility: N/A

Beneficiary Eligibility: N/A

Award Range/Average: No more than 20 awards.

Funding: FY 17 $3,000,000; FY 18 est $3,000,000; FY 19 est $0; FY 16 $2,936,000.

HQ: 409 3rd Street SW, 6th Floor

Washington, DC 20416

Phone: 202-710-5163
Email: brittany.sickler@sba.gov
http://www.sbir.gov

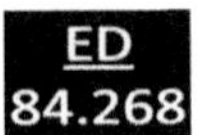

ED 84.268 FEDERAL DIRECT STUDENT LOANS

Award: Direct Loans

Purpose: To provide loan support directly from the Federal government to vocational, undergraduate, and graduate postsecondary school students and their parents.

Applicant Eligibility: The applicant must be a U.S. citizen, national, or person in the United States for other than a temporary purpose. A student borrower must be enrolled or accepted for enrollment in a degree or certificate program on at least a half-time basis as an undergraduate, graduate, or professional student at a participating postsecondary institution.

Beneficiary Eligibility: Vocational, undergraduate, and graduate postsecondary school students and their parents.

Award Range/Average: N/A

Funding: (Direct Loans) FY 17 $93,812,654,000; FY 18 est $96,674,634,000; FY 19 est $99,013,780,000; FY 16 $95,462,059,000; (Direct Loans) FY 17 $48,762,128,000; FY 18 est $50,295,066,000; FY 19 est $51,848,235,000; FY 16 $45,633,297,000.

HQ: Federal Student Aid Information Center Department of Education, P.O. Box 84
Washington, DC 20044-0084
Phone: 800-433-3243
http://studentaid.ed.gov/sa/types/loans

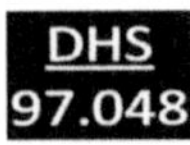

DHS 97.048 FEDERAL DISASTER ASSISTANCE TO INDIVIDUALS & HOUSEHOLDS IN PRESIDENTIAL DECLARED DISASTER AREAS "IHP"

Award: Project Grants; Direct Payments for Specified Use

Purpose: The program primarily focuses on the financial assistance for housing construction or renovation for people whose shelters are affected due to natural disasters or terrorist acts.

Applicant Eligibility: Individuals and households, in areas declared an emergency or major disaster by the President, who have necessary expenses and serious needs they are unable to meet through insurance or other means, are eligible to apply for this program. All needs must be caused by the disaster.

Beneficiary Eligibility: Individual/Family; Homeowner (located within an area which has been designated as a disaster area by Presidential declaration).

Award Range/Average: FY 18: Range- $50 - $34,000; Average- $8,905.16

Funding: (Project Grants) FY 17 $1,537,114,703,522; FY 18 est $2,648,834,819; FY 19 est $0; FY 16 $1,048,419,969.

HQ: Department of Homeland Security 500 C Street SW, 6th Floor
Washington, DC 20472-3100
Phone: 202-212-1000
http://www.fema.gov/individual-disaster-assistance

FEDERAL OIL & GAS ROYALTY MANAGEMENT STATE & TRIBAL COORDINATION "FOGRMA"

Award: Project Grants

Purpose: To assure that all oil, gas, and solid minerals originated on the public lands and on the Outer Continental Shelf are properly accounted for under the direction of the Secretary of the Interior, and for other purposes.

Applicant Eligibility: State and Tribal Governments as specified in Title II of the Federal Oil and Gas Royalty Management Act of 1982, as amended.

Beneficiary Eligibility: States and Federally recognized Tribal Governments that receive funds collected as a result of the compliance activities on Federal and Indian mineral leases.

Award Range/Average: Awards range from $230,000 to $3.0 million. Average is $892,000.

Funding: (Project Grants) FY 19 est $13,548,000; FY 17 $13,548,000; FY 18 est $13,548,000.

HQ: Office of Natural Resources Revenue
Washington, DC 20240
Phone: 202-513-0600
http://www.onrr.gov

FEDERAL PELL GRANT PROGRAM

Award: Direct Payments for Specified Use

Purpose: To demonstrate financial need for undergraduate postsecondary students with grant assistance to help meet educational expenses.

Applicant Eligibility: Undergraduate students and students pursuing a teaching certificate enrolled as regular students in an eligible program at an eligible institution of higher education and making satisfactory academic progress. The applicants must be U.S. citizens or eligible noncitizens and have a high school diploma (or its equivalent); or, for students enrolled prior to July 1, 2012, a demonstrated ability to benefit from the program offered; or, have successfully completed six credits.

Beneficiary Eligibility: Same as Applicant Eligibility.

Award Range/Average: $609- $6,095; the average grant is $4,115.

Funding: (Direct Payments for Specified Use) FY 17 $29,031,160,000; FY 18 est $30,617,995,000; FY 19 est $31,059,260,000; FY 16 $26,861,935,000.

HQ: Federal Student Aid Information Center Department of Education, P.O. Box 84
Washington, DC 20044-0084
Phone: 800-433-3243
http://studentaid.ed.gov/sa/types/grants-scholarships/pell

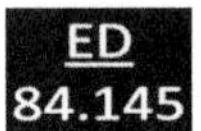

FEDERAL REAL PROPERTY ASSISTANCE PROGRAM

Award: Sale, Exchange, or Donation of Property and Goods

Purpose: To convey surplus Federal Real Property for educational purposes at fair market value.

Applicant Eligibility: Those groups, organizations, entities, or institutions providing educational programs including: States; their political subdivisions and instrumentalities; and tax supported organizations or private nonprofit institutions held exempt from taxation under Section 501(C)(3) of the Internal Revenue Code of 1954 may apply.

Beneficiary Eligibility: Program participants receiving educational opportunities will benefit.

Award Range/Average: N/A

Funding: N/A

HQ: Office of the Administrator for Management Services Department of Education 400 Maryland Avenue SW

Washington, DC 20202

Phone: 202-260-4558

http://www.frpa@ed.gov

FEDERAL SUPPLEMENTAL EDUCATIONAL OPPORTUNITY GRANTS "FSEOG"

Award: Direct Payments for Specified Use

Purpose: To provide need-based grant aid to eligible undergraduate postsecondary students to meet their educational expenses.

Applicant Eligibility: Higher education institutions (public, private nonprofit, postsecondary vocational, and proprietary) meeting eligibility requirements may apply.

Beneficiary Eligibility: Undergraduate students enrolled or accepted for enrollment as regular students; are maintaining satisfactory academic progress in accordance with the standards and practices of the institution, have financial need, do not owe a refund on a Title IV grant, are not in default on a Title IV loan, file a statement of educational purpose, file a statement of registration compliance (Selective Service) and meet citizen/resident requirements may benefit.

Award Range/Average: The average award is estimated to be $649.

Funding: (Direct Payments for Specified Use) FY 17 $992,875,000; FY 18 est $1,137,609,000; FY 19 est $1,137,609,000; FY 16 $992,875,000.

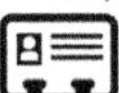

HQ: Federal Student Aid Information Center Department of Education, P.O. Box 84

Washington, DC 20044-0084

Phone: 800-433-3243

http://studentaid.ed.gov/sa/types/grants-scholarships/fseog

FEDERAL SURPLUS PROPERTY TRANSFER PROGRAM

Award: Sale, Exchange, or Donation of Property and Goods

Purpose: To facilitate the possible no cost conveyance, by the Federal Government, to State and local governments, of surplus real and related personal property for correctional facility use, under programs or projects for the care or rehabilitation of criminal offenders, and for law enforcement purposes.

Applicant Eligibility: Eligible applicants include states, or political subdivisions or instrumentalities of states, proposing to use the subject property for law enforcement purposes or correctional facility purposes. The 50 States, the District of Columbia, the Commonwealth of Puerto Rico, Guam, American Samoa, the Virgin Islands, the Federated States of Micronesia, the Marshall Islands, Palau, and the Northern Mariana Islands.

Beneficiary Eligibility: State, local and territorial governments, that are engaged in activities to control or reduce crime and juvenile delinquency or the enforcement of criminal law including investigative activities as well as training or for the care or rehabilitation of criminal offenders.

Award Range/Average: N/A

Funding: (Sale, Exchange, or Donation of Property and Goods) Through the Federal Surplus Property Public Benefit Conveyance Program (Program), surplus federal land and buildings are conveyed to public entities at no cost.

HQ: US Department of Justice Bureau of Justice Assistance 810 7th Street NW
Washington, DC 20351
Phone: 202-616-6500
Email: laura.mizhir@usdoj.gov
http://www.bja.gov/programdetails.aspx?program_id=61

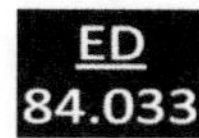

FEDERAL WORK-STUDY PROGRAM

Award: Direct Payments for Specified Use

Purpose: To provide part-time employment for the eligible postsecondary students to meet educational expenses and to encourage students for participating in community service activities.

Applicant Eligibility: Higher education institutions (public, private nonprofit, postsecondary vocational, and proprietary) meeting eligibility requirements may apply.

Beneficiary Eligibility: Undergraduate, graduate, or professional students enrolled or accepted for enrollment as regular students; are maintaining satisfactory academic progress in accordance with the standards and practices of the institution; have financial need; do not owe a refund on a Title IV grant; are not in default on a Title IV loan; file a statement of educational purpose; file a statement of registration compliance (Selective Service); and meet citizen/resident requirements may benefit.

Award Range/Average: The average award is at $1,726.

Funding: (Direct Payments for Specified Use) FY 17 $1,096,080,000; FY 18 est $1,251,425,000; FY 19 est $1,251,425,000; FY 16 $1,096,080,000.

HQ: Department of Education, P.O. Box 84
Washington, DC 20044-0084
Phone: 800-433-3243
http://studentaid.ed.gov/sa/types/work-study

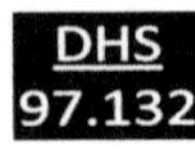

FINANCIAL ASSISTANCE FOR COUNTERING VIOLENT EXTREMISM "CVE"

Award: Project Grants

Purpose: Offers community-based support to curb extremism recruitment and radicalization to violence.

Applicant Eligibility: Please refer to program guidance.

Beneficiary Eligibility: The CVE Grant Program restricts Eligible Applicants to specific CVE focus areas. Applicants representing States, Local governments, Tribal government, and non-profit organizations are invited to apply for funding to implement the following program priorities: Developing resilience; Training and engagement with community members; Managing intervention activities; and Applicants representing non-profit organizations and institutions of higher education are invited to apply for funding to implement the following program priorities: Challenging the narrative; and Building capacity of community-level non-profit organizations active in CVE.

Award Range/Average: TBD

Funding: (Project Grants) FY 17 est $10,000,000; FY 18 est $0; FY 19 est $0; FY 16 est $10,000,000.

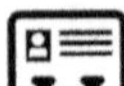

HQ: US Department of Homeland Security Office of Terrorism Prevention Partnerships880 Second Street SW
Washington, DC 20528
Phone: 202-786-0816
http://www.fema.gov

FIRE MANAGEMENT ASSISTANCE GRANT "FMAG"

Award: Project Grants; Provision of Specialized Services

Purpose: Grants from this process are provided to the local and State governments for the management and control of any fire in a public place. The grant money is also used for other purposes such as fire suppression services and for getting emergency protective measure equipment and supplies.

Applicant Eligibility: State governments and Indian tribal governments are eligible for fire management assistance grants. The State or Indian tribal government may be the Recipient.

Beneficiary Eligibility: The State Government and/or Indian tribal government, acting as the Recipient is the government to which the grant is awarded and which is accountable for the use of the funds provided. Other State entities, Indian tribal governments and local governments are eligible to apply as subrecipients.

Award Range/Average: 17 year average is $68,522,000/year

Funding: (Project Grants) FY 17 $56; FY 18 est $240; FY 19 est $110; FY 16 $22,663,963.

HQ: Department of Homeland Security Public Assistance Division Control Desk, 6th Floor 500 C Street SW
Washington, DC 20523
Phone: 800-368-6498
http://www.fema.gov

FLOOD CONTROL ACT LANDS

Award: Direct Payments for Specified Use

Purpose: Shares 75 percent of mineral leasing revenue with the State, paid monthly and is subject to late disbursement interest.

Applicant Eligibility: Revenue from acquired Flood Control land leasing will trigger automatic payment distribution computed in accordance with the law.

Beneficiary Eligibility: ONRR distributes these funds to state governments for leased lands within a state, and the State governments has sole discretion in their use in accordance with the enabling legislation.

Award Range/Average: N/A

Funding: (Direct Payments with Unrestricted Use) FY 17 $12,512,000; FY 19 est $51,342,000; FY 18 est $47,625,000.

HQ: Office of Natural Resources Revenue 1849 C Street NW, P.O. Box 4211
Washington, DC 20240
Phone: 202-513-0600
http://www.onrr.gov

FLOOD INSURANCE

Award: Insurance

Purpose: Offers flood insurance coverage to property owners in low and high-risk flood zones to reduce federal disaster assistance and to promote smarter floodplain management practices.

Applicant Eligibility: Federal flood insurance can be made available in any community (a State or political subdivision thereof with authority to adopt and enforce floodplain management measures for the areas within its jurisdiction) that adopts and enforces floodplain management measures consistent with the National Flood Insurance Program regulations.

Beneficiary Eligibility: Residential and business property owners, renters and state owned property.

Award Range/Average: Claims paid: $1 to $1,900,000; $31,802.

Funding: FY 17 $17,705,769; FY 18 est $0; FY 19 est $0; FY 16 $117,363,039.

HQ: 400 C Street SW
Washington, DC 20024
Phone: 800-621-3363
Email: paul.huang@fema.dhs.gov
http://www.fema.gov/national-flood-insurance-program

FLOOD MITIGATION ASSISTANCE "FMA"

Award: Project Grants

Purpose: The program supports tribal and State governments to help reduce the loss of lives and destruction to property during natural hazards thereby reducing claims under the National Flood Insurance Program.

Applicant Eligibility: The 50 States, the District of Columbia, American Samoa, Guam, the U.S. Virgin Islands, Puerto Rico, the Northern Mariana Islands, and Federally - recognized Indian Tribal governments shall serve as the Applicant to FEMA for FMA assistance.

Beneficiary Eligibility: State agencies, Indian Tribal governments, and local governments and communities are eligible to apply as sub applicants for assistance under the FMA program. All interested sub applicants must apply to the Applicant.

Award Range/Average: N/A.

Funding: (Project Grants) FY 17 $191; FY 18 est $75,000,000; FY 19 est $75,000,000; FY 16 $137,809,485.

HQ: 400 C Street SW
Washington, DC 20472
Phone: 202-646-3458
Email: kayed.lakhia@fema.dhs.gov
http://www.fema.gov/flood/mitigation/assistance/grant/program

FOOD & AGRICULTURE SERVICE LEARNING PROGRAM "FASLP"

Award: Project Grants

Purpose: This program promotes education on food and nutrition in the premises of educational institutions and organizations. It introduces the efforts of the farm to school programs. It implements through the food authorities the school lunch program. It introduces nutrition education in elementary and secondary schools, and supports the efforts of national service.

Applicant Eligibility: The Secretary may make grants to carry out research, extension, and education under this subsection to- (A) State agricultural experiment stations; (B) colleges and universities; (C) university research foundations; (D) other research institutions and organizations; (E) Federal agencies; (F) national laboratories; (G) private organizations, foundations, or corporations; (H) individuals; or (I) any group consisting of 2 or more of the entities described in subparagraphs (A) through (H).

Beneficiary Eligibility: Same as Applicant Eligibility.

Award Range/Average: If minimum or maximum amounts of funding per competitive and/or capacity project grant, or cooperative agreement are established, these amounts will be announced in the annual Competitive Request for Application (RFA). The most current RFA is available via: https://nifa.usda.gov/funding-opportunity/food-and-agriculture-service-learning-program

Funding: Project Grants (Discretionary) FY 17 $0; FY 18 est $881,900; FY 19 est $0.

HQ: 1400 Independence Avenue SW, P.O. Box 2225
Washington, DC 20250-2225
Phone: 202-720-5004
Email: dnchester@nifa.usda.gov
http://nifa.usda.gov/funding-opportunity/food-and-agriculture-service-learning-program

USDA 10.518

FOOD ANIMAL RESIDUE AVOIDANCE DATABANK "FARAD"

Award: Project Grants

Purpose: The FARAD provides information for the veterinarians and livestock producers on food animal products that are contaminant with drugs and pesticides.

Applicant Eligibility: Title VI Section 604 of the Agricultural Research, Extension, and Education Reform Act of 1998 (7 U.S.C. 7642) states that -The Secretary of Agriculture shall continue operation of the Food Animal Residue Avoidance Database program (referred to in this section as the "FARAD program") through contracts, grants, or cooperative agreements with appropriate colleges or universities.

Beneficiary Eligibility: Same as Applicant Eligibility.

Award Range/Average: If minimum or maximum amounts of funding per competitive and/or capacity project grant, or cooperative agreement are established, these amounts will be announced in the annual Request for Application (RFA).

Funding: (Project Grants) FY 17 $0; FY 18 est $0; FY 19 est $1,242,000; FY 16 $0.

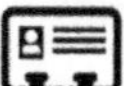

HQ: 1400 Independence Avenue SW, P.O. Box 2240
Washington, DC 20250-2220
Phone: 202-401-4892
Email: rsmith@nifa.usda.gov
http://nifa.usda.gov/food-animal-residue-avoidance-databank

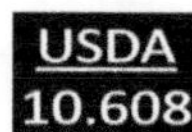

FOOD FOR EDUCATION "McGovern-Dole International Food for Education and Children Nutrition Program"

Award: Direct Payments for Specified Use; Sale, Exchange, or Donation of Property and Goods

Purpose: The purpose of the McGovern-Dole Program is to promote health and dietary practices. It also provides school meals and other essential assistance.

Applicant Eligibility: FAS will set forth specific eligibility information, including any factors or priorities that will affect the eligibility of an applicant or application for selection, in the full text of the applicable notice of funding opportunity posted on the U.S. Government web site for grant opportunities.

Beneficiary Eligibility: The McGovern-Dole Program focuses on developing countries in which the national government of the recipient country is fully committed to achieving the goals of the World Declaration on Education for All and is taking steps to improve the quality and availability of education.

Award Range/Average: FAS encourages proposals for 5-year implementation periods, which are expected to range from $20-35 million.

Funding: (Sale, Exchange, or Donation of Property and Goods) FY 19 N/A FY 18 est $193,000,000; FY 17 $193,000,000.

HQ: 1400 Independence Avenue SW, P.O. Box 1030
Washington, DC 20250
Phone: 202-720-4221
Email: ppded@fas.usda.gov
http://www.fas.usda.gov/programs/mcgovern-dole-food-education-program

USDA 10.606 FOOD FOR PROGRESS "FFPr"

Award: Direct Payments for Specified Use; Sale, Exchange, or Donation of Property and Goods

Purpose: The Food for Progress program compensates for the U.S. agricultural commodities and also funds for the proceeds of the monetization. It maximizes productivity and expands trade of agricultural products.

Applicant Eligibility: A private voluntary organization, a nonprofit agricultural organization or cooperative, a nongovernmental organization, or any other private entity is eligible to submit an application under this part to become a recipient under the Food for Progress Program. CCC will set forth specific eligibility information, including any factors or priorities that will affect the eligibility of an applicant or application for selection, in the full text of the applicable notice of funding opportunity posted on the U.S. Government web site for grant opportunities.

Beneficiary Eligibility: The Food for Progress programs focuses on developing countries and emerging democracies that are committed to introducing or expanding free enterprise in their agricultural economies.

Award Range/Average: 3-5-year implementation periods and awards ranging from $20-30 million.

Funding: (Sale, Exchange, or Donation of Property and Goods) FY 17 $141,247,000; FY 18 est $155,044,000; FY 19 est $155,000,000; FY 16 $161,362,494; - FY 19 is subject to continuation of program authority.

HQ: 1400 Independence Avenue SW, P.O. Box 1030
Washington, DC 20250
Phone: 202-720-4221
Email: ppded@fas.usda.gov
http://www.fas.usda.gov/programs/food-progress

USDA 10.331 FOOD INSECURITY NUTRITION INCENTIVE GRANTS PROGRAM "Food Insecurity Nutrition Incentive Program (FINI)"

Award: Project Grants

Purpose: The Food Insecurity Nutrition Incentive program compensates for low-income consumers and the supplemental nutrition assistance program support State agencies that serve in the rural areas.

Applicant Eligibility: Eligible entities include governmental agencies and nonprofit organizations.

Beneficiary Eligibility: Same as Applicant Eligibility.

Award Range/Average: If minimum or maximum amounts of funding per competitive and/or capacity project grant, or cooperative agreement are established, these amounts will be announced in the annual Competitive Request for Application (RFA).

Funding: (Project Grants) FY 17 $16,758,000; FY 18 est $21,015,000; FY 19 est $0; FY 16 $16,776,000.

HQ: 1400 Independence Avenue SW, P.O. Box 2255
Washington, DC 20024
Phone: 202-720-0740
Email: iwalls@nifa.usda.gov
http://nifa.usda.gov/program/food-insecurity-nutrition-incentive-fini-grant-program

FOREIGN MARKET DEVELOPMENT COOPERATOR PROGRAM "FMD"

Award: Direct Payments for Specified Use

Purpose: To maximize exporting markets for U.S. agricultural products to work closely with FAS and its overseas offices.

Applicant Eligibility: The Commodity Credit Corporation (CCC) enters into agreements with those nonprofit U.S. trade organizations that have the broadest possible producer representation of the commodity being promoted. To be approved, an applicant's proposal must indicate how it can effectively contribute to the creation, expansion, or maintenance of markets abroad.

Beneficiary Eligibility: Preference is given to nonprofit U.S. trade organizations which are nationwide in membership and scope.

Award Range/Average: $11,000 to $7,000,000; $1,243,000.

Funding: Formula Grants (Apportionments) FY 17 $35,000,000; FY 18 est $35,000,000; FY 19 est $35,000,000; FY 15 $32,016,000; FY 16 est $35,000,000.

HQ: 1400 Independence Avenue SW
Washington, DC 20250
Phone: 202-720-4327
Email: curt.alt@fas.usda.gov
http://www.fas.usda.gov/programs/foreign-market-development-program-fmd

FOREIGN PUBLIC HEALTH CONSTRUCTION

Award: Project Grants

Purpose: Authorizes the award of grants or cooperative agreements to public or nonprofit private institutions or agencies in foreign countries to acquire, lease, construct, alter, or renovate facilities in their country in furtherance of activities authorized under Public Health Service Act Section 307(a).

Applicant Eligibility: An eligible applicant must: (1) Be a public or nonprofit private institution or agency in a foreign country; and (2) Be located in the same foreign country as the Project. An eligible project must: (1) Be located in the same foreign country as the Recipient; (2) Be limited to approved Construction, Modernization, and Minor Alteration and Renovation activities; and (3) Result upon completion is a facility that is for use by recipient personnel only, and not for use by any U.S. Government personnel; and (4) Fulfill a purpose of Public Health Service Act Section 307(a).

Beneficiary Eligibility: Same as Applicant Eligibility.

Award Range/Average: New program with no awards to date.

Funding: (Cooperative Agreements) FY 17 $0; FY 18 N/A FY 19 est $0; FY 16 $0; - Potential funding considered for FY 18.

HQ: 1600 Clifton Road, P.O. Box E29
Atlanta, GA 30329
Phone: 404-639-4276
Email: ctg8@cdc.gov
http://www.cdc.gov

HHS 93.658 FOSTER CARE TITLE IV-E "Title IV-E Foster Care"

Award: Formula Grants; Project Grants

Purpose: The Title IV-E Foster Care program helps states, Indian tribes, tribal organizations and tribal consortia to provide safe and stable out-of-home care for children under the jurisdiction of the state or tribal child welfare agency until the children are returned home safely, placed with adoptive families, or placed in other planned arrangements for permanency.

Applicant Eligibility: Funds are available to states (including the District of Columbia, Puerto Rico, the U.S. Virgin Islands, Guam, and American Samoa) and to tribes with approved title IV-E plans.

Beneficiary Eligibility: Children meeting eligibility criteria for the former Aid to Families with Dependent Children program (except for up to a 12-month period for those children placed with a parent residing in a licensed residential family-based treatment facility for substance abuse treatment) whose removal and placement in foster care are in accordance with a voluntary placement agreement or judicial determinations to the effect that continuation in the home would be contrary to the child's welfare and that reasonable efforts were made to prevent the removal (or that such efforts were not necessary), and whose placement and care are the responsibility of the state or tribal agency administering the title IV-E program. See section 472 of the Social Security Act and the Code of Federal Regulations at 45 CFR Part 1356.

Award Range/Average: FY 2016 Formula Grants: $58,993 to $2,496,685 with an average of $77,434,135. FY 2016 Plan Development/Implementation Grants: $67,891 to $1,470,700 with an average of $487,676.

Funding: (Formula Grants) FY 17 $5,363,945,064; FY 18 est $5,502,000,181; FY 19 est $5,400,000,000; FY 16 $4,797,115,524; - Project Grants (Discretionary) FY 17 $2,424,630; FY 18 est $1,170,700; FY 19 est $1,700,000; FY 16 $2,438,381.

HQ: 330 C Street SW, Room 3512
Washington, DC 20201
Phone: 225-654-2527
Email: jennifer.butler-hembree@acf.hhs.gov
http://www.acf.hhs.gov/programs/cb

ED 84.116 FUND FOR THE IMPROVEMENT OF POSTSECONDARY EDUCATION "FIPSE"

Award: Project Grants

Purpose: To assist and support institutional reforms and innovative strategies designed to improve postsecondary instruction, quality, and to expand postsecondary opportunities.

Applicant Eligibility: Eligible applicants include institutions of higher education, other public and private non-profit institutions and agencies and combinations of these institutions and agencies.

Beneficiary Eligibility: Postsecondary educational institutions and their students will benefit.

Award Range/Average: In 2017, no funding was provided for this program.

Funding: (Project Grants) FY 17 $0; FY 18 est $6,000,000; FY 19 est $0.

HQ: 400 Maryland Avenue SW
Washington, DC 20202

Phone: 202-453-6150
Email: stacey.slijepcevic@ed.gov
http://www2.ed.gov/about/offices/list/ope/fipse/index.html

FUNDING IN SUPPORT OF THE PENNSYLVANIA RURAL HEALTH MODEL

Award: Cooperative Agreements

Purpose: The purpose of this funding opportunity for the Funding in Support of Pennsylvania's Rural Health Model cooperative agreement is to provide Pennsylvania with the start-up and initial implementation funding component of the Model to assist Pennsylvania in accomplishing the health outcomes, financial, and rural hospital scale targets required of Pennsylvania under the Model.

Applicant Eligibility: This single source funding opportunity provides Pennsylvania with the necessary start-up funding for the Model and is open to Pennsylvania's Department of Health and later the Rural Health Redesign Center. First, the Pennsylvania Department of Health is uniquely positioned as the initial applicant under this funding opportunity to meet the objectives of this funding opportunity based on its existing knowledge of the Model, its regulatory authority over healthcare in Pennsylvania, and its capacity to administer the Pennsylvania Rural Health Model including operationalizing the Rural Health Redesign Center, and its existing partnerships and collaborations with Pennsylvania providers.

Beneficiary Eligibility: CMS is committed to achieving better care for individuals, better health for populations, and reduced expenditures for Medicare, Medicaid, and CHIP. Through the Innovation Center, CMS strives towards these goals by testing innovative payment and service delivery models.

Award Range/Average: In 2017, up to $10M will be awarded to Pennsylvania Department of Health. In 2018, up to $7M will be awarded to the Rural Health Redesign Center. In 2019, up to $5M will be awarded to the Rural Health Redesign Center. Finally, in 2020 up to $3M will be awarded to the Rural Health Redesign Center.

Funding: (Cooperative Agreements) FY 17 $10,000,000; FY 18 est $0; FY 19 est $7,000,000; FY 16 $0.

HQ: 7500 Security Boulevard
Baltimore, DC 21244
Phone: 410-786-8984
Email: theresa.dreyer@cms.hhs.gov
http://www.innovations.cms.gov

GAINING EARLY AWARENESS & READINESS FOR UNDERGRADUATE PROGRAMS "GEAR-UP"

Award: Project Grants

Purpose: To provide 6-or 7-year grants to States and Partnerships to provide support, and maintain a commitment, to eligible low-income students, including students with disabilities.

Applicant Eligibility: A State, or a partnership consisting of one or more local educational agencies one or more degree granting institutions of higher education.

Beneficiary Eligibility: Low-income students and students in high-poverty schools.

Award Range/Average: State grants: Average award in FY 17, $3,328,109. Partnership grants: Average award in FY 17, $1,701,679.

Funding: (Project Grants) FY 17 est $338,831,000; FY 16 $322,588,000; FY 18 est $218,817,000.

HQ: 400 Maryland Avenue SW
Washington, DC 20202
Phone: 202-453-7197
Email: karmon.simms-coates@ed.gov
http://www.ed.gov/programs/gearup/index.html

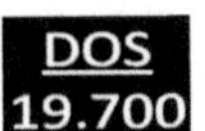

DOS 19.700

GENERAL DEPARTMENT OF STATE ASSISTANCE "General Assistance Programs"

Award: Cooperative Agreements; Project Grants

Purpose: Fulfills the mission of The United States Department of State.

Applicant Eligibility: The General Assistance Programs provide information of Department of State programs that are not elsewhere classified.

Beneficiary Eligibility: Same as Applicant Eligibility.

Award Range/Average: Various

Funding: N/A

HQ: Federal Assistance Policy Federal Assistance 2201 C Street
Washington, DC 20522
Phone: 703-516-1684

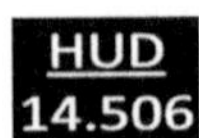

HUD 14.506

GENERAL RESEARCH & TECHNOLOGY ACTIVITY

Award: Provision of Specialized Services

Purpose: To improve the operations of the Department's programs.

Applicant Eligibility: Researchers, research organizations, State and local governments, academic institutions, public and/or private profit and nonprofit organizations which have authority and capacity to carry out projects.

Beneficiary Eligibility: Same as Applicant Eligibility.

Award Range/Average: $15,000 - $20,000,000

Funding: (Provision of Specialized Services) FY 17 $60,121,878; FY 18 est $65,331,205; FY 19 est $62,596,412; FY 16 $58,312,095.

HQ: 451 7th Street, Room 8230
Washington, DC 20410
Phone: 202-402-3852
Email: susan.s.brunson@hud.gov

GEOSCIENCES "GEO"

Award: Project Grants

Purpose: To strengthen and enhance the national scientific enterprise through the expansion of fundamental knowledge and increased understanding of the integrated Earth system through the support of basic research in the atmospheric, earth, and ocean sciences.

Applicant Eligibility: Except where a program solicitation establishes more restrictive eligibility criteria, individuals and organizations in the following categories may submit proposals: Universities and colleges; Non-profit, non-academic organizations; For-profit organizations; State and local governments; and unaffiliated individuals. See the NSF Grant Proposal Guide, Chapter I.

Beneficiary Eligibility: N/A

Award Range/Average: Range Low $1,093 Range High $14,846,730 Average $224,843

Funding: (Project Grants) FY 17 est $1,223,116,000; FY 18 est $1,121,490,000; FY 16 $1,257,859,000; - 1) FY 2016 Obligation projections are the FY 2016 NSF Current Plan 2) FY 2016 Obligations are the FY 2016 NSF Appropriations Actual 3) FY 2017 Obligations estimates are the FY 2017 NSF Current Plan 4) FY 2018 Obligations estimates are the FY 2018 NSF Congressional Request. Starting in FY 2018 GEO will be reported separate from Polar Programs.

HQ: 4201 Wilson Boulevard Stafford I, Suite 705
Arlington, VA 22230
Phone: 703-292-8500
Email: mlane@nsf.gov
http://nsf.gov/dir/index.jsp?org=geo

GEOTHERMAL RESOURCES

Award: Direct Payments for Specified Use

Purpose: Shares 50 percent of mineral leasing revenue with the State, and 25 percent with the county.

Applicant Eligibility: Revenue from government owned land leasing will trigger automatic payment distribution computed in accordance with the law.

Beneficiary Eligibility: ONRR distributes these funds to state and county governments for leased lands within the state or county and the state or county government has sole discretion in their use in accordance with the enabling legislation.

Award Range/Average: N/A

Funding: (Direct Payments for Specified Use) FY 19 est $9,117,000; FY 18 est $11,810,000; FY 17 $10,445,000.

HQ: 1849 C Street NW, P.O. Box 4211
Washington, DC 20240
Phone: 202-513-0600
http://www.onrr.gov

DOJ 16.830 GIRLS IN THE JUVENILE JUSTICE SYSTEM
"Delinquent Girls program, Girls in the Juvenile Justice system"

Award: Project Grants

Purpose: To provide support for girls from entering the juvenile justice system and improve services and treatment for girls at risk, to protect victims of child sexual exploitation or domestic sex trafficking, and other efforts for the welfare of women.

Applicant Eligibility: Eligible applicants are limited to states (including territories), units of local government, federally recognized tribal governments as determined by the Secretary of the Interior, nonprofit organizations, and for-profit organizations (including tribal nonprofit and for-profit organizations), as well as institutions of higher education (including tribal institutions of higher education). For-profit organizations (as well as other recipients) must agree to forgo any profit or management fee.

Beneficiary Eligibility: See applicable program announcement.

Award Range/Average: $400,000- $2,000,000

Funding: Project Grants (Discretionary) FY 17 $1,666,643; FY 18 FY 19 FY 16 $1,689,366.

HQ: Office of Juvenile Justice and Delinquency Prevention
Washington, DC 20531
Phone: 202-353-9093
http://www.ojjdp.gov

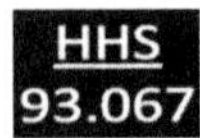

GLOBAL AIDS

Award: Project Grants

Purpose: To help save the lives of those suffering from HIV/AIDS around the world.

Applicant Eligibility: Competition is open, limited, or single eligibility by authorizing legislation.

Beneficiary Eligibility: This is only for non-research and research activities supported by CDC/ATSDR.

Award Range/Average: $25,000 to $48,000,000. Average $2,700,000

Funding: (Cooperative Agreements) FY 17 $1,511,170,959; FY 18 est $1,099,877,957; FY 19 est $1,300,000,000; FY 16 $2,354,719,081.

HQ: 1600 Clifton Road NE, P.O. Box E-29
Atlanta, GA 30333
Phone: 404-639-4276
Email: ctg8@cdc.gov
http://www.cdc.gov

GLOBAL ENGAGEMENT
"Special Representative to Muslim Communities"

Award: Project Grants

Purpose: Supports projects that fulfills U.S. government global engagement goals to strengthen civil society and counter extremism, including social media training, media empowerment, leadership and social entrepreneurship development that establishes civil society capacity in Muslim communities around the world.

Applicant Eligibility: N/A

Beneficiary Eligibility: N/A

Award Range/Average: $10,000 - $100,000 dollars, average $20,000

Funding: (Project Grants)

HQ: H Street Building 2201 C Street
Washington, DC 20520
Phone: 202-736-7884
Email: kifayata@state.gov

GLOBAL PEACE OPERATIONS INITIATIVE "GPOI"

Award: Project Grants

Purpose: Global Peace Operations Initiative (GPOI) was initially envisioned as a five-year program (FY 2005-2009) to help address major gaps in international capacity to conduct peace support operations (PSOs), with a focus on Africa. Through GPOI, the United States further provides deployment support, obligating $ 76.6 million to date to facilitate the equipping, transportation, and sustainment of troops deploying to various UN and regional missions.

Applicant Eligibility: N/A

Beneficiary Eligibility: N/A

Award Range/Average: No Data Available.

Funding: N/A

HQ: 2201 C Street NW, Suite 2811
Washington, DC 20520
Phone: 202-647-0904
Email: hoytlv@state.gov
http://www.state.gov/t/pm/gpi/gpoi/index.htm

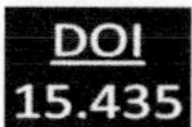

GOMESA

Award: Direct Payments for Specified Use

Purpose: Shares 37.5 percent of selected revenue with Gulf producing states and political subdivisions; payable annually during the year after receipt in accordance with 30 CFR Section 519.418.

Applicant Eligibility: Revenue from selected leases will automatically trigger distribution to states and political subdivisions.

Beneficiary Eligibility: Eligible states and political subdivisions with Louisiana, Texas, Alabama, and Mississippi.

Award Range/Average: N/A

Funding: (Direct Payments for Specified Use) FY 17 $957,000; FY 19 est $268,014,000; FY 18 est $187,989,000.

HQ: Office of Natural Resources Revenue 1849 C Street NW, P.O. Box 4211
Washington, DC 20240
Phone: 202-513-0600
http://www.onrr.gov

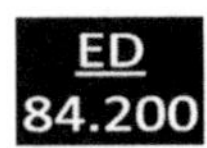

GRADUATE ASSISTANCE IN AREAS OF NATIONAL NEED

Award: Project Grants

Purpose: To provide fellowships through graduate academic departments, programs, and units of institutions of higher education to graduate students of superior ability who demonstrate financial need for the purpose of teaching and research in academic areas designated by the Secretary.

Applicant Eligibility: Academic departments and programs of IHEs that provide courses of study leading to a graduate degree may apply. Nondegree granting institutions may submit joint proposals with degree-granting IHEs.

Beneficiary Eligibility: Graduate students receiving fellowships must demonstrate financial need, have excellent academic records, plan to pursue the highest degree in the field, and be a U.S. citizen or a National, or a permanent resident of the U.S., or intend to become a U.S. citizen, be a permanent resident of the Trust Territory of the Pacific Islands, or a citizen of any one of the Freely Associated States.

Award Range/Average: No Data Available.

Funding: (Project Grants) FY 17 $28,047,000; FY 18 est $23,047,000; FY 19 est $0; FY 16 $29,293,000.

HQ: Teacher and Student Development Programs Service Graduate Assistance in Areas of National Need Program, Department of Education 400 Maryland Avenue SW
Washington, DC 20202
Phone: 202-453-6348
Email: rebecca.ell@ed.gov
http://www2.ed.gov/programs/gaann/index.html

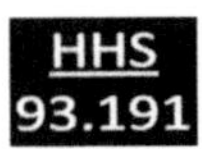

GRADUATE PSYCHOLOGY EDUCATION
"Graduate Psychology Education (GPE) Program"

Award: Project Grants

Purpose: To provide behavioral healthcare, including substance abuse prevention and treatment services, in a setting that provides integrated primary and behavioral health services to underserved and/or rural populations.

Applicant Eligibility: Public or private nonprofit schools, universities, or other educational entities which provide for graduate psychology education and training or other public or private nonprofit entities capable, as determined by the Secretary, of carrying out the objectives of the project. Eligible entities are American Psychological Association (APA)-accredited doctoral-level schools and programs of health service psychology, APA-accredited doctoral internships in professional psychology, and APA-accredited post-doctoral residency programs in practice psychology.

Beneficiary Eligibility: Doctoral students, doctoral interns, and post-doctoral residents receiving a stipend in the GPE Program must be in an APA-accredited program, a citizen of the United States, a non-citizen national of the United States, or a foreign national who possesses a visa permitting permanent residence in the United States. Individuals on temporary or student visas are not eligible participants.

Award Range/Average: FY 18: est Range: $94,506 - $350,000; Average award: $269,458

Funding: (Project Grants) FY 17 $8,160,438; FY 18 est $8,353,211; FY 19 est $0; FY 16 $7,900,000.

HQ: Division 5600 Fishers Lane Parklawn Building, Room 11N138
Rockville, MD 20857
Phone: 301-443-7661
Email: charne@hrsa.gov
http://www.hrsa.gov

GRADUATE RESEARCH OPPORTUNITIES FOR MINORITY STUDENTS (MINORITIES & RETIREMENT SECURITY PROGRAM)

Award: Project Grants

Purpose: To support competitive post-graduate grants to apprentice scholars at selected minority-serving graduate institutions in the area of retirement security for low- to moderate-income individuals.

Applicant Eligibility: Eligible institutions include institutions of higher education (IHE) grantees receiving grants from the Historically Black Graduate Institutions (HBGIs) program (84.031B); the Master's Degrees Programs at Historically Black Colleges and Universities (HBCUs) (84.

Beneficiary Eligibility: Researchers and graduate students researching retirement security will benefit.

Award Range/Average: $60,000- $120,000. Average $90,000.

Funding: (Project Grants) FY 17 $480,000; FY 18 est $0; FY 19 est $0; FY 16 $480,000.

HQ: 400 Maryland Avenue SW
Washington, DC 20202
Phone: 202-453-6337
Email: sheryl.wilson@ed.gov
http://www2.ed.gov/programs/mrs

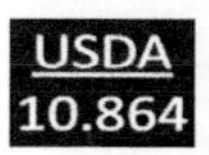

GRANT PROGRAM TO ESTABLISH A FUND FOR FINANCING WATER & WASTEWATER PROJECTS "RFP Program"

Award: Project Grants

Purpose: To compensate nonprofit organizations to establish short-term loans for pre-development and water or waste disposal projects.

Applicant Eligibility: An applicant must be a private organization, organized as a non-profit corporation. The applicant must have the legal capacity and authority to perform the obligations of the grant.

Beneficiary Eligibility: Municipalities, counties, and other political subdivisions of a State, such as districts and authorities, associations, cooperatives, corporations operated on a not-for-profit basis, Indian tribes on Federal and State reservations and other Federally recognized Indian tribes. Facilities shall primarily serve rural residents and rural businesses.

Award Range/Average: $250,000 to $500,00. Average grant: $333,333

Funding: (Project Grants) FY 17 $1,000,000; FY 18 est $1,000,000; FY 19 est $0; FY 16 $1,000,000.

HQ: 1400 Independence Avenue SW, P.O. Box 1548
Washington, DC 20250
Phone: 202-690-2670
Email: edna.primrose@wdc.usda.gov
http://www.rd.usda.gov/programs-services/all-programs/water-environmental-programs

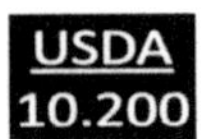

GRANTS FOR AGRICULTURAL RESEARCH, SPECIAL RESEARCH GRANTS

"Special Research Grants (SRGP)"

Award: Project Grants

Purpose: To enhance and expand food and agricultural research programs.

Applicant Eligibility: Special Research Grants: State agricultural experiment stations, all colleges and universities, other research institutions and organizations, Federal agencies, private organizations or corporations and individuals having a demonstrable capacity to conduct research activities to facilitate or expand promising breakthroughs in areas of the food and agricultural sciences of importance to the United States.

Beneficiary Eligibility: For Special Research Grants

Award Range/Average: If minimum or maximum amounts of funding per competitive and/or capacity project grant, or cooperative agreement are established, these amounts will be announced in the annual Competitive Request for Application (RFA).

Funding: (Project Grants) FY 17 $20,162,542; FY 18 est $21,349,723; FY 19 est $0; FY 16 $20,712,503.

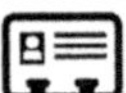

HQ: Institute of Bioenergy Climate and Environment Division of Bioenergy 1400 Independence Avenue SW, P.O. Box 2210
Washington, DC 20250-2210
Phone: 202-401-5244
Email: rmelnick@nifa.usda.gov
http://nifa.usda.gov/grants

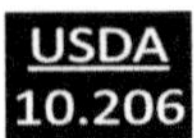

GRANTS FOR AGRICULTURAL RESEARCH_COMPETITIVE RESEARCH GRANTS

"National Research Initiative Competitive Grants Program (NRI)"

Award: Project Grants

Purpose: To support all components of agriculture and implement modern ideas to sustain agriculture for various purposes.

Applicant Eligibility: For research projects, the eligibility requirements for the NRI were as follows: except where otherwise prohibited by law, State agricultural experiment stations, all colleges and universities, other research institutions and organizations, Federal agencies, national laboratories, private organizations or corporations, and individuals were eligible to apply for and to receive a competitive grant. The Agricultural Research Enhancement Awards (AREA) have some notable differences from these requirements.

Beneficiary Eligibility: For research grants eligibility includes State Agricultural Experiment Stations, U.S. colleges/universities, other U.S. research institutions and organizations, Federal agencies, national laboratories, private organizations or corporations, and individuals. For integrated research, education and extension grants eligibility includes State Agricultural Experiment Stations, U.S. colleges/universities, research foundations maintained by colleges or universities, private research organizations with established and demonstrated capacities to perform research or technology transfer, Federal research agencies and national laboratories.

Award Range/Average: Minimum and maximum amounts of funding per grant were established by the annual program announcement or RFA.

Funding: N/A

HQ: 1400 Independence Avenue SW
Washington, DC 20024
Phone: 202-401-1782
Email: jwilliams@nifa.usda.gov
http://nifa.usda.gov

HHS 93.526 GRANTS FOR CAPITALL DEVELOPMENT IN HEALTH CENTERS "Capital Development Grants"

Award: Project Grants

Purpose: To award Health Center Capital Development Grants for immediate facility improvements or building capacity.

Applicant Eligibility: Eligibility is limited to currently-funded health centers (see applicable Notice of Funding Opportunity available through Grants.gov for additional eligibility information).

Beneficiary Eligibility: Populations in medically underserved areas.

Award Range/Average: Varies. See applicable notice of funding opportunity.

Funding: (Project Grants) FY 17 $0; FY 18 est $0; FY 19 est $0; FY 16 $262,000,000.

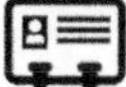

HQ: Bureau of Primary Health Care 5600 Fishers Lane, Room 16N20
Rockville, MD 20857
Phone: 301-594-4300
http://www.hrsa.gov

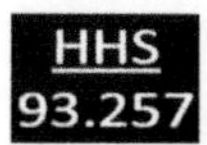

HHS 93.257 GRANTS FOR EDUCATION, PREVENTION, AND EARLY DETECTION OF RADIOGENIC CANCERS & DISEASES "Radiation Exposure Screening and Education Program"

Award: Project Grants

Purpose: To screen individuals described under section 4 (a) (1)(A)(i) or 5(a)(1)(A) of the Radiation Exposure Compensation Act (42 U.S.C. 2210 note) for cancer as a preventative health measure.

Applicant Eligibility: The following entities, (located within the approved states of Arizona, Colorado, Idaho, Nevada, New Mexico, North Dakota, Oregon, South Dakota, Texas, Utah, Washington or Wyoming) are eligible to apply for the funds: (1) National Cancer Institute-designated cancer centers; (2) Department of Veterans Affairs hospitals or medical centers; (3) Federally Qualified Health Centers (FQHC), community health centers or hospitals; (4) agencies of any state or local government, includes any state department of health that currently provide direct health care services; (5) IHS health care facilities, including programs provided through tribal contracts, compacts, grants, or cooperative agreements with the IHS and which are determined appropriate to raising the health status of Indians; including federally-recognized Tribal Government and Native American Organizations, and (6) nonprofit organizations.

Beneficiary Eligibility: For purposes of the Radiation Exposure Screening and Education Program (RESEP), individuals eligible for health screening, education, medical referral, and appropriate follow-up services include an individual who either: (1) was employed in a uranium mine or uranium mill (including any individual who was employed in the transport of uranium ore or vanadium-uranium ore from such mine or mill) located in Colorado, New Mexico, Arizona, Wyoming, South Dakota, Washington, Utah, Idaho, North Dakota, Oregon, and Texas at any time during the period beginning on January 1, 1942, and ending on December 31, 1971; (2) was a miner exposed to 40 or more working level months of radiation or worked for at least 1 year during the period beginning on January 1, 1942 and ending on December 31, 1971; (3) was a miller or ore transporter who worked for at least 1 year during the period beginning on January 1, 1942, and ending on December 31, 1971; (4) was physically present in the nuclear arms affected area (which includes, in the state of Utah, the counties of Beaver, Garfield, Iron, Kane, Millard, Piute, San Juan, Sevier, Washington, and Wayne; in the state of Nevada, the counties of Eureka, Lander, Lincoln, Nye, White Pine, and that portion of Clark County that consists of townships 13 through 16 at ranges 63 through 71; and in the state of Arizona, the counties of Apache, Coconino, Gila, Navajo, and Yavapai) for a period of at least 2 years during the period beginning on January 21, 1951, and ending on October 31, 1958; (5) was physically present in the nuclear arms testing area, cited in 4. above, for the period beginning on June 30, 1962, and ending on July 31, 1962, or (6) participated onsite in a nuclear arms test involving the atmospheric detonation of a nuclear device.

Award Range/Average: Range = $100,995 to $242,525. $200,590 (average).

Funding: FY 17 $1,834,000; FY 18 est $1,834,000; FY 19 est $1,834,000.

HQ: 5600 Fishers Lane
Rockville, MD 20857
Phone: 301-443-2702
Email: mlincoln@hrsa.gov
http://www.hrsa.gov/ruralhealth/about/community/resepgrant.html

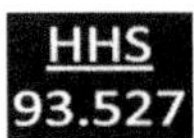

GRANTS FOR NEW & EXPANDED SERVICES UNDER THE HEALTH CENTER PROGRAM

"Grants for New and Expanded Services under the Health Center Program"

Award: Project Grants

Purpose: To provide for expanded and sustained national investment in health centers funded under section 330 of the Public Health Service Act.

Applicant Eligibility: Eligible applicants for funding for new access points are public and private non-profit entities, including federally recognized Indian Tribal governments and Native American, faith-based, and community-based organizations that have the capacity to effectively administer the grant in alignment with the requirements outlined in Section 330 of the Public Health Services Act, as amended. Refer to the applicable notice of funding opportunity under this CFDA program for additional information.

Beneficiary Eligibility: Population groups in medically underserved areas, medically underserved populations, and special populations such migratory and seasonal agricultural workers and their families, people experiencing homelessness, and public housing residents.

Award Range/Average: Varies. See applicable notice of funding opportunity.

Funding: (Project Grants) FY 17 $0; FY 18 est $0; FY 19 est $0; (Project Grants) FY 17 $36,300,000; FY 18 est $36,000,000; FY 19 est $36,000,000; (Project Grants) FY 17 $0; FY 18 est $0; FY 19 est $0; (Project Grants) FY 17 $50,000,000; FY 18 est $0; FY 19 est $0

HQ: Bureau of Primary Health Care HRSA
Rockville, MD 20857
Phone: 301-594-4300
http://www.hrsa.gov

GRANTS FOR PRIMARY CARE TRAINING & ENHANCEMENT
"Primary Care Training and Enhancement; PCTE"

Award: Project Grants

Purpose: The purpose of the PCTE program is to strengthen the primary care workforce by supporting enhanced training for future primary care. The focus of this grant is to produce primary care providers who will be well prepared to practice in and lead transforming healthcare systems aimed at improving access, quality of care, and cost effectiveness.

Applicant Eligibility: Eligible entities include accredited public or nonprofit private hospitals, schools of allopathic or osteopathic medicine, academically affiliated physician assistant training programs, or a public or nonprofit private entity that the Secretary has determined is capable of carrying out such grants. Federally Recognized Indian Tribal Government and Native American Organizations may apply if they are otherwise eligible.

Beneficiary Eligibility: Beneficiaries include physician and physician assistant training programs that train medical students, physician assistant students, medical residents, practicing physician and physician assistants, and physician and physician assistant faculty.

Award Range/Average: Primary Care Training and Enhancement Program (PCTE): FY 2017 Range Actual: $169,995 to $580,000; Average award $366,669 for PCTE Program; Range: $1,487 to $80,000, Average MAT supplement: $69,210 FY 2018 est Range $169,826 to $500,000. Average award est. $367,394.79 Academic Units for Primary Care Training and Enhancement Program: FY 2017 Range actual: $703,396 to $749,897; Average award : $737,043 FY 2018 Range actual $727,702 to $749,802 Average award $744,446FY 2019 Range est $727,702 to $749,802 Average award $744,446 Physician Assistant Training in Primary Care: FY 2018 est range: $194,827- $274,037; Average Award - $238,859 Interdisciplinary and Interprofessional Joint Degree Program: FY 2017 $0 FY 2018 $0 FY 2019 est $0

Funding: (Cooperative Agreements) FY 17 $4,536,029; FY 18 est $4,466,667; FY 19 est $0; (Project Grants) FY 17 $0; FY 18 est $0; FY 19 est $0; (Project Grants) FY 17 $0; FY 18 est $716,579; FY 19 est $0; (Project Grants) FY 17 $29,155,360; FY 18 est $24,982,846.

HQ: Bureau of Health Workforce For the Academic Units for PCTE Awards 5600 Fishers Lane, Room 15N152
Rockville, MD 20857
Phone: 301-443-2295
Email: isandvold@hrsa.gov
http://bhpr.hrsa.gov

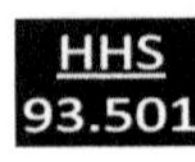

GRANTS FOR SCHOOL-BASED HEALTH CENTER CAPITAL EXPENDITURES "SBHCC"

Award: Project Grants

Purpose: To award funds made available to expand school-based health center capacity to provide primary healthcare services for school-aged children. This competitive funding opportunity is available for school-based health centers to address significant and pressing capital improvement needs, including: alteration, renovation, and the purchase of equipment.

Applicant Eligibility: To be eligible for a grant under this subsection, an entity shall be a school-based health center or a sponsoring facility of a school-based health center as defined in section 2110(c)(9) of the Social Security Act (42 USC 1397jj(c)(9)).

Beneficiary Eligibility: School-based health centers or a sponsoring facility of a school-based health center.

Award Range/Average: N/A

Funding: (Project Grants) FY 17 $0; FY 18 est $0; FY 19 est $10,000,000; FY 16 $0.

HQ: Bureau of Primary Health Care HRSA, Room 16N20 5600 Fishers Lane
Rockville, MD 20857
Phone: 301-594-4300
http://www.hrsa.gov

GRANTS FOR STATE ASSESSMENTS & RELATED ACTIVITIES

Award: Formula Grants

Purpose: To pay the costs of developing the standards and high-quality assessments required by Title I of the ESEA.

Applicant Eligibility: State educational agencies.

Beneficiary Eligibility: States and local educational agencies.

Award Range/Average: FY 2019 range of awards to States: $3,306,849- $28,444,134 average $7,027,096.

Funding: (Formula Grants) FY 17 $369,051,480; FY 18 est $369,100,000; FY 19 est $369,100,000; FY 16 $369,051,480.

HQ: Department of Education 400 Maryland Avenue SW
Washington, DC 20202
Phone: 202-453-5514
Email: patrick.rooney@ed.gov
http://www2.ed.gov/admins/lead/account/saa.html

GRANTS TO INCREASE ORGAN DONATIONS

Award: Cooperative Agreements

Purpose: To support grants for the purpose of increasing public commitment to organ donation and ultimately the number of organs recovered and transplanted.

Applicant Eligibility: Reimbursement of Travel and Subsistence Expenses toward Living Organ Donation: As specified in Section 377 of the Public Health Service Act, as amended, eligible applicants include States, transplant centers, qualified organ procurement organizations under section 371, or other public or private entities. Faith-based, community organizations and Federally Recognized Indian Tribal Government and Native American Organizations are eligible to apply.

Beneficiary Eligibility: Reimbursement of Travel and Subsistence Expenses toward Living Organ Donation: Primary beneficiaries are low/moderate income living organ donors and recipients. Increasing Organ Donation Awareness Grant Program: Beneficiaries of the grant efforts are patients on the national transplant waiting list.

Award Range/Average: Reimbursement of Travel and Subsistence Expenses toward Living Organ Donation: one award up to $3,500,000 Increasing Organ Donation Awareness Grant Program: $184,192 to $601,373; $467,561. Lost Wages Support for Living Organ Donors one award up to $2,000,000.

Funding: (Project Grants) FY 17 $3,508,854; FY 18 est $4,359,978; FY 19 est $1,198,498; FY 16 $4,857,109; - Increasing Organ Donation Awareness(Cooperative Agreements) FY 17 $2,790,204; FY 18 est $2,744,196; FY 19 est $3,200,000; FY 16 $1,795,729.

HQ: Division of Transplantation 5600 Fishers Lane 08W49
Rockville, MD 20857
Phone: 301-443-7578
http://www.hrsa.gov

GRANTS TO PROVIDE OUTPATIENT EARLY INTERVENTION SERVICES WITH RESPECT TO HIV DISEASE "Ryan White HIV/AIDS Program (RWHAP) Part C Early Intervention Services (EIS)"

Award: Project Grants

Purpose: The RWHAP Part C Early Intervention Services Program provides comprehensive HIV primary care and support services in an outpatient setting for low income, uninsured, and underserved people living with HIV (PLWH). The RWHAP Part C Capacity Development Program strengthens organizational infrastructure to respond to the changing healthcare landscape and to increase capacity to develop, enhance, or expand access to high quality HIV primary healthcare services.

Applicant Eligibility: Public and private nonprofit entities that are: federally qualified health centers under Section 1905(1)(2)(B) of the Social Security Act; recipients under Section 1001 of the PHS Act (regarding family planning) other than States; comprehensive hemophilia diagnostic and treatment centers; rural health clinics; health facilities operated by or pursuant to a contract with the Indian Health Service; community-based organizations, clinics, hospitals and other health facilities that provide early intervention services to those persons infected with HIV/AIDS through intravenous drug use; or nonprofit private entities that provide comprehensive primary care services to populations at-risk of HIV/AIDS, including faith-based and community-based organizations. Eligible applicants for the Capacity Development Program include public and nonprofit private entities, including faith-based and community-based organizations, and Tribes and tribal organizations.

Beneficiary Eligibility: Low income, uninsured, and underserved PLWH.

Award Range/Average: $2,597 to $1,495,123; Average $516,803. Capacity Development grants are $150,000

Funding: (Project Grants) FY 17 $3,798,106; FY 18 est $2,250,000; FY 19 est $2,250,000; FY 16 $1,500,000; - Capacity Development.(Project Grants) FY 17 $181,747,027; FY 18 est $181,914,492; FY 19 est $181,914,492; FY 16 $186,586,879; - Early Intervention Services.

HQ: 5600 Fishers Lane, Room 09N16
Rockville, MD 20857
Phone: 301-443-1326
Email: hendale@hrsa.gov
http://www.hrsa.gov

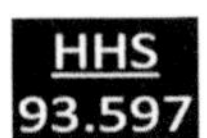

GRANTS TO STATES FOR ACCESS & VISITATION PROGRAMS

Award: Formula Grants

Purpose: Enables States to create programs which support and facilitate access and visitation by non-custodial parents with their children.

Applicant Eligibility: All States, the District of Columbia, Puerto Rico, Virgin Islands and Guam.

Beneficiary Eligibility: Custodial and non-custodial parents.

Award Range/Average: The amount of funding provided to each grantee is based on an allocation formula with a designated minimum amount provided in statute.

Funding: (Formula Grants) FY 17 $10,000,000; FY 18 est $10,000,000; FY 19 est $10,000,000; FY 16 $10,000,000.

HQ: 330 C Street SW
Washington, DC 20201
Phone: 202-401-5651
Email: michael.hayes@acf.hhs.gov
http://www.acf.dhhs.gov/programs/cse

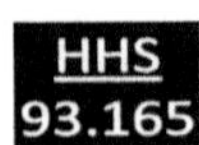

GRANTS TO STATES FOR LOAN REPAYMENT PROGRAM "State Loan Repayment Program (SLRP)"

Award: Project Grants; Direct Payments for Specified Use

Purpose: To increase the availability of primary healthcare in health professional shortage areas (HPSAs) by assisting States in operating programs for the repayment of educational loans of health professionals.

Applicant Eligibility: Eligible entities include the 50 States, the District of Columbia, Guam, the Commonwealth of Puerto Rico, the Northern Mariana Islands, the U.S. Virgin Islands, American Samoa, the Federated States of Micronesia, the Republic of the Marshall Islands, and the Republic of Palau

Beneficiary Eligibility: Applicants for State programs must have completed a course of study required to practice independently without supervision as one of the following health care professionals: Doctor of Allopathic Medicine or Osteopathic Medicine, General Practice Dentist (D.D.

Award Range/Average: $80,000 to $1,000,000, average of $333,444

Funding: (Project Grants) FY 17 $12,633,936; FY 18 est $15,000,000; FY 19 est $15,000,000; FY 16 $13,070,603.

HQ: Division of National Health Service Corps Bureau of Health Workforce Department of Health and Human Services, 5600 Fishers Lane Room 14N58

Rockville, MD 20857

Phone: 301-594-4400

http://nhsc.hrsa.gov

GRANTS TO STATES FOR OPERATION OF QUALIFIED HIGH-RISK POOLS

Award: Formula Grants

Purpose: Assists States in the operation of a qualified high-risk health insurance pool by providing Federal funding of losses incurred by the pool for a given State fiscal year.

Applicant Eligibility: A State must meet all of the following requirements to be eligible for a grant: 1) the State is operating a qualified high-risk pool as defined in section 2744(c)(2) of the Public Health Service Act; 2) the pool restricts premium charged under the pool to no more than 200 percent for applicable standard risk rates for the State; 3) the pool offers a choice of two or more coverage options through the pool; 4) the pool has in effect a mechanism reasonably designed to ensure continued funding of losses incurred by the State; and 5) Grant Awards: FY 2012 - The Consolidated Appropriations Act, 2012. (Public Law 112-74), provided $43.

Beneficiary Eligibility: State Agency.

Award Range/Average: None

Funding:N/A

HQ: 200 Independence Avenue SW, Room 739H

Washington, DC 20201

Phone: 301-492-4482

Email: gabriel.nah@cms.hhs.gov

http://www.cms.hhs.gov/highriskpools

GRANTS TO STATES FOR OPERATION OF STATE OFFICES OF RURAL HEALTH
"The State Offices of Rural Health (SORH) Program"

Award: Project Grants

Purpose: The Rural Outreach Benefits Counseling Program seeks to expand outreach, education and enrollment efforts to eligible uninsured individuals and families, and newly insured individuals and families in rural communities.

Applicant Eligibility: Grants: All fifty states may apply. Each state may only submit one application.

Beneficiary Eligibility: Underserved populations in rural areas; facilities and services in rural areas.

Award Range/Average: $165,521 - $179,871.

Funding: (Project Grants) FY 17 $8,587,983; FY 18 est $8,955,261; FY 19 est $8,955,355.

HQ: The Federal Office of Rural Health Policy 5600 Fishers Lane, Room 17W45C

Rockville, MD 20857

Phone: 301-443-0835
Email: sstack@hrsa.gov
http://www.hrsa.gov/ruralhealth

GRANTS TO STATES TO SUPPORT ORAL HEALTH WORKFORCE ACTIVITIES

"Grants to States to Support Oral Health Workforce Activities"

Award: Project Grants

Purpose: To Support Oral Health Workforce Activities assists states to develop and implement innovative programs to address the dental workforce needs of designated Dental Health Professional Shortage Areas.

Applicant Eligibility: Eligible applicants include Governor appointed, state government entities. In addition to U.S. states, eligible applicants include: District of Columbia, Guam, the Commonwealth of Puerto Rico, the Northern Mariana Islands, the U.S. Virgin Islands, American Samoa, the Federated States of Micronesia, the Republic of the Marshall Islands, and the Republic of Palau.

Beneficiary Eligibility: Beneficiaries include Governor appointed, State government entities.

Award Range/Average: FY 16 Range: $287,883 to $500,000 Average award: $457,558 FY 17 Range: $287,000 to $500,000 Average award: $457,000 FY 18 (estimate) Range: $121,698 to $400,000 Average award: $367,514

Funding: (Project Grants) FY 17 $11,206,376; FY 18 est $11,589,816; FY 19 est $0; FY 16 $14,014,185.

HQ: Division of Medicine and Dentistry Bureau of Health Workforce 5600 Fishers Lane, Room 15N-120
Rockville, MD 20857
Phone: 301-443-5260
Email: srogers@hrsa.gov
http://www.hrsa.gov

GROWTH ACCELERATOR FUND COMPETITION

Award: Direct Payments for Specified Use

Purpose: To help entrepreneurs start and scale their businesses.

Applicant Eligibility: For-profit and nonprofit organizations and the general public. Funds are intended for accelerators and other entrepreneurial ecosystem models to fund operating budgets.

Beneficiary Eligibility: For-profit and nonprofit organizations, Small Businesses and the general public. Organizations which provide networking opportunities, mentorship, space (can be physical or virtual) and sometimes equity to start-ups.

Award Range/Average: $2,500,000 to $4,000,000 cumulative. $50,000 to $80,000 for individual awards.

Funding: (Direct Payments for Specified Use) FY 17 est $5,000,000; FY 15 $3,950,000; FY 16 est $1,000,000.

HQ: 409 3rd Street SW, 6th Floor
Washington, DC 20416

Phone: 202-205-7576
Email: nareg.sagherian@sba.gov
http://www.sba.gov

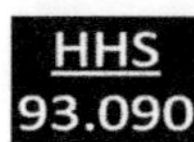

GUARDIANSHIP ASSISTANCE

Award: Formula Grants

Purpose: To provide Federal financial participation (FFP) to states, Indian tribes, tribal organizations and tribal consortia (tribes) who opt to provide guardianship assistance payments to relatives who have assumed legal guardianship of eligible children that they previously cared for as foster parents.

Applicant Eligibility: Funds are available to states (including the District of Columbia, Puerto Rico, the U.S. Virgin Islands, Guam and American Samoa) and to tribes with approved Title IV-E plans.

Beneficiary Eligibility: Beneficiaries are children who meet the following requirements: (1) the child has been eligible for Title IV-E foster care maintenance payments while residing for at least six consecutive months in the home of the prospective relative guardian; (2) the state or tribe has determined that the permanency options of being returned home or adoption are not appropriate for the child; (3) the child demonstrates a strong attachment to the prospective relative guardian and the prospective guardian is committed to caring permanently for the child; and (4) for children who have attained the age of 14, the child has been consulted regarding the kinship guardianship arrangement. Beneficiaries may also be siblings of eligible children placed in the same kinship guardianship arrangement.

Award Range/Average: Fiscal Year 2017: Grants to states and tribes ranged from $3,964 to $54,898,970 with an average of $4,125,583.

Funding: (Formula Grants) FY 17 $147,808,681; FY 18 est $181,000,000; FY 19 est $181,000,000; FY 16 $122,631,572.

HQ: 330 C Street SW, Room 3507A
Washington, DC 20201
Phone: 202-205-8086
Email: liliana.hernandez@acf.hhs.gov
http://www.acf.hhs.gov/programs/cb

GULF COAST ECOSYSTEM RESTORATION COUNCIL COMPREHENSIVE PLAN COMPONENT PROGRAM "RESTORE Council-Selected Restoration Component"

Award: Project Grants

Purpose: To disburse funds to eligible entities for the purpose of restoring and protecting the natural resources, ecosystems, fisheries, marine and wildlife habitats, beaches, coastal wetlands, and economy of the Gulf Coast region using the best available science.

Applicant Eligibility: The Council will periodically request proposals from its eleven state and federal members. The Council members are the only entities eligible to submit proposals.

Beneficiary Eligibility: Beneficiaries are the people, wildlife, and natural resources of the Gulf Coast region.

Award Range/Average: No Data Available.

Funding: (Project Grants) FY 17 $81,704,027; FY 18 est $55,039,432; FY 19 est $55,500,000; FY 16 $7,759,216.

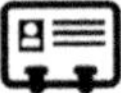

HQ: 500 Poydras Street, Suite 1117
New Orleans, LA 70130
Phone: 504-444-3558
Email: kristin.smith@restorethegulf.gov
http://www.restorethegulf.gov

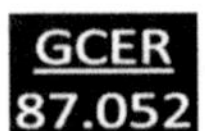

GULF COAST ECOSYSTEM RESTORATION COUNCIL OIL SPILL IMPACT PROGRAM
"RESTORE Council Oil Spill Impact Program"

Award: Project Grants

Purpose: To disburse funds to eligible entities for the purpose of restoring and protecting the natural resources, ecosystems, fisheries, marine and wildlife habitats, beaches, coastal wetlands, and economy of the Gulf Coast region.

Applicant Eligibility: Eligible applicants are specified by the RESTORE Act and regulations at 31 C.F.R. Part 34 as the five Gulf Coast States or their administrative agents, as defined in 33 U.S.C. 1321(a)(34), Alabama, Florida, Louisiana, Mississippi, and Texas. For the development of the State Expenditure Plan, the eligible entities for each Gulf Coast State are as follows: in Alabama, the Alabama Gulf Coast Recovery Council; in Florida, a consortia of local political subdivisions that includes at a minimum 1 representative of each affected county; in Louisiana, the Coastal Protection and Restoration Authority of Louisiana; in Mississippi, the Office of the Governor or an appointee of the Office of the Governor; and in Texas, the Office of the Governor or an appointee of the Office of the Governor [33 U.S.C. 1321(t)(3)(B)(iii)]. Only the above-named entities are eligible applicants who may apply for funding. The RESTORE Council does not make Spill Impact Program grants directly to other entities or individuals. States may select subrecipients to carryout approved projects in the State Expenditure Plan. Interested third parties may contact their jurisdiction listed above to learn more about how the eligible entities select proposed activities.

Beneficiary Eligibility: The principal beneficiaries are the people, wildlife, economy/businesses, and natural resources of the Gulf Coast region.

Award Range/Average: No Data Available.

Funding: (Project Grants (for specified projects) FY 17 $19,760,358; FY 18 est $35,597,956; FY 19 est $152,000,000; FY 16 $6,015,287; - Financial assistance is provided as grants to eligible State entities to carry out projects and programs contained within an approved State Expenditure Plan.

HQ: 500 Poydras Street, Suite 1117
New Orleans, LA 70130
Phone: 504-444-3558
Email: kristin.smith@restorethegulf.gov
http://www.restorethegulf.gov

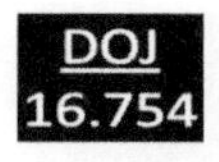

HAROLD ROGERS PRESCRIPTION DRUG MONITORING PROGRAM "PDMP"

Award: Project Grants

Purpose: To support law enforcement agencies in enhancing prescription drug monitoring programs to safeguard public health and enhance public safety data sets and develop interventions.

Applicant Eligibility: N/A

Beneficiary Eligibility: Category 1: Implementation and Enhancement: Applicants are limited to state governments that have a pending or enacted enabling statute or regulation requiring the submission of controlled substance prescription data to an authorized state agency. Category 2: Tribal PDMP Data Sharing Grants: Applicants are limited to federally recognized tribal governments as defined under the Indian Self Determination Act, 25 U.S.C.

Award Range/Average: N/A

Funding: FY 17 $12,841,705; FY 18 est $30,000,000; FY 19 est $12,000,000; FY 16 $11,162,933.

HQ: Office of Justice Programs Bureau of Justice Assistance 810 7th Street NW
Washington, DC 20531
Phone: 202-616-6500
http://www.bja.gov/programdetails.aspx?program_id=72

HAZARD MITIGATION GRANT "HMGP"

Award: Project Grants

Purpose: The program's objective is to provide a fund for Indian tribal, local and State governments against the loss of life or property affected by natural hazards and also to be prepared and prevent any such further losses.

Applicant Eligibility: State and local governments, other political subdivisions such as a special districts, Federally-recognized Indian tribal governments, Alaska Native villages or organizations, but not Alaska Native Corporations, and certain Private Non-Profit organizations in designated emergency or major disaster areas shall serve as the Applicant to FEMA for HMGP assistance. A State is defined as any State of the United States, the District of Columbia, Puerto Rico, the Virgin Islands, Guam, American Samoa, the Northern Marianna Islands, the Marshall Islands and Micronesia.

Beneficiary Eligibility: State and local governments; other political subdivisions such as a special districts, Private, non-profit organizations that own or operate a private, non-profit public facility; certain qualified conservation organizations may apply for acquisition or relocation for open space projects; Indian tribes or authorized tribal organizations and Alaska Native villages or organizations, but not Alaska native corporations with ownership vested in private individuals in designated emergency or major disaster areas are eligible to apply as sub applicants for assistance. All interested sub applicants must apply to the Applicant, who then applies to FEMA.

Award Range/Average: Refer to HMA program guidance.

Funding: FY 17 $5; FY 18 est $435; FY 19 est $500; FY 16 $609,957,698.

HQ: 400 C Street SW

Washington, DC 20472
Phone: 202-646-3458
Email: kayed.lakhia@fema.dhs.gov
http://www.fema.gov/government/mitigation.shtm

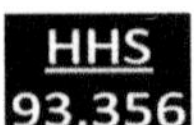

HEAD START DISASTER RECOVERY FROM HURRICANES HARVEY, IRMA, AND MARIA

Award: Project Grants

Purpose: Funds Head Start programs for necessary expenses directly related to the consequences of Hurricanes Harvey, Irma, and Maria, including making payments under the Head Start Act.

Applicant Eligibility: Funding for Head Start programs, for necessary expenses directly related to the consequences of Hurricanes Harvey, Irma, and Maria, including making payments under the Head Start Act.

Beneficiary Eligibility: Head Start/Early Head Start programs are for children from birth up to the age when the child enters the school system. Head Start programs serve preschool age children while Early Head Start programs serve children from birth to age three as well as pregnant women.

Award Range/Average: The range of award amounts could vary as there is not a set maximum threshold of financial assistance a grantee may request.

Funding: Project Grants (Discretionary) FY 17 $0; FY 18 est $15,000,000; FY 19 est $200,000,000.

HQ: 330 C Street SW
Washington, DC 20201
Phone: 202-205-7378
Email: colleen.rathgeb@acf.hhs.gov
http://acf.hhs.gov/programs/ohs

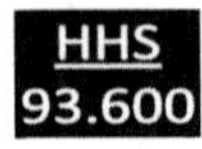

HEAD START

Award: Project Grants; Direct Payments for Specified Use

Purpose: Promotes school readiness by enhancing the social and cognitive development of low-income children, including children on federally recognized reservations and children of migratory farm workers, through the provision of comprehensive health, educational, nutritional, social and other services; and to involve parents in their children's learning and to help parents make progress toward their educational, literacy and employment goals.

Applicant Eligibility: Any government, federally-recognized Indian tribe, or public or private nonprofit or for profit agency which meets the requirements may apply for a grant.

Beneficiary Eligibility: Head Start/Early Head Start programs are for children from birth up to the age when the child enters the school system; however, Head Start programs only serve pre-school age children while Early Head Start programs serve children from birth through age three as well as pregnant women. The Early Head Start-Child Care Partnership programs are expanding access to high quality early learning and development opportunities for infants and toddlers from birth through age four.

Award Range/Average: $214,489 - $144,283,203; average is $4,490,093

Funding: (Project Grants) FY 17 $9,357,741,817; FY 18 est $9,414,718,228; FY 19 est $9,437,248,659; FY 16 $8,934,669,231.

HQ: 330 C Street SW
Washington, DC 20024
Phone: 202-205-7378
Email: colleen.rathgeb@acf.hhs.gov
http://www.acf.hhs.gov/programs/ohs

HEALTH CARE & PUBLIC HEALTH (HPH) SECTOR INFORMATION SHARING & ANALYSIS ORGANIZATION (ISAO)

Award: Cooperative Agreements

Purpose: The purpose of this cooperative agreement is to build the capacity of an information sharing and analysis organization to share information bi-directionally with the Health and Public Health sector and HHS about cyber threats and provide outreach and education surrounding cybersecurity awareness.

Applicant Eligibility: In order to be eligible for funding, the entity needs to be performing some of the functions of an Information Sharing and Analysis Organizations (i.e.

Beneficiary Eligibility: As health care delivery impacts everyone, the beneficiary eligibility includes all of the listed groups as provided in the reference manual.

Award Range/Average: No Data Available.

Funding: (Cooperative Agreements) FY 17 $0; FY 18 est $500,000; FY 19 est $500,000.

HQ: 330 C Street SW
Washington, DC 20201
Phone: 202-720-2919
Email: carmel.halloun@hhs.gov
http://www.healthit.gov

HEALTH CARE INNOVATION AWARDS (HCIA)

Award: Cooperative Agreements

Purpose: In HCIA, Round One, CMS funded 107 Awardees who proposed compelling new models of service delivery/ payment improvements that showed substantial promise of delivering the Three-Part Aim of better health, better healthcare, and lower costs through improved quality for Medicare, Medicaid, and Children's Health Insurance Program beneficiaries.

Applicant Eligibility: Round One of HCIA sought to attract a wide variety of health care innovators and organizations, including: provider groups, health systems, payers and other private sector organizations, faith-based organizations, local governments, and public-private partnerships. In addition, certain organizations (such as professional associations) were eligible to apply as conveners assembling and coordinating the efforts of a group of participants.

Beneficiary Eligibility: The Health Care Innovation Awards initiative will fund applicants who propose the most compelling new service delivery and payment models that will drive system transformation and deliver better outcomes for Medicare, Medicaid, and CHIP beneficiaries. Proposals should be focused on innovative approaches to improving health and lowering costs for high risk/high opportunity populations, including Medicare, Medicaid, and CHIP beneficiaries.

Award Range/Average: In Round Two of the Health Care Innovation Awards, the Innovation Center expects to make up to $900 million in funding available to support a diverse portfolio of new and innovative payment and service delivery models that will reduce the cost of health care and improve its quality in Medicare, Medicaid, and/or CHIP. CMS has approximately 100 awards, with a range of approximately $1 million to $30 million per award. Cooperative agreements will be awarded with consideration to the criteria listed above under Award Procedure. Awardees might not receive the award amount requested and might be asked to adjust the service delivery model, payment model, work plan, budget, or other application deliverable. In Round One, the Innovation Center made 107 awards ranging from approximately $1 million to $26.5 million for a three-year period. Cooperative agreements were awarded with consideration to: (1) available funding; (2) geographic diversity; and (3) the quality of each application and the ability to meet the goals of the project. In the first round, less than 5% percent of applications were funded.

Funding: (Salaries and Expenses) FY 17 $26,715,516; FY 18 est $0; FY 19 est $0; FY 16 $119,108,914.

HQ: 7500 Security Boulevard
Baltimore, MD 21207
Phone: 410-786-7724
http://innovation.cms.gov

HEALTH CAREERS OPPORTUNITY PROGRAM "HCOP: National HCOP Academies"

Award: Project Grants

Purpose: The healthcareers Opportunity Program strives to develop a more competitive applicant pool to build diversity in the health professions. The program's goal is to provide students from economically and educationally disadvantaged backgrounds who are interested in pursuing a health profession to develop the needed skills to compete for, enter, and graduate from a health or allied health professions program, graduate program in behavioral and mental health, and/or programs for the training of physician assistants.

Applicant Eligibility: Eligible applicants include accredited schools of medicine, osteopathic medicine, public health, dentistry, veterinary medicine, optometry, pharmacy, allied health, chiropractic, podiatric medicine, public and nonprofit private schools that offer graduate programs in behavioral and mental health, programs for the training of physician assistants, and other public or private nonprofit health or educational entities including community, technical and tribal colleges. HCOP grant programs may only operate in the fifty (50) states, the District of Columbia, Commonwealth of Puerto Rico, Commonwealth of Northern Mariana Islands, the U.S. Virgin Islands, Guam, American Samoa, the Republic of Palau, Republic of the Marshall Islands, and the Federated States of Micronesia.

Beneficiary Eligibility: Eligible participants of the HCOP grant program must a) meet the definition of economically disadvantaged; b) be from an "educationally disadvantaged" background; and c) express an interest in pursuing a health degree program. Individuals must be U.S. citizens, non-citizen nationals, or foreign nationals who possess a visa permitting permanent residence in the United States.

Award Range/Average: $619,989 to $640,000 Average award $635,000

Funding: (Project Grants) FY 17 $12,794,324; FY 18 est $13,027,065; FY 19 est $0; FY 16 $10,776,373.

HQ: Bureau of Health Workforce Health Resources and Services Administration, Department of Health and Human Services Room 15N38D 5600 Fishers Lane
Rockville, MD 20857
Phone: 301-443-0827

Email: tmayo-blake@hrsa.gov
http://bhw.hrsa.gov/grants/healthcareers

HEALTH CENTER PROGRAM (COMMUNITY HEALTH CENTERS, MIGRANT HEALTH CENTERS, HEALTH CARE FOR THE HOMELESS, AND PUBLIC HOUSING PRIMARY CARE) "Health Center Program"

Award: Project Grants

Purpose: To improve the health of the Nation's underserved communities and vulnerable populations by assuring continued access to affordable, quality primary healthcare services.

Applicant Eligibility: Eligible applicants are domestic public and non-profit private entities, including federally recognized Indian tribal governments and Native American, faith-based, and community-based organizations that have the capacity to effectively administer the grant.

Beneficiary Eligibility: Population groups in medically underserved areas, medically underserved populations, and special populations such as migratory and seasonal agricultural workers, people experiencing homelessness, and public housing residents.

Award Range/Average: $116,000 to $22,600,000; average $3,000,000.

Funding: (Project Grants) FY 17 $4,263,000,000; FY 18 est $4,300,000,000; FY 19 est $4,300,000,000; FY 16 $3,862,636,832.

HQ: Bureau of Primary Health Care 5600 Fishers Lane, Room 16N09
Rockville, MD 20857
Phone: 301-594-4300
Email: dmarx@hrsa.gov
http://bphc.hrsa.gov/programopportunities/fundingopportunities/sac/index.html

HEALTH INFORMATION TECHNOLOGY REGIONAL EXTENSION CENTERS PROGRAM

Award: Cooperative Agreements

Purpose: Establish Health Information Technology Regional Extension Centers to identify and disseminate best practices and provide technical assistance supporting the adoption and meaningful use of health IT to improve care quality while protecting patient privacy.

Applicant Eligibility: N/A

Beneficiary Eligibility: N/A

Award Range/Average: Awards for regional centers are expected to average $8.5M.

Funding: Cooperative Agreements (Discretionary Grants) FY 17 est $0; FY 16 est $222,566; FY 18 est $0.

HQ: Office of the National Coordinator for Health Information Technology
Washington, DC 20201
Phone: 202-690-7151
http://healthit.gov

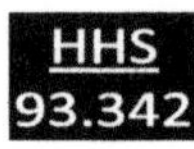

HEALTH PROFESSIONS STUDENT LOANS, INCLUDING PRIMARY CARE LOANS/LOANS FOR DISADVANTAGED STUDENTS "HPSL, PCL, LDS"

Award: Project Grants

Purpose: To increase educational opportunities by providing long-term, low-interest loans to students in need of financial assistance.

Applicant Eligibility: Any accredited public or other nonprofit private school of medicine, dentistry, osteopathic medicine, optometry, podiatry, pharmacy, or veterinary medicine which provides a course of study leading to a degree of Doctor of Medicine or Doctor of Osteopathic Medicine for PCL and LDS borrowers, Doctor of Dentistry (or an equivalent degree), Doctor of Optometry (or an equivalent degree), Doctor of Podiatric Medicine (or an equivalent degree), Bachelor of Science in Pharmacy (or an equivalent degree), Doctor of Pharmacy (or an equivalent degree), or Doctor of Veterinary Medicine (or an equivalent degree) for HPSL and LDS borrowers. Additionally, the school must be located in the United States, the District of Columbia, the Commonwealth of Puerto Rico, the Northern Mariana Islands, the U.S. Virgin Islands, Guam, American Samoa, the Republic of Palau, the Republic of the Marshall Islands, or the Federated States of Micronesia.

Beneficiary Eligibility: Student applicants must display financial need and be enrolled or accepted for enrollment in a health professions school to pursue a full-time course of study leading to a degree as specified above. Students must also be citizens, nationals or lawful permanent residents of the United States, the District of Columbia, the Commonwealths of Puerto Rico, the Northern Mariana Islands, the U.S. Virgin Islands, Guam, American Samoa, the Republic of Palau, the Republic of the Marshall Islands, or the Federated States of Micronesia.

Award Range/Average: $1,780 to $5,545,683 Average: $369,796 per institution

Funding: Project Grants (to capitalize loan funds) FY 17 $20,599,308; FY 18 est $5,551,875; FY 19 est $13,075,592; FY 16 $9,773,066; - LDS Project Grants (to capitalize loan funds)Project Grants (to capitalize loan funds) FY 17 $406,845; FY 18 est $9,854,161.

HQ: Department of Health and Human Services 5600 Fishers Lane, Room 15N58
Rockville, MD 20857
Phone: 301-443-1173
Email: jim.essel@hrsa.hhs.gov
http://bhw.hrsa.gov/scholarshipsloans/index.html

HEALTH PROMOTION & DISEASE PREVENTION RESEARCH CENTERS: PPHF – AFFORDABLE CARE ACT PROJECTS "Prevention Research Centers"

Award: Cooperative Agreements

Purpose: To maintain, and operate academic-based centers for high-quality research and demonstration with respect to health promotion and disease prevention.

Applicant Eligibility: Only applicants who have applied for and have been selected as Prevention Research Centers under CDC Program Announcement DP-14-001 are eligible to apply for the annual continuation funding for the core award and Special Interest Project (SIPS) awards. Funding is limited to Prevention

Research Centers under CDC Program Announcement PA DP-14-001 because they are uniquely positioned to perform, oversee, and coordinate community-based participatory research that promotes the field of prevention research due to their established relationships with community partners.

Beneficiary Eligibility: Academic health centers, scientist/researchers, operational public health programs, targeted high risk groups, selected demonstration areas, and the general public.

Award Range/Average: No Data Available.

Funding: (Cooperative Agreements) FY 17 $19,083,950; FY 18 est $19,084,000; FY 19 est $0; FY 16 $19,084,000.

HQ: 4770 Buford Highway
Atlanta, GA 30341
Phone: 770-488-6384
Email: ijh9@cdc.gov
http://www.cdc.gov

HHS 93.266

HEALTH SYSTEMS STRENGTHENING & HIV/AIDS PREVENTION, CARE & TREATMENT UNDER THE PRESIDENT'S EMERGENCY PLAN FOR AIDS RELIEF "Global HIV/AIDS Program"

Award: Cooperative Agreements

Purpose: To offer training and technical assistance to build and strengthen care programs and health systems.

Applicant Eligibility: Eligibility varies depending on the specific program. Applicants should review the individual HRSA notice of funding opportunity issued under this CFDA for specific eligibility requirements.

Beneficiary Eligibility: Beneficiaries are foreign governments, foreign public or private institutions or organizations, or foreign individuals.

Award Range/Average: International Twinning Center - $500,000 to $10,000,000; Average $10,000,000 Quality Improvement Capacity for Impact Project - $6,000,000 to $20,000,000; Average $10,000,000 International AIDS Education & Training Center $1,000,000 to $60,000,000; Average $55,000,000 Resilient and Responsive Health Systems Initiative (CoAg) - $1,500,000 to $2,000,000; Average $1,500,000 Resilient and Responsive Health Organizations Initiative: Sustainability Communities of Practice Initiative (CoAg) - $750,000 Health Workforce for HIV and Chronic Disease Service Delivery Global Initiative (CoAg) - $30,000,000 Optimizing Momentum Toward Sustainable Epidemic Control (CoAg) - $10,000,000.

Funding: (Cooperative Agreements) FY 17 $38,000,000; FY 18 est $40,000,000; FY 19 est $40,000,000; FY 16 $30,000,000.

HQ: Office of Training and Capacity Development
Rockville, MD 20857
Phone: 301-443-8109
Email: hphillips@hrsa.gov
http://www.hrsa.gov

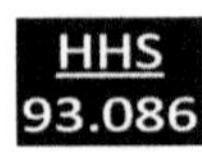

HEALTHY MARRIAGE PROMOTION & RESPONSIBLE FATHERHOOD GRANTS "HMRF"

Award: Project Grants; Dissemination of Technical Information

Purpose: To fund Healthy Marriage Promotion activities that will help couples, who have chosen marriage for themselves, gain greater access to marriage education services on a voluntary basis.

Applicant Eligibility: The Healthy Marriage and Relationship Education Grant Program (HMRE) is part of the U.S. Department of Health and Human Services (HHS), Administration for Children and Families (ACF) efforts to promote HMRE at the community level. The Healthy Marriage program funds organizations that combine marriage and relationship education efforts with a robust effort to address participation barriers and the economic stability needs of their participants.

Beneficiary Eligibility: Persons who may benefit from the assistance includes, families, couples, and individuals in need of assistance with Healthy Marriage services. Services include marriage enhancement and relationship education.

Award Range/Average: $350,000 to $2,000,000

Funding: Project Grants (Discretionary) FY 17 $108,704,468; FY 18 est $108,704,468; FY 19 est $108,713,468; FY 16 $113,460,060.

HQ: 330 C Street SW
Washington, DC 20447
Phone: 202-401-5587
Email: robin.mcdonald@acf.hhs.gov
http://hmrf.acf.hhs.gov

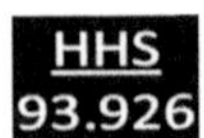

HEALTHY START INITIATIVE "Healthy Start"

Award: Project Grants

Purpose: The program's purpose is to improve perinatal health outcomes by using community-based approaches to service delivery, and to facilitate access to comprehensive health and social services for women, infants, and their families.

Applicant Eligibility: Eligible Project Area All applicants applying for funding under this grant notice must identify themselves as serving an urban, rural, or border community project area. A project area is defined as a geographic community in which the proposed services are to be implemented.

Beneficiary Eligibility: Service area residents, particularly women and infants in areas with significant perinatal health disparities.

Award Range/Average: $750,000- $2,000,000 per year.

Funding: FY 17 $109,028,547; FY 18 est $101,749,283; FY 19 est $100,800,000.

HQ: 5600 Fishers Lane, Room 18N29
Rockville, MD 20857
Phone: 301-443-0543
Email: dcruz@hrsa.gov
http://www.hrsa.gov

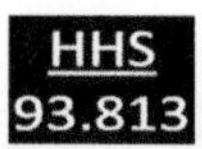

HEART DISEASE & STROKE PREVENTION PROGRAM & DIABETES PREVENTION – STATE & LOCAL PUBLIC HEALTH ACTIONS TO PREVENT OBESITY, DIABETES, AND HEART DISEASE & STROKE

Award: Cooperative Agreements

Purpose: The program's purpose is to support implementation of population-wide and priority population approaches to prevent obesity, diabetes, and heart disease and stroke and reduce health disparities in these areas among adults.

Applicant Eligibility: Eligible Applicants: State Departments of Health or their Bona Fide Agents (includes the District of Columbia) 2. Large city health departments or their bona fide agents, with populations of at least 900,000

Beneficiary Eligibility: States and communities will benefit from this assistance in many ways including through improved clinical and other preventive services for self-management of hypertension, diabetes, overweight and obesity

Award Range/Average: $1,300,000 to $1,760,000 for component 1 and $1,3000 to $1,760,000 for component 2, and $2,600,000 to $3,520,000 per applicant

Funding: (Cooperative Agreements) FY 17 $69,500,000; FY 18 est $69,500,000; FY 19 est $69,500,000; FY 16 $69,500,000.

HQ: 4770 Buford Highway, P.O. Box F75
Atlanta, GA 30341
Phone: 770-488-1431
Email: rnh2@cdc.gov
http://www.cdc.gov

HIGH IMPACT PILOT AWARDS "HIP Awards"

Award: Cooperative Agreements

Purpose: The purpose of these pilots is to advance a scalable process of interoperable exchange of electronic health data using standards that will improve the delivery of how and where healthcare is delivered, improve patient outcomes, and reduce cost. All awardees will be expected to measure the progress of their pilots and the level of impact towards the advancement of interoperability and produce a final evaluation report that includes lessons learned.

Applicant Eligibility: The objective of this award is to advance a scalable process of interoperable exchange of electronic health data using standards that will improve the delivery of how and where health care is delivered, improve patient outcomes, and reduce cost. Collaborative groups of multiple stakeholders across different organizations will be considered, as well as encouraged, to support widespread interoperability.

Beneficiary Eligibility: As health care delivery impacts everyone, the beneficiary eligibility includes all of the listed groups.

Award Range/Average: There has been $1,250,000 for FY 16-17 for this award. We estimate that we would award no more than four (4) awards total; the award amounts would be no less than $250,000 and may not exceed $500,000 per awardee.

Funding: N/A

HQ: 330 C Street SW
Washington, DC 20201
Phone: 202-720-2919
Email: carmel.halloun@hhs.gov
http://www.healthit.gov

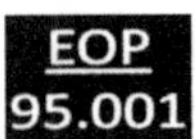

HIGH INTENSITY DRUG TRAFFICKING AREAS PROGRAM "HIDTA"

Award: Project Grants

Purpose: The program works on reducing drug trafficking and drug production in the country by sharing information and implementing enforcement activities among tribal, local and State law enforcement agencies; support law enforcement agencies to help reduce the supply of illegal drugs in the country.

Applicant Eligibility: In order to apply for and receive funds, the law enforcement initiatives must be located and operate in an area designated as a HIDTA by the Director of ONDCP. The request for funding must be supported by the Executive Board of the regional HIDTA under which they will operate.

Beneficiary Eligibility: Law enforcement drug task forces; drug-related law enforcement initiatives; drug-related intelligence or information centers located in designated HIDTAs.

Award Range/Average: Award amounts vary by HIDTA.

Funding: FY 17 $228,300,000; FY 18 est $252,300,000; FY 19 est $252,300,000.

HQ: 750 17th Street NW
Washington, DC 20503
Phone: 202-395-6739
Email: phuong_desear@ondcp.eop.gov
http://www.whitehouse.gov/ondcp

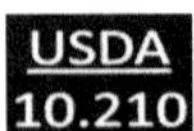

HIGHER EDUCATION – GRADUATE FELLOWSHIPS GRANT PROGRAM

"Institution Challenge, Multicultural Scholars & Graduate Fellowships Grant Program (Graduate Fellowships)"

Award: Project Grants

Purpose: To support students pursuing doctorates in food and agriculture sciences and studies suggested by USDA.

Applicant Eligibility: Proposals may be submitted by all U.S. colleges and universities that confer a master's or doctoral degree in at least one area of the food and agricultural sciences targeted for national needs fellowships. As defined in Section 1404 of the National Agricultural Research, Extension, and Teaching Policy Act of 1977, as amended (7 U.S.C.

Beneficiary Eligibility: Funds awarded in this program are used to support the training of graduate students to obtain either a master's or doctoral degree in one of the targeted specializations of the food and agricultural sciences.

Award Range/Average: If minimum or maximum amounts of funding per competitive and/or capacity project grant, or cooperative agreement are established, these amounts will be announced in the annual Competitive Request for Application (RFA).

Funding: (Project Grants) FY 17 $3,099,600; FY 18 est $3,099,600; FY 19 est $0; FY 16 $3,103,400.

HQ:

Washington, DC 20250-2250

Phone: 202-720-2324

http://nifa.usda.gov/program/national-needs-graduate-and-postgraduate-fellowship-grants-program-funding-opportunity-nnf

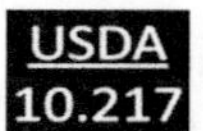

HIGHER EDUCATION – INSTITUTION CHALLENGE GRANTS PROGRAM

"Institution Challenge, Multicultural Scholars & Graduate Fellowships Grant Program (Institution Higher Education Challenge) [Formerly, Challenge or HEC Grants]"

Award: Project Grants

Purpose: Responding to State, regional, national, or international educational needs by strengthening college and university teaching programs in the food and agricultural sciences, and thereby increasing institutional capacities.

Applicant Eligibility: All U.S. public and private nonprofit colleges and universities offering a baccalaureate or first professional degree in at least one discipline or area of the food and agricultural sciences.

Beneficiary Eligibility: All U.S. colleges and universities having a demonstrable capacity to teach the food and agricultural sciences.

Award Range/Average: If minimum or maximum amounts of funding per competitive and/or capacity project grant, or cooperative agreement are established, these amounts will be announced in the annual Competitive Request for Application (RFA).

Funding: (Project Grants) FY 17 $4,565,475; FY 18 est $4,549,875; FY 19 est $0; FY 16 $4,570,425.

HQ: Institute of Youth Family and Community Division of Community and Education 1400 Independence Avenue SW, P.O. Box 2250

Washington, DC 20250-2250

Phone: 202-720-2324

Email: elewis@nifa.usda.gov

http://nifa.usda.gov/program/higher-education-challenge-grants-program

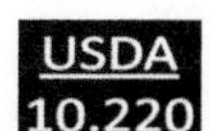

HIGHER EDUCATION – MULTICULTURAL SCHOLARS GRANT PROGRAM

"Institution Challenge, Multicultural Scholars & Graduate Fellowships Grant Program (Multicultural Scholars)"

Award: Project Grants

Purpose: Providing grants to colleges and universities to increase the ethnic and cultural diversity of the food and agricultural scientific and professional work force, and to advance the educational achievement of minority Americans.

Applicant Eligibility: Proposals may be submitted by all U.S. colleges and universities with baccalaureate or higher degree programs in agriculture, natural resources, forestry, veterinary medicine, home economics, and disciplines closely allied to the food and agricultural system, including land-grant colleges and universities, colleges and universities having significant minority enrollments and a demonstrable capacity to carry out the teaching of food and agricultural sciences, and other colleges and universities having a demonstrable capacity to carry out the teaching of food and agricultural sciences.

Beneficiary Eligibility: Funds awarded under this program are used to support full-time undergraduate students pursing a baccalaureate degree in an area of the food and agricultural sciences or a closely allied field. Persons eligible to receive scholarships under this program are students who either are enrolled or have been accepted as full-time baccalaureate or DVM degree candidates, and who are members of groups traditionally under-represented in food and agricultural scientific and professional fields.

Award Range/Average: If minimum or maximum amounts of funding per competitive and/or capacity project grant, or cooperative agreement are established, these amounts will be announced in the annual Competitive Request for Application (RFA).

Funding: (Project Grants) FY 17 $944,775; FY 18 est $944,775; FY 19 est $0; FY 16 $945,400.

HQ: Institute of Youth Family and Community Division of Community and Education 1400 Independence Avenue SW, P.O. Box 2250

Washington, DC 20250-2250

Phone: 202-720-2324

http://nifa.usda.gov/program/higher-education-multicultural-scholars-program-msp

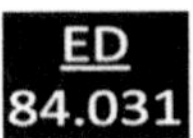

ED 84.031

HIGHER EDUCATION INSTITUTIONAL AID

Award: Project Grants

Purpose: To help eligible colleges and universities to strengthen their management and fiscal operations and to assist them to plan, develop, or implement activities for strengthening the academic quality of their institutions.

Applicant Eligibility: An institution of higher education (IHE) that qualifies as eligible using criteria as specified in the regulations. Under Part A, specific and basic requirements as stated in the program regulations must be met.

Beneficiary Eligibility: Applicant institutions of higher education, including those in the territories and possessions that meet statutory eligibility requirements will benefit.

Award Range/Average: Varies by competition

Funding: (Project Grants) FY 17 $63,281,000; FY 18 est $72,314,000; FY 19 est $63,281,000; FY 16 $63,281,000.

HQ: Department of Education Office of Higher Education Programs Institutional Service

Washington, DC 20202

Phone: 202-453-7348

Email: james.laws@ed.gov

http://www.ed.gov/about/offices/list/ope/idues

USDA 10.223 HISPANIC SERVING INSTITUTIONS EDUCATION GRANTS "HSI Grants"

Award: Project Grants

Purpose: To promote and strengthen the ability of Hispanic-Serving Institutions to carry out higher education programs in the food and agricultural sciences that aim to attract outstanding students. Grants under this program will be awarded to enhance educational equity for underrepresented students; strengthen institutional educational capacities; to prepare students for careers related to the food, agricultural, and natural resource systems of the United States; and to maximize the development and use of resources to improve food and agricultural sciences teaching programs.

Applicant Eligibility: Hispanic serving institutions are eligible to receive funds under this program. "Hispanic serving institutions" means an institution of higher education which, at the time of application, has an enrollment of undergraduate full-time equivalent students that is at least 25 percent Hispanic students, and which (1) admits as regular students only persons having a certificate of graduation from a school providing secondary education, or the recognized equivalent of such certificate; (2) is a public or other nonprofit institutions accredited by a nationally recognized accrediting body; and (3) is legally authorized to provide a program of education beyond the secondary level for which a 2-year associate, baccalaureate, or higher degree is awarded.

Beneficiary Eligibility: Hispanic serving institutions, as identified above, are eligible to receive funds under this program.

Award Range/Average: If minimum or maximum amounts of funding per competitive and/or capacity project grant, or cooperative agreement are established, these amounts will be announced in the annual Competitive Request for Application (RFA).

Funding: (Project Grants) FY 17 $8,806,013; FY 18 est $8,808,579; FY 19 est $8,801,920; FY 16 $8,840,842.

HQ: Institute of Youth Family and Community Division of Community and Education 1400 Independence Avenue SW, P.O. Box 2250
Washington, DC 20250-2250
Phone: 202-720-2324
Email: ilawrence@nifa.usda.gov
http://nifa.usda.gov/funding-opportunity/hispanic-serving-institutions-education-grants-program-hsi

HISTORICALLY BLACK COLLEGES & UNIVERSITIES PROGRAM

Award: Project Grants

Purpose: To help Historically Black Colleges and Universities (HBCUs) expand their role and strength in addressing community development needs in their localities.

Applicant Eligibility: Historically Black Colleges and Universities as determined by the Department of Education in 34 CFR 608.2 pursuant to that Department's responsibilities under Executive Order 13256, dated February 12, 2002.

Beneficiary Eligibility: The principal beneficiaries of the Historically Black Colleges and Universities program will include any city, county, town, township, parish, village, or other general political subdivision of a State within which the HBCU is located. A HBCU located in a metropolitan statistical area, as established by the Office of Management and Budget, may consider its locality to be one or more of these entities within the entire area.

Award Range/Average: The maximum amount a Previously Funded HBCU applicant can request for award is $800,000 for a maximum three-year (36 months) grant performance period. The maximum amount a Previously Unfunded HBCU applicant can request for award is $500,000 for a maximum three-year (36 months) grant performance period.

Funding: Project Grants (Discretionary) FY 11 est $9,780,000; FY 10 est $9,682,200; FY 09 $9,000,000.

HQ: 451 7th Street, Room 8226
Washington, DC 20410
Phone: 202-402-3852
Email: susan.s.brunson@hud.gov
http://www.oup.org/ or www.hud.gov/grants

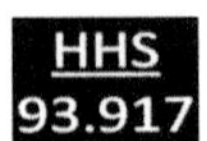

HIV CARE FORMULA GRANTS

Award: Formula Grants

Purpose: To enable States to improve the quality, availability, and organization HIV/AIDS healthcare and support services for eligible individuals living with Human Immunodeficiency Virus disease.

Applicant Eligibility: All 50 States of the United States, and the District of Columbia and U.S. Territories including, the Commonwealth of Puerto Rico, Commonwealth of the Northern Mariana Islands, the Virgin Islands, Guam, American Samoa, the Republic of the Marshall Islands, Federated States of Micronesia, and the Republic of Palau.

Beneficiary Eligibility: Individuals living with HIV.

Award Range/Average: $23,877 to $181,550,889; Average $23,856,580

Funding: (Project Grants) FY 17 $1,407,538,207; FY 18 est $1,500,000,000; FY 19 est $1,500,000,000; FY 16 $1,385,561,174.

HQ:
Rockville, MD 20857
Phone: 301-443-0917
Email: rsterling@hrsa.gov
http://www.hrsa.gov

HIV DEMONSTRATION, RESEARCH, PUBLIC & PROFESSIONAL EDUCATION PROJECTS

Award: Cooperative Agreements

Purpose: To develop and test improved HIV prevention strategies.

Applicant Eligibility: States, political subdivisions of States, other public including American Indian/Alaska Native tribal governments or tribal organizations located wholly or in part within their boundaries, and nonprofit private entities.

Beneficiary Eligibility: Same as Applicant Eligibility.

Award Range/Average: No Data Available.

Funding: (Cooperative Agreements) FY 17 $9,923,758; FY 18 est $9,845,942; FY 19 est $5,925,000; FY 16 $5,781,877.

HQ: 1600 Clifton Road NE, P.O. Box E-07
Atlanta, GA 30333
Phone: 404-639-1877
Email: lrw3@cdc.gov
http://www.cdc.gov/hiv

HIV EMERGENCY RELIEF PROJECT GRANTS

Award: Project Grants

Purpose: Provides financial assistance to Eligible Metropolitan Areas (EMAs) and Transitional Grant Areas (TGAs) that are severely affected by the Human Immunodeficiency Virus (HIV) epidemic to enhance access to high quality, community-based care for low-income individuals and families with HIV and to strengthen strategies to reach minority populations.

Applicant Eligibility: RWHAP Part A recipients that were classified as an EMA or as a TGA in fiscal year (FY) 2007 and continue to meet the statutory requirements are eligible to apply for these funds. For an EMA, this is more than 2,000 cases of AIDS reported and confirmed during the most recent five calendar years, and for a TGA, this is at least 1,000, but fewer than 2,000 cases of AIDS reported and confirmed during the most recent period of five calendar years for which such data are available.

Beneficiary Eligibility: Individuals and families living with HIV disease

Award Range/Average: $2,810,586 to $95,799,060; Average $12,006,679.

Funding: FY 17 $629,697,949; FY 18 est $624,346,301; FY 19 est $624,346,301.

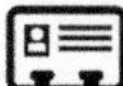

HQ: 5600 Fishers Lane, Room 9W12
Rockville, MD 20857
Phone: 301-443-7136
Email: syoung@hrsa.gov
http://www.hrsa.gov

HIV PREVENTION ACTIVITIES HEALTH DEPARTMENT BASED "HIV Prevention Program: PS12-1201; PS15-1506; PS15-1509; PS17-1711; PS18-1802"

Award: Cooperative Agreements

Purpose: To assist States in meeting the cost of establishing and maintaining HIV prevention programs.

Applicant Eligibility: States, and in consultation with State health authorities, political subdivisions of States including American Indian/Alaska Native tribal governments or tribal organizations located wholly or in part within their boundaries and U.S. territories and possessions.

Beneficiary Eligibility: Same As Applicant Eligibility

Award Range/Average: No Data Available.

Funding: (Cooperative Agreements) FY 17 $349,730,904; FY 18 est $399,583,909; FY 19 est $383,083,909; FY 16 $355,286,556.

HQ: 1600 Clifton Road NE, P.O. Box E-07
Atlanta, GA 30333
Phone: 404-639-8531
Email: eow1@cdc.gov
http://www.cdc.gov/hiv

HIV PREVENTION ACTIVITIES NON-GOVERNMENTAL ORGANIZATION BASED

Award: Cooperative Agreements

Purpose: To provide assistance to nonprofit organizations to develop and implement effective community-based HIV prevention programs related to achieving national goals.

Applicant Eligibility: Nongovernmental public and nonprofit private entities are eligible, including American Indian/Alaska Native tribal governments or tribal organizations located wholly or in part within their boundaries.

Beneficiary Eligibility: Public and nonprofit private entities.

Award Range/Average: No Data Available.

Funding: (Cooperative Agreements) FY 18 est $67,545,000; FY 17 est $78,829,335; FY 16 $74,165,683.

HQ: 1600 Clifton Road NE, P.O. Box E-07
Atlanta, GA 30333
Phone: 404-639-1877
Email: lrw3@cdc.gov
http://www.cdc.gov/hiv

HIV-RELATED TRAINING & TECHNICAL ASSISTANCE

Award: Cooperative Agreements; Project Grants

Purpose: To assess Ryan White HIV/AIDS Program recipients' technical assistance needs and/or provide technical assistance related to building capacity and increasing their ability to provide high quality HIV care and treatment services along the HIV care continuum.

Applicant Eligibility: Entities eligible to apply include public and nonprofit entities (including faith-based and community based organizations) and school and academic health science centers involved in addressing HIV related issues at a national level. Federally Recognized Indian Tribal Government and Native American Organizations are eligible to apply.

Beneficiary Eligibility: Persons living with HIV.

Award Range/Average: FY19: $1,000,000 to $4,145,278; Average $2,728,640

Funding: (Cooperative Agreements) FY 17 $33,371,581; FY 18 est $33,896,488; FY 19 est $32,896,488; - (Project Grants) FY 17 $1,375,460; FY 18 N/A FY 19 N/A.

HQ: 5600 Fishers Lane, Room 9N-160
Rockville, MD 20857
Phone: 301-443-8109
Email: sgagne@hrsa.gov
http://www.hrsa.gov

HUD 14.183 HOME EQUITY CONVERSION MORTGAGES "Section 255"

Award: Guaranteed/Insured Loans

Purpose: To facilitate the elderly homeowners to convert equity in their homes to monthly income or lines of credit.

Applicant Eligibility: Eligible borrowers are persons 62 years of age or older and eligible non-borrowing spouses who are identified at the time of closing. Eligible borrowers and eligible non-borrowing spouses must complete HECM counseling from a HUD-approved agency prior to obtaining the loan.

Beneficiary Eligibility: Individuals.

Award Range/Average: No Data Available.

Funding: (Sale, Exchange, or Donation of Property and Goods) FY 17 est $18,468,953,952; FY 16 est $15,137,995,710; FY 15 $15,988,470,296.

HQ: 451 7th Street SW
Washington, DC 20410
Phone: 800-225-5342
http://portal.hud.gov/hudportal/hud?src=/program_offices/housing/sfh/hecm/hecmhome

HUD 14.239 HOME INVESTMENT PARTNERSHIPS PROGRAM "HOME Program"

Award: Formula Grants

Purpose: To enlarge the supply of affordable housing for low and very low income Americans; to strengthen the abilities of State and local governments for designing and implementing strategies to achieve adequate supplies of affordable housing; and to increase and strengthen partnerships among all levels of government and the private sector.

Applicant Eligibility: States, cities, urban counties, and consortia (of contiguous units of general local governments with a binding agreement) are eligible to receive formula allocations; funds are also set aside for grants to Insular Areas.

Beneficiary Eligibility: For rental housing, at least 90 percent of HOME funds must benefit low and very low income families at 60 percent of the area median income; the remaining ten percent must benefit families below 80 percent of the area median. Assistance to homeowners and homebuyers must be to families below 80 percent of the area median.

Award Range/Average: $205,547 to $75,481,734; $2,117,854 average.

Funding: (Formula Grants) FY 17 $950,000,000; FY 18 est $1,362,000,000; FY 19 est $0.

HQ: 451 7th Street SW, Room 7164
Washington, DC 20410
Phone: 202-708-2684
Email: peter.h.huber@hud.gov
http://www.hud.gov/homeprogram

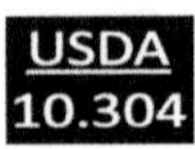

HOMELAND SECURITY AGRICULTURAL "Food and Agriculture Defense Initiative (FADI) (Homeland Security Program)"

Award: Cooperative Agreements

Purpose: To compensate for the agricultural products through cooperative agreements such as national animal health, plant diagnostic network, pest information platform, etc.

Applicant Eligibility: In accordance with section 1472(c) of the National Agricultural Research, Extension, and Teaching Policy Act of 1977, (NARETPA) applicant may be: State agricultural experiment stations, State cooperative extension services, all colleges and universities, other research or education institutions and organizations, Federal and private agencies and organizations, individuals, and any other contractor or recipient, either foreign or domestic, to further research, extension, or teaching programs in the food and agricultural sciences of the Department of Agriculture.

Beneficiary Eligibility: Same as Applicant Eligibility.

Award Range/Average: If minimum or maximum amounts of funding per Capacity, Competitive, and/or Non-Competitive project grant, or cooperative agreement are established, these amounts will be announced in the annual Capacity, Competitive, and/or Non-Competitive Request for Application (RFA).

Funding: (Cooperative Agreements) FY 17 $7,680,000; FY 18 est $7,680,000; FY 19 est $0; FY 16 $6,432,000.

HQ: 1400 Independence Avenue SW, P.O. Box 2201
Washington, DC 20250-2201
Phone: 202-401-1112
http://nifa.usda.gov/grants

HOMELAND SECURITY BIOWATCH PROGRAM

Award: Project Grants; Use of Property, Facilities, and Equipment

Purpose: The BioWatch program is an aerosolized biological agent detection and warning system that helps to prevent bioterrorist events in the country.

Applicant Eligibility: Generally, State and local governments or as specified by U.S. Appropriation Statute. Specific applicant eligibility will be identified in the funding opportunity announcement and program guidance.

Beneficiary Eligibility: State and local governments.

Award Range/Average: Specified in the announcement.

Funding: (Salaries and Expenses) FY 17 $27,000,000; FY 18 est $27,842,000; FY 19 est $27,810,000.

HQ: DHS 245 Murray Lane SW, P.O. Box 0115
Washington, DC 20528
Phone: 703-647-8052
Email: daniel.yereb@hq.dhs.gov
http://www.dhs.gov

DHS 97.067 HOMELAND SECURITY GRANT PROGRAM "HSGP"

Award: Formula Grants

Purpose: The program's objective is to fund for the local and state's preparedness against natural calamities and terrorist and cyber terrorist activities.

Applicant Eligibility: All 56 states and territories, which includes any state of the United States, the District of Columbia, the Commonwealth of Puerto Rico, the U.S. Virgin Islands, Guam, American Samoa, and the Commonwealth of the Northern Mariana Islands, are eligible to apply for SHSP funds. The State Administrative Agency (SAA) is the only entity eligible to submit HSGP applications to DHS/FEMA, including those applications submitted on behalf of UASI and OPSG applicants.

Beneficiary Eligibility: U.S. Territories, State, Local THSGP: In order to be eligible to receive THSGP funding, recipients must be directly eligible Tribes. Directly eligible Tribes are Federally recognized Tribes that meet the criteria set forth in Section 2001 of the Homeland Security Act of 2002, as amended (6 U.S.C.

Award Range/Average: For more information, refer to the FY 2018 HSGP and THSGP Notice of Funding Opportunity.

Funding: FY 17 $1,037,000,000; FY 18 est $1,067,000,000; FY 19 est $1,067,000,000.

HQ: Department of Homeland Security 400 C Street SW
Washington, DC 20523
Phone: 800-368-6498
http://www.fema.gov/homeland-security-grant-program

HOMELAND SECURITY PREPAREDNESS TECHNICAL ASSISTANCE PROGRAM "HSPTAP"

Award: Cooperative Agreements

Purpose: The Homeland Security Technical Assistance Program builds State and local capabilities to detect, prevent, protect, respond and recover from threats and acts of terrorism.

Applicant Eligibility: Eligible Applicants: DHS Preparedness Homeland Security Grant Program grantees and sub-grantees.

Beneficiary Eligibility: State and local units of government.

Award Range/Average: Refer to program guidance document.

Funding: (Cooperative Agreements) FY 16 $525,000; FY 18 est $525,000; FY 17 est $525,000.

HQ: FEMA DHS/FEMA 500 C Street, 7th Floor
Washington, DC 20472-3100
Phone: 202-786-0849
Email: john.allen5@fema.dhs.gov
http://www.fema.gov

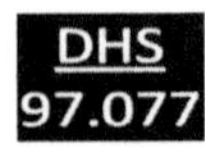

HOMELAND SECURITY RESEARCH, DEVELOPMENT, TESTING, EVALUATION, AND DEMONSTRATION OF TECHNOLOGIES RELATED TO NUCLEAR THREAT DETECTION "Countering Weapons of Mass Destruction (CWMD)"

Award: Cooperative Agreements

Purpose: The program's objective is to prevent nuclear or radiological terrorist attacks in the country.

Applicant Eligibility: State (includes District of Columbia, public institutions of higher education and hospitals), Local (includes State-designated Indian Tribes, excludes institutions of higher education and hospitals, Public nonprofit institution/organization (includes institutions of higher education and hospitals), Other public institution/organization Eligible Applicants: The ARI is limited to State, public or private accredited institutions of higher education. The ER Program supports State, Public nonprofit institution/ organizations; Private nonprofit institution/organizations; Small businesses; Profit organizations and Other private institution/organizations.

Beneficiary Eligibility: ARI: State, public or private accredited institutions of higher education; Scientists/ Researcher; Graduate Student; Education (13+). Exploratory Research: Public Nonprofit Institution/ Organization; Small Business; Profit Organization; Private Organization; Other Private Institution/ organization; Scientists/Researcher; State, public or private accredited institutions of higher education.

Award Range/Average: See announcement and program guidance.

Funding: FY 17 $10,802,277; FY 18 est $5,661,247; FY 19 est $8,108,503.

HQ: 245 Murray Lane SW DNDO, P.O. Box 0550
Washington, DC 20528
Phone: 202-254-7109
http://www.dhs.gov/about-domestic-nuclear-detection-office

HOMELAND SECURITY, RESEARCH, TESTING, EVALUATION, AND DEMONSTRATION OF TECHNOLOGIES

Award: Cooperative Agreements

Purpose: Provides funding and/or property to conduct research and check the readiness of homeland security agencies to respond to the terrorist threats.

Applicant Eligibility: States, local governments, private, public, profit or nonprofit organizations, Indian Tribal governments, or individuals specified by U.S. Appropriation Statute, including U.S. and international institutions of higher education and educational laboratories.

Beneficiary Eligibility: Federal, State, and local governments, private, public, profit or nonprofit organizations, Indian tribal governments, and individuals.

Award Range/Average: Refer to program guidance.

Funding: (Salaries and Expenses) FY 16 $1,548,332; FY 17 est $2,716,638; FY 18 est $2,000,000.

HQ: S and T Directorate 245 Murray Lane SW
Washington, DC 20528
Phone: 202-254-6748
http://www.dhs.gov

HUD 14.261 HOMELESS MANAGEMENT INFORMATION SYSTEMS TECHNICAL ASSISTANCE "HMIS TA"

Award: Cooperative Agreements

Purpose: See HUD Community Compass CFDA14.259

Applicant Eligibility: This is now included in HUD Community Compass

Beneficiary Eligibility: Same as Applicant Eligibility.

Award Range/Average: $750,000 award minimum

Funding: (Cooperative Agreements) FY 16 est $0; FY 17 est $0; FY 18 est $0.

HQ: Office of Special Needs Assistance Programs Office of Community Planning and Development, Department of Housing and Urban Development Room 7262
Washington, DC 20410
Phone: 202-708-1226
http://www.onecpd.info

HHS 93.074 HOSPITAL PREPAREDNESS PROGRAM (HPP) & PUBLIC HEALTH EMERGENCY PREPAREDNESS (PHEP) ALIGNED COOPERATIVE AGREEMENTS "HPP/PHEP"

Award: Formula Grants

Purpose: The purpose of the 2017-2018 HPP-PHEP aligned programs cooperative agreement is to provide resources that support state, local, territorial, and tribal public health departments and healthcare systems/ organizations.

Applicant Eligibility: N/A

Beneficiary Eligibility: N/A

Award Range/Average: FY 2018: Range: $579,108 to $65,814,534 Average: $13,552,419

Funding: Formula Grants (Cooperative Agreements) FY 17 $840,250,000; FY 18 est $851,750,000; FY 19 est $851,750,000; FY 16 $840,250,000.

HQ: 1600 Clifton Road
Atlanta, GA 30333
Phone: 404-639-0817
Email: lss1@cdc.gov
http://www.cdc.gov

HHS 93.817 HOSPITAL PREPAREDNESS PROGRAM (HPP) EBOLA PREPAREDNESS & RESPONSE ACTIVITIES

Award: Formula Grants

Purpose: The program covers two separate, but related projects which are Part A – healthcare System Preparedness for Ebola and Part B – Development of a Regional Network for Ebola Patient Care.

Applicant Eligibility: Eligible applicants are the 62 Hospital Preparedness Program (HPP) awardees, which include health departments in all 50 States, the District of Columbia, the nation's three largest municipalities (Chicago, Los Angeles County, and New York City, the Commonwealths of Puerto Rico and the Northern Mariana Islands, the territories of American Samoa, Guam, and the United States Virgin Islands, the Federated States of Micronesia, and the Republics of Palau and the Marshall Islands.

Beneficiary Eligibility: Health departments listed above, hospitals and supporting health care systems

Award Range/Average: Part A - Health Care System Preparedness for Ebola: Range: $202,989 - $15,229,780 Est. Average Amount: $2,612,903 Part B - Development of a Regional Network for Ebola Patient Care: Range: $3,250,000 - $4,600,000 Est. Average Amount: $3,250,000

Funding: Formula Grants (Cooperative Agreements) FY 17 $21,670,730; FY 18 est $21,670,730; FY 19 est $21,670,730; FY 16 est $4,738,688; - Part A - Health Care System Preparedness for Ebola: $162,000,000 Part B - Development of a Regional Network for Ebola Patient

HQ: Division of National Healthcare Preparedness Programs Office of the Assistant Secretary for Preparedness and Response, US Department of Health and Human 200 C Street SW RM C4K12

Washington, DC 20024

Phone: 202-245-0732

Email: robert.dugas@hhs.gov

http://www.phe.gov

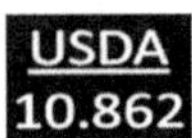

HOUSEHOLD WATER WELL SYSTEM GRANT PROGRAM "HWWS"

Award: Project Grants

Purpose: To assist nonprofit organizations in construction, refurbishing, and household water well systems in rural areas for those with low-income.

Applicant Eligibility: An applicant must be a private organization, organized as a non-profit corporation. The applicant must have the legal capacity and authority to perform the obligations of the grant.

Beneficiary Eligibility: An individual in a household in which the combined income of all household members (for the most recent 12 months) does not exceed 100 percent of the median non-metropolitan household income for the State or territory in which the individual resides.

Award Range/Average: $75,000 to $350,000. Avg. $198680

Funding: (Project Grants) FY 17 $993,000; FY 18 est $993,000; FY 19 FY 16 $1,192,081.

HQ: Department of Agriculture 1400 Independence Avenue SW, P.O. Box 1548

Washington, DC 20250

Phone: 202-690-2670

http://www.rd.usda.gov/programs-services/all-programs/water-environmental-programs

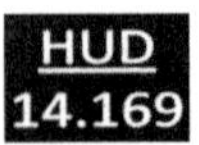

HOUSING COUNSELING ASSISTANCE PROGRAM

Award: Project Grants

Purpose: To advocate homeowners, homebuyers, potential renters and tenants under HUD and other government programs in improving their housing conditions and meeting the responsibilities of tenancy and homeownership.

Applicant Eligibility: Qualified public or private nonprofit organizations. There are four categories of eligible applicants: (1) HUD-approved local housing counseling agency; (2) HUD-approved national or regional intermediary; (3) State housing finance agency; and (4) multi-state organizations.

Beneficiary Eligibility: Individuals, groups of individuals, and families who are renters, tenants, homeowners, and home buyers under HUD, conventional and other government programs.

Award Range/Average: Range and average of financial assistance: For Fiscal Year 2012, the minimum request from a local agency was $15,000 and the maximum request from an intermediary was $3,000,000. The average local agency counseling grant was approximately $20,500. The average intermediary award was approximately $990,000.

Funding: Project Grants (Cooperative Agreements) FY 17 est $43,000,000; FY 16 est $45,000,000; FY 15 $42,000,000.

HQ: 451 7th Street SW
Washington, DC 20410
Phone: 800-225-5342
http://portal.hud.gov/hudportal/hud?src=/program_offices/housing/sfh/hcc/hcc_home

HOUSING COUNSELING TRAINING PROGRAM

Award: Project Grants

Purpose: To support the delivery of training activities for counselors from agencies participating in HUD's Housing Counseling program, and thereby improving the quality of counseling provided by housing counselors.

Applicant Eligibility: Applicants must be public or private nonprofit organizations with a least two years of experience providing housing counseling training services nationwide.

Beneficiary Eligibility: Housing Counselors from HUD-approved housing counseling agencies.

Award Range/Average: Average award size is $666,666.

Funding: (Project Grants) FY 16 est $4,000,000; FY 17 est $4,000,000; FY 15 $3,000,000.

HQ: 451 7th Street SW
Washington, DC 20410
Phone: 800-225-5342
http://portal.hud.gov/hudportal/hud?src=/program_offices/housing/sfh/hcc/hcc_home

HOUSING FINANCE AGENCIES (HFA) RISK SHARING "542(c) Risk Sharing Program)"

Award: Guaranteed/Insured Loans

Purpose: To provide credit enhancement for mortgages for multifamily housing projects whose loans are underwritten, processed, serviced, and disposed of.

Applicant Eligibility: Eligible mortgagors, who include investors, builders, developers, public entities, and private nonprofit corporations or associations, may apply to a qualified HFA. To be eligible for HUD's approval, the HFA must: (1) carry the designation of "top tier" or its equivalent as evaluated by Standard and Poors or another nationally recognized rating agency; (2) receive an overall rating of "A" for the HFA for its general obligation bonds from a nationally recognized rating agency; and (3) otherwise demonstrate its capacity as a sound, well-managed agency that is experienced in financing multifamily housing.

Beneficiary Eligibility: Individuals, families, and property owners may be eligible for affordable housing.

Award Range/Average: No Data Available.

Funding: (Guaranteed/Insured Loans) FY 16 est $430,586,683; FY 14 est $325,000,000; FY 17 est $458,350,159; FY 13 $355,000,000; FY 15 $409,997,152.

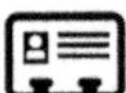

HQ: 451 7th Street SW
Washington, DC 20410
Phone: 202-402-2579
Email: carmelita_a._james@hud.gov
http://www.hud.gov/offices/hsg/mfh/progdesc/progdesc.cfm

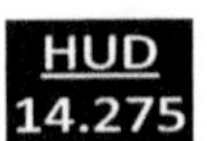

HOUSING TRUST FUND
"Housing Trust Fund"

Award: Formula Grants

Purpose: To expand and preserve the supply of affordable housing, particularly rental housing, for extremely low-income and very low income households.

Applicant Eligibility: States as defined in 24 CFR 93.2 are eligible to receive formula allocations.

Beneficiary Eligibility: At least 75 percent of funds must be used for extremely low-income families, or families with incomes at or below the poverty line (whichever is greater), unless the allocation is below $1 billion, at which point 100 percent of the funds must be used for extremely low-income families.

Award Range/Average: $11,349 to $35,619,586; average is $4,763,846.

Funding: (Formula Grants) FY 17 $217,084,000; FY 18 est $187,940,000; FY 19 est $0.

HQ: 451 7th Street SW, Room 7164
Washington, DC 20410
Phone: 202-402-3941
Email: peter.h.huber@hud.gov
http://www.hudexchange.info/program/htf

HUBZONE PROGRAM

Award: Provision of Specialized Services

Purpose: To provide federal contracting assistance for qualified small business concerns (SBCs) located in Historically Underutilized Business Zones in an effort to increase employment opportunities, investment, and economic development in such areas.

Applicant Eligibility: To be eligible to participate in the program, a firm must (1) be a small business (as defined by SBA Size Standards), (2) be at least 51% owned and controlled by one or more U.S. citizens, a Community Development Corporation, an agricultural cooperative, a Native Hawaiian Organization, or an Indian tribe, (3) be located (principal office) in a HUBZone, and (4) certify that least 35 percent of its employees are residents of a HUBZone.

Beneficiary Eligibility: The HUBZone Program is precisely targeted to provide contract opportunities - revenue sources - to firms located in approximately 19,467 qualified census tracts, 767 qualified non-metropolitan counties, 593 qualified Indian Lands, 108 qualified base closure areas, and 37 Qualified Disaster Areas.

Award Range/Average: N/A

Funding: (Salaries and Expenses) FY 17 $2,792,000; FY 18 est $3,000,000; FY 19 est $2,500,000.

HQ: 409 3rd Street SW, 8th Floor
Washington, DC 20410
Phone: 202-205-2985
Email: mariana.pardo@sba.gov
http://www.sba.gov/hubzone

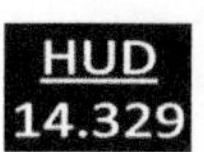

HUD MULTIFAMILY PFS PILOT
"Multifamily Assisted Housing Pay For Success Energy and Water Conservation Pilot"

Award: Direct Payments for Specified Use

Purpose: To save taxpayer money; develop a Pay For Success model for funding and delivering energy and water conservation improvements; evaluate the effectiveness of energy and water conservation retrofits; and identify lessons learned and best practices in order to assess the feasibility of scaling up and replicating this approach to achieving energy and water conservation.

Applicant Eligibility: HUD will make performance-based payments to entities serving as Intermediaries under a cooperative agreement executed with the agency. Payments will be contingent on utility consumption and cost savings associated with energy and water conservation measures installed by the Intermediary at HUD-assisted multifamily properties.

Beneficiary Eligibility: Same as Applicant Eligibility.

Award Range/Average: No Data Available.

Funding: N/A

HQ: US Department of Housing and Urban Development, Office of the Deputy Assistant Secretary for Multifamily Housing Programs 451 7th Street SW Room 6106
Washington, DC 20410
Phone: 202-402-3372
Email: mark.a.kudlowitz@hud.gov
http://portal.hud.gov/hudportal/hud?src=/program_offices/housing/mfh

HUMAN GENOME RESEARCH
"Human Genome Project"

Award: Project Grants

Purpose: To support the development of resources and technologies that will accelerate genome research and its application to human health and genomic medicine.

Applicant Eligibility: Research Projects: Awards can be made to any public or private, for-profit or nonprofit university, college, hospital, laboratory, or other institution, including State and local units of government, qualifying small businesses (through the Small Business Innovation Research/STTR Programs, and to individuals. SBIR grants can be awarded only to domestic small businesses (entities that are independently owned and operated for profit, are not dominant in the field in which research is proposed, and have no more than 500 employees).

Beneficiary Eligibility: Any nonprofit or for-profit organization, company, or institution engaged in biomedical research can apply for research support.

Award Range/Average: $26,000 – $19,996,553.

Funding: (Project Grants) FY 18 est $287,953,000; FY 16 $377,186,406; FY 17 est $389,196,000.

HQ: 6700B Rockledge Drive, Room 3186
Bethesda, MD 20892
Phone: 301-496-7531
Email: grahambj@exchange.nih.gov
http://www.genome.gov

HHS 93.944 HUMAN IMMUNODEFICIENCY VIRUS (HIV)/ACQUIRED IMMUNODEFICIENCY VIRUS SYNDROME (AIDS) SURVEILLANCE "HIV/AIDS Surveillance"

Award: Cooperative Agreements

Purpose: To continue and strengthen effective human immunodeficiency virus (HIV) and acquired immunodeficiency syndrome (AIDS) surveillance programs and to affect, maintain, measure and evaluate the extent of HIV/AIDS incidence and prevalence throughout the United States and its territories.

Applicant Eligibility: The governments, or their agents or instrumentalities, of any of the States of the United States, the District of Columbia, the Commonwealth of Puerto Rico, territories or possessions of United States, including American Indian/Alaska Native tribal governments or tribal organizations located wholly or in part within their boundaries, and local governments who are current recipients of HIV/AIDS surveillance cooperative agreements.

Beneficiary Eligibility: Official health agencies will benefit.

Award Range/Average: No Data Available.

Funding: (Cooperative Agreements) FY 17 $81,670,365; FY 18 est $26,150,317; FY 19 est $24,166,107; FY 16 $78,939,621.

HQ: 1600 Clifton Road NE, P.O. Box E-07
Atlanta, GA 30333
Phone: 404-639-1877
Email: lrw3@cdc.gov
http://www.cdc.gov

HURRICANE SANDY COMMUNITY DEVELOPMENT BLOCK GRANT DISASTER RECOVERY GRANTS (CDBG-DR) "Community Development Block Grant Disaster Recovery program for Hurricane Sandy and other qualifying disasters occurring in 2011, 2012 and 2013"

Award: Formula Grants

Purpose: To develop viable urban communities for persons of low and moderate income.

Applicant Eligibility: CDBG Disaster Recovery funds are made available to States and units of general local governments designated by the President of the United States as disaster areas. These communities must have significant unmet recovery needs and the capacity to carry out a disaster recovery program (usually these are governments that already receive HOME or Community Development Block Grant allocations).

Beneficiary Eligibility: The principal beneficiaries of CDBG DR funds are low- and moderate-income persons (generally defined as a member of a family having an income equal to or less than the Section 8 low income limit established by HUD) in communities that have experienced a disaster event. At least 50 percent of each grantee's CDBG-DR grant award must be used for activities that benefit low- and moderate-income (LMI) persons.

Award Range/Average: From low of $5,061,000 a high of $4,416,882,000

Funding: (Formula Grants) FY 17 $5,424,129,914; FY 18 est $0; FY 19 est $0; FY 16 $8,757,761,836; - These funds represent obligations to the thirty four (34) currently identified state and local government grantees during each of the named fiscal years for disaster recovery from Hurricane Sandy and other federally declared disasters that occurred in 2011, 2012, and 2013.

HQ: DRSI 451 7th Street SW, Room 7272
Washington, DC 20410
Phone: 817-978-5948
Email: phyllis.j.foulds@hud.gov
http://portal.hud.gov/hudportal/hud?src=/program_offices/comm_planning/communitydevelopment/programs/drsi

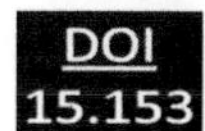

HURRICANE SANDY DISASTER RELIEF – COASTAL RESILIENCY GRANTS

Award: Project Grants

Purpose: The main objective of this program is to provide grants for disaster assistance for Hurricane Sandy. Funds shall be used by recipients to assist Interior and its bureaus/offices to restore and rebuild national parks, national wildlife refuges, and enhance the resiliency and capacity of coastal habitat and infrastructure to withstand storms and bring down the amount of damage caused by such storms.

Applicant Eligibility: Anyone / general public

Beneficiary Eligibility: Anyone / general public.

Award Range/Average: New program, have not allocated yet

Funding: N/A

HQ: Department of the Interior 1849 C Street NW, Room 4257
Washington, DC 20240
Phone: 202-513-0692
Email: megan_olsen@ios.doi.gov

IAF ASSISTANCE FOR OVERSEAS PROGRAMS

Award: Project Grants

Purpose: To strengthen the bonds of friendship and understanding among the peoples in the Western Hemisphere.

Applicant Eligibility: N/A

Beneficiary Eligibility: N/A

Award Range/Average: The range of financial assistance is up to $400,000 per grant award.

Funding: (Project Grants) FY 18 est $12,149,235; FY 17 est $16,657,463; FY 16 $11,930,945.

HQ: 1331 Pennsylvania Avenue NW, Suite 1200N
Washington, DC 20004
Phone: 202-803-6098
Email: cwood@iaf.gov
http://www.iaf.gov

IIP – AMERICAN SPACES "U.S. Department of State, Bureau of International Information Programs, Office of American Spaces"

Award: Project Grants

Purpose: American Spaces are publicly accessible facilities designed to build and strengthen relationships with foreign audiences, showcase the American culture and values, and provide information about the United States in an environment that inspires dialogue. Users get to enjoy access to physical collections and also explore the many electronic resources available.

Applicant Eligibility: The State Department's Public Diplomacy Strategic Framework calls for the revitalization of existing American Spaces and the establishment of new ones. American Spaces support one of the Secretary of State's five strategic imperatives for 21st century public diplomacy – that of building mutual trust and respect through expanded public diplomacy platforms.

Beneficiary Eligibility: Foreign audiences.

Award Range/Average: N/A

Funding: (Project Grants) FY 16 est $15,000,000.

HQ: 2200 C Street NW
Washington, DC 20037
Phone: 202-632-9204
Email: bairdem@state.gov

IIP INDIVIDUAL GRANTS
"U.S. Speaker Program Grants, Bureau of International Information Programs (IIP)"

Award: Project Grants

Purpose: The Office of the U.S. Speaker Program of the Department of State's Bureau of International Information Programs awards grants to cooperating organizations with experience in international exchanges for the administration of projects that enable U.S. experts to present lectures, serve as consultants, or conduct workshops and seminars for professional audiences worldwide.

Applicant Eligibility: N/A

Beneficiary Eligibility: N/A

Award Range/Average: N/A

Funding: (Project Grants (including individual awards) FY 17 $3,900,000; FY 18 est $4,201,000; FY 19 N/A FY 16 est $3,500,000; FY 15 est $3,500,000; FY 14 $3,407,036.

HQ: 2200 C Street NW
Washington, DC 20037
Phone: 202-632-9204
Email: bairdem@state.gov

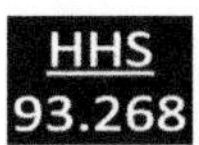

IMMUNIZATION COOPERATIVE AGREEMENTS
"Immunizations CoAg and Vaccines for Children Program previously published as Immunization Grants and Vaccines for Children Program"

Award: Project Grants

Purpose: To assist states and communities in establishing and maintaining preventive health service programs to immunize individuals against vaccine-preventable diseases.

Applicant Eligibility: Any U.S. state, and in consultation with state health authorities, political subdivisions of states and other public entities and U.S. territories may apply; private individuals and private nonprofit agencies are not eligible for immunization grants.

Beneficiary Eligibility: Any U.S. state, political subdivision (as described above), and other public entities will benefit.

Award Range/Average: 317 Grants: From $252,725 to $48,568,982; $6,870,723 VFC Grants: From $1,649,229 to $368,026,903; $52,334,322.

Funding: (Cooperative Agreements) FY 17 $145,052,647; FY 18 est $330,791,211; FY 19 est $329,486,648; FY 16 $151,109,102.

HQ: 1600 Clifton Road, P.O. Box 19
Atlanta, GA 30333
Phone: 404-639-7824
Email: ibr0@cdc.gov
http://www.cdc.gov/vaccines

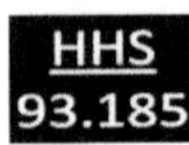

IMMUNIZATION RESEARCH, DEMONSTRATION, PUBLIC INFORMATION & EDUCATION TRAINING & CLINICAL SKILLS IMPROVEMENT PROJECTS

Award: Cooperative Agreements

Purpose: Assists states, political subdivisions of states, and other public and private nonprofit entities to conduct research, demonstration projects, and provide public information on vaccine-preventable diseases and conditions.

Applicant Eligibility: Under Section 317(k) of the Public Health Service Act: States, political subdivision of states, and other public and private nonprofit entities.

Beneficiary Eligibility: Same As Applicant Eligibility.

Award Range/Average: Varies

Funding: FY 17 $8,407,817; FY 18 est $14,948,051; FY 19 est $14,948,051.

HQ: NCIRD 1600 Clifton Road, P.O. Box A-27
Atlanta, GA 30333
Phone: 404-639-2110
Email: ezs8@cdc.gov
http://www.cdc.gov

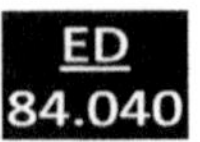

IMPACT AID FACILITIES MAINTENANCE

Award: Project Grants

Purpose: To maintain school facilities used to serve federally connected military dependent students that are owned by the Department of Education and operated by local educational agencies (LEAs), and to transfer those facilities to the LEAs, where appropriate.

Applicant Eligibility: LEAs that operate school facilities owned by the Department of Education.

Beneficiary Eligibility: Public elementary and secondary school children benefit.

Award Range/Average: N/A.

Funding: FY 17 $4,835,000; FY 18 est $4,835,000; FY 19 est $4,835,000.

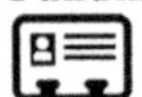
HQ: Department of Education 400 Maryland Avenue SW, Room 3E105
Washington, DC 20202
Phone: 202-205-8724
Email: marilyn.hall@ed.gov
http://www.ed.gov/about/offices/list/oese/impactaid/index.htmlsa

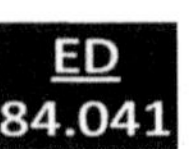

IMPACT AID

Award: Formula Grants; Project Grants

Purpose: To provide financial assistance to local educational agencies (LEAs) affected by Federal activities through 7002, 7003, and 7007 ESEA sections.

Applicant Eligibility: Local educational agencies that provide free public elementary or secondary education may apply. Under Section 7002, generally, assistance is provided to districts where an aggregate of 10 percent or more of the assessed valuation of all real property in the school district as of the time(s) of acquisition has been acquired by the Federal Government since 1938 and the district is not being substantially compensated by revenue from activities on the eligible Federal property.

Beneficiary Eligibility: Public elementary and secondary school children benefit.

Award Range/Average: Basic Support payments is expected to be between $50- $57,000,000 with an average award of $1,200,000; for Payments for Children With Disabilities, $500- $1,100,000 with an average award of $57,000.

Funding: Project Grants (Discretionary) FY 17 $17,406,000; FY 18 est $0; FY 19 est $17,406,000; FY 16 $0; (Formula Grants) FY 17 $1,189,233,000; FY 18 est $1,287,648,000; FY 19 est $1,294,242,000; FY 16 $1,233,955,000; (Formula Grants) FY 17 $66,813,000.

HQ: Department of Education 400 Maryland Avenue SW, Room 3E105
Washington, DC 20202
Phone: 202-205-8724
Email: marilyn.hall@ed.gov
http://www.ed.gov/about/offices/list/oese/impactaid/index.html

IMPROVING EPILEPSY PROGRAMS, SERVICES, AND OUTCOMES THROUGH NATIONAL PARTNERSHIPS
"Epilepsy Programs"

Award: Cooperative Agreements

Purpose: The purpose of this program is to reduce the treatment gap by improving professional education about epilepsy diagnosis, treatment, and management.

Applicant Eligibility: Open and full competition. However, to fulfill the requirements of the cooperative agreement, applicants must be able to demonstrate that their organization has specialized knowledge and experience addressing the complex and challenging health and social needs of individuals with epilepsy and their families.

Beneficiary Eligibility: Individual/Family Racial/ethnic minority groups People with disabilities Specialty group Children Adults Older adults Schools Health Professional Educational Professional Student/trainee Low income Moderate income Rural Urban Suburban Education (0-13+) Nonprofit groups

Award Range/Average: 1 award expected for $3,200,000;

Funding: (Cooperative Agreements) FY 17 $3,525,691; FY 18 est $3,567,141; FY 19 est $3,567,141; FY 16 $3,175,691; - 1 award.

HQ: 4770 Buford Highway NE, P.O. Box F-78
Atlanta, GA 30341
Phone: 770-488-5598
Email: mmoore6@cdc.gov
http://www.cdc.gov

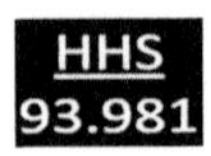

IMPROVING STUDENT HEALTH & ACADEMIC ACHIEVEMENT THROUGH NUTRITION, PHYSICAL ACTIVITY & THE MANAGEMENT OF CHRONIC CONDITIONS IN SCHOOLS

Award: Cooperative Agreements

Purpose: This program helps children and adolescents reduce their risk of developing any chronic or long-term disease. The program strives to achieve this by increasing the number of students who consume nutritious food and beverages, increasing the number of students who take part in a daily physical activity and prevent the outbreak of chronic illnesses at educational areas.

Applicant Eligibility: The intent of this funding opportunity announcement (FOA) is to improve the health and educational outcomes of youth/adolescents through the implementation of evidence-based strategies and activities within school settings. Funding eligibility is limited to state education agencies or equivalents since these agencies have the greatest likelihood of reaching Local Education Areas, schools and the youth/adolescents they serve.

Beneficiary Eligibility: The intent of this FOA is to improve the health and educational outcomes of youth/adolescents through the implementation of evidence-based strategies and activities within school settings. Funding eligibility is limited to state education agencies or equivalents since these agencies have the greatest likelihood of reaching Local Education Areas, schools and the youth/adolescents they serve.

Award Range/Average: Estimated floor of award: $300,000 Estimated average award: $355,000 Estimated ceiling of award: $375,000

Funding: (Cooperative Agreements) FY 17 $0; FY 18 est $6,693,000; FY 19 est $6,693,000; FY 16 $0; - This funding amount support a new program for FY 18. FY 19 will be the continuation year.

HQ: 4770 Buford Highway NE
Atlanta, GA 30341
Phone: 770-488-6103
http://www.cdc.gov

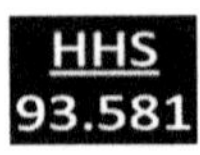

IMPROVING THE CAPABILITY OF INDIAN TRIBAL GOVERNMENTS TO REGULATE ENVIRONMENTAL QUALITY "Environmental Regulatory Enhancement (ERE)"

Award: Project Grants

Purpose: To provide funding for the costs of planning, developing, and implementing programs designed to improve the capability of tribal governing bodies to regulate environmental quality pursuant to federal and tribal environmental laws.

Applicant Eligibility: Eligible applicants include, federally recognized Indian tribes; consortia of Indian tribes; incorporated non-federally recognized tribes; incorporated state-recognized tribes; Alaska Native villages, as defined in the Alaska Native Claims Settlement Act (ANCSA) and/or non-profit village consortia; non-profit Alaska Native regional corporation/associations in Alaska with village specific projects; other tribal or village organizations or consortia of Indian tribes; and Tribal governing bodies (IRA or traditional councils) as recognized by the Bureau of Indian Affairs.

Beneficiary Eligibility: Federally recognized Indian tribes; Consortia of Indian tribes; Incorporated non-federally recognized tribes; Incorporated state-recognized tribes; Alaska Native villages, as defined in the ANCSA and/or non-profit village consortia; Non-profit Alaska Native Regional Corporation/Associations in Alaska with village specific projects; Other tribal or village organizations or consortia of Indian tribes; and Tribal governing bodies (IRA or traditional councils) as recognized by the Bureau of Indian Affairs.

Award Range/Average: $100,000 - $300,000; average $182,000 per budget period

Funding: FY 17 $1,694,325; FY 18 est $1,981,267; FY 19 est $1,981,267.

HQ: Department of Health and Human Services Mary E Switzer Building 330 C Street SW
Washington, DC 20024
Phone: 877-922-9262
Email: carmelia.strickland@acf.hhs.gov
http://www.acf.hhs.gov/ana

IMPROVING THE HEALTH OF AMERICANS THROUGH PREVENTION & MANAGEMENT OF DIABETES & HEART DISEASE & STROKE-FINANCED IN PART BY 2018 PREVENTION & PUBLIC HEALTH FUNDS

Award: Cooperative Agreements

Purpose: To implement and evaluate evidence-based strategies to address the challenges and systemic barriers that contribute to prevention and management of cardiovascular disease and diabetes in high-burden populations.

Applicant Eligibility: State Governments or their Bona Fide Agents (includes the District of Columbia) are eligible

Beneficiary Eligibility: Beneficiaries of this program include: State, Local, Individual/Family, Minority Group, Anyone/General Public, Black American, American Indian, Spanish Origin, Oriental, Other Nonwhite, Women, Handicapped, Physically Afflicted, Senior Citizen, Rural

Award Range/Average: Awards ranged from $980,000 to $3,800,000. Awards we based on per-capita population and the burden of disease of diabetes and heart disease and stroke in each individual state.

Funding: (Project Grants) FY 17 $0; FY 18 est $120,769,531; FY 19 est $0.

HQ: 4770 Buford Highway, P.O. Box F75
Atlanta, GA 30341
Phone: 770-488-1431

IMPROVING THE INVESTIGATION & PROSECUTION OF CHILD ABUSE & THE REGIONAL & LOCAL CHILDREN'S ADVOCACY CENTERS "VOA"

Award: Cooperative Agreements

Purpose: To Improve the investigation and prosecution of child abuse cases, to train criminal justice system professionals, to limit the number of child victims, and to enhance medical support.

Applicant Eligibility: May be limited to national organizations with broad membership among attorneys who prosecute criminal cases in state courts and have demonstrated experience in providing training and technical assistance to prosecutors.

Beneficiary Eligibility: N/A

Award Range/Average: Range and average of financial assistance varies by project.

Funding: (Cooperative Agreements) FY 17 $18,053,892; FY 18 est $21,000,000; FY 19 est $20,000,000.

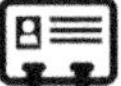

HQ: US Department of Justice Office of Juvenile Justice and Delinquency Prevention 810 7th Street NW
Washington, DC 20531
Phone: 202-514-5335
Email: jacqueline.oreilly@ojp.usdoj.gov

HHS 93.980 INCREASING PUBLIC AWARENESS & PROVIDER EDUCATION ABOUT PRIMARY IMMUNODEFICIENCY DISEASE

Award: Project Grants

Purpose: The program helps healthcare providers and educators to carry out public health activities in areas affected by primary immunodeficiency diseases through public awareness activities.

Applicant Eligibility: This FOA will be full and open competition. The ideal applicant will have ten years of experience in: conducting effective physician education and public awareness campaigns for primary immunodeficiency diseases, collaborating effectively with health care and public health partners, and maximizing resources dedicated to campaign materials development and distribution to meet outcome goals.

Beneficiary Eligibility: The general public will benefit from outcome of this FOA. The ideal applicant will have ten years of experience in: conducting effective physician education and public awareness campaigns for primary immunodeficiency diseases, collaborating effectively with health care and public health partners, and maximizing resources dedicated to campaign materials development and distribution to meet outcome goals.

Award Range/Average: FY 2018 Estimated at 921, 500 FY2019 Estimated at 921, 500 FY2020 Estimated at 921, 500 FY2021 Estimated at 921, 500 Total anticipated funding is $4,607,500.

Funding: (Salaries and Expenses) FY 17 $921,500; FY 18 est $921,500; FY 19 est $921,500.

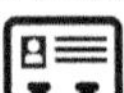

HQ: 1600 Clifton Road
Altanta, GA 30329
Phone: 404-498-0068
Email: sbowen1@cdc.gov
http://www.cdc.gov

HHS 93.808 INCREASING THE IMPLEMENTATION OF EVIDENCE-BASED CANCER SURVIVORSHIP INTERVENTIONS TO INCREASE QUALITY & DURATION OF LIFE AMONG CANCER PATIENTS "DP15-1501"

Award: Cooperative Agreements

Purpose: Funds up to six National Comprehensive Cancer Control Programs grantees to implement core surveillance activities to improve cancer survivor health in their populations.

Applicant Eligibility: No additional eligibility requirements – All eligible applicants should be current recipients of funds under DP12-1205 – Component 2 – The National Comprehensive Cancer Control Program.

Beneficiary Eligibility: Same as Applicant Eligibility.

Award Range/Average: $341,509 for each award

Funding: (Cooperative Agreements) FY 17 $2,049,055; FY 18 est $0; FY 19 est $0; FY 16 $2,049,055. No dollar amounts are available.

HQ: 4770 Buford Highway, P.O. Box F-76
Altanta, GA 30341
Phone: 770-488-4879
Email: nnh1@cdc.gov

INDIAN COMMUNITY DEVELOPMENT BLOCK GRANT PROGRAM "ICDBG program"

Award: Project Grants

Purpose: To develop viable Indian and Alaska Native communities, along with the creation of decent housing, suitable living environments, and economic opportunities especially for persons with low- and moderate-incomes.

Applicant Eligibility: Eligible applicants are any Indian tribe, band, group, or nation, including Alaska Indians, Aleuts, and Eskimos, and any Alaska native village of the United States which is considered an eligible recipient under Title I of the Indian Self-Determination and Education Assistance Act or which had been an eligible recipient under the State and Local Fiscal Assistance Act of 1972.

Beneficiary Eligibility: The principal beneficiaries of ICDBG funds are low and moderate income persons. Low and moderate income beneficiary means a family, household, or individual whose income does not exceed 80 percent of the median income for the area, as determined by HUD, with adjustments for smaller and larger households or families.

Award Range/Average: $25,000 to $4,100,000 Average of $605,000

Funding: Project Grants (Discretionary) FY 17 $58,474,277; FY 18 est $65,000,000; FY 19 est $65,000,000; FY 16 $56,582,132.

HQ: 451 7th Street SW, Room 5156
Washington, DC 20410
Phone: 202-402-3057
Email: marco.c.santos@hud.gov
http://www.hud.gov/program_offices/public_indian_housing/ih/grants/icdbg

INDIAN COUNTRY ALCOHOL & DRUG PREVENTION "Indian Alcohol and Substance Abuse Program"

Award: Project Grants

Purpose: To assist tribal governments in the development and enhancement of tribal justice strategies to address crime issues related to alcohol and substance abuse.

Applicant Eligibility: Same As Beneficiary Eligibility.

Beneficiary Eligibility: Federally recognized Tribal governments.

Award Range/Average: N/A

Funding: (Project Grants) FY 17 $18,224,169; FY 18 FY 19 FY 16 $13,632,104.

HQ: US Department of Justice Bureau of Justice Assistance
Washington, DC 20531
Phone: 202-616-6500
http://www.bja.gov/programdetails.aspx?program_id=63

INDIAN EDUCATION -- SPECIAL PROGRAMS FOR INDIAN CHILDREN

Award: Project Grants

Purpose: To develop, test, and demonstrate the effectiveness of services and programs to improve educational opportunities and achievement of Indian children.

Applicant Eligibility: For Demonstration grants (84.299A), eligible applicants include State educational agencies (SEAs); local educational agencies (LEAs), including charter schools that are considered LEAs under State law; Indian tribes; Indian organizations; federally supported elementary or secondary schools for Indian students (including Department of the Interior/Bureau of Indian Education-funded schools); Indian institutions (including Indian institutions of higher education); or a consortium of any of these entities.

Beneficiary Eligibility: SEAs, LEAs, Indian students, and teachers and administrators will benefit.

Award Range/Average: No Data Available.

Funding: (Project Grants) FY 17 $57,993,000; FY 18 est $57,993,000; FY 19 est $57,993,000.

HQ: 400 Maryland Avenue SW
Washington, DC 20202
Phone: 202-205-1909
Email: angela.hernandez-marshall@ed.gov
http://www.ed.gov/programs/indiandemo/index.html

INDIAN EDUCATION GRANTS TO LOCAL EDUCATIONAL AGENCIES

Award: Formula Grants

Purpose: To address the unique educational and culturally related academic needs of Indian students; to ensure that Indian students gain knowledge and understanding of Native communities, languages, tribal histories, traditions, and cultures; and to ensure that teachers, principals, other school leaders and other staff who serve Indian students have that ability to provide culturally appropriate and effective instruction.

Applicant Eligibility: Local educational agencies (LEAs) that enroll at least 10 Indian children or in which Indians constitute at least 25 percent of the total enrollment. These requirements do not apply to LEAs serving Indian children in Alaska, California, and Oklahoma or located on, or in proximity to, an Indian reservation.

Beneficiary Eligibility: Eligible Indian children enrolled in eligible local educational agencies, BIE-funded schools, Indian organizations, and Indian Community Based Organizations.

Award Range/Average: $4,000- $2,854,289; Average $81,125

Funding: FY 17 $100,381,000; FY 18 est $105,381,000; FY 19 est $100,381,000.

HQ: Office of Indian Education Department of Education 400 Maryland Avenue SW
Washington, DC 20202
Phone: 202-453-6459
Email: kimberly.smith@ed.gov
http://www.ed.gov/about/offices/list/oese/oie/programs.html

INDIAN HOUSING BLOCK GRANTS

Award: Formula Grants

Purpose: To recognize the right of tribal self-governance, and for other purposes.

Applicant Eligibility: Indian tribes or tribally designated housing entities (TDHE)

Beneficiary Eligibility: Primarily low-income families and in limited cases, over-income families may be eligible.

Award Range/Average: $50,282 to $86,438,873; Median grant $867,063

Funding: FY 17 $645,986,672; FY 18 est $646,000,000; FY 19 est $598,000,000.

HQ: 451 7th Street SW, Room 4126
Washington, DC 20410
Phone: 202-402-6321
Email: heidi.j.frechette@hud.gov
http://www.hud.gov

INDIGENT DEFENSE

Award: Cooperative Agreements; Project Grants

Purpose: To enhance the capacity to deliver high-quality, fair, and comprehensive legal services to youth, to improve juvenile courts' data collection, to analyze juvenile defense system and other defense services.

Applicant Eligibility: Applicants are limited to states (including territories and the District of Columbia), federally recognized tribal governments (as determined by the Secretary of the Interior), nonprofit and for-profit organizations (including tribal nonprofit and for-profit organizations) and institutions of higher education (including tribal institutions of higher education).

Beneficiary Eligibility: The beneficiary of these funds would be juvenile delinquents and youth.

Award Range/Average: Varies by project

Funding: Project Grants (Discretionary) FY 17 $1,666,316; FY 18 est $2,000,000; FY 19 est $2,500,000; FY 16 $2,152,950.

HQ: 810 7th Street NW
Washington, DC 20531
Phone: 202-598-6892
Email: julia.alanen@usdoj.gov
http://www.ojjdp.gov

DOD 12.902 INFORMATION SECURITY GRANTS
"Information Assurance Scholarship Program"

Award: Project Grants

Purpose: To increase the number of qualified students entering the cybersecurity field to meet the DoD's increasing dependence on information technology for war fighting and the security of its information infrastructure.

Applicant Eligibility: Investigators must be an employee of a U.S. college or university. The principal investigator and supported graduate students must be a U.

Beneficiary Eligibility: This will benefit researchers in the information security field of computer science that are permanent residents of the United States (U.S.) as well as their students that are permanent residents of the U.S. or U.S. citizens. Scholarships will benefit those pursuing a Bachelor's, Master's or Doctoral Degree in one of the academic areas cited under the DoD Information Assurance Scholarship Program.

Award Range/Average: IASP Grants: $40,000 to $312,000 Average Award: $67,000

Funding: (Salaries and Expenses) FY 17 FY 18 FY 19 est $3,000,000; FY 14 $3,000,000; FY 15 est $3,000,000; FY 16 N/A.

HQ: 9800 Savage Road, Suite 6623
Fort George G. Meade, MD 20755
Phone: 443-479-7660
Email: diboyer@nsa.gov
http://cio-nii.defense.gov/sites/iasp2/index.html

HHS 93.136 INJURY PREVENTION & CONTROL RESEARCH & STATE & COMMUNITY BASED PROGRAMS
"National Center for Injury Prevention and Control"

Award: Cooperative Agreements

Purpose: To support injury control research on priority issues.

Applicant Eligibility: For INJURY PREVENTION AND CONTROL RESEARCH PROGRAMS, AND INJURY CONTROL RESEARCH CENTERS: Eligible applicants may include any nonprofit or for-profit organization; for STATE AND COMMUNITY PROGRAM GRANTS/COOPERATIVE AGREEMENTS: State and local governments or their Bona Fide Agents (this includes the District of Columbia, the Commonwealth of Puerto Rico, the Virgin Islands, the Commonwealth of the Northern Marianna Islands, American Samoa, Guam, the Federated States of Micronesia, the Republic of the Marshall Islands, and the Republic of Palau) and political subdivisions of States (in consultation with States),Federally recognized or state-recognized American Indian/Alaska Native tribal governments, American Indian/Alaska native tribally designated organizations, Alaska Native health corporations, Urban Indian health organizations, Tribal epidemiology centers; for COMMUNITY-BASED PROGRAMS: public, private, nonprofit and for-profit organizations may be eligible.

Beneficiary Eligibility: FOR RESEARCH GRANTS: Academic health centers, scientist/researchers, operational public health programs, State and local governments, and public and private organizations involved in injury research. FOR STATE AND COMMUNITY-BASED GRANTS AND COOPERATIVE AGREEMENTS: State and local health departments, and community-based organizations.

Award Range/Average: Injury Control Research Centers: $802,300. Injury Control Research Projects: $200,000 to $300,000; $250,000. State and Community Based Injury Control Programs: $40,000 to

$300,000; $170,000. Violence Prevention Programs: $80,609 to $1,946,399; $1,013,504. Motor Vehicle Prevention Programs: $247,500 to $803,000; $525,250. Prescription Drug Overdose Programs: $200,000 to $350,716; $288,586. National Violent Death Reporting System: $148,000 to $352,500; $244,985

Funding: (Cooperative Agreements) FY 17 $186,532,989; FY 18 est $223,311,180; FY 19 est $223,311,180; FY 16 $146,139,227.

HQ: NCIPC 4770 Buford Highway NE, P.O. Box F63
Atlanta, GA 30341
Phone: 770-488-0143
Email: dcameron@cdc.gov
http://www.cdc.gov

INNOVATIONS IN APPLIED PUBLIC HEALTH RESEARCH "Applied Public Health Research"

Award: Cooperative Agreements; Project Grants

Purpose: To foster the new knowledge necessary to develop, enhance, and disseminate effective public health services, programs, and policies.

Applicant Eligibility: Applications may be submitted by public and private nonprofit and for profit organizations and by governments and their agencies, such as: Public nonprofit organizations Private nonprofit organizations, For profit organizations, Small, minority, women-owned businesses, Universities, Colleges, Research institutions, Hospitals, Community-based organizations, Faith-based organizations, Federally Recognized Indian Tribal Governments, Indian tribes, Indian tribal organizations, State and local governments or their Bona Fide Agents (this includes the District of Columbia, the Commonwealth of Puerto Rico, the Virgin Islands, the Commonwealth of the Northern Marianna Islands, American Samoa, Guam, the Federated States of Micronesia, the Republic of the Marshall Islands, and the Republic of Palau), Political subdivisions of States (in consultation with States).

Beneficiary Eligibility: Same As Applicant Eligibility.

Award Range/Average: No Data Available.

Funding: (Cooperative Agreements) FY 17 $16,468,158; FY 18 est $16,468,158; FY 19 est $16,488,158.

HQ: Deputy Director Office of Science Quality 1600 Clifton Rd
Atlanta, GA 30333
Phone: 404-639-4639
Email: jcyril@cdc.gov
http://www.cdc.gov

INNOVATIONS IN COMMUNITY-BASED CRIME REDUCTION "CBCR"

Award: Project Grants

Purpose: The CBCR reduces crime and improves community safety and provides technical assistance by increasing law enforcement and supports agencies that are promoting public safety through all the disciplines possible.

Applicant Eligibility: See the current solicitation available at the Office of Justice Programs.

Beneficiary Eligibility: Eligible entities to serve as fiscal agent include states, unit of local governments, non-profit organizations, and federally recognized Indian tribal governments as determined by the Secretary of the Interior.

Award Range/Average: Category 1 (Implementation) Award: up to $850,000 Category 2 (Planning and Implementation) Award: up to $1 million

Funding: Project Grants (Discretionary) FY 17 $14,618,292; FY 18 est $17,500,000.

HQ: 810 7th Street NW
Washington, DC 20531
Phone: 202-616-6500
Email: askbja@usdoj.gov
http://www.bja.gov

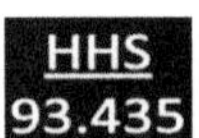

HHS 93.435 INNOVATIVE STATE & LOCAL PUBLIC HEALTH STRATEGIES TO PREVENT & MANAGE DIABETES & HEART DISEASE & STROKE

Award: Cooperative Agreements

Purpose: To design, test, and evaluate novel approaches to addressing a set of evidence based strategies aimed at reducing risks, complications, and/or barriers to prevention and control of diabetes and cardiovascular disease among high-burden populations.

Applicant Eligibility: State or local health departments or their Bona Fide Agents (includes the District of Columbia) Eligibility will be limited to state and local/city/county governments with a population of 900,000 or more with the greatest potential to reach and impact large numbers of high risk/high burden populations, or their bona fide agents. Consortia of smaller local/city/county health departments may collaborate to submit one application that, collectively, represents a population of 900,000 or more.

Beneficiary Eligibility: Beneficiaries of this program include: State, Local, Individual/Family, Minority Group, Anyone/General Public, Black American, American Indian, Spanish Origin, Oriental, Other Nonwhite, Women, Handicapped, Physically Afflicted, Senior Citizen, Rural

Award Range/Average: Awards for this new program are expected to range from $1,000,000 to $3,500,000. Awards will be based on activities proposed by the applicant, the burden of disease of diabetes and heart disease and stroke, and the recipient's potential reach and effect outcomes for large numbers of adults.

Funding: (Cooperative Agreements) FY 17 $0; FY 18 est $39,928,477; FY 19 est $39,928,477.

HQ: 4770 Buford Highway, P.O. Box F75
Atlanta, GA 30341
Phone: 770-488-1431
Email: rnh2@cdc.gov
http://www.cdc.gov

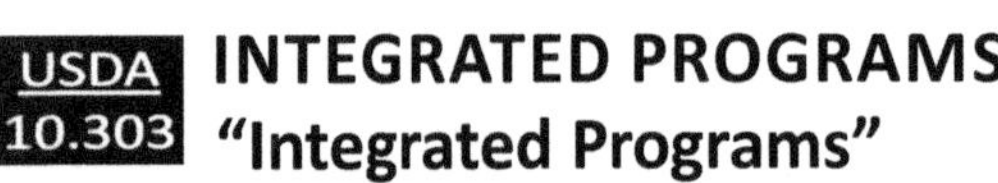

USDA 10.303 INTEGRATED PROGRAMS
"Integrated Programs"

Award: Project Grants

Purpose: To compensate for research to address agricultural requirements such as conservation of water, food safety, pest management, and critical organic farming issues.

Applicant Eligibility: State agricultural experiment stations, State cooperative extension services, all colleges and universities, other research and extension institutions and organizations, Federal agencies, private organizations or corporations, and individuals to facilitate or expand promising breakthroughs in areas of the food and agricultural sciences of importance to the United States.

Beneficiary Eligibility: Same as Applicant Eligibility.

Award Range/Average: If minimum or maximum amounts of funding per competitive and/or capacity project grant, or cooperative agreement are established, these amounts will be announced in the annual Competitive Request for Application (RFA).

Funding: (Project Grants) FY 17 $7,571,059; FY 18 est $8,482,607; FY 19 est $0; FY 16 $6,616,405.

HQ: 1400 Independence Avenue SW, P.O. Box 2210
Washington, DC 20250
Phone: 202-720-5229
http://nifa.usda.gov/grants

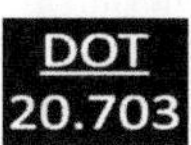

INTERAGENCY HAZARDOUS MATERIALS PUBLIC SECTOR TRAINING & PLANNING GRANTS

"Hazardous Materials Emergency Preparedness Training and Planning Grants, (HMEP) Hazardous Materials Instructor Training Grants (HMIT) Supplemental Public Sector Training Grants (SPST) Assistance for Local Emergency Response Training Grants (ALERT) Hazardous Materials Community Safety Grants (HMCS)"

Award: Project Grants

Purpose: To increase State, local, territorial and Native American tribal effectiveness to safely and efficiently handle hazardous materials accidents and incidents; enhance implementation of the Emergency Planning and Community Right-to-Know Act of 1986 (EPCRA); and encourage a comprehensive approach to emergency planning and training by incorporating response to transportation standards.

Applicant Eligibility: States, U. S.

Beneficiary Eligibility: HMEP: State, Local, Federally Recognized Indian Tribal Governments, U.S. Territories, Student/Trainee HMIT: Public nonprofit institution/organization, Private nonprofit institution/organization SPST: Public nonprofit institution/organization, Private nonprofit institution/organization ALERT: Public nonprofit institution/organization, Private nonprofit institution/organization HMCS: Public nonprofit institution/organization, Private nonprofit institution/organization All segments of the U.S. including Territories and Native American tribal populations that are involved with management of or possible exposure to hazardous materials benefit. Specifically Federal, State, and local authorities are assisted through the HMEP grant program with their responsibilities.

Award Range/Average: HMEP grant $24,000 - $1,500,000. State and Territory HMEP awards are allocated based on a formula that accounts for risk and population. HMIT grant award ranges are $250,000-$1,000,000. SPST grant award ranges are $100,000- $3,500,000. ALERT grant are $500,000- $2,500,00. HMCS grant are $200,000- $1,000,000

Funding: Project Grants (Discretionary) FY 17 $28,276,087; FY 18 est $26,092,844; FY 19 est $26,433,000; FY 16 $24,460,000.

HQ: 1200 New Jersey Avenue SE
Washington, DC 20590
Phone: 202-366-0579
Email: aaron.mitchell@dot.gov
http://www.phmsa.dot.gov

INTERCITY BUS SECURITY GRANTS "Intercity Bus Security"

Award: Cooperative Agreements

Purpose: The program's objective is to strengthen the nation's preparedness and resilience against natural calamities and terrorist and cyber terrorist activities.

Applicant Eligibility: This program is limited to applicants meeting one or both of the following criteria: (1) own/operate a fixed-route intercity bus service using over-the-road buses and providing services to a defined Urban Area Security Initiative (UASI) jurisdiction; or (2) own/operate a charter bus service using over-the-road buses providing a minimum of 50 trips annually to a defined UASI jurisdiction.

Beneficiary Eligibility: General public.

Award Range/Average: Refer to program guidance.

Funding: (Project Grants) FY 17 $2,000,000; FY 18 est $2,000,000; FY 19 est $2,000,000.

HQ: 400 C Street SW, 3rd Floor N Control Desk
Washington, DC 20472
Phone: 800-368-6498
http://www.fema.gov

INTEREST REDUCTION PAYMENTS RENTAL & COOPERATIVE HOUSING FOR LOWER INCOME FAMILIES "236"

Award: Direct Payments for Specified Use; Guaranteed/Insured Loans

Purpose: To provide quality rental and cooperative housing for persons of low- and moderate-income.

Applicant Eligibility: Eligible mortgagors included nonprofit, cooperative, builder-seller, investor-sponsor, and limited-distribution sponsors. Public bodies did not qualify as mortgagors under this program.

Beneficiary Eligibility: Families and individuals, including the elderly and handicapped or those displaced by government action or natural disaster, eligible to receive the benefits of the subsidies must at the time of admission fall within certain locally determined income limits. Families with higher incomes may occupy apartments, but may not benefit from subsidy payments.

Award Range/Average: No Data Available.

Funding:N/A

HQ: 451 7th Street SW
Washington, DC 20410
Phone: 202-402-2492
Email: stephen.a.martin@hud.gov
http://www.hud.gov/offices/hsg/mfh/progdesc/progdesc.cfm

USDA 10.767 INTERMEDIARY RELENDING PROGRAM "IRP"

Award: Direct Loans

Purpose: To facilitate for community and business development.

Applicant Eligibility: Eligible intermediaries may include: Private nonprofit organizations, State or local governments, and Federally recognized Indian tribes and cooperatives.

Beneficiary Eligibility: Ultimate recipients may include: For profit organizations, individuals, public and private nonprofit organizations.

Award Range/Average: This program has no statutory formula. Matching requirements are not applicable to this program. However, Intermediaries may not use IRP funds to finance more than 75 percent of the cost of an ultimate recipient's project MOE requirements are not applicable to this program

Funding: FY 17 est $18,889,000; FY 18 est $18,889,000; FY 19 N/A FY 16 est $19,000,000.

HQ: 1400 Independence Avenue SW Room 4204, P.O. Box 3226
Washington, DC 20250
Phone: 202-720-1400
Email: lori.hood@wdc.usda.gov
http://www.rd.usda.gov/programs-services/intermediary-relending-program

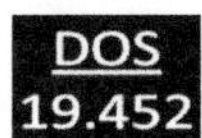

INTERNATIONAL EXCHANGE ALUMNI PROGRAMS "International Exchange Alumni Programs include International Exchange Alumni Enrichment Seminars"

Award: Cooperative Agreements; Project Grants

Purpose: The Bureau of Educational and Cultural Affairs seeks to increase mutual understanding between the people of the United States and the people of other countries by means of educational and cultural exchange programs, including the exchange of scholars, researchers, professionals, students, and educators.

Applicant Eligibility: Pursuant to the Mutual Educational and Cultural Exchange Act of 1961, as amended (Fulbright-Hays Act) the Bureau of Educational and Cultural Affairs of the U.S. Department of State awards grants and cooperative agreements to educational and cultural public or private nonprofit foundations or institutions. Applications may be submitted by public and private non-profit organizations meeting the provisions described in Internal Revenue Code section 26 USC 501(c)(3).

Beneficiary Eligibility: Beneficiaries include recipient organizations, educational institutions, other non-government organizations (NGOs) that meet the provisions described in Internal Revenue Code section 26 USC 501(c)(3), as well as sponsored participants, and the American people and the people of participating countries who interact with the international participants.

Award Range/Average: 2600000

Funding: Project Grants (Cooperative Agreements) FY 17 $2,600,000; FY 18 est $2,600,000; FY 19 est $2,600,000; FY 16 $750,000.

HQ: 2200 C Street NW SA 05 01 Z03
Washington, DC 20037
Phone: 202-632-6183
Email: bistranskysj@state.gov
http://alumni.state.gov

DOL 17.007 INTERNATIONAL LABOR PROGRAMS
"International Labor Programs"

Award: N/A

Purpose: The Bureau of International Labor Affairs promotes trade commitments, strengthens labor standards, and combats child labor and human trafficking.

Applicant Eligibility: N/A

Beneficiary Eligibility: N/A

Award Range/Average: No Data Available.

Funding: N/A

HQ: 200 Constitution Avenue
Washington, DC 20210
Phone: 202-693-4770
Email: yoon.bruce@dol.gov
http://www.dol.gov

DOS 19.019 INTERNATIONAL PROGRAMS TO COMBAT HUMAN TRAFFICKING
"International Programs to Combat Human Trafficking"

Award: Cooperative Agreements; Project Grants

Purpose: Prevents trafficking in persons, protecting and assisting trafficking victims, and prosecuting traffickers and others who profit from trafficking in persons.

Applicant Eligibility: Foreign NGOs are eligible for awards under this program.

Beneficiary Eligibility: Same as Applicant Eligibility.

Award Range/Average: $50,000 to $750,000

Funding: N/A

HQ: 1800 G Street NW, Suite 2201 (SA 22)
Washington, DC 20006
Phone: 202-312-9893
Email: forstromma@state.gov
http://www.state.gov

DOS 19.345 INTERNATIONAL PROGRAMS TO SUPPORT DEMOCRACY, HUMAN RIGHTS & LABOR

Award: Project Grants

Purpose: Funds targeted democracy and human rights programs to address human rights abuses globally, where fundamental rights are threatened; open political space in struggling or nascent democracies and countries ruled by authoritarian regimes; support civil society activists worldwide; and protect at-risk populations.

Applicant Eligibility: N/A

Beneficiary Eligibility: N/A

Award Range/Average: N/A

Funding: N/A

HQ: 2201 C Street NW
Washington, DC 20520
Phone: 202-663-3672
Email: mulladydk@state.gov
http://www.state.gov

INTERNATIONAL RESEARCH & RESEARCH TRAINING "Global Health Research and Research Training"

Award: Project Grants; Training

Purpose: The John E. Fogarty International Center provides research and research training on global health and to foster a knowledge-sharing relationship between the U.S. and other scientists living abroad. It helps in conducting biological, behavioral, social science and career development researches.

Applicant Eligibility: In general, universities, colleges, hospitals, laboratories, Federal institutions and other public or private non-profit and for-profit domestic and foreign institutions, and State and local units of government are eligible to submit applications for research grants, research training grants, cooperative agreements, and career development awards. The grantee institution must agree to administer the grant in accordance with prevailing regulations and policies.

Beneficiary Eligibility: Usually any non-profit or for-profit organization, company or institution engaged in health and biomedical research.

Award Range/Average: No Data Available.

Funding: (Project Grants (including individual awards) FY 17 $51,379,157; FY 18 est $53,485,107; FY 19 est $54,019,955; FY 16 $50,563,458.

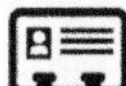

HQ: Building 31 Room B2C39 31 Center Drive, P.O. Box 2220
Bethesda, MD 20892
Phone: 301-496-1653
Email: flora.katz@nih.gov
http://www.fic.nih.gov

INTERNATIONAL RESEARCH & STUDIES

Award: Project Grants

Purpose: To improve foreign language, area, and other international studies training through research, studies, development and publication of specialized instructional materials developed from the result of research conducted under this program.

Applicant Eligibility: Public and private agencies, organizations, institutions, and individuals may apply.

Beneficiary Eligibility: Public and private agencies, organizations, institutions, and individuals will benefit.

Award Range/Average: Varies by competition.

Funding: (Project Grants) FY 17 $712,329; FY 18 est $712,329; FY 19 est $0; FY 16 $0.

HQ: Maryland Avenue SW
Washington, DC 20202
Phone: 202-453-5690
Email: cheryl.gibbs@ed.gov
http://www.ed.gov

INTEROPERABILITY ROADMAP: PUBLIC/PRIVATE PARTNERSHIP

HHS 93.830

Award: Cooperative Agreements

Purpose: To help identify best practices in privacy law to improve interoperable exchange of health information consistent with ONC's Interoperability Roadmap.

Applicant Eligibility: This is a non-competitive funding opportunity and is restricted to the National Governors Association (NGA), a private non-profit organization that is uniquely qualified because of its unique relationship with senior health policy leaders in executive branches of state government; its long prior collaborations with parallel organizations that support state legislator; expanded support of gubernatorial initiatives to improve health outcomes and reduce health costs in states; and first-hand experience with the complex health privacy rules environment that exists today for patients, providers and state health policy makers. Eligible applicant is uniquely situated to lead a collaboration among high-level state health policy-making officials and ONC for the purpose of harmonizing state health privacy law to support nationwide interoperable exchange of health information for patient care.

Beneficiary Eligibility: Beneficiaries will belong to the following stakeholder groups: Federal; State; Local; Health care covered entities that conduct interstate health transactions; Health Care Consumers; Health Professionals; Scientists/Researchers; and EHR Developers.

Award Range/Average: Total funding $406,250 ($325,000 plus $81,250 supplemental funding).

Funding: N/A

HQ: 330 C Street SW
Washington, DC 20201
Phone: 202-720-2919
Email: carmel.halloun@hhs.gov

INTEROPERABLE EMERGENCY COMMUNICATIONS

DHS 97.055

Award: Project Grants

Purpose: It provides planning and training and flexibility to local and State governments to carry out interoperable emergency communications during natural disasters and acts of terrorism.

Applicant Eligibility: Applicant Eligibility - All 56 states and territories.

Beneficiary Eligibility: States, territories, and local and tribal governments.

Award Range/Average: N/A

Funding: (Project Grants) FY 17 $0; FY 18 est $0; FY 19 est $0; FY 16 $0.

HQ: 400 C Street SW
Washington, DC 20523
Phone: 800-368-6498
Email: askcsid@dhs.gov
http://www.fema.gov

INTRAMURAL RESEARCH TRAINING AWARD "IRTA"

Award: Direct Payments for Specified Use

Purpose: To provide opportunities for developmental training and practical research experience in a variety of disciplines related to biomedical research, medical library research, and related fields.

Applicant Eligibility: Candidates for the IRTA Program must be U.S. Citizens or Permanent Resident Aliens: 1) Postdoctoral IRTA participants must possess a Ph.D., M.D., D.D.S., D.M.D., D.V.M. or equivalent degree in biomedical, behavioral, or related sciences; or certification by a university as meeting all the requirements leading to such a doctorate; 5 or fewer years of relevant postdoctoral experience and up to 2 additional years of experience not oriented toward research (i.e., clinical training for physicians); 2) predoctoral IRTA participants must be: a) students enrolled in Ph.D., M.D., D.D.S., D.M.D., D.V.M., or equivalent degree programs at any accredited U.S. or foreign university, which frequently involves dissertation research. The research experience is undertaken as an integral part of the student's ongoing academic preparation and is credited toward completion of degree requirements; or b) students who have been accepted into graduate or medical degree programs and who have written permission from their school to interrupt their current schooling and to return within 1 year to their degree granting programs; 3) postbaccalaureate IRTA participants are individuals who have received a bachelor's degree no more than 3 years prior to the activation date of the traineeship or a master's degree no more than 6 months prior to the activation date of the traineeship, and who intend to apply to graduate or medical school in biomedical research within the next year or students who have been accepted into graduate, other doctoral, or medical degree programs and who have written permission of their school to delay entrance for up to 1 year; and 4) student IRTA participants are at least 16 years of age and are enrolled at least half-time in high school or have been accepted for or are enrolled as an undergraduate or graduate in an accredited college or university and are in good academic standing. U.S. citizens may be enrolled anywhere in the world; permanent residents must be enrolled in the U.S.

Beneficiary Eligibility: The IRTA Program benefits the participants by combining an opportunity for study with practical work experience and valuable research training experience at the NIH.

Award Range/Average: No Data Available.

Funding: (Direct Payments for Specified Use) FY 17 $113,993,420; FY 18 est $116,615,268; FY 19 est $117,781,421.

HQ:
Bethesda, MD 20892
Phone: 301-594-2053
Email: milgrams@od.nih.gov
http://www.training.nih.gov

INVESTING IN PEOPLE IN THE MIDDLE EAST & NORTH AFRICA
"Investing in people/ cultural/educational/alumni/information and media efforts in the Middle East and North Africa."

Award: Cooperative Agreements

Purpose: Support programs, projects and activities to include (but not limited to) cultural, educational, alumni, information and media efforts in the Middle East and North Africa.

Applicant Eligibility: Not-For-Profit organizations subject to 501(c)(3) or registered as a non-profit organization in the entity's home country. Organizations that have and have not previously received international program funding from the U.S. Government.

Beneficiary Eligibility: Local organizations, citizens of countries in the Middle East and North Africa, and the U.S.

Award Range/Average: $10,000 to over 5 Million Avg: $500,000

Funding: N/A

HQ: 2201 C Street NW H Street Building
Washington, DC 20520
Phone: 202-647-6397
Email: hollandly@state.gov

INVITATIONAL GRANTS FOR MILITARY-CONNECTED SCHOOLS
"DoDEA Grant"

Award: Project Grants

Purpose: To enhance student learning opportunities, student achievement, educator professional development, and to ease the challenges students who are military dependents face due to their parents' military station transfers or deployments.

Applicant Eligibility: These DoDEA grants are awarded to military-connected local educational agencies (LEAs) by invitation only.

Beneficiary Eligibility: K-12 students are the primary beneficiaries, although grants may also fund teacher professional development.

Award Range/Average: $100,000 to $2,500,000

Funding: Project Grants (Discretionary) FY 17 FY 18 est $20,000,000; FY 19 N/A FY 15 est $20,000,000; FY 13 $0; FY 14 est $32,150,595.

HQ: 4040 N Fairfax Drive, 9th Floor
Arlington, VA 22203
Phone: 703-588-3345
Email: brian.pritchard@hq.dodea.edu

JAVITS GIFTED & TALENTED STUDENTS EDUCATION

Award: Project Grants

Purpose: To identify talented students through a coordinated program of evidence-based research, demonstration projects, innovative strategies, and similar activities designed to build and enhance the ability of elementary and secondary schools nationwide.

Applicant Eligibility: State and local educational agencies, the Bureaus of Indian Education, institutions of higher education, and other public and private agencies and organizations may apply for project grants.

Beneficiary Eligibility: Students (including gifted and talented students) and their teachers benefit.

Award Range/Average: No Data Available.

Funding: (Project Grants) FY 17 $12,000,000; FY 18 est $12,000,000; FY 19 est $0; FY 16 $12,000,000.

HQ: 400 Maryland Avenue SW
Washington, DC 20202
Phone: 202-205-3783
Email: theda.zawaiza@ed.gov
http://www.ed.gov

JOBS-PLUS PILOT INITIATIVE
"Jobs-Plus"

Award: Project Grants

Purpose: Jobs Plus Pilot is a locally-designed program implemented aiming at significantly increasing employment and income of public housing residents.

Applicant Eligibility: Public Housing Authorities(PHA)

Beneficiary Eligibility: Individuals and families who are residents of conventional public housing are eligible to receive benefits under the Job Plus program.

Award Range/Average: The range for financial assistance is $2,666,667 to $3,000,000 per grantee award.

Funding: (Project Grants) FY 17 $15,000,000; FY 18 est $15,000,000; FY 19 est $10,000,000; FY 16 $29,398,000.

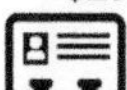

HQ: 451 7th Street SW, Room 4116
Washington, DC 20410
Phone: 202-402-6230
Email: tobey.j.zimber@hud.gov

JOHN R. JUSTICE PROSECUTORS & DEFENDERS INCENTIVE ACT
"JRJ Grant Program"

Award: Project Grants

Purpose: To encourage qualified attorneys to choose careers as prosecutors and defenders for a minimum of thirty-six (36) months.

Applicant Eligibility: Applicants are limited to state and U.S. territory government agencies, designated by their Governor, and the District of Columbia, designated by the Mayor, to manage this program. The States, Territories, and the District of Columbia will make loan payments directly to the institutions holding eligible beneficiary loans on behalf of eligible beneficiaries.

Beneficiary Eligibility: For purposes of this program the following persons shall be considered eligible: Prosecutor - full-time employee of a State or unit of local government (including tribal government) who is continually licensed to practice law and prosecutes criminal or juvenile delinquency cases at the state or unit of local government level (including supervision, education, or training of other persons prosecuting such cases).

Award Range/Average: N/A

Funding: Project Grants (Discretionary) FY 17 $1,806,643; FY 18 est $2,000,000; FY 19 est $2,000,000; FY 16 $1,773,891.

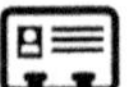

HQ: 451 7th Street SW, Room 4116
Washington, DC 20410
Phone: 202-402-6230
Email: tobey.j.zimber@hud.gov

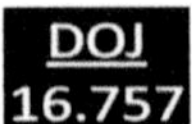

JUDICIAL TRAINING ON CHILD MALTREATMENT FOR COURT PERSONNEL JUVENILE JUSTICE PROGRAMS

Award: Cooperative Agreements

Purpose: To assist the judicial system's handling of child abuse and victims of commercial sexual exploitation including sex trafficking.

Applicant Eligibility: Certain national organizations as specified in the individual program announcement.

Beneficiary Eligibility: N/A

Award Range/Average: Range and average of financial assistance vary by project.

Funding: (Cooperative Agreements) FY 17 $1,666,643; FY 18 est $2,000,000; FY 19 est $2,000,000.

HQ: 810 7th Street NW
Washington, DC 20531
Phone: 202-616-3646
Email: darian.hanrahan@usdoj.gov
http://ojjdp.gov

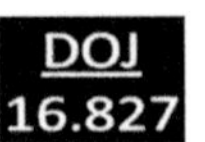

JUSTICE REINVESTMENT INITIATIVE "JRI"

Award: Project Grants

Purpose: The Justice Reinvestment Initiative helps to respond to crime and other public safety problems. It responds to crime and cost drivers.

Applicant Eligibility: Justice Reinvestment Initiative: TTA -- national scope private and nonprofit organizations (including tribal nonprofit or for-profit organizations) and colleges and universities, both public and private (including tribal institutions of higher education). All recipients and sub-recipients (including any for-profit organization) must forgo any profit or management fee.

Beneficiary Eligibility: N/A

Award Range/Average: N/A

Funding: Project Grants (Discretionary) FY 17 $17,151,490; FY 18 est $22,000,000; FY 19 est $20,000,000; FY 16 $24,224,613.

HQ: 810 7th Street NW
Washington, DC 20531
Phone: 202-514-1158
Email: heather.tubman-carbone@usdoj.gov
http://www.bja.gov/jri

JUSTICE SYSTEM INFRASTRUCTURE PROGRAM FOR INDIAN TRIBES

"Justice System Infrastructure Program for Indian Tribes"

Award: Project Grants

Purpose: Providing grant funding to support the physical tribal justice infrastructure capacity needs of Indian Country.

Applicant Eligibility: Federally recognized Indian tribes may apply.

Beneficiary Eligibility: Same as Applicant Eligibility.

Award Range/Average: Approximately $9,000,000 is available under this program each FY. Suggested award amounts range between $1,000,000 (single jurisdiction projects) and $4,000,000 (multiple jurisdictional projects).

Funding: (Project Grants) FY 17 $8,684,426; FY 18 est $7,777,796; FY 19 - 7% Tribal Set-Aside (also known as Indian Country Prison Grants) in FY 17; Indian Assistance budget line item in FY 18.

HQ: 810 Seventh Street NW
Washington, DC 20531
Phone: 202-616-6500
Email: askbja@usdoj.gov
http://www.bja.gov

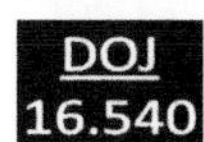

JUVENILE JUSTICE & DELINQUENCY PREVENTION

"Title II, Part B Formula Grants"

Award: Formula Grants; Project Grants; Training

Purpose: To provide grants to states to assist them in planning, establishing, operating, coordinating, and evaluating projects for the development of more effective juvenile delinquency prevention; to support technical assistance grants to facilitate state compliance; to support training and technical assistance to benefit the formula grant program; and to support research, evaluation, and statistics activities designed to benefit the formula grant program.

Applicant Eligibility: N/A

Beneficiary Eligibility: Units of a State and its local government, public and private organizations, Indian tribes performing law enforcement functions, and agencies involved in juvenile delinquency prevention, treatment, and rehabilitation.

Award Range/Average: Allocation of formula grants to States and territories are based on relative populations under the age of 18. Amounts awarded for discretionary technical assistance, training, and research grants vary depending on the particular program or project being funded.

Funding: (Formula Grants) FY 17 $45,945,125; FY 18 est $60,000,000; FY 19 est $55,000,000.

HQ: 810 7th Street NW
Washington, DC 20531
Phone: 202-532-0020
http://www.ojjdp.gov

JUVENILE JUSTICE EDUCATION COLLABORATION ASSISTANCE

Award: Project Grants

Purpose: To support the Department of Justice/OJJDP to respond to student mental health and behavioral needs and it supports with education in case of any violence.

Applicant Eligibility: N/A

Beneficiary Eligibility: N/A

Award Range/Average: Between $400,000-2,000,000

Funding: Project Grants (Discretionary) FY 17 $0; FY 18 est $35,000,000; FY 19 FY 16 $0.

HQ: 810 Seventh Street NW 2136
Washington, DC 20531
Phone: 202-307-9963
Email: robin.delany-shabazz@usdoj.gov
http://www.ojjdp.gov

JUVENILE MENTORING PROGRAM "Mentoring"

Award: Project Grants

Purpose: To improve outcomes for at-risk and high-risk youth, and reduce negative outcomes through the provision of mentoring services.

Applicant Eligibility: Eligible applicants are limited to states (including territories), units of local government, federally recognized tribal governments as determined by the Secretary of the Interior, nonprofit organizations, and for-profit organizations (including tribal nonprofit and for-profit organizations), as well as institutions of higher education (including tribal institutions of higher education). For-profit organizations (as well as other recipients) must agree to forgo any profit or management fee.

Beneficiary Eligibility: N/A

Award Range/Average: Award amounts vary according to solicitation.

Funding: (Project Grants) FY 17 $66,685,734; FY 18 est $94,000,000; FY 19 est $58,000,000.

HQ:
Washington, DC 20531
Phone: 202-616-9135
Email: jennifer.yeh@usdoj.gov
http://www.ojjdp.ncjrs.gov

KEEP YOUNG ATHLETES SAFE

Award: Cooperative Agreements; Project Grants

Purpose: To safeguard young athletes in organized sports from sexual and emotional abuse and ensures prosecution for all forms of abuse to support victims of abuse.

Applicant Eligibility: Eligible applicants are nonprofit, nongovernmental entities with nationally recognized expertise in preventing and investigating sexual, physical and emotional abuse in the athletic programs of the United States Olympic Committee, each national governing body, and each Paralympic sports organization. Applicants must have a recognized background investigating allegations of abuse and reporting to law enforcement in order to inform training and prevention activities.

Beneficiary Eligibility: The program will safeguard amateur athletes through the prevention of sexual, physical and emotional abuse in the athletic programs of the United States Olympic Committee, each national governing body, and each Paralympic sports organization.

Award Range/Average: Range and average of financial assistance varies by project.

Funding: (Cooperative Agreements) FY 17 $0; FY 18 est $2,500,000; FY 19 N/A.

LABORATORY LEADERSHIP, WORKFORCE TRAINING & MANAGEMENT DEVELOPMENT, IMPROVING PUBLIC HEALTH LABORATORY INFRASTRUCTURE
"APHL-CDC Partnership for Quality Lab Practice"

Award: Cooperative Agreements

Purpose: To improve public health laboratory infrastructure, maintain a competent and trained laboratory workforce.

Applicant Eligibility: Assistance will be provided only to APHL. CDC approved single eligibility of this award.

Beneficiary Eligibility: This project represents the front line defense against health threats to the nation's public. The nation's public is the ultimate recipient of benefits from this program.

Award Range/Average: N/A

Funding: (Cooperative Agreements) FY 17 $1,711,259; FY 18 est $1,810,677; FY 19 est $1,810,677; FY 16 $1,711,259.

HQ: 4770 Buford Highway, P.O. Box F45
Atlanta, GA 30341
Phone: 770-488-0563
http://www.cdc.gov

LABORATORY TRAINING, EVALUATION, AND QUALITY ASSURANCE PROGRAMS
"Quality Assurance in Pathology and Laboratory Medicine"

Award: Cooperative Agreements

Purpose: To improve the quality of laboratory testing practices relevant to clinical and public health settings and to determine standardized approaches to quality assurance in pathology and laboratory medicine.

Applicant Eligibility: Applications may be submitted by public and private nonprofit organizations and by governments and their agencies, such as: Public nonprofit organizations, private nonprofit organizations, universities, colleges, research institutions, hospitals, community and faith based organizations, State and local governments or their Bona Fide Agents (this includes the District of Columbia, the Commonwealth of Puerto Rico, the Virgin Islands, the Commonwealth of the Northern Marianna Islands, American Samoa, Guam, the Federated States of Micronesia, the Republic of the Marshall Islands, and the Republic of Palau).

Beneficiary Eligibility: Applicants must have experience in the administration and evaluation of standardized quality assurance programs in multiple, diverse laboratory sites (including community hospitals and academic medical centers). This experience is required for an applicant to be able to assess the effectiveness of these quality assurance programs and to determine best practices.

Award Range/Average: $100,000 to $500,000; $250,000

Funding: FY 17 $1,617,208; FY 18 est $1,816,175; FY 19 est $2,000,000.

HQ: 2400 Century Pkwy NE
Atlanta, GA 30345
Phone: 404-498-0899
http://www.cdc.gov

DOI 15.152

LAND BUY-BACK FOR TRIBAL NATIONS
"Buy-Back Program"

Award: Cooperative Agreements

Purpose: To work in partnership with the tribes to minimize the number of fractional interests in trust or restricted lands by purchasing fractional interests from willing sellers and transferring them to the tribe of jurisdiction for purposes benefitting the community.

Applicant Eligibility: Eligibility is restricted to federally recognized Indian tribal governments with jurisdiction over fractionated lands as identified in the Land Buy-Back Program for Tribal Nation's November 2016 Status Report.

Beneficiary Eligibility: Federally recognized Indian tribal governments as identified in the Land Buy-Back Program for Tribal Nation's November 2016 Status Report.

Award Range/Average: There is no minimum or maximum award amount. Awards have averaged less than $400,000.

Funding: (Cooperative Agreements) FY 19 est $3,400,000; FY 17 $1,160,122; FY 18 est $2,800,000.

HQ: 1849 C Street NW, Room 3543
Washington, DC 20240
Phone: 703-235-3811
Email: katherine_feiring@ios.doi.gov
http://www.doi.gov/buybackprogram

LANGUAGE RESOURCE CENTERS

Award: Project Grants

Purpose: To provide grants for establishing, strengthening, and operating centers for teaching and learning foreign languages through teacher training, research, materials development, and dissemination projects.

Applicant Eligibility: An institution of higher education or a consortia of institutions of higher education is eligible to receive an award.

Beneficiary Eligibility: Institutions of higher education or combinations of such institutions and individuals will benefit.

Award Range/Average: To be determined.

Funding: (Project Grants) FY 17 $2,746,768; FY 18 est $2,746,768; FY 19 est $0; FY 16 $2,746,768.

HQ: 4800 Mark Center Drive
Alexandria, VA 22350
Phone: 571-256-0716
Email: shirley.t.rapues.civ@mail.mil
http://www.dodltc.org

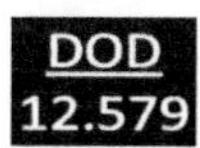

LANGUAGE TRAINING CENTER
"Language Training Center Program"

Award: Project Grants

Purpose: A DOD-funded initiative that seeks to accelerate the development of foundational or higher-level expertise in critical and strategic languages and regional studies for DOD personnel.

Applicant Eligibility: Any accredited U.S. institutions of higher education (defined in 20 U.S.C. 1001 of the Higher Education Act of 1965) is eligible for a grant.

Beneficiary Eligibility: Accredited U.S. institutions of higher education.

Award Range/Average: Grant range from $150,000 to $2,000,000 annually for a single year project

Funding: FY 17 $8,755,000; FY 18 est $5,800,000; FY 19 est $5,800,000; FY 16 $3,396,000.

HQ: 1849 C Street NW, P.O. Box 4211
Washington, DC 20240
Phone: 202-513-0600
http://www.onrr.gov

LATE DISBURSEMENT INTEREST

Award: Direct Payments with Unrestricted Use

Purpose: Pays late disbursement interest on subject payments made to States after the due date.

Applicant Eligibility: Late disbursements will trigger automatic payment distribution computed in accordance with the Law.

Beneficiary Eligibility: ONRR pays late disbursement interest on subject payments made to States after the due date.

Award Range/Average: N/A

Funding: (Direct Payments with Unrestricted Use) FY 18 est $100,000; FY 17 $85,000; FY 19 est $111,000.

HQ: 955 L'Enfant Plaza N SW, Suite 4000
Washington, DC 20024
Phone: 202-653-4730
Email: mball@imls.gov
http://www.imls.gov

HUD 14.888 LEAD-BASED PAINT CAPITAL FUND PROGRAM

Award: Project Grants

Purpose: To assist Public Housing Authorities identify and eliminate lead-based paint hazards in public housing.

Applicant Eligibility: Only Public Housing Authorities (PHA) with the legal authority to develop, own, modernize and operate a public housing development in accordance with the 1937 Housing Act.

Beneficiary Eligibility: Public housing residents

Award Range/Average: $0- $1,000,000; average award $500,000

Funding: (Project Grants) FY 16 N/A FY 17 est $25,000,000; FY 18 N/A.

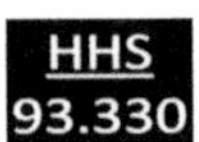

HQ: 451 7th Street SW, Room 8236
Washington, DC 20410
Phone: 202-380-7369
Email: tara.j.radosevich@hud.gov
http://www.hud.gov

HHS 93.330 LEADERSHIP IN PUBLIC HEALTH SOCIAL WORK EDUCATION GRANT PROGRAM

"Public Health Social Work Education Grant Program, LPHSWE"

Award: Project Grants

Purpose: Provides training and education, faculty development, and curriculum enhancement to prepare students for leadership roles in public health social work through enrollment in a dual master's degree program in social work and public health.

Applicant Eligibility: Eligible applicants include accredited schools of social work/programs that 1) offer a dual master's degree in an accredited graduate program in social work with a macro-level concentration in management and administration and in an accredited graduate program in public health; and 2) previously received HRSA support for dual degree enrollment, education, and graduation in the Leadership in Public Health Social Work Education program. Eligible applicants include accredited schools of social work/ programs that 1) offer a dual master's degree in an accredited graduate program in social work with a macro-level concentration in management and administration and in an accredited graduate program in public health; and 2) previously received HRSA support for dual degree enrollment, education, and graduation in the Leadership in Public Health Social Work Education program.

Beneficiary Eligibility: A student receiving a stipend in the LPHSWE Program must be a citizen of the United States, a non-citizen national of the United States, or a foreign national who possesses a visa permitting permanent residence in the United States. Individuals on temporary or student visa are not eligible participants.

Award Range/Average: Range: $296,865 - $300,000; average $300,000

Funding: (Project Grants) FY 17 $900,000; FY 18 est $0; FY 19 est $0; FY 16 $900,000.

HQ: 451 7th Street SW, Room 8236
Rockville, MD 20857
Phone: 301-443-6760
Email: mgerdine@hrsa.gov
http://www.hrsa.gov

LEADING EDGE ACCELERATION PROJECTS (LEAP) IN HEALTH INFORMATION TECHNOLOGY "LEAP"

Award: N/A

Purpose: Seeks to partner with innovative organizations that can look to the future and develop leading solutions and innovations to some of these vexing problems.

Applicant Eligibility: Public or non-profit private institutions, such as a university, college, or a faith-based or community-based organization; units of local or state government, eligible agencies of the federal government, Indian/Native American Tribal Governments (federally recognized, other than federally recognized, and tribally designated organizations).

Beneficiary Eligibility: N/A

Award Range/Average: There has been $2,00,000 allocated for FY 18 for this program. We estimate that we will award two (2) total; the award amounts will be $1,000,000 for each.

Funding: Cooperative Agreements (Discretionary Grants) FY 17 FY 18 est $2,000,000.

HQ: 330 C Street SW
Washington, DC 20201
Phone: 202-969-3369
Email: kevin.chaney@hhs.gov
http://www.healthit.gov

LEGACY RESOURCE MANAGEMENT PROGRAM "DoD Legacy Program"

Award: Cooperative Agreements; Project Grants

Purpose: A DoD Legacy Program is to provide funding to help manage and sustain DoD land in the United States.

Applicant Eligibility: Cultural Resources/Historic Preservation

Beneficiary Eligibility: Successful applicants must have the ability to accept funds from DOD via cooperative agreement, contract, or MIPR.

Award Range/Average: Most funded projects range between $40,000 and $150,000.

Funding: (Cooperative Agreements) FY 14 $4,478,500; FY 16 est $4,668,000; FY 15 est $2,624,000.

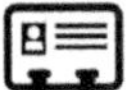

HQ: 4800 Mark Center Drive, Suite 16G14
Alexandria, VA 22352
Phone: 571-372-6905
Email: l.p.boice.civ@mail.mil
http://www.dodlegacy.org

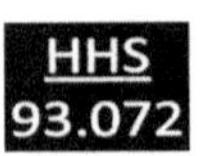

LIFESPAN RESPITE CARE PROGRAM "Lifespan Respite"

Award: Cooperative Agreements

Purpose: To expand and enhance respite care services to family caregivers; improve the statewide dissemination and coordination of respite care; and to provide, supplement, or improve access and quality of respite care services to family caregivers, thereby reducing family caregiver strain.

Applicant Eligibility: N/A

Beneficiary Eligibility: N/A

Award Range/Average: FY 2017 - 2 New State Grants ($200,000 per grant); 1 Continuation Award for Lifespan Respite Technical Assistance Resource Center ($239,010); 12 Advancing State Lifespan Respite Care System Awards (Range: $86,867 - $261,953) FY 2018 – 12 Advancing State Lifespan Respite Care System and 1 Technical Assistance Resource Center Continuation Awards (Range: $84,275 - $254,135), 13 Supplemental Awards to all 12 Advancing State Care System and Technical Assistance Resource Center (Range: $8,597 - $25,792); 4 Additional Advancing State Lifespan Respite Care System Awards that were approved but not funded in the 2017 Funding Opportunity (Range: $88,333 - $265,000)

Funding: (Cooperative Agreements) FY 17 $3,360,000; FY 18 est $4,110,000; FY 19 N/A FY 16 $3,360,000.

HQ: 330 C Street SW
Washington, DC 20201
Phone: 202-795-7473
Email: victoria.wright@acl.hhs.gov
http://www.acl.gov

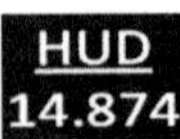

LOAN GUARANTEES FOR NATIVE HAWAIIAN HOUSING "Section 184A"

Award: Guaranteed/Insured Loans

Purpose: To provide greater access to private mortgage resources to eligible Native Hawaiian families by guaranteeing loans for one-to-four family housing located on Hawaiian Home Lands.

Applicant Eligibility: A Native Hawaiian family; the Department of Hawaiian Home Lands; the Office of Hawaiian Affairs; a private nonprofit organization experienced in the planning and development of affordable housing for Native Hawaiians.

Beneficiary Eligibility: Native Hawaiian homeowners are the beneficiaries of the program.

Award Range/Average: The average loan amount in FY 2017 was $227,882.

Funding: (Guaranteed/Insured Loans) FY 17 $360,432; FY 18 est $556,262; FY 19 est $650,000; FY 16 $82,000.

HQ: ONAP 451 7th Street SW, Room 5156
Washington, DC 20410
Phone: 202-402-4978
Email: thomas.c.wright@hud.gov
http://www.hud.gov/offices/pih/ih/codetalk/onap/program184a.cfm

HHS
93.232

LOAN REPAYMENT PROGRAM FOR GENERAL RESEARCH "NIH General Research Loan Repayment Program; GR-LRP"

Award: Direct Payments for Specified Use

Purpose: To recruit and retain health professionals performing research in fields required by the NIH to carry out its mission.

Applicant Eligibility: Eligible applicants must: (1) Be a citizen, national, or permanent resident of the United States; (2) possess a M.D.

Beneficiary Eligibility: NIH researchers who possess substantial unpaid educational debt relative to income will benefit from this program.

Award Range/Average: (Loan Repayment) For initial 3-year contracts, loan repayment awards may range from $7,800 to $105,000; Tax reimbursements range from $3,679 to $48,825. The average contract cost which includes loan and tax reimbursement is $102,000.

Funding: (Direct Payments for Specified Use) FY 17 $4,000,036; FY 18 est $3,917,457; FY 19 est $4,000,000; FY 16 $3,548,000.

HQ: Building 2, Room 2E18 2 Center Drive
Bethesda, MD 20892
Phone: 301-402-1283
Email: colep@mail.nih.gov
http://www.lrp.nih.gov

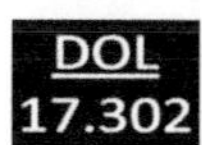

DOL
17.302

LONGSHORE & HARBOR WORKERS' COMPENSATION

Award: Direct Payments with Unrestricted Use

Purpose: Provides compensation for disability or death resulting from injury, including occupational disease, to eligible private employees.

Applicant Eligibility: Longshore workers, harbor workers, and certain other employees engaged in maritime employment on the navigable waters of the United States and adjoining pier and dock areas, employees engaged in activities on the Outer Continental Shelf, employees of Nonappropriated Fund Instrumentalities, employees of private employers engaged in work outside the United States under contracts with the United States Government, and others as specified, including survivors of the above. Employees of private concerns in the District of Columbia and their survivors are eligible for benefits under an extension of the Act, applicable to injuries or deaths based upon employment events that occurred prior to July 26, 1982.

Beneficiary Eligibility: Same as Applicant Eligibility.

Award Range/Average: Disability - 66-2/3 percent of average weekly wage; death benefits 50 percent average wages of deceased to such widow or widower, plus 16-2/3 percent for one or more surviving children with 66-2/3 percent limit. Average benefit unknown. Weekly compensation payments limited to between 50-200 percent of national average weekly wage.

Funding: (Direct Payments with Unrestricted Use) FY 17 $111,233,689; FY 18 est $118,004,000; FY 19 est $117,179,000; FY 16 $119,491,000.

HQ: Division of Longshore and Harbor Workers Compensation 200 Constitution Avenue NW
Washington, DC 20210
Phone: 202-693-0038
http://www.dol.gov/owcp/dlhwc

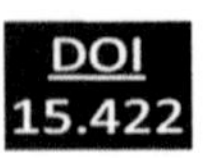

LOUISIANA STATE UNIVERSITY (LSU) COASTAL MARINE INSTITUTE (CMI) "LSU CMI"

Award: Cooperative Agreements

Purpose: The Bureau of Ocean Energy Management (BOEM) provides major economic and energy benefits on a national and local level to the taxpayers, States and the American Indian community. The purpose of the Louisiana State University Coastal Marine Institute (CMI) is to use highly qualified scientific expertise at local levels to collect and disseminate environmental information needed for OCS oil and gas and marine minerals decisions; address local and regional OCS-related environmental and resource issues of mutual interest; and strengthen the BOEM-State partnership in addressing OCS oil and gas and marine minerals information needs.

Applicant Eligibility: To apply for a research award, the recipient is asked to provide the name of the Principal Investigator. If an applicant other than LSU wants to apply, they must do so in collaboration with an LSU research scientist.

Beneficiary Eligibility: Research scientists, Federal, State and local decision-makers, Native American Organizations, and the general public will ultimately benefit from the program.

Award Range/Average: Range is $100,000 to $450,000; Average $250,000.

Funding: (Cooperative Agreements) FY 17 $570,000; FY 18 N/A FY 19 N/A FY 16 $913,809.

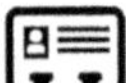

HQ: 45600 Woodland Road
Sterling, VA 20166
Phone: 703-787-1087
Email: rodney.cluck@boem.gov
http://www.boem.gov

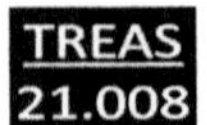

LOW INCOME TAXPAYER CLINICS "Low Income Taxpayer Clinic"

Award: Project Grants

Purpose: To provide matching grants to organizations providing representation of low income taxpayers in controversies with the Internal Revenue Service (IRS).

Applicant Eligibility: The Low income Taxpayer Clinic programs awards matching grants to qualifying organizations that represent low income taxpayers involved in controversies with the IRS and organizations that provide education and outreach on the taxpayer rights and responsibilities of U.S. taxpayers to individuals who speak English as a second language. IRC Section 7526 requires clinics to provide services for free or for no more than a nominal fee.

Beneficiary Eligibility: Low-income taxpayers are those with incomes which do not exceed 250 percent of the Federal Poverty Guidelines published annually by the Department of Health and Human Services, or taxpayers for whom English is a second language.

Award Range/Average: Range of grant: $10,000 to $100,000.

Funding: (Project Grants) FY 17 $11,800,000; FY 18 est $12,000,000; FY 19 est $12,000,000.

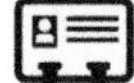

HQ: 24000 Avila Road
Laguna Niguel, CA 92677
Phone: 949-575-6200
Email: beard.william@irs.gov
http://www.irs.gov/advocate

LOWER INCOME HOUSING ASSISTANCE PROGRAM SECTION 8 MODERATE REHABILITATION

"Section 8 Housing Assistance Payments Program for Very Low Income Families-Moderate Rehabilitation"

Award: Direct Payments for Specified Use

Purpose: To assist very low income families in obtaining decent rental housing.

Applicant Eligibility: An authorized Public Housing Agency (any State, county, municipality or other governmental entity or public body (or agency or instrumentality thereof).

Beneficiary Eligibility: Very low income families (whose income does not exceed 50 percent of the median income for the area as determined by the Secretary with adjustments for smaller and larger families) and, on an exception basis, lower income families (whose income does not exceed 80 percent of the median income for the area adjusted for small and large families). A very low income or, on an exception basis, lower income single person who is elderly, disabled or handicapped, displaced, or the remaining member of an eligible tenant family is also eligible.

Award Range/Average: $4,426 to $19,549,245: Average of $1,135,021

Funding: (Direct Payments for Specified Use) FY 17 $148,539,213; FY 18 est $161,800,000; FY 19 est $154,417,000; FY 16 $107,177,925.

HQ: 451 7th Street SW, Room 4210
Washington, DC 20410
Phone: 202-708-6050
Email: becky.l.primeaux@hud.gov
http://www.hud.gov/progdesc/pihindx.html

LOW-INCOME HOME ENERGY ASSISTANCE

Award: Formula Grants

Purpose: To make Low Income Home Energy Assistance Program (LIHEAP) grants available to States District of Columbia, U.S. Territories and Native American Tribes and to assist eligible households to meet the costs of home energy.

Applicant Eligibility: Energy Assistance Block Grants: All States, the District of Columbia, federally-and State-recognized Indian Tribal governments which request direct funding, and specified Territories may receive direct grants. The prospective grantee must submit an annual application.

Beneficiary Eligibility: Energy Assistance Block Grants: All States, the District of Columbia, federally-and State-recognized Indian Tribal governments that request direct funding, and specified Territories may provide assistance to households with incomes up to the greater of 150 percent of the poverty level or 60 percent of the State median income. Grantees may establish lower income eligibility levels, but they may not set the limit below 110 percent of the poverty level.

Award Range/Average: Average is $16,053,630.

Funding: (Training) FY 17 $2,391,345; FY 18 est $2,186,021; FY 19 est $0; FY 16 $2,418,568; - (Formula Grants) FY 17 $3,393,585,459; FY 18 est $3,637,316,000; FY 19 est $0; FY 16 $3,369,018,056; - (Competitive Grants) FY 2016 act. 0; FY 2017 est. 0; FY 2018 est. 0; In both FY 2016 and FY 2017 there were 211 formula grants.

HQ: 330 C Street SW 5th Floor W, P.O. Box 5425
Washington, DC 20201
Phone: 202-401-4870
Email: lauren.christopher@acf.hhs.gov
http://www.acf.hhs.gov/programs/ocs/programs/liheap

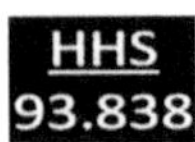

LUNG DISEASES RESEARCH

Award: Project Grants

Purpose: The Division of Lung Diseases supports research and research training on the causes, diagnosis, prevention, and treatment of lung diseases and sleep disorders. Research is funded through investigator-initiated and Institute-initiated grant programs and through contract programs in areas including asthma, bronchopulmonary dysplasia, chronic obstructive pulmonary disease, cystic fibrosis, respiratory neurobiology, sleep-disordered breathing, critical care and acute lung injury, developmental biology and pediatric pulmonary diseases, immunologic and fibrotic pulmonary disease, rare lung disorders, pulmonary vascular disease, and pulmonary complications of AIDS and tuberculosis.

Applicant Eligibility: Any nonprofit organization engaged in biomedical research and institutions or companies organized for profit may apply for almost any kind of grant. Only domestic, non-profit, private or public institutions may apply for NRSA Institutional Research Training Grants.

Beneficiary Eligibility: Any nonprofit or for-profit organization, company or institution engaged in biomedical research. Only domestic for-profit small business firms may apply for SBIR and STTR programs.

Award Range/Average: Grants: $5,000 to $9,234,634; $459,620. SBIR Phase I - $150,000; Phase II - up to $1,000,000; STTR Phase I - $150,000; Phase II $1,000,000.

Funding: (Project Grants) FY 17 $607,437,335; FY 18 est $654,547,092; FY 19 est $654,547,092.

HQ: National Heart Lung and Blood Institute (NHLBI) 6701 Rockledge Drive, Room 7176
Bethesda, MD 20892
Phone: 301-827-7968
Email: pharesda@nhlbi.nih.gov
http://www.nhlbi.nih.gov/about/scientific-divisions/division-lung-diseases

MAINSTREAM VOUCHERS

Award: Direct Payments for Specified Use

Purpose: To aid persons with disabilities in getting decent, safe, and hygienic rental housing.

Applicant Eligibility: Public housing agencies (PHA)that is defined as any State, county, municipality or other governmental entity or public body (or agency or instrumentality thereof) which is authorized to engage in or assist in the development or operation of housing for very low income families; and a consortium of PHAs; any other nonprofit entity that was administering a Section 8 tenant-based program on October 21, 1998; or, for an area outside the jurisdiction of a PHA administering a voucher program, a private nonprofit entity or a governmental entity or public body that would otherwise lack jurisdiction to administer the program in such area and non-profit organization that provide services to the disabled as defined in 42 U.S.C.

Beneficiary Eligibility: Disabled family that is income-eligible under the Housing Choice Voucher program regulations at 24 CFR 982.201(b)(1)as well as other wise eligible under the regulations at 24CFR 982.

Award Range/Average: $26,758 to $2,499,026; Average $530,237

Funding: (Direct Payments for Specified Use) FY 17 est $120,000,000; FY 16 $108,041,000; FY 18 est $107,074,000.

HQ: 451 7th Street SW, Room 4210
Washington, DC 20410
Phone: 202-708-6050
Email: becky.l.primeaux@hud.gov
http://www.hud.gov/offices/pih/programs/hcv/about/fact_sheet.cfm

MANUFACTURED HOME DISPUTE RESOLUTION

Award: Provision of Specialized Services

Purpose: To provide for a dispute resolution program for the timely resolution of disputes between manufacturers, retailers, and installers of manufactured homes.

Applicant Eligibility: Refer to HUD's website at www.hud.

Beneficiary Eligibility: The program may only address disputes between manufacturers, retailers, and installers of manufactured homes regarding responsibility for the correction or repair of defects in manufactured homes that are reported during the 1-year period beginning on the date of installation. Manufactured home owners may initiate action under, and be observers to, the HUD Manufactured Home Dispute Resolution Program, as provided regulation.

Award Range/Average: This program does not provide direct financial assistance.

Funding: (Provision of Specialized Services) FY 15 FY 17 FY 16 - Dispute resolution is a program within the comprehensive Manufactured Housing Construction and Safety Standards program.

HQ: 451 7th Street SW
Washington, DC 20410
Phone: 202-402-7112
Email: pamela.b.danner@hud.gov
http://portal.hud.gov

MANUFACTURED HOME LOAN INSURANCE FINANCING PURCHASE OF MANUFACTURED HOMES AS PRINCIPAL RESIDENCES OF BORROWERS "Title I"

Award: Guaranteed/Insured Loans

Purpose: To provide reasonable funding of manufactured home purchases.

Applicant Eligibility: All persons are eligible to apply.

Beneficiary Eligibility: Individuals/families.

Award Range/Average: The maximum loan amount is $69,678. The average loan amount is $47,146.

Funding: (Sale, Exchange, or Donation of Property and Goods) FY 17 est $30,000,000; FY 16 est $30,000,000; FY 15 $32,000,000.

HQ: 451 7th Street SW
Washington, DC 20410
Phone: 800-225-5342
http://portal.hud.gov/hudportal/hud?src=/program_offices/housing/sfh/title/manuf1414.117

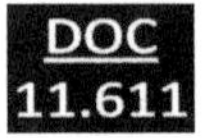

MANUFACTURING EXTENSION PARTNERSHIP

Award: Cooperative Agreements; Dissemination of Technical Information

Purpose: To assist in productivity and technological performance in United States manufacturing and to help Manufacturing Extension Centers and services.

Applicant Eligibility: For MEP Center projects applicants shall be U.S. based nonprofit institutions or organizations or a consortium thereof; institutions of higher education; or a State, U.S. territory, local or tribal government, or groups thereof.

Beneficiary Eligibility: Beneficiary shall be U.S.-based manufacturing firms, especially smaller companies.

Award Range/Average: Individual awards for extension service planning and pilot testing and special project agreements generally range between $25,000 and $100,000. Awards for Manufacturing Extension Centers generally range between of $500,000 to $15,000,000 annually. Competitive awards generally range between $500,000 and $1,000,000 annually.

Funding: (Cooperative Agreements) FY 17 $124,845,000; FY 18 est $125,965,000; FY 19 est $0; FY 16 $121,363,000.

HQ: 100 Bureau Drive, P.O. Box 4800
Gaithersburg, MD 20899
Phone: 301-975-4676
Email: carroll.thomas@nist.gov
http://www.mep.nist.gov

MAP MODERNIZATION MANAGEMENT SUPPORT "MMMS"

Award: Project Grants

Purpose: Helps prepare and maintain flood hazard maps for the National Flood Insurance Program.

Applicant Eligibility: All States and Commonwealths (including the District of Columbia and territories and possessions of the United States), regional agencies, and communities may apply. All applicants must be communities participating and in good standing in the NFIP or agencies which service participating NFIP communities.

Beneficiary Eligibility: State; local; U.S. Territory & Possession; other public institution/organization; small business; engineer/architect; builder, contractor, developer; land/property owner; general public.

Award Range/Average: Refer to program guidance

Funding: (Salaries and Expenses) FY 17 $0; FY 18 est $0; FY 19 est $0; FY 16 $0; - Program not funded in Fiscal Year 2009. This program remains open due to open awards.

HQ: 400 C Street SW
Washington, DC 20523
Phone: 800-621-3363
Email: patrick.sacbibit@fema.dhs.gov
http://www.dhs.gov

MARINE CORPS SYSTEMS COMMAND FEDERAL ASSISTANCE PROGRAM

Award: Project Grants

Purpose: To reduce the demand for illegal drugs among America's youth by providing standardized Drug Demand Reduction (DDR) training.

Applicant Eligibility: Other private/public nonprofit organizations which are operated primarily for educational or similar purposes in the public interest, and commercial concerns.

Beneficiary Eligibility: The beneficiaries for this program are American youth ranging from age eight through the completion of high school, not to exceed twenty years old.

Award Range/Average: No Data Available.

Funding: (Salaries and Expenses) FY 18 N/A FY 17 est $4,000,000; FY 16 est $4,000,000.

HQ: 2200 Lester Street
Quantico, VA 22134
Phone: 703-432-3147
Email: angela.gorman@usmc.mil

MARINE GAS HYDRATE RESEARCH ACTIVITIES

Award: Cooperative Agreements

Purpose: To characterize and oversee gas hydrate deposits and environmental conditions on OCS Block Mississippi Canyon 118 (MC-118) in the Gulf of Mexico.

Applicant Eligibility: Proposals are received from the CMRET (and qualified subcontractors through CMRET) for research and scientific sensory equipment for the monitoring station. Applicants must have expertise in marine gas hydrates.

Beneficiary Eligibility: Organizations participating in the project, as well as the general public.

Award Range/Average: $0 to $100,000

Funding: (Cooperative Agreements) FY 17 $95,000; FY 18 est $0; FY 19 N/A FY 16 $0.

HQ: 381 Elden Street, P.O. Box 4070
Herndon, VA 20170
Phone: 703-787-1514
Email: matthew.frye@boem.gov
http://www.boem.gov

MARINE MINERALS ACTIVITIES
"Marine Minerals Activities"

Award: Cooperative Agreements

Purpose: To assess OCS sand deposits for coastal restoration and beach nourishment needs, and to cultivate good working relationships regarding OCS mineral issues with coastal States due to effects from hurricanes and coastal erosion.

Applicant Eligibility: Proposals are received from coastal States in need of coastal restoration.

Beneficiary Eligibility: State agencies and organizations participating in the project, as well as the general public.

Award Range/Average: Range is $500,000 to $600,000.

Funding: (Cooperative Agreements) FY 17 $500,000; FY 18 N/A FY 19 N/A.

HQ: 381 Elden Street, P.O. Box E3313
Herndon, VA 20170
Phone: 703-787-1851
Email: keith.good@bsee.gov
http://www.boem.gov/marinemineralsprogram

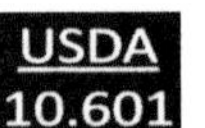

MARKET ACCESS PROGRAM
"MAP"

Award: Formula Grants; Direct Payments for Specified Use

Purpose: To maximize the expansion of commercial exporting markets for U.S. agricultural commodities to organizations that develop foreign marketing.

Applicant Eligibility: To be approved, applicants must be: (1) A nonprofit U.S. agricultural trade organization; (2) a nonprofit State regional trade group; (3) a U.S. agricultural cooperative; or (4) a State agency.

Beneficiary Eligibility: CCC will enter into MAP agreements only where the eligible agricultural commodity is comprised of at least 50 percent U.S. origin content by weight, exclusive of added water.

Award Range/Average: From $22,000 to $9,611,000; $1,375,000.

Funding: Formula Grants (Cooperative Agreements) FY 17 $200,000,000; FY 18 est $200,000,000; FY 19 est $200,000,000; FY 16 est $200,000,000; FY 15 $185,600,000.

HQ: 1400 Independence Avenue SW
Washington, DC 20250
Phone: 202-720-4327
Email: curt.alt@fas.usda.gov
http://www.fas.usda.gov/programs/market-access-program-map

MATERNAL & CHILD HEALTH FEDERAL CONSOLIDATED PROGRAMS

"Special Projects of Regional and National Significance (SPRANS), including the Community Integrated Service Systems (CISS); and the Heritable Disorders Program"

Award: Project Grants

Purpose: To carry out special maternal and child health (MCH) projects of regional and national significance.

Applicant Eligibility: Training grants may be made to public or private nonprofit institutions of higher learning. Research grants may be made to public or private nonprofit institutions of higher learning and public or private nonprofit private agencies and organizations engaged in research or in Maternal and Child Health (MCH) or Children with Special Health Care Needs (CSHCN) programs.

Beneficiary Eligibility: For training grants: (1) Trainees in the health professions related to MCH; and (2) mothers and children who receive services through training programs. For research grants: public or private nonprofit agencies and organizations engaged in research in MCH or CSHCN programs.

Award Range/Average: $3,419 to $3,996,711; $387,145

Funding: Project Grants (Discretionary) FY 17 $132,166,263; FY 18 est $155,592,453; FY 19 est $147,365,163; FY 16 $133,938,299; - FY 2017 includes $20M for Zika response.

HQ: 5600 Fishers Lane, Room 18W37
Rockville, MD 20857
Phone: 301-443-2170
Email: lkavanagh@hrsa.gov
http://www.hrsa.gov

HHS 93.994 MATERNAL & CHILD HEALTH SERVICES BLOCK GRANT TO THE STATES "MCH Block Grants"

Award: Formula Grants

Purpose: Enables States to enhance the health of the people, especially the vulnerable population such as mothers and children by developing and enhancing the systems of healthcare in the region.

Applicant Eligibility: Title V MCH Block Grants are limited to States and insular areas.

Beneficiary Eligibility: Mothers, infants, children, including CSHCN, and their families, particularly those of low-income.

Award Range/Average: $145,466 - $39,113,905; Average $9,217,188

Funding: (Formula Grants) FY 17 $537,371,166; FY 18 est $543,814,110; FY 19 est $545,175,782; FY 16 $538,256,696.

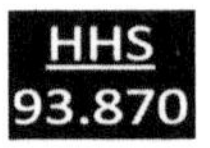
HQ: 5600 Fishers Lane, Room 18N110
Rockville, MD 20857
Phone: 301-443-2170
Email: mlawler@hrsa.gov
http://www.hrsa.gov

HHS 93.870 MATERNAL, INFANT & EARLY CHILDHOOD HOME VISITING GRANT PROGRAM "MIECHV Program"

Award: Formula Grants

Purpose: "The goals of the Maternal, Infant, and Early Childhood Home Visiting Program (MIECHV Program) are to improve coordination of services for at-risk communities; and identify and provide comprehensive services to improve outcomes for eligible families who reside in at-risk communities.

Applicant Eligibility: Eligible entities include those currently funded under the MIECHV Program: 47 states, 3 nonprofit organizations serving Florida, North Dakota, and Wyoming, and 6 territories and jurisdictions serving District of Columbia, Puerto Rico, Guam, the U.S. Virgin Islands, the Commonwealth of the Northern Mariana Islands, and American Samoa. For those states that have elected not to participate in MIECHV, nonprofit organizations with an established record of providing early childhood home visiting programs or initiatives in a state or several states are eligible to apply to carry out programs in those states.

Beneficiary Eligibility: As directed in statute, awardees must give priority in providing services under the MIECHV program to the following: Eligible families who reside in communities in need of such services, as identified in the statewide needs assessment required under subsection 511(b)(1)(A); Low-income eligible families Eligible families with pregnant women who have not attained age 21; Eligible families that have a history of child abuse or neglect or have had interactions with child welfare service Eligible families that have a history of substance abuse or need substance abuse treatment; Eligible families that have users of tobacco products in the home Eligible families that are or have children with low student achievement; Eligible families with children with developmental delays or disabilities; an Eligible families that include individuals who are serving or formerly served in the Armed Forces, including such families that have members of the Armed Forces who have had multiple deployments outside of the United States.

Award Range/Average: Formula (2016): $1,000,000 – $22,201,618 Formula (2017): Ceiling amount ranges: $992,000 - $22,024,005; Competitive (2017): $949,664 - $3,957,620

Funding: (Formula Grants) FY 17 $344,717,896; FY 18 est $363,343,165; FY 19 est $351,000,000; FY 16 $344,717,896; (Project Grants) FY 17 FY 18 est $1,375,000; FY 19 est $1,300,000; - Home Visiting Research Project Grants(Project Grants) FY 17 $1,200,000; FY 18 est

HQ: 5600 Fishers Lane, Room 18N110
Rockville, MD 20857
Phone: 301-594-4149
Email: mbezuneh@hrsa.gov
http://mchb.hrsa.gov/programs/homevisiting

MATERNAL, INFANT, AND EARLY CHILDHOOD HOME VISITING RESEARCH PROGRAMS "Home Visiting Research Programs; MIECHV TA"

Award: Cooperative Agreements; Project Grants

Purpose: The Maternal, Infant, and Early Childhood Home Visiting Research Programs are designed to increase knowledge about the implementation and effectiveness of voluntary home visiting programs, using random assignment designs to the maximum extent feasible.

Applicant Eligibility: As cited in 42 CFR Part 51a.3(b), only public or nonprofit institutions of higher learning and public or private nonprofit agencies engaged in research or in programs relating to maternal and child health and/or services for children with special health care needs may apply for grants, contracts or cooperative agreements for research in maternal and child health services or in services for children with special health care needs.

Beneficiary Eligibility: Funded research should benefit MIECHV awardees by increasing knowledge about the implementation and effectiveness of home visiting programs.

Award Range/Average: Home Visiting Research: Awards of up to $300,000 per year.

Funding: (Project Grants) FY 17 $0; FY 18 est $0; FY 19 est $0; FY 16 $0; - Home Visiting Research (Project Grants)(Cooperative Agreements) FY 17 $0; FY 18 est $0; FY 19 est $0; FY 16 $299,000; - Home Visiting Research Network.

HQ: 5600 Fishers Lane, Room 18N160
Rockville, MD 20857
Phone: 301-443-7758
Email: kpeplinski@hrsa.gov
http://mchb.hrsa.gov/programs/homevisiting

MATHEMATICAL & PHYSICAL SCIENCES "MPS"

Award: Project Grants

Purpose: To promote the progress of the mathematical and physical sciences and thereby strengthen the Nation's scientific enterprise; to increase the store of scientific knowledge and enhance understanding of major problems confronting the Nation.

Applicant Eligibility: Except where a program solicitation establishes more restrictive eligibility criteria, individuals and organizations in the following categories may submit proposals: Universities and colleges; Non-profit, non-academic organizations; for-profit organizations; State and local governments; and unaffiliated individuals. See the NSF Grant Proposal Guide, Chapter I.

Beneficiary Eligibility: N/A

Award Range/Average: Range Low $4,30; Range High $50,478,909 Average $157,941

Funding: (Project Grants) FY 18 est $1,219,430,000; FY 17 est $1,356,025,000; FY 16 $1,348,784,00.

HQ: 2415 Eisenhower Avenue
Alexandria, VA 22314
Phone: 703-292-8800
Email: ccooper@nsf.gov
http://nsf.gov/dir/index.jsp?org=mps

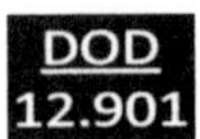

MATHEMATICAL SCIENCES GRANTS

Award: Project Grants

Purpose: Program seeks to stimulate new and important developments in the field areas of algebra, discrete mathematics, number theory, probability and statistics.

Applicant Eligibility: All those receiving support from our grants must be U.S. citizens or permanent residents of the United States. Investigators must be an employee of a U.S. college or university.

Beneficiary Eligibility: This will benefit researchers in the mathematical sciences who are U.S. citizens or permanent residents as well as their students who are U. S.

Award Range/Average: Research Grants: Range: $5,000 - $40,000 Average Award: $26,000 Conferences: Range: $5,000 - $50,000 Average Award: $15,000 Research Experiences for Undergraduates: Range: $33,000 - $125,000 Average Award: $125,000

Funding: (Salaries and Expenses) FY 17 $2,263,987; FY 18 est $533,957; FY 19 N/A FY 13 est $13,814,759; FY 16 $4,139,272; FY 15 $3,671,533; N/A FY 14 $4,800,000.

HQ: 1401 Constitution Avenue NW
Washington, DC 20230
Phone: 202-482-0065
Email: nchambers@mbda.gov
http://www.mbda.gov

MEASUREMENT & ENGINEERING RESEARCH & STANDARDS

Award: Cooperative Agreements; Project Grants

Purpose: To support scientific and engineering research for technology transfer.

Applicant Eligibility: Institutions of higher education

Beneficiary Eligibility: Universities, colleges, professional institutes and associations, nonprofit organizations, State and local governments, and commercial organizations.

Award Range/Average: No Data Available.

Funding: (Project Grants) FY 17 $84,360,992; FY 18 est $94,429,081; FY 19 est $33,598,000.

HQ: 100 Bureau Drive, P.O. Box 1650
Gaithersburg, MD 20899
Phone: 301-975-3086
Email: leon.sampson@nist.gov

MEASURING INTEROPERABILITY PROGRESS THROUGH INDIVIDUALS' ACCESS & USE OF THE ELECTRONIC HEALTH DATA

Award: Cooperative Agreements

Purpose: To establish a mechanism of collaboration with the National Partnership for Women & Families to support the development of consumer survey questions for the Health Information National Trends Survey and associated reports.

Applicant Eligibility: This is a non competitive agreement being awarded to the National Partnership for Women and Families (NPWF)

Beneficiary Eligibility: The beneficiaries will include all health care organizations and patients using electronic health records

Award Range/Average: No Data Available.

Funding: N/A

HQ: 330 C Street SW
Washington, DC 20201
Phone: 202-720-2919
Email: carmel.halloun@hhs.gov

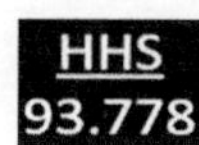

MEDICAL ASSISTANCE PROGRAM "Medicaid; Title XIX"

Award: Formula Grants

Purpose: Provides financial assistance to States for payments of medical assistance on behalf of cash assistance recipients, children, pregnant women, and the aged who meet income and resource requirements, and other categorically-eligible groups.

Applicant Eligibility: State and local welfare agencies must operate under an HHS-approved Medicaid State Plan and comply with all Federal regulations governing aid and medical assistance to the needy.

Beneficiary Eligibility: Low-income persons who are over age 65, blind or disabled, members of families with dependent children, low- income children and pregnant women, certain Medicare beneficiaries and, in many States, medically-needy individuals may apply to a State or local welfare agency for medical assistance. At the State's option, eligibility to non-elderly individuals with family incomes up to 133 percent of the federal poverty level will start in calendar year 2014.

Award Range/Average: $16,828,000 TO $60,223,130,000. Average assistance is $7,012,811,340

Funding: Formula Grants (Apportionments) FY 17 $422,044,667,089; FY 18 est $430,443,422,832; FY 19 est $464,462,125,954; FY 16 $393,054,311,000.

HQ: 7500 Security Boulevard
Baltimore, MD 21244
Phone: 410-786-3870
Email: sean.danus@cms.hhs.gov
http://www.cms.hhs.gov/contracts

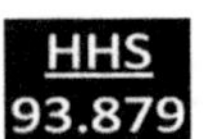

MEDICAL LIBRARY ASSISTANCE

Award: Project Grants

Purpose: To meet a growing need for investigators trained in biomedical informatics research and data science by training qualified pre- and post-doctoral candidates; to conduct research in biomedical informatics, bioinformatics and related computer, information and data sciences; to facilitate management of electronic health records and clinical research data; and to advance biocomputing and bioinformatics.

Applicant Eligibility: Any individual(s) with the skills, knowledge, and resources necessary to carry out the proposed research as the project director/principal investigator (PD/PI) is invited to work with his/her organization to develop an application for support. Individuals from underrepresented racial and ethnic groups as well as individuals with disabilities are always encouraged to apply for NIH support.

Beneficiary Eligibility: Research Grants are available to public or private, domestic or foreign, for profit or not-for-profit institutions or organizations with research capabilities in biomedical informatics, bioinformatics, computer sciences, information sciences, data sciences and related disciplines. Training Grants may be made to nonfederal public and nonprofit private institutions.

Award Range/Average: $20,000 to $750,000 (range) $406,540 – average cost for Research Grant (R01) $97,351 – average cost for Information Resource Grant (G08) $45,435 - average total cost for Scholarly Works Grant (G13)

Funding: (Project Grants) FY 17 $56,629,037; FY 18 est $61,240,485; FY 19 est $54,728,283; FY 16 $42,276,400.

HQ: 6705 Rockledge Drive, Suite 301
Baltimore, MD 20892
Phone: 301-496-4621
Email: alicia.ross@nih.gov
http://www.nlm.nih.gov/ep/index.html

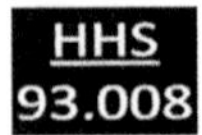

MEDICAL RESERVE CORPS SMALL GRANT PROGRAM "MRC"

Award: Cooperative Agreements

Purpose: To support the development of Medical Reserve Corps (MRC) units in communities throughout the United States.

Applicant Eligibility: Eligible applicants for this funding opportunity are national-level nonprofit organizations with significant local, state and national networking connections.

Beneficiary Eligibility: General public.

Award Range/Average: Only one Cooperative Agreement awarded at the amount of $3,000,000

Funding: (Cooperative Agreements) FY 16 est $3,000,000; FY 18 N/A FY 17 est $4,000,000.

HQ: 200 C Street ONeill Building
Washington, DC 20024
Phone: 202-260-0400
Email: virginia.simmons@hhs.gov
http://www.medicalreservecorps.gov/homepage

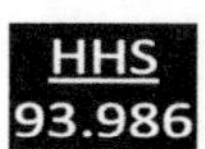

MEDICARE ACCESS & CHIP REAUTHORIZATION ACT (MACRA) FUNDING OPPORTUNITY: MEASURE DEVELOPMENT FOR THE QUALITY PAYMENT PROGRAM

Award: Formula Grants

Purpose: The Medicare Access and CHIP Reauthorization Act (MACRA) Funding Opportunity: Measure Development for the Quality Payment Program develops, improves or updates the quality measures to help structure a pay based on a merit-based incentive system.

Applicant Eligibility: Clinical specialty societies, clinical professional organizations, patient advocacy organizations, educational institutions, independent research organizations, health systems, and other entities engaged in quality measure development. For this funding opportunity, the above categories are referenced collectively as entity or entities.

Beneficiary Eligibility: Quality Payment Program provides new opportunities to improve care delivery by supporting and rewarding clinicians as they find new ways to engage patients, families, and caregivers and to improve care coordination and population health management. The quality measures in MIPS and APMs serve as the mechanism of measuring the improved care delivery.

Award Range/Average: The Medicare Access and CHIP Reauthorization Act (MACRA) Funding Opportunity: Measure Development for the Quality Payment Program Cooperative Agreements expect to award 5-10 agreements with a range of $0- $2,000,000 a year for up to 3 years. The expected total funding is $10,000,000 a years for 3 years totaling $30,000,000

Funding: (Salaries and Expenses) FY 17 $0; FY 18 est $30,000,000; FY 19 est $0.

HQ: 7500 Security Boulevard
Woodlawn, MD 21244
Phone: 410-786-4399
Email: wilfred.agbenyikey@cms.hhs.gov
http://www.cms.gov

MEDICARE ENROLLMENT ASSISTANCE PROGRAM "MIPPA"

Award: Formula Grants; Project Grants

Purpose: To provide outreach to eligible Medicare beneficiaries regarding the benefits available under title XVIII of the Social Security Act.

Applicant Eligibility: Formula grants: State governments and U.S. Territories, with distribution to designated area agencies on aging and Indian Tribal Organizations through an approved State plan. Project grants: Grants may be made to any public or nonprofit private agency, organization, or institution.

Beneficiary Eligibility: Individuals eligible for Medicare benefits, including Part D drug benefits, and older persons eligible for benefits and services provided under Federal and state programs.

Award Range/Average: Formula Grants – Based on Statutory formula Discretionary Grant – one award not more than 12M

Funding: (Project Grants) FY 17 $34,912,500; FY 18 est $37,500,000; FY 19 est $37,500,000; FY 16 $37,500,000.

HQ: 330 C Street SW
Washington, DC 20201
Phone: 202-795-7350
Email: katherine.glendening@acl.hhs.gov
http://www.acl.gov

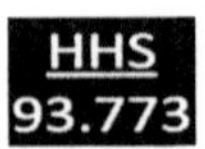

MEDICARE HOSPITAL INSURANCE "Medicare Part A"

Award: Direct Payments for Specified Use

Purpose: Provides hospital insurance protection for covered services to persons age 65 or above, to certain disabled persons and to individuals with chronic renal disease.

Applicant Eligibility: Persons age 65 or over and certain disabled persons are eligible to receive hospital insurance benefits. Nearly all individuals who had reached the age of 65 before 1968 are eligible for Part A, including people not eligible for cash Social Security benefits.

Beneficiary Eligibility: Persons age 65 or over and qualified disabled persons.

Award Range/Average: Benefits may be paid based on the prospective payment amount or the reasonable costs of covered inpatient hospital services and based on the reasonable costs of covered post-hospital extended care services, which are incurred during a benefit period. For benefit periods beginning in calendar year 2018 the beneficiary is responsible for $1,340 inpatient hospital deductible, a $335 per day coinsurance amount for 61 through 90 days of inpatient hospital care, a $670 per day coinsurance amount for inpatient hospital care during the 60 lifetime reserve days, and a $167.50 per day coinsurance amount for days 21 through 100 of care in a skilled nursing facility. Home health services are paid in full.

Funding: (Insurance) FY 17 $291,122,000,000; FY 18 est $297,842,000,000; FY 19 est $323,801,000,000; FY 16 $291,248,000,000; - These figures represent benefit outlays, not including QIO or Health IT payments to medical providers.

HQ: 7500 Security Boulevard
Baltimore, MD 21244
Phone: 410-786-4724
Email: tiffany.walker@cms.hhs.gov
http://www.cms.hhs.gov

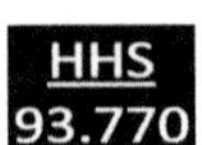

MEDICARE PRESCRIPTION DRUG COVERAGE "Medicare Part D"

Award: Direct Payments for Specified Use

Purpose: Provides prescription drugs to Medicare beneficiaries through their voluntary participation in prescription drug plans, with an additional subsidy provided to lower-income beneficiaries.

Applicant Eligibility: An entity organized and licensed under State law as a risk-bearing entity eligible to offer health insurance in each State in which it is to offer a plan, meeting the requirements in 42 CFR 423.504 and 42 CFR 423.

Beneficiary Eligibility: Eligible beneficiaries include individuals who are entitled to Medicare benefits under Part A or enrolled in Part B and who reside in the plan's service area. Individuals in a Medicare Advantage Plan with Part D coverage may not be separately enrolled in a stand alone prescription drug plan.

Award Range/Average: Determined by plan offerings, number of enrollees, and utilization.

Funding: (Insurance) FY 17 $88,263,000,000; FY 18 est $82,340,000,000; FY 19 est $85,996,000,000; FY 16 $89,102,000,000.

HQ: 7500 Security Boulevard
Baltimore, MD 21244
Phone: 410-786-4724
Email: lori.levine@cms.hhs.gov
http://www.cms.hhs.gov

MEDICARE SUPPLEMENTARY MEDICAL INSURANCE "Medicare Part B"

Award: Direct Payments for Specified Use

Purpose: Provides medical insurance protection for covered services to persons age 65 or over, to certain disabled persons and to individuals with end-stage renal disease.

Applicant Eligibility: All persons who are eligible for premium-free hospital insurance benefits (see 93.773), and persons age 65 and older who reside in the United States and are either citizens or aliens lawfully admitted for permanent residence who have resided in the United States continuously during the five years immediately preceding the month in which the application for enrollment is filed, may voluntarily enroll for Part B supplementary medical insurance (SMI).

Beneficiary Eligibility: All persons who qualify for hospital insurance, and those who do not qualify for hospital insurance but meet eligibility requirements and choose to purchase Part "B".

Award Range/Average: Generally, with exceptions of certain services, the beneficiary is responsible for meeting the annual $183 deductible before you may begin. Thereafter, Medicare pays a percent of the approved amount of the covered service. This percentage is 80 percent for most services.

Funding: (Insurance) FY 17 $314,543,000,000; FY 18 est $326,044,000,000; FY 19 est $362,687,000,000.

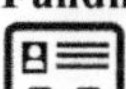

HQ: 7500 Security Boulevard
Baltimore, MD 21207
Phone: 410-786-5995
Email: inga.feldmanayte@cms.hhs.gov
http://www.cms.hhs.gov

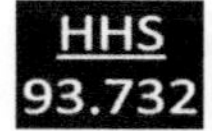

MENTAL & BEHAVIORAL HEALTH EDUCATION & TRAINING GRANTS "Behavioral Health Workforce Education and Training (BHWET)"

Award: Project Grants

Purpose: The BHWET Program develops and expands the behavioral health workforce serving populations across the lifespan, especially in rural and medically underserved areas.

Applicant Eligibility: Professional Track • Accredited institutions of higher education or accredited behavioral health professional training programs in behavioral pediatrics, social work, school social work, substance use disorder prevention and treatment, marriage and family therapy, occupational therapy, school counseling, or professional counseling. Programs must require a pre-degree clinical field placement in behavioral health as part of the training and a prerequisite for graduation.

Beneficiary Eligibility: In both the Professional and Paraprofessional Certificate Tracks, students must be enrolled in the school or program receiving the grant award in order to receive stipend and tuition support in the BHWET Program. In addition, students/interns must be U.S. citizens, U.S. nationals, or foreign nationals who possess a visa permitting permanent residence in the United States.

Award Range/Average: FY 16 Range: $57,142- $480,000; Average $307,637 FY 17 Range: $83,320- $480,000; Average $343,126 FY 18 est Range: $83,324- $480,000; Average $364,033

Funding: (Project Grants) FY 17 $44,000,000; FY 18 est $50,000,000; FY 19 est $0; FY 16 $43,078,630; - FY 16 $43,078,630 (via SAMHSA).

HQ: 5600 Fishers Lane, Room 11N94A
Rockville, MD 20857
Phone: 301-443-7759
http://www.hrsa.gov

MENTAL HEALTH DISASTER ASSISTANCE & EMERGENCY MENTAL HEALTH "Mental Health Disaster Assistance"

Award: Project Grants

Purpose: The program provides mental health counseling to individuals who are affected due to severe disasters.

Applicant Eligibility: Applicants may be State or local nonprofit agencies as recommended by the State Governor and accepted by the Secretary.

Beneficiary Eligibility: Individuals who were victims of major disasters.

Award Range/Average: $694,600 to $2,134,752; $1,305,100

Funding: Project Grants (Discretionary) FY 17 $8,018,395; FY 18 est $0; FY 19 est $0; FY 16 $19,459,721.

HQ: 5600 Fishers Lane
Rockville, MD 20857
Phone: 240-276-1418
Email: roger.george@samhsa.hhs.gov
http://www.samhsa.gov

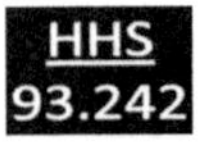

MENTAL HEALTH RESEARCH GRANTS

Award: Cooperative Agreements; Project Grants; Training

Purpose: To transform the understanding and treatment of mental illnesses through basic and clinical research, paving the way for prevention, recovery, and cure.

Applicant Eligibility: Public, private, -profit, or nonprofit agencies (including State and local government agencies), eligible Federal agencies, universities, colleges, hospitals, and academic or research institutions may apply for research grants. SBIR grants can be awarded only to domestic small businesses, and STTR grants can be awarded only to domestic small businesses which "partner" with a research institution in cooperative research and development.

Beneficiary Eligibility: Individuals and public, private, profit, or nonprofit organizations.

Award Range/Average: FY 2017 range: $1 to $9,957,606 Average Cost: $450,033

Funding: (Project Grants) FY 17 $1,274,043,961; FY 18 est $1,365,511,296; FY 19 N/A - These figures represent total base dollars for Research Grants, SBIR/STTR, and NRSA training grants.

HQ: 6001 Executive Boulevard
Rockville, MD 20892
Phone: 301-443-3367
Email: nimhreferral@mail.nih.gov
http://www.nimh.nih.gov

MICROBIOLOGY & INFECTIOUS DISEASES RESEARCH

Award: Project Grants

Purpose: To assist public and private nonprofit institutions and individuals to establish, expand and improve biomedical research and research training in infectious diseases and related areas; to conduct developmental research, to produce and test research materials.

Applicant Eligibility: Universities, colleges, hospitals, laboratories and other public or private nonprofit domestic institutions, including State and local units of government. Individuals are eligible to make application for grant support of research by a named principal investigator or a research career development candidate.

Beneficiary Eligibility: Any nonprofit or for-profit organization, company, or institution engaged in biomedical research.

Award Range/Average: $2,500 to $6,395,901 and the average $426,165.

Funding: N/A

HQ: Fishers Lane, Suite 5E39
Rockville, MD 20852
Phone: 301-761-7870
Email: kevin.richardson@nih.gov
http://www.niaid.nih.gov

MICROLOAN PROGRAM

Award: Formula Grants; Direct Loans

Purpose: To assist women, low-income, and minority entrepreneurs, business owners, and other individuals possessing the capability to operate successful business concerns and to assist small business concerns in those areas suffering from a lack of credit due to economic downturns.

Applicant Eligibility: An applicant is considered eligible to apply if it meets the definition of an intermediary lender as published in program materials, 13 CFR, and PL 102-140, and meets published minimum experience and capability requirements.

Beneficiary Eligibility: Small businesses, minority entrepreneurs, nonprofit entities, business owners, women and low-income, and other individuals possessing the capability to operate successful business concerns.

Award Range/Average: No Data Available.

Funding: (Direct Loans) FY 17 $44,000,000; FY 18 est $44,000,000; FY 19 est $42,000,000; FY 16 $35,000,000; - (Advisory Services and Counseling) FY 17 $23,535,000; FY 18 est $31,000,000; FY 19 est $25,000,000; FY 16 $24,340,000.

HQ: 409 3rd Street SW, 5th Floor
Washington, DC 20416
Phone: 202-205-7001
Email: daniel.upham@sba.gov
http://www.sba.gov

MIDDLE EAST PARTNERSHIP INITIATIVE "MEPI"

Award: Cooperative Agreements; Project Grants

Purpose: Supports organizations and individuals in their efforts to promote political, economic, and social engagement in the Middle East and North Africa.

Applicant Eligibility: U.S. or foreign non-profit organizations; for-profit organizations; private institutions of higher education, public or state institutions of higher education; public international organizations; and small businesses with functional and regional experience. Each solicitation outlines who is eligible and what types of experience are needed to apply for funding.

Beneficiary Eligibility: MEPI supports projects in Algeria, Bahrain, Israel, Iraq, Jordan, Kuwait, Lebanon, Libya, Morocco, Qatar, Saudi Arabia, Syria, Tunisia, West Bank and Gaza, and Yemen. Regional and multi-country projects may include Iraqi participants, but we currently do not fund Iraq-specific projects.

Award Range/Average: From $10,000 to $9,600,000; average approximately $3,100,000.

Funding: N/A

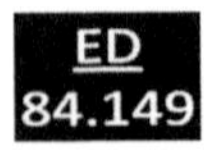

MIGRANT EDUCATION COLLEGE ASSISTANCE MIGRANT PROGRAM "CAMP"

Award: Project Grants

Purpose: To assist students whose background in migrant and other seasonal farm work, are enrolled or are admitted for enrollment on a full-time basis, at institutions of higher education and are in the first academic year at such an institution.

Applicant Eligibility: Institutions of higher education or private nonprofit agencies in cooperation with institutions of higher education may apply.

Beneficiary Eligibility: First-year college students who are engaged, or whose immediate family member is engaged, in migrant and other seasonal formwork or who have participated or been eligible to participate in the Title I, Migrant Education Program, or the Department of Labor's National Farmworker Jobs Program.

Award Range/Average: $180,000 - $425,000. Average is $410,615.

Funding: (Project Grants) FY 17 $22,212,961; FY 18 est $22,073,297; FY 19 est $22,199,943; FY 16 $22,199,943.

HQ: 400 Maryland Avenue S W, Room 3E311
Washington, DC 20202
Phone: 202-260-1426
Email: lisa.gillette@ed.gov
http://www.ed.gov/program/hep/index.html

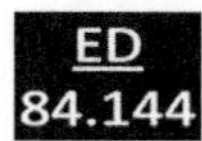

MIGRANT EDUCATION COORDINATION PROGRAM

Award: Project Grants

Purpose: To provide financial incentives to State Educational Agencies (SEAs) to participate in consortia that provide high-quality project designs and services to improve the interstate or intrastate coordination of migrant education programs for migratory children who have their education interrupted.

Applicant Eligibility: SEAs receiving MEP State Formula grants, in a consortium with another State or other appropriate entities.

Beneficiary Eligibility: Migratory children of migratory agricultural workers or migratory fishers, or individuals under 21 years old who are migratory agricultural workers or migratory fishers, or spouses of such workers or fishers whose education is interrupted benefit.

Award Range/Average: $60,000 - $120,000

Funding: FY 17 $3,000,000; FY 18 est $3,000,000; FY 19 est $3,000,000.

HQ: 400 Maryland Avenue S W, Room 3E311
Washington, DC 20202
Phone: 202-260-1426
Email: lindsay.booth@ed.gov
http://www.ed.gov/about/offices/list/oese/ome/index.html

MIGRANT EDUCATION HIGH SCHOOL EQUIVALENCY PROGRAM "HEP"

Award: Project Grants

Purpose: To assist students whose background from migrant and other seasonal farm-work to obtain the equivalent of a secondary school diploma and to gain employment or be placed in an institution of higher education or other postsecondary education or training.

Applicant Eligibility: Institutions of higher education or private nonprofit agencies in cooperation with institutions of higher education may apply.

Beneficiary Eligibility: Persons who are engaged or whose immediate family is engaged in migrant and other seasonal farm work or who have participated or have been eligible to participate in the Title I, Migrant Education Program or the Department of Labor's National Farmworker Jobs Program. Eligible beneficiaries also must be age 16 and older or beyond the age of compulsory school attendance, and lacking a high school diploma or its equivalent.

Award Range/Average: Range: $180,000- $475,000 Average: $446,438.

Funding: FY 17 $22,212,961; FY 18 est $21,928,478; FY 19 est $22,199,943.

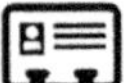

HQ: Avenue S W, Room 3E311
Washington, DC 20202
Phone: 202-260-1426
Email: lisa.gillette@ed.gov
http://www.ed.gov/program/hep/index.html

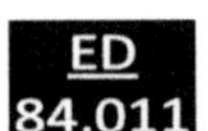

MIGRANT EDUCATION STATE GRANT PROGRAM

Award: Formula Grants

Purpose: To assist States with the migratory children to meet the same challenging State content and performance standards.

Applicant Eligibility: State educational agencies or consortia of State educational agencies.

Beneficiary Eligibility: Children, ages 0 through 21, of migratory agricultural workers or migratory fishers, including children

Award Range/Average: The range of awards in FY 2017 was $0 - $114,481,469.

Funding: (Formula Grants) FY 17 $364,751,000; FY 18 est $364,079,000; FY 19 est $364,079,000; FY 16 $364,751,000.

HQ: Avenue S W, Room 3E311
Washington, DC 20202
Phone: 202-260-1426
Email: lisa.gillette@ed.gov
http://www.ed.gov/programs/mep/index.html

MINERALS LEASING ACT

Award: Direct Payments for Specified Use

Purpose: Office of Natural Resources Revenue (ONRR) shares 50 percent (90 percent for Alaska) of mineral leasing revenue with States.

Applicant Eligibility: Revenue from public land leasing will trigger automatic payment distribution computed in accordance with the Law.

Beneficiary Eligibility: State governments in which Federal leased lands and minerals are located.

Award Range/Average: N/A

Funding: (Direct Payments for Specified Use) FY 18 est $1,647,867,000; FY 17 $1,395,081,000; FY 19 est $1,824,498,000.

HQ: 1849 C Street NW, P.O. Box 4211
Washington, DC 20240
Phone: 202-513-0600
http://www.onrr.gov

MINORITY HEALTH & HEALTH DISPARITIES RESEARCH

Award: Project Grants

Purpose: To support basic, clinical, social, and behavioral research; promote research infrastructure and training; foster emerging programs; disseminate information; and reach out to minority and other health disparity communities.

Applicant Eligibility: Individuals and public and private institutions, both non-profit and for-profit, who propose to establish, expand, and conduct research, promote or engage in research training, and outreach activities that contribute to improving minority health and/or eliminating health disparities. Endowment grants: Only NIMHD Centers of Excellence or Section 736 health professional schools (see 42 U.S.C.

Beneficiary Eligibility: Any non-profit or for-profit organization, company, or institution engaged in biomedical and behavioral research. Endowment grants: NIMHD Centers of Excellence or Section 736 institutions.

Award Range/Average: (1) Centers of Excellence (COE) grants: 14 total awards made by the NIMHD ranged from $1,091,427 to $1,563,465; average $1,412,022. (2) Endowment grants: 5 total awards made by the NIMHD ranged from $1,900,000 to $2,000,000; average $1,980,000. (3) Centers of Excellence on Environmental Health Disparities Research (P50): 2 total awards made by the NIMHD ranged from $700,000 to $799,178; average $749,589. (4) Minority Health and Health Disparities Research International Research Training (MHIRT) grants: 22 total awards made by the NIMHD ranged from $106,508 to $269,872; average $251,063. (5) Small Business Innovation Research (SBIR) grants: 21 total awards made by the NIMHD ranged from $187,157 to $755,980; average $406,131. (6) Small Business Technology Transfer (STTR) Grants: 3 total awards made by the NIMHD ranged from $220,560 to $689,032; average $394,288. (7) Health Disparities Research Project grants and cooperative agreements (RPG): 205 total awards made by the NIMHD ranged from $74,761 to $2,005,661; average $510,887. (8) Research Centers in Minority Institutions (RCMI): 18 total awards made ranged from $455,263 to $4,849,098; average $2,379,637. (9) RCMI Infrastructure for Clinical and Translational Research (RCTR): 5 total awards made ranged from $2,206,313 to $3,152,326; average $2,776,705. (10) RCMI Translational Research Network (RTRN): single award made was $2,170,006. (11) Clinical Research Education and Career Development (CRECD) Awards: 4 total awards ranged from $534,513 to $540,000; average $537,625. (12) Resource-Related and Research Capacity Building grants: 2 total awards made by the NIMHD ranged from $345,595 to $534,789; average $440,192. (13) Pathway to Independence Awards: 3 total awards made by the NIMHD ranged from $90,386 to $132,943; average $117,355. (14) NIH Research Conference Grants: 10 total awards made ranged from $49,718 to $110,000; average $58,857. (15) Transdisciplinary Collaborative Centers: 11 total awards made ranged from $1,594,338 to $3,000,000; average $2,382,557. (16) Disparities Research and Education Advancing Mission (DREAM) Career Transition Awards: single award made was $235,337. (17) Ruth L. Kirschstein NRSA Individual Fellowships: 9 total awards ranged from $28,044 to $44,044; average $40,958. (18) NIH BD2K Enhancing Diversity in Biomedical Data Science: 7 total awards ranged from $210,072 to $323,443; average $246,235. (19) NIH Director's New Innovator Award Program (DP2): single award made was $2,542,500.

Funding: (Project Grants) FY 17 $245,071,212; FY 18 N/A FY 19 FY 16 $235,912,124.

HQ: 7201 Wisconsin Avenue, Suite 533
Bethesda, MD 20892
Phone: 301-594-1788
Email: joan.wasserman@nih.gov
http://www.nimhd.nih.gov

MINORITY SCIENCE & ENGINEERING IMPROVEMENT "MSEIP"

Award: Project Grants

Purpose: To effect long-range improvement in science and engineering education at predominantly minority institutions; and to increase the participation of underrepresented ethnic minorities, particularly minority women, in scientific and technological careers.

Applicant Eligibility: Private and public nonprofit accredited (or successfully working toward accreditation) institutions of higher education that award baccalaureate degrees; and are minority institutions; public or private accredited (or successfully working toward accreditation) nonprofit institutions of higher education that award associate degrees, and are minority institutions that have a curriculum that includes science and engineering subjects; and enters into a partnership with public or private nonprofit institutions of higher education that award baccalaureate degrees in science or engineering. Applications may also be submitted by nonprofit science-oriented organizations, professional scientific societies, and institutions of higher education that award baccalaureate degrees, that provide a needed service to a group of minority institutions; or provide in-service training for project directors, scientists, and engineers from minority institutions; or consortia of organizations, that provide needed services to one or more minority institutions, the membership of which may include: institutions of higher education which have a curriculum in science or engineering; institutions of higher education that have graduate or professional programs in science or engineering; research laboratories of, or under contract with the Department of Energy; private organizations that have science or engineering facilities; or quasi-governmental entities that have a significant scientific or engineering mission.

Beneficiary Eligibility: Private or public accredited (or successfully working toward accreditation) 2- and 4-year institutions of higher education whose enrollments of a single minority or a combination of minorities exceed 50 percent of the total enrollment. The term minorities refers to American Indian; Alaskan Native; Native Hawaiian, Black (not of Hispanic origin); Hispanic (including persons of Mexican, Puerto Rican, Cuban, and Central or South American origin); Pacific Islander; or other ethnic group who are underrepresented in science and engineering.

Award Range/Average: FY 2017: Average new award was $236,700; Average continuation award was $242,900. Awards ranged from approximately $164,000 to $250,000.

Funding: (Project Grants) FY 17 $9,648,000; FY 18 est $11,052,000; FY 19 est $11,052,000; FY 16 $8,971,000.

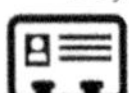

HQ: 400 Maryland Avenue SW
Washington, DC 20202
Phone: 202-453-7913
Email: bernadette.hence@ed.gov
http://www.ed.gov/programs/iduesmsi

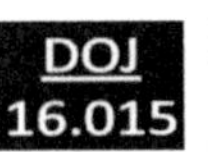

MISSING ALZHEIMER'S DISEASE PATIENT ASSISTANCE PROGRAM "Alzheimer's Initiatives"

Award: Cooperative Agreements

Purpose: To assist law enforcement agencies search for missing persons with Alzheimer disease.

Applicant Eligibility: N/A

Beneficiary Eligibility: All funds must be focused solely on initiatives to benefit those with Alzheimer's disease or other forms of dementia.

Award Range/Average: BJA may make one or more awards under this category.

Funding: N/A

HQ: 810 7th Street NW
Washington, DC 20531
Phone: 202-616-6500
Email: david.p.lewis@usdoj.gov
http://www.bja.gov

MISSING CHILDREN'S ASSISTANCE "Missing and Exploited Children (MEC) Program"

Award: Project Grants

Purpose: To coordinate missing and exploited children activities and to support research, training, technical assistance, and demonstration programs to enhance the overall response to missing and exploited children and as well as their families.

Applicant Eligibility: Eligible applicants are limited to states (including territories), units of local government, federally recognized tribal governments as determined by the Secretary of the Interior, nonprofit and for-profit organizations (including tribal nonprofit and for-profit organizations), and institutions of higher education (including tribal institutions of higher education). For-profit organizations (as well as other recipients) must forgo any profit or management fee.

Beneficiary Eligibility: State and local units of government, private nonprofit agencies, organizations, institutions or individuals.

Award Range/Average: No Data Available.

Funding: (Project Grants) FY 17 $65,690,610; FY 18 est $76,000,000; FY 19 est $72,000,000.

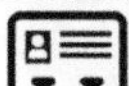

HQ: 810 7th Street NW
Washington, DC 20531
Phone: 202-514-5533
Email: james.antal@usdoj.gov
http://www.ojjdp.gov

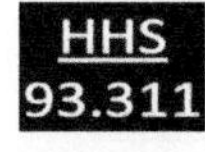

MOBILIZATION FOR HEALTH: NATIONAL PREVENTION PARTNERSHIP AWARDS "NPPA"

Award: Project Grants

Purpose: To provide strategic direction for the coordination of the vaccine and immunization enterprise for the National Vaccine Plan (NVP) implementation.

Applicant Eligibility: Public (including city, county, regional, and State government) organizations and private nonprofit entities.

Beneficiary Eligibility: All children, women (including pregnant women), and adults, including those underserved and minority populations in the US.

Award Range/Average: Program ended June, 2018

Funding: (Project Grants) FY 17 N/A FY 18 N/A FY 19 FY 16 $2,428,998.

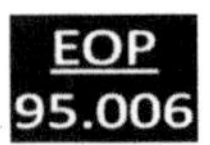

HQ: 1101 Wootton Parkway Tower Building, Suite 550
Rockville, MD 20852
Phone: 240-453-8442
Email: alice.bettencourt@hhs.gov
http://www.hhs.gov/ash/public_health/indexph.html

EOP 95.006

MODEL STATE DRUG LAWS INITIATIVE

Award: Project Grants

Purpose: ONDCP's Model State Drug Laws Initiative helps to create comprehensive laws, policies and programs on current and emerging drug and alcohol issues in different States and localities.

Applicant Eligibility: Applicants must have expert knowledge and extensive experience in conducting research and analysis, providing technical assistance, and drafting model state drug and alcohol laws, policies and programs as established by PL109-469, Section 1105, MODEL ACTS and in accordance with the President's Commission on Model State Drug Laws in 1993.

Beneficiary Eligibility: N/A

Award Range/Average: range varies based upon appropriated amount

Funding: (Cooperative Agreements) FY 17 $2,500,000; FY 18 est $0; FY 19 est $2,500,000; FY 16 $0.

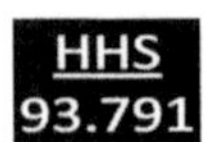

HQ: 750 17th Street NW
Washington, DC 20503
Phone: 202-395-6739
Email: phuong_desear@ondcp.eop.gov
http://www.whitehouse.gov/ondcp

HHS 93.791

MONEY FOLLOWS THE PERSON REBALANCING DEMONSTRATION

"Money Follows the Person Demonstration"

Award: Project Grants

Purpose: The Money Follows the Person Rebalancing Demonstration program was designed to assist States to balance their long-term care systems and help Medicaid enrollees transition from institutions to the community.

Applicant Eligibility: Applicants for this Demonstration Grant must be any single State Medicaid Agency, State Mental Health Agency, or instrumentality of the State. Only one application can be submitted for a given State.

Beneficiary Eligibility: As defined in the Affordable Care Act, the term "eligible individual" means an individual in the State who, immediately before beginning participation in the MFP demonstration project: (i) resides (and has resided, for a period of not less than 90 consecutive days in an inpatient facility; (ii) is receiving Medicaid benefits for inpatient services furnished by such inpatient facility; and (iii) with respect to whom a determination has been made that, but for the provision of home and community-based long- term care services, the individual would continue to require the level of care provided in an inpatient facility and, in any case in which the State applies a more stringent level of care standard as a result of implementing the State plan option permitted under section 1915 (i) of the Social Security Act, the individual must continue to require at least the level of care which had resulted in admission to the institution.

Award Range/Average: There is not a prescribed or predetermined maximum floor or ceiling grant award. Each State is unique in the number of individuals that will be projected for transition under the demonstration grant. In addition, the costs of individuals transitioning to community settings may vary, by targeted population. Applicants are advised to request a grant award that is sufficient in the amount needed to transition the projected individuals into community settings. CMS reserves the right to reduce the requested grant award, based on the number and size of additional grant awards given under this demonstration, as well as because of concerns contained within a State's application (i.e., concerns with the number of costs of individuals projected for transition by the individual State.

Funding: N/A

HQ: 7500 Security Boulevard
Baltimore, MD 21244
Phone: 410-786-8287
Email: cathy.cope@cms.hhs.gov
http://www.cms.gov/communityservices/20_mfp.asp

HUD 14.162 MORTGAGE INSURANCE COMBINATION & MANUFACTURED HOME LOT LOANS "Title I"

Award: Guaranteed/Insured Loans

Purpose: To make reasonable financing for the purchase of a manufactured home and a lot.

Applicant Eligibility: All persons are eligible to apply.

Beneficiary Eligibility: Individuals/families.

Award Range/Average: The maximum mortgage amount is $92,904 for a manufactured home on a suitably developed lot and $23,226 for a developed lot only.

Funding: (Sale, Exchange, or Donation of Property and Goods) FY 17 FY 16 FY 15 - Reported Under 14.110 for Fiscal Years 2009 through present.

HQ: 451 7th Street SW
Washington, DC 20410
Phone: 800-225-5342
http://portal.hud.gov/hudportal/hud?src=/program_offices/housing/sfh/title/manuf146

HUD 14.126 MORTGAGE INSURANCE COOPERATIVE PROJECTS "213 Cooperatives"

Award: Guaranteed/Insured Loans

Purpose: Enabling nonprofit cooperative ownership housing corporations or trusts to develop or sponsor the development of housing projects to be operated as cooperatives.

Applicant Eligibility: Eligible mortgagors are nonprofit cooperatives, ownership housing corporations or trusts which may either sponsor projects directly, sell individual units to cooperative members, or purchase projects from investor-sponsors (builders, developers, or others who meet HUD requirements).

Beneficiary Eligibility: Members of the cooperative are eligible to occupy a dwelling in the structure whose mortgage is insured under the program.

Award Range/Average: No Data Available.

Funding: (Guaranteed/Insured Loans) FY 15 est $15,000,000; FY 14 est $15,000,000; FY 16 FY 13 $16,700,000; FY 17.

HQ: 451 7th Street SW
Washington, DC 20410
Phone: 202-402-2579
Email: carmelita_a._james@hud.gov
http://www.hud.gov/offices/hsg/hsgmulti.cfm

MORTGAGE INSURANCE FOR THE PURCHASE OR REFINANCING OF EXISTING MULTIFAMILY HOUSING PROJECTS "Section 223(f)/207)"

Award: Guaranteed/Insured Loans

Purpose: To provide mortgage insurance to HUD-approved lenders for the purchase or refinancing of existing multifamily housing projects.

Applicant Eligibility: Mortgagors may be either profit and non-profit.

Beneficiary Eligibility: All persons are eligible to occupy such projects subject to normal occupancy restrictions.

Award Range/Average: No Data Available.

Funding: (Guaranteed/Insured Loans) FY 13 $7,700,000,000; FY 17 FY 14 est $7,000,000,000; FY 15 est $70,000,000,000.

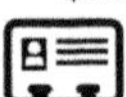

HQ: 451 7th Street SW
Washington, DC 20410
Phone: 202-402-2579
Email: carmelita_a._james@hud.gov
http://www.hud.gov/offices/hsg/hsgmu

MORTGAGE INSURANCE HOMES FOR DISASTER VICTIMS "203(h))"

Award: Guaranteed/Insured Loans

Purpose: To help victims of a disaster declared by the President undertake homeownership on a solid basis.

Applicant Eligibility: Anyone that is a victim of a major disaster as designated by the President is eligible to apply.

Beneficiary Eligibility: Families or individuals that are victims of a major disaster as designated by the President.

Award Range/Average: No Data Available.

Funding: (Sale, Exchange, or Donation of Property and Goods) FY 17 FY 15 FY 16 - Reported Under 14.117 for all fiscal years.

HQ: 451 7th Street SW
Washington, DC 20410
Phone: 800-225-5342
http://portal.hud.gov/hudportal/hud?src=/program_offices/housing/sfh/ins/203h-dft

MORTGAGE INSURANCE HOMES IN URBAN RENEWAL AREAS "220 Homes"

Award: Guaranteed/Insured Loans

Purpose: To assist qualified entities to purchase and/or rehabilitate homes in urban renewal areas.

Applicant Eligibility: Eligible mortgagors include private profit motivated entities, public bodies and others who meet HUD requirements for mortgagors.

Beneficiary Eligibility: Families and Individuals

Award Range/Average: No Data Available.

Funding: (Guaranteed/Insured Loans) FY 16 FY 17 FY 15 est $100,000,000; FY 14 est $100,000,000; FY 13 - Reported under 14.117.

HQ: 451 7th Street SW
Washington, DC 20410
Phone: 202-402-2579
Email: carmelita_a._james@hud.gov
http://www.hud.gov/offices/hsg/hsgmulti.cfm

MORTGAGE INSURANCE HOMES "203(b))"

Award: Guaranteed/Insured Loans

Purpose: To assist people undertake home ownership.

Applicant Eligibility: All persons with a valid Social Security Number are eligible to apply. State and local government agencies, HUD approved non-profit organizations and individuals employed by the Work Bank or a foreign embassy are not required to provide a Social Security number.

Beneficiary Eligibility: Individuals/families.

Award Range/Average: Maximum insurable loans are as follows: In areas where 125 percent of the median house price is less than 65 percent of the National Conforming Loan Limit ($417,000), FHA "floor" limits are set at the 65 percent limit as follows: one-family $271,050; two-family $347,000; three-family $419,425; and four-family $521,250. Any area where the limits exceed the floor is known as a "high cost" area. In areas where 115 percent of the median house price exceeds 150 percent of the National

Conforming Loan Limit for a one unit property, the mortgage limits are set at the 150 percent amount (ceiling)as follows: one-unit $625,500; two-unit $800,775; three-unit $967,950; and four-unit $1,202,925.

Funding: (Sale, Exchange, or Donation of Property and Goods) FY 15 $212,961,411,747; FY 17 est $204,000,000,000; FY 16 est $209,000,000,000.

HQ: 451 7th Street SW
Washington, DC 20410
Phone: 800-225-5342
http://portal.hud.gov/hudportal/hud?src=/program_offices/housing/sfh/ins/203h-dft

MORTGAGE INSURANCE HOSPITALS
"Section 242 – Mortgage Insurance for Hospitals"

Award: Guaranteed/Insured Loans

Purpose: To facilitate the affordable financing of hospitals for the care and treatment of persons who are acutely ill or who otherwise require medical care.

Applicant Eligibility: Qualified applicants can be either profit or not-for-profit hospitals licensed or regulated by the State, municipality, or other political subdivision. At least 50 percent of the care must be for general acute patients as of June 2012.

Beneficiary Eligibility: Persons needing the services of these hospitals benefit by using the modernized facilities supported by the insured mortgages.

Award Range/Average: No Data Available.

Funding: (Guaranteed/Insured Loans) FY 16 est $665,000,000; FY 15 $160,000,000; FY 17 est $300,000,000.

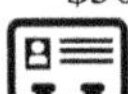

HQ: 451 7th Street SW, Room 6264
Washington, DC 20410
Phone: 202-402-2333
Email: ivy.m.jackson@hud.gov
http://www.fha.gov/healthcare

MORTGAGE INSURANCE HOUSING IN OLDER, DECLINING AREAS
"223(e))"

Award: Guaranteed/Insured Loans

Purpose: To aid in the acquisition or rehabilitation of housing in older, declining urban areas.

Applicant Eligibility: HUD-approved mortgagees.

Beneficiary Eligibility: For single family purposes, an individual or family is eligible to apply through HUD approved mortgagees. Multifamily sponsorship is determined by applicable program requirements.

Award Range/Average: No Data Available.

Funding: (Sale, Exchange, or Donation of Property and Goods) FY 17 FY 16 FY 15 - Reported under 14.117.

HQ: 451 7th Street
Washington, DC 20410
Phone: 800-225-5342
http://portal.hud.gov/hudportal/hud?src=/program_offices/housing/sfh/ins/sfh203b

MORTGAGE INSURANCE NURSING HOMES, INTERMEDIATE CARE FACILITIES, BOARD & CARE HOMES & ASSISTED LIVING FACILITIES "232"

Award: Guaranteed/Insured Loans

Purpose: To assist the construction or rehabilitation of nursing homes, intermediate care facilities, board and care homes and assisted-living facilities, to allow purchase or refinancing with/without repairs of projects not requiring significant rehabilitation, and to provide loan insurance to install fire safety equipment.

Applicant Eligibility: Eligible mortgagors include investors, builders, developers, public entities, nursing homes and private nonprofit corporations or associations.

Beneficiary Eligibility: Residents requiring skilled nursing, custodial care, and assistance with activities of daily living are eligible to live in a structure whose mortgage is insured under the program.

Award Range/Average: No Data Available.

Funding: (Guaranteed/Insured Loans) FY 16 est $2,765,000,000; FY 15 $2,770,000,000; FY 17 est $2,765,000,000.

HQ: 451 7th Street SW, Room 6264
Washington, DC 20410
Phone: 202-402-2333
Email: ivy.m.jackson@hud.gov
http://www.hud.gov/healthcare

MORTGAGE INSURANCE PURCHASE OF UNITS IN CONDOMINIUMS "203(b)"

Award: Guaranteed/Insured Loans

Purpose: To enable individuals and families to buy or refinance qualified units in FHA-approved home projects.

Applicant Eligibility: All individuals and families are eligible to apply.

Beneficiary Eligibility: Individuals/families.

Award Range/Average: No Data Available.

Funding: (Sale, Exchange, or Donation of Property and Goods) FY 17 FY 15 FY 16 - Reported under 14.117.

HQ: 451 7th Street
Washington, DC 20410
Phone: 800-225-5342
http://portal.hud.gov/hudportal/hud?src=/program_offices/housing/sfh/ins/sfh203b

MORTGAGE INSURANCE RENTAL & COOPERATIVE HOUSING FOR MODERATE INCOME FAMILIES & ELDERLY, MARKET INTEREST RATE
"221(d)(4) Multifamily - Market Rate Housing)"

Award: Guaranteed/Insured Loans

Purpose: To provide quality rental or cooperative housing for moderate-income families, elderly, and disabled.

Applicant Eligibility: Public, profit-motivated sponsors, limited distribution, nonprofit cooperative, builder-seller, investor-sponsor, and general mortgagors.

Beneficiary Eligibility: All families are eligible to occupy dwellings in a structure whose mortgage is insured under the program, subject to normal tenant selection. There are no income limits.

Award Range/Average: No Data Available.

Funding: (Guaranteed/Insured Loans) FY 13 $2,470,000,000; FY 16 est $3,541,142,939; FY 17 est $3,786,731,323; FY 14 est $2,400,000,000; FY 15 $3,362,376,350.

HQ: 451 7th Street SW
Washington, DC 20410
Phone: 202-402-2579
Email: carmelita_a._james@hud.gov
http://www.hud.gov

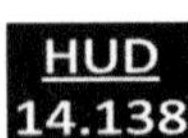

MORTGAGE INSURANCE RENTAL HOUSING FOR THE ELDERLY
"231"

Award: Guaranteed/Insured Loans

Purpose: To provide quality rental housing for the elder people.

Applicant Eligibility: Eligible mortgagors include private profit-motivated developers, and nonprofit sponsors.

Beneficiary Eligibility: All elderly or handicapped persons are eligible to occupy apartments in a project whose mortgage is insured under the program.

Award Range/Average: No Data Available.

Funding: (Guaranteed/Insured Loans) FY 14 est $15,000,000; FY 15 $53,212,283; FY 13 $17,000,000; FY 17 est $59,494,779; FY 16 est $55,170,497.

HQ: 1200 New Jersey Avenue SE NRO-100
Washington, DC 20590
Phone: 202-366-2121
Email: maggi.gunnels@dot.gov
http://www.nhtsa.gov

HUD 14.139

MORTGAGE INSURANCE RENTAL HOUSING IN URBAN RENEWAL AREAS "220 Multifamily"

Award: Guaranteed/Insured Loans

Purpose: To provide quality rental housing in urban renewal areas, code enforcement areas, and areas designated for overall revitalization.

Applicant Eligibility: Eligible mortgagors include private profit motivated entities, public bodies, and others who meet HUD requirements for mortgagors.

Beneficiary Eligibility: All families eligible to occupy a dwelling in a structure whose mortgage is insured under the program, subject to normal tenant selection.

Award Range/Average: No Data Available.

Funding: (Guaranteed/Insured Loans) FY 17 est $22,006,608; FY 13 $111,300,000; FY 15 $19,694,500; FY 16 est $20,387,968; FY 14 est $100,000,000.

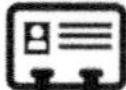

HQ: 451 7th Street SW
Washington, DC 20410
Phone: 202-402-2579
Email: carmelita_a._james@hud.gov
http://www.hud.gov

MORTGAGE INSURANCE RENTAL HOUSING "Section 207"

Award: Guaranteed/Insured Loans

Purpose: To increase supply of quality rental housing for middle-income families.

Applicant Eligibility: Eligible mortgagors include investors, builders, developers, and others who meet HUD requirements for mortgagors.

Beneficiary Eligibility: All families eligible to occupy dwellings in a structure whose mortgage is insured under the program, subject to normal tenant selection.

Award Range/Average: No Data Available.

Funding: (Guaranteed/Insured Loans) FY 14 est $0; FY 16 est $5,916,508,274; FY 15 $6,422,666,988; FY 17 est $5,831,984,488; FY 13 $0.

HQ: 451 7th Street SW
Washington, DC 20410
Phone: 202-402-2579
Email: carmelita_a._james@hud.gov
http://www.hud.gov

MOVING TO WORK DEMONSTRATION PROGRAM

Award: Formula Grants

Purpose: To provide public housing agencies and the Secretary of Housing and Urban Development the flexibility to design and test different approaches for providing and administering housing assistance.

Applicant Eligibility: Public housing agencies administering the public housing program and/or the section 8 housing assistance payments program may be selected by the Secretary to participate.

Beneficiary Eligibility: Low-income public housing residents.

Award Range/Average: N/A

Funding: (Formula Grants) FY 17 est $3,912,687,996; FY 18 est $3,912,687,996; FY 16 $3,703,906,074.

HQ: 451 7th Street SW
Washington, DC 20410
Phone: 202-402-4306
Email: marianne.nazzaro@hud.gov
http://www.hud.gov/offices/pih/programs/ph/mtw

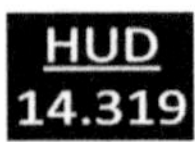

MULTIFAMILY ENERGY INNOVATION FUND
"Multifamily Energy Innovation Fund"

Award: Cooperative Agreements

Purpose: Increasing the energy efficiency of existing multifamily residential properties that can be copied by others.

Applicant Eligibility: This program is directed at the multifamily housing market, to catalyze innovations in the residential energy efficiency sector that have promise of replicability and to help create a standardized home energy efficient retrofit market.

Beneficiary Eligibility: Must be related to eligible multifamily housing.

Award Range/Average: We expect to make awards ranging from $2.5 to $7 million. For the total amount we expect to make between five and 10 awards.

Funding: (Cooperative Agreements) FY 12 est $24,750,000; FY 10 $0; FY 11 est $0.

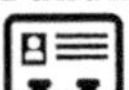

HQ: 451 7th Street SW, Room 6230
Washington, DC 20410
Phone: 202-402-8395
Email: beverly.n.rudman@hud.gov
http://www.hud.gov

MULTIFAMILY HOUSING SERVICE COORDINATORS

Award: Project Grants

Purpose: To link elderly or disabled non-elderly assisted housing and neighborhood residents, prevent premature and unnecessary institutionalization, and assess individual service needs, determine eligibility for public services, and make resource allocation decisions that enable residents to stay in the community longer.

Applicant Eligibility: Eligible applicants are owners of Section 8 developments with project-based subsidy (including Rural Housing Service Section 515/8 developments); Section 202 developments as defined under 24 CFR Sections 277 and 885, and 221(d)(3) below-market interest rate and 236 developments which are insured or assisted (funded under Sections 24 CFR 221 Subpart C, 236, 277, 880, 881, 883, 885 and 886). To be eligible, developments must also be current in mortgage payments.

Beneficiary Eligibility: Eligible beneficiaries are residents of eligible housing or community residents who live in the vicinity of such housing. Service Coordination may be provided to elderly or disabled families.

Award Range/Average: $88,825 to $402,196; $171,064.

Funding: (Project Grants) FY 17 est $75,000,000; FY 15 $86,000,000; FY 16 est $77,000,000; - Reported under program 14.157 for FY 10, FY 11, and FY 12.

HQ: 451 7th Street SW, Room 6146
Washington, DC 20410
Phone: 202-708-3000
Email: carissa.l.janis@hud.gov
http://portal.hud.gov/hudportal/hud?src=/program_offices/housing/mfh/scp/scphome

HHS
93.373

MULTIPLE APPROACHES TO SUPPORT YOUNG BREAST CANCER SURVIVORS & METASTATIC BREAST CANCER PATIENTS "CDC-RFA-DP19-1906"

Award: N/A

Purpose: To offer support for caregivers and families for these individuals, increased awareness of clinical trials by both young women diagnosed with cancer and individuals diagnosed with metastatic breast cancer, increased financial support, and improved quality of life among young breast cancer survivors.

Applicant Eligibility: Government organizations, non-governmental organizations, private colleges and universities, community-based organizations, faith-based organizations, for-profit organizations (other than small business), and small businesses can apply.

Beneficiary Eligibility: N/A

Award Range/Average: DP11-1111: $180,000 (Average award) DP14-1408: Component 1 ($200,000 - $450,000); Component 2 ($150,000 to $350,000) DP19-1906: TBD

Funding: Formula Grants (Cooperative Agreements) FY 17 $180,000; FY 18 est $800,000; FY 19 est $0.

HQ: 4770 Buford Highway Chamblee Campus, Building 107/4th Floor
Atlanta, GA 30341
Phone: 770-488-3094
Email: armoore@cdc.gov
http://cdc.gov

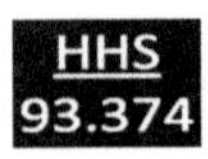

MULTIPLE APPROACHES TO SUPPORT YOUNG BREAST CANCER SURVIVORS & METASTATIC BREAST CANCER PATIENTS "CDC-RFA-DP19-1906"

Award: N/A

Purpose: To offer support for caregivers and families for these individuals, increased awareness of clinical trials by both young women diagnosed with cancer and individuals diagnosed with metastatic breast cancer, increased financial support, and improved quality of life among young breast cancer survivors.

Applicant Eligibility: Government organizations, non-governmental organizations, private colleges and universities, community-based organizations, faith-based organizations, for-profit organizations (other than small business), and small businesses can apply.

Beneficiary Eligibility: n/a

Award Range/Average: DP11-1111: $180,000 (Average award) DP14-1408: Component 1 ($200,000 - $450,000); Component 2 ($150,000 to $350,000) DP19-1906: TBD

Funding: Cooperative Agreements (Discretionary Grants) FY 17 $180,000; FY 18 est $449,998; FY 19 est $0.

HQ: 4770 Buford Highway Chamblee Campus, Building 107/4th Floor
Atlanta, GA 30341
Phone: 770-488-3094
Email: armoore@cdc.gov
http://cdc.gov

MULTI-STATE INFORMATION SHARING & ANALYSIS CENTER "MS-ISAC"

Award: Cooperative Agreements

Purpose: Serves as a cyber threat monitoring center to help local and State governments to address cybersecurity issues. It also acts as a cyber security center for the nation's elections community.

Applicant Eligibility: This funding opportunity is restricted to the Multi-State Information Sharing and Analysis Center (MS-ISAC). Specific information on applicant eligibility is identified in the funding opportunity announcement.

Beneficiary Eligibility: State Governments, local government, territorial governments, tribal governments and territories

Award Range/Average: N/A

Funding: (Salaries and Expenses) FY 17 $9,500,000; FY 18 est $9,500,000; FY 19 est $9,500,000; FY 16 $9,500,000.

HQ: 245 Murray Lane SW
Washington, DC 20528
Phone: 703-705-6213
Email: donnalee.beach@hq.dhs.gov
http://www.dhs.gov

NATIONAL BIOTERRORISM HOSPITAL PREPAREDNESS PROGRAM "HPP"

Award: Formula Grants

Purpose: To ready hospitals and other healthcare systems to deliver coordinated and effective care to victims of terrorism and other public health emergencies.

Applicant Eligibility: State health departments of all 50 States, the District of Columbia, the nation's three largest municipalities (New York City, Chicago and Los Angeles County), the Commonwealths of Puerto Rico and the Northern Mariana Islands, the territories of American Samoa, Guam and the United States Virgin Islands, the Federated States of Micronesia, and the Republics of Palau and the Marshall Islands.

Beneficiary Eligibility: All State health departments listed above, hospitals and supporting health care systems.

Award Range/Average: Range in FY 13: $270,000 - to $27,000,000. FY 13 Average: $5,351,000

Funding: Formula Grants (Cooperative Agreements) FY 17 $150,000; FY 18 est $150,000; FY 19 est $150,000; FY 16 $150,000.

HQ: 200 C E Street Concourse C4K17
Washington, DC 20024
Phone: 202-245-0732
Email: robert.dugas@hhs.gov
http://www.phe.gov

NATIONAL CENTER FOR ADVANCING TRANSLATIONAL SCIENCES "NCATS"

Award: Cooperative Agreements

Purpose: To catalyze the generation of innovative methods and technologies that will enhance the development, testing, and implementation of diagnostics and therapeutics across a wide range of human diseases and conditions.

Applicant Eligibility: Biomedical investigators at any nonprofit or for-profit organization, company, or institution engaged in biomedical research.

Beneficiary Eligibility: Same as Applicant Eligibility.

Award Range/Average: Clinical and Translational Science Award program: $1 - $24,600,001, Therapeutics for Rare and Neglected Diseases: $49,209 - $92,677

Funding: (Project Grants) FY 17 $579,953,132; FY 18 est $613,648,522; FY 19 est $561,194,638.

HQ: 6701 Democracy Boulevard, Room 970
Bethesda, MD 20892-4874
Phone: 301-435-0860
Email: parsonss@mail.nih.gov
http://www.ncats.nih.gov

NATIONAL CENTER FOR CAMPUS PUBLIC SAFETY "National Center"

Award: Cooperative Agreements

Purpose: The National Center identifies and examines safety and security and develops resources to expand services to those who are charged with providing a safe environment on the campuses of the nation's colleges and universities.

Applicant Eligibility: A demonstrated knowledge of campus public safety needs and demonstrated experience and infrastructure for successfully carrying out a multi-faceted initiative with multiple campus stakeholder groups is required.

Beneficiary Eligibility: State, local, and tribal criminal justice agencies are the primary beneficiaries of this program.

Award Range/Average: See the current fiscal year's solicitation available at the Office of Justice Programs

Funding:N/A

HQ: 810 Seventh Street NW
Washington, DC 20531
Phone: 202-514-5309
http://www.bja.gov

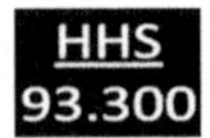

NATIONAL CENTER FOR HEALTH WORKFORCE ANALYSIS "Health Workforce Research Centers; NCHWA HWRC"

Award: Cooperative Agreements

Purpose: To provide for the development of information describing and analyzing the healthcare workforce and workforce related issues in order to provide necessary information for decision-making regarding future directions in health professions in response to societal and professional needs.

Applicant Eligibility: Those eligible to apply are: state or local governments, a state workforce investment board, public health or health professions schools, schools of medicine, schools of nursing, universities, academic health centers, community-based health facilities, and other appropriate public or private nonprofit entities, including faith based and community based organizations. Federally Recognized Indian Tribal Government and Native American Organizations may apply if they are otherwise eligible.

Beneficiary Eligibility: Those who will ultimately benefit from these grants are the local, state, and federal legislators, planners, and policy makers, as well as the public, who will receive the information needed to better understand health workforce issues and trends and to make evidenced-based health workforce decisions.

Award Range/Average: $549,795 to $666,716; average award of $569,412.

Funding: (Cooperative Agreements) FY 17 $3,646,754; FY 18 est $3,650,379; FY 19 est $3,279,031; FY 16 $2,989,303; - Not included: SAMHSA IAA for $886,093 to fund Behavioral Health Workforce Research Center.

HQ: 5600 Fishers Lane, Room 11N78
Rockville, MD 20857
Phone: 301-443-1304
Email: rstreeter@hrsa.gov
http://bhw.hrsa.gov/health-workforce-analysis/research/research-centers

HHS 93.702 NATIONAL CENTER FOR RESEARCH RESOURCES, RECOVERY ACT CONSTRUCTION SUPPORT

Award: Project Grants

Purpose: To renovate existing research facilities and build new research facilities to meet basic and clinical space requirements, laboratory safety, biohazard containment, and animal care standards to support the facility demands of NIH research programs.

Applicant Eligibility: Construction/Renewal/Rehabilitation

Beneficiary Eligibility: Public nonprofit institution/organization

Award Range/Average: Awards will range from $2M to $20M total costs. The average award is expected to be $10M.

Funding: (Project Grants) FY 16 $0; FY 17 est $0; FY 18 est $0; - There will be no available funds for competing awards after 2010.

HQ: 6701 Democracy Boulevard, Room 960
Bethesda, MD 20892
Phone: 301-435-0877
Email: farberg@mail.nih.gov
http://www.ncrr.nih.gov

NATIONAL CENTER ON SLEEP DISORDERS RESEARCH

Award: Project Grants

Purpose: To support research and research training related to sleep disordered breathing, and the fundamental functions of sleep and circadian rhythms.

Applicant Eligibility: Any nonprofit organization engaged in biomedical research and institutions or companies organized for profit may apply for almost any kind of grant. Only domestic, non-profit, private or public institutions may apply for NRSA Institutional Research Training Grants.

Beneficiary Eligibility: Any nonprofit or for-profit organization, company or institution engaged in biomedical research. Only domestic for-profit small business firms may apply for SBIR and STTR programs.

Award Range/Average: Grants: $25,416 to $2,620,576: $502,736. SBIR Phase I - $150,000; Phase II - up to $1,000,000; STTR Phase I - $150,000; Phase II - $1,000,000.

Funding: (Project Grants) FY 17 $62,180,387; FY 18 est $67,002,782; FY 19 est $67,002,782.

HQ: 6701 Rockledge Drive, Room 7176
Bethesda, MD 20892
Phone: 301-827-7968
Email: pharesda@nhlbi.nih.gov
http://www.nhlbi.nih.gov/about/scientific-divisions/national-center-sleep-disorders-research

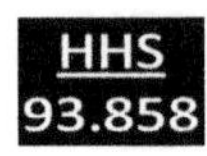

HHS 93.858 NATIONAL COLLABORATION TO SUPPORT HEALTH, WELLNESS & ACADEMIC SUCCESS OF SCHOOL-AGE CHILDREN

Award: Cooperative Agreements

Purpose: The purpose of this announcement is to fund applicants to improve the health of youth by funding NGOs to assist CDC funded grantees and the organizations' constituents to implement environmental and systems changes that support and reinforce healthful behaviors and reduce disparities. The program places a strong emphasis on training and professional development, technical assistance, dissemination and communication, and program implementation and evaluation, and all activities are to be developed and delivered within the whole school, whole community, and whole child framework.

Applicant Eligibility: - Eligibility is limited to Community-Based Organizations, Faith Based Organizations, American Indian or Alaska Native Tribally-Designated organizations, Nonprofit without or with 501C3 IRS Status (other than Institution of Higher Education) are eligible.

Beneficiary Eligibility: Nonprofit, Community-based, Faith based, American Indian/Alaska Native

Award Range/Average: Funding range $300,000 - $450,000 for FY 16

Funding: (Cooperative Agreements) FY 17 $2,099,750; FY 18 est $2,099,750; FY 19 est $2,099,750; FY 16 $1,775,000.

HQ: 4770 Buford Highway
Atlanta, GA 30341
Phone: 770-488-6167
http://www.cdc.gov

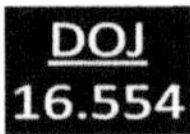

DOJ 16.554 NATIONAL CRIMINAL HISTORY IMPROVEMENT PROGRAM (NCHIP)

Award: Cooperative Agreements

Purpose: To enhance the quality and completeness of the nation's criminal history record systems.

Applicant Eligibility: Applicants are limited to the agency designated by the governor in each state to administer the NCHIP program, and federally recognized tribal entities. States and tribes may choose to submit applications as part of a multi-state consortium, multi-tribe consortium, or other entity.

Beneficiary Eligibility: Funds awarded to the state or tribe may be allocated for use in state or local/tribal agencies or the courts, but should have an impact on national record systems. Private organizations may receive funds under contract arrangements with a state/tribal agency or its subgrantees to which NCHIP funds are allocated by the state/tribe.

Award Range/Average: See the current fiscal year's solicitation guidelines posted on the Office of Justice Programs.

Funding: (Project Grants) FY 17 $31,941,079; FY 18 est $50,000,000; FY 19 est $51,000,000; FY 16 $33,965,029.

HQ: 810 7th Street NW
Washington, DC 20531
Phone: 202-307-0765
Email: devon.adams@usdoj.gov
http://www.bjs.gov

NATIONAL CYBER SECURITY AWARENESS

Award: Cooperative Agreements

Purpose: The program helps to create a public awareness on cybersecurity and on safe ways on Internet browsing.

Applicant Eligibility: N/A

Beneficiary Eligibility: N/A

Award Range/Average: Refer to the funding opportunity announcement.

Funding: (Salaries and Expenses) FY 17 $550,000; FY 18 est $550,000; FY 19 est $550,000; FY 16 $550,000.

HQ: 245 Murray Lane SW, P.O. Box 0640
Arlington, VA 20598-0640
Phone: 703-705-6275
Email: daniel.stein@hq.dhs.gov
http://dhs.gov/stopthinkconnect

NATIONAL DAM SAFETY PROGRAM

Award: Project Grants

Purpose: The National Dam Safety Program allows the State and local governments to conduct dam safety checks through supervision of a dam's construction, operation and maintenance and by preparing for hazard mitigation of lives and property during the failure of dams.

Applicant Eligibility: All States and U.S. territories with a legislated and approved dam safety program are eligible for the National Dam Safety Program Assistance.

Beneficiary Eligibility: The State Dam Safety Program Office of eligible States.

Award Range/Average: Refer to program guidance.

Funding: (Project Grants) FY 17 $7,500,000; FY 18 est $6,800,000; FY 19 est $7,000,000; FY 16 $7,500,000.

HQ: 4th Floor, Room 427 500 C Street SW
Washington, DC 20472
Phone: 202-646-3435
Email: james.demby@fema.dhs.gov
http://www.fema.gov

NATIONAL DISASTER RESILIENCE COMPETITION "Community Development Block Grant P. L. 113-2"

Award: Project Grants

Purpose: To provide decent housing and a suitable living environment and expand economic opportunities mainly for persons of low and moderate income.

Applicant Eligibility: CDBG DR competitive funds are made available to States and units of general local governments designated by the President of the United States as disaster areas. These communities must have significant unmet recovery needs and the capacity to carry out a disaster recovery program (usually these are governments that already receive HOME or Community Development Block Grant allocations).

Beneficiary Eligibility: The principal beneficiaries of CDBG DR funds are low- and moderate-income persons (generally defined as a member of a family having an income equal to or less than the Section 8 low income limit established by HUD) in communities that have experienced a disaster event. Generally, grantees must use at least half of Disaster Recovery funds for activities that principally benefit low-and moderate-income persons.

Award Range/Average: Thirteen (13) grants were awarded. The smallest award amount was $15 million (New Jersey) and the largest was $176 million (New York City). The average award amount was $76.8 million.

Funding: Project Grants (Discretionary) FY 17 $791,723,730; FY 18 est $0; FY 19 est $0.

HQ: 801 Cherry Street, Suite 2800
Fort Worth, TX 76102
Phone: 817-978-5948
Email: phyllis.j.foulds@hud.gov
http://www.hudexchange.info/programs/cdbg-dr/resilient-recove

HHS 93.825 NATIONAL EBOLA TRAINING & EDUCATION CENTER (NETEC) "NETEC"

Award: Project Grants

Purpose: The program helps to increase the competency of healthcare and public health workers and the capability of healthcare facilities to deliver efficient and effective Ebola patient care through the nationwide, regional network for Ebola and other infectious diseases.

Applicant Eligibility: Eligible applicants are limited to health care facilities that have safely and successfully evaluated and treated patients with Ebola in the U.S. The lead applicant will collaborate, coordinate, plan, and work directly with the other facilities on appropriate activities described in the individual funding opportunity announcement, as well as distribute the funds from the funding opportunity announcement to support those activities.

Beneficiary Eligibility: Public health departments, hospitals and supporting health care systems

Award Range/Average: 12000000

Funding: Project Grants (Cooperative Agreements) FY 17 $5,431,430; FY 18 est $5,431,430; FY 19 est $5,431,430; FY 16 $3,506,523.

HQ: 200 C Street SW
Washington, DC 20024
Phone: 202-692-4673
Email: melissa.harvey@hhs.gov
http://www.phe.gov

NATIONAL FAMILY CAREGIVER SUPPORT, TITLE III, PART E

Award: Formula Grants

Purpose: To assist States, Territories in providing multifaceted systems of support services for family caregivers; and older relative caregivers.

Applicant Eligibility: Formula grants: State governments and U.S. Territories, with distribution to designated area agencies on aging through an approved State plan and intrastate funding formula.

Beneficiary Eligibility: Family caregivers, grandparents and older individuals who are relative caregivers will benefit.

Award Range/Average: No Data Available.

Funding: (Formula Grants) FY 17 $150,299,736; FY 18 est $180,586,000; FY 19 est $150,586,000; FY 16 $150,586,000.

HQ: 330 C Street SW
Washington, DC 20201
Phone: 202-795-7386
Email: greg.link@acl.hhs.gov
http://www.acl.gov

NATIONAL FAMILY CAREGIVER SUPPORT, TITLE VI, PART C, GRANTS TO INDIAN TRIBES & NATIVE HAWAIIANS
"Native American Caregiver Support Program, Title VI, Part C"

Award: Project Grants

Purpose: To assist Indian Tribal and Native Hawaiian Organizations in providing multifaceted systems of support services for family caregivers; and grandparents or older individuals who are relative caregivers.

Applicant Eligibility: Indian Tribal and Native Hawaiian Organizations with approved applications under Title VI, Parts A and B.

Beneficiary Eligibility: Family caregivers, grandparents, and older individuals who are relative caregivers will benefit.

Award Range/Average: FY 16 Ranges for Part C - $14,270- $58,547 FY 17 Ranges for Part C - $13,820- $56,560

Funding: (Formula Grants) FY 17 est $7,478,530; FY 16 $7,468,657; FY 18 N/A.

HQ: 330 C Street SW
Washington, DC 20201
Phone: 202-795-7380
http://www.acl.gov

DHS 97.018 NATIONAL FIRE ACADEMY TRAINING ASSISTANCE "Student Stipend Reimbursement Program"

Award: Direct Payments for Specified Use

Purpose: The program offers stipends to first responders and emergency managers attending the National Fire Academy courses to prepare and respond to man-made and natural disasters at a local or regional level.

Applicant Eligibility: Any student who is a member of a fire department or has significant responsibility for fire prevention and control and has been accepted into an eligible course at NFA may apply for stipend reimbursement. Federal or private industry employees or foreign students may be accepted into NFA courses but are not eligible for stipend reimbursement.

Beneficiary Eligibility: Student or sponsoring organization.

Award Range/Average: N/A

Funding: (Salaries and Expenses) FY 17 $1,775,000; FY 18 est $1,775,000; FY 19 est $1,775,000; FY 16 $1,640,758.

HQ: 500 C Street SW
Washington, DC 20472
Phone: 800-238-3828
http://www.usfa.fema.gov

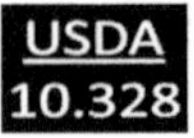

NATIONAL FOOD SAFETY TRAINING, EDUCATION, EXTENSION, OUTREACH, AND TECHNICAL ASSISTANCE COMPETITIVE GRANTS PROGRAM "National Food Safety Training, Education, Extension, Outreach, and Technical Assistance (aka FSMA)"

Award: Project Grants

Purpose: The National Food Safety training promotes education, technical assistance, food safety methods, organic agriculture production, and other environmental practices for conservation. These programs to be promoted to all agencies that serve those eligible people.

Applicant Eligibility: The Cooperative Extension Service for a U.S. state or territory; A non-profit community-based or non-governmental organization representing owners and operators of farms, small food processors, or small fruit and vegetable merchant wholesalers that has a commitment to public health and expertise in administering programs that contribute to food safety; An institution of higher education or a foundation maintained by an institution of higher education; Federal, State, Local, or Tribal Agencies, A collaboration of two or more eligible entities; or Such other appropriate entity, as determined by the Secretary of Agriculture.

Beneficiary Eligibility: Same as Applicant Eligibility.

Award Range/Average: If minimum or maximum amounts of funding per competitive and/or capacity project grant, or cooperative agreement are established, these amounts will be announced in the annual Competitive Request for Application (RFA).

Funding: Project Grants (Discretionary) FY 17 $4,760,653; FY 18 est $6,646,621; FY 19 est $0; FY 16 $4,758,326.

HQ: 1400 Independence Avenue SW
Washington, DC 20024
Phone: 202-205-0250
http://nifa.usda.gov/program/food-safety

NATIONAL FOREST ACQUIRED LANDS

Award: Direct Payments for Specified Use

Purpose: Shares 25 percent of minerals leasing revenue with the State in which such National Forest is situated.

Applicant Eligibility: Revenue from acquired National Forest land leasing will trigger automatic payment distribution computed in accordance with the Law.

Beneficiary Eligibility: ONRR distributes these funds to State governments for leased lands within the state and the State government had sole discretion in their use in accordance with the enabling legislation.

Award Range/Average: N/A

Funding: (Direct Payments for Specified Use) FY 18 est $8,471,000; FY 19 est $9,144,000; FY 17 $6,165,000.

HQ: 1849 C Street NW
Washington, DC 20240
Phone: 202-513-0600
http://www.onrr.gov

NATIONAL FORUM FOR STATE & TERRITORIAL CHIEF EXECUTIVES
"National Forum"

Award: Cooperative Agreements

Purpose: To collaborate on the development and implementation of innovative strategies and best practices related to health workforce issues, health systems, and access to healthcare.

Applicant Eligibility: Eligible applicants include public and nonprofit entities. Faith-based and community-based organizations, and tribes and tribal organizations as those terms are defined in 25 U.S.C.

Beneficiary Eligibility: Same as Applicant Eligibility.

Award Range/Average: Approximately $600,000 is expected to be available annually to fund one (1) recipient. There will be a New and Competing Continuation funding opportunity in FY 18 for a 5-year project period (FY 18-FY23).

Funding: (Cooperative Agreements) FY 17 $649,800; FY 18 est $600,000; FY 19 est $0; FY 16 $563,000.

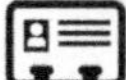
HQ: 5600 Fishers Lane
Rockville, MD 20857
Phone: 301-443-6204
Email: laraki@hrsa.gov
http://www.hrsa.gov

DOJ 16.819 NATIONAL FORUM ON YOUTH VIOLENCE PREVENTION "the Forum"

Award: Project Grants

Purpose: To assist localities by participating in the Forum to address youth violence.

Applicant Eligibility: 1) US Territories; state; local; public nonprofits; other public institutions; private nonprofits 2) law, justice, legal services; youth development 3) Contact program office for additional information.

Beneficiary Eligibility: 1) family/individual; youth; child, local 2) Contact program office for additional information.

Award Range/Average: capacity building awards: varied training and technical assistance award: varied

Funding: Project Grants (Discretionary) FY 17 $0; FY 18 est $0; FY 19 est $0; - While this has not been any funding under this program since FY 16, there are still open awards that had been made with Forum funds.

HQ: 810 7th Street NW
Washington, DC 20531
Phone: 202-514-3913
Email: robin.delany-shabazz@ojp.usdoj.gov
http://ojjdp.gov

NATIONAL HEALTH PROMOTION "APTR"

Award: Cooperative Agreements

Purpose: This program is no longer funded. The previous grant award ended on August 13, 2017.

Applicant Eligibility: This program is no longer funded. The grant award ended on August 31, 2017.

Beneficiary Eligibility: Same as Applicant Eligibility.

Award Range/Average: Up to $200,000

Funding: (Cooperative Agreements) FY 16 $100,000; FY 18 N/A FY 17 est $100,000; - Grant program ending 8/31/2017.

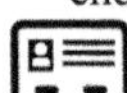

HQ: 1101 Wootton Parkway, Suite 550
Rockville, MD 20852
Phone: 240-453-8822
Email: eric.west@hhs.gov
http://www.healthypeople.gov

NATIONAL HEALTH SERVICE CORPS LOAN REPAYMENT PROGRAM "NHSC Loan Repayment Program (LRP)"

Award: Direct Payments for Specified Use

Purpose: To increase the supply of primary care physicians, dentists, dental hygienists, behavioral and mental health professionals, certified nurse midwives, primary care nurse practitioners, physician assistants and, if needed by the NHSC, other health professionals in Health Professional Shortage Areas.

Applicant Eligibility: Individuals are eligible to apply if they have (1) U.S. citizenship; (2) a health professions degree or are in professional practice (they must hold an unrestricted health professions license from the State in which they will be working, and be eligible for selection for a Federal civil service appointment, or hold an appointment as a commissioned officer in the Regular or Reserve Corps of the U.S. Public Health Service); (3) not had any judgment liens arising from Federal debt ; (4) not been excluded, debarred, suspended, or disqualified by a Federal agency; (5) not been in breach of a health professional service obligation to the Federal, State or local government and (6) no conflicting service obligation. Individuals must also participate or be eligible to participate as a provider in the Medicare, Medicaid, and Children's Health Insurance Programs, as appropriate.

Beneficiary Eligibility: Primary care, oral health, and mental and behavioral health professionals are eligible for the Loan Repayment Program (LRP). Specific specialties within these professions are selected for LRP awards based on community demand for health services.

Award Range/Average: N/A.

Funding: N/A

HQ: 5600 Fishers Lane, Room 14N56
Rockville, MD 20857
Phone: 301-594-4400
http://nhsc.hrsa.gov

NATIONAL HEALTH SERVICE CORPS SCHOLARSHIP PROGRAM
"NHSC Scholarship Program (SP)"

Award: Direct Payments for Specified Use

Purpose: To increase the supply of primary care physicians, dentists, certified nurse midwives, primary care nurse practitioners, and physician assistants and, if needed by the National Health Service Corps, other health professionals in Health Professional Shortage Areas (HPSAs) within the United States by providing service-obligated scholarships to health professions students.

Applicant Eligibility: At the time of application, the applicant must be a U.S. citizen or national. The applicant must be enrolled and/or accepted for enrollment and in good academic standing in an accredited school in a State, the District of Columbia, or a U.S. Territory as a full-time student in a course of study leading to a health professional degree.

Beneficiary Eligibility: The participant must maintain full-time enrollment, with good academic standing in an accredited school in a State, the District of Columbia, or a U.S. Territory as a full-time student in a course of study leading to a health professional degree. The participant must maintain eligibility for Federal employment, be free of any Federal judgment liens, not be excluded, debarred, suspended or disqualified by a Federal agency, and have no conflicting service obligation.

Award Range/Average: No Current Data Available

Funding: (Direct Payments for Specified Use) FY 17 $0; FY 18 est $0; FY 19 est $0; FY 16 $0.

HQ: 5600 Fishers Lane, Room 14N56
Rockville, MD 20857
Phone: 301-594-4400
http://nhsc.hrsa.gov

NATIONAL HEALTH SERVICE CORPS
"ACA National Health Service Corps - NHSC Loan Repayment Program (LRP), NHSC Scholarship Program (SP), The Students to Service (S2S) Loan Repayment Program, and State Loan Repayment Program (SLRP)"

Award: Project Grants; Direct Payments for Specified Use

Purpose: To assists Health Professional Shortage Areas (HPSAs) in every State, Territory, and Possession of the United States to meet their primary care medical, oral, and mental and behavioral health service needs by increasing the supply of clinicians.

Applicant Eligibility: For specific program and eligibility requirements, please see: http://nhsc.hrsa.gov/ SLRP: Entities eligible to apply for this grant program include the 50 States, the District of Columbia, Guam, the Commonwealth of Puerto Rico, the Northern Mariana Islands, the U.S. Virgin Islands, American Samoa, the Federated States of Micronesia, the Republic of the Marshall Islands, and the Republic of Palau. Federally Recognized Indian Tribal Government and Native American Organizations may apply if they are otherwise eligible.

Beneficiary Eligibility: Health professional, U.S. citizen Education, (13+)

Award Range/Average: NHSC LRP $556 to $50,000; with an average of $43,281. NHSC S2S $19,965 to $120,000; with an average of $116,000. NHSC SP $33,868 to $462,670; with an average of $205,580.

Funding: (Direct Payments for Specified Use) FY 17 $149,888,000; FY 18 est $164,349,000; FY 19 est $167,000; FY 16 $164,997,994; - NHSC LRP(Direct Payments for Specified Use) FY 17 $33,722,000; FY 18 est $38,000,000; FY 19 est $38,000,000; FY 16 $42,877,908; - NHSC

HQ: 5600 Fishers Lane, Room 14N56
Rockville, MD 20857
Phone: 301-594-4400
http://nhsc.hrsa.gov

NATIONAL IMPLEMENTATION & DISSEMINATION FOR CHRONIC DISEASE PREVENTION
"National Organizations"

Award: Cooperative Agreements

Purpose: To support national organizations and their chapters/affiliates' (sub-recipients) coalitions in implementing Socio-Ecological Model informed multi-level approaches to improve communities' health.

Applicant Eligibility: This cooperative agreement is limited to national organizations (to include public and private nonprofit organizations) that serve communities across the nation.

Beneficiary Eligibility: Any U.S. state, political subdivision and U.S. territories and other public entities will benefit.

Award Range/Average: Category A = $2,000,000 - $3,000,000 and Category B = $200,000 - $500,000

Funding: FY 17 $2,050,000; FY 18 est $2,653,000; FY 19 est $2,653,000.

 **HQ:** 4770 Buford Highway
Atlanta, GA 30341
Phone: 770-488-8438
http://www.cdc.gov

NATIONAL INCIDENT MANAGEMENT SYSTEM (NIMS)

Award: Project Grants

Purpose: It helps NIMS to develop a consistent system on national preparedness against terrorist threats.

Applicant Eligibility: Specific information on applicant eligibility is identified in the funding opportunity announcement and program guidance.

Beneficiary Eligibility: State, local, Public Nonprofit Institution/Organization, Federal Recognized Indian Tribal Government, U.S. Territory/Possession, Private Organization, Other Public Institution/Organization.

Award Range/Average: N/A

Funding: (Cooperative Agreements) FY 17 $2,000,000; FY 18 est $2,000,000; FY 19 est $2,000,000; FY 16 $2,000,000.

 **HQ:** 400 C Street SW
Washington, DC 20742-3620
Phone: 202-384-5008
http://www.fema.gov/national-incident-management-system

NATIONAL INFRASTRUCTURE INVESTMENTS "TIGER Discretionary Grants"

Award: Project Grants

Purpose: Offers grants for capital investments in surface transportation infrastructure grants to be awarded to a State, local, or Tribal governments.

Applicant Eligibility: State, local, and tribal governments, including U.S. territories, transit agencies, port authorities, metropolitan planning organizations (MPOs), other political subdivisions of State or local governments, and multi-State or multi-jurisdictional groups applying through a single lead applicant (for multi-jurisdictional groups, each member of the group, including the lead applicant, must be an otherwise eligible applicant as defined in this paragraph.

Beneficiary Eligibility: The ultimate benefits of this program may be received by, among others, States or local governments, transit agencies, major metropolises, and other urban, suburban, or rural areas.

Award Range/Average: Grants provided under this were generally not less than $5,000,000 and not greater than $25,000,000, however, projects located in rural areas will have a minimum grant size of $1,000,000 and the Secretary may increase the Federal share of costs above 80 percent.

Funding: Project Grants (Discretionary) FY 17 $484,400,000; FY 18 est $0; FY 19 est $0; FY 16 $484,400,000.

 **HQ:** 1200 New Jersey Avenue
Washington, DC 20590
Phone: 202-366-0301

Email: howard.hill@dot.gov

http://www.dot.gov/tiger

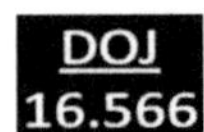

NATIONAL INSTITUTE OF JUSTICE W.E.B. DUBOIS FELLOWSHIP PROGRAM

"W.E.B. Du Bois Program of Research on Race and Crime"

Award: Project Grants

Purpose: To advance the field of knowledge regarding the confluence of crime, justice, and culture in various societal contexts. The secondary objective is to provide early career researchers an opportunity to elevate independently generated research and ideas to the level of national discussion.

Applicant Eligibility: Fellowship grants are awarded to individuals or to their parent agencies or organizations. IPA appointments also may be negotiated with Fellows' parent agencies.

Beneficiary Eligibility: Generally, researchers and academicians with research experience in criminal-justice or criminal-justice relevant fields are eligible for grants; those working for law enforcement related branches of State or local government units are eligible for grants or IPA appointments. Each prospective candidate must possess a terminal degree in their respective field.

Award Range/Average: No Data Available.

Funding: N/A

HQ: 810 7th Street NW

Washington, DC 20531

Phone: 202-307-2942

Email: christine.crossland@ojp.usdoj.gov

http://nij.gov/funding/fellowships/dubois-fellowship/pages/welcome.aspx

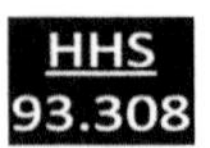

NATIONAL INSTITUTE ON MINORITY HEALTH & HEALTH DISPARITIES (NIMHD) EXTRAMURAL LOAN REPAYMENT PROGRAMS

"NIMHD Loan Repayment Programs"

Award: Direct Payments for Specified Use

Purpose: To lead scientific research to improve minority health and eliminate health disparities.

Applicant Eligibility: The following eligibility requirements apply to both: (1) Extramural Loan Repayment Program for Health Disparities Research (LRP-HDR):. and (2) Extramural Clinical Research Loan Repayment Program for Individuals from Disadvantaged Backgrounds (LRP-IDB).

Beneficiary Eligibility: (1) Extramural Loan Repayment Program for Health Disparities Research (LRP-HDR), and (2) Extramural Clinical Research Loan Repayment Program for Individuals from Disadvantaged Backgrounds (LRP-IDB) contracts: Qualified health professionals who conduct minority health or other health disparities research or highly qualified health professionals from disadvantaged backgrounds who will conduct clinical research and who possess substantial unpaid educational debt relative to income.

Award Range/Average: No Data Available.

Funding: (Direct Payments for Specified Use) FY 17 $6,579,794; FY 18 N/A FY 19 N/A FY 16 $13,655,192.

HQ: 7301 Wisconsin Avenue, Suite 533
Bethesda, MD 20892
Phone: 301-594-1788
Email: joan.wasserman@nih.gov
http://www.nimhd.nih.gov

NATIONAL INSTITUTES OF HEALTH ACQUIRED IMMUNODEFICIENCY SYNDROME RESEARCH LOAN REPAYMENT PROGRAM
"NIH AIDS Research Loan Repayment Program; AIDS LRP"

Award: Direct Payments for Specified Use

Purpose: To recruit trained researcher volunteers (physicians, registered nurses and scientists) with respect to AIDS at the National Institutes of Health (NIH) and helping them with repayment of their educational loans.

Applicant Eligibility: Eligible applicants must: (1) Be a citizen, national, or permanent resident of the United States; (2) possess a M.D.

Beneficiary Eligibility: AIDS researchers who have unpaid educational loans will benefit from this program.

Award Range/Average: For initial 2-year contracts, loan repayment awards may range from $4,000 to $70,000; tax reimbursements range from $1,977 to $34,598. The average contract cost which includes loan and tax reimbursement is $53,162. There were no new awards in 2009. There 4 renewal awards.

Funding: (Project Grants) FY 17 $27,845; FY 18 est $148,020; FY 19 est $153,825; FY 16 $226,093.

HQ: Building 2, Room 2E18 2 Center Drive
Bethesda, MD 20892
Phone: 301-402-1283
Email: colep@mail.nih.gov
http://www.lrp.nih.gov

NATIONAL INSTITUTES OF HEALTH LOAN REPAYMENT PROGRAM FOR CLINICAL RESEARCHERS
"NIH Clinical Research Loan Repayment Program; LRP-CR"

Award: Direct Payments for Specified Use

Purpose: To attract and retain health professionals to clinical research careers by offering educational loan repayment.

Applicant Eligibility: (1) A U.S. citizen, U.S. national, or permanent resident of the United States; (2) Have a Ph.D., M.D., D.O., D.D.S., D.M.D., D.P.M., Pharm.D., D.C., N.D., O.D. or equivalent doctoral degree from an accredited institution; (3) Have total qualifying educational loan debt equal to or in excess of 20 percent of their institutional base salary on the date of program eligibility (the effective date that a loan repayment contract has been executed by the Secretary of Health and Human Services or designee); (4) Conduct qualifying research supported by a domestic nonprofit foundation, nonprofit professional association, or other nonprofit institution, or a U.S. or other government agency (State or local); (5)

Engage in qualified clinical research. Clinical research is patient-oriented clinical research conducted with human subjects, or research on the causes and consequences of disease in human populations involving material of human origin (such as tissue specimens and cognitive phenomena) for which an investigator or colleague directly interacts with human subjects in an outpatient or inpatient setting to clarify a problem in human physiology, pathophysiology or disease, or epidemiologic or behavioral studies, outcomes research or health services research, or developing new technologies, therapeutic interventions, or clinical trials; (6) Engage in qualified clinical research for at least 50 percent of their time, i.e., not less than 20 hours per week based on a 40 hour week; (7) Agree to conduct research for which funding is not prohibited by Federal law, regulation, or HHS/NIH policy, and in accordance with applicable Federal, State and local law (e.g., applicable human subject protection regulations); and (8) Sign and submit to the Secretary of Health and Human Services, at the time of application submission, a contract agreeing to engage in clinical research in a qualifying institution for a minimum of 2 years. Full-time employees of Federal Government agencies are ineligible to apply for LRP benefits. Part-time Federal employees who engage in qualifying research as part of their nonfederal duties for at least 20 hours per week based on a 40 hour week, and who are not compensated as a Federal employee for their research, are eligible to apply for loan repayment if they meet all other eligibility requirements.

Beneficiary Eligibility: Health professionals who are interested in pursuing clinical research careers and who have unpaid educational loans will benefit from this program.

Award Range/Average: For initial two-year contract periods, loan repayment of 50 percent of education debt up to $70,000. For renewal contracts, loan repayment of 50 percent of education debt per year up to $35,000 per year.

Funding: (Direct Payments for Specified Use) FY 17 $43,571,347; FY 18 est $44,000,000; FY 19 est $44,000,000; FY 15 $43,757,421; FY 16 $44,254,056.

HQ: 6700B Rockledge Drive, Suite 2300
Bethesda, MD 20817
Phone: 240-380-3062
Email: matthew.lockhart@nih.gov
http://www.lrp.nih.gov

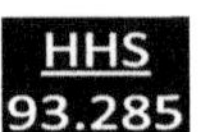

NATIONAL INSTITUTES OF HEALTH PEDIATRIC RESEARCH LOAN REPAYMENT PROGRAM
"NIH Pediatric Research Loan Repayment Program; LRP-PR"

Award: Direct Payments for Specified Use

Purpose: To attract and retain health professionals to pediatric research careers by offering educational loan repayment for participants.

Applicant Eligibility: Eligible applicants must: (1) be a U.S. citizen, U.S. national, or permanent resident of the United States; (2) have a Ph.D., M.D., D.O., D.D.S., D.M.D., D.P.M., Pharm.D., D.C., N.D., O.D. or equivalent doctoral degree from an accredited institution; (3) have total qualifying educational loan debt equal to or in excess of 20 percent of their institutional base salary on the date of program eligibility (the effective date that a loan repayment contract has been executed by the Secretary of Health and Human Services or designee); (4) conduct qualifying research supported by a domestic nonprofit foundation, nonprofit professional association, or other nonprofit institution, or a U.S. or other government agency (Federal, State, or local); (5) engage in qualified pediatric research (pediatric research is research that is directly related to diseases, disorders, and other conditions in children); (6) engage in qualified pediatric research for at least 50 percent of their time, i.e., not less than 20 hours per week based on a 40 hour week; (7) agree to conduct research for which funding is not prohibited by Federal law, regulation, or

HHS/NIH policy, and in accordance with applicable Federal, State and local law (e.g., applicable human subject protection regulations); and (8) sign and submit to the Secretary of Health and Human Services, at the time of application submission, a contract agreeing to engage in pediatric research in a qualifying institution for a minimum of 2 years. Full-time employees of Federal Government agencies are ineligible to apply for LRP benefits. Part-time Federal employees who engage in qualifying research as part of their non-Federal duties for at least 20 hours per week based on a 40 hour week, and who are not compensated as Federal employees for their research, are eligible to apply for loan repayment if they meet all other eligibility requirements.

Beneficiary Eligibility: Health professionals who are interested in pursuing pediatric research careers who have unpaid educational loans will benefit from this program.

Award Range/Average: For initial 2-year contract periods, loan repayment of 50 percent of education debt up to $70,000 plus tax payments. For renewal contracts, loan repayment of 50 percent of education debt per year up to $35,000 per year.

Funding: (Direct Payments for Specified Use) FY 16 $16,175,369; FY 17 est $17,000,000; FY 18 est $17,000,000.

HQ: 6700B Rockledge Drive, Suite 2300
Bethesda, MD 20817
Phone: 240-380-3062
Email: matthew.lockhart@nih.gov
http://www.lrp.nih.gov

NATIONAL NUCLEAR FORENSICS EXPERTISE DEVELOPMENT PROGRAM "NNFEDP"

Award: Cooperative Agreements; Project Grants

Purpose: The program provides a strong foundation to develop the nuclear forensics workforce and a strong resilience against nuclear terrorism by anticipating threats and protecting the country's Chemical, Biological, Radiological and Nuclear materials from enemy access.

Applicant Eligibility: N/A

Beneficiary Eligibility: N/A

Award Range/Average: Refer to the funding opportunity announcements.

Funding: (Project Grants) FY 17 $685,000; FY 18 est $500,000; FY 19 est $700,000; FY 16 $1,895,349.

HQ: 245 Murray Lane SW
Washington, DC 20528-0550
Phone: 202-254-7437
Email: sandra.gogol@hq.dhs.gov
http://www.dhs.gov

NATIONAL ORGANIZATIONS FOR CHRONIC DISEASE PREVENTION & HEALTH PROMOTION

Award: Cooperative Agreements

Purpose: Develops effective state chronic disease prevention and health promotion programs through cross-cutting activities supportive of all chronic disease programs, focusing on Training and Technical Assistance, Performance Monitoring and Evaluation, Innovation and Leadership and Development.

Applicant Eligibility: Eligible applicants that can apply for this funding opportunity are national organizations whose primary focus is on health education, chronic disease prevention and health promotion, and related public health training and who are of the type listed below: National organizations that work specifically with state and territorial health departments and that have organizational units focusing on state-based public health issues and reducing chronic diseases and their associated risk factors, are uniquely qualified to successfully implement the activities of this FOA because they have the knowledge, experience, and skills in working on reducing the burden of chronic diseases and on implementing policy, systems, and environmental changes that address chronic disease risk factors in states and community settings that no other national organization entities have. Focusing on these types of national organizations provides CDC the greatest potential to successfully implement the activities of this FOA.

Beneficiary Eligibility: This cooperative agreement will support the development of effective state chronic disease prevention and health promotion programs through cross-cutting activities supportive of all chronic disease programs. This FOA will serve to improve the effectiveness of chronic disease prevention and health promotion programs by focusing on cross-cutting activities that are supportive of all Chronic Disease Programs; better identify major components/priority areas based on the needs of the NCCDPHP that will serve as the core functions; increase the effectiveness of CDC's work with state chronic disease programs, so that work with state programs is more effective; and to experience the collective benefit of having strong state chronic disease programs by allowing for better coordination of efforts and greater utilization of resources, increase efficiency and minimize duplication of efforts.

Award Range/Average: No Data Available.

Funding: (Cooperative Agreements) FY 17 $2,500,000; FY 18 est $2,500,000; FY 19 est $2,500,000; FY 16 $2,500,000; - FY 18 reflects a new program funding amount. DP18-1812.

HQ: 4770 Buford Highway, P.O. Box F78
Atlanta, GA 30341
Phone: 770-488-5659
Email: tnb9@cdc.gov
http://www.cdc.gov

NATIONAL ORGANIZATIONS OF STATE & LOCAL OFFICIALS "NOSLO"

Award: Cooperative Agreements

Purpose: To support technical assistance, promotion of best practices and innovative solutions to emerging and ongoing national health priorities such as communicable disease prevention and suppression, childhood obesity, substance use disorders and/or mental health.

Applicant Eligibility: Eligible applicants include nonprofit service and/or membership organizations that can provide training and technical assistance on a national level to strengthen the infrastructure capacities of states and local government entities. Applicants must be national in scope with a broad reach, and have established long-term relationships with at least one of the following groups: state and local health departments; state government entities such as state PCOs, SRHAs, and SORHs; state Medicaid Offices; state policymakers; state legislatures; and local county and city government entities.

Beneficiary Eligibility: Eligible beneficiaries include the following entities: Federal; Interstate; Intrastate; State; Local; Public nonprofit institution/organization; Other public institution/organization; Non-Governmental –General; Minority group; Specialized group (e.g.

Award Range/Average: In FY 2017, approximately $3,500,000 is expected to fund four (4) recipients. Applicants can request funding for a ceiling amount of up to $875,000 total costs (includes both direct and indirect/facilities and administrative costs).

Funding: (Cooperative Agreements) FY 17 $3,263,575; FY 18 est $3,128,575; FY 19.

HQ: 5600 Fishers Lane Parklawn, Room 14W06
Rockville, MD 20857
Phone: 301-443-6204
Email: laraki@hrsa.gov

HHS 93.422 NATIONAL PARTNERSHIPS TO PROMOTE CANCER SURVEILLANCE STANDARDS & SUPPORT DATA QUALITY & OPERATIONS OF NATIONAL PROGRAM OF CANCER REGISTRIES "NPCR National Partnerships"

Award: Cooperative Agreements

Purpose: To enhance the data quality and operational efficiency of CDC's National Program of Cancer Registries (NCPR).

Applicant Eligibility: State governments County governments City or township governments Special district governments Independent school districts Public and State controlled institutions of higher education Native American tribal governments (Federally recognized) Public housing authorities/Indian housing authorities Native American tribal organizations (other than Federally recognized tribal governments) Nonprofits having a 501(c)(3) status with the IRS, other than institutions of higher education Nonprofits without 501(c)(3) status with the IRS, other than institutions of higher education Private institutions of higher education For profit organizations other than small businesses Small businesses Unrestricted (i.e.

Beneficiary Eligibility: Benefits the general public

Award Range/Average: No Data Available.

Funding: (Cooperative Agreements) FY 17 $0; FY 18 est $995,000; FY 19 est $995,000; FY 16 $0; - This number supports a new FY 18 NOFO (DP18-1802).

HQ: 4770 Buford Highway, P.O. Box F 76
Atlanta, GA 30341
Phone: 770-488-8430
Email: eoi9@cdc.gov
http://www.cdc.gov

DOI 15.439 NATIONAL PETROLEUM RESERVE – ALASKA

Award: Direct Payments for Specified Use

Purpose: Shares 50 percent of NPR-A oil and gas mineral leasing revenue with the State of Alaska.

Applicant Eligibility: Revenue from public land leasing will trigger automatic payment distribution computed in accordance with the Law.

Beneficiary Eligibility: Lease lands must be located in the National Petroleum Reserve-Alaska.

Award Range/Average: N/A

Funding: (Direct Payments for Specified Use) FY 18 est $21,191,000; FY 19 est $23,548,000; FY 17 $1,667,000.

HQ: 1849 C Street NW, P.O. Box 4211
Washington, DC 20240
Phone: 202-513-0600
http://www.onrr.gov

NATIONAL PRISON RAPE STATISTICS PROGRAM "PREA"

Award: Cooperative Agreements

Purpose: To collect and examine data on the incidence of sexual assault among individuals held in Federal and State prisons, local jails, and juvenile facilities as well as former inmates.

Applicant Eligibility: The Bureau of Justice Statistics is authorized to award grants and cooperative agreements to State and local governments, private nonprofit organizations, public nonprofit organizations, profit organizations, institutions of higher education, and qualified individuals.

Beneficiary Eligibility: Eligible beneficiaries are State and local governments, private nonprofit organizations, public nonprofit organizations, profit organizations, institutions of higher education, and qualified individuals.

Award Range/Average: $1,000,000 to $10,000,000

Funding: N/A

HQ: 810 7th Street NW
Washington, DC 20531
Phone: 202-598-7610
Email: jessica.stroop@usdoj.gov
http://bjs.gov

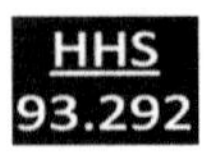

NATIONAL PUBLIC HEALTH IMPROVEMENT INITIATIVE "National Public Health Improvement Initiative (NPHII) - Capacity Building Assistance to Strengthen Public Health Infrastructure and Performance; CDC-RFA-CD10-1011"

Award: Formula Grants

Purpose: To provide support for accelerating public health accreditation readiness activities; to provide additional support for performance management and improvement practices; and, for the development, identification and dissemination of evidence-based policies and practices.

Applicant Eligibility: This award will be a continuation of funds intended only for grantees previously awarded.

Beneficiary Eligibility: State health departments, large local health departments supporting cities with populations of 1 million or more inhabitants, the District of Columbia, U.S. Territories, tribal health organizations and the general public.

Award Range/Average: Component I: This amount is based on population and will continue for each year of the cooperative agreement: Below 1.5 million = $100,000 1.5 million - 5 million = $200,000 5 million - 8 million = $300,000 Above 8 million = $400,000 Component II: $1 million - $2.95 million

Funding: Formula Grants (Cooperative Agreements) FY 17 FY 18 est $0; FY 19 est $0; FY 16 $0.

HQ: 4770 Buford Highway
Atlanta, GA 30341
Phone: 404-498-6792
Email: ayw3@cdc.gov

NATIONAL RESEARCH SERVICE AWARD IN PRIMARY CARE MEDICINE
"Ruth L. Kirschstein National Research Service Award Institutional Research Training Grant (NRSA)"

Award: Project Grants

Purpose: To prepare qualified individuals for careers that will have significant impact on the nation's primary care research agenda and ensure that a diverse and highly trained workforce is available to assume leadership roles in the area of primary healthcare research.

Applicant Eligibility: Eligible applicants are those entities that have received a grant under Title VII, sections 736, 739, or 747 of the Public Health Service (PHS) Act designed to prepare the primary health care workforce. Federally Recognized Indian Tribal Government and Native American Organizations may apply if they are otherwise eligible.

Beneficiary Eligibility: Individuals and public or private nonprofit organizations or institutions, including state or local governments and U.S. Territories. Participants must be U.S. Citizens, non-citizen nationals, or foreign nationals who possess visas permitting permanent residence in the United States.

Award Range/Average: The range of awards in FY 2017 is $159,362 to $400,000. The average award is $365,889. The est range of awards in FY 2018 is $175,600 to 416,238. The average award is $393,743.

Funding: (Project Grants) FY 17 $7,485,782; FY 18 est $7,874,869; FY 19 est $0; FY 16 $7,969,505.

HQ: 5600 Fishers Lane, Room 15N130D
Rockville, MD 20857
Phone: 301-443-7271
Email: scicale@hrsa.gov
http://www.hrsa.gov

NATIONAL RESEARCH SERVICE AWARDS HEALTH SERVICES RESEARCH TRAINING

Award: Training

Purpose: To provide predoctoral and postdoctoral training opportunities in health services research. Individual fellowships will be awarded directly to applicants for postdoctoral research training.

Applicant Eligibility: Domestic public or private nonprofit organizations or institutions may apply for training grants. The applicant institutions must have or expand training programs designed to develop competent investigators in the methods and techniques of conducting health services research.

Beneficiary Eligibility: Individuals and public or private nonprofit organizations or institutions are the beneficiaries of this program.

Award Range/Average: (Individual Fellowships) $58,562 to $74,921; $64,855 average. (Institutions) $160,424 to $613,880; $426,181 average. These figures are total costs.

Funding: (Training) FY 17 $8,060,380; FY 18 est $8,559,640; FY 19 est $8,559,640; FY 16 $7,974,677; - Grants for recipients to provide training to fellows or trainees.

HQ: 5600 Fishers Lane
Rockville, MD 20857
Phone: 301-427-1528
Email: shelley.benjamin@ahrq.hhs.gov
http://www.ahrq.gov

HHS 93.057 NATIONAL RESOURCE CENTER FOR HIV PREVENTION AMONG ADOLESCENTS

"National Resource Center for HIV Prevention Among Adolescents"

Award: Cooperative Agreements

Purpose: To facilitate online access to practical tools and resources for service providers, community-based organizations, professionals and peer educators who serve adolescents who reside in communities with high HIV prevalence and are at-risk based on a variety of issues.

Applicant Eligibility: Public organizations (including city, county, regional and State government) and private nonprofit entities

Beneficiary Eligibility: Service providers, community-based organizations, and professionals who serve adolescents who reside in communities with high HIV prevalence and are at-risk. Public organizations and private nonprofit entities and institutes of higher education.

Award Range/Average: OAH awarded one (1) cooperative agreement up to $350,000 per year in FY 15 for up to three (3) years contingent upon the availability of funds. No new grant awarded in FY 18.

Funding: (Cooperative Agreements) FY 16 $350,000; FY 17 est $350,000; FY 18 N/A.

HQ: 1101 Wootton Parkway Tower Building, Suite 550
Rockville, MD 20852
Phone: 240-453-8822
Email: roscoe.brunson@hhs.gov
http://www.hhs.gov/ash/oah

NATIONAL RESOURCE CENTERS PROGRAM FOR FOREIGN LANGUAGE & AREA STUDIES OR FOREIGN LANGUAGE & INTERNATIONAL STUDIES PROGRAM & FOREIGN LANGUAGE & AREA STUDIES FELLOWSHIP PROGRAM

Award: Project Grants

Purpose: To promote instruction in modern foreign languages and international studies that are critical to national needs to support such programs at colleges and universities.

Applicant Eligibility: Centers: U.S. institutions of higher education or consortia of institutions of higher education are eligible to apply. Applying institutions provide evidence of existing resources and institutional commitment to language and area and international studies through a curriculum that provides instruction dealing with a particular country or world area and its languages, or with international studies and modern foreign languages, including the international aspects of professional or other fields of study.

Beneficiary Eligibility: Centers: U.S. institutions of higher education or consortia of institutions of higher education will benefit. Fellowships: Undergraduate and graduate students enrolled in funded centers and programs will benefit.

Award Range/Average: Varies by competition.

Funding: (Project Grants) FY 17 $30,343,000; FY 18 est $30,343,000; FY 19 est $0; FY 16 $30,343,000; - For Fellowships.(Project Grants) FY 17 $22,743,107; FY 18 est $22,743,107; FY 19 est $0; FY 16 $22,743,107; - For Centers.

HQ: 400 Maryland Avenue SW
Washington, DC 20202
Phone: 202-453-5690
Email: cheryl.gibbs@ed.gov
http://www.ed.gov/programs/iegpsnrc

NATIONAL SECURITY EDUCATION PROGRAM DAVID L. BOREN FELLOWSHIPS "Boren Fellowships Program"

Award: Cooperative Agreements

Purpose: To provide the necessary resources, accountability and flexibility to meet the national security education needs of the United States.

Applicant Eligibility: The award for this program is made to a nonprofit organization that administers this assistance program on behalf of DoD.

Beneficiary Eligibility: Any U.S. citizen enrolled in an accredited public or private U.S. institution of higher education (defined in the Higher Education Act of 1965) is eligible to apply for a graduate fellowship.

Award Range/Average: Assistance to beneficiaries range: $0 - $30,000. Average for 2015: $23,000.

Funding: (Project Grants (Fellowships) FY 17 $3,430,000; FY 18 est $2,330,000; FY 19 N/A FY 16 $2,330,000.

HQ: 4800 Mark Center Drive, Suite 08 G 08
Alexandria, VA 22350

Phone: 571-256-0771

Email: alison.m.patz.civ@mail.mil

http://www.borenawards.org

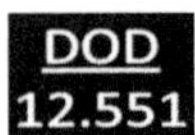

NATIONAL SECURITY EDUCATION PROGRAM DAVID L. BOREN SCHOLARSHIPS "Boren Scholarships Program"

Award: Cooperative Agreements

Purpose: To provide the necessary resources, accountability and flexibility to meet the national security education needs of the United States, especially as such needs change over time.

Applicant Eligibility: The award for this program is made to a nonprofit organization that administers this assistance program on behalf of DoD.

Beneficiary Eligibility: Any U.S. citizen enrolled in a degree seeking program at an accredited two- or four-year public or private U.S. institution of higher education (defined in the Higher Education Act of 1965) is eligible to apply for an undergraduate scholarship.

Award Range/Average: Assistance to beneficiaries range: $0 - $20,000. Average for 2015 - $18,000

Funding: (Cooperative Agreements) FY 17 $3,430,000; FY 18 est $2,330,000; FY 19 N/A FY 16 $2,330,000.

HQ: 4800 Mark Center Drive, Suite 08 G 08

Alexandria, VA 22350

Phone: 571-256-0771

Email: alison.m.patz.civ@mail.mil

http://www.borenawards.org

NATIONAL SEXUAL ASSAULT KIT INITIATIVE "SAKI"

Award: Cooperative Agreements

Purpose: To promote government initiatives to support children of incarcerated parents and their caregivers.

Applicant Eligibility: Eligible applicants for Purpose Areas 1, 3 and 4 are law enforcement agencies of states, units of local government, and federally recognized Indian tribal governments (as determined by the Secretary of the Interior), prosecutor's offices, or a governmental non-law enforcement agency acting as fiscal agent for one of the previously listed types of eligible applicants. Eligible applicants for Purpose Area 2 are limited to Small Law Enforcement Agencies with less than 250 sworn officers OR consortia of small law enforcement agencies.

Beneficiary Eligibility: U.S. Citizen.

Award Range/Average: See the current fiscal year's solicitation guidelines posted on the Office of Justice Programs web site at https://ojp.gov/funding/Explore/CurrentFundingOpportunities.htm.

Funding: (Project Grants) FY 17 $37,450,080; FY 18 est $47,500,000; FY 19 est $45,000,000; FY 16 $38,393,725.

HQ: 810 7th Street NW

Washington, DC 20531

Phone: 202-307-5831

Email: angela.williamson@usdoj.gov
http://www.bja.gov

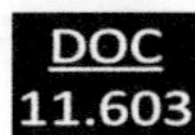

NATIONAL STANDARD REFERENCE DATA SYSTEM "SRD"

Award: Sale, Exchange, or Donation of Property and Goods

Purpose: To assure scientific and technical data to scientists, engineers, and the public.

Applicant Eligibility: Federal agencies, universities, industrial laboratories, institutions, firms, corporations, other research establishments, and individuals may purchase databases. Data compilations published and databases established by the program are owned by the Federal government and are subject to copyright restrictions.

Beneficiary Eligibility: Same as Applicant Eligibility.

Award Range/Average: No Data Available.

Funding: (Sale, Exchange, or Donation of Property and Goods) FY 17 $7,686,380; FY 18 est $8,679,300; FY 19 est $8,680,000; FY 16 $9,543,700.

HQ: 100 Bureau Drive, P.O. Box 6410
Gaithersburg, MD 20899
Phone: 844-374-0183
Email: robert.hanisch@nist.gov
http://www.nist.gov/srd

NATIONAL SYNDROMIC SURVEILLANCE PROGRAM COMMUNITY OF PRACTICE (NSSP COP)

Award: Cooperative Agreements

Purpose: Funds an organization with extensive experience developing and supporting syndromic surveillance practice to develop, implement and maintain a community of practice for CDC's National Syndromic Surveillance Program.

Applicant Eligibility: Organizations with more than a decade of experience in advancing the science and practice of syndromic surveillance and managing a distributed community of practice.

Beneficiary Eligibility: States, political subdivisions of States, local health authorities, and individuals or organizations with specialized health interests will benefit. Colleges, universities, private non-profit and public nonprofit domestic organizations, research institutions, faith-based organizations, and managed care organizations for some specific programs such as Diabetes.

Award Range/Average: Average award depends on funding opportunity announcement.

Funding: (Cooperative Agreements) FY 17 $400,000; FY 18 est $400,000; FY 19 est $0; FY 16 $400,000.

HQ: 2960 Brandywine Road
Atlanta, GA 30341
Phone: 404-498-2441
Email: mpr3@cdc.gov
http://www.cdc.gov

DHS 97.025 NATIONAL URBAN SEARCH & RESCUE (US&R) RESPONSE SYSTEM "US&R"

Award: Project Grants

Purpose: The program offers development and maintenance of the national urban search and rescue capability among the 28 task forces that conducts search and rescue operations to locate people in distress.

Applicant Eligibility: Only the 28 sponsoring agencies currently designated by FEMA as members of the National Urban Search and Rescue Response System are eligible for readiness and response cooperative agreements.

Beneficiary Eligibility: Only the 28 sponsoring jurisdictions currently designated by FEMA as members of the National Urban Search and Rescue Response System are eligible for readiness and response cooperative agreements.

Award Range/Average: FY 2016: $1,158,582 - $1,418,582

Funding: (Project Grants) FY 17 $27,513,000; FY 18 est $34; FY 19 est $27; FY 16 $35,508,524.

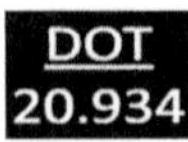

HQ: 500 C Street SW
Washington, DC 20472
Phone: 202-646-4013
Email: wanda.casey@fema.dhs.gov
http://www.fema.gov

DOT 20.934 NATIONALLY SIGNIFICANT FREIGHT & HIGHWAY PROJECTS "Infrastructure For Rebuilding America"

Award: Project Grants

Purpose: To provide Federal financial assistance to projects of national or regional significance.

Applicant Eligibility: Eligible applicants for NSFHP grants are 1) a State or group of States; 2) a metropolitan planning organization that serves an urbanized area (as defined by the Bureau of the Census) with a population of more than 200,000 individuals; 3) a unit of local government or group of local governments; 4) a political subdivision of a State or local government; 5) a special purpose district or public authority with a transportation function, including a port authority; 6) a Federal land management agency that applies jointly with a State or group of States; 7) a tribal government or a consortium of tribal governments; or 8) a multi-State or multijurisdictional group of public entities. Multiple States or jurisdictions that submit a joint application must identify a lead applicant as the primary point of contact.

Beneficiary Eligibility: Same as Applicant Eligibility.

Award Range/Average: For a large project, the FAST Act specifies that an INFRA grant must be at least $25 million. The FAST Act specifies that not more than $500 million in aggregate of the $4.5 billion authorized for INFRA grants over fiscal years 2016 to 2020 may be used for grants to freight rail, water (including ports), or other freight intermodal projects that make significant improvements to freight movement on the National Highway Freight Network. After accounting for FY 2016 and previous FY 2017 INFRA selections, approximately $326 million within this constraint remains available. Only the non-highway portion(s) of multimodal projects count toward the $500 million maximum. Grade crossing and grade separation projects do not count toward the $500 million maximum for freight rail, port, and intermodal projects. The FAST Act directs that at least 25 percent of the funds provided for INFRA grants must be used for projects located in rural areas, as defined in Section C.3.iv. The Department may elect to go above that threshold if the appropriate projects are submitted. The USDOT must consider geographic diversity among grant recipients, including the need for a balance in addressing the needs of urban and rural areas.

Funding: (Project Grants) FY 17 $788,880,000; FY 18 est $8,100,000,000; FY 19 N/A FY 16 $759,200,000.

HQ: 1200 New Jersey Avenue SE
Washington, DC 20590
Phone: 202-366-7687
http://www.transportation.gov/nsfhp

NATIVE AMERICAN COMMUNITY RESEARCH, DEMONSTRATION, AND PILOT PROJECTS
"Native Language Community Coordination Program (NLCC)"

Award: Cooperative Agreements

Purpose: To promote economic and social self-sufficiency for American Indians, Alaska Natives, Native Hawaiians, and other Native American Pacific Islanders from American Samoa, Guam, and the Commonwealth of the Northern Mariana Islands.

Applicant Eligibility: Federally-recognized Indian Tribes, as recognized by the Bureau of Indian Affairs; Incorporated non-federally recognized Tribes; Incorporated state-recognized Indian Tribes; Consortia of Indian Tribes; Incorporated nonprofit multi-purpose community-based Indian organizations; Urban Indian Centers; Alaska Native villages as defined in the Alaska Native Claims Settlement Act (ANSCA) and/or non-profit village consortia; Non-profit Alaska Native Regional Corporations/Associations in Alaska with village-specific projects; Non-profit Alaska Native community entities or tribal governing bodies (Indian Reorganization Act or Traditional Councils) as recognized by the Bureau of Indian Affairs; National or regional incorporated non-profit Native American organizations with Native American community-specific objectives; Public and nonprofit private agencies serving native peoples from Guam, American Samoa, or the Commonwealth of the Northern Mariana Islands, Tribal Colleges and Universities, and colleges and universities located in Hawaii, Guam, American Samoa, or the Tribal Colleges and Universities, and colleges and universities located in Hawaii, Guam, American Samoa, or the Commonwealth of the Northern Mariana Islands which serve Native American Pacific Islanders.

Beneficiary Eligibility: American Indians, Alaska Natives, Native Hawaiians, and Native American Pacific Islanders will benefit.

Award Range/Average: Range $100,000 - $400,000; average award: $387,027.

Funding: (Cooperative Agreements) FY 17 $1,914,209; FY 18 est $1,917,264; FY 19 est $1,917,264; FY 16 $1,854,290.

HQ: Mary E Switzer Building 330 C Street SW, P.O. Box 4126
Washington, DC 20024
Phone: 877-922-9262
Email: carmelia.strickland@acf.hhs.gov
http://www.acf.hhs.gov/programs/ana

NATIVE AMERICAN OUTREACH

Award: Advisory Services and Counseling

Purpose: Funds economic development projects that will provide small business opportunities and empower American Indians, Alaska Natives and Native Hawaiian entrepreneurs located in disadvantaged and underserved Native American communities nationwide.

Applicant Eligibility: Organizations must have experience in effectively training, counseling, developing and measuring small business development in Indian Country, Alaska and Hawaii.

Beneficiary Eligibility: Native American entrepreneurs who are starting their own business or expanding their existing business.

Award Range/Average: No Data Available.

Funding: (Advisory Services and Counseling) FY 17 $1,541,000; FY 18 est $2,000,000; FY 19 est $1,500,000; FY 16 $1,778,000.

HQ: 409 3rd Street SW, 8th Floor
Washington, DC 20416
Phone: 202-205-7094
Email: carol.walker@sba.gov
http://www.sba.gov/naa

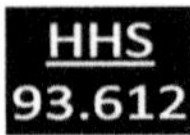

NATIVE AMERICAN PROGRAMS
"Social and Economic Development Strategies (SEDS)"

Award: Project Grants

Purpose: The Social and Economic Development Strategies program promotes economic and social self-sufficiency for American Indians, Alaska Natives, Native Hawaiians, and Native American Pacific Islanders from American Samoa, Guam, and the Commonwealth of the Northern Mariana Islands.

Applicant Eligibility: Federally-recognized Indian Tribes, as recognized by the Bureau of Indian Affairs; Incorporated non-federally recognized Tribes; Incorporated state-recognized Indian Tribes; Consortia of Indian Tribes; Incorporated nonprofit multi-purpose community-based Indian organizations; Urban Indian Centers; Alaska Native villages as defined in the Alaska Native Claims Settlement Act (ANSCA) and/or nonprofit village consortia; Nonprofit native organizations in Alaska with village specific projects; Incorporated non-profit Alaska Native multi-purpose, community-based organizations; Non-profit Alaska Native Regional Corporations/Associations in Alaska with village-specific projects; Non-profit Alaska Native community entities or tribal governing bodies (Indian Reorganization Act or Traditional Councils) as recognized by the Bureau of Indian Affairs; Public and nonprofit private agencies serving Native Hawaiians; National or regional incorporated nonprofit Native American organizations with Native American community-specific objectives; Public and nonprofit private agencies serving native peoples from Guam, American Samoa, or the Commonwealth of the Northern Mariana Islands; Tribal Colleges and Universities, and colleges and universities located in Hawaii, Guam, American Samoa, or the Commonwealth of the Northern Mariana Islands which serve Native American Pacific Islanders.

Beneficiary Eligibility: American Indians, Alaska Natives, Native Hawaiians, and Native American Pacific Islanders will benefit.

Award Range/Average: $100,000 to $400,000; average = $259,215 per budget period.

Funding: Project Grants (Discretionary) FY 17 $29,960,978; FY 18 est $31,624,179; FY 19 est $31,624,179; FY 16 $27,689,780.

HQ: 330 C Street Switzer Building, P.O. Box 4126
Washington, DC 20447
Phone: 877-922-9262
Email: carmelia.strickland@acf.hhs.gov
http://www.acf.hhs.gov/ana

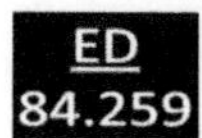

NATIVE HAWAIIAN CAREER & TECHNICAL EDUCATION

Award: Project Grants

Purpose: To make grants to organizations primarily serving and representing Native Hawaiians programs authorized by, and consistent with, the Carl D. Perkins Career and Technical Education Act of 2006.

Applicant Eligibility: Community-based organizations primarily serving and representing Native Hawaiians may apply.

Beneficiary Eligibility: Native Hawaiians individuals will benefit.

Award Range/Average: Estimated range: $250,000- $500,000; Estimated average: $289,827; Actual range: $258,219- $513,638; Actual average: $362,220

Funding: FY 17 $2,793,955; FY 18 est $2,981,495; FY 19 est $2,793,955.

HQ: 400 Maryland Avenue SW
Washington, DC 20202-7241
Phone: 202-245-7792
Email: linda.mayo@ed.gov
http://cte.ed.gov/grants/discretionary-grants

NATIVE HAWAIIAN EDUCATION

Award: Project Grants

Purpose: To develop innovative educational programs to assist Native Hawaiians, and to supplement and expand programs and authorities in the area of education.

Applicant Eligibility: Eligible applicants include: (1) Native Hawaiian educational organizations and community-based organizations; (2) public and private nonprofit organizations, agencies, and institutions with experience in developing or operating Native Hawaiian programs or programs of instruction in the Native Hawaiian language; (3) charter schools; or (4) consortia of the organizations, agencies, and institutions described above.

Beneficiary Eligibility: Native Hawaiian children and adults.

Award Range/Average: Range of New Awards: $250,000- $950,000; Average New Award: $425,000.

Funding: (Project Grants) FY 17 $33,397,000; FY 18 est $36,397,000; FY 19 est $0; FY 16 $33,397,000.

HQ: 400 Maryland Avenue S W, Room 3W215
Washington, DC 20202
Phone: 202-260-1265

Email: joanne.osborne@ed.gov
http://www.ed.gov/programs/nathawaiian/index.html

NATIVE HAWAIIAN HEALTH CARE SYSTEMS
"Native Hawaiian Health Care Systems"

Award: Project Grants

Purpose: To raise the health status of Native Hawaiians to the highest possible level through comprehensive health promotion and disease prevention services, as well as primary health services.

Applicant Eligibility: Eligible entities include Papa Ola Lokahi and the Native Hawaiian Health Care Systems (Systems). The Systems: (1) organized under the laws of the State of Hawaii; (2) provide or arrange for health care services through practitioners licensed by the State of Hawaii, where licensure requirements are applicable; (3) are public or nonprofit private entities; (4) involve Native Hawaiian health practitioners significantly in the planning, management, monitoring, and evaluation of health care services; (5) are recognized by Papa Ola Lokahi (a consortium of Hawaiian and Native Hawaiian organizations) for the purpose of planning, conducting, or administering programs or portions of programs, authorized by this act for the benefit of Native Hawaiians; and (6) are certified by Papa Ola Lokahi as having the qualifications and the capacity to provide the services and meet the requirements of this Act for the benefit of Native Hawaiians.

Beneficiary Eligibility: Hawaiian natives will benefit.

Award Range/Average: $1,108,201 to $2,674,268; Average $2,161,259.

Funding: (Project Grants) FY 17 $12,339,016; FY 18 est $15,624,696; FY 19 est $12,967,553; FY 16 $12,339,016.

HQ: 5600 Fishers Lane, Room 16N09
Rockville, MD 20857
Phone: 301-594-4300
http://bphc.hrsa.gov/programopportunities/fundingopportunities/nhhcs/index.html

NATIVE HAWAIIAN HOUSING BLOCK GRANTS

Award: Project Grants

Purpose: To provide housing assistance to low-income Native Hawaiian families who are entitled to reside on Hawaiian Home Lands.

Applicant Eligibility: The Department of Native Hawaiian Home Lands (DHHL) is the only eligible grant recipient.

Beneficiary Eligibility: Native Hawaiian families who are eligible to reside on the Hawaiian Home Lands.

Award Range/Average: N/A

Funding: (Project Grants) FY 17 $771; FY 18 est $2,000,000; FY 19 est $2,000,000; FY 16 $539,000.

HQ: 500 Ala Moana Boulevard, Suite 3A
Honolulu, HI 96813
Phone: 808-522-8175 x-223
Email: claudine.c.allen@hud.gov
http://www.hud.gov/offices/pih/ih/codetalk/onap/nhhbgprogram.cfm

TREAS 21.012

NATIVE INITIATIVES "NACA Program"

Award: Project Grants

Purpose: Promotes economic revitalization and community development through financial and technical assistance to Native Community Development Financial Institutions (CDFIs).

Applicant Eligibility: Only certified CDFIs that demonstrate the majority of its activities are targeted to a Native Community are eligible to apply for Financial Assistance awards. Organizations that are Native CDFIs, Emerging CDFIs, or Sponsoring Entities and demonstrate the majority of its activities are target to a Native Community may apply for Technical Assistance awards.

Beneficiary Eligibility: Investment Areas and Targeted Populations as defined in 12 C.F.

Award Range/Average: Range of Technical Assistance Awards were $127,430 to $150,000; Average Financial Assistance Awards were $577,000 and capped at $1,000,000.

Funding: FY 17 $15,464,710; FY 18 est $16,200,000; FY 19 est $16,200,000.

HQ: 1500 Pennsylvania Avenue NW
Washington, DC 20036
Phone: 202-653-0300
http://www.cdfifund.gov

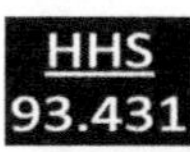

NETWORKING2SAVE": CDC'S NATIONAL NETWORK APPROACH TO PREVENTING & CONTROLLING TOBACCO-RELATED CANCERS IN SPECIAL POPULATIONS "Networking2Save"

Award: Cooperative Agreements

Purpose: Seek to build on the progress of the previously funded networks and expand work to address tobacco-and cancer- related health disparities among populations particularly vulnerable to tobacco industry marketing tactics and with higher cancer incidence and death rates.

Applicant Eligibility: Open competition no eligibility

Beneficiary Eligibility: Federal, State and Local

Award Range/Average: No Data Available.

Funding: (Cooperative Agreements) FY 17 $0; FY 18 est $3,999,345; FY 19 est $3,999,345.

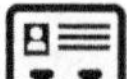

HQ: 4770 Buford Highway, P.O. Box F50
Atlanta, GA 30341
Phone: 770-488-8119
Email: crecasner@cdc.gov
http://www.cdc.gov

DOJ 16.813 NICS ACT RECORD IMPROVEMENT PROGRAM "NARIP"

Award: Cooperative Agreements

Purpose: To assist the FBI's National Instant Criminal Background Check System to improve the automation of criminal history records, records of felony convictions, records of protective orders, records of mental health adjudications, and others to reduce delays for law-abiding gun purchasers.

Applicant Eligibility: Applications must be submitted by (a) the agency designated by the Governor to administer the National Criminal History Improvement Program (NCHIP); (b) the state or territory central administrative office or similar entity designated by statute or regulation to administer federal grant funds on behalf of the jurisdiction's court system; or (c) a federally recognized Indian tribal government.

Beneficiary Eligibility: In accordance with the NICS Improvement Amendments Act there are two specific conditions that each state must satisfy.

Award Range/Average: N/A

Funding: (Cooperative Agreements) FY 17 $11,209,680; FY 18 est $25,000,000; FY 19 est $10,000,000; FY 16 $0.

HQ: 810 7th Street NW
Washington, DC 20531
Phone: 202-307-0765
Email: devon.adams@usdoj.gov
http://bjs.gov/index.cfm?ty=tp&tid=49

HHS 93.142 NIEHS HAZARDOUS WASTE WORKER HEALTH & SAFETY TRAINING

"Superfund Worker Training Program (WTP)"

Award: Project Grants

Purpose: To provide cooperative agreements and project grant support for the development and administration of model worker health and safety training programs.

Applicant Eligibility: A public or private nonprofit entity, including tribal governments, that provide worker health and safety education and training, may submit an application and receive a cooperative agreement or project grant for support of waste worker education and training by a named principal investigator. Recipients/grantees may use services, as appropriate, of other public or private organizations necessary to develop, administer, or evaluate proposed worker training programs, as long as the requirement for awards to nonprofit organizations is not violated.

Beneficiary Eligibility: Any public or private entity providing worker safety and health education and training will benefit from this program.

Award Range/Average: Range: $26,960 to $2,742,081 Average: $833,895

Funding: (Cooperative Agreements) FY 17 $35,857,495; FY 18 est $35,778,048; FY 19 est $27,702,595; FY 16 $35,762,223; - Reimbursable funding from the Department of Energy has been included.

HQ: 111 TW Alexander Drive
Research Triangle Park, NC 27709
Phone: 984-287-3784
Email: encarna1@niehs.nih.gov
http://www.niehs.nih.gov/careers/hazmat/about_wetp/index.cfm

NIEHS SUPERFUND HAZARDOUS SUBSTANCES_BASIC RESEARCH & EDUCATION "NIEHS Superfund Research Program"

Award: Project Grants

Purpose: To establish a unique program linking biomedical research with engineering, geoscience and ecological research.

Applicant Eligibility: An accredited institution of higher education, as defined in the Higher Education Act, 20 U.S.C. (annotated) 3381, may submit an application and receive a grant for support of research by a named principal investigator.

Beneficiary Eligibility: Any accredited institution of higher education engaged in biomedical research and/or engineering and ecological research. SBIR awards are restricted to small business that meet NIH's criteria for SBC.

Award Range/Average: Range: $7,440 to $2,998,492 Average: $850,527.

Funding: (Project Grants) FY 17 $46,779,000; FY 18 est $46,479,000; FY 19 est $32,039,405; FY 16 $46,546,000.

HQ: 111 TW Alexander Drive
Research Triangle Park, NC 27709
Phone: 984-287-3258
Email: encarna1@niehs.nih.gov
http://www.niehs.nih.gov/research/supported/centers/srp/index.cfm

NIH OFFICE OF RESEARCH ON WOMEN'S HEALTH "NIH/ORWH"

Award: Project Grants

Purpose: To identify projects on women's health that should be conducted or supported by national research institutes.

Applicant Eligibility: Awards can be made to domestic, public or private, non-profit or profit organization, university, hospital, laboratory, or other institution including state and local units of government and individuals. Some initiatives will accept applications from foreign organizations.

Beneficiary Eligibility: See information above.

Award Range/Average: No Data Available.

Funding: (Project Grants) FY 17 est $34,000,000; FY 18 est $32,000,000; FY 19.

HQ: 6707 Democracy Boulevard, Suite 400
Bethesda, MD 20892
Phone: 301-496-3975
Email: beggl@od.nih.gov

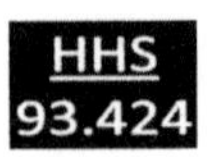

NON-ACA/PPHF—BUILDING CAPACITY OF THE PUBLIC HEALTH SYSTEM TO IMPROVE POPULATION HEALTH THROUGH NATIONAL NONPROFIT ORGANIZATIONS "CBA to Strengthen the Public Health Infrastructure and Performance"

Award: Cooperative Agreements

Purpose: To cover NON-ACA/PPHF-funded capacity building assistance projects under CDC-RFA-OT13-1302.

Applicant Eligibility: 1. Eligible Applicants: Organizations with nonprofit 501(c)(3) or nonprofit 501(c)(6) IRS status (other than institutions of higher education).

Beneficiary Eligibility: Beneficiaries include state health departments; tribal health organizations; local health departments; the District of Columbia; U.S. Territories; and other components of the public health system. The general public will also serve as beneficiaries.

Award Range/Average: The range is $4 million to up to $20 million for Category A, $1 million to up to $15 million for Category B and $100,000 to up to $5 million for Category C. The approximate average award ranges for the 12-month budget period are up to $15 million for Category A, up to $5 million for Category B and up to $2 million for Category C.

Funding: (Cooperative Agreements) FY 17 $88,119,908; FY 18 est $0; FY 19 est $0; FY 16 $99,246,021.

HQ: 1600 Clifton Road, P.O. Box E70
Atlanta, GA 30333
Phone: 770-488-1523
Email: syt2@cdc.gov
http://www.cdc.gov/stltpublichealth/funding/rfaot13.html

NON-PROFIT SECURITY PROGRAM "NSGP"

Award: Project Grants

Purpose: The Nonprofit Security Grant Program provides preparedness activities for nonprofit organizations against terrorist attacks.

Applicant Eligibility: The SAA is the only entity eligible to apply for FY 20187 NSGP funds on behalf of eligible nonprofit organizations (as described under section 501(c)(3) of the Internal Revenue Code of 1986) determined to be at high risk of terrorist attack and for NSGP-UA, organizations must be located within one of the designated FY 2018 UASI-designated Urban areas. Eligible nonprofit organizations must provide their applications to their respective SAA in order to be considered for FY 2018 funding.

Beneficiary Eligibility: The FY 2018 NSGP provides funding support for physical security enhancements and other security activities to nonprofit organizations that are at high risk of a terrorist attack.

Award Range/Average: No Data Available.

Funding: (Formula Grants) FY 17 $25,000,000; FY 18 est $60,000,000; FY 19 est $60,000,000; FY 16 $20,000,000.

HQ: 500 C Street SW
Washington, DC 20523
Phone: 800-368-6498
http://www.fema.gov/government/grant/index

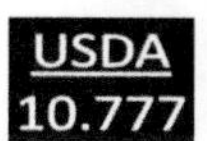

NORMAN E. BORLAUG INTERNATIONAL AGRICULTURAL SCIENCE & TECHNOLOGY FELLOWSHIP "Borlaug Fellowship Program"

Award: Cooperative Agreements; Direct Payments for Specified Use

Purpose: The Borlaug International Agricultural Science and Technology Fellowship Program promotes food security and economic growth, educates a new generation of agricultural scientists, increases scientific knowledge, improves agricultural productivity, provides collaborative research opportunities, and reduces the barriers to technology adoption.

Applicant Eligibility: The Borlaug Fellowship Program solicits proposals from U.S. universities and state cooperative institutions.

Beneficiary Eligibility: Technical assistance and research collaboration provided through these agreements benefit foreign governments and related agricultural institutions in their countries.

Award Range/Average: $38,000 - $50,000 per fellow.

Funding: (Project Grants (Fellowships) FY 17 $2,275,203; FY 18 est $1,600,000; FY 19 est $1,000,000; FY 16 $2,275,203.

HQ: 1400 Independence Avenue SW #3226, P.O. Box 1030
Washington, DC 20250
Phone: 202-690-1940
Email: tim.sheehan@fas.usda.gov
http://www.fas.usda.gov/programs/borlaug-fellowship-program

NOT FOR PROFIT

Award: Cooperative Agreements

Purpose: The Bureau of Ocean Energy Management provides major economic and energy benefits on a national and local level to the taxpayers, states and the American Indian community. The purpose of the Environmental Studies Program is to obtain the information needed for the assessment and the management of environmental impacts; to predict impacts on marine biota; and to monitor the human, marine, and coastal environments to provide time series and data trend information.

Applicant Eligibility: State or political subdivision (including any agency thereof), or any not-for-profit organization if: (1) the agreement will serve a mutual interest of the parties to the agreement in carrying out the programs administered by BOEM; and (2) all parties will contribute resources to the accomplishment of these objectives.

Beneficiary Eligibility: Research scientists, Federal, State and local decision-makers, Native American Organizations, and the general public will ultimately benefit from the program.

Award Range/Average: Range is $25,000 to $100,000; Average $250,000.

Funding: (Cooperative Agreements) FY 17 $5,742,696; FY 18 est $6,400,000; FY 19 N/A.

HQ: 45600 Woodland Road
Sterling, VA 20166
Phone: 703-787-1087
Email: rodney.cluck@boem.gov
http://www.boem.gov

NURSE ANESTHETIST TRAINEESHIP "NAT"

Award: Formula Grants

Purpose: Awarded to accredited institutions that educate registered nurses to become nurse anesthetists; recipient institutions in turn disburse funds to students in the form of traineeship support.

Applicant Eligibility: Eligible applicants are collegiate schools of nursing, academic health centers, and other private or public nonprofit entities accredited by a recognized body or bodies or State agency, approved for the purpose of nursing education by the Secretary of Education, which provide registered nurses with full-time, graduate-level nurse anesthesia master's or doctoral education and have evidence of accreditation from the American Association of Nurse Anesthetists (AANA) Council on Accreditation of Nurse Anesthesia Educational Programs. The school must be located in the 50 states, the District of Columbia, Guam, the Commonwealth of Puerto Rico, the Northern Mariana Islands, American Samoa, Guam, the U.S. Virgin Islands, the Federated States of Micronesia, the Republic of the Marshall Islands, and the Republic of Palau.

Beneficiary Eligibility: NAT funds are awarded to institutions, not individuals. Traineeship recipients are selected by the participating institutions.

Award Range/Average: $11,487- $274,539; Average award: $69,406

Funding: (Formula Grants) FY 17 $229,066; FY 18 est $4,850,000; FY 19 est $0; FY 16 $2,250,000; - FY 18 includes One-time funds ($2,600,000) to address the opioid epidemic.

HQ: 5600 Fishers Lane, Room 11N74B
Rockville, MD 20857
Phone: 301-443-5787
Email: kbreeden@hrsa.gov
http://www.hrsa.gov

NURSE CORPS LOAN REPAYMENT PROGRAM "NURSE Corps Loan Repayment Program (NURSE Corps LRP)"

Award: Direct Payments for Specified Use

Purpose: The NURSE Corps Loan Repayment Program provides loan repayment assistance to professional registered nurses, including advanced practice registered nurses, in return for a commitment to work full-time in eligible healthcare facilities with a critical shortage of nurses or serve as a nurse faculty in an eligible schools of nursing.

Applicant Eligibility: Individuals who satisfy the following criteria are eligible to apply: (1) have received a bachelor's degree, a master's degree, an associate degree, a diploma, or a doctoral degree in nursing; (2) have outstanding qualifying educational loans leading to a degree or diploma in nursing; (3) a U.S.

citizen (either U.S. born or naturalized), U.S., national or a lawful permanent resident of the United States; (4) employed full-time (32 hours or more per week) at a critical shortage facility (CSF) or employed as a full-time nurse faculty member at an accredited, public or private nonprofit school of nursing; (5) have completed the nursing education program for which the loan balance applies; (6) have a current, full, permanent, unencumbered, unrestricted license in the State in which they intend to practice or be authorized to practice in the State under the Nurse Licensure Compact; and (7) submit a complete application, including a signed contract to work full-time as a registered or advanced practice nurse for 2 years at an eligible health care facility with a critical shortage of nurses or an accredited, eligible school of nursing. Federally Recognized Indian Tribal Government and Native American Organizations may apply if they are otherwise eligible.

Beneficiary Eligibility: Beneficiaries include registered nurses who have received a diploma, an associate degree, a baccalaureate degree or a graduate degree in nursing from an accredited school of nursing.

Award Range/Average: $10,038 to $259,190; Average new award - $78,135

Funding: FY 17 $48,870,088; FY 18 est $48,452,829; FY 19 est $48,452,829.

HQ: Division of Health Careers and Financial Support 5600 Fishers Lane
Rockville, MD 20857
Phone: 301-594-4130
Email: cmahlmann@hrsa.gov
http://bhw.hrsa.gov/loansscholarships/nursecorps/lrp

NURSE CORPS SCHOLARSHIP PROGRAM
"NURSE Corps Scholarship Program"

Award: Direct Payments for Specified Use

Purpose: To increase the supply and maldistribution of registered nurses (RN) and nurse practitioners (NPs) in eligible healthcare facilities across the nation, with a critical shortage of nurses by providing service-obligated scholarships to nursing students.

Applicant Eligibility: The applicant must be a U.S. citizen or national, enrolled or accepted for enrollment in a fully accredited academic institution with a graduate, baccalaureate, associate degree or diploma nursing program located in a State, the District of Columbia, or a U.S. Territory. The applicant must be free of any Federal judgment liens, not have breached a prior service obligation, is not excluded, debarred, suspended, or disqualified by a Federal agency, and have no conflicting service obligations.

Beneficiary Eligibility: United States citizens or nationals enrolled or accepted for enrollment in a fully accredited graduate, baccalaureate, associate degree or diploma nursing program.

Award Range/Average: Average $110,065; Range $7,000 - $280,000.

Funding: (Direct Payments for Specified Use) FY 17 $22,154,211; FY 18 est $21,792,814; FY 19 est $23,864,826; FY 16 $24,584,049.

HQ: Division of Health Careers and Financial Support 5600 Fishers Lane
Rockville, MD 20857
Phone: 301-594-4130
Email: cmahlmann@hrsa.gov
http://bhw.hrsa.gov/loansscholarships/nursecorps/lrp

HHS 93.359 NURSE EDUCATION, PRACTICE QUALITY & RETENTION GRANTS "NEPQR"

Award: Cooperative Agreements; Project Grants

Purpose: Provides grant support for academic, service, and continuing education projects designed to enhance nursing education, improve the quality of patient care, increase nurse retention, and strengthen the nursing workforce.

Applicant Eligibility: NEPQR – Veterans' Bachelor of Science in Nursing Program (NEPQR-VBSN), NEPQR – Interprofessional Collaborative Practice: Behavioral Health Integration (NEPQR-IPCP:BHI), and NEPQR – Registered Nurses in Primary Care (NEPQR-RNPC): Eligible applicants are: accredited schools of nursing, health care facilities, a partnership of such a school and a health care facility. A health care facility may include a nurse-managed health center, Indian Health Service health center, Native Hawaiian health center, hospital, Federally-qualified health center, rural health clinic, nursing home, home health agency, hospice program, public health clinic, State or local department of public health, skilled nursing facility, ambulatory surgical center, or any other facility designated by the Secretary (see PHS Act section 801(11)).

Beneficiary Eligibility: Project participants, or students in the program, must be U.S. Citizens, non-citizen nationals, or foreign nationals who possess visas permitting permanent residence in the United States. Individuals on temporary student visas are not eligible.

Award Range/Average: NEPQR-VBSN: FY 17 Range: $131,830- $350,000, Average: $310,955; FY 18 Range: $131,830- $350,000, Average $310,955; NEPQR-IPCP:BHI: FY 17 Range: $350,000- $500,000, Average: $487,935; FY 18 Range: $431,718- $500,000, Average $492,441; NEPQR-RNPC: FY 18 Range: $279,104- $700,000, Average: $617,093;

Funding: (Project Grants) FY 17 $9,611,566; FY 18 est $3,368,154; FY 19 est $0; FY 16 $9,639,618; - NEPQR-VBSN (Cooperative Agreements) FY 17 $9,642,645; FY 18 est $9,622,941; FY 19 est $0; FY 16 $4,321,275; - NEPQR-IPCP:BHI(Project Grants) FY 17 $0; FY 18 est $25,6

HQ: Division of Nursing and Public Health
Rockville, MD 20857
Phone: 301-443-4926
Email: kkoyama@hrsa.gov
http://www.hrsa.gov

NURSE FACULTY LOAN PROGRAM (NFLP) "NFLP"

Award: Formula Grants

Purpose: To increase the number of qualified nursing faculty.

Applicant Eligibility: Eligible applicants are accredited public or private collegiate schools of nursing or departments within an academic institution, that offer graduate degree nursing education programs (master's or doctoral) that will prepare the graduate student to serve as nurse faculty. The school must be located in the 50 States, the Commonwealth of Puerto Rico, the District of Columbia, the Commonwealth of the Northern Mariana Islands, Guam, American Samoa, the U.S. Virgin Islands, the Republic of the Marshall Islands, the Federated States of Micronesia, or the Republic of Palau.

Beneficiary Eligibility: Eligible nursing students must: (1) be a citizen or national of the United States, or a lawful permanent resident of the United States, the Commonwealth of Puerto Rico, the District of Columbia, the Commonwealth of the Northern Mariana Islands, Guam, American Samoa, the U.S. Virgin Islands, the Republic of the Marshall Islands, the Federated States of Micronesia, or the Republic of Palau; (2) be enrolled in an advanced degree program in nursing to become qualified nursing faculty; (3) not be in default on a Federal debt; and (4) maintain good academic standing.

Award Range/Average: 84 total awards: Range is $14,842 to $2,351,957; Average is $294.,230

Funding: (Formula Grants) FY 17 $24,715,373; FY 18 est $26,825,131; FY 19 est $0; FY 16 $24,405,295.

HQ: Division of Nursing and Public Health 5600 Fishers Lane, Room 11N-104A
Rockville, MD 20857
Phone: 301-443-4301
Email: ewroblewski@hrsa.gov
http://www.hrsa.gov

NURSING RESEARCH

Award: Project Grants

Purpose: To promote and improve the health of individuals, families, and communities.

Applicant Eligibility: Research Grants: Any corporation, public or private institution or agency, or other legal entity, either nonprofit or for-profit, may apply. NRSAs (Individual): An applicant must be a registered professional nurse with either a baccalaureate and/or a master's degree in nursing and must be a citizen of the United States or lawfully admitted for permanent residence.

Beneficiary Eligibility: Individuals and public or private institutions.

Award Range/Average: Research Grants: $38,740 to $1,912,959; Average cost $442,807; NRSA Individual Awards: $2,337 to $60,834; Average cost of FTTP/Award $35,385; NRSA Institutional Awards: $1,293 to $500,721; Average cost of FTTP $51,491/Average cost of Award $288,350

Funding: (Training) FY 17 $7,438,885; FY 18 est $7,896,000; FY 19 est $7,288,000; FY 16 $7,998,401; - National Research Service Awards (NRSA)(Project Grants) FY 17 $109,058,689; FY 18 est $117,092,000; FY 19 est $107,528,000; FY 16 $106,770,328; - Research Grants.

HQ: Division of Extramural Science Programs 5600 Fishers Lane 11N104B
Bethesda, MD 20892
Phone: 301-402-7932
Email: marguerite.kearney@nih.gov
http://www.ninr.nih.gov

NURSING STUDENT LOANS "NSL"

Award: Direct Loans

Purpose: To increase educational opportunities by providing long-term, low-interest loans to students in need of financial assistance and in pursuit of a course of nursing program.

Applicant Eligibility: All accredited public and nonprofit private schools of nursing that prepare students for practice as registered or graduate nurses, and that do not discriminate against students because of race, color, origin, sex, or handicapping conditions, are eligible to apply for funds to be disbursed to qualified nursing students. Federally Recognized Indian Tribal Government and Native American Organizations may apply if they are otherwise eligible.

Beneficiary Eligibility: The Nursing Student Loan Program provides financial assistance to nursing students who are citizens, nationals or lawful permanent residents of the United States or the District of Columbia, the Commonwealth of Puerto Rico, the Northern Mariana Islands, the U.S. Virgin Islands, Guam, American Samoa, the Republic of Palau, the Republic of the Marshall Islands, and the Federated States of Micronesia.

Award Range/Average: Range: $6,501 to $401,893,196; Average: $203,093.07 per institution.

Funding: (Direct Loans) FY 17 $9,342,281; FY 18 est $7,773,916; FY 19 N/A FY 16 $5,055,338.

HQ: Division of Health Careers and Financial Support 31 Center Drive
Rockville, MD 20857
Phone: 301-443-1173
Email: cgrosso@hrsa.gov
http://bhw.hrsa.gov/scholarshipsloans/index.html

NURSING WORKFORCE DIVERSITY "NWD"

Award: Project Grants

Purpose: To support projects that assist underrepresented students throughout the educational pipeline to become registered nurses, facilitate diploma or associate degree registered nurses becoming baccalaureate-prepared registered nurses, and prepare practicing registered nurses for advanced nursing education.

Applicant Eligibility: Eligible applicants are collegiate schools of nursing, nursing centers, academic health centers, State or local governments, and other private or public entities accredited by a recognized body or bodies or state agency, approved for the purpose of nursing education by the Secretary of Education. In addition to schools in the 50 states, only those in the District of Columbia, the Commonwealth of Puerto Rico, the Northern Mariana Islands, American Samoa, Guam, the U.S. Virgin Islands, the Federated States of Micronesia, the Republic of the Marshall Islands, and the Republic of Palau are eligible to apply.

Beneficiary Eligibility: Accredited public and nonprofit private schools of nursing and other public or nonprofit private entities. Project participants must be in an accredited program, a citizen of the United States, a non-citizen national of the United States or a foreign national who possesses a visa permitting permanent residence in the United States.

Award Range/Average: $241,752- $500,000; Average award: $463,774

Funding: (Project Grants) FY 17 $13,857,483; FY 18 est $16,065,986; FY 19 est $0; FY 16 $13,867,000.

HQ: Division of Nursing and Public Health 5600 Fishers Lane, Room 15N58B
Rockville, MD 20857
Phone: 301-443-3192
Email: tspencer@hrsa.gov
http://www.hrsa.gov

NUTRITION & PHYSICAL ACTIVITY PROGRAM FUNDED SOLELY BY PREVENTION & PUBLIC HEALTH FUNDS (PPHF) "Nutrition and Physical Activity"

Award: Cooperative Agreements

Purpose: Purpose of this program is to provide leadership of strategic public health efforts to prevent and control obesity, chronic disease, and other health conditions through regular physical activity and good nutrition.

Applicant Eligibility: : Food and Nutrition, Health/Medical, Environment, Higher Education, Training, Transportation, Regional Development, Youth Development

Beneficiary Eligibility: Eligible applicants may include: States, Interstate, Intrastate, Local, Sponsored organizations, Public/Non Profit organizations, Federally-recognized Indian Tribal Governments, U.S Territories or possessions, or Specialized groups that will be identified in individual funding opportunities.

Award Range/Average: Expected $150,000 - $1,000,000.

Funding: (Cooperative Agreements) FY 17 $0; FY 18 est $0; FY 19 est $0; FY 16 $0.

HQ: 4770 Buford Highway 5600 Fishers Lane, Room 11N94B
Atlanta, GA 30341
Phone: 404-867-9697
Email: lbarnes@cdc.gov
http://www.cdc.gov

NUTRITION & PHYSICAL ACTIVITY PROGRAMS "Micronutrient"

Award: Cooperative Agreements

Purpose: The purpose of the program is to achieve two goals related to risk factors for illness, disability, and premature death as follows: Improve dietary quality to support healthy child development and reduce chronic disease and Decrease prevalence of obesity through prevention of weight gain and maintenance of healthy weight.

Applicant Eligibility: Additional eligibility requirements may apply for funding opportunities that address high needs/risks and disparate populations.

Beneficiary Eligibility: Same as Applicant Eligibility.

Award Range/Average: Average award depends on funding opportunity announcement.

Funding: (Cooperative Agreements) FY 17 $750,000; FY 18 est $750,000; FY 19 est $749,996; FY 16 $750,000.

HQ: 4770 Buford Highway
Atlanta, GA 30341
Phone: 404-867-9697
Email: lbarnes@cdc.gov
http://www.cdc.gov

HHS 93.053 NUTRITION SERVICES INCENTIVE PROGRAM "NSIP"

Award: Formula Grants

Purpose: To reward effective performance by States and Tribes in the efficient delivery of nutritious meals to older adults.

Applicant Eligibility: State Units on Aging (SUA) and Indian Tribal Organizations (ITO) that receive funding through Titles III and VI of the OAA may receive grants of cash from the Administration for Community Living, and/or USDA Foods.

Beneficiary Eligibility: For Title III congregate meals, persons who are older adults (age 60 years and above) or a spouse of an older adult, regardless of age; disabled adults who live in housing facilities primarily occupied by older adults where a congregate site is located; disabled adults under age 60, who reside at home with older adults; and volunteers, regardless of age, who assist in meal service during meal hours. For Title III home-delivered meals, an older individual (age 60 years and above) must be assessed to be homebound.

Award Range/Average: Range: $72 to $16,439,201; Average $475,000

Funding: (Formula Grants) FY 17 $160,069,000; FY 18 est $159,795,000; FY 19 est $160,069,000; FY 16 $160,069,000.

HQ: 330 C Street SW
Washington, DC 20201
Phone: 202-795-7355
Email: holly.greuling@acl.hhs.gov
http://www.acl.gov

OCCUPATIONAL SAFETY & HEALTH PROGRAM

Award: Project Grants; Training

Purpose: To develop specialized professional and paraprofessional personnel in the occupational safety and health field with training in occupational medicine, occupational health nursing, industrial hygiene, occupational safety, and other priority training areas.

Applicant Eligibility: Eligible applicants include for-profit or non-profit organizations, public or private institutions, such as universities, colleges, hospitals, and laboratories, units of State and local governments, eligible agencies of the Federal government, domestic or foreign institutions/organizations, faith-based organizations, Indian Tribes, Tribal Government, College and/or Organizations. Racial/ethnic minority individuals, women, and persons with disabilities are encouraged to apply as Principal Investigators.

Beneficiary Eligibility: Research institutions and agencies as well as workers affected by occupational hazards.

Award Range/Average: General Grants and Cooperative Agreements: $15,000 to $4,924,000. Training Grants: $29,000 to $1,770,000. SBIR Grants: Phase I -up to $150,000; Phase II - up to $1,000,000.

Funding: (Project Grants) FY 17 $109,857,961; FY 18 est $100,000,000; FY 19 est $100,000,000; FY 16 $112,305,445; - Occupational Safety and Health Program.

HQ: 1600 Clifton Road NE Cubicle 4201 23, P.O. Box E 74
Atlanta, GA 30329
Phone: 404-498-2530
Email: sshack@cdc.gov
http://www.cdc.gov/niosh/oep

DOD 12.582 OFFICE FOR REINTEGRATION PROGRAMS
"Yellow Ribbon Reintegration Program"

Award: Cooperative Agreements; Project Grants

Purpose: Conducts data collection, trend analysis, and curriculum development and to prepare reports in support of activities under Section 582 of Public Law 110-181, Sec. 582 (2008), as amended by Public Law 114-92 (2016).

Applicant Eligibility: The Yellow Ribbon Reintegration Program is a DoD-wide effort to promote the well-being of National Guard and Reserve members, their families and communities, by connecting them with resources throughout the deployment cycle. Through Yellow Ribbon events, Service members and loved ones connect with local resources before, during, and after deployments.

Beneficiary Eligibility: Beneficiaries must be able to conduct data collection, trend analysis, and curriculum development and to prepare reports in support of activities of the Yellow Ribbon Reintegration Program.

Award Range/Average: No Data Available.

Funding: N/A

HQ: 4800 Mark Center Drive, Suite 05E22
Alexandria, VA 22350
Phone: 703-571-3183
Email: daniel.j.meshel.civ@mail.mil
http://www.yellowribbon.mil

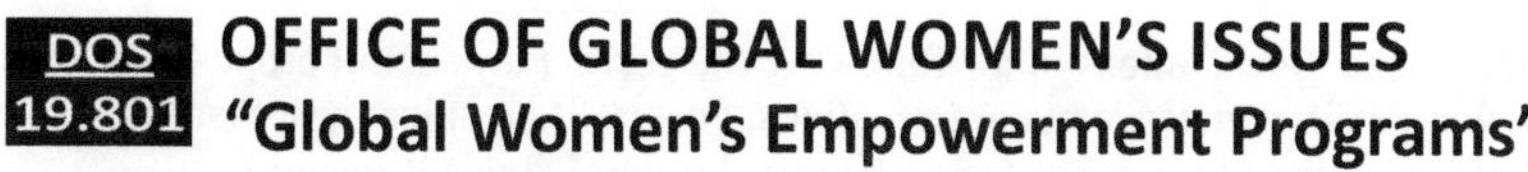

DOS 19.801 OFFICE OF GLOBAL WOMEN'S ISSUES
"Global Women's Empowerment Programs"

Award: Project Grants

Purpose: To promote sustained peace and development by empowering women around the world.

Applicant Eligibility: See individual announcements in grants.gov for further information.

Beneficiary Eligibility: Same as Applicant Eligibility.

Award Range/Average: See individual announcements in grants.gov for further information

Funding: (Cooperative Agreements) FY 14 $8,000,000; FY 17 est $10,000,000; FY 15 est $22,000,000; FY 16 $8,250,000; FY 18 est $10,000,000.

HQ: 2201 C Street NW, Room 7532
Washington, DC 20520
Phone: 202-647-5896
Email: fotovatki@state.gov

NSF 47.083 OFFICE OF INTEGRATIVE ACTIVITIES
"OIA"

Award: Project Grants

Purpose: To enhance the competitiveness of the Nation's research through activities that build capacity for science and engineering and broaden participation in research and education.

Applicant Eligibility: For non-EPCOR grants, except where a program solicitation establishes more restrictive eligibility criteria, individuals and organizations in the following categories may submit proposals: Universities and colleges; Non-profit, non-academic organizations; For-profit organizations; State and local governments; and unaffiliated individuals. See the NSF Grant Proposal Guide, Chapter I.

Beneficiary Eligibility: Except where a program solicitation establishes more restrictive eligibility criteria, individuals and organizations in the following categories may submit proposals: Universities and colleges; Non-profit, non-academic organizations; for-profit organizations; State and local governments; and unaffiliated individuals.

Award Range/Average: Range Low $41,259 Range High $16,367,828 Average $578,630

Funding: (Project Grants) FY 16 $426,570,000; FY 17 est $432,250,000; FY 18 est $315,740,000.

HQ: 2415 Eisenhower Avenue, Suite W17100
Alexandria, VA 22314
Phone: 703-292-8040
Email: ppage@nsf.gov

OFFICE OF INTERNATIONAL SCIENCE & ENGINEERING "OISE"

Award: Project Grants

Purpose: To enable the U.S. to maintain its leadership within the global scientific community by strengthening international partnerships to advance scientific discovery and contribute to the scientific strength and welfare of the Nation.

Applicant Eligibility: Individuals and organizations in the following categories may submit proposals: Universities and colleges; Non-profit, non-academic organizations; For-profit organizations; State and local governments; and unaffiliated individuals. See the NSF Grant Proposal Guide, Chapter I.

Beneficiary Eligibility: N/A

Award Range/Average: Range Low $5,400; Range High $5,678,833 Average $91,872

Funding: (Project Grants) FY 18 est $44,020,000; FY 16 $49,070,000; FY 17 est $48,980,000.

HQ: 2415 Eisenhower Avenue, Suite W17220
Alexandria, VA 22314
Phone: 703-292-7216
Email: sgilbert@nsf.gov
http://nsf.gov/dir/index.jsp?org=oise

OFFICE OF NATIVE AMERICAN PROGRAMS TRAINING & TECHNICAL ASSISTANCE FOR INDIAN HOUSING BLOCK GRANT PROGRAM

Award: Training

Purpose: To provide technical assistance for Indian tribes, Alaska Native villages, and tribally-designated housing entities (TDHEs) to develop viable communities.

Applicant Eligibility: Depending on the component, any national or regional T&TA provider, or any organization with the capacity to provide services.

Beneficiary Eligibility: N/A

Award Range/Average: $9,000- $50,000; $18,000 Average

Funding: (Training) FY 17 $5,842,285; FY 18 est $3,500,000; FY 19 est $3,500,000; FY 16 $5,048,000.

HQ: 451 7th Street SW
Washington, DC 20410
Phone: 202-402-4507
Email: nicholas.c.zolkowski@hud.gov
http://portal.hud.gov/hudportal/hud?src=/program_offices/administration/grants/fundsavail

OFFICE OF NATIVE AMERICAN PROGRAMS TRAINING & TECHNICAL ASSISTANCE FOR NATIVE HAWAIIAN HOUSING BLOCK GRANT PROGRAM

Award: Training

Purpose: To provide technical assistance for Native Hawaiians to develop viable communities.

Applicant Eligibility: Depending on the component, any national or regional T&TA provider, or any organization with the capacity to provide services.

Beneficiary Eligibility: N/A

Award Range/Average: $30,000- $100,000; $20,000 Average

Funding: (Training) FY 17 est $0; FY 16 $0; FY 18 est $0.

HQ: 451 7th Street SW
Washington, DC 20410
Phone: 202-402-4507
Email: nicholas.c.zolkowski@hud.gov
http://portal.hud.gov/hudportal/hud?src=/program_offices/administration/grants/fundsavail

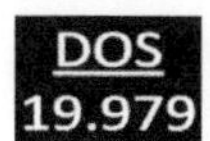

OFFICE OF SECURITY AFFAIRS
"African Regional Security Affairs"

Award: Cooperative Agreements; Project Grants

Purpose: To support U.S. foreign policy goals in sub-Saharan Africa through a variety of programs and policies designed to bolster peace and security.

Applicant Eligibility: If you are interested in implementing AF/SA security-related assistance programs that promote peace and stability on the continent, please see www.Grants.

Beneficiary Eligibility: AF/SA security-related assistance grants bolster our African partners' capacity to provide peace and security.

Award Range/Average: N/A

Funding: (Project Grants) FY 17 N/A FY 16 est $31,000,000; FY 15 est $28,400,000; FY 18 N/A.

HQ: 2201 C Street NW
Washington, DC 20520
Phone: 202-647-7158
Email: pommerercj@state.gov

DOI 15.155 OFFICE OF THE SPECIAL TRUSTEE FOR AMERICAN INDIANS, FIELD OPERATIONS "OST- Field Ops"

Award: Project Grants

Purpose: The goal of these OST grants will be to assist and initiate a wide range of projects that facilitate Trust Improvement and Reform, including but not limited to the areas of Probate/Estates, Individual and Tribal Financial Empowerment, Trust Asset Management, Investments, and Trust administration processes generally.

Applicant Eligibility: Eligible applicants are: Indian tribes; Alaska Native Corporations; Indian or Alaska Native Foundations; Indian or Alaska Native non-profits; qualifying corporations; qualifying contractors; qualifying individual consultants, Law Schools accredited by a recognized body or bodies or state agency, Legal Aid organizations and ULCs. Schools must be located in the 50 states or the District of Columbia.

Beneficiary Eligibility: Beneficiaries will include organizations that will provide direct and defined service to Tribal and Individual beneficiaries. Eligible beneficiaries are: Alaska Native Corporations; Indian or Alaska Native Foundations; Indian or Alaska Native non-profits; qualifying corporations; qualifying contractors; Law Schools accredited by a recognized body or bodies or state agency, Legal Aid organizations and ULCs.

Award Range/Average: $6000 - $149,000

Funding: N/A

HQ: 1849 C Street NW, Room 4257
Washington, DC 20240
Phone: 202-513-0692
Email: megan_olsen@ios.doi.gov
http://www.doi.gov/ost

HHS 93.961 ONE-TIME FUNDING IN SUPPORT OF THE VERMONT ALL-PAYER ACO MODEL

Award: Cooperative Agreements

Purpose: The purpose of this single source funding opportunity for the One-Time Funding in Support of Vermont's All-Payer ACO Model cooperative agreement is to provide Vermont with the start-up costs of the Model to assist Vermont in accomplishing the health outcomes, financial and ACO scale targets required of Vermont under the Model.

Applicant Eligibility: This single source funding opportunity provides Vermont with the necessary start-costs of the Model and is open to Vermont's Agency for Human Services ("Agency"). The Agency is uniquely positioned to meet the objectives of this funding opportunity based on its existing knowledge of the Model, its regulatory authority over healthcare in Vermont and its role in administering the Vermont All-payer ACO Model, its existing partnerships and collaborations with Vermont providers, and its resources and ability to deploy the funding immediately.

Beneficiary Eligibility: CMS is committed to achieving better care for individuals, better health for populations, and reduced expenditures for Medicare, Medicaid, and CHIP. Through the Innovation Center, CMS strives towards these goals by testing innovative payment and service delivery models.

Award Range/Average: The lowest and highest amount is $9.5M - it is only 1 grant.

Funding: (Cooperative Agreements) FY 17 $9,500,000; FY 18 est $0; FY 19 est $0; FY 16 $0.

HQ: 7500 Security Boulevard
Baltimore, MD 21244
Phone: 041-786-8901
Email: akash.shah@cms.hhs.gov
http://www.innovation.cms.gov

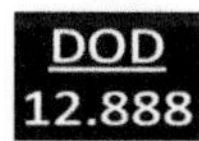

OPA RESEARCH FELLOWSHIP PROGRAM
"OPA Research Fellowship Program"

Award: Cooperative Agreements

Purpose: To solicit offers from interested applicants to establish partnership/relationship which includes a program for university students, post-doctoral researchers and faculty members to conduct mutually-benefitting research which supports OPA's research programs.

Applicant Eligibility: To facilitate the Fellow selection, the Applicant should propose a competitive application process that incorporates OPA evaluation of the research and capability provided. It is important that a research application be consistent and complimentary with OPA facilities and interests, supporting or stimulating OPA basic and applied research programs.

Beneficiary Eligibility: a) Provide appropriately trained and experienced undergraduate and graduate students, Post-doctoral researchers, and faculty for conducting mutually-benefitting research that is compatible with, and contributes to, OPA research, analysis, and studies; b) Match faculty expertise to mutually-benefitting research and study needs within OPA; c) Facilitate a mentoring relationship between OPA researchers and undergraduate and graduate students and post-doctoral researchers; d) Provide a structured approach for OPA researchers to collaborate with university* faculty and graduate students on mutually-benefiting research projects; and e)Provide research space (to include laboratory space when applicable) for conducting research to support the OPA program if proposed by faculty.

Award Range/Average: No Data Available.

Funding: (Salaries and Expenses) FY 18 est $100,000; FY 17 est $500,000; FY 16 $0; - FY 2017 O&M, DW.

HQ: 4800 Mark Center Drive, Suite 06E22
Alexandria, VA 22350
Phone: 571-372-2271
Email: lindsey.r.schaefer.civ@mail.mil

OPIOD AFFECTED YOUTH INITIATIVE

Award: Project Grants

Purpose: To support states and tribal government to respond to the opioid epidemic to promote public safety, to develop multi-disciplinary working groups, to prevent opioid addiction, etc.

Applicant Eligibility: The Opioid Affected Youth Initiative supports states, local units of government, and Tribal Governments in 1) the development multi-disciplinary working groups; 2) the collection and interpretation of data to assist the working group in developing strategies and programming that will be used to better coordinate efforts; and 3) the implementation of services that will address public safety concerns, intervention, prevention and diversion services for children, youth and their families that are directly impacted by opioid addiction.

Beneficiary Eligibility: A training and technical assistance provider will: 1) assist sites with developing data sharing agreements; 2) interpreting data; 3) developing tools that can assist the sites with identifying trends, gaps in services and coordination, targeted demographics and public safety needs; 4) assist sites with developing performance and outcome measurements to improve service delivery and coordination, results and sustainability strategies; and 5) compare performance and outcome measurements across the sites to highlight changed outcomes, program impacts and lessons learned throughout the initiative to the Office of Juvenile Justice and Delinquency Prevention (OJJDP).

Award Range/Average: The Opioid Affected Youth Initiative is new this Fiscal Year (2018) and has appropriated $8,000,000 to the Office of Juvenile Justice and Delinquency Prevention.

Funding: Project Grants (Cooperative Agreements or Contracts) FY 17 $0; FY 18 est $8,000,000.

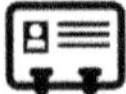

HQ: 810 7th Street NW
Washington, DC 20531
Phone: 202-307-5911
http://www.ojp.gov

OPIOID STR
"State Targeted Response to the Opioid Crisis Grants"

Award: Formula Grants

Purpose: Used for carrying out activities that supplement activities pertaining to opioids undertaken by the State agency responsible for administering the substance abuse prevention and treatment block grant.

Applicant Eligibility: N/A

Beneficiary Eligibility: N/A

Award Range/Average: No Data Available.

Funding: (Formula Grants) FY 17 $484,491,946; FY 18 est $474,729,556; FY 19 est $0; FY 16 $0.

HQ: 5600 Fishers Lane
Rockville, MD 20857
Phone: 240-276-1078
Email: odessa.crocker@samhsa.hhs.gov
http://www.samhsa.gov

ORAL DISEASES & DISORDERS RESEARCH
"Dental, Oral and Craniofacial Research."

Award: Cooperative Agreements; Project Grants

Purpose: Supports basic research examining the role of the oral microbiota in dental health and disease as well as preclinical studies aimed at developing new prevention and treatment options for dental infections.

Applicant Eligibility: Research Project Grants: Scientists at universities, medical and dental schools, hospitals, laboratories, and other public or private nonprofit and for-profit institutions. NRSA and career development awards: (1) Nonprofit domestic organizations may apply for institutional awards.

Beneficiary Eligibility: Health professionals, graduate students, undergraduate students, health professional students, scientists, researchers, and any nonprofit or for-profit organization, company or institution engaged in biomedical research.

Award Range/Average: Research project grants: range $8042- $9,224,715, average $445,599; NRSA: range $363- $568,952, average $77,309; SBIR/STTR: range $27,916- $1,046,856, average $540,253; Career development: range $9,369- $346,329, average $134,492.

Funding: (Project Grants) FY 17 $310,249,153; FY 18 est $335,999,832; FY 19 est $323,332,633; FY 16 $292,486,346.

HQ: 6701 Democracy Boulevard
Bethesda, MD 20892
Phone: 301-594-4890
Email: adombroski@nidcr.nih.gov
http://www.nidcr.nih.gov

ORGANIC AGRICULTURE RESEARCH & EXTENSION INITIATIVE "OREI"

Award: Project Grants

Purpose: To promote organic agriculture, a systematic approach to saving crops, analyzing channels for marketing products, developing international trade, understanding relationship between organic and conventional crops, and analyzing other barriers to organic farming.

Applicant Eligibility: Applications may be submitted by State agricultural experiment stations, all colleges and universities, other research institutions and organizations, Federal agencies, national laboratories, private organizations or corporations, and individuals. For both ORG and OREI, all award recipients may subcontract to organizations not eligible to apply provided such organizations are necessary for the conduct of the project.

Beneficiary Eligibility: State agricultural experiment stations, all colleges and universities, other research institutions and organizations, Federal agencies, national laboratories, private organizations or corporations, and individuals.

Award Range/Average: If minimum or maximum amounts of funding per competitive and/or capacity project grant, or cooperative agreement are established, these amounts will be announced in the annual Competitive Request for Application (RFA).

Funding: (Project Grants) FY 17 $17,580,428; FY 18 est $17,601,735; FY 19 est $18,900,519; FY 16 $17,640,143.

HQ: 1400 Independence Avenue SW, P.O. Box 2240
Washington, DC 20250-2240
Phone: 202-401-6134
http://nifa.usda.gov/program/organic-agriculture-program

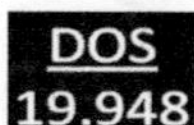

ORGANIZATION OF AMERICAN STATES PROGRAMS "Organization of American States Programs"

Award: Cooperative Agreements; Project Grants

Purpose: Funds shall be for Organization of American States development assistance programs; building of Democracy and restoration of Peace; and Congress reaffirms its support for the work of the Inter-American Commission on Human Rights.

Applicant Eligibility: All funds may only be provided to the Organization of American States, a public international organization.

Beneficiary Eligibility: Public International Organization

Award Range/Average: 500,000 to $4,500,000

Funding: (Salaries and Expenses) FY 17 $9,500,000; FY 19 est $9,000,000; FY 18 est $9,500,000.

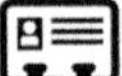

HQ: 2201 C Street NW
Washington, DC 20520
Phone: 202-647-9908
Email: kodiakt@state.gov
http://usoas.usmission.gov

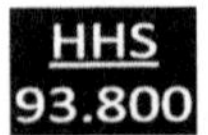

ORGANIZED APPROACHES TO INCREASE COLORECTAL CANCER SCREENING

"Organized Approaches to Increase Colorectal Cancer Screening Program – DP15-1502"

Award: Cooperative Agreements

Purpose: The program's purpose is to increase CRC screening rates among an applicant-defined target population of persons 50-75 years of age within partner health system(s), defined geographical areas, or disparate populations.

Applicant Eligibility: Eligible applicants are the official State/Territorial health agencies of the United States or their bona fide agents; Tribes/Tribal Organizations and Private/Public Colleges and Universities.

Beneficiary Eligibility: Same as Applicant Eligibility.

Award Range/Average: Component 1 annual awards will range from $350,000 to $800,000. Component 2 annual awards will range from $500,000 to $1,000,000.

Funding: FY 17 $23,251,826; FY 18 est $22,659,654; FY 19 est $22,659,654; FY 16 $19,510,684.

HQ: 4770 Buford Highway
Atlanta, GA 30341
Phone: 770-488-1074
Email: dcm0@cdc.gov

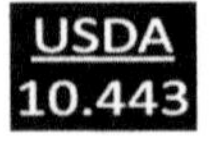

OUTREACH & ASSISTANCE FOR SOCIALLY DISADVANTAGED & VETERAN FARMERS & RANCHERS

"USDA 2501 Grant Program"

Award: Project Grants

Purpose: The U.S. Department of Agriculture assists socially disadvantaged veteran farmers by providing education, training, and technical assistance.

Applicant Eligibility: Organizations that may apply: Any community-based organization, network, or coalition of community-based organizations with documented evidence of working with and on behalf of socially disadvantaged and veteran farmers and ranchers during the 3-year period preceding this application cycle and does not or has not engaged in activities prohibited under Section 501(c)(3) of the Internal Revenue Code of 1986; an 1890 or 1994 institution of higher education (as defined in 7 U.S.C. § 7601); a Hispanic-Serving Institution of higher education (as defined in 7 U.S.C.

Beneficiary Eligibility: A farmer or rancher who is a member of one or more of the following groups whose members have been subjected to racial or ethnic prejudice because of their identity as members of a group without regard to their individual qualities: African-Americans, American Indians, Alaskan Natives, Hispanics, Asians, and Pacific Islanders. The Secretary of Agriculture will determine on a case-by-case basis whether additional groups qualify under this definition.

Award Range/Average: $50,000 to $200,000 Average is $200,000 per award

Funding: (Project Grants) FY 17 $9,000,000; FY 18 est $10,000,000; FY 19 est $10,000,000.

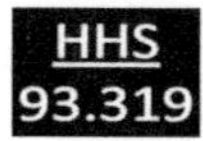

HQ: 1400 Independence Avenue SW, P.O. Box 0601
Washington, DC 20250-9600
Phone: 202-720-6350
http://www.outreach.usda.gov/grants/index.htm

HHS 93.319

OUTREACH PROGRAMS TO REDUCE THE PREVALENCE OF OBESITY IN HIGH RISK RURAL AREAS "High Risk Obesity"

Award: Project Grants

Purpose: To assist Land-Grant institutions to conduct pilot programs through existing extension and outreach services to enhance and expand efforts to combat the prevalence of obesity in areas where the problem is worst, particularly rural areas.

Applicant Eligibility: Must conduct activities in eligible counties (defined as having an obesity prevalence of 40%+ (based on 2006–2008 data from BRFSS, CDC County-Level Map.

Beneficiary Eligibility: Individual/Family (residents) in local counties/rural areas will benefit from this assistance through increased access and opportunities to healthy, affordable foods and beverages, safe and convenient places for physical activity and breastfeeding duration and support.

Award Range/Average: No Data Available.

Funding: (Project Grants) FY 17 $6,843,000; FY 18 est $10,873,643; FY 19 est $10,873,643.

HQ: 4770 Buford Highway NE
Atlanta, GA 30341
Phone: 404-867-9697
Email: lbarnes@cdc.gov

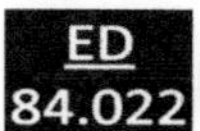

ED 84.022

OVERSEAS PROGRAMS – DOCTORAL DISSERTATION RESEARCH ABROAD

Award: Project Grants

Purpose: To provide opportunities for graduate students to engage in full-time dissertation research abroad in modern foreign language and area studies with the exception of Western Europe.

Applicant Eligibility: Institutions of higher education may apply.

Beneficiary Eligibility: A candidate for Doctoral Dissertation Research Abroad Fellowship must: (1) be a (a) citizen or national of the United States; or (b) permanent resident of the United States; (2) be a graduate student in good standing at an institution of higher education who, when the fellowship period begins, has been admitted to candidacy in a doctoral degree program in modern foreign languages and area studies at that institution; (3) plan a teaching career in the United States upon graduation; (4) possess adequate skills in the foreign language(s) necessary to carry out the dissertation research project.

Award Range/Average: N/A.

Funding: FY 17 $3,397,151; FY 18 est $3,408,151; FY 19 est $0; FY 16 $3,477,313.

HQ: 400 Maryland Avenue SW
Washington, DC 20202
Phone: 202-453-6891
Email: ddra@ed.gov
http://www.ed.gov/programs/iegpsddrap

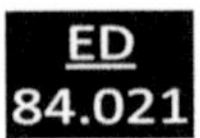

OVERSEAS PROGRAMS – GROUP PROJECTS ABROAD

Award: Project Grants

Purpose: To support the development and improvement of the study of modern foreign languages and area studies in the United States by providing grants to support overseas projects in training, research, and curriculum development in modern foreign languages and area studies for teachers, students, and faculty engaged in a common endeavor.

Applicant Eligibility: Institutions of higher education, State departments of education, private nonprofit educational organizations, and a consortium of institutions, departments, and organizations.

Beneficiary Eligibility: A participant must be: a citizen, or permanent resident of the United States, currently employed full-time in a United States school system, institution of higher education, local education agency or state education agency (not applicable to students), and at least one of the following: A teacher in an elementary or secondary school (please see note below); A faculty member who teaches modern foreign languages or area studies; An experienced education administrator responsible for planning, conducting, or supervising programs in modern foreign languages or area studies at the elementary, secondary, or postsecondary levels; A graduate student or junior or senior in an institution of higher education, who is a prospective teacher in the areas of social sciences, humanities and foreign languages. The student should meet the provisions set by his or her local and state education agencies; or For the Advanced Overseas Intensive Language Training project, the participating student, other than those planning a teaching career, should be planning to apply their language skills and knowledge of countries vital to the United States national security in fields outside teaching, including government, the professions, or international development.

Award Range/Average: Varies by competition.

Funding: (Project Grants) FY 17 $2,792,439; FY 18 est $2,792,439; FY 19 est $0; FY 16 $32,792,439.

HQ: 400 Maryland Avenue SW
Washington, DC 20202
Phone: 202-453-6391
Email: tanyelle.richardson@ed.gov
http://www.ed.gov/programs/iegpsgpa

OVERSEAS PROGRAMS SPECIAL BILATERAL PROJECTS

Award: Project Grants

Purpose: To increase mutual understanding and knowledge between the people of the United States and other countries, to participate in short-term study seminars abroad on topics in the social sciences and the humanities through qualified U.S. educators.

Applicant Eligibility: Applicants must (1) be U.S. citizens or have permanent resident status; (2) hold at least a bachelor's degree from an accredited college or university; (3) have at least 3 years full-time in teaching, administering or supervising in the humanities, the social sciences or social studies subjects; (4) be currently employed full-time in teaching, administering or supervising in the aforementioned areas; (5) meet any language requirements if applicable (see the application booklet for details). If selected, awardees must furnish evidence of good health and emotional maturity.

Beneficiary Eligibility: (1) Undergraduate faculty members of 4 year colleges/universities and 2-year community colleges in the fields of the humanities and social sciences; (2) supervisors and secondary (grades 9 through 12) and elementary and junior high school (grades K through 8) teachers of social studies and humanities; and (3) curriculum development specialists, administrators of local and State education agencies who have direct responsibility for developing curriculum in the subject areas encompassed by the social sciences and the humanities.

Award Range/Average: Varies by competition.

Funding: (Project Grants) FY 17 $532,300; FY 18 est $552,300; FY 19 est $0; FY 16 $532,300.

HQ: 400 Maryland Avenue SW
Washington, DC 20202
Phone: 202-453-6080
Email: maria.chang@ed.gov
http://www.ed.gov/programs/iegpssap

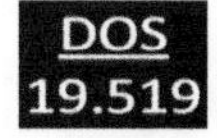

OVERSEAS REFUGEE ASSISTANCE PROGRAM FOR NEAR EAST
"Overseas Refugee Assistance Program for Near East"

Award: Cooperative Agreements

Purpose: Providing protection and assistance to Syrian and Iraqi refugees, conflict victims, internally displaced persons and returnees remains a high priority. Programs will assist refugee populations in neighboring countries.

Applicant Eligibility: United Nations, international and non- governmental organizations. MRA designates primary UN or IO recipient organizations.

Beneficiary Eligibility: Refugees and victims of conflict requiring assistance.

Award Range/Average: No Data Available.

Funding: (Salaries and Expenses) FY 18 est $23,100,000; FY 19 est $23,100,000; FY 17 $23,099,109.

HQ: 2025 E Street NW, 8th Floor SA 9
Washington, DC 20520
Phone: 202-453-9292
Email: terharvs@state.gov
http://www.state.gov/j/prm/index.htm

DOS 19.523 OVERSEAS REFUGEE ASSISTANCE PROGRAM FOR SOUTH ASIA

Award: Cooperative Agreements

Purpose: The Bureau continues to support for the return and reintegration programs for Afghan refugees and Internally Displaced Persons. The Bureau will also continue supporting protection and assistance activities for refugees who remain in Pakistan and Iran and who may not repatriate.

Applicant Eligibility: United Nations (UN), international organization (IO), and non-governmental organizations(NGO). MRA designates primary UN or IO recipient organizations.

Beneficiary Eligibility: Refugees and victims of conflict requiring assistance.

Award Range/Average: No Data Available.

Funding: (Salaries and Expenses) FY 18 est $23,100,000; FY 19 est $23,100,000; FY 17 $23,099,109.

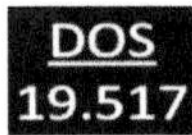

HQ: 2025 E Street NW, 8th Floor SA 9
Washington, DC 20520
Phone: 202-453-9282
Email: mestetskyea@state.gov
http://www.state.gov/j/prm/index.htm

DOS 19.517 OVERSEAS REFUGEE ASSISTANCE PROGRAMS FOR AFRICA
"Overseas Refugee Assistance Programs for Africa"

Award: Project Grants

Purpose: Provides assistance to the basic needs of refugees and conflict victims spread across the African continent. NGOs are key partners of international organizations in Africa, often in specialized areas such as healthcare, water, sanitation, food distribution, and education.

Applicant Eligibility: International and non- governmental organizations. MRA designates primary UN or IO recipient organizations.

Beneficiary Eligibility: Refugees and victims of conflict requiring assistance.

Award Range/Average: No Data Available.

Funding: (Cooperative Agreements) FY 17 est $93,000,000; FY 12 $75,434,648; FY 14 $65,628,490; N/A FY 16 $93,759,300; FY 18 est $93,000,000; FY 13 $60,739,119.

HQ: 2025 E Street NW
Washington, DC 20522-0908
Phone: 202-453-9239
Email: hembreeel@state.gov
http://www.state.gov/j/prm/index.htm

DOS 19.511 OVERSEAS REFUGEE ASSISTANCE PROGRAMS FOR EAST ASIA
"Overseas Refugee Assistance Programs for East Asia"

Award: Cooperative Agreements

Purpose: The Bureau of Population, Refugees, and Migration supports humanitarian assistance and protection programs for vulnerable populations in Australia, Bangladesh, Burma, Cambodia, Indonesia, Laos, Malaysia, Mongolia, the Philippines, Thailand, and Vietnam.

Applicant Eligibility: Non-governmental organizations. The Migration and Refugee Assistance Account (MRA) designates primary UN or IO recipient organizations.

Beneficiary Eligibility: Refugees and victims of conflict requiring assistance.

Award Range/Average: No Data Available.

Funding: (Cooperative Agreements) FY 13 $20,718,964; FY 16 $18,264,778; FY 14 $20,073,554; FY 18 est $18,300,000; FY 17 est $18,300,000; FY 12 $19,982,796.

HQ: 2025 E Street NW
Washington, DC 20522-0908
Phone: 202-453-9289
Email: tranht3@state.gov
http://www.state.gov/j/prm/index.htm

OVERSEAS REFUGEE ASSISTANCE PROGRAMS FOR EUROPE
"Overseas Refugee Assistance Programs for Europe"

Award: Cooperative Agreements

Purpose: Provides funding for organizations that assist refugees and internally displaced persons in Europe and Central Asia.

Applicant Eligibility: United Nations, international and non- governmental organizations. MRA designates primary UN or IO recipient organizations.

Beneficiary Eligibility: Refugees and victims of conflict requiring assistance.

Award Range/Average: N/A.

Funding: (Cooperative Agreements) FY 12 $4,424,719; FY 14 $2,893,233; FY 17 est $3,100,000; FY 13 $9,275,661; FY 18 est $3,100,000; FY 16 $3,098,439.

HQ: 2025 E Street NW, 8th Floor SA 9
Washington, DC 20520
Phone: 202-453-9297
Email: irisnr@state.gov
http://www.state.gov/j/prm/index.htm

OVERSEAS REFUGEE ASSISTANCE PROGRAMS FOR STRATEGIC GLOBAL PRIORITIES
"Overseas Refugee Assistance Programs for Strategic Global Priorities"

Award: Cooperative Agreements

Purpose: Bureau support under this program includes mostly contributions to the headquarters and global program costs of the United Nations High Commissioner for Refugees, the headquarters budget of the International Committee of the Red Cross and to a smaller extent, the multiregional activities of other international and non-governmental organizations assisting refugees and other conflict victims.

Applicant Eligibility: United Nations, international and non-governmental organizations. MRA designates primary UN or IO recipient organizations.

Beneficiary Eligibility: Refugees and victims of conflict requiring assistance.

Award Range/Average: N/A.

Funding: (Cooperative Agreements) FY 17 est $6,700,000; FY 13 $2,520,151; FY 14 $8,929,407; FY 16 $6,717,762; FY 12 $3,259,693; FY 18 est $6,700,000.

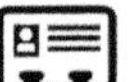

HQ: 2025 E Street NW
Washington, DC 20522-0908
Phone: 202-453-9239
Email: hembreeel@state.gov
http://www.state.gov/j/prm/index.htm

OVERSEAS REFUGEE ASSISTANCE PROGRAMS FOR WESTERN HEMISPHERE

"Overseas Refugee Assistance Programs for Western Hemisphere"

Award: Cooperative Agreements

Purpose: PRM provides assistance to internally displaced persons and refugees in Colombia and neighboring countries. PRM's assistance strategy includes ensuring adequate protection for vulnerable IDPs, filling gaps in the provision of emergency humanitarian assistance, and building local government and community capacity to meet the needs of IDPs.

Applicant Eligibility: United Nations, international and non-governmental organizations. MRA designates primary UN or IO recipient organizations.

Beneficiary Eligibility: Refugees and victims of conflict requiring assistance.

Award Range/Average: No Data Available.

Funding: (Cooperative Agreements) FY 16 $22,864,159; FY 12 $17,371,720; FY 18 est $22,800,000; FY 13 $17,706,876; FY 14 $16,051,526; FY 17 est $22,800,000.

HQ: 2025 E Street NW, 8th Floor SA 9
Washington, DC 20520
Phone: 202-453-9297
Email: irisnr@state.gov
http://www.state.gov/j/prm/index.htm

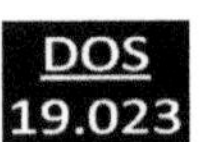

OVERSEAS SCHOOLS PROGRAM

Award: Project Grants

Purpose: Promotes quality educational opportunities at the elementary and secondary school levels for dependents of American citizens carrying out programs and interests of the U.S. Government abroad. It also works to increase mutual understanding between the people of the United States and the people of other countries through educational institutions which demonstrates American educational practices, principles and methods employed in the United States.

Applicant Eligibility: Grants are generally restricted to selected overseas schools.

Beneficiary Eligibility: Dependents of American citizens carrying out programs and interests of the U.S. Government abroad are the primary beneficiaries.

Award Range/Average: Grants range from $5000 to $400,000. Majority of grants are less than $40,000.

Funding: (Project Grants) FY 17 est $1,200,000; FY 16 est $11,500,000; FY 18 est $12,000,000; FY 15 $12,000,000.

HQ: 2401 C Street NW, Room H328
Washington, DC 20522-0103
Phone: 202-261-8203
Email: lyleswm2@state.gov
http://www.state.gov/m/a/os

PACKAGING & SPREADING PROVEN PEDIATRIC WEIGHT MANAGEMENT INTERVENTIONS FOR USE BY LOW-INCOME FAMILIES
"Childhood Obesity Research Demonstration"

Award: N/A

Purpose: To increase the availability and number of packaged effective pediatric weight management interventions (PWMI) that can be used by healthcare, community or public health organizations to serve low-income children and their caregivers.

Applicant Eligibility: Eligibility will not be limited.

Beneficiary Eligibility: N/A

Award Range/Average: $3750000

Funding: N/A

HQ: 4770Buford Highway NE NCCDPHP
Atlanta, GA 30341
Phone: 404-867-9697
Email: lbarnes@cdc.gov
http://cdc.gov

PARALYSIS RESOURCE CENTER
"Paralysis Resource Center & National Limb Loss Resource Center (PRC)"

Award: Cooperative Agreements

Purpose: Grant is awarded to the Christopher & Dana Reeve Foundation.

Applicant Eligibility: Eligible applicants will include public and private nonprofit entities, including universities, university-affiliated systems, not-for-profit medical centers, research institutions and rehabilitation hospitals, disability service groups such as advocacy and voluntary organizations, and independent living centers, and federally recognized Indian Tribal Governments.

Beneficiary Eligibility: In addition to the eligible applicants, other groups who will receive benefits from the programs include persons individuals living with disabilities paralysis and family members of persons with disabilities, persons individuals living with limb loss, minority populations, refugees, infants, children, youth, adults, senior citizens, women, all educational levels, all income levels, urban, suburban, and rural populations, health/ rehabilitation professionals, scientists, educators, and researchers.

Award Range/Average: No Data Available.

Funding: (Project Grants) FY 17 $7,700,000; FY 18 est $7,700,000; FY 19 FY 16 $7,700,000.

HQ: 330 C Street SW
Washington, DC 20201
Phone: 202-795-7401
Email: ophelia.mclain@acl.hhs.gov
http://www.acl.gov

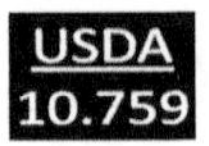

PART 1774 SPECIAL EVALUATION ASSISTANCE FOR RURAL COMMUNITIES & HOUSEHOLDS PROGRAM (SEARCH) "SEARCH Grant Program"

Award: Project Grants

Purpose: To make development grants for financially distressed communities in rural areas with water disposal projects.

Applicant Eligibility: Applicants must be (1) public bodies or governmental entities such as states, municipalities, counties, districts, authorities, and other political subdivisions of a State; (2) nonprofit organizations such as associations, cooperatives, private nonprofit corporations, and institutions of higher education and hospitals; (3) Native American Indian tribes on Federal and State reservations, other federally recognized Indian tribes, and Native American Organizations (includes Indian groups, cooperatives, corporations, partnerships, and associations.

Beneficiary Eligibility: Beneficiaries are the entities or organizations eligible to develop projects under the Water and Waste Disposal Loan and Grant Program. Eligible entities include (1) public bodies or governmental entities such as municipalities, counties, districts, authorities, and other political subdivisions of a State, (2) nonprofit organizations such as associations, cooperatives, and private nonprofit corporations, (3) Native American Indian tribes on Federal and State reservations and other federally recognized Indian tribes.

Award Range/Average: $7,500 to $30,000. Average is $25,918

Funding: (Project Grants) FY 17 $2,410,383; FY 18 est $4,000,000; FY 19 est $0; FY 16 $3,515,212.

HQ: 1400 Independence Avenue SW, P.O. Box 1570
Washington, DC 20005
Phone: 202-690-2525
Email: stephen.saulnier@wdc.usda.gov
http://www.rd.usda.gov/programs-services/all-programs/water-environmental-programs

PARTNER ACTIONS TO IMPROVE ORAL HEALTH OUTCOMES

Award: Cooperative Agreements; Project Grants

Purpose: To establish oral health leadership and program guidance, oral health data collection and interpretation, multi-dimensional delivery system for oral and physical health, and to implement science-based programs (including dental sealants and community water fluoridation) to improve oral and physical health.

Applicant Eligibility: Eligible applicants are the official State and territorial health agencies of the United States, the District of Columbia, tribal organizations, the Commonwealth of Puerto, the Virgin Islands, Guam, the Northern Mariana Islands, the Federated States of Micronesia, the Republic of the Marshall Islands, the Republic of Palau, and American Samoa, or their Bona Fide Agents.

Beneficiary Eligibility: States, political subdivisions of States, local health authorities, and individuals or organizations with specialized health interests will benefit.

Award Range/Average: 350000

Funding: (Cooperative Agreements) FY 17 $350,000; FY 18 est $350,000; FY 19 est $350,000.

HQ: 4770 Buford Highway NE, P.O. Box F80
Atlanta, GA 30341
Phone: 770-488-6075

PARTNER SUPPORT FOR HEART DISEASE & STROKE PREVENTION "Partner Support"

Award: Cooperative Agreements

Purpose: The program provides partner support around cardiovascular disease prevention activities.

Applicant Eligibility: Government and non-governmental organizations, including state, local, tribal and territorial governments or their bona fide agents.

Beneficiary Eligibility: non-governmental organizations, including state, local, tribal and territorial governments or their bona fide agents

Award Range/Average: The award range is $250,000- $500,000, with an average of $400,000 per budget year.

Funding: (Cooperative Agreements) FY 17 $500,000; FY 18 est $500,000; FY 19 est $500,000; FY 16 $500,000.

HQ: 4770 Buford Highway NE, P.O. Box F 72
Atlanta, GA 30341
Phone: 770-488-5108
Email: sij9@cdc.gov
http://www.cdc.gov

PARTNERSHIPS TO IMPROVE COMMUNITY HEALTH "PICH"

Award: Cooperative Agreements

Purpose: To support implementation of evidenced- and practice-based strategies that address previously-identified community gaps and needs within a defined jurisdiction in order to reduce the prevalence of chronic disease and related risk factors.

Applicant Eligibility: Eligible applicants are considered responsive if providing: Evidence of being a member of or working through a functioning multi-sector community coalition of organizations and agencies that are committed to improving the health of their community (of 2 or more years).

Beneficiary Eligibility: Anyone/General Public

Award Range/Average: $100,000 - $5,000,000

Funding: (Cooperative Agreements) FY 16 $34,498,309; FY 17 est $0; FY 18 est $0; - Program ended 2017.

HQ: 4770 Buford Highway, P.O. Box F81
Atlanta, GA 30341
Phone: 770-488-5266
Email: dyu9@cdc.gov
http://www.cdc.gov

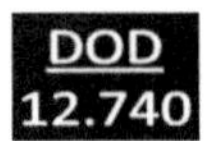

PAST CONFLICT ACCOUNTING
"Defense POW/MIA Accounting Agency (DPAA) Past Conflict Accounting Grants and Cooperative Agreements Program (DPAAGCAP)"

Award: Cooperative Agreements; Project Grants

Purpose: Is responsible for determining the fate of our missing and, where possible, recovering and identifying those who have made the ultimate sacrifice on behalf of a grateful nation.

Applicant Eligibility: Applicants can be any private entity. A private entity is defined as any self-sustaining, non-Federal person or organization, established, operated, and controlled by any individual(s) acting outside the scope of any official capacity as officers, employees, or agents of the Federal Government.

Beneficiary Eligibility: Beneficiaries of an assistance award can be any private entity which is defined as any self-sustaining, non-Federal person or organization, established, operated, and controlled by any individual(s) acting outside the scope of any official capacity as officers, employees, or agents of the Federal Government.

Award Range/Average: Not yet defined as this is a new program.

Funding: Cooperative Agreements (Discretionary Grants) FY 19 est $500,000; FY 17 N/A FY 18 est $250,000; - As this is a new program, DPAA will need to evaluate the usefulness of grants and cooperative agreement to develop refined plans and budgets.

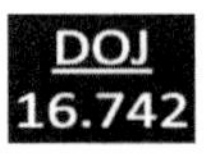

PAUL COVERDELL FORENSIC SCIENCES IMPROVEMENT GRANT PROGRAM
"Coverdell Program"

Award: Formula Grants; Project Grants

Purpose: To fund for analysis of forensic evidence and forensic laboratory, to improve the quality and timeliness of forensic science, to address emerging forensic science issues, to educate and train forensic pathologists, and to assist medicolegal death investigators.

Applicant Eligibility: Under the Coverdell program, SAAs may apply for both "base" (formula) and competitive funds. Units of local government may apply for competitive funds.

Beneficiary Eligibility: Eligible applicants must be State or local.

Award Range/Average: In amounts consistent with the applicant's proposed project and NIJ's plans, priorities and levels of financing.

Funding: (Formula Grants) FY 17 $10,690,702; FY 18 FY 19.

HQ: 810 7th Street NW
Washington, DC 20531
Phone: 202-514-1287
Email: luther.schaeffer@usdoj.gov
http://nij.gov

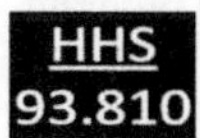

PAUL COVERDELL NATIONAL ACUTE STROKE PROGRAM NATIONAL CENTER FOR CHRONIC DISEASE PREVENTION & HEALTH PROMOTION "Coverdell"

Award: Cooperative Agreements

Purpose: The program works to improve the quality of acute stroke care and health outcomes for acute stroke patients.

Applicant Eligibility: State governments (this includes the District of Columbia) are eligible to apply

Beneficiary Eligibility: Eligibility is limited to state health departments (to include the District of Columbia) with heart disease and stroke prevention programs for this cooperative agreement. State health departments are the only agencies who are uniquely positioned to develop strong state level task forces to develop these stroke systems of care that can be used to focus on an comprehensive approach to improving quality of care at all points along the continuum of care that will have the largest reach and impact on decreasing morbidity and mortality from stroke, reducing disparities in the delivery of care, and improving outcomes.

Award Range/Average: 700,000 -800,000

Funding: (Cooperative Agreements) FY 17 $6,740,000; FY 18 est $674,000; FY 19 est $674,000; FY 16 $6,740,000.

HQ: 4770 Buford Highway NE, P.O. Box F72
Atlanta, GA 30341
Phone: 770-488-6093
Email: sweagle@cdc.gov
http://www.cdc.gov

PAY FOR SUCCESS PERMANENT SUPPORTIVE HOUSING DEMONSTRATION "Pay for Success Demonstration"

Award: Project Grants

Purpose: To prevent and end homelessness and reduce avoidable incarceration by increasing the provision of Permanent Supportive Housing (PSH). The PFS Demonstration is an opportunity to equip communities for funding PSH projects that will prevent returns to homelessness and reduce recidivism among the reentry population.

Applicant Eligibility: The grantee will use grant funds for assessing the feasibility of a PFS project and/or structuring PFS operations, including: partnership building, capital-raising activities, program design for the target population at the Demonstration Site, managing contracts with service providers, making Success Payments on behalf of the government entity, and managing third-party evaluators. Intermediaries may carry out all activities directly and/or subaward funds to subrecipients or procure the services of contractors to carry out PFS activities.

Beneficiary Eligibility: See program's Notice of Funding Availability

Award Range/Average: Range of awards is: $881,376 to $1.3 million. The average award is: $1.24 million.

Funding: (Project Grants) FY 17 est $0; FY 18 est $0; FY 16 $8,679,000; - $8,679,000 was awarded through federal grants. The remainder of the $10,000,000 appropriation is for administration and program evaluation of the PFS Demonstration.

HQ: 451 7th Street SW, Room 7260
Washington, DC 20410
Phone: 202-402-4773
Email: karen.m.deblasio@hud.gov
http://hudexchange.info

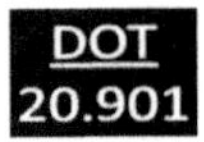

DOT 20.901 PAYMENTS FOR ESSENTIAL AIR SERVICES "EAS"

Award: Project Grants; Direct Payments for Specified Use

Purpose: To assure that air transportation is provided to eligible communities by subsidizing air carriers.

Applicant Eligibility: Air carrier must be found fit and be selected by the Department to perform the subsidized service.

Beneficiary Eligibility: Air carriers and eligible local communities.

Award Range/Average: For continental United States: range from $491,205 to $4,710,683 annually; an average of $2,189,355 annually per community per year.

Funding: (Direct Payments for Specified Use) FY 17 $275,000,000; FY 18 est $317,000,000; FY 19 est $315,000,000; FY 16 $288,172,731.

HQ: 1200 New Jersey Avenue SE
Washington, DC 20590
Phone: 202-366-3176
Email: kevin.schlemmer@dot.gov
http://www.dot.gov/policy/aviation-policy/small-community-rural-air-service/essential-air-service

DOT 20.930 PAYMENTS FOR SMALL COMMUNITY AIR SERVICE DEVELOPMENT

"Small Community Program or SCASDP Payments for Small Community Air Service Development"

Award: Project Grants

Purpose: To assist small communities enhance their air service and increase access to the national transportation system.

Applicant Eligibility: In order to qualify for a SCASDP grant: 1. The airport serving the community is not larger than a small hub airport, according to FAA hub classifications effective on the date of service of the Department's Solicitation (RFP) Order or as of calendar year 1997, the airport serving the community was not larger than a small hub airport; 2.

Beneficiary Eligibility: The legal sponsor of the proposed project must be a government entity. If the applicant is a public-private partnership, a public government member of the organization must be identified as the community's sponsor to receive project cost reimbursements.

Award Range/Average: Range: $50,000 to $1,000,000 Average: $620,000

Funding: (Project Grants) FY 17 $9,925,000; FY 18 est $10,000,000; FY 19 N/A FY 16 $5,150,000.

HQ: 1200 New Jersey Avenue SE W86 307
Washington, DC 20590
Phone: 202-366-0577
Email: brooke.chapman@dot.gov
http://www.dot.gov/policy/aviation-policy/small-community-rural-air-service/scasdp

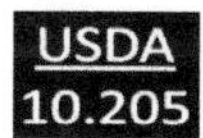

PAYMENTS TO 1890 LAND-GRANT COLLEGES & TUSKEGEE UNIVERSITY

"Evans-Allen Research and/or Agricultural Research at 1890 Land-Grant Institutions, Including Tuskegee University, West Virginia State University and Central State University"

Award: Formula Grants

Purpose: To support agricultural research, agriculture, and rural life.

Applicant Eligibility: Applications may be submitted by 1890 Land-Grant Universities, including Tuskegee University, West Virginia State University and Central State University.

Beneficiary Eligibility: Same as Applicant Eligibility.

Award Range/Average: If minimum or maximum amounts of funding per competitive and/or capacity project grant, or cooperative agreement are established, these amounts will be announced in the annual Capacity, Competitive, and/or Non-Competitive Request for Application (RFA).

Funding: Formula Grants (Apportionments) FY 17 $50,780,008; FY 18 est $50,877,548; FY 19 est $50,683,295; FY 16 $50,910,586.

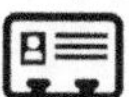

HQ: 1400 Independence Avenue SW, P.O. Box 2250
Washington, DC 20250-2250
Phone: 202-720-9278
http://nifa.usda.gov/program/agricultural-research-1890-land-grant-institutions

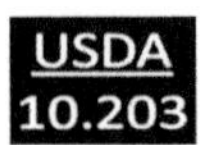

PAYMENTS TO AGRICULTURAL EXPERIMENT STATIONS UNDER THE HATCH ACT "Hatch Act and The Hatch Act of 1887"

Award: Formula Grants

Purpose: To promote agriculture and rural life, provide support for agricultural research and compensations for agriculture research.

Applicant Eligibility: (A) The Hatch Act of 1887 (Regular Research) Hatch Act funds are provided for agricultural research on an annual basis to the State Agricultural Experiment Stations (SAES's) which were established under the direction of the college or university or agricultural departments of the college or university in each State in accordance with the act approved July 2, 1862 (7 U.S.C. 301 et seq.

Beneficiary Eligibility: Funds under the Hatch Act are allocated in accordance with the statutory formula stated in the Act to the State agricultural experiment stations of the 50 States, the District of Columbia, Guam, Puerto Rico, the Virgin Islands, American Samoa, Micronesia, and Northern Mariana Islands. These institutions have been identified and declared eligible by their respective State legislatures.

Award Range/Average: N/A

Funding: Formula Grants (Apportionments) FY 17 $228,105,022; FY 18 est $229,053,592; FY 19 est $227,669,828; FY 16 $228,687,214.

HQ: 1400 Independence Avenue SW, P.O. Box 2250
Washington, DC 20250-2240
Phone: 202-401-4939
http://nifa.usda.gov/grants

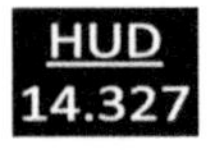

PERFORMANCE BASED CONTRACT ADMINISTRATOR PROGRAM "PBCA Program"

Award: Direct Payments for Specified Use

Purpose: To implement the policy of the United States, as established in section 2 of the 1937 Act, of assisting States and their political subdivisions for aiding lower income families.

Applicant Eligibility: HUD will accept applications to provide contract administration services for the 42 "States," which are listed in Appendix A of the program Notice of Funding Availability (NOFA). State is defined in the ACC as one of the fifty United States, the District of Columbia, the United States Virgin Islands, or the Commonwealth of Puerto Rico.

Beneficiary Eligibility: Families currently receiving assistance as long as their income does not exceed 80 percent of area median income adjusted for family size.

Award Range/Average: estimated $20 million per month for entire program.

Funding: (Salaries and Expenses) FY 16 est $338,000,000; FY 17 est $295,000,000; FY 15 $273,000,000.

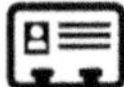

HQ: 451 7th Street SW
Washington, DC 20410
Phone: 202-402-2768

Email: deborah.k.lear@hud.gov
http://portal.hud.gov/hudportal/hud?src=/program_offices/housing/mfh/rfp/sec8rfp

DOD 12.355 PEST MANAGEMENT & VECTOR CONTROL RESEARCH

Award: Cooperative Agreements; Project Grants

Purpose: To develop new interventions for protection of deployed military personnel from diseases caused by arthropod-borne pathogens and to improve control of filth flies.

Applicant Eligibility: Applicants must be a public or private educational institution, nonprofit organizations operated for purposes in the public interest and commercial firms.

Beneficiary Eligibility: Beneficiaries are relatively independent investigators associated with an applicant organization.

Award Range/Average: $100- $250K per year/per award.

Funding: (Cooperative Agreements) FY 17 $145,000; FY 18 est $500,000; FY 19 est $1,479,376.

HQ: 110 Thomas Johnson Drive
Frederick, MD 21702
Phone: 301-619-2446
Email: richard.w.totten2.civ@mail.mil
http://www.3.natick.army.mil

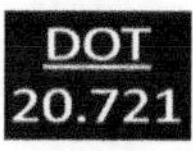

DOT 20.721 PHMSA PIPELINE SAFETY PROGRAM ONE CALL GRANT

Award: Project Grants

Purpose: Provides funding to State agencies in promoting damage prevention, including changes with their State underground damage prevention laws, related compliance activities, training and public education.

Applicant Eligibility: A state is eligible if it qualifies under section 49 USC 6104 (b).

Beneficiary Eligibility: State (Includes District of Columbia and Puerto Rico) Also, State agency with a Certification or Agreement under 60105 or 60106 of Title 49 USC.

Award Range/Average: The range for grants awarded $10,000 to $45,000

Funding: Project Grants (Discretionary) FY 17 $1,237,942; FY 18 est $1,058,000; FY 19 est $1,051,000.

HQ: 1200 New Jersey Avenue SE
Washington, DC 20590
Phone: 405-834-8344
Email: zach.barrett@dot.gov
http://www.phmsa.dot.gov

DOT 20.723 PHMSA PIPELINE SAFETY RESEARCH & DEVELOPMENT "OTHER TRANSACTION AGREEMENTS"

Award: Project Grants

Purpose: Sponsors research and development projects focused on providing near-term solutions that will improve the safety, reduce environmental impact, and enhance the reliability of the Nation's pipeline transportation system.

Applicant Eligibility: Universities and other academic institutions, individual, profit organization, nonprofit organization, State (includes D.C.), U.S. Territories and possessions, Indian tribes, local government, other entities are eligible to apply.

Beneficiary Eligibility: Anyone/general public can receive benefits from the eligible applicant.

Award Range/Average: $40,000 to $856,000. Average is $189,000.

Funding: FY 17 $644,695; FY 18 est $13,000,000; FY 19 est $6,000,000.

HQ: 1200 NJ Avenue SE
Washington, DC 20590
Phone: 919-238-4759
Email: robert.w.smith@dot.gov
http://www.phmsa.dot.gov

DOT 20.725 PHMSA PIPELINE SAFETY UNDERGROUND NATURAL GAS STORAGE GRANT

Award: Formula Grants

Purpose: Through annual Certification/Agreements with PHMSA, inspects and enforces the federal underground storage regulations for intrastate underground natural gas storage facilities located within the state.

Applicant Eligibility: State must have a 60105 Certification or 60106 Agreement with PHMSA. The Department provides Federal funds, up to 80 percent of the State's total program costs to any State agency with a certificate under Section 60105 of Title 49, United States Code, an agreement under Section 60106 of Title 49, United States Code, or to any State acting as a DOT agent on interstate pipelines.

Beneficiary Eligibility: State (Includes District of Columbia and Puerto Rico) Also, State agency with a Certification or Agreement under 60105 or 60106 of Title 49 USC.

Award Range/Average: No Data Available.

Funding: (Formula Grants) FY 17 $0; FY 18 est $4,000,000; FY 19 est $6,000,000.

HQ: 1200 New Jersey Avenue SE
Washington, DC 20590
Phone: 405-834-8344
Email: zach.barrett@dot.gov
http://www.phmsa.dot.gov

PIMA AGRICULTURE COTTON TRUST FUND
"Pima Agriculture Cotton Trust Fund"

Award: Direct Payments with Unrestricted Use

Purpose: The Pima Agriculture Cotton Trust compensates for accidents to the domestic textile manufacturers resulting from U.S. import tariffs on cotton fabric.

Applicant Eligibility: Payments to reduce the injury to domestic textile manufacturers resulting from U.S. import tariffs on cotton fabric that are higher than tariffs on certain apparel articles made of cotton fabric.

Beneficiary Eligibility: Beneficiaries limited to: one or more nationally recognized associations established for the promotion of pima cotton in apparel; yarn spinners of pima cotton that produce ring spun cotton yarns in the United States, and manufacturers who cut and sew cotton shirts in the United States who certify that they used imported cotton fabric in 2013.

Award Range/Average: Range: $273,000 to $4,285,000. Average: $1,800,000.

Funding: (Direct Payments with Unrestricted Use) FY 17 $16,000,000; FY 18 est $16,000,000; FY 19 FY 16 $16,000,000.

HQ: 1400 Independence Avenue SW
Washington, DC 20250
Phone: 202-720-3538
Email: amy.harding@fas.usda.gov
http://www.fas.usda.gov

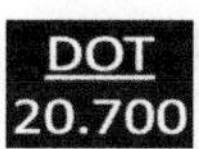

PIPELINE SAFETY PROGRAM STATE BASE GRANT

Award: Formula Grants

Purpose: Develops, supports, and maintains inspection and enforcement activities for State gas and hazardous liquid pipeline safety programs.

Applicant Eligibility: State must have a 60105 Certification or 60106 Agreement with PHMSA. The Department provides Federal funds (limited to congressional appropriations), up to 80 percent of the State's total program costs to any State agency with a certificate under Section 60105 of Title 49, United States Code, an agreement under Section 60106 of Title 49, United States Code, or to any State acting as a DOT agent on interstate pipelines.

Beneficiary Eligibility: State, District of Columbia, and Puerto Rico.

Award Range/Average: $16,283 - $5,023,033 and average award $769,976

Funding: (Formula Grants (Health Incentive Grants) FY 17 $54,203,187; FY 18 est $55,952,000; FY 19 est $52,202,000; FY 16 $47,882,989.

HQ: 1200 New Jersey Avenue SE
Washington, DC 20590
Phone: 405-834-8344
Email: zach.barrett@dot.gov
http://www.phmsa.dot.gov

DOT 20.724 PIPELINE SAFETY RESEARCH COMPETITIVE ACADEMIC AGREEMENT PROGRAM (CAAP)

Award: Project Grants

Purpose: To spur innovation by enabling an academic research focus on high-risk and high pay-off solutions for the many pipeline safety challenges.

Applicant Eligibility: Applicants must be non-profit institutions of higher education located in the United States or a U.S. territory or possession.

Beneficiary Eligibility: Solutions from academic research agreements to non-profit institutions of higher education will benefit the American public who has a stake in safe, reliable and environmentally friendly pipeline transportation of hydrocarbons.

Award Range/Average: The current program level of $2,000,000 (six individual awards at up to $300,000 each) is anticipated.

Funding: (Cooperative Agreements) FY 17 $47,351; FY 18 est $2,000,000; FY 19 est $2,000,000; FY 16 $1,828,846.

HQ: 1200 New Jersey Avenue SE
Washington, DC 20590
Phone: 202-366-6085
Email: joshua.arnold@dot.gov
http://www.phmsa.dot.gov/pipeline

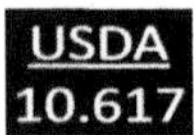

PL-480 MARKET DEVELOPMENT & TECHNICAL ASSISTANCE "Section 108"

Award: Project Grants

Purpose: The Foreign Agricultural Service promotes a grant program to assist in the implementation of market development and agricultural technical assistance activities.

Applicant Eligibility: The program aims to expand or maintain U.S. agricultural exports.

Beneficiary Eligibility: U.S. agricultural entities are expected to benefit from the growth of U.S. export markets.

Award Range/Average: Awards generally fall between $0 and $1 million.

Funding: Project Grants (Discretionary) FY 17 $300,000; FY 18 est $3,000,000; FY 19 est $3,000,000.

HQ: 1400 Independence Avenue
Washington, DC 20050
Phone: 202-720-8557
Email: lona.powell@fas.usda.gov
http://www.fsa.usda.gov

HHS 93.835 PLANNING GRANT FOR HEALTHCARE & PUBLIC HEALTH SECTOR CYBERSECURITY INFORMATION SHARING

Award: Cooperative Agreements

Purpose: The objectives of this award are to gain an understanding of the cybersecurity threat information needs and to increase organizational capacity and develop a strategy to expand cybersecurity threat information sharing.

Applicant Eligibility: N/A

Beneficiary Eligibility: Select as many that apply (see pages 11 through 14 of the Reference Manual); Nonprofit with 501(c)3 IRS status (other than institution of higher education), Nonprofit without 501(c)3 IRS status (other than institution of higher education), Universities; Colleges, Research institutions, Hospitals, Community-based organizations, Faith-based organizations.

Award Range/Average: $150000

Funding: Cooperative Agreements (Discretionary Grants) FY 17 $200,000; FY 18 est $200,000; FY 19 est $20,000; FY 16 $100,000.

HQ: 200 C Street SW
Washington, DC 20024
Phone: 202-260-0400
Email: virginia.simmons@hhs.gov
http://phe.gov

HHS 93.253 POISON CENTER SUPPORT & ENHANCEMENT GRANT PROGRAM
"Poison Control Centers (PCCs)"

Award: Project Grants

Purpose: To support PCCs' efforts to prevent, and provide treatment recommendations, for poisonings.

Applicant Eligibility: U.S. accredited Poison Control Centers. Unaccredited centers are eligible for a grant waiver if such centers can reasonably demonstrate that they will obtain such accreditation within a reasonable period of time.

Beneficiary Eligibility: Residents of the 50 United States, Puerto Rico, the District of Columbia, the U.S. Virgin Islands, Guam, American Samoa, and the Federated States of Micronesia.

Award Range/Average: Range: $12,466 to $2,185,501. Average: $356,711.

Funding: (Project Grants) FY 17 $17,140,752; FY 18 est $18,549,001; FY 19 N/A FY 16 $17,018,338.

HQ: 5600 Fishers Lane, Room 08W 26
Rockville, MD 20857
Phone: 301-443-8177
Email: sstevenson1@hrsa.gov
http://www.hrsa.gov

NSF 47.078 POLAR PROGRAMS "OPP"

Award: Project Grants

Purpose: To strengthen and enhance the national scientific enterprise through the expansion of fundamental knowledge and increased understanding of the polar regions.

Applicant Eligibility: Except where a program solicitation establishes more restrictive eligibility criteria, individuals and organizations in the following categories may submit proposals: Universities and colleges; Non-profit, non-academic organizations; For-profit organizations; State and local governments; and unaffiliated individuals. See the NSF Grant Proposal Guide Chapter I.

Beneficiary Eligibility: N/A

Award Range/Average: Range Low $6,318 Range High $17,254,128 Average $355,937

Funding: (Project Grants) FY 16 est $0; FY 15 $0; FY 17 est $0.

HQ: 4201 Wilson Boulevard Stafford I, Suite 740
Arlington, VA 22230
Phone: 703-292-8033
Email: wreuning@nsf.gov
http://nsf.gov/dir/index.jsp?org=opp

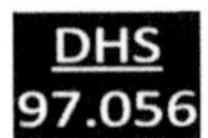

PORT SECURITY GRANT PROGRAM "PSGP"

Award: Project Grants

Purpose: The Port Security Grant Program's function is to enhance the nation's preparedness and resilience against natural calamities and terrorist and cyber terrorist activities.

Applicant Eligibility: Pursuant to the Maritime Transportation Security Act of 2002, as amended (MTSA), DHS established a risk-based grant program to support maritime security risk management. Funding is directed towards the implementation of AMSPs, Facility Security Plans (FSP), and Vessel Security Plans (VSPs) among port authorities, facility operators, and state and local government agencies that are required to provide port security services.

Beneficiary Eligibility: Critical national seaports and terminals.

Award Range/Average: No Data Available.

Funding: (Project Grants) FY 17 $100,000,000; FY 18 est $100,000,000; FY 19 est $100,000,000.

HQ: 400 C Street SW
Washington, DC 20523
Phone: 800-368-6498
http://www.fema.gov/government/grant/index.shtm

DOJ 16.820 POSTCONVICTION TESTING OF DNA EVIDENCE "Kirk Bloodsworth Program"

Award: Project Grants

Purpose: To fund projects that assist States with postconviction DNA testing in cases of violent offenses to ensure fair and impartial administration of justice for all citizens.

Applicant Eligibility: Eligible applicants are States, units of local government, and public institutions of higher education (including tribal institutions of higher education). For the purposes of agency program announcements, the term "State" includes the District of Columbia, the Commonwealth of Puerto Rico, the U.S. Virgin Islands, American Samoa, Guam, and the Northern Mariana Islands.

Beneficiary Eligibility: Ensures the availability of fair and impartial administration of justice to Americans who may have been unjustly convicted.

Award Range/Average: N/A

Funding: Project Grants (Discretionary) FY 17 $3,333,287; FY 18 FY 19.

HQ: 810 7th Street NW
Washington, DC 20531
Phone: 202-307-2942
http://www.nij.gov

POSTSECONDARY EDUCATION SCHOLARSHIPS FOR VETERAN'S DEPENDENTS "Iraq and Afghanistan Service Grant (IASG)"

Award: Direct Payments for Specified Use

Purpose: Provides eligible veteran's dependent undergraduate postsecondary students with non-need based grant assistance to help meet educational expenses.

Applicant Eligibility: The student must be an eligible veteran's dependent whose parent or guardian was a member of the Armed Forces of the United States and died as a result of performing military service in Iraq or Afghanistan after September 11, 2001. At the time of the parent or guardian's death, the student was less than 24 years of age or enrolled at an institution of higher education.

Beneficiary Eligibility: Eligible veteran's dependent undergraduate students, and students pursuing a teaching certificate that are U.S. citizens or eligible noncitizens. Students must be: regular students in an eligible program and enrolled in institutions of higher education, making satisfactory academic progress.

Award Range/Average: $572- $5,717, the average grant is $5,019.

Funding: (Formula Grants) FY 17 $455,000; FY 18 est $490,000; FY 19 est $566,000; FY 16 $432,000.

HQ: P.O. Box 84
Washington, DC 20044-0084
Phone: 800-433-3243
http://studentaid.ed.gov/sa

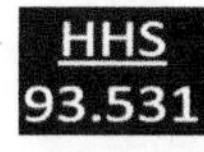

PPHF – COMMUNITY TRANSFORMATION GRANTS & NATIONAL DISSEMINATION & SUPPORT FOR COMMUNITY TRANSFORMATION GRANTS – FINANCED SOLELY BY PREVENTION & PUBLIC HEALTH FUNDS

Award: Cooperative Agreements

Purpose: To reduce death and disability from the five leading causes of death through the prevention and control these conditions and their risk factors.

Applicant Eligibility: Applications may be submitted by State or local governments or their Bona Fide Agents (this includes the District of Columbia, the Commonwealth of Puerto Rico, the Virgin Islands, the Commonwealth of the Northern Marianna Islands, American Samoa, Guam, the Federated States of Micronesia, the Republic of the Marshall Islands, and the Republic of Palau). Eligible applicants also include public and private nonprofit organizations, for profit organizations, small, minority, women-owned businesses, universities, colleges, research institutions, hospitals, community-based organizations, faith-based organizations, Federally recognized Indian tribal governments, Indian tribes, and Indian tribal organizations.

Beneficiary Eligibility: The general public will benefit from the objectives of this program.

Award Range/Average: Community Transformation Grants Expected: $50,000 - $500,000 National Dissemination and Support for Community Transformation Grants Expected - $350,000 - 3,500,000

Funding: N/A

HQ: 4770 Buford Highway NE
Atlanta, GA 30333
Phone: 770-488-2524
Email: rrb7@cdc.gov
http://www.cdc.gov

HHS 93.749 PPHF – PUBLIC HEALTH LABORATORY INFRASTRUCTURE – FINANCED SOLELY BY PREVENTION & PUBLIC HEALTH FUND

Award: Cooperative Agreements

Purpose: The Association of Public Health Laboratories (APHL) will engage in activities to strengthen public health infectious disease laboratory infrastructure by addressing gaps in public health laboratory practice, and assist with development, implementation and ongoing support of laboratory technologies for use in public health.

Applicant Eligibility: Eligibility is limited to the Association of Public Health Laboratories (APHL), a private nonprofit organization and the current grantee. CDC approved single eligibility of this award.

Beneficiary Eligibility: Students/trainees and any U.S. state, political subdivision and U.S. territories (as described above), and other public entities will benefit.

Award Range/Average: Awards will range from approximately $1 million to $3 million with an average of approximately $2 million.

Funding: N/A

HQ: 1600 Clifton Road NE, P.O. Box E94
Atlanta, GA 30333
Phone: 404-498-6451
Email: atc4@cdc.gov
http://www.cdc.gov

PPHF 2018: OFFICE OF SMOKING & HEALTH-NATIONAL STATE-BASED TOBACCO CONTROL PROGRAMS-FINANCED IN PART BY 2018 PREVENTION & PUBLIC HEALTH FUNDS (PPHF) "National Tobacco Control Program"

Award: Cooperative Agreements

Purpose: Addresses tobacco use and secondhand smoke exposure in the United States and supports four National Tobacco Control Program goals.

Applicant Eligibility: State departments of health are essential for coordinating the public health response to prevent tobacco use and protect the population from second hand smoke exposure. They have experience with implementing evidence-based interventions and strategies that use environment, policy, and system approaches that have the potential to reach large numbers of people in the state.

Beneficiary Eligibility: General Public would benefit

Award Range/Average: No Data Available.

Funding: (Cooperative Agreements) FY 17 $54,997,853; FY 18 est $54,442,137; FY 19 est $54,442,137.

HQ: 4770 Buford Highway NE, P.O. Box F79
Atlanta, GA 30341
Phone: 770-488-5218
Email: ksneegas@cdc.gov
http://www.cdc.gov

PPHF 2018: PREVENTION HEALTH & HEALTH SERVICES – STRENGTHENING PUBLIC HEALTH SYSTEMS & SERVICES THROUGH NATIONAL PARTNERSHIPS TO IMPROVE & PROTECT THE NATION'S HEALTH – FINANCED IN PART BY PREVENTION & PUBLIC HEALTH FUNDS (PPHF) "CDC-RFA-OT18-1802"

Award: Cooperative Agreements

Purpose: To announce a program to strengthen the nation's public health infrastructure, ensure a competent, current and connected public health system, and improve delivery of essential services through capacity building assistance (CBA).

Applicant Eligibility: Organizations deemed eligible to apply must also meet responsiveness criteria as outlined in the "Additional Information on Eligibility" in CDC-RFA-OT18-1802.

Beneficiary Eligibility: Beneficiaries include state health departments; tribal health organizations; local health departments; the District of Columbia; U.S. Territories; and other components of the public health system. The general public will also serve as beneficiaries.

Award Range/Average: The approximate average award ranges for the 12-month budget period are $2 million for Category A, up to $1 million for Category B and up to $500,000 for Category C.

Funding: (Salaries and Expenses) FY 17 $0; N/A FY 19 est $120,000,000; FY 18 est $120,000,000.

HQ: 4770 Buford Highway NE, P.O. Box K 90
Atlanta, GA 30345
Phone: 770-488-1523
http://www.cdc.gov/stltpublichealth/partnerships/index.html

PPHF CAPACITY BUILDING ASSISTANCE TO STRENGTHEN PUBLIC HEALTH IMMUNIZATION INFRASTRUCTURE & PERFORMANCE FINANCED IN PART BY PREVENTION & PUBLIC HEALTH FUNDS
"Prevention and Public Health Fund (Affordable Care Act) – Immunization Program"

Award: Cooperative Agreements

Purpose: To support efforts to transition immunization programs supported by Section 317 funding to the healthcare environment being transformed by the Affordable Care Act (ACA).

Applicant Eligibility: Eligibility is limited to existing grantees under the Immunization Program (CFDA 93.268) which includes all 50 U.S. states, the District of Columbia, local health departments (Chicago, Houston, New York City, Philadelphia, San Antonio) and U.S. territories (Commonwealth of Puerto Rico, Virgin Islands, Commonwealth of the Northern Mariana Islands, American Samoa, Guam, Federated States of Micronesia, Republic of the Marshall Islands, Republic of Palau).

Beneficiary Eligibility: Any U.S. state, political subdivision and U.S. territories (as described above), and other public entities will benefit.

Award Range/Average: Award ranges and averages vary based on program areas and supplemental projects funded through these cooperative agreements.

Funding: N/A

HQ: 1600 Clifton Road, P.O. Box A19
Atlanta, GA 30333
Phone: 404-639-7824
Email: ibr0@cdc.gov
http://www.cdc.gov

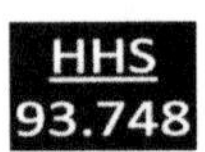

PPHF COOPERATIVE AGREEMENTS FOR PRESCRIPTION DRUG MONITORING PROGRAM ELECTRONIC HEALTH RECORD (EHR) INTEGRATION & INTEROPERABILITY EXPANSION
"PPHF-2012: PDMP EHR Integration and Interoperability (TI-12-011)"

Award: Cooperative Agreements

Purpose: Purpose of this program is to improve real-time access to PDMP data by integrating PDMPs into existing technologies like EHRs, in order to improve the ability of State PDMPs to reduce the nature, scope, and extent of prescription drug abuse.

Applicant Eligibility: Grant funds will enable States to integrate their PDMPs into EHR and other health information technology systems to expand utilization by increasing the production and distribution of unsolicited reports and alerts to prescribers and dispensers of prescription data. Grant funds will also be used by States to allow for modification of their systems to expand interoperability.

Beneficiary Eligibility: Eligible applicants are the immediate office of the Chief Executive.

Award Range/Average: No Data Available.

Funding: (Cooperative Agreements) FY 16 $0; FY 17 est $0; FY 18 est $0; - Multi-year funding for a total of two 12 month incremental periods within a two year/24 month project period.

HQ: 5600 Fishers Lane
Rockville, MD 20857
Phone: 240-276-1418
Email: roger.george@samhsa.hhs.gov
http://www.samhsa.gov

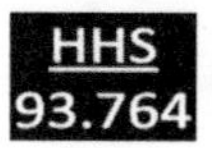

PPHF- COOPERATIVE AGREEMENTS TO IMPLEMENT THE NATIONAL STRATEGY FOR SUICIDE PREVENTION (SHORT TITLE: NATIONAL STRATEGY GRANTS)

Award: Cooperative Agreements

Purpose: Supports states in implementing the 2012 National Strategy for Suicide Prevention (NSSP) goals and objectives focused on preventing suicide and suicide attempts among adults aged 25-64 years old in order to reduce the overall suicide rate and number of suicides in the U.S. nationally.

Applicant Eligibility: Eligibility is limited to the Mental Health Authority in states, territories, and the District of Columbia. The purpose of this program is to support states in implementing the 2012 National Strategy for Suicide Prevention (NSSP) goals and objectives focused on preventing suicide and suicide attempts among working-age adults 25-64 years old in order to reduce the overall suicide rate and number of suicides in the U.S. nationally.

Beneficiary Eligibility: Consumers that are working-age adults between 25-64 years old.

Award Range/Average: up to $587,524 per year

Funding: (Cooperative Agreements) FY 18 est $0; FY 16 $2,350,097; FY 17 est $0.

HQ: 5600 Fishers Lane
Rockville, MD 20857
Phone: 240-276-1418
Email: roger.george@samhsa.hhs.gov
http://www.samhsa.gov

PPHF GERIATRIC EDUCATION CENTERS "Geriatric Workforce Enhancement Program (GWEP)"

Award: Cooperative Agreements

Purpose: The cooperative agreement program's purpose is to establish and operate geriatric education centers that will implement the Geriatric Workforce Enhancement Program to develop a healthcare workforce that maximizes patient and family engagement and improves health outcomes for older adults by integrating geriatrics with primary care. These centers improves the training of health professionals and individuals in geriatrics, including geriatric residencies, traineeships or fellowships and develops and disseminates curricula relating to the treatment of the health problems of elderly individuals.

Applicant Eligibility: Eligible applicants are accredited health professions schools and programs. The following entities are eligible applicants: Schools of Allopathic Medicine; Schools of Veterinary Medicine; Schools of Dentistry; Schools of Public Health; Schools of Osteopathic Medicine; Schools of Chiropractic; Schools of Pharmacy; Physician Assistant Programs; Schools of Optometry; Schools of Allied Health; Schools of Podiatric Medicine; and Schools of Nursing The following accredited graduate programs are also eligible applicants: Health Administration; and Behavioral Health and Mental Health Practice, including: Clinical Psychology, Clinical Social Work, Professional Counseling, and Marriage and Family Therapy.

Beneficiary Eligibility: Accredited health professions schools

Award Range/Average: $714,739 - $850,000; Average is $825,676

Funding: (Project Grants) FY 17 $35,839,723; FY 18 est $37,729,921; FY 19 est $0; FY 16 $35,872,006.

HQ: Division of Medicine and Dentistry 5600 Fishers Lane, Room 15N194B
Rockville, MD 20857
Phone: 301-443-5626
Email: ntumosa@hrsa.gov
http://www.hrsa.gov

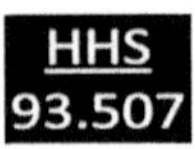

PPHF NATIONAL PUBLIC HEALTH IMPROVEMENT INITIATIVE

Award: Cooperative Agreements

Purpose: To increase the performance management capacity of public health departments in order to ensure that public health goals are effectively and efficiently met.

Applicant Eligibility: Eligible applicants include all 50 states, Washington, DC., 9 large local health departments supporting cities with populations of 1 million or more inhabitants (Chicago, Illinois; Dallas, Texas; Houston Texas; Los Angeles, California; New York City, New York; Philadelphia, Pennsylvania; Phoenix, Arizona; San Antonio, Texas; San Diego, California), 5 U.S. Territories 3 U.S. Affiliated Pacific Islands, and up to 7 federally-recognized tribes with an established public health departments structure (or their equivalent) that provide public health services to their tribal members or their bona fide agents.

Beneficiary Eligibility: State health departments, large local health departments supporting cities with populations of 1 million or more inhabitants, the District of Columbia, U.S. Territories, tribal health organizations and the general public.

Award Range/Average: Component I: This amount is based on population and will continue for each year of the cooperative agreement: Below 1.5 million = $100,000, 1.5 million - 5 million = $200,000, 5 million - 8 million = $300,000, Above 8 million = $400,000. Component II: $1M - $2.95M.

Funding: N/A

HQ: 2500 Century Parkway
Atlanta, GA 30329
Phone: 404-498-6792
Email: ayw3@cdc.gov
http://www.cdc.gov

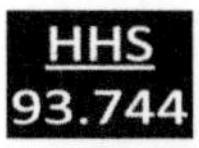

PPHF: BREAST & CERVICAL CANCER SCREENING OPPORTUNITIES FOR STATES, TRIBES & TERRITORIES SOLELY FINANCED BY PREVENTION & PUBLIC HEALTH FUNDS

"Breast and Cervical Cancer Screening Opportunities through the National Breast and Cervical Cancer Early Detection Program (NBCCEDP) - PPHF Funds (DP12-1218)"

Award: Cooperative Agreements

Purpose: Purpose of the FOA is to enhance and leverage existing organized systems for breast and cervical cancer screening to provide high quality screening with tracking and follow-up including patient navigation to low income, uninsured and under-insured women.

Applicant Eligibility: Eligibility is limited to the currently funded states or their bona fide agents, tribal and territorial recipients under CDC-RFA-DP12-1205. Cancer Prevention and Control Programs for State, Territorial and Tribal Organizations.

Beneficiary Eligibility: The general public will benefit from the objectives of this program. Additionally states, tribes and territories funded under DP12-1205 will benefit from this program.

Award Range/Average: $15,000 - $700,000

Funding: N/A

HQ: 4770 Buford Highway, P.O. Box F76
Atlanta, GA 30341
Phone: 770-488-4880
Email: fwong@cdc.gov
http://www.cdc.gov

PPHF: CHRONIC DISEASE INNOVATION GRANTS – FINANCED SOLELY BY PUBLIC PREVENTION HEALTH FUNDS

"National Diabetes Prevention Program Evidence-Based Lifestyle Intervention to Prevent Type 2 Diabetes in Underserved Communities"

Award: Cooperative Agreements

Purpose: The purpose of the program is to expand the National Diabetes Prevention Program, an evidence-based lifestyle change program in populations at high-risk for developing type 2 diabetes that includes African American; American Indian/Alaska Native; Hispanic/Latino, Low Social Economic Status; and women with a history of Gestational Diabetes.

Applicant Eligibility: Nonprofits with 501(c)(3) IRS Status (Other than Institutions of Higher Education); For-Profit Organizations; Small, minority, and women-owned businesses; Indian/Native American Tribal Governments (Federally Recognized); Hospitals; Regional Organizations; Faith-based or Community-based Organizations.

Beneficiary Eligibility: The general public will benefit from the objectives of this program. More specifically, populations at high-risk for developing type 2 diabetes (African American; American Indian/

Alaska Native; Hispanic/Latino, Low Social Economic Status; Women with a history of Gestational Diabetes) will benefit from the objectives of this program.

Award Range/Average: N/A

Funding: N/A

HQ: 4770 Buford Highway NE, P.O. Box K10 NCCDPHP
Atlanta, GA 30333
Phone: 770-488-1097
Email: djt4@cdc.gov
http://www.cdc.gov

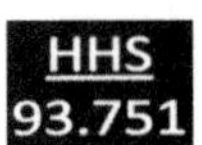

PPHF: CONSORTIUM FOR TOBACCO USE CESSATION TECHNICAL ASSISTANCE FINANCED BY SOLELY BY PREVENTION & PUBLIC HEALTH FUNDS "PPHF2013: Consortium for Tobacco Use Cessation Technical Assistance"

Award: Cooperative Agreements

Purpose: Develops a consortium for tobacco use cessation technical assistance. The aim of the consortium is to provide technical assistance to state tobacco control programs and other partners by translating the science of tobacco control cessation into public health action to further increase the rate of cessation among tobacco users in the United States.

Applicant Eligibility: A Bona Fide Agent is an agency/organization identified by the state as eligible to submit an application under the state eligibility in lieu of a state application. If applying as a bona fide agent of a state or local government, a legal, binding agreement from the state or local government as documentation of the status is required.

Beneficiary Eligibility: The general public will benefit from the objectives of this program.

Award Range/Average: Awards will range from approximately $75,000 to $450,000 with an average of approximately $112,500.

Funding: (Cooperative Agreements) FY 17 $450,000; FY 18 est $450,000; FY 19 est $0; FY 16 $450,000.

HQ: 4770 Buford Highway NE, P.O. Box K50
Atlanta, GA 30341
Phone: 770-488-1172
Email: sbabb@cdc.gov
http://www.cdc.gov

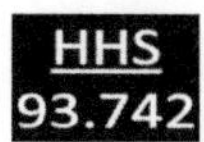

PPHF: EARLY CHILDCARE & EDUCATION OBESITY PREVENTION PROGRAM – OBESITY PREVENTION IN YOUNG CHILDREN – FINANCED SOLELY BY PUBLIC PREVENTION & HEALTH FUNDS

"Early Care and Education Statewide Collaboratives to Improve Nutrition, Breastfeeding Support, Physical Activity and Screen Time Practices for Obesity Prevention in Young Children"

Award: Cooperative Agreements

Purpose: The Program is an obesity prevention effort targeting the early care and education setting (ECE) to reach most children in the U.S. to reverse obesity trends through helping ECE providers across the nation to adopt healthier policies and practices around physical activity and nutrition, including limiting screen time and supporting breastfeeding.

Applicant Eligibility: Selected applicant under initial solicitations are eligible applicants for future years.

Beneficiary Eligibility: N/A

Award Range/Average: est $4,000,000

Funding: (Cooperative Agreements) FY 17 $3,294,900; FY 18 est $0; FY 19 est $0; FY 16 $3,796,359; - Project Period ends 9/29/2017. Program was extended for one year with funds project/budget period will end 9/2018.

HQ: 4770 Buford Highway NE, P.O. Box F77
Atlanta, GA 30341
Phone: 770-488-6042
Email: lit2@cdc.gov
http://www.cdc.gov

PPHF: HEALTH CARE SURVEILLANCE/HEALTH STATISTICS – SURVEILLANCE PROGRAM ANNOUNCEMENT: BEHAVIORAL RISK FACTOR SURVEILLANCE SYSTEM FINANCED IN PART BY PREVENTION & PUBLIC HEALTH FUND

"Behavioral Risk Factor Surveillance System (BRFSS)"

Award: Cooperative Agreements

Purpose: Provides assistance to State and Territorial Health Departments to maintain and expand: Specific health surveillance using telephone and multi-mode survey methodology for the behaviors of the general population that contribute to the occurrences and prevention of chronic diseases, injuries, and other public health threats.

Applicant Eligibility: Eligibility includes all 50 states, Washington D.C., Puerto Rico, the U.S. Virgin Islands, Guam, American Samoa, Palau, and the Federated States of Micronesia, who are currently funded through the Behavioral Risk Factor Surveillance System (BRFSS) Funding Opportunity Announcements (CDC-RFA-SO11-1101 and CDC-RFA-SO11-1102).

Beneficiary Eligibility: Any U.S. State, political subdivision, and U.S. Territories as described above.

Award Range/Average: Awards will range from approximately $50,000 through $100,000 with an average award of approximately $68,000

Funding: (Cooperative Agreements) FY 17 $15,795,015; FY 18 est $17,278,605; FY 19 est $0; FY 16 $4,000,000.

HQ: 4602 Buford Highway, P.O. Box F 78
Atlanta, GA 30341
Phone: 770-488-4588
Email: aii9@cdc.gov
http://www.grants.gov

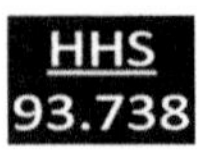

PPHF: RACIAL & ETHNIC APPROACHES TO COMMUNITY HEALTH PROGRAM FINANCED SOLELY BY PUBLIC PREVENTION & HEALTH FUNDS

"Racial and Ethnic Approaches to Community Health (REACH)"

Award: Cooperative Agreements

Purpose: The proposed FY2012 REACH program supports the implementation of projects to reduce racial and ethnic health disparities.

Applicant Eligibility: Applications may be submitted by State or local governments or their Bona Fide Agents (this includes the District of Columbia, the Commonwealth of Puerto Rico, the Virgin Islands, the Commonwealth of the Northern Marianna Islands, American Samoa, Guam, the Federated States of Micronesia, the Republic of the Marshall Islands, and the Republic of Palau). Eligible applicants also include public and private nonprofit organizations, for profit organizations, small, minority, women-owned businesses, universities, colleges, research institutions, hospitals, community-based organizations, faith-based organizations, Federally recognized Indian tribal governments, Indian tribes, and Indian tribal organizations.

Beneficiary Eligibility: The general public will benefit from the objectives of this program. Additionally, colleges, universities, private non-profit and public nonprofit domestic organizations, research institutions, and faith-based organization, states, political subdivisions of states, local health authorities, and individuals or organizations with specialized health interests will benefit.

Award Range/Average: No Data Available.

Funding: (Cooperative Agreements) FY 17 $23,243,874; FY 18 est $0; FY 19 est $0; FY 16 $34,298,752; - This program was extended with funds budge/project period will end 2018.

HQ: 4770 Buford Highway NE, P.O. Box K30
Atlanta, GA 30333
Phone: 404-498-3058
Email: scoulberson@cdc.gov
http://www.cdc.gov

PPHF: STATE NUTRITION, PHYSICAL ACTIVITY, AND OBESITY PROGRAMS – FINANCED IN PART BY PPHF
"Nutrition, Physical Activity, and Obesity Programs - financed solely by PPHF funds"

Award: Cooperative Agreements

Purpose: To provide leadership of strategic public health efforts to prevent and control obesity, chronic disease, and other health conditions through regular physical activity and good nutrition.

Applicant Eligibility: N/A

Beneficiary Eligibility: N/A

Award Range/Average: $50,000 to $16M

Funding: N/A

 **HQ:** 4770Buford Highway NE NCCDPHP
Atlanta, GA 30341
Phone: 404-867-9697
Email: lbarnes@cdc.gov
http://www.grants.gov

PPHF2018-NATIONAL ORGANIZATION FOR CHRONIC DISEASE PREVENTION & HEALTH PROMOTION-FINANCED IN PART BY 2018 PREVENTION & PUBLIC HEALTH FUNDS

Award: Cooperative Agreements

Purpose: Supports the development of effective state chronic disease programs to strengthen public health science and practice by addressing crosscutting functions, domains, settings, risk factors and diseases.

Applicant Eligibility: The intent of this funding is to support the development of effective state chronic disease programs by disseminating effective chronic disease prevention and health promotion approaches to strengthen public health science and practice. Funding eligibility is limited to national, public non-profit organizations, that work with state and territorial health departments and whose primary focus is chronic disease prevention and health promotion.

Beneficiary Eligibility: Same as Applicant Eligibility.

Award Range/Average: No Data Available.

Funding: (Cooperative Agreements) FY 18 est $2,500,000; FY 19 est $2,500,000; FY 17 $0.

HQ: 477 Buford Highway NE
Atlanta, GA 30341
Phone: 770-488-0877
Email: cmw@cdc.gov
http://www.cdc.gov

HHS 93.765 PPHF-CDC PARTNERSHIP: STRENGTHENING PUBLIC HEALTH LABORATORIES

Award: Formula Grants

Purpose: The major objective is to enhance and strengthen the work and functionality of public health laboratories both domestically and abroad. The overall goal of the program is to improve several aspects of public health laboratories.

Applicant Eligibility: Eligible applicants that can apply for this funding opportunity are listed below: Nonprofit organizations, Small, minority, and women-owned businesses, Universities, Colleges, Research institutions, Hospitals, Community-based organizations, Faith-based organizations, Federally recognized or state-recognized American Indian/Alaska Native tribal governments, American Indian/Alaska native tribally designated organizations, Alaska Native health corporations, Urban Indian health organizations, Tribal epidemiology centers, State and local governments or their Bona Fide Agents (this includes the District of Columbia, the Commonwealth of Puerto Rico, the Virgin Islands, the Commonwealth of the Northern Marianna Islands, American Samoa, Guam, the Federated States of Micronesia, the Republic of the Marshall Islands, and the Republic of Palau), Political subdivisions of States (in consultation with States). A Bona Fide Agent is an agency/organization identified by the state as eligible to submit an application under the state eligibility in lieu of a state application. If applying as a bona fide agent of a state or local government, a legal, binding agreement from the state or local government as documentation of the status is required.

Beneficiary Eligibility: Applicants must have experience with enhancing and strengthening the work and functionality of public health laboratories both domestically and abroad. The overarching goal is to improve several aspects of public health laboratories.

Award Range/Average: FY 2019 estimated PPHF award $4,000,000 ; FY 2020 estimated PPHF award amount $4,000,000. Total anticipated PPHF award from FY 2015 - FY 2020 : $ 19,046,800.

Funding: Formula Grants (Cooperative Agreements) FY 17 $24,626,569; FY 18 est $27,552,526; FY 19 est $28,000,000.

HQ: 1600 Clifton Road NE, P.O. Box E92
Atlanta, GA 30333
Phone: 404-498-6451
Email: atc4@cdc.gov
http://www.cdc.gov

DOJ 16.735 PREA PROGRAM: STRATEGIC SUPPORT FOR PREA IMPLEMENTATION "Prison Rape Elimination Act (PREA)"

Award: Cooperative Agreements; Project Grants

Purpose: To support efforts in the confinement facilities that are covered by the PREA Standards to achieve compliance with the standards.

Applicant Eligibility: Eligible applicants include states, units of local government, and federally-recognized Indian tribes, as well as any national nonprofit organization, for-profit (commercial) organization (including tribal nonprofit or for-profit organizations), or institution of higher education (including tribal institutions of higher education) that have expertise and experience managing and delivering training and technical assistance on complex corrections or criminal justice issues at the national and local levels.

For-profit organizations (as well as other recipients) (including tribal institutions of higher education) must forgo any profit or management fee.

Beneficiary Eligibility: Local agencies that oversee small- and medium-sized jails.

Award Range/Average: No Data Available.

Funding: (Project Grants) FY 17 $10,500,000; FY 18 est $15,500,000; FY 19 N/A.

HQ: 810 7th Street NW
Washington, DC 20531
Phone: 202-616-6500
http://www.bja.gov

PRE-DISASTER MITIGATION "PDM"

Award: Project Grants

Purpose: The program provides funds for Indian tribal governments, communities and territories to prepare for pre-disaster mitigation by addressing the natural hazards at an early stage.

Applicant Eligibility: Applications are reviewed by DHS/FEMA program and administrative staff. Any issues or concerns noted in the application will be negotiated with the successful applicant prior to the award being issued.

Beneficiary Eligibility: State agencies, Indian Tribal governments, and local governments and communities are eligible to apply as sub applicants for assistance under the PDM program. All interested sub applicants must apply to the Applicant.

Award Range/Average: No Data Available.

Funding: (Project Grants) FY 17 $61,446,767; FY 18 est $124,600,000; FY 19 est $124,600,000.

HQ: 400 C Street
Washington, DC 20472
Phone: 202-646-3458
Email: kayed.lakhia@fema.dhs.gov
http://www.fema.gov/pre-disaster/mitigation/grant/program

PRE-EXISTING CONDITION INSURANCE PROGRAM (PCIP)

Award: Direct Payments for Specified Use

Purpose: The Patient Protection and Affordability Care Act, was enacted on March 23, 2010. The healthcare and Education Reconciliation Act Public Law 111-152, was enacted on March 30, 2010. Collectively, these laws are known as the "Affordable Care Act." Section 1101 of the Affordable Care Act requires that the Secretary of the Department of Health and Human Services (HHS) establish, either directly or through contracts with States or nonprofit private entities, a temporary high risk health insurance program to provide access to coverage for uninsured Americans with pre-existing conditions.

Applicant Eligibility: The applicants must meet the terms and conditions outlined in the model contract. See the State PCIP Model contract at www.

Beneficiary Eligibility: Eligibility and enrollment rules for the Federal and state-operated PCIP programs can be found at www.healthcare.

Award Range/Average: No Data Available.

Funding: (Direct Payments for Specified Use) FY 17 $0; FY 18 est $0; FY 19 est $0; FY 16 $0.

HQ: 200 Independence Avenue SW
Washington, DC 20201
Phone: 301-492-4312
Email: michelle.feagins@hhs.gov
http://www.pcip.com

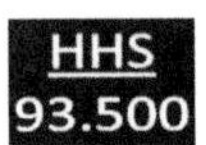

PREGNANCY ASSISTANCE FUND PROGRAM "PAF"

Award: Project Grants

Purpose: Provides support for States and Tribes to develop and implement programs to improve the educational, health, and social outcomes for expectant and parenting teens, women, fathers, and their families.

Applicant Eligibility: Eligible applicants are from States, which include the District of Columbia, any commonwealth, possession, or other territory of the of the United States and any Federally-recognized Indian tribe, reservation or consortium or council (referred to as "States or tribes"), for the development and implementation of programs for expectant and parenting teens, women, fathers and their families. The authorized representative from the State or tribe must apply for grant funds available through this announcement to assist expectant and parenting teens, women, fathers and their families.

Beneficiary Eligibility: States, which include the District of Columbia, any commonwealth, possession, or other territory of the United States, and any Federally-recognized Indian Tribe, reservation, consortium or council.

Award Range/Average: $250,000 - $1,000,000 per year.

Funding: (Project Grants) FY 17 $23,300,000; FY 18 N/A FY 19 FY 16 $23,300,000.

HQ: 1101 Wootton Parkway Tower Building, Suite 550
Rockville, MD 20852
Email: alice.bettencourt@hhs.gov
http://www.hhs.gov/ash/oah

PREPARING FOR EMERGING THREATS & HAZARDS

Award: Project Grants

Purpose: Provides federal assistance to communities to help prepare for new and emerging threats and hazards.

Applicant Eligibility: Please refer to the FY2016 Funding Opportunity Announcement.

Beneficiary Eligibility: Preparedness is the shared responsibility of our entire nation. Each community contributes to achieving the National Preparedness Goal by assessing and preparing for the risks that are most relevant and urgent for them individually, which in turn strengthens our collective security and resilience as a Nation.

Award Range/Average: TBD

Funding: (Project Grants) FY 17 N/A FY 18 N/A FY 19 est $0; FY 16 $35,940,000.

HQ: FEMA 500 C Street SW
Washington, DC 20472
Phone: 800-368-6498
http://www.fema.gov

PRESIDENTIAL DECLARED DISASTER ASSISTANCE TO INDIVIDUALS & HOUSEHOLDS – OTHER NEEDS "ONA"

Award: Direct Payments for Specified Use

Purpose: The program offers financial support for disaster survivors whose financial needs aren't met by the insurance.

Applicant Eligibility: Individuals and households, in areas declared an emergency or major disaster by the President, who have necessary expenses and serious needs they are unable to meet through insurance or other means, are eligible for Other Needs Assistance. Basic conditions of eligibility include: the individual or a member of the household must be a citizen of the United States, a non-citizen national, or a qualified alien.

Beneficiary Eligibility: Individual/Family; expenses/losses must have occurred within an area which has been designated as a disaster area by Presidential declaration.

Award Range/Average: Range: $50 - $33,300; Average is $2,559.92

Funding: (Direct Payments for Specified Use) FY 17 est $300,000; FY 16 $26,368,942; FY 18 N/A.

HQ: FEMA 500 C Street SW
Washington, DC 20472
Phone: 800-368-6498
http://www.dhs.gov

PRESIDENTIAL RESIDENCE PROTECTION SECURITY GRANT "PRPA Grant"

Award: Project Grants

Purpose: The Fiscal Year 2018 Presidential Residence Protection Assistance Grant provides reimbursement to law enforcement agencies from Federal funds for any law enforcement personnel costs that incurs while protecting the President during any non-governmental residential tenure.

Applicant Eligibility: Eligible applicants are limited to state and local law enforcement agencies, directly or through the State Administrative Agency, that conducted protection activities associated with any non-governmental residence of the President of the United States designated or identified to be secured by the United States Secret Service.

Beneficiary Eligibility: Eligible applicants are limited to state and local law enforcement agencies that conducted protection activities associated with any non-governmental residence of the President of the United States designated or identified to be secured by the United States Secret Service.

Award Range/Average: This was a new program in FY 2017, so there were no previous program budgets.

Funding: (Project Grants) FY 17 $20,500,000; FY 18 est $41,000,000; FY 19 est $41,000,000; FY 16 N/A - This is a new program in FY 2017 so there are not previous program budgets.

HQ: 400 C Street SW
Washington, DC 20472
Phone: 866-927-5646
Email: elise.alexander@fema.dhs.gov
http://fema.gov/grants

PRESIDENT'S COMMITTEE FOR PEOPLE WITH INTELLECTUAL DISABILITIES (PCPID) "PCPID"

Award: Dissemination of Technical Information

Purpose: The President's Committee for People with Intellectual Disabilities provides advice to the President and to the Secretary of Health and Human Services, concerning a broad range of topics relating to people with intellectual disabilities.

Applicant Eligibility: General public.

Beneficiary Eligibility: Same as Applicant Eligibility.

Award Range/Average: N/A

Funding: (Formula Grants) FY 17 $248,294; FY 18 est $242,916; FY 19 N/A FY 16 est $166,142.

HQ: 330 C Street SW
Washington, DC 20201
Phone: 202-795-7309
Email: melissa.oritiz@acl.hhs.gov
http://www.acl.gov

PREVENTING HEART ATTACKS & STROKES IN HIGH NEED AREAS

Award: Cooperative Agreements

Purpose: The purpose of the program is to support implementation of population-wide and priority population approaches to prevent and control high blood pressure, and reduce health disparities associated with high blood pressure, among adults in Mississippi's 18-county Delta Region, which is an underserved and rural area.

Applicant Eligibility: The Mississippi Department of Health / Mississippi Delta Health Collaborative is uniquely qualified to carry out the activities outlined. To meet Congressional intent detailed in the Appropriations language, CDC needs to continue supporting the Mississippi Department of Health / Mississippi Delta Health Collaborative's work related to policy, systems, and environmental approaches, as well as community-clinical linkages for the prevention and control of chronic diseases, such as heart disease and stroke. The Mississippi Department of Health's mission is to promote and protect the health of the citizens of Mississippi.

Beneficiary Eligibility: The ultimate benefits of this program will be received by the general and priority adult populations in a local, rural area of Mississippi.

Award Range/Average: $1,058,464 to $ $4,000,000

Funding: (Cooperative Agreements) FY 17 $3,000,000; FY 18 est $3,150,000; FY 19 est $0; FY 16 $3,150,000.

HQ: 4770 Buford Highway NE
Atlanta, GA 30341
Phone: 770-488-5519
Email: rmoeti@cdc.gov
http://www.cdc.gov

PREVENTION & CONTROL OF CHRONIC DISEASE & ASSOCIATED RISK FACTORS IN THE U.S. AFFILIATED PACIFIC ISLANDS, U.S. VIRGIN ISLANDS, AND PUERTO RICO

Award: N/A

Purpose: The five-year program reduces the rates of disability and death associated with chronic disease in the U.S. Affiliated Pacific Islands, U.S. Virgin Islands, and Puerto Rico.

Applicant Eligibility: Applicants much provide proof of ability to serve populations in one of the following jurisdictions: Commonwealth of the Northern Mariana Islands (CNMI), American Samoa, Guam, Federated States of Micronesia (FSM), Republic of the Marshall Islands (RMI), Republic of Palau, U.S. Virgin Islands, Puerto Rico.

Beneficiary Eligibility: N/A

Award Range/Average: Awards are expected to range from $250,000 to $1,500,000 (total award for both Core and Competitive Components, where applicable).

Funding: Cooperative Agreements (Discretionary Grants) FY 17 $0; FY 18 est $0; FY 19 est $0.

HQ: 4770 Buford Highway, P.O. Box F80
Atlanta, GA 30341
Phone: 770-488-6393
Email: sdejesus@cdc.gov
http://cdc.gov

PREVENTION & CONTROL OF CHRONIC DISEASE & ASSOCIATED RISK FACTORS IN THE U.S. AFFILIATED PACIFIC ISLANDS, U.S. VIRGIN ISLANDS, AND PUERTO RI

Award: N/A

Purpose: To reduce the rates of disability and death associated with chronic disease in the U.S. Affiliated Pacific Islands, U.S. Virgin Islands, and Puerto Rico.

Applicant Eligibility: State governments, county governments, city or township governments, special district governments, independent school districts, public and state controlled institutions of higher education, Native American tribal governments (Federally recognized), Public housing authorities/Indian housing authorities, Native American tribal organizations (other than Federally recognized tribal governments), Nonprofits having 501(c)(3) status with the IRS, other institutions of higher education; Nonprofits without 501 (c)(3) status with the IRS, other than institutions of higher education, private institutions of higher education, For profit organizations other than small businesses, small businesses, Territorial governments or their bona fide agents in the Commonwealth of Puerto Rico, the Virgin Islands, the Commonwealth of the Northern Mariana Islands, American Samoa, Guam, Federated States of Micronesia, Republic of the Marshall Islands, and the Republic of Palau, State Controlled institutions of higher education, American Indian or Alaska Native tribal governments, American Indian or Alaska Native tribally designated organizations, Ministries of Health Applicants must provide proof of ability to serve populations in one of the following jurisdictions: Commonwealth of the Northern Mariana Islands (CNMI), American Samoa, Guam, Federated States of Micronesia (FSM), Republic of the Marshall Islands (RMI), Republic of Palau, U.S. Virgin Islands, Puerto Rico.

Beneficiary Eligibility: Beneficiaries of this NOFO are anyone/general public currently living in the Commonwealth of the Northern Mariana Islands, American Samoa, Guam, Federated States of Micronesia, Republic of the Marshall Islands, Republic of Palau, U.S. Virgin Islands, Puerto Rico.

Award Range/Average: Awards are expected to range from $250,000 to $1,500,000 (total award for both Core and Competitive Components, where applicable).

Funding: (Cooperative Agreements) FY 17 FY 18 FY 19 est $4,000,000.

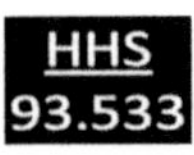

HQ: 4770 Buford Highway, P.O. Box F80
Atlanta, GA 30341
Phone: 770-488-6393
Email: sdejesus@cdc.gov
http://cdc.gov

HHS 93.533 PREVENTION & PUBLIC HEALTH FUND (AFFORDABLE CARE ACT): ENHANCED SURVEILLANCE FOR NEW VACCINE PREVENTABLE DISEASE "NVSN"

Award: Cooperative Agreements

Purpose: To support a network of sites that provide surveillance and data collection on new vaccine use, the impact of new and upcoming vaccines and other immunoprophylaxis, new vaccine policies / policies under consideration, through enhanced inpatient and Emergency Department(ED) surveillance, applied epidemiologic research, and investigator-initiated investigations.

Applicant Eligibility: Higher Education Institutions: Public/State Controlled Institutions of Higher Education, Private Institutions of Higher Education. The following types of Higher Education Institutions are always encouraged to apply for CDC support as Public or Private Institutions of Higher Education: Hispanic-serving Institutions, Historically Black Colleges and Universities (HBCUs), Tribally Controlled Colleges and Universities (TCCUs), Alaska Native and Native Hawaiian Serving Institutions Nonprofits Other Than Institutions of Higher Education, Nonprofits (Other than Institutions of Higher Education), Governments, State Governments, County Governments, City or Township Governments, Special District Governments, Indian/Native American Tribal Governments (Federally Recognized), Indian/ Native American Tribal Governments (Other than Federally Recognized), Eligible Agencies of the Federal Government, U.S. Territory or Possession Other, Independent School Districts, Public Housing Authorities/Indian Housing Authorities, Native American tribal organizations (other than Federally recognized tribal governments), Faith-based or Community-based Organizations, Regional Organizations, Bona Fide Agents Entities must be States (or bona fide agents of States), political subdivision of States, or other public or non-profit private entities.

Beneficiary Eligibility: Any U.S. state, political subdivision and U.S. territories (as described above), and other public entities will benefit.

Award Range/Average: $450,000 to $550,000 with an average of approximately $500,000.

Funding: (Cooperative Agreements) FY 17 $8,200,000; FY 18 est $9,788,642; FY 19 est $9,788,642; FY 16 $6,699,986.

HQ: 1600 Clifton Road
Atlanta, GA 30329
Phone: 404-639-1305
Email: tlockhart@cdc.gov

PREVENTION OF DISEASE, DISABILITY, AND DEATH BY INFECTIOUS DISEASES

Award: Cooperative Agreements

Purpose: To prevent disease, disability and death by infectious diseases.

Applicant Eligibility: Dependent upon the individual NOFO, eligibility may range from open competition, limited competition, single-source, domestic and/or international in accordance with the authorizing legislation.

Beneficiary Eligibility: N/A

Award Range/Average: $100,000 - $5,000,000; Average $2,000,000

Funding: Cooperative Agreements (Discretionary Grants) FY 17 $60,252,755; FY 18 est $18,999,998; FY 19 est $19,999,999; FY 16 $60,836,631.

HQ: 1600 Clifton Road, P.O. Box E60
Atlanta, GA 30333
Phone: 404-718-8832
Email: bsg2@cdc.gov

PREVENTION OF DISEASE, DISABILITY, AND DEATH THROUGH IMMUNIZATION & CONTROL OF RESPIRATORY & RELATED DISEASES

Award: Project Grants

Purpose: To strengthen capacity to prevent disease, disability, and death through immunization and control of respiratory and related diseases.

Applicant Eligibility: Dependent on the NOFO, eligibility may range from open competition, limited competition, single-source, domestic and/or international in accordance with the authorizing language.

Beneficiary Eligibility: N/A

Award Range/Average: $500,000 - $2,000,000, Average $1,000,000

Funding: (Cooperative Agreements) FY 17 $7,370,314; FY 18 est $7,040,000; FY 19 est $8,000,000; FY 16 $6,082,761.

HQ: 1600 Clifton Road, P.O. Box E60
Atlanta, GA 30333
Phone: 404-718-8832
Email: bsg2@cdc.gov

PREVENTIVE HEALTH & HEALTH SERVICES BLOCK GRANT FUNDED SOLELY WITH PREVENTION & PUBLIC HEALTH FUNDS (PPHF) "PHHS Block Grant"

Award: Formula Grants

Purpose: Provides States with the resources to improve the health status of the population of each grantee by conducting activities leading to the accomplishment of the most current Healthy People objectives for the nation; rapidly responding to emerging health threats; providing emergency medical services, excluding most equipment purchases; and providing services for sex offense victims including prevention activities.

Applicant Eligibility: All fifty States, the District of Columbia, eight US Pacific Territorial governments, and two Native American tribes - the Kickapoo in Kansas and the Santee Sioux in Nebraska are eligible for Preventive Health and Health Services Block Grants.

Beneficiary Eligibility: Preventive Health and Health Services Block Grant grantees utilize this assistance to address the public health priorities in their state, aligning their Programs to the latest Healthy People objectives. As a critical public health resource, the Preventive Health and Health Services Block Grant supports activities that benefits states by (1)Addressing basic health concerns such as tooth decay among children, food sanitation, and injuries to older adults from falling, (2) Allowing states to respond rapidly to emerging health threats they experience, (3) Funding critical prevention efforts to address health concerns such as skin cancer, child safety, and untreated dental decay that lack specific state funding, (4) Protecting investments in and enhancing the effectiveness of funded programs that address specific health problems and (5) Leveraging other resources to increase the benefit of preventive health measures.

Award Range/Average: Estimated amounts for FY 14 are $38,812 to $10,126,018.

Funding: (Formula Grants) FY 18 est $150,000,000; FY 17 est $151,121,365; FY 16 $146,339,574.

HQ: 2500 Century Parkway
Atlanta, GA 30329
Phone: 404-498-6792
Email: ayw3@cdc.gov
http://www.cdc.gov

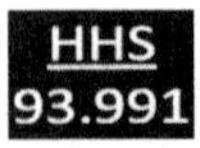

PREVENTIVE HEALTH & HEALTH SERVICES BLOCK GRANT "PHHS Block Grants"

Award: Formula Grants

Purpose: The program supports the healthcare of regions to improve the health status of the people by conducting activities, responding quickly to emerging health threats, providing medical emergency services to nearby locations and by administrating, educating, monitoring and evaluating the activities.

Applicant Eligibility: Only State and U.S. Pacific Territorial governments, the District of Columbia, the Kickapoo Tribe of Kansas and the Santee Sioux Tribe of Nebraska are eligible for Preventive Health and Health Services Block Grants.

Beneficiary Eligibility: The general public will benefit from the objectives of this program with special attention to disparately affected populations.

Award Range/Average: $21,258 to $7,026,219; $1,572,013.

Funding: N/A

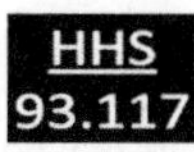

HQ: 2500 Century Parkway
Atlanta, GA 30329
Phone: 404-498-6792
Email: ayw3@cdc.gov
http://www.cdc.gov

HHS 93.117 PREVENTIVE MEDICINE & PUBLIC HEALTH RESIDENCY TRAINING PROGRAM, INTEGRATIVE MEDICINE PROGRAM, AND NATIONAL CENTER FOR INTEGRATIVE PRIMARY HEALTHCARE

Award: Project Grants

Purpose: To promote postgraduate medical education in the specialty of preventive medicine and to enhance preventive medicine education through incorporation of evidence-based integrative medicine curricula into such programs.

Applicant Eligibility: Eligible Preventive Medicine and Public Health Residency program grants, and those enhancing their programs with integrative health care applicants are: (1) an accredited school of public health or school of medicine or osteopathic medicine; (2) an accredited public or private nonprofit hospital; (3) a State, local, or tribal health department; or (4) a consortium of 2 or more entities described in (1) through (3). Eligible applicants for the NCIPH are (1) a health professions school, including an accredited school or program of public health, health administration, preventive medicine, or dental public health or a school providing health management programs; (2) an academic health center; (3) a State or local government; (4) any other appropriate public or private nonprofit entity.

Beneficiary Eligibility: For Preventive Medicine and Public Health Residency program grants, and for those enhancing their programs with integrative health care, each trainee receiving stipend support must: (a) be a citizen of the United States, a non-citizen U.S. national, or a foreign national having in his or her possession a visa permitting permanent residence in the United States; (b) be a physician who has graduated from an accredited school of medicine or osteopathic medicine in the United States; or if a graduate from a foreign school, meet the criteria of the Educational Commission for Foreign Medical Graduates, for entry into the program supported by this grant; and (c) plan to complete the grant-supported program and engage in the practice and/or teaching of preventive medicine, especially in positions which meet the needs of medically underserved populations.

Award Range/Average: Range $234,439 to $400,000; Average award $382,352 Preventive Medicine Residency with Integrative Healthcare Range: $120,484 to $135,253; Average Award: $133,376

Funding: (Cooperative Agreements) FY 17 $0; FY 18 est $0; FY 19 est $0; FY 16 $0; - National Center for Integrative Primary Health Care.(Project Grants) FY 17 $2,000,654; FY 18 est $0; FY 19 est $0; FY 16 $5,928,992; - Preventive Medicine Residency with Integrative Healthcare(Project Grants) FY 17 $4,469,058; FY 18 est $6,499,989; FY 19 est $0; FY 16 $4,623,648; - Preventive Medicine Residency Grants.

HQ: 5600 Fishers Lane, Room 15N 144A
Rockville, MD 20857
Phone: 301-945-3336
Email: scoulter@hrsa.gov
http://www.hrsa.gov

PRIMARY CARE MEDICINE & DENTISTRY CLINICIAN EDUCATOR CAREER DEVELOPMENT AWARDS PROGRAM
"Career Development Awards (CDA)"

Award: Project Grants

Purpose: The career development awards are targeted towards physicians, dentists and dental hygienists who act as role models by improving the standards of primary care medicine and dentistry faculty and also plan to teach in primary care fields.

Applicant Eligibility: Eligible applicant organizations include schools of allopathic or osteopathic medicine, academically affiliated physician assistant training programs, dental and dental hygiene schools, accredited public or nonprofit private hospitals, or a public or nonprofit private entity that the Secretary has determined is capable of carrying out such grants. If the applicant organization is not a medical school, physician assistant training program, dental or dental hygiene school, they must be affiliated with one of the listed schools or training programs and provide a letter of agreement from the relevant organization.

Beneficiary Eligibility: Eligible junior faculty candidates (Project Directors/Principal Investigators) are identified individuals who are applying to HRSA for a clinician educator faculty award through the applicant organization. Candidates must hold a non-tenured faculty appointment.

Award Range/Average: Range $89,549 to $200,000; Average: $186,074; Oral Health: Range: $178,752 to $199,673; Average is $192,117.

Funding: (Project Grants) FY 17 $3,161,510; FY 18 est $3,131,597; FY 19 est $0.

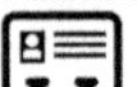

HQ: 5600 Fishers Lane, Room 15N186A
Rockville, MD 20857
Phone: 301-443-6822
http://www.hrsa.gov

PRIME TECHNICAL ASSISTANCE
"Prime"

Award: Project Grants

Purpose: To increase the number of microenterprises and to enhance the management capability of microentrepreneurs in starting, expanding and/or growing their business.

Applicant Eligibility: Grant recipients shall be non-profit microenterprise development or program (or a collaborative thereof) that has a demonstrated record of delivering microenterprise services to disadvantaged entrepreneurs, an intermediary, a microenterprise development organization or program that is accountable to a local community, working in conjunction with a State or local government or Indian tribe, or an Indian tribe acting on its' own, if the tribe can certify that no private organization or program referred to in this paragraph exists within its' jurisdiction.

Beneficiary Eligibility: Disadvantaged entrepreneurs, microenterprises, and microenterprise development organizations as defined in the Act.

Award Range/Average: No Data Available.

Funding: (Project Grants) FY 17 $4,700,000; FY 18 est $5,000,000; FY 19 est $0; FY 16 $5,000,000.

HQ: 409 3rd Street SW, 5th Floor
Washington, DC 20416
Phone: 202-401-6365
Email: manuel.hidalgo@sba.gov
http://www.sba.gov

USIP 91.005 PRIORITY GRANT COMPETITION

Award: Project Grants

Purpose: To seek and develop the international conflict resolution and peacebuilding field.

Applicant Eligibility: Nonprofit or public institutions are eligible to apply. USIP does not accept applications from individuals who are not affiliated with an eligible institution.

Beneficiary Eligibility: N/A

Award Range/Average: Range $30,000 - $150,000. Average ~ $60,000.

Funding: (Salaries and Expenses) FY 18 N/A FY 16 $1,384,555; FY 17 est $1,359,342.

HQ: 2301 Constitution Avenue NW
Washington, DC 20037
Phone: 202-429-3841
Email: seisenberg@usip.gov
http://www.usip.org

HUD 14.418 PRIVATE ENFORCEMENT INITIATIVES "FHIP PEI"

Award: Cooperative Agreements

Purpose: To develop, implement, and carry out, related activities and enforcement under the or State or local laws that provide substantially equivalent rights and remedies for alleged discriminatory housing practices. Objectives include carrying out testing and other investigative activities.

Applicant Eligibility: Eligible applicants are other private institutions/organizations with at least one year of enforcement related experience.

Beneficiary Eligibility: Any person or group of persons aggrieved by discriminatory housing practices because of race, color, religion, sex disability familial status or national origin. Also, any person or group of persons, including landlords or real estate agents, to prevent discriminatory housing practices because of race, color, religion, sex, disability, familial status or national origin.

Award Range/Average: $300,000 per project period. $900,000 total funding for multi-year (3 years)

Funding: (Cooperative Agreements) FY 17 $16,013,813; FY 18 est $30,750,000; FY 19 est $30,350,000; FY 16 $30,350,000.

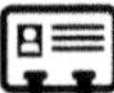

HQ: 451 7th Street SW, Room 5222
Washington, DC 20410
Phone: 202-402-7054
Email: paula.stone@hud.gov
http://www.hud.gov/offices/fheo/partners/fhip/fhip.cfm

PROFESSIONAL & CULTURAL EXCHANGE PROGRAMS – CITIZEN EXCHANGES

Award: Cooperative Agreements; Project Grants

Purpose: Seeks to increase mutual understanding between the people of the United States and the people of other countries by means of educational and cultural exchange programs, including the exchange of scholars, researchers, professionals, students, and educators.

Applicant Eligibility: Pursuant to the Mutual Educational and Cultural Exchange Act of 1961, as amended (Fulbright-Hays Act) the Bureau of Educational and Cultural Affairs of the U.S. Department of State awards grants and cooperative agreements to educational and cultural public or private nonprofit foundations or institutions. Applications may be submitted by public and private non-profit organizations meeting the provisions described in Internal Revenue Code section 26 USC 501(c)(3).

Beneficiary Eligibility: Beneficiaries include recipient organizations, educational institutions, other non-government organizations (NGOs) that meet the provisions described in Internal Revenue Code section 26 USC 501(c)(3), as well as sponsored participants, and the American people and the people of participating countries who interact with the international participants.

Award Range/Average: $119,875 to $16,673,716.

Funding: (Project Grants) FY 17 $120,595,927; FY 18 est $120,595,927; FY 19 est $120,595,927.

HQ: 2200 C Street NW SA 05, Room 3B13
Washington, DC 20037
Phone: 202-632-6070
Email: hadjigeorgalisea@state.gov
http://eca.state.gov/about-bureau-0/organizational-structure/office-citizen-exchanges

PROFESSIONAL & CULTURAL EXCHANGE PROGRAMS – INTERNATIONAL VISITOR LEADERSHIP PROGRAM "International Visitor Leadership Program"

Award: Project Grants

Purpose: Seeks to increase mutual understanding between the people of the United States and the people of other countries by means of educational and cultural exchange programs, including the exchange of scholars, researchers, professionals, students, and educators.

Applicant Eligibility: Pursuant to the Mutual Educational and Cultural Exchange Act of 1961, as amended (Fulbright-Hays Act) the Bureau of Educational and Cultural Affairs of the U.S. Department of State awards grants and cooperative agreements to educational and cultural public or private nonprofit foundations or institutions. Applications may be submitted by public and private non-profit organizations meeting the provisions described in Internal Revenue Code section 26 USC 501(c)(3).

Beneficiary Eligibility: Beneficiaries include recipient organizations, educational institutions, other non-government organizations (NGOs) that meet the provisions described in Internal Revenue Code section 26 USC 501(c)(3), as well as sponsored participants, the American people and the people of participating countries who interact with the international participants.

Award Range/Average: $300,000 to $18,106,089.

Funding: (Cooperative Agreements) FY 17 $65,947,690; FY 18 est $65,947,690; FY 19 est $65,947,690.

HQ: 2200 C Street NW SA 05, Room 03BB06
Washington, DC 20037
Phone: 202-632-9384
Email: rathburntg@state.gov
http://eca.state.gov/ivlp

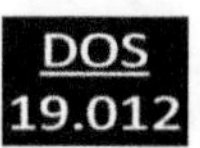

PROFESSIONAL & CULTURAL EXCHANGE PROGRAMS – SPECIAL PROFESSIONAL & CULTURAL PROGRAMS

"Special Professional and Cultural Programs include the Ngwang Choephel Fellows Program."

Award: Project Grants

Purpose: Seeks to increase mutual understanding between the people of the United States and the people of other countries by means of educational and cultural exchange programs. The purpose of the Special Professional and Cultural Programs is to carry out Congressionally-directed initiatives that support professional exchanges between the United States and select countries through grants to American non-profit, non-governmental institutions and organizations, including community organizations, professional associations, and universities.

Applicant Eligibility: Pursuant to the Mutual Educational and Cultural Exchange Act of 1961, as amended (Fulbright-Hays Act) the Bureau of Educational and Cultural Affairs of the U.S. Department of State awards grants and cooperative agreements to educational and cultural public or private nonprofit foundations or institutions. Applications may be submitted by public and private non-profit organizations meeting the provisions described in Internal Revenue Code section 26 USC 501(c)(3).

Beneficiary Eligibility: Beneficiaries include recipient organizations, educational institutions, other non-government organizations (NGOs) that meet the provisions described in Internal Revenue Code section 26 USC 501(c)(3), as well as sponsored participants, and the American people and the people of participating countries who interact with the international participants.

Award Range/Average: 287500

Funding: (Project Grants) FY 17 $575,000; FY 18 est $575,000; FY 19 est $575,000; FY 16 $575,000.

HQ: 3101 Park Center Drive
Alexandria, VA 22302
Phone: 703-305-2590
Email: cndinternet@fns.usda.gov
http://www.fns.usda.gov

PROGRAM OF PROTECTION & ADVOCACY OF INDIVIDUAL RIGHTS

ED 84.240

Award: Formula Grants

Purpose: To provide grants for States to support systems for protection and advocacy for the rights of individuals with disabilities who are ineligible for advocacy services from the other protection and advocacy programs or whose problems fall outside the scope of services available from the Client Assistance Program (CAP).

Applicant Eligibility: Only designated protection and advocacy agencies in each State and Territory, and the protection and advocacy system serving the American Indian Consortium, may apply. With the exception of the protection and advocacy system serving the American Indian Consortium, the Governor designates the protection and advocacy agency.

Beneficiary Eligibility: Individuals with disabilities will benefit.

Award Range/Average: Range of State awards (including the District of Columbia and Puerto Rico) under the distribution formula is $225,000 to $3,373,204, with a median award of $421,728. The statutory amount for each of the four outlying areas is $40,000.

Funding: (Formula Grants) FY 17 $17,650,000; FY 18 est $17,650,000; FY 19 est $17,650,000.

HQ: 400 Maryland Avenue SW
Washington, DC 20202
Phone: 202-245-6493
Email: jessica.smith@ed.gov
http://www.rsa.ed.gov/programs.cfm

PROJECT GRANTS & COOPERATIVE AGREEMENTS FOR TUBERCULOSIS CONTROL PROGRAMS

HHS 93.116

Award: Cooperative Agreements

Purpose: To assist State, local health agencies, political subdivisions, and other government entities to conduct TB preventive health service programs to assist in carrying out tuberculosis (TB) control activities designed to prevent transmission of infection and disease.

Applicant Eligibility: Under Section 317 of the Public Health Service Act, official public health agencies or their bona fide agents of State and local governments, including the District of Columbia, the Commonwealth of Puerto Rico, the Virgin Islands, Guam, the Northern Mariana Islands, the Federated States of Micronesia, the Republic of the Marshall Islands, the Republic of Palau, and American Samoa.

Beneficiary Eligibility: Official public health agencies of State and local governments, including the District of Columbia, the Commonwealth of Puerto Rico, the Virgin Islands, Guam, the Northern Mariana Islands, the Federated States of Micronesia, the Republic of the Marshall Islands, the Republic of Palau, and American Samoa.

Award Range/Average: $86,938 to $9,9,317,764 with an average of $1,454,714

Funding: (Cooperative Agreements) FY 17 $79,830,700; FY 18 est $79,486,233; FY 19 est $80,863,811; FY 16 $80,863,811; - It should be noted that for PS13-1304, RTMCCs, the funding in TAGGS is being reported under 93.116 when the NOFO itself shows 93.947. OGS corrected the NoAs by doing deobligation/reobligation for FY 13 and FY 14; however for FY 15 funding is showing under 93.116.

HQ: Division of Tuberculosis Elimination 1600 Clifton Road, P.O. Box E-10
Atlanta, GA 30333
Phone: 404-639-5259
Email: kak4@cdc.gov
http://www.cdc.gov/tb

PROJECT RENTAL ASSISTANCE DEMONSTRATION (PRA DEMO) PROGRAM OF SECTION 811 SUPPORTIVE HOUSING FOR PERSONS WITH DISABILITIES

Award: Project Grants

Purpose: Implementing the new requirements for the new project rental assistance authority rendered by the Melville Act.

Applicant Eligibility: Any housing agency currently allocating Low Income Housing Tax Credits (LIHTC) under IRS Section 42 or any housing or Community Development Agency currently allocating and overseeing in good standing HOME Funds or the Section 8 Program or a similar program are eligible applicants, and only one housing agency per state is eligible. Only states that are developing partnerships or that have existing partnerships with State Health Care and Human Service Agency or agencies and the state Medicaid Agency for supportive services are eligible.

Beneficiary Eligibility: Extremely low-income non-elderly (18-62 years of age) persons with disabilities that are eligible for community-based, long-term care as provided through Medicaid waivers, Medicaid state plan options or other appropriate services. Eligible applicants will provide these PRA Demo project-based rental assistance funds to not more than 25% of the units in multifamily developments for extremely low-income persons with disabilities which are the beneficiaries.

Award Range/Average: tbd

Funding: (Project Grants) FY 16 est $67,000,000; FY 17 est $3,000,000; FY 15 $82,000,000.

HQ: 451 7th Street SW
Washington, DC 20410
Phone: 202-708-3000
Email: lessie.p.evans@hud.gov

PROJECT SAFE NEIGHBORHOODS "PSN"

Award: Project Grants

Purpose: To create and foster safer neighborhoods through a sustained diminution in violent crime, including, but not limited to, addressing criminal gangs and the felonious possession and use of firearms.

Applicant Eligibility: Eligible applicants are PSN Task Force fiscal agents for the U.S. Attorney districts and federally recognized Indian tribal governments (as determined by the Secretary of the Interior). All fiscal agents must be certified by the relevant U.S. Attorney's Office (USAO).

Beneficiary Eligibility: State and local governments, public and private organizations, Indian Tribal government, prosecutor offices.

Award Range/Average: Prior awards have ranged from approximately $200,000 to $500,000.

Funding: (Project Grants) FY 17 $5,871,591; FY 18 est $20,000,000; FY 19 est $140,000,000.

HQ: 810 7th Street NW
Washington, DC 20735
Phone: 202-598-5248
http://www.bja.gov

PROJECTS FOR ASSISTANCE IN TRANSITION FROM HOMELESSNESS (PATH) "PATH"

Award: Formula Grants

Purpose: To provide financial assistance to States to support services for individuals who are suffering from serious mental illness or serious mental illness and substance abuse; and are homeless or at imminent risk of becoming homeless.

Applicant Eligibility: States, District of Columbia, Guam, American Samoa, the Commonwealths of Puerto Rico and the Northern Mariana Islands, and the Virgin Islands.

Beneficiary Eligibility: Individuals who have a serious mental illness or serious mental illness and substance abuse; and are homeless or are at imminent risk of becoming homeless.

Award Range/Average: Range - $50,000 to $8,812,865; Average is $1,099,933.96

Funding: (Formula Grants) FY 17 $61,578,634; FY 18 est $61,596,302; FY 19 est $61,581,202; FY 16 $61,626,502.

HQ: 5600 Fishers Lane
Rockville, MD 20857
Phone: 240-276-1078
Email: odessa.crocker@samhsa.hhs.gov
http://www.samhsa.gov

PROMOTE THE SURVIVAL & CONTINUING VITALITY OF NATIVE AMERICAN LANGUAGES "Native American Language Preservation and Maintenance (P&M) and the Esther Martinez Immersion (EMI)"

Award: Project Grants

Purpose: Provides financial assistance to eligible applicants for the purpose of promoting the survival and continued vitality of native languages.

Applicant Eligibility: Federally-recognized Indian Tribes, as recognized by the Bureau of Indian Affairs, Incorporated non-federally recognized Tribes Incorporated state-recognized Indian Tribes Consortia of Indian Tribes Incorporated nonprofit multi-purpose community-based Indian organizations Urban Indian Centers Alaska Native villages as defined in the Alaska Native Claims Settlement Act (ANSCA) and/or nonprofit village consortia Nonprofit native organizations in Alaska with village specific projects Incorporated non-profit Alaska Native multi-purpose, community-based organizations Non-profit Alaska Native Regional Corporations/Associations in Alaska with village-specific projects Non-profit Alaska

Native community entities or tribal governing bodies (Indian Reorganization Act or Traditional Councils) as recognized by the Bureau of Indian Affairs, Public and nonprofit private agencies serving Native Hawaiians, National or regional incorporated nonprofit Native American organizations with Native American community-specific objectives, Public and nonprofit private agencies serving native peoples from Guam, American Samoa, or the Commonwealth of the Northern Mariana Islands, Tribal Colleges and Universities, and colleges and universities located in Hawaii, Guam, American Samoa, or the Tribal Colleges and Universities, and colleges and universities located in Hawaii, Guam, American Samoa, or the Commonwealth of the Northern Mariana Islands which serve Native American Pacific Islanders.

Beneficiary Eligibility: American Indians, Alaska Natives, Native Hawaiians, and Native American Pacific Islanders will benefit.

Award Range/Average: $100,000- $300,000. Average per Budget Period: $278,000

Funding: (Project Grants) FY 17 $10,142,892; FY 18 est $10,158,441; FY 19 est $10,158,441.

HQ: Division of Program Operations 330 C Street SW
Washington, DC 20201
Phone: 877-922-9262
Email: carmelia.strickland@acf.hhs.gov
http://www.acf.hhs.gov/programs/ana

PROMOTING EVIDENCE INTEGRATION IN SEX OFFENDER MANAGEMENT DISCRETIONARY GRANT PROGRAM

Award: Project Grants; Training

Purpose: To support the Adam Walsh Act (AWA) by administering grant programs related to sex offender registration and notification as authorized under AWA or directed by the Attorney General and provide technical assistance to states, the District of Columbia, principal U.S. territories, units of local government, tribal governments, and other public and private entities involved in activities related to sex offender registration or notification or to other measures for the protection of children or other members of the public from sexual abuse or exploitation. To assist states, the District of Columbia, the principal U.S. territories, local, and tribal jurisdictions in improving their adult and/or juvenile sex offender management policies and practices by supporting training, technical assistance, demonstration projects, and fellowships in the Office of Sex Offender Sentencing, Monitoring, Apprehending, Registering and Tracking (SMART).

Applicant Eligibility: Non-profit organizations (including tribal organizations), institutions of higher education (including tribal institutions of higher education), for-profit organizations, states, the District of Columbia, the Commonwealth of Puerto Rico, the Virgin Islands, America Samoa, Guam, the Commonwealth of the Northern Mariana Islands, local, and tribal communities who are interested in addressing the management of juvenile, adult, or a mixed population of sex offenders are eligible to apply for this grant program. Applicants must coordinate their proposal with others in their jurisdiction to ensure a collaborative response to this solicitation as well as to ensure that agencies within a single jurisdiction are not competing against one another in the grant process.

Beneficiary Eligibility: State, local, and tribal agencies.

Award Range/Average: Up to $500,000 for sex offender management enhancement programs, up to $1,000,000 for training and technical assistance, and up to $250,000 per fellowship opportunity.

Funding: (Project Grants) FY 17 $853,266.

HQ: 810 Seventh Street NW
Washington, DC 20531
Phone: 202-307-5762
http://www.smart.gov

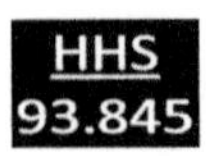

PROMOTING POPULATION HEALTH THROUGH INCREASED CAPACITY IN ALCOHOL EPIDEMIOLOGY "Alcohol Epidemiology"

Award: Cooperative Agreements

Purpose: The purpose of this FOA is to support the building of capacity in alcohol epidemiology in state and large city Health Departments and help provide the tools needed to perform core public health functions. This increased epidemiologic capacity will help build the public health infrastructure that is needed to address excessive alcohol use in the U.S.

Applicant Eligibility: Eligibility will be limited to State and District of Columbia Health Departments, large city health departments (900,00 residents or more), or their Bona Fide Agents.

Beneficiary Eligibility: State and local health departments' work may benefit work may benefit others outside the institution including health professionals, non-profit organizations, and the general public.

Award Range/Average: No Data Available.

Funding: (Cooperative Agreements) FY 17 $741,957; FY 18 est $750,000; FY 19 est $750,000; FY 16 $731,260.

HQ: 4770 Buford Highway, P.O. Box F78
Atlanta, GA 30341
Phone: 770-488-8063
Email: gla5@cdc.gov
http://www.cdc.gov

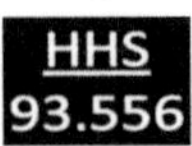

PROMOTING SAFE & STABLE FAMILIES

Award: Formula Grants; Project Grants

Purpose: To prevent child maltreatment among families at risk through the provision of supportive family services.

Applicant Eligibility: (1) Formula Grants: States, the District of Columbia, Puerto Rico, the U. S.

Beneficiary Eligibility: Families and children who need services to assist them to stabilize their lives, strengthen family functioning, prevent out-of-home placement of children, enhance child development and increase competence in parenting abilities, facilitate timely reunification of the child, and promote appropriate adoptions.

Award Range/Average: Formula grants for main grant program: states, territories, and tribes ranged from $1,935 to $26,939,151 with an average of $1,333,355.

Funding: (Formula Grants) FY 17 $326,671,996; FY 18 est $322,718,755; FY 19 est $325,000,000; FY 16 $269,891,000; - Cooperative Agreements (Discretionary Grants) FY 17 $2,349,912; FY 18 est $2,349,921; FY 19 est $2,400,000; FY 16 $59,692,755.

HQ: 330 C Street SW, Room 3509B
Washington, DC 20201
Phone: 202-205-8438
Email: eileen.west@acf.hhs.gov
http://www.acf.hhs.gov/programs/cb

HHS 93.832 PROMOTING THE CANCER SURVEILLANCE WORKFORCE, EDUCATION & DATA USE

Award: Cooperative Agreements

Purpose: The purpose of this program is to expand the capacity of CDC-funded National Program of Cancer Registries through external partners, to pursue activities that impact the national cancer surveillance workforce.

Applicant Eligibility: Nonprofit with 501C3 IRS status (other than institution of higher education) Nonprofit without 501C3 IRS status (other than institution of higher education) Private colleges and universities

Beneficiary Eligibility: Same as Applicant Eligibility.

Award Range/Average: $200,000 per budget year for five years.

Funding: (Cooperative Agreements) FY 17 $200,000; FY 18 est $200,000; FY 19 est $200,000; FY 16 $200,000.

HQ: 4770 Buford Highway, P.O. Box F 76
Atlanta, GA 30341
Phone: 770-488-8430
Email: eoi9@cdc.gov
http://www.cdc.gov

NEA 45.024 PROMOTION OF THE ARTS GRANTS TO ORGANIZATIONS & INDIVIDUALS

Award: Project Grants

Purpose: To support public engagement with, and access to, various forms of excellent art across the nation, the creation of art that meets the highest standards of excellence.

Applicant Eligibility: Tax-exempt organizations meeting the following conditions may apply: (1) No part of any earnings may benefit a private stockholder or individual, and (2) donations to the organization are allowable as charitable deductions under Section 170(c) of the Internal Revenue Code. Examples of eligible organizations are arts institutions, arts service organizations, local arts agencies, official units of state and local governments, federally recognized tribal communities and Indian tribes.

Beneficiary Eligibility: Through activities and services supported, beneficiaries include the general public and artists as well as nonprofit organizations, state and local governments, local arts agencies, local education agencies (school districts), federally recognized tribal communities and Indian tribes, literary artists, and master artists.

Award Range/Average: In the past few years, well over half of our grants have been for amounts less than $25,000.

Funding: Project Grants (Discretionary) FY 17 $75,224,919; FY 18 est $70,605,191; FY 19 N/A.

HQ: 400 7th Street SW
Washington, DC 20506
Phone: 202-682-5441
Email: chauveauxt@arts.gov
http://www.arts.gov

PROMOTION OF THE ARTS PARTNERSHIP AGREEMENTS

Award: Project Grants; Advisory Services and Counseling

Purpose: To develop and maintain partnerships with the state and jurisdictional arts agencies (SAAs) and their regional arts organizations (RAOs) to advance the mission of the National Endowment for the Arts.

Applicant Eligibility: Agencies that are officially designated as the state arts agency by the state government in each of the 50 States and six special U.S. jurisdictions, and that meet the National Endowment for the Arts' eligibility requirements for SAAs as outlined in the Partnership Agreements guidelines on our website; regional arts organizations that represent state arts agencies and that meet the National Endowment for the Arts' eligibility requirements for RAOs as outlined in the Partnership Agreements guidelines on our website; and organizations providing support services to state and regional arts agencies at a national level.

Beneficiary Eligibility: The official arts agencies of the 50 states and six U.S. jurisdictions, regional arts organizations, and organizations providing support services to SAAs and RAOs at the national level. Through activities and services supported, beneficiaries include the general public, local arts agencies, nonprofit organizations, and artists.

Award Range/Average: Partnership Agreements for SAAs range from $296,700 to $1,155,300, averaging $750,000. RAO awards is $1,088,400 to $1,687,800, averaging $1,384,000.

Funding: Project Grants (with Formula Distribution) FY 17 $51,991,405; FY 18 est $50,666,790.

HQ: 400 7th Street SW
Washington, DC 20506
Phone: 202-682-5430
Email: mathisa@arts.gov
http://www.arts.gov

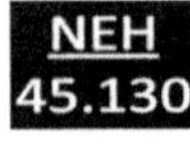

PROMOTION OF THE HUMANITIES CHALLENGE GRANTS

Award: Project Grants

Purpose: To strengthen the institutional base of the humanities by supporting infrastructure development and capacity building.

Applicant Eligibility: U.S. public and nonprofit 501(c)(3) organizations (including institutions of higher education), state and local governmental agencies, and federally recognized Native American tribal governments. The following eligible entities are subject to the one-to-one matching requirement: public and 501(c)(3) nonprofit community colleges and post-secondary two-year institutions of higher education; public and nonprofit 501(c)(3) U.S. historically black colleges or universities, as defined by Executive Order 13532; public and nonprofit 501(c)(3) Hispanic-serving institutions of higher education; and U.S. tribal college or university, as defined by Executive Order 13270.

Beneficiary Eligibility: All applicant organizations and institutions and all users of their humanities resources, programs, or activities; humanities scholars, and the general public.

Award Range/Average: Applicants may request up to $750,000. Average award was approximately $72,240.

Funding: (Project Grants) FY 17 $7,414,400; FY 18 est $4,216,500; FY 19 N/A FY 16 $8,836,549.

HQ: 400 Seventh Street SW
Washington, DC 20506
Phone: 202-606-8309
http://www.neh.gov

PROMOTION OF THE HUMANITIES DIVISION OF PRESERVATION & ACCESS

Award: Project Grants

Purpose: To ensure the long-term and wide availability of primary resources in the humanities by funding projects that promote preserving, creating, and providing intellectual access to resources held in libraries, museums, archives, historical organizations, and other collections.

Applicant Eligibility: U.S. public and nonprofit 501(c)(3) organizations (including institutions of higher education), state and local governmental agencies, and federally recognized Native American tribal governments.

Beneficiary Eligibility: Same as Applicant Eligibility.

Award Range/Average: $6,000 to $350,000; Average is $98,850

Funding: (Project Grants) FY 17 $14,700,000; FY 18 est $19,810,000; FY 19 FY 16 $16,054,272.

HQ: 400 Seventh Street SW
Washington, DC 20506
Phone: 202-606-8570
http://www.neh.gov/divisions/preservation

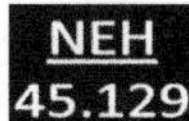

PROMOTION OF THE HUMANITIES FEDERAL/STATE PARTNERSHIP

Award: Formula Grants

Purpose: To promote local, statewide, and regional humanities programming through annual grants to humanities councils in each of the 50 States, the District of Columbia, Puerto Rico, the U.S. Virgin Islands, Northern Mariana Islands, Guam, and American Samoa.

Applicant Eligibility: Nonprofit 501(c)(3) state and jurisdictional humanities councils which conform to the requirements of 20 U.S.C. 956(f).

Beneficiary Eligibility: State and local governments; sponsored organizations; public and private nonprofit institutions/organizations; other public institutions/organizations; Federally recognized Indian tribal governments; Native American organizations; U.S. Territories; non-government general; minority organizations; other specialized groups; and quasi-public nonprofit institutions which apply directly to the State Humanities Council.

Award Range/Average: $384,160 to $2,446,300. Average $823,747.

Funding: (Project Grants) FY 17 $46,875,190; FY 18 est $47,500,660; FY 19 N/A FY 16 $43,014,272.

HQ: 400 Seventh Street SW
Washington, DC 20506
Phone: 202-606-8254
http://www.neh.gov/divisions/fedstate

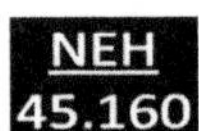

PROMOTION OF THE HUMANITIES FELLOWSHIPS & STIPENDS

Award: Project Grants

Purpose: To provide support for scholars to undertake full-time independent research and writing in the humanities. Grants are available for six to-12-month fellowships and two months of summer study.

Applicant Eligibility: All applicants must be U.S. citizens, native residents of U.S. jurisdictions, foreign nationals who have been legal residents in the U.S. or its jurisdictions for at least the three years immediately preceding the application deadline. Fellowships: Faculty members at colleges and universities, individuals affiliated with other institutions, independent scholars, and others who work in the humanities are eligible.

Beneficiary Eligibility: Fellowships and Stipends: College and university faculty and staff, individuals affiliated with institutions other than colleges and universities, and scholars and writers working independently. Awards for Faculty: faculty members at Historically Black Colleges and Universities, Hispanic-Serving Institutions, and Tribal Colleges and Universities.

Award Range/Average: Fellowships and Awards for Faculty: An award of $5,000 per month for a grant period of from 3 to 12 months. Summer Stipends: All awards are $6,000 for a grant period of 8 weeks.

Funding: Project Grants (Fellowships) FY 17 $5,925,000; FY 18 est $5,750,000; FY 19 N/A FY 16 $5,812,170.

HQ: Division of Research Programs 400 Seventh Street SW
Washington, DC 20506
Phone: 202-606-8200
http://www.neh.gov

PROMOTION OF THE HUMANITIES OFFICE OF DIGITAL HUMANITIES

Award: Project Grants

Purpose: Supports innovative humanities projects that utilize or study the impact of digital technology for research, preservation, access, education, and public programming.

Applicant Eligibility: U.S. public and 501(c)(3) nonprofit organizations (including institutions of higher education); state and local governmental agencies and Native American tribal organizations.

Beneficiary Eligibility: U.S. public and nonprofit organizations (including institutions of higher education); state and local governmental agencies and Native American tribal organizations; U.S. citizens; and humanities scholars.

Award Range/Average: FY 18 from $25200 to $325000.

Funding: (Project Grants) FY 17 $4,742,350; FY 18 est $4,600,000; FY 19 N/A FY 12 $43,014,272; FY 11 $4,334,509; FY 13 $4,412,557; FY 16 $4,747,437.

HQ: 400 Seventh Street SW
Washington, DC 20506
Phone: 202-606-8400
http://www.neh.gov

PROMOTION OF THE HUMANITIES PROFESSIONAL DEVELOPMENT

Award: Project Grants

Purpose: Seminars and Institutes promote better teaching and research in the humanities through faculty development.

Applicant Eligibility: Distinguished scholar/teachers in the humanities may apply through a sponsoring institution to direct a seminar or institute for college teachers or school teachers. For Landmarks in American History and Culture, the following may apply: U.S. public and nonprofit 501(c)(3) organizations (including institutions of higher education), state and local governmental agencies, and federally recognized Native American tribal governments.

Beneficiary Eligibility: U.S. public and nonprofit 501(c)(3) organizations (including institutions of higher education), state and local governmental agencies, federally recognized Native American tribal governments, humanities scholars, and the general public. For Seminars and Institutes and Landmarks of American History and Culture--primarily K-12 or college teachers, depending on the particular project--as well as their colleagues and students.

Award Range/Average: N/A

Funding: (Project Grants) FY 17 $9,429,550; FY 18 est $8,644,000; FY 19 N/A.

HQ: Division of Education Programs 400 Seventh Street SW
Washington, DC 20506
Phone: 202-606-8463
http://www.neh.gov

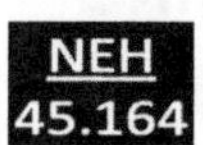

PROMOTION OF THE HUMANITIES PUBLIC PROGRAMS

Award: Project Grants

Purpose: To provide opportunities for the American public to explore human history and culture through humanities programs in museums, historical organizations, libraries, community centers, and other gathering places.

Applicant Eligibility: U.S. public and private 501(c)(3) nonprofit institutions/organizations (including institutions of higher education); state and local governmental agencies; and Federally recognized Indian tribal governments.

Beneficiary Eligibility: Same as Applicant Eligibility.

Award Range/Average: FY 18 from $1,000 to $460,000.

Funding: (Project Grants) FY 17 $14,586,200; FY 18 est $15,400,000; FY 19 N/A FY 16 $16,938,857.

HQ: Division of Public Programs 400 7th Street SW
Washington, DC 20506

Phone: 202-606-8269

http://www.neh.gov/divisions/public

PROMOTION OF THE HUMANITIES RESEARCH

Award: Project Grants

Purpose: To advance knowledge and understanding of the humanities, and strengthen the intellectual foundations of the humanities.

Applicant Eligibility: For Collaborative Research and Scholarly Editions and Translations, U.S. public and 501(c)(3) nonprofit organizations (including institutions of higher education), state and local governments, federally recognized Native American tribal governments, and individuals (U.S. citizens and foreign nationals who have been living in the United States or its jurisdictions for at least the three years immediately prior to the time of application). For Fellowship Programs at Independent Research Institutions (FPIRI), U.S. nonprofit 501(c)(3) organizations, a state or local governmental agency, or a federally recognized Indian tribal government with existing fellowship programs may apply.

Beneficiary Eligibility: U.S. citizens and residents, State and local governments, sponsored organizations, public and private nonprofit institutions/organizations, other public institutions/ organizations, Federally recognized Indian tribal governments, Native American organizations, U.S. territories; non-governmental-general; minority organizations, other specialized groups; and quasi-public nonprofit institutions benefit.

Award Range/Average: FY 17 from $50,400 to $330,000; $177,300 average.

Funding: (Project Grants) FY 17 $9,850,000; FY 18 est $7,785,000; FY 19 N/A FY 16 $10,203,370.

HQ: Division of Research Programs 400 Seventh Street SW

Washington, DC 20506

Phone: 202-606-8200

http://www.neh.gov/divisions/research

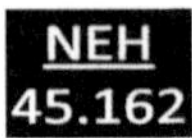

PROMOTION OF THE HUMANITIES TEACHING & LEARNING RESOURCES & CURRICULUM DEVELOPMENT

Award: Project Grants

Purpose: Humanities Initiatives at Historically Black, Hispanic-Serving Institutions, and Tribal Colleges and Universities are designed to strengthen humanities teaching and learning at these institutions.

Applicant Eligibility: Public and nonprofit U.S. Historically Black Colleges or Universities (HBCU) as defined by Executive Order 13532, Hispanic-serving institutions of higher education (HSI) recognized by the U.S. Department of Education, tribal colleges or universities as defined by Executive Order 13270, and public and nonprofit 501(c)(3) community colleges.

Beneficiary Eligibility: U.S. public and nonprofit 501(c)(3) organizations (including institutions of higher education), state and local governmental agencies, federally recognized Native American tribal governments, humanities scholars, and the general public.

Award Range/Average: Do not exceed $100,000.

Funding: (Project Grants) FY 17 $2,772,500; FY 18 est $2,900,000; FY 19 N/A FY 16 $15,339,908.

HQ: Division of Education Programs 400 Seventh Street SW
Washington, DC 20506
Phone: 202-606-8463
http://www.neh.gov

PROPERTY IMPROVEMENT LOAN INSURANCE FOR IMPROVING ALL EXISTING STRUCTURES & BUILDING OF NEW NONRESIDENTIAL STRUCTURES "Title I"

Award: Guaranteed/Insured Loans

Purpose: To assist the financing of improvements to homes and other property types.

Applicant Eligibility: Eligible borrowers include the owner of the property to be improved, a lessee having a lease extending at least 6 months beyond maturity of the loan, or a purchaser of the property under a land installment contract.

Beneficiary Eligibility: Individuals/families.

Award Range/Average: No Data Available.

Funding: (Sale, Exchange, or Donation of Property and Goods) FY 15 $90,000,000; FY 16 est $90,000,000; FY 17 est $90,000,000.

HQ: 451 7th Street SW
Washington, DC 20410
Phone: 800-225-5342
http://portal.hud.gov/hudportal/hud?src=/program_offices/housing/sfh/title/ti_home

PROTECTING & IMPROVING HEALTH GLOBALLY: BUILDING & STRENGTHENING PUBLIC HEALTH IMPACT, SYSTEMS, CAPACITY & SECURITY "Global Health"

Award: Cooperative Agreements

Purpose: To assist Ministries of Health and other international partners to plan, manage effectively, and evaluate public health programs.

Applicant Eligibility: Dependent on the FOA, eligibility may range from open, competitive, limited, or single eligibility in accordance with authorizing legislation.

Beneficiary Eligibility: This will benefit individuals worldwide, including in the U.S., through collaborations with national Ministries of Health and other organizations/institutions. This is only for non-research activities supported by CDC/ATSDR.

Award Range/Average: No Data Available.

Funding: (Cooperative Agreements) FY 17 $97,771,052; FY 18 est $77,987,031; FY 19 est $0.

HQ: 1600 Clifton Road, P.O. Box 29
Atlanta, GA 30329
Phone: 404-639-7276
Email: ctg8@cdc.gov
http://www.cdc.gov

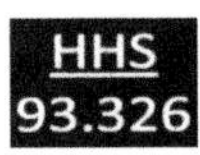

PROTECTING & IMPROVING HEALTH GLOBALLY: STRENGTHENING PUBLIC HEALTH THROUGH SURVEILLANCE, EPIDEMIOLOGIC RESEARCH, DISEASE DETECTION & PREVENTION "Global Health Research"

Award: Cooperative Agreements

Purpose: To assist Ministries of Health and other international partners to plan, effectively manage and conduct public health research in the intent of public health protection; achieve U.S. Government program and international organization goals to improve health; including surveillance, intervention and prevention in global health programs.

Applicant Eligibility: Dependent on the FOA, eligibility may range from open, competitive, limited or single eligibility in accordance with authorizing legislation. May include non-profit organizations who may be domestic, international or Ministries of Health.

Beneficiary Eligibility: This will benefit individuals worldwide, including in the U.S., through collaborations with the national Ministries of Health and other organizations/institutions. This is only for research activities supported by CDC/ATSDR.

Award Range/Average: No Data Available.

Funding: (Cooperative Agreements) FY 17 N/A FY 18 N/A FY 19 est $0; FY 16 $189,100.

HQ: 1600 Cliton Road
Atlanta, GA 30047
Phone: 404-639-7618
Email: lek7@cdc.gov

PROTECTION & ADVOCACY FOR INDIVIDUALS WITH MENTAL ILLNESS "PAIMI"

Award: Formula Grants

Purpose: To enable the expansion of the Protection and Advocacy system established in each State.

Applicant Eligibility: State, local, and territory government agencies, public or private organizations designated by the Governor under Part C of the Developmental Disabilities Assistance and Bill of Rights Acts as systems to protect and advocate the rights of persons with developmental disabilities in that State.

Beneficiary Eligibility: Individuals with significant mental illness or severe emotional impairment (children) who are at risk for abuse, neglect, or civil rights violations while residing in care or treatment facilities have service priority. Persons with significant mental illness and severe emotional impairment living in the community, including their own home, may be served as determined by their state protection and advocacy systems PAIMI program funded priorities and objectives and available resources includes persons who are in the process of being admitted to a facility rendering care or treatment, persons being transported to such a facility, or persons who are involuntarily confined in a municipal detention facility, jails, or prisons.

Award Range/Average: $229,300 to $3,140,635; Average is $619,645

Funding: (Formula Grants) FY 17 $35,319,775; FY 18 est $35,329,908; FY 19 est $35,335,604.

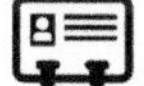

HQ: 5600 Fishers Lane
Rockville, MD 20857
Phone: 240-276-1078
Email: odessa.crocker@samhsa.hhs.gov
http://www.samhsa.gov

PROVISION OF TECHNICAL ASSISTANCE & TRAINING ACTIVITIES TO ASSURE COMPREHENSIVE CANCER CONTROL OUTCOMES

Award: Cooperative Agreements

Purpose: To fund up to two national organizations with proven capacities and expertise in chronic disease prevention and health promotion to provide technical assistance and training to National Comprehensive Cancer Control Program awardees and their coalitions to implement evidence-based and promising comprehensive cancer control interventions in the areas of primary prevention, screening and survivorship.

Applicant Eligibility: Eligible applicants: National 501(c) 3 organizations; Public Non-for profits National 501(c)3 organizations comprised of affiliates or chapters at state and/or local levels or universities with national reach who have the capacity to provide technical assistance and training to all funded grantees of the National Comprehensive Cancer Control Program.

Beneficiary Eligibility: Federal, State, Local

Award Range/Average: No Data Available.

Funding: (Cooperative Agreements) FY 17 $0; FY 18 est $1,325,000; FY 19 est $1,325,000.

HQ: Public Health Advisor 4770 Buford Highway, P.O. Box 76
Atlanta, GA 30341
Phone: 770-488-4296
Email: jfonseka@cdc.gov
http://www.cdc.gov

PUBLIC & INDIAN HOUSING INDIAN LOAN GUARANTEE PROGRAM

"Loan Guarantees for Indian Housing"

Award: Guaranteed/Insured Loans

Purpose: With the help of a guaranteed mortgage loan program available through private financial institutions, homeownership opportunities are provided to the Native Americans, Tribes, Indian Housing Authorities including Tribally Designated Housing Entities (TDHEs), and Indian Housing Authorities on Indian land.

Applicant Eligibility: The loan applicant must be members of a federally recognized Indian tribe, band or community, which includes Native Americans, Alaska Natives, or an Indian Housing Authority including a Tribally Designated Housing Authority (TDHE) or a Tribe which meets certain requirements. Applicant eligibility is validated by current enrollment in a federally recognized tribe.

Beneficiary Eligibility: The homeowner is the ultimate beneficiary of the program. When the Indian Housing Authority, TDHE or Tribe is the homebuyer, they may then rent the property.

Award Range/Average: The average loan amount in FY 2014 was $176,000.

Funding: (Guaranteed/Insured Loans) FY 18 est $4,006,000; FY 16 $4,492,000; FY 17 est $4,999,000.

HQ: 7th Street SW, Room 5156
Washington, DC 20410
Phone: 202-402-4978
Email: thomas.c.wright@hud.gov
http://www.hud.gov/offices/pih/ih/homeownership/184

PUBLIC & INDIAN HOUSING TRANSFORMATION INITIATIVE (TI) TECHNICAL ASSISTANCE (TA)

Award: Provision of Specialized Services

Purpose: To increase the operational efficiency of PIH processes, which is a key step toward capacity building and technical awareness of HUD's mission.

Applicant Eligibility: Increasing the operation efficiency of PIH processes is a key step toward capacity building and technical awareness that are at the heart of HUD's mission.

Beneficiary Eligibility: Public and Indian Housing Transformation Initiatives Technical Assistance ultimate beneficiaries are those who receive assistance. These initiatives will improve the way the Department operates.

Award Range/Average: Range $34,000 - $5,320,000 Average $2,130,000

Funding: (Provision of Specialized Services) FY 17 est $0; FY 18 est $0; FY 16 $0.

HQ: 451 7th Dt SW, Room 4246
Washington, DC 20410
Phone: 202-402-4307
Email: gary.f.vanbuskirk@hud.gov

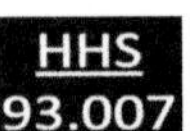

PUBLIC AWARENESS CAMPAIGNS ON EMBRYO ADOPTION "Embryo Donation/Adoption"

Award: Project Grants

Purpose: To increase public awareness of embryo adoption as a method of family building and to provide services to infertile individuals.

Applicant Eligibility: Eligible applicants include public agencies, nonprofit organizations, and for-profit organizations. Eligibility to compete for this announcement is limited to particular applicant organizations.

Beneficiary Eligibility: The beneficiaries for this program are potential donors and/or recipients of frozen embryos.

Award Range/Average: $100,000 - $300,000

Funding: (Project Grants) FY 16 $680,000; FY 17 est $688,000; FY 18 N/A.

HQ: 1101 Wootton Parkway Tower Building, Suite 550
Rockville, MD 20852
Phone: 240-453-8822
Email: eric.west@hhs.gov
http://www.opa.gov

PUBLIC DIPLOMACY PROGRAMS

Award: Project Grants

Purpose: To support the achievement of U.S. foreign policy goals and objectives, advance national interests, and enhance national security by informing and influencing foreign publics.

Applicant Eligibility: See specific announcement in www.grants.

Beneficiary Eligibility: Local organizations, See specific announcement in www.grants.

Award Range/Average: Range between $10,000 and $5,000,000. Average $50,000.

Funding: (Project Grants) FY 17 FY 18 FY 16 - Public Diplomacy funds are for use by Embassies worldwide.

HQ: 2200 C Street NW R/PPR/R, 5th Floor
Washington, DC 2052
Phone: 202-632-3341

PUBLIC HEALTH CONFERENCE SUPPORT
"Centers for Disease Control and Prevention (CDC) National Center for HIV, Viral Hepatitis, Sexually Transmitted Disease and Tuberculosis Prevention (NCHHSTP) Public Health Conference Support"

Award: Cooperative Agreements

Purpose: Allows state and local governments, their Bona Fide Agents, non-governmental organizations and the general public to request funds for partial support for public health conferences related to the health promotion, education and prevention of HIV, Viral Hepatitis, STD and TB Prevention.

Applicant Eligibility: N/A

Beneficiary Eligibility: N/A

Award Range/Average: $25,000 to $125,000 with an average of $30,000.

Funding: Formula Grants (Cooperative Agreements) FY 17 $500,000; FY 18 est $500,000; FY 19 FY 16 $500,000.

HQ: 1600 Clifton Road NE, P.O. Box E-07
Atlanta, GA 30333
Phone: 404-639-1877
Email: lrw3@cdc.gov
http://www.cdc.gov

PUBLIC HEALTH EMERGENCY PREPAREDNESS

Award: Cooperative Agreements

Purpose: To offer critical source of funding, guidance, and technical assistance for state, territorial, and local public health departments.

Applicant Eligibility: State health departments of all 50 States, the District of Columbia, the nation's three largest municipalities (New York City, Chicago and Los Angeles County), the Commonwealths of Puerto Rico and the Northern Mariana Islands, the territories of American Samoa, Guam and the U.S. Virgin Islands, the Federated States of Micronesia, and the Republics of Palau and the Marshall Islands.

Beneficiary Eligibility: All State, County, and Local Health Departments.

Award Range/Average: No Data Available.

Funding: (Cooperative Agreements) FY 18 est $0; FY 16 $25,100,000; FY 17 est $24,577,907.

HQ: 1600 Clifton Road, P.O. Box D29
Atlanta, GA 30329
Phone: 404-639-5276
Email: vbk5@cdc.gov
http://www.cdc.gov

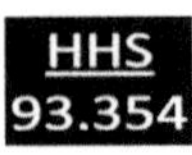

PUBLIC HEALTH EMERGENCY RESPONSE: COOPERATIVE AGREEMENT FOR EMERGENCY RESPONSE: PUBLIC HEALTH CRISIS RESPONSE
"Public Health Crisis Response Awards"

Award: Cooperative Agreements

Purpose: To fund state, local, and territorial public health departments for HHS Secretarial declared and non-declared public health emergencies having an overwhelming impact on jurisdictional resources.

Applicant Eligibility: State government public health departments or their bona fide agents (N=50), Local health departments or their bona fide agents (N=6) (city or county) consistent with PHEP and ELC awardees, which include: Chicago Department of Public Health, District of Columbia Department of Health, Houston Department of Health and Human Services, Los Angeles County Department of Health Services - Public Health, New York City Department of Health and Mental Hygiene, and Philadelphia Department of Public Health, Territorial governments or their bona fide agents (N=8) in the Commonwealth of Puerto Rico, the US Virgin Islands, the Commonwealth of the Northern Marianna Islands, American Samoa, Guam, the Federated States of Micronesia, the Republic of the Marshall Islands, and the Republic of Palau, Tribal Public Health Departments – (N=5) Federally recognized tribal governments meeting the core criteria outlined for all eligible applicants and that serve, through their own PH infrastructure, at least 50,000 people and have demonstrable PH capacity.

Beneficiary Eligibility: Same as Applicant Eligibility.

Award Range/Average: Due to the nature of the issues that would trigger CDC to activate this NOFO as designed, it is difficult to project the total funding amount that would be made available. While CDC will use this NOFO, it is expected to be for the time necessary to respond to the emergency and that long-term recovery needs and/or emergencies that shift from an epidemic to an endemic nature would be addressed by other NOFOs as appropriate.

Funding: N/A

HQ: 1600 Clifton Road NE, P.O. Box D29
Atlanta, GA 30329
Phone: 404-639-0817
Email: ssharpe@cdc.gov

PUBLIC HEALTH PREPAREDNESS & RESPONSE SCIENCE, RESEARCH, AND PRACTICE
"Public Health Preparedness Science"

Award: Cooperative Agreements; Project Grants

Purpose: To conduct research and related public health preparedness and response (PHPR) program activities to build the scientific evidence base for public health preparedness, response, and recovery (PHPRR).

Applicant Eligibility: Eligible applicants may include public and private nonprofit and for profit organizations and governments and their agencies, such as: public nonprofit organizations private nonprofit organizations, for-profit organizations, small, minority, women-owned businesses, universities, colleges, research institutions, hospitals, community-based organizations, faith-based organizations, Federally Recognized Indian Tribal Governments, Indian tribes, Indian tribal organizations, state and local governments or their bona fide agents (this includes the District of Columbia, the Commonwealth of Puerto Rico, the Virgin Islands, the Commonwealth of the Northern Marianna Islands, American Samoa, Guam, the Federated States of Micronesia, the Republic of the Marshall Islands, and the Republic of Palau), political subdivisions of states (in consultation with States)

Beneficiary Eligibility: Same as Applicant Eligibility

Award Range/Average: No Data Available.

Funding: (Cooperative Agreements) FY 17 $0; FY 18 est $0; FY 19 est $0; FY 16 $0.

HQ: Resource Management 1600 Clifton Road, P.O. Box D-29
Atlanta, GA 30329
Phone: 404-639-5276
http://www.cdc.gov/phpr/science/research.htm

PUBLIC HEALTH SERVICE EVALUATION FUNDS
"PHS Evaluation Funds"

Award: Cooperative Agreements

Purpose: To carry out evaluations of teen pregnancy prevention approaches.

Applicant Eligibility: Nonprofit, for profit, small businesses, community based organizations, faith based organizations, universities, hospitals, state and local governments, US territories and possessions, tribal entities, native American organizations are eligible to apply.

Beneficiary Eligibility: Researchers, Policymakers, Teens, Parents

Award Range/Average: $357,345 awarded for a fully funded 2 year project period from FY 16-FY 18

Funding: (Cooperative Agreements) FY 17 $1,500,000; FY 18 N/A FY 19 N/A FY 16 $357,345.

HQ: 1101 Wootton Parkway, Suite 550
Rockville, MD 20852
Phone: 240-453-8822
Email: alice.bettencourt@hhs.gov
http://www.hhs.gov/oah

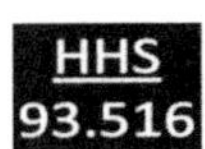

PUBLIC HEALTH TRAINING CENTERS PROGRAM "Regional Public Health Training Center (PHTC) and the National Coordinating Center for Public Health Training (NCCPHT) Programs"

Award: Cooperative Agreements; Project Grants

Purpose: To improve the Nation's public health system by strengthening the technical, scientific, managerial and leadership competencies of the current and future public health workforce through the provision of education, training and consultation services.

Applicant Eligibility: Accredited school of public health, or another public or nonprofit private institution accredited for the provision of graduate or specialized training in public health. This program also includes a statutory funding preference for accredited schools of public health.

Beneficiary Eligibility: Each trainee receiving stipend support must be a citizen of the United States, a non-citizen U.S. national, or a foreign national having in his or her possession a visa permitting permanent residence in the United States.

Award Range/Average: Range: NCCPHT: - $845,000. Regional PHTCs: - $780,000 to $1,105,000 (Dependent on Region)

Funding: (Cooperative Agreements) FY 17 $8,250,000; FY 18 est $9,100,000; FY 19 est $0; FY 16 $8,250,000; - Regional PHTCs(Cooperative Agreements) FY 17 $845,000; FY 18 N/A FY 19 est $0.

HQ: Department of Health and Human Services 5600 Fishers Lane 11N94D
Rockville, MD 20857
Phone: 301-443-1057
Email: mjenkins@hrsa.gov
http://www.hrsa.gov

PUBLIC HOUSING CAPITAL FUND "CFP"

Award: Formula Grants

Purpose: To provide funds annually to Public Housing Agencies (PHAs) for capital and management activities and permit PHAs to use Capital Funds for financing activities, in standard PHA developments and in mixed-finance developments.

Applicant Eligibility: The PHA must demonstrate that it has the legal authority to develop, own, modernize and operate a public housing development in accordance with the 1937 Act.

Beneficiary Eligibility: Low-income public housing residents.

Award Range/Average: $5,527 to $300,862,746; Average: $583,427

Funding: (Formula Grants) FY 17 $1,785,565,332; FY 18 est $2,750,000,000; FY 19 est $0; FY 16 $1,799,528,000.

HQ: 451 7th Street
Washington, DC 20410
Phone: 202-402-2488
Email: ivan.m.pour@hud.gov
http://www.hud.gov/offices/pih/programs/ph/capfund/index.cfm

PUBLIC HOUSING FAMILY SELF-SUFFICIENCY UNDER RESIDENT OPPORTUNITY & SUPPORTIVE SERVICES "Public Housing Family Self-Sufficiency (PH FSS))"

Award: Project Grants

Purpose: To promote the development of local strategies and enable participating families to achieve economic independence and housing self-sufficiency.

Applicant Eligibility: Public Housing Authorities (PHAs) and Tribes and tribally designated housing entities (TDHEs).

Beneficiary Eligibility: Individuals and families who are residents of conventional public or Indian housing are eligible to receive benefits from the ROSS program.

Award Range/Average: The average financial assistance was $60,036.

Funding: (Project Grants) FY 16 est $0; FY 17 est $0; FY 15 $0.

HQ: 451 7th Street SW, Room 4238
Washington, DC 20410
Phone: 202-402-2341
Email: anice.m.schervish@hud.gov
http://www.hud.gov/offices/pih/programs/ph/ross

PUBLIC SAFETY OFFICERS' BENEFITS PROGRAM "PSOB"

Award: Direct Payments with Unrestricted Use

Purpose: To provide death benefits to the eligible survivors of federal, state, or local public safety officers whose deaths are the direct and proximate result of a traumatic injury sustained in the line of duty.

Applicant Eligibility: Public safety officer means-- (A) an individual serving a public agency in an official capacity, with or without compensation, as a law enforcement officer, as a firefighter, or as a chaplain; (B) an employee of the Federal Emergency Management Agency who is performing official duties of the Agency in an area, if those official duties— (i) are related to a major disaster or emergency that has been, or is later, declared to exist with respect to the area under the Robert T. Stafford Disaster Relief and Emergency Assistance Act; and (ii) are determined by the Administrator of the Federal Emergency Management Agency to be hazardous duties; (C) an employee of a State, local, or tribal emergency management or civil defense agency who is performing official duties in cooperation with the Federal Emergency Management Agency in an area, if those official duties.

Beneficiary Eligibility: The Public Safety Officers' Benefits (PSOB) Act, enacted in 1976, was designed to offer peace of mind to men and women seeking careers in public safety and to make a strong statement about the value American society places on the contributions of those who serve their communities in potentially dangerous circumstances. The PSOB Program provides a one-time financial benefit to the eligible survivors of public safety officers whose deaths are the direct and proximate result of a traumatic injury sustained in the line of duty.

Award Range/Average: N/A.

Funding: (Direct Payments with Unrestricted Use) FY 17 $16,300,000; FY 18 est $16,300,000; FY 19 FY 16 $13,770,525; - (Direct Payments with Unrestricted Use) FY 17 $136,780,600; FY 18 est $24,800,000; FY 19 est $16,300,000.

HQ: 810 7th Street NW
Washington, DC 20531
Phone: 888-744-6513
Email: askpsob@usdoj.gov
http://www.psob.gov

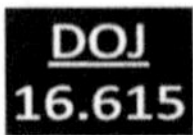

DOJ 16.615 PUBLIC SAFETY OFFICERS' EDUCATIONAL ASSISTANCE "PSOEA"

Award: Direct Payments with Unrestricted Use

Purpose: To provide financial assistance for higher education to the spouses and children of public safety officers killed in line of duty.

Applicant Eligibility: Spouses and children who attend a program of education at an eligible institution and are the spouse and/or surviving children under the age of 27 of federal, state, and local public safety officers whose deaths or permanent and totally disabling injuries are covered by the Public Safety Officers' Benefits (PSOB) Program (34 U.S.C. §§ 10281-10288) are eligible for this program.

Beneficiary Eligibility: The spouse and surviving children of federal, state, and local public safety officers receive the ultimate benefits from this program. The children may receive benefits for classes taken before their 27th birthday.

Award Range/Average: For classes taken since October 1, 2016, the rates of assistance are $1024 per month for full-time students, $767 for three-quarter-time students, $510 for half-time students, and $256 for less-than-half-time students.

Funding: (Direct Payments with Unrestricted Use) FY 17 $4,602,215; FY 18 FY 19 FY 16 $4,000,000.

HQ: 810 7th Street NW
Washington, DC 20531
Phone: 202-616-6500
Email: askpsob@usdoj.gov
http://www.bja.gov/programdetails.aspx?program_id=78

DOC 11.550 PUBLIC TELECOMMUNICATIONS FACILITIES PLANNING & CONSTRUCTION "PTFP"

Award: Project Grants

Purpose: To compensate for installation and modernization of public telecommunication facilities, to extend delivery of public telecommunications services and non-broadcast technologies, to increase public telecommunication services operated by minorities and women, and to provide telecommunication services to the public.

Applicant Eligibility: A public or noncommercial educational broadcast station; a noncommercial telecommunications entity; a system of public telecommunications entities; a nonprofit foundation, corporation, institution or association organized primarily for educational or cultural purposes; State, local, and Indian Tribal governments (or an agency thereof); or a political or special purpose subdivision of a State. Special consideration is given to applications which would increase minority and women's ownership of, operation of, and participation in public telecommunications entities.

Beneficiary Eligibility: General public and students.

Award Range/Average: $5,122 to $731,924. Average $177,889

Funding: N/A

HQ: 1401 Constitution Avenue NW, Room 4888 NTIA/OPCM
Washington, DC 20230
Phone: 202-482-5515
Email: writchie@ntia.doc.gov
http://www.ntia.doc.gov/ptfp

QUALIFIED PARTICIPATING ENTITIES (QPE) RISK SHARING "542(b) Risk Sharing Program)"

Award: Guaranteed/Insured Loans

Purpose: To provide reinsurance on multifamily housing projects whose loans are originated, underwritten, serviced, and disposed of.

Applicant Eligibility: Eligible mortgagors include investors, builders, developers, public entities, and private nonprofit corporations or associations may apply to a qualified QPE and/or its lender.

Beneficiary Eligibility: Individuals, families, and property owners may be eligible for affordable housing.

Award Range/Average: No Data Available.

Funding: (Guaranteed/Insured Loans) FY 17 est $66,633,349; FY 15 $14,352,529; FY 16 est $40,873,150; FY 14 est $300,000,000; FY 13 $315,000,000.

HQ: 451 7th Street SW
Washington, DC 20410
Phone: 202-402-2579
Email: carmelita_a._james@hud.gov
http://www.hud.gov/offices/hsg/hsgmulti.cfm

USDA 10.605 QUALITY SAMPLES PROGRAM "QSP"

Award: Direct Payments for Specified Use

Purpose: The Quality Samples Program maximizes exporting of U.S. agricultural commodities by assisting U.S. entities to promote a high quality of U.S. agricultural commodities.

Applicant Eligibility: To be approved, an applicant must be a U.S. private or government entity.

Beneficiary Eligibility: The Quality Samples Program is intended to benefit a represented U.S. industry rather than a specific company or brand.

Award Range/Average: range $15,000 to $75,000

Funding: (Project Grants) FY 17 $1,223,975; FY 18 est $2,000,000; FY 19 FY 16 est $1,381,344.

HQ: 1400 Independence Avenue SW
Washington, DC 20050
Phone: 202-720-8557
Email: lona.powell@fas.usda.gov
http://www.fas.usda.gov/programs/quality-samples-program-qsp

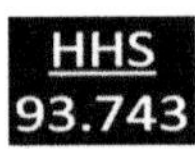

RACIAL & ETHNIC APPROACHES TO COMMUNITY HEALTH: OBESITY & HYPERTENSION DEMONSTRATION PROJECTS FINANCED SOLELY BY PREVENTION & PUBLIC HEALTH FUNDS "Racial and Ethnic Approaches to Community Health (REACH)"

Award: Cooperative Agreements

Purpose: Supports the implementation of projects to reduce racial and ethnic health disparities.

Applicant Eligibility: Applications may be submitted by State or local governments or their Bona Fide Agents (this includes the District of Columbia, the Commonwealth of Puerto Rico, the Virgin Islands, the Commonwealth of the Northern Marianna Islands, American Samoa, Guam, the Federated States of Micronesia, the Republic of the Marshall Islands, and the Republic of Palau). Eligible applicants also include public and private nonprofit organizations, for profit organizations, small, minority, women-owned businesses, universities, colleges, research institutions, hospitals, community-based organizations, faith-based organizations, Federally recognized Indian tribal governments, Indian tribes, and Indian tribal organizations.

Beneficiary Eligibility: The general public will benefit from the objectives of this program. Additionally, colleges, universities, private non-profit and public nonprofit domestic organizations, research institutions, and faith-based organization, states, political subdivisions of states, local health authorities, and individuals or organizations with specialized health interests will benefit.

Award Range/Average: Range $1,500,000 – $4,000,000

Funding: N/A

HQ: 4770 Buford Highway NE, P.O. Box K40 NCCDPHP
Atlanta, GA 30333
Phone: 770-488-2524

RACIAL & ETHNIC APPROACHES TO COMMUNITY HEALTH "REACH National Networks"

Award: Cooperative Agreements

Purpose: To fund National Networks to fund, manage, support, and monitor sub-recipients to address health disparities and implement evidence- and practice-based strategies that reduce health disparities for intervention population(s) experiencing high burden of disease or risk factors.

Applicant Eligibility: In continuation years, eligibility is limited to the six (6) existing original awardees: Asian and Pacific Islander American Health Forum, Hidalgo Medical Services, National Council of Young Men's Christian Association of the USA, National REACH Coalition, Regents of the University of California, Los Angeles, University of Colorado Denver

Beneficiary Eligibility: The general public will benefit from the objectives of this program.

Award Range/Average: No Data Available.

Funding: (Cooperative Agreements) FY 17 $23,230,732; FY 18 est $23,197,325; FY 19 est $23,197,325.

HQ: 4770 Buford Highway, P.O. Box F-81
Atlanta, GA 30341
Phone: 770-488-8438
http://www.cdc.gov

RAIL & TRANSIT SECURITY GRANT PROGRAM "TSGP/IPR (AMTRAK)"

Award: Project Grants

Purpose: The TSGP and IPR lay a few sets of measures for the Homeland Security to strengthen the nation's preparedness and resilience against terrorist and cyber attacks.

Applicant Eligibility: Agencies eligible for FY 2018 TSGP are determined based upon daily unlinked passenger trips (ridership) and transit systems that serve historically eligible Urban Area Security Initiative (UASI) jurisdictions. Certain ferry systems are eligible to participate in the FY 2018 TSGP and receive funds.

Beneficiary Eligibility: Specialized group; general public.

Award Range/Average: For more information, refer to the FY 2018 TSGP and IPR Program Notice of Funding Opportunity (NOFO).

Funding: (Project Grants) FY 17 $10,000,000; FY 18 est $10,000,000; FY 19 est $9,999,997.

HQ: 400 C Street SW
Washington, DC 20523
Phone: 800-368-6498
http://www.fema.gov/government/grant/index.shtm

RARE DISORDERS: RESEARCH, SURVEILLANCE, HEALTH PROMOTION, AND EDUCATION "Rare Disorders and Health Outcomes"

Award: Cooperative Agreements

Purpose: To promote public health capacity by conducting research to expand the knowledge base around people with complex disabling conditions, including muscular dystrophy, fragile X syndrome and spina bifida across the lifespan.

Applicant Eligibility: N/A

Beneficiary Eligibility: State; Local; Public nonprofit institution/organization; Federally Recognized Indian Tribal Governments; Individuals/Families affected by rare disorder/conditions; Private nonprofit institution/organizations, minority populations including Spanish speaking populations.

Award Range/Average: $20,530 to $500,000.

Funding: (Cooperative Agreements) FY 17 $6,044,277; FY 18 est $5,818,927; FY 19 est $5,818,927; FY 16 $5,754,724.

HQ: 1600 Clifton Road NE, P.O. Box E88
Atlanta, GA 30329
Phone: 404-498-3042

REFUGEE & ENTRANT ASSISTANCE DISCRETIONARY GRANTS

Award: Project Grants

Purpose: Grant programs seeks to decrease the numbers of refugees on public assistance and the length of time refugees require such assistance.

Applicant Eligibility: Public and private nonprofit agencies may apply for these grants.

Beneficiary Eligibility: Refugees, certain Amerasians, Cuban and Haitian entrants, asylees, certified victims of a severe form of trafficking, and Special Immigrants from Iraq and Afghanistan.

Award Range/Average: Refugee Health Promotion grants range from a minimum of $83,055 to a maximum of $203,055. TAG and SS Discretionary grants range from a minimum of $23,500 to a maximum of $10,384,000

Funding: (Project Grants) FY 17 $4,600,000; FY 18 est $4,600,000; FY 19 est $4,600,000; FY 16 $4,600,000; - Refugee Health PromotionProject Grants (Discretionary) FY 17 $33,263,046; FY 18 est $42,619,000; FY 19 est $40,000,000; FY 16 $45,036,000; - SS Discretionary

HQ: Mary E Switzer Building 330 C Street SW
Washington, DC 20201
Phone: 202-401-4559
Email: anastasia.brown@acf.hhs.gov
http://www.acf.hhs.gov/programs/orr/programs

REFUGEE & ENTRANT ASSISTANCE STATE/REPLACEMENT DESIGNEE ADMINISTERED PROGRAMS

"Refugee Cash and Medical Assistance Program and Refugee Social Services Program"

Award: Formula Grants

Purpose: Reimburses States and State Replacement Designees for the cost of cash and medical assistance provided to refugees, certain Amerasians from Vietnam, Cuban and Haitian entrants, asylees, victims of a severe form of trafficking, and Iraqi and Afghan Special Immigrants during the first eight months after their arrival in this country or grant of asylum.

Applicant Eligibility: State agencies, State Replacement Designees, and Wilson/Fish Alternative projects are eligible to apply for these funds.

Beneficiary Eligibility: Refugees, certain Amerasians from Vietnam, Cuban and Haitian entrants, asylees, victims of a severe form of trafficking, and Iraqi and Afghan Special Immigrants are eligible for benefits and services.

Award Range/Average: Refugee Cash and Medical Assistance program ranged from $17,197 to $106,841,265; the average was $6,189,740. Grants for the Refugee Social Services program ranged from $75,000 to $45,033,129; the average was $2,429,000. In FY 2018, Refugee Social Services is renamed to Refugee Support Services.

Funding: (Formula Grants) FY 17 $121,359,160; FY 18 est $159,982,000; FY 19 est $116,221,000; FY 16 $121,870,000; - Social Services Formula Grants(Formula Grants) FY 17 $377,574,141; FY 18 est $236,500,000; FY 19 est $257,100,000; FY 16 $409,600,000; - Refugee Cas

HQ: Mary E Switzer Building 330 C Street SW, 8th Floor W
Washington, DC 20201
Phone: 202-205-5933
Email: carl.rubenstein@acf.hhs.gov
http://www.acf.hhs.gov/programs/orr

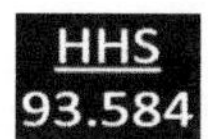

REFUGEE & ENTRANT ASSISTANCE TARGETED ASSISTANCE GRANTS
"Targeted Assistance Grants Program"

Award: Formula Grants

Purpose: The Targeted Assistance Grant program provides funding for employment-related and other social services for refugees that includes certain Amerasians from Vietnam, Cuban and Haitian entrants.

Applicant Eligibility: (includes District of Columbia), State agencies, State Replacement Designees, and Wilson/Fish Alternative Projects are eligible to receive funding for assistance to counties and Targeted Assistance areas where, because of factors such as large refugee population, there exists a need for supplementation of available resources for services to refugees.

Beneficiary Eligibility: Beneficiaries include refugees, certain Amerasians from Vietnam, Cuban and Haitian entrants, asylees, victims of a severe form of trafficking, and Iraqi and Afghan Special Immigrants. Potential beneficiaries must be within five years of arrival in this country or grant of asylum to be eligible for services.

Award Range/Average: In FY 2017, Awards ranged from $48,268 to $9,384,988. The average award was $683,094.

Funding: (Formula Grants) FY 17 $41,196,858; FY 18 est $0; FY 19 est $0; FY 16 $47,872,000.

HQ: Mary E Switzer Building 330 C Street SW 8th Floor W, 8th Floor W
Washington, DC 20201
Phone: 202-205-5933
Email: carl.rubenstein@acf.hhs.gov
http://www.acf.hhs.gov/programs/orr

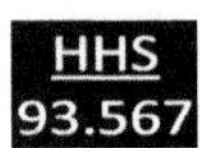

REFUGEE & ENTRANT ASSISTANCE VOLUNTARY AGENCY PROGRAMS
"Matching Grant Program"

Award: Formula Grants

Purpose: Assists refugees in becoming self-supporting and independent members of American society by providing grant funds to private nonprofit organizations to support case management, transitional assistance, and social services for new arrivals.

Applicant Eligibility: Grant awards are limited to private nonprofit organizations that have a Reception and Placement Cooperative Agreement with the Department of State or Department of Homeland Security.

Beneficiary Eligibility: Enrollment must occur within 31 days of the individual's date of eligibility. The date of eligibility for Matching Grant Services is counted from the date of arrival into the country for refugees and Amerasians; the date a Cuban/Haitian becomes an entrant; the date of the final grant of asylum for asylees; the date of the certification or eligibility letter for Victims of Severe Forms of Trafficking; and the date an SIV arrives in the U.S. or the date of adjustment of status if applying for Special Immigrant Status within the U.S. At least one member of the case unit must be deemed 'employable' for the case to be enrolled in the Matching Grant Program, and all other members must be otherwise Program eligible.

Award Range/Average: $1,786,400 to $19,406,200 with an average of $7,577,778.

Funding: (Formula Grants) FY 17 $68,200,000; FY 18 est $55,000,000; FY 19 est $60,000,000; FY 16 $76,309,200.

HQ: Mary E Switzer Building 330 C Street SW
Washington, DC 20201
Phone: 202-401-4559
Email: anastasia.brown@acf.hhs.gov
http://www.acf.hhs.gov/programs/orr/programs

REFUGEE & ENTRANT ASSISTANCE WILSON/FISH PROGRAM
"Wilson-Fish Program"

Award: Cooperative Agreements

Purpose: To develop alternative projects which promote early employment of refugees, certain Amerasians from Vietnam, Cuban and Haitian entrants, asylees, victims of a severe form of trafficking, and Iraqi and Afghan Special Immigrants.

Applicant Eligibility: Beginning in FY2015/2016, funding under this program is open only to those agencies that currently administer a Wilson-Fish project. ORR requires that appropriate proposals and applications are submitted and that a determination is made that the grantees are the ones that can "best perform" the services in accordance with 8 U.S.C.

Beneficiary Eligibility: Refugees, certain Amerasian immigrants from Vietnam, Cuban/Haitian entrants, asylees, victims of a severe of trafficking, and Iraqi and Afghan Special Immigrants are eligible for services and assistance through funded projects in a community. Cash assistance is transitional for up to 8 months; services may be provided for up to five years.

Award Range/Average: In FY 2017 awards ranged from $295,996 to $7,364,452

Funding: (Cooperative Agreements) FY 17 $30,546,996; FY 18 est $19,000,000; FY 19 est $26,500,000.

HQ: Mary E Switzer Building 330 C Street SW
Washington, DC 20201
Phone: 202-205-5266
Email: colleen.mahar-piersma@acf.hhs.gov
http://www.acf.hhs.gov/programs/orr

REGIONAL DEMOCRACY PROGRAM "Iran Assistance"

Award: Cooperative Agreements; Cooperative Agreements; Project Grants

Purpose: Supports democracy and human rights in the Near East region.

Applicant Eligibility: Non-profit, for-profit organizations or state and local governments interested in partnering with the NEA/AC to promote democratic change in the Near East.

Beneficiary Eligibility: Any award made using State/NEA funds requires the full complement of standard federal forms and budget documents, CVs of main program staff, as dictated by the U.S. Department of State, Bureau of Administration, and the relevant OMB circulars.

Award Range/Average: The range is $500,000 to $2,500,000 with an average of $1,500,000.

Funding: N/A

HQ: 2430 E Street NW
Washington, DC 20037
Phone: 202-776-8691
Email: curleysl@state.gov

REGIONAL INFORMATION SHARING SYSTEMS "RISS"

Award: Project Grants

Purpose: To assist agencies in reducing violent crime and support law enforcement through officer safety, enhance the ability to identify, target, and remove criminal conspiracies and activities spanning multi-jurisdictional, multi-state, and sometime international boundaries.

Applicant Eligibility: Six RISS Centers are authorized as eligible to receive funding to provide services to law enforcement agencies throughout the nation. The Centers are: The Middle Atlantic Great-Lakes Organized Crime Law Enforcement Center (MAGLOCLEN), the Mid-States Organized Crime Information Center (MOCIC), the New England State Police Information Network (NESPIN), the Regional Organized Crime Information Center (ROCIC), the Rocky Mountain Information Network (RMIN), and the Western States Information Network (WSIN).

Beneficiary Eligibility: State and local criminal justice agencies; Federal, State, local, tribal, and territorial law enforcement agencies and personnel benefit from this program.

Award Range/Average: N/A

Funding: (Project Grants) FY 17 $31,616,261; FY 18 est $36,000,000; FY 19 est $10,000,000.

HQ: Bureau of Justice Assistance 810 7th Street NW
Washington, DC 20531

Phone: 202-616-6500

Email: david.p.lewis@usdoj.gov

http://www.riss.net

REGIONAL INNOVATION CLUSTERS

Award: Direct Payments for Specified Use

Purpose: To connect and enhance regional cluster initiatives so that small businesses can effectively leverage them to commercialize new technologies and expand into new markets, thereby positioning themselves and their regional economies for growth.

Applicant Eligibility: Educational institutions, public or private organizations and businesses, individuals, State and local governments, Indian tribes and lending and financial institutions and sureties that have the capability to provide the required business assistance.

Beneficiary Eligibility: Small business concerns as defined by industry size standards established by the U.S. Small Business Administration.

Award Range/Average: $5,000,000 to $6,000,000 cumulative.

Funding: (Direct Payments for Specified Use) FY 17 $3,259,000; FY 18 est $5,000,000; FY 19 est $0.

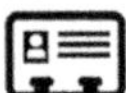

HQ: 409 3rd Street SW, 5th Floor

Washington, DC 20416

Phone: 202-205-7699

Email: matthew.stevens@sba.gov

http://www.sba.gov/clusters

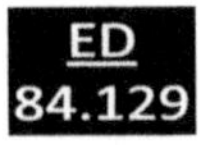

REHABILITATION LONG-TERM TRAINING

Award: Project Grants

Purpose: To support academic training project in areas of personnel shortages identified by the Secretary and to increase the number of personnel trained in vocational rehabilitation services to individuals with disabilities.

Applicant Eligibility: States and public or private nonprofit agencies and organizations, including Indian tribes and institutions of higher education.

Beneficiary Eligibility: Individuals preparing for employment in the field of rehabilitation counseling of individuals with disabilities.

Award Range/Average: to be determined.

Funding: (Project Grants) FY 17 $17,802,835; FY 18 est $18,610,980; FY 19 est $17,000,000.

HQ: OSERS Rehabilitation Services Administration 400 Maryland Avenue SW

Washington, DC 20202

Phone: 202-245-7343

Email: tom.finch@ed.gov

http://www.ed.gov/about/offices/list/osers/rsa/index.html

HUD 14.108

REHABILITATION MORTGAGE INSURANCE "203(k)"

Award: Guaranteed/Insured Loans

Purpose: To rehabilitate and repair single family properties. The program will allow a purchase or refinance transaction along with the loan amount the cost of making repairs and/or nonluxury improvements.

Applicant Eligibility: Individual and families.

Beneficiary Eligibility: Individuals and families.

Award Range/Average: No Data Available.

Funding: (Sale, Exchange, or Donation of Property and Goods) FY 16 FY 17 FY 15 - Reported Under 14.117.

HQ: Federal Housing Administration 451 Seventh Street SW
Washington, DC 20410
Phone: 800-225-5342

REHABILITATION SERVICES AMERICAN INDIANS WITH DISABILITIES

Award: Project Grants

Purpose: To provide vocational rehabilitation services to American Indians with disabilities that reside on or near Federal or State reservations.

Applicant Eligibility: Service projects: Governing bodies of Indian tribes, consortia of such governing bodies, or tribal organizations established and controlled by the governing bodies of Indian tribes, located on or near Federal and State reservations may apply. Training and technical assistance: State, local, or tribal governments, non-profit organizations, or institutions of higher education that have experience in the operation of AIVRS programs.

Beneficiary Eligibility: American Indians with disabilities residing on or near a Federal or State reservation who meet the definition of an individual with a disability in Section 7 (8) (A) of the Rehabilitation Act.

Award Range/Average: Range of new awards in FY 2016 was $365,000 to $1,550,000; Median new award: $550,000.

Funding: (Project Grants) FY 17 $43,000,000; FY 18 est $40,188,809; FY 19 est $43,300,000.

HQ: OSERS Rehabilitation Services Administration 400 Maryland Avenue SW
Washington, DC 20202
Phone: 202-245-7410
Email: august.martin@ed.gov
http://www.ed.gov/about/offices/list/osers/rsa/index.html

ED 84.161 REHABILITATION SERVICES CLIENT ASSISTANCE PROGRAM "CAP"

Award: Formula Grants

Purpose: To establish client assistance programs that provide information for clients and client-applicants of available benefits under the Rehabilitation Act; to assist clients and client-applicants in their relationships with projects and programs providing services under this Act; to inform individuals with disabilities in the State, of the services and benefits available under the Act and under Title I of the Americans with Disabilities Act.

Applicant Eligibility: States and Territories (through the Governor) and the protection and advocacy system serving the American Indian Consortium, are eligible for awards. With the exception of the protection and advocacy system serving the American Indian Consortium, the Governor designates a public or private agency to conduct the State's program.

Beneficiary Eligibility: Clients and client-applicants receiving services or interested in seeking assistance under the Rehabilitation Act of 1973, as amended, will benefit from CAP services.

Award Range/Average: For FY 2018, the estimated range of State awards (including the District of Columbia and Puerto Rico) under the distribution formula is $131,917 to $1,324,362, with a median award of $143,916. The FY 2018 amount for each of the four outlying areas and the American Indian Consortium is $59,477.

Funding: (Formula Grants) FY 17 $13,000,000; FY 18 est $13,000,000; FY 19 est $13,000,000.

HQ: OSERS Rehabilitation Services Administration 400 Maryland Avenue SW
Washington, DC 20202
Phone: 202-245-6769
Email: sandy.derobertis@ed.gov

ED 84.235 REHABILITATION SERVICES DEMONSTRATION & TRAINING PROGRAMS

Award: Project Grants

Purpose: To provide financial assistance to projects that expands and improve the provision of rehabilitation and research and evaluation activities authorized under the Act.

Applicant Eligibility: Eligible applicants are States and public or nonprofit organizations. Grants cannot be made directly to individuals.

Beneficiary Eligibility: Individuals with disabilities.

Award Range/Average: To be determined.

Funding: (Project Grants) FY 16 $5,796,000; FY 17 est $5,796,000; FY 18 est $5,796,000.

HQ: OSERS Rehabilitation Services Administration 400 Maryland Avenue SW
Washington, DC 20202
Phone: 202-245-7423
Email: mary.lovley@ed.gov

REHABILITATION SERVICES INDEPENDENT LIVING SERVICES FOR OLDER INDIVIDUALS WHO ARE BLIND

Award: Project Grants

Purpose: To provide any independent living services that are described in 34 CFR Section 367.3(b) to older individuals who are blind that improve or expand services for these individuals.

Applicant Eligibility: Any State agency in the 50 States and the District of Columbia and territories (Commonwealth of Puerto Rico and Virgin Islands) and outlying areas (Guam, American Samoa, and the Commonwealth of the Northern Mariana Islands) designated by the State as the State agency and authorized to provide rehabilitation services to blind individuals may apply. In order to receive assistance under this program, a designated state agency (DSA) must- submit in a timely manner and obtain approval from the Department of an application containing the agreements, assurances, and information that the Department determines to be necessary to carry out this program.

Beneficiary Eligibility: Older individuals who are blind, as defined in 34 C.F.

Award Range/Average: For FY 2018, the estimated range of State awards (including the District of Columbia and Puerto Rico) under the distribution formula is $225,000 to $3,373,204, with a median award of $421,728. The statutory amount for each of the four outlying areas is $40,000.

Funding: (Project Grants) FY 17 $33,317,000; FY 18 est $33,317,000; FY 19 est $33,317,000.

HQ: 400 Maryland Avenue SW
Washington, DC 20202
Phone: 202-245-7273
Email: james.billy@ed.gov

REHABILITATION SERVICES VOCATIONAL REHABILITATION GRANTS TO STATES

Award: Formula Grants

Purpose: To assist States in operating comprehensive, coordinated, effective, efficient and accountable programs of vocational rehabilitation (VR); to assess, plan, develop, and provide VR services for individuals with disabilities and engage in competitive integrated employment.

Applicant Eligibility: State agencies in all States (including territories/possessions) designated as the State agency to administer the VR program may receive funds with the submission and approval a VR services portion of the Unified or Combined State plan in accordance with section 101(a) of the Rehabilitation Act of 1973, as amended.

Beneficiary Eligibility: In order to be eligible for VR services, an individual must have a physical and/or mental impairment, which, for such an individual, constitutes or results in a substantial impediment to employment, and requires VR services to achieve an employment outcome.

Award Range/Average: In FY 2018 initial annual allotments to States, including D.C. and Puerto Rico ranged from $10.6 million to $296.3 million, with a median award of $44.4 million. Grants to outlying areas ranged from $0.8 million to $2.9 million.

Funding: (Formula Grants) FY 17 $3,121,053,774; FY 18 est $3,184,848,745; FY 19 est $3,260,626,620.

HQ: 400 Maryland Avenue SW
Washington, DC 20202
Phone: 202-245-7454
Email: suzanne.mitchell@ed.gov

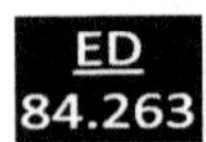

REHABILITATION TRAINING EXPERIMENTAL & INNOVATIVE TRAINING

Award: Project Grants

Purpose: To develop new types and methods of training programs for rehabilitation personnel to individuals with disabilities by designated State rehabilitation units or other public or non-profit rehabilitation service agencies or organizations.

Applicant Eligibility: States and public or private nonprofit agencies and organizations, including Indian tribes and institutions of higher education may apply.

Beneficiary Eligibility: Individuals preparing for or employed in positions relating to the rehabilitation of individuals with disabilities will benefit.

Award Range/Average: To be determined.

Funding: (Project Grants) FY 17 $0; FY 18 est $500,000; FY 19 est $500,000; FY 16 $0.

HQ: OSERS Rehabilitation Services Administration 400 Maryland Avenue SW
Washington, DC 20202
Phone: 202-245-7343
Email: tom.finch@ed.gov
http://www2.ed.gov/programs/rsatrain/index.html

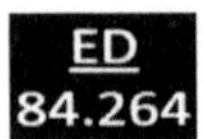

REHABILITATION TRAINING TECHNICAL ASSISTANCE CENTERS

Award: Project Grants

Purpose: To improve the capacity of State Vocational Rehabilitation agencies and their partners to equip individuals with disabilities to help them obtain high quality competitive integrated employment.

Applicant Eligibility: States and public or nonprofit agencies and organizations, including Indian tribes and institutions of higher education.

Beneficiary Eligibility: Individuals employed in positions related to the rehabilitation of individuals with disabilities will benefit.

Award Range/Average: No Data Available.

Funding: (Project Grants) FY 17 $5,541,391; FY 18 est $6,170,000; FY 19 est $7,500,000.

HQ: OSERS Rehabilitation Services Administration 400 Maryland Avenue SW
Washington, DC 20202
Phone: 202-245-7343
Email: tom.finch@ed.gov
http://www.ed.gov/offices/osers/rsa

USDA 10.515

RENEWABLE RESOURCES EXTENSION ACT & NATIONAL FOCUS FUND PROJECTS
"RREA and RREA-NFF"

Award: Formula Grants; Project Grants

Purpose: To assist forest and range landowners in making resource management decisions and also to support during rangeland resource issues. Rangeland management includes vegetation, water, fisheries, wildlife, etc.

Applicant Eligibility: In accordance with the Renewable Resources Extension Act of 1978, applications may only be submitted by the following State colleges and universities. Auburn University; Alabama A&M University; Tuskegee University; University of Alaska - Fairbanks; University of Arizona; University of Arkansas; University of Arkansas at Pine Bluff; University of California; Central State University; Colorado State University; University of Connecticut; University of Delaware; Delaware State University; University of the District of Columbia; University of Florida; Florida A&M University; University of Georgia; Fort Valley State University; University of Guam; University of Hawaii; University of Idaho; University of Illinois; Purdue University; Iowa State University; Kansas State University; University of Kentucky; Kentucky State University; Louisiana State University; Southern University; University of Maine; University of Maryland (College Park); University of Maryland (Eastern Shore); University of Massachusetts; Michigan State University; University of Minnesota; Mississippi State University; Alcorn State University; University of Missouri; Lincoln University; Montana State University; University of Nebraska; University of Nevada; University of New Hampshire; Rutgers University; New Mexico State University; Cornell University; North Carolina State University; North Carolina A&T State University; North Dakota State University; The Ohio State University; Oklahoma State University; Langston University; Oregon State University; Pennsylvania State University; University of Puerto Rico; University of Rhode Island; Clemson University; South Carolina State University; South Dakota State University; University of Tennessee; Tennessee State University; Texas A&M University; Prairie View A&M University; Utah State University; University of Vermont; University of the Virgin Islands; Virginia Polytechnic Institute and State University Virginia State University; Washington State University; West Virginia University; West Virginia State University; University of Wisconsin; and University of Wyoming.

Beneficiary Eligibility: Same as Applicant Eligibility.

Award Range/Average: If minimum or maximum amounts of funding per competitive and/or capacity project grant, or cooperative agreement are established, these amounts will be announced in the annual Competitive Request for Application (RFA).

Funding: N/A

HQ: Institute of Bioenergy Climate and Environment (IBCE) Division of Environmental Systems Forest Resource Management 1400 Independence Avenue SW, P.O. Box 2210

Washington, DC 20250-2210

Phone: 202-720-0740

Email: enorland@nifa.usda.gov

http://nifa.usda.gov/program/renewable-resources-extension-act-capacity-grant

RENT SUPPLEMENTS RENTAL HOUSING FOR LOWER INCOME FAMILIES
"Rent Supplement Program"

Award: Direct Payments for Specified Use

Purpose: To provide quality rental housing to low income families at a cost they can afford.

Applicant Eligibility: Eligible sponsors included nonprofit, cooperative, builder-seller, investor-sponsor, and limited-distribution mortgagors.

Beneficiary Eligibility: Families incomes must be within the income limits prescribed for admission to Section 8 housing in order to qualify for benefits under this program. Families may continue in occupancy if 30 percent of monthly income exceeds the market rent.

Award Range/Average: No Data Available.

Funding: (Direct Payments for Specified Use) FY 15 $11,000,000; FY 16 est $12,000,000; FY 17 est $4,000,000; - Salaries and Expenses not separately identifiable.

HQ: 451 7th Street SW
Washington, DC 20410
Phone: 202-402-2614
Email: brandt.t.witte@hud.gov

REPETITIVE FLOOD CLAIMS "RFC"

DHS 97.092

Award: Project Grants

Purpose: Assists the local and State governments to reduce the long-term risk of flood damage to structures by removing them from flood hazard areas.

Applicant Eligibility: Entities eligible to apply for HMA grants include the emergency management agency or a similar office of the 50 States, the District of Columbia, American Samoa, Guam, the U.S. Virgin Islands, Puerto Rico, the Northern Mariana Islands, and Indian Tribal governments. Each State, Territory, Commonwealth, or Indian Tribal government shall designate one agency to serve as the Applicant for each HMA program.

Beneficiary Eligibility: State agencies, Indian Tribal governments, and local governments and communities are eligible to apply as sub applicants for assistance under the RFC program. All interested sub applicants must apply to the Applicant.

Award Range/Average: Refer to HMA program guidance.

Funding: N/A

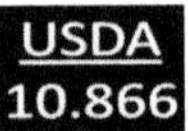

HQ: 400 C Street SW
Washington, DC 20472
Phone: 202-646-3458
Email: kayed.lakhia@fema.dhs.gov
http://www.fema.gov

REPOWERING ASSISTANCE "Section 9004 Repowering Assistance"

USDA 10.866

Award: Direct Payments for Specified Use

Purpose: To assist biorefineries for restoring fossil fuels with renewable biomass.

Applicant Eligibility: A Biorefinery facility (including equipment and processes) that converts renewable biomass into biofuels and biobased products, and may produce electricity. An eligible biorefinery producer, whose primary production is biofuels; that meets all requirements of this program.

Beneficiary Eligibility: For biorefineries in existence on June 18, 2008 Primary production is biofuels

Award Range/Average: Determined on a project bases.

Funding: (Direct Payments with Unrestricted Use) FY 17 $0; FY 18 est $5,000,000; FY 19 est $0; FY 16 $0.

HQ: 1400 Independence Avenue SW, P.O. Box 3225
Washington, DC 20250-3225
Phone: 202-690-0784
Email: frederick.petok@wdc.usda.gov
http://www.rd.usda.gov/programs-services/repowering-assistance-program

RESEARCH & DATA ANALYSIS

Award: Cooperative Agreements

Purpose: The program involves research and analysis of data pertaining to drug policy.

Applicant Eligibility: Applicants must have expert knowledge and extensive experience in conducting research and analysis.

Beneficiary Eligibility: Same as Applicant Eligibility.

Award Range/Average: No Data Available.

Funding: (Cooperative Agreements) FY 17 $100,000; FY 18 est $0; FY 19 FY 16 $0.

HQ: 750 17th Street NW
Washington, DC 20503
Phone: 202-395-6739
Email: phuong_desear@ondcp.eop.gov

RESEARCH & EVALUATIONS, DEMONSTRATIONS, AND DATA ANALYSIS & UTILIZATION

Award: Cooperative Agreements

Purpose: Through Notice of Funding Availability (NOFA), HUD plans to solicit applications for cooperative agreements to engage in research, evaluations, demonstrations, and data analysis and utilization activities.

Applicant Eligibility: N/A

Beneficiary Eligibility: N/A

Award Range/Average: $100,000 minimum funding amount for successful applicants.

Funding: (Cooperative Agreements) FY 17 $2,900,000; FY 18 est $890,661; FY 19 est $3,200,000.

HQ: 451 7th Street, Room 8230
Washington, DC 20410
Phone: 202-402-3852
Email: susan.s.brunson@hud.gov

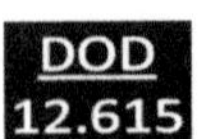

RESEARCH & TECHNICAL ASSISTANCE

Award: Cooperative Agreements; Project Grants

Purpose: To make awards to, or conclude cooperative agreements with States or local governments, or any nongovernmental or other private entity, to conduct research, and provide technical assistance related to community economic adjustment needs and assistance under 10 U.S.C. Section 2391(c), or Executive Order 12788, as amended.

Applicant Eligibility: Eligible respondents include any governmental or private entity. A "private entity" is defined for purposes of this listing as any entity that is non-governmental.

Beneficiary Eligibility: States and communities, including workers, businesses, and other community interests that may be affected by Department of Defense activity.

Award Range/Average: $400,000-550,000; $477,247

Funding: Project Grants (Cooperative Agreements) FY 15 $609,556; FY 17 N/A FY 16 est $954,493.

HQ: 2231 Crystal Drive, Suite 520
Arlington, VA 22202-3711
Phone: 703-697-2130

RESEARCH & TRAINING IN COMPLEMENTARY & INTEGRATIVE HEALTH
"National Center for Complementary and Integrative Health"

Award: Project Grants; Training

Purpose: To evaluate complementary and integrative health approaches.

Applicant Eligibility: Universities, colleges, hospitals, laboratories, and other public or private nonprofit domestic institutions, including State and local units of government, and individuals are eligible to make application for grant support of research by a named principal investigator or a research career development candidate. For-profit organizations are also eligible, with the exception of NRSA.

Beneficiary Eligibility: Any nonprofit or for-profit organization, company, or institution engaged in biomedical research.

Award Range/Average: R13 - $20,000 to DP2 - $2,234,425; average financial assistance is: $445,512.

Funding: (Project Grants) FY 16 $93,982,220; FY 17 est $97,133,393; FY 18 est $71,057,000.

HQ: NCCIH 6707 Democracy Boulevard, Suite 401
Bethesda, MD 20892
Phone: 301-594-3462
Email: partap.khalsa@nih.gov
http://nccih.nih.gov

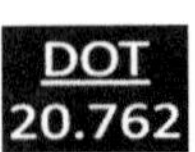

RESEARCH GRANTS

Award: Project Grants

Purpose: Carries various research grants on improving transportation field by funding for research such as the Rural Transportation Research Initiative by North Dakota State University's Upper Great Plains

Transportation Institute, Hydrogen-Powered Transportation Research Initiative by the University of Montana, Cold Region and Rural Transportation Research, Maintenance, and Operations by Montana State University's Western Transportation Institute, Advanced Vehicle Technology by the University of Kansas Transportation Research Institute, Renewable Transportation Systems Research by University of Vermont, Alternative Fuels and Life Cycle Engineering by Rochester Institute of Technology, and National Cooperative Freight Research Program by National Academy of Sciences.

Applicant Eligibility: N/A

Beneficiary Eligibility: All listed beneficiaries will benefit from results produced by these research efforts.

Award Range/Average: $500K to $22M. Averaged $2.25M

Funding: N/A

HQ: 1200 New Jersey Avenue E33-464
Washington, DC 20590
Phone: 202-366-7253
Email: dawn.tucker-thomas@dot.gov
http://www.rita.dot.gov

RESEARCH IN SPECIAL EDUCATION

Award: Project Grants

Purpose: Supports scientifically rigorous research contributing to the solution of specific early intervention and education problems associated with children with disabilities.

Applicant Eligibility: Applicants that have the ability and capacity to conduct scientifically valid research are eligible to apply. Eligible applicants include, but are not limited to, non-profit and for-profit organizations and public and private agencies and institutions, such as colleges and universities.

Beneficiary Eligibility: Infants, toddlers, and children with disabilities or at risk for disabilities benefit from this research.

Award Range/Average: $250,000 to $4,000,000 for 1 to 5 years projects. Award maximums vary depending on the type of project.

Funding: (Project Grants) FY 17 $53,889,236; FY 18 est $54,510,225; FY 19 est $54,000,000.

HQ: National Center for Special Education Research 550 12th Street SW, Room 4144
Washington, DC 20202
Phone: 202-245-8201
Email: joan.mclaughlin@ed.gov
http://ies.ed.gov/ncser

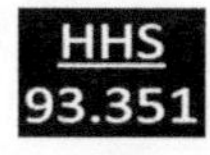

RESEARCH INFRASTRUCTURE PROGRAMS "Comparative Medicine, Instrumentation, Research Infrastructure"

Award: Project Grants

Purpose: To supporting research infrastructure and related research programs. ORIP consists of the Division of Comparative Medicine (DCM); and Division of Construction and Instruments (DCI).

Applicant Eligibility: Comparative Medicine: Institutions of higher education, hospitals, and other institutions and organizations, both nonprofit and for-profit, seeking to establish, continue, or enlarge programs consistent with the objectives of the program. Applicants for NRSA must be citizens of the United States or be admitted to the United States for permanent residency.

Beneficiary Eligibility: Biomedical investigators at any nonprofit or for-profit organization, company, or institution engaged in biomedical research.

Award Range/Average: Awards vary in range depending on the particular activity codes. Research Centers grants have much larger ranges - from hundreds of thousands to several million dollars. All costs are shown on a single year basis. Awards may be for up to five years.

Funding: (Project Grants) FY 17 $248,984,521; FY 18 est $259,702,053; FY 19 est $259,702,053; FY 16 $265,638,377; - (Project Grants) FY 15 $264,543,192; FY 16 est $264,187,662; and FY 17 est $264,187,662- Amounts shown are actual/estimated amounts available for research grants including SBIR/STTR, centers, research career awards, and research project grants. Amounts for research training grants, R&D contracts, and research management support are not included.(Project Grants (Capacity Building and Complaint Processing, Training) FY 17 $7,537,974; FY 18 est $7,503,531; FY 19 est $7,503,531; FY 16 $7,659,219; - (Project Grants (Training) FY 15 $6,514,392; FY 16 est $7,787,235; and FY 17 est $7,787,235 - Amounts shown are for individual and institutional research training awards.

HQ: 6701 Democracy Boulevard Room 956, P.O. Box 4874
Bethesda, MD 20892-4874
Phone: 301-435-0864
Email: pnewman@mail.nih.gov
http://orip.nih.gov

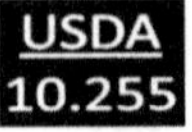

RESEARCH INNOVATION & DEVELOPMENT GRANTS IN ECONOMIC (RIDGE)

Award: Dissemination of Technical Information

Purpose: ERS provides help for development, administration, and evaluation of agricultural and rural policies.

Applicant Eligibility: Any individual or organization in the U.S. and U.S. Territories is eligible to receive the popular or technical research publications that convey the research results, although there may be a fee.

Beneficiary Eligibility: Same as Applicant Eligibility.

Award Range/Average: No Data Available.

Funding: Formula Grants (Cooperative Agreements) FY 17 $600,000; FY 18 est $600,000; FY 19 est $0.

HQ: 355 E Street SW, Room 5-254
Washington, DC 20024-3231
Phone: 202-694-5008
Email: nthomas@ers.usda.gov
http://www.ers.usda.gov

RESEARCH ON CHEMICAL & BIOLOGICAL DEFENSE

Award: Cooperative Agreements; Project Grants

Purpose: To improve the capability to prevent, detect, diagnose and treat the effects of chemical, radiological and biological warfare agents.

Applicant Eligibility: Applicants must be a public or private educational institution, a nonprofit organizations operated for purposes in the public interest, or a commercial firm.

Beneficiary Eligibility: Beneficiaries are relatively independent investigators associated with an applicant organization.

Award Range/Average: No Data Available.

Funding: (Project Grants) FY 17 $0; FY 18 est $1,000,000; FY 19 est $336,754.

HQ: 110 Thomas Johnson Drive
Frederick, MD 21702
Phone: 301-619-2446
Email: richard.w.totten2.civ@mail.mil

RESEARCH ON HEALTHCARE COSTS, QUALITY & OUTCOMES

Award: Project Grants

Purpose: To support research and evaluations, demonstration projects, research networks, and multidisciplinary centers and to disseminate information on healthcare and on systems for the delivery.

Applicant Eligibility: Federal, State or local government agencies, federally-recognized Indian Tribal Governments, U.S. Territories, non-government organizations, public or private institutions of higher education, and other public or nonprofit private agencies, institutions, or organizations. For-profit organizations are eligible to apply for these grants only if "cooperative agreement" is the designated funding mechanism.

Beneficiary Eligibility: Federal, State or local government agencies, federally-recognized Indian Tribal Governments, public or private nonprofit institutions, U.S. territories, Native American organizations, consumers, students, minority groups, specialized groups, health or education professionals, individuals, scientist/researchers, and the general public.

Award Range/Average: $21,349 to $1,182,529; $284,741 average. These are total cost figures.

Funding: (Project Grants) FY 17 $104,007,785; FY 18 est $109,068,185; FY 19 est $77,372,171.

HQ: 5600 Fishers Lane
Rockville, MD 20857
Phone: 301-427-1447
Email: george.gardner@ahrq.hhs.gov
http://www.ahrq.gov

RESEARCH ON RESEARCH INTEGRITY

Award: Project Grants

Purpose: To solicit applications for competing grant awards for the planning and implementation of conferences or workshops.

Applicant Eligibility: Public, private or nonprofit agencies (including State and local government agencies) eligible Federal agencies, universities, colleges, hospitals and academic or research institutions may apply for research grants.

Beneficiary Eligibility: Individuals and public, private, profit or nonprofit organizations

Award Range/Average: $48321 - $50,000 Total $98,321

Funding: Project Grants (Discretionary) FY 17 $249,971; FY 18 est $98,321; FY 19 N/A FY 16 $1,113,008.

HQ: 1101 Wootton Parkway Tower Building, Suite 550
Rockville, MD 20852
Phone: 240-453-8822
Email: roscoe.brunsont@hhs.gov
http://ori.hhs.gov

RESEARCH RELATED TO DEAFNESS & COMMUNICATION DISORDERS

Award: Project Grants

Purpose: To investigate solutions to problems directly relevant to individuals with deafness or disorders of human communication in the areas of hearing, balance, smell, taste, voice, speech, and language.

Applicant Eligibility: Project Grants and Centers Grants: Any public, private, nonprofit, or for-profit institution is eligible to apply. For-profit institutions are not eligible for institutional National Research Service Awards.

Beneficiary Eligibility: Health professionals; student/trainee; scientists/researchers; consumer.

Award Range/Average: Ranged from $100 to $2,509,086; Average was $339,886.

Funding: (Project Grants) FY 17 $353,820,813; FY 18 est $377,474,000; FY 19 est $347,943,000.

HQ: 6001 Executive Boulevard Room 8328, P.O. Box 9670
Bethesda, MD 20892-9670
Phone: 301-496-8693
Email: holmesd@mail.nih.gov
http://www.nidcd.nih.gov

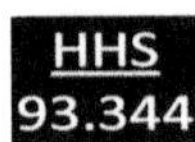

RESEARCH, MONITORING & OUTCOMES DEFINITIONS FOR VACCINE SAFETY

"Vaccine Safety Research"

Award: Cooperative Agreements

Purpose: Collaborates with federal partners to provide strategic direction for the coordination of the vaccine and immunization enterprise for the National Vaccine Plan (NVP) implementation.

Applicant Eligibility: Public (including city, county, regional, and State government) organizations and private nonprofit entities.

Beneficiary Eligibility: Improving vaccine safety for adults.

Award Range/Average: Estimated Funds Available for Competition $750,000

Funding: (Cooperative Agreements) FY 18 N/A FY 17 est $750,000; FY 16 $250,000.

HQ: 1101 Wootton Parkway Tower Building, Suite 550
Rockville, MD 20852
Phone: 240-453-8822
Email: eric.west@hhs.gov
http://www.hhs.gov/nvpo

RESEARCH, PREVENTION, AND EDUCATION PROGRAMS ON LYME DISEASE IN THE UNITED STATES
"Lyme Disease"

Award: Cooperative Agreements

Purpose: To develop, implement and evaluate measures for the prevention of Lyme disease in the United States.

Applicant Eligibility: Public and nonprofit organizations able to provide services to geographical areas where Lyme disease is endemic or found to be newly emerging in the continental United States. Thus, universities, colleges, research institutions, State and local health departments, and private nonprofit organizations are eligible.

Beneficiary Eligibility: States, political subdivisions of states, and other public and nonprofit private entities and the general public who may be exposed to the threat of Lyme disease in certain geographical areas.

Award Range/Average: $250,000 to $500,000; Average award depends on Notice of Funding Opportunity (NOFO).

Funding: Cooperative Agreements (Discretionary Grants) FY 17 $522,087; FY 18 est $462,404; FY 19 est $300,000; FY 16 $299,992.

HQ: Extramural Research Program Office CDC 1600 Clifton Road E60
Atlanta, GA 30329-4018
Phone: 404-718-8845
Email: cmorrison@cdc.gov
http://www.cdc.gov

RESETTLEMENT SUPPORT CENTERS (RSCS) FOR U.S. REFUGEE RESETTLEMENT

Award: Cooperative Agreements

Purpose: Assists the Bureau in preparing the necessary casework for persons eligible for interview by United States Citizenship and Immigration Services (USCIS) of the Department of Homeland Security (DHS) under the U.S. Refugee Admissions Program and, for those approved, to provide assistance in completing the additional requirements for refugee admission under Section 207 of the Immigration and Nationality Act.

Applicant Eligibility: International and non-governmental organizations.

Beneficiary Eligibility: Refugees approved under the U.S. Refugee Admissions Program will benefit.

Award Range/Average: No Data Available.

Funding: (Cooperative Agreements) FY 16 $52,847,676; FY 17 est $53,000,000; FY 18 est $53,000,000.

HQ: 2025 E Street NW, 8th Floor SA 9
Washington, DC 20520
Phone: 202-453-9253
Email: smithjl1@state.gov
http://www.state.gov/j/prm/index.htm

RESIDENT INSTRUCTION GRANTS FOR INSULAR AREA ACTIVITIES
"Grants for Insular Areas - Resident Instruction Grants for Insular Areas (RIIA)"

Award: Project Grants

Purpose: The secretary of agriculture shall fund for education infrastructure with required equipment, encourage UG and PG students to pursue studies in agriculture sciences, support organizations in the private sector, and provide training for agricultural scientists.

Applicant Eligibility: The Secretary of Agriculture shall ensure that each eligible institution, prior to receiving grant funds under subsection (a), shall have a significant demonstrable commitment to higher education programs in the food and agricultural sciences and to each specific subject area for which grant funds under this section are to be used. The Secretary of Agriculture may require that any grant awarded under this section contain provisions that require funds to be targeted to meet the needs identified in section 1402.

Beneficiary Eligibility: Same as Applicant Eligibility.

Award Range/Average: If minimum or maximum amounts of funding per competitive and/or capacity project grant, or cooperative agreement are established, these amounts will be announced in the annual Competitive Request for Application (RFA).

Funding: (Project Grants) FY 17 $1,150,200; FY 18 est $1,200,000; FY 19 est $0; FY 16 $1,150,425.

HQ: Institute of Youth Family and Community Division of Community and Education 1400 Independence Avenue SW, P.O. Box 2250

Washington, DC 20250-2250

Phone: 202-720-2324

Email: elewis@nifa.usda.gov

http://nifa.usda.gov/program/resident-instruction-grants-riia-and-distance-education-grants-deg-institutions-higher

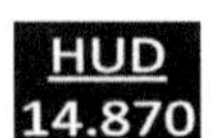

RESIDENT OPPORTUNITY & SUPPORTIVE SERVICES – SERVICE COORDINATORS
"ROSS Service Coordinators"

Award: Project Grants

Purpose: To provide service coordinator positions to organize supportive services, resident empowerment activities and/or assisting residents in becoming economically self-sufficient or age-in-place.

Applicant Eligibility: Public Housing Authorities (PHAs), Tribes and tribally designated housing entities (TDHEs), resident councils and nonprofit entities supported by residents. Applicants must establish partnerships to leverage resources.

Beneficiary Eligibility: Individuals, families, children, youth, adults as well as elderly/persons with disabilities who are residents of conventional public or Indian housing are eligible to receive benefits from the ROSS program.

Award Range/Average: Average $360,000

Funding: (Project Grants) FY 17 $45,962,000; FY 18 est $35,000,000; FY 19 est $0; FY 16 $45,962,000.

HQ: 451 7th Street SW, Room 4130
Washington, DC 20410
Phone: 202-402-2341
Email: anice.m.schervish@hud.gov

RESIDENTIAL SUBSTANCE ABUSE TREATMENT FOR STATE PRISONERS
"RSAT"

Award: Formula Grants

Purpose: To assist states and units of local and tribal governments to break the cycle of incarceration for drug addiction and violence by reducing the demand for, use, and trafficking of illegal drugs.

Applicant Eligibility: States, the District of Columbia, the Commonwealth of Puerto Rico, the Virgin Islands, America Samoa, Guam, and the Northern Mariana Islands are eligible to apply. By statute 42 U.S.C.

Beneficiary Eligibility: State and local correctional agencies will implement programs to provide treatment to incarcerated offenders.

Award Range/Average: Individual state and territory awards ranged from $35,000 to $908,000.

Funding: (Formula Grants) FY 17 $12,646,502; FY 18 est $30,000,000; FY 19 est $12,000,000.

HQ: Bureau of Justice Assistance 810 7th Street NW
Washington, DC 20531
Phone: 202-616-7385
Email: timothy.jeffries@usdoj.gov
http://www.bja.gov

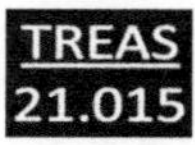

RESOURCES & ECOSYSTEMS SUSTAINABILITY, TOURIST OPPORTUNITIES, AND REVIVED ECONOMIES OF THE GULF COAST STATES
"Gulf RESTORE - Direct Component and Centers of Excellence Research Grant Programs"

Award: Formula Grants

Purpose: To disburse funds to eligible entities for the ecological and economic restoration of the Gulf Coast Region.

Applicant Eligibility: The RESTORE Act specifies who may apply to receive funds under the Direct Component Grant Program. Treasury's regulations list the Direct Component eligible states, counties, and parishes who may apply as follows: in Alabama, the Alabama Gulf Coast Recovery Council or such administrative agent as it may designate; in Florida, the Florida counties of Bay, Charlotte, Citrus, Collier, Dixie, Escambia, Franklin, Gulf, Hernando, Hillsborough, Jefferson, Lee, Levy, Manatee, Monroe, Okaloosa, Santa Rosa, Pasco, Pinellas, Sarasota, Taylor, Wakulla, and Walton; in Louisiana, the Coastal Protection and Restoration Authority Board of Louisiana through the Coastal Protection and Restoration

Authority of Louisiana; in Louisiana, the Louisiana parishes of Ascension, Assumption, Calcasieu, Cameron, Iberia, Jefferson, Lafourche, Livingston, Orleans, Plaquemines, St.

Beneficiary Eligibility: The beneficiaries are the coastal communities of the Gulf Coast Region.

Award Range/Average: No Data Available.

Funding: (Formula Grants) FY 17 $53,699,007; FY 18 est $54,000,000; FY 19 N/A.

HQ: 1500 Pennsylvania Avenue NW
Washington, DC 20220
Phone: 202-622-0904
Email: restoreact@treasury.gov

ROSS SUPPORTIVE SERVICES PROGRAMS
"ROSS Supportive Services Programs"

Award: Project Grants

Purpose: To address the needs of public housing residents by providing supportive services, resident empowerment activities, and/or assisting residents of all ages in becoming economically self-sufficient through a variety of innovative programs/initiatives.

Applicant Eligibility: Public Housing Authorities (PHAs), Tribes and tribally designated housing entities (TDHEs), resident councils and nonprofit entities supported by residents. Applicants must establish partnerships to leverage resources.

Beneficiary Eligibility: Individuals, families, children, youth, adults as well as elderly/persons with disabilities who are residents of conventional public or Indian housing are eligible to receive benefits from the ROSS program.

Award Range/Average: TBD by each individual program/initiative in accordance with the NOFA.

Funding: (Project Grants) FY 17 est $3,000,000; FY 18 est $0; FY 16 $1,753,464.

HQ: 451 7th Street SW
Washington, DC 20410
Phone: 202-402-2430
Email: dina.lehmann-kim@hud.gov

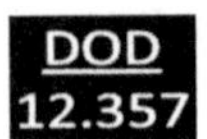

ROTC LANGUAGE & CULTURE TRAINING GRANTS
"ROTC Project GO (Global Officers)"

Award: Project Grants

Purpose: A DoD-funded initiative that promotes critical language education, study abroad, and intercultural dialogue opportunities within the ROTC student population in order to develop future military officers.

Applicant Eligibility: Any accredited U.S. institution of higher education (defined in 20 U.S.C. 1001 of the Higher Education Act of 1965, is eligible to apply for a grant.

Beneficiary Eligibility: Accredited U.S. institutions of higher education and their ROTC students.

Award Range/Average: Grants range from $150,000 to $350,000 annually for multi-year projects.

Funding: (Salaries and Expenses) FY 17 $8,550,000; FY 18 est $7,000,000; FY 19 est $19,109,834.

HQ: 4800 Mark Center Drive, Suite 8G08
Alexandria, VA 22350-7000
Phone: 571-256-0716
Email: shirley.t.rapues.civ@mail.mil

RURAL ACCESS TO EMERGENCY DEVICES GRANT & PUBLIC ACCESS TO DEFIBRILLATION DEMONSTRATION GRANT "Rural Access to Emergency Devices (RAED) The Public Access Defibrillation Demonstration Project (PADDP) Rural Opioid Overdose Reversal (ROOR) Program"

Award: Project Grants

Purpose: To purchase automated external defibrillators (AEDs) that have been approved, or cleared for marketing, by the Food and Drug Administration.

Applicant Eligibility: RAED program: Awards will be made to community partnerships for purchase, placement and training for AEDs in eligible rural areas. These partnerships are defined as a consortium of first responders (e.

Beneficiary Eligibility: Same as Applicant Eligibility

Award Range/Average: Rural Access to Emergency Devices Program: $93,603 to $200,000, $152,429 (average); Public Access Defibrillation Demonstration Project: $85,752 to $146,997, $116,375 (average); Rural Opioid Overdose Reversal Program: $100,000 to $100,000, $100,000 (average).

Funding: (Project Grants) FY 17 $0; FY 18 est $0; FY 19 est $0; - Rural Opioid Overdose Reversal (Project Grants) FY 17 $0; FY 18 est $0; FY 19 est $0; - Rural Access to Emergency Devices (Project Grants) FY 17 $0; FY 18 est $0; FY 19 est $0; - Public Access Defibri

HQ: Office of Rural Health Policy 5600 Fishers Lane
Rockville, MD 20857
Phone: 301-443-7320
Email: mgibson@hrsa.gov
http://www.hrsa.gov

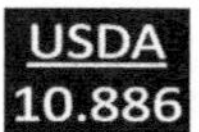

RURAL BROADBAND ACCESS LOANS & LOAN GUARANTEES "Farm Bill Broadband Loans & Loan Guarantees"

Award: Direct Loans; Guaranteed/Insured Loans

Purpose: To assure that people in rural communities have access to broadband services.

Applicant Eligibility: (a) To be eligible for a broadband loan, an applicant may be either a nonprofit or for-profit organization, and must take one of the following forms: (1) Corporation; (2) Limited liability company (LLC); (3) Cooperative or mutual organization; (4) Indian tribe or tribal organization as defined in 25 U.S.C. 450b; or (5) State or local government, including any agency, subdivision, or instrumentality thereof.

Beneficiary Eligibility: Residents and businesses of eligible rural areas.

Award Range/Average: $8,700,000 to $15,308,000 with an average of $12,004,000

Funding: (Direct Loans) FY 17 $0; FY 18 est $0; FY 19 est $0; FY 16 $0; - Four (4) Percent Loans (Guaranteed/Insured Loans) FY 17 $0; FY 18 est $0; FY 19 est $0; FY 16 $0; - (Direct Loans) FY 17 $24,008,000; FY 18 est $20,000,000; FY 19 est $2,000,000; FY 16 $19,43

HQ: Telecommunications Program 1400 Independence Avenue SW, P.O. Box 1590
Washington, DC 20250
Phone: 202-720-9564
Email: chad.parker@wdc.usda.gov
http://www.rd.usda.gov/programs-services/farm-bill-broadband-loans-loan-guarantees

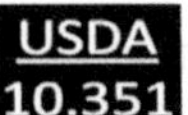

RURAL BUSINESS DEVELOPMENT GRANT "RBDG"

Award: Project Grants

Purpose: To support economic development in various disciplines and businesses in rural communities.

Applicant Eligibility: Applicants eligible for RBDG grants are government entities, Indian tribes or nonprofit corporations serving rural areas such as States, counties, cities, townships, and incorporated towns and villages, boroughs, authorities, districts and Indian tribes on Federal and State reservations which will serve rural areas. Applicants eligible for TD grants are statewide, private, nonprofit, public television systems whose coverage is predominantly rural.

Beneficiary Eligibility: Rural communities and small and emerging private business enterprises which will employ 50 or less new employees and have less than $1.0 million in projected gross revenue.

Award Range/Average: $25,000 to $500,000. Average is less than $100,000.

Funding: (Formula Grants) FY 17 $33,000,000; FY 18 est $34,000,000; FY 19 N/A FY 16 est $28,000,000.

HQ: 1400 Independence Avenue SW, P.O. Box 3226
Washington, DC 20250
Phone: 202-720-1400
Email: sami.zarour@wdc.usda.gov
http://www.rd.usda.gov/programs-services/rural-business-development-grants

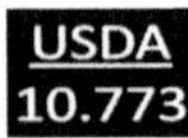

RURAL BUSINESS OPPORTUNITY GRANTS "RBOG) Combined with RBEG 10.769 and RBDG 10.351"

Award: Project Grants

Purpose: To promote economic development in rural communities.

Applicant Eligibility: Grants may be made to public bodies, nonprofit corporations, Federally-Recognized Native American Tribes, and cooperatives with members that are primarily rural residents and that conduct activities for the mutual benefit of the members.

Beneficiary Eligibility: Rural communities and businesses in rural areas.

Award Range/Average: Varies from year to year

Funding: (Cooperative Agreements) FY 17 $30,000,000; FY 18 est $28,000,000; FY 19 est $0.

HQ: 1400 Independence Avenue
Washington, DC 20250
Phone: 202-720-1400

Email: sami.zarour@wdc.usda.gov

http://www.rd.usda.gov/programs-services/rural-business-development-grants

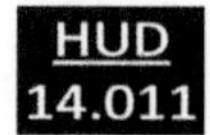

RURAL CAPACITY BUILDING FOR COMMUNITY DEVELOPMENT & AFFORDABLE HOUSING GRANTS "Rural Capacity Building (RCB)"

Award: N/A

Purpose: The Rural Capacity Building program.

Applicant Eligibility: Only National Organizations that are 503(c)(3) nonprofits, other than institutions of higher education, can apply for RCB funding. For the purpose of the RCB program, a National Organization must be a single organization that has experience conducting RCB eligible activities with RCB eligible beneficiaries within the last ten years in at least seven Federal HUD regions.

Beneficiary Eligibility: RCB program Eligible Beneficiaries are limited to a local organization serving rural areas that are one of the following types of organizations: Rural housing development organization, Community Development Corporation (CDC), Community Housing Development Organization (CHDO), Local government, and/or Indian tribe. RCB program Eligible Beneficiaries must serve rural areas.

Award Range/Average: The minimum grant award is $1,000,000 and the maximum grant award is $2,500,000.

Funding: (Project Grants) FY 17 $5,000,000; FY 18 est $5,000,000; FY 19 est $5,000,000.

HQ: 451 7th Street SW
Washington, DC 20410
Phone: 202-402-4385
Email: diane.m.schmutzler@hud.gov
http://www.hudexchange.info

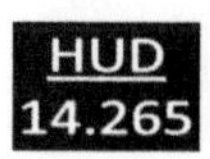

RURAL CAPACITY BUILDING FOR COMMUNITY DEVELOPMENT & AFFORDABLE HOUSING GRANTS "Rural Capacity Building Program"

Award: Project Grants

Purpose: The capacity of rural housing development organizations, Community Development Corporations (CDCs), Community Housing Development Organizations (CHDOs), local governments, and the eligible beneficiaries of the Indian tribes are built by the Rural Capacity Building program in order to serve their communities and low- and moderate-income families with community development and low-cost housing activities.

Applicant Eligibility: Only National Organizations that are 503(c)(3) nonprofits, other than institutions of higher education, can apply for RCB funding. For the purpose of the RCB program, a National Organization must be a single organization that has experience conducting RCB eligible activities with RCB eligible beneficiaries within the last ten years in at least seven Federal HUD regions.

Beneficiary Eligibility: RCB program Eligible Beneficiaries are limited to a local organization serving rural areas that are one of the following types of organizations: Rural housing development organization, Community Development Corporation (CDC), Community Housing Development Organization (CHDO), Local government, and/or Indian tribe. RCB program Eligible Beneficiaries must serve rural areas.

Award Range/Average: The minimum grant award is $1,000,000 and the maximum grant award is $2,500,000.

Funding: (Project Grants) FY 17 $5,000,000; FY 18 est $5,000,000; FY 19 est $5,000,000.

HQ: 451 7th Street SW
Washington, DC 20410
Phone: 202-402-4385
Email: diane.m.schmutzler@hud.gov
http://www.hudexchange.info/programs/rural-capacity-building

RURAL COMMUNITY DEVELOPMENT INITIATIVE "RCDI"

Award: Project Grants

Purpose: To assist low-income rural communities to improve housing, economic development, and other essential facilities for standard living.

Applicant Eligibility: Rural Community Development Initiative grants may be made to a legally qualified private or public (including tribal) organization that provides technical assistance to nonprofit community-based housing and community development organizations, and low income rural communities. The grantee must provide a program of technical assistance to the recipient entity.

Beneficiary Eligibility: Recipient entities must be legally organized private, nonprofit community-based housing and community development organizations, low income rural communities, and Federally recognized Indian Tribes.

Award Range/Average: FY 2017 grant range: $50,000 to $250,000. Average: $194,691

Funding: (Project Grants) FY 17 $4,000,000; FY 18 est $4,000,000; FY 19 est $4,000,000.

HQ: 1400 Independence Avenue SW
Washington, DC 20250
Phone: 202-205-9685
Email: shirley.stevenson@wdc.usda.gov
http://www.rd.usda.gov/had-rcdi_grants.html

RURAL COOPERATIVE DEVELOPMENT GRANTS "RCDG"

Award: Project Grants

Purpose: To assist people and businesses in rural areas for improving economic condition through Cooperative Development Centers.

Applicant Eligibility: Applicants are not eligible if they have been debarred or suspended or otherwise excluded from participation in Federal assistance programs under Executive Order 12549, "Debarment and Suspension." Applicants are not eligible if they have an outstanding judgement obtained by the U.S. in a Federal Court (other than U.S. Tax Court), are delinquent on the payment of Federal income taxes, or are delinquent on a Federal debt.

Beneficiary Eligibility: Ultimate beneficiaries must be located in rural areas.

Award Range/Average: Average = $180,000 Range = $70,000 (minimum) to $200,000 (maximum)

Funding: (Project Grants) FY 17 $6,000,000; FY 18 est $5,800,000; FY 19 N/A FY 16 $6,000,000; - President has not included in budget yet.

HQ: Grants Division 1400 Independence Avenue SW Room 4208-S, P.O. Box 3253
Washington, DC 20250-3253
Phone: 202-690-1374
http://www.rd.usda.gov/programs-services/rural-cooperative-development-grant-program

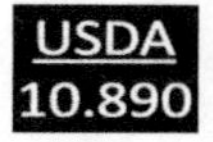

RURAL DEVELOPMENT COOPERATIVE AGREEMENT PROGRAM "RCAP"

Award: Project Grants

Purpose: To maximize effectiveness of Federal programs affecting the rural areas.

Applicant Eligibility: Applicants are not eligible if they have been debarred or suspended or otherwise excluded from participation in Federal assistance programs under Executive Order 12549, "Debarment and Suspension." Applicants are not eligible if they have an outstanding judgement obtained by the U.S. in a Federal Court (other than U.S. Tax Court), are delinquent on the payment of Federal income taxes, or are delinquent on a Federal debt.

Beneficiary Eligibility: Ultimate beneficiaries must be located in rural areas.

Award Range/Average: Average = $130,000 Range = $30,000 (minimum) to $1,000,000 (maximum)

Funding: (Project Grants) FY 17 $785,981; FY 18 est $864,580; FY 19 N/A FY 16 $2,498,776.

HQ: Grants Division 1400 Independence Avenue SW Room 4208-S, P.O. Box 3253
Washington, DC 20250-3253
Phone: 202-690-1374
http://www.rd.usda.gov/programs-services/all-programs

RURAL DEVELOPMENT MULTI-FAMILY HOUSING RURAL HOUSING VOUCHER DEMONSTRATION PROGRAM "Rural Development Voucher Demonstration Program"

Award: Direct Payments for Specified Use

Purpose: The Rural Housing Voucher Demonstration program assists the tenants to prepay their rural development mortgage through rental housing assistance vouchers. Prepaying opportunities are located in Puerto Rico, the U.S. Virgin Islands, and Guam.

Applicant Eligibility: Applicants must (a) be residing in the Section 515 project on the date of the prepayment of the Section 515 loan or upon foreclosure by Rural Development; (b) the date of the prepayment or foreclosure must be after September 30, 2005; (c) as required by 42 U.S.C. 1436a the tenant must be a citizen, U.S. non-citizen national or qualified alien and will so provide proof of citizenship.

Beneficiary Eligibility: Applicants must be citizens, U.S. non-citizen nationals or qualified aliens and have an adjusted household income at or below 80 percent of area median income as determined annually by the U.S. Department of Housing and Urban Development (HUD) to be eligible for a rural housing voucher.

Award Range/Average: No Data Available.

Funding: (Direct Payments for Specified Use) FY 17 $22,000,000; FY 18 est $25,000,000; FY 19 est $19,000,000; FY 16 $17,530,138.

HQ: USDA Rural Development 1400 Independence Avenue SW, P.O. Box 0782
Washington, DC 20250-0782
Phone: 202-720-9728
Email: janet.stouder@wdc.usda.gov
http://www.rd.usda.gov

RURAL ECONOMIC DEVELOPMENT LOANS & GRANTS "REDLG"

Award: Project Grants; Direct Loans

Purpose: To promote rural economic development and job creation projects.

Applicant Eligibility: Electric and telephone utilities that have current loans with the Rural Utilities Service (RUS), Rural Telephone Bank loans, or guarantees outstanding and are not delinquent on any Federal debt or in bankruptcy proceedings.

Beneficiary Eligibility: Rural/General Public.

Award Range/Average: Loans and Grants to establish Revolving Loan Fund Programs.

Funding: (Loan Guarantees/Grants) FY 17 $85,000,000; FY 18 est $0; FY 19 FY 16 $33,000,000; - REDLG is a loan and grant program. Amounts listed for FY 2015, 2016, and 2017, are loan obligations. Grant obligations are: FY 2015 - $9,213,000, FY 2016 estimate - $12,000,000, FY 2016 estimate - $12,000,000. (Project Grants) FY 17 FY 18 est $10,000,000; FY 19 N/A - (Direct Loans) FY 17 FY 18 est $58,000,000.

HQ: 1400 Independence Avenue SW, P.O. Box 3226
Washington, DC 20250
Phone: 202-720-1400
Email: sami.zarour@wdc.usda.gov
http://www.rd.usda.gov/programs-services/rural-economic-development-loan-grant-program

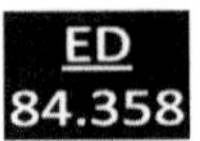

RURAL EDUCATION

Award: Formula Grants

Purpose: Provides financial assistance to rural districts to carry out activities to help improve the quality of teaching and learning in their schools.

Applicant Eligibility: For SRSA, eligible recipients are local educational agencies (LEAs) in which (1) the total number of students in average daily attendance at all of the schools served by the LEA is less than 600 or where each school in the LEA is located in a county with a total population density of less than 10 persons per square mile; and (2) all of the schools served by the LEA are designated as rural by the U.S. Department of Education's National Center for Education Statistics (NCES) using the NCES school locale methodology in place at the time of enactment of the Every Student Succeeds Act (ESSA) or the

LEA is located in an area of the State defined as rural by a State governmental agency. For RLIS, eligible recipients are State educational agencies (SEAs).

Beneficiary Eligibility: Elementary and secondary schools, students, and teachers in rural schools.

Award Range/Average: For Fiscal Year 2018: Range of new awards for SRSA: $140 - $51,294; Average new award for SRSA: $22,478. Estimated range of new subgrants for RLIS: $17 - $266,500; Average new subgrants for RLIS: $34,102.

Funding: (Formula Grants) FY 17 $175,840,000; FY 18 est $180,840,000; FY 19 est $175,840,000.

HQ: Department of Education 400 Maryland Avenue SW
Washington, DC 20202
Phone: 202-260-7349
Email: reap@ed.gov
http://www2.ed.gov/nclb/freedom/local/reap.html

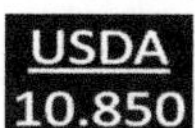

USDA 10.850 RURAL ELECTRIFICATION LOANS & LOAN GUARANTEES "Electric Loans and Loan Guarantees"

Award: Direct Loans; Guaranteed/Insured Loans

Purpose: To assist with electric services in rural areas and provide awareness on-grid and off-grid renewable energy systems.

Applicant Eligibility: Rural electric cooperatives, public utility districts, municipalities, corporations, and other qualified power suppliers including those located in the U.S. Territories, the Federated States of Micronesia, the Republic of the Marshall Islands, and the Republic of Palau.

Beneficiary Eligibility: Persons, businesses, public bodies, tribal entities, and other entities in rural areas (as defined in program regulations) or those currently served through RUS electric loans.

Award Range/Average: Average Guaranteed FFB: $32,668,948 Average.

Funding: (Direct Loans) FY 17 $0; FY 18 est $0; FY 19 FY 16 $0; Hardship (Guaranteed/Insured Loans) FY 17 $2,776,979,000; FY 18 est $5,500,000,000; FY 19 est $5,500,000,000; FY 16 $3,165,750,000; Guaranteed Federal Financing Bank Loans.

HQ: Electric Programs 1400 Independence Avenue, P.O. Box 1560
Washington, DC 20250
Phone: 202-720-9545
Email: christopher.mclean@wdc.usda.gov
http://www.rd.usda.gov/programs-services/all-programs/electric-programs

DHS 97.120 RURAL EMERGENCY MEDICAL COMMUNICATIONS DEMONSTRATION PROJECT "REMCDP"

Award: Project Grants

Purpose: This grant provides training and education and also helps to improve the communication infrastructure and operational effectiveness on rural medical services.

Applicant Eligibility: Please refer to the Notice of Funding Opportunity Announcement.

Beneficiary Eligibility: Refer to program guidance for further information.

Award Range/Average: Refer to program guidance.

Funding: (Salaries and Expenses) FY 17 $0; FY 18 est $2,000,000; FY 19 est $0; FY 16 $0.

HQ: Cyber Security and Communications (CS and C)/Office of Emergency Communications (OEC) NPPD, 4200 Wilson Boulevard
Arlington, VA 22201
Phone: 703-235-4025
http://www.dhs.gov

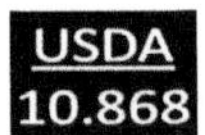

RURAL ENERGY FOR AMERICA PROGRAM "REAP"

Award: Loan Guarantees/grants

Purpose: To compensate for agricultural producers and rural small businesses to promote renewable energy systems and to compensate government entities, educational institutions, and public power entities to assist agricultural producers and rural small businesses with renewable energy systems.

Applicant Eligibility: To be eligible for renewable energy systems or energy efficiency improvement assistance, an applicant must be an agricultural producer or rural small business. Rural small businesses must be located in a rural area.

Beneficiary Eligibility: For energy efficiency improvements and renewable energy systems the program is for agricultural producers and rural small businesses. For energy audits and renewable energy development assistance grants, units of State, tribal, and local governments; land-grant colleges, universities, and other institutions of higher education; rural electric cooperatives and public power entities; instrumentalities of a state, tribal, and local governments; and Resource Conservation and Development Councils are eligible for the assistance.

Award Range/Average: Grant Range $2,500 to $500,000; Average $45,000 Guaranteed Loan Range $5,000 to $25,000,000; Average $85,000.

Funding: (Loan Guarantees/Grants) FY 17 $299,030,000; FY 18 est $0; FY 19 FY 16 $159,000,000; - (Project Grants) FY 17 FY 18 est $25,000,000; FY 19 N/A - (Guaranteed/Insured Loans) FY 17 FY 18 est $530,000,000; FY 19 N/A.

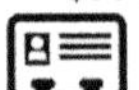

HQ: Energy Division 511 W 7th Street
Atlantic, IA 50022
Phone: 712-243-2107
Email: lisa.noty@wdc.usda.gov

USDA 10.751

RURAL ENERGY SAVINGS PROGRAM (RESP) "RESP"

Award: Direct Loans

Purpose: To assist in cost savings for the rural and small business families.

Applicant Eligibility: N/A

Beneficiary Eligibility: N/A

Award Range/Average: Range of loan size is from $200,000 to $13,000,000. The average is $3,034,147

Funding: (Direct Loans) FY 17 $24,273,000; FY 18 est $153,750,777; FY 19 est $60,000,000.

HQ: Electric Programs 1400 Independence Avenue, P.O. Box 1560
Washington, DC 20250
Phone: 202-720-9545
Email: christopher.mclean@wdc.usda.gov
http://www.rd.usda.gov/programs-services/rural-energy-savings-program

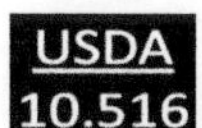

RURAL HEALTH & SAFETY EDUCATION COMPETITIVE GRANTS PROGRAM

"Rural Health and Safety Education Competitive Grants Program-RHSE"

Award: Project Grants

Purpose: The Rural Health and Safety Education provide programs for individuals and families, promotes rural health leadership development, farm safety, information and training to farm workers.

Applicant Eligibility: Applications may be submitted by 1862 and 1890 Land Grant colleges and universities that are eligible to receive funds under the Act of July 2, 1862.

Beneficiary Eligibility: Same as Applicant Eligibility.

Award Range/Average: If minimum or maximum amounts of funding per competitive and/or capacity project grant, or cooperative agreement are established, these amounts will be announced in the annual Competitive Request for Application (RFA).

Funding: Project Grants (Discretionary) FY 17 $0; FY 18 est $0; FY 19 est $0; FY 16 $0.

HQ: Institute of Youth Family and Community (IYFC) Division of Family and Consumer Sciences 1400 Independence Avenue SW, P.O. Box 2250
Washington, DC 20250-2250
Phone: 202-720-2324
Email: ashipley@nifa.usda.gov
http://nifa.usda.gov/program/rural-health-and-safety

RURAL HEALTH CARE SERVICES OUTREACH, RURAL HEALTH NETWORK DEVELOPMENT & SMALL HEALTH CARE PROVIDER QUALITY IMPROVEMENT PROGRAM

Award: Project Grants

Purpose: The Rural healthcare Coordination Network Partnership Program supports the development of formal and mature rural health networks that focus on care coordination activities for the following chronic conditions: diabetes, congestive heart failure and chronic obstructive pulmonary disease. Care coordination in the primary care practice involves deliberately organizing patient care activities and sharing information among all of the participants concerned with a patient's care to achieve safer and more effective care.

Applicant Eligibility: Rural Health Care Services Outreach, Rural Health Network Development and Rural Health Network Development Planning Programs: Applicants applying to these programs can be rural public or rural nonprofit private entities. These include faith-based organizations, health departments,

Tribal governments whose grant-funded activities are conducted in a federally recognized Tribal area, organizations that serve migrant and seasonal farm- workers in rural areas etc.

Beneficiary Eligibility: Medically underserved populations in rural areas will receive expanded services in rural communities where they did not previously exist.

Award Range/Average: Program: Rural Health Care Services Outreach Program; Maximum award: $200,000; Minimum award: $191,755; Average Award: $199,352. Program: Rural Health Network Development Planning Program; Maximum award: $100,000; Minimum award: $ $94,698; Average Award: $95,653. Program: Rural Health Network Development Program; Maximum award: $300,000; Minimum award: $199,562; Average Award: $295,072. Program: Delta States Rural Development Network Program; Maximum award: $945,000; Minimum award: $584,999; Average Award: $839,995. Program: Small Health Care Provider Quality Improvement Program; Maximum award: $200,000; Minimum award: $137,070; Average Award: $192,365. Program: Rural Health Opioid Program; Maximum award: $250,000; Minimum award: $179,934; Average Award: $245,980. Program: Delta Region Community Health Systems Development; Maximum award $4,000,000; Minimum award $4,000,000. Average Award: $4,000,000. Program: Rural Communities Opioid Response Program-Planning: Maximum award $200,000; Minimum award $200,000. Average award: $200,000

Funding: (Project Grants) FY 17 $2,000,000; FY 18 est $4,000,000; FY 19 N/A FY 16 $0.

HQ: Community-Based Division 5600 Fishers Lane
Rockville, MD 20857
Phone: 301-443-7444
Email: kumali@hrsa.gov
http://www.hrsa.gov/ruralhealth

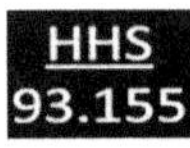

RURAL HEALTH RESEARCH CENTERS

Award: Cooperative Agreements

Purpose: To increase the amount of publically available, high quality, impartial, policy-relevant research to assist decision makers at the federal, state and local levels to better understand the challenges faced by rural communities and providers.

Applicant Eligibility: The Rural Health Research Center and Telehealth Focused Rural Health Research Center cooperative agreements are open to domestic public, for-profit, and non-profit entities. Institutions of higher education, faith-based and community based organizations, Tribes, and tribal organizations are eligible to apply.

Beneficiary Eligibility: The entities that will benefit from this program are health care personnel, health research personnel, policy makers, and the general public. Underserved populations in rural areas; facilities and services in rural areas States with at least one hospital located in a non-metropolitan statistical area or county and provides CMS with necessary assurances.

Award Range/Average: For Rural Health Research Centers (eight awards): Range $699,363- $700,000 For Telehealth Research Center (one award): $750,0000 For Rural Health Research Dissemination (one award): $120,000- $135,000 For Frontier Community Health Integration Project Technical Assistance, Tracking and Analysis (one award): $484,097- $497,734 For Rural Policy Analysis (one award): $224,986- $225,000 For Rapid Response Rural Data Analysis and Issue Specific Rural Research Studies (one award) : $450,000 For National Rural Health Best Practice and Community Development Program (one award): $1,799,843- $1,799,997 For Rural Health Value (one award): $500,000 For the Information Services to Rural Hospital Flexibility Program Awardees: $957,510- $1,100,000 For the Medicare Rural Hospital Flexibility Program Evaluation Cooperative Agreement: $1,500,000 (one award) For the State

Rural Health Coordination and Development Cooperative Agreement (SRHCD-CA): - $750,000 (one award) For Rural Quality Improvement Technical Assistance Cooperative Agreement: $ $500,000 (one award) For Rural Health Clinic Technical Assistance Cooperative Agreement (one award): $100,000 For Rural Residency Technical Assistance and Development Cooperative Agreement (one award): $666,666 For Vulnerable Rural Hospitals Assistance Program Cooperative Agreement (one award): $800,000 The Rural Residency Planning and Development Program (up to sixteen awards): FY '19 $12,550,000 (anticipated total), up to $750,000 per award (estimated)

Funding: (Cooperative Agreements) FY 17 $1,000,000; FY 18 est $1,500,000; FY 19 est $1,500,000; FY 16 $1,000,000; - Medicare Rural Hospital Flexibility Program Evaluation Cooperative Agreement(Cooperative Agreements) FY 17 $5,472,360; FY 18 est $5,599,848; FY 19 est $5,599,848; FY 16 $4,898,583; - Rural Health Research Center Cooperative Agreement(Cooperative Agreements) FY 17 $484,097; FY 18 est $494,209; FY 19 est $494,209; FY 16 $497,734; - Frontier Community Health Integration Project Technical Assistance, Tracking and Analysis Program Cooperative Agreement. (Cooperative Agreements) FY 17 $500,000; FY 18 est $500,000; FY 19 N/A FY 16 $500,000; - Rural Quality Improvement Technical Assistance Cooperative Agreement.(Cooperative Agreements) FY 17 $1,100,000; FY 18 est $1,100,000; FY 19 N/A FY 16 $957,510; - Information Services to Rural Hospital Flexibility Program Awardees(Cooperative Agreements) FY 17 $450,000; FY 18 est $450,000; FY 19 N/A FY 16 $450,000; - Rapid Response Rural Data Analysis and Issue Specific Rural Research Studies Cooperative Agreement(Cooperative Agreements) FY 17 $1,799,997; FY 18 est $1,799,997; FY 19 N/A FY 16 $1,799,843; - National Rural Health Best Practices and Community Development Program.

HQ: 5600 Fishers Lane, P.O. Box 17W59-D
Rockville, MD 20857
Phone: 301-945-3985
Email: jburges@hrsa.gov
http://www.hrsa.gov/ruralhealth

RURAL HOUSING & ECONOMIC DEVELOPMENT "CFDA Number: 14:250"

Award: N/A

Purpose: To support capacity building at the State and local level for rural housing and economic development and modern housing and economic development activities in rural areas.

Applicant Eligibility: n/a

Beneficiary Eligibility: n/a

Award Range/Average: n/a

Funding: (Project Grants) FY 17 $0; FY 18 est $0; FY 19 est $0; - RHED program was archived in 2010.

HQ: 451 7th Street SW, Room 7240
Washington, DC 20410
Phone: 202-402-4464
Email: thann.young@hud.gov
http://www.hudexchange.info

HUD 14.250 RURAL HOUSING & ECONOMIC DEVELOPMENT
"Rural Housing and Economic Development"

Award: Project Grants

Purpose: To build capacity at the State and local level for rural housing and economic development, and to assist innovative housing and economic development activities.

Applicant Eligibility: Local rural nonprofit organizations, community development corporations, Federally recognized Indian Tribes, State Housing Financing Agencies and State Community and/or Economic Development Agencies.

Beneficiary Eligibility: Local and rural communities.

Award Range/Average: The maximum amount awarded to a successful applicant is $300,000.

Funding: (Project Grants) FY 18 est $0; FY 17 est $0; FY 16 $0.

HQ: Department of Housing and Urban Development Office of Rural Housing and Economic Development
Washington, DC 20410
Phone: 202-708-2290
Email: thann.young@hud.gov

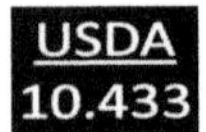

RURAL HOUSING PRESERVATION GRANTS

Award: Project Grants

Purpose: To support low-income rural residents to renovate their houses and develop standard living.

Applicant Eligibility: Must be a State or political subdivision, public nonprofit corporation, Indian tribal corporations, authorized to receive and administer housing preservation grants, private nonprofit corporation, or a consortium of such eligible entities. Applicants must provide assistance under this program to persons residing in open country and communities with a population of 10,000 that are rural in character and places with a population of up to 20,000 under certain conditions.

Beneficiary Eligibility: Very low and low-income rural individuals and families who are homeowners and need resources to bring their housing up to code standards, rental property owners, or co-ops.

Award Range/Average: No Data Available.

Funding: (Project Grants) FY 17 $4,890,755; FY 18 est $5,000,000; FY 19 est $0; FY 16 $3,800,000.

HQ: Multi-Family Housing Preservation and Direct Loan Division 1400 Independence Avenue SW
Washington, DC 20250-0788
Phone: 202-720-1604
https://www.rd.usda.gov/programs-services/housing-preservation-grants

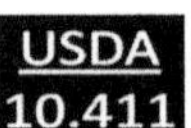

RURAL HOUSING SITE LOANS & SELF HELP HOUSING LAND DEVELOPMENT LOANS
"Section 523 and 524 Site Loans"

Award: Direct Loans

Purpose: To support public and private nonprofit organization with sites for development and provide families those who have low-income with loans.

Applicant Eligibility: A private or public nonprofit organization that will provide the developed sites to qualified borrowers on a cost of development basis in open country and towns of 10,000 population or less and places up to 25,000 population under certain conditions. Applicants from towns of 10,000 to 25,000 population should check with local RD office to determine if agency can serve them.

Beneficiary Eligibility: Sites developed with Section 524 loans must be for housing low and very low income families and may be sold to families, nonprofit organizations, public agencies and cooperatives eligible for assistance under any Section of Title V of the Housing Act of 1949, or under any other law which provides financial assistance. Sites developed with Section 523 loans must be for housing to be built by the self-help method.

Award Range/Average: Loan amounts vary based on proposed project size.

Funding: (Direct Loans) FY 17 $1,000,000; FY 18 est $0; FY 19 est $5,000,000; FY 16 N/A - (523 Site Loans) FY 19 Estimates based on the President's Budget(Direct Loans) FY 17 $0; FY 18 est $0; FY 19 est $5,000,000.

HQ: 1400 Independence Avenue SW
Washington, DC 20250
Phone: 804-287-1559
Email: myron.wooden@usda.gov
http://www.rd.usda.gov

RURAL HOUSING STABILITY ASSISTANCE PROGRAM

Award: Project Grants; Direct Payments for Specified Use

Purpose: To provide aid for rural counties to re-house or improve the housing situations of individuals and families who are homeless, at risk of homelessness, or in the worst housing situations, stabilize them, and improve their ability afford stable housing.

Applicant Eligibility: Counties, that meet the definition of a rural county (a county that has no part of it within an area designated as a standard metropolitan statistical area by OMB; a county that is within an area designated as a metropolitan statistical area or considered as part of a metropolitan statistical area and at least 75 percent of its population is located on U.S. Census blocks classified as non-urban; a county that is located in a State that has population density of less than 30 persons per square mile [as reported in the most recent decennial census], and of which at least 1.25 percent of the total acreage of such State is under Federal jurisdiction, provided that no metropolitan city in such State is the sole beneficiary of the grant amounts awarded under this part.

Beneficiary Eligibility: Individuals and families who are homeless, at risk of homelessness or are in a worst housing situation. Worst housing situation is defined as housing that has serious health and safety defects and at least one major system that has failed or is failing.

Award Range/Average: No Data Available.

Funding: (Project Grants) FY 18 est $0; FY 16 $0; FY 17 est $0.

HQ: Community Planning and Development Office of Special Needs Assistance Programs, 451 7th Street SW Room 7260
Washington, DC 20410
Phone: 202-402-4773
Email: karen.m.deblasio@hud.gov
http://www.hudexchange.info/rural

USDA 10.870 RURAL MICROENTREPRENEUR ASSISTANCE PROGRAM "RMAP"

Award: Project Grants; Direct Loans

Purpose: To provide financial assistance for operations of rural microenterprises. Microenterprise Development Organizations support rural microenterprise development. These grants are known as technical assistance and used by an MDO to provide marketing, management, and other technical assistance to microentrepreneurs.

Applicant Eligibility: To be eligible to apply for Microlender status under the Rural Microentrepreneur Assistance Program, an applicant must be a non-profit entity, an Indian tribe, or a public institution of higher education. Applicants must be at least 51 percent controlled by persons who are either (i) citizens of the United States, the Republic of Palau, the Federated States of Micronesia, the Republic of the Marshall Islands, or American Samoa; or (ii) legally admitted permanent residents residing in the U.S. The applicant or owner must not have an outstanding judgment, be delinquent on any Federal debt or debarred from receiving Federal assistance.

Beneficiary Eligibility: Microentrepreneur is defined as an owner and operator, or prospective owner and operator, of a rural microenterprise who is unable to obtain sufficient training, technical assistance, or as determined by the Secretary. All microentrepreneurs must be located in a rural area.

Award Range/Average: Range of financial assistance is outlined in the Notice of Funding Availability published in the federal register, however prior loans has ranged from $131,250 to $500,000.

Funding: (Direct Loans) FY 17 $29,467,000; FY 18 est $7,000,000; FY 19 N/A FY 16 $7,000,000; - RMAP is a loan and grant program. Amounts listed for FY 2015, 2016, and 2017 are loan obligations. Grant obligations are: FY 2015 - $3,474834, FY 2016 estimate - $2,000,000, FY 2017 estimate - $4,250,000. (Direct Loans) FY 17 FY 18 est $2,500,000; FY 19 N/A.

HQ: Speciality Program 1400 Independence Avenue
Washington, DC 20250
Phone: 202-720-1400
Email: sami.zarour@wdc.usda.gov
http://www.rd.usda.gov/programs-services/rural-microentrepreneur-assistance-program

USDA 10.427 RURAL RENTAL ASSISTANCE PAYMENTS "Rental Assistance"

Award: Direct Payments for Specified Use

Purpose: The Rural Housing Service reduced the rent for less-income families in rural areas based on the sections 515, 514, and 516.

Applicant Eligibility: To be eligible to participate in the rental assistance program, borrowers must have an eligible project. All projects must convert to Interest Credit Plan II before they are eligible, except direct RRH and insured RRH loans approved prior to August 1, 1968, and LH loans and grants.

Beneficiary Eligibility: Any very low and low-income family, handicapped or senior citizen that is unable to pay the approved rental rate for an eligible RHS rental assistance unit within 30 percent of their adjusted monthly income. Households eligible for rental assistance are those 1) whose net tenant contribution to rent, determined in accordance with 3560.

Award Range/Average: From 30 to 90 days from the time Form RD 3560-25, "Request for Rental Assistance is filed.

Funding: (Direct Payments for Specified Use) FY 17 $1,365,018,600; FY 18 est $1,395,000,000; FY 19 est $1,351,000,000; FY 16 $1,389,695,000.

HQ: Multi-Family Housing Portfolio Management Division Rural Housing Service, Department of Agriculture 1400 Independence Avenue SW

Washington, DC 20250

Phone: 202-720-9728

Email: janet.stouder@wdc.usda.gov

http://www.rd.usda.gov

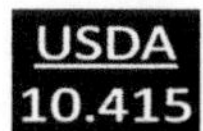

RURAL RENTAL HOUSING LOANS

Award: Project Grants; Direct Loans

Purpose: To provide rural residents with rental and housing related facilities.

Applicant Eligibility: Applicants may be individuals, cooperatives, nonprofit organizations, State or local public agencies, profit corporations, trusts, partnerships, limited partnerships, and be unable to finance the housing either with their own resources or with credit obtained from private sources. However, applicants must be able to assume the obligations of the loan, furnish adequate security, and have sufficient income for repayment.

Beneficiary Eligibility: Occupants must be very low-, low- or moderate-income families households, elderly, handicapped, or disabled persons.

Award Range/Average: No Data Available.

Funding: (Direct Loans) FY 17 $33,204,553; FY 18 est $39,000,000; FY 19 est $0; FY 16 $33,000,000.

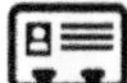

HQ: Multi-Family Housing Direct Loan Division Rural Development

Washington, DC 20250

Phone: 202-720-1604

Email: dsandison@agr.wa.gov

http://beta.sam.gov/fal/4fea7568bf0d411f96b5bd98be6c3515/view?keywords=10.415&sort=-relevance&index=&is_active=true&page=1

RURAL SELF-HELP HOUSING TECHNICAL ASSISTANCE "Section 523 Technical Assistance"

Award: Project Grants

Purpose: The Self-help Technical Assistance Grants financial support to those with less income to construct homes with the self-help method and assistance to nonprofit organizations. Section 523 provides up to $10,000 for qualified organizations.

Applicant Eligibility: Must be a State or political subdivision, public nonprofit corporation or a private nonprofit corporation. Assistance is authorized for eligible applicants in the United States, Puerto Rico, Virgin Islands, Guam, and the Northern Marianas.

Beneficiary Eligibility: Very low and low-income rural families, usually in groups of 6 to 10 families.

Award Range/Average: FY 2017 average grant assistance $800,000. FY 2018 average grant assistance $824,766 FY 2018 average amount is estimated.

Funding: (Project Grants) FY 17 $27,626,751; FY 18 est $29,000,000; FY 19 est $0; FY 16 $22,148,496; - Fiscal Year 2019 estimates are based on the President's proposed budget.

HQ: 1400 Independence Avenue SW
Washington, DC 20250
Phone: 804-287-1559
Email: myron.wooden@wdc.usda.gov

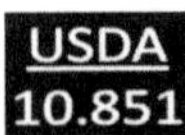

RURAL TELEPHONE LOANS & LOAN GUARANTEES "Telecommunications Infrastructure Loan Program"

Award: Direct Loans; Guaranteed/Insured Loans

Purpose: To assist those in rural areas to have telecommunications services.

Applicant Eligibility: Telephone companies or cooperatives, nonprofit associations, limited dividend associations, mutual associations or public bodies including those located in the U.S. Territories and countries included in the Compact of Free Association Act of 1985, providing or proposing to provide telecommunications service to meet the needs of rural areas.

Beneficiary Eligibility: Residents and businesses of eligible rural areas.

Award Range/Average: Direct Loans - $2,000,000 to $59,356,000 Avg. $20,369,417 Guaranteed Loans - $2,000,000 to $59,775,000 Avg. $16,629,091

Funding: (Guaranteed/Insured Loans) FY 17 $182,920,000; FY 18 est $57,021,000; FY 19 est $1,000,000; FY 16 $96,222,000; - FFB Treasury Loans (Direct Loans) FY 17 $0; FY 18 est $0; FY 19 est $0; FY 16 $0; - Hardship Loans (Direct Loans) FY 17$244,433,000; FY 18 est

HQ: 1400 Independence Avenue SW Room 5151, P.O. Box 1590
Washington, DC 20250
Phone: 202-720-9554
Email: chad.parker@wdc.usda.gov
http://www.rd.usda.gov/programs-services/telecommunications-infrastructure-loans-loan-guarantees

RYAN WHITE HIV/AIDS DENTAL REIMBURSEMENT & COMMUNITY BASED DENTAL PARTNERSHIP GRANTS

Award: Formula Grants; Project Grants

Purpose: The Dental Reimbursement Program partially compensates accredited dental schools, postdoctoral dental education programs, and dental hygiene education programs for unreimbursed costs they have incurred in providing oral health services to low income, uninsured, and underserved people living with HIV (PLWH). The Community Based Dental Partnership Program aims to improve access to oral healthcare services for low income, uninsured and underserved PLWH in underserved geographic areas.

Applicant Eligibility: Applicants are limited to accredited dental schools and other accredited dental education programs such as dental hygiene programs or those sponsored by a school of dentistry, a hospital, or a public or private institution that offers postdoctoral training in the specialties of dentistry, advanced education in general dentistry, or a dental general practice residency.

Beneficiary Eligibility: Low income, uninsured, and underserved people living with HIV.

Award Range/Average: Dental Reimbursement: $1,901 to $ 1,134,333; Average $155,737. Community-Based Dental Partnership grants: $219,230 to $364,172; Average $289,999.

Funding: (Project Grants) FY 17 $3,189,991; FY 18 est $3,475,672; FY 19 est $3,475,672; FY 16 $3,189,991; - Community Based Dental Partnership Program (Formula Grants) FY 17$8,721,326; FY 18 est $8,500,000; FY 19 est $8,500,000; FY 16 $9,342,411; - Dental Reimburs

HQ: 5600 Fishers Lane, Room 09N09
Rockville, MD 20857
Phone: 301-443-2075
Email: mmofidi@hrsa.gov
http://www.hrsa.gov

SAFETY & ENVIRONMENTAL ENFORCEMENT RESEARCH & DATA COLLECTION FOR OFFSHORE ENERGY & MINERAL ACTIVITIES
"Office of Offshore Regulatory Programs (OORP)"

Award: Cooperative Agreements

Purpose: The Agency oversees the exploration and development of oil, natural gas and other materials and renewable energy alternatives on the Nation's outer continental shelf. Bureau of Safety and Environmental Enforcement continues to look for better ways to serve the American people and to ensure that the nation receives the best oversight and regulation of National resource development now and into the future. The purposes of the Office of Offshore Regulatory Program (OORP) is to obtain the information needed to improve the knowledge, practices, and technologies used to promote operational safety and pollution prevention for offshore oil and gas activities and alternate energy projects.

Applicant Eligibility: State agencies and public universities may apply. More than one institution may collaborate in the preparation of an application for assistance.

Beneficiary Eligibility: Research scientists, Federal, State and local decision-makers, and the general public will ultimately benefit from the program.

Award Range/Average: Range is $100,000 to $5,000,000; Average $350,000.

Funding: (Cooperative Agreements) FY 17 $501,000; FY 18 N/A FY 19 N/A FY 16 $907,024.

HQ: 45600 Woodland Road
Sterling, VA 20164
Phone: 703-787-1844
Email: andre.king@bsee.gov
http://www.bsee.gov

SBA EMERGING LEADERS INITIATIVE
"Emerging Leaders"

Award: Direct Payments for Specified Use

Purpose: Provides executives with the organizational framework and resources to build sustainable businesses and support economic development within underserved communities.

Applicant Eligibility: Existing small business owners that meet criteria, this training is for established business owners and is not for start-ups or people who are thinking about starting a business. The Emerging Leaders Initiative advanced training series is open to small business owners and executives that:

Have annual revenues of at least $400,000; Have been in business for at least 3 years; Have at least one employee, other than self

Beneficiary Eligibility: Existing small business owners

Award Range/Average: N/A

Funding: (Direct Payments for Specified Use) FY 17 est $2,675,421; FY 15$2,555,067; FY 16 est $2,732,421.

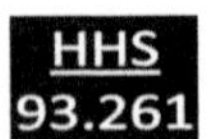
HQ: 409 3rd Street SW, 6th Floor
Washington, DC 20416
Phone: 202-205-6052
Email: john.bienko@sba.gov
http://www.sba.gov

HHS 93.261 SCALING THE NATIONAL DIABETES PREVENTION PROGRAM TO PRIORITY POPULATIONS "National Diabetes Prevention Program"

Award: Cooperative Agreements

Purpose: To scale (expand) and sustain the National Diabetes Prevention Program (National DPP).

Applicant Eligibility: Nonprofit Organizations, For-Profit Organizations, Indian/Native American Tribal Governments, Faith-based Organizations

Beneficiary Eligibility: Any U.S. state, political subdivision and U.S. territories and other public entities will benefit.

Award Range/Average: $750,000 - $ 2 million

Funding: (Cooperative Agreements) FY 17 $14,165,149; FY 18 est $14,165,143; FY 19 est $14,165,143; FY 16 $7,017,715. FY 17 funding is reflective of a new NOFO which is a follow on that supports DP17-1705.

HQ: 4770 Buford Highway, P.O. Box K75
Atlanta, GA 30341
Phone: 770-488-8330
http://www.cdc.gov/diabetes/prevention

HHS 93.925 SCHOLARSHIPS FOR HEALTH PROFESSIONS STUDENTS FROM DISADVANTAGED BACKGROUNDS "Scholarships for Disadvantaged Students (SDS)"

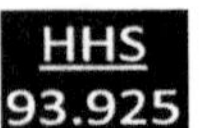

Award: Project Grants

Purpose: The SDS program promotes service in primary care and in medically underserved communities by providing grants to eligible health professions and nursing schools for use in awarding scholarships to students from disadvantaged backgrounds who have financial need for such scholarships.

Applicant Eligibility: Accredited public or non-profit private schools of medicine, nursing, osteopathic medicine, dentistry, pharmacy, podiatric medicine, optometry, veterinary medicine, chiropractic, allied health, public health, a school offering a graduate program in behavioral and mental health practice, or an entity providing programs for the training of physician assistants. 1) At least 20 percent of the total enrollment (full-time enrolled) of a program during the specified academic year must be students from disadvantaged backgrounds; and 2) At least 20 percent of the total graduates (who were full-time students) of a program during the specified academic year must have been from disadvantaged backgrounds.

Beneficiary Eligibility: Students who are citizens, nationals, or lawful permanent residents of the United States or the District of Columbia, the Commonwealths of Puerto Rico or the Northern Mariana Islands, the U.S. Virgin Islands, Guam, the American Samoa, the Republic of Palau, the Republic of the Marshall Islands, the Federated States of Micronesia; and enrolled full-time in health professions or nursing schools.

Award Range/Average: Range FY est 2018: $28,000 to $650,000; Average est $578,812.

Funding: (Project Grants) FY 17 $43,120,389; FY 18 est $45,991,614; FY 19 est $0; FY 16 $42,621,413.

HQ: Bureau of Health Workforce 5600 Fishers Lane, Room 15N78
Rockville, MD 20857
Phone: 301-443-1173
Email: dsorrell@hrsa.gov
http://bhw.hrsa.gov/loansscholarships/schoolbasedloans

SCHOOL SAFETY NATIONAL ACTIVITIES (FORMERLY, SAFE & DRUG-FREE SCHOOLS & COMMUNITIES-NATIONAL PROGRAMS)

Award: Project Grants

Purpose: To improve safety and well-being for students during and after the school day.

Applicant Eligibility: Public and private entities, and individuals.

Beneficiary Eligibility: State educational agencies, local educational agencies, institutions of higher education, public and private organizations and institutions will benefit.

Award Range/Average: No Data Available.

Funding: (Project Grants) FY 17 $68,000,000; FY 18 est $90,000,000; FY 19 est $43,000,000.

HQ: LBJ Building, Room 3E330
Washington, DC 20202
Phone: 202-453-6727
Email: paul.kesner@ed.gov
http://www2.ed.gov/about/offices/list/oese/oshs/index.html

SCIENCE, TECHNOLOGY, BUSINESS AND/OR EDUCATION OUTREACH

Award: Cooperative Agreements

Purpose: To assist in the efforts innovative approaches and various methods of development measures of NIST research. It also supports small businesses and other research programs.

Applicant Eligibility: Public and private institutions of higher education, public and private hospitals, and other quasi-public and private non-profit organizations such as, but not limited to, community action agencies, research institutes, educational associations, and health centers. The term may include commercial organizations, foreign or international organizations (such as agencies of the United Nations) which are recipients, subrecipients, or contractors or subcontractors of recipients or subrecipients at the discretion of the DoC.

Beneficiary Eligibility: Same as Applicant Eligibility.

Award Range/Average: Dependent upon nature and type of grant

Funding: (Cooperative Agreements) FY 17 $19,740,065; FY 18 est $23,521,919; FY 19 est $49,907,000; FY 16 $18,424,889.

HQ: 100 Bureau Drive, P.O. Box 1090
Gaithersburg, MD 20899
Phone: 301-975-2371
Email: brandi.toliver@nist.gov
http://www.nist.gov

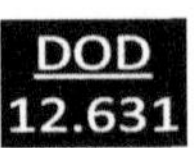

SCIENCE, TECHNOLOGY, ENGINEERING & MATHEMATICS (STEM) EDUCATIONAL PROGRAM: SCIENCE, MATHEMATICS & RESEARCH FOR TRANSFORMATION (SMART)
"Science, Technology, Engineering and Mathematics (STEM)"

Award: Cooperative Agreements; Project Grants

Purpose: To increase the intellectual capacity and proficiency of future scientists and engineers in disciplines critical to defense.

Applicant Eligibility: Subject to language in any announcement for competitive procedures.

Beneficiary Eligibility: All applicants for scholarships must be at least 18 years of age and U.S. citizens. Applicants must be an undergraduate or graduate student majoring in a DoD-relevant STEM field.

Award Range/Average: See above.

Funding: (Project Grants) FY 17 $30,000,000; FY 18 est $35,000,000; FY 19 est $30,419,552; FY 16 $27,000,000; FY 15$2,576,362; FY 14 est $10,000,000; - These figures are for scholarships to non-DoD personnel.

HQ: 800 Park Office Drive, Suite 4229
Research Triangle Park, NC 27709
Phone: 919-549-4338
Email: andrew.l.fiske.civ@mail.mil

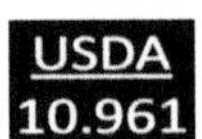

SCIENTIFIC COOPERATION & RESEARCH
"Scientific Cooperation Research Program (SCRP)"

Award: Cooperative Agreements; Direct Payments for Specified Use

Purpose: To leverage resources to advance cooperative research extension in agriculture.

Applicant Eligibility: Institutions of higher education in the United States, including state cooperative institutions.

Beneficiary Eligibility: Beneficiaries will be specified in the Notice of Funding Opportunities, and are generally nationals of an eligible beneficiary country.

Award Range/Average: Research projects up to 18 months. Individual projects may not exceed $40,000 of program funding.

Funding: (Cooperative Agreements) FY 17 $240,000; FY 18 est $280,000; FY 19 est $280,000; FY 16 $240,000.

HQ: 1400 Independence Avenue SW #3226, P.O. Box 1030
Washington, DC 20250
Phone: 202-690-1940
Email: tim.sheehan@fas.usda.gov
http://www.fas.usda.gov/programs/scientific-cooperation-research-program

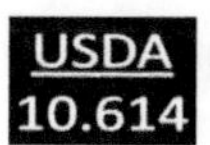

SCIENTIFIC COOPERATION EXCHANGE PROGRAM WITH CHINA "SCEP"

Award: Project Grants; Direct Payments for Specified Use

Purpose: To encourage agricultural research between the United States and China through mutual cooperation.

Applicant Eligibility: U.S. Institutions of higher-learning, and public and private nonprofit organizations whose primary purpose is agriculture, natural resources management and/or rural development (including those located in U.S. territories).

Beneficiary Eligibility: U.S. institutions from the public, private, and academia sectors.

Award Range/Average: Exchange visits last approximately two weeks. Average cost per participant is $8,000.

Funding: Project Grants (Cooperative Agreements or Contracts) FY 17 $345,000; FY 18 est $300,000; FY 19 est $300,000; FY 16 $371,979.

HQ: 1400 Independence Avenue SW #3226, P.O. Box 1030
Washington, DC 20250
Phone: 202-690-1940
Email: tim.sheehan@fas.usda.gov

SCIENTIFIC LEADERSHIP AWARDS

Award: Project Grants; Direct Payments for Specified Use

Purpose: The program helps attract highly talented students and other professionals such as scholars and fellows to work on emerging areas of science and technology that is of high importance to the homeland security.

Applicant Eligibility: US accredited MSIs are eligible to apply. Student recipients must be U.S. citizens studying in one of the following areas including: computer science, engineering, life sciences, math, physical sciences, psychology, social sciences.

Beneficiary Eligibility: Undergraduate Student, Graduate Student, and Minority Serving Institution Faculty.

Award Range/Average: Refer to program guidance.

Funding: (Project Grants) FY 17 $3,396,347; FY 18 est $3,500,000; FY 19 est $3,396,347.

HQ: Office of University Programs S and T 245 Murray Lane Building 410, P.O. Box 0217
Washington, DC 20523
Phone: 202-254-5695
http://www.hsuniversityprograms.org

DOD 12.351 SCIENTIFIC RESEARCH – COMBATING WEAPONS OF MASS DESTRUCTION

Award: Cooperative Agreements; Project Grants

Purpose: To support and stimulate basic, applied and advanced research at educational or research institutions, non-profit organizations, and commercial firms.

Applicant Eligibility: As stated in individual program BAAs. Generally, competitions are open to private and public educational accredited institutions of higher education that carry out science and engineering research and/or related science and engineering education on a non-profit basis.

Beneficiary Eligibility: See above.

Award Range/Average: No Data Available.

Funding: (Project Grants) FY 17 $67,822,327; FY 18 est $67,000,000; FY 19 est $78,850,816; FY 16 $66,330,338.

HQ: 8725 Mr. John J. Kingman Road, P.O. Box 6201
Fort Belvoir, VA 22060
Phone: 703-767-5853
Email: ato.b.andoh.civ@mail.mil

SBA 59.026 SCORE "SHOP"

Award: Project Grants

Purpose: To use the management experience of retired and active business professionals to counsel and train potential and existing small business owners.

Applicant Eligibility: All existing and potential small business owners are eligible. The business must be independently owned and operated, not dominant in its field, and must conform to SBA size standards.

Beneficiary Eligibility: Current and potential small business persons.

Award Range/Average: FY 15 $8,000,000 FY 16 $10,500,000 FY 17 $10,300,000

Funding: (Project Grants) FY 17 $10,500,000; FY 18 est $10,500,000; FY 19 est $9,900,000.

HQ: 409 3rd Street SW, 6th Floor
Washington, DC 20416
Phone: 202-205-7007
Email: nvbishop@sba.gov
http://www.sba.gov

DOJ 16.812 SECOND CHANCE ACT REENTRY INITIATIVE "Second Chance Act (SCA)"

Award: Cooperative Agreements; Project Grants

Purpose: To compensate for the programs that assist those individuals from prison to the community is successful.

Applicant Eligibility: See current solicitation at the Office of Justice Programs website http://ojp.gov/funding/Explore/CurrentFundingOpportunities.

Beneficiary Eligibility: N/A

Award Range/Average: Varies, see solicitation guidelines posted on the Office of Justice Programs web site at http://www.ojp.gov/funding/solicitations.htm or www.bja.gov.

Funding: (Cooperative Agreements) FY 17 $49,045,026; FY 18 est $85,000,000; FY 19 est $58,000,000.

HQ: Bureau of Justice Assistance 810 7th Street NW
Washington, DC 20531
Phone: 202-616-6500
Email: askbja@usdoj.gov
http://www.bja.gov

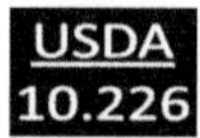

SECONDARY & TWO-YEAR POSTSECONDARY AGRICULTURE EDUCATION CHALLENGE GRANTS "SPECA Grants Program"

Award: Project Grants

Purpose: To encourage agricultural education for the students to promote agribusiness and agriscience.

Applicant Eligibility: Public secondary schools or public or private nonprofit junior and community colleges.

Beneficiary Eligibility: Same as Applicant Eligibility.

Award Range/Average: If minimum or maximum amounts of funding per competitive and/or capacity project grant, or cooperative agreement are established, these amounts will be announced in the annual Competitive Request for Application (RFA). The most current RFA is available via: https://nifa.usda.gov/funding-opportunity/secondary-education-two-year-postsecondary-education-and-agriculture-k-12

Funding: (Project Grants) FY 17 $855,255; FY 18 est $839,625; FY 19 est $0; FY 16 $852,300; - The difference between the appropriation and obligation numbers reflects legislative authorized set-asides deducted as appropriate, and in some cases the availability of obligational authority from prior years. NOTE: Funding associated with this program has been transferred to the Department of Education or the National Science Foundation in the President's FY 2016 Budget proposal. Therefore, FY 2019 funds are not reported for the NIFA program.

HQ: National Program Leader Institute of Youth Family and Community Division of Community and Education 1400 Independence Avenue SW, P.O. Box 2250
Washington, DC 20250-2250
Phone: 202-720-2324
Email: rali@nifa.usda.gov
http://nifa.usda.gov/program/secondary-education-two-year-postsecondary-education-and-agriculture-k-12-classroom

SECTION 223 DEMONSTRATION PROGRAMS TO IMPROVE COMMUNITY MENTAL HEALTH SERVICES
"Section 223 Behavioral Health Demonstration"

Award: Project Grants

Purpose: Funding to support development of proposals to participate in time-limited demonstration programs described in subsection (d) of section 223 of P.L. 113-93 Protecting Access to Medicare Act of 2014, 42 USC 1396(a) note.

Applicant Eligibility: The statutory authority limits eligibility to states including the District of Columbia. Eligible applicants are either the State Mental Health Authority (SMHSA) or the Single State Agency for Substance Abuse Services (SSA) or the State Medicaid Agency (SMAs).

Beneficiary Eligibility: Individual/Family; Non-profit organization; Consumer; Mentally Disabled; Drug Addict; Alcoholic; Child; Youth; Senior Citizen

Award Range/Average: Up to $3 Million.

Funding: (Project Grants) FY 17 $0; FY 18 est $0; FY 19 est $0; FY 16 $22,959,820.

HQ: 1 Choke Cherry Road, Room 7-1097
Rockville, MD 20850
Phone: 240-276-1418
Email: roger.george@samhsa.hhs.gov
http://www.samhsa.gov

SECTION 4 CAPACITY BUILDING FOR COMMUNITY DEVELOPMENT & AFFORDABLE HOUSING
"Section 4 Capacity Building"

Award: N/A

Purpose: To serve low- and moderate-income families with community development and low-cost housing activities.

Applicant Eligibility: By law, there are only three eligible applicants for the Section 4 program. The competition is limited to the organizations identified in Section 4 of the HUD Demonstration Act of 1993 (Pub.

Beneficiary Eligibility: Community Development Corporations (CDCs) and Community Housing Development Organizations (CHDOs) are the only eligible beneficiaries.

Award Range/Average: There have been three grant awards made each fiscal year ranging from $5 million to $15 million over the past three years.

Funding: (Project Grants) FY 17 $35,000,000; FY 18 est $35,000,000; FY 19 est $35,000,000.

HQ: 451 7th Street SW
Washington, DC 20410
Phone: 202-402-4385
Email: diane.m.schmutzler@hud.gov
http://www.hudexchange.info

SECTION 4 CAPACITY BUILDING FOR COMMUNITY DEVELOPMENT & AFFORDABLE HOUSING
"Section 4 Capacity Building"

Award: Project Grants

Purpose: To build the capacity of Community Development Corporations (CDCs) and Community Housing Development Organizations (CHDOs) to serve their communities and low- and moderate-income families.

Applicant Eligibility: By law, there are only three eligible applicants for the Section 4 program. The competition is limited to the organizations identified in Section 4 of the HUD Demonstration Act of 1993 (Pub.

Beneficiary Eligibility: Community Development Corporations (CDCs) and Community Housing Development Organizations (CHDOs) are the only eligible beneficiaries.

Award Range/Average: There have been three grant awards made each fiscal year ranging from $5 million to $15 million over the past three years.

Funding: (Project Grants) FY 17 $35,000,000; FY 18 est $35,000,000; FY 19 est $35,000,000.

HQ: 451 7th Street SW
Washington, DC 20410
Phone: 202-402-4385
Email: diane.m.schmutzler@hud.gov
http://www.hudexchange.info/programs/section-4-capacity-building

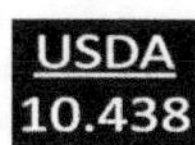

SECTION 538 RURAL RENTAL HOUSING GUARANTEED LOANS
"Rural Rental Housing Guaranteed Loans"

Award: Guaranteed/Insured Loans

Purpose: To support by providing loans for multifamily housing in rural areas.

Applicant Eligibility: The applicant in this program is the lender. The lender must be approved and currently active with Fannie Mae, Freddie Mac, HUD/FHA insurance programs, Ginnie Mae or be a State or local Housing Finance Agency.

Beneficiary Eligibility: Occupants must be families or persons with income not in excess of 115 percent of the Median Income at the time of initial occupancy.

Award Range/Average: N/A

Funding: (Guaranteed/Insured Loans) FY 17 $176,969,693; FY 18 est $230,000,000; FY 19 est $230,000,000; FY 16 $186,935,103.

HQ: 1400 Independence Avenue SW
Washington, DC 20250
Phone: 202-720-1604
Email: michael.steininger@wdc.usda.gov
http://www.rd.usda.gov

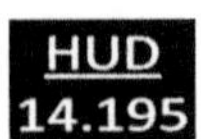

HUD 14.195 SECTION 8 HOUSING ASSISTANCE PAYMENTS PROGRAM "Project-based Section 8"

Award: Direct Payments for Specified Use

Purpose: To provide rental aid to very low income individuals and families helping them live in low-cost, decent, safe, and sanitary housing.

Applicant Eligibility: No funding is available to new applicants. Funding is currently available only for the owners of record of projects with an existing expiring project-based Section 8 contract.

Beneficiary Eligibility: Families currently receiving assistance as long as their income does not exceed 80 percent of area median income adjusted for smaller or larger families.

Award Range/Average: Eligible tenants pay no more than 30 percent of their monthly adjusted income for rent.

Funding: (Direct Payments for Specified Use) FY 17 est $10,707,000,000; FY 15$9,537,000,000; FY 16 est $10,393,000,000.

HQ: 451 7th Street SW
Washington, DC 20410
Phone: 202-402-6732
Email: catherine.m.brennan@hud.gov

HUD 14.871 SECTION 8 HOUSING CHOICE VOUCHERS

Award: Direct Payments for Specified Use

Purpose: Aiding very low-income families in obtaining decent, safe, and sanitary rental housing.

Applicant Eligibility: Applicants are limited to public housing agencies. A public housing agency (PHA) is defined as any State, county, municipality or other governmental entity or public body (or agency or instrumentality thereof) which is authorized to engage in or assist in the development or operation of housing for very low income families; and, a consortium of PHAs; any other nonprofit entity that was administering a Section 8 tenant-based program on October 21, 1998; or, for an area outside the jurisdiction of a PHA administering a voucher program, a private nonprofit entity or a governmental entity or public body that would otherwise lack jurisdiction to administer the program in such area.

Beneficiary Eligibility: Very low income families (whose income does not exceed 50 percent of the median income for the area as determined by the Secretary with adjustments for smaller and larger families) and, on an exception basis, lower income families (whose income does not exceed 80 percent of the median income for the area, adjusted for smaller and larger families). At least 75 percent of families admitted to the voucher program during the PHA fiscal year must be extremely low income families (whose income does not exceed 30 percent of the median income for the area).

Award Range/Average: $5,618 to $1,074,563,247 average of 7,142,148

Funding: (Direct Payments for Specified Use) FY 17 $16,740,888,987; FY 18 est $17,211,712,441; FY 19 est $16,425,500,023; FY 16 $16,548,277,187.

HQ: 451 7th Street SW
Washington, DC 20410
Phone: 202-402-6050
Email: becky.l.primeaux@hud.gov

HUD 14.249 SECTION 8 MODERATE REHABILITATION SINGLE ROOM OCCUPANCY

Award: Project Grants

Purpose: To provide rental assistance to homeless individuals.

Applicant Eligibility: An eligible applicant is a PHA or private nonprofit organization. Private nonprofits have to contract with a PHA to administer the rental assistance.

Beneficiary Eligibility: Homeless individuals.

Award Range/Average: No Data Available.

Funding: (Project Grants) FY 16 $0; FY 17 est $0; FY 18 est $0.

HQ: Office of Special Needs Assistance Programs 400 Maryland Avenue SW 451 7th Street SW, Room 7266
Washington, DC 20410
Phone: 202-402-4080
Email: brian.p.fitzmaurice@hud.gov
http://www.hudexchange.info/sro

DHS 97.106 SECURING THE CITIES PROGRAM "STC"

Award: Cooperative Agreements; Use of Property, Facilities, and Equipment; Dissemination of Technical Information

Purpose: The program seeks to prevent the smuggling of nuclear and radiological components and weaponry into the country by enhancing the nuclear detection capabilities of the local, State and Federal territorial agencies.

Applicant Eligibility: Specific information on applicant eligibility is identified in the funding opportunity announcement and program guidance, or as specified by U.S. Appropriation Statute.

Beneficiary Eligibility: State, and local governments, Interstate or intrastate governmental organizations, and Indian tribal governments.

Award Range/Average: See Program Guidance.

Funding: (Salaries and Expenses) FY 17 $2,500,000; FY 18 est $19,350,000; FY 19 est $34,640,000; FY 16 $19,885,000.

HQ: DNDO 245 Murray Lane, P.O. Box 0550
Washington, DC 20528
Phone: 202-254-7223
Email: kimberly.patten@hq.dhs.gov
http://www.dhs.gov

HUD 14.009 SELF-HELP HOMEOWNERSHIP OPPORTUNITY PROGRAM "SHOP"

Award: N/A

Purpose: Granting funds to purchase home sites and develop or improve the infrastructure for low-income persons and families.

Applicant Eligibility: SHOP grant funds are made available through HUD's annual SHOP NOFA competition. The SHOP NOFA is published on HUD's e-grant portal.

Beneficiary Eligibility: Low and moderate income families and individuals.

Award Range/Average: 450,000 - 10,000,000

Funding: (Project Grants) FY 17 $10,000,000; FY 18 est $100,000,000; FY 19 est $10,000,000.

HQ: 451 7th Street SW, Room 7240
Washington, DC 20410
Phone: 202-708-2290
Email: thann.young@hud.gov
http://www.hudexchange.info

SELF-HELP HOMEOWNERSHIP OPPORTUNITY PROGRAM

Award: Project Grants

Purpose: To assist and support innovative home-ownership opportunities through the provision of self-help home-ownership.

Applicant Eligibility: Funds are awarded competitively to national or regional nonprofit organizations or consortia that have capacity and experience in providing or facilitating self-help housing homeownership opportunities. Grantees must use a significant amount of SHOP grant funds in at least two states.

Beneficiary Eligibility: Eligible homebuyers are low-income families, (including individuals) who are otherwise unable to afford to purchase a dwelling, and who provide significant amounts of sweat equity towards the development of the dwellings.

Award Range/Average: Four grants were awarded with FY 2014 & 2015 funds. They ranged from $562,500 to $6,211,368. The average grant was $1,693,342.

Funding: (Project Grants) FY 17 $10,000,000; FY 18 est $10,000,000; FY 19 est $0; FY 16 $10,000,000.

HQ: 451 7Th Street SW
Washington, DC 20410
Phone: 202-402-4464
Email: thann.young@hud.gov

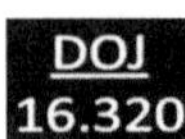

SERVICES FOR TRAFFICKING VICTIMS

Award: Project Grants; Direct Payments for Specified Use

Purpose: To provide comprehensive and specialized services to victims of human trafficking; to develop multidisciplinary task forces with federal, state, and local law enforcement, service providers, and community-

and faith-based organizations to ensure that trafficking victims are identified and referred for appropriate services; to conduct training, technical assistance and public awareness activities for professionals and community members in order to improve their knowledge of human trafficking and their ability to identify and respond to victims; and to conduct data collection and evaluation activities to determine if the program is meeting stated goals and objectives.

Applicant Eligibility: The Attorney General may make grants to States, Indian tribes, units of local government, and nonprofit, non- governmental victim service organizations.

Beneficiary Eligibility: Eligible victim assistance agencies. Eligibility depends on the nature of they may vary depending on specific grant types but generally includes victims and potential victims of human trafficking, as defined in TVPA, but may include a wide variety of public and private nonprofit agencies.

Award Range/Average: OJP anticipates awarding grants of up to $925,000 (depending on the program) for 3 years to support enhanced services to trafficking victims, training and technical assistance, and research and evaluation.

Funding: (Project Grants) FY 17 $40,465,886; FY 18 est $74,690,000; FY 19 est $44,500,000.

HQ: Office of Victims of Crime Department of Justice Office of Justice Programs Office of Victims of Crime, 810 Seventh Street NW

Washington, DC 20531

Phone: 202-305-2601

http://www.ovc.gov

HHS 93.598 SERVICES TO VICTIMS OF A SEVERE FORM OF TRAFFICKING

Award: Project Grants; Direct Payments for Specified Use

Purpose: Provides outreach to, identification of, and service referrals to individuals who may be victims of a severe form of trafficking. To provide comprehensive case management services to alien victims of a severe form of trafficking.

Applicant Eligibility: Eligible organizations includes: state governments, tribes, units of local government, and non-profit, non-governmental victim service organizations. Victim service organizations include those who by nature of their current operations serve victims of sexual assault, sexual violence, domestic violence, human trafficking, and youth homelessness.

Beneficiary Eligibility: Under the TVPA, as amended, alien victims of a severe form of trafficking in persons are eligible for benefits and services to the same extent as refugees. Beneficiaries are adult alien victims of a severe form of trafficking who have been certified by the Department of Health and Human Services (HHS)/OTIP.

Award Range/Average: In FY 2017, grants ranged from $90,000 to $3,491,385. The average grant amount was $490,605.

Funding: (Project Grants) FY 17 $10,126,252; FY 18 est $13,800,000; FY 19 est $13,250,000; FY 16 $10,727,355; - (Direct Payments for Specified Use) FY 17 FY 18 FY 19 FY 16 - (Salaries and Expenses) FY 17$354,000; FY 18 est $380,000; FY 19 est $400,000; FY 16 $440,

HQ: 330 C Street SW, 4th Floor

Washington, DC 20201

Phone: 202-401-9372

Email: katherine.chon@acf.hhs.gov

http://www.acf.hhs.gov/otip

DHS 97.110 SEVERE REPETITIVE LOSS PROGRAM "SRL"

Award: Project Grants

Purpose: It assists local and State governments to help reduce the long-term risk of flood damage to insured properties by removing such structures from flood hazard areas in the shortest time possible.

Applicant Eligibility: Entities eligible to apply for HMA grants include the emergency management agency or a similar office of the 50 States, the District of Columbia, American Samoa, Guam, the U.S. Virgin Islands, Puerto Rico, the Northern Mariana Islands, and Indian Tribal governments. Each State, Territory, Commonwealth, or Indian Tribal government shall designate one agency to serve as the Applicant for each HMA program.

Beneficiary Eligibility: State agencies, Indian Tribal governments, and local governments and communities are eligible to apply as sub applicants for assistance under the SRL program. All interested sub applicants must apply to the Applicant.

Award Range/Average: N/A

Funding: (Project Grants) FY 17 $0; FY 18 est $0; FY 19 FY 16 $0.

HQ: Risk Reduction Branch 1800 S Bell Street
Arlington, VA 20595-3015
Phone: 202-646-3428
Email: lloyd.hake@dhs.gov

SEXUAL RISK AVOIDANCE EDUCATION "SRAE"

Award: Project Grants

Purpose: To promote sexual risk avoidance education, as defined by section 1110 of the Social Security Act, for adolescents.

Applicant Eligibility: Grants made under the authority of section 1110 of the Social Security Act, 42 U.S.C. § 1310 grants shall be made only to public and private entities that agree to use medically accurate information referenced to peer-reviewed publications by educational, scientific, governmental, or health organizations; implement an evidence-based approach integrating research findings with practical implementation that aligns with the needs and desired outcomes for the intended audience; and teach the benefits associated with self-regulation, success sequencing for poverty prevention, healthy relationships, goal setting, and resisting sexual coercion, dating violence, and other youth risk behaviors such as underage drinking or illicit drug use without normalizing teen sexual activity.

Beneficiary Eligibility: Vulnerable populations of youth with a focus on those that are most likely to bear children out-of-wedlock or who live in areas with high teen birth rates.

Award Range/Average: $350,000 to $450,000. The average estimate award amount is $450,000.

Funding: Project Grants (Discretionary) FY 17 $13,447,039; FY 18 est $24,341,891; FY 19 est $24,341,891; FY 16 $8,981,973.

HQ: Mary E Switzer Building 330 C Street SW, Room #3614
Washington, DC 20024
Phone: 202-205-9605
Email: lebretia.white@acf.hhs.gov
http://www.acf.hhs.gov/programs/fysb

HHS 93.977 SEXUALLY TRANSMITTED DISEASES (STD) PREVENTION & CONTROL GRANTS

"Sexually Transmitted Diseases (STD) Prevention and Control Grants: PS13-1306, PS14-1402, PS18-1808"

Award: Project Grants

Purpose: The program provides grants to the State and local STD prevention programs under Section 318 to implement prevention and control programs against sexually transmitted diseases.

Applicant Eligibility: Any State, and, in consultation with the appropriate State Health Authority, any political subdivision of a State, including American Indian/Alaska Native tribal governments or tribal organizations located wholly or in part within their boundaries; academic institutions, and national and public health organizations.

Beneficiary Eligibility: Same as Applicant Eligibility.

Award Range/Average: Range: $149,560 to $2,817,271; Average: $3,571,002

Funding: (Cooperative Agreements) FY 17 $98,380,591; FY 18 est $92,734,652; FY 19 est $96,934,652; FY 16 $93,895,559; - Cooperative Agreement.

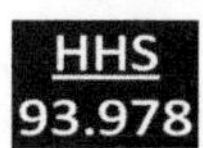

HQ: 1600 Clifton Road NE, P.O. Box E-07
Atlanta, GA 30333
Phone: 404-639-8531
Email: eow1@cdc.gov
http://www.cdc.gov/std

HHS 93.978 SEXUALLY TRANSMITTED DISEASES (STD) PROVIDER EDUCATION GRANTS

"STD Prevention Training Centers: PS14-1407, PS14-1408, PS15-1504, PS17-1707, PS17-1708"

Award: Project Grants

Purpose: The programs funds clinical and public health organizations to develop, deliver and evaluate the educational and clinical skill improvement activities for the healthcare professionals to prevent, control or clinically manage sexually transmitted diseases.

Applicant Eligibility: Academic institutions and national, state and Tribal clinical and public health training organizations.

Beneficiary Eligibility: Private and public clinical providers, such as physicians, nurse practitioners, nurses, physician assistants, pharmacists, and others. Any academic institutions and national, state and Tribal clinical and public health training organizations may apply for assistance.

Award Range/Average: Range: $83,800 to $6,188,272; Average: $2,781,692

Funding: (Cooperative Agreements) FY 17 $7,323,683; FY 18 est $7,342,786; FY 19 est $7,342,786; FY 16 $4,284,914; - STD Prevention Grants = Acct. No. 75-0943-0-1-550 Prevention Training Centers Grants = Acct. No. 75-0950-0-1-550.

HQ: 1600 Clifton Road NE, P.O. Box E-07
Atlanta, GA 30333

Phone: 404-639-8531
Email: eow1@cdc.gov
http://www.cdc.gov/std

SHELTER PLUS CARE

Award: Project Grants

Purpose: To assist through Tenant-based Rental Assistance (TRA), Sponsor-based Rental Assistance (SRA), Project-based Rental Assistance (PRA), (4) and Single Room Occupancy for Homeless Individuals (SRO).

Applicant Eligibility: An eligible applicant is a State, unit of general local government, or public housing agency (PHA).

Beneficiary Eligibility: Homeless persons with disabilities and their families. Except in single room occupancy dwellings that are only for homeless individuals with disabilities.

Award Range/Average: No Data Available.

Funding: (Project Grants) FY 18 est $0; FY 16 $0; FY 17 est $0.

HQ: Office of Special Needs Assistance Programs 451 7th Street SW, Room 7262
Washington, DC 20410
Phone: 202-402-4080
Email: brian.p.fitzmaurice@hud.gov
http://www.hudexchange.info/spc

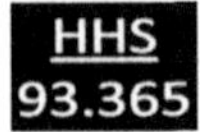

SICKLE CELL TREATMENT DEMONSTRATION PROGRAM "SCDTDP"

Award: Cooperative Agreements

Purpose: To improve the prevention and treatment of sickle cell disease complications, including the coordination of service delivery for individuals with sickle cell disease; genetic counseling and testing; bundling of technical services.

Applicant Eligibility: Eligible entities include, Federally-qualified health center, as defined in section 1905(10(2)(B) of the Social Security Act (42 U.S.C. 1396d(10(2)(B), nonprofit hospital or clinic, or university health center that provides primary health care, that: (1) has a collaborative agreement with a community-based Sickle Cell Disease organization or a nonprofit entity with experience in working with individuals who have Sickle Cell Disease; and (2) demonstrates that either the Federally-qualified health center, the nonprofit hospital or clinic, the university health center, the community-based Sickle Cell Disease organization or the Sickle Cell Disease experts who serve as consultants to the project have at least 5 years of experience in working with individuals who have Sickle Cell Disease.

Beneficiary Eligibility: Projects will benefit individuals with Sickle Cell Disease and health professionals who provide care for individuals with Sickle Cell Disease.

Award Range/Average: FY 18 $357,500 - $1,072,497; $714,998.

Funding: (Cooperative Agreements) FY 17 $3,457,018; FY 18 est $3,457,025; FY 19 est $3,457,025.

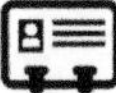
HQ: 5600 Fishers Lane, Room 18W56
Rockville, MD 20857
Phone: 301-443-9775
Email: eivy@hrsa.gov
http://www.hrsa.gov

SINGLE FAMILY PROPERTY DISPOSITION

Award: Sale, Exchange, or Donation of Property and Goods

Purpose: To sell the inventory of HUD-acquired properties, and expand home ownership opportunities, strengthen neighborhoods and communities, and guarantee a maximum return to the FHA mortgage insurance fund.

Applicant Eligibility: Local Governments and Nonprofit Organizations: HUD contractors in the specific area should be contacted regarding eligibility requirements. Contact HUD at Toll free: (800) CALL FHA or (800) 225-5342 for a listing of nationwide HUD contractors.

Beneficiary Eligibility: Individual, governmental and organizational homebuyers.

Award Range/Average: No Data Available.

Funding: (Sale, Exchange, or Donation of Property and Goods) FY 17 est $10,777,393,429; FY 16 est $1,571,887,224.

HQ: 451 7th Street SW
Washington, DC 20410
Phone: 800-225-5342

SKILLS TRAINING & HEALTH WORKFORCE DEVELOPMENT OF PARAPROFESSIONALS GRANT PROGRAM
"Paraprofessionals Training Grant Program"

Award: Project Grants

Purpose: To assist individuals from economically and educationally disadvantaged backgrounds to develop the skills needed to compete for, enter, and graduate from a paraprofessional training program.

Applicant Eligibility: Eligible applicants include accredited schools of medicine, allopathic medicine, osteopathic medicine, public health, dentistry, veterinary medicine, optometry, pharmacy, allied health, chiropractic, podiatric medicine, public and nonprofit private schools that offer graduate programs in behavioral and mental health, programs for the training of physician assistants, two-year community colleges, technical colleges, tribal colleges, and other public or private nonprofit health or educational entities. Each applicant must specifically state its eligibility information in the project abstract.

Beneficiary Eligibility: Beneficiaries include individuals who a) meet the definition of either educationally or economically disadvantaged, b) express an interest in pursuing a health degree program c) have completed at a minimum a high school diploma or GED, or d) individuals who are already practicing in a health-related paraprofessional field and who want additional credentials to advance their employability.

Award Range/Average: FY 16 actual: $136.851- $200,000; average award $192.097 FY 17: $0 FY 18: $0

Funding: (Project Grants) FY 17 $0; FY 18 est $0; FY 19 est $0; FY 16 $2,497,258.

HQ: Bureau of Health Workforce Department of Health and Human Services, Room 15N38D 5600 Fishers Lane
Rockville, MD 20857
Phone: 301-443-0827
Email: tmayo-blake@hrsa.gov
http://bhw.hrsa.gov/grants/healthcareers

SMALL BUSINESS DEVELOPMENT CENTERS "SBDC"

Award: Project Grants; Provision of Specialized Services; Advisory Services and Counseling; Dissemination of Technical Information

Purpose: Provides management counseling, training, and technical assistance to the small business community through Small Business Development Centers (SBDCs).

Applicant Eligibility: SBA is authorized to make grants (including contracts and cooperative agreements) to any public or private institution of higher education, including but not limited to any land- grant college or university, any college or school of business, engineering, commerce, or agriculture, community college or junior college. SBA is also authorized to renew the funding of other entities currently funded as SBDCs providing SBA affirmatively determines that such applicants have their own budget and will primarily utilize institutions of higher education to provide the services to the small business community.

Beneficiary Eligibility: Current and potential Small business persons.

Award Range/Average: No Data Available.

Funding: (Formula Grants) FY 17 $126,532,000; FY 18 est $125,000,000; FY 19 est $110,000,000.

HQ: 409 3rd Street SW, 6th Floor
Washington, DC 20416
Phone: 202-205-7176
Email: victoria.mundt@sba.gov
http://www.sba.gov/sbdc

SMALL BUSINESS INNOVATION RESEARCH "SBIR Program - Phase I and II"

Award: Project Grants

Purpose: To implement technological creations in all businesses and in other research and development aspects.

Applicant Eligibility: Applicant Eligibility (1) is organized for profit, with a place of business located in the United States, which operates primarily within the United States, or which makes a significant contribution to the United States economy through the payment of taxes or use of American products, materials or labor; (2) is in the legal form of an individual proprietorship, partnership, limited liability company, corporation, joint venture, association, trust or cooperative, except that where the form is a joint venture, there can be no more than 49 percent participation by foreign business entities in the joint venture; (3) is at least 51 percent owned and controlled by one or more individuals who are citizens of, or permanent resident aliens in, the United States, except in the case of a joint venture, where each entity in the venture must be 51 percent owned and controlled by one or more individuals who are citizens of, or permanent resident aliens in the United States; and (4) has, including its affiliates, not more than 500 employees. The term "affiliates" is defined in greater detail in 13 CFR 121.

Beneficiary Eligibility: Small businesses.

Award Range/Average: If minimum or maximum amounts of funding per competitive and/or capacity project grant, or cooperative agreement are established, these amounts will be announced in the annual Competitive Request for Application (RFA).

Funding: (Project Grants) FY 17 $22,893,330; FY 18 est $24,209,624; FY 19 est $17,151,241; FY 16 $21,813,069; - The difference between the appropriation and obligation numbers reflects legislative authorized set-asides deducted as appropriate, and in some cases the availability of obligational authority from prior years.

HQ: National Program Leader Institute of Bioenergy Climate and Environment – Division of Environmental Systems 1400 Independence Avenue SW, P.O. Box 2210

Washington, DC 20250-2210

Phone: 202-720-5229

Email: dcassidy@nifa.usda.gov

http://nifa.usda.gov/grants

SMALL BUSINESS INVESTMENT COMPANIES "SBIC; SSBIC"

Award: Guaranteed/Insured Loans

Purpose: To establish privately owned and managed investment companies, which are licensed and regulated by the U.S. Small Business Administration.

Applicant Eligibility: Any chartered small business investment company having private capital of not less than $5 million, having qualified management, giving evidence of sound operation, and establishing the need for SBIC financing in the geographic area in which the applicant proposes to operate.

Beneficiary Eligibility: Individual businesses (single proprietorship, partnership or corporation) which satisfy the established criteria of a small business. SSBICs beneficiary must also be a business owned and operated by socially or economically disadvantaged individuals.

Award Range/Average: Additional information available at SBA's website

Funding: (Guaranteed/Insured Loans) FY 17 $196,000,000; FY 18 est $4,000,000,000; FY 19 est $4,000,000,000; FY 16 $2,514,000,000.

HQ: 409 3rd Street SW, 6th Floor

Washington, DC 20416

Phone: 202-619-0384

http://www.sba.gov

SMALL RURAL HOSPITAL IMPROVEMENT GRANT PROGRAM "Small Rural Hospital Improvement Program"

Award: Project Grants

Purpose: Supports small rural hospitals in their quality improvement efforts and with adapting to changing payment systems through investments in hardware, software, and related trainings.

Applicant Eligibility: The State Office of Rural Health (SORH) in each state will be the official awardee of record, as they will act as a fiscal intermediary for all hospitals within their state. Each SORH will be charged with organizing the distribution of funds to eligible hospitals.

Beneficiary Eligibility: Small rural hospitals must meet the following eligibility requirements in order to be eligible for SHIP funds: "Small" is a facility with 49 or fewer available beds, as reported on the hospital's most recent Medicare Cost Report. "Rural area" is either (a) being located outside of a Metropolitan Statistical Area (MSA); (b) being located within a rural census tract of a MSA, as determined under the Goldsmith Modification or the Rural Urban Commuting Areas; or (c) being treated as if it is located in a rural area pursuant to 42 U.S.C.

Award Range/Average: Range = $20,340 to $1,118,700. $351,970 (average award amount).

Funding: (Project Grants) FY 17 $15,288,642; FY 18 est $16,190,640; FY 19 N/A FY 16 $14,757,796; - Small Hospital Improvement Program.

HQ: The Small Rural Hospital Improvement Program 5600 Fishers Lane
Rockville, MD 20857
Phone: 301-443-3822
Email: bware@hrsa.gov
http://www.hrsa.gov

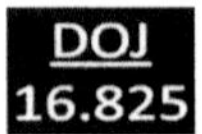

SMART PROSECUTION INITIATIVE "IPI"

Award: Project Grants

Purpose: The Innovative Prosecution Initiative helps prosecutors to develop practices to evaluate new solutions for public safety concerns.

Applicant Eligibility: Site-based-- Eligible applicants are limited to state, local, and tribal prosecutor agencies or a government agency acting as fiscal agent for the applicant. TTA-- Eligible applicants are limited to for-profit (commercial) organizations, nonprofit organizations, and institutions of higher learning that support national initiatives to improve the functioning of the criminal justice system.

Beneficiary Eligibility: N/A

Award Range/Average: See the current fiscal year's solicitation guidelines posted on the Office of Justice Programs web site at https://ojp.gov/funding/Explore/CurrentFundingOpportunities.htm.

Funding: Project Grants (Discretionary) FY 17 $2,258,302; FY 18 est $2,242,009; FY 19 est $5,000,000; FY 16 $2,211,852.

HQ: Bureau of Justice Assistance 810 7th Street NW
Washington, DC 20531
Phone: 202-514-5309
Email: askbja@usdoj.gov
http://www.smartprosecution.apainc.org

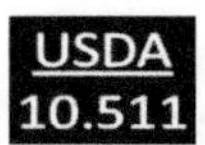

SMITH-LEVER FUNDING (VARIOUS PROGRAMS) "1862 LGI's: 1862 CES (Smith-Lever) and DCPPERA, 1862 Smith-Lever Special Needs, and Smith-Lever Special Needs-Competitive"

Award: Formula Grants; Project Grants

Purpose: To increase agricultural extension activities, education, emergency preparedness for natural and human-made disasters.

Applicant Eligibility: 1862 CES Capacity & DCPPERA: Joint Cooperative Extension Programs at 1862 Land-Grant Institutions applications may only be submitted by the following 1862 Land-grant Institutions: Auburn University, University of Alaska-Fairbanks, American Samoa Community College, University of Arizona, University of Arkansas, University of California, Colorado State University, University of Connecticut, University of Delaware, University of Florida, University of Georgia, University of Guam, University of Hawaii, University of Idaho, University of Illinois, Purdue University, Iowa State University, Kansas State University, University of Kentucky, Louisiana State University, University of Maine, University of Maryland-College Park, University of Massachusetts, Michigan State University, College of Micronesia, University of Minnesota, Mississippi State University, University of Missouri, Montana State University, University of Nebraska, University of Nevada-Reno, University of New Hampshire, Rutgers University, New Mexico State University, Cornell University, North Carolina State University, North Dakota State University, Northern Marianas College, Ohio State University, Oklahoma State University, Oregon State University, Pennsylvania State University, University of Puerto Rico, University of Rhode Island, Clemson University, South Dakota State University, University of Tennessee, Texas A & M University, Utah State University, University of Vermont, Virginia Polytechnic Institute & State University, University of the Virgin Islands, Washington State University, West Virginia University, University of Wisconsin, and University of Wyoming. University of the District of Columbia Public Postsecondary Education Reorganization Act Program (DCPPERA): Applications may only be submitted by the University of the District of Columbia.

Beneficiary Eligibility: Same As Applicant Beneficiary

Award Range/Average: If minimum or maximum amounts of funding per capacity project grant, or cooperative agreement are established, these amounts will be announced in the annual Request for Application (RFA).

Funding: Project Grants (Discretionary) FY 17 $0; FY 18 est $0; FY 19 est $0; FY 16 $0.

HQ: National Program Leader Institute of Food and Production and Sustainability Division of Agricultural Systems 1400 Independence Avenue SW, P.O. Box 2240

Washington, DC 20250-2220

Phone: 202-720-6059

Email: wesley.dean@nifa.usda.gov

http://nifa.usda.gov/program/district-columbia-public-postsecondary-education-reorganization-act-program-cooperative

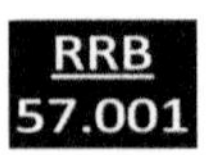

SOCIAL INSURANCE FOR RAILROAD WORKERS
"Railroad retirement and railroad unemployment-sickness insurance programs"

Award: Direct Payments with Unrestricted Use

Purpose: Provide income security for retired and disabled railroad workers, their family members, and survivors, and financial benefits for railroad workers who are unemployed or unable to work due to illness or injury.

Applicant Eligibility: Under the Railroad Retirement Act, for employee, spouse and survivor benefits, the employee must have had 10 or more years of railroad service or, for annuities beginning January 2002 or later, 5 years of railroad service rendered after 1995. For survivors to be eligible for benefits, the employee must also have been insured at death.

Beneficiary Eligibility: Individuals, families, pension recipients.

Award Range/Average: Amounts for 2017: Employee initially awarded age annuities – monthly maximum $5,037, average $2,806; employee disability – monthly maximum $4,992, average $2,744; employee supplemental annuities – monthly maximum $70, average $42; married spouse benefits – monthly maximum $2,405, average $1,047; widows and widowers – monthly maximum $4,805, average $1,696; children – monthly maximum $2,780, average $1,109; unemployment and sickness – weekly maximum for benefit year 2017-2018 $361, expected average $361.

Funding: (Direct Payments with Unrestricted Use) FY 17 $12,667,000,000; FY 18 est $12,841,000,000; FY 19 est $13,148,000,000; FY 16 $12,594,000,000; - (Salaries and Expenses) FY 17$141,500,000; FY 18 est $142,100,000; FY 19 est $143,200,000.

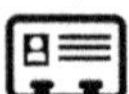

HQ: 844 N Rush Street 4NE
Chicago, IL 60611-1275
Phone: 312-751-4932
Email: bruce.rodman@rrb.gov
http://www.rrb.gov

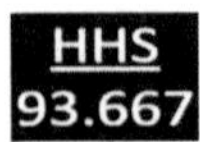

SOCIAL SERVICES BLOCK GRANT
"SSBG Program"

Award: Formula Grants

Purpose: Enables each State to furnish social services best suited to the needs of the individuals residing in the State. Federal block grant funds may be used to provide services directed toward one of the following five goals specified in the law: (1) Prevent, reduce, or eliminate dependency; (2) Achieve or maintain self-sufficiency; (3) Prevent neglect, abuse, or exploitation of children and adults; (4) Prevent or reduce inappropriate institutional care; and (5) Secure admission or referral for institutional care when other forms of care are not appropriate.

Applicant Eligibility: The 50 States, the District of Columbia, Puerto Rico, Guam, the Virgin Islands, the Commonwealth of the Northern Mariana Islands, and American Samoa are eligible entities.

Beneficiary Eligibility: Under Title XX, each eligible jurisdiction determines the services that will be provided and the individuals that will be eligible to receive services.

Award Range/Average: $36,087 to $194,063,454 ; $28,303,508 on average.

Funding: (Formula Grants) FY 17 $1,582,700,000; FY 18 est $1,587,800,000; FY 19 est $0; FY 16 $1,584,400,000.

HQ: Division of Social Services 330 C Street SW 5th Floor W, P.O. Box 5425
Washington, DC 20201
Phone: 202-401-5591
Email: yolanda.butler@acf.hhs.gov
http://www.acf.hhs.gov/programs/ocs/ssbg

SOCIAL SERVICES RESEARCH & DEMONSTRATION "SSRD"

Award: Project Grants

Purpose: Promotes research and demonstrations related to the prevention and reduction of dependency or the administration and effectiveness of programs related to that purpose.

Applicant Eligibility: Grants and cooperative agreements may be made to or with governmental entities, colleges, universities, nonprofit and for-profit organizations (if fee is waived), and faith-based and community organizations. Grants and cooperative agreements cannot be made directly to individuals.

Beneficiary Eligibility: Children, youth, and families, especially low-income families, will benefit.

Award Range/Average: Range from $24,918 to $100,000; Average being $70,772.75

Funding: (Project Grants) FY 17 $849,273; FY 18 est $624,577; FY 19 est $150,000; FY 16 $842,073.

HQ: 330 C Street SW, Room 4625A
Washington, DC 20201
Phone: 202-401-5803
Email: sheila.celentano@acf.hhs.gov
http://www.acf.hhs.gov/programs/opre

SOCIAL, BEHAVIORAL, AND ECONOMIC SCIENCES "SBE"

Award: Project Grants

Purpose: To contribute to the scientific strength and welfare of the Nation through the promotion of basic research and education in the social, behavioral and economic sciences and through monitoring and understanding the resources invested in science and engineering in the United States.

Applicant Eligibility: Except where a program solicitation establishes more restrictive eligibility criteria, individuals and organizations in the following categories may submit proposals: Universities and colleges; Non-profit, non-academic organizations; For-profit organizations; State and local governments; and unaffiliated individuals. See the NSF Grant Proposal Guide, Chapter I.

Beneficiary Eligibility: N/A

Award Range/Average: Range Low $377 Range High $15,777,424 Average $104,193

Funding: (Project Grants) FY 17 est $269,820,000; FY 16 $272,200,000; FY 18 est $244,020,000.

HQ: Senior Information Technology 2415 Eisenhower Avenue
Alexandria, VA 22314
Phone: 703-292-8700
Email: dlivings@nsf.gov
http://nsf.gov/dir/index.jsp?org=sbe

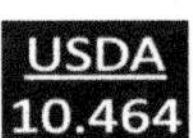

SOCIALLY DISADVANTAGED FARMERS & RANCHERS POLICY RESEARCH CENTER "Policy Research Center"

Award: Project Grants

Purpose: The Policy Research Center assists socially disadvantaged farmers and ranchers. The program also creates awareness of socially disadvantaged farmers and ranchers.

Applicant Eligibility: Only 1890 Institutions as defined in 7 U.S.C. 7601, including Tuskegee University, may apply and are eligible to receive funds under the Act of August 30, 1890

Beneficiary Eligibility: Minority Farmers and Ranchers

Award Range/Average: 400000

Funding: (Salaries and Expenses) FY 17 $400,000; FY 18 est $400,000; FY 19 est $400,000; FY 16 est $400,000; FY 15$400,000.

HQ: 1400 Independence Avenue SW Room 520-A, P.O. Box 0601
Washington, DC 20250
Phone: 202-720-6350
http://www.outreach.usda.gov/education/index.htm

SOCIALLY-DISADVANTAGED GROUPS GRANT "SSDG"

Award: Project Grants

Purpose: To assist financially distressed groups through Cooperative Development Centers.

Applicant Eligibility: Eligible applicants are cooperatives, groups of cooperatives, and cooperative development centers that serve socially-disadvantaged groups and whose governing board is comprised of a majority of individuals who are members of a socially-disadvantaged group. Applicants are not eligible if they have been debarred or suspended or otherwise excluded from participation in Federal assistance programs under Executive Order 12549, "Debarment and Suspension.

Beneficiary Eligibility: Ultimate beneficiaries must be located in rural areas, as defined by 7 U.S.C. 1991(a).

Award Range/Average: Average = $150,000 Range = $37,000 (minimum) to $175,000 (maximum)

Funding: (Project Grants) FY 17 $3,000,000; FY 18 est $3,000,000; FY 19 N/A FY 16 $3,000,000; - Project usually fund with $3,000,000 annually.

HQ: Cooperative Programs Grants Division 1400 Independence Avenue SW Room 4208-S, P.O. Box 3253
Washington, DC 20250
Phone: 202-690-1374
http://www.rd.usda.gov/programs-services/socially-disadvantaged-groups-grant

SODIUM REDUCTION IN COMMUNITIES

Award: Cooperative Agreements

Purpose: To reduce Americans' sodium intake to limits recommended by the Dietary Guidelines.

Applicant Eligibility: a. An official state health department (or its bona fide agent), or its equivalent, as designated by the Governor, is to serve as the lead/fiduciary agency for Small City and Rural Community applications.

Beneficiary Eligibility: Any U.S. state, political subdivision and U.S. territories (as described above), and other public entities will benefit.

Award Range/Average: 250,000 for Large City Applicants; $350,000 for state coordinated applicants (this amount is subject to the availability of funds

Funding: (Cooperative Agreements) FY 17 $2,999,949; FY 18 est $2,999,949; FY 19 est $299,949.

HQ: 4770 Buford Highway, P.O. Box F72
Atlanta, GA 30341
Phone: 770-488-2047
Email: kmugavero@cdc.gov
http://www.cdc.gov

SOFT TARGET PROGRAM FOR OVERSEAS SCHOOLS "Soft Target Program"

Award: Project Grants

Purpose: Improves physical security of overseas schools to prevent or lessen the impact of terrorism and/or violent crime.

Applicant Eligibility: N/A

Beneficiary Eligibility: N/A

Award Range/Average: Range: $1K - $1.5M Avg: $800K

Funding: (Project Grants)

HQ: 1701 Ft Myer Drive
Arlington, VA 22209
Phone: 703-516-1615
Email: adamsmr@state.gov

SOLID WASTE MANAGEMENT GRANTS

Award: Project Grants

Purpose: To minimize pollution of water and management of solid waste disposal facilities in rural areas.

Applicant Eligibility: Entities eligible for grants are nonprofit organizations, including: Private, nonprofit organizations that have been granted tax exempt status by the Internal Revenue Service (IRS); and public bodies including local governmental-based multijurisdictional organizations. Applicants must have the proven ability, background, experience, legal authority, and actual capacity to provide technical assistance and/or training on a regional basis to eligible beneficiaries.

Beneficiary Eligibility: The entities that receive assistance are: (1) municipalities, counties, districts, authorities, and other political subdivisions of a State; (2) organizations operated on a not-for-profit basis, such as associations, cooperatives, and private nonprofit corporations; (3) and, Indian tribes on Federal and State reservations and other federally recognized Indian tribes.

Award Range/Average: $16540 to $815,000. Average: $127,765

Funding: (Project Grants) FY 17 $4,343,994; FY 18 est $4,202,873; FY 19 est $0; FY 16 $4,284,791.

HQ: Water and Environmental Programs Department of Agriculture 1400 Independence Avenue SW, P.O. Box 1548

Washington, DC 20250

Phone: 202-720-0986

Email: edna.primrose@wdc.usda.gov

http://www.rd.usda.gov/programs-services/all-programs/water-environmental-programs

SOUTH HALF OF THE RED RIVER

Award: Direct Payments for Specified Use

Purpose: Shares 37.5 percent of mineral leasing revenue with the State of Oklahoma paid monthly and is subject to late disbursement interest.

Applicant Eligibility: Revenue from public land leasing will trigger automatic payment distribution computed in the accordance with the Law.

Beneficiary Eligibility: ONRR distributes these funds to the State of Oklahoma for leased lands located within the south half of the Red River.

Award Range/Average: N/A

Funding: (Direct Payments for Specified Use) FY 17 $9,000; FY 18 est $11,000; FY 19 est $12,000.

HQ: Department of the Interior Office of Natural Resources Revenue 1849 C Street NW, P.O. Box 4211

Washington, DC 20240

Phone: 202-513-0600

http://www.onrr.gov

DOJ
16.734

SPECIAL DATA COLLECTIONS & STATISTICAL STUDIES "Statistics"

Award: Cooperative Agreements

Purpose: To make grants to or enter into cooperative agreements or contracts with public agencies, institutions of higher education, private organizations, or private individuals for purposes of collecting and analyzing criminal justice statistics.

Applicant Eligibility: The Bureau of Justice Statistics is authorized to award grants and cooperative agreements to State and local governments, private nonprofit organizations, public nonprofit organizations, profit organizations, institutions of higher education, and qualified individuals. Applicants from the Territories of the United States and federally recognized Indian Tribal Governments are also eligible to participate in this program.

Beneficiary Eligibility: Eligible beneficiaries are State and local governments, private nonprofit organizations, public nonprofit organizations, profit organizations, institutions of higher education, and qualified individuals.

Award Range/Average: $50,000 to $1,000,000

Funding: (Cooperative Agreements) FY 17 $41,755,090; FY 18 est $48,000,000; FY 19 est $41,000,000.

HQ: Bureau of Justice Statistics 810 7th Street NW
Washington, DC 20531
Phone: 202-307-0765
Email: allina.lee@usdoj.gov
http://www.bjs.gov

SPECIAL EDUCATION -- OLYMPIC EDUCATION PROGRAMS

Award: Project Grants

Purpose: To promote the expansion of Special Olympics and the design and implementation of Special Olympics education programs.

Applicant Eligibility: Special Olympics is the only eligible recipient of funds.

Beneficiary Eligibility: Individuals with and without intellectual disabilities.

Award Range/Average: One award for $12,583,000 in FY 17 and one award for $15,083,000 in FY 18.

Funding: (Project Grants) FY 17 $12,583,000; FY 18 est $15,083,000; FY 19 est $15,083,000.

HQ: OSERS Office of Special Education Programs 400 Maryland Avenue SW
Washington, DC 20202
Phone: 202-245-6039
Email: terry.jackson@ed.gov
http://www2.ed.gov/programs/osepoly/index.html

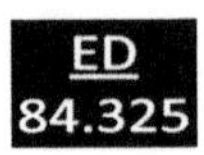

SPECIAL EDUCATION – PERSONNEL DEVELOPMENT TO IMPROVE SERVICES & RESULTS FOR CHILDREN WITH DISABILITIES

Award: Project Grants

Purpose: To help address State identified needs for highly qualified personnel in special education, related services, early intervention, and regular education to work with infants, toddlers, and children with disabilities.

Applicant Eligibility: State educational agencies, local education agencies, public charter schools that are LEAs under State law, institutions of higher education, other public agencies, private nonprofit organizations, outlying areas, Indian tribes or tribal organizations, and, if approved by the Secretary, for-profit organizations.

Beneficiary Eligibility: Infants, toddlers, and children with disabilities are the primary beneficiaries under this program.

Award Range/Average: The range and average vary by competition.

Funding: (Project Grants) FY 17 $83,700,000; FY 18 est $83,700,000; FY 19 est $83,700,000.

HQ: OSERS Office of Special Education Programs Potomac Center Plaza 550 12th Street SW
Washington, DC 20202
Phone: 202-245-7875
Email: sarah.allen@ed.gov
http://www.ed.gov/about/offices/list/osers/osep/index.html

SPECIAL EDUCATION – STATE PERSONNEL DEVELOPMENT

Award: Project Grants

Purpose: To assist State educational agencies in reforming and improving their systems for personnel preparation and professional development in early intervention, educational and transition services, to improve results for children with disabilities.

Applicant Eligibility: State Educational Agencies. A State educational agency of one of the 50 States, the District of Columbia, the Commonwealth of Puerto Rico, and the outlying areas (U.S. Virgin Islands, Guam, American Samoa, and the Commonwealth of the Northern Mariana Islands) may apply.

Beneficiary Eligibility: Infants and toddlers with disabilities as defined in the IDEA and their families, and children with disabilities as defined in the IDEA and their parents benefit from this program.

Award Range/Average: $500,000 and $1,750,000; the average is expected to be about $1,000,000.

Funding: (Project Grants) FY 17 $38,630,000; FY 18 est $38,630,000; FY 19 est $38,630,000.

HQ: OSERS Office of Special Education Programs 400 Maryland Avenue SW
Washington, DC 20202
Phone: 202-245-6673
Email: jennifer.coffey@ed.gov
http://www.ed.gov/about/offices/list/osers/osep/index.html

SPECIAL EDUCATION EDUCATIONAL TECHNOLOGY MEDIA, AND MATERIALS FOR INDIVIDUALS WITH DISABILITIES

Award: Project Grants

Purpose: To improve results for children with disabilities by promoting the development, demonstration, and use of technology.

Applicant Eligibility: State educational agencies (SEAs), local educational agencies (LEAs), public charter schools that are LEAs under State law, institutions of higher education (IHEs), other public agencies, private nonprofit organizations, outlying areas, freely associated States, Indian tribes or tribal organizations, and, if approved by the Secretary, for-profit organizations.

Beneficiary Eligibility: Infants, toddlers, children, and other individuals with disabilities, their families, as well as practitioners and service providers benefit from this program.

Award Range/Average: The range and average vary by competition.

Funding: (Project Grants) FY 16 $30,047,000; FY 18 est $28,047,000; FY 17 est $28,047,000.

HQ: Office of Special Education Programs, Room 5158 Potomac Center Plaza
Washington, DC 20202
Phone: 202-245-6039
Email: terry.jackson@ed.gov
http://www2.ed.gov/programs/oseptms/index.html

SPECIAL EDUCATION GRANTS TO STATES

Award: Formula Grants

Purpose: To provide grants to States to assist them in providing special education and related services to all children with disabilities.

Applicant Eligibility: State educational agencies in the 50 States, District of Columbia, Puerto Rico, American Samoa, Commonwealth of the Northern Mariana Islands, Guam and Virgin Islands, the Department of the Interior, and freely associated States. Local educational agencies apply to their State educational agency for subgrants.

Beneficiary Eligibility: Children with disabilities will benefit.

Award Range/Average: In FY 2017, regular annual allotments to States, including DC and Puerto Rico, ranged from $18.9 million to $1.2 billion, with an average award of $228 million. Grants to outlying areas ranged from $4.8 million to $14 million. The Department of Interior received $95 million.

Funding: (Formula Grants) FY 17 $12,002,848,000; FY 18 est $12,002,848,000; FY 19 est $12,002,848,000.

HQ: Department of Education 401 Maryland Avenue SW
Washington, DC 20202
Phone: 202-245-7309
Email: gregg.corr@ed.gov
http://www.ed.gov/about/offices/list/osers/osep/index.html

SPECIAL EDUCATION PARENT INFORMATION CENTERS

Award: Project Grants

Purpose: To ensure that parents of children with disabilities receive training and information to help improve results for their children.

Applicant Eligibility: Parent organizations, as defined in Section 671(a)(2) of the Individuals with Disabilities Education Act are eligible for parent center awards under IDEA sections 671 and 672. For section 672 funding, these parent centers must meet additional conditions set forth in section 672.

Beneficiary Eligibility: Infants, toddlers, children and youth with disabilities, and their families, benefit from this program.

Award Range/Average: The range and average vary by competition.

Funding: (Project Grants) FY 17 $27,411,000; FY 18 est $27,411,000; FY 19 est $27,411,000.

HQ: Department of Education OSERS Office of Special Education Programs, 400 Maryland Avenue SW Room 5175 PCP

Washington, DC 20202

Phone: 202-245-6595

Email: carmen.sanchez@ed.gov

http://www2.ed.gov/programs/oseppic/index.html

SPECIAL EDUCATION PRESCHOOL GRANTS

Award: Formula Grants

Purpose: To provide grants to States to assist them in providing special education and related services to children with disabilities ages 3 through 5 years, and to 2- year- old children with disabilities who will reach age three during the school year.

Applicant Eligibility: State educational agencies in the 50 States, the District of Columbia, and the Commonwealth of Puerto Rico. Local educational agencies apply to their State educational agency for sub-grants.

Beneficiary Eligibility: Children aged 3 through 5 with disabilities, and (at the State's option) 2-year- old children with disabilities that will reach age 3 during the school year, that require special education and related services.

Award Range/Average: For FY 2018, regular annual allotments to States, including DC and Puerto Rico, ranged from $241,030 to $38,332,578, with an average award of $7,329,231.

Funding: (Formula Grants) FY 17 $368,238,000; FY 18 est $381,120,000; FY 19 est $381,120,000.

HQ: Department of Education 402 Maryland Avenue SW

Washington, DC 20202

Phone: 202-245-7309

Email: gregg.corr@ed.gov

http://www.ed.gov/about/offices/list/osers/osep/programs.html

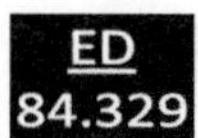

SPECIAL EDUCATION STUDIES & EVALUATIONS

Award: Project Grants

Purpose: To provide free appropriate public education to children with disabilities; and early intervention services to infants and toddlers with disabilities who would be at risk of having substantial developmental delays if early intervention services were not provided.

Applicant Eligibility: Applicants that have the ability and capacity to conduct scientifically valid evaluations are eligible to apply. Eligible applicants include, but are not limited to, non-profit and for-profit organizations.

Beneficiary Eligibility: Infants, toddlers, and children with disabilities, and other individuals with disabilities, and their families benefit from this program.

Award Range/Average: No Data Available.

Funding: Project Grants (Contracts) FY 17 $10,818,000; FY 18 est $10,818,000; FY 19 est $10,818,000.

HQ: 550 12th Street SW, Room 4104
Washington, DC 20208
Phone: 202-245-7474
Email: lauren.angelo@ed.gov
http://ies.ed.gov/ncee

SPECIAL EDUCATION TECHNICAL ASSISTANCE & DISSEMINATION TO IMPROVE SERVICES & RESULTS FOR CHILDREN WITH DISABILITIES

Award: Project Grants

Purpose: To improve Services and Results for Children with Disabilities program is to promote academic achievement and to improve results for children with disabilities by providing technical assistance (TA).

Applicant Eligibility: State educational agencies (SEAs), local educational agencies (LEAs), public charter schools that are LEAs under State law, institutions of higher education (IHEs), other public agencies, private nonprofit organizations, outlying areas, freely associated States, Indian tribes or tribal organizations, and, if approved by the Secretary, for-profit organizations.

Beneficiary Eligibility: Infants, toddlers, children, and other individuals with disabilities, their families as well as practitioners and service providers benefit from this program.

Award Range/Average: The range and average vary by competition.

Funding: (Project Grants (Capacity Building and Complaint Processing, Training) FY 17 est $44,345,000; FY 18 est $44,345,000; FY 16 $44,345,000.

HQ: Office of Special Education Programs, Room 5136 Potomac Center Plaza
Washington, DC 20202
Phone: 202-245-6674
Email: tina.diamond@ed.gov
http://www.ed.gov/about/offices/list/osers/osep/index.html

ED 84.373 SPECIAL EDUCATION TECHNICAL ASSISTANCE ON STATE DATA COLLECTION

Award: Project Grants

Purpose: Provides technical assistance needed, to improve the capacity of States to meet the data collection requirements of the IDEA.

Applicant Eligibility: Public and private agencies and organizations, including for profit and non-profit agencies and organizations.

Beneficiary Eligibility: Infants, toddlers, and children with disabilities benefit from this program.

Award Range/Average: No Data Available.

Funding: (Project Grants) FY 17 $21,400,000; FY 18 est $21,000,000; FY 19 est $21,000,000.

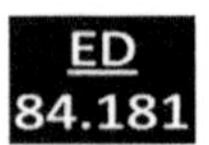

HQ: OSERS Office of Special Education Programs 400 Maryland Avenue SW
Washington, DC 20202
Phone: 202-245-7334
Email: david.egnor@ed.gov
http://www.ed.gov/about/offices/list/osers/osep/index.html

ED 84.181 SPECIAL EDUCATION-GRANTS FOR INFANTS & FAMILIES

Award: Formula Grants

Purpose: To provide grants to States to assist them to implement and maintain a Statewide, comprehensive, coordinated, multidisciplinary, interagency system to make available early intervention services to infants and toddlers with disabilities and their families.

Applicant Eligibility: Eligible applicants are the following 57 entities: the 50 States, the District of Columbia, the Commonwealth of Puerto Rico, the Secretary of the Interior and the following four outlying area jurisdictions: Guam, American Samoa, the Virgin Islands, and the Commonwealth of the Northern Mariana Islands.

Beneficiary Eligibility: The beneficiaries are infants and toddlers with disabilities aged birth through 2 and their families and at the State's option, children with disabilities ages three through five and their families.

Award Range/Average: For 2018, regular annual allotments to States, including DC and Puerto Rico, ranged from, $2,301,533 to $55,507,072; with an average award of $8,860,943.

Funding: (Formula Grants) FY 17 $458,556,000; FY 18 est $470,000,000; FY 19 est $470,000,000.

HQ: Office of Special Education Programs Department of Education 400 Maryland Avenue SW
Washington, DC 20202
Phone: 202-245-7309
Email: gregg.corr@ed.gov
http://www2.ed.gov/about/offices/list/osers/osep/programs.html

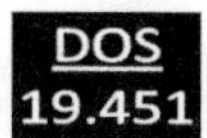

DOS 19.451 SPECIAL INTERNATIONAL EXCHANGE GRANT PROGRAMS

Award: Cooperative Agreements; Project Grants

Purpose: Provides special grants for international exchanges and other activities that support and address current and emerging issues of mutual interest to the United States and other countries, consistent with the program criteria established in the Department's annual appropriation.

Applicant Eligibility: Pursuant to the Mutual Educational and Cultural Exchange Act of 1961, as amended (Fulbright-Hays Act) the Bureau of Educational and Cultural Affairs of the U.S. Department of State awards project grants and cooperative agreements to educational and cultural public or private nonprofit foundations or institutions. Applications may be submitted by public and private non-profit organizations.

Beneficiary Eligibility: Same as Applicant Eligibility.

Award Range/Average: 8401984

Funding: (Cooperative Agreements) FY 17 $8,401,984; FY 18 est $8,401,984; FY 19 est $8,401,984; FY 16 $6,690,877;

HQ: Office of Academic Exchanges E Asia and Pacific Branch 2200 C Street NW SA-05 4-L11
Washington, DC 20037
Phone: 202-632-3216
Email: marshallt@state.gov

HHS 93.044 SPECIAL PROGRAMS FOR THE AGING, TITLE III, PART B, GRANTS FOR SUPPORTIVE SERVICES & SENIOR CENTERS

Award: Formula Grants

Purpose: To encourage State Agencies on Aging and Area Agencies on Aging to concentrate resources to develop and implement comprehensive and coordinated community-based systems of service for older individuals.

Applicant Eligibility: Only State and U.S. Territories which have State Agencies on Aging designated by the Governors are eligible to receive these grants.

Beneficiary Eligibility: Individuals age 60 and over, targeting those older individuals with the greatest economic needs, the greatest social needs, and those residing in rural areas.

Award Range/Average: Average $6,511,854

Funding: (Formula Grants) FY 17 $357,063,000; FY 18 est $385,074,000; FY 19 est $350,224,000.

HQ: 330 C Street SW
Washington, DC 20201
Phone: 202-795-7386
Email: greg.link@acl.hhs.gov
http://acl.gov

HHS 93.045 SPECIAL PROGRAMS FOR THE AGING, TITLE III, PART C, NUTRITION SERVICES

Award: Formula Grants

Purpose: To provide grants to States and U.S. Territories to support nutrition services including nutritious meals, nutrition education and other appropriate nutrition services for older adults.

Applicant Eligibility: Only States and U.S. Territories which have State Units on Aging designated by the governors are eligible to receive these grants.

Beneficiary Eligibility: For Title III congregate meals, persons who are older adults (age 60 years and above) or a spouse of an older adult, regardless of age; disabled adults who live in housing facilities primarily occupied by older adults where a congregate site is located; disabled adults under age 60, who reside at home with older adults; and volunteers, regardless of age, who assist in meal service during meal hours. For Title III home-delivered meals, an older individual must be assessed to be homebound.

Award Range/Average: Congregate Nutrition Services: FY 18 Range $302,513 to $50,682, 482, AVERAGE: $ 8,643,237; Home-Delivered Nutrition Services: FY 18: Range $151,968- $25,494,622, Average: $4,341,937

Funding: (Formula Grants) FY 17 $688,488,000; FY 18 est $688,684,000; FY 19 N/A FY 16 $669,721,620; - Congregate Nutrition Services: FY 18 Range $302,513 to $50,682, 482 AVERAGE: $ 8,643,237; - Home-Delivered Nutrition Services: FY 18: Range $151,968- $25,494,622, Average: $4,341,937.

HQ: Office of Nutrition and Health Promotion Programs Administration on Aging DHHS 330 C Street SW
Washington, DC 20201
Phone: 202-795-7355
Email: holly.greuling@acl.hhs.gov

HHS 93.043 SPECIAL PROGRAMS FOR THE AGING, TITLE III, PART D, DISEASE PREVENTION & HEALTH PROMOTION SERVICES

Award: Formula Grants

Purpose: To develop or strengthen preventive health service and health promotion systems through designated State Agencies on Aging and Area Agencies on Aging.

Applicant Eligibility: Only States and U.S. Territories which have State Agencies on Aging designated by the governors are eligible to receive these grants.

Beneficiary Eligibility: Older individuals, age sixty and older, especially those living in areas of States which are medically underserved and in which there are a large number of older individuals who have the greatest economic need for the services.

Award Range/Average: FY 17 est $12,281 - $1,992,449; $350,884

Funding: (Formula Grants) FY 17 $19,664,255; FY 18 est $24,599,520; FY 19 est $24,599,520.

HQ: 330 C Street SW
Washington, DC 20201
Phone: 617-565-1170
Email: casey.dicocco@acl.hhs.gov
http://www.acl.gov/programs/health-wellness/disease-prevention

HHS 93.048 SPECIAL PROGRAMS FOR THE AGING, TITLE IV, AND TITLE II, DISCRETIONARY PROJECTS

Award: Cooperative Agreements

Purpose: To support the development and testing of innovative programs, services and systems of support that respond to the needs of the nation's growing elderly population and those individuals in need of long term services and supports (LTSS).

Applicant Eligibility: Grants may be made to any public or nonprofit private agency, organization, or institution. Contracts may be awarded to any agency, organization or institution.

Beneficiary Eligibility: Older individuals aged 60 and older, family caregivers and grandparents, and older individuals who are relative caregivers, individuals at high-risk of institutional placement, and individuals in need of assistance with or planning ahead for their long-term care needs.

Award Range/Average: N/A

Funding: Cooperative Agreements (Discretionary Grants) FY 17 $36,323,928; FY 18 est $36,323,928; FY 19 est $35,323,928; FY 16 $36,323,928.

HQ: Department of Health and Human Services 330 C Street SW, Room 1144
Washington, DC 20201
Phone: 202-795-7386
Email: greg.link@acl.hhs.gov
http://www.acl.gov

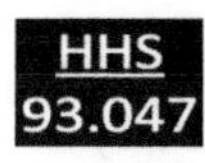

HHS 93.047 SPECIAL PROGRAMS FOR THE AGING, TITLE VI, PART A, GRANTS TO INDIAN TRIBES, PART B, GRANTS TO NATIVE HAWAIIANS

Award: Formula Grants

Purpose: To promote the delivery of supportive services, including nutrition services, to American Indians, Alaskan natives, and Native Hawaiians.

Applicant Eligibility: Tribal organizations of Indian tribes eligible for assistance under Section 4 of the Indian Self-Determination and Education Assistance Act (25 U.S.C. 450b), and public or nonprofit private organizations which serve Native Hawaiian Elders, which represent at least 50 Indians or Hawaiians 60 years of age or older.

Beneficiary Eligibility: Indians who are 60 years of age and older, and in the case of nutrition services, their spouses. Tribes also have the authority to define Indians under 60 years of age as "older Indian" making them eligible for services.

Award Range/Average: FY 16 Ranges for Part A - $75,540- $186,042; Part B - $1,505,000 FY 17 Ranges for Part A - $73,990- $181,831; Part B - $1,505,000

Funding: (Formula Grants) FY 17 $31,158,000; FY 18 est $31,923,872; FY 19 N/A FY 16 $29,773,242.

HQ: 330 C Street SW
Washington, DC 20201
Phone: 202-357-0148
Email: cynthia.lacounte@acl.hhs.gov
http://www.acl.gov

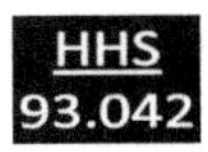

SPECIAL PROGRAMS FOR THE AGING, TITLE VII, CHAPTER 2, LONG TERM CARE OMBUDSMAN SERVICES FOR OLDER INDIVIDUALS
"State Grants for Long Term Care Ombudsman Services"

Award: Formula Grants

Purpose: To investigate and resolve complaints made by or on behalf of residents of nursing homes or other long-term care facilities.

Applicant Eligibility: All States and U.S. Territories which have State Agencies on Aging designated by the governors.

Beneficiary Eligibility: Individuals residing in long-term care facilities or requiring assistance in entering or transferring from such facilities.

Award Range/Average: FY 15 Range: $9,829 - $1,618,546; Average: $280,824

Funding: (Formula Grants) FY 17 $15,885,000; FY 18 est $16,885,000; FY 19 FY 16 $15,837,665.

HQ: Dept of Health and Human Services 330 C Street SW
Washington, DC 20201
Phone: 206-615-2514
Email: louise.ryan@acl.hhs.gov
http://www.acl.gov

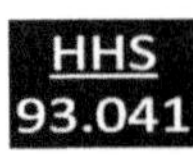

SPECIAL PROGRAMS FOR THE AGING, TITLE VII, CHAPTER 3, PROGRAMS FOR PREVENTION OF ELDER ABUSE, NEGLECT, AND EXPLOITATION

Award: Formula Grants

Purpose: To develop, strengthen, and carry out programs for the prevention, detection, assessment, and treatment of, intervention in, investigation of, and response to elder abuse, neglect, and exploitation.

Applicant Eligibility: All States and U.S. Territories which have State Agencies on Aging designated by the governors.

Beneficiary Eligibility: Individuals 60 years of age and older, targeting those older individuals with the greatest social needs and those with the greatest economic needs.

Award Range/Average: Average: $84,500 FY 16 Range $2,958- $471,073.

Funding: (Formula Grants) FY 18 N/A FY 17 est $4,742,357; FY 16 $4,751,881.

HQ: 330 C Street SW
Washington, DC 20201
Phone: 202-795-7467
Email: stephanie.whittiereliason@acl.hhs.gov
http://www.acl.gov

HHS 93.928 SPECIAL PROJECTS OF NATIONAL SIGNIFICANCE "SPNS"

Award: Cooperative Agreements; Project Grants

Purpose: To respond to the care and treatment needs of individuals receiving assistance under the Ryan White HIV/AIDS program (RWHAP). Special Projects of National Significance (SPNS) also supports the development and implementation of innovative delivery models of HIV care, services, and capacity development initiatives.

Applicant Eligibility: Academic institutions, non-profit organizations including faith-based organizations, and those eligible for funding under Parts A-D authorized by Title XXVI of the Public Health Service (PHS) Act as amended by the Ryan White HIV/AIDS Treatment Extension Act of 2009. Additionally, federally recognized Indian Tribal Governments and tribal organizations are also eligible to apply for these funds.

Beneficiary Eligibility: Individuals living with HIV.

Award Range/Average: Project Grants: $263,206 to $482,500; Average $300,000; Coop. Agreements: $ 500,000 to $3,049,198. Average $550,000.

Funding: (Project Grants) FY 17 $11,728,612; FY 18 est $7,155,077; FY 19 est $4,173,757; FY 16 $17,098,752; - (Cooperative Agreements) FY 17$10,976,665; FY 18 est $15,786,011; FY 19 est $18,817,687; FY 16 $6,231,128.

HQ: 5600 Fishers Lane, Room 9N-114
Rockville, MD 20857
Phone: 301-443-8109
Email: hphillips@hrsa.gov
http://www.hrsa.gov

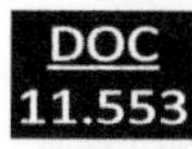

DOC 11.553 SPECIAL PROJECTS

Award: Project Grants

Purpose: To assist organizations and new sources of advanced telecommunications.

Applicant Eligibility: Organizations specifically identified by Congress in agency appropriations legislation or other authority that provides for non-competitive grants.

Beneficiary Eligibility: Beneficiaries are those served by the organizations receiving awards.

Award Range/Average: N/A

Funding: N/A

HQ: 1401 Constitution Avenue NW, Room 4888 NTIA/OPCM
Washington, DC 20230
Phone: 202-482-5515
Email: writchie@ntia.doc.gov
http://www.ntia.doc.gov/home

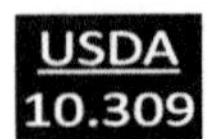

SPECIALTY CROP RESEARCH INITIATIVE "SCRI"

Award: Project Grants

Purpose: The Specialty Crop Research Initiative resolves issues of industries. It promotes projects that address innovations and technology for advancing agriculture, management of pests, food safety, etc.

Applicant Eligibility: Applications may be submitted by Federal agencies, national laboratories, colleges and universities, research institutions and organizations, private organizations or corporations, State agricultural experiment stations, individuals, or groups consisting of two or more of these entities.

Beneficiary Eligibility: Same as Applicant Eligibility.

Award Range/Average: If minimum or maximum amounts of funding per competitive and/or capacity project grant, or cooperative agreement are established, these amounts will be announced in the annual Competitive Request for Application (RFA).

Funding: Project Grants (Cooperative Agreements) FY 17 $69,578,033; FY 18 est $69,796,077; FY 19 est $74,795,599; FY 16 $70,197,495.

HQ: National Program Leader Institute of Food Production and Sustainability Division of Plant Systems-Production 1400 Independence Avenue SW, P.O. Box 2240

Washington, DC 20250-2240

Phone: 202-401-4202

Email: skwok@nifa.usda.gov

http://nifa.usda.gov/program/specialty-crop-research-initiative

STAFFING FOR ADEQUATE FIRE & EMERGENCY RESPONSE (SAFER) "SAFER ACT"

Award: Project Grants

Purpose: SAFER grant program assists the local fire departments with staffing and deployment to respond quickly to emergencies. The program also ensures that communal areas have adequate protection from fire and fire-related hazards.

Applicant Eligibility: This program is restricted to the jurisdictions/organizations described in program guidance documents. For specific information, refer to the Notice of Funding Opportunity.

Beneficiary Eligibility: Local or tribal communities serviced by the fire department including, local businesses, homeowners and property owners.

Award Range/Average: Refer to Notice of Funding Opportunity document.

Funding: (Project Grants) FY 17 $345,000,000; FY 18 est $350,000,000; FY 19 est $0; FY 16 $345,000,000.

HQ: Department of Homeland Security/FEMA Grant Programs Directorate Assistance to Firefighters Grant, 400 C Street SW 3N

Washington, DC 20742-3635

Phone: 866-274-0960

http://www.fema.gov/firegrants

DOC 11.604

STANDARD REFERENCE MATERIALS "SRM"

Award: Sale, Exchange, or Donation of Property and Goods

Purpose: Standard Reference Materials are issued by NIST for analysis, strategies for quality control and to assess material performance, steps to measure materials, etc.

Applicant Eligibility: Federal agencies, State and local governments, societies, institutions, firms, corporations, and individuals may purchase the materials.

Beneficiary Eligibility: N/A

Award Range/Average: No Data Available.

Funding: (Sale, Exchange, or Donation of Property and Goods) FY 17 $22,159,227; FY 18 est $24,526,000; FY 19 est $24,530,000; FY 16 $18,649,000.

HQ: 100 Bureau Drive, P.O. Box 2300
Gaithersburg, MD 20899
Phone: 301-975-3096
Email: steven.choquette@nist.gov
http://www.nist.gov/srm

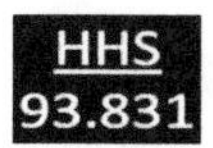

STANDARDS DEVELOPMENT ORGANIZATION COLLABORATION TO ENHANCE STANDARDS ALIGNMENT, TESTING, AND MEASUREMENT

Award: Cooperative Agreements

Purpose: To establish a mechanism for ongoing collaboration among ONC and various SDOs. It aims to provide support to these organizations for standards and interoperability within these organizations portfolio's that is of mutual interest to ONC.

Applicant Eligibility: Applicants must be a United States-based non-profit institution or organization, state or local government, agency or group.

Beneficiary Eligibility: The beneficiaries will include all health care organizations and patients using electronic health records.

Award Range/Average: Average of $100,000.

Funding: (Cooperative Agreements) FY 17 $100,000; FY 18 est $100,000; FY 19 est $100,000.

HQ: 330 C Street SW
Washington, DC 20201
Phone: 202-720-2919
Email: carmel.halloun@hhs.gov
http://www.healthit.gov

STANDARDS EXPLORATION AWARD

Award: Cooperative Agreements

Purpose: The Office of the National Coordinator for Health Information Technology funds up to four pilot programs that will advance a scalable process of interoperable exchange of electronic health data using standards that will improve the delivery of how and where healthcare is delivered, improve patient outcomes, and reduce cost.

Applicant Eligibility: The objective of this award is to advance a scalable process of interoperable exchange of electronic health data using standards that will improve the delivery of how and where health care is delivered, improve patient outcomes, and reduce cost. Collaborative groups of multiple stakeholders across different organizations will be considered, as well as encouraged, to support widespread interoperability.

Beneficiary Eligibility: As health care delivery impacts everyone, the beneficiary eligibility includes all of the listed groups as provided in the reference manual.

Award Range/Average: There has been $250,000 for FFY 16-17 for this award. We estimate that we would award no more than four (4) awards total; the award amounts would be no less than $20,000 and may not exceed $75,000 per awardee. The award amount will be determined upon the scope and strength the awardee's proposal.

Funding: N/A

HQ: 330 C Street SW
Washington, DC 20201
Phone: 202-720-2919
Email: carmel.halloun@hhs.gov
http://www.healthit.gov/topic/grants-contracts/standards-exploration-award-sea-cooperative-agreement-program

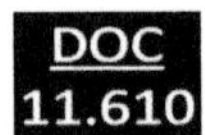

STANDARDS INFORMATION CENTER "SIC"

Award: Dissemination of Technical Information

Purpose: To assist information center and referral services and guidance on standards to provide regulatory and certification information to U.S. exporters and manufacturers.

Applicant Eligibility: State and local government, private, public, profit organizations, nonprofit institutions and individuals.

Beneficiary Eligibility: State and local government, private, public, profit organizations, nonprofit institutions and individuals will benefit.

Award Range/Average: No Data Available.

Funding: (Formula Grants) FY 17 $250,000; FY 18 est $250,000; FY 19 est $250,000; FY 16 $250,000.

HQ: 100 Bureau Drive, P.O. Box 2100
Gaithersburg, MD 20899
Phone: 301-975-5571
Email: kerry.miles@nist.gov
http://www.nist.gov/standardsgov/what-we-do/trade-regulatory-programs/standards-information-center

DOJ 16.614 STATE & LOCAL ANTI-TERRORISM TRAINING "SLATT"

Award: Advisory Services and Counseling; Dissemination of Technical Information; Training

Purpose: To prevent terrorism and promote the Nation's Security Consistent with the Rule of Law by assisting state, local, and tribal law enforcement in identifying, investigating, and preventing criminal acts of terror through training, technical assistance, and resources that build law enforcement's knowledge and capacity to identify and respond to possible domestic terrorism.

Applicant Eligibility: For-profit (commercial) organizations; nonprofit organizations; faith-based and community organizations; institutions of higher education; and consortiums with significant and demonstrated experience in terror prevention strategies and in delivering training and technical assistance to law enforcement and tribal communities are eligible to apply. For-profit organizations must agree to waive any profit or fees for services.

Beneficiary Eligibility: State, local, and tribal criminal justice agencies are the primary beneficiaries of this program.

Award Range/Average: One cooperative agreement for up to $2 million for a project period of 24 months.

Funding: (Project Grants) FY 17 $0; FY 18 est $2,000,000; FY 19 est $0; FY 16 $0.

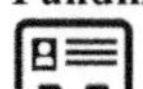

HQ: Bureau of Justice Assistance 810 7th Street NW
Washington, DC 20531
Phone: 202-616-6500

DHS 97.005 STATE & LOCAL HOMELAND SECURITY NATIONAL TRAINING PROGRAM "Homeland Security National Training Program National Domestic Preparedness Consortium (NDPC) and Continuing Training Grants (CTG)"

Award: Project Grants

Purpose: The Homeland Security National Training Program together with the National Domestic Preparedness Consortium and Continuing Training Grants program helps in implementing the National Preparedness System to help build a secure and resilient nation against terrorist attacks and natural disasters.

Applicant Eligibility: The HSNTP/NDPC is a closed solicitation, available only to eligible organizations. Non-Federal members that make up the National Domestic Preparedness Consortium (NDPC) which consist of the following institutions: Louisiana State University, Texas A&M, New Mexico Institute of Mining and Technology, and the University of Hawaii.

Beneficiary Eligibility: State and Local units of government, public non-profits, and Federally recognized tribal entities.

Award Range/Average: Refer to FOA.

Funding: (Cooperative Agreements) FY 17 $87,000,000; FY 18 est $87,000,000; FY 19 est $87,000,000; FY 16 $87,521,000; - FY2015 – HSNTP/NDPC $76,000,000 and CTG $11,521,000 = $87,521,000 FY 2016 – HSNTP/NDPC $76,000,000 and CTG $11,521,000 = $87,521,000 FY 2017 – H

HQ: National Preparedness Directorate (NPD) Grants Program Directorate (GPD), FEMA Department of Homeland Security National Training and Education Division 400 C Street SW
Washington, DC 20472
Phone: 800-368-6498

DOC 11.549 STATE & LOCAL IMPLEMENTATION GRANT PROGRAM "SLIGP"

Award: Project Grants

Purpose: To assist State and local jurisdictions in implementing effective ways for utilizing equipment and architecture for safety broadband network and wireless communications.

Applicant Eligibility: Grants were awarded to eligible States and Territories.

Beneficiary Eligibility: Indirect beneficiaries of the grants are law enforcement officers, fire fighters, emergency medical professionals and other public safety officials, as well as the general public, who will receive improved communications capabilities from the creation of the single, nationwide interoperable public safety broadband network that these grants will facilitate.

Award Range/Average: SLIGP 2.0 awards for the first increment of funding ranged from $200,000 to $425,000.

Funding: (Project Grants) FY 17 $80,000; FY 18 est $12,630,000; FY 19 est $20,755,000.

HQ: Office of Public Safety Communications US Department of Commerce, 1401 Constitution Avenue NW Room 4078

Washington, DC 20230

Phone: 202-482-1181

Email: mdame@ntia.doc.gov

http://www.ntia.doc.gov/category/state-and-local-implementation-grant-program

HHS 93.757 STATE & LOCAL PUBLIC HEALTH ACTIONS TO PREVENT OBESITY, DIABETES, HEART DISEASE & STROKE (PPHF)

Award: Cooperative Agreements

Purpose: The purpose of this program is to support statewide implementation of cross-cutting, evidence-based approaches to promote health and prevent and control chronic diseases and their risk factors.

Applicant Eligibility: Eligible Applicants: State Departments of Health or their Bona Fide Agents.

Beneficiary Eligibility: States and communities will benefit from this assistance in many ways including through improved clinical and other preventive services for self management of hypertension, diabetes, overweight and obesity

Award Range/Average: $550,000 for basic component and $1,000,000 to $1,700,000 per applicant

Funding: (Cooperative Agreements) FY 17 $51,239,531; FY 18 est $0; FY 19 est $0; FY 16 $49,700,889; This program ended in FY 18 and not re-announced.

HQ: 4770 Buford Highway NE, P.O. Box K-10

Atlanta, GA 30341

Phone: 770-488-5007

Email: rif6@cdc.gov

http://www.cdc.gov

HHS 93.699

STATE & NATIONAL TOBACCO CESSATION SUPPORT SYSTEMS
"Quitlines"

Award: N/A

Purpose: The program supports state quitline capacity in order to respond to federal initiatives such as the National Tobacco Education Campaign. This program addresses the "Healthy People 2020" focus area of tobacco use and the goal of reducing illness, disability, and death related to tobacco use and secondhand smoke exposure.

Applicant Eligibility: Eligible applicants that can apply for this funding are listed below: State Governments, County Governments, City or township governments, Special district governments, Independent school districts, Public and State controlled institutions of higher education, Native American tribal governments (Federally recognized tribal governments), Nonprofit with 501C3 IRS status (other than institution of higher education), Nonprofit without 501C3 IRS status (other than institution of higher education), Private Institutions of higher education, For profit organizations other than small businesses, Small Businesses Government Organizations:, State (includes the District of Columbia) Local governments or their bona fide agents, Territorial governments or their bona fide agents in the Commonwealth of Puerto Rico, the Virgin Islands, the Commonwealth of the Northern Marianna Islands, American Samoa, Guam, the Federated States of Micronesia, the Republic of the Marshall Islands, and the Republic of Palau, State controlled institutions of higher education, American Indian or Alaska Native tribal governments (federally recognized or state-recognized),

Beneficiary Eligibility: Public Housing Authorities/Indian Housing Authorities] Non-government Organizations: American Indian or Alaska native tribally designated organizations Other: Private colleges and universities Community-based organizations Faith-Based organizations.

Award Range/Average: N/A Pending FY 19 funding

Funding: (Cooperative Agreements) FY 17 N/A FY 18 N/A FY 19 est $18,000,000.

HQ: 4770 Buford Highway NE
Atlanta, GA 30341
Phone: 770-488-5941
Email: hyu1@cdc.gov
http://cdc.gov

STATE ACTIONS TO IMPROVE ORAL HEALTH OUTCOMES & PARTNER ACTIONS TO IMPROVE ORAL HEALTH OUTCOMES
"Oral Health"

Award: Cooperative Agreements; Project Grants

Purpose: To establish oral health leadership and program guidance, oral health data collection and interpretation, multi-dimensional delivery system for oral and physical health, and to implement science-based programs to improve oral and physical health.

Applicant Eligibility: States, political subdivisions of States, local health authorities, and individuals or organizations with specialized health interests will benefit.

Beneficiary Eligibility: Same as Applicant Eligibility.

Award Range/Average: No Data Available.

Funding: (Cooperative Agreements) FY 17 $0; FY 18 est $8,400,000; FY 19 est $8,400,000; FY 16 $0; - This is a new FY 18 NOFO no funding was obligated in FY 16 and FY 17.

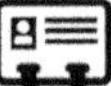

HQ: 4770 Buford Highway NE, P.O. Box F80
Atlanta, GA 30341
Phone: 770-488-6075
Email: kuv7@cdc.gov
http://www.cdc.gov

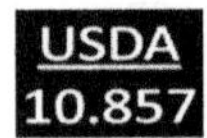

STATE BULK FUEL REVOLVING FUND GRANTS
"State Bulk Fuel Grants"

Award: Project Grants

Purpose: To compensate for cost-effective fuel purchases to the communities where fuel cannot be shipped by surface transportation.

Applicant Eligibility: Applicants are limited to State entities and to entities of any Territory, possession or other area authorized to receive the services and programs of the Rural Utilities Service or the Rural Electrification Act of 1936, as amended. Entities must be in existence as of November 9, 2000.

Beneficiary Eligibility: Assistance must be used to improve the cost-effectiveness of fuel purchasing for communities that are dependent on fuel deliveries by water or air.

Award Range/Average: $500,000 to $5 million

Funding: (Project Grants) FY 17 $0; FY 18 est $0; FY 19 est $0; FY 16 $0.

HQ: 1400 Independence Avenue, P.O. Box 1560
Washington, DC 20250
Phone: 202-720-9545
Email: christopher.mclean@wdc.usda.gov
http://www.rd.usda.gov/programs-services/state-bulk-fuel-revolving-loan-fund

STATE COURT IMPROVEMENT PROGRAM
"State and Tribal Court Improvement Programs"

Award: Formula Grants; Project Grants

Purpose: Provides three grant opportunities to state courts to improve court efficiency and the quality of legal representation; a basic grant for assessment work; a grant for data collection and analysis; and a grant to increase training of court personnel, including cross training with agency staff.

Applicant Eligibility: The highest state courts in each of the 50 states, the District of Columbia, Puerto Rico and the U.S. Virgin Islands are eligible to apply for funding. The term "highest state court" means the judicial tribunal which is the ultimate court of appeals in the state.

Beneficiary Eligibility: Families and children who are served by state and tribal courts in proceedings related to foster care, guardianship and adoption.

Award Range/Average: FY 2017: State grant awards ranged from $86,408 to $571,308 with an average of $158,094. FY 2017: Tribal grant awards ranged from $31,282 to $140,000 with an average of $103,444.

Funding: Project Grants (Discretionary) FY 17 $19,551,000; FY 18 est $19,614,000; FY 19 est $19,600,000; - (Formula Grants) FY 17$8,379,000; FY 18 est $8,406,000; FY 19 est $8,400,000.

HQ: 330 C Street SW, Room 3508A
Washington, DC 20201
Phone: 202-205-8709
Email: david.kelly@acf.hhs.gov
http://www.acf.hhs.gov/programs/cb

STATE CRIMINAL ALIEN ASSISTANCE PROGRAM "SCAAP"

DOJ 16.606

Award: Direct Payments for Specified Use

Purpose: The goal of the program is to refund state and local jurisdictions for housing criminal noncitizens in the state and local jails.

Applicant Eligibility: Eligible applicants include States, the District of Columbia, Puerto Rico, Guam, the Virgin Islands and localities or local jurisdictions exercising authority with respect to the incarceration of an undocumented criminal alien. This covers state prison facilities and local jails, whether operated by counties or cities.

Beneficiary Eligibility: States, the District of Columbia, Puerto Rico, Guam, the Virgin Islands and localities or local jurisdictions.

Award Range/Average: Contact Bureau of Justice Assistance for funding information or see the SCAAP Guidelines at https://www.bja.gov/ProgramDetails.aspx?Program_ID=86.

Funding: (Direct Payments with Unrestricted Use) FY 17 $390,000; FY 18 est $240,000,000; FY 19 est $0.

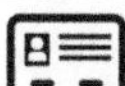
HQ: Bureau of Justice Assistance 810 7th Street NW
Washington, DC 20531
Phone: 202-353-4411
Email: joseph.husted@usdoj.gov
http://www.bja.gov

STATE DAMAGE PREVENTION PROGRAM GRANTS

DOT 20.720

Award: Project Grants

Purpose: Improves State Damage Prevention programs, which are intended to protect underground facilities from excavation damage.

Applicant Eligibility: Any State (including U.S. Territory or possessions) authority designated by the Governor is eligible to apply for a grant as long an agency within the State (including U.S. Territory or possessions) has an annual Section 60105 (49 U.S.C.) certification or Section 60106 (49 U.S.C.

Beneficiary Eligibility: State Government, U.S. Territory and possessions would receive the ultimate benefit from this program.

Award Range/Average: The grants awarded range $30,000- $100,000. The average is $88,231.

Funding: Project Grants (Discretionary) FY 17 $1,499,939; FY 18 est $1,500,000; FY 19 est $1,490,000.

HQ: 1200 New Jersey Avenue SE
Washington, DC 20590

Phone: 202-366-0568
Email: hung.nguyen@dot.gov
http://www.phmsa.dot.gov

STATE FIRE TRAINING SYSTEMS GRANTS "National Fire Academy State Fire Training Grants"

Award: Project Grants

Purpose: The program supports training programs to the fire and emergency response community irrespective of local or State agencies to meet individual training standards based on NFA course guidelines.

Applicant Eligibility: Representatives from the 50 State Fire Training Systems.

Beneficiary Eligibility: Specialized Group; fire and emergency response personnel.

Award Range/Average: Refer to program guidance.

Funding: (Project Grants) FY 17 $960,000; FY 18 est $960,000; FY 19 est $960,000; FY 16 $960,000.

HQ: United States Fire Administration FEMA16825 S Seton Avenue
Emmitsburg, MD 21727
Phone: 301-447-1376
Email: diane.close@fema.dhs.gov
http://www.usfa.fema.gov

STATE GRANTS FOR PROTECTION & ADVOCACY SERVICES "Protection and Advocacy for Traumatic Brain Injury"

Award: Formula Grants

Purpose: To make grants to Protection and Advocacy systems established in each State to provide services to individuals with traumatic brain injury which may include: information, referrals, and advice; and individual and family advocacy.

Applicant Eligibility: State Grant Agencies

Beneficiary Eligibility: Individuals with disabilities and family members

Award Range/Average: Range is $20,000 to $145,583; Average is $50,000

Funding: (Formula Grants) FY 17 $3,099,589; FY 18 est $4,000,000; FY 19 FY 16 $3,099,589.

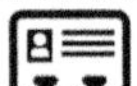

HQ: 330 C Street SW, P.O. Box 1104-B
Washington, DC 20201
Phone: 202-795-7474
Email: yi-hsin.yan@acl.hhs.gov

STATE HEALTH INSURANCE ASSISTANCE PROGRAM "SHIP"

Award: Cooperative Agreements

Purpose: Provides information, counseling, and assistance relating to obtaining adequate and appropriate health insurance coverage to individuals eligible to receive benefits under the Medicare program.

Applicant Eligibility: Grants or cooperative agreements may be made to States and U.S. Territories with approved State regulatory programs under section 1882 of the Social Security Act.

Beneficiary Eligibility: Individuals eligible for Medicare benefits, including Part D drug benefits, and older persons eligible for benefits and services provided under Medicare, their families, and caregivers.

Award Range/Average: FY 17: 54 awards that range from $50,000 to $5,003,012 per budget period

Funding: Cooperative Agreements (Discretionary Grants) FY 17 $52,115,000; FY 18 est $49,115,000; FY 19 est $49,115,000.

HQ: 330 C Street SW, P.O. Box 1104-B
Washington, DC 20201
Phone: 202-795-7375
Email: rebecca.kinney@acl.hhs.gov

DOJ 16.550

STATE JUSTICE STATISTICS PROGRAM FOR STATISTICAL ANALYSIS CENTERS "SACs"

Award: Cooperative Agreements

Purpose: To give financial and technical help to state governments for the establishment and operation of Statistical Analysis Centers (SACs) to collect, analyze, and disseminate justice statistics.

Applicant Eligibility: Eligible applicants are state agencies whose responsibilities include statistical activities consistent with the goals of the specific programs and are designated as the state Statistical Analysis Center through an Executive Order or legislation.

Beneficiary Eligibility: Eligible beneficiaries are state agencies whose responsibilities include statistical activities consistent with the goals of the specific programs.

Award Range/Average: See the current fiscal year's solicitation guidelines posted on the Office of Justice Programs web site at https://ojp.gov/funding/Explore/CurrentFundingOpportunities.htm.

Funding: (Cooperative Agreements) FY 17 $3,400,000; FY 18 est $5,500,000; FY 19 est $6,000,000.

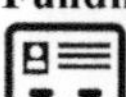

HQ: Bureau of Justice Statistics 810 7th Street NW
Washington, DC 20531
Phone: 202-307-0765
Email: stephanie.burroughs@usdoj.gov
http://www.bjs.gov/index.cfm?ty=tp&tipd=48

HHS 93.775

STATE MEDICAID FRAUD CONTROL UNITS "SMFCU's"

Award: Formula Grants

Purpose: Strives to eliminate fraud and patient abuse in the State Medicaid Programs.

Applicant Eligibility: An established State Medicaid Fraud Control Unit must be a single identifiable entity of the State government which the Secretary certifies (and the Office of Inspector General annually re-certifies) as complying with the requirements of 1903(q) of the Social Security Act (42 CFR 1007) regarding location, function and procedure. Applicants must also comply with section 1902 (a)(61) of the Act as amended by the Omnibus Budget Reconciliation Act of 1993.

Beneficiary Eligibility: Grantees are State entities.

Award Range/Average: FY 2018: Range $355,016 to $46,128,256; Average $5,282,322

Funding: (Formula Grants) FY 17 $255,000,000; FY 18 est $270,000,000; FY 19 est $278,000,000.

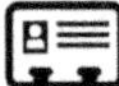

HQ: 330 Independence Avenue SW Cohen Building
Washington, DC 20201
Phone: 202-619-0480
Email: richard.stern@oig.hhs.gov
http://www.oig.hhs.gov

STATE PARTNERSHIP GRANT PROGRAM TO IMPROVE MINORITY HEALTH

Award: Project Grants

Purpose: To facilitate the improvement of minority health and eliminate health disparities.

Applicant Eligibility: Any state, which includes the District of Columbia, any commonwealth possession, or other territory of the United States. If the applicant is a state, the application must include the state office of minority health/healthy equity (or other state entity with similar function) and the state health agency as partners.

Beneficiary Eligibility: Targeted populations: Alaskan Natives; American Indians; Asians; Blacks/African Americans; Hispanics/Latinos; Native Hawaiians and other Pacific Islanders; or subgroups of these populations. However, services may not be denied to any individual on the basis of race or ethnicity.

Award Range/Average: Range from $175,000 to $200,000

Funding: (Project Grants) FY 18 est $4,150,105; FY 16 $4,150,105; FY 17 est $4,150,105.

HQ: 1101 Wootton Parkway Tower Building, Suite 550
Rockville, MD 20852
Phone: 240-453-8822
Email: eric.west@hhs.gov
http://www.fta.dot.gov

STATE PHYSICAL ACTIVITY & NUTRITION (SPAN

Award: Project Grants

Purpose: To implement state and local nutrition and physical activity interventions that support healthy nutrition, safe and accessible physical activity, and breastfeeding within states and/or the District of Columbia.

Applicant Eligibility: Applicants must provide evidence of the authority to direct work on government public health systems at the state and local levels to readily implement this state based program.

Beneficiary Eligibility: Same as Applicant Eligibility.

Award Range/Average: Base funding level is $13,000,000 with potential for up to $15,000,000 annually for each of the five year budget periods. Based on available funding. $600,000 - $1,250,000 annually.

Funding: (Project Grants) FY 17 $0; FY 18 est $14,088,691; FY 19 est $14,088,691.

HQ: 4770Buford Highway NE NCCDPHP
Atlanta, GA 30341
Phone: 404-867-9697
Email: lbarnes@cdc.gov
http://www.cdc.gov

STATE PLANNING & ESTABLISHMENT GRANTS FOR THE AFFORDABLE CARE ACT (ACA)'S EXCHANGES

Award: Cooperative Agreements

Purpose: To provide assistance for activities related to establishing a Health Insurance Exchange that facilitates the purchase of qualified health plans.

Applicant Eligibility: Eligible applicants for the FOA "State Planning and Establishments Grants for the Affordable Care Act's Exchanges" include the 50 States and the District of Columbia. Eligible applicants for the FOA "Limited Competition for State Planning and Establishment Grants for the Affordable Care Act's Exchanges" include States which did not receive an award under the prior FOA "State Planning and Establishment Grants for the Affordable Care Act's Exchanges".

Beneficiary Eligibility: Projects will benefit States and Territories or entities authorized by the State or Territory that will set up Exchanges in States or Territories.

Award Range/Average: No floor or ceiling for award. Amounts are provided based on the wide range and complexity of applications.

Funding: (Project Grants) FY 17 $0; FY 18 est $0; FY 19 est $0; FY 16 $0.

HQ: 200 Independence Avenue SW
Washington, DC 20201
Phone: 301-492-4312
Email: michelle.feagins@hhs.gov
http://www.cciio.cms.gov

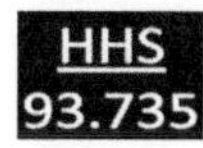

STATE PUBLIC HEALTH APPROACHES FOR ENSURING QUITLINE CAPACITY – FUNDED IN PART BY PREVENTION & PUBLIC HEALTH FUNDS (PPHF)

Award: Cooperative Agreements

Purpose: The program addresses the "Healthy People 2020" focus area of tobacco use and the goal of reducing illness, disability, and death related to tobacco use and secondhand smoke exposure.

Applicant Eligibility: Eligible applicants that can apply for this funding opportunity are listed below: Eligibility is limited to currently funded recipients under RFA-DP09-901 and RFA-DP09-902. These include state, District of Columbia, and the U.S. territorial health departments of Guam and Puerto Rico because they are the only entities with the authority to prevent and control tobacco use and which provide Quitline services within the states and territories.

Beneficiary Eligibility: Any State and territorial health department, and other public entities will benefit.

Award Range/Average: $50,000- $2,771,803.

Funding: Cooperative Agreements (Discretionary Grants) FY 17 $15,395,971; FY 18 est $15,395,970; FY 19 FY 16 $15,395,970.

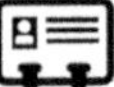

HQ: 4770 Buford Highway NE, P.O. Box K-50
Atlanta, GA 30341
Phone: 770-488-1221
Email: ksneegas@cdc.gov
http://www.cdc.gov

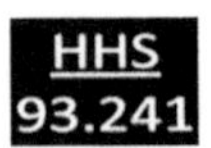

STATE RURAL HOSPITAL FLEXIBILITY PROGRAM
"The Rural Hospital Flexibility Program (Flex) The Rural Veterans Health Access Program"

Award: Project Grants

Purpose: Engages state designated entities in activities relating to planning and implementing rural healthcare plans and networks; designating facilities as Critical Access Hospitals; providing support for CAHs for quality improvement, quality reporting, performance improvements, and benchmarking; and integrating rural emergency medical services.

Applicant Eligibility: Flex and Rural Veterans Awardees: Only states with certified Critical Access Hospitals are eligible for this Program. The Governor designates the eligible applicant from each state.

Beneficiary Eligibility: States with at least one hospital located in a non-metropolitan statistical area or county and provides CMS with necessary assurances.

Award Range/Average: Medicare Rural Hospital Flexibility Program $316,735 to $968,815; Average, $592,440 Rural Veterans Health Access Program: $300,000

Funding: (Project Grants) FY 17 $23,659,822; FY 18 est $26,659,822; FY 19 N/A FY 16 $23,659,822; - Medicare Rural Hospital Flexibility Grant Program.(Project Grants) FY 17$900,000; FY 18 est $600,000; FY 19 N/A FY 16 $900,000; - Rural Veterans Health Access Prog

HQ: 5600 Fishers Lane
Rockville, MD 20857
Phone: 301-443-5905
Email: syoung@hrsa.gov
http://www.hrsa.gov/ruralhealth

STATE SELECT

Award: Direct Payments with Unrestricted Use

Purpose: Shares 90 percent of oil and gas royalties with the State to be paid monthly subject to late disbursement interest.

Applicant Eligibility: Revenue from public land leasing will trigger automatic payment distribution computed in accordance with the law.

Beneficiary Eligibility: ONRR distributes these funds to state governments for leased lands within the State and the State government has sole discretion in their use in accordance with the enabling legislation.

Award Range/Average: N/A

Funding: (Direct Payments with Unrestricted Use) FY 17 $263,000; FY 18 est $311,000; FY 19 est $344,000.

HQ: Office of Natural Resources Revenue 1849 C Street NW, P.O. Box 4211
Washington, DC 20240
Phone: 202-513-0600
http://www.onrr.gov

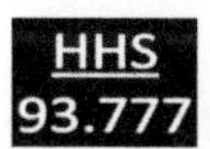

STATE SURVEY & CERTIFICATION OF HEALTH CARE PROVIDERS & SUPPLIERS (TITLE XVIII) MEDICARE

Award: Formula Grants

Purpose: Provides financial assistance to any State which is able to determine through an appropriate State agency that providers and suppliers of healthcare services are in compliance with Federal regulatory health and safety standards and conditions of participation.

Applicant Eligibility: Under Title XVIII, States enter into Section 1864 agreements with the Secretary of Health and Human Services whereby the designated agency of the State will be supported or reimbursed for on-site inspection of health care providers and suppliers. The designated State agency is usually that unit performing licensure activities within the State health department.

Beneficiary Eligibility: NA

Award Range/Average: $558,610 to $46,266,103 and an average of $6,523,464 (includes IMPACT Act funding).

Funding: (Direct Payments for Specified Use) FY 17 $365,054,041; FY 18 est $363,975,955; FY 19 est $366,784,147; FY 16 $363,816,174.

HQ: 7500 Security Boulevard
Baltimore, MD 21244
Phone: 410-786-9493
Email: david.wright@cms.hhs.gov

STATE SURVEY CERTIFICATION OF HEALTH CARE PROVIDERS & SUPPLIERS (TITLE XIX) MEDICAID

Award: Formula Grants

Purpose: Provides Medicaid financial assistance to any State which is able and willing to determine through its State health agency or other appropriate State agency that providers and suppliers of healthcare services are in compliance with Federal regulatory health and safety standards and conditions of participation.

Applicant Eligibility: The Federal government reimburses States for the Federal Financial Participation share for costs of inspection. Such participation is dependent on an approved State activity plan.

Beneficiary Eligibility: NA

Award Range/Average: FY 12 range is from $411,833 to $25,578,617 and an average of $3,941,426. FY 13 range is from $458,382 to $28,355,355 and an average of $3,888,836. FY 14 range is from $411,961 to $37,611,130 with an average of $4,245,492.

Funding: (Formula Grants) FY 17 N/A FY 18 N/A FY 19 est $308,315,000; FY 16 $291,000,000.

HQ: 7500 Security Boulevard
Baltimore, MD 21244
Phone: 410-786-9493
Email: david.wright@cms.hhs.gov

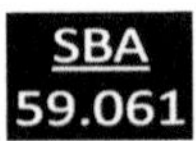

STATE TRADE EXPANSION
"State Trade Expansion Program"

Award: Cooperative Agreements; Project Grants

Purpose: To increase the number of small businesses that are exporting and increase the value of exports for those small businesses that are currently exporting.

Applicant Eligibility: States, defined as the 50 states, District of Columbia, Puerto Rico, US Virgin Islands, Guam, American Samoa, and the Commonwealth of Northern Mariana Islands.

Beneficiary Eligibility: N/A

Award Range/Average: No Data Available.

Funding: (Cooperative Agreements) FY 17 $18,000,000; FY 18 est $18,000,000; FY 19 est $10,000,000.

HQ: 409 3rd Street SW, 2nd Floor
Washington, DC 20416
Phone: 202-205-3644
Email: james.parker@sba.gov

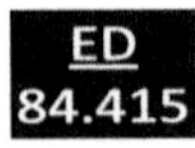

STATE TRIBAL EDUCATION PARTNERSHIP (STEP)

Award: Project Grants

Purpose: To promote tribal self-determination in education.

Applicant Eligibility: Eligible entities include an Indian tribe or tribal organization approved by an Indian tribe, or a tribal educational agency.

Beneficiary Eligibility: TEAs, SEAs, LEAs, Indian students, and teachers will benefit.

Award Range/Average: The average award is expected to be $240,000 for a single TEA or $400,000 for a consortium of TEAs.

Funding: (Project Grants) FY 17 $2,000,000; FY 18 est $2,000,000; FY 19 est $2,000,000.

HQ: Office of Indian Education Department of Education 400 Maryland Avenue SW
Washington, DC 20202
Phone: 202-453-5602
Email: shahla.ortega@ed.gov
http://www2.ed.gov/about/offices/list/oese/oie/index.html

STATE VITAL STATISTICS IMPROVEMENT PROGRAM

Award: Cooperative Agreements

Purpose: To enhance the performance of the National Vital Statistics System (NVSS) by convening states to aid in improving vital statistics data quality, timeliness and public health utility, increasing the competencies of the vital statistics workforce, and promoting accreditation of jurisdictional vital statistics programs consistent with National Center for Health Statistics goals.

Applicant Eligibility: Any application requesting an award higher than the funded amount is considered nonresponsive and will receive no further review. In addition, application will be considered non-responsive if they do not contain a letter of support written on behalf of the 57 jurisdictions' vital statistics offices.

Beneficiary Eligibility: An organization with demonstrated support of the 57 jurisdiction vital statistics offices. (See eligibility requirements.

Award Range/Average: $694,500 per year (5-year Cooperative Agreement)

Funding: (Cooperative Agreements) FY 17 $694,038; FY 18 est $694,500; FY 19 est $694,500.

HQ: 3210 Ea Street Highway 54 RTP
, NC 27709
Phone: 919-541-4414
http://www.cdc.gov

STATEWIDE FAMILY ENGAGEMENT CENTERS

Award: Project Grants

Purpose: To provide financial support to statewide organizations that conduct parent education and family engagement programs to support family-school partnerships.

Applicant Eligibility: Statewide organizations or consortia of such organizations may apply.

Beneficiary Eligibility: State educational agencies, local educational agencies, schools, and families will benefit.

Award Range/Average: Varies by competition.

Funding: (Project Grants) FY 17 $0; FY 18 est $10,000,000; FY 19 est $0; FY 11 est $0; FY 12 est $0.

HQ: 400 Maryland Avenue SW
Washington, DC 20202
Phone: 202-453-6620
Email: jane.hodgdon@ed.gov
http://www.ed.gov/programs/pirc/index.html

STATEWIDE LONGITUDINAL DATA SYSTEMS

Award: Project Grants

Purpose: To design, develop, and implement statewide, longitudinal data systems to efficiently and accurately manage, analyze, disaggregate, and use individual student data, consistent with the Elementary and

Secondary Education Act of 1965 and to facilitate analyses and research to improve student academic achievement and close achievement gaps.

Applicant Eligibility: State educational agencies.

Beneficiary Eligibility: State educational agencies, local educational agencies, non-profit and for-profit organizations, and individuals involved with education will benefit.

Award Range/Average: The 2015 grant awards ranged in size from approximately $3.5 million to $7 million for 4-year projects.

Funding: Project Grants (Contracts) FY 17 $4,850,238; FY 18 est $6,000,000; FY 19 est $0; (Project Grants) FY 17$27,287,085; FY 18 est $22,757,781; FY 19 est $0.

HQ: 550 12th Street SW, Room 9101
Washington, DC 20006
Phone: 202-245-7689
Email: nancy.sharkey@ed.gov
http://nces.ed.gov/programs/slds

STEPHANIE TUBBS JONES CHILD WELFARE SERVICES PROGRAM

Award: Formula Grants

Purpose: Purpose of the Stephanie Tubbs Jones Child Welfare Services program is to promote state and tribal flexibility in the development and expansion of a coordinated child and family services program that utilizes community-based agencies and ensures all children are raised in safe, loving families.

Applicant Eligibility: Territories and possessions include only Puerto Rico, U.S. Virgin Islands, Northern Marianas, Guam, and American Samoa.

Beneficiary Eligibility: Families and children in need of child welfare services will benefit.

Award Range/Average: Awards for states and territories ranged from $107,236 to $29,787,966 with an average of $4,661,994. Awards for Tribes ranged from $1,162 to $927,457 with an average of $32,847.

Funding: Formula Grants (Apportionments) FY 17 $267,871,118; FY 18 est $268,735,000; FY 19 est $268,000,000; FY 16 $268,735,000.

HQ: 330 C Street SW, Room 3509B
Washington, DC 20201
Phone: 202-205-8438
Email: eileen.west@acf.hhs.gov
http://www.acf.hhs.gov/programs/cb

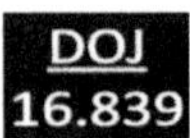

STOP SCHOOL VIOLENCE

Award: Project Grants

Purpose: To promote education for students on preventing violence and assists officials in responding to mental health crises.

Applicant Eligibility: The STOP School Violence Act of 2018 describes those who are eligible to apply are States, local units of government, and Indian tribes.

Beneficiary Eligibility: The STOP School Violence Act of 2018 states that training for teachers and education of students to prevent violence against others and self. This will include specialized training for school officials responding to mental health crisis.

Award Range/Average: Award amounts will range from $100,000 up to $500,000. See solicitation for specifics at https://ojp.gov/funding/Explore/CurrentFundingOpportunities.htm

Funding: (Cooperative Agreements) FY 17 $0; FY 18 est $75,000,000; FY 19 N/A.

HQ: 810 7th Street N West
Washington, DC 20351
Phone: 202-616-6500
http://bja.gov

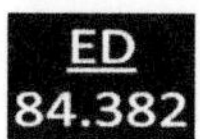

STRENGTHENING MINORITY-SERVING INSTITUTIONS

Award: Project Grants

Purpose: To strengthen Predominantly Black Institutions (PBI); Asian American and Native American Pacific Islander-Serving Institutions (AANAPISI); and Native American-Serving Nontribal Institutions (NASNTI) that propose to carry out activities to improve and expand such institution's capacity to serve low-income and minority students.

Applicant Eligibility: At the time of application, PBIs must have an enrollment of undergraduate students that is at least 40 percent African American students. AANAPISI and NASNTI applicants must have, at the time of application, an enrollment of undergraduate students not less than 10 percent Asian American and Native American Pacific Islanders and Native Americans, respectively.

Beneficiary Eligibility: The authorized beneficiaries are underrepresented; low-income; first-generation; minority; undergraduate students.

Award Range/Average: No Data Available.

Funding: (Project Grants) FY 17 $4,655,000; FY 18 est $4,670,000; FY 19 est $5,000,000; NASNTI (Project Grants) FY 17$7,500,000; FY 18 est $8,571,000; FY 19 est $7,500,000; Strengthening Master's Degree Program at HBCUs(Project Grants) FY 17$13,965,000; FY 18 est

HQ:
Washington, DC 20202
Phone: 202-453-7605
Email: winston.skerrett@ed.gov
http://www2.ed.gov/about/offices/list/ope/idues/index.html

STRENGTHENING PUBLIC HEALTH SYSTEMS & SERVICES THROUGH NATIONAL PARTNERSHIPS TO IMPROVE & PROTECT THE NATION'S HEALTH "CDC-RFA-OT18-1802"

Award: Cooperative Agreements

Purpose: To fund nongovernmental organizations with demonstrated capability, expertise, resources, national reach, and track record to strengthen governmental public health system's infrastructure and core services through provision of capacity building assistance.

Applicant Eligibility: Organizations deemed eligible to apply must also meet responsiveness criteria as outlined in the "Additional Information on Eligibility" in CDC-RFA-OT18-1802.

Beneficiary Eligibility: Beneficiaries include state health departments; tribal health organizations; local health departments; the District of Columbia; U.S. Territories; and other components of the public health system. The general public will also serve as beneficiaries.

Award Range/Average: The approximate average award ranges for the 12-month budget period are $2 million for Category A, up to $1 million for Category B and up to $500,000 for Category C.

Funding: (Salaries and Expenses) FY 18 est $120,000,000; FY 19 est $120,000,000; FY 17 est $0.

HQ: 4770 Buford Highway NE, P.O. Box K-90
Altanta, GA 30345
Phone: 770-488-1523
http://www.cdc.gov/stltpublichealth/partnerships/index.html

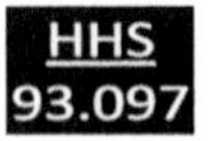

STRENGTHENING THE NATION'S PUBLIC HEALTH SYSTEM THROUGH A NATIONAL VOLUNTARY ACCREDITATION PROGRAM FOR STATE, TRIBAL, LOCAL & TERRITORIAL HEALTH DEPARTMENTS

"A National Voluntary Accreditation Program for State, Tribal, Local and Territorial Health Departments"

Award: Cooperative Agreements

Purpose: To support the operations and continuous improvement of a national accreditation program for state, tribal, local and territorial public health departments.

Applicant Eligibility: Public Health Accreditation Board (PHAB), a nonprofit with 501(c)3 IRS status.

Beneficiary Eligibility: State, Tribal, Local and Territorial Public Health Departments via a National Voluntary Accreditation Program administered by the Public Health Accreditation Board (PHAB), a 501(c)3 independent accrediting entity.

Award Range/Average: 1 award at an approximate average award of: $900,000.

Funding: (Cooperative Agreements) FY 17 $1,085,000; FY 18 est $900,000; FY 19 est $900,000.

HQ: 1600 Clifton Road, P.O. Box E70
Altanta, GA 30333
Phone: 770-488-1523
http://www.cdc.gov

STRENGTHENING THE PUBLIC HEALTH SYSTEM IN US-AFFILIATED PACIFIC ISLANDS (NON-PPHF)

"CBA to Strengthen Public Health Infrastructure and Performance in USAPIs (Non-PPHF)"

Award: Cooperative Agreements

Purpose: The purpose of this funding initiative is to ensure provision of capacity building assistance (CBA) to the USAPI's public health officials and public health systems by the formation of sound policies, strengthened organizational structures, effective management and revenue control, and address important cross-cutting issues such as health equity programs and services, and improved accountability measures for performance effectiveness and efficiency.

Applicant Eligibility: The only eligible applicant for this award is the Pacific Island Health Officers Association (PIHOA), a 501(c)3 independent accrediting body that administers the national voluntary public health department accreditation program.

Beneficiary Eligibility: Governmental public health departments, workforce segments across governmental public health departments, and/or nongovernmental public health professionals in the US-Affiliated Pacific Islands (USAPI). The US-Affiliated Pacific Islands (USAPI) consist of three U.S. Flag Territories of American Samoa, Guam, and the Commonwealth of the Northern Mariana Islands, as well as three sovereign states that have a Compact of Free Association with the United States (US)---Freely Associated States of the Republic of the Marshall Islands, Republic of Palau, and Federated States of Micronesia.

Award Range/Average: 1 award at approximate average award of 2,000,000

Funding: (Cooperative Agreements) FY 17 $2,232,125; FY 18 est $2,000,000; FY 19 est $2,000,000.

HQ: 4770 Buford Highway NE, P.O. Box K-90
Altanta, GA 30345
Phone: 770-488-1523
http://www.cdc.gov/stltpublichealth

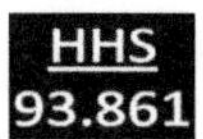

STRENGTHENING THE PUBLIC HEALTH SYSTEM IN US-AFFILIATED PACIFIC ISLANDS (PPHF)
"CBA to Strengthen Public Health Infrastructure and Performance in USAPIs"

Award: Cooperative Agreements

Purpose: The purpose of this funding initiative is to ensure provision of capacity building assistance to the USAPI's public health officials and public health systems through the formation of sound policies, strengthened organizational structures, effective management and revenue control, building jurisdictional partnerships, and by addressing important cross-cutting issues such as health equity programs and services, and improved accountability measures for performance effectiveness and efficiency.

Applicant Eligibility: The only eligible applicant for this award is the Pacific Island Health Officers Association (PIHOA), a 501(c)3 independent accrediting body that administers the national voluntary public health department accreditation program.

Beneficiary Eligibility: Governmental public health departments, workforce segments across governmental public health departments, and/or nongovernmental public health professionals in the US-Affiliated Pacific Islands (USAPI). The US-Affiliated Pacific Islands (USAPI) consist of three U.S. Flag Territories of American Samoa, Guam, and the Commonwealth of the Northern Mariana Islands, as well as three sovereign states that have a Compact of Free Association with the United States (US)---Freely Associated States of the Republic of the Marshall Islands, Republic of Palau, and Federated States of Micronesia.

Award Range/Average: 1 award at approximate average award of $2,000,000

Funding: (Cooperative Agreements) FY 17 $0; FY 18 est $2,000,000; FY 19 est $2,000,000; FY 16 $0.

HQ: 4770 Buford Highway NE, P.O. Box K-90
Altanta, GA 30345
Phone: 770-488-1523
http://www.cdc.gov/stltpublichealth

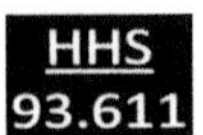

STRONG START FOR MOTHERS & NEWBORNS

Award: Cooperative Agreements

Purpose: Tests new care and payment models that have the potential to improve perinatal outcomes for women enrolled in Medicaid or CHIP who are at high-risk for adverse pregnancy outcomes.

Applicant Eligibility: The target applicants for this solicitation are providers (e.g., specific service providers, clinician groups and/or hospitals); States applying in partnership with providers; managed care organizations (MCOs) applying in partnership with providers; and conveners applying in partnership with providers.

Beneficiary Eligibility: Women enrolled in Medicaid and/or CHIP

Award Range/Average: Approximately $40.2 million may be awarded over the four-year plus period of performance (overlapping FFY 2013 into FFY 2017) to implement the approved models. This includes a minimum three year period for service delivery and up to an additional year for data collection and submission.

Funding: (Cooperative Agreements) FY 17 $1,254,197; FY 18 est $0; FY 19 est $0; FY 16 $2,066,898.

HQ: 200 Independence Avenue SW, Room 733H-02
Washington, DC 20201
Phone: 301-492-4312
Email: michelle.feagins@cms.hhs.gov
http://innovations.cms.gov/initiatives/strong-start/index.html

SUBSTANCE ABUSE & MENTAL HEALTH SERVICES PROJECTS OF REGIONAL & NATIONAL SIGNIFICANCE "PRNS"

Award: Project Grants

Purpose: To address priority substance abuse treatment, prevention and mental health needs of regional and national significance through assistance (grants and cooperative agreements) to States, political subdivisions of States, Indian tribes and tribal organizations, and other public or nonprofit private entities.

Applicant Eligibility: Public organizations, such as units of State and local governments and to domestic private nonprofit organizations such as community-based organizations, universities, colleges and hospitals.

Beneficiary Eligibility: other non-profits

Award Range/Average: $17,692 to $7,099,783; $417,410

Funding: (Project Grants) FY 17 $791,216,652; FY 18 est $444,885,477; FY 19 est $250,792,827.

HQ: 5600 Fishers Lane
Rockville, MD 20857
Phone: 240-276-1418
Email: roger.george@samhsa.hhs.gov
http://www.samhsa.gov

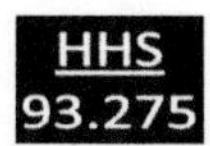

SUBSTANCE ABUSE & MENTAL HEALTH SERVICES-ACCESS TO RECOVERY "ATR I, ATR II, ATRIII"

Award: Project Grants

Purpose: To implement voucher programs for substance abuse clinical treatment and recovery support services pursuant to sections 501 (d)(5) and 509 of Public Health Service Act (42 U.S.C. sections 290aa(d)(5) and 290bb-2).

Applicant Eligibility: Eligibility for Access to Recovery (ATR) grants is limited to the immediate office of the Chief Executive (e.g.

Beneficiary Eligibility: Same as Applicant Eligibility.

Award Range/Average: No Data Available.

Funding: (Project Grants) FY 16 $0; FY 17 est $0; FY 18 est $0.

HQ: 5600 Fishers Lane
Rockville, MD 20857
Phone: 240-276-1418
Email: roger.george@samhsa.hhs.gov
http://www.samhsa.gov

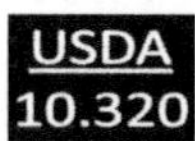

SUN GRANT PROGRAM

Award: Project Grants

Purpose: To promote biobased energy technology and related research and to provide funds for promoting educational programs to implement biobased technology in the rural U.S.

Applicant Eligibility: Only the Sun Grant Centers and Subcenter as specifically designated in 7 U.S.C. 8114 are eligible to apply for funding under this program.

Beneficiary Eligibility: Same as Applicant Eligibility.

Award Range/Average: If minimum or maximum amounts of funding per competitive and/or capacity project grant, or cooperative agreement are established, these amounts will be announced in the annual Competitive Request for Application (RFA).

Funding: Project Grants (Cooperative Agreements) FY 17 $2,787,840; FY 18 est $2,815,488; FY 19 est $0; FY 16 $2,328,000.

HQ: 1400 Independence Avenue SW, P.O. Box 2210
Washington, DC 20250-2210
Phone: 202-401-5244
http://nifa.usda.gov/funding-opportunity/sun-grant-program

HUD 14.151 SUPPLEMENTAL LOAN INSURANCE MULTIFAMILY RENTAL HOUSING "241(a)"

Award: Guaranteed/Insured Loans

Purpose: To provide quality rental housing.

Applicant Eligibility: Owners of a multifamily project or facility already subject to a mortgage insured by HUD or held by HUD.

Beneficiary Eligibility: Individuals/families and owners of multifamily projects.

Award Range/Average: No Data Available.

Funding: (Guaranteed/Insured Loans) FY 16 FY 14 est $15,000,000; FY 13$16,900,000; FY 15 est $15,000,000; FY 17.

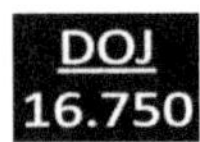

HQ: 451 7th Street SW
Washington, DC 20410
Phone: 202-402-2579
Email: carmelita_a._james@hud.gov
http://www.hud.gov/offices/hsg/hsgmulti.cfm

DOJ 16.750 SUPPORT FOR ADAM WALSH ACT IMPLEMENTATION GRANT PROGRAM "Adam Walsh Act"

Award: Project Grants

Purpose: To assist U.S. territories, tribes and local jurisdictions with developing programs to implement requirements of the Sex Offender Registration and Notification Act, where the offender lives, works and goes to school.

Applicant Eligibility: States, the District of Columbia, the Commonwealth of Puerto Rico, the Virgin Islands, America Samoa, Guam, the Northern Mariana Islands, and Federally recognized Indian tribes who have elected to carry out the requirements of SORNA. Only applicant jurisdictions that are enhancing, maintaining, or working towards substantial implementation of SORNA are eligible to apply for AWA Implementation Grants.

Beneficiary Eligibility: State (including the District of Columbia), local governments (through funds granted to States), U.S. territory and tribal government agencies that have sex offender registry and tracking responsibilities. For training and technical assistance funds: nonprofit and for-profit organizations with experience in SORNA implementation and sex offender management practices.

Award Range/Average: Up to $400,000 each for Adam Walsh Act (AWA) Implementation grants, up to $1,000,000 for the National Sex Offender Public Website (NSOPW), up to $1,000,000 for tribal training and technical assistance and $150,000 per fellowship opportunity

Funding: (Project Grants) FY 17 $16,883,370; FY 18 est $20,000,000; FY 19 est $20,000,000.

SUPPORT TO THE WORLD HEALTH ORGANIZATION (WHO) FOR RESPONSE TO THE EBOLA VIRUS DISEASE OUTBREAK IN WESTERN AFRICA

Award: Cooperative Agreements

Purpose: The project's objective is to contribute to on-going efforts to reduce the morbidity, mortality and to break the chain of transmission of EVD by strengthening capacities at the district level of affected countries in western Africa to actively find, investigate and refer cases, register all potential contacts and monitor them for symptom development.

Applicant Eligibility: World Health Organization (WHO). For purposes of this document, the term "WHO" includes its regional offices.

Beneficiary Eligibility: Individuals worldwide, including the U.S.

Award Range/Average: Range and Average Award for FY 2015: Approx. $50M

Funding: (Cooperative Agreements) FY 17 N/A FY 18 N/A FY 19 est $0; FY 16 $16,466,287.

HQ: 1600 Clifton Road
Atlanta, GA 30329
Phone: 404-639-4276
Email: ctg8@cdc.gov
http://www.cdc.gov

SUPPORTED EMPLOYMENT SERVICES FOR INDIVIDUALS WITH THE MOST SIGNIFICANT DISABILITIES "Supported Employment State Grants"

Award: Formula Grants

Purpose: To provide grants for time limited services leading to supported employment for individuals with the most severe disabilities.

Applicant Eligibility: The State VR agency designated in the VR services portion of the Unified or Combined State plan to administer the VR program is eligible to receive Federal funds under this program.

Beneficiary Eligibility: Individuals with the most significant disabilities who have been determined eligible for VR services under Title I of the Rehabilitation Act and whose individualized plan for employment identifies supported employment as the employment outcome.

Award Range/Average: In FY 2018, the estimated range of awards is $28,185 (territories) to $2,052,838, with a median State award, excluding outlying, areas of $300,000.

Funding: (Formula Grants) FY 17 $27,548,000; FY 18 est $22,548,000; FY 19 est $22,548,000.

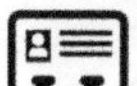

HQ: 400 Maryland Avenue SW
Washington, DC 20202
Phone: 202-245-7454
Email: suzanne.mitchell@ed.gov
http://www2.ed.gov/about/offices/list/osers/rsa/index.html

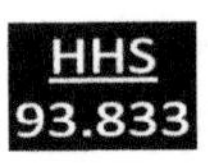

SUPPORTING & MAINTAINING A SURVEILLANCE SYSTEM FOR CHRONIC KIDNEY DISEASE (CKD) IN THE UNITED STATES "Chronic Kidney Disease (CKD)"

Award: Cooperative Agreements

Purpose: The award will build upon previous work to continue developing, supporting and enhancing the CKD Surveillance System in the United States, to monitor the burden and trends of CKD and its risk factors over time, and monitor and evaluate trends in achieving Healthy People 2020 objectives.

Applicant Eligibility: Public nonprofit organizations, Private nonprofit organizations, For profit organizations, Small, minority, and women-owned businesses, Universities, Colleges, Research institutions, Hospitals, Community-based organizations, Faith-based organizations, Indian/Native American Tribal Governments (Federally Recognized), Indian/Native American Tribal Governments (other than Federally recognized), Indian/Native American Tribally Designated Organizations State and local governments or their Bona Fide Agents (this includes the District of Columbia, the Commonwealth of Puerto Rico, the Virgin Islands, the Commonwealth of the Northern Marianna Islands, American Samoa, Guam, the Federated States of Micronesia, the Republic of the Marshall Islands, and the Republic of Palau). Note: A Bona Fide Agent is an agency/organization identified by the state as eligible to submit an application under the state eligibility in lieu of a state application.

Beneficiary Eligibility: The general public will benefit from the objectives of this program. Kidney diseases are the ninth leading cause of death in the United States and more than 1 of 10 US adults may have CKD.

Award Range/Average: 200000 – 400000; new FY 16 will fund two range is contingent upon funding request.

Funding: (Cooperative Agreements) FY 17 $1,200,000; FY 18 est $1,311,429; FY 19 est $1,311,429.

HQ: 4770 Buford Highway, P.O. Box F 75
Atlanta, GA 30341
Phone: 770-488-1057
Email: nmr0@cdc.gov
http://www.cdc.gov

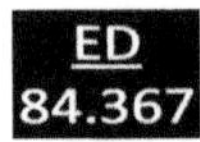

SUPPORTING EFFECTIVE INSTRUCTION STATE GRANTS (FORMERLY, IMPROVING TEACHER QUALITY STATE GRANTS)

Award: Formula Grants

Purpose: To provide grants to State Educational Agencies (SEAs), to increase student academic achievement consistent with challenging State academic standards.

Applicant Eligibility: SEAs

Beneficiary Eligibility: Elementary and secondary schools, teachers, paraprofessionals, principals and other school leaders; and students will benefit.

Award Range/Average: FY 17: Range: $9,722,812 - $227,942,395; Average: $38,944,141. FY 18: Range: $9,789,945 to $230,422,543; Average: $38,944,141 FY 19: N/A

Funding: (Formula Grants) FY 17 $2,055,830,000; FY 18 est $2,055,830,000; FY 19 est $0.

HQ: 400 Maryland Avenue SW
Washington, DC 20202

Phone: 202-453-7019
Email: roberta.miceli@ed.gov
http://www.ed.gov/programs/teacherqual/index.html

SUPPORTIVE HOUSING FOR PERSONS WITH DISABILITIES "Section 811"

Award: Direct Payments for Specified Use

Purpose: To enlarge the supply of supportive housing for very low-income disabled persons.

Applicant Eligibility: Eligible Sponsors are nonprofit organizations with a Section 501(c)(3) tax exemption from the Internal Revenue Service. Eligible Owner entities are nonprofit organizations with a 501(c)(3) tax exemption from the Internal Revenue Service and, if the proposed project involves mixed financing, for-profit limited partnerships with a nonprofit entity as the sole general partner.

Beneficiary Eligibility: Beneficiaries of housing developed under this program must be very low-income (equal to or less than 50% AMI) adults (18 or older) with a physical, mental, or emotional impairment that is expected to be of long-continued and indefinite duration, that substantially impedes his or her ability to live independently, and is of a nature that such ability could be improved by more suitable housing conditions.

Award Range/Average: $422,600 to $4,092,000 (FY 10/11)

Funding: (Direct Payments for Specified Use) FY 15 $125,000,000; FY 16 est $129,000,000; FY 17 est $146,000,000.

HQ: 451 7th Street SW, Room 6142
Washington, DC 20410
Phone: 202-708-3000
Email: marvis.s.hayward@hud.gov
http://portal.hud.gov/hudportal/hud?src=/program_offices/housing/mfh/progdesc/disab811

SUPPORTIVE HOUSING FOR THE ELDERLY "Section 202"

Award: Direct Payments for Specified Use

Purpose: To enlarge the supply of multifamily housing for very low income elderly persons.

Applicant Eligibility: Eligible Sponsors include private nonprofit organizations and nonprofit consumer cooperatives. Eligible Owner entities include private nonprofit corporations, nonprofit consumer cooperatives, and if the proposed project involves mixed-financing, for-profit limited partnerships with a nonprofit entity as the sole general partner.

Beneficiary Eligibility: Beneficiaries of housing developed under this program must be elderly (62 years of age or older) and have very low-incomes.

Award Range/Average: No Data Available.

Funding: (Direct Payments for Specified Use) FY 15 $354,000,000; FY 17 est $430,000,000; FY 16 est $356,000,000.

HQ: 451 7th Street SW, Room 6152
Washington, DC 20410

Phone: 202-708-3000
Email: alicia.anderson@hud.gov
http://portal.hud.gov/hudportal/hud?src=/program_offices/housing/mfh/progdesc/eld202

SURETY BOND GUARANTEES

Award: Insurance

Purpose: To guarantee surety bonds issued by commercial surety companies for small businesses unable to obtain a bond without an SBA guarantee.

Applicant Eligibility: Guarantees are limited to those surety companies holding certificates of authority from the Secretary of the Treasury as an acceptable surety for bonds on Federal contracts. Specific criteria apply to the Prior Approval and PSB Sureties.

Beneficiary Eligibility: For Federal contracts, a small business is eligible for the surety bond program if it qualifies as a small business under Code of Federal Regulations Subpart 121, Size Eligibility Provisions and Standards.

Award Range/Average: Additional information available on SBA's website at www.sba.gov.

Funding: (Insurance (Guaranteed Surety Bonds) FY 17 $1,392,000,000; FY 18 est $6,000,000,000; FY 19 est $6,000,000,000; FY 16 $1,424,000,000.

HQ: 409 3rd Street SW, 8th Floor
Washington, DC 20416
Phone: 202-205-6548
Email: peter.gibbs@sba.gov
http://www.sba.gov/osg

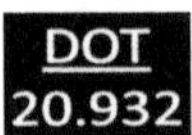

SURFACE TRANSPORTATION DISCRETIONARY GRANTS FOR CAPITAL INVESTMENT "TIGER Grants (Transportation Investment Generating Economic Recovery)"

Award: Project Grants

Purpose: To preserve and create jobs and promote economic recovery.

Applicant Eligibility: The Federal share of the costs for which an expenditure is made under this program may have been up to 100 percent, however, the Department gave priority to projects that required a contribution of Federal funds in order to complete an overall financing package, and to projects that are expected to be completed by February 17, 2012.

Beneficiary Eligibility: The ultimate benefits of this program may have been received by, among others, State or local governments, transit agencies, builders/contractors/developers, major metropolises, and other urban, suburban, or rural areas.

Award Range/Average: Grants provided under this program generally were not less than $20,000,000 and not greater than $300,000,000.

Funding: (Salaries and Expenses) FY 18 est $0; FY 16 $0; FY 17 est $0.

HQ: 1200 New Jersey Avenue SE
Washington, DC 20590
Phone: 202-366-0301
Email: tigergrants@dot.gov
http://www.dot.gov/tiger

SURPLUS PROPERTY UTILIZATION "Federal Real Property Assistance Program"

Award: Sale, Exchange, or Donation of Property and Goods

Purpose: To convey or lease all surplus Federal real properties made available by the disposal agency which are needed and usable by eligible organizations and institutions to carry out health programs.

Applicant Eligibility: States, their political subdivisions and instrumentalities; tax-supported public health institutions, and nonprofit institutions which (except for institutions which lease property to assist the homeless under Title V of Public Law 100-77) have been held exempt from taxation under Section 501 (c) (3) of the 1986 Internal Revenue Code.

Beneficiary Eligibility: Anyone attending, working with or for, or served by the eligible applicants. Examples of potentially eligible use programs are hospitals, public health clinics, water and sewer systems, institutions for the rehabilitation of mentally or physically disabled, health research institutions, homeless assistance facilities, and other institutions with basic health programs.

Award Range/Average: No Data Available.

Funding: N/A

HQ: 7700 Wisconsin Avenue, Suite 8216
Bethesda, MD 20814
Phone: 301-443-2265
Email: theresa.ritta@psc.hhs.gov
http://www.psc.gov/additional-resources/real-property-management

SURVEILLANCE FOR DISEASES AMONG IMMIGRANTS & REFUGEES FINANCED IN PART BY PREVENTION & PUBLIC HEALTH FUNDS (PPHF)

Award: Cooperative Agreements

Purpose: Conducts surveillance to detect, prevent and control diseases and evaluate existing health programs to improve the health of refugees and/or immigrants that are newly arrived in the United States.

Applicant Eligibility: Eligibility is limited to any domestic entity providing health care services to immigrants and refugees newly arrived in the United States.

Beneficiary Eligibility: Any U.S. state, political subdivision and U.S. territories and other public entities providing healthcare services to newly arrived refugees and immigrants will benefit

Award Range/Average: Awards will range from approximately $25,000 to $150,000 with an average of approximately $80,000.

Funding: (Cooperative Agreements) FY 17 $0; FY 18 est $0; FY 19 est $0; FY 16 $480,000.

HQ: 1600 Clifton Road
Atlanta, GA 30333
Phone: 404-639-0712
http://www.cdc.gov/immigrantrefugeehealth

SUSTAINABLE AGRICULTURE RESEARCH & EDUCATION "SARE"

Award: Project Grants

Purpose: To support agriculture products, sustain domestic and wildlife habitat, conservation of land and natural resources, and provide employment opportunities.

Applicant Eligibility: Land-grant colleges or universities, other universities, State agricultural experiment stations, State cooperative extension services, nonprofit organizations, and individuals with demonstrable expertise, or Federal or State governmental entities.

Beneficiary Eligibility: Same as Applicant Eligibility.

Award Range/Average: If minimum or maximum amounts of funding per competitive and/or capacity project grant, or cooperative agreement are established, these amounts will be announced in the annual Competitive Request for Application (RFA).

Funding: (Project Grants) FY 17 $25,297,920; FY 18 est $32,770,088; FY 19 est $0; FY 16 $23,147,513.

HQ: 1400 Independence Avenue SW
Washington, DC 20250
Phone: 202-401-0151
http://nifa.usda.gov/program/sustainable-agriculture-program

SWIFT, CERTAIN, AND FAIR (SCF) SUPERVISION PROGRAM: INCLUDING PROJECT HOPE "SCF"

Award: Cooperative Agreements; Project Grants

Purpose: The SCF Program reduces crimes. It implements strategies to respond to offender behavior and reduces recidivism. It develops supervision strategies and reduces violence.

Applicant Eligibility: Eligible applicants for project grants under the SCF Program include states, units of local government, and federally recognized Indian tribal governments (as determined by the Secretary of the Interior). Eligible applicants for a cooperative agreement to operate the SCF Resource Center are limited to national-scope private and nonprofit organizations (including tribal nonprofit or for-profit organizations), and colleges and universities, both public and private (including tribal institutions of higher education).

Beneficiary Eligibility: See goals and objectives for additional information. Also, view the current fiscal year's solicitation available at the Office of Justice Programs web site

Award Range/Average: Award amounts may be up to $600,000.

Funding: (Project Grants) FY 17 $3,378,658; FY 18 est $3,614,134; FY 19 est $3,614,134.

HQ: 810 7th Street NW
Washington, DC 20531
Phone: 202-305-9317
Email: emily.n.chonde@usdoj.gov
http://www.bja.gov

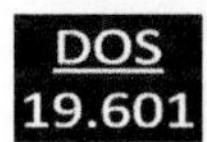

SYRIA ASSISTANCE PROGRAM "NEA Syria"

Award: Cooperative Agreements; Cooperative Agreements; Project Grants

Purpose: Supports the foreign assistance goals and objectives of the Department of State, Bureau of Near Eastern Affairs, as delineated in the Fiscal Year Bureau Strategic and Resource Plan. This program is for all grant awards for the entire fiscal year funded through State/NEA for Syria programming.

Applicant Eligibility: U.S. or foreign non-profit organizations; for-profit organizations; private institutions of higher education, public or state institutions of higher education; public international organizations; and small businesses with functional and regional experience. Each solicitation outlines who is eligible and what types of experience are needed to apply for funding.

Beneficiary Eligibility: Same as Applicant Eligibility.

Award Range/Average: Depends on specific grant award. See www.grants.gov for specific announcement.

Funding: N/A

HQ: 2430 E Street NW
Washington, DC 20037
Phone: 202-776-8691
Email: curleysl@state.gov
http://www.state.gov

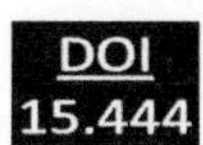

TAKE PRIDE

Award: Cooperative Agreements

Purpose: The Bureau of Ocean Energy Management (BOEM) oversees the exploration and development of oil, natural gas and other minerals and renewable energy alternatives on the Nation's outer continental shelf. The purpose of the Environmental Studies Program is to obtain the information needed for the assessment and the management of environmental impacts; to predict impacts on marine biota; and to monitor the human, marine, and coastal environments to provide time series and data trend information.

Applicant Eligibility: Public and private organizations.

Beneficiary Eligibility: Research scientists, Federal, State and local decision-makers, Native American Organizations, and the general public will ultimately benefit from the program.

Award Range/Average: Range is $25,000 to $100,000; Average $250,000.

Funding: (Cooperative Agreements) FY 17 $5,742,696; FY 18 est $6,400,000; FY 19 N/A.

HQ: 45600 Woodland Road
Sterling, VA 20166

Phone: 703-787-1087
Email: rodney.cluck@boem.gov
http://www.boem.gov

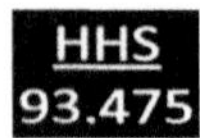

TANF POLICY ACADEMY FOR INNOVATIVE EMPLOYMENT STRATEGIES (PAIES) "PAIES"

Award: Cooperative Agreements

Purpose: Work with successful state TANF applicants to design, plan and refine components and strategies to improve employment outcomes for TANF program participants.

Applicant Eligibility: State (including the District of Columbia, Guam, Puerto Rico, and the Virgin Islands) human services agencies are eligible to receive assistance.

Beneficiary Eligibility: State (including the District of Columbia, Guam, Puerto Rico, and the Virgin Islands) human services agencies are eligible to receive assistance to participate in the PAIES to design, plan and refine components and strategies to improve employment outcomes for TANF program participants.

Award Range/Average: For Fiscal Year 2018, the grants awarded will range from $100,000 to $150,000.

Funding: (Cooperative Agreements) FY 17 $0; FY 18 est $770,000; FY 19 est $0; FY 16 $0.

HQ: 330 C Street SW, Suite 3026
Washington, DC 20002
Phone: 202-401-5141
Email: lwashington-thomas@acf.hhs.gov
http://www.acf.hhs.gov/ofa

TAX COUNSELING FOR THE ELDERLY

Award: Project Grants

Purpose: To authorize the Internal Revenue Service to enter into agreements with private or public nonprofit agencies or organizations.

Applicant Eligibility: Tax Counseling for the Elderly sponsors must be private or public nonprofit organizations with experience in coordinating volunteer programs. Federal, State, and local governmental agencies are not eligible to sponsor a program.

Beneficiary Eligibility: Elderly taxpayers, age 60 or older.

Award Range/Average: No Data Available.

Funding: Cooperative Agreements (Discretionary Grants) FY 18 est $8,890,000; FY 19 est $8,890,000; FY 17$6,500,000.

HQ: 5000 Ellin Road NCFB C4 110
Lanham, MD 20706
Phone: 404-338-7894
http://www.irs.gov/individuals/tax-counseling-for-the-elderly

TEACHER EDUCATION ASSISTANCE FOR COLLEGE & HIGHER EDUCATION GRANTS (TEACH GRANTS)

Award: Direct Payments for Specified Use

Purpose: To provide annual grants of up to $4,000 to eligible undergraduate and graduate students who agree to teach specified high-need subjects at schools serving primarily disadvantaged populations for four years within eight years of graduation.

Applicant Eligibility: Undergraduate and graduate students completing coursework or other requirements necessary to begin a career in teaching. Students must attend an institution of higher education that provides high-quality teacher preparation and professional development services; is financially sound; provides, or assists in the provision, of pedagogical coursework; and provides, or assists in the provision, of supervision and support services to teachers.

Beneficiary Eligibility: Students must have a grade-point-average (GPA) comparable to a 3.25 on a scale of zero to 4.

Award Range/Average: No Data Available.

Funding: (Direct Payments for Specified Use) FY 17 $90,955,000; FY 18 est $91,978,000; FY 19 est $98,833,000; FY 16 $91,000,000.

HQ: P.O. Box 84
Washington, DC 20044
Phone: 800-433-3243
http://www2.ed.gov/programs/tqpartnership/index.html

TEACHING HEALTH CENTER GRADUATE MEDICAL EDUCATION PAYMENT "THCGME Payment Program"

Award: Formula Grants

Purpose: To expand primary care and dental residency training programs in community based settings.

Applicant Eligibility: Eligible entities include community-based ambulatory patient care centers that operate a primary care residency program. Specific examples of eligible entities include, but are not limited to: Federally qualified health centers, as defined in section 1905(l)(2)(B) of the Social Security Act, Community mental health centers, as defined in section 1861(ff)(3)(B) of the Social Security Act, Rural health clinics, as defined in section 1861(aa) of the Social Security Act, Health centers operated by the Indian Health service, an Indian tribe, or tribal organization, or an urban Indian organization, as defined in section 4 of the Indian Health Care Improvement Act, An entity receiving funds under Title X of the Public Health Service Act.

Beneficiary Eligibility: The program supports high-quality primary care residency training in community based settings. Eligible entities include community-based ambulatory patient care centers that operate a primary care residency program.

Award Range/Average: The annual FTE payment rate is determined by the availability of funds.

Funding: (Formula Grants) FY 17 $55,860,000; FY 18 est $60,000,000; FY 19 est $122,000,000.

HQ: 5600 Fishers Lane, Room 15N142
Rockville, MD 20857

Phone: 301-443-6190
Email: mlee1@hrsa.gov
http://www.hrsa.gov

TECHNICAL & NON-FINANCIAL ASSISTANCE TO HEALTH CENTERS
"State and Regional Primary Care Associations and National Cooperative Agreements"

Award: Cooperative Agreements

Purpose: To provide necessary technical and non-financial assistance to potential and existing health centers, including training and assistance.

Applicant Eligibility: Eligible applicants include public, non-profit, and for-profit entities, including federally recognized Indian Tribal governments and Native American and faith-based organizations, that can provide training and technical assistance on a national or state/regional level to health centers and other community-based organizations with similar missions. Applications may be submitted by current State and Regional Primary Care Associations, National Cooperative Agreements, or new organizations that care to provide training and technical assistance to potential and existing health centers.

Beneficiary Eligibility: Population groups in medically underserved areas, medically underserved populations, and special populations such migratory and seasonal agricultural workers, people experiencing homelessness, and public housing residents.

Award Range/Average: $448,662 to $6,375,000; Average $1,909,130

Funding: (Cooperative Agreements) FY 17 $54,000,000; FY 18 est $57,000,000; FY 19 est $57,000,000; FY 16 $67,348,597; - State and Regional Primary Care Associations(Cooperative Agreements) FY 17$19,000,000; FY 18 est $21,000,000; FY 19 est $21,000,000; FY 16 $20,8

HQ: 5600 Fishers Lane, Room 16N16
Rockville, MD 20857
Phone: 301-594-4300
http://www.hrsa.gov/about/contact/bphc.aspx

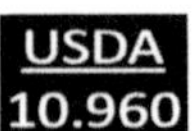

TECHNICAL AGRICULTURAL ASSISTANCE
"International Capacity Building and Development Assistance Programs"

Award: Cooperative Agreements; Direct Payments for Specified Use

Purpose: To identify agricultural issues and problems and to maximize the capabilities of U.S. educational institutions and nonprofit agencies in agricultural technical assistance and research.

Applicant Eligibility: Institutions of higher education, state cooperative institutions, non-profit organizations, and public international organizations.

Beneficiary Eligibility: Technical assistance provided through these agreements generally benefits agricultural institutions in specified locations, or supports programming that does so.

Award Range/Average: $10,000 - $2,000,000

Funding: (Cooperative Agreements) FY 17 $23,408,866; FY 18 est $25,757,319; FY 19 est $24,200,000.

HQ: 1400 Independence Avenue SW Room 3016 S, P.O. Box 1033
Rockville, MD 20250
Phone: 202-720-5337
Email: lawrence.trouba@fas.usda.gov
http://www.hrsa.gov/about/contact/bphc.aspx

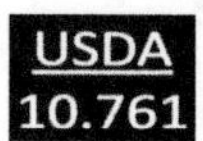

TECHNICAL ASSISTANCE & TRAINING GRANTS "TAT Grants"

Award: Project Grants

Purpose: To identify water and waste disposal problems in rural areas and to provide maintenance facilities.

Applicant Eligibility: Eligible entities must be private nonprofit organizations. Applicants must have proven ability, background, experience, legal authority and actual capacity to provide technical assistance and/or training on a regional basis to associations.

Beneficiary Eligibility: Entities that may be eligible for water and waste disposal loans and grants (10.760) such as municipalities, counties, districts, authorities, and other political subdivisions of a State, organizations operated on a not-for-profit basis, such as associations, cooperatives, or private corporations, Indian tribes on Federal and State reservations and other federally recognized Indian tribes.

Award Range/Average: $50,000 to $9,100,000. Average: $914,028

Funding: (Project Grants) FY 17 $20,108,621; FY 18 est $41,164,931; FY 19 est $0.

HQ: 1400 Independence Avenue SW, P.O. Box 1548
Washington, DC 20250
Phone: 202-720-0986
Email: edna.primrose@wdc.usda.gov
http://www.rd.usda.gov/programs-services/water-waste-disposal-technical-assistance-training-grants

TECHNICAL ASSISTANCE FOR SPECIALTY CROPS PROGRAM "TASC"

Award: Direct Payments for Specified Use

Purpose: The Technical Assistance for Specialty Crops Program is for U.S. organizations to address sanitary, phytosanitary, and technical barriers that threaten the export of U.S. specialty crops.

Applicant Eligibility: To be approved, an applicant must be a: (1) U.S. government agency; (2) U.S. State government agency; (3) U.S. non-profit trade association; (4) U.S. university; (5) U.S. agricultural cooperative; (6) U.S. private company or (7) any other U.S. organization.

Beneficiary Eligibility: The Technical Assistance for Specialty Crops Program is intended to benefit the represented U.S. industry rather than a specific company or brand.

Award Range/Average: Projects funded on a project by project basis for up to $500,000 per year.

Funding: Formula Grants (Apportionments) FY 17 $3,005,104; FY 18 est $6,000,000.

HQ: 1400 Independence Avenue SW
Washington, DC 20050
Phone: 202-720-8557
Email: lona.powell@fas.usda.gov
http://www.fas.usda.gov/programs/technical-assistance-specialty-crops-tasc

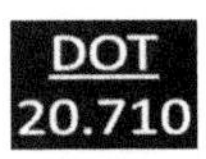

TECHNICAL ASSISTANCE GRANTS "Information Grants to Communities- Technical Assistance Grant"

Award: Project Grants

Purpose: Promotes development of engineering or other scientific analysis of pipeline safety issues, including the promotion of public participation in official proceedings.

Applicant Eligibility: As well as private nonprofit institutions/organizations and public nonprofit institutions/organizations.

Beneficiary Eligibility: N/A

Award Range/Average: The range is $0 - $100,000

Funding: Project Grants (Discretionary) FY 17 $1,500,000; FY 18 est $1,500,000; FY 19 est $0; FY 16 $0.

HQ: 1200 New Jersey Avenue SE E22 105
Washington, DC 20590
Phone: 202-366-6855
Email: karen.lynch@dot.gov
http://primis.phmsa.dot.gov/tag

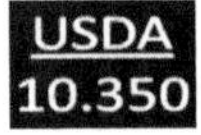

TECHNICAL ASSISTANCE TO COOPERATIVES "TAC"

Award: Provision of Specialized Services; Advisory Services and Counseling; Dissemination of Technical Information; Training

Purpose: To promote research, technical assistance, educational programs in various disciplines, especially on farmer and farming aspects in rural areas.

Applicant Eligibility: Farmer and rural cooperatives and rural residents in all U.S. States and Territories.

Beneficiary Eligibility: Ultimate beneficiaries must be located in rural areas.

Award Range/Average: Non-monetary

Funding: (Advisory Services on Compliance) FY 17 $0; FY 18 est $0; FY 19 est $0.

HQ: 1400 Independence Avenue SW Room 5803 S, P.O. Box 3201
Washington, DC 20250
Phone: 202-690-1374
http://www.rd.usda.gov/about-rd/agencies/rural-business-cooperative-service

HHS 93.348 TECHNICAL ASSISTANCE TO INCREASE TOBACCO CESSATION

Award: N/A

Purpose: To provide technical assistance to state tobacco control programs and national and state partners.

Applicant Eligibility: N/A

Beneficiary Eligibility: N/A

Award Range/Average: DP13-1316 $450K

Funding: (Cooperative Agreements) FY 17 $450; FY 18 N/A FY 19 est $400.

HQ: 4770 Buford Highway NE, P.O. Box S107 7
Atlanta, GA 30341
Phone: 770-488-2499
Email: zho7@cdc.gov
http://www.cdc.gov

DOC 11.616 TECHNOLOGY INNOVATION PROGRAM (TIP) "TIP"

Award: Project Grants

Purpose: The Technology Innovation Program supports innovation in the United States especially in the areas of critical national need.

Applicant Eligibility: A U.S.-owned, single, small-sized or medium-sized company doing a majority of its business in the United States or a joint venture may apply for TIP funding. Members of joint ventures that are companies must also be doing a majority of their business in the United States.

Beneficiary Eligibility: Same As Applicant Eligibility

Award Range/Average: New program; therefore, no range and average available.

Funding: Project Grants (Cooperative Agreements) FY 17 $106,000; FY 18 est $4,000; FY 19 est $0.

HQ: 100 Bureau Drive
Gaithersburg, MD 20899
Phone: 301-975-4429
Email: heather.mayton@nist.gov
http://www.nist.gov

HHS 93.297 TEENAGE PREGNANCY PREVENTION PROGRAM "TPP"

Award: Cooperative Agreements

Purpose: To support competitive grants to public and private entities to replicate evidence-based teen pregnancy prevention program models that have been shown to be effective through rigorous evaluation and research and demonstration projects to develop and test additional models and innovative strategies to prevent teen pregnancy.

Applicant Eligibility: Nonprofit with or without 501C3 IRS status ; For profit organizations; Small, minority, and women owned businesses; Universities and colleges; Research institutions; Hospitals; Community-based organizations; Faith-based organizations; Federally recognized or state-recognized American Indian/ Alaska Native tribal governments; American Indian/Alaska Native tribally designated organizations; Alaska Native health corporations; Urban Indian health organizations; Tribal epidemiology centers; State and local governments or their Bona Fide Agents; Political subdivisions of States

Beneficiary Eligibility: Teenagers in the US

Award Range/Average: $250,000 - $2,000,000 per year. TPP Program grants in FY 18 are funded through 6 different Funding Opportunity Announcements.

Funding: (Cooperative Agreements) FY 17 est $101,000,000; FY 16 $101,000,000; FY 18 N/A - Fiscal year amounts include total for grants and contracts to support replication of evidence-based teen pregnancy prevention programs and research and demonstration projects to develop and test new and innovative approaches to prevent teen pregnancy, as well as program support costs.

HQ: 1101 Wootton Parkway Tower Building, Suite 550
Rockville, MD 20852
Phone: 240-453-8822
Email: alice.bettencourt@hhs.gov
http://www.hhs.gov/ash/oah

TELEHEALTH PROGRAMS

Award: Project Grants

Purpose: To fund programs that demonstrate how telehealth networks improve healthcare services in rural communities. The current cohort is focused on telehealth services delivered through school-based health centers/clinics (SBHC), particularly those serving high-poverty populations.

Applicant Eligibility: Telehealth Network Grant Program (TNGP) - Eligible applicants include public and private non-profit entities, including faith-based and community organizations, as well as federally-recognized tribal governments and organizations. National Telehealth Resource Center Program (TNRC) and Regional Telehealth Resource Center Program (RTRC) - Eligible applicants include public and private non-profit entities.

Beneficiary Eligibility: Telehealth Network Grant Program (TNGP) - Health care providers in rural areas, in medically underserved areas, in frontier communities, and for medically underserved populations. TNGP grantees include in the network at least two (2) of the following entities (at least one (1) of which shall be a community-based health care provider: (a) community or migrant health centers or other federally qualified health centers; (b) health care providers, including pharmacists, in private practice; (c) entities operating clinics, including rural health clinics; (d) local health departments; (e) nonprofit hospitals, including community (critical) access hospitals; (f) other publicly funded health or social service agencies; (g) long-term care providers; (h) providers of health care services in the home; (i) providers of outpatient mental health services and entities operating outpatient mental health facilities; (j) local or regional emergency health care providers; (k) institutions of higher education; or (l) entities operating dental clinics; and (m) school based health centers/clinics.

Award Range/Average: No Data Available.

Funding: (Project Grants) FY 17 $6,240,582; FY 18 est $6,242,829; FY 19 est $6,246,073; - Telehealth Network Program (Project Grants) FY 17$1,299,552; FY 18 est $0; FY 19 N/A; - The Rural Child Poverty Telehealth Network Program (Project Grants) FY 17$3,900,000.

HQ: 5600 Fishers Lane
Rockville, MD 20857
Phone: 301-443-0835
Email: cmena@hrsa.gov
http://www.hrsa.gov/ruralhealth/telehealth/index.html

TEMPORARY ASSISTANCE FOR NEEDY FAMILIES "TANF"

Award: Formula Grants; Dissemination of Technical Information

Purpose: To provide grants to States, Territories, the District of Columbia, and Federally-recognized Indian Tribes.

Applicant Eligibility: In general, all States, Territories, the District of Columbia, and all Federally-recognized Tribes in the lower 48 States and 13 specified entities in Alaska are eligible. State and local agencies and Tribes that operate TANF programs must do so under plans determined to be complete (or for Tribes approved) by the Department of Health and Human Services (HHS).

Beneficiary Eligibility: Needy families with children, as determined eligible by the State, Territory, or Tribe in accordance with the State or Tribal plan submitted to HHS.

Award Range/Average: State and Tribal Family Assistance grants are estimated from $77,195 to $3,637,503,251 with an average of $125,451,428.

Funding: (Formula Grants) FY 17 $608,000,000; FY 18 est $608,000,000; FY 19 est $608,000,000; - TANF Contingency Fund (Formula Grants) FY 17$77,617,558; FY 18 est $77,617,558; FY 19 est $77,617,558.

HQ: 330 C Street SW, 3rd Floor
Washington, DC 20201
Phone: 202-401-4731
Email: susan.golonka@acf.hhs.gov
http://www.acf.hhs.gov/programs/ofa

TENANT RESOURCE NETWORK PROGRAM "TRN"

Award: Cooperative Agreements

Purpose: To make grants to applicant organizations to help, communicate, educate and engage tenants of eligible project-based Section 8-assisted properties.

Applicant Eligibility: Eligible applicants are non profit organizations with current IRS 501(c)(3) tax-exempt status. Eligible applicants shall demonstrate a minimum of five years of tenant outreach and organizing work, and may not have an identity of interest with any owner or management entity of any property where TRN activities are proposed.

Beneficiary Eligibility: Tenants in identified TRN eligible properties will ultimately benefit from the program.

Award Range/Average: 200000 to 720000

Funding: (Cooperative Agreements) FY 14 est $0; FY 15 est $0; FY 13$0.

HQ: 451 7th Street SW, Room 6178
Washington, DC 20410
Phone: 202-402-3263
Email: carol.schrader@hud.gov
http://portal.hud.gov/hudportal/hud?src=/program_offices/housing/mfh/grants/trn

HHS 93.609 THE AFFORDABLE CARE ACT – MEDICAID ADULT QUALITY GRANTS
"Measuring and Improving the Quality of Maternity Care in Medicaid"

Award: Project Grants

Purpose: Supports State Medicaid agencies in testing, collecting, and reporting the Initial Core Set of healthcare Quality Measures for Adults Enrolled in Medicaid to CMS. Additionally, the grant funding will also support States' efforts to use these data for improving the quality of care for adults covered by Medicaid.

Applicant Eligibility: Grant applicants are limited to the 51 State Medicaid Agencies and the Medicaid Agencies in the US Territories.

Beneficiary Eligibility: N/A

Award Range/Average: Grant awards up to $1 million for each 12-month budget period, with an estimated total of up to $2 million per Grantee over the two-year project period.

Funding: (Project Grants) FY 17 N/A FY 18 est $0; FY 19 est $0; FY 16 $0.

HQ: 200 Independence Avenue SW, Room 733H 02
Washington, DC 20201
Phone: 301-492-4312
Email: michelle.feagins@cms.hhs.gov
http://www.medicaid.gov/medicaid-chip-program-information/by-topics/quality-of-care/adult-medicaid-quality-grants.html

HHS 93.536 THE AFFORDABLE CARE ACT MEDICAID INCENTIVES FOR PREVENTION OF CHRONIC DISEASE DEMONSTRATION PROJECT
"MIPCD Program"

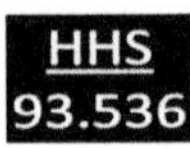

Award: Project Grants

Purpose: Award grants to States to carry out initiatives to provide incentives to Medicaid beneficiaries.

Applicant Eligibility: Applicants should review the eligibility information of the individual funding opportunity announcement issued under this CFDA program.

Beneficiary Eligibility: Applicants should review the funding opportunity description of the funding opportunity announcement issued under this CFDA program for information on participant eligibility requirements.

Award Range/Average: Grantees receive between $250,000 baseline - $1.1 million.

Funding: (Salaries and Expenses) FY 17 $0; FY 18 est $0; FY 19 est $0; FY 16 $0.

HQ: 7500 Security Boulevard
Baltimore, MD 21244
Phone: 410-786-6616
Email: grant@cms.hhs.gov
http://www.grants.gov

THE AFFORDABLE CARE ACT: BUILDING EPIDEMIOLOGY, LABORATORY, AND HEALTH INFORMATION SYSTEMS CAPACITY IN THE EPIDEMIOLOGY & LABORATORY CAPACITY FOR INFECTIOUS DISEASE (ELC) & EMERGING INFECTIONS PROGRAM (EIP) COOPERATIVE AGREEMENTS; PPHF

Award: Cooperative Agreements

Purpose: To provide for expanded and sustained national investment in prevention and public health programs to improve health and help restrain the rate of growth in private and public sector healthcare costs.

Applicant Eligibility: Eligible applicants include the current ELC and EIP grantees which consists of all U.S. states, 6 large local health departments (Los Angeles County, Philadelphia, New York City, Chicago, Houston, and the District of Columbia), U.S. territories (Puerto Rico, Guam, U.S. Virgin Islands) and other U.S. affiliates in the Pacific (American Samoa, the Republic of Palau, Federated States of Micronesia, Marshall Islands, Mariana Islands and American Samoa).

Beneficiary Eligibility: State health departments, large local health departments, the District of Columbia, U.S. Territories, and the general public.

Award Range/Average: No Data Available.

Funding: (Cooperative Agreements) FY 17 $60,145,113; FY 18 est $18,845,332; FY 19 est $18,845,332.

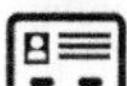

HQ: 1600 Clifton Road NE, P.O. Box C18
Atlanta, GA 30333
Phone: 404-639-7379
Email: amoconnor@cdc.gov
http://www.cdc.gov

THE HEALTH INSURANCE ENFORCEMENT & CONSUMER PROTECTIONS GRANT PROGRAM

Award: Project Grants

Purpose: The Health Insurance Enforcement and Consumer Protections grants will provide states with the opportunity to ensure their laws, regulations, and procedures are in line with federal requirements and that states are able to effectively oversee and enforce the PHS Act's title XXVII Part A provisions with respect to health insurance issuers.

Applicant Eligibility: The Health Insurance Enforcement and Consumer Protections grant is open to all states that are currently enforcing the ACA market reforms and also for those states who are not currently enforcing the ACA market reforms to assist with their respective transition to an active enforcement role for all the market reforms and consumer protections under Part A of Title XXVII of the Public Health Service Act.

Beneficiary Eligibility: Grants to States (including the District of Columbia) for planning and/or implementing the market reforms and consumer protections in Part A of title XXVII of the PHS Act.

Award Range/Average: Grantees will receive a minimum of $476,998 as a baseline award amount.

Funding: (Project Grants) FY 17 $25,547,052; FY 18 est $8,600,000; FY 19 N/A FY 15$0.

HQ: 200 Independence Avenue

Washington, DC 20201

Phone: 301-492-4182

Email: james.taing@cms.hhs.gov

http://www.cms.gov/cciio/programs-and-initiatives/health-insurance-market-reforms/health_insurance_enforcement_and_consumer_protections-grants-.html

HHS 93.334

THE HEALTHY BRAIN INITIATIVE: TECHNICAL ASSISTANCE TO IMPLEMENT PUBLIC HEALTH ACTIONS RELATED TO COGNITIVE HEALTH, COGNITIVE IMPAIRMENT, AND CAREGIVING AT THE STATE & LOCAL LEVELS "Healthy Brain Initiative"

Award: Cooperative Agreements

Purpose: To implement public health actions through engagement of national partners and public health networks at national, state and local levels to apply public health strategies to promote cognitive health; address cognitive impairment, including Alzheimer's disease; and support the needs of care partners.

Applicant Eligibility: Eligible applicants are limited to national, non-profit professional public health or cognitive health/cognitive impairment mission organizations with experience and expertise providing technical assistance and support to governmental and non-governmental components of the public health system

Beneficiary Eligibility: Anyone/General Public

Award Range/Average: No Data Available.

Funding: (Cooperative Agreements) FY 17 $1,366,098; FY 18 est $1,366,098; FY 19 est $1,366,098.

HQ: 4770 Buford Highway, P.O. Box F7

Atlanta, GA 30341

Phone: 770-488-5998

http://www.cdc.gov

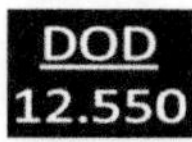

THE LANGUAGE FLAGSHIP GRANTS TO INSTITUTIONS OF HIGHER EDUCATION
"The Language Flagship"

Award: Cooperative Agreements; Project Grants

Purpose: To establish centers for the teaching of critical languages that enable students to reach or exceed Level 3 in proficiency based on the Interagency Language Roundtable (ILR) scale in African Languages, Arabic, Chinese, Hindi/Urdu, Korean, Persian, and Russian.

Applicant Eligibility: The award for this program is made to a nonprofit organization that administers this assistance program on behalf of DoD.

Beneficiary Eligibility: Any accredited U.S. institution of higher education (defined in 20 U.S.C. 1001 of the Higher Education Act of 1965) is eligible to apply for assistance (subaward) under this program.

Award Range/Average: Subawards range from $200,000 to $500,000 depending on type of project. The average award is estimated at $325,000 per subaward for each budget period. The core program has four-year project periods pending availability of funds.

Funding: (Salaries and Expenses) FY 17 $24,494,000; FY 18 est $18,330,000; FY 19 est $41,730,948.

HQ: 4800 Mark Center Drive, Suite 08 G 08
Alexandria, VA 22350
Phone: 571-256-0756
Email: g.e.mcdermott.civ@mail.mil
http://www.thelanguageflagship.org

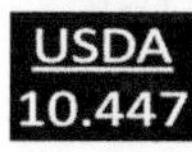

THE RURAL DEVELOPMENT (RD) MULTI-FAMILY HOUSING REVITALIZATION DEMONSTRATION PROGRAM (MPR)
"Restructuring Program"

Award: Project Grants

Purpose: The RHS under Section 515 provides for the low-income residents with affordable housing.

Applicant Eligibility: Owners or buyers of financially viable Section 515 financed rental or Section 514/516 labor housing properties.

Beneficiary Eligibility: Low-income rural residents needing safe, decent, and sanitary rental housing are eligible.

Award Range/Average: The underwriting guidelines include, but are not limited to, the following: The maximum soft-second loan will be limited to no more than $5,000 per unit; revitalization grants limited to $5,000 per unit; total assistance provided from a revitalization grant, revitalization zero percent loan, and/or a soft-second loan is limited to $10,000 per unit; and the maximum Section 515 loan or Section 514/516 loan and grant is limited to no more than $20,000 per unit.

Funding: (Direct Loans) FY 17 $37,000,000; FY 18 est $40,000,000; FY 19 est $0; FY 16 $67,000,000.

HQ: 1400 Independence Avenue SW, P.O. Box 0782
Washington, DC 20250
Phone: 202-720-1604
http://www.rd.usda.gov

HHS 93.413 THE STATE FLEXIBILITY TO STABILIZE THE MARKET GRANT PROGRAM

Award: Project Grants

Purpose: To provide a funding source to enhance the role of states in the implementation and planning for several of the Federal market reforms and consumer protections under Part A of Title XXVII of the Public Health Service Act (PHS Act).

Applicant Eligibility: This Funding Opportunity Announcement is open to all fifty States and the District of Columbia for planning and/or implementing one or more of the three pre-selected market reforms and consumer protections in Part A of title XXVII of the PHS Act. Only one application per state is permitted, except in a state in which there is more than one regulating entity, each with a primary responsibility over the regulation of a portion of the private health insurance market.

Beneficiary Eligibility: Grants to States (including the District of Columbia) for planning and/or implementing the market reforms and consumer protections in Part A of title XXVII of the PHS Act.

Award Range/Average: Grantees will receive a minimum of $156,000 as a baseline award amount.

Funding: (Cooperative Agreements) FY 17 est $0; FY 19 N/A FY 18 est $8,000,000.

HQ: 200 Independence Avenue
Washington, DC 20201
Phone: 301-492-4182
Email: james.taing@cms.hhs.gov
http://www.cms.gov/cciio/index.html

DOS 19.029 THE U.S. PRESIDENT'S EMERGENCY PLAN FOR AIDS RELIEF PROGRAMS "PEPFAR"

Award: Cooperative Agreements; Project Grants

Purpose: The Office of the U.S. Global AIDS Coordinator coordinates and oversees the U.S. global response to HIV/AIDS through the U.S. President's Plan for Emergency AIDS Relief (PEPFAR). The key aspect of the program is to provide support in achieving the HIV/AIDS care, treatment, and prevention goals of PEPFAR as detailed in the PEPFAR Blueprint.

Applicant Eligibility: N/A

Beneficiary Eligibility: N/A

Award Range/Average: No Data Available.

Funding: N/A

HQ: 2100 Pennsylvania Avenue NW, Room 200
Washington, DC 20037
Phone: 202-663-2109
Email: ewingwf@state.gov
http://www.pepfar.gov

HHS 93.966 THE ZIKA HEALTH CARE SERVICES PROGRAM
"The Zika Health Care Services Program"

Award: Formula Grants

Purpose: The purpose of the Zika healthcare Services Program is to support prevention activities and treatment services for men, women (including pregnant women) and children adversely or potentially impacted by the Zika virus.

Applicant Eligibility: The funds available for states, territories, tribes or tribal organizations with active or local transmission of the Zika virus, as confirmed by the CDC. Active transmission refers to geographic areas for intervention and issuance of travel guidance in a setting where local Zika virus transmission is occurring.

Beneficiary Eligibility: State, Intrastate, Local, Sponsored Organization, Public Nonprofit Institution/ Organization, Other Public Institution/organization, Federally Recognized Indian Tribal Government, U.S. territory/possession, individual/family, Specialized group, Small business, Private organization, Profit organization, Quasi-public nonprofit organization, Other private institution/organization, Anyone/general public, Health professional, Infant, Low Income, Welfare Recipient, Unemployed

Award Range/Average: $1,100,000 - $60,600,000

Funding: Formula Grants (Cooperative Agreements) FY 17 $71,355,000; FY 18 est $0; FY 19 est $0.

HQ: 7500 Security Boulevard
Baltimore, MD 21244
Phone: 410-786-0426
Email: elizabeth.garbarczyk@cms.hhs.gov
http://www.cms.gov

DOS 19.013 THOMAS R. PICKERING FOREIGN AFFAIRS FELLOWSHIP PROGRAM
"Pickering Fellowship Program"

Award: Cooperative Agreements; Cooperative Agreements; Project Grants

Purpose: The program offers only graduate fellowships. The purpose of the program is to attract outstanding students who represent all ethnic and social backgrounds and who have an interest in pursuing a Foreign Service career in the U.S. Department of State. This program encourages the application of members of minority groups historically underrepresented in the Foreign Service, women, and those with financial need.

Applicant Eligibility: N/A

Beneficiary Eligibility: N/A

Award Range/Average: N/A

Funding: (Salaries and Expenses)

HQ: 2401 E Street NW
Washington, DC 20522
Phone: 202-261-8892
Email: georgecm@state.gov

TITLE I GRANTS TO LOCAL EDUCATIONAL AGENCIES "Title I Basic, Concentration, Targeted and Education Finance Incentive Grants"

Award: Formula Grants

Purpose: To improve teaching and learning in high-poverty schools in particular for children falling through local educational agencies (LEAs).

Applicant Eligibility: SEAs including for the Outlying Areas and the Secretary of the Interior. Local educational agencies (LEAs) and Indian tribal schools are subgrantees.

Beneficiary Eligibility: In a targeted assistance program, children who are failing, or most at risk of failing, to meet challenging State academic standards. In a schoolwide program, all children in the school.

Award Range/Average: $1,000,000 - $2,028,646,221. The average award is $266,462,103.

Funding: (Formula Grants) FY 17 $15,459,802,000; FY 18 est $154,759,802,000; FY 19 est $15,459,802,000; FY 16 $14,905,581,800.

HQ: 400 Maryland Avenue SW
Washington, DC 20202
Phone: 202-453-5514
Email: patrick.rooney@ed.gov
http://www.ed.gov/programs/titleiparta/index.html

TITLE I STATE AGENCY PROGRAM FOR NEGLECTED & DELINQUENT CHILDREN & YOUTH

Award: Formula Grants

Purpose: To provide educational continuity for neglected and delinquent children and youth in State-run institutions for juveniles and in adult correctional institutions.

Applicant Eligibility: SEAs. State agencies responsible for providing free public education for children and youth (1) in institutions for neglected or delinquent children and youth; (2) attending community day programs for neglected or delinquent children and youth; or (3) in adult correctional institutions may apply to their SEA for subgrants.

Beneficiary Eligibility: Children and youth in institutions for neglected or delinquent children and youth, community day programs for neglected or delinquent children and youth, and adult correctional institutions.

Award Range/Average: $106,792-2,176,848; Average: $892,763.

Funding: (Formula Grants) FY 17 $47,614,000; FY 18 est $47,614,000; FY 19 est $47,614,000.

HQ: 400 Maryland Avenue SW, Room 3E244
Washington, DC 20202
Phone: 202-453-6716
Email: earl.myers@ed.gov
http://www.ed.gov/programs/titleipartd/index.html

DOJ 16.548 TITLE V DELINQUENCY PREVENTION PROGRAM
"Delinquency Prevention Program"

Award: Formula Grants

Purpose: To reduce risks and enhancing protective factors to prevent youth at risk of becoming delinquent from entering the juvenile justice system and to intervene with first-time and nonserious offenders to keep them out of the juvenile justice system.

Applicant Eligibility: N/A

Beneficiary Eligibility: N/A

Award Range/Average: Available in the OJP Program Announcement.

Funding: (Formula Grants) FY 18 est $17,000,000; FY 16 $9,014,278; FY 17 est $14,500,000.

HQ: 810 7th Street NW
Washington, DC 20531
Phone: 202-616-9135
http://www.ojjdp.ncjrs.org/titlev

HHS 93.787 TITLE V SEXUAL RISK AVOIDANCE EDUCATION PROGRAM (DISCRETIONARY GRANTS)
"Title V SRAE - Discretionary Grants"

Award: Project Grants

Purpose: The program provides messages to youth that normalizes the optimal health behavior of avoiding non-marital sexual activity.

Applicant Eligibility: Faith-based and community organizations that meet the eligibility requirements are eligible to receive awards under the Competitive Title V SRAE Discretionary Grants and National SRA Resource Center funding opportunity announcements.

Beneficiary Eligibility: Title V SRAE Discretionary Grant Program will fund States and other entities to provide youth ages 10 to 19 with education on sexual risk avoidance (meaning voluntarily refraining from sexual activity).

Award Range/Average: The range of awards for each discretionary funding stream as follows: Title V Competitive SRAE is $13,500 to $850,000. National SRARC is $1.8 million to $2.3 million.

Funding: Project Grants (Discretionary) FY 19 est $75,000,000; FY 18 est $75,000,000; FY 17$0; - Title V SRAE funding will be used to award competitive grants. A set-aside of 20% ($15,000,000) of the $75,000,000 appropriation will fund program support activities and $60,000,000 for formula and competitive grants. Funds (approximately $10,000,000) allocated for states that do not apply for Title V State SRAE funding shall be used to fund Title V Competitive SRAE grants.

HQ: 330 C Street SW
Washington, DC 20021
Phone: 202-205-9605
Email: lebretia.white@acf.hhs.gov
http://www.acf.hhs.gov/programs/fysb

TITLE V STATE SEXUAL RISK AVOIDANCE EDUCATION (TITLE V STATE SRAE) PROGRAM
"Title V State Sexual Risk Avoidance Education (Title V State SRAE) Program"

Award: Formula Grants

Purpose: To provide messages to youth that normalizes the optimal health behavior of avoiding non-marital sexual activity.

Applicant Eligibility: Eligible applicants include all 50 States, the District of Columbia, Puerto Rico, U.S. Virgin Islands, Guam, American Samoa, Commonwealth of the Northern Mariana Islands, Federate States of Micronesia, the Republic of the Marshall Islands, and Republic of Palau.

Beneficiary Eligibility: Title V State SRAE will fund states to provide youth ages 10 to 19 with education on sexual risk avoidance (meaning voluntarily refraining from sexual activity).

Award Range/Average: The range of awards for Title V SRAE is $13,500 to $7,358,829.

Funding: (Formula Grants) FY 19 est $75,000,000; FY 18 est $75,000,000; FY 17$63,372,499.

HQ: 330 C Street SW
Washington, DC 20021
Phone: 202-205-9605
Email: lebretia.white@acf.hhs.gov
http://www.acf.hhs.gov/programs/fysb

HUD 14.869

TITLE VI FEDERAL GUARANTEES FOR FINANCING TRIBAL HOUSING ACTIVITIES

Award: Guaranteed/Insured Loans

Purpose: To obtain financing for affordable housing activities.

Applicant Eligibility: The applicant must be a Federally recognized Indian tribe or TDHE that is either a beneficiary or recipient of Indian Housing Block Grants (IHBG) funds.

Beneficiary Eligibility: Indian tribes and their members are the beneficiaries. A TDHE acts on behalf of a tribe, as authorized by Tribal and TDHE resolutions.

Award Range/Average: A borrower's guaranteed obligations may not exceed an amount equal to the borrower's IHBG, less the amount needed to operate and maintain current assisted stock (CAS), times five (IHBG - CAS X 5 = maximum guaranteed amount).

Funding: (Guaranteed/Insured Loans) FY 18 est $2,000,000; FY 17 est $2,000,000; FY 16 $5,760,000.

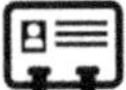

HQ: 451 7th Street SW, Room 5156
Washington, DC 20410
Phone: 202-402-4978
Email: thomas.c.wright@hud.gov
http://www.hud.gov/offices/pih/ih/homeownership/titlevi

TOBACCO PREVENTION & CONTROL LEGAL TECHNICAL ASSISTANCE "Legal TA"

Award: Cooperative Agreements

Purpose: To provide legal technical assistance and consultation to OSH and NTCP grantees awardees on questions related to the identification, development, adoption, and implementation of evidence-based interventions and policies nationwide.

Applicant Eligibility: In addition to the above list, legal centers are eligible for this FOA. Due to the strategies, activities and approaches required by this cooperative agreement, it is essential that the potential awardee has a) deep institutional knowledge specific to current and historical U.S. tobacco control issues, b) is an experienced national organization with capacity to work at the national level in tobacco control legal TA, and c) does not have any present or historical links to the tobacco industry and should provide a statement to such effect.

Beneficiary Eligibility: The immediate beneficiaries of the program include the federal government, state, local, territorial and Federally Recognized Indian Tribal Governments, as well as other CDC Office on Smoking and Health Awardees such as the National Networks, which include a range of non profit organizations. The ultimate beneficiary of the program is the general public, as the program seeks to support population-wide environmental changes that help to transform the nation's health and provide individuals with equitable opportunities to take charge of their health.

Award Range/Average: $250,000 per year for 5 years

Funding: Cooperative Agreements (Discretionary Grants) FY 17 $235,000; FY 18 est $235,000; FY 19 est $235,000; FY 16 $235,000.

HQ: 4770 Buford Highway
Atlanta, GA 30341
Phone: 770-488-6204
Email: sedwards2@cdc.gov
http://www.cdc.gov

TRACKING ELECTRONIC HEALTH RECORD ADOPTION & CAPTURING RELATED INSIGHTS IN U.S. HOSPITALS

Award: Cooperative Agreements

Purpose: Significant federal investments to accelerate the adoption of electronic health records and exchange of clinical data are now in place. It is critical to continue to track the adoption and use of EHRs. The data generated under this funding opportunity will enable ONC and researchers to carry out these important activities for inpatient settings.

Applicant Eligibility: This is a non-competitive funding opportunity and is restricted to a designated organization. Organizations not designated as such are not eligible to apply for this opportunity, and therefore should not submit an application.

Beneficiary Eligibility: The beneficiaries will include the Office of the National Coordinator for Health Information Technology, the American Hospital Association, and any researchers or members of the general public interested in survey data on the adoption and use of health IT by U.S. hospitals.

Award Range/Average: No Data Available.

Funding: (Cooperative Agreements) FY 17 $105,000; FY 18 est $105,000; FY 19 FY 16 $0.

HQ: 330 C Street SW
Washington, DC 20201
Phone: 202-720-2919
Email: carmel.halloun@hhs.gov

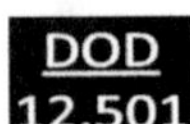

TRAINING & SUPPORT – COMBATING WEAPONS OF MASS DESTRUCTION

Award: Cooperative Agreements

Purpose: Offers support and stimulate training and collaborative efforts for solutions to combat or counter weapons of mass destruction (WMD).

Applicant Eligibility: Applicant eligibility is specified in individual program announcements, funding opportunities, award documents, and codified regulations applicable to award.

Beneficiary Eligibility: Competitions are open to private and public accredited institutions of higher education, non-profit organizations, non-Federal government entities and other qualified organizations as listed in the appropriate funding opportunity.

Award Range/Average: No Data Available.

Funding: (Salaries and Expenses) FY 18 est $10,000,000; FY 16 $0; FY 17$0; FY 19 est $10,000,000.

HQ: 8725 John J Kingman Road
Fort Belvoir, VA 22060
Phone: 703-767-3527
Email: mary.k.chase2.civ@mail.mil

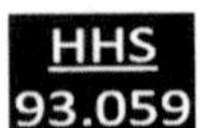

TRAINING IN GENERAL, PEDIATRIC, AND PUBLIC HEALTH DENTISTRY

"General, Pediatric, and Public Health Dentistry and Dental Hygiene"

Award: Project Grants

Purpose: To improve access to and the delivery of oral healthcare services for all individuals, particularly low income, underserved, uninsured, minority, health disparity, and rural populations.

Applicant Eligibility: Eligible applicants are accredited dental or dental hygiene schools, public or private not-for-profit hospitals, or other pubic or not for profit entities, which the Secretary has determined is capable of carrying out such a grant. Eligible entities include entities that have programs in dental or dental hygiene schools, or approved residency or advanced education programs in the practice of general, pediatric, or public health dentistry.

Beneficiary Eligibility: Beneficiaries include a full range of trainees: dental or dental hygiene students, dental hygienists, dental residents, practicing dentists, and other approved primary care dental trainees and dental faculty.

Award Range/Average: Predoctoral Training in General, Pediatric and Public Health Dentistry and Dental Hygiene: FY 18 est.: Range: $315,000 to $350,000; Average award: $344,000 Postdoctoral Training in General, Pediatric and Public Health Dentistry: FY 18 est: Range: $242,000 to $749,000; Average award: $549,000 Faculty Development in General, Pediatric and Public Health Dentistry and Dental Hygiene: Average award: $457,418. Dental Faculty Development and Loan Repayment Program: Average award: $180,959. FY 18 est: Range: $236,765 to $300,000; Average award: $285,367 Dental Faculty Loan Repayment Program: FY 18 est.: Range: $79,715 to $150,000; Average award: $115,780

Funding: (Project Grants) FY 17 $884,922; FY 18 est $2,199,834; FY 19 est $0; - Dental Faculty Loan Repayment Program (Project Grants) FY 17$11,232,162; FY 18 est $12,645,256; FY 19 est $0; - Postdoctoral Training in General, Pediatric and Public Health Dentistry

HQ: 5600 Fishers Lane, Room 15N 120
Rockville, MD 20857
Phone: 301-443-5260
Email: srogers@hrsa.gov
http://www.hrsa.gov

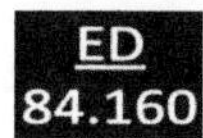

TRAINING INTERPRETERS FOR INDIVIDUALS WHO ARE DEAF & INDIVIDUALS WHO ARE DEAF-BLIND

Award: Project Grants

Purpose: To support projects that improve the skills of manual, tactile, oral, and cued speech interpreters providing services to individuals who are deaf and individuals who are deaf-blind.

Applicant Eligibility: Public or private nonprofit agencies and organizations, including institutions of higher education are eligible for assistance.

Beneficiary Eligibility: Individuals preparing for employment as interpreters for individuals who are deaf and individuals who are deaf- blind individuals who are presently serving as interpreters and wish to maintain or raise the level of their skills, and the persons who will receive the services of interpreters are beneficiaries of this program.

Award Range/Average: To be determined.

Funding: (Project Grants) FY 17 $2,399,805; FY 18 est $2,399,507; FY 19 est $2,399,996.

HQ: 400 Maryland Avenue SW
Washington, DC 20202
Phone: 202-245-7343
Email: tom.finch@ed.gov
http://rsa.ed.gov/programs.cfm?pc=traindeaf

TRANSFORMATION INITIATIVE RESEARCH GRANTS: DEMONSTRATION & RELATED SMALL GRANTS

Award: Project Grants

Purpose: To enhance the demonstrations of Office of Policy Development and Research by providing a vehicle for conducting a number of small research projects.

Applicant Eligibility: Nonprofit organizations, for profit organizations located in the U.S (HUD will not pay fee or profit for the work conducted under this program), foundations, think tanks, consortia, Institutions of higher education accredited by a national or regional accrediting agency recognized by the U.S. Department of Education and other entities that will sponsor a researcher, expert and analyst.

Beneficiary Eligibility: Eligibility of tribes and tribal organizations applies only to the small grant program associated with the Sustainable Construction in Indian Country demonstration.

Award Range/Average: $25,000- $500,000 per grant for a maximum three-grant performance period.

Funding: (Project Grants) FY 17 $0; FY 18 est $0; FY 19 est $0.

HQ: 451 7th Street, Room 8230
Washington, DC 20410
Phone: 202-402-3852
Email: susan.s.brunson@hud.gov

HUD 14.524 TRANSFORMATION INITIATIVE RESEARCH GRANTS: NATURAL EXPERIMENTS

Award: Project Grants

Purpose: To provide funding to support scientific research to evaluate the impact on local, state, and federal policies.

Applicant Eligibility: Nonprofit organizations, for profit organizations located in the U.S (HUD will not pay fee or profit for the work conducted under this program), foundations, think tanks, consortia, Institutions of higher education accredited by a national or regional accrediting agency recognized by the U.S. Department of Education and other entities.

Beneficiary Eligibility: The research funded by these HUD grants should be state-of-the-art natural experiments and result in substantive contributions to the existing pool of scientific theory and evidence on the effectiveness of public policies. It should also yield methodological advances to evaluating public policy – preference will be given to proposals aimed at developing general solutions that may be applied to additional problems.

Award Range/Average: An applicant can request $100,000 to $250,000 per award.

Funding: (Project Grants) FY 17 $0; FY 18 est $0; FY 19 est $0.

HQ: 451 7th Street, Room 8230
Washington, DC 20410
Phone: 202-402-3852
Email: susan.s.brunson@hud.gov

HUD 14.523 TRANSFORMATION INITIATIVE RESEARCH GRANTS: SUSTAINABLE COMMUNITY RESEARCH GRANT PROGRAM

Award: Cooperative Agreements

Purpose: To fill key data and information gaps and to develop and evaluate policy alternatives that communities can choose to facilitate decision making about various community investments.

Applicant Eligibility: Nationally recognized and accredited institutes of higher education; non-profit foundations, research consortia or policy institutes; for-profit organizations located in the U.S. and contract research institutions or academic entities that will sponsor a researcher or experts as the applicant. However, the sponsored researcher assumes the sole responsibility for the completion of the application and conducting the research.

Beneficiary Eligibility: HUD is primarily interested in sponsoring cutting edge research in the areas of affordable housing development and preservation; transportation-related issues; economic development and job creation; land use planning and urban design; green and sustainable energy practices; and a range of issues related to sustainability.

Award Range/Average: $150,000, up to $500,000 for an award.

Funding: (Cooperative Agreements) FY 17 $0; FY 18 est $0; FY 19 est $0.

HQ: 451 7th Street, Room 8230
Washington, DC 20410
Phone: 202-402-3852
Email: susan.s.brunson@hud.gov

TRANSFORMATION INITIATIVE: CHOICE NEIGHBORHOODS DEMONSTRATION SMALL RESEARCH GRANT PROGRAM

Award: Cooperative Agreements

Purpose: To fund research related to Choice Neighborhoods that complements the work already being funded by HUD through the Choice baseline research project.

Applicant Eligibility: Since one purpose of this NOFA is to broaden the community of researchers working on Choice Neighborhoods, HUD will not directly fund entities or individuals already involved in HUD-funded Choice Neighborhoods research under Task Order C-CHI-01127/TO001.

Beneficiary Eligibility: The goal of this research program is to fund research related to Choice Neighborhoods that complements the work already being funded by HUD through the Choice baseline research project (C-CHI-01127/TO001). Since the Choice baseline research project will focus on implementation grants in Boston, Chicago, and New Orleans, applicants are encouraged to identify research projects in other Choice Neighborhood implementation or planning grant sites.

Award Range/Average: An applicant may request up to $200,000 for an award. A Cooperative Agreement means that HUD will have substantial involvement during performance of the contemplated research project.

Funding: (Cooperative Agreements) FY 17 $0; FY 18 est $0; FY 19 est $0.

HQ: 451 7th Street, Room 8230
Washington, DC 20410
Phone: 202-402-3852
Email: susan.s.brunson@hud.gov

"TRANSFORMING CLINICAL PRACTICE INITIATIVE (TCPI) – SUPPORT & ALIGNMENT NETWORK (SAN) 2.0"

Award: Cooperative Agreements

Purpose: Works to leverage primary and specialist care transformation work and learning in the field. SAN 2.0 awardees add a valuable technical assistance asset to TCPI that will catalyze the accelerated adoption of Alternative Payment Models, prior to 2019, at very large scale, and with very low cost.

Applicant Eligibility: Applications will be screened for completeness and adherence to eligibility. Applications received late or that fail to meet the eligibility requirements or do not include the required forms will not be reviewed.

Beneficiary Eligibility: The Beneficiary eligibility includes the list as noted above with the exception of: Federal, Interstate; Intrastate; Student/Trainee and Graduate Students; Artist/Humanist; Engineer/Architect, Builder/Contractor/Developer; Farmer/Rancher/Agriculture Producer; Industrialist/Business Person; Small Business Person; Homeowner -Property Owner; Anyone/General Public

Award Range/Average: Budget Fiscal Year 2017: $700,000 - $110,000

Funding: Formula Grants (Cooperative Agreements) FY 17 $1,712,720; FY 18 est $0; FY 19 est $0.

HQ: LT 7500 Security Boulevard
Baltimore, MD 21207
Phone: 410-786-8834
Email: fred.butler@cms.hhs.gov
http://www.cms.hhs.gov

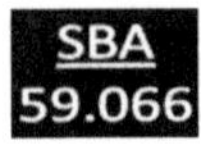

SBA 59.066 TRANSITION ASSISTANCE – ENTREPRENEURSHIP TRACK (BOOTS TO BUSINESS)

"Boots to Business"

Award: Cooperative Agreements

Purpose: Funds eligible organizations to provide follow-on online entrepreneurship training, information and resources, and domestic and global delivery of the B2B.

Applicant Eligibility: Eligible applicants may be a non-profit organization, a state, local, or tribal government agency, an institution of higher learning, a for-profit organization, or collaboration between such entities.

Beneficiary Eligibility: First beneficiaries are eligible transitioning service members, spouses and family members, and veterans, as defined by DOD policy

Award Range/Average: 3500000

Funding: (Advisory Services and Counseling) FY 17 $12,572,000; FY 18 est $12,300,000; FY 19 est $11,250,000; FY 16 $12,808,000.

HQ: 409 3rd Street SW, 5th Floor
Washington, DC 20416
Phone: 202-205-7034
Email: dena.moglia@sba.gov
http://www.sba.gov/bootstobusiness

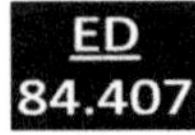

ED 84.407 TRANSITION PROGRAMS FOR STUDENTS WITH INTELLECTUAL DISABILITIES INTO HIGHER EDUCATION

Award: Project Grants

Purpose: To support competitive grants to institutions of higher education (IHEs) (as defined under section 101(a) of the Higher Education Act of 1965, as amended (HEA)), or consortia of IHEs, to create or expand high-quality, inclusive model comprehensive transition and postsecondary programs for students with intellectual disabilities.

Applicant Eligibility: Institutions of higher education (IHEs) (as defined under section 101(a) of the Higher Education Act of 1965, as amended) and consortia of IHEs are eligible to receive grants under the TPSID program. All grant recipients must partner with one or more local educational agencies to support students with intellectual disabilities who are still eligible for special education and related services under the Individuals with Disabilities Education Act (IDEA).

Beneficiary Eligibility: Grant funds establish model comprehensive transition and postsecondary programs for students with intellectual disabilities at institutions of higher education. Funds also support a Coordinating Center that: provides technical assistance for all comprehensive transition and postsecondary programs for students with intellectual disabilities; conducts and disseminates research to the public on strategies to promote academic, social, employment, and independent living outcomes for students with intellectual disabilities; and builds capacity of Kindergarten through Grade 12 transition services and supports of local and State education agencies.

Award Range/Average: Not currently available

Funding: (Project Grants) FY 17 $11,800,000; FY 18 est $11,800,000; FY 19 est $11,800,000.

HQ: 400 Maryland Avenue S W 4C144
Washington, DC 20202
Phone: 202-453-7090
Email: shedita.alston@ed.gov
http://www2.ed.gov/programs/tpsid/index.html

TRANSITIONAL LIVING FOR HOMELESS YOUTH
"Transitional Living Program (TLP) and Maternity Group Homes (MGH)"

Award: Project Grants

Purpose: To help runaway and homeless youth between the ages of 16 to under 22 establish sustainable living and well-being for themselves and if applicable, their dependent child(ren).

Applicant Eligibility: States, localities, private entities, and coordinated networks of such entities are eligible to apply for a Transitional Living Program grant unless they are part of the law enforcement structure or the juvenile justice system. Federally recognized Indian organizations are also eligible to apply for grants as private, nonprofit agencies.

Beneficiary Eligibility: Homeless youth (ages 16 to under 22) are the beneficiaries.

Award Range/Average: Range of grant is $100,000 to $200,000; the average grant is $193,910.

Funding: (Project Grants) FY 17 $43,274,791; FY 18 est $51,086,900; FY 19 est $43,274,791.

HQ: 330 C Street SW
Washington, DC 20201
Phone: 202-205-9560
Email: christopher.holloway@acf.hhs.gov
http://www.acf.hhs.gov

HHS 93.840 TRANSLATION & IMPLEMENTATION SCIENCE RESEARCH FOR HEART, LUNG, BLOOD DISEASES, AND SLEEP DISORDERS

Award: Project Grants

Purpose: To foster late–stage translation phase 4 research and facilitate the understanding of multi-level processes and factors associated with successful and sustainable integration of evidence-based interventions within specific clinical and public health settings related to heart, lung, and blood diseases and sleep diseases and disorders for diverse populations across the lifespan, including those that reduce health inequities within the U.S. and globally.

Applicant Eligibility: Any nonprofit organization engaged in biomedical research and institutions or companies organized for profit may apply for almost any kind of grant. Only domestic, non-profit, private or public institutions may apply for NRSA Institutional Research Training Grants.

Beneficiary Eligibility: Any nonprofit or for-profit organization, company or institution engaged in biomedical research. Only domestic for-profit small business firms may apply for SBIR and STTR programs.

Award Range/Average: Range of Dollar Amount: $30,000 - $821,921. Average Dollar Amount: $194,768.

Funding: (Project Grants) FY 17 $4,674,437; FY 18 est $5,036,963; FY 19 est $5,036,963.

HQ: 6701 Rockledge Drive, Room 7176
Bethesda, MD 20892
Phone: 301-827-7968
http://www.nhlbi.nih.gov/about/scientific-divisions/center-translation-research-and-implementation-science

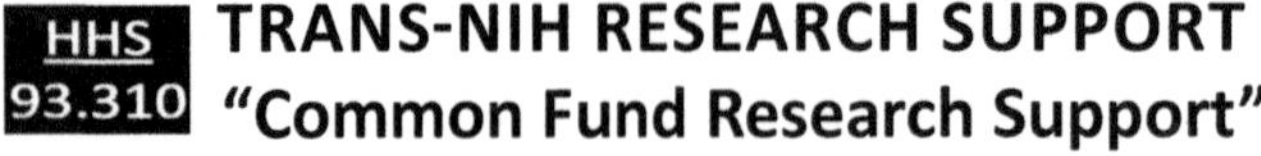

HHS 93.310 TRANS-NIH RESEARCH SUPPORT "Common Fund Research Support"

Award: Project Grants; Training

Purpose: To provide support for new initiatives designed to address major opportunities and gaps in biomedical research.

Applicant Eligibility: Awards can be made to domestic, public or private, for-profit or nonprofit organization, university, college, hospital, laboratory, or other institution, including State and local units of government, and individuals. Some initiatives will accept applications from foreign organizations.

Beneficiary Eligibility: Institutions as described above.

Award Range/Average: $10,000 to $15,462,500 with the average being $737,000

Funding: (Project Grants) FY 17 $623,900,000; FY 18 est $495,047,357; FY 19 est $486,896,365; FY 16 $613,925,000.

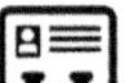

HQ: 6001 Executive Boulevard Room 8180D, P.O. Box 9500
Bethesda, MD 20892
Phone: 301-402-7617
Email: elizabeth.wilder@nih.gov
http://commonfund.nih.gov

DOT 20.931

TRANSPORTATION PLANNING, RESEARCH & EDUCATION
"Innovative and Advanced Transportation Research"

Award: Project Grants

Purpose: Provides funds to conduct research and development on innovative transportation systems and related applied technologies.

Applicant Eligibility: These grants are mandated by Congress in US DOT's Annual Appropriation Legislation. Therefore, only those organizations specifically identified in the appropriation legislation can apply.

Beneficiary Eligibility: Public Non-Profit Institutions/Organizations; Sponsored Organizations; State; Local; Other Public Institutions; Federal Recognized Indian Tribal Government; US Territory or Possession; Private Non-Profit Institutions/Organizations; Quasi-Public Non-Profit Institutions/Organizations; Native American Organizations.

Award Range/Average: No funding beyond FFY 2014.

Funding: (Project Grants) FY 17 $0; FY 18 est $0; FY 19 est $0; FY 16 $0.

HQ: 1200 New Jersey Avenue SE
Washington, DC 20950
Phone: 202-366-3252
Email: caesar.singh@dot.gov

TRAUMATIC BRAIN INJURY STATE DEMONSTRATION GRANT PROGRAM
"TBI State Implementation grants"

Award: Project Grants

Purpose: To improve access to rehabilitation and other services for individuals with Traumatic Brain Injury (TBI) and their families.

Applicant Eligibility: State, Territorial governments, and Federally recognized Indian Tribal government and Native American organizations are eligible to apply for funding under the TBI grant program. The application for Implementation Partnership funds may only come from the State agency designated as the lead for TBI services.

Beneficiary Eligibility: Individuals with TBI and their families, including those in high risk groups, such as children and youth, the elderly, Native Americans and Alaska Natives, military service members and veterans.

Award Range/Average: $100,000 to $250,000; average $249,252

Funding: (Project Grants) FY 17 $4,734,432; FY 18 est $5,090,467; FY 19 FY 16 $4,984,432.

HQ: 330 C Street SW
Washington, DC 20201
Phone: 202-475-2482
Email: elizabeth.leef@acl.hhs.gov
http://www.acl.gov

TRIBAL CIVIL & CRIMINAL LEGAL ASSISTANCE GRANTS, TRAINING & TECHNICAL ASSISTANCE

"Tribal Civil and Criminal Legal Assistance (TCCLA)"

Award: Project Grants

Purpose: To enhance tribal justice systems and technical assistance for the development and enhancement of tribal justice systems.

Applicant Eligibility: Applicants for Tribal Legal Assistance Grants are limited to non-profit organizations, as defined by (Internal Revenue Code § 501(c)(3)), including tribal enterprises and educational institutions (public, private, and tribal colleges and universities), with experience providing legal assistance services to eligible individuals pursuant to federal poverty guidelines, federally-recognized Indian tribes, or tribal justice systems. Tribal Justice Training and Technical Assistance (TTA) Grants: Applicants are limited to national or regional membership organizations and associations whose membership or a membership section consists of judicial system personnel within tribal justice systems.

Beneficiary Eligibility: N/A

Award Range/Average: The awards vary by fiscal year and resources appropriated.

Funding: (Project Grants) FY 17 $1,200,000; FY 18 est $1,200,000; FY 19 FY 16 $1,200,000.

HQ: 810 7th Street NW
Washington, DC 20531
Phone: 202-927-5657
http://www.bja.gov

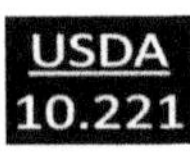

TRIBAL COLLEGES EDUCATION EQUITY GRANTS

"Higher Education Native American Formula and/or Higher Education Native American Institutions"

Award: Project Grants

Purpose: To promote and strengthen higher education instruction in the food and agricultural sciences at the 34 Tribal Colleges. The purpose of the TCEG Program is to fund and enhance educational opportunities for Native Americans in the food and agricultural sciences. The TCEG program also strengthens institutional capacity to deliver relevant formal education opportunities.

Applicant Eligibility: Applications may be submitted by any of the Tribal colleges and universities designated as 1994 Land-Grant Institutions under the Educational Land-Grant Status Act of 1994, as amended. This Act, as amended in Section 533(a), requires that each 1994 Land-Grant Institution be accredited or making progress towards accreditation and be recognized as a legal entity.

Beneficiary Eligibility: Current Listing of 1994 Land-Grant Institutions (aka Tribal Colleges).

Award Range/Average: N/A

Funding: (Project Grants) FY 17 $3,439,000; FY 18 est $3,439,000; FY 19 est $3,432,000; FY 16 $3,439,000; - Based on current legislation there are no set-asides for the Higher-Ed Native American Institutions program. Further, federal administration is not deducted from the program.

HQ: 1400 Independence Avenue SW, P.O. Box 2250
Washington, DC 20250
Phone: 202-720-2324
http://nifa.usda.gov/program/tribal-equity-grants-program

TRIBAL COLLEGES ENDOWMENT PROGRAM
"Tribal Colleges Endowment Interest Program aka 1994 Institutions Endowment Interest Program"

Award: Formula Grants

Purpose: Strengthening the thirty-four (34) Land Grant Institutions' teaching programs in the food and agricultural sciences in targeted need areas, and thereby, enhancing their educational opportunities.

Applicant Eligibility: Eligibility is defined by legislation. An institution must be an accredited 1994 Land Grant Institution with current accreditation from a recognized accreditation organization.

Beneficiary Eligibility: Same as Applicant Eligibility.

Award Range/Average: The highest amount awarded was in 2009 was $299,509 and the lowest amount was $57,866. Three Institutions received amounts over $200,000; 11 Institutions received amounts over $100,000 and 18 Institutions received amounts under $99,000.

Funding: Formula Grants (Apportionments) FY 17 $4,629,955; FY 18 est $4,376,381; FY 19 est $4,473,600; FY 16 $4,517,676.

HQ: 1400 Independence Avenue SW, P.O. Box 2250
Washington, DC 20250
Phone: 202-720-2324
http://nifa.usda.gov/program/tribal-equity-grants-program

TRIBAL COLLEGES EXTENSION PROGRAMS
"Tribal Colleges Extension Program Special Emphasis (TCEP-SE); Tribal Colleges Extension Program (TCEP); Federally Recognized Tribes Extension Program (FRTEP) (formerly Extension Indian Reservation Program)"

Award: Project Grants

Purpose: The TCEP-SE promotes the development of sustainable energy, global food security, adaptation of natural resources to global change, minimizing childhood and adolescent obesity, increasing food safety, energy conservation, adapting tribal culture, etc.

Applicant Eligibility: TCEP-SE and TCEP: The Educational Land-Grant Status Act of 1994, as amended in Section 533(a), requires that each 1994 Land-Grant Institution be accredited or making progress towards accreditation and be recognized as a legal entity. If accreditation is being sought, a college must demonstrate its progress towards accreditation by a letter from a nationally recognized accreditation agency affirming receipt of application for an accreditation site visit or other such documentation.

Beneficiary Eligibility: Same as Applicant Eligibility.

Award Range/Average: If minimum or maximum amounts of funding per competitive and/or capacity project grant, or cooperative agreement are established, these amounts will be announced in the annual Competitive Request for Application (RFA).

Funding: Project Grants (Discretionary) FY 17 $0; FY 18 est $0; FY 19 est $7,160,210; FY 16 $0.

HQ: 1400 Independence Avenue SW, P.O. Box 2250
Washington, DC 20250

Phone: 202-690-0402
Email: erin.riley@nifa.usda.gov
http://nifa.usda.gov

TRIBAL HUD-VA SUPPORTIVE HOUSING PROGRAM "Tribal HUD-VASH Program"

Award: Project Grants

Purpose: To provide rental assistance and supportive services to Native American veterans who are homeless or at risk of homelessness living on or near a reservation or other Indian areas.

Applicant Eligibility: Housing assistance under this program is made available by grants to tribes and tribally designated housing entities (TDHEs) that are eligible to receive Indian Housing Block Grant funding under the Native American Housing Assistance and Self-Determination Act of 1996 (NAHASDA).

Beneficiary Eligibility: Beneficiaries of the Tribal HUD-VASH program are Native American veterans who are Homeless or At Risk of Homelessness.

Award Range/Average: $100,000- $400,000

Funding: Project Grants (Discretionary) FY 17 est $7,000,000; FY 16 $5,878,516; FY 18 N/A FY 19 N/A.

HQ: 451 7th Street SW, Room 5156
Washington, DC 20410
Phone: 202-402-3057
Email: marco.c.santos@hud.gov
http://www.hud.gov/program_offices/public_indian_housing/ih/headquarters/gm

TRIBAL JUSTICE SYSTEMS & ALCOHOL & SUBSTANCE ABUSE "TCAP"

Award: Project Grants

Purpose: To develop, support, and enhance adult and juvenile tribal justice systems and the prevention of violent crime and crime related to opioid, alcohol, and other substance abuse. The main objective is to support the critical and priority needs of tribal justice systems, to prevent crime and to ensure tribal safety through the development, implementation, and enhancement of strategies.

Applicant Eligibility: Federally recognized Indian Tribal governments are eligible to apply for and receive funds under this program.

Beneficiary Eligibility: Indian Tribal governments.

Award Range/Average: N/A

Funding: (Project Grants) FY 17 $18,224,169; FY 18 est $20,803,997; FY 19 est $0.

HQ: 810 Seventh Street NW
Washington, DC 20531
Phone: 202-307-0581
http://www.bja.gov

TRIBAL MATERNAL, INFANT, AND EARLY CHILDHOOD HOME VISITING
"Tribal MIECHV, Tribal Home Visiting Tribal Research Center for Early Childhood (TRCEC)"

Award: Cooperative Agreements

Purpose: The Tribal Maternal, Infant, and Early Childhood Home Visiting Program offers assistance to eligible Tribes (or consortia of Tribes), Tribal Organizations, and Urban Indian Organizations, to strengthen and improve maternal and child health programs, improve service coordination for at-risk communities, and identify and provide comprehensive evidence-based home visiting services to families who reside in at-risk communities. The program's goal is to support the development of happy, healthy, and successful American Indian and Alaska Native children and families through a coordinated home visiting strategy that addresses critical maternal and child health, development, early learning, family support, and child abuse and neglect prevention needs.

Applicant Eligibility: Specifically: Only Tribes (or a consortium of Indian Tribes), Tribal Organizations, or Urban Indian Organizations, as defined by Section 4 of the Indian Health Care Improvement Act, Public Law 94-437, are eligible applicants for the Tribal MIECHV Grant Program.

Beneficiary Eligibility: Eligible families in at-risk AIAN communities include pregnant women, expectant fathers, parents, and primary caregivers of children aged birth through kindergarten entry, including grandparents or other relatives of the child, foster parents who are serving as the child's primary caregiver, and non-custodial parents who have an ongoing relationship with, and at times provide physical care for, the child. Specifically: Eligible families residing in at-risk American Indian/Alaskan Native communities in need of such services, as identified in a needs assessment; Low-income eligible families; Eligible families who are pregnant women under age 21; Eligible families with a history of child abuse or neglect or have had interactions with child welfare services; Eligible families with a history of substance abuse or need substance abuse treatment; Eligible families that have users of tobacco products in the home; Eligible families that are or have children with low student achievement; Eligible families with children with developmental delays or disabilities; and Eligible families who, or that include individuals serving or formerly serving in the Armed Forces, including those with members who have had multiple deployments outside the US.

Award Range/Average: The range of funding is $250,000- $895,000 per budget period for Tribal MIECHV grants. For the TRCEC, the range of funding is up to $600,000 per budget period and the average is $250,000.

Funding: (Cooperative Agreements) FY 17 $8,870,000; FY 18 est $12,000,000; FY 19 est $12,000,000.

HQ: Mary E Switzer Building 330 C Street SW, Suite 3014F
Washington, DC 20201
Phone: 202-260-8515
Email: anne.bergan@acf.hhs.gov
http://www.acf.hhs.gov/ecd/home-visiting/tribal-home-visiting

TRIBAL PUBLIC HEALTH CAPACITY BUILDING & QUALITY IMPROVEMENT UMBRELLA COOPERATIVE AGREEMENT
"Tribal Umbrella CoAg"

Award: Cooperative Agreements

Purpose: This program's ultimate outcomes are decreased morbidity and mortality among American Indians and Alaska Natives and advanced capacity of Indian Country to identify, respond to, and mitigate public health threats.

Applicant Eligibility: Executive Order 13175, "Consultation and Coordination with Indian Tribal Governments."

Beneficiary Eligibility: Eligible applicants should be able to demonstrate tribal affiliation including (1) a record of effectively working with American Indian and Alaska Native populations (2) an ability to methodically and efficiently reach tribal members in American Indian and Alaska Native communities and (3), if recipient is a tribally owned and operated organization, it should provide a letter of approval from Tribal council for the proposed program.

Award Range/Average: No Data Available.

Funding: (Cooperative Agreements) FY 17 $550,000; FY 18 est $13,050,000; FY 19 est $12,500,000.

HQ: 1825 Century Boulevard NE
Atlanta, GA 30345
Phone: 404-498-2208
Email: yur3@cdc.gov
http://www.cdc.gov/tribal

TRIBAL PUBLIC HEALTH CAPACITY BUILDING & QUALITY IMPROVEMENT

"Tribal Public Health Capacity Building and Quality Improvement (CBQI)"

Award: Cooperative Agreements

Purpose: To provide funding to improve tribal health systems' quality, effectiveness, and efficiency in the delivery of public health services to American Indians/Alaska Natives (AI/AN).

Applicant Eligibility: This program will provide funding to improve tribal health systems' quality, effectiveness, and efficiency in the delivery of public health services to American Indians/Alaska Natives (AI/AN). The intent is to provide support to optimize the quality and performance of tribal public health systems, tribal public health practice and services, tribal public health partnerships, and tribal public health resources.

Beneficiary Eligibility: Tribal Public Health Capacity Building and Quality Improvement Infrastructure and Tribal Entities and Organizations as described/listed in Section (080) Eligibility Requirements, above.

Award Range/Average: Subject to the availability of Funds; Fiscal Year: 2013-2018, Approximate Total Fiscal Year Funding: $587274, Approximate Average Award: $97,500, Approximate Total Project Period Funding: $2,925,000.

Funding: (Cooperative Agreements) FY 17 $550,000; FY 18 est $550,000; FY 19 est $0.

HQ: 1825 Century Boulevard NE
Atlanta, GA 30345
Phone: 404-498-2208
Email: yur3@cdc.gov
http://www.cdc.gov/tribal

HHS 93.594 TRIBAL WORK GRANTS "Native Employment Works; NEW"

Award: Formula Grants

Purpose: Allows eligible Indian Tribes and Alaska Native organizations to operate a program to make work activities available.

Applicant Eligibility: An Indian Tribe or Alaska Native organization that conducted a Tribal JOBS (Job Opportunities and Basic Skills Training) Program in fiscal year 1995.

Beneficiary Eligibility: Service areas and populations as designated by the eligible Indian Tribe or Alaska Native organization.

Award Range/Average: From $5,187 to $1,752,666; $96,000, on average.

Funding: (Formula Grants) FY 17 $7,535,110; FY 18 est $7,535,110; FY 19 est $7,535,110; FY 16 $7,535,110.

HQ: 330 C Street SW
Washington, DC 20201
Phone: 202-401-5457
Email: stanley.koutstaal@acf.hhs.gov
http://www.acf.hhs.gov/programs/ofa/programs/tribal/new

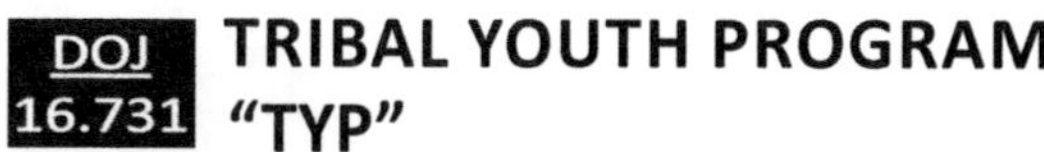

DOJ 16.731 TRIBAL YOUTH PROGRAM "TYP"

Award: Project Grants

Purpose: To assist tribes in responding to myriad issues facing tribal nations. It includes creating, expanding, or strengthening tribally-driven approaches along the juvenile justice continuum that can range from prevention to intervention and treatment.

Applicant Eligibility: Only federally recognized Indian tribes, as determined by the Secretary of Interior, may apply. This includes Alaska Native villages and tribal consortia consisting of two or more federally recognize Indian tribes.

Beneficiary Eligibility: N/A

Award Range/Average: No Data Available.

Funding: Project Grants (Discretionary) FY 17 $9,666,150; FY 18 est $5,000,000; FY 19 est $0; - 7% Tribal set aside.

HQ: 810 7th Street NW
Washington, DC 20531
Phone: 202-514-1289
Email: jennifer.yeh@usdoj.gov
http://www.ojjdp.gov

ED 84.245 TRIBALLY CONTROLLED POSTSECONDARY CAREER & TECHNICAL INSTITUTIONS

Award: Project Grants

Purpose: To provide career and technical education (CTE) services and basic support for the education and training of Indian students through tribally controlled postsecondary career and technical institutions.

Applicant Eligibility: A tribally controlled postsecondary career and technical institution that: (1) Is formally controlled, or has been formally sanctioned or chartered, by the governing body of an Indian tribe or Indian tribes; (2) offers a technical degree- or certificate-granting program; (3) is governed by a board of directors or trustees, a majority of whom are Indians; (4) demonstrates adherence to stated goals, a philosophy, or a plan of operation, that fosters individual Indian economic and self-sufficient opportunity, including programs that are appropriate to stated tribal goals of developing individual entrepreneurships and self-sustaining economic infrastructures on reservations; (5) has been in operation for at least 3 years; (6) holds accreditation with or is a candidate for accreditation by a nationally recognized accrediting authority for postsecondary vocational and technical education; (7) enrolls the full-time equivalent of not less than 100 students, of whom a majority are Indians; and (8) receives no Federal funds under the Tribally Controlled College or University Act of 1978 or the Navajo Community College Act may apply.

Beneficiary Eligibility: Indian students and tribally controlled postsecondary career and technical institutions not receiving Federal funds under the Tribally Controlled College or University Act of 1978 or the Navajo Community College Act may benefit.

Award Range/Average: Estimated range: $2,500,000- $5,000,000; Estimated average: $3,000,000

Funding: (Project Grants) FY 17 $8,286,000; FY 18 est $9,469,000; FY 19 est $8,286,000.

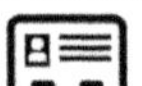

HQ: 400 Maryland Avenue SW
Washington, DC 20202
Phone: 202-245-7790
Email: gwen.washington@ed.gov
http://www2.ed.gov/about/offices/list/ovae/programs.html

TRIO EDUCATIONAL OPPORTUNITY CENTERS

Award: Project Grants

Purpose: To provide information on financial and academic assistance available for qualified adults to pursue postsecondary education program and to assist them in applying for admission to institutions of postsecondary education.

Applicant Eligibility: Institutions of Higher Education, public and private agencies and organizations including community-based organizations with experience in serving disadvantaged youth, combinations of such institutions, agencies and organizations, and as appropriate to the purposes of the program; secondary schools.

Beneficiary Eligibility: Persons residing in the target area who need one or more of the services provided by the project in order to pursue a program of postsecondary education and who desire to pursue or who are pursuing a program of postsecondary education. Two-thirds of the participants must be low-income individuals who are also potential first-generation college students.

Award Range/Average: Varies by competition. In 2017, awards ranged from $141,575 to $1,201,831; the average award was approximately $356,688.

Funding: (Project Grants) FY 17 $50,650,000; FY 18 est $49,661,000; FY 19 est $49,661,000.

HQ: 400 Maryland Avenue SW
Washington, DC 20202
Phone: 202-502-7655
Email: rachel.couch@ed.gov
http://www.ed.gov/programs/trioeoc

TRIO MCNAIR POST-BACCALAUREATE ACHIEVEMENT

Award: Project Grants

Purpose: To provide grants for institutions of higher education to prepare participants for doctoral studies through involvement in research and other scholarly activities.

Applicant Eligibility: Institutions of higher education or combinations of institutions of higher education may apply.

Beneficiary Eligibility: 2/3 of participants must be low-income first generation college students. The remaining participants must be students from groups underrepresented in graduate education.

Award Range/Average: $225,064 to $388,253; the average $245,434.

Funding: (Project Grants) FY 17 $45,665,000; FY 18 est $45,886,000; FY 19 est $45,665,000.

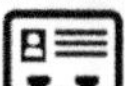

HQ: 400 Maryland Avenue SW
Washington, DC 20202
Phone: 202-453-7095
Email: katie.blanding@ed.gov
http://www.ed.gov/programs/triomcnair

TRIO STAFF TRAINING PROGRAM

Award: Project Grants

Purpose: To provide training for staff and leadership personnel employed in, or preparing for employment in, projects funded under the Federal TRIO Programs (program numbers 84.042, 84.044, 84.047, 84.066, and 84.217.

Applicant Eligibility: Institutions of higher education and other public and private nonprofit institutions and organizations.

Beneficiary Eligibility: Leadership personnel, full-time and part- time staff members of projects under the Federal TRIO Programs, and individuals preparing for employment as staff or leadership personnel in projects under the Federal TRIO Special Programs will benefit.

Award Range/Average: $97,230 to $343,119. The average $215,769.

Funding: (Project Grants) FY 17 $2,805,000; FY 18 est $2,873,402; FY 19 est $2,873,402; FY 16 $2,737,000.

HQ: 400 Maryland Avenue SW
Washington, DC 20202
Phone: 202-502-7789
Email: suzanne.ulmer@ed.gov
http://www.ed.gov/programs/triotrain

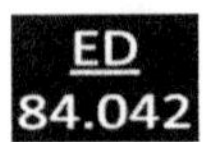

TRIO STUDENT SUPPORT SERVICES

Award: Project Grants

Purpose: To support disadvantaged college students and to enhance their potential for successfully completing the postsecondary education programs in which they are enrolled and increase their transfer rates from 2-year to 4-year institutions.

Applicant Eligibility: Institutions of higher education and combinations of institutions of higher education may apply.

Beneficiary Eligibility: Low-income, first generation college students or disabled students who are enrolled or accepted for enrollment at the institution that is the recipient of the grant and who are in need of academic support in order to successfully pursue a program of postsecondary education. At least two-thirds of the project participants must be disabled or must be low-income individuals who are first generation college students.

Award Range/Average: $116,111 to $1,464,591; the average $290,030.

Funding: (Project Grants) FY 17 $303,355,000; FY 18 est $303,361,000; FY 19 est $306,457,000.

HQ: 400 Maryland Avenue SW
Washington, DC 20202
Phone: 202-453-7814
Email: james.davis@ed.gov
http://www.ed.gov

TRIO TALENT SEARCH

Award: Project Grants

Purpose: To identify qualified disadvantaged youths and to encourage them in completing secondary school and in enrolling in programs of postsecondary education.

Applicant Eligibility: Institutions of higher education (IHEs), public and private agencies and organizations including community-based organizations with experience in serving disadvantaged youth, combinations of such institutions, agencies and organizations, and as appropriate to the purposes of the program, secondary schools.

Beneficiary Eligibility: Individuals residing in the target area or attending a target school who have potential for education at the postsecondary level and who can benefit from one or more of the services provided by the project. Two-thirds must be low-income individuals who are also potential first generation college students.

Award Range/Average: $185,152 to $914,012; the average award was $320,873. The statutory minimum is $200,000, unless the applicant requests a smaller amount.

Funding: (Project Grants) FY 17 $151,773,000; FY 18 est $151,817,000; FY 19 est $151,817,000.

HQ: 400 Maryland Avenue SW
Washington, DC 20202
Phone: 202-453-6195
Email: craig.pooler@ed.gov
http://www.ed.gov

TRIO UPWARD BOUND

Award: Project Grants

Purpose: To increase the academic performance and motivational levels of low-income and potential first-generation college students and veterans to complete secondary and postsecondary school.

Applicant Eligibility: Institutions of higher education, public and private agencies and organizations including community-based organizations with experience in serving disadvantaged youth, combinations of such institutions, agencies and organizations, and as appropriate to the purposes of the program, secondary schools.

Beneficiary Eligibility: Low-income individuals and potential first generation college students who have a need for academic support in order to successfully pursue a program of postsecondary education. Two-thirds of the participants must be low-income individuals who are also potential first generation college students.

Award Range/Average: Varies by competition. In FY 2017, the smallest award was $226,637 and the largest award was $900,511. The average award was $326,415.

Funding: (Project Grants) FY 17 $388,495,000; FY 18 est $387,364,000; FY 19 est $387,364,000.

HQ: 400 Maryland Avenue SW
Washington, DC 20202
Phone: 202-453-6273
Email: ken.waters@ed.gov
http://www.ed.gov

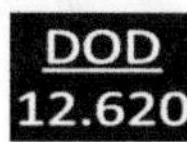

TROOPS TO TEACHERS GRANT PROGRAM
"Troops to Teachers Program"

Award: Project Grants

Purpose: To facilitate employment of eligible members of the armed forces in schools identified in 10 U.S.C. 1154.

Applicant Eligibility: Grant opportunity is for one or more, or a consortia of such States, to receive grant funding to develop and implement a replicable model for attracting and assisting eligible members and former members of the armed forces to obtain employment as teachers.

Beneficiary Eligibility: Beneficiaries of the program are eligible members of the armed forces, as specified in 10 U.S.C. 1154.

Award Range/Average: $100,000 to $400,000 annually for multi-year projects. Average is $200,000.

Funding: (Salaries and Expenses) FY 17 $5,000,000; FY 18 est $5,000,000; FY 19 est $3,581,414.

HQ: 6490 Saufley Field Road
Pensacola, FL 32508
Phone: 850-452-1940
Email: kim.h.day@navy.mil
http://www.proudtoserveagain.com

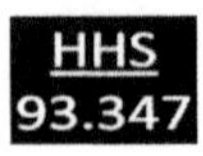

TRUSTED EXCHANGE FRAMEWORK & COMMON AGREEMENT (TEFCA) RECOGNIZED COORDINATING ENTITY (RCE) COOPERATIVE AGREEMENT "TEFCA RCE Cooperative Agreement"

Award: N/A

Purpose: To advance the establishment of an interoperable health system that empowers individuals to use their electronic health information to the fullest extent.

Applicant Eligibility: Any entity applying for a cooperative agreement must satisfy the following criteria: 1. Be a United States-based not-for-profit entity; 2.

Beneficiary Eligibility: N/A

Award Range/Average: There has been $500,000 allocated for FY 18 for this award. We estimate that we will award one (1) total.

Funding: (Cooperative Agreements) FY 17 FY 18 est $499,997; FY 19.

HQ: 330 C Street SW
Washington, DC 20201
Phone: 202-774-2466
Email: hibah.qudsi@hhs.gov
http://www.healthit.gov

HHS 93.947 TUBERCULOSIS DEMONSTRATION, RESEARCH, PUBLIC & PROFESSIONAL EDUCATION

Award: Cooperative Agreements

Purpose: Assists States and other public and nonprofit private entities in conducting research into prevention and control of tuberculosis nationally and internationally.

Applicant Eligibility: States, political subdivisions of States, and other public and nonprofit private entities.

Beneficiary Eligibility: States, political subdivisions of States, other public and nonprofit private entities, serving persons with TB infection and disease.

Award Range/Average: $100,000 to $1,000,000 with an average of $120,000.

Funding: (Cooperative Agreements) FY 17 $5,303,518; FY 18 est $5,388,040; FY 19 est $5,388,040.

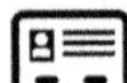

HQ: 1600 Clifton Road, P.O. Box E10
Atlanta, GA 30333
Phone: 404-639-5259
Email: kak4@cdc.gov
http://www.cdc.gov/tb

ED 84.287 TWENTY-FIRST CENTURY COMMUNITY LEARNING CENTERS

Award: Formula Grants

Purpose: To provide opportunities for communities to establish community learning centers high-poverty and low-performing school students.

Applicant Eligibility: State educational agencies (SEAs) are eligible for funds under this program. Local educational agencies, community-based organizations, and other public or private entities are eligible to apply to the SEA in state in which they are located for subgrants.

Beneficiary Eligibility: School-aged children and their families.

Award Range/Average: $708,746 - $139,212,692; Average: $21,044,847.

Funding: (Project Grants) FY 17 $1,179,756,270; FY 18 est $1,199,556,270; FY 19 est $0.

HQ: 400 Maryland Avenue SW
Washington, DC 20202
Phone: 202-260-2551
Email: sylvia.lyes@ed.gov
http://www.ed.gov/programs/21stcclc/index.html

DOS 19.025 U.S. AMBASSADORS FUND FOR CULTURAL PRESERVATION "AFCP, USAFCP"

Award: Project Grants

Purpose: Supports the preservation of cultural heritage overseas, shows respect for the cultural heritage of other countries and supports U.S. diplomatic objectives and foreign policy goals.

Applicant Eligibility: The U.S. Ambassadors Fund for Cultural Preservation supports the preservation of cultural heritage in more than 130 eligible countries around the world. Eligible entities may apply through U.S. embassies for fund support for the preservation of cultural sites, cultural objects and collections, and forms of traditional cultural expression (intangible heritage).

Beneficiary Eligibility: Eligible countries: Afghanistan, Albania, Algeria, Angola, Antigua & Barbuda, Armenia, Azerbaijan, Bangladesh, Barbados, Belarus, Belize, Benin, Bhutan, Bolivia, Bosnia & Herzegovina, Botswana, Brazil, Bulgaria, Burkina Faso, Burma, Burundi, Cambodia, Cameroon, Cape Verde, Central African Republic, Chad, China, Colombia, Comoros, Congo (Democratic Republic of the), Congo (Republic of), Costa Rica, Cote d'Ivoire, Cuba, Djibouti, Dominica, Dominican Republic, Ecuador, Egypt, El Salvador, Equatorial Guinea, Eritrea, Ethiopia, Fiji, Gabon, Gambia, Georgia, Ghana, Grenada, Guatemala, Guinea, Guinea-Bissau, Guyana, Haiti, Honduras, India, Indonesia, Iraq, Jamaica, Jordan, Kazakhstan, Kenya, Kiribati, Kosovo, Kyrgyzstan, Laos, Lebanon, Lesotho, Liberia, Libya, Macedonia, Madagascar, Malawi, Malaysia, Maldives, Mali, Marshall Islands, Mauritania, Mauritius, Mexico, Micronesia, Moldova, Mongolia, Montenegro, Morocco, Mozambique, Namibia, Nauru, Nepal, Nicaragua, Niger, Nigeria, Oman, Pakistan, Palau, Panama, Papua New Guinea, Paraguay, Peru, Philippines, Romania, Russian Federation, Rwanda, Saint Kitts & Nevis, Saint Lucia, Saint Vincent & the Grenadines, Samoa, Sao Tome & Principe, Senegal, Serbia, Seychelles, Sierra Leone, Solomon Islands, South Africa, South Sudan, Sri Lanka, Sudan, Suriname, Swaziland, Syria, Tajikistan, Tanzania, Thailand, Timor-Leste, Togo, Tonga, Trinidad & Tobago, Tunisia, Turkey, Turkmenistan, Tuvalu, Uganda, Ukraine, Uzbekistan, Vanuatu, Venezuela, Vietnam, Yemen, Zambia, and Zimbabwe.

Award Range/Average: $10,000 to $695,000 with an average of $154,000.

Funding: (Project Grants) FY 17 est $5,750,000; FY 16 est $5,750,000.

HQ: SA 5 C2 Department of State
Washington, DC 20522
Phone: 202-632-6308
Email: perschlermj@state.gov
http://www.state.gov

U.S. REFUGEE ADMISSIONS PROGRAM
"U.S. Refugee Admissions Program"

Award: Cooperative Agreements

Purpose: Provides initial reception and placement program for refugees approved for admission in the United States. Program objectives include: arranging for refugees' placement by ensuring that approved refugees are sponsored and offered appropriate assistance upon arrival in the United States; providing them with basic necessities and core services during their initial resettlement period in the United States; and by promoting refugee self-sufficiency through employment as soon as possible after arrival in the United States in coordination with other refugee service and assistance programs.

Applicant Eligibility: private non-profit organizations

Beneficiary Eligibility: Refugees approved under the U.S. Refugee Admissions Program will benefit.

Award Range/Average: No Data Available.

Funding: (Cooperative Agreements) FY 18 est $227,000,000; FY 16 $227,636,918; FY 17 est $227,000,000.

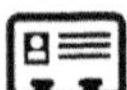

HQ: 2025 E Street NW
Washington, DC 20522
Phone: 202-453-9261
Email: daybj@state.gov
http://www.state.gov/j/prm/index.htm

U.S. REPATRIATION
"Repatriation Program"

Award: Cooperative Agreements

Purpose: To provide temporary assistance to U.S. citizens and their dependents who have been identified by the Department of State (DOS) as having returned, or been brought from a foreign country to the U.S. because of destitution, illness, war, threat of war, or a similar crisis, and are without available resources immediately accessible to meet their needs.

Applicant Eligibility: Social service organizations with expertise in mental health, child welfare, the criminal justice system, and emergency assistance.

Beneficiary Eligibility: ORR authorized staff determines eligibility for citizens and their dependents who have been identified by the Department of State (DOS) as having returned, or been brought from a foreign country to the U.S. because of destitution, illness, war, threat of war, or a similar crisis, and are without resources immediately accessible to meet their needs. In addition, U.S. nationals who are determined eligible by an authorized ORR staff in accordance to 211.

Award Range/Average: One Cooperative Agreement is awarded each year of the project period and other applicable reimbursement is provided to states for emergency plans whenever funds are available.

Funding: (Cooperative Agreements) FY 17 $2,249,983; FY 18 est $24,934,000; FY 19 est $1,000,000.

HQ: 330 C Street SW
Washington, DC 20201
Phone: 202-401-4845
Email: elizabeth.russell@acf.hhs.gov
http://www.acf.hhs.gov/programs/orr

UNACCOMPANIED ALIEN CHILDREN PROGRAM

Award: Project Grants

Purpose: The Unaccompanied Alien Children's program is designed to provide for the care and placement of unaccompanied alien minors who are apprehended in the U.S. by Homeland Security agents, Border patrol agents, or other federal law enforcement agencies and are taken into care pending resolution of their claims for relief under U.S. immigration law or release to parent, adult family members or another responsible adult.

Applicant Eligibility: Also, State and Local governments, private non-profit organizations. Faith-based and private for-profit organizations who can provide state licensed residential capacity or other requisite services.

Beneficiary Eligibility: Beneficiaries are unaccompanied alien children who are in Federal custody by reason of their immigration status.

Award Range/Average: $524,764 to $123,962,310. Average of Awards: $9,968,989.

Funding: Project Grants (Cooperative Agreements) FY 17 $829,398,723; FY 18 est $1,303,245,000; FY 19 est $1,048,000,000; FY 16 $642,000,000.

HQ: 330 C Street SW
Washington, DC 20201
Phone: 202-401-4997
Email: jallyn.sualog@acf.hhs.gov
http://www.acf.hhs.gov

UNDERGRADUATE INTERNATIONAL STUDIES & FOREIGN LANGUAGE PROGRAMS

Award: Project Grants

Purpose: To assist institutions of higher education to plan, develop, and carry out a program to strengthen and improve undergraduate instruction in international studies and foreign languages.

Applicant Eligibility: Accredited colleges and universities, and public and nonprofit private agencies and organizations.

Beneficiary Eligibility: Same as Applicant Eligibility.

Award Range/Average: No Data Available.

Funding: (Project Grants) FY 17 $2,862,833; FY 18 est $2,193,144; FY 19 est $0; FY 16 $3,492,716.

HQ: 400 Maryland Avenue SW
Washington, DC 20202
Phone: 202-453-6391
Email: tanyelle.richardson@ed.gov
http://www2.ed.gov

UNDERGRADUATE SCHOLARSHIP PROGRAM FOR INDIVIDUALS FROM DISADVANTAGED BACKGROUNDS "NIH Undergraduate Scholarship Program (UGSP)"

Award: Direct Payments for Specified Use

Purpose: To provide service-conditioned scholarships to individuals from disadvantaged backgrounds who agree to pursue undergraduate education at accredited institutions.

Applicant Eligibility: An eligible applicant must be (1) A U.S. citizen, national, or permanent resident; (2) enrolled or accepted for enrollment as a full-time student at an accredited undergraduate institution (4 year school) of higher education; (3) from a disadvantaged background as determined by the Secretary of Health and Human Services; (4) in good academic standing (minimum GPA of 3.3 or be in the top 5 percent) with his/her educational institution; and (5) submit an application to participate in the Undergraduate Scholarship (UGS) Program; (6) agree to serve as a full-time NIH employee for not less than 10 consecutive weeks of each year during which the individual is attending the educational institution and receiving a scholarship; (7) agree to serve as a full-time NIH employee for 12 months for each academic year during which the scholarship was provided, not later than 60 days after obtaining his or her academic degree, unless a service deferment is granted.

Beneficiary Eligibility: Undergraduate students from disadvantaged backgrounds pursuing academic programs supporting professions needed by the NIH.

Award Range/Average: Scholarship awards over the past seven years have ranged from $2,000- $20,000, with the average award amount of $9,000.

Funding: (Direct Payments for Specified Use) FY 17 $4,150,531; FY 18 est $4,100,542; FY 19 est $3,550,000.

HQ: Dr Building 2, Room 2E20 Two Center Drive
Bethesda, MD 20892
Phone: 301-594-2222
Email: murrayda@mail.nih.gov
http://www.training.nih.gov/programs/ugsp

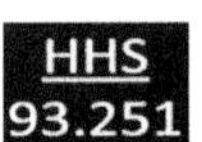

UNIVERSAL NEWBORN HEARING SCREENING

Award: Project Grants

Purpose: To support state and territory programs in developing a comprehensive and coordinated system of care targeted toward ensuring that newborns and infants receive appropriate timely services including continuous screening, evaluation, diagnosis and early intervention services.

Applicant Eligibility: Grants to states/territories and cooperative agreements to two organizations that will provide technical assistance.

Beneficiary Eligibility: Infants and newborns who are deaf or hard of hearing and their families/caretakers.

Award Range/Average: Grants to states and territories: FY 18 est $195,000- $250,000. Average award of $248,000 Grants to LEND Audiology Programs FY 18 est $942, 259. $62, 624- $80,000. Average award of $78,521 Cooperative Agreements: FY 18 est $1,200,000/ $500,000 Average Award of $850,000.

Funding: (Project Grants) FY 17 $15,221,419; FY 18 est $15,327,470; FY 19 est $16,382,200.

HQ: 5600 Fishers Lane, Room 18W57
Rockville, MD 20857
Phone: 301-443-0133
Email: ssilcott@hrsa.gov
http://www.hrsa.gov

HHS 93.632 UNIVERSITY CENTERS FOR EXCELLENCE IN DEVELOPMENTAL DISABILITIES EDUCATION, RESEARCH, AND SERVICE "University Centers (UCEDD))"

Award: Project Grants

Purpose: To pay the Federal share of the cost of administration and operation of interdisciplinary centers that (1) provide interdisciplinary training for personnel concerned with developmental disabilities; (2) provide community service activities that include training and technical assistance and may include direct services, e.g., family support, individual support, educational, vocational, clinical, health and prevention; (3) conduct research, evaluation and analysis of public policy in areas affecting individuals with developmental disabilities; and (4) disseminate information as a national and international resource.

Applicant Eligibility: Existing Centers; A public or nonprofit entity which is associated with, or is an integral part of a college or university and which provides at least: interdisciplinary training; demonstration of exemplary services, technical assistance, research and dissemination of findings.

Beneficiary Eligibility: Individuals of all ages with developmental disabilities attributable to a mental and/or physical impairment, their families, and personnel and trainees providing services to them.

Award Range/Average: All Centers receive the same award amount. $547,000 per Center.

Funding: Project Grants (Discretionary) FY 17 $38,619,000; FY 18 N/A FY 19 FY 16 $38,619,000.

HQ: 330 C Street SW
Washington, DC 20201
Phone: 202-795-7417
Email: pamela.o'brien@acl.hhs.gov
http://www.acl.gov/programs/aidd/programs/ucedd/index.aspx

DOT 20.701 UNIVERSITY TRANSPORTATION CENTERS PROGRAM "UTC Program"

Award: Project Grants

Purpose: To provide grants to nonprofit institutions of higher learning for the purpose of establishing and operating university transportation centers that conduct research, education, and technology transfer programs.

Applicant Eligibility: For the program's competitive grants, public and private nonprofit institutions of higher learning that have established transportation research programs. Non-competitive grants must also be to public and private nonprofit institutions of higher learning but may or may not have established programs.

Beneficiary Eligibility: Same as Applicant Eligibility.

Award Range/Average: Funding for FFY 2017 UTCs is based on the type of UTC: National Center = 5 @ $2,833,700 ea.; *Regional =7 @ $2,606,200 ea. ; Tier 1= 20 @ $1,416,900. The average award equals $6,855.800

Funding: (Project Grants) FY 17 $69,600,000; FY 18 est $69,600,000; FY 19 est $75,000,000.

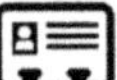

HQ: 1200 New Jersey Avenue SE
Washington, DC 20590
Phone: 202-366-4985
Email: denise.e.dunn@dot.gov
http://www.transportation.gov/utc

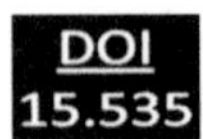

DOI 15.535

UPPER COLORADO RIVER BASIN FISH & WILDLIFE MITIGATION
"Section 314c Projects"

Award: Cooperative Agreements

Purpose: Protects, restores and enhances wetland and upland ecosystems for the conservation of fish and wildlife resources in the upper Colorado River Basin.

Applicant Eligibility: Under Section 314(c) projects, state and local government agencies, Federally recognized Indian Tribal governments, private nonprofit institutions/organizations; public nonprofit institutions/organizations; for-profit organizations, interstate and intras

Beneficiary Eligibility: Same as Applicant Eligibility.

Award Range/Average: Range $ 3,000 - $ 582,881 Average $ $356,049

Funding: Cooperative Agreements (Discretionary Grants) FY 18 est $385,000; FY 19 est $391,000; FY 17$421,000.

HQ: 1849 C Street NW
Washington, DC 20240
Phone: 801-379-1254
Email: rswanson@uc.usbr.gov
http://www.cupcao.gov

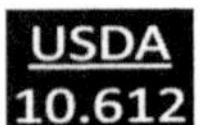

USDA 10.612

USDA LOCAL & REGIONAL FOOD AID PROCUREMENT PROGRAM
"Local and Regional Food Aid Procurement Program"

Award: Cooperative Agreements

Purpose: The FAS compensates for the purchase of commodities through the U.S. Department of Agriculture. The FAS also provides food assistance in the form of emergency response.

Applicant Eligibility: N/A

Beneficiary Eligibility: Only food-insecure populations in developing countries are eligible beneficiaries under the USDA LRP Program.

Award Range/Average: Individual applications may be valued between $2 and $4 million.

Funding: Project Grants (Cooperative Agreements) FY 17 $5,000,000; FY 18 est $10,000,000.

HQ: 1400 Independence Avenue SW, P.O. Box 1030
Washington, DC 20250
Phone: 202-720-4221
Email: ppded@fas.usda.gov
http://www.fas.usda.gov/programs/local-and-regional-food-aid-procurement

VALUE-ADDED PRODUCER GRANTS "VAPG"

Award: Project Grants

Purpose: To support agricultural producers in expanding marketing opportunities and to have increased income by providing new products.

Applicant Eligibility: Applicants are not eligible if they have been debarred or suspended or otherwise excluded from participation in Federal assistance programs under Executive Order 12549, "Debarment and Suspension." Applicants are not eligible if they have an outstanding judgement obtained by the U.S. in a Federal Court (other than U.S. Tax Court), are delinquent on the payment of Federal income taxes, or are delinquent on a Federal debt.

Beneficiary Eligibility: Agricultural producers

Award Range/Average: Average = $120,000 Range = $5,000 (minimum) to $250,000 (maximum)

Funding: (Project Grants) FY 17 $11,000,000; FY 18 est $11,250,000; FY 19 N/A FY 16 est $11,000,000.

HQ: Cooperative Programs Grants Division 1400 Independence Avenue
Washington, DC 20250
Phone: 202-690-1374
http://www.rd.usda.gov/programs-services/value-added-producer-grants

VERY LOW TO MODERATE INCOME HOUSING LOANS "Section 502 Rural Housing Loans"

Award: Direct Loans; Guaranteed/Insured Loans

Purpose: To support those who receive low-income with permanent housing and essential requirements.

Applicant Eligibility: Applicants must have very low-, low- or moderate incomes. Very low-income is defined as below 50 percent of the area median income (AMI); low-income is between 50 and 80 percent of AMI; moderate income is below 115 percent of AMI.

Beneficiary Eligibility: Applicants must meet eligibility requirements. Guaranteed Loan Low and Moderale income eligible.

Award Range/Average: FY 17 Average: 502 Direct Loans ($139,158) Guaranteed Loans ($143,804) FY 18 Average: 502 Direct Loans ($151,469) Guaranteed Loans ($147,318) FY 18 are estimates. Loans in high cost areas may be higher.

Funding: (Guaranteed/Insured Loans) FY 17 $19,279,916,900; FY 18 est $17,416,823,972; FY 19 est $24,000,000,000; - Fiscal Year 2019 figures are based on the President's proposed budget.(Direct Loans) FY 17$999,991,163; FY 18 est $1,000,000,000; FY 19 est $0.

HQ: 1400 Independence Avenue SW
Washington, DC 20250
Phone: 202-720-1532
Email: myron.wooden@wdc.usda.gov
http://www.rurdev.usda.gov

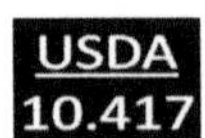

VERY LOW-INCOME HOUSING REPAIR LOANS & GRANTS "Section 504 Rural Housing Loans and Grants"

Award: Project Grants; Direct Loans

Purpose: Section 504 compensates for those in rural areas to repair their properties.

Applicant Eligibility: Applicants must own and occupy a home in a rural area; and be a citizen of the United States or reside in the United States after having been legally admitted for permanent residence or on indefinite parole. Loan recipients must have sufficient income to repay the loan.

Beneficiary Eligibility: Same as Applicant Eligibility.

Award Range/Average: Average loan amount is $6,154. Average grant amount is $6,172

Funding: (Project Grants) FY 17 $28,873,909; FY 18 est $26,000,000; FY 19 est $0; (Direct Loans) FY 17$19,637,606; FY 18 est $19,000,000; FY 19 est $0.

HQ: 1400 Independence Avenue SW
Washington, DC 20250
Phone: 804-287-1559
Email: myron.wooden@wdc.usda.gov
http://www.rurdev.usda.gov

VETERANS HOUSING REHABILITATION & MODIFICATION PILOT PROGRAM "CFDA Number: 14.278"

Award: N/A

Purpose: To look into the potential benefits of awarding grants to nonprofit organizations to rehabilitate and change the primary residence of low-income and disabled veterans.

Applicant Eligibility: Nonprofits organizations that provide nationwide or statewide programs that primarily serve veterans or low-income individuals. Applicants that are nonprofits organizations as described in section 501(c) (3) or 501 (a) (19) of the Internal Revenue Code of 1986 and exempt from tax under section 501 (a) of such Code.

Beneficiary Eligibility: Eligible recipients for use of the Veterans Housing Rehabilitation and Modification program include disabled and low-income veterans.

Award Range/Average: Up to $1,000,000

Funding: (Project Grants) FY 17 $0; FY 18 est $8,000,000; FY 19 est $5,000,000.

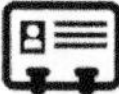

HQ: 451 7th Street SW, Room 7240
Washington, DC 20410
Phone: 202-402-4464
Email: thann.young@hud.gov
http://www.hud.gov

VETERANS OUTREACH PROGRAM "Veterans Business Outreach Center Program (VBOC)"

Award: Cooperative Agreements

Purpose: Organizations provide information on small business ownership to service members and military spouses by facilitating and instructing the U.S. Small Business Administration's "Introduction to Entrepreneurship" known as "Boots to Business" which is a course offered within the Department of Defense Transition Assistance Program in accordance with Public Law of 110-186.

Applicant Eligibility: Eligible applicants may be education institutions, private businesses, veterans' nonprofit community-based organizations, and Federal, State, local and tribal government agencies.

Beneficiary Eligibility: First beneficiaries are eligible veterans, active duty service members, Guard & Reserve members and military spouses who seek to start and manage a small business; second beneficiaries are all others.

Award Range/Average: No Data Available.

Funding: (Project Grants) FY 17 $12,572,000; FY 18 est $12,500,000; FY 19 est $11,250,000; FY 16 $12,808,000.

HQ: 409 3rd Street SW, 5th Floor
Washington, DC 20416
Phone: 202-205-6777
Email: raymond.milano@sba.gov
http://www.sba.gov

VETERINARY MEDICINE LOAN REPAYMENT PROGRAM "VLMRP"

Award: Direct Payments for Specified Use

Purpose: To encourage veterinarians to serve in socially disadvantaged areas and the SCA shall provide them with loans and necessary assistance.

Applicant Eligibility: The Secretary may enter into agreements with veterinarians under which the veterinarians agree to provide, for a period of time as determined by the Secretary and specified in the agreement, veterinary services in veterinarian shortage situations.

Beneficiary Eligibility: Same as Applicant Eligibility.

Award Range/Average: N/A

Funding: (Direct Payments for Specified Use) FY 17 $5,850,000; FY 18 est $7,200,000.

HQ: 1400 Independence Avenue SW, P.O. Box 2240
Washington, DC 20250-2240
Phone: 202-401-6134
http://nifa.usda.gov

USDA 10.336 VETERINARY SERVICES GRANT PROGRAM "VSGP"

Award: Cooperative Agreements; Project Grants

Purpose: The Veterinary Services Grant Program is to support and promote veterinary services and to encourage education, training, and expand veterinary practices.

Applicant Eligibility: A qualified entity shall be eligible to receive a grant described in paragraph (1) if the entity carries out programs or activities that the Secretary determines will: (A) Substantially relieve veterinarian shortage situations; (B) Support or facilitate private veterinary practices engaged in public health activities; or (C) support or facilitate the practices of veterinarians who are providing or have completed providing services under an agreement entered into with the Secretary under section 1415A(a)(2). The term 'qualified entity' means: (A) A for-profit or nonprofit entity located in the United States that, or an individual who, operates a veterinary clinic providing veterinary services: (i) In a rural area, as defined in section 343(a) of the Consolidated Farm and Rural Development Act (7 U.S.C.

Beneficiary Eligibility: Same as Applicant Eligibility.

Award Range/Average: If minimum or maximum amounts of funding per competitive and/or capacity project grant, or cooperative agreement are established, these amounts will be announced in the annual Competitive Request for Application (RFA).

Funding: Cooperative Agreements (Discretionary Grants) FY 17 $2,350,736; FY 18 est $2,354,305; FY 19 est $0; - The Veterinary Services Grant Program (VSGP) was recently authorized in the Agricultural Act of 2014.

HQ: 1400 Independence Avenue SW, P.O. Box 2240
Washington, DC 20024
Phone: 202-401-6802
http://nifa.usda.gov

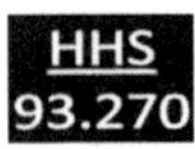

HHS 93.270 VIRAL HEPATITIS PREVENTION & CONTROL "Viral Hepatitis Prevention, Screening, Linkage to Care, and Education"

Award: Cooperative Agreements

Purpose: Funding will allow for CDC to partner with multiple organizations to benefit individuals by substantially reducing viral hepatitis transmission, identifying those that are acutely and chronically infected, and linking infected individuals with treatment if appropriate.

Applicant Eligibility: Applicants include State or local governments or their Bona Fide Agents, public and private nonprofit organizations, for profit organizations, small, minority, women-owned businesses, universities, colleges, research institutions, hospitals, community-based organizations, faith based organizations, Federally recognized Indian tribal governments, Indian tribes, and Indian tribal organizations. Additional guidance may be provided in individual program announcements.

Beneficiary Eligibility: The individual will benefit from the objectives of this program as well as the community at large, and society from the savings realized from treating those who are infected with viral hepatitis.

Award Range/Average: $30,000 to $500,000, with an average award of $150,000.

Funding: (Cooperative Agreements) FY 17 $17,034,281; FY 18 est $19,979,265; FY 19 est $19,979,265; FY 16 $16,815,000; - Funding is provided to state and local health departments to increase testing and linkage to care if necessary for chronically infected individuals with viral hepatitis B and C.

HQ: 1600 Clifton Road NE, P.O. Box G-37
Atlanta, GA 30333
Phone: 404-718-8504
Email: jle1@cdc.gov
http://www.cdc.gov

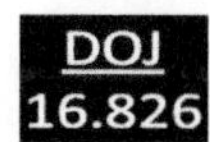

VISION 21

Award: Project Grants

Purpose: To assist victims of violence and help jurisdictions to build the technological infrastructure to improve services to victims of crime.

Applicant Eligibility: N/A

Beneficiary Eligibility: N/A

Award Range/Average: $250,000 to $1,000,000

Funding: (Project Grants) FY 17 $385,621; FY 18 est $0; FY 19 est $25,000,000; FY 16 $47,762,871.

HQ: Office for Victims of Crime 810 7th Street NW
Washington, DC 20531
Phone: 800-363-0441
Email: katherine.darke@ojp.usdoj.gov
http://ojp.gov/ovc

VISION RESEARCH

Award: Project Grants

Purpose: To support eye and vision research projects that address the leading causes of blindness and impaired vision in the U.S.

Applicant Eligibility: Public/State-controlled institutions of higher education, private institutions of higher education, Hispanic-serving institutions, Historically Black Colleges and Universities, tribally-controlled colleges and universities, Alaska Native- and Native Hawaiian-serving Institutions, nonprofits with or without 501(c)(3) IRS status, Small Businesses, for-profit organizations, federal institutions, and State and local units of government are eligible to make application for research grants, cooperative agreements, and career development awards. Foreign institutions may apply for research grants and cooperative agreements only.

Beneficiary Eligibility: Any nonprofit or for-profit organization, company, or institution engaged in biomedical research.

Award Range/Average: Grants and Cooperative Agreements: $13,587 to $4,500,000; $777,643. NRSA (Institutional): $25,240 to $505,935; $162,521. NRSA (Individual): $10,576 to $63,078; $ 45,562. SBIR Phase I: $136,774 to $299,999; $216,691. SBIR Phase II: $171,203 to $1,165,695; $499,120. STTR Phase I: $147,349 to $299,999; $206,034 STTR Phase II: $136,774 to $899,580; $684,190.

Funding: (Project Grants) FY 17 $572,203,845; FY 18 est $602,608,017; FY 19 est $562,363,947.

HQ: 6700B Rockledge Drive, Room 3438
Bethesda, MD 20892
Phone: 301-451-2020
Email: paul.sheehy@nih.gov
http://www.nei.nih.gov

VOCA TRIBAL VICTIM SERVICES SET-ASIDE PROGRAM "VOCA Tribal Set-Aside Program"

Award: Project Grants

Purpose: To provide support to Indian tribes through the Tribal Set-Aside Training and Technical Assistance Program to assist crime victims and provide technical assistance for Indian tribes and tribal consortia.

Applicant Eligibility: Indian tribes and tribal consortia (NOTE: eligible applicants may also include tribal organizations and organizations that directly serve Indian tribes).

Beneficiary Eligibility: The following will receive the ultimate benefits of the funding: Federally-Recognized Indian Tribal Governments Native American Organizations American Indians/Alaska Natives

Award Range/Average: Tribal Set-Aside: Up to $720,000 Training and Technical Assistance: Up to $1.3 million

Funding: Cooperative Agreements (Discretionary Grants) FY 17 $0; FY 18 est $133,080,000; FY 19 est $115,000,000.

HQ: 810 7th Street NW
Washington, DC 20531
Phone: 202-307-5983
http://www.ovc.gov

VOLUNTEER INCOME TAX ASSISTANCE (VITA) MATCHING GRANT PROGRAM

Award: Project Grants

Purpose: To provide direct funding that will enable VITA initiatives to extend services to underserved populations and hardest-to-reach areas, both urban and non-urban; specific objectives as they relate to the VITA Program.

Applicant Eligibility: Non-profit organization or state or government entity

Beneficiary Eligibility: Providing assistance to low to moderate income individuals and families

Award Range/Average: No Data Available

Funding: Project Grants (Discretionary) FY 17 $15,000,000; FY 19 est $15,000,000; FY 18 est $15,000,000.

HQ: 401 W Peachtree Street NW, P.O. Box 420-D
Atlanta, GA 30308
Phone: 404-338-7894
http://www.irs.gov

VOTING ACCESS FOR INDIVIDUALS WITH DISABILITIES-GRANTS FOR PROTECTION & ADVOCACY SYSTEMS "PAVA"

Award: Formula Grants; Project Grants

Purpose: Section 291 of HAVA provides that funds be made available to Protection and Advocacy Systems to: ensure full participation in the electoral process for individuals with disabilities.

Applicant Eligibility: States and Territories who have a Protection and Advocacy System in place in accordance with the Developmental Disabilities Assistance and Bill of Rights Act of 2000 with the exception of the Commonwealth of the Northern Mariana Islands and Native Americans.

Beneficiary Eligibility: Individuals with a full-range of disabilities.

Award Range/Average: $35,000 to $348,000. The average is $144,000.

Funding: (Formula Grants) FY 16 $4,963,000; FY 18 N/A FY 17 est $4,963,000.

HQ: 330 C Street SW
Washington, DC 20201
Phone: 202-795-7472
Email: melvenia.wright@acl.hhs.gov
http://www.acl.gov

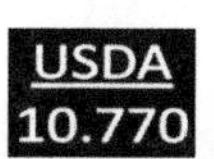

WATER & WASTE DISPOSAL LOANS & GRANTS (SECTION 306C) "Section 306C"

Award: Project Grants; Direct Loans

Purpose: To provide for the low-income rural communities who face significant health risks with water and waste disposal facilities.

Applicant Eligibility: Local level governments, Indian Tribes on Federal and State reservations, and other federally recognized Indian Tribes, U.S. Territories and possessions, and nonprofit associations can receive assistance under this program. Except for rural areas known as "Colonia" along the U.S./Mexico border, the projects funded under this program must primarily provide water and/or waste disposal services to residents of a county where the per capita income of the residents is not more than 70 percent of the most recent national average per capita income, as determined by the U.S. Department of Commerce, and unemployment rate of the residents is not less than 125 percent of the most recent national average unemployment rate, as determined by the Bureau of Labor Statistics.

Beneficiary Eligibility: Users of the applicant systems, which are previously described as public bodies, private nonprofit corporations, Indian tribes, and individuals.

Award Range/Average: Colonias Grants - $374,000 to $5,327,190 Average: $1,963,826. Native American Tribe Grants - $573,620to $2,000,000 Average: $1,388,647

Funding: Project Grants (Discretionary) FY 17 $24,995,648; FY 18 est $25,000,000; FY 19 est $0; - Native American Tribe GrantsProject Grants (Discretionary) FY 17$23,565,914; FY 18 est $25,000,000; FY 19 est $0; - Colonias Grants.

HQ: 1400 Independence Avenue SW
Washington, DC 20250

Phone: 202-720-0986
Email: edna.primrose@wdc.usda.gov
http://www.rd.usda.gov

USDA 10.760 WATER & WASTE DISPOSAL SYSTEMS FOR RURAL COMMUNITIES

Award: Project Grants; Direct Loans; Guaranteed/Insured Loans

Purpose: To compensate for financially distressed communities for water and waste projects.

Applicant Eligibility: Municipalities, counties, other political subdivisions of a State such as districts and authorities, associations, cooperatives, corporations operated on a not-for-profit basis, Indian tribes on Federal and State reservations and other Federally recognized Indian tribes. The applicant must: (1) be unable to finance the proposed project from its own resources or through commercial credit at reasonable rates and terms; and (2) have the legal authority necessary for constructing, operating, and maintaining the proposed facility or service, and for obtaining, giving security for, and repaying the proposed loan.

Beneficiary Eligibility: Users of the applicant systems, which are previously described as public bodies, private nonprofit corporations, Indian tribes, and individuals.

Award Range/Average: (Direct Loans) $22,000 to $17,900,000; average $2,096,294 (Grants) $34,682 to $14,307,000; average $952,987 (Guaranteed/Insured Loans) $210,000 to $3,200,000; average $845,057

Funding: (Project Grants) FY 17 $443,139,085; FY 18 est $851,913,500; FY 19 est $0; - (Direct Loans) FY 17$1,307,533,636; FY 18 est $141,176,471; FY 19 est $1,200,000,000; - (Guaranteed/Insured Loans) FY 17$5,070,341; FY 18 est $50,000,000; FY 19 est $0.

HQ: 1400 Independence Avenue SW, P.O. Box 1548
Washington, DC 20250
Phone: 202-690-2670
Email: edna.primrose@wdc.usda.gov
http://www.rd.usda.gov

DOS 19.800 WEAPONS REMOVAL & ABATEMENT "PM/WRA"

Award: Cooperative Agreements; Project Grants

Purpose: Reduces the threats posed to civilian security by at-risk, illicitly proliferated, and indiscriminately used conventional weapons.

Applicant Eligibility: All projects must have a clear focus on CWD program goals and objectives.

Beneficiary Eligibility: N/A

Award Range/Average: Grants range from $25,000 to $30,000,000.

Funding: Project Grants (Discretionary) FY 17 est $189,000,000; FY 16 $179,532,000; FY 18 est $196,900,000.

HQ: 2121 Virginia Avenue NW, Suite 6100
Washington, DC 20037
Phone: 202-663-0085
Email: murguiace@state.gov
http://www.state.gov

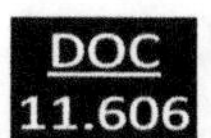

WEIGHTS & MEASURES SERVICE

Award: Provision of Specialized Services; Advisory Services and Counseling; Dissemination of Technical Information; Training

Purpose: To assist with technical resources in all commercial transactions in the U.S. by harmonizing national and international metrology standards to facilitate the metric system.

Applicant Eligibility: States, political subdivisions of States, private industry, and the general public.

Beneficiary Eligibility: States, political subdivisions of States, private industry, and the general public.

Award Range/Average: N/A

Funding: (Sale, Exchange, or Donation of Property and Goods) FY 17 $5,034,683; FY 18 est $5,093,400; FY 19 est $4,943,400; FY 16 $4,925,000.

HQ: 100 Bureau Drive, P.O. Box 8400
Gaithersburg, MD 20899
Phone: 301-975-4290
Email: patrick.hovis@nist.gov
http://www.nist.gov/pml/wmd/index.cfm

WELFARE REFORM RESEARCH, EVALUATIONS & NATIONAL STUDIES
"Welfare Research"

Award: Project Grants

Purpose: Supports research on the benefits, effects, and costs of operating different State welfare programs, including studies on the effects of different programs and the operation of such programs on welfare dependency, employment rates, child well-being, family formation and healthy marriage, illegitimacy, teen pregnancy, and others.

Applicant Eligibility: Grants and cooperative agreements may be made to or with governmental entities, colleges, universities, nonprofit and for-profit organizations (if fee is waived), and faith- and community-based organizations. Grants or cooperative agreements cannot be made directly to individuals.

Beneficiary Eligibility: Children, youth, and families, especially low-income families, will benefit.

Award Range/Average: Range of $350,000 to $599,961, with an average of $474,981

Funding: (Project Grants) FY 17 $949,961; FY 18 est $50,000; FY 19 est $0; FY 16 $1,553,995.

HQ: 330 C Street SW 4625A
Washington, NY 20201
Phone: 202-401-5803
Email: sheila.celentano@acf.hhs.gov
http://www.acf.hhs.gov/programs/opre

WELL-INTEGRATED SCREENING & EVALUATION FOR WOMEN ACROSS THE NATION (WISEWOMAN) "WISEWOMAN"

Award: Cooperative Agreements

Purpose: To fund state health departments and tribal organizations to extend services to improve prevention, detection, and control of CVD risk factors for low-income, uninsured, or underinsured women by offering CVD screening, risk reduction counseling, referral to medical services, referral to programs, and resources to support positive cardiovascular health.

Applicant Eligibility: State and the District of Columbia government; local government or their Bona Fide Agent; U.S. Territory or Possession; Federally Recognized Indian Tribal Government; Native American Organization (American Indian/Alaska native tribally designated organization). 1 Eligible Applicants: State and local governments or their Bona Fide Agents (this includes the District of Columbia, the Commonwealth of Puerto Rico, the Virgin Islands, the Commonwealth of the Northern Marianna Islands, American Samoa, Guam, the Federated States of Micronesia, the Republic of the Marshall Islands, and the Republic of Palau).

Beneficiary Eligibility: Beneficiaries of this program include: Women who are ages 40-64 and eligible through the National Breast and Cervical Cancer Early Detection Program criteria.

Award Range/Average: Awards are expected to range from $500,000 to $2,500,000 (total award for both Core and innovation Components, were applicable). All activities supported through this NOFO must contribute to health improvements across the target population and across population subgroups. Award recipients must demonstrate significant disease burden to allow the strategies supported by this NOFO to reach a significant proportion of the target population. Funding strategy will also include the awardees' proposed activities and goals, estimated population reach, and program capacity as described in the application.

Funding: Cooperative Agreements (Discretionary Grants) FY 17 $14,549,174; FY 18 est $16,296,500; FY 19 est $16,296,500.

HQ: 4770 Buford Highway
Atlanta, GA 30341
Phone: 770-488-6215
http://www.cdc.gov

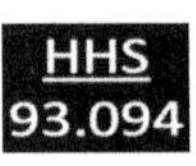

WELL-INTEGRATED SCREENING & EVALUATION FOR WOMEN ACROSS THE NATION "WISEWOMAN"

Award: Cooperative Agreements

Purpose: To improve the cardiovascular health of low-income, uninsured and under-insured women, ages 40-64, who are participants in the National Breast and Cervical Cancer Early Detection Program (NBCCEDP).

Applicant Eligibility: Applicants must be recipients of the National Breast and Cervical Cancer Early Detection Program (NBCCEDP)

Beneficiary Eligibility: Low Income, uninsured or under-insured women

Award Range/Average: Awards will range from approximately $500,000 to $2,000,000 with an average of approximately $780,000.

Funding: (Cooperative Agreements) FY 17 $14,548,574; FY 18 est $0; FY 19 FY 16 $13,778,401.

HQ: 4770 Buford Highway, P.O. Box F 72
Atlanta, GA 30341
Phone: 770-488-8404
Email: dvc2@cdc.gov
http://www.cdc.gov

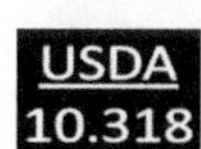

WOMEN & MINORITIES IN SCIENCE, TECHNOLOGY, ENGINEERING, AND MATHEMATICS FIELDS "WAMS; Women and Minorities in Science, Technology, Engineering, and Mathematics Fields (STEM) program"

Award: Project Grants

Purpose: The WAMS supports women by providing them the education in the fields such as Science, Technology, Engineering, and Mathematics. STEM supports women in rural areas by providing them with career and other skills necessary.

Applicant Eligibility: State agricultural experiment stations; colleges and universities; university research foundations; other research institutions and organizations; Federal agencies; national laboratories; private organizations or corporations; individuals; or any group consisting of 2 or more of these entities.

Beneficiary Eligibility: Same as Applicant Eligibility.

Award Range/Average: If minimum or maximum amounts of funding per competitive and/or capacity project grant, or cooperative agreement are established, these amounts will be announced in the annual Competitive Request for Application (RFA).

Funding: Cooperative Agreements (Discretionary Grants) FY 17 $378,600; FY 18 est $363,000; FY 19 est $0; FY 16 $382,650.

HQ: 1400 Independence Avenue SW, P.O. Box 2250
Washington, DC 20024-2250
Phone: 202-720-2324
http://nifa.usda.gov/program/women-and-minorities-science-technology-engineering-and-mathematics-fields-grant-program

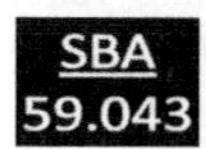

WOMEN'S BUSINESS OWNERSHIP ASSISTANCE "Women's Business Center"

Award: Project Grants

Purpose: To fund private, nonprofit organizations to assist, through training and counseling, small business concerns owned and controlled by women, and to remove.

Applicant Eligibility: Private, nonprofit organizations having experience in effectively training and counseling business women. Public educational institutions and State and local governments are not eligible.

Beneficiary Eligibility: Women entrepreneurs starting their own business or expanding their existing business.

Award Range/Average: No Data Available.

Funding: (Project Grants) FY 17 $15,849,000; FY 18 est $18,000,000; FY 19 est $16,000,000.

HQ: 409 3rd Street SW, 5th Floor
Washington, DC 20416
Phone: 202-205-7532
Email: bruce.purdy@sba.gov
http://www.sba.gov/wbc

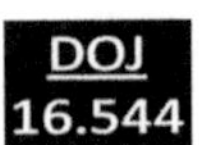

YOUTH GANG PREVENTION
"Gangs and youth violence prevention"

Award: Project Grants

Purpose: To provide funding to states, local units of government, and federal recognized tribes to implement programs and strategies to prevent and intervene youth-gang-related violence.

Applicant Eligibility: Part D funds are available under the Juvenile Justice and Delinquency Prevention Act of 1974, as amended, to public or private nonprofit agencies, organizations or individuals.

Beneficiary Eligibility: Contact program office for additional information

Award Range/Average: Varies.

Funding: (Formula Grants) FY 17 $3,333,287; FY 18 est $0; FY 19 est $0.

HQ: 810 7th Street NW
Washington, DC 20351
Phone: 202-514-4817
Email: kellie.dressler@usdoj.gov
http://www.ojjdp.gov

YOUTH HOMELESSNESS DEMONSTRATION PROGRAM
"Youth Homelessness Demonstration Program"

Award: Direct Payments for Specified Use

Purpose: To promote a community-wide commitment to the goal of ending youth homelessness and promote access and effective utilization of mainstream programs and optimizes self-sufficiency among youth experiencing homelessness.

Applicant Eligibility: Homeless unaccompanied youth (age 24 and younger) and homeless youth (age 24 and younger) with children.

Beneficiary Eligibility: Same as Applicant Eligibility.

Award Range/Average: The allocation for selected communities ranges between $1 million and $15 million. The allocation is abased upon a formula that considers the number of youth in the community and the local poverty rate.

Funding: Project Grants (Discretionary) FY 17 $43,000,000; FY 18 est $80,000,000; FY 19 N/A.

HQ: Division Director U S Department of Housing and Urban Development 451 7th Street SW, Room 7256
Washington, DC 20410
Phone: 202-402-5183
Email: lisa.a.hill@hud.gov
http://www.hudexchange.info/programs/yhdp

PROGRAMS ADMINISTERED BY REGIONAL - STATE - LOCAL OFFICES

ADVANCED RESEARCH PROJECTS AGENCY
Regional - State - Local Offices

USA Cold Regions Research and Engineering Laboratory
Mr. Peter Smallidge | 72 Lynn Road, Hanover, NH 03755-1290 603-646-4445

USA Construction Engineering Research Laboratories
Ms. Bea Shahim | 2902 Newmark Drive, Champaign, IL 61821-1075 800-872-2375

USA Topographic Engineering Center
Mr. Charles McKenna | Cude Building No. 2592, Ft. Belvoir, VA 22060-5546 703-355-3133

USAE Hydrologic Engineering Center
Mr. Arlen Feldman | 609 Second Street, Davis, CA 95616-4887 916-756-1104

USAE Institute for Water Resources
Casey Building No. 2594, Ft. Belvoir, VA 22060-5586 703-355-3084

USAE Waterways Experiment Station
Mr. William McGleese | 3909 Falls Ferry Road, Vicksburg, MI 39180-6199 601-634-2512

DOD 12.910 RESEARCH AND TECHNOLOGY DEVELOPMENT

Award: Cooperative Agreements

Purpose: To assist and induce the basic research, applied research, and advanced research at educational institutions, nonprofit organizations, and commercial firms.

Applicant Eligibility: For grants, eligibility is limited to public and private educational institutions and nonprofit organizations operated for purposes in the public interest. For cooperative agreements, eligibility is limited to educational institutions, nonprofit organizations, and commercial firms.

Beneficiary Eligibility: Public and private educational institutions. Nonprofit organizations operated for purposes in the public interest and commercial firms.

Award Range/Average: No Data Available.

Funding: (Project Grants) FY 17 $207,024,175; FY 18 est $265,566,513; FY 19 N/A FY 16 $235,374,638.

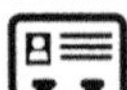

HQ: 675 N Randolph Street
Arlington, VA 22203
Phone: 703-526-2103
Email: anthony.cicala@darpa.mil

AGRICULTURAL MARKETING SERVICE

COTTON DIVISION

Standardization and Quality Assurance Branch
Don West, Chief | 3275 Appling Road, Memphis, TN 38133 901-384-3015

Tennessee
J. Jerome Boyd | 3275 Appling Road, Memphis, TN 38133 901-384-3000

DAIRY DIVISION

Illinois
Dairy Division | 800 Roosevelt Road, Building A, Suite 370, Glen Ellyn, IL 60137 708-790-6920

USDA, AMS, Dairy Division
2811 Agricultural Drive, Madison, WI 53704-6777 608-224-5080

FRUIT AND VEGETABLE DIVISION

Alabama

Robert Spann, Federal Supervisor, In-Charge | 1557 Reeves Street, For Mail: P.O. Box 1368, Dothan, AL 36302 334-792-5185

Arizona

James E. Nowlin | 1688 W. Adams, Room 415, Phoenix, AZ 85007 602-542-0880

Jerry W. Taylor, Regional Director | Tucson Federal Building, Box FB30 300 West Congress Street, Room 7, Tucson, AZ 85701-1319 520-670-4793

Stephen Skuba, In-Charge | 522 North Central Avenue, Room 106, Phoenix, AZ 85004 602-379-3066

Baltimore/Washington

Nathaniel Taylor IV, In-Charge | USDA, AMS, F&VD Baltimore-Washington Terminal Market Office 8610 Baltimore-Washington Boulevard, Suite 212, Jessup, MD 20794 301-317-4387, 4587

California

Clifton Harada, In-Charge | 1320 East Olympic Avenue, Room 212, Los Angeles, CA 90021 213-894-2489, 6553

Dale I. Scarborough, Inspector | Inspection Point of Fresno, CA 45-116 Commerce Street, Suite 15, Indio, CA 92201-3440 619-347-1057

Frederick Teensma, In-Charge | 630 Sansome Street, Room 727, San Francisco, CA 94111 415-705-1300

John Henry, In-Charge | 1320 East Olympic Boulevard, Room 212, Los Angeles, CA 90021-1948 213-894-3173

Kevin Morris, In-Charge | 2202 Monterey Street, Suite 104-A, Fresno, CA 93721 209-487-5178

Kurt J. Kimmel, In-Charge | USDA, AMS, MFO 2202 Monterey Street, Suite 102-B, Fresno, CA 93721 209-487-5901

Michael Shine, In-Charge | 1320 East Olympic Boulevard, Suite 212, Los Angeles, CA 90021-1907 213-894-3077

Michael V. Morrelli, Federal Supervisor | In-Charge 1220 N Street, Room A-270 For Mail: P.O. 942871, Sacramento, CA 94271-0001 916-654-0810, 13,15

Yoshiki (Junior) Kagawa, In-Charge | 2202 Monterey Street, Suite 102-A, Fresno, CA 93721-3129 209-487-5210

Colorado

Ronald D. Nightengale, Federal Supervisor | In-Charge 2331 West 31st Avenue, Denver, CO 80211 303-844-4570

Tom Guttierrez, In-Charge | Greeley Producers Building 711 "O" Street, Greeley, CO 80631 970-351-7097, 351-8256

Connecticut

Peter Bucci, Federal Supervisor, In-Charge Connecticut Regional Market | 101 Reserve Road, Room 5, Hartford, CT 06114 860-240-3446

Delaware

Clifford W. Hudson, In-Charge | State of Delaware Department of Agriculture 2320 South DuPont Highway, Dover, DE 19901 302-736-4811

Terry B. Bane, Director 800 Roosevelt Road, Building A, Suite 380, Glen Ellyn, IL 60137-5875 630-790-6957

Florida

775 Warner Lane, Orlando, FL 32803 407-897-5950

Ann S. Pinner, In-Charge | 98 Third Street, SW, Winter Haven, FL 33880-2909 941-294-7416

Christian Nissen, In-Charge | For mail: P.O. Box 2276 301 3rd Street, N.W., Suite 206, Winterhaven, FL 33881 941-299-4770, 4886

Clyde Thornhill, In-Charge | 6966 NW 36th Avenue, Miami, FL 33147-6506 305-835-7626

James Dunn, In-Charge | Techniport Building, Room 556 5600 N.W. 36 Street, Miami, FL 33122 305-870-9542

Jim Cunningham, In-Charge | Brickell Plaza Building 909 S.E. 1st Avenue, Suite 424, Miami, FL 33131 305-373-2955

Georgia

John Kerrens, In-Charge | 203 Administration Building 16 Forest Parkway, Forest Park, GA 30050 404-763-7297

John Pollard, In-Charge | 1555 St. Joseph Avenue, East Point, GA 30344-2591 404-763-7495

Larry Ivaska, In-Charge | Administration Building, Room 205 16 Forest Parkway, Forest Park, GA 30050 404-366-7522

Richard DeMenna, In-Charge | For mail: P.O. Box 1447 Georgia State Farmers Market, Stall 39 502 Smith Avenue, U.S. Highway 84, Thomasville, GA 31799 912-228-1208

Hawaii

Walter T. Mitsui, Federal Supervisory Inspector | State of Hawaii Department of Agriculture 1428 South King Street For mail: P.O. Box 22159, Honolulu, HI 96823-2159 808-973-9566

Warren Maeda, Assistant Federal Supervisor | In-Charge 1428 South King Street For mail: P.O. Box 22159, Honolulu, HI 96823-2159 808-973-9566

Idaho

Scott P. Brubaker, Federal Supervisor, In-Charge | Idaho State Department of Agriculture 2270 Old Penitentiary Road, Boise, ID 83712 208-332-8670

Thomas L. Cooper, In-Charge | 1820 East 17th Street, Suite 130, Idaho Falls, ID 83404 208-526-0166

Illinois

Greg Braun, Regional Director | USDA, AMS, F&V PACA Branch 800 Roosevelt Road, Building A, Suite 360, Glen Ellyn, IL 60137-5832 630-790-6929

Steven D. Dailey, In-Charge | J.C. Kluczynski Building 230 South Dearborn Street, Room 512, Chicago, IL 60604 312-353-0111

Indiana

Anthony Chartrand, In-Charge | 4318 Technology Drive, South Bend, IN 46628-9752 219-287-5407

Richard Barlow, Federal Supervisor, In-Charge | P.O. Box 427, Greenfield, IN 46140-0427 317-462-5897

Kentucky

Jesse M. Stockton, Federal Supervisor, In-Charge | No. 1 Produce Terminal, Louisville, KY 40218 502-595-4266, 4278

John Crose, Federal Supervisor, In-Charge | U.S. Postal Service Building 701 Loyola Avenue, Room 11036, New Orleans, LA 70113 504-589-6741, 6742

Louisiana

Thomas Clominger, USDA Inspector | (Inspection Point of East Point, GA) Commerce Building, Suite 3 1942 Williams Boulevard, Kenner, LA 70062-6285 504-466-0343

Maine

Ed Margeson, Federal Supervisor, In-Charge | For mail: P.O. Box 1058 744 Main Street, Suite 4, Presque Isle, ME 04769 207-764-2100

Wallace Fengler, In-Charge | 165 Lancaster Street, Portland, ME 04101-2499 207-772-1588

Maryland

Holly R. Mozal, In-Charge | Maryland Wholesale Produce Market Building B, Room 101 7460 Conowingo Avenue, Jessup, MD 20794

Norman Upton, In-Charge | Hunt Valley Professional Building 9 Schilling Road, Hunt Valley, MD 21031-1106 410-962-4946

William V. Kaier, Inspector | (Inspector Point of Hunt Valley, MD) 102 Maryland Avenue, Easton, MD 21601-3409 410-822-3383

Massachusetts

James Calnan, In-Charge | Boston Market Terminal 34 Market Street, Room 10, Everett, MA 02149 617-387-4498, 4615, 4681

Susan Taylor, Federal Supervisor, In-Charge | Boston Market Terminal Building 34 Market Street, Room 1, Everett, MA 02149 617-389-2480, 2481

Michigan

Charles W. Hackensmith II, In-Charge | For mail: P.O. Box 1204 Federal Building 175 Territorial Road, Room 201, Benton Harbor, MI 49023 616-925-3270, 3271

Gary Reij, USDA Inspector | (Inspection Point of South Bend, IN) c/o Vroom Cold Storage Russell Road, Hart, MI 49420-0113 616-873-5654

Michael Rann, In-Charge Union Produce Terminal | 7201 West Fort Street, Room 53, Detroit, MI 48209 313-841-1111

Michael W. Moore, Federal Supervisor | 90 Detroit Union Produce Terminal 7201 West Fort Street, Detroit, MI 48209 313-226-6059, 6225

Minnesota

Gregory Stevens, USDA Inspector | (Inspection Point of Ripon, WI) 2126 Hoffman Road, Mankato, MN 56001-5863 507-387-6101

Mark Inverson, Federal Supervisor, In-Charge | 90 West Plato Boulevard, St. Paul, MN 55107 612-296-8557, 0593

Missouri

Arne Stokke, In-Charge | Gumble Building, Room 502 801 Walnut Street, Kansas City, MO 64106 816-374-6273

Charles M. Gore, In-Charge | Unit 1, Produce Row, Room 101, St. Louis, MO 63102-1418 314-425-4520

Francis Allard, Federal Supervisor, In-Charge | Fresh Fruit & Vegetable Division Ohio Dept. of Agriculture Division of Food, Dairy & Drugs 8995 East Main Street, Bldg. 2, Reynoldsburg, OH 43068 614-728-6350

Larry Wenger, In-Charge | Unit 1 Produce Row, 1st Floor, Room 100, St. Louis, MO 63102 314-425-4514, 4515

Randall T. Edwards, In-Charge | 3716 Croton Avenue, Cleveland, OH 44115 216-522-2135

New Jersey

Michiko F. Shaw, Regional Director | PACA Branch USDA, AMS, F&V, Division 622 Georges Road, Suite 303, North Brunswick, NJ 08902-3303 908-846-8222

Park Plaza, Professional Building, Suite 304 622 Georges Road, North Brunswick, NJ 08902-3313 908-545-0939

Tom Robertson, In-Charge | Federal Building 970 Broad Street, Room 1430, Newark, NJ 07102 201-645-2636

New York

Bruce Copeland | (Inspection Point of North Brunswick, NJ) Genesee Valley Regional Market 900 Jefferson Road, Room 110, Rochester, NY 14623-3289 716-424-2092, 2096

C. Michael Wells, In-Charge | 465B Hunts Point Market, Bronx, NY 10474 718-991-7665, 7669

Paul Beattie, Federal Supervisor, In-Charge | Division of Food Safety & Inspection Service Department of Agriculture Capital Plaza, 1 Winners Circle Building No. 2, Second Floor, Albany, NY 12235 518-457-1211, 457-2090, 457-1982

Philip H. Montgomery, In-Charge 5A NYC Terminal Market | Halleck Street at Edgewater Road, Bronx, NY 10474-7355 718-542-2225

Oklahoma

716 South 2nd Street, Suite 106, Stilwell, OK 74960-4806 918-696-6333

James W. Goodson, In-Charge | 2800 North Lincoln Boulevard, Oklahoma City, OK 73105 405-521-3864

Oregon

Dick C. Harms, Federal Supervisor, In-Charge | 635 Capitol Street, NE, Salem, OR 97310-0110 503-986-4629

Gary Olson, In-Charge | 1220 S.W. 3rd Avenue, Room 369, Portland, OR 97204 503-326-2724, 2725

Gary Sheltor, USDA Inspector | (Inspection Point of Yakima, WA) 111 South Main Street, Milton-Freewater, OR 97862-1342 541-938-3251

Jack Whitt, In-Charge | 340 High Street, NE, Salem, OR 97301-3631 503-399-5761

Pennsylvania

Armia Lawandy, In-Charge | 210 Produce Building 3301 South Galloway Street, Philadelphia, PA 19148 215-336-0845, 0846

Dennis Jemmerson, In-Charge | 2100 Smallman Street, Room 207, Pittsburgh, PA 15222 412-644-5847

James Prady, In-Charge | Pittsburgh Produce Terminal Building, Room 206 2100 Smallman Street, Pittsburgh, PA 15222 412-261-6435

Michael Cramer, In-Charge | Room 261 3301 South Galloway Street, Philadelphia, PA 19148 215-597-4536

Thomas Yawman, Federal Supervisor, In-Charge | 2301 North Cameron Street, Room 112, Harrisburg, PA 17110 717-787-5107, 5108

Puerto Rico

Luis Aponte, Federal Supervisor, In-Charge | Federal-State Inspection, GSA Service Center 651 Federal Drive, Suite 103-05, Guaynabo, PR 00965 787-783-2230, 4116

Luis Aponte, In-Charge | Federal State Inspection Service, GSA Center 651 Federal Drive, Suite 103-05, Guaynabo, PR 00965-1030 809-783-2230, 4116

Tennessee

Jerry L. Cook, In-Charge | 3211 Alcoa Highway, Knoxville, TN 37920 423-577-2633

Michael W. Golightly, Federal Supervisor | In-Charge For mail: P.O. Box 40627 Melrose Station, Nashville, TN 37204 615-360-0169

Texas

350 North Redwood Road Room 217, Salt Lake City, UT 84116 801-538-7187

Alfonso T. Briones, USDA Inspector | 319 Market Street, Laredo, TX 78040-8529 210-726-2258

Belinda G. Garza, In-Charge | McAllen Marketing Field Office Fruit & Vegetable Division Agricultural Marketing Services, USDA 1313 East Hackberry, McAllen, TX 78501 956-682-2833

Byron E. White, Regional Director | PACA Branch USDA, AMS, F&U 1200 E. Copeland Road, Suite 404, Arlington, TX 76011-4938 817-885-7805

Calvin Harvey, In-Charge | 8001 E N. Mesa, Suite 303, El Paso, TX 79932 505-589-3753

D.C. Benavides, In-Charge | Administration Building, Room 244 1500 South Zarzamora Street, San Antonio, TX 78207 210-222-2751

Daniel Frey, Inspector | 2320 La Branch Street Federal Building, Room 1011, Houston, TX 77004-1036 713-659-3836

Desiree Shaw, In-Charge | 1406 Parker Street, Room 201, Dallas, TX 75215 214-767-5375, 5376, 5377

Dwain Parrish, In-Charge | 117 So. Westgate, Weslaco, TX 78596-2701 210-968-2772, 2126

Gary Verheek, Federal Supervisor, In-Charge | 1301 West Expressway P.O. Box 107, San Juan, TX 78589 210-787-4091, 6881

Ken Edwards, In-Charge | 3100 Produce Row, Room 1A, Houston, TX 77023 713-923-2557, 2558

Timothy J. Peppel, In-Charge | 1406 Parker Street, Suite 203, Dallas, TX 75215 214-767-5337, 5338

Virginia

8700 Centerville Road, Suite 206, Manassas, VA 22110 703-330-4455

Raymond Oliver, In-Charge | No. 1 North 14th Street, Room 332, Richmond, VA 23219-3691 804-786-0930

Washington

Dale Guyant, Federal Supervisor, In-Charge | For Mail: P.O. Box 42560 National Resources Building, 2nd Floor 1111 Washington Street, Olympia, WA 98504-2560 360-902-1831

Frank V. Warren, In-Charge | 32 North 3rd Street, Room 212, Yakima, WA 98901-2791 509-575-5869

Jeffrey Main, In-Charge | Agricultural Service Center 2015 South 1st Street, Room 4, Yakima, WA 98903 509-575-2492, 2493

Peter Echanove, In-Charge | Interwest Savings Bank 15111 8th Avenue, S.W., Suite 302 P.O. Box 48099, Seattle, WA 98148-0099 206-764-3804, 3753

Western Region | Romeo V. Villaluz, Regional Director 2202 Monterey Street, Suite 102-C, Fresno, CA 93721-3175 209-487-5891

Wisconsin

Milborn Beaty, In-Charge | 742 East Fond du Lac Street, Ripon, WI 54971-9555 414-748-2287

LIVESTOCK DIVISION

Alabama

F. David Gonsoulin | 1445 Federal Drive, Room 107 P.O. Box 3336, Montgomery, AL 36109-0336 334-223-7488

Arizona

Donald W. Perkins | Stockyards Building 5001 East Washington Street, Room 102, Phoenix, AZ 85034-2010 602-379-4376

Arkansas

Steve R. Cheney | P.O. Box 391 2301 S. University, Room 110-B, Little Rock, AR 72203-3910 501-671-2203

Colorado

Dale Krows | 400 Livestock Exchange Building, Denver, CO 80216-2139 303-294-7676

Keith L. Padgett | 711 "O" Street, Greeley, CO 80631-9540 970-353-9750

Florida

Ronald Carpenter | 775 Warner Lane, Orlando, FL 32803 407-897-2708

Georgia

Terry Harris | Georgia State Farmers Market P.O. Box 86 502 Smith Avenue, Stall 38, Thomasville, GA 31792-0086 912-226-2198

Illinois

James Epstein | Illinois Department of Agriculture Division of Marketing State Fairgrounds, Box 19281, Springfield, IL 62794-9281 217-782-4925

Richard Johnson | 800 Roosevelt Road Building A, Suite 330, Glen Ellyn, IL 60137-5832 708-790-6905

Iowa

C. Thomas Sandau | P.O. Box 2437 800 Cunningham Drive, Room 225, Sioux City, IA 51107-2437 712-252-3286

Michael Sheats | 210 Walnut Street, Room 767, Des Moines, IA 50309-2106 515-284-4460

Richard Jones | 210 Walnut Street, Room 575-A, Des Moines, IA 50309-2106 515-284-7166

Kansas

R. Gary Mills | 100 Military Avenue, Suite 217, Dodge City, KS 67801-4945 316-227-8881

Kentucky

Jack L. Colley | 1321 Story Avenue, Louisville, KY 40206-1884 502-582-5287

Louisiana

David H. Foster | P.O. Box 3334, Capitol Station 5825 Florida Boulevard, Baton Rouge, LA 70821-3334 504-922-1328

Minnesota

Robert Brommer | New Livestock Exchange Building, Suite 208, South St. Paul, MN 55075-5598 612-451-1565

Missouri

Phil B. McFall | 601 Illinois Avenue, Room 210, St. Joseph, MO 64504-1396 816-238-0678

Montana

Russ Travelute | P.O Box 1191 Public Auction Yards Building 112 South 18th & Minnesota Avenue, Room 206, Billings, MT 59103-1191 406-657-6285

Nebraska
Evan Stachowicz | 204 Livestock Exchange Building 29th & O Streets, Omaha, NE 68107-2603 402-733-4833

Gary R. Kinder | 213 Livestock Exchange Building 29th & "O" Street, Omaha, NE 68107-2603 402-731-4520

Oklahoma
Robert P. Miles | Livestock Exchange Building, Room 140 2501 Exchange Avenue, Oklahoma City, OK 73108-2477 405-232-5425

Oregon
Lowell C. Serfling | 1220 S.W., 3rd Avenue, Room 1772, Portland, OR 97204-2899 503-326-2237

Pennsylvania
James L. Anderson | c/o New Holland Sales Stables 101 W. Fulton Street, P.O. Box 155, New Holland, PA 17557 717-354-2391

South Carolina
Daniel Schussler | P.O. Box 13405 Youngblood Building 1001 Bluff Road, Columbia, SC 29201-3405 803-737-4491

South Dakota
Charles E. McIntyre | 803 East Rice Street, Room 103, Sioux Falls, SD 57103-0193 605-338-4061

Tennessee
Lewis Langell | P.O. Box 40627 Melrose Station, Ellington Agriculture Center, Hogan Road, Nashville, TN 37204-0627 615-781-5406

Texas
Cecil R. Rains | P.O. Box 30217 Livestock Exchange Building 101 South Manhattan Street, Amarillo, TX 79104 806-373-7111

John Langenegger | 2507 N. Telshor Boulevard, Suite 4, Las Cruces, NM 88001 505-521-4928

Kenneth Gladney | Livestock Exchange Building P.O. Box 30217 101 South Manhattan Street, 1st Floor, Amarillo, TX 79104-0217 806-372-6361

Rebecca Saunder | Producer's Livestock Auction Building P.O. Box 30160, San Angelo, TX 76903-0160 915-653-1778

Washington
Vern Larson | 988 Juniper Street, Moses Lake, WA 98837-2250 509-765-3611

Wyoming
Ray Leach | 1834 East A Street, Torrington, WY 82240-1813 307-532-4146

POULTRY DIVISION

Arkansas
Larry Poldrack | 1 Natural Resources Drive, Room 110 P.O. Box 8521, Little Rock, AR 72215-8521 501-324-5955

California
Gerald Brockman | 2909 Coffee Road, Suite 4, Modesto, CA 95355-3188 209-522-5251

James Derby | 5600 Rickenbacker Road Building 6 Section E, Bell, CA 90201-6418 213-269-4154

Connecticut
Patricia Bussy, Administrative Assistant | Connecticut Department of Agriculture Marketing Division, 165 Capital Avenue State Office Building, Room 263, Hartford, CT 06106-1688 860-566-3671

District of Columbia
AMS, PY Division | USDA National Poultry Supervisor/National Egg Supervisor Richard Parsons/David Bowden, Jr. South Building, Room 3960 P.O. Box 96456, Washington, DC 20090-6456 202-720-6911

Georgia
Johnny Freeman | 60 Forsyth Street, S.W., Room 6M80, Atlanta, GA 30303

Iowa
Jerry Mason | Room 777, Federal Building 210 Walnut Street, Des Moines, IA 50309-2100 515-284-4581

Mary Adkins | 210 Walnut Street, Room 951, Des Moines, IA 50309-2103 515-284-4545

Louisiana
Dave Foster, Director | Louisiana Department of Agriculture P.O. Box 3334, H.J. Wilson Building, Baton Rouge, LA 70821-3334 504-922-1328

Mississippi
Gary Brown | 352 East Woodrow Wilson P.O. Box 4629, Jackson, MS 39296-4629 601-965-4662

North Carolina
Douglas N. Lecher | 635 Cox Road, Suite G, Gastonia, NC 28054-3441 704-867-3871

Spurgeon Hyder, Manager | North Carolina Department of Agriculture P.O. Box 27647 State Agriculture Building, Room 402 2 West Edenton Street, Raleigh, NC 27611-7647 919-733-7252

Texas
Neal Alexander, Director of Market Information | Texas Department of Agriculture P.O. Box 12847,

Capitol Station 1700 North Congress Avenue, Austin, TX 78711-2847 512-463-7628

Virginia
Linda M. Kelley, Reporter | Virginia Department of Agriculture and Consumer Services, Market News 116 Reservoir Street, Harrisonburg, VA 22801-4232 540-434-0779

SCIENCE DIVISION

Alabama
Bobby L. Joyner, Supervisory Chemist | Aflatoxin Laboratories 3119 Wesley Way, Dothan, AL 36301-2020 334-794-5070

Melvin C. Ginn, Laboratory Supervisor | For mail: P.O. Box 1368 1557 Reeves Street, Dothan, AL 36302 334-792-5185

Florida
James Carson, Supervisory Chemist | Eastern Laboratories 98 Third Street, S.W., Suite 211, Winter Haven, FL 33880-2909 941-299-7958

Georgia
Donald Johnson, Laboratory Supervisor | 610 North Main Street, Blakely, GA 31723 912-723-4570

Lorine Lewis, Laboratory Supervisor | For mail: P.O. Box 488, Ashburn, GA 31714 912-567-3703

Thomas E. Parris, Laboratory Supervisor | 1211 Schley Avenue, Albany, GA 31707 912-430-8490

Walter K. Wills, Laboratory Supervisor | For mail: P.O. Box 272, Dawson, GA 31742 912-995-7257

Illinois
Dr. Fred Pepper, Laboratory Director | Midwestern Laboratory 3570 No. Avondale Avenue, Chicago, IL 60618-5391 312-353-6525

North Carolina
James G. Hess, Laboratory Director | Eastern Laboratory 2311-B Aberdeen Boulevard, Gastonia, NC 28054-0614 704-867-3873

Laboratory Address 645 Cox Road, Gastonia, NC 28054-0614 704-867-1882

Michael S. Lyons, Laboratory Supervisor | For mail: P.O. Box 279 301 West Pearl Street, Aulander, NC 27805 919-345-1661, Ext 156

Oklahoma
John Mangham, Laboratory Supervisor | 107 South 4th Street, Madill, OK 73446 405-795-5615

Virginia
Bonnie Poli, Branch Chief | Pesticide Records Branch 8700 Centreville Road, Suite 200, Manassas, VA 22110-0031 703-330-7826

Robert L. Epstein, Acting Branch Chief | Residue Branch 8700 Centreville Road, Suite 200, Manassas, VA 22110-0031 703-330-2300

Virginia L. Meeks, Laboratory Supervisor | For mail: P.O. Box 1130 308 Culloden Street, Suffolk, VA 23434 757-925-2286

TOBACCO DIVISION

Kentucky
Everette B. Mace | 771 Corporate Drive, Suite 500, Lexington, KY 40503 606-224-1088

North Carolina
Ralph W. Lowery | 1306 Annapolis Drive, Room 205, Raleigh, NC 27608-0001 919-856-4584

MARKET NEWS

Award: Dissemination of Technical Information

Purpose: To give the exact fare list to the State department of agriculture on all U.S. agricultural products.

Applicant Eligibility: State Departments of Agriculture may subscribe to existing market news reports or bulletins pertaining to specific agricultural commodities and markets.

Beneficiary Eligibility: State Departments of Agriculture

Award Range/Average: N/A

Funding: (Information) FY 17 $33,659,000; FY 18 est $33,659,000; FY 19 est $28,281,000; FY 16 $33,219,000

HQ: 1400 Independence Avenue SW
Washington, DC 20250
Phone: 202-690-4024
Email: erin.morris@ams.usda.gov
http://www.ams.usda.gov

USDA 10.155 MARKETING AGREEMENTS AND ORDERS

Award: Provision of Specialized Services; Advisory Services and Counseling

Purpose: To increase infrastructure of the marketing facilities by providing quality commodities.

Applicant Eligibility: Marketing orders are issued by the Secretary of Agriculture only after a public hearing where milk, fruit and vegetable producers, marketers, and consumers testify, and after farmers vote approval through a referendum. Growers of certain fruits, vegetables, and specialty crops (like nuts, raisins, olives, and hops).

Beneficiary Eligibility: The beneficiaries are producers of milk, fruit and vegetable products.

Award Range/Average: N/A

Funding: (Salaries and Expenses) FY 17 $20,705,000; FY 18 est $20,489,000; FY 19 est $20,489,000; FY 15 $18,843,000; FY 16 $20,489,000

HQ: 1400 Independence Avenue SW
Washington, DC 20250
Phone: 202-690-4024
Email: erin.morris@ams.usda.gov
http://www.ams.usda.gov

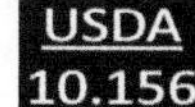

USDA 10.156 FEDERAL-STATE MARKETING IMPROVEMENT PROGRAM "FSMP"

Award: Project Grants

Purpose: To increase the market value for the U.S. agriculture products and enhance the marketing system in the U.S.

Applicant Eligibility: State Departments of Agriculture, State Agricultural Experiment Stations and other appropriate State agencies including State universities, State colleges, and State government entities such as State departments of forestry, natural resources, or energy.

Beneficiary Eligibility: Producers, processors, marketing agencies, and general public.

Award Range/Average: $25,000 to $1,000,000. Average: $148,000.

Funding: (Project Grants (for specified projects)) FY 17 $981,682; FY 18 est $1,109,000; FY 19 est $0; FY 16 $1,235,000

HQ: 1400 Independence Avenue SW, P.O. Box 0234
Washington, DC 20250
Phone: 202-260-8449
Email: martin.rosier@ams.usda.gov
http://www.ams.usda.gov/services/grants/fsmip

USDA 10.162 INSPECTION GRADING AND STANDARDIZATION "Agricultural Fair Practices Act"

Award: Provision of Specialized Services

Purpose: To provide qualitative infrastructure for the agriculture commodities and egg hatcheries.

Applicant Eligibility: Any owner of or dealer in agricultural commodities who (a) has a financial interest in the commodity to be graded and (b) is located within the United States and its Territories. All hatcheries and shell egg handlers having an annual production from 3,000 or more hens who pack for the retail consumer and are located within the U.S. or its Territories.

Beneficiary Eligibility: Buyers and sellers of agricultural commodities. Shell egg handlers having an annual production from 3,000 or more hens who pack for the retail consumer and are located in the U.S. or its Territories.

Award Range/Average: N/A

Funding: (Salaries and Expenses) FY 17 $157,759,000; FY 18 est $160,473,000; FY 19 est $160,473,000; FY 16 $155,357,000

HQ: 1400 Independence Avenue SW
Washington, DC 20250
Phone: 202-690-4024
Email: erin.morris@ams.usda.gov
http://www.ams.usda.gov

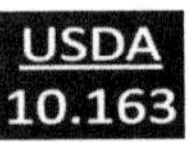

MARKET PROTECTION AND PROMOTION

Award: Provision of Specialized Services; Advisory Services and Counseling; Training

Purpose: To reduce misbranding of seeds and to analyze pesticide usage in the agriculture commodities.

Applicant Eligibility: Any State government, public and private organization and institution, business and industry, or individual may apply for technical assistance or service. State, trade associations, and universities may be eligible for cooperative agreements.

Beneficiary Eligibility: Any State government, public and private organization and institution, business and industry, or individual may apply for technical assistance or service.

Award Range/Average: N/A

Funding: (Salaries and Expenses) FY 17 $63,000,000; FY 18 est $65,000,000; FY 19 est $35,000,000; FY 16 $17,338,000

HQ: 1400 Independence Avenue SW
Washington, DC 20250
Phone: 202-690-4024
Email: erin.morris@ams.usda.gov
http://www.ams.usda.gov

USDA 10.164 WHOLESALE FARMERS AND ALTERNATIVE MARKET DEVELOPMENT

Award: Advisory Services and Counseling; Training

Purpose: To create apt infrastructure for the U.S. marketing.

Applicant Eligibility: Other government agencies and private industry. State, trade associations, universities, and other nonprofit organizations are eligible to apply for cooperative agreements.

Beneficiary Eligibility: Producers, processors, marketing agencies, and general public.

Award Range/Average: N/A

Funding: (Advisory Services and Counseling) FY 17 $5,246,000; FY 18 est $4,254,000; FY 19 est $4,250,000; FY 16 $5,216,000.

HQ: 1400 Independence Avenue SW
Washington, DC 20250
Phone: 202-690-1300
Email: arthur.neal@ams.usda.gov
http://www.ams.usda.gov

USDA 10.165 PERISHABLE AGRICULTURAL COMMODITIES ACT

Award: Investigation of Complaints

Purpose: To detect fraud practices of supplying unreliable agricultural products and reduce wastage of the products.

Applicant Eligibility: Business and industry or individuals may apply for a PACA license.

Beneficiary Eligibility: Same as Applicant Eligibility.

Award Range/Average: N/A

Funding: (Investigation of Complaints) FY 17 $10,423,000; FY 18 est $10,590,000; FY 19 est $10,733,000; FY 16 $11,452,000

HQ: 1400 Independence Avenue SW
Washington, DC 20250
Phone: 202-690-4024
Email: erin.morris@ams.usda.gov
http://www.ams.usda.gov

USDA 10.167 TRANSPORTATION SERVICES

Award: Advisory Services and Counseling; Training

Purpose: To increase income for rural Americans by providing agricultural transportation facilities.

Applicant Eligibility: Any State government, public and private organization and institution, business and industry, or individual may apply for technical assistance or service. State, trade associations, universities, and nonprofit organizations may be eligible for cooperative agreements.

Beneficiary Eligibility: Producers, processors, and general public.

Award Range/Average: N/A

Funding: (Advisory Services and Counseling) FY 17 $3,928,999; FY 18 est $2,929,000; FY 19 est $2,933,000; FY 16 $2,901,000

HQ: 1400 Independence Avenue SW
Washington, DC 20250
Phone: 202-690-1300
Email: arthur.neal@ams.usda.gov
http://www.ams.usda.gov

FARMERS MARKET PROMOTION PROGRAM "FMPP"

Award: Project Grants

Purpose: To promote better marketing facilities and infrastructure for increasing marketing opportunities.

Applicant Eligibility: Agricultural cooperatives, local governments, nonprofit corporations, producer networks, producer associations, community supported agriculture networks, community supported agriculture associations, public benefit corporations, economic development corporations, regional farmers market authorities, and Tribal governments. Projects and applicants must be owned, operated, and located within the 50 States, the District of Columbia, and the U.S. territories (American Samoa, Commonwealth of the Northern Mariana Islands, Guam, Puerto Rico, and U.S. Virgin Islands.

Beneficiary Eligibility: Projects that benefit producers, direct marketing enterprises, and consumers.

Award Range/Average: Capacity Building (CB) - $50,000- $250,000 Community Development, Training, and Technical Assistance (CDTTA) - $250,000-500,000

Funding: (Project Grants) FY 17 $13,965,000; FY 18 est $14,010,000; FY 19 est $0; FY 16 $15,000,000

HQ: USDA FMPP 1400 Independence Avenue SW
Washington, DC 20250
Phone: 202-720-8317
http://www.ams.usda.gov/services/grants/fmpp

SPECIALTY CROP BLOCK GRANT PROGRAM - FARM BILL "SCBGP"

Award: Project Grants

Purpose: To increase the productivity of specialty crops such as nuts, dry fruits, nursery crops, etc., and address issues such as pests, food safety, and marketing issues.

Applicant Eligibility: The State department of agriculture, agency, commission, or department of a State government responsible for agriculture within any of the 50 States, the District of Columbia, the Commonwealth of Puerto Rico, Guam, American Samoa, the U.S. Virgin Islands, and the Commonwealth of the Northern Mariana Islands are eligible to receive grants under this program.

Beneficiary Eligibility: Producers, processors, growers, state agencies, beginning and socially disadvantaged farmers, and general public.

Award Range/Average: As provided for in the applicable request for applications.

Funding: (Project Grants) FY 17 $4,000,000; FY 18 est $5,000,000; FY 19 est $0; FY 16 $3,000,000; - SCMS Only(Formula Grants) FY 17 $60,932,292; FY 18 est $78,829,891; FY 19 est $85,000,000

HQ: 1400 Independence Avenue SW Room 4534, P.O. Box 0269
Washington, DC 20250
Phone: 202-260-8702
Email: carlym.borgmeier@ams.usda.gov
http://www.ams.usda.gov/scbgp

LOCAL FOOD PROMOTION PROGRAM "LFPP"

Award: Project Grants

Purpose: To enhance marketing opportunities for regionally produced agricultural products.

Applicant Eligibility: Agricultural businesses and cooperatives, local governments, nonprofit corporations, producer networks, producer associations, community supported agriculture networks, community supported agriculture associations, public benefit corporations, economic development corporations, regional farmers market authorities, and Tribal governments. Projects and applicants must be owned, operated, and located within the 50 States, the District of Columbia, and the U.S. territories (American Samoa, Commonwealth of the Northern Mariana Islands, Guam, Puerto Rico, and U.S. Virgin Islands.

Beneficiary Eligibility: Projects that benefit producers, local and regional food business enterprises, and consumers.

Award Range/Average: For planning grants, the minimum grant request is $25,000; maximum grant request is $100,000. For implementation grants, the minimum grant request is $100,000; maximum grant request is $500,000.

Funding: (Project Grants) FY 17 $13,965,000; FY 18 est $14,010,000; FY 19 est $0; FY 16 $15,000,000

HQ: 1400 Independence Avenue SW Room 4543, P.O. Box 0234
Washington, DC 20250
Phone: 202-720-8713
http://www.ams.usda.gov

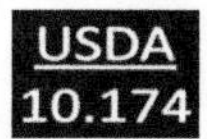

ACER ACCESS DEVELOPMENT PROGRAM

Award: Project Grants

Purpose: To assist the research institutions, producers, and States to increase products based on maple.

Applicant Eligibility: State agencies, tribal governments, and research institutions.

Beneficiary Eligibility: Producers, processors, marketing agencies, and general public.

Award Range/Average: $100,000 to $500,000. Average $350,000.

Funding: FY 17 $1,000,000; FY 18 est $993,000; FY 19 est $0; FY 16 N/A

Programs Administered by Regional - State - Local Offices

HQ: 1400 Independence Avenue SW Room 4534, P.O. Box 0234
Washington, DC 20250
Phone: 202-720-1403
Email: john.miklozek@ams.usda.gov
http://www.ams.usda.gov/services/grants

AGRICULTURAL RESEARCH SERVICE

Beltsville Area
Building 003, Room 203, BARC-West, Beltsville, MD 20705 301-504-7019

Midsouth Area
Delta States Research Center P.O. Box 225, Stoneville, MS 38776

Midwest Area
Northern Regional Research Center 1815 North University Street, Peoria, IL 61604

North Atlantic Area
Eastern Regional Research Center 600 E. Mermaid Lane, Philadelphia, PA 19118

Northern Plains Area
1201 Oakridge Drive, Suite 150, Fort Collins, CO 80525-5526 303-229-5513

Pacific West Area
Western Regional Research Center 800 Buchanan Street, Albany, CA 94710

South Atlantic Area
Richard B. Russell Research Center College Station Road, Athens, GA 30604-5677 706-546-3532

Southern Plains Area
7607 Eastmark Drive, Suite 230, College Station, TX 77840 979-960-9444

Virginia
5601 Sunnyside Avenue, Room 3-2172C Mail Stop 5110, Beltsville, MD 20705-5110 301-504-1147

USDA 10.001 AGRICULTURAL RESEARCH BASIC AND APPLIED RESEARCH "Extramural Research"

Award: Project Grants

Purpose: To attain other possible ways of agricultural techniques and scientific information on agriculture.

Applicant Eligibility: Usually nonprofit institutions of higher education or other nonprofit research organizations, whose primary purpose is conducting scientific research.

Beneficiary Eligibility: Same as Applicant Eligibility.

Award Range/Average: $1,000 to $25,000. Average $15,000

Funding: FY 17 $45,381,885; FY 18 est $35,000,000; FY 19 est $35,000,000; FY 16 $45,381,885.

HQ: 5601 Sunnyside Avenue, P.O. Box 5110
Beltsville, MD 20705
Phone: 301-504-1702
Email: kathleen.townson@ars.usda.gov
http://www.ars.usda.gov

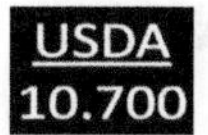

NATIONAL AGRICULTURAL LIBRARY

Award: Dissemination of Technical Information

Purpose: To provide agricultural information on products to agencies of the USDA, public organizations, and individuals.

Applicant Eligibility: Individuals, State and local governments, educational organizations, research societies, business and industry including those located in the U.S. Territories.

Beneficiary Eligibility: Same as Applicant Eligibility.

Award Range/Average: No Data Available.

Funding: (Cooperative Agreements) FY 17 $24,000,000; FY 18 est $24,000,000; FY 19 est $22,000,000; FY 16 $23,000,000; FY 15 $23,992,000; FY 14 $23,771,425

HQ: 5601 Sunnyside Avenue, P.O. Box 5110
Betsville, MD 20705
Phone: 301-504-1702
Email: kathleen.townson@ars.usda.gov
http://www.nal.usda.gov

ANIMAL AND PLANT HEALTH INSPECTION SERVICE

Central Region

3505 Boca Chica Boulevard, Suite 360, Brownsville, TX 78521-4065 956-504-4150

Dr. R. Harrington, Regional Director | 100 West Pioneer Parkway, Suite 100, Arlington, TX 76010 817-276-2201

Eastern Region

Gary E. Larson, Regional Director | 3322 West End Avenue, Suite 301, Nashville, TN 37203 615-736-2007

Jerry L. Fowler, Regional Director | Blason II, Second Floor 505 South Lenola Road, Moorestown, NJ 08057-1549 609-968-4970

Northern Region

Thomas Holt, Acting Regional Director | 1 Winner's Circle, Suite 100, Albany, NY 12205 518-453-0103

Southeastern Region

Harold McCoy, Assistant Regional Director | 500 E. Zack Street, Suite 410, Tampa, FL 33602-3945 813-228-2952

Jerry L. Fowler, Regional Director | 3505 25th Avenue Building 1, Gulfport, MS 39501

Western Region

James R. Reynolds, Regional Director | 9580 Micron Avenue, Suite I, Sacramento, CA 95827 916-857-6065

Michael Worthen, Regional Director | 12345 West Alameda Parkway, Suite 204, Lakewood, CO 80228

W.W. Buisch, Acting Regional Director | 384 Inverness Drive South, Suite 150, Englewood, CO 80112 303-784-6202

NATIONAL WILDLIFE RESEARCH CENTER

Richard Curnow
1201 Oakridge Drive, Ft. Collins, CO 80525

USDA 10.025 PLANT AND ANIMAL DISEASE, PEST CONTROL, AND ANIMAL CARE

Award: Project Grants

Purpose: To ensure the safety of U.S. agriculture including plants and animals.

Applicant Eligibility: Foreign, State, local, and U.S. Territorial government agencies, nonprofit institutions of higher education, and nonprofit associations or organizations requiring Federal support to eradicate, control, or assess the status of injurious plant and animal diseases and pests that are a threat to regional or national agriculture and conduct related demonstration projects.

Beneficiary Eligibility: Farmers, ranchers, agriculture producers, State, local, U.S. Territorial government agencies, public and private institutions and organizations benefit from Federal assistance to eradicate or control injurious plant and animal diseases and pests that are a threat to regional or national agriculture.

Award Range/Average: No Data Available.

Funding: (Salaries and Expenses) FY 17 $243,631,584; FY 18 est $256,467,514; FY 19 est $193,289,258; FY 16 $239,406,515

HQ: 4700 River Road, Unit 55
Riverdale, MD 20737
Phone: 301-851-2856
Email: eileen.m.berke@aphis.usda.gov
http://www.aphis.usda.gov

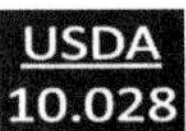

USDA 10.028 WILDLIFE SERVICES

Award: Project Grants

Purpose: To implement human methods to safeguard from zoonotic disease.

Applicant Eligibility: State and local governments, federally recognized Indian tribal governments, public/private nonprofit organizations, nonprofit institutions of higher education, and individuals.

Beneficiary Eligibility: States, local jurisdictions, U.S. Territorial government agencies, federally recognized Indian tribal governments, public and private institutions and organizations, farmers, ranchers, agricultural producers, and land/property owners benefit from Federal assistance in the control of nuisance mammals and birds and those mammal and bird species that are reservoirs for zoonotic diseases.

Award Range/Average: No Data Available.

Funding: (Salaries and Expenses) FY 17 $8,583,390; FY 18 est $8,755,058; FY 19 est $5,003,582;

HQ: 4700 River Road Unit 55, Suite 3B06 3
Riverdale, MD 20737
Phone: 301-851-2856
Email: eileen.m.berke@aphis.usda.gov
http://www.aphis.usda.gov

USDA 10.030 INDEMNITY PROGRAM

Award: Direct Payments with Unrestricted Use

Purpose: The animal and plant health inspection service provide compensation for the destroyed agriculture crops and cattle under the section 415 Plant Protection Act.

Applicant Eligibility: N/A

Beneficiary Eligibility: N/A

Award Range/Average: No Data Available.

Funding: (Direct Payments with Unrestricted Use) FY 17 $6,794,055; FY 18 est $5,988,018; FY 19 est $6,560,683; FY 16 $30,472,730

HQ: 100 N 6th Street, Suite 510C
Minneapolis, MN 55403
Phone: 612-336-3261
Email: donna.r.cichy@aphis.usda.gov

BUREAU OF INDIAN AFFAIRS AND BUREAU OF INDIAN EDUCATION

Alaska

1675 C Street, Anchorage, AK 99501 907-271-4115

1675 C Street, Suite 211, Anchorage, AK 99501-5198 907-271-4088

1675 C Street, Suite 279, Anchorage, AK 99501-5198 907-271-4086

P.O. Box 25520, Juneau, AK 99802-5520 907-586-7177

Arizona

10000 E. McDowell Road, Scottsdale, AZ 85256 602-640-2168

2800 Cottage Way, Sacramento, CA 95825 916-979-2560, Ext. 234

400 North 5th Street P.O. Box 10, Phoenix, AZ 85001 602-379-3944

Building 38, Blue Canyon Highway 110 P.O. Box 110, Fort Defiance, AZ 86504-0110 520-729-7251

Highway 160 and Warrior Drive Building 407 PO Box 746, Tuba City, AZ 86045 520-283-2218

Highway 264 P.O. Box 568, Keams Canyon, AZ 86034 520-738-2262

Highway 73 and Elm Street P.O. Box 920, White River, AZ 85941 520-338-5441

Navjo Route 7 P.O. Box 6003, Chinle, AZ 86503 520-674-5130, Ext. 201

P.O. Box 11000, Yuma, AZ 85366-1000 760-572-0248

P.O. Box 127, Tuba City, AZ 86045 520-283-2254, 2252

P.O. Box 158, Keams Canyon, AZ 86034 520-738-2228

P.O. Box 209, San Carlos, AZ 85550 520-475-2321

P.O. Box 37, Valentine, AZ 86437 520-769-2286

P.O. Box 560, Whiteriver, AZ 85941 520-338-5353

P.O. Box 578, Sells, AZ 85634 520-383-3286

P.O. Box 619, Fort Defiance, AZ 86504 520-729-7217, 7218

P.O. Box 7H, Chinle, AZ 86503 520-674-5100

P.O. Box 8, Sacaton, AZ 85247 520-562-3326

Route 1, Box 9-C, Parker, AZ 85344 520-669-7111

South Building #49 P.O. Box 38, Sells, AZ 85634 520-383-3292

Two Arizona Center, 12th Floor P.O. Box 10, MS-100, Phoenix, AZ 85001-0010 602-379-6600

California

1824 Tribute Road, Suite J, Sacramento, CA 95815 916-566-7121

1900 Churn Creek Road, Suite 300, Redding, CA 96002

2038 Iowa Avenue, Suite 101, Riverside, CA 92507-0001 909-276-6624

Federal Office Building 2800 Cottage Way, Sacramento, CA 95825-1846 916-979-2600

P.O. Box 2245 650 E. Tahquitz Canyon Way, Suite A, Palm Springs, CA 92262 760-416-2133

Programs Administered by Regional - State - Local Offices

Colorado

P.O. Box 315, Ignacio, CO 81137 970-563-4511

P.O. Box KK, Towaoc, CO 81334 970-565-8473
, Fairbanks, AK 99701-6270 907-456-0222

Eastern Region

1849 C Street N.W., MS-4140 MIB, Washington, DC 20240 202-208-5116

Metlakatla Field Office P.O. Box 450, Metlakatla, AK 99926 907-886-3791

Florida

6075 Sterling Road, Hollywood, FL 33024 954-356-7288

Idaho

P.O. Box 220, Fort Hall, ID 83203 208-238-2301

P.O. Box 408 850 A Street, Plummer, ID 83851 208-686-1887

P.O. Drawer 277, Lapwai, ID 83540 208-843-2300

Kansas

155 Indian Avenue #1305, Lawrence, KS 66046-4800 785-749-8404

155 Indian Avenue, Lawrence, KS 66046 785-749-8404

Michigan

2901.5 I-75 Business Spur Sault, Ste Marie, MI 49783 906-632-6809

P.O. Box 31, Horton, KS 66439 785-486-2161
, Red Lake, MN 56671 218-679-3361

Minnesota

331 South Second Avenue, Minneapolis, MN 55401-2241 612-373-1000, Ext. 1090

One Federal Drive, Room 550, St. Snelling, MN 55111 612-713-4400, Ext. 1020

Room 418, Federal Building 522 Minnesota Avenue, NW, Bemidji, MN 56601-3062 218-751-2011

Mississippi

421 Powell Street, Philadelphia, MS 39350 601-656-1522
, MT 59022 406-638-2672

Montana

316 North 26th Street, Billings, MT 59101-1397 406-247-7943

316 North 26th Street, Billings, MT 59101-1397 406-247-7953

Blackfeet Agency P.O. Box 880, Browning, MT 59417 406-338-7544

P.O. Box #1060, Gallup, NM 87305 505-863-8314

P.O. Box 40, Lame Deer, MT 59043 406-477-8242

P.O. Box 40, Pablo, MT 59855-5555 406-675-0242

P.O. Box 637, Poplar, MT 59255 406-768-5312

RR 1, Box 542, Box Elder, MT 59521 406-395-4476

RR 1, Box 980, Harlem, MT 59526 406-353-2901, Ext. 23

Nebraska

P.O. Box 18, Winnebago, NE 68071 402-878-2502

Nevada

1555 Shoshone Circle, Elko, NV 89801 775-738-0569

1677 Hot Springs Road, Carson City, NV 89706 775-887-3500

New Mexico

1 Main Street, Building 222 P.O. Box 328, Crownpoint, NM 87313

1000 Indian School Road NW P.O. Box 1667, Albuquerque, NM 87103 505-346-2431

1Mile North of Espanola Highway 68 P.O. Box 4269 Fairview Station, Espanola, NM 87533 505-753-1465

615 1st Street, N.W. P.O. Box 26567, Albuquerque, NM 87125-6567 505-346-7590

Highway 666N P.O. Box 3239, Shiprock, NM 87420-3239 505-368-4427, Ext. 360

P.O. Box 1448, Laguna, NH 87026 505-552-6001

P.O. Box 1667, Albuquerque, NM 87103 505-346-2424

P.O. Box 167, Dulce, NM 87528 505-759-3951

P.O. Box 189, Mescalero, NM 88340 505-671-4423

P.O. Box 328, Crownpoint, NM 87313 505-786-6100

P.O. Box 369, Zuni, NM 87327 505-782-5591

P.O. Box 4269 Fairview Station, Espanola, NM 87533 505-753-1400

P.O. Box 966, Shiprock, NM 87420 505-368-3300

Route 2, Box 14, Ramah, NM 87321 505-775-3235

New York

P.O. Box 7366, Syracuse, NY 13261-7366 315-448-0620
, Cherokee, NC 28719

North Carolina

North Dakota

4149 Highline Boulevard, Suite 380, Oklahoma City, OK 73108 605-945-6051, Ext. 301

9169 Coors Road NW P.O. Box 10146-9196, Albuquerque, NM 87184 505-346-2343

Main Street off Highway 106 Agency Avenue PO Box E, Fort Yates, ND 58538 701-854-3497

P.O. Box 270, Fort Totten, ND 58335 701-766-4545

P.O. Box 370, New Town, ND 58763 701-627-4707

P.O. Box 60, Belcourt, ND 58316 701-477-3191

P.O. Box E, Fort Yates, ND 58538 701-854-3433

PO Box 30, Belcourt, ND 58316 701-477-6471, Ext. 211

Oklahoma

1500 N. Country Club Road P.O. Box 2240, Ada, OK 74821 580-436-0784

624 West Independence, Suite 114, Shawnee, OK 74801 405-273-0317

Bureau of Indian Affairs 101 North 5th Street, Muskogee, OK 74401-6206 918-687-2295

Drawer H, Talihina, OK 74571 918-567-2207

P.O. Box 1060, Wewoka, OK 74884 405-257-6259

P.O. Box 1539, Pawhuska, OK 74056 918-287-1032

P.O. Box 309, Anadarko, OK 73005 405-247-6677

P.O. Box 368, Anadarko, OK 73005-0368 405-247-6673, Ext. 257

P.O. Box 370, Okmulgee, OK 74447 918-756-3950

P.O. Box 391, Miami, OK 74355 918-542-3396

P.O. Box 440, Pawnee, OK 74058-0440 918-762-2585

P.O. Box 569, Siletz, OR 97380 541-444-2679

P.O. Box 68, El Reno, OK 73036-0068 405-262-7481

Oregon

911 N.E. 11th Avenue, Portland, OR 97232-4169 503-231-6702

911 North East 11 Avenue, Portland, OR 97232-4169 503-872-2743

P.O. Box 1239, Warm Springs, OR 97761

P.O. Box 520, Pendleton, OR 97801 541-278-3786

South Dakota

100 North Main P.O. Box 2020, Eagle Butte, SD 51625 605-964-8722

1001 Avenue D P.O. Box 669, Mission, SD 57555 605-856-4478, Ext. 261

101 Main Street P.O. Box 333, Pine Ridge, SD 57770 605-867-1306

140 Education Avenue P.O. Box 139, Fort Thompson, SD 57339 605-245-2398

Bureau of Indian Affairs 115 4th Avenue, SE, Aberdeen, SD 57401-4382 605-226-7343

P.O. Box 1203, Pine Ridge, SD 57770 605-867-5125

P.O. Box 139, Ft. Thompson, SD 57339 605-245-2311

P.O. Box 190, Lower Brule, SD 57548 605-473-5512

P.O. Box 325, Eagle Butte, SD 57625 605-964-6611

P.O. Box 550, Rosebud, SD 57570 605-747-2224

P.O. Box 577, Wagner, SD 57380 605-384-3651

P.O. Box 688, Agency Village, SD 57262 605-698-3001

Utah

P.O. Box 130, Fort Duchesne, UT 84026 435-722-4300

P.O. Box 720, St. George, UT 84771 435-674-9720

Virginia

3701 North Fairfax Drive Suite 260, Arlington, VA 22203 703-235-3006

3701 North Fairfax Drive, Suite 260, Arlington, VA 22203 703-235-3233

Washington

2707 Colby Avenue, Suite 1101, Everett, WA 98201 425-258-2651

P.O. Box 111, Nespelem, WA 99155-0111 509-634-2316

P.O. Box 115, Neah Bay, WA 98357 360-645-3232

P.O. Box 151 (Tribal) P.O. Box 632 (BIA), Toppenish, WA 98948 509-865-5121

P.O. Box 389, Wellpinit, WA 99040 509-258-4561

P.O. Box 48, Aberdeen, WA 98520 360-533-9100

Wisconsin

615 Main Street, West P.O. Box 273, Ashland, WI 54806-0273

Wyoming

Cross-references denote which area or offices provide services to eligible Indians within the State.

P.O. Box 158, Fort Washakie, WY 82514 307-332-7810

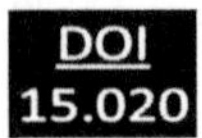

AID TO TRIBAL GOVERNMENTS

Award: Direct Payments for Specified Use

Purpose: To provide funds to Indian tribal governments to support general tribal government operations; to maintain up-to-date tribal registration; to conduct tribal elections; and to develop appropriate tribal policies, legislation, and regulations.

Applicant Eligibility: Federally Recognized Indian Tribal Governments.

Beneficiary Eligibility: Federally Recognized Indian Tribal Governments and members of American Indian Tribes.

Award Range/Average: Range is $10,000 to $700,000; average $80,000.

Funding: FY 16 FY 17 FY 18.

HQ: Sovereignty in Indian Education Program 1849 C Street NW, P.O. Box MIB-3610
Washington, DC 20240
Phone: 202-208-6123
Email: juanita.mendoza@bie.edu
http://www.bia.gov

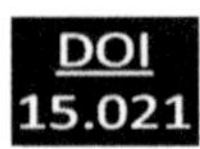

CONSOLIDATED TRIBAL GOVERNMENT

Award: Direct Payments for Specified Use

Purpose: To promote Indian self-determination and improve the quality of life in Tribal communities by providing greater flexibility in planning programs and meeting the needs of communities.

Applicant Eligibility: Federally Recognized Indian Tribal Governments.

Beneficiary Eligibility: Federally Recognized Indian Tribal Governments and members of American Indian Tribes.

Award Range/Average: The range is $1,300 to $2,400,000; average $500,000.

Funding: (Direct Payments for Specified Use) FY 17 FY 16 FY 18

HQ: 1849 C Street NW, P.O. Box 4657-MIB
Washington, DC 20240
Phone: 202-208-3559
Email: juanita.mendoza@bie.edu
http://www.bia.gov

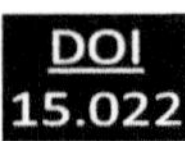

TRIBAL SELF-GOVERNANCE

Award: Direct Payments for Specified Use

Purpose: To promote Indian self-determination by providing funds to administer a wide range of programs with broad administrative and programmatic flexibility.

Applicant Eligibility: Federally Recognized Indian Tribal Governments and tribal consortia authorized by the Federally Recognized Indian Tribal Governments to be served.

Beneficiary Eligibility: Federally Recognized Indian Tribal Governments and their Members.

Award Range/Average: $9,705 to $27,537,488; Average $434,655.

Funding: (Direct Payments for Specified Use) FY 16 FY 18 FY 17

HQ: 1849 C Street NW Bureau of Indian Education, P.O. Box 4657-MIB
Washington, DC 20240
Phone: 202-208-3559
Email: juanita.mendoza@bie.edu
http://www.doi.gov/bureau-indian-affairs.html

INDIAN SELF-DETERMINATION CONTRACT SUPPORT "Contract Support"

Award: Direct Payments for Specified Use

Purpose: To provide funds to Federally-recognized Indian Tribal Governments and to tribal organizations to fund the indirect costs incurred in administering Federal programs.

Applicant Eligibility: Federally Recognized Indian Tribal Governments and tribal organizations authorized by Indian Tribal Governments.

Beneficiary Eligibility: Federally Recognized Indian Tribal Governments.

Award Range/Average: The range is $10,000 to $8,000,000; average $190,000.

Funding: (Direct Payments for Specified Use) FY 16 FY 18 FY 17

HQ: 1849 C Street NW, P.O. Box 4657-MIB
Washington, DC 20240
Phone: 202-208-3559
Email: juanita.mendoza@bie.edu

SERVICES TO INDIAN CHILDREN, ELDERLY AND FAMILIES "Social Services"

Award: Direct Payments for Specified Use

Purpose: To provide funds to Federally-recognized Indian Tribal Governments to administer welfare assistance programs for American Indians; to support caseworkers and counselors; and to support tribal programs to reduce the incidence of substance abuse and alcohol abuse in Indian country.

Applicant Eligibility: Federally Recognized Indian Tribal Governments.

Beneficiary Eligibility: Federally Recognized Indian Tribal Governments, adult American Indians in need of financial assistance or social services counseling, American Indian children who require foster care services, and American Indian youth requiring temporary, emergency shelter.

Award Range/Average: The range is $10,000 to $4,800,000; average $100,000.

Funding: N/A

HQ: 1849 C Street NW, P.O. Box 4657-MIB

Washington, DC 20240
Phone: 202-208-3559
Email: juanita.mendoza@bie.edu
http://www.bia.gov

INDIAN ADULT EDUCATION

Award: Direct Payments for Specified Use

Purpose: To improve the educational opportunities for Indian adults who lack the level of literacy skills necessary for effective citizenship and productive employment, and to encourage the formation of adult education programs.

Applicant Eligibility: Federally Recognized Indian Tribal Governments.

Beneficiary Eligibility: Federally Recognized Indian Tribal Governments and members of American Indian Tribes.

Award Range/Average: Range is $100 to $297,000; Average $35,900.

Funding: N/A

HQ: 1849 C Street
Washington, DC 20240
Phone: 202-208-5810
Email: james.martin@bie.edu
http://www.bie.gov

ASSISTANCE TO TRIBALLY CONTROLLED COMMUNITY COLLEGES AND UNIVERSITIES

Award: Project Grants

Purpose: To provide funds for the operation and improvement of Tribal Colleges and Universities (TCUs) to insure continued and expanded educational opportunities for Indian students, and to allow for the improvement and expansion of their physical resources.

Applicant Eligibility: Colleges chartered by Federally Recognized Indian Tribes or tribal organizations which are governed by a board of directors, are in operation more than one year, admit students with a certificate of graduation from a secondary institution or equivalent, provide certificates, associate, baccalaureate and graduate degrees, are nonprofit and nonsectarian, and are accredited by a nationally recognized agency or association.

Beneficiary Eligibility: Indian students who are a member of or are at least a one-fourth degree Indian blood descendant of a member of an Indian tribe which is eligible for the special programs and services provided by the United States through the Bureau of Indian Affairs to Indians because of their status as Indians.

Award Range/Average: FY 2015: Range is $273,790 to $13,598,820; Average $2,467,250. The amount of the award is determined by the number of eligible Indian students enrolled in the college. Indian Tribes may choose to supplement the funding provided by the grant program by identifying additional amounts in the Tribal Priority Allocations portion of the Bureau of Indian Affairs budget.

Funding: FY 18 FY 17 FY 16 est $68,084,000.

HQ: 1849 C Street NW Bureau of Indian Education, P.O. Box 4657-MIB
Washington, DC 20240
Phone: 202-208-3559
Email: juanita.mendoza@bie.edu
http://www.bie.edu

TRIBALLY CONTROLLED COMMUNITY COLLEGE ENDOWMENTS

Award: Project Grants

Purpose: To provide funds to establish endowments for the Tribally Controlled Community Colleges and Universities.

Applicant Eligibility: Colleges chartered by Federally Recognized Indian Tribes which are governed by an Indian board of directors, are in operation more than one year, admit students with a certificate of graduation from a secondary institution or equivalent, provide certificates, associate, baccalaureate and graduate degrees, are nonprofit and nonsectarian, and are accredited by a nationally recognized agency or association.

Beneficiary Eligibility: Indian students who are a member of or are at least a one-fourth degree Indian blood descendant of a member of an Indian tribe which is eligible for the special programs and services provided by the United States through the Bureau of Indian Affairs to Indians because of their status as Indians.

Award Range/Average: Range is $0 to $5,700; Average $5,700

Funding: (Project Grants) FY 17 FY 16 est $109,000; FY 18

HQ: 1849 C Street NW
Washington, DC 20240
Phone: 202-208-3559
Email: juanita.mendoza@bie.edu
http://www.bie.edu

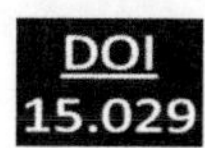

TRIBAL COURTS

Award: Direct Payments for Specified Use

Purpose: To provide grants to Federally-recognized Indian Tribal Governments to operate a judicial branch of government.

Applicant Eligibility: Federally Recognized Indian Tribal Governments exercising law enforcement jurisdiction on their reservation.

Beneficiary Eligibility: Federally Recognized Indian Tribal Governments.

Award Range/Average: The range is $15,000 to $800,000; average $50,000.

Funding: (Direct Payments for Specified Use) FY 17 FY 18 FY 16 FY 15 FY 14 est $23,241,000

HQ: 1849 C Street NW Bureau of Indian Education, P.O. Box 4657-MIB
Washington, DC 20240

Phone: 202-208-3559
Email: juanita.mendoza@bie.edu
http://www.bia.gov

DOI 15.030 INDIAN LAW ENFORCEMENT
"Law Enforcement"

Award: Direct Payments for Specified Use

Purpose: To provide grants to Indian Tribal Governments to operate police departments and detention facilities.

Applicant Eligibility: Federally Recognized Indian Tribal Governments exercising Federal criminal law enforcement authority over crimes under the Major Crimes Act (18 U.S.C. 1153) and other Federal statutes on their reservations and operating a Law Enforcement Services program.

Beneficiary Eligibility: Federally Recognized Indian Tribal Governments.

Award Range/Average: The range is $20,000 to $20,000,000; average $200,000.

Funding: N/A

HQ: 1849 C Street NW, P.O. Box 4657-MIB
Washington, DC 20240
Phone: 202-208-3559
Email: juanita.mendoza@bie.edu

DOI 15.031 INDIAN COMMUNITY FIRE PROTECTION
"Community Fire Protection"

Award: Direct Payments for Specified Use

Purpose: To provide grants to perform fire protection services for Indian Tribal Governments that do not receive fire protection support from State or local government.

Applicant Eligibility: Federally Recognized Indian Tribal Governments performing fire protection services on their reservation.

Beneficiary Eligibility: Federally Recognized Indian Tribal Governments.

Award Range/Average: $200 to $138,000; $10,000.

Funding: N/A

HQ: 1849 C Street NW, P.O. Box 4657-MIB
Washington, DC 20240
Phone: 202-208-3559
Email: juanita.mendoza@bie.edu
http://www.bia.gov

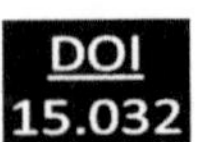

DOI 15.032 INDIAN ECONOMIC DEVELOPMENT

Award: Direct Payments for Specified Use

Purpose: To aid Federally Recognized Indian Tribal Governments by catering the resources necessary to develop a self-sustaining economic base. The program provides opportunities for business development, the coordination and integration of programs through out the Federal government, and the partnering of Federally Recognized Indian Tribal Governments with local government and the public and private business sector.

Applicant Eligibility: Federally Recognized Indian Tribal Governments.

Beneficiary Eligibility: Federally Recognized Indian Tribal Governments and their members.

Award Range/Average: $5,000 to $300,000; $215,000.

Funding: (Direct Payments for Specified Use) FY 17 FY 18 FY 16

HQ: 1849 C Street NW, P.O. Box 4657-MIB
Washington, DC 20240
Phone: 202-208-3559
Email: juanita.mendoza@bie.edu

DOI 15.033 ROAD MAINTENANCE INDIAN ROADS

Award: Direct Payments for Specified Use

Purpose: To issue limited routine and preventive maintenance on BIA transportation facilities as described below: (1) BIA road systems and related road appurtenances such as signs, traffic signals, pavement striping, trail markers, guardrails, etc.; (2) Highway bridges and drainage structures; (3) Airport runways and heliport pads, including runway lighting; (4) Boardwalks; (5) Adjacent parking areas; (6) Maintenance yards; (7) Bus stations; (8) System public pedestrian walkways, paths, bike and other trails; (9) Motorized vehicle trails; (10) Public access roads to heliports and airports; (11) BIA and tribal post-secondary school roads and parking lots built with IRR Program funds; and (12) Public ferry boats and boat ramps.

Applicant Eligibility: Federally Recognized Indian Tribal Governments with BIA transportation facilities qualifying for this program.

Beneficiary Eligibility: Federally Recognized Indian Tribal Governments; individual tribal members and the public that use the BIA transportation system on Indian Reservation and lands.

Award Range/Average: No Data Available.

Funding: (Direct Payments for Specified Use) FY 18 FY 17 FY 16

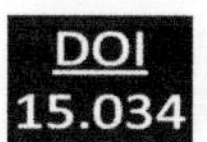

HQ: 1849 C Street NW, P.O. Box 4657-MIB
Washington, DC 20240
Phone: 202-208-3559
Email: juanita.mendoza@bie.edu

DOI 15.034 AGRICULTURE ON INDIAN LANDS

Award: Direct Payments for Specified Use; Provision of Specialized Services; Advisory Services and Counseling

Purpose: To safeguard and restore the agricultural (cropland and rangeland) resources on trust lands and ease the development of renewable agricultural resources.

Applicant Eligibility: Native American individuals, tribal governments and native organizations authorized by tribal governments, and individuals and entities authorized to make use of Indian agricultural lands and resources.

Beneficiary Eligibility: Native American landowners, Indian tribes and their members, native organizations authorized by tribal governments, and individuals and entities authorized to make use of Indian agricultural lands and resources. Agricultural grant programs (Rangeland Inventory and Noxious Weed Control) are not currently available to individuals or to non-tribal land-user entities.

Award Range/Average: Agriculture: $200 to $575,000; $50,000. Noxious Weed Eradication: $500 to $300,000; $6,200.

Funding: (Direct Payments for Specified Use) FY 16 FY 18 FY 17

HQ: 1849 C Street NW, P.O. Box 4657-MIB
Washington, DC 20240
Phone: 202-208-3559
Email: juanita.mendoza@bie.edu

FORESTRY ON INDIAN LANDS

Award: Direct Payments for Specified Use; Provision of Specialized Services; Advisory Services and Counseling

Purpose: To preserve, protect, strengthen, and develop Indian forest resources through the execution of forest management activities.

Applicant Eligibility: Federally Recognized Indian Tribal Governments and Native American Organizations authorized by Indian tribal governments.

Beneficiary Eligibility: Federally Recognized Indian Tribal Governments and their members and Native American Organizations.

Award Range/Average: Range is $10,000 to $1,000,000: Average $100,000.

Funding: (Direct Payments for Specified Use) FY 16 FY 18 FY 17

HQ: Office of Trust Services Division of Forestry and Wildland Fire Management 1849 C Street NW, P.O. Box 4513 MIB
Washington, DC 20240
Phone: 202-208-4620
Email: bill_downes@bia.gov

INDIAN RIGHTS PROTECTION

Award: Direct Payments for Specified Use

Purpose: To secure Indian rights guaranteed through treaty or statute by acquiring the services or information needed to litigate challenges to these rights.

Applicant Eligibility: Federally Recognized Indian Tribal Governments and Native American Organizations authorized by Indian tribal governments.

Beneficiary Eligibility: Federally Recognized Indian Tribal Governments and their members.

Award Range/Average: Range is $1,000 to $100,000; Average $25,000.

Funding: N/A

HQ: 1849 C Street NW, P.O. Box 4657-MIB
Washington, DC 20240
Phone: 202-208-3559
Email: juanita.mendoza@bie.edu

DOI 15.037 WATER RESOURCES ON INDIAN LANDS

Award: Direct Payments for Specified Use; Provision of Specialized Services; Advisory Services and Counseling

Purpose: To assist Indian tribes in the effective and efficient management, planning, and use of their water resources.

Applicant Eligibility: Federally Recognized Indian Tribal Governments and Native American Organizations authorized by Indian tribal governments.

Beneficiary Eligibility: Same as Applicant Eligibility.

Award Range/Average: The range is $10,000 to $200,000.

Funding: (Direct Payments for Specified Use) FY 17 FY 16 FY 18

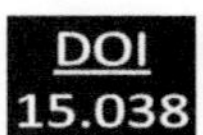

HQ: 1849 C Street NW
Washington, DC 20240
Phone: 202-083-5590
Email: juanita.mendoza@bie.edu

DOI 15.038 MINERALS AND MINING ON INDIAN LANDS

Award: Direct Payments for Specified Use; Provision of Specialized Services; Dissemination of Technical Information

Purpose: The key aspect of the Energy and Mineral Development Program are to provide funds to Tribes to perform technical evaluations of the energy (both renewable and conventional) and mineral resource potential of Indian reservations and provide Tribes with geological, geophysical and engineering reports, maps, and other data concerning their energy and mineral resources; and technical assistance on using and interpreting assessment information so that Tribes can understand and plan for the potential development of these resources; and with an outreach vehicle to promote their lands and resources to potential partners if they so desire. Those projects that fell into economic development categories will be considered for funding through the Office of Indian Energy and Economic Development.

Applicant Eligibility: Federally Recognized Indian Tribes and Individual American Indian mineral owners.

Beneficiary Eligibility: Federally Recognized Indian Tribal Governments and their members, Native American Organizations, and/or individual American Indian mineral property owners.

Award Range/Average: Minerals and Mining: Currently not contracted by any of the tribal governments. Mineral Assessments range is $10,000 to $250,000; average $75,000.

Funding: N/A

HQ: 1849 C Street NW Bureau of Indian Education, P.O. Box 4657-MIB
Washington, DC 20240
Phone: 202-208-3559
Email: juanita.mendoza@bie.edu
http://www.doi.gov/whoweare/as-ia/ieed

REAL ESTATE PROGRAMS INDIAN LANDS

Award: Direct Payments for Specified Use

Purpose: To render real property management, counseling, and land use planning services to individual Indian allottees and Indian tribal and Alaska Native entities who own an interest in almost 56 million acres of trust land; to provide real estate appraisal services required in processing land transactions, and to safeguard and enhance the Indian leasehold estate by providing individual Indian landowners and Indian tribes with lease compliance activities.

Applicant Eligibility: Federally Recognized Indian Tribal Governments, Native American Organizations authorized by tribes, and individual American Indians.

Beneficiary Eligibility: Federally Recognized Indian Tribal Governments and their members.

Award Range/Average: For Real Estate Services, tribal award amounts vary from approximately $1,000 to $500,000. For Real Estate Appraisals, the cost of most appraisals is less than $500 but can range up to approximately $2,500 or more for large or complex properties; the average is $1000. Lease Compliance awards range from $250 to $30,000 with most awards less than $5,000.

Funding: (Direct Payments for Specified Use) FY 16 FY 18 FY 17

HQ: 1849 C Street NW
Washington, DC 20240
Phone: 202-208-3559
Email: juanita.mendoza@bie.edu

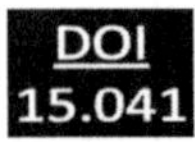

ENVIRONMENTAL MANAGEMENT INDIAN

Award: Direct Payments for Specified Use

Purpose: To calculate environmental impacts of Federal projects on Indian lands; to conduct surveys of Bureau of Indian Affairs controlled Federal lands and facilities, and of Indian lands, in order to recognize hazardous waste sites, evaluate the potential threat to health and the environment, and develop the necessary remedial actions; to train area, agency and tribal staff in waste management principles; and to respond to emergencies and alleviate adverse health or environmental impacts.

Applicant Eligibility: Federally Recognized Indian Tribal Governments and Native American Organizations authorized by the Tribes.

Beneficiary Eligibility: Federally Recognized Indian tribes.

Award Range/Average: Range is $5,000 to $250,000; Average $25,000.

Funding: (Direct Payments for Specified Use) FY 18 FY 17 FY 16

HQ: 1849 C Street NW Bureau of Indian Education, P.O. Box 4657-MIB
Washington, DC 20240
Phone: 202-208-3559
Email: juanita.mendoza@bie.edu
http://www.doi.gov/bureau-indian-affairs.html

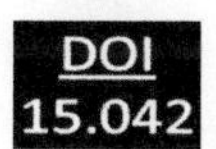

INDIAN SCHOOL EQUALIZATION "ISEP"

Award: Direct Payments for Specified Use

Purpose: To allocate funding for primary and secondary education.

Applicant Eligibility: Federally Recognized Indian Tribes or tribal organizations currently served by a Bureau of Indian Education funded school.

Beneficiary Eligibility: Children between the ages of 5 and 21 who are a member of or are at least a one-fourth degree Indian blood descendant of a member of an Indian tribe which is eligible for the special programs and services provided by the United States through the Bureau of Indian Affairs to Indians because of their status as Indians.

Award Range/Average: $161,000 to $8,930,300. Average $2,007,600

Funding: (Direct Payments for Specified Use) FY 17 FY 16 est $391,857,000; FY 18 - FY 16 est. $391,857,000/$240,908,000

HQ: 1849 C Street NW, P.O. Box 4657-MIB
Washington, DC 20240
Phone: 202-208-7658
Email: joe.herrin@bie.edu
http://www.bie.edu

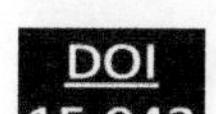

INDIAN CHILD AND FAMILY EDUCATION "FACE"

Award: Project Grants; Training

Purpose: The Family And Child Education (FACE) program is aimed to serve families with children from prenatal to age five in home and center-based settings. Families may receive services in one or both settings. The program provides early childhood for all children from birth to age five and adult education for their parents through family literacy, parental involvement, increasing school readiness, high school graduation rates among Indian parents, and encouraging life-long learning.

Applicant Eligibility: Federally Recognized Indian Tribal Governments and tribal organizations authorized by Indian tribal governments on reservations with Bureau of Indian Education funded elementary schools may apply to administer the program.

Beneficiary Eligibility: Parents and their Indian children under 5 years of age who live on a reservation with a Bureau-funded school.

Award Range/Average: Each site receives approximately $289,910.

Funding: (Project Grants) FY 17 FY 18 FY 16 est $8,177,500; - (Appropriations/Project Grants) FY 16 est. $15,520,000/$8,177,500.

HQ: Division of Performance and Accountability BIA Building 2 1011 Indian School Road NW, 3rd Floor
Albuquerque, NM 87104
Phone: 505-563-5260
Email: jeffrey.hamley@bie.edu
http://www.bie.edu

INDIAN SCHOOLS STUDENT TRANSPORTATION "Student Transportation"

Award: Direct Payments for Specified Use

Purpose: To assign funds to each Bureau of Indian Education (BIE) funded school for the round trip transportation of students between home and the school site.

Applicant Eligibility: Federally Recognized Indian Tribes or tribal organizations currently served by a BIE-funded school.

Beneficiary Eligibility: Children between the ages of 5 and 21 who are members of or are at least a one-fourth degree Indian blood descendant of a member of an Indian tribe which is eligible for the special programs and services provided by the United States through the Bureau of Indian Affairs to Indians because of their status as Indians.

Award Range/Average: Range is $2,870 to $1,630,820; Average $328,061.

Funding: (Direct Payments for Specified Use) FY 18 FY 16 est $53,145,000; FY 17

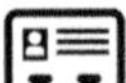

HQ: 1849 C Street NW, P.O. Box 4657-MIB
Washington, DC 20240
Phone: 202-208-7658
Email: joe.herrin@bie.edu
http://www.bie.edu

ADMINISTRATIVE COST GRANTS FOR INDIAN SCHOOLS

Award: Project Grants

Purpose: To allocate grants to tribes and tribal organizations operating schools for the purpose of paying administrative and indirect costs.

Applicant Eligibility: Federally Recognized Indian Tribal Governments or Tribal Organizations operating a Bureau of Indian Education funded school.

Beneficiary Eligibility: Indian Tribal Governments or tribal organizations operating a Bureau funded elementary or secondary school under a Public Law 100.297 grant or Public Law 93-638 Self-determination Contract with the Bureau of Indian Education.

Award Range/Average: Range is $127,600 to $1,166,200; Average $405,967.

Funding: FY 17 FY 16 est $75,335,000.

HQ: Department of the Interior 1849 C Street NW, P.O. Box 3609-MIB
Washington, DC 20240
Phone: 202-208-6123
Email: joe.herrin@bie.edu
http://bie.edu

DOI 15.047 INDIAN EDUCATION FACILITIES, OPERATIONS, AND MAINTENANCE

Award: Direct Payments for Specified Use

Purpose: To allocate funds to BIE funded elementary schools, secondary schools and peripheral dormitories for facilities operations and maintenance.

Applicant Eligibility: Federally Recognized Indian Tribal Governments or tribal organizations currently served by a Bureau of Indian Education (BIE) funded elementary school, secondary school or peripheral dormitory.

Beneficiary Eligibility: Federally Recognized Indian Tribal Governments and occupants and visitors of BIE funded elementary or secondary schools or peripheral dormitories.

Award Range/Average: $58,374 to $2,385,121; Average $533,888

Funding: (Direct Payments for Specified Use) FY 18 FY 16 est $124,985,000; FY 17 - Direct Payments for Specified Use - Appropriation/Grant) FY 16 est. $124,985,000/S74,991,000 FY 2014 Operations $55,668,000/;32,856,345 Maintenance $48,396,000/26,272,194; FY 2015 est. Operations $55,865,000/33,591,000;Maintenance $48,591,000/29,754,000; FY 2016 est. Operations $66.0980/$39,659,000;Maintenance $58,887,000/$35,332,000

HQ: 1849 C Street NW
Washington, DC 20240
Phone: 202-208-7658
Email: joe.herrin@bie.edu
http://www.bie.edu

DOI 15.048 BUREAU OF INDIAN AFFAIRS FACILITIES OPERATIONS AND MAINTENANCE

Award: Direct Payments for Specified Use

Purpose: To assign funds for basic operating services to Bureau-owned or Bureau-operated non-education facilities and to maintain these facilities in a safe operating condition for the conduct of Bureau programs.

Applicant Eligibility: Federally Recognized Indian Tribal Governments who have Bureau-owned or Bureau-operated facilities on their reservation.

Beneficiary Eligibility: Same as Applicant Eligibility.

Award Range/Average: N/A.

Funding: N/A

HQ: 1849 C Street NW Bureau of Indian Education, P.O. Box 4657-MIB
Washington, DC 20240

Phone: 202-208-3559

Email: juanita.mendoza@bie.edu

http://www.indianaffairs.gov/as-ia/ofpsm/dfmc/om

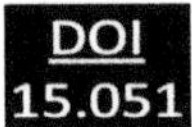

ENDANGERED SPECIES ON INDIAN LANDS

Award: Direct Payments for Specified Use; Advisory Services and Counseling; Dissemination of Technical Information

Purpose: To adhere with the Endangered Species Act, the Northern Spotted Owl Recovery plan, and to carry out the Endangered Species Recovery on Indian lands.

Applicant Eligibility: Federally Recognized Indian Tribal Governments and Native American Organizations authorized by Indian tribal governments whose reservations are in areas inhabited by these specific endangered species.

Beneficiary Eligibility: Same as Applicant Eligibility.

Award Range/Average: Range is $20,000 to $140,000; Average $50,000.

Funding: (Direct Payments for Specified Use) FY 16 FY 17 FY 18

HQ: 1849 C Street NW, P.O. Box 4657-MIB
Washington, DC 20240
Phone: 202-208-3559
Email: juanita.mendoza@bie.edu

LITIGATION SUPPORT FOR INDIAN RIGHTS

Award: Direct Payments for Specified Use

Purpose: To implement or safeguard the Indian property or treaty rights through judicial, administrative, or settlement actions.

Applicant Eligibility: Federally Recognized Indian Tribal Governments and Native American Organizations authorized by these Tribes.

Beneficiary Eligibility: Federally Recognized Indian Tribes and their members.

Award Range/Average: Funding range and average is not available. Approximately 30 funding requests are received on an annual basis; between 20 and 25 are funded each year.

Funding: N/A

HQ: 1849 C Street NW, P.O. Box 4657-MIB
Washington, DC 20240
Phone: 202-208-3559
Email: juanita.mendoza@bie.edu

ATTORNEY FEES INDIAN RIGHTS

Award: Direct Payments for Specified Use

Purpose: To help or aid Federally Recognized Tribes in protecting their treaty rights and other rights established through Executive Order or court action.

Applicant Eligibility: Federally Recognized Indian Tribal Governments.

Beneficiary Eligibility: Federally Recognized Indian Tribes and their members.

Award Range/Average: Information not available.

Funding: FY 17 FY 16 FY 18.

HQ: 1849 C Street NW Bureau of Indian Education, P.O. Box 4657-MIB
Washington, DC 20240
Phone: 202-208-3559
Email: juanita.mendoza@bie.edu

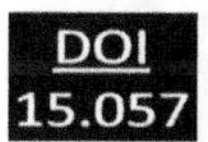

NAVAJO-HOPI INDIAN SETTLEMENT

Award: Direct Payments for Specified Use; Provision of Specialized Services

Purpose: To carry out those provisions of the Navajo-Hopi Settlement Act of 1974, as amended, which are allocated to the Department of the Interior; and to introduce conservation practices and methods to restore the grazing potential of rangelands lying within the former Navajo/Hopi Joint Use Area.

Applicant Eligibility: Federally Recognized Indian Tribal Governments of the Navajo and Hopi Tribes and Native American Organizations authorized by either Tribe.

Beneficiary Eligibility: Same as Applicant Eligibility.

Award Range/Average: No Data Available.

Funding: (Direct Payments for Specified Use) FY 17 FY 18 FY 16

HQ: 1849 C Street NW, P.O. Box 4657-MIB
Washington, DC 20240
Phone: 202-208-3559
Email: juanita.mendoza@bie.edu
http://www.doi.gov/bureau-indian-affairs.html

INDIAN POST SECONDARY SCHOOLS "Haskell Indian Nations University (Haskell) and Southwestern Indian Polytechnic Institute (SIPI)"

Award: Training

Purpose: To arrange or layout postsecondary educational opportunities for American Indian Students.

Applicant Eligibility: American Indians and Alaskan Natives.

Beneficiary Eligibility: Same as Applicant Eligibility.

Award Range/Average: Not identifiable.

Funding: (Training) FY 16 est $19,900,000; FY 17 FY 18

HQ: 1849 C Street NW, P.O. Box 4657-MIB
Washington, DC 20240
Phone: 202-208-3559
Email: juanita.mendoza@bie.edu

INDIAN GRADUATE STUDENT SCHOLARSHIPS "Special Higher Education Scholarships"

DOI 15.059

Award: Project Grants

Purpose: To assign financial aid to eligible Indian students to enable them to obtain advanced degrees.

Applicant Eligibility: Individual applicants must be Indian students who are members of Federally Recognized Indian Tribes, who have been admitted to a graduate program and have unmet financial need.

Beneficiary Eligibility: Members of Federally Recognized Indian Tribes who are a member of or are at least one-fourth degree Indian blood descendant of a member of an Indian tribe which is eligible for the special programs and services provided by the United States through the Bureau of Indian Affairs to Indians because of their status as Indians.

Award Range/Average: Range is $250 to $4,000; Average $3,947.

Funding: (Project Grants) FY 16 est $2,992,000; FY 18 FY 17

HQ: 1849 C Street NW, P.O. Box 4657-MIB
Washington, DC 20240
Phone: 202-208-3559
Email: juanita.mendoza@bie.edu

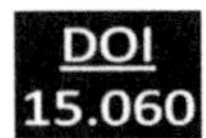

INDIAN VOCATIONAL TRAINING UNITED TRIBES TECHNICAL COLLEGE

DOI 15.060

Award: Direct Payments with Unrestricted Use; Training

Purpose: To render vocational training to individual American Indians through the United Tribes Technical College, located in Bismarck, North Dakota.

Applicant Eligibility: Application to administer the program is limited to the United Tribes Technical College. Individual American Indian applicants must be a member of a Federally Recognized Indian Tribe, be in need of financial assistance, and reside on or near an Indian reservation under the jurisdiction of the Bureau of Indian Affairs.

Beneficiary Eligibility: Individual American Indians who are members of a Federally Recognized Indian Tribe and reside on or near an Indian reservation under the jurisdiction of the Bureau of Indian Affairs.

Award Range/Average: Range is between $500 to $3,000; Average $2,500.

Funding: N/A

HQ: 1849 C Street NW, P.O. Box 4657-MIB
Washington, DC 20240

Phone: 202-208-3559

Email: juanita.mendoza@bie.edu

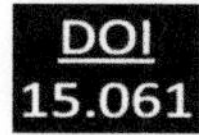

INDIAN JOB PLACEMENT UNITED SIOUX TRIBES DEVELOPMENT CORPORATION "United Sioux Tribes"

Award: Direct Payments with Unrestricted Use; Advisory Services and Counseling

Purpose: To render job development, counseling, social adjustment guidance, and referrals to job training programs and other assistance programs through the United Sioux Tribes Development Corporation, located in Pierre, South Dakota.

Applicant Eligibility: Application to administer the program is limited to the United Sioux Tribes Development Corporation. Individual American Indian applicants must be a member of a Federally Recognized Indian Tribe, be in need of financial assistance, and reside on or near an Indian reservation under the jurisdiction of the Bureau of Indian Affairs.

Beneficiary Eligibility: Must be an American Indian member of a Federally Recognized Indian Tribe and reside on or near an Indian reservation under the jurisdiction of the Bureau of Indian Affairs.

Award Range/Average: No Data Available.

Funding: N/A

HQ: 1849 C Street NW, P.O. Box 4657-MIB

Washington, DC 20240

Phone: 202-208-3559

Email: juanita.mendoza@bie.edu

REPLACEMENT AND REPAIR OF INDIAN SCHOOLS

Award: Direct Payments for Specified Use

Purpose: To provide safe, functional, code-compliant, economical, and energy efficient education facilities for American Indian students attending Bureau of Indian Affairs owned or funded primary and secondary schools and/or residing in Bureau owned or funded dormitories. Additional objectives for ARRA funded projects comprises of having a demonstrated or potential ability to deliver programmatic results, optimizing economic activity and the number of jobs created or saved, obtaining long-term public benefits from improved school infrastructure, fostering energy independence or improving educational quality.

Applicant Eligibility: Federally Recognized Indian Tribal Governments and Tribal Organizations, including School Boards, who have a prioritized Replacement School Construction or Facilities Improvement and Repair, for which funds have been specifically approved through the appropriation process, or for which ARRA funds have been allocated.

Beneficiary Eligibility: American Indian children attending Bureau owned or funded primary and secondary schools and/or American Indian children residing in Bureau owned or funded dormitories.

Award Range/Average: The amount of financial assistance can range from approximately $6 million to $25 million depending on the size of the school, both grade level and student enrollment, the program requirements, and the location. For the higher amounts, funding may be incremental over 2, 3, or even 5 years. Because of the limited number of schools that have received funding in the last few years and the increasing costs for construction, there is no way to determine a true representative "average" of financial assistance. Facilities Improvement and Repair: The amount of financial assistance can range significantly from a few thousand dollars to approximately $7 million. There are several categories of projects that are included under Facilities Improvement and Repair, such as, Emergency, Roofing, Replacement/Repair, and Portable Classrooms. The average amount of financial assistance can vary depending on the category. An average amount is not calculable.

Funding: (Direct Payments for Specified Use) FY 18 FY 16 FY 17 - School Construction and Facility Repair

HQ: 1849 C Street NW
Washington, DC 20240
Phone: 202-208-3559
Email: juanita.mendoza@bie.edu
http://www.bia.gov

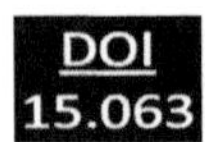

IMPROVEMENT AND REPAIR OF INDIAN DETENTION FACILITIES

Award: Direct Payments for Specified Use

Purpose: To help in providing a safe, functional, code and standards compliant, economical, and energy-efficient adult and/or juvenile detention facilities. Additional objectives for ARRA-funded projects consists of having a demonstrated or potential ability to deliver programmatic results, optimizing economic activity and the number of jobs created or saved, achieving long-term public benefits from improved detention facilities, infrastructure, fostering energy independence.

Applicant Eligibility: Federally Recognized Indian Tribal Governments or Tribal Organizations who have a prioritized Facilities Improvement and Repair and for which funds have been specifically approved through the appropriation process or for which ARRA funds have been allocated.

Beneficiary Eligibility: Federally Recognized Indian Tribal Governments in Bureau owned or funded Law Enforcement/Detention Facilities.

Award Range/Average: Facilities Improvement and Repair: The amount of financial assistance can range significantly from a few thousand dollars to approximately $3 million. There are several categories of projects that are included under Facilities Improvement and Repair, such as, Emergency, Roofing and Environmental. The average amount of financial assistance can vary depending on the category. ARRA-funded projects range from less than $1.1 million to $1.6 Million.

Funding: Direct Payments for Specified Use

HQ: 1849 C Street NW Bureau of Indian Education, P.O. Box 4657-MIB
Washington, DC 20240
Phone: 202-208-3559
Email: juanita.mendoza@bie.edu

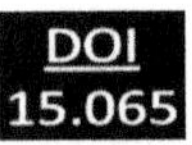

SAFETY OF DAMS ON INDIAN LANDS

Award: Direct Payments for Specified Use

Purpose: To enhance the structural integrity of dams on Indian lands, including operations and maintenance of these dams.

Applicant Eligibility: Federally Recognized Indian Tribal Governments and Native American Organizations authorized by Indian tribal governments to be benefited by the award.

Beneficiary Eligibility: Federally Recognized Indian Tribal Governments and their members and Native American Organizations.

Award Range/Average: Awards are commonly awarded for various phases of the safety program. For example, conception design $100,000 to $300,000; final design $300,000 to $1,000,000; and construction repair $1,000,000 to $17,000,000. For the non-construction portion, awards can be from $10,000 up to $250,000.

Funding: (Direct Payments for Specified Use) FY 18 FY 16 FY 17

HQ: PE Office of Trust Services Division of Water and Power Branch of Safety of Dams, 13922 Denver W Parkway

Lakewood, CO 80401

Phone: 303-231-5222

Email: jack.byers@bia.gov

TRIBAL GREAT LAKES RESTORATION INITIATIVE "Tribal GLRI"

Award: Project Grants

Purpose: The BIA Tribal GLRI Program offers financial assistance to Great Lakes tribes to protect, enhance, and restore the Great Lakes. Priority actions are to identify, protect, conserve, manage, enhance, or restore species or habitat, as well as to build tribal capacity to oversee natural resources within the Great Lakes Basin.

Applicant Eligibility: Federally-recognized Indian Tribes and Native American Organizations authorized by Indian tribal governments

Beneficiary Eligibility: Same as Applicant Eligibility.

Award Range/Average: Projects may range from $1,000 to $500,000, or greater. Average over two years is $162,000.

Funding: (Project Grants (Discretionary)) FY 16 est $5,180,000; FY 17 FY 18

HQ: 5600 W American Boulevard, Suite 500

Bloomington, MN 55437

Phone: 612-725-4529

Email: merben.cebrian@bia.gov

STRENGTHENING TRIBAL NATIONS

Award: Cooperative Agreements; Advisory Services and Counseling; Dissemination of Technical Information; Training

Purpose: To allocate funding to advance nation-to-nation relationships, support Indian families and protect Indian country, support sustainable stewardship of trust resources, and advance Indian education.

Applicant Eligibility: N/A

Beneficiary Eligibility: American Indians/Alaska Natives will be the ultimate beneficiaries of the funded projects either directly or indirectly depending upon the nature of the project.

Award Range/Average: No Data Available.

Funding: (Cooperative Agreements (Discretionary Grants)) FY 17 FY 18 FY 16 est $200,000.

HQ: 1849 C Street NW, P.O. Box 4657-MIB
Washington, DC 20240
Phone: 202-208-3559
Email: juanita.mendoza@bie.edu
http://www.bia.gov

INDIAN EMPLOYMENT ASSISTANCE "Employment Assistance Program"

Award: Direct Payments for Specified Use

Purpose: To render vocational training and employment opportunities to eligible American Indians and Alaska Natives to reduce Federal dependence.

Applicant Eligibility: Federally Recognized Indian Tribal Governments and Native American Organizations authorized by Indian Tribal Governments may apply to administer the program. Individual American Indian and Alaska Native applicants must be a member of a Federally Recognized Indian Tribe, be in need of financial assistance, and reside on or near an Indian reservation or in Alaska under the jurisdiction of the Bureau of Indian Affairs.

Beneficiary Eligibility: Members of Federally Recognized Indian Tribes who are unemployed, underemployed, or in need of training to obtain reasonable and gainful employment.

Award Range/Average: N/A.

Funding: N/A

HQ: 1849 C Street NW, P.O. Box 4657-MIB
Washington, DC 20240
Phone: 202-208-3559
Email: juanita.mendoza@bie.edu

INDIAN SOCIAL SERVICES WELFARE ASSISTANCE

Award: Direct Payments for Specified Use

Purpose: To offer financial assistance for basic needs of needy eligible American Indians who reside on or near reservations, including those American Indians living under Bureau of Indian Affairs service area jurisdictions, when such backing is not available from State or local public agencies.

Applicant Eligibility: An American Indian who is a member of a federally recognized Indian Tribe, who resides on or near a federally recognized Indian reservations, who is in need of financial assistance and who meets the eligibility criteria in 25 CFR Part 20.

Beneficiary Eligibility: American Indians who are members of federally recognized Indian Tribes.

Award Range/Average: May range from a few hundred to several hundred dollars monthly depending upon the assistance provided.

Funding: N/A

HQ: 1849 C Street NW, P.O. Box 4657-MIB
Washington, DC 20240
Phone: 202-208-3559
Email: juanita.mendoza@bie.edu

INDIAN EDUCATION HIGHER EDUCATION GRANT "Higher Education"

Award: Project Grants

Purpose: To offer financial aid to eligible Indian students to enable them to attend accredited institutions of higher education.

Applicant Eligibility: Federally Recognized Indian Tribal Governments and tribal organizations authorized by Indian Tribal Governments may apply to administer the program. Individuals who are members of Federally Recognized Indian Tribes may submit applications for benefits directly to the Bureau of Indian Affairs if the Bureau agency serving their reservation provides direct services for this program.

Beneficiary Eligibility: Members of a Federally Recognized Indian Tribe who are enrolled or accepted for enrollment in an accredited college and have financial need as determined by the institution's financial aid office.

Award Range/Average: Range is $300 to $5,000; Average $2,700.

Funding: (Project Grants) FY 17 FY 16 est $0; FY 18

HQ: 1849 C Street NW, P.O. Box 4657 MIB
Washington, DC 20240
Phone: 202-208-7658
Email: joe.herrin@bie.edu
http://www.bie.edu

INDIAN LOANS ECONOMIC DEVELOPMENT "Loan Guaranty, Insurance, and Interest Subsidy Program"

Award: Guaranteed/insured Loans

Purpose: To render assistance to Federally Recognized Indian Tribal Governments, Native American Organizations, and individual American Indians in acquiring financing from private sources to promote business development initiatives to improve the economies of Federally Recognized Indian Reservations.

Applicant Eligibility: Federally Recognized Indian Tribal Governments, Native American Organizations authorized by Indian tribal governments, and individual American Indians.

Beneficiary Eligibility: Federally Recognized Indian Tribal Governments, Native American Organizations, and individual American Indians or Alaska natives. Complete information on beneficiary eligibility is found in 25 CFR, Part 103.

Award Range/Average: For individuals and tribal enterprises, $150,000 to 10,500,000. For Federally Recognized Tribal Governments and Native American Organizations, $10,000,000 to $38,000,000.

Funding: N/A

HQ: 1849 C Street NW, P.O. Box 4657-MIB
Washington, DC 20240
Phone: 202-208-3559
Email: juanita.mendoza@bie.edu

INDIAN EDUCATION ASSISTANCE TO SCHOOLS "Johnson-O'Malley"

Award: Direct Payments for Specified Use

Purpose: To finance programs that meets the unique and specialized needs of eligible Indian students.

Applicant Eligibility: Tribal organizations, Indian Corporations, school districts or States which have eligible Indian children attending public school districts and have established Indian Education Committees to approve supplementary or operational support programs beneficial to Indian students. Current funding is calculated with the 1995 JOM student count.

Beneficiary Eligibility: Children who are enrolled members of, or at least one-fourth or more degree of Indian blood descendant of a member of a federally recognized Indian tribal government eligible for service by the Bureau, and are between age 3 through grade 12 with priority given to those residing on or near Indian reservations.

Award Range/Average: Range is $100 to $3,360,980; TPA Average $77,300

Funding: (Direct Payments for Specified Use) FY 18 FY 17 FY 16 est $24,683,892

HQ: 1849 C Street NW, P.O. Box 4657 MIB
Washington, DC 20240
Phone: 202-208-4397
Email: jennifer.davis@bie.edu
http://www.bie.edu

NATIVE AMERICAN BUSINESS DEVELOPMENT INSTITUTE "NABDI"

Award: Formula Grants

Purpose: Under its Native American Business Development Institute (NABDI) conceived in FY 2006, IEED has established partnerships with U.S. graduate schools to help tribal business evaluate financial opportunities and prepare economic feasibility studies. Assistance by way of Public Law 93-638 agreements between tribes and participating business schools. During FY 2006- 2010, NABDI assisted tribes to estimate the potential of economic opportunities as diverse as a business park, a meat packing plant, a wind energy project, a security business, a medical supply business, upland bird hunting, new uses for a dormat tribal wellness/recreation center, and a greenhouse heated by way of woody biomass. Starting in FY 2011, NABDI funding will be dispersed on a competitive basis following notice in the Federal Register. Applicants will be free to choose private consultants in addition to graduate schools.

Applicant Eligibility: Federally Recognized Indian Tribal governments.

Beneficiary Eligibility: Federally Recognized Indian Tribal governments and their members.

Award Range/Average: Determined on an annual basis, subject to appropriations.

Funding: (Formula Grants) FY 18 FY 16 FY 17

HQ: 1849 C Street NW, P.O. Box 4657-MIB
Washington, DC 20240
Phone: 202-208-3559
Email: juanita.mendoza@bie.edu
http://bie.edu

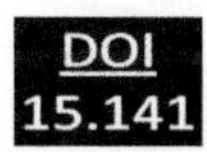

INDIAN HOUSING ASSISTANCE

Award: Project Grants; Dissemination of Technical Information

Purpose: To utilize the Housing Improvement Program (HIP) resources of the Bureau of Indian Affairs to remove substantially substandard Indian owned and inhabited housing for very low income eligible Indians living in approved tribal service areas. This effort is assisted by the Indian Health Service (Department of Health and Human Services) which provides water and sanitary systems for houses repaired or built with HIP funds.

Applicant Eligibility: Federally Recognized Indian Tribal Governments and tribal organizations to administer the program who have eligible applicants with identified housing needs. Individual members of Federally recognized Indian tribes living in approved tribal service areas in need of housing assistance who are unable to obtain assistance from any other source, and who meet the eligibility criteria of the HIP regulations.

Beneficiary Eligibility: Individual members of Federally recognized Indian tribes.

Award Range/Average: For HIP, maximum of $35,000 for repairs and renovations; $2,500 for interim improvements. The average cost of repair has been approximately $17,500. New housing does not have a specified maximum amount but is intended to provide only a modest standard dwelling. Average new housing construction cost has been approximately $100,000.

Funding: N/A

HQ: 1849 C Street NW
Washington, DC 20240
Phone: 202-208-3559
Email: juanita.mendoza@bie.edu

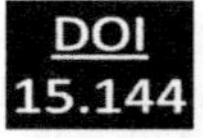

INDIAN CHILD WELFARE ACT TITLE II GRANTS

Award: Project Grants

Purpose: To foster the stability and security of American Indian tribes and families by protecting American Indian children and avert the separation of American Indian families and providing assistance to Indian tribes in the operation of child and family service programs designed to prevent the break up families.

Applicant Eligibility: Federally Recognized Indian Tribal Governments.

Beneficiary Eligibility: American Indian children and families.

Award Range/Average: $26,449 to $750,000; $60,000.

Funding: N/A

HQ: 1849 C Street NW, P.O. Box 4657-MIB
Washington, DC 20240
Phone: 202-208-3559
Email: juanita.mendoza@bie.edu

IRONWORKER TRAINING

Award: Project Grants

Purpose: To render ironworker vocational training, apprenticeships, and job placement to eligible American Indians through the National Ironworkers Training Program, located in Broadview, Illinois.

Applicant Eligibility: Applicants must be an American Indian who is a member of a Federally Recognized Indian Tribe, at least 18 years old, possess a high school diploma or General Equivalency Development (GED) Certificate, be in good physical health, and reside on or near an Indian reservation under the jurisdiction of the Bureau of Indian Affairs.

Beneficiary Eligibility: American Indian who is a member of a Federally Recognized Indian Tribal Government, at least 18 years old, possess a high school diploma or General Equivalency Development (GED) Certificate, be in good physical health, and reside on or near an Indian reservation under the jurisdiction of the Bureau of Indian Affairs.

Award Range/Average: Students receive $185 per week for the duration of the program for room and board and miscellaneous expenses. Work clothes and tools are also provided.

Funding: N/A

HQ: 1849 C Street NW, P.O. Box 4657-MIB
Washington, DC 20240
Phone: 202-208-3559
Email: juanita.mendoza@bie.edu

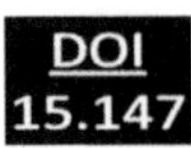

TRIBAL COURTS TRUST REFORM INITIATIVE

Award: Project Grants

Purpose: To allocate grant funds to Federally Recognized Indian Tribal Governments that operate a judicial branch of government which has assumed the increased responsibilities required by Trust Funds for Individual Indians Money accounts.

Applicant Eligibility: Federally Recognized Indian Tribal Governments that operate a judicial branch of government which has assumed the increased responsibilities required by 25 CFR Part 115.

Beneficiary Eligibility: Same as Applicant Eligibility.

Award Range/Average: $3,000 to $216,000; $50,000

Funding: (Project Grants) FY 16 FY 18 FY 17

HQ: 1849 C Street NW Bureau of Indian Education, P.O. Box 4657-MIB
Washington, DC 20240
Phone: 202-208-3559

Email: juanita.mendoza@bie.edu

http://www.bia.gov

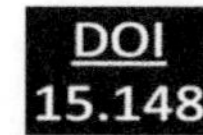

TRIBAL ENERGY DEVELOPMENT CAPACITY GRANTS "TEDC "

Award: Direct Payments for Specified Use

Purpose: To allocate development grants to Indian tribes for use in developing and sustaining the managerial and technical capacity needed to enhance their energy resources, and to properly account for resulting energy production and revenues. Proposals from tribes should strive to obtain the following stated goals: To evaluate the type and range of energy development activities that a tribe way want to assume under a TERA; To determine the current level of scientific, technical, administrative, for financial management capacity of the tribe to assume responsibility for the identified development activities; and to determine which scientific, technical, administrative, or financial management capacities needs enhancement and what process and/or procedures the grantee may use to eliminate these capacity gaps.

Applicant Eligibility: Federally Recognized Indian Tribal Governments.

Beneficiary Eligibility: Federally Recognized Tribal Governments and their members.

Award Range/Average: Determined on an annual basis, subject to appropriations.

Funding: (Direct Payments for Specified Use) FY 16 FY 17 FY 18

HQ: 1849 C Street NW Bureau of Indian Education, P.O. Box 4657-MIB

Washington, DC 20240

Phone: 202-208-3559

Email: juanita.mendoza@bie.edu

FOCUS ON STUDENT ACHIEVEMENT "FOCUS"

Award: Project Grants

Purpose: The FOCUS program focuses on schools where student achievement is close to achieving annual measurable objectives as set by their state's achievement test and where additional resources could facilitate achievement of Adequate Yearly Progress (AYP) as required by Public Law 107-110, the No Child Left Behind Act of 2001.

Applicant Eligibility: Federally Recognized Indian Tribal Governments and tribal organizations authorized by Indian tribal governments on reservations with Bureau-funded schools may apply to administer the program.

Beneficiary Eligibility: Children between the ages of 5 and 21 who are members of or are at least a one-fourth degree Indian blood descendant of a member of an Indian tribe which is eligible for the special programs and services provided by the United States through the Bureau of Indian Affairs to Indians because of their status as Indians.

Award Range/Average: Range is $100,000 to $225,000; Average $153,333.

Funding: (Project Grants) FY 16 FY 18 FY 17

HQ: Division of Performance and Accountability BIA Building 2 1011 Indian School Road NW 3rd Floor, Suite 332

Albuquerque, NM 87104

Phone: 505-563-5250
Email: joel.longie@bie.edu
http://www.bie.edu

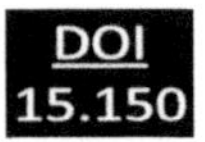

JUVENILE DETENTION EDUCATION

Award: Project Grants

Purpose: The Juvenile Detention Education Program offers education services to detained and incarcerated youth in the 24 Bureau of Indian Affairs funded juvenile detention centers.

Applicant Eligibility: Federally Recognized Indian Tribal Governments and tribal organizations authorized by Indian tribal governments on reservations with BIA-funded JDCs.

Beneficiary Eligibility: Children between the ages of 5 and 21 who are members of or are at least a one-fourth degree Indian blood descendant of a member of an Indian tribe which is eligible for the special programs and services provided by the United States through the Bureau of Indian Affairs to Indians because of their status as Indians.

Award Range/Average: Average grant/and contract was $34,444, minimum $19,000, maximum $56,000.

Funding: N/A

HQ: BIA Building 2 1011 Indian School Road NW 3rd Floor, Suite 332
Albuquerque, NM 87104
Phone: 505-563-5250
Email: jeffrey.hamley@bie.edu

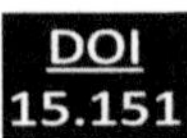

EDUCATION ENHANCEMENTS

Award: Cooperative Agreements

Purpose: Education Program Enhancements offers resources for special studies, projects, new activities, and other costs associated with enhancing the basic educational programs provided to students. These funds allow BIE to provide specialized assistance to schools struggling to make Adequate Yearly Progress (AYP) that is focused to address the schools' unique needs and specific gaps in achievement. Typically, assistance comprises of implementation of specialized programs in reading and math, and staff development for principals, teachers and support staff.

Applicant Eligibility: Federally Recognized Indian Tribal Governments and tribal organizations authorized by Indian tribal governments on reservations with Bureau-funded schools may apply to administer the program.

Beneficiary Eligibility: Children between the ages of 5 and 21 who are members of or are at least a one-fourth degree Indian blood descendant of a member of an Indian tribe which is eligible for the special programs and services provided by the United States through the Bureau of Indian Affairs to Indians because of their status as Indians.

Award Range/Average: In Fiscal Year 2012 the average Reads grant was $23,052, and the maximum Reads grant was $176,038; the average Math Counts grant was $17,353 and the maximum Math Counts grant was 232,507.

Funding: (Project Grants (Cooperative Agreements)) FY 18 FY 16 FY 17

HQ: Division of Performance and Accountability BIA Building 2 1011 Indian School Road NW 3rd Floor, Suite 332
Albuquerque, NM 87104
Phone: 505-563-5250
Email: joel.longie@bie.edu

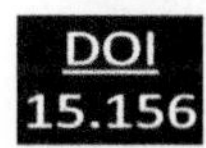

TRIBAL CLIMATE RESILIENCE "Climate Change"

Award: Direct Payments for Specified Use

Purpose: The Cooperative Landscape Conservation (CLC) program allocates funds and technical support to enable tribal governments and trust land managers to better understand potential impacts and vulnerabilities of communities, ecosystems and built systems to climate-related change, to enable them to develop information and tools to support planning and decision making, to establish strategies that elevates the preparedness and resilience of communities in the face of a changing climate and address the potential for increased peak weather events. The program also enables tribal participation in ocean and coastal planning.

Applicant Eligibility: Direct Support Awards: Federally Recognized Indian Tribal Governments, Native American Organizations authorized by Indian tribal governments and Native American non-profit organizations, federally/tribally chartered tribal colleges and universities. Providers of Training and Technical Support Awards: Native American Organizations authorized by Indian tribal governments, federally/tribally chartered tribal colleges and universities, Native American tribal and non-profit organizations, and public universities.

Beneficiary Eligibility: Federally Recognized Indian Tribal Governments and consortia, tribal and public colleges and universities, and Native American organizations.

Award Range/Average: N/A

Funding: N/A

HQ: 1849 C Street NW, P.O. Box 4635 MIB
Washington, DC 20240
Phone: 202-513-0337
Email: sean.hart@bia.gov
http://www.bia.gov

CULTURAL RESOURCES MANAGEMENT

Award: Project Grants; Direct Payments for Specified Use

Purpose: To verify the proper management, protection, and preservation of cultural resources over which the BIA maintains responsibility; furnish secure, short-term housing and care for cultural resources regained during investigations; provide for the curation, stewardship, and public access to BIA museum collections and other cultural resources, including the increase of public awareness, appreciation, and knowledge of these resources.

Applicant Eligibility: State and local agencies, sponsored organizations, public nonprofit institutions/organizations, other public institutions/organizations, Federally-recognized Indian Tribal governments, specialized groups, small businesses, profit organizations, private nonprofit institutions/organizations, quasi-public nonprofit institutions/organizations, other private institutions/organizations, and Native American Organizations, educational or scientific organization, or any institution, corporation, association, or individual that possesses the requisite professional expertise. Applicant eligibility will be specified in the Funding Opportunity Announcement, if applicable.

Beneficiary Eligibility: State and local governments, Federally recognized Indian Tribal governments, nonprofit organizations, educational or scientific institutions, universities, associations, and entities that have an education mission or mission-component, and museums and/or repositories that meet the standards of the Department of the Interior, Department Manual, Part 411.

Award Range/Average: No Data Available.

Funding: (Direct Payments for Specified Use) FY 18 FY 16 FY 17(Project Grants (Discretionary)) FY 16 FY 17 FY 18

HQ: 12220 Sunrise Valley Drive, Room 6084
Reston, VA 20191
Phone: 703-390-6343
Email: anna.pardo@bia.gov
http://www.bia.gov

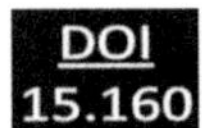

DOI 15.160 BIA WILDLAND URBAN INTERFACE COMMUNITY FIRE ASSISTANCE

Award: Cooperative Agreements; Use of Property, Facilities, and Equipment; Dissemination of Technical Information; Training

Purpose: To establish the National Fire Plan and help communities at risk from catastrophic wildland fires by providing assistance in the following areas: Community programs that develop local capability including; assessment and planning, mitigation activities, and community and homeowner education and action; plan and implement hazardous fuels reduction activities, including the training, monitoring or maintenance associated with such hazardous fuels reduction activities, on federal land, or on adjacent nonfederal land for activities that mitigate the threat of catastrophic fire to communities and natural resources in high risk areas; improve local and small business employment opportunities for rural communities; enhance the knowledge and fire protection capability of rural fire districts by providing aid in education and training; assist with the prevention and detection of wildfires to minimize the risk and impact to communities and their values.

Applicant Eligibility: States and local governments at risk as published in the Federal Register, Indian Tribes, public and private education institutions, nonprofit organizations, and rural fire departments serving a community with a population of 10,000 or less in the wildland/urban interface.

Beneficiary Eligibility: Same as Applicant Eligibility.

Award Range/Average: N/A

Funding: (Cooperative Agreements (Discretionary Grants)) FY 18 est $0; FY 16 $0; N/A FY 17 est $0; - New Program

HQ: 12220 Sunrise Valley Drive, Room 6084
Reston, VA 20191
Phone: 703-390-6343
Email: anna.pardo@bia.gov

DOI 15.161 NATIVE LANGUAGE IMMERSION GRANT "Native Language Immersion Grant"

Award: Direct Payments for Specified Use

Purpose: Offers capacity building grants for Bureau-funded schools to amplify existing language immersion programs, or create new programs that will lead to oral Native language proficiency.

Applicant Eligibility: Specialized group: Bureau of Indian Education Funded Schools

Beneficiary Eligibility: American Indian Student

Award Range/Average: Range: $1,000 - $95,000, or greater. Average: $48,500 over one year.

Funding: (Direct Payments for Specified Use) FY 17 est $0; FY 18 est $2,000,000; FY 19 N/A - New Program

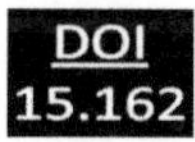

HQ: 1849 C Street NW, P.O. Box MIB 3610
Washington, DC 20240
Phone: 202-208-6123
Email: juanita.mendoza@bie.edu
http://bie.edu

DOI 15.162 TIWAHE HOUSING

Award: Project Grants

Purpose: According to the FY 17 Appropriations Bill, to enhance tribal communities in Indian country by leveraging programs and resources; to maximize the number of single families and veterans assisted; and to address the dilapidated and overcrowded housing conditions in Tribes' service.

Applicant Eligibility: Tribe must hold status as an active Tiwahe Initiative Tribe with an approved Tiwahe Initiative Plan that includes a plan and budget for Tiwahe housing funds

Beneficiary Eligibility: Federally Recognized Indian Tribal Government

Award Range/Average: At the present time, $1,688,304 has been allotted. However, additional funds may become available.

Funding: (Project Grants) FY 18 est $281,384; FY 17 N/A FY 19 N/A - New Program

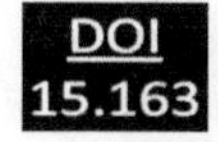

HQ: 1849 C Street NW
Washington, DC 20240
Phone: 202-513-7712
Email: meredes.garcia@bia.gov
http://www.bia.gov/bia/ois

DOI 15.163 TRIBAL EDUCATION DEPARTMENTS "TED"

Award: N/A

Purpose: Allocates grants and offers technical assistance to tribes for the development and operation of tribal departments or divisions of education for the purpose of planning and coordinating all education programs of the tribe.

Applicant Eligibility: Specialized group: Indian tribes which are federally recognized as eligible by the U.S. Government through the Secretary of the Interior for the special programs and services provided by the Secretary because of their status as Indians.

Beneficiary Eligibility: Same as Applicant Eligibility.

Award Range/Average: $50,000 - $300,000

Funding: (Direct Payments for Specified Use) FY 17 N/A FY 18 est $2,500,000; FY 19 N/A

HQ: 1849 C Street NW, P.O. Box MIB-3610
Washington, DC 20240
Phone: 505-563-5397
Email: maureen.lesky@bie.edu
http://www.bie.edu

BUREAU OF LABOR STATISTICS

REGIONAL OFFICES

Atlanta
Room 7T50 61 Forsyth Street, SW, Atlanta, GA 30303 404-893-8300

Boston/New York
JFK Federal Building, Room E-310, Boston, MA 02203 617-565-2331

Chicago
JCK Federal Office Building, 9th Floor 230 South Dearborn Street, Chicago, IL 60604 312-353-7226

Dallas/Kansas City
Federal Office Building 525 Griffin Street, Room 221, Dallas, TX 75202 972-850-4882

Kansas City
Two Pershing Square Building 2300 Main Street, Room 1190, Kansas City, MO 64108 816-285-7018

New York
201 Varick Street, Room 808, New York, NY 10014 212-337-2500

Philadelphia
The Curtis Center, Suite 610 East 170 South Independence Mall West, Philadelphia, PA 19106 215-861-5600

San Francisco
SF Federal Building, 14th Floor 90 7th Street, San Francisco, CA 94103 415-625-2245

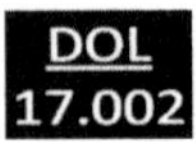

LABOR FORCE STATISTICS

Award: Project Grants; Dissemination of Technical Information

Purpose: To provide payroll employment and occupational employment and provide regular wages.

Applicant Eligibility: SWAs designated under Section 4 of the Wagner-Peyser Act (as amended by the Workforce Investment Act and subsequently the Workforce Innovation and Opportunity Act) are eligible to apply for cooperative agreement funding to operate the Current Employment Statistics (CES), Local Area Unemployment Statistics (LAUS), Quarterly Census of Employment and Wages (QCEW), and Occupational Employment Statistics (OES) programs in the states. BLS may select an alternative applicant if a SWA declines to apply for cooperative agreement funding or otherwise substantially fails to meet BLS application and performance requirements.

Beneficiary Eligibility: General public may request information from the SWAs and the Bureau of Labor Statistics.

Award Range/Average: The size of each cooperative agreement reflects the staff and non-personal resources required to operate the programs in a state. The range $57,000 to $7,623,000 average $1,337,000

Funding: (Salaries and Expenses) FY 17 $267,571,094; FY 18 est $272,912,000; FY 19 N/A FY 16 $262,746,958; - (Grants) FY 17 $72,203,000; FY 18 est 70,626,000; and FY 19 est N/A

HQ: 2 Massachusetts Avenue NE
Washington, DC 20212
Phone: 202-691-6400
https://www.bls.gov

PRICES AND COST OF LIVING DATA

Award: Dissemination of Technical Information

Purpose: To provide assistance in export and import price changes and consumer expenditures.

Applicant Eligibility: Request for information may be made by the general public.

Beneficiary Eligibility: General public.

Award Range/Average: N/A

Funding: (Salaries and Expenses) FY 17 $210; FY 18 est $209; FY 19 N/A FY 16 $213,317,666

HQ: 2 Massachusetts Avenue NE
Washington, DC 20212
Phone: 202-691-6960
Email: friedman.david@bls.gov
http://www.bls.gov

PRODUCTIVITY AND TECHNOLOGY DATA

Award: Dissemination of Technical Information

Purpose: To assist in productivity trends in the U.S. economy and examines the factors for productivity change.

Applicant Eligibility: N/A

Beneficiary Eligibility: N/A

Award Range/Average: N/A

Funding: (Salaries and Expenses) FY 17 $10,932,451; FY 18 est $10,798,000; FY 19 N/A FY 16 $10,749,905

HQ: 2 Massachusetts Avenue NE
Washington, DC 20212
Phone: 202-691-5600
Email: eldridge.lucy@bls.gov
http://www.bls.gov

COMPENSATION AND WORKING CONDITIONS

Award: Project Grants; Dissemination of Technical Information

Purpose: To assist in the measures of employee compensation, including cost, wages and to improve the measurement process.

Applicant Eligibility: State agencies or designated local governments are eligible to apply for cooperative agreement funding to share costs in operating statistical programs dealing with occupational safety and health statistics. Request for copies of published studies and reports may be made by the general public.

Beneficiary Eligibility: General public.

Award Range/Average: The size of each cooperative agreement reflects the staff and nonpersonal resources required to operate the program. The range of awards in fiscal year 2017 was from $5,000 (Idaho) to $755,000 (California). The average was $120,000.

Funding: (Salaries and Expenses) FY 17 $84; FY 18 est $82; FY 19 N/A FY 16 $85,682,556; - (Grants) FY 17 $6,743,000; FY 18 est $7,093,000; and FY 19 est N/A.

HQ: 2 Massachusetts Avenue NE
Washington, DC 20212
Phone: 202-691-7527
Email: monaco.kristen@bls.gov
http://www.bls.gov

BUREAU OF LAND MANAGEMENT

REGIONAL OFFICES

Alaska
227 W. 7th Ave 13, Anchorage, AK 99513 907-267-4323

Arizona
One Central Ave, Ste 800, Phoenix, AZ 85004-4427 602-417-9296

Branch of Procurement Management
20 M Street South East, Washington, DC 20003-0047

California
2800 Cottage Way, Suite W-1834, Sacramento, CA 85825-1886

Colorado
2850 Youngfield Street, Lakewood, CO 80215-7076

Nevada
1340 Financial Boulevard, Reno, NV 89520-0006 702-861-6559

New Mexico
100 Sun Avenue North East Pan American Building, Suite 300, Albuquerque, NM 87109 505-761-8917

Oregon
1515 SW 5th Avenue, Portland, OR 97208 503-952-6220

Utah
440 West 200 South, Ste 500, Salt Lake City, UT 84101 801-539-4177

Wyoming
5353 Yellowstone Road P.O. Box 1828, Cheyenne, WY 82005 307-775-6056

RESEARCH HEADQUARTERS

Idaho
1387 S. Vinnell Way, Boise, ID 83709-1657 208-373-3909

Montana
5001 Southgate Drive, Billings, MT 59101

DOI 15.214 NON-SALE DISPOSALS OF MINERAL MATERIAL

Award: Sale, Exchange, or Donation of Property and Goods

Purpose: To allow free use of certain mineral material from federally owned lands under the jurisdiction of the Bureau of Land Management by governmental units and nonprofit organizations.

Applicant Eligibility: Any Federal or State agency, unit, or subdivision, including municipalities, where material will be used for public project; or any nonprofit association or corporation. A free use permit will not be issued upon the determination that the applicant owns or control an adequate supply of suitable mineral materials that are readily available and can be mined in a manner which is economically and environmentally acceptable.

Beneficiary Eligibility: Federal or State agencies, units, or subdivisions, including municipalities, where material will be used for public project; or any nonprofit association or corporation.

Award Range/Average: N/A

Funding: FY 17 $14,391,000; FY 18 N/A FY 19 N/A FY 16 $6,071,882

HQ: 1849 C Street NW, Room 2134 LM
Washington, DC 20240
Phone: 570-593-8659
Email: gbrown@blm.gov
http://www.blm.gov/nhp/index.htm

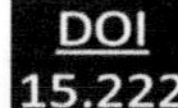

DOI 15.222 COOPERATIVE INSPECTION AGREEMENTS WITH STATES AND TRIBES

"Section 202 Agreements"

Award: Cooperative Agreements

Purpose: Assists the Bureau of Land Management (BLM) to enter into cooperative agreements with Tribes so that authorized Tribal inspectors can perform inspection activities on Indian oil and gas leases within Tribal jurisdiction.

Applicant Eligibility: Indian tribes with producing tribal oil and gas leases for which with Federal government has trust responsibility. State may enter into a cooperative agreement for inspection of tribal oil and gas leases with the permission of the Tribe.

Beneficiary Eligibility: Indian tribes with producing tribal oil and gas leases for which the Federal government has trust responsibility. States that have tribal permission to enter into cooperative agreements to conduct inspections on tribal oil and gas leases.

Award Range/Average: Past partnership projects have ranged from $200,000 to $494,708. Average amount is $273,064 or less.

Funding: (Cooperative Agreements (Discretionary Grants)) FY 17 $418,435; FY 18 N/A FY 19 N/A FY 16 $1,092,254

HQ: Division of Lands and Realty Bureau of Land Management (WO 350) 20 M Street SE, Room 2134
Washington, DC 20003
Phone: 202-912-7350
http://www.blm.gov/nhp/index.htm

DOI 15.224 CULTURAL AND PALEONTOLOGICAL RESOURCES MANAGEMENT

Award: Cooperative Agreements

Purpose: To organize and safeguard cultural resources on the public lands and to increase public awareness and appreciation of these resources. Most of these lands are located in the Western United States and Alaska.

Applicant Eligibility: Anyone/general public.

Beneficiary Eligibility: All Public Land users.

Award Range/Average: Past partnership projects have ranged from $3,000 to $100,000. Average amount is $45,000 or less.

Funding: (Cooperative Agreements (Discretionary Grants)) FY 17 $3,938,237; FY 18 est $2,500,000; FY 19 N/A FY 16 $7,428,219,219

HQ: Division of Lands and Realty (WO 350) 20 M Street SE, Room 2134
Washington, DC 20003
Phone: 202-912-7350
http://www.blm.gov

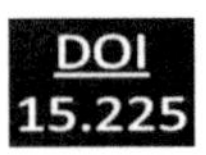

RECREATION AND VISITOR SERVICES

Award: Cooperative Agreements

Purpose: Public lands administered by the BLM that offers some of the most diverse outdoor recreation opportunities on Federal lands in the western United States. The BLM's Recreation and Visitor Services Program manages a broad and complex set of recreation related and social management activities and programs. Recreation Management activities support efforts to provide resource-related recreational opportunities for a wide range of activities and furnish quality visitor services; and also to provide diversity of recreational facilities and visitor centers. Objective of this program are to provide: recreation planning and visitor use monitoring; trails, access, and rivers management including: off-highway vehicle, public access, and comprehensive travel and transportation management; visitor services, information, interpretation and stewardship education; visitor health, safety, and accessibility for persons with disabilities; trail maintenance, including visitor centers; and recreation and community support partnerships including tourism and marketing.

Applicant Eligibility: Anyone/general public.

Beneficiary Eligibility: All Public Land users.

Award Range/Average: Past partnership projects have ranged from $2000 to $552,400. Average amounts approximately $60,000 or less.

Funding: (Cooperative Agreements (Discretionary Grants)) FY 17 $8,267,453; FY 18 N/A FY 19 N/A

HQ: 1849 C Street NW, Room 2134
Washington, DC 20240
Phone: 202-912-7256
Email: jmccusker@blm.gov
http://www.blm.gov/nhp/index.htm

DOI 15.228 BLM WILDLAND URBAN INTERFACE COMMUNITY FIRE ASSISTANCE

Award: Cooperative Agreements; Use of Property, Facilities, and Equipment; Dissemination of Technical Information; Training

Purpose: To implement the National Fire Plan and assist communities at risk from catastrophic wildland fires by providing assistance in developing local capability including; assessment and planning, mitigation activities, and community and homeowner education and action; plan and implement hazardous fuels reduction activities, including the training, monitoring or maintenance associated with such hazardous fuels reduction activities, on federal land, or on adjacent nonfederal land for activities that mitigate the threat of catastrophic fire to communities and natural resources in high risk areas.

Applicant Eligibility: States and local governments at risk as published in the Federal Register, Indian Tribes, public and private education institutions, nonprofit organizations, and rural fire departments serving a community with a population of 10,000 or less in the wildland/urban interface.

Beneficiary Eligibility: Same as Applicant Eligibility.

Award Range/Average: Past partnership projects have ranged from $5,000 to $686,000. Average amount is $47,400 or less.

Funding: (Cooperative Agreements (Discretionary Grants)) FY 17 $6,895,026; FY 18 est $2,100,000; FY 19 N/A FY 16 $3,708,000

HQ: Division of Fire Planning and Fuels Management (FA-600) 83705 National Interagency Fire Center, 3833 S Development Avenue

Boise, ID 83705

Phone: 208-387-5321

Email: jskinner@blm.gov

http://www.nifc.gov

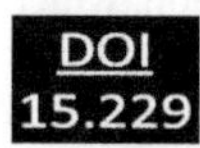

DOI 15.229 WILD HORSE AND BURRO RESOURCE MANAGEMENT

Award: Cooperative Agreements

Purpose: The objective of the Wild Horses and Burro Resource Management program is to manage wild horses and burros as an integral part of the natural system of the public lands under the principle of multiple use.

Applicant Eligibility: Anyone/general public.

Beneficiary Eligibility: All Public Land users.

Award Range/Average: $85,000 to $3,180,000. Average amounts are $532,300 or less.

Funding: (Cooperative Agreements (Discretionary Grants)) FY 17 $5,990,730; FY 18 N/A FY 19 N/A

HQ: Division of Wild Horses and Burros 1849 C Street NW

Washington, DC 20244

Phone: 202-912-7350

Email: brittenh@blm.gov

http://www.wildhorseandburro.blm.gov

INVASIVE AND NOXIOUS PLANT MANAGEMENT

Award: Cooperative Agreements; Training

Purpose: Develop and implement projects that foster consultation and cooperation among stakeholders, interested parties, and the public and to organize, finalize, and develop projects to implement IPM plans for noxious weeds or invasive species within a specific geographic area.

Applicant Eligibility: N/A

Beneficiary Eligibility: State and local governments.

Award Range/Average: $1,000 to $567,000. Average $31,600 or less.

Funding: (Cooperative Agreements (Discretionary Grants)) FY 17 $7,685,772; FY 18 est $2,400,000; FY 19 N/A FY 16 $7,258,967

HQ: 20 M Street SE

Washington, DC 20240

Phone: 202-912-7226

Email: gramos@blm.gov

http://www.blm.gov/wo/st/en/prog/more/weeds/html

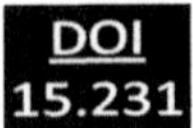

FISH, WILDLIFE AND PLANT CONSERVATION RESOURCE MANAGEMENT

Award: Cooperative Agreements; Training

Purpose: Provides national leadership to promote conservation of fish, wildlife and plant conservation, which will help restore and protect lands containing noteworthy resource values for regionally significant species of management concern or wetland and riparian areas; restore and protect crucial habitat through vegetation treatments, installation of wildlife friendly fences, and creating fish passages or barriers to protect aquatic species.

Applicant Eligibility: Anyone/general public.

Beneficiary Eligibility: All Public Land users.

Award Range/Average: $10,000 to $1,000,000. Average amounts $68,300 or less.

Funding: (Cooperative Agreements (Discretionary Grants)) FY 17 $60,960,949; FY 18 est $67,000,000; FY 19 FY 16 $67,344,390

HQ: Fish Wildlife and Plant Conservation 1849 C Street NW, P.O. Box 5115

Washington, DC 20240-9998

Phone: 202-912-7230

http://www.blm.gov/nhp/index.htm

WILDLAND FIRE RESEARCH AND STUDIES

Award: Cooperative Agreements

Purpose: To encourage interested parties to perform research and studies pertaining to wildland fire and resource management, to develop products and tools for all levels of decision making to meet the objectives of the National Fire Plan, and to seek information to improve decision making in wildland fire management.

Applicant Eligibility: Anyone/General Public.

Beneficiary Eligibility: Same as Applicant Eligibility.

Award Range/Average: Past partnership projects range from $15,000 to $90,000. Average amounts are $30,000 or less. For the Joint Fire Science Program awards range from $60,000 to $500,000. Average amounts are $350,000 or less.

Funding: (Cooperative Agreements (Discretionary Grants)) FY 17 $5,374,206; FY 18 est $650,000; FY 19 est $950,000

HQ: WO 350) 20 M Street SE, Room 2134

Washington, DC 20003

Phone: 202-912-7350

Email: kim_berns@blm.gov

http://www.forestsandrangelands.gov

FORESTS AND WOODLANDS RESOURCE MANAGEMENT

Award: Cooperative Agreements

Purpose: The Forest and Woodland Management program provides financial assistance, through grants or cooperative agreements, to public or private organizations for the improvement of forests on public lands. Stewardship Authority provides financial assistance for Stewardship projects that achieve land management goals for the public lands that meet local and rural community needs. Good Neighbor Authority provides financial assistance for Good Neighbor projects that consist of Authorized Restoration Services which include: treatment of insect and disease infected trees, hazardous fuels reduction, or any other activities to restore or improve forest, rangeland, and watershed health, including fish and wildlife habitat.

Applicant Eligibility: Anyone/General public. State Government only (Good Neighbor Authority).

Beneficiary Eligibility: Anyone/General public.

Award Range/Average: $1,000 to $450,900. Average amounts $50,000 or less.

Funding: (Cooperative Agreements (Discretionary Grants)) FY 17 $774,228; FY 18 N/A FY 19 N/A FY 16 $1,447,356

HQ: 20 M Street SE, Room 2134

Washington, DC 20003

Phone: 202-912-7222

Email: kim_berns@blm.gov

http://www.blm.gov/wo/st/en/prog/more/forests_and_woodland.html

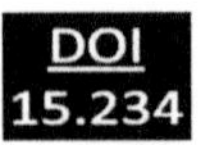

SECURE RURAL SCHOOLS AND COMMUNITY SELF-DETERMINATION

Award: Cooperative Agreements; Training

Purpose: To reinstate stability and predictability to the annual payments made to States and counties containing National Forest System lands and Oregon and California and Coos Bay Wagon Road lands managed by the Bureau of Land Management.

Applicant Eligibility: State and local governments, public nonprofit institutions/organizations, other public institution/organization, private nonprofit institution/organization, other private institution/organization and landowners.

Beneficiary Eligibility: Anyone/General public.

Award Range/Average: Past partnership projects have run between $1,100 to $596,700. Average amounts run about $83,600 or less.

Funding: (Cooperative Agreements (Discretionary Grants)) FY 17 N/A FY 18 N/A FY 19 N/A FY 16 $2,868,160

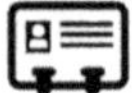

HQ: 20 M Street SE, Room 2134
Washington, DC 20003
Phone: 202-912-7350
Email: kim_berns@blm.gov
http://www.blm.gov/or/rac/ctypayhistory.php

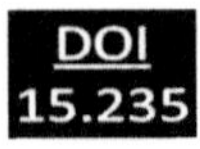

SOUTHERN NEVADA PUBLIC LAND MANAGEMENT

Award: Cooperative Agreements

Purpose: To contribute for the acquisition of environmentally sensitive lands in the State of Nevada.

Applicant Eligibility: Local governments and regional government entities within the State of Nevada as specifically identified in Public Law 105-263, as amended.

Beneficiary Eligibility: N/A

Award Range/Average: Past partnership projects have been between $30,000 to $30,500,000. Average project amount is $2,500,000 or less.

Funding: (Cooperative Agreements (Discretionary Grants)) FY 17 $79,617,609; FY 18 est $20,000,000; FY 19 N/A FY 16 $72,973,176

HQ: 20 M Street SE, Room 2134
Washington, DC 20003
Phone: 202-912-7350

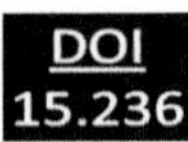

ENVIRONMENTAL QUALITY AND PROTECTION

Award: Cooperative Agreements

Purpose: To render financial assistance, through grants or cooperative agreements as a partnership to reduce or remove pollutants in the environment for the protection of human health, water and air resources; to restore damaged or degraded watersheds; and to respond to changing climate. Objectives are implemented through core programs such as: the Abandoned Mine Land program, Hazmat program and the Soil, Water and Air (SWA) program.

Applicant Eligibility: Anyone/General public.

Beneficiary Eligibility: Same as Applicant Eligibility.

Award Range/Average: Past partnership projects have ranged from $1,000 to 1,762,000. Average amount is $62,700 or less.

Funding: (Cooperative Agreements (Discretionary Grants)) FY 17 $7,172,688; FY 18 N/A FY 19 N/A FY 16 $10,814,674.

HQ: Division of Lands and Realty Bureau of Land Management (WO 350) 20 M Street SE, Room 2134

Washington, DC 20003

Phone: 202-912-7350

http://www.blm.gov

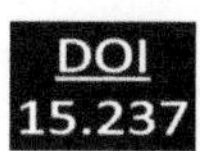

RANGELAND RESOURCE MANAGEMENT

Award: Cooperative Agreements

Purpose: Provides financial assistance to manage, develop and protect public lands and enhance the understanding of rangeland and watershed resources, their ecological processes, and capabilities in order to meet rangeland and water quality standards for the improvement of rangelands on public lands. Projects and livestock administration for the management of rangeland ecosystems are conducted in a coordinated manner and consider the interrelationships of living organisms of plants and animals, the physical environment of soil, water, air, and landscape characteristics when developing and implementing resource objectives and management actions.

Applicant Eligibility: N/A

Beneficiary Eligibility: N/A

Award Range/Average: $7,000 to $501,000. Average amounts $57,891 or less.

Funding: (Cooperative Agreements (Discretionary Grants)) FY 18 est $0; FY 16 $3,439,748; FY 17 est $2,000,000

HQ: Division of Lands and Realty

Washington, DC 20003

Phone: 202-912-7350

Email: kim_berns@blm.gov

http://www.blm.gov/programs/natural-resources

CHALLENGE COST SHARE

Award: Cooperative Agreements

Purpose: Works through cooperative partners to help accomplish high priority work to support habitat improvement, comprehensive travel management, recreation and cultural projects.

Applicant Eligibility: N/A

Beneficiary Eligibility: N/A

Award Range/Average: Past partnership projects have been between $5,000 to $182,000 depending on the policies of that particular state and the money available. Average amounts are $25,100 or less.

Funding: (Cooperative Agreements (Discretionary Grants)) FY 16 $4,804,450

HQ: Bureau of Land Management (WO 350) 20 M Street SE, Room 2134 2025 E Street NW
Washington, DC 20003
Phone: 202-912-7350
Email: kim_berns@blm.gov
http://www.blm.gov

MANAGEMENT INITIATIVES

Award: Cooperative Agreements

Purpose: Supports mission program efforts for the management, protection, and development of public lands managed by the Bureau of Land Management. Awards are typically supported by funding one-time specific legislation and internal projects and programs.

Applicant Eligibility: Anyone/General public.

Beneficiary Eligibility: Same as Applicant Eligibility.

Award Range/Average: Past partnerships have been between $2,900 to $800,000. Average amounts are $117,400 or less.

Funding: (Cooperative Agreements (Discretionary Grants)) FY 16 $616,490; FY 17 est $0; FY 18 est $0

HQ: 20 M Street SE, Room 2134
Washington, DC 20003
Phone: 202-912-7040
Email: kim_berns@blm.gov
http://www.blm.gov

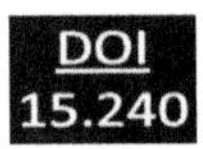

HELIUM RESOURCE MANAGEMENT

Award: Cooperative Agreements

Purpose: To ensure that the U.S. Government can upgrade and deliver crude helium from an underground storage field.

Applicant Eligibility: N/A

Beneficiary Eligibility: N/A

Award Range/Average: $720,000 and $6,000,000. Average is $336,000 or less.

Funding: (Cooperative Agreements (Discretionary Grants)) FY 17 $827,005; FY 18 est $416,760; FY 19 N/A FY 16 $10,774,064

HQ: Division of Lands and Realty
Washington, DC 20003
Phone: 202-912-7350
http://www.blm.gov/programs/energy-and-minerals/helium/federal-helium-operations

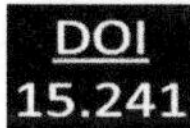

INDIAN SELF-DETERMINATION ACT CONTRACTS, GRANTS AND COOPERATIVE AGREEMENTS

Award: Cooperative Agreements; Training

Purpose: To provide the full participation of the Indian tribes in programs and services conducted by the Bureau of Land Management for Indians and to encourage the development of human resources of the Indian people; and to establish program assistance to upgrade Indian education that will support the right of Indian citizens and for other purposes.

Applicant Eligibility: Federally recognized Indian tribal governments and any Alaska Native Village, or regional or village corporation.

Beneficiary Eligibility: Federally recognized Indian tribal governments and American Indians.

Award Range/Average: $12,600 to $1,302,100. Average is $244,300 or less.

Funding: (Cooperative Agreements (Discretionary Grants)) FY 17 $3,838,581; FY 18 N/A FY 19 N/A FY 16 $7,652,468

HQ: 20 M Street SE, Room 2134
Washington, DC 20003
Phone: 202-912-7245
Email: kim_berns@blm.gov
http://www.blm.gov

BLM RURAL FIRE ASSISTANCE

Award: Cooperative Agreements; Use of Property, Facilities, and Equipment; Provision of Specialized Services; Advisory Services and Counseling; Dissemination of Technical Information; Training

Purpose: Supports mission program efforts for the management, protection, and development of public lands managed by the Bureau of Land Management. Awards are typically supported by funding one-time specific legislation and internal projects and programs.

Applicant Eligibility: Rural and Volunteer Fire Departments and Rangeland Fire Protection Association with an existing cooperative fire response agreement with BLM. State and local government, Public nonprofit institution/organizations, Other public institution/organization, Federally Recognized Indian Tribal Government, Private nonprofit institution/organization, Native American Organization, and rural fire departments serving a community with a population of 10,000 or less in the wildland/urban interface.

Beneficiary Eligibility: State, Local, Public Nonprofit Institution/Organization, Other Public Institution/ Organization, Federally Recognized Indian Tribal Government, Small Business, Profit Organization,

Private Organization, Anyone/General Public, Native American Organization, Farmer/Rancher/Agriculture Producer, Homeowner, Land/Property Owner, Suburban, and Rural.

Award Range/Average: Past partnership projects have ranged from $1,600 to $125,000. Average amount is $28,600 or less.

Funding: (Cooperative Agreements (Discretionary Grants)) FY 17 $0; FY 18 est $600,000; FY 19 FY 16 $186,100

HQ: Division of Fire Planning and Fuels Management (FA-600) 83705 National Interagency Fire Center, 3833 S Development Avenue

Boise, ID 83705

Phone: 208-387-5685

Email: sacarregui@blm.gov

http://www.nal.usda.gov/ric/15242

DOI 15.243 YOUTH CONSERVATION OPPORTUNITIES ON PUBLIC LANDS

Award: Cooperative Agreements

Purpose: Promotes and stimulate public purposes such as education, job training, development of responsible citizenship, productive community involvement, and further the understanding and appreciation of natural and cultural resources through the involvement of youth and young adults in the care and enhancement of public resources.

Applicant Eligibility: Any qualified youth or conservation corps that supports youth career training and development in the areas of appropriate natural and cultural resource conservation projects. A qualified service and conservation corps means any program established by a State, or local government, by the governing body of any Indian tribe, or by a nonprofit organization.

Beneficiary Eligibility: Youth and local communities that benefit from conservation improvements and involvement in youth programs activities on Bureau of Land Management public lands and facilities.

Award Range/Average: $2,500 to $250,000. Average amounts approximately $150,000 or less.

Funding: (Cooperative Agreements (Discretionary Grants)) FY 17 $3,439,772; FY 18 N/A

HQ: Division of Education Interpretation and Partnerships 01849 C Street NW, Room 2134LM

Washington, DC 20240-9998

Phone: 202-912-7454

http://www.blm.gov/nhp/index.htm

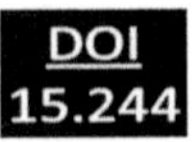

DOI 15.244 FISHERIES AND AQUATIC RESOURCES MANAGEMENT

Award: Cooperative Agreements

Purpose: Bureau of Land Management (BLM) provides national leadership to promote conservation of aquatic habitats, healthy aquatic ecosystems, and the fish, aquatic wildlife, and invertebrate species that are dependent upon them including native, non-native, subsistence, sportfish and aquatic invasive species. Aquatic resources on BLM-managed public lands support the nation's aquatic biodiversity, support public recreation, and help sustain Native American cultural heritages. The BLM works to ensure the resiliency of public trust aquatic species and habitats through on the ground programs and activities including conducting instream habitat and riparian vegetation treatments; removing passage barriers to aquatic organisms; preserving water quantity and quality; taking actions that prevent the introduction, spread, and establishment of aquatic invasive species; conducting family, youth and veterans education and outreach programs; and inventorying, assessing and monitoring aquatic organisms and habitats. The BLM manages these resources in cooperation with states, tribes, other federal agencies, and non-governmental organizations.

Applicant Eligibility: N/A

Beneficiary Eligibility: All Public Land users.

Award Range/Average: Past partnership projects have ranged from $10,000 to $1,000,000. Average amounts approximately $68,300 or less.

Funding: (Cooperative Agreements (Discretionary Grants)) FY 19 est $0; FY 18 est $0; FY 17 $1,643,111; - New Program

HQ: 1849 C Street NW, P.O. Box 5115
Washington, DC 20240-9998
Phone: 202-912-7230
http://www.blm.gov/nhp/index.htm

PLANT CONSERVATION AND RESTORATION MANAGEMENT

Award: Cooperative Agreements; Training

Purpose: Bureau of Land Management (BLM) Plant Conservation & Restoration Program provides national leadership to support field office habitat management efforts to restore sage grouse, mule deer, desert tortoise, and wild game species habitats; and increase on-the-ground project work to restore and reduce the threats to sage-grouse, mule deer, and other sensitive species in high priority habitats; conduct seed collection through the Seeds of Success (SOS) Program within priority species habitat; continue to work with growers to develop genetically appropriate native plant material for use in habitat restoration; continue to support and increase labor and operations of the BLM National Seed Warehouse System to assist field offices with seed procurement; support studies to improve the effectiveness of seed and seeding treatments through partners, State Offices, and Eco regional Programs; continue to monitor and protect more than 1,700 rare plant species, ~400 of which are found exclusively on BLM lands; continue to work with partners to prioritize and implement priority species conservation actions; continue to assist Emergency Stabilization & Restoration in identifying imminent post-wildfire threats, managing unacceptable risks, and restoring public lands with the use of native plant materials.

Applicant Eligibility: Anyone/general public.

Beneficiary Eligibility: All Public Land users.

Award Range/Average: Past partnership projects have ranged from $10,000 to $1,000,000.

Funding: (Cooperative Agreements (Discretionary Grants)) FY 18 est $0; FY 19 est $0; FY 17 $15,900,000

HQ: 1849 C Street NW, P.O. Box 5115
Washington, DC 20240-9998
Phone: 202-912-7230
http://www.blm.gov/programs/natural-resources/native-plant-communities

DOI 15.246 THREATENED AND ENDANGERED SPECIES

Award: Cooperative Agreements

Purpose: The Bureau of Land Management (BLM) implements tasks identified in T&E recovery plans developed by the U.S. Fish and Wildlife Service (USFWS) and National Marine Fisheries Service. It also implements conservation actions for sensitive and candidate species to preclude the need for federal listing. The Threatened and Endangered Species Program works to conserve and recover federally-listed animal and plant species and their habitat on public lands and shares cooperative responsibility with other BLM programs and partners for conservation of candidate and sensitive species.

Applicant Eligibility: Anyone/general public with the exception of other federal agencies. Applicants must competitively apply to postings on Grants.

Beneficiary Eligibility: All Public Land users.

Award Range/Average: $5,000 to $2,000,000. Average amounts approximately $68,300 or less.

Funding: (Cooperative Agreements (Discretionary Grants)) FY 18 est $0; FY 19 est $0; FY 17 $3,200,000.

WILDLIFE RESOURCE MANAGEMENT

Award: Cooperative Agreements

Purpose: The Bureau of Land Management's Wildlife Program manages wildlife habitat to help ensure self-sustaining, abundant and diverse populations of wildlife on public lands. In order to provide for the long-term conservation of wildlife resources, it supports numerous habitat maintenance and restoration activities. BLM-managed lands are vital to thousands of mammal, reptile, avian, and amphibian species. Managing more wildlife habitat than any other federal agency, the wildlife program helps ensure self-sustaining populations and a natural abundance and diversity of wildlife (a publically owned resource) on public lands.

Applicant Eligibility: Anyone/general public with the exception of other federal agencies. Applicants must competitively apply to postings on Grants.

Beneficiary Eligibility: All Public Land users.

Award Range/Average: Past partnership projects have ranged from $10,000 to $1,000,000. Average amounts approximately $68,300 or less.

Funding: (Cooperative Agreements (Discretionary Grants)) FY 18 est $0; FY 17 $27,411,958; FY 19 est $0; - New Program

HQ:

Washington, DC 20240-9998

BUREAU OF RECLAMATION

Commissioner's Office, Denver, Colorado

Denver Federal Center, Building 53, PO Box 45047, Denver, CO 80225-0047 303-236-6309

Great Plains Regional Office

5001 Southgate Drive, Billings, MT 59101 406-896-5188

Lower Colorado Regional Office

1340 Financial Boulevard, Reno, NV 89520-0006 702-861-6559

Mid-Pacific Regional Office

2800 Cottage Way, Suite W-1834, Sacramento, CA 85825-1886 916-978-4527

Pacific Northwest Regional Office
1387 S. Vinnell Way, Boise, ID 83709-1657
208-373-3909

Upper Colorado Regional Office
440 West 200 South, Ste 500, Salt Lake City, UT 84101
801-539-4177

TITLE XVI WATER RECLAMATION AND REUSE "Title XVI Program"

Award: Formula Grants

Purpose: Directs the Secretary of Interior to undertake a program to identify and investigate opportunities to reclaim and reuse wastewaters and naturally impaired ground and surface water in the 17 Western States and Hawaii. It also provides authority for the Secretary to provide up to the lesser of 25 percent of, or the Federal appropriations ceiling (typically $20 million), for the cost of planning, design, and construction of specific water recycling projects, as well as up to 50 percent of the cost of Title XVI feasibility studies and 25 percent of the cost of Title XVI water reclamation and reuse research studies.

Applicant Eligibility: Eligible recipients of Title XVI funding are identified under the 1902 Act and include State, regional, or local authorities; Indian tribes or tribal organizations; or other entities such as a water conservation or conservancy district, wastewater district, rural water district, all located within the 17 Western States or Hawaii. To be eligible to receive funding for construction activities, a water reclamation and reuse project must be specifically authorized under Title XVI or eligible under the amendments in section 4009(c) of the Water Infrastructure Improvements for the Nation (WIIN) Act.

Beneficiary Eligibility: Water users, including municipal, industrial, and agricultural, that benefit from the additional drought resistant water source created.

Award Range/Average: Range: $75,000 to $5,250,000 Average: $1,000,000

Funding: (Cooperative Agreements) FY 19 est $3,000,000; FY 18 est $21,500,000; FY 17 $23,619,391.

HQ: Denver Federal Center, P.O. Box 25007
Denver, CO 80225
Phone: 303-445-3577
Email: aerath@usbr.gov
http://www.usbr.gov/watersmart/title/index.html

WATER DESALINATION RESEARCH AND DEVELOPMENT

Award: Cooperative Agreements

Purpose: Goals of the program: augment the supply of usable water in the United States; understand the environmental impacts of desalination and develop approaches to minimize these impacts relative to other water supply alternatives; develop approaches to lower the financial costs of desalination so that it is an attractive option relative to other alternatives in locations where traditional sources of water are inadequate.

Applicant Eligibility: Any responsible source, to include individuals, State and local entities, public nonprofit institutions/organizations, other public institutions/organizations, Federally recognized Indian Tribal Governments, small businesses, profit organizations, private nonprofit institutions/organizations, quasi-public nonprofit institutions/organizations, and other private institutions/organizations may submit a proposal which will be considered by Reclamation. Foreign entities are not eligible for funding.

Beneficiary Eligibility: Individuals, State and local entities, public nonprofit institutions/organizations, other public institutions/organizations, Federally recognized Indian Tribal Governments, small businesses, profit organizations, private nonprofit institutions/organizations, quasi-public nonprofit institutions/organizations and other private institutions/organizations.

Award Range/Average: Range is $100,000 - $500,000, Average $150,000.

Funding: (Cooperative Agreements) FY 18 est $1,250,000; FY 17 $3,610,000; FY 19 est $1,250,000;

HQ: Denver Federal Center, P.O. Box 25007
Denver, CO 25007
Phone: 303-445-2265
Email: yporrasmendoza@usbr.gov
http://www.usbr.gov

WATER SMART (SUSTAINING AND MANAGE AMERICA'S RESOURCES FOR TOMORROW)
"Water SMART Grants"

Award: Cooperative Agreements

Purpose: Makes funding available for eligible applicants to leverage their money and resources by cost sharing with Reclamation on projects that save water; mitigate conflict risk in areas at a high risk of water conflict; and accomplish other benefits to increase the reliability of existing supplies; development of water marketing strategies that will help prevent water conflicts and will contribute to water supply reliability; and small-scale water efficiency projects to that have been identified through previous planning efforts to conserve and use water more efficiently.

Applicant Eligibility: In accordance with P.L. 111-11, Section 9502, eligible applicants include any: university, nonprofit research institution, or other organization with water or power delivery authority. Applicants must also be located in the western U.S. or Territories as identified in the Reclamation Act of June 17, 1902, as amended and supplemented; specifically, Arizona, California, Colorado, Idaho, Kansas, Montana, Nebraska, Nevada, New Mexico, North Dakota, Oklahoma, Oregon, South Dakota, Texas, Utah, Washington, Wyoming, American Samoa, Guam, the Northern Mariana Islands, and the Virgin Islands.

Beneficiary Eligibility: The general public, agricultural, municipal and industrial water users; irrigation or water districts; and state governmental entities with water or power delivery authority, located in the states identified in the Act of June 17, 1902.

Award Range/Average: Range: $75,000- $1,000,000 Average: $300,000

Funding: (Cooperative Agreements (Discretionary Grants)) FY 19 est $10,000,000; FY 18 est $23,365,000; FY 17 $27,500,000;

HQ: P.O. Box 25007
Denver, CO 80225
Phone: 303-445-2839
Email: jgerman@usbr.gov
http://www.usbr.gov

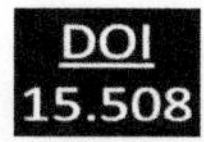

PROVIDING WATER TO AT-RISK NATURAL DESERT TERMINAL LAKES
"Desert Terminal Lakes Program"

Award: Project Grants

Purpose: Under this authority, Reclamation will fund various activities for the benefit of at-risk terminal lakes to provide water and assistance to a terminal lake to carry out research, support, and conservation activities for associated fish, wildlife, plant, and habitat resources in Nevada and California.

Applicant Eligibility: All funding allocated for grants, interagency agreements and 93-638 grants and contracts has been obligated, if additional funding is realized, the following would apply: State and local public agencies, Indian tribes, nonprofit organizations, educational institutions, and individuals may submit a proposal which will be considered by Reclamation. Foreign entities and Federal agencies are not eligible to apply.

Beneficiary Eligibility: Same as Applicant Eligibility.

Award Range/Average: Range: $168,236 to $3,000,000 in FY 17 Average: $1,047,081.89 in FY 17

Funding: (Cooperative Agreements (Discretionary Grants)) FY 18 est $1,850,000; FY 19 est $0; FY 17 $4,188,327

HQ: Lahontan Basin Area 705 N Plaza Street, Room 320

Carson City, NV 89701-4015

Phone: 775-882-3436

Email: abrinnand@usbr.gov

http://www.usbr.gov/mp/lbao

TITLE II, COLORADO RIVER BASIN SALINITY CONTROL
"Basinwide Program"

Award: Cooperative Agreements

Purpose: Provides financial and technical assistance to identify salt source areas; develop project plans to carry out conservation practices to reduce salt loads; install conversation practices to reduce salinity levels; carry out research, education, and demonstration activities; carry out monitoring and devaluation activities; and to decrease salt concentration and salt loading which causes increased salinity levels within the Colorado River and to enhance the supply and quality of water available for use in the United States and the Republic of Mexico.

Applicant Eligibility: Any legal entity that is the owner or operator of the features to be replaced and/or to be constructed and capable of contracting with Reclamation.

Beneficiary Eligibility: Any person who uses or reuses Colorado River water for irrigation, domestic, municipal or industrial water supply, or for fish and wildlife habitat will benefit.

Award Range/Average: Range $11,962,857 to $12,210,000 Average $10,914,762

Funding: (Cooperative Agreements (Discretionary Grants)) FY 18 est $3,588,857; FY 17 $3,663,000; FY 19 est $2,571,429; - Basin(Cooperative Agreements (Discretionary Grants)) FY 19 est $6,000,000; FY 18 est $8,374,000; FY 17 $8,547,000.

HQ: 2764 Compass Drive

Grand Junction, CO 20240

Phone: 970-248-0637

Email: tstroh@usbr.gov

http://www.usbr.gov/uc/progact/salinity/index.html

COLORADO UTE INDIAN WATER RIGHTS SETTLEMENT ACT "Colorado Ute Settlement Act/Animas La Plata"

Award: Cooperative Agreements; Project Grants; Direct Payments for Specified Use

Purpose: Provides municipal and industrial water supply to the Ute Mountain Ute, Southern Ute Indian Tribe, the Navajo Nation and non-Tribal participants from the Animas-La Plata Project in settlement of water rights claims for the Tribes, and also fulfill other project activities that may be required as a result of the construction, such as relocation of roads and moving powerlines.

Applicant Eligibility: Federally Recognized Indian Tribal Government - Projects shall be subject to the provisions of the Indian Self-Determination and Education Assistance Act (ii Stat. 2203; 25 U.S.C.

Beneficiary Eligibility: Federally recognized Indian Tribal Government members and the general public in southwestern Colorado and northwestern New Mexico.

Award Range/Average: Range: $4,128,239.07 Average: $ 1,592,746.36

Funding: (Direct Payments for Specified Use) FY 19 est $0; FY 18 est $0; FY 17 $250,000

HQ: FCCO 100 Four Corners Construction Office 1235 La Plata Highway

Farmington, NM 87401

Phone: 505-324-5000

CULTURAL RESOURCES MANAGEMENT

Award: Cooperative Agreements

Purpose: Manages and protects cultural resources on Reclamation land; provide for the curation of and public access to collectible heritage assets, including the increase of public awareness, appreciation, and knowledge of these resources; and provide for the protection and preservation of the tribal cultural resources impacted by operations of some Reclamation projects.

Applicant Eligibility: State and local agencies, sponsored organizations, public nonprofit institutions/ organizations, other public institutions/organizations, Federally-recognized Indian Tribal governments, minority groups, specialized groups, small businesses, profit organizations, private nonprofit institutions/ organizations, quasi-public nonprofit institutions/organizations, other private institutions/organizations, and Native American Organizations, educational or scientific organization, or any institution, corporation, association, or individual that possesses the requisite professional requirements.

Beneficiary Eligibility: State and local governments, Tribes, universities, anyone/general public, entities that have an education mission or mission-component, and repositories that meet the standards of the Department of the Interior, Department Manual, Part 411: Identifying and Managing Museum Property, for facilities managing Federal museum property. Further information regarding the general purpose and scope of the Department Manual (DM) is included in Part 001, Chapter 1, of the DM.

Award Range/Average: Range $ 15,144 - $ 69,342 Average $ 42,243

Funding: (Cooperative Agreements (Discretionary Grants)) FY 18 est $168,827; FY 17 $247,798; FY 19 est $151,247

HQ: P.O. Box 25007
Denver, CO 80225-0007
Phone: 303-445-3206
Email: jgiliberti@usbr.gov
http://www.usbr.gov/cultural

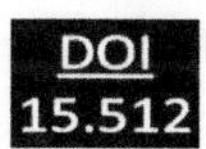

CENTRAL VALLEY IMPROVEMENT ACT, TITLE XXXIV

Award: Cooperative Agreements

Purpose: Central Valley Project Improvement Act (CVPIA) protects, restores, and enhances fish, wildlife, and associated habitats in the Central Valley and Trinity River basins of California; to address impacts of the Central Valley Project on fish, wildlife, and associated habitats; to improve the operational flexibility of the Central Valley Project; to increase water-related benefits provided by the Central Valley Project to the State of California through expanded use of voluntary water transfers and improved water conservation; to contribute to the State of California's interim and long-term efforts to protect the San Francisco Bay/ Sacramento-San Joaquin Delta Estuary and to achieve a reasonable balance among competing demands for use of Central Valley Project water, including the requirements of fish and wildlife, agricultural, municipal and industrial and power contractors.

Applicant Eligibility: State of California or an agency or subdivision thereof, Indian tribes, or nonprofit entities concerned with restoration, protection, or enhancement of fish, wildlife, habitat, or environmental values that are able to assist in implementing any action authorized by the title in an efficient, timely, and cost effective manner.

Beneficiary Eligibility: Anyone/General Public

Award Range/Average: Range is $10,000,000 to $12,000,000; Average $ 10,750,000

Funding: (Cooperative Agreements (Discretionary Grants)) FY 19 est $12,000,000; FY 18 est $12,000,000; FY 17 $10,024,159

HQ: Mid-Pacific Regional Office Federal Office Building 2800 Cottage Way
Sacramento, CA 95825-1898
Phone: 916-978-5001
http://www.usbr.gov/mp/cvpia

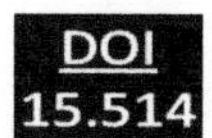

RECLAMATION STATES EMERGENCY DROUGHT RELIEF "Emergency Drought Relief and Drought Contingency Planning"

Award: Cooperative Agreements; Project Grants

Purpose: Develops and updates comprehensive drought contingency plans and implements projects that will build long-term resiliency to drought.

Applicant Eligibility: 1) Drought contingency planning: Applicants eligible to apply for funding to develop or update drought contingency plans include: States, cities, or sub-divisions of a state or city; Indian tribes or tribal water organizations; irrigation and water districts, water conservancy districts and other organizations with water or power delivery authority located within the following 17 Western U.S. States: Arizona, California, Colorado, Idaho, Kansas, Montana, Nebraska, Nevada, New Mexico, North Dakota,

Oklahoma, Oregon, South Dakota, Texas, Wyoming, Utah, and Washington; and Hawaii. 2) Drought resiliency projects: Applicants eligible to apply for funding for drought resiliency projects include: States, cities, or sub-divisions of a state or city; Indian tribes or tribal water organizations; irrigation and water districts, water conservancy districts, and other organizations with water or power delivery authority.

Beneficiary Eligibility: General public; Federal, State and local governments; and Federally Recognized Indian Tribal Governments.

Award Range/Average: Range is $ 35,000 - $ 750,000; Average $270,000.

Funding: (Cooperative Agreements (Discretionary Grants)) FY 18 est $3,250,000; FY 19 est $2,900,000; FY 17 $6,900,000

HQ: Mail Code 84-51000, P.O. Box 25007
Denver, CO 80225-0007
Phone: 303-445-3121
Email: dmayhorn@usbr.gov
http://www.usbr.gov/drought

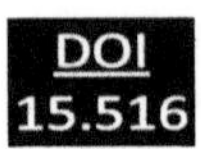

DOI 15.516

FORT PECK RESERVATION RURAL WATER SYSTEM "Fort Peck Water Supply Project"

Award: Project Grants; Direct Payments for Specified Use

Purpose: Ensures a safe and adequate municipal, rural and industrial water supply and assist the citizens in developing safe and adequate municipal, rural, and industrial water supplies.

Applicant Eligibility: The Fort Peck Tribal Executive Board, Dry Prairie Rural Water Association Incorporated (or any successor non-Federal entity).

Beneficiary Eligibility: Same as Applicant Eligibility.

Award Range/Average: No Data Available.

Funding: (Project Grants (Cooperative Agreements or Contracts)) FY 17 $15,250,000; FY 18 est $6,000,000; FY 19 est $4,731,000

HQ: P.O. Box 36900
Billings, MT 59107
Phone: 406-247-7710
Email: douglasdavis@usbr.gov

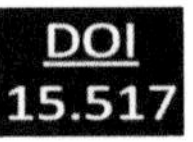

DOI 15.517

FISH AND WILDLIFE COORDINATION ACT

Award: Cooperative Agreements

Purpose: Provides financial assistance through grants or cooperative agreements and to public or private organizations for the improvement of fish and wildlife habitat associated with water systems or water supplies affected by Bureau of Reclamation projects.

Applicant Eligibility: State and local governments, nonprofit organizations and institutions, public and private institutions and organizations, Federally recognized Indian Tribal Governments, individuals, small businesses, for-profit organizations, and Native American Organizations.

Beneficiary Eligibility: Anyone/general public, governmental entities, Tribal governments, Native American organizations, and/or public or private organizations in the specific project area.

Award Range/Average: Range $10,0000 to $11,000,000 Average $430,000

Funding: (Cooperative Agreements (Discretionary Grants)) FY 19 est $20,000,000; FY 17 $31,227,958; FY 18 est $20,000,000

HQ: 1849 C Street NW
Washington, DC 20240
Phone: 202-208-3100
http://www.usbr.gov

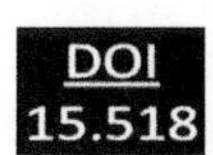

GARRISON DIVERSION UNIT
"Garrison Diversion Unit Project"

Award: Project Grants

Purpose: Provides funds on a non-reimbursable basis for the planning and construction of a multi-purpose water resource development project for irrigation; municipal, rural, and industrial water; fish, wildlife, and other natural resource conservation and development; recreation; flood control; augmented stream flows; ground water recharge; and other project purposes.

Applicant Eligibility: The State of North Dakota, the Garrison Conservancy District, the Standing Rock Sioux, the Three Affiliated Tribes, the Spirit Lake Nation, the Turtle Mountain Band of Chippewa and the Trenton Indian Service Area

Beneficiary Eligibility: The citizens of the State of North Dakota and the Standing Rock Sioux, the Three Affiliated Tribes, the Spirit Lake Nation, the Turtle Mountain Band of Chippewa and the Trenton Indian Service Area.

Award Range/Average: Range $2,000 to $40,000,000 Average $567,000

Funding: (Project Grants (Cooperative Agreements or Contracts)) FY 17 $22,676,904; FY 19 est $4,980,000; FY 18 est $9,600,000

HQ: 2021 4th Avenue N, P.O. Box 36900
Billings, MT 59101
Phone: 406-247-7789
Email: lparker@usbr.gov
http://www.usbr.gov/gp

INDIAN TRIBAL WATER RESOURCES DEVELOPMENT, MANAGEMENT, AND PROTECTION
"Indian Tribal Water Resources"

Award: Cooperative Agreements; Direct Payments for Specified Use

Purpose: Increases the opportunities for Indian tribes to develop, manage, and protect their water resources.

Applicant Eligibility: Federally recognized Indian tribes, institutions of higher education, national Indian organizations, and tribal organizations located in the 17 western States identified in the Act of June 17, 1902, as amended; specifically, Arizona, California, Colorado, Idaho, Kansas, Montana, Nebraska,

Nevada, New Mexico, North Dakota, Oklahoma, Oregon, South Dakota, Texas, Utah, Washington, and Wyoming.

Beneficiary Eligibility: Federally recognized Indian tribes in the 17 western states.

Award Range/Average: $2,000 to $1,300,000; Average is $125,000

Funding: Cooperative Agreements (Discretionary Grants) FY 19 est $3,500,000; FY 18 est $3,500,000; FY 17 $3,600,000

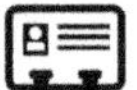

HQ: Native American and International Affairs Office 1849 C Street NW
Washington, DC 20240
Phone: 202-513-0550
http://www.usbr.gov/native

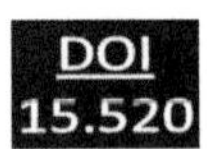

DOI 15.520 LEWIS AND CLARK RURAL WATER SYSTEM "Lewis and Clark Project"

Award: Cooperative Agreements

Purpose: Provides safe and adequate municipal, rural, and industrial water supplies, mitigation of wetland areas and water conservation for the Lewis and Clark Rural Water System.

Applicant Eligibility: The Lewis and Clark Rural Water Supply System, Inc., and its member entities (rural water systems and municipalities the meet the requirements for membership in the Lewis and Clark Rural Water Supply System, Inc.

Beneficiary Eligibility: Fifteen communities and 5 rural water systems in Lake, McCook, Minnehaha, Turner, Lincoln, Clay, and Union Counties, in southeastern South Dakota; Rock and Nobles Counties, in Southwestern Minnesota; and Lyon, Sioux, Osceola, O'Brien Dickinson, and Clay Counties, in northwestern Iowa.

Award Range/Average: $2,432,000 to $ 8,775,000 Average $5,000,000

Funding: (Cooperative Agreements) FY 18 est $3,650,000; FY 17 $9,522,000; FY 19 est $100,000

HQ: 316 N 26th Street, P.O. Box 36900
Billings, MT 59101
Phone: 406-247-7684
Email: lnafts@usbr.gov
http://www.lcrws.org

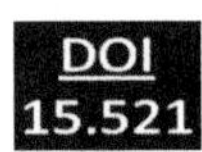

DOI 15.521 LOWER RIO GRANDE VALLEY WATER RESOURCES CONSERVATION AND IMPROVEMENT "Lower Rio Grande Valley Irrigation Projects"

Award: Cooperative Agreements

Purpose: Program includes the review of studies and planning reports, conduct of or participation in funding engineering work, infrastructure construction, and improvements for the purpose of conserving and transporting raw water.

Applicant Eligibility: The State of Texas, water users in the program area, specified irrigation districts, and other non-Federal entities.

Beneficiary Eligibility: The general public located in the state of Texas.

Award Range/Average: $0 - $435,000; Average 140,449

Funding: (Cooperative Agreements) FY 19 est $50,000; FY 17 $321,348; FY 18 est $50,000

HQ: 316 N 26th Street, P.O. Box 36900
Billings, MT 59101
Phone: 406-247-7710
Email: kbanks@gp.usbr.gov
http://www.usbr.gov/gp

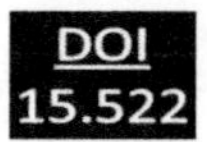

MNI WICONI RURAL WATER SUPPLY PROJECT "Mni Wiconi Project"

Award: Project Grants

Purpose: Ensures a safe and adequate municipal, rural, and industrial water supply for the residents of the Pine Ridge Indian, Rosebud Indian, and Lower Brule Indian Reservations in South Dakota; to assist the citizens of Haakon, Jackson, Jones, Lyman, Mellette, Pennington, and Stanley Counties, South Dakota, to develop safe and adequate municipal, rural, and industrial water supplies to promote the implementation of water conservation programs at these locations.

Applicant Eligibility: West River/Lyman-Jones Water Systems; the Oglala, Rosebud, and Lower Brule Sioux Tribes; and non-Federal entity or entities. Section 3(b) of Public Law 100-516 states "the Secretary, with the concurrence of the Oglala Sioux Tribal Council, shall enter into agreements with the appropriate non-Federal entity or entities for planning, designing, constructing, operating, maintaining and replacing the Oglala Sioux Rural Water Supply System.

Beneficiary Eligibility: The citizens of the southwest quarter of the State of South Dakota, including the Oglala, Rosebud, and Lower Brule Indian Reservations.

Award Range/Average: Range $ 50,000 to $ 20,000,000; Average $ 12,000,000

Funding: (Project Grants (Cooperative Agreements or Contracts)) FY 18 est $0; FY 17 $0; FY 19 est $0

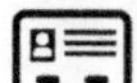

HQ: 2021 4th Avenue N, P.O. Box 36900
Billings, MN 59107
Phone: 406-247-7789
Email: lparker@usbr.gov
http://www.usbr.gov

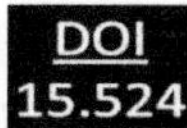

RECREATION RESOURCES MANAGEMENT "Title XXVIII"

Award: Cooperative Agreements

Purpose: Provides cost-share opportunities with non-Federal recreation partners to assist in planning, development, operation, maintenance, and replacement of recreation and fish and wildlife resource facilities at partner managed Reclamation project recreation areas.

Applicant Eligibility: Non-Federal managing partners (e.g.

Beneficiary Eligibility: Non-Federal recreation management partners.

Award Range/Average: Range $485,000 to $2,500,000; Average $3,398,215

Funding: (Cooperative Agreements (Discretionary Grants)) FY 18 est $8,960,439; FY 17 $7,490,397; FY 19 est $6,288,761

HQ: P.O. Box 25007 (84-57000)
Denver, CO 80225-0007
Phone: 303-445-2712
Email: jljackson@usbr.gov
http://www.usbr.gov/recreation

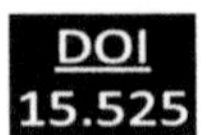

ROCKY BOY'S/NORTH CENTRAL MONTANA REGIONAL WATER SYSTEM
"North Central Montana Rural Water Supply Project"

Award: Project Grants

Purpose: Ensures a safe and adequate rural, municipal, and industrial water supply for the residents of the Rocky Boy's Reservation in the State of Montana.

Applicant Eligibility: The Chippewa-Cree of the Rocky Boy's Indian Reservation and the North Central Montana Regional Water Authority.

Beneficiary Eligibility: The Chippewa-Cree of the Rocky Boy's Indian Reservation and inhabitants of the areas served by the North Central Montana Regional Water Authority in Chouteau, Glacier, Hill, Liberty, Pondera, Teton, and Toole Counties, Montana.

Award Range/Average: N/A

Funding: (Project Grants (Cooperative Agreements or Contracts)) FY 17 $13,091,919; FY 19 est $3,984,000; FY 18 est $4,850,000

HQ: Great Plains Regional Office, P.O. Box 36900
Billings, MT 59101
Phone: 406-247-7710
Email: douglasdavis@usbr.gov

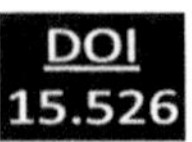

SAN GABRIEL BASIN RESTORATION

Award: Project Grants

Purpose: Designs, constructs, operates, and maintains water quality projects within the San Gabriel Basin, Los Angeles County, California.

Applicant Eligibility: San Gabriel Basin Water Quality Authority (or its successor agency) and/or the Central Basin Municipal Water District.

Beneficiary Eligibility: General public, all users and indirect users of groundwater supplies in the San Gabriel Basin.

Award Range/Average: Range $0 to $0 Average $0.

Funding: (Project Grants) FY 19 est $0; FY 17 $0; FY 18 est $0

HQ:
Washington, DC
http://www.usbr.gov/lc/socal

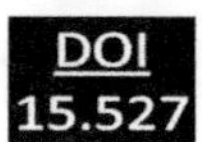

SAN LUIS UNIT, CENTRAL VALLEY

Award: Cooperative Agreements

Purpose: Provides drainage service to lands within the San Luis Unit of the Central Valley Project of central California.

Applicant Eligibility: Any responsible source, to include irrigation and/or water districts, State and local entities, public nonprofit institutions/organizations, other public institutions/organizations, Federally recognized Indian Tribal Governments, small businesses, profit organizations, private nonprofit institutions/organizations, quasi-public nonprofit institutions/organizations, and other private institutions/organizations.

Beneficiary Eligibility: Irrigation and/or water districts, State and local entities, farmers and ranchers, agricultural producers, and owners of drainage impacted land within the San Luis Unit of the Central Valley Project.

Award Range/Average: $32,600 - $122,700, Average $124,014.67

Funding: (Project Grants (Cooperative Agreements)) FY 19 est $3,000,000; FY 17 $3,047,817; FY 18 est $2,000,000

HQ:
Washington, DC
http://www.usbr.gov/mp

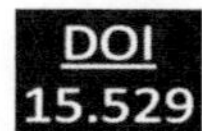

UPPER COLORADO AND SAN JUAN RIVER BASINS ENDANGERED FISH RECOVERY
"Upper Colorado and San Juan River Recovery Implementation Program"

Award: Project Grants

Purpose: Authorizes the U.S. Bureau of Reclamation (USBR) to provide cost sharing for the endangered fish recovery implementation programs for the Upper Colorado and San Juan River Basins.

Applicant Eligibility: Federal, Interstate, Intrastate, State and Local governments; Public Institution/Organizations, and Federally Recognized Indian Tribal Governments and private contractors.

Beneficiary Eligibility: Indian Tribes in the location of the San Juan River Basin and in the Duchesne River Basin, and the general public in the Colorado River Basin.

Award Range/Average: Range $5,000 to $1,800,000 per award Average $1,208,532

Funding: (Project Grants (Cooperative Agreements)) FY 18 est $2,825,785; FY 19 est $2,910,559; FY 17 $2,634,704; - SJRIP(Project Grants (Cooperative Agreements)) FY 18 est $5,651,571; FY 19 est $5,821,118; FY 17 $5,700,251; - UCRIP

HQ:

http://www.usbr.gov/uc/wcao/rm/sjrip

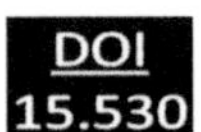

WATER CONSERVATION FIELD SERVICES (WCFS)

Award: Cooperative Agreements

Purpose: Encourages water conservation in the operations of recipients of water from Federal water projects, to assist agricultural and urban water districts in preparing and implementing water conservation plans in accordance with the Reclamation Reform Act of 1982 (RRA).

Applicant Eligibility: Eligible applicants include any State, Indian tribe, irrigation district, water district, or other organization with water or power delivery authority. Applicants must also be located in the western U.S. or Territories as identified in the Reclamation Act of June 17, 1902, as amended and supplemented; specifically, Arizona, California, Colorado, Idaho, Kansas, Montana, Nebraska, Nevada, New Mexico, North Dakota, Oklahoma, Oregon, South Dakota, Texas, Utah, Washington, Wyoming, American Samoa, Guam, the Northern Mariana Islands, and the Virgin Islands.

Beneficiary Eligibility: The general public and irrigation or water districts located in the 17 western States identified in the Act of June 17, 1902, as amended; specifically, Arizona, California, Colorado, Idaho, Kansas, Montana, Nebraska, Nevada, New Mexico, North Dakota, Oklahoma, Oregon, South Dakota, Texas, Utah, Washington, and Wyoming.

Award Range/Average: Range $6,938 - $100,000 Average $50,000

Funding: (Cooperative Agreements (Discretionary Grants)) FY 19 est $1,750,000; FY 17 $4,179,000; FY 18 est $4,038,000;

HQ:

http://www.usbr.gov

YAKIMA RIVER BASIN WATER ENHANCEMENT (YRBWE)

Award: Cooperative Agreements

Purpose: Within the Yakima River Basin to safeguard, mitigate, and enhance fish and wildlife through improved water management; improved instream flows; improved water quality; protection, creation and enhancement of wetlands; and by other appropriate means of habitat improvement; to improve the reliability of water supply for irrigation; to authorize a Yakima River basin water conservation program that will improve the efficiency of water delivery and use; enhance basin water supplies; improve water quality; protect, create and enhance wetlands, and determine the amount of basin water needs that can be met by water conservation measures.

Applicant Eligibility: State of Washington, and Federally Recognized Indian Tribal Governments, water and irrigation districts, and water rights owners located in the project area.

Beneficiary Eligibility: Anyone/General Public, Intrastate, Local, Individual/Family, and Federally Recognized Indian Tribal Governments within the project area.

Award Range/Average: Range $ 5,000 to $ 44,700,000 Average $ 6,687,907

Funding: (Cooperative Agreements) FY 17 $8,401,840; FY 19 est $4,544,458; FY 18 est $3,490,000;

HQ: 1849 C Street NW
Washington, DC 20240
Phone: 202-208-3100
http://www.usbr.gov/pn

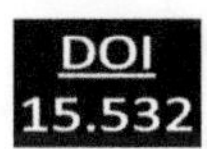

CENTRAL VALLEY, TRINITY RIVER DIVISION, TRINITY RIVER FISH AND WILDLIFE MANAGEMENT
"Trinity River Restoration Program"

Award: Cooperative Agreements

Purpose: Addresses the impacts of the Central Valley Project (CVP) on fish, wildlife, and associated habitats by protecting, restoring, and enhancing such habitats and to address other identified adverse environmental impacts.

Applicant Eligibility: State and local entities, public nonprofit institutions/organizations, other public institutions/organizations, Federally recognized Indian Tribal governments, small businesses, profit organizations, private nonprofit institutions/organizations, quasi- public nonprofit institutions/ organizations, and other private institutions/organizations.

Beneficiary Eligibility: General public, public institutions/organizations, Federally recognized Indian Tribal Governments, small businesses, profit organizations, private nonprofit institutions/organizations, quasi-public nonprofit institutions/organizations, and other private institutions/organizations.

Award Range/Average: Range $48,652- $3,862,051 Average $1,115,849

Funding: (Cooperative Agreements (Discretionary Grants)) FY 17 $7,707,625; FY 18 est $8,875,640; FY 19 est $9,117,640

HQ: 1313 S Main Street, P.O. Box 1300
Weaverville, CA 96093
Phone: 530-623-1800
Email: info@trrp.net
http://www.trrp.net

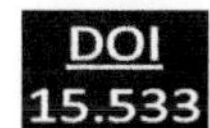

CALIFORNIA WATER SECURITY AND ENVIRONMENTAL ENHANCEMENT
"California Bay-Delta Authorization Act (CALFED)"

Award: Cooperative Agreements

Purpose: Primary objectives of the program are to expand water supplies to ensure efficient use through an array of projects and approaches, to improve water quality from source to tap, improve the health of the Bay-Delta system through restoring and protecting habitats and native species, and improve the Bay-Delta levees to provide flood protection, ecosystem benefits, and protect water supplies.

Applicant Eligibility: Agencies of the state of California.

Beneficiary Eligibility: State agencies within the CALFED solution area as defined in the CALFED Bay-Delta Program Record of Decision.

Award Range/Average: Range: $438,640 to $750,000 Average: $3,753,144

Funding: 432FY 18 est $0; FY 19 est $589,975; FY 17 $521,36

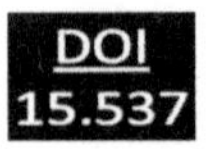

DOI 15.537 MIDDLE RIO GRANDE ENDANGERED SPECIES COLLABORATIVE "Collaborative Program"

Award: Cooperative Agreements

Purpose: A collaborative effort consisting of 16 stakeholders including federal, state, and local governmental entities; Indian tribes and pueblos; and non-governmental organizations representing diverse interests working to support compliance with the Endangered Species Act (ESA). The purpose of the Program is to protect and improve the status of endangered listed species along the Middle Rio Grande (MRG) by implementing certain recovery activities to benefit those species and their associated habitats.

Applicant Eligibility: Federal, Interstate, Intrastate, State, Local, Public nonprofit institution/organization, Other public institution/organization, Federally Recognized Tribal Government, Specialized Group, Private Non-profit Institution/Organization.

Beneficiary Eligibility: Same as Applicant Eligibility.

Award Range/Average: $25,000 to $200,000 Average is $ 125,000

Funding: (Cooperative Agreements (Discretionary Grants)) FY 17 $155,301; FY 19 est $404,278; FY 18 est $405,960

HQ: 555 Broadway Boulevard
Albuquerque, NM 87102
Phone: 505-462-3540
http://www.usbr.gov

DOI 15.538 LOWER COLORADO RIVER MULTI-SPECIES CONSERVATION "MSCP"

Award: Cooperative Agreements

Purpose: Protects the lower Colorado River environment while ensuring the certainty of existing river water and power operations, address the needs of threatened and endangered wildlife under the Endangered Species Act, and reduce the likelihood of listing additional species along the lower Colorado River.

Applicant Eligibility: State and local governments, nonprofit organizations and institutions, public and private institutions and organizations, Federally recognized Indian Tribal Governments, individuals, small businesses, for-profit organizations, and Native American Organizations.

Beneficiary Eligibility: Anyone/general public, governmental entities, Tribal governments, Native American organizations, and/or public or private organizations in the specific project area.

Award Range/Average: $1,739 to $285,374; Average $ 1,613,317

Funding: (Cooperative Agreements (Discretionary Grants)) FY 17 $1,509,950; FY 18 est $1,665,000; FY 19 est $1,665,000

HQ: P.O. Box 61470
Boulder City, NV 89006
Phone: 702-293-8555
http://www.lcrmscp.gov

EQUUS BEDS DIVISION ACQUIFER STORAGE RECHARGE
"Equus Beds Aquifer Storage Recharge Project"

Award: Cooperative Agreements

Purpose: Designs and constructs the City of Wichita's Aquifer Storage and Recovery project to divert flood flows from the Little Arkansas River into the Equus Beds Aquifer in order to recover depleted storage and protect the Aquifer.

Applicant Eligibility: The City of Wichita.

Beneficiary Eligibility: M & I and agricultural waters users of South-central Kansas.

Award Range/Average: No Data Available.

Funding: FY 19 est $0; FY 18 est $0; FY 17 $0

HQ: Great Plains Regional Office 316 N 26th Street, P.O. Box 36900

Billings, MT 59101-6900

Phone: 406-247-7684

Email: lnafts@usbr.gov

http://www.usbr.gov/gp

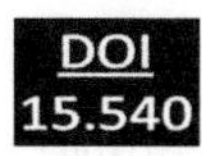

LAKE MEAD/LAS VEGAS WASH
"Las Vegas Wash (LVW Program)"

Award: Cooperative Agreements

Purpose: Develops and implements management strategies to improve water quality, habitat integrity, and reduce the salinity and sediment transport while providing environmental enhancement and recreational opportunities.

Applicant Eligibility: The Southern Nevada Water Authority (SNWA), a Special District Government.

Beneficiary Eligibility: The Southern Nevada Water Authority (SNWA) and the General Public.

Award Range/Average: $384,510.93; Average $101,106.40

Funding: Cooperative Agreements (Discretionary Grants) FY 19 est $300,000; FY 17 $300,000; FY 18 est $300,000

HQ:

Boulder City, NV 89006

Phone: 702-293-8109

http://www.usbr.gov

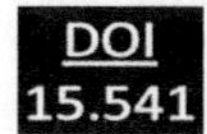

COLORADO RIVER BASIN ACT OF 1968
"Colorado River Basin Projects Act"

Award: Cooperative Agreements

Purpose: Provides a program for the further comprehensive development of water resources of the Colorado River Basin and for the provision of additional and adequate water supplies for the use in the upper as well as in the lower Colorado Basin.

Applicant Eligibility: Must have a water allocation and water delivery from a Reclamation water resource project or State responsibility for various project purposes.

Beneficiary Eligibility: The general public in the state of Arizona and southwestern New Mexico, irrigation and water districts and local entities.

Award Range/Average: N/A

Funding: (Cooperative Agreements) FY 18 est $0; FY 17 $0; FY 19 est $0

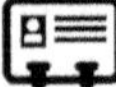

HQ: 6150 W Thunderbird Road
Glendale, AZ 85306-4001
Phone: 623-773-6215
http://www.usbr.gov/lc/phoenix

ARIZONA WATER SETTLEMENT ACT OF 2004
"Arizona Water Settlement Act"

Award: Project Grants; Direct Payments for Specified Use

Purpose: Provide for adjustments to the Central Arizona Project in Arizona, to authorize the Gila River Indian Community water rights settlement, to reauthorize and amend the Southern Arizona Water Rights settlement Act of 1982.

Applicant Eligibility: Must be authorized to receive funds by Congress in the statute.

Beneficiary Eligibility: Authorized beneficiaries are identified in the statute and include the state of Arizona, state of New Mexico, various irrigation and water districts, local entities and municipalities and Tribal Governments.

Award Range/Average: Range: $25,000,000 to $100,000,000 Average: $69,300,000

Funding: (Project Grants (Cooperative Agreements or Contracts)) FY 17 $0; FY 18 est $0; FY 19 est $0

HQ: Phoenix Area Office 6150 W Thunderbird Road
Glendale, AZ 85306-4001
Phone: 623-773-6200
http://www.usbr.gov/lc/phoenix

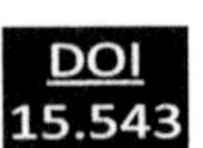

LAKE TAHOE REGIONAL WETLANDS DEVELOPMENT

Award: Cooperative Agreements

Purpose: Assists in addressing the past degradation of Lake Tahoe and its watershed by undertaking projects to meet the environmental thresholds as defined in the Tahoe Regional Planning Agency's Environmental Improvement Program (EIP). The environmental thresholds of interest include water quality, soil conservation, wildlife, fisheries and vegetation.

Applicant Eligibility: State and local agencies, public nonprofit institutions/organizations, other public institutions/organizations, Federally-recognized Indian Tribal governments, profit organizations, private nonprofit institutions/organizations, other private institutions/organizations, and educational or scientific organizations may apply.

Beneficiary Eligibility: Awards made under this program are intended to benefit the public by maintaining and improving the environmental quality in general, and water quality in particular, of the Lake Tahoe Basin.

Award Range/Average: Range: $0 to $ 320,029 Average: $ 106,676

Funding: (Cooperative Agreements (Discretionary Grants)) FY 19 est $0; FY 18 est $0; FY 17 $150,000. There are only funds to administer existing financial assistance agreements for this program.

HQ: 2800 Cottage Way
Sacramento, CA 95825
Phone: 916-978-5045
http://www.usbr.gov/mp

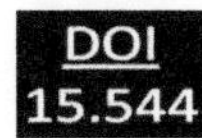

PLATTE RIVER RECOVERY IMPLEMENTATION "PRRIP"

Award: Cooperative Agreements

Purpose: Implements certain aspects of the U.S. Fish and Wildlife Service's recovery plans for four target species (interior least tern, whooping crane, piping plover and pallid sturgeon) listed as threatened or endangered pursuant to the Endangered Species Act.

Applicant Eligibility: Legislation authorizes the agreement. The term "Agreement" means the Platte River Recovery Implementation Program Cooperative Agreement entered into by the Governors of the States of Wyoming, Nebraska, and Colorado and the Secretary.

Beneficiary Eligibility: General public, irrigation and/or water districts, State and local entities, farmers and ranchers, agricultural producers, property owners, municipal water users, and power users.

Award Range/Average: Range $1,000,000 to $22,000,000 Average $16,605,536

Funding: (Cooperative Agreements (Discretionary Grants)) FY 18 est $12,959,000; FY 19 est $11,959,000; FY 17 $19,674,308

HQ: P.O. Box 36900
Billings, MT 59107-6900
Phone: 307-261-5671
http://www.platteriverprogram.org

BUNKER HILL GROUNDWATER BASIN, RIVERSIDE-CORONA FEEDER "Riverside Corona Feeder"

Award: Cooperative Agreements

Purpose: Directs the Secretary of the Interior to participate in the planning, design, and construction of the Riverside-Corona Feeder Project.

Applicant Eligibility: The Secretary is authorized to cooperate with the Western Municipal Water District, Riverside County, California, in the planning, design, and construction of the Riverside-Corona Feeder Project.

Beneficiary Eligibility: Water users serviced by the Western Municipal Water District.

Funding: FY 19 est $0; FY 17 $0; FY 18 est $0; - No FY2014 new obligations, but work continues on prior year financial assistance agreements.

HQ: Office of Policy and Administration Denver Federal Center, P.O. Box 25007 P.O. Box 84-51000
Denver, CO 80225
Phone: 303-445-3577
http://www.usbr.gov/lc/socal

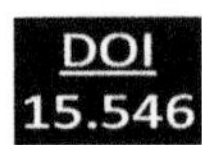

YOUTH CONSERVATION

Award: Cooperative Agreements

Purpose: Promotes and stimulates the public purposes such as education, job training, development of responsible citizenship, productive community involvement, and furthering the understanding and appreciation of natural and cultural resources.

Applicant Eligibility: Eligibility for conservation activities is limited to qualified youth or conservation corps that are able to involve youth ages 15-25 in the 17 states west of the Mississippi river. Eligibility for the Intern Program is limited to non-profit organizations other than institutions of higher education that are capable of recruiting qualified youth interns for positions located at Reclamation offices and facilities.

Beneficiary Eligibility: Youth and local communities that benefit from conservation improvements and involvement in youth programs activities on Reclamation-owned lands and facilities.

Award Range/Average: Range: $4,000 to $500,000 Average: $50,000

Funding: (Cooperative Agreements (Discretionary Grants)) FY 19 est $0; FY 18 est $0; FY 17 $0;

HQ: P.O. Box 25007
Denver, CO 80255
Phone: 303-445-2632
Email: rfarrell@usbr.gov
http://www.usbr.gov/youth

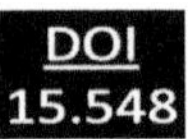

RECLAMATION RURAL WATER SUPPLY
"Rural Water Program"

Award: Cooperative Agreements

Purpose: Provides the basic requirements and framework for conducting water and related resource feasibility studies in order to formulate, evaluate, and select project plans for implementation.

Applicant Eligibility: Eligible applicants include states and political subdivisions of states, such as departments, agencies, municipalities, counties, and other regional or local authorities; Indian tribes and tribal organizations; and entities created under state law that have water management or water delivery authority, such as irrigation or water districts, canal companies, water users associations, rural water associations or districts, joint powers authorities, and other qualifying entities; and any combination of the entities listed above. Applicants must be located in the 17 Western States as identified in the Reclamation Act of June 17, 1902, as amended.

Beneficiary Eligibility: Eligible beneficiaries include small communities or group of small communities, including Indian tribes and tribal organizations. For the purpose of the Rural Water Supply Program, a small community is defined as having a population of no more than 50,000 people.

Award Range/Average: N/A

Funding: N/A

HQ: Water and Environmental Resources Division Building 67, P.O. Box 25007 (84-55000)
Denver, CO 80225-0007
Phone: 303-445-2711
http://www.usbr.gov/ruralwater

FISHING EVENTS FOR DISADVANTAGED CHILDREN

Award: Cooperative Agreements

Purpose: Provide opportunities for disabled and disadvantaged children to use and enjoy public waters and related lands; to assist Reclamation in meeting its goal to provide accessible programs, facilities and activities to create a positive outdoor experience for all citizens; to increase awareness of all the participants to the capabilities of disabled and disadvantaged children; and to provide educational opportunities for disabled and disadvantaged children to learn more about fish and water as natural resources.

Applicant Eligibility: Eligible applicants are State governments, County governments, City or townships governments, Special districts governments, Independent school districts, Public and State controlled institutions of higher education, Native American tribal governments(federally recognized), Public Housing Authorities/Indian Housing Authorities, Native American tribal organization(other than Federally recognized tribal governments) Non-Profits having a 501(c)(3) status with the Internal Revenue Survive (IRS), other than institutions of higher education, Private institutions of higher education, Individuals, Small businesses.

Beneficiary Eligibility: Disabled and disadvantaged children

Award Range/Average: Range: $50,000 - 118,000 Average: $136,000

Funding: Cooperative Agreements (Discretionary Grants) FY 19 est $0; FY 18 est $0; FY 17 $132,000

HQ: Financial Assistance Services 87-27850, P.O. Box 25007
Denver, CO 80255
Phone: 303-445-2025
Email: ihoiby@usbr.gov

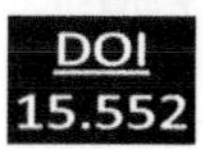

NAVAJO-GALLUP WATER SUPPLY

Award: Project Grants

Purpose: Provides financial aid to design and construct portions of the Navajo-Gallup Water Supply Project.

Applicant Eligibility: Native American Organization (Navajo Nation) Local governments (City of Gallup New Mexico) Profit organization(s) Private nonprofit institution(s)/organization(s)

Beneficiary Eligibility: Federally Recognized Indian Tribal Government (Navajo Nation) Local Governments (City of Gallup New Mexico)

Award Range/Average: Range: $499,985 - $32,409,679 Average: $14,647,328 Average from FY 11-FY 17

Funding: (Project Grants (Cooperative Agreements)) FY 18 est $60,000,000; FY 19 est $20,300,000; FY 17 $1,806,336

HQ: 103 Everett Street

Durango, CO 81303

Phone: 505-325-1794

Email: blongwell@usbr.gov

EASTERN NEW MEXICO RURAL WATER SYSTEM "ENMRWS"

Award: Project Grants

Purpose: Provides potable surface water to communities in Eastern New Mexico.

Applicant Eligibility: Eastern New Mexico Water Utility Authority (Authority) was formed for the sole purpose of administration of this new water supply project for the surrounding communities.

Beneficiary Eligibility: The Project would pipe 16,450 acre-feet of surface water per year from Ute Reservoir to the eastern New Mexico municipalities of Clovis, Elida, Grady, Melrose, Portales, and Texico currently relying on the declining quantity and quality of the Ogallala Aquifer. Curry County, Roosevelt County, and Cannon Air Force Base (CAFB) are also beneficiaries of the Project.

Award Range/Average: Range: $ 1,875,000 Average:N/A

Funding: (Project Grants (Cooperative Agreements)) FY 19 est $0; FY 17 $5,000,000; FY 18 est $1,875,000

HQ: 555 Broadway Boulevard NE

Albuquerque, NM 87102

Phone: 505-462-3655

Email: jirizarrynazario@usbr.gov

http://www.enmwua.com

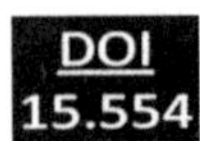

COOPERATIVE WATERSHED MANAGEMENT "CWMP"

Award: Project Grants

Purpose: Enhances water conservation, uses; improve water quality and ecological resiliency of a river or stream; and to reduce conflicts over water at the watershed level by supporting the formation of watershed groups to develop local solutions to address water management issues.

Applicant Eligibility: Watershed Group Development and Restoration Planning (Phase I): Applicants eligible to receive financial assistance through Phase I of the Cooperative Watershed Management Program include: States and Indian tribes.

Beneficiary Eligibility: The Cooperative Watershed Management Program benefits a diverse array of stakeholders, which may include but is not limited to, private property owners, Federal, State, or local agencies, and Indian tribes that are located in the 17 western States identified in the Act of June 17, 1902, as amended, and have authority with respect to the watershed.

Award Range/Average: Range: $20,000 - $100,000 Average: $80,000

Funding: (Project Grants (Cooperative Agreements)) FY 17 $560,000; FY 19 est $250,000; FY 18 est $3,250,000

 **HQ:** Office of Policy and Administration Denver Federal Center, P.O. Box 25007 P.O. Box 84-51000
Denver, CO 20191
Phone: 303-445-2906
Email: aomorgan@usbr.gov
http://www.usbr.gov/watersmart/cwmp/index.html

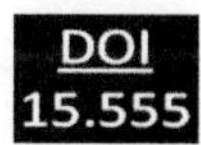

SAN JOAQUIN RIVER RESTORATION

Award: Project Grants

Purpose: Implements the Stipulation of Settlement in NRDC, which is consistent with and as supplement by, the San Joaquin River Restoration Settlement Act. It restores and maintains fish populations in "good condition" in the main stem of the San Joaquin River below Friant Dam to the confluence of the Merced River, including naturally-reproducing and self-sustaining populations of salmon and other fish.

Applicant Eligibility: State, tribal, and local governmental agencies, and with private parties, including agreements related to construction, improvement, and operation and maintenance of facilities, subject to any terms and conditions that the Secretary deems necessary to achieve the purposes of the Settlement.

Beneficiary Eligibility: State, tribal, and local governmental agencies, private parties, and the general public

Award Range/Average: Range: $ 5,000,000 Average: $ 2,294,246

Funding: (Project Grants (Cooperative Agreements)) FY 19 est $6,600,000; FY 18 est $21,101,965; FY 17 $4,339,481

 **HQ:** 2800 Cottage Way MP-170
Sacramento, CA 95825
Phone: 916-978-5464
Email: alubaswilliams@usbr.gov
http://www.restoresjr.net

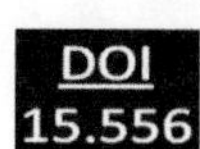

CROW TRIBE WATER RIGHTS SETTLEMENT "Crow Tribe Water Rights Settlement Act of 2010"

Award: Direct Payments for Specified Use

Purpose: Rehabilitates and improves the water diversion and delivery features of the Crow Irrigation Project (CIP) and to construct a new municipal, rural and industrial (MR&I) water system for the benefit of the Crow Tribe and its members.

Applicant Eligibility: The Crow Tribe of Montana.

Beneficiary Eligibility: Irrigable lands within the Crow Reservation. Drinking water for people on the reservation.

Award Range/Average: Range: $2,000,000 to $12,772,000 Average: $9,361,286

Funding: FY 18 est $12,772,000; FY 19 est $12,772,000; FY 17 $12,772,000.

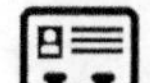 **HQ:** 2021 4th Avenue N
Billings, MT 59101

Phone: 406-247-7710

Email: douglasdavis@usbr.gov

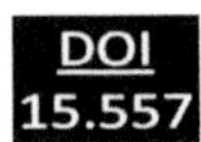

APPLIED SCIENCE GRANTS "Landscape Conservation Cooperatives (LCC)"

Award: Project Grants

Purpose: Enhances the management of natural and cultural resources that have a nexus to water resource management. It also includes developing tools to assess and adapt to the impacts of climate change and other landscape scale stressors within the geographic boundaries.

Applicant Eligibility: Eligible applicants include any: States; Tribes; Irrigation districts; Water districts; Organizations with water or power delivery in the Western United States or Territories as identified in the Reclamation Act of June 17, as amended and supplemented; specifically, Arizona, California, Colorado, Idaho, Kansas, Montana, Nebraska, Nevada, New Mexico, North Dakota, Oklahoma, Oregon, South Dakota, Texas, Utah, Washington, Wyoming, American Samoa, Guam, the Northern Mariana Islands, and the Virgin Islands); Universities located in the United States; Non-profit research institutions located in the United States; or Non-profit organizations (Non-profit organizations are eligible to apply for funding under all three task areas so long as the proposal addresses fish or wildlife habitat in wetland, riparian, or aquatic areas and there is a nexus to a Reclamation project.)

Beneficiary Eligibility: The general public; agricultural, municipal and industrial water users; irrigation or water districts; state governmental entities with water or power delivery authority; tribes; non-profit research institutions; and non-profit organizations located in the states identified in the Act of June 17, 1902.

Award Range/Average: Range: $25,000 $150,000 Average: $100,000

Funding: (Project Grants (Cooperative Agreements)) FY 17 est $700,000; FY 16 $15,649; FY 18 est $700,000; - FY 16: $15,649 (award was for an inter-agency agreement to provide capacity support for the LCCs, not to fund applied science projects).

HQ: Office of Policy and Administration Denver Federal Center, P.O. Box 25007 P.O. Box 84-51000 Denver, CO 80225

Phone: 303-445-2906

Email: aomorgan@usbr.gov

http://www.usbr.gov/watersmart/lcc/index.html

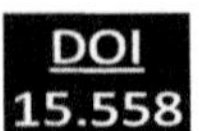

WHITE MOUNTAIN APACHE TRIBE RURAL WATER SYSTEM "Miner Flat Project"

Award: Direct Payments for Specified Use

Purpose: Assists in planning, engineering, design and construction of the Miner Flat Project.

Applicant Eligibility: White Mountain Apache Tribe

Beneficiary Eligibility: White Mountain Apache Tribe

Award Range/Average: Range: $ 0 Average: $ 0

Funding: (Direct Payments for Specified Use (Cooperative Agreements)) FY 17 $0; FY 19 est $0; FY 18 est $0;

HQ: 6150 W Thunderbird Road
Glendale, AZ 85306-4001
Phone: 623-773-6200
http://www.usbr.gov/lc/phoenix

NEW MEXICO RIO GRANDE BASIN PUEBLOS IRRIGATION INFRASTRUCTURE
"New Mexico Pueblos Irrigation Project"

Award: Project Grants; Direct Payments for Specified Use

Purpose: Rehabilitates and repairs the irrigation infrastructure of the Rio Grande Pueblos and helps in conserving water and addressing potential conflicts over water in the Rio Grande Basin.

Applicant Eligibility: Federally Recognized Indian Tribal Government—New Mexico Rio Grande Pueblos only: Taos, Picuris, Ohkay Owingeh, Santa Clara, San Ildefonso, Tesuque, Pojoaque, Nambe, Cochiti, Santo Domingo, San Felipe, Santa Ana, Sandia, Isleta, Acoma, Laguna, Jemez, Zia.

Beneficiary Eligibility: Same as Applicant Eligibility.

Award Range/Average: Range: $12,000 - $400,000 Average: $130,000

Funding: (Direct Payments for Specified Use (Cooperative Agreements)) FY 17 $300,000; FY 19 est $1,000,000; FY 18 est $1,000,000

HQ: 1849 C Street NW
Washington, DC 20240-0001
Phone: 202-513-0558
http://www.usbr.gov/uc/albuq/progact/nmpueblos/index.html

SECURE WATER ACT – RESEARCH AGREEMENTS

Award: Project Grants

Purpose: Research activities designed to conserve water resources, increases the efficiency of the use of water resources, and enhances the management of water resources, including increasing the use of renewable energy in the management and delivery of water.

Applicant Eligibility: In accordance with P.L.

Beneficiary Eligibility: The general public; agricultural, municipal and industrial water users; irrigation or water districts; and state governmental entities with water or power delivery authority.

Award Range/Average: Range: $36,000 - $420,000 Average: $105,000

Funding: (Project Grants (Cooperative Agreements)) FY 19 est $3,000,000; FY 17 $3,466,553; FY 18 est $3,000,000

HQ: Acquisition and Assistance Management Division Denver Federal Center, P.O. Box 84-27850 P.O. Box 25007
Denver, CO 80225
Phone: 303-445-2490
Email: jablack@usbr.gov

DOI 15.564 CENTRAL VALLEY PROJECT CONSERVATION "CVPCP"

Award: Project Grants

Purpose: Provides financial support for activities to benefit federally listed endangered and threatened species to compensate for impacts to species resulting from the operation and maintenance of the Central Valley Project (CVP).

Applicant Eligibility: Any person(s) without regard to specified eligibility criteria.

Beneficiary Eligibility: Anyone/General Public

Award Range/Average: Range: $ 25,000 to $1,000,000 Average: $ 1,132,347

Funding: FY 17 $1,142,000; FY 18 est $1,122,000; FY 19 est $1,130,000.

HQ: 1849 C Street NW, P.O. Box MIB6640
Washington, DC 20240
Phone: 202-208-3100
Email: rswanson@uc.usbr.gov
http://www.usbr.gov/mp/cvpcp

IMPLEMENTATION OF THE TAOS PUEBLO INDIAN WATER RIGHTS SETTLEMENT

Award: Project Grants

Purpose: The Act authorizes and directs the Bureau of Reclamation to provide financial assistance in the form of grants on a non-reimbursable basis to plan, permit, design, engineer, and construct Mutual-Benefit Projects that will minimize adverse effects on the Pueblo's water resources by moving future non-Indian ground water pumping away from the Pueblo's Buffalo Pasture, a culturally sensitive wetland.

Applicant Eligibility: Only the eligible non-Pueblo entities identified in section 503(1) of the Settlement Act are eligible to receive financial assistance.

Beneficiary Eligibility: Only the eligible non-Pueblo entities identified in section 503(1) are eligible to receive financial assistance.

Award Range/Average: $8,000 to $12.5 million

Funding: (Project Grants (Cooperative Agreements)) FY 19 est $12,500,000; FY 17 $4,000,000; FY 18 est $6,000,000

HQ: Denver Federal Center Building 56, Room 1000 25007
Denver, CO 80225
Phone: 303-445-2490
http://beta.sam.gov/fal/6413f3faab7a51ea0c978e1409f1f5f0/view?keywords=15.565&sort=-relevance&index=&is_active=true&page=1

UPPER KLAMATH BASIN HYDROLIC ANALYSES

Award: Formula Grants; Project Grants; Direct Payments for Specified Use; Dissemination of Technical Information

Purpose: Studies the hydrologic characteristics of Upper Klamath Basin to include the quantity, quality and distribution of all water, both above and below ground surface, and the geologic environment in which the water resides.

Applicant Eligibility: Federal - Department and establishment of the Federal government which are responsible for enforcement and the fulfillment of public policy. These departments and establishments directly administer and exercise jurisdiction over matters assigned to them, and are the administering agencies of Federal domestic assistance programs.

Beneficiary Eligibility: N/A

Award Range/Average: Range: $50,000 – $1,500,000 Average: 300,000

Funding: (Formula Grants) FY 19 est $500,000; FY 17 $511,000; FY 18 est $576,000;

DOI 15.567

COLORADO RIVER CONSERVATION SYSTEM (PILOT))

Award: Cooperative Agreements

Purpose: Conservation projects that creates "system water" through voluntary compensated reductions in water use. All water conserved as a result of the SCPP becomes system water with the sole purpose of increasing storage levels in Lakes Powell and Mead and does not accrue to the benefit of any individual user.

Applicant Eligibility: Eligibility of the Upper Colorado River Commission established through PL 113-235.

Beneficiary Eligibility: Pursuant to PL 113-235, participation in the Pilot Program is limited to Entitlement Holders in the Lower Colorado Division States and Colorado River Water Users in the Upper Colorado River Basin.

Award Range/Average: Range: $1,065,000 Average: $1,065,000

Funding: FY 19 est $0; FY 17 $1,000,000; FY 18 est $0.

CORPORATION FOR NATIONAL AND COMMUNITY SERVICE

Alabama

Nancy Reeder, Director | Medical Forum 950 22nd Street, North, Suite 428, Birmingham, AL 35203 205-731-0027

Alaska

Billy Joe Caldwell, Director | Jackson Federal Building 915 Second Avenue, Suite 3190, Seattle, WA 98174-1103 206-220-7736

Altantic Cluster (CT,DE,MA,MD,ME,NH,NJ,NY,PA,PR,RI,VT)

Rocco Gaudio, Director | 801 Arch Street, Suite 103, Philadelphia, PA 19107-2416 215-597-9972

Arizona

Richard Persely, Director | 522 North Central, Room 205A, Phoenix, AZ 85004-2190 602-379-4825

Arkansas

Opal Sims, Director | Federal Building, Room 2506 700 West Capitol Street, Little Rock, AR 72201 501-324-5234

California

Javies Lafianza, Director | 11150 W. Olympia Boulevard, Suite 170, Los Angeles, CA 90064 310-235-7421

Colorado

James Byrnes Cacting, Director | 999 18th Street, Suite 1440 South, Denver, CO 80202 303-312-7950

Connecticut

Romero A. Cherry, Director | 1 Commercial Plaza, 21st Floor, Hartford, CT 06103-3510 860-240-3237

Delaware (and MD)

Jerry E. Yates, Director Fallen Federal Building | 31 Hopkins Plaza, Suite 400B, Baltimore, MD 21201 410-962-4443

District of Columbia (and VA)
Thomas Harmon, Director | 400 North 8th Street, Suite 446 P.O. Box 10066, Richmond, VA 23240-1832 804-771-2197

Florida
Warren Smith, Director | 3165 McCrory Street, Suite 115, Orlando, FL 32803-3750 407-648-6117

Georgia
Daryl James, Director | 75 Piedmont Avenue, N.E., Suite 982, Atlanta, GA 30303-2587 404-331-4646

Hawaii/Guam/American Samoa
Lynn Dunn, Director | Federal Building, Room 6213 300 Ala Moana Boulevard, Honolulu, HI 96850-0001 808-541-2832

Idaho
Van Kent Griffitts, Director | 304 North 8th Street, Room 344, Boise, ID 83702-5835 208-334-1707

Illinois
Timothy Krieger, Director | 77 West Jackson Boulevard, Suite 442, Chicago, IL 60604-3511 312-353-3622

Indiana
Thomas L. Haskett, Director | 46 East Ohio Street, Room 457, Indianapolis, IN 46204-1922 317-226-6724

Iowa
Joel Weinstein, Director | Federal Building, Room 917 210 Walnut Street, Des Moines, IA 50309-2195 515-284-4816

Kansas
James M. Byrnes, Director | 444 S.E. Quincy, Room 260, Topeka, KS 66683-3572 785-295-2540

Kentucky
Betsy Irvin Wells, Director | Federal Building, Room 372-D 600 Martin Luther King Place, Louisville, KY 40202-2230 502-582-6384

Louisiana
Willard L. Labrie, Director | 707 Florida Street, Suite 316, Baton Rouge, LA 70801-1910 504-389-0473

Maine (NH and VT)
Mal Coles, Director (Acting) | 1 Pillsbury Street, Suite 201, Concordina, MN 03301-3556 603-225-1450

Maryland (and DE)
Jerry E. Yates, Director | Fallon Federal Building 31 Hopkins Plaza, Suite 400B, Baltimore, MD 21201-3418 410-962-4443

Massachusetts
Mal Coles, Director | 10 Causeway Street, Room 473, Boston, MA 02222-1038 617-565-7000

Michigan
Mary Pfeiler, Director | 211 West Fort Street, Suite 1408, Detroit, MI 48226-2799 313-226-7848

Minnesota
Robert Jackson, Director | 431 South 7th Street, Room 2480, Minneapolis, MN 55415-1854 612-334-4083

Mississippi
Roktabija Abdul-Azeez, Director | 100 West Capitol Street, Room 1005A, Jackson, MS 39269-1092 601-965-5664

Missouri
John J. McDonald, Director | 801 Walnut Street, Suite 504, Kansas City, MO 64106-2009 816-374-6300

Montana
Junn Allen, Director | Capitol One Center 208 North Montana Avenue, Suite 206, Helena, MT 59601-3837 406-449-5404

Nebraska
Anne C. Johnson, Director | Federal Building, Room 156 100 Centennial Mall North, Lincoln, NE 68508-3896 402-437-5493

Nevada
Craig Warner, Director | 4600 Kietzke Lane, Suite E-141, Reno, NV 89502-5033 702-784-5314

New Hampshire (ME and VT)
Mal Coles, Acting Director | 1 Pillsbury Street, Suite 201, Concord, NH 03301-3556 603-225-1450

New Jersey
Stanley Gorland, Director | 44 South Clinton Avenue, Room 702, Trenton, NJ 08609-1507 609-989-2243

New Mexico
Ernesto Ramos, Director | 120 S. Federal Place, Room 315, Santa Fe, NM 87501-2026 505-988-6577

New York
Donna Smith, Director | Leo O'Brien Federal Building Room 818, Clinton Avenue and Pearl Street, Albany, NY 12207 518-431-4150

North Carolina
Robert L. Winston, Director | 300 Fayetteville Street Mall, Room 131, Raleigh, NC 27601-1739 919-856-4731

North Central Cluster
Mary Lubertozzi, Director | 77 West Jackson Boulevard, Suite 442, Chicago, IL 60604-3511 312-353-7705

North Dakota (and SD)
John Pohlman, Director | 225 S. Pierre Street, Room 225, Pierre, SD 57501-2452 605-224-5996

Ohio
Paul Schrader, Director | 51 North High Street, Suite 451, Columbus, OH 43215

Oklahoma
H. Zeke Rodriguez, Director | 215 Dean A. McGee, Suite 324, Oklahoma City, OK 73102 405-231-5201

Oregon
Robin Sutherland, Director | 2010 Lloyd Center, Portland, OR 97232 503-231-2103

Pacific Cluster
Lee Spencer, Director | P.O. Box 29996, Presidio of San Francisco, CA 94129-0996 415-561-5960

Pennsylvania
Jorina Ahmed, Director | Robert Nic Nix Federal Building 900 Market Street, Suite 229, Philadelphia, PA 19107 215-597-2806

Puerto Rico/Virgin Island
Loretta de Cordova, Director | U.S. Federal Building, Suite 662 150 Carlos Chardon Avenue, Hato Rey, PR 00918-1737 787-766-5314

Rhode Island
Vincent Marzullo, Director | 400 Westminister Street, Room 203, Providence, RI 02903 401-528-5424

South Carolina
Jerome J. Davis, Director | 1835 Assembly Street, Suite 872, Columbia, SC 29201-2430 803-765-5771

South Dakota (and ND)
John Pohlman, Director | 225 S. Pierre Street, Room 225, Pierre, SD 57501-2452 605-224-5996

Southern Cluster
Harold Williams, Director | 60 Forsyih Street, SW, Suite 3M40, Atlanta, GA 30323-2301 404-562-4055

Southest Cluster
James Parker, Director | 1999 Bryan Street, Room 2050, Dallas, TX 75201 214-880-7050

Tennessee
Jerry Herman, Director | 265 Cumberland Bend Drive, Nashville, TN 37228 615-736-5561

Texas
Jerry G. Thompson, Director | 903 San Jacinto, Suite 130, Austin, TX 78701-3747 512-916-5671

Utah
Rick Crawford, Director | 350 South Main Street, Room 504, Salt Lake City, UT 84101-2198 801-524-5411

Vermont (ME and NH)
Mal Coles, Director | 10 Causeway Street, Room 473, Boston, MA 02222-1038 617-565-7001

Virginia (and DC)
Thomas Harmon, Director | 400 North 8th Street, Suite 446 P.O. Box 10066, Richmond, VA 23240-1832 804-771-2197

Washington
John Miller, Director | Jackson Federal Building, Suite 3190 915 Second Avenue, Seattle, WA 98174-1103 206-220-7745

West Virginia
Judith Russell, Director | 10 Hale Street, Suite 203, Charleston, WV 25301-1409 304-347-5246

Wisconsin
Linda Sunde, Director | Henry Reuss Federal Plaza 310 W. Wisconsin Avenue, Room 1240, Milwaukee, WI 53203-2211 414-297-1118

Wyoming
Patrick Gallizzi, Director | Federal Building, Room 1110 2120 Capitol Avenue, Cheyenne, WY 82001-3649 307-772-2385

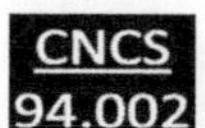

RETIRED AND SENIOR VOLUNTEER PROGRAM "RSVP"

Award: Project Grants

Purpose: The Retired and Senior Volunteer Program provides grants for volunteers aged 55 and older who serve in various community programs and respond to the National Performance Measures.

Applicant Eligibility: See the program's Notice of Funding Availability/Opportunity.

Beneficiary Eligibility: Persons age 55 and older who are willing to volunteer on a regular basis by serving in a diverse range of activities that meet specific community needs. See the program's Notice of Federal Funding for additional information.

Award Range/Average: $0 to $728,668. The average is $80,239.

Funding: (Project Grants (Discretionary)) FY 17 $46,508,000; FY 18 est $45,031,000; FY 19 N/A.

HQ: RSVP 250 E Street SW
Washington, DC 20525
Phone: 202-606-5000
Email: tbecton@cns.gov
http://www.nationalservice.gov/programs/senior-corps

CNCS 94.007 PROGRAM DEVELOPMENT AND INNOVATION GRANTS "Basic Innovative Grants"

Award: Project Grants

Purpose: Innovation grants program supports other service programs such as the Day of Service grants, September 11th and Disability Outreach grants which help to build service ethics amongst all Americans.

Applicant Eligibility: See program's Notice of Federal Funding.

Beneficiary Eligibility: Same as Applicant Eligibility.

Award Range/Average: See program's Notice of Federal Funding for matching information.

Funding: (Project Grants) FY 17 N/A FY 18 est $0; FY 19 est $0; FY 16 est $1,384,482

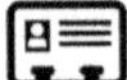

HQ: 250 E Street SW
Washington, DC 20525
Phone: 202-606-6667
Email: jbastresstahmasebi@cns.gov
http://www.nationalservice.gov

FOSTER GRANDPARENT PROGRAM "FGP"

Award: Project Grants

Purpose: The Foster Grandparent Program provides grants to volunteers with limited income from agencies and organizations that take care of critical community needs. The program also provides supportive services to children with special needs that might otherwise limit their social or emotional development.

Applicant Eligibility: See the program's Notice of Funding Availability/Opportunity.

Beneficiary Eligibility: Foster Grandparents must be: 55 years of age or older, with an income of up to 200 percent of poverty, based on the Department of Health and Human Services Poverty Guidelines, and interested in serving infants, children, and youth with special or exceptional needs. (However, individuals who are not income eligible may serve as non-stipend volunteers under certain conditions.

Award Range/Average: The range of financial assistance is from $0 to $1,917,775. The average of financial assistance is $310,711.

Funding: (Project Grants (Discretionary)) FY 17 $100,953,000; FY 18 est $99,093,000; FY 19 N/A FY 16 $102,534,738

HQ: Senior Corps - FGP 250 E Street SW
Washington, DC 20525
Phone: 202-606-5000
Email: tbecton@cns.gov
http://www.nationalservice.gov/programs/senior-corps/foster-grandparents

VOLUNTEERS IN SERVICE TO AMERICA
"AmeriCorps VISTA, VISTA, or Volunteers In Service To America"

Award: Provision of Specialized Services

Purpose: AmeriCorps Volunteers in Service to America (VISTA) is a service program that takes efforts to eradicate poverty by engaging volunteers aged 18 and older to develop or expand programs that helps to bring individuals and communities out of poverty.

Applicant Eligibility: The proposed project must have a clear anti-poverty focus, include the involvement of the low-income community, and the activities must lead towards sustainability of the project. The activities of the VISTA members may not supplant staff or current volunteers.

Beneficiary Eligibility: VISTA activities must benefit low-income persons and communities by building the capacity of the sponsoring organization to find permanent solutions to poverty. VISTAs live and serve in some of our nation's poorest areas.

Award Range/Average: See program's Notice of Funding Opportunity for information.

Funding: (Provision of Specialized Services) FY 17 $92,364,000; FY 18 est $92,364,000; FY 19 est $92,364,000; FY 16 est $92,364,000; -

HQ: 250 E Street SW
Washington, DC 20525
Phone: 202-606-6849
http://www.nationalservice.gov

SENIOR COMPANION PROGRAM
"SCP"

Award: Project Grants

Purpose: The Senior Companion Program provides grants to volunteers with limited income and aged 55 and above from agencies and organizations that take care of adults with special needs.

Applicant Eligibility: See the program's Notice of Funding Availability/Opportunity.

Beneficiary Eligibility: Senior Companions must be: 55 years of age or older, with an income of up to 200 percent of poverty, based on the Department of Health and Human Services Poverty Guidelines; interested in serving special-needs adults, especially the frail elderly, and must be physically, mentally and emotionally capable, and willing to serve on a person-to-person basis. However, non-income eligible individuals may serve as non-stipend volunteers under certain conditions.

Award Range/Average: $0 to $779,169. The average is $228,258.

Funding: (Project Grants) FY 17 $42,277,000; FY 18 est $41,692,000; FY 19 N/A FY 16 $43,710,959

HQ: Senior Corps - SCP 250 E Street SW
Washington, DC 20525
Phone: 202-606-5000
Email: tbecton@cns.gov
http://www.nationalservice.gov/programs/senior-corps/senior-companions

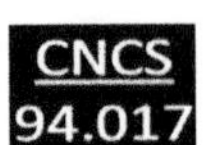

SENIOR DEMONSTRATION PROGRAM "SDP"

Award: Project Grants

Purpose: The program provides grants to agencies that involve older Americans as volunteers to carry out innovative activities in their community.

Applicant Eligibility: See program's Notice of Federal Funding or Invitation to Apply.

Beneficiary Eligibility: Persons age 55 and older who are willing to volunteer by serving in a diverse range of activities that meet specific community needs. See the program's Notice of Federal Funding/ Opportunity for additional information.

Award Range/Average: The range and average are not applicable to this program.

Funding: (Project Grants (Discretionary)) FY 17 $0; FY 18 est $0; FY 19 N/A FY 16 $0.

HQ: Senior Demonstration Program 250 E Street SW
Washington, DC 20525
Phone: 202-606-5000
Email: tbecton@cns.gov
http://www.seniorcorps.gov

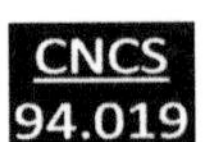

SOCIAL INNOVATION FUND "Social Innovation Fund (SIF)"

Award: Cooperative Agreements

Purpose: The Corporation for National and Community Service rolls out the Social Innovation Fund to non-profit community organizations that are high-performing and provides promising solutions to their community problems.

Applicant Eligibility: See program's Notice of Funding Opportunity.

Beneficiary Eligibility: Same as Applicant Eligibility.

Award Range/Average: No Data Available.

Funding: (Direct Payments for Specified Use (Cooperative Agreements)) FY 17 $0; FY 18 est $0; FY 19 est $0; FY 16 $40,000,000; - No new grants will be made.

HQ: 250 E Street SW
Washington, DC 20525
Phone: 202-606-6961
Email: lcook@cns.gov
http://www.nationalservice.gov/programs/social-innovation-fund

CNCS 94.020 CNCS DISASTER RESPONSE COOPERATIVE AGREEMENT "CNCS AmeriCorps Disaster Response Team"

Award: Cooperative Agreements

Purpose: The CNCS Disaster Response Cooperative Agreement is an initiative which helps the national service programs provide physical support to communities affected by a disaster and monetary reimbursements for any expense during such times.

Applicant Eligibility: N/A

Beneficiary Eligibility: N/A

Award Range/Average: Variable depending on levels of disaster activity across the country.

Funding: (Direct Payments for Specified Use (Cooperative Agreements)) N/A

HQ: 250 E Street SW, Suite 300
Washington, DC 20525
Phone: 202-606-3906
Email: jmurphy@cns.gov
http://www.nationalservice.gov/focus-areas/disaster-services

AMERICORPS VISTA TRAINING & LOGISTICS SUPPORT "VISTA (Volunteers in Service to America)"

Award: Dissemination of Technical Information; Training

Purpose: The program offers training and technical assistance to members of the AmeriCorps VISTA program and the staff at community-based organizations.

Applicant Eligibility: The use of this cooperative agreement is limited to overall support of VISTA Training.

Beneficiary Eligibility: Any US Citizen or legal resident, 18 years of age or older, with no history of crime against a minor, is eligible to serve as a VISTA member and therefore be trained through the assistance of this cooperative agreement. Equally any organization whose mission is to eradicate poverty in the US may apply to "sponsor" a VISTA member or members, and as such is eligible to be trained through assistance of this cooperative agreement.

Award Range/Average: Currently not active.

Funding: (Salaries and Expenses) FY 17 $0; FY 18 est $0; FY 19 est $0; FY 16 $0; - Currently not active.

HQ: 250 E Street SW
Washington, DC 20525
Phone: 202-606-3774
http://www.nationalservice.gov

SOCIAL INNOVATION FUND PAY FOR SUCCESS "Pay for Success"

Award: Project Grants

Purpose: Pay for Success program conducts grant competitions that implement Pay for Success strategies to improve the low-income community areas and people living in it.

Applicant Eligibility: See program's Notice of Federal Funding.

Beneficiary Eligibility: Same as Applicant Eligibility.

Award Range/Average: No Data Available.

Funding: (Project Grants) FY 17 FY 18 est $0; FY 19 est $0; FY 16 $10,000; - No new grants will be made.

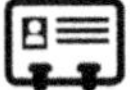

HQ: 250 E Street SW
Washington, DC 20525
Phone: 202-606-6961
Email: lcook@cns.gov
http://www.nationalservice.gov/programs/social-innovation-fund/our-programs/pay-success

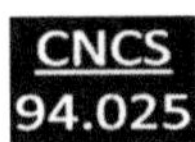

OPERATION AMERICORPS
"Operation AmeriCorps"

Award: Project Grants

Purpose: The Corporation for National and Community Service partners with all 3 streams of AmeriCorps members to address high-priority problems put forward by the tribal and local leaders.

Applicant Eligibility: See program's Notice of Federal Funding.

Beneficiary Eligibility: Same as Applicant Eligibility.

Award Range/Average: See program's Notice of Federal Funding for matching information.

Funding: (Project Grants) FY 17 N/A FY 18 N/A FY 19 N/A FY 16 $4,600,019

HQ: 250 E Street SW
Washington, DC 20525
Phone: 202-606-6745
Email: pstengel@cns.gov
http://www.nationalservice.gov/programs/americorps/operation-americorps

NATIONAL SERVICE AND CIVIC ENGAGEMENT RESEARCH COMPETITION

Award: Cooperative Agreements

Purpose: The program conducts research, addresses gaps and provides new ideas and approaches on effective strategies for national and community service and volunteering.

Applicant Eligibility: N/A

Beneficiary Eligibility: N/A

Award Range/Average: See program's Notice of Funding Opportunity for matching information.

Funding: (Cooperative Agreements) FY 17 $1,300,000; FY 18 est $1,500,000; FY 19 N/A - A second year of funding is being offered for 2017 cohort. A new competition was initiated in 2018 for a new cohort.

HQ: 250 E Street SW
Washington, DC 20525
Phone: 202-606-6687
Email: arobles@cns.gov
http://www.nationalservice.gov

DEPARTMENT OF EDUCATION

RESEARCH HEADQUARTERS

Eastern Zone Regions I, II, III, IV, V
Peter Wieczorek | McCormack P. O. and Courthouse, Room 536, Boston, MA 02109-4557 617-223-9321

Federal Real Property Assistance Program
David B. Hakola, Office of Administrator for | Management Services, Director for the Western Zone (VI, VII, VIII, IX, X) 400 Maryland Avenue, S.W., Room 2C107, Washington, DC 20202 202-401-0506

Region I
Jan Pashcal | McCormack P.O. and Courthouse Room 540, Boston, MA 02109 617-223-9317

Mr. David C. Bayer, Regional Director (I-III) | 5 Post Office Square, MS 01-0070 McCormack P.O. and Courthouse, Room 502, Boston, MA 02109 617-223-9328

Mr. John J. Szufnarowski | McCormack P.O. and Courthouse, Room 232, Boston, MA 02109-4557 617-223-4085

Region II
John Mahoney | 75 Park Place, 12th Floor, New York, NY 10007 212-637-6283

Mr. John J. Szufarowski, Acting | 75 Park Place, 12th Floor, New York, NY 10007 212-264-4016

Mr. Robert J. McKiernan, Chief | Institutional Review Branch 75 Park Place, 12th Floor, New York, NY 10007 212-637-6423

Region III
Dr. Ralph Pacinelli | 100 Penn Square East, Suite 512 Nancy Klingler, Acting Regional Director 3535 Market Street, Room 16200, MS 03-2080, Philadelphia, PA 19104 215-596-1018

Wilson Goode | 100 Penn Square East, Suite 505, Philadelphia, PA 19107 215-656-6010

Region IV
Dr. Ralph Pacinelli | 61 Forsyth Street, S.W., Room 18T91, Atlanta, GA 30303 404-562-6330

Ms. Judith G. Brantley, Acting Regional Director | P.O. Box 1692, Atlanta, GA 30301 404-331-0556

Stan Williams | 61 Forsyth Street S.W., Room 19T40, Atlanta, GA 30303 404-562-6225

Region IX
Loni Hancock | 50 United Nations Plaza, Room 205, San Francisco, CA 94102-4987 415-437-7520

Mr. Gilbert (Doc) Williams | Federal Office Building 50 United Nations Plaza, Room 215, San Francisco, CA 94102 415-437-7840

Ms. Jane Bryson, Regional Director (VIII-X) | 50 United Nations Plaza, Room 227, MS 09-8080, San Francisco, CA 94102-4987 415-556-8382

Region V
Dr. Douglas L. Burleigh | 10220 N. Executive Hills Boulevard, Kansas City, MO 64153-1367 816-880-4107

Mr. Douglas Parrott, Chief | 401 South State Street, Room 700-D, MS 05-4080, Chicago, IL 60605 312-353-0375

Stephanie Jones | 111 North Canal Street, Room 1094, Chicago, IL 60606 312-553-8192

Region VI
Mr. Loerance Deaver | 1999 Bryan Street, Room 2740, Dallas, TX 75202 214-808-4927

Sally Cain | 1999 Bryan Street, Suite 2700, Dallas, TX 75201-6817 214-880-3011

W. Carl Hammack, Regional Director (IV-VII) | 1200 Main Tower Building, Room 2150, MS 06-5080, Dallas, TX 75202 214-767-3811

Region VII
Douglas Burleigh | 111 N. Canal Street, Suite 510, Chicago, IL 60606 816-880-4107

Mr. Steve Dorssom, Chief | Institutional Review Branch 10220 North Executive Hills Boulevard, 9th Floor, Kansas City, MO 64153 816-880-4054

Sandra Walker | 10220 North Executive Hills Boulevard, Suite 720, Kansas City, MO 64153-1367 816-880-4000

Region VIII
Lynn Simons | Federal Regional Office Building 1244 Speer Boulevard, Room 310, Denver, CO 80204-3582 303-844-3544

Mr. Harry Shriver, Chief | Institutional Review Branch 1244 Speer Boulevard, Room 322, Denver, CO 80204 303-844-3676

Mr. Loerance Deaver | Harwood Center 1999 Byran Street, Dallas, TX 75201-6817 214-880-4927

Region X
Carla Nuxoll | 915 Second Avenue, Room 3362, Seattle, WA 98174-1099 206-220-7800

Richard Corbridge, Assistant Regional | Commissioner 915 Second Avenue, Room 2848, Seattle, WA 98174-1099 206-220-7840

Susan Bowder, Regional Director | 1000 Second Avenue, Room 1200, Seattle, WA 98174-1099 206-287-1770

MAGNET SCHOOLS ASSISTANCE

Award: Project Grants

Purpose: To provide grants to eligible local educational agencies (LEAs) to establish and operate magnet schools to eliminate, reduce, or prevent minority-group isolation in elementary and secondary schools under court-ordered, agency-ordered, or federally approved voluntary desegregation plans.

Applicant Eligibility: LEAs that are implementing court-ordered, agency-ordered or federally approved voluntary desegregation plans that include magnet schools are eligible to apply.

Beneficiary Eligibility: LEAs and participating students will benefit.

Award Range/Average: Range of awards: $350,000- $3,000,000

Funding: FY 17 $97,647,000; FY 18 est $105,000,000; FY 19 est $97,647,000

HQ: 400 Maryland Avenue SW
Washington, DC 20202
Phone: 202-260-1816
Email: anna.hinton@ed.gov
http://www.ed.gov/programs/magnet/index.html

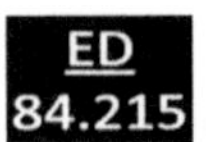

INNOVATIVE APPROACHES TO LITERACY, FULL-SERVICE COMMUNITY SCHOOLS; AND PROMISE NEIGHBORHOODS "Innovative Approaches to Literacy (IAL); Full-service Community Schools (FSCA); Promise Neighborhoods (PN)"

Award: Project Grants

Purpose: To conduct nationally significant programs for all elementary and secondary students to quality education and assist them to meet challenging State content standards.

Applicant Eligibility: Local educational agencies, the Bureau of Indian Education, institutions of higher education, Indian tribes or tribal organizations, public and private organizations and institutions may apply.

Beneficiary Eligibility: Local educational agencies, institutions of higher education, Indian tribes or tribal organizations, public and private organizations and institutions will benefit.

Award Range/Average: Varies by competition.

Funding: FY 17 $110,254,000; FY 18 est $122,754,000; FY 19 est $0; FY 16 $53,815,000

HQ: Office of Elementary and Secondary Education (OESE) 400 Maryland Avenue SW
Washington, DC 20202
Phone: 202-260-2551
Email: sylvia.lyles@ed.gov
http://innovation.ed.gov/what-we-do/parental-options/promise-neighborhoods-pn

CHARTER SCHOOLS

Award: Project Grants

Purpose: To support startup of new charter schools and the replication and expansion of high-quality charter schools.

Applicant Eligibility: State entities, including State educational agencies, State charter school boards, Governors, and statewide charter school organizations, in States in which State law authorizes charter schools are eligible. If no State entity in a State receives a grant, charter school developers in the State that have applied to an authorized public chartering authority to operate a charter school, and provided adequate and timely notice to that authority, may apply directly to the Secretary.

Beneficiary Eligibility: School administrators, teachers, and students and their parents are beneficiaries.

Award Range/Average: Range of awards: $100,000 - $45,000,000

Funding: FY 17 $285,922,000; FY 18 est $360,000,000; FY 19 est $425,000,000; FY 16 $304,961,000.

HQ: Office of Innovation and Improvement Parental Options and Information 400 Maryland Avenue SW

Washington, DC 20202

Phone: 202-453-6384

Email: stefan.huh@ed.gov

http://www.ed.gov/programs/charter/index.html

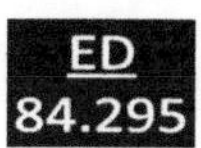

READY-TO-LEARN TELEVISION

Award: Project Grants

Purpose: To provide educational program with accompanying educational support materials, for preschool and early elementary school children and their families.

Applicant Eligibility: To be eligible to receive a grant, contract, or cooperative agreement, an entity shall be a public telecommunications entity that can demonstrate a capacity to: (1) develop and disseminate educational and instructional television programming nationwide; (2) contract with the producers of children's television programming; (3) negotiate such contracts in a manner that returns an appropriate share of ancillary income from sales of program-related products; and (4) localize programming and materials to meet specific State and local needs.

Beneficiary Eligibility: Programming is to be made widely available, with support materials as appropriate, to young children, their parents, child care workers, and Head Start and Even Start providers.

Award Range/Average: No Data Available.

Funding: (Project Grants) FY 17 $25,741,000; FY 18 est $27,741,000; FY 19 est $0; FY 16 $25,741,000

HQ: 400 Maryland Avenue SW

Washington, DC 20202

Phone: 202-205-5633

Email: brian.lekander@ed.gov

http://www.ed.gov/programs/rtltv/index.html

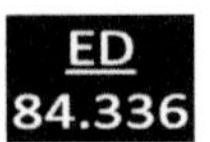

TEACHER QUALITY PARTNERSHIP GRANTS

Award: Project Grants

Purpose: To improve the quality of new and prospective teachers by improving the preparation of prospective teachers and enhancing professional development activities for new teachers.

Applicant Eligibility: States and partnerships that consist of at least one institution of higher education, a school, department or program of education within the partner institution, one school of arts and sciences within the partner institution, one high-need local educational agency, and a high-need school or a consortium of high-need schools served by the high-need local educational agency. A high-need local educational agency; is an agency that serves an elementary school or secondary school located in an area containing: (1) A high percentage of individuals or families with incomes below the poverty line, (2) a high percentage of secondary teachers not teaching in the content area that they were trained to teach, or (3) a high teacher turnover rate.

Beneficiary Eligibility: Students in high-need schools and school districts are the primary beneficiaries.

Award Range/Average: An average award is $1.5 million per year.

Funding: (Project Grants) FY 17 $43,092,000; FY 18 est $43,092,000; FY 19 est $0; FY 16 $43,092,000

HQ: 400 Maryland Avenue SW
Washington, DC 20202
Phone: 202-260-2614
Email: venita.richardson@ed.gov
http://www2.ed.gov/programs/tqpartnership/index.html

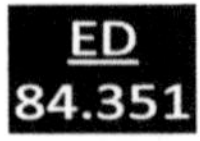

ARTS IN EDUCATION

Award: Project Grants

Purpose: Provides competitive grants that support the integration of the arts into the elementary and secondary school curriculum, with particular focus on improving the academic achievement of low-income students.

Applicant Eligibility: State educational agencies; local educational agencies in which 20 percent or more of the students served are from low-income families; institutions of higher education; museums and other cultural institutions; the Bureau of Indian Education; a national nonprofit organization; and any other public or private agencies, institutions, or organizations.

Beneficiary Eligibility: Arts educators and administrators, and their students benefit.

Award Range/Average: Range of new awards: $100,000 to $6,700,000.

Funding: FY 17 $27,000,000; FY 18 est $29,000,000; FY 19 est $0; FY 16 $27,000,000.

HQ: Office of Innovation and Improvement 400 Maryland Avenue SW
Washington, DC 20202
Phone: 202-260-1816
Email: anna.hinton@ed.gov
http://www2.ed.gov/programs/artsnational/index.html

CREDIT ENHANCEMENT FOR CHARTER SCHOOL FACILITIES

Award: Project Grants

Purpose: Provides grants to eligible entities to leverage funds through credit enhancement initiatives in order to assist charter schools in using private-sector capital to acquire, construct, renovate, or lease academic facilities.

Applicant Eligibility: A public entity, such as a State or local government entity, a private nonprofit entity, or a consortium of such entities may apply.

Beneficiary Eligibility: Public charter schools as defined in Section 5210, ESEA.

Award Range/Average: Range: $8,000,000- $12,000,000. Average: $10,000,000.

Funding: FY 17 $56,250,000; FY 18 est $40,000,000; FY 19 est $75,000,000; FY 16 $16,000,000.

HQ: 400 Maryland Avenue SW 4W244

Washington, DC 20202

Phone: 202-205-2204

Email: clifton.jones@ed.gov

http://innovation.ed.gov/what-we-do/charter-schools/credit-enhancement-for-charter-school-facilities-program

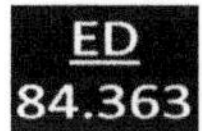

SCHOOL LEADER RECRUITMENT AND SUPPORT (FORMERLY SCHOOL LEADERSHIP)

Award: Project Grants

Purpose: Improves the recruitment, preparation, placement, support, and retention of effective principals and other school leaders in high-need schools.

Applicant Eligibility: Eligible entities include: (1) local educational agencies (LEAs) that serve high-need schools; (2) State educational agencies (SEAs); SEAs in partnership with LEAs that serve high-need schools; (3) the Bureau of Indian Education; or (4) any of those entities in partnership with nonprofit organizations or institutions of higher education.

Beneficiary Eligibility: Local educational agencies and school leaders in high-need schools.

Award Range/Average: FY 2017: Range $212,000 to $2,208,000; (continuation awards); FY 2018: $0.

Funding: (Project Grants) FY 17 $14,500,000; FY 18 est $0; FY 19 est $0; FY 16 $16,368,000

HQ: Department of Education Office of Innovation and Improvement Teacher Quality Programs, 400 Maryland Avenue SW

Washington, DC 20202

Phone: 202-205-3548

Email: margarita.melendez@ed.gov

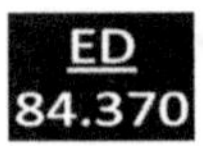

DC SCHOOL CHOICE INCENTIVE PROGRAM

Award: Project Grants

Purpose: To provide low-income parents residing in the District of Columbia (District) with expanded options for the education of their children.

Applicant Eligibility: An educational entity of the District of Columbia Government; a nonprofit organization; or a consortium of nonprofit organizations.

Beneficiary Eligibility: To receive an award under this program, an applicant must ensure that a majority of the members of its voting board or governing organization are residents of the District of Columbia. The Secretary gives priority to applications from eligible entities that will most effectively provide students and families with the widest range of educational options; to applications from eligible entities that will most effectively target resources to students and families who lack the financial resources to take advantage of available educational options.

Award Range/Average: Average new awards: $13,000,000.

Funding: (Project Grants) FY 17 $13,000,000; FY 18 est $13,939,394; FY 19 est $13,939,394; FY 16 $13,000,000

HQ: 400 Maryland Avenue SW 4W231

Washington, DC 20202-6140

Phone: 202-260-1816

Email: anna.hinton@ed.gov

http://innovation.ed.gov/what-we-do/parental-options/district-of-columbia-opportunity-scholarship-program

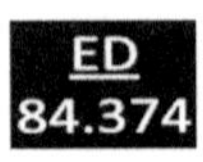

TEACHER AND SCHOOL LEADER INCENTIVE GRANTS (FORMERLY THE TEACHER INCENTIVE FUND) "TSL"

Award: Project Grants

Purpose: To help eligible entities develop, implement, improve, or expand human capital management systems or performance-based compensation systems for teachers, principals, or other school leaders in schools (and especially those in high-need schools) served by the grantees.

Applicant Eligibility: Eligible applicants are local educational agencies (LEAs), including charter schools that are LEAs in their State; State educational agencies (SEAs) or other State agencies; the Bureau of Indian Education (BIE); and partnerships of (1) one or more LEAs, State agencies, or the BIE and, (2) and at least one nonprofit or for-profit entity. An LEA may receive a grant, whether individually or as part of a partnership, only twice.

Beneficiary Eligibility: SEAs, LEAs, the BIE, non-profit and for profit organizations, and students, teachers, principals, and other school leaders in an LEA's high-need schools.

Award Range/Average: FY 17 Range $830,000 to $18,720,000 (continuation awards) and $535,000 to $12,880,000 (new awards). FY 18 $799,000 to $14,576,000 (continuation awards).

Funding: (Project Grants) FY 17 $200,000,000; FY 18 est $200,000,000; FY 19 est $0; FY 16 $230,000,000.

HQ: 400 Maryland Avenue SW
Washington, DC 20202
Phone: 202-453-6921
Email: orman.feres@ed.gov
http://www2.ed.gov/programs/teacherincentive/index.html

EDUCATION INNOVATION AND RESEARCH (FORMERLY INVESTING IN INNOVATION (I3) FUND)

Award: Project Grants

Purpose: To support the creation, development, implementation, replication, and scaling up of evidence-based, field-initiated innovations designed to improve student achievement.

Applicant Eligibility: (1) Local educational agencies (LEAs); (2) State educational agencies (SEAs); (3) the Bureau of Indian Education (BIE); (4) consortia of LEAs or SEAs; (5) nonprofit organizations; or (6) SEAs, LEAs, or the BIE in consortia with a nonprofit organization, a business, an educational service agency, or an institution of higher education.

Beneficiary Eligibility: High-need students in LEAs will benefit.

Award Range/Average: Range: $3,000,000- $25,000,000; Average: $7,727,000.

Funding: (Project Grants) FY 17 $100,000,000; FY 18 est $120,000,000; FY 19 est $180,000,000.

HQ: 400 Maryland Avenue SW
Washington, DC 20202
Phone: 202-205-3010
Email: margo.anderson@ed.gov
http://www.ed.gov/programs/innovation/index.html

DIRECTED GRANTS AND AWARDS

Award: Direct Payments for Specified Use

Purpose: Awards are made to specified institutions for purposes specified in the appropriations or authorization bills.

Applicant Eligibility: The use of the grants varies based on the appropriation and authorization language.

Beneficiary Eligibility: The National Technical Institute for the Deaf (NTID), American Printing House for the Blind (APHB), Gallaudet University, Howard University, and other institutions and organization will benefit.

Award Range/Average: No Data Available.

Funding: N/A

HQ: 400 Maryland Avenue SW, Room 5W327
Washington, DC 20202
Phone: 202-401-0292
Email: nancy.martin@ed.gov

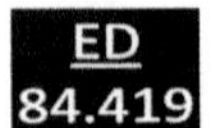

PRESCHOOL DEVELOPMENT GRANTS

Award: Project Grants

Purpose: Supports effort to build, develop, and expand voluntary, high-quality preschool programs.

Applicant Eligibility: Eligible applicants are States.

Beneficiary Eligibility: Children age 4 from families at or below 200 percent of the Federal poverty line.

Award Range/Average: Range of awards $5- $35 million; average award est. $20 million.

Funding: (Project Grants) FY 16 $250,000,000; FY 18 est $0; FY 17 est $250,000,000; - The Every Student Succeeds Act authorizes the Department of Health and Human Services (HHS) to award Preschool Development grants to States jointly with the Department of Education.

HQ: 400 Maryland Avenue SW
Washington, DC 20202
Phone: 202-260-7803
Email: tammy.proctor@ed.gov
http://www.ed.gov/earlylearing

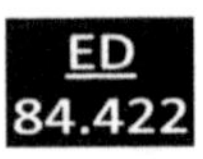

AMERICAN HISTORY AND CIVICS EDUCATION "American History and Civics Academies: National Activities Grants"

Award: Project Grants

Purpose: The program supports American History and Civics Academies grants and National Activities grants.

Applicant Eligibility: N/A

Beneficiary Eligibility: N/A

Award Range/Average: American History and Civics Academies: Anticipated range of awards is $300,000-$700,000 per year. National Activities: Anticipated range of awards is $200,000- $700,000 per year.

Funding: (Project Grants (Discretionary)) FY 17 $3,515,000; FY 18 est $3,515,000; FY 19 est $0; FY 16 $1,815,000

HQ: Office of Innovation and Improvement 400 Maryland Avenue SW LBJ Building, Room 4W205
Washington, DC 20202-5960
Phone: 202-260-7350
Email: christine.miller@ed.gov
http://innovation.ed.gov/what-we-do/american-history-and-civics-academies

ED 84.423

SUPPORTING EFFECTIVE EDUCATOR DEVELOPMENT PROGRAM "SEED"

Award: Project Grants

Purpose: To support pathways that allow teachers, principals, or other school leaders with nontraditional preparation and certification to obtain employment in traditionally underserved local educational agencies (LEAs).

Applicant Eligibility: Eligible applicants include institutions of higher education and nonprofit entities meeting specific statutory requirements, the Bureau of Indian Education, and partnerships of one or more of those entities and a for-profit entity.

Beneficiary Eligibility: Educators and prospective educators benefit from this program.

Award Range/Average: The Department held two competitions for new awards in FY 2017 and made 12 awards; the range of funding for the 3 year project was $4.9 to $17 million. The Department is holding one competition in FY 2018; the notice inviting applications was published in the Federal Register on March 21, 2018. The Department estimates making 10 to 12 awards that average $3.5 million per project year.

Funding: (Project Grants) FY 17 $65,000,000; FY 18 est $75,000,000; FY 19 est $0; FY 16 $93,993,000

HQ: 400 Maryland Avenue SW

Washington, DC 20202

Phone: 202-453-6709

Email: seed@ed.gov

http://innovation.ed.gov/what-we-do/teacher-quality/supporting-effective-educator-development-grant-program

STUDENT SUPPORT AND ACADEMIC ENRICHMENT PROGRAM "SSAE"

Award: Formula Grants

Purpose: To provide all students with access to a well-rounded education; and improve school conditions for student learning.

Applicant Eligibility: SEAs must submit a program or consolidated state plan to the Secretary for review and approval.

Beneficiary Eligibility: LEAs, schools, and their community stakeholders will benefit directly by improving students' academic achievement by increasing the capacity to: (1) provide all students with access to a well-rounded education; (2) improve school conditions for student learning: and (3) improve the use of technology in order to improve the academic achievement and digital literacy for all students.

Award Range/Average: FY 17 range: $1,940,000- $46,418,059; FY 17 average: $7,000,000. FY 18 est range: $5,308,325- $127,291,818; FY 18 est average: $19,153,750.

Funding: (Formula Grants) FY 17 $392,000,000; FY 18 est $1,072,610,000; FY 19 est $0; FY 16 $0

HQ: 400 Maryland Avenue SW
Washington, DC 20202
Phone: 202-453-6727
Email: paul.kesner@ed.gov
http://www2.ed.gov/programs/ssae/index.html

HURRICANE EDUCATION RECOVERY

Award: Formula Grants; Project Grants

Purpose: Assists in meeting the educational needs of individuals affected by a 2017 Presidentially declared major disaster or emergency related to the consequences of Hurricanes Harvey, Irma, and Maria and the 2017 California wildfires.

Applicant Eligibility: State educational agencies (SEAs) and institutions of higher education (IHEs) in affected areas or which enrolled students displaced from an affected area. Local educational agencies (LEAs) and public and non-public schools in affected areas are subgrantees.

Beneficiary Eligibility: State educational agencies, local educational agencies, postsecondary institutions and students in areas affected by Hurricanes Harvey, Irma, and Maria and the 2017 California wildfires will benefit.

Award Range/Average: N/A

Funding: (Formula Grants) FY 17 $0; FY 18 est $2,700,000,000; FY 19 est $0

HQ: 400 Maryland Avenue SW, Room 3E-330
Washington, DC 20202
Phone: 202-453-6727
Email: paul.kesner@ed.gov
http://www.ed.gov/disasterrelief

DEPARTMENT OF ENERGY

REGIONAL OFFICES

Colorado
PO Box 281213, Lakewood, CO 80228-2802 720-962-7160

Golden Field Office
Golden Field Office 15013 Denver West Parkway, Golden, CO 80401 240-562-1800

Idaho
850 Energy Drive (MS-1221), Idaho Falls, ID 83401-1563 208-526-5277

Illinois
9800 South Cass Avenue, Argonne, IL 60439 630-252-2339

Nevada
1551 Hillshire Drive, Las Vegas, NV 89143-6321 702-794-1301

Ohio
Ohio Field Office 250 E. Fifth Street, Suite 500, Cincinnati, OH 45202 513-246-0550

Tennessee
P.O. Box 2001, Oak Ridge, TN 37831 865-576-0795

Washington
825 Jadwin Avenue P.O. Box 550, A7-80, Richland, WA 99352 509-376-7271

West Virginia and Pennsylvania
3610 Collins Ferry Road (MS-002) P.O. Box 880, Morgantown, WV 26507-0880 412-386-6073

SERVICE CENTER

New Mexico
National Nuclear Security Administration (NNSA) Service Center P.O. Box 5400, Albuquerque, NM 87185-5400

Office of Headquarters Procurement Services
1000 Independence Ave, SW, Washington, DC 20585

South Carolina
P.O. Box A, Aiken, SC 29802 803-952-9345

DOE 81.005 ENVIRONMENTAL MONITORING, INDEPENDENT RESEARCH, TECHNICAL ANALYSIS

Award: N/A

Purpose: To provide technical and financial assistance to State of New Mexico Environment Department and the Regents of New Mexico State University/Carlsbad Environmental Monitoring and Research Center (NMSU/CEMRC) for the conduct of projects/activities to support DOE's and the Waste Isolation Pilot Plant (WIPP) mission and to provide the public assurances that implemented DOE programs are protective of human health and the environment.

Applicant Eligibility: Eligibility for this program is restricted to the following: The Board of Regents New Mexico State University - Carlsbad Environmental Monitoring and Research Center and the State of New Mexico

Beneficiary Eligibility: N/A

Award Range/Average: 500,000 to 3,300,000 per fiscal year

Funding: (Cooperative Agreements (Discretionary Grants)) FY 17 FY 18 FY 19 est $3,287,000

HQ: 1000 Independence Avenue SW
Washington, DC 20585
Phone: 301-903-8466
Email: alton.harris@em.doe.gov
http://www.energy.gov

DOE 81.036 INVENTIONS AND INNOVATIONS "I&I"

Award: Project Grants; Advisory Services and Counseling; Dissemination of Technical Information

Purpose: To provide financial and technical assistance to projects that have a potential for significant energy savings and future commercialization markets through a competitive solicitation process.

Applicant Eligibility: N/A

Beneficiary Eligibility: N/A

Award Range/Average: $500,000 to $1,000,000

Funding: (Project Grants (Discretionary)) FY 17 $0; FY 18 est $0; FY 19 FY 16 $0; - This program has not been regularly funded since 2012, and it is unlikely that it will receive significant funding in future periods.

HQ: 15013 Denver W Parkway
Golden, CO 80401
Phone: 240-562-1456
Email: james.cash@ee.doe.gov
http://www.eere.energy.gov

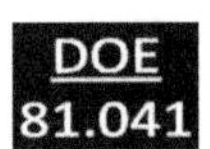

STATE ENERGY PROGRAM "SEP"

Award: Formula Grants; Dissemination of Technical Information

Purpose: To increase market transformation of energy efficiency and renewable energy technologies; and to provide financial and technical assistance to State governments to create and implement a variety of energy efficiency and conservation projects.

Applicant Eligibility: All States plus the District of Columbia, the U.S. Virgin Islands, Puerto Rico, Guam, Samoa, and the Commonwealth of the Northern Mariana Islands.

Beneficiary Eligibility: The ultimate potential beneficiaries will be the people affected by the plan that each State develops. This is anticipated to be the State's population.

Award Range/Average: $1- $5,000,000

Funding: (Formula Grants) FY 17 $37,286,640; FY 18 est $27,510,345.

HQ: 15013 Denver W Parkway
Golden, CO 80401
Phone: 240-562-1456
Email: james.cash@ee.doe.gov
http://www.eere.energy.gov

WEATHERIZATION ASSISTANCE FOR LOW-INCOME PERSONS "WAP"

Award: Formula Grants

Purpose: To improve home energy efficiency by reducing fossil fuel emissions and reducing the total energy usage.

Applicant Eligibility: States and Territories, including the District of Columbia, Puerto Rico, U.S. Virgin Islands, American Samoa, Guam, Commonwealth of the Northern Marianas, and, Native American tribal organizations (Navajo Nation, Northern Cheyenne, Intertribal Council of Arizona). In the event a State does not apply, a unit of general purpose local government, or community action agencies and/or other nonprofit agencies within that State becomes eligible to apply.

Beneficiary Eligibility: All low-income households are eligible to receive weatherization assistance. A low-income household is one whose combined income falls at or below 200 percent of the Federal poverty level determined by the Office of Management and Budget's poverty income guidelines or the basis on which Federal, State, or local cash assistance payments have been made.

Award Range/Average: $2,500 to $7,500 per dwelling unit.

Funding: (Formula Grants) FY 17 $221,066,797; FY 18 est $112,524,592; FY 19 -

HQ: 15013 Denver W Parkway
Golden, CO 80401
Phone: 240-562-1456
Email: james.cash@ee.doe.gov
http://www.eere.energy.gov

DOE 81.049

OFFICE OF SCIENCE FINANCIAL ASSISTANCE PROGRAM "Advanced Scientific Computing Research (ASCR), Basic Energy Sciences (BES), Biological and Environmental Research (BER), Fusion Energy Sciences (FES), High Energy Physics (HEP), Nuclear Physics (NP), Workforce Development for Teachers and Scientists (WDT)

Award: Project Grants

Purpose: To deliver scientific discoveries and major scientific tools to transform the understanding of nature and advance the energy, economic and national security of the United States.

Applicant Eligibility: Except where a program solicitation establishes more restrictive eligibility criteria, individuals and organizations in the following categories may submit proposals: Institutions of higher education; National Laboratories; Nonprofit and for-profit private entities; State and local governments; and consortia of entities described above.

Beneficiary Eligibility: N/A

Award Range/Average: $10,000 to $2,500,000; $250,000.

Funding: (Project Grants (Cooperative Agreements)) FY 17 $1,134,577,949; FY 18 est $1,125,000,000; FY 19 est $1,125,000,000; FY 16 $1,152,471,037

HQ: 19901 Germantown Road
Germantown, MD 20874
Phone: 301-903-4946
Email: michael.zarkin@science.doe.gov
http://science.energy.gov/grants

DOE 81.057

UNIVERSITY COAL RESEARCH

Award: Project Grants

Purpose: To fund Fossil Energy's coal-related programs and improve scientific and technical understanding of the chemistry and physics involved in the conversion and utilization of coal.

Applicant Eligibility: Only US colleges and universities can apply.

Beneficiary Eligibility: U.S. colleges, universities, and university-affiliated research institutions.

Award Range/Average: Maximum funding for 36 month project is $400,000.

Funding: (Project Grants) FY 17 $2,400,000; FY 18 est $3,250,000; FY 19 est $5,300,000

HQ:
Morgantown, WV 26507
Phone: 304-285-5297
Email: anthony.provenzano@netl.doe.gov
http://www.netl.doe.gov/technologies/coalpower/advresearch

NUCLEAR LEGACY CLEANUP PROGRAM "Consultation and Cooperation Financial Assistance"

Award: Project Grants; Direct Payments for Specified Use

Purpose: To carry out the purposes of the Nuclear Waste Policy Act of 1982, Public Law 97–425, as amended (NWPA); to conduct and participate in licensing activities in accordance with the NWPA.

Applicant Eligibility: Local governments, elected officials and affected Indian tribes surrounding DOE facilities. Designation of a local government or tribe as an "Affected Unite of Local Government" or "Affected Tribe is done pursuant to the NWPA.

Beneficiary Eligibility: States, affected units of local government and affected American Indian tribes will benefit, as well as the cleanup work at the Department of Energy.

Award Range/Average: No Data Available.

Funding: (Direct Payments for Specified Use (Cooperative Agreements)) FY 19 est $750,000; FY 17 $730,000; FY 18 est $535,000

HQ: 1000 Independence Avenue SW
Washington, DC 20585
Phone: 202-586-2904
Email: elizabeth.lisann@em.doe.gov

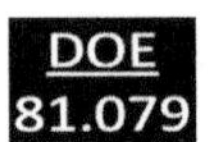

REGIONAL BIOMASS ENERGY PROGRAMS

Award: Project Grants

Purpose: To help meet the goal by significantly increasing America's use of fuels, chemicals, materials, and power made from domestic biomass on a sustainable basis.

Applicant Eligibility: Profit organizations; private nonprofit institutions/organizations; intrastate, interstate, State and local government agencies, and universities may apply.

Beneficiary Eligibility: Same as Applicant Eligibility.

Award Range/Average: Varies

Funding: (Project Grants) FY 17 $0; FY 18 est $0; FY 19

HQ: 15013 Denver W Parkway
Golden, CO 80401
Phone: 240-562-1456
Email: james.cash@ee.doe.gov
http://www.eere.energy.gov

DOE 81.086 CONSERVATION RESEARCH AND DEVELOPMENT "Energy Efficiency (EE)"

Award: Project Grants

Purpose: To conduct a balanced, long-term research effort in Buildings Technologies, Industrial Technologies, Vehicle Technologies, Solid State Lighting Technologies, and Advanced Manufacturing Technologies.

Applicant Eligibility: For-profit organizations, private nonprofit institutions/organizations, State and local governments may apply.

Beneficiary Eligibility: Same as Applicant Eligibility.

Award Range/Average: Varies.

Funding: (Cooperative Agreements) FY 17 $102,628,015; FY 18 est $18,791,390; FY 19

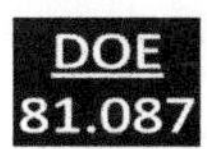

HQ: 15013 Denver W Parkway
Golden, CO 80401
Phone: 240-562-1456
Email: james.cash@ee.doe.gov
http://www.eere.energy.gov

DOE 81.087 RENEWABLE ENERGY RESEARCH AND DEVELOPMENT "Renewable Energy (RE)"

Award: Project Grants

Purpose: To conduct balanced research and development efforts in the fields like solar, biomass, hydrogen fuel cells and infrastructure, wind and hydropower, and geothermal.

Applicant Eligibility: For-profit organizations, private nonprofit institutions/organizations, intrastate, interstate, and local agencies and universities may apply.

Beneficiary Eligibility: For-profit organizations, private nonprofit institutions/organizations, intrastate, interstate, State and local agencies and universities will benefit.

Award Range/Average: Varies

Funding: (Cooperative Agreements) FY 17 $384,753,603; FY 18 FY 19

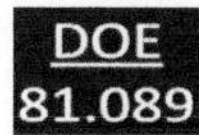

HQ: 15013 Denver W Parkway
Golden, CO 80401
Phone: 240-562-1456
Email: james.cash@ee.doe.gov
http://www.eere.doe.gov

DOE 81.089 FOSSIL ENERGY RESEARCH AND DEVELOPMENT

Award: Cooperative Agreements

Purpose: To promote the development and use of environmentally and economically superior technologies for supply, conversion, delivery, utilization and reliability constraints of producing and using fossil fuels.

Applicant Eligibility: States, local governments, universities, governmental entities, consortia, nonprofit institutions, commercial corporations, joint Federal/Industry corporations, U.S. Territories, and individuals are eligible to apply.

Beneficiary Eligibility: Federal, State, local governments, universities, consortia, nonprofit institutions, commercial corporations, joint Federal/Industry corporations, and individuals will benefit.

Award Range/Average: $200,000 to $10,000,000+.

Funding: (Cooperative Agreements) FY 17 $485,747,344; FY 18 est $481,100,000; FY 19 est $343,300,000; FY 16 est $357,945,926; FY 15 $441,763,487

HQ: 1000 Independence Avenue SW

Washington, DC 20623

Phone: 202-586-7661

Email: miranda.johnson@hq.doe.gov

ENVIRONMENTAL REMEDIATION AND WASTE PROCESSING AND DISPOSAL "Environmental Management"

Award: Cooperative Agreements; Project Grants

Purpose: To support the development of technologies to safely expedite tank waste processing and tank closure, remediation of contaminated groundwater and soil, disposition of nuclear materials and spent (used) nuclear fuel, and deactivation and decommissioning of contaminated excess facilities.

Applicant Eligibility: Public, quasi-public, private industry, individuals, groups, educational institutions, organizations, and nonprofit organizations may apply including State or local level governments, federally recognized Indian tribal governments, and institutions in U.S. Territories and possessions may apply. Determinations are made by DOE EM Headquarters or EM Field Offices, or both.

Beneficiary Eligibility: States, affected Indian tribes, regional organizations, (including U.S. Territories) local governments, and the public will benefit.

Award Range/Average: No Data Available.

Funding: (Cooperative Agreements) FY 17 $24,152,574; FY 18 est $33,722,500; FY 19 est $25,000,000; FY 16 $15,924,295

HQ: EM-412 1000 Independence Avenue SW

Washington, DC 20585

Phone: 301-903-7654

Email: latrincy.bates@em.doe.gov

http://www.em.doe.gov

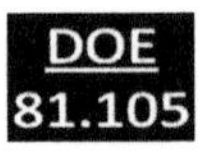

NATIONAL INDUSTRIAL COMPETITIVENESS THROUGH ENERGY, ENVIRONMENT, AND ECONOMICS "NICE3) or NICE Cubed"

Award: Project Grants

Purpose: This program is in close-out. Financial assistance will not be provided in the future.

Applicant Eligibility: N/A

Beneficiary Eligibility: Both state and local governments benefited from these grants. Commercial firms with expertise in waste reduction and pollution prevention, large and small businesses, and others in the business of preventing pollution and energy conserving technologies also benefited.

Award Range/Average: No Data Available.

Funding: (Project Grants) FY 17 $0; FY 18 est $0; FY 19 est $0

HQ: 15013 Denver W Parkway
Golden, CO 80401
Phone: 240-562-1456
Email: james.cash@ee.doe.gov
http://www.eere.energy.gov

TRANSPORT OF TRANSURANIC WASTES TO THE WASTE ISOLATION PILOT PLANT: STATES AND TRIBAL CONCERNS, PROPOSED SOLUTIONS

"Transport of Transuranic Waste to the Waste Isolation Pilot Plant (WIPP): States and Tribal Concerns, Proposed Solutions"

Award: Project Grants

Purpose: To enlist cooperation among the Tribal and the Southern, Western, and Midwest state governments along the Waste Isolation Pilot Plant (WIPP) shipping corridors for the safe and uneventful transportation of transuranic waste from storage facilities to the WIPP.

Applicant Eligibility: Eligibility is restricted by action of the Western Governors' Association, Southern States Energy Board, the State of New Mexico, Council of State Governments (Midwest region), and tribal governments along WIPP transportation routes. DOE administers agreements with 10 southern State governments, and two Midwest state governments.

Beneficiary Eligibility: Benefits from this program will go to DOE and the State and tribal governments located on the WIPP disposal phase shipping corridor.

Award Range/Average: $50,000 to $3,000,000 per year

Funding: (Project Grants (Cooperative Agreements or Contracts)) FY 17 $9,301,475; FY 18 est $8,031,210; FY 19 est $9,302,500

HQ: 1000 Independence Avenue SW
Washington, DC 20585
Phone: 301-903-8466
Email: alton.harris@em.doe.gov
http://www.wipp.energy.gov

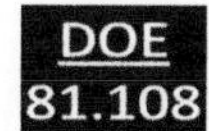

EPIDEMIOLOGY AND OTHER HEALTH STUDIES FINANCIAL ASSISTANCE PROGRAM

"Health Studies"

Award: Project Grants

Purpose: To provide financial support for research, education, conferences, communication, and other activities relating to the health of Department of Energy workers and others who are exposed to health hazards associated with energy production, transmission, and use.

Applicant Eligibility: Colleges and universities, businesses, and nonprofit institutions may apply.

Beneficiary Eligibility: Colleges and universities, businesses, and nonprofit institutions will benefit.

Award Range/Average: $10,000 to $6,500,000. Average about $2.0 Million.

Funding: (Project Grants) FY 17 $14,447,254; FY 18 est $26,910,000; FY 19 est $26,910,000; FY 16 $25,361,000

HQ: 1000 Independence Avenue SW
Washington, DC 20585
Phone: 301-903-1244
Email: ron.barnes@hq.doe.gov
http://energy.gov/ehss/environment-health-safety-security

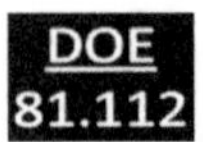

STEWARDSHIP SCIENCE GRANT PROGRAM
"Stewardship Science Academic Alliances Programs (SSAP)"

Award: Cooperative Agreements; Project Grants

Purpose: To grow the U.S. scientific community through the areas of fundamental science and technology; to promote and sustain scientific interactions between the academic community and scientists at the NNSA laboratories; to train scientists in specific areas; to increase the availability of unique experimental facilities sited at NNSA's laboratories; and to develop and maintain a long-term recruiting pipeline to NNSA's laboratories.

Applicant Eligibility: Some solicitations are open to institutions of higher education only and others include nonprofit organizations and for profit commercial organizations. See individual funding opportunity announcements for details on eligibility.

Beneficiary Eligibility: Depending upon the eligibility requirements of the individual solicitation, U.S. public and private institutions of higher education and/or nonprofit organizations and for profit commercial organizations will benefit. The Federal government will also benefit from the research of these grants.

Award Range/Average: grants $50,000 - $750,000 per year Cooperative agreements $1,000,000-$68,000,000 per year

Funding: (Project Grants (Cooperative Agreements)) FY 17 $108,277,283; FY 18 est $118,587,000; FY 19 est $90,372,000; FY 16 $110,269,150

HQ: 19901 Germantown Road
Germantown, MD 20874
Phone: 301-903-7423
Email: terri.stone@nnsa.doe.gov
http://www.nnsa.energy.gov

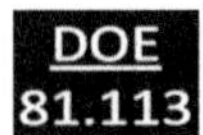

DEFENSE NUCLEAR NONPROLIFERATION RESEARCH
"Defense Nuclear Nonproliferation Research and Development"

Award: Project Grants

Purpose: To conduct basic and applied research and development that enhances U.S. national security and reduces the global danger from the proliferation of weapons of mass destruction and special nuclear materials.

Applicant Eligibility: Universities (public and private), institutions of higher education, whose activities benefit the general public through results which are available to the National Nuclear Security Administration (NNSA), other U.S. government agencies, and universities and institutions of higher learning may apply

Beneficiary Eligibility: The NNSA, other U.S. government agencies, universities and institutions of higher learning will benefit.

Award Range/Average: The expected range of Awards is approximately $25,000,000; $5,000,000/year for five years for the lifecycle of the project.

Funding: FY 16 $15,000,000; FY 17 est $15,000,000; FY 18 est $15,000,000.

HQ: 1000 Independence Avenue SW
Washington, DC 20585
Phone: 202-586-2246
Email: ivy.martin@nnsa.doe.gov
http://www.nnsa.doe.gov/na-20

DOE 81.117 ENERGY EFFICIENCY AND RENEWABLE ENERGY INFORMATION DISSEMINATION, OUTREACH, TRAINING AND TECHNICAL ANALYSIS/ASSISTANCE

Award: Project Grants

Purpose: To provide financial assistance for information dissemination, outreach, training and related technical analysis/assistance for the Department of Energy (DOE).

Applicant Eligibility: Profit organizations, individuals, private nonprofit institutions/organizations, public nonprofit institutions/organizations, State and local governments, Native American organizations, Alaskan Native corporations and universities may apply. DOE Laboratories are not eligible.

Beneficiary Eligibility: Profit organizations, individuals, private nonprofit institutions/organizations, public nonprofit institutions/organizations, State and local governments, Native American organizations, Alaskan Native corporations and universities benefit.

Award Range/Average: Vary

Funding: (Cooperative Agreements) FY 17 $41,019,057; FY 18 est $8,794,742; FY 19

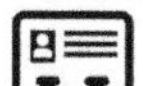

HQ: 15013 Denver W Parkway
Golden, CO 80401
Phone: 240-562-1456
Email: james.cash@ee.doe.gov
http://www.eere.energy.gov

DOE 81.119 STATE ENERGY PROGRAM SPECIAL PROJECTS "SEP Competitive Grants"

Award: Project Grants

Purpose: To allow States to submit proposals to implement specific Department of Energy (DOE) Office of Energy Efficiency and Renewable Energy deployment activities and initiatives as Special Projects under the State Energy Program.

Applicant Eligibility: All States plus the District of Columbia, the U.S. Virgin Islands, Puerto Rico, Guam, American Samoa, and the Commonwealth of the Northern Mariana Islands may apply.

Beneficiary Eligibility: States, territories, and their project partners will benefit.

Award Range/Average: 500,000 - 1,000,000

Funding: (Cooperative Agreements) FY 17 $4,493,256; FY 18 est $0.

HQ: 15013 Denver W Parkway
Golden, CO 80402
Phone: 240-562-1457
Email: james.cash@ee.doe.gov
http://www.eere.energy.gov

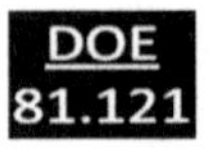

NUCLEAR ENERGY RESEARCH, DEVELOPMENT AND DEMONSTRATION "NE RD&D"

Award: Project Grants

Purpose: To provide financial assistance to address key issues affecting the worldwide use of nuclear energy through the research, development, and demonstration of science and technology fields.

Applicant Eligibility: Federal, State, local governments, universities, consortia, nonprofit institutions, commercial corporations, and individuals may apply.

Beneficiary Eligibility: Any individual, partnership, corporation, association, joint venture, institution of higher education, or nonprofit organization will benefit.

Award Range/Average: The range of awards vary per funding opportunity. Awards are typically in the range of $400,000 to $1,000,000, but can be more or less as described per individual opportunity.

Funding: (Project Grants (Cooperative Agreements)) FY 17 $158,806,998; FY 18 est $130,000,000; FY 19 est $130,000,000; FY 16 $136,079,605

HQ: 1000 Independence Avenue SW
Washington, DC 20585
Phone: 301-903-3723
Email: kenny.osborne@nuclear.energy.gov
http://www.ne.doe.gov

ELECTRICITY DELIVERY AND ENERGY RELIABILITY, RESEARCH, DEVELOPMENT AND ANALYSIS

Award: Project Grants

Purpose: To develop cost-effective technology that enhances the reliability, efficiency, and resiliency of the electric grid for the effective utilization of emerging and renewable generation sources.

Applicant Eligibility: All types of domestic entities are eligible to apply, such as profit organizations, private nonprofit institutions/organizations, universities, research organizations, and state and local governments.

Beneficiary Eligibility: Profit organizations, private nonprofit institutions/organizations, universities, research organizations, and state and local governments benefit.

Award Range/Average: Varies.

Funding: (Cooperative Agreements) FY 17 $0; FY 18 est $0; FY 19 est $0

HQ: 15013 Denver W Parkway
Golden, CO 80401
Phone: 240-562-1456
Email: james.cash@ee.doe.gov
http://www.oe.energy.gov

NATIONAL NUCLEAR SECURITY ADMINISTRATION (NNSA) MINORITY SERVING INSTITUTIONS (MSI) PROGRAM "Minority Serving Institutions Partnership Program (MSIPP)"

Award: Project Grants

Purpose: To focus on building sustainable pipeline between DOE/NNSA's sites/labs and MSIs in STEM disciplines, and bring a awareness of NNSA plants and laboratories to MSIs.

Applicant Eligibility: Historically Black Colleges and Universities (HBCUs), Hispanic Serving Institutions (HSIs), Tribal Colleges and Universities (TCUs) and non-profit institutions servicing HBCUs, HSIs and TCUs.

Beneficiary Eligibility: The general public, scientists, researchers, student/trainee, graduate students, institutions of higher learning, NNSA, and other US government agencies will benefit. Elementary, Middle and high school students will also benefit due to the institutions of higher learning's programs supported by NNSA.

Award Range/Average: Grant awards range from $750K to $5M annually over either a three or five year period.

Funding: (Project Grants) FY 17 $18,956,000; FY 18 est $18,832,000; FY 19 est $18,832,000; FY 16 $16,500,000; - A competitive solicitation is anticipated in Fiscal Year 2018.

HQ: 1000 Independence Avenue SW
Washington, DC 20585
Phone: 202-586-6019
Email: jonathan.jackson@nnsa.doe.gov
http://www.nnsa.doe.gov

PREDICTIVE SCIENCE ACADEMIC ALLIANCE PROGRAM "Office of Advanced Simulation and Computing (ASC)"

Award: Project Grants

Purpose: To focus on code validation and verification in the predictive science; to promote scientific interactions between the academic community and scientists at the NNSA laboratories; and to train scientists in specific areas.

Applicant Eligibility: Only U.S. Public and Private Education Institutions with Ph.D. granting programs can apply.

Beneficiary Eligibility: Only U.S Public and Private Education Institutions with Ph.

Award Range/Average: $17M for each award for 5 project years ranging from mid-FY 08 to mid-FY 13 (under a one year no cost time extension, with $3.4 M as the average annual award amount. The 6 new Centers that started in FY 14 will receive $4M each year for 5 years for 3 Multidisciplinary Simulation Centers (MSC) and $2M each year for 5 years for 3 Single-Discipline Centers (SDC). The latter 6 Centers will receive this money annually for 5 years. We will request an additional sixth year for the Centers to receive awards out of FY 19 funds.

Funding: (Project Grants) FY 17 $18,000,000; FY 18 est $18,000,000; FY 19 est $20,000,000; FY 16 est $18,000,000

HQ: 1000 Independence Avenue SW
Washington, DC 20585
Phone: 202-586-8081
Email: david.etim@nnsa.doe.gov
http://www.sandia.gov/psaap/index.html

DOE 81.126 FEDERAL LOAN GUARANTEES FOR INNOVATIVE ENERGY TECHNOLOGIES

"Loan Programs Office"

Award: Direct Loans; Guaranteed/Insured Loans

Purpose: To promote the new or significantly improved technologies in energy projects and their commercial use in the United States of America.

Applicant Eligibility: For innovative clean energy projects: including advanced fossil energy, nuclear energy, renewable energy, and energy efficiency. Eligible projects must utilize a new or significantly improved technology, avoid, reduce or sequester greenhouse gases, be located in the United States, and have a reasonable prospect of repayment.

Beneficiary Eligibility: Small businesses, profit organizations, quasi-public nonprofits, public institutions and interstate, intrastate, State and local governments will benefit from the loan guarantee program. For ATVM, DOE has promulgated regulations defining the eligibility requirements for automobile manufacturers.

Award Range/Average: The value of the loan or guarantee will be determined on a project by project basis.

Funding: (Guaranteed/Insured Loans) FY 17 $0; FY 18 est $0; FY 19 est $5; FY 16 $24,942,000,000. FY 16 Loan Authority: $24.9B FY 17 Loan Authority: $24.9B FY 18 Loan Authority: ~$21.4B(Guaranteed/Insured Loans) FY 17 $0; FY 18 est $0; FY 19 est $0; FY 16 $16,680,000,000. FY 16 Loan Authority: $16.7B FY 17 Loan Authority: $13.3B FY 18 Loan Authority: ~$13.3B (Guaranteed/Insured Loans) FY 17 $0; FY 18 est $0; FY 19 est $0.

HQ: 1000 Independence Avenue SW
Washington, DC 20585
Phone: 202-586-5059
Email: jeffrey.walker@hq.doe.gov
http://www.energy.gov/lpo/loan-programs-office

DOE 81.127 ENERGY EFFICIENT APPLIANCE REBATE PROGRAM (EEARP) "EEARP"

Award: Formula Grants

Purpose: To provide financial and technical assistance to States for establishing residential energy star rated appliance rebate programs.

Applicant Eligibility: Assistance available to States and US Territories and possessions.

Beneficiary Eligibility: Individuals and families are the ultimate beneficiaries.

Award Range/Average: Range: 500k-6 million

Funding: (Project Grants) FY 17 $0; FY 18 est $0; FY 19 est $0.

HQ: 15013 Denver W Parkway
Golden, CO 80401
Phone: 240-562-1456
Email: james.cash@ee.doe.gov
http://energy.gov/eere/office-energy-efficiency-renewable-energy

DOE 81.128 ENERGY EFFICIENCY AND CONSERVATION BLOCK GRANT PROGRAM (EECBG) "EECBG"

Award: Formula Grants; Project Grants

Purpose: To provide financial and technical assistance to State and local governments for creating and implementing a variety of energy efficiency and conservation projects.

Applicant Eligibility: State and local governments including US Territories and Possessions.

Beneficiary Eligibility: Individuals and families.

Award Range/Average: Varies.

Funding: (Project Grants) FY 17 $0; FY 18 est $0; FY 19 est $0; - Project Grants - This program was funded by the American Recovery and Reinvestment Act (ARRA) of 2009. All ARRA funds expired on 09/30/2015. This program may, or may not receive funding in future periods.

HQ: 15013 Denver W Parkway
Golden, CO 80401
Phone: 240-562-1456
Email: james.cash@ee.doe.gov
http://www.eere.energy.gov

DOE 81.129 ENERGY EFFICIENCY AND RENEWABLE ENERGY TECHNOLOGY DEPLOYMENT, DEMONSTRATION AND COMMERCIALIZATION

Award: Cooperative Agreements; Project Grants

Purpose: To provide financial assistance for the technology deployment, demonstration, and commercialization of Energy Efficiency and Renewable Energy technologies.

Applicant Eligibility: Anyone who meets the requirements specified in the funding opportunity announcement.

Beneficiary Eligibility: Beneficiaries are states and local governments and other public and private institutions.

Award Range/Average: None

Funding: FY 17 $0; FY 18 est $0; FY 19 est $0; FY 16 $0.

HQ: 15013 Denver W Parkway
Golden, CO 80401
Phone: 240-562-1456
Email: james.cash@ee.doe.gov
http://www.eere.energy.gov

ADVANCED RESEARCH PROJECTS AGENCY - ENERGY "ARPA-E"

Award: Cooperative Agreements

Purpose: To support the President's National Objectives for the Department of Energy.

Applicant Eligibility: As described in the Funding Opportunity Announcement.

Beneficiary Eligibility: General public

Award Range/Average: $250,000 to $10,000,000 (average range is $2 million)

Funding: (Cooperative Agreements) FY 17 $204,480,148; FY 18 N/A FY 19 N/A FY 16 $266,955,201; - Energy Transformation Acceleration Fund

HQ: 1000 Independence Avenue SW
Washington, DC 20585
Phone: 202-287-6583
Email: hai.duong@hq.doe.gov
http://www.arpa-e.energy.gov

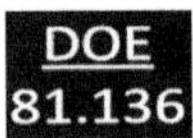

LONG-TERM SURVEILLANCE AND MAINTENANCE

Award: Project Grants

Purpose: To ensure the future protection of human health and the environment through Office of Legacy Management department.

Applicant Eligibility: N/A

Beneficiary Eligibility: N/A

Award Range/Average: The range us $4,000 to $450,000. The average is ~ $89,736

Funding: (Project Grants (Cooperative Agreements)) FY 17 $27; FY 18 est $16; FY 19 N/A FY 16 $3,039,278

HQ: 1000 Independence Avenue SW
Washington, DC 20585
Phone: 202-586-1431
Email: ingrid.colbert@hq.doe.gov
http://www.lm.doe.gov

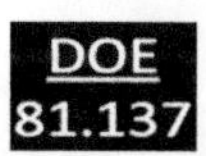

MINORITY ECONOMIC IMPACT
"Minority Education Awards and Minority Business and Economic Development Programs"

Award: Cooperative Agreements

Purpose: To engage minority serving institutions (MSIs) in DOE mission activities, collaborative research projects throughout the DOE, and future workforce development.

Applicant Eligibility: Historically Black Colleges and Universities (HBCUs), Hispanic Serving Institutions (HSIs), Tribal Colleges and Universities (TCUs), Asian American Pacific Islander (AAPI) Serving Institutions, and non-profit institutions servicing HBCUs, HSIs, TCUs, and AAPIs. Additionally, minority business enterprises, and organizations the primary purpose which is to assist in the development of those communities will be able to participate in the research, development, demonstration, and contract activities of the Department.

Beneficiary Eligibility: The general public, scientists, researchers, student/trainee, graduate students, institutions of higher learning, DOE, minority business enterprises, and organizations the primary purpose which is to assist in the development of those communities and other US government agencies will benefit. Middle and high school will also benefit due to the institutions of higher learning's programs supported by DOE.

Award Range/Average: N/A

Funding: (Formula Grants (Cooperative Agreements)) FY 17 $1,370,961; FY 18 est $1,009,000; FY 19 est $1,500,000; FY 16 $75,000; FY 15 $1,000,000

HQ: 1000 Independence Avenue SW
Washington, DC 20585
Phone: 202-586-8383
http://energy.gov/diversity

STATE HEATING OIL AND PROPANE PROGRAM
"SHOPP"

Award: Cooperative Agreements

Purpose: To enable a joint data collection effort between heating oil and propane consuming States across the United States and the U.S. Department of Energy/U.S. Energy Information Administration (EIA).

Applicant Eligibility: SHOPP is a joint data collection effort between States that consume heating oil and propane for residential heating purposes across the United States and the U.S. Department of Energy/ Energy Information Administration (EIA).

Beneficiary Eligibility: Beneficiaries are States and their agencies that have the resources to conduct the program, and whose residents consume heating oil and/or propane for residential purposes.

Award Range/Average: The range of individual awards is from $1,900 to $24,000. $250,000 is allocated annually for financial assistance to States for SHOPP.

Funding: (Salaries and Expenses) FY 17 $198,507; FY 18 est $200,347; FY 19 est $188,814; FY 16 $223,575

HQ: 1000 Independence Avenue SW
Washington, DC 20585
Phone: 202-586-4412
Email: marcela.rourk@eia.gov
http://www.eia.gov

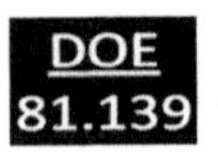

ENVIRONMENTAL MANAGEMENT R&D AND VALIDATION TESTING ON HIGH EFFICIENCY PARTICULATE AIR (HEPA) FILTERS
"Environmental Management R&D"

Award: Cooperative Agreements

Purpose: To support the safety and quality of permanent containment and confinement ventilation systems as well as modular worksite and breathing-zone ventilation systems used to support nuclear, radiological, chemical, and other high-consequence facility and environmental operations.

Applicant Eligibility: A publicly-owned agency or organization established to perform specialized functions or services for the benefit of all or part of the general public either without charge or at cost, making no profits and having no shareholders to receive dividends. Includes institutions of higher education and hospitals.

Beneficiary Eligibility: The following organizations will significantly benefit from improved, more reliable, and safer advanced HEPA filters: Federal/ State radioactive treatment and/or storage facilities, commercial nuclear power industry, workers in a radioactive environment, industrial, military or medical processes that require very stringent filtering and the general public, particularly landowners or homeowners in proximity to radioactive facilities. Indirect benefits include more accurate known and understood HEPA filter failure mechanisms and limits, margins, and operational constraints, especially in emergency situations such as fire or a seismic event.

Award Range/Average: No Data Available.

Funding: (Salaries and Expenses) FY 17 $3,533,767; FY 18 est $5,000,000; FY 19 est $5,000,000; FY 16 $219,500.

HQ: Office of Technology Development 1000 Independence Avenue SW
Washington, DC 20585
Phone: 202-287-1348
Email: rodrigo.rimando@em.doe.gov
http://www.energy.gov

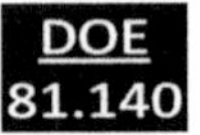

LOS ALAMOS NATIONAL LABORATORY - FIRE PROTECTION
"Los Alamos Fire Department Cooperative Agreement"

Award: Project Grants

Purpose: To provide an enhanced level of fire department services, including advanced nuclear facility capable, industrial fire suppression, advanced emergency medical, rescue, hazardous materials response, and other services for County of Los Alamos through its municipal fire department.

Applicant Eligibility: EMERGENCY PREPAREDNESS: The fire department has an authorized staffing level of 139 fire fighters and officers and 11 civilian support staff. The fire department staff, in addition to being trained as conventional fire fighters responding to fires in residence and businesses, is also trained to respond to fires and other emergencies at nuclear and high hazard facilities.

Beneficiary Eligibility: Los Alamos Fire Department is an agency within Los Alamos County. Los Alamos County is a political subdivision of the State of New Mexico.

Award Range/Average: $19,216,331 to $21,266,489

Funding: (Project Grants (Cooperative Agreements)) FY 17 $18,236,558; FY 18 est $19,083,838; FY 19 est $19,216,331; FY 16 $17,747,975

HQ: 3747 W Jamez Road
Los Alamos, NM 87544
Phone: 505-665-0838
Email: james.rast@nnsa.doe.gov
http://nnsa.energy.gov

ENERGY POLICY AND SYSTEMS ANALYSIS

Award: Cooperative Agreements

Purpose: To enhance intergovernmental coordination and collaboration on key analytical and policy issues; and to provide technical assistance and guidance to states and local governments on energy planning and measures.

Applicant Eligibility: State, local, and/or tribal nonprofit institutions/organizations and "instrumentalities of the states" are eligible.

Beneficiary Eligibility: State, local, and tribal government officials benefit.

Award Range/Average: $100,000 to $1,000,000 per year per award (maximum of 6 awards)

Funding: (Cooperative Agreements) FY 17 $500,000; FY 18 N/A FY 19 FY 16 est $465,000; - FY 2016 NCSL: $137,500 NASEO: $137,500 NARUC: $92,500 NGA: $97,500 FY 2017: NCSL: $0 NASEO: $125,000 NARUC: $75,000 NGA: $83,850

HQ: 1000 Independence Avenue SW
Washington, DC 20585
Phone: 202-586-9842
Email: kate.marks@hq.doe.gov
http://www.blm.gov

ECONOMIC DEVELOPMENT ADMINISTRATION

Atlanta Regional Office

William J. Day, Regional Director | 401 West Peachtree Street, N.W., Suite 1820, Atlanta, GA 30308-3510 404-730-3002

Austin Regional Office

903 San Jacinto Suite 206, Austin, TX 78701-5595 512-381-8144

Chicago Regional Office

C. Robert Sawyer, Regional Director | 111 North Canal Street Suite 855, Chicago, IL 60606-7204 312-353-8143

Denver Regional Office

Robert Olsen, Regional Director | 1244 Speer Boulevard Room 670, Denver, CO 80204 303-844-4715

Philadelphia Regional Office
Paul M. Raetsch, Regional Director | Curtis Center, Independence Square West Suite 140 South, Philadelphia, PA 19106 215-597-4603

Seattle Regional Office
A. Leonard Smith, Regional Director | 915 Second Avenue Jackson Federal Building, Suite 1856, Seattle, WA 98174 206-220-7660

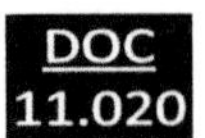

CLUSTER GRANTS

Award: Project Grants

Purpose: The Regional Innovation Strategies program assists innovators and entrepreneurs and provides operational support for organizations.

Applicant Eligibility: N/A

Beneficiary Eligibility: N/A

Award Range/Average: For the 2018 i6 Challenge the maximum Federal share of each i6 Challenge grant is $500,000 and EDA plans to award up to 32 grants. The average size of an i6 grant has been approximately $477,000. For the 2018 SFS Grant Competition the maximum Federal share of each SFS Grant is $300,000, and EDA plans to award up to 16 grants. The average size of an SFS grant has been approximately $249,600.

Funding: (Project Grants) FY 17 $17,000,000; FY 18 est $21,000,000; FY 19 est $0

HQ: Office of Innovation and Entrepreneurship 1401 Constitution Avenue NW
Washington, DC 20230
Phone: 202-482-8001
http://www.eda.gov/oie/ris/seed

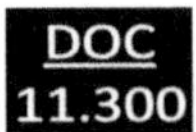

INVESTMENTS FOR PUBLIC WORKS AND ECONOMIC DEVELOPMENT FACILITIES

Award: Project Grants

Purpose: The Public Works program helps distressed communities and facilities to implement regional development strategies, regional prosperity, water and sewer system improvements, industrial parks, shipping and logistics facilities, workforce training facilities, etc. Public Works program follows the standards of EDA.

Applicant Eligibility: EDA is not authorized to provide grants or cooperative agreements under its Public Works or EAA programs to individuals or to for-profit entities. Requests from such entities will not be considered for funding.

Beneficiary Eligibility: N/A

Award Range/Average: The average $1.4 million, and range from $600,000 to $3,000,000. 80 and 150 projects a year.

Funding: (Project Grants) FY 17 $100,000,000; FY 18 est $117,500,000; FY 19 est $0; FY 16 $110,897,917

HQ: 1401 Constitution Avenue NW, Room 71030
Washington, DC 20230
Phone: 202-400-0662
Email: psaputo@eda.gov
http://www.eda.gov

DOC 11.302 ECONOMIC DEVELOPMENT SUPPORT FOR PLANNING ORGANIZATIONS
"Planning Investments and Comprehensive Economic Development Strategies"

Award: Project Grants

Purpose: The Planning program provides assistance to create regional economic development plans in order to stimulate and guide the economic development efforts of a community or region by helping to create and retain higher-skill, higher-wage jobs, particularly for the unemployed and underemployed in the Nation's most economically distressed regions. In addition, EDA provides Partnership Planning grants to Indian Tribes to help organize and assist with the implementation of economic development activities within their areas.

Applicant Eligibility: Pursuant to PWEDA, eligible applicants for and recipients of EDA investment assistance include a(n): (a) District Organization (as defined in 13 CFR 304.2); (b) Indian Tribe or a consortium of Indian Tribes; (c) State, city, or other political subdivision of a State, including a special purpose unit of a State or local government engaged in economic or infrastructure development activities, or a consortium of political subdivisions; (d) institution of higher education or a consortium of institutions of higher education; or (e) public or private non-profit organization or association acting in cooperation with officials of a political subdivision of a State.

Beneficiary Eligibility: EDA Planning investments provide support to Planning Organizations for the development, implementation, revision, or replacement of a CEDS. They also may provide support for related short-term planning investments and State plans designed to create and retain higher-skill, higher-wage jobs, particularly for the unemployed and underemployed in the nation's most economically distressed regions.

Award Range/Average: The average size has been approximately $70,000, and range from $40,000 to $200,000.

Funding: (Project Grants) FY 17 $30,000,000; FY 18 est $33,000,000; FY 19 est $0; FY 16 $29,955,674

HQ: 1401 Constitution Avenue NW, Room 71030
Washington, DC 20230
Phone: 202-482-0529
Email: dives@eda.gov
http://www.eda.gov

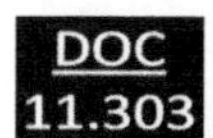

ECONOMIC DEVELOPMENT TECHNICAL ASSISTANCE
"National Technical Assistance"

Award: Project Grants

Purpose: EDA's NTA supports projects that provide technical assistance at a national scope to solve problems related to economic development and provides training, information, and implementation of economic development practices.

Applicant Eligibility: Pursuant to PWEDA, eligible applicants for and eligible recipients of EDA investment assistance under this NOFO include a(n): a. District Organization; b.

Beneficiary Eligibility: • Description of the technical assistance that will be provided to stakeholders; Description of how the proposed project increases the economic development capacity of individuals, firms, or communities; Discussion of how the project will stimulate economic development in distressed regions; and Explanation of how the proposed project supports EDA's mission to lead the Federal economic development agenda by promoting innovation and competitiveness, preparing and supporting American regions for growth and success in the global economy.

Award Range/Average: Average size of R&E and NTA investments has been $350,000, and investments range from $200,000 to $500,000. Historically, EDA has funded five R&E projects per year and three NTA projects. EDA anticipates making similar awards in FY 2018-2020.

Funding: FY 17 $1,000,000; FY 18 est $1,000,000; FY 19 est $0; FY 16 $10,321,215.

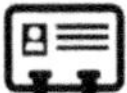

HQ: 1401 Constitution Avenue NW, Room 71030
Washington, DC 20230
Phone: 202-482-0529
Email: dives@eda.gov
http://www.eda.gov

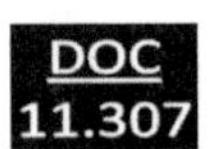

ECONOMIC ADJUSTMENT ASSISTANCE "Economic Adjustment"

Award: Project Grants

Purpose: The EAA supports a wide range of construction and non-construction activities. It provides resources to help communities by advancing economic development, job creation, foster collaboration, attract investment, support the construction of a publicly-owned multi-tenant business, and support the regions that have been negatively impacted by changes in the coal economy.

Applicant Eligibility: EDA is not authorized to provide grants or cooperative agreements under its Public Works or EAA programs to individuals or to for-profit entities. Requests from such entities will not be considered for funding.

Beneficiary Eligibility: Beneficiaries of investments made under Economic Adjustment are those communities who satisfy one or more of the economic distress and/or "Special Need" criteria set forth in 13 C.F.

Award Range/Average: The average size of an EAA investment has been approximately $650,000, and investments range from $150,000 to $1,000,000. EDA has awarded funds for between 70 and 140 EAA projects a year.

Funding: (Project Grants (Cooperative Agreements)) FY 18 N/A FY 16 $53,787,463; FY 17 est $48,000,000

HQ: 1401 Constitution Avenue NW, Room 71030
Washington, DC 20230
Phone: 202-400-0662
Email: psaputo@eda.gov
http://www.eda.gov

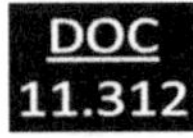

RESEARCH AND EVALUATION PROGRAM

Award: Project Grants

Purpose: The R&E program supports the development of tools, recommendations, and resources that shape Federal economic development policies to implement economic development throughout the country. EDA also regularly evaluates the impacts and outcomes of its various programs.

Applicant Eligibility: Pursuant to PWEDA, eligible applicants for and eligible recipients of EDA investment assistance under this NOFO include District Organization;

Beneficiary Eligibility: Research and Evaluation investments are designed to finance projects for research into techniques that promote competitiveness and innovation in urban and rural regions throughout the United States.

Award Range/Average: In recent years, the average size of R&E and NTA investments has been approximately $350,000, and investments generally range from $200,000 to $500,000. Historically, EDA has funded approximately five R&E projects per year.

Funding: (Project Grants (Cooperative Agreements)) FY 17 $1,500,000; FY 18 est $1,500,000; FY 19 est $0.

HQ: 1401 Constitution Avenue NW, Room 71030
Washington, DC 20230
Phone: 202-482-1464
Email: rsmith2@eda.gov
http://www.eda.gov

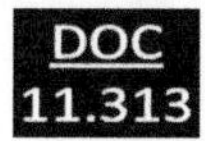

TRADE ADJUSTMENT ASSISTANCE FOR FIRMS
"Trade Adjustment Assistance for Firms"

Award: Cooperative Agreements

Purpose: The Trade Adjustment Assistance for Firms program assists economically distressed U.S. business in building strategies to increase exports.

Applicant Eligibility: Section 253 of the Trade Act (19 U.S.C. § 2343(b)) provides that grants may be awarded to "intermediary organizations (including Trade Adjustment Assistance Centers)" to provide assistance to trade-injured firms.

Beneficiary Eligibility: Only firms certified by EDA on behalf of the Secretary of Commerce are eligible for assistance under the TAAF program. Industries that can demonstrate they have been injured by imports and have a substantial number of Trade Act certified firm or worker groups may also benefit.

Award Range/Average: Awards range between $1M- $1.6M.

Funding: (Cooperative Agreements) FY 17 $13,309,066; FY 18 est $13,000,000; FY 19 est $0.

HQ: 1401 Constitution Avenue NW, Suite 71030
Washington, DC 20230
Phone: 202-482-0556
Email: mkearse@eda.gov
http://www.eda.gov

EMPLOYEE BENEFITS SECURITY ADMINISTRATION

California

Crisanta Johnson, Director | 1055 East Colorado Blvd Suite 200, Pasadena, CA 91106 626-229-1000

Jean Ackerman, Director | 90 7th St Suite 11-300, San Francisco, CA 94105 415-625-2481

District of Columbia

Elizabeth Bond, Supervisor | 1335 East-West Highway Suite 200, Silver Spring, MD 20910-3225 202-693-8700

Florida

Norman Rivera, Supervisor | 1000 S Pine Island Road Suite 100, Plantation, FL 33324 954-424-4022

Georgia

Isabel Colon, Director | 61 Forsyth Street, SW Suite 7B54, Atlanta, GA 30303 404-302-3900

Programs Administered by Regional - State - Local Offices

Illinois
Donna Seermon, Acting Director | John C. Kluczynski Federal Bldg 230 S. Dearborn Street, Ste 2160, Chicago, IL 60604 312-353-0900

Kentucky
Joe Rivers, Director | 1885 Dixie Hwy Suite 210, Fort Wright, KY 41011-2664 859-578-4680

Massachusetts
Susan Hensley, Director | J.F.K. Building 15 New Sudbury St, Suite 575, Boston, MA 02203 617-565-9600

Michigan
211 West Fort St Suite 1310, Detroit, MI 48226-3211 313-226-7450

Missouri
Frank Wilson, Acting Supervisor Robert A. Young Federal Bldg. | 1222 Spruce St Suite 6310, St. Louis, MO 63103-2818 314-539-2693

James Purcell, Director | 2300 Main St Suite 1100, Kansas City, MO 64108 816-285-1800

New York
Jonathan Kay - Director | 33 Whitehall St Suite 1200, New York, NY 10004 212-607-8600

Pennsylvania
Marc Machiz, Director | 170 S Independence Mall West Suite 870 West, Philadelphia, PA 19106-3317 215-861-5300

Texas
Deborah Perry, Director | 525 South Griffin St Suite 900, Dallas, TX 75202-5025 972-850-4500

Washington
Judy Owen, Supervisor | 300 Fifth Avenue Suite 1110, Seattle, WA 98101-3212 206-757-6781

REGISTERED APPRENTICESHIP "Fitzgerald Act"

Award: Project Grants; Advisory Services and Counseling; Training

Purpose: To assist industry in the development and improvement of Registered Apprenticeship and ensure equal employment opportunities.

Applicant Eligibility: Employers, unions, and other workforce intermediaries can be eligible to start and maintain Registered Apprenticeship programs. The vast majority of programs are not funded by Federal grant funds.

Beneficiary Eligibility: Registered Apprenticeship program sponsors identify the minimum qualifications to apply into their apprenticeship programs. Individuals applying for acceptance into an apprenticeship program must be at least 16 years old.

Award Range/Average: N/A

Funding: (Salaries and Expenses) FY 17 $36,000,000; FY 18 est $36,000,000; FY 19 est $36,000,000; FY 16 $34,000,000; - (Project Grants) FY 17 $0; FY 18 est $0; FY 19 est $0; FY 16 $2,000,000; - Women in Apprenticeship and Non-traditional Occupations (WANTO)

HQ: 200 Constitution Avenue NW C-5311
Washington, DC 20210
Phone: 202-693-3748
Email: jordan.alexander@dol.gov
http://www.doleta.gov/oa

DOL 17.207 EMPLOYMENT SERVICE/WAGNER-PEYSER FUNDED ACTIVITIES
"Wagner- Peyser Act of 1933."

Award: Formula Grants; Project Grants

Purpose: The Employment Service program provides a variety of services including labor exchange services, job search assistance, workforce information, referrals to employment, and other assistance to obtain qualified employment.

Applicant Eligibility: For Wagner-Peyser Employment Service grants and Labor Market Information grants, eligible applicants include all 50 States, the District of Columbia, the Virgin Islands, Puerto Rico, and Guam.

Beneficiary Eligibility: The system affords universal access to all job seekers. In addition, services are available to employers seeking to hire workers.

Award Range/Average: Wagner-Peyser Formula Grants vary by year.

Funding: (Formula Grants) FY 17 $701,000,000; FY 18 est $695,000,000; FY 19 est $446,000,000; FY 16 $710,000,000; - (Project Grants) FY 17 $31,000,000; FY 18 est $32,000,000; FY 19 est $36,000,000; FY 16 $23,000,000

DOL 17.225 UNEMPLOYMENT INSURANCE
"UI"

Award: Formula Grants; Direct Payments With Unrestricted Use

Purpose: To assist eligible workers with unemployment compensation for federal employees or ex-service members, Disaster Unemployment Assistance through Trade Adjustment Assistance programs.

Applicant Eligibility: State workforce agencies, including those in the District of Columbia, Puerto Rico and Virgin Islands.

Beneficiary Eligibility: All workers whose wages are subject to state unemployment insurance laws, federal civilian employees, ex-service members, and workers whose unemployment is caused by a presidentially declared disaster under the Robert T. Stafford Disaster Relief and Emergency Assistance Act, are eligible if they are involuntarily unemployed, able to work, available for work, meet the eligibility and qualifying requirements of the state law, and are free from disqualifications.

Award Range/Average: Minimum award is $1.7 million and the maximum award is $338 million. The estimated average award is $47 million

Funding: (Direct Payments with Unrestricted Use) FY 17 $30,664,000,000; FY 18 est $29,591,000,000; FY 19 est $29,434,000,000; - (Formula Grants) FY 17 $2,707,000,000; FY 18 est $2,734,000,000; FY 19 est $2,555,000,000

HQ: 200 Constitution Avenue NW, Room S4524
Washington, DC 20210
Phone: 202-693-3029
Email: gilbert.gay@dol.gov
http://ows.doleta.gov

DOL 17.235 SENIOR COMMUNITY SERVICE EMPLOYMENT PROGRAM "Senior Community Employment Program (SCSEP)"

Award: Formula Grants; Project Grants

Purpose: To provide low-income persons with training at community service employment to gain work experience for self-sufficiency.

Applicant Eligibility: The following types of organizations are eligible to receive grants: (1) States; (2) U.S. territories; (3) Public and nonprofit private agency and organizations; and (4) Public or nonprofit national Indian aging organizations and public or nonprofit Pacific Island and Asian American aging organizations. Unless otherwise stipulated, entities carrying out the project are subject to Uniform Administrative Requirements, Cost Principles, and Audit Requirements for Federal Awards found at 2 CFR Part 200 along with the OMB approved exceptions for DOL at 2 CFR Part 2900 published on December 19, 2014 in the Federal Register; Older Americans Act Reauthorization Act of 2016 published April 22, 2016; Interim Final Rule published December 1, 2017); Final Rule published December 26, 2010; and Training and Employment Guidance Letters available via https://www.

Beneficiary Eligibility: SCSEP applicants must be unemployed adults 55 years or older with a family income that is not more than 125 percent of the Department of Health and Human Services (DHHS) poverty level. Prospective participants must provide documentation relevant to age and income, which is required to determine whether the individual is program eligible.

Award Range/Average: For Program Year 2013, grants ranged from $318,604 to $82.8M. For Program Year 2014, grants ranged from $324,965 to $84.2M.

Funding: (Formula Grants) FY 17 $87,000,000; FY 18 est $87,000,000; FY 19 est $0; FY 16 $95,000,000; - State Grants(Formula Grants) FY 17 $478,000,000; FY 18 est $314,000,000; FY 19 est $0; FY 16 $222,000,000; - National Programs

HQ: 200 Constitution Avenue NW, Room C-4510
Washington, DC 20210
Phone: 202-693-3356
Email: chapman.lamia@dol.gov
http://www.doleta.gov/seniors

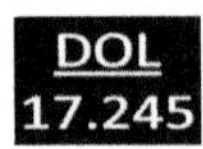

TRADE ADJUSTMENT ASSISTANCE

Award: Formula Grants

Purpose: The Trade Adjustment Assistance for Workers Program provides employment-related benefits and services.

Applicant Eligibility: For a worker to be eligible to apply for TAA, the worker must be part of a group of workers that are the subject of a petition filed with the Department. Three workers of a company, a company official, a union or other duly authorized representative, or an AJC operator or partner may file that petition with the Department.

Beneficiary Eligibility: Once a member of a worker group is covered by a certification for eligibility to apply for TAA, the workers individually apply for benefits and services through the American Job Centers. TAA benefits and services have specific individual eligibility criteria that must be met, such as previous work history, unemployment insurance eligibility, and individual skill levels.

Award Range/Average: This amount is published yearly in the Report to the Committee on Finance of the Senate and Committee on Ways and Means of the House of Representatives, which can be found on the program website at www.doleta.gov/tradeact.

Funding: (Formula Grants) FY 17 $391,000,000; FY 18 est $398,000,000; FY 19 est $450,000,000.

HQ: 200 Constitution Avenue NW
Washington, DC 20210
Phone: 202-693-3628
Email: herrmann.erica@dol.gov
http://www.doleta.gov/tradeact

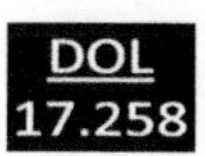

WIOA ADULT PROGRAM
"Workforce Innovation and Opportunity Act (WIOA), Adult Programs"

Award: Formula Grants

Purpose: The Adult Program serves individuals and helps employers meet their workforce needs and provides them with job search assistance and training opportunities. It also assists low-income individuals and disabled persons with employment.

Applicant Eligibility: Under WIOA, the entities eligible to receive funding from the Department are the 50 States, Puerto Rico, the District of Columbia and the outlying areas. Funds are allotted based on a statutory formula.

Beneficiary Eligibility: All adults 18 years of age and older are eligible to receive career services. Several populations receive priority, with States and local areas being responsible for establishing procedures for applying the priority requirements.

Award Range/Average: WIOA formula grant amounts vary annually and are published in the Federal Register.

Funding: (Formula Grants) FY 17 $813,000,000; FY 18 est $843,000,000; FY 19 est $811,000,000;

HQ: 200 Constitution Avenue NW, Room S 4203
Washington, DC 20210
Phone: 202-693-3937
Email: kight.robert@dol.gov
http://www.doleta.gov

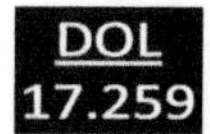

WIOA YOUTH ACTIVITIES
"WIOA Formula Youth"

Award: Formula Grants

Purpose: To assist low-income youth to acquire the educational and occupational skills and successfully transition into careers and productive adulthood.

Applicant Eligibility: Under WIOA, 50 states, Puerto Rico, the District of Columbia, and the outlying areas are identified as the recipients of youth training activities funds. For a state to be eligible to receive youth funds, the governor of the state will submit a Unified or Combined State Plan to the Secretary of DOL that outlines a 4-year strategy for the State's workforce development system.

Beneficiary Eligibility: To be eligible to participate in the WIOA youth program, an individual must be an Out-of-School Youth or an In-School Youth. Under WIOA, an out-of-school youth is an individual who is: (a) Not attending any school (as defined under State law); (b) Not younger than age 16 or older than age 24 at time of enrollment.

Award Range/Average: Formula grant award amounts vary annually and are published in the Federal Register.

Funding: (Formula Grants) FY 17 $853,000,000; FY 18 est $886,000,000; FY 19 est $514,000,000

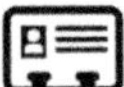

HQ: 200 Constitution Avenue NW
Washington, DC 20210
Phone: 202-693-3377
Email: kemp.jennifer.n@dol.gov
http://www.doleta.gov/youth_services

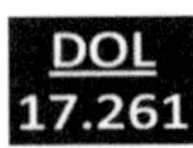

WIOA PILOTS, DEMONSTRATIONS, AND RESEARCH PROJECTS "PDR (including WDQI)"

Award: Project Grants

Purpose: To address national employment and training issues for continuous improvement of the public workforce system.

Applicant Eligibility: State and local governments, Federal agencies, private non-profit and for-profit organizations, including faith-based and community-based organizations, and educational institutions. Note: Applicant eligibility may be restricted to one or more applicant classes under the particular announcement or solicitation.

Beneficiary Eligibility: Generally limited to the economically disadvantaged and those who are underemployed, unemployed, need to upgrade their skills in order to retain jobs, at-risk youth, and/or to those who have barriers to employ ability. With WDQI funding, states are required to develop a scorecard, using their longitudinal administrative database, that will display information in a consumer-friendly manner.

Award Range/Average: Grant amounts vary and are influenced by the complexity of the initiative being studied. A general range of grant amounts would be $200,000 to $1 million and an average $500,000. WDQI grant award amounts are influenced by the total amount available funding as determined by the appropriation.

Funding: (Project Grants) FY 17 $6,000,000; FY 18 est $6,000,000; FY 19 est $6,000,000

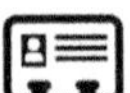

HQ: 200 Constitution Avenue NW, Room N 5641
Washington, DC 20210
Phone: 202-693-2746
Email: leonetti.ann@dol.gov
http://www.doleta.gov

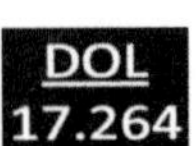

NATIONAL FARMWORKER JOBS PROGRAM "NFJP"

Award: Formula Grants

Purpose: To assist individuals and their dependents in agricultural and fish farming labor and provide housing assistance and other related assistance.

Applicant Eligibility: The provisions of WIOA, Section 167(b), describe entities eligible to receive a grant as those that have: 1) an understanding of the problems of eligible migrant and seasonal farmworkers (including their dependents); 2) a familiarity with the area to be served; and 3) the ability to demonstrate a capacity to administer and deliver effectively a diversified program of workforce investment activities (including youth workforce investment activities) and related assistance for eligible migrant and seasonal farmworkers. Entities such as state government agencies, state workforce investment boards, local government agencies, local workforce investment boards, faith-based and community-based organizations, institutions of higher learning, and other entities are examples of organizations that could be eligible to apply for NFJP grants.

Beneficiary Eligibility: Beneficiaries are low-income individuals and their dependents who, for 12 consecutive months out of the 24 months prior to application for the program, have been primarily employed in agricultural or fish farming labor that is characterized by chronic unemployment or underemployment, and who face multiple barriers to economic self-sufficiency. Male NFJP Participants must not have violated section 3 of the Military Selective Service Act.

Award Range/Average: The range and average varies by year according to appropriation levels. State allocations are published annually in the Federal Register.

Funding: (Formula Grants) FY 17 $81,000,000; FY 18 est $88,000,000; FY 19 est $0; FY 16 $81,000,000

HQ: 200 Constitution Avenue NW, Room C-4510
Washington, DC 20201
Phone: 202-693-3912
Email: rietzke.steven@dol.gov
http://www.doleta.gov/farmworker/html/nfjp.cfm

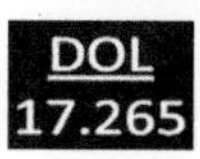

NATIVE AMERICAN EMPLOYMENT AND TRAINING "WIA / WIOA, Section 166, Native American Employment and Training Program"

Award: Formula Grants

Purpose: To support employment and training services for Native Americans to develop more fully in academic, occupational, and literacy skills achieve academic and employment success and transition to careers and productive adulthood.

Applicant Eligibility: Federally-recognized Indian Tribal Governments, bands or groups, Alaska Native villages or groups (as defined in the Alaska Native Claims Settlement Act), Native Hawaiian organizations meeting the eligibility criteria, and Native American Organizations (public bodies or private nonprofit agencies) are selected by the Secretary on a competitive basis.

Beneficiary Eligibility: Eligibility requirements for the adult program in the WIOA Final Rule at 684.300.

Award Range/Average: The range and average of financial assistance varies by year. Amounts are published annually in a Training Employment Guidance Letter (TEGL) Grant awards range from $1,000 to $5,000,000. Funding is based on a formula which is based on the percentage of low-income and unemployed Native Americans living in a geographic service area requested by the applicant in the competitive proposal. Federally Recognized tribes are typically awarded funds based on their reservation area (land base) but may also apply for "off-reservation" areas.

Funding: FY 17 $63,000,000; FY 18 est $67,000,000; FY 19 est $8,000,000; FY 16 $63,000,000

HQ: 200 Constitution Avenue NW, Room S 4209
Washington, DC 20210
Phone: 972-850-4637
Email: hall.duane@dol.gov
http://www.doleta.gov/dinap

DOL 17.267 INCENTIVE GRANTS - WIA SECTION 503 "WIA Incentive Grants"

Award: Project Grants

Purpose: To compensate for programs consistent with the purposes of Title I of Workforce Investment Systems, Title II of WIA Adult Education and Family Literacy Act.

Applicant Eligibility: A listing of States eligible to receive incentive grants for Program Year 2013 performance was published in the Federal Register on May 1, 2015. This is the last year that incentive grants will be awarded to states.

Beneficiary Eligibility: Regulations at 20 CFR 666.210 authorize the state to use its incentive grant award to carry out an innovative program consistent with the requirements of any one or more of the programs within Title IB or Title II of WIA or the Perkins Act.

Award Range/Average: For PY13 awards, each eligible state received $3,000,000.

Funding: (Project Grants) FY 17 $0; FY 18 est $0; FY 19 est $0; FY 16 $0

HQ: Frances Perkins Building 200 Constitution Avenue NW, Room N-5641
Washington, DC 20210
Phone: 202-693-3733
Email: murren.luke@dol.gov
http://www.doleta.gov/performance

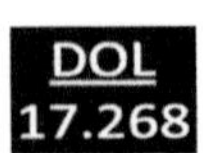

DOL 17.268 H-1B JOB TRAINING GRANTS

Award: Project Grants

Purpose: The H-1B Job Training Grant Program funds projects to provide training and related activities to workers in gaining the skills and competencies to work in economic sectors.

Applicant Eligibility: Grants may be awarded to a partnership of private and public sector entities as defined in the American Competitiveness and Workforce Improvement Act (ACWIA). Applicants may generally be public and non-profit organizations.

Beneficiary Eligibility: The scope of potential trainees under these programs can be very broad. Please review the Funding Opportunity Announcement (FOA) for specific requirements.

Award Range/Average: $1,000,000 to $5,000,000.

Funding: FY 17 $115,000,000; FY 18 est $0; FY 19 est $150,000,000; FY 16 $321,000,000

HQ: 200 Constitution Avenue NW, Room C-4518
Washington, DC 20210
Phone: 202-693-2822

Email: baird.megan@dol.gov
http://www.doleta.gov

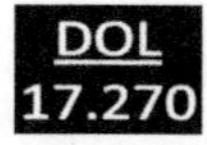

REENTRY EMPLOYMENT OPPORTUNITIES "Prisoner Re-entry"

Award: Project Grants

Purpose: To compensate for youth who are involved in crime and violence. It prevents school youth from dropping out of school and provides employment.

Applicant Eligibility: Eligible applicants for Reentry Employment Opportunities (REO) grants are community-based organizations (CBOs) that are located in, or have a staff presence in the community being served. Eligible applicants for youth focused grants vary depending on the solicitation.

Beneficiary Eligibility: Reentry Employment Opportunities (REO) Adult grants serve individuals, 18 years old and older, who have been convicted as an adult and have been imprisoned for violating a state or federal law, and who have never been convicted of a sex-related offense. Depending on the solicitation, enrollment may be limited based on whether the presenting offense was violent or whether the individual has previously committed a violent crime.

Award Range/Average: Adult focused grants have recently varied from $680,000 to $1.4 million for two years of operation. Youth offender grants have recently varied from $800,000 to $5 million for two years of operation.

Funding: (Project Grants) FY 17 $78,000,000; FY 18 est $84,000,000; FY 19 est $85,000,000

HQ: 200 Constitution Avenue NW, Room N-4511
Washington, DC 20210
Phone: 202-693-3603
Email: morris.richard@dol.gov
http://www.doleta.gov

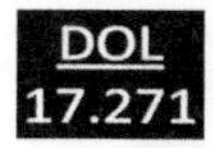

WORK OPPORTUNITY TAX CREDIT PROGRAM (WOTC) "WOTC"

Award: Formula Grants

Purpose: The federal tax helps individuals to face significant barriers and gain self-sufficiency to claim tax credits against the wages paid during the first year of employment.

Applicant Eligibility: States (not individuals), the District of Columbia, the Virgin Islands, and Puerto Rico.

Beneficiary Eligibility: Beneficiaries are all employers seeking WOTC target group workers and members of those target groups seeking employment. The members of the different target groups have statutory definitions (per Public Law 104-188, as amended) with specific eligibility requirements that must be verified by the State Workforce Agencies before a new hire certification can be issued to an employer or his/her representative.

Award Range/Average: FY 2016 grants to states ranged from $66,000 to $2,518,373

Funding: (Formula Grants) FY 17 $18,000,000; FY 18 est $18,000,000; FY 19 est $18,000,000;

HQ: 200 Constitution Avenue NW, Room C 4510
Washington, DC 20210-0001

Phone: 202-693-3912
Email: rietzke.steven@dol.gov
http://www.doleta.gov/wotc

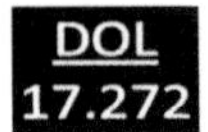

PERMANENT LABOR CERTIFICATION FOR FOREIGN WORKERS

Award: Provision of Specialized Services

Purpose: To ensure that the admission of foreign labor does not adversely affect the wages and employment opportunities for the U.S. workers.

Applicant Eligibility: Under Section 212 (a)(5)(A) of the Immigration and Nationality Act, foreign workers who seek to immigrate to the United States for employment shall be excluded from admission unless the Secretary of Labor determines and certifies to the Secretary of State and Secretary of Homeland Security that there are not sufficient U.S. workers available for the position and that the employment of such foreign workers will not adversely affect the wages and working conditions of similarly-employed U.S. workers. The certified employer must hire the foreign worker as a full-time employee; there must be a bona fide job opening available to U.S. workers; and job requirements must adhere to what is customarily required for the occupation in the U.S. and may not be tailored to the foreign worker's qualifications.

Beneficiary Eligibility: Any employer who is unable to find qualified U.S. workers to meet his or her needs and seeks to hire a foreign worker to fill a given job vacancy on a permanent basis is eligible to file an application for permanent labor certification with the Department of Labor. An employer who seeks to employ a foreign worker whose category of employment is included in the Department of Labor, Schedule A list of pre-certified occupations contained in Part 656, Title 20, Code of Federal Regulations is eligible to file an application directly with the appropriate U.S. Citizenship and Immigration Services Office.

Award Range/Average: No Data Available.

Funding: (Salaries and Expenses) FY 17 $12,000,000; FY 18 est $12,000,000; FY 19 est $12,000,000; FY 16 $12,000,000

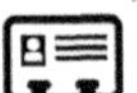

HQ: 200 Constitution Avenue NW
Washington, DC 20210
Phone: 202-513-7350
Email: ake.john@dol.gov
http://www.foreignlaborcert.doleta.gov

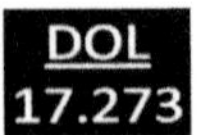

TEMPORARY LABOR CERTIFICATION FOR FOREIGN WORKERS

Award: Formula Grants; Provision of Specialized Services; Federal Employment

Purpose: To ensure adequate working and living conditions are provided for foreign and domestic workers and to assist U.S. employers seeking to hire temporary foreign workers.

Applicant Eligibility: H-2A Program: An agricultural employer who anticipates a shortage of U.S. workers needed to perform agricultural labor or services of a temporary or seasonal nature may apply to the Department of Labor under the H-2A program. The employer may be an individual proprietorship, a partnership, or a corporation.

Beneficiary Eligibility: N/A

Award Range/Average: No Data Available.

Funding: (Provision of Specialized Services) FY 17 $36,000,000; FY 18 est $36,000,000; FY 19 est $36,000,000; - Congressional funding for temporary labor certification programs is not appropriated separately from funds for other federal labor certification activities.(Formula Grants) FY 17 $14,000,000; FY 18 est $14,000,000; FY 19 est $14,000,000.

HQ: 200 Constitution Avenue NW, P.O. Box 12200
Washington, DC 20210
Phone: 202-513-7350
Email: ake.john@dol.gov
http://www.foreignlaborcert.doleta.gov

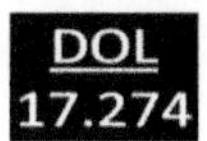

YOUTHBUILD

Award: Project Grants

Purpose: To compensate for the disadvantaged youth with education and employment skills to achieve self-sufficiency.

Applicant Eligibility: Eligible applicants for these grants are public or private nonprofit agency or organization (including a consortium of such agencies or organizations), including: a community-based organization; a faith-based organization; an entity carrying out activities under this title, such as a local board; a community action agency; a State or local housing development agency; an Indian tribe or other agency primarily serving Indians; a community development corporation; a State or local youth service or conservation corps; and any other entity eligible to provide education or employment training under a Federal program other than Youth Build.

Beneficiary Eligibility: Under WIOA, an eligible youth is an individual who is (i) not less than age 16 and not more than age 24 on the date of enrollment; (ii) a member of a low-income family, a youth in foster care (including youth aging out of foster care), a youth offender, a youth who is an individual with a disability, a child of incarcerated parents, or a migrant youth; and (iii) a school dropout or an individual who was a school dropout and has subsequently reenrolled. Up to (but not more than) 25 percent of the participants in the program may be youth who do not meet the education and disadvantaged criteria above but who are: (1) basic skills deficient, despite attainment of a secondary school diploma or its recognized equivalent (including recognized certificates of attendance or similar documents for individuals with disabilities); or (2) have been referred by a local secondary school for participation in a YouthBuild program leading to the attainment of a secondary school diploma.

Award Range/Average: Grants range from $700,000 to $1.1 million.

Funding: (Project Grants) FY 17 $80,000,000; FY 18 est $85,000,000; FY 19 est $56,000,000;

HQ: 200 Constitution Avenue NW, Room N 4508
Washington, DC 20210
Phone: 202-693-3597
Email: smith.jenn@dol.gov
http://www.doleta.gov

HEALTH CARE TAX CREDIT (HCTC) NATIONAL EMERGENCY GRANTS (NEGS)

"HCTC Infrastructure National Dislocated Worker Grants (NDWG) (formerly called HCTC NEGs)"

Award: Project Grants

Purpose: To provide health insurance and related services through Trade Adjustment Assistance.

Applicant Eligibility: N/A

Beneficiary Eligibility: N/A

Award Range/Average: $45,422 - $500,000. Average $217,083

Funding: (Project Grants) FY 17 $1,000,000; FY 18 est $0; FY 19 est $0; FY 16 $1,000,000

HQ: 200 Constitution Avenue NW
Washington, DC 20210
Phone: 202-693-3401
Email: donvan.dominica@dol.gov
http://www.doleta.gov/tradeact

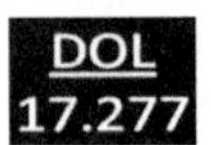

WIOA NATIONAL DISLOCATED WORKER GRANTS / WIA NATIONAL EMERGENCY GRANTS

"National Dislocated Worker Grants"

Award: Project Grants

Purpose: To temporarily expand service capacity at the state and local levels by providing time-limited funding assistance in response to significant dislocation events.

Applicant Eligibility: Entities that are generally eligible to receive a National Dislocated Worker Grant include: designated state Workforce Innovation and Opportunity Act (WIOA) program grantee agencies; a Local Workforce Investment Area; a consortium of local boards for adjoining local areas; a designated organization receiving WIOA funding through the Native American Program provisions of WIOA; and a consortium of states. Funds can be used to provide employment and training services (including some supportive services) to eligible participants.

Beneficiary Eligibility: Individuals who are eligible for assistance vary by type of National Dislocated Worker Grant project; however, they must meet the criteria provided in the Workforce Investment Act: National Emergency Grants - Application Procedures, 69 Federal Register (April 27, 2004).

Award Range/Average: Grant amounts awarded PY2016/FY 2017 ranged from $500,000 - $12,000,000. The average was $2,559.552. Grant amounts awarded PY2017/FY 2018 ranged from $210,000 - $12,000,000.

Funding: (Project Grants) FY 17 $120,000,000; FY 18 est $161,000,000; FY 19 est $177,000,000;

HQ: 200 Constitution Avenue NW, Room C 4526
Washington, DC 20210
Phone: 202-693-3937
Email: kight.robert@dol.gov
http://www.doleta.gov/dwgs

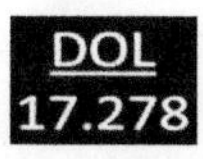

WIOA DISLOCATED WORKER FORMULA GRANTS "Workforce Innovation and Opportunity Act (WIOA) Dislocated Worker Program"

Award: Formula Grants

Purpose: The purpose of the WIOA Dislocated Worker program is to help dislocated workers become reemployed.

Applicant Eligibility: Under WIOA, the entities eligible to receive formula-based funding from the Department are the 50 states, Puerto Rico, the District of Columbia and the outlying areas. Funds are allotted based on a statutory formula and states, in turn, allocate funds to local workforce development boards (approximately 600), which are responsible for operating comprehensive American Job Centers (approximately 2,400 nationwide).

Beneficiary Eligibility: Individuals eligible for assistance through the Act are workers who have lost their jobs, including those dislocated as a result of plant closings or mass layoffs, and are unlikely to return to their previous industry or occupation; formerly self-employed individuals; and displaced homemakers who depend on income of another family member, but are no longer supported by that income. Priority of Service is given to veterans and other covered persons.

Award Range/Average: N/A

Funding: (Formula Grants) FY 17 $1,020,000,000; FY 18 est $1,041,000,000; FY 19 est $1,020,000,000;

HQ: 200 Constitution Avenue NW, Room S 4203
Washington, DC 20210
Phone: 202-693-3937
Email: kight.robert@dol.gov
http://www.doleta.gov

WIOA DISLOCATED WORKER NATIONAL RESERVE DEMONSTRATION GRANTS "Workforce Innovation and Opportunity Act (WIOA) Dislocated Worker National Reserve Demonstration Grants"

Award: Project Grants

Purpose: To carry out demonstration and pilot projects for the purpose of developing and implementing techniques and approaches, and demonstrating the effectiveness of specialized methods.

Applicant Eligibility: Eligible applicants include: State and local governments, Federal agencies, private non-profit and for profit organizations, including faith-based and community-based organizations, and educational institutions. Note: Applicant eligibility may be restricted to one or more applicant classes under the particular announcement or solicitation.

Beneficiary Eligibility: Project participants are dislocated workers and incumbent workers.

Award Range/Average: Six grants were awarded for this CFDA number. The grant award range $1,975,085 - $5,000,000. The average award is $3,670,516.

Funding: (Project Grants) FY 17 $0; FY 18 est $22,000,000; FY 19 est $22,000,000;

HQ: 200 Constitution Avenue NW
Washington, DC 20210
Phone: 202-693-3937
Email: kight.robert@dol.gov
http://www.doleta.gov

WIOA DISLOCATED WORKER NATIONAL RESERVE TECHNICAL ASSISTANCE AND TRAINING

Award: Project Grants

Purpose: To support the coordination, development, and provision of appropriate training, technical assistance, staff development, and other activities, including assistance in replicating programs of demonstrated effectiveness to States, local areas, and other entities.

Applicant Eligibility: Eligible applicants include: State and local governments, Federal agencies, private non-profit and for profit organizations, including faith-based and community-based organizations, and educational institutions. Note: Applicant eligibility may be restricted to one or more applicant classes under the particular announcement or solicitation.

Beneficiary Eligibility: Funds are used to promote the continuous improvement of assistance provided to dislocated workers.

Award Range/Average: Ranged from $55,000 to $2.3 million

Funding: (Project Grants) FY 17 $10,000,000; FY 18 est $9,000,000; FY 19 est $10,000,000;

HQ: 200 Constitution Avenue NW, Room C 4526
Washington, DC 20210
Phone: 202-693-3937
Email: kight.robert@dol.gov
http://www.doleta.gov

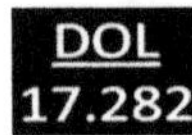

TRADE ADJUSTMENT ASSISTANCE COMMUNITY COLLEGE AND CAREER TRAINING (TAACCCT) GRANTS

Award: Project Grants

Purpose: The TAACCCT program seeks to increase the number of workers who attain certificates, degrees, and other industry-recognized credentials, helping to meet the college graduation goal of increasing the percentage of adults with a post-secondary credential by 2020.

Applicant Eligibility: See Uses Section Above

Beneficiary Eligibility: See Information Above

Award Range/Average: There are currently no new awards being made for this program.

Funding: (Project Grants (Discretionary)) FY 16 $0; FY 18 est $0; FY 17 est $0.

HQ: 200 Constitution Avenue NW, Room C 4518
Washington, DC 20210
Phone: 202-693-3644

Email: martin.cheryl.l@dol.gov
http://www.doleta.gov/taaccct

WORKFORCE INNOVATION FUND

Award: Project Grants

Purpose: Funds projects that demonstrate innovative strategies or replicate effective evidence-based strategies that align and strengthen the workforce investment system in order to improve program delivery and education and employment outcomes for program beneficiaries.

Applicant Eligibility: Eligible institutions are: (i) State Workforce Agencies; (ii) Local Workforce Investment Boards; (iii) entities eligible to apply for WIA Section 166 grants; (iv) consortia of State Workforce Agencies; (v) consortia of Local Workforce Investment Boards; and (vi) consortia of entities eligible to apply for WIA Section 166 grants (Tribal entities).

Beneficiary Eligibility: The scope of potential beneficiaries under these programs can be very broad.

Award Range/Average: See SGAs.

Funding: (Project Grants) FY 17 $0; FY 18 est $0; FY 19 est $0; FY 16 $0; - No new applications are being accepted.

HQ: Division Chief Division of National Programs
Washington, DC 20210
Phone: 202-693-2618
Email: havenstrite.wendy@dol.gov
http://www.doleta.gov/workforce_innovation

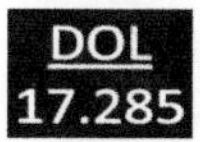

APPRENTICESHIP USA GRANTS
"Apprenticeship USA Expansion and Innovation Grants"

Award: Project Grants

Purpose: The objectives for grant funding are to make registered apprenticeship a mainstream education and career pathway option, one that can help each state, and the country as a whole, maintain its prominence in building the strongest, most adaptable, and most credentialed workforce in the world.

Applicant Eligibility: - Apprenticeship USA State Expansion.

Beneficiary Eligibility: States and US Territories are the recipients of this funding.

Award Range/Average: Average grant will be approximately $1.55 million with a range of $700,000 - $3,000,000 depending on a combination of factors including but not limited to state size and level of commitment to innovate and expand Registered Apprenticeship in the State.

Funding: (Project Grants (Discretionary)) FY 17 $51,000,000; FY 18 est $49,000,000; FY 19 est $0; FY 16 $10,000,000; - FY 2016 is the first year of funding. Future funding is conditional upon congressional approval.

HQ: 200 Constitution Avenue NW, Room C5321
Washington, DC 20210
Phone: 202-693-2796
Email: velez.anna@dol.gov
http://www.dol.gov/apprenticeship

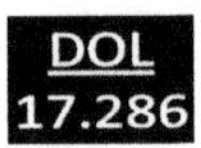

HURRICANES AND WILDFIRES OF 2017 SUPPLEMENTAL–NATIONAL DISLOCATED WORKER GRANTS
"Hurricanes and Wildfires Supplemental– NDWG"

Award: N/A

Purpose: The purpose of the National Dislocated Worker Grant program is to temporarily expand service capacity at the state and local levels by providing time-limited funding assistance in response to significant dislocation events.

Applicant Eligibility: Entities that are eligible to receive a Disaster Recovery National Dislocated Worker Grant include: designated state Workforce Innovation and Opportunity Act (WIOA) program grantee agencies; and a designated organization receiving WIOA funding through the Native American Program provisions of WIOA. Funds can be used to provide disaster relief employment as well as employment and training services (including some supportive services) to eligible participants.

Beneficiary Eligibility: N/A

Award Range/Average: N/A

Funding: (Project Grants (for specified projects)) FY 17 $0; FY 18 est $40,000,000; FY 19 est $60,000,000

HQ: 200 Constitution Avenue NW, Room C-4526
Washington, DC 20210
Phone: 202-693-3937
Email: kight.robert@dol.gov
http://www.dol.gov

ENVIRONMENTAL PROTECTION AGENCY

REGIONAL OFFICES

(Alaska, Idaho, Oregon, Washington)
Deborah Flood, Manager | Grants Administration Unit 1200 6th Avenue, Seattle, WA 98101

Branch
Paula VanHaagen | 1200 Sixth Avenue M/C-OMP-173, Seattle, WA 98101 206-553-6977

Grants
Cheryll Scott | 5 Post Office Square Boston, MA M/C - OARM05-5, Boston, MA 03109-3912 617-981-1174

Craig Wills | 75 Hawthorne Street M/C - EMD-6-1, San Francisco, CA 94105 415-972-3663

Dany Levergne | 4220 South Maryland Parkway Bldg. C - Suite 503 M/C - LVFC, Las Vegas, NV 89119

Debbie Titus | 11201 Renner Blvd. M/C - PLMGGRMS, Lenexa, KS 66219 913-551-7712

Donna Miller | 1445 Ross Avenue Suite 1200 M/C-6MD, Dallas, TX 75202-2733

James Hageman | 1595 Wynkoop Street M/C-R08-OTMS, Denver, CO 80202-1129

Keva Lloyd | 61 Forsyth Street M/C-9T 25, Atlanta, GA 30303-8960 404-562-8420

Lisa White | 1650 Arch Street Philadelphia, PA M/C - 3PM70, Philadelphia, PA 19103-2029

Mike Osinski | 1300 Pennsylvania Ave 3903R, Washington, DC 20460

Rudnell O'Neal | 290 Broadway M/C-27th FL, New York, NY 10007-1866

Sharon Green | 77 West Jackson Boulevard M/C - 105, Chicago, IL 60604-3507 312-353-5661

Tony Fournier | 1300 Pennsylvania Avenue, N.W, MC/3093-R, Washington, DC 20460

Headquarters
Jill Young | 1300 Pennsylvania Avenue, N.W. M/C-3903-R, Washington, DC 20460

Region I
Cheryl Scott | 1 Congress Street Suite 1100, Mail Code MGM, Boston, MA 02114-2023 617-918-1972

Region II
Donna Vivian-McCabe, Chief | Grants Administration Branch, (OPM-GRA) 290 Broadway, New York, NY 10007-1866

Rudnell O'Neal | Grants Administration Branch, New York, NY 10007 212-637-3427

Region III
Robert G. Reed | Grants Management Section Office of the Comptroller, (3PM70) 1650 Arch Street, Philadelphia, PA 19103-2029

Region IX
Melinda Taplin, Chief | 75 Hawthorne Street Grants and Finance Branch, San Francisco, CA 94105

Region V
Sharon Green | Acquisition and Assistance Branch (MC-10J) 77 W. Jackson Boulevard, Chicago, IL 60604-3507 312-886-2400

Region VI
Brenda Durden, Chief | 1445 Ross Avenue Grants Audit Section (6M-PG) Management Division, Dallas, TX 75202-2733 214-665-6510

Region VII
Debbie Titus | 901 North 5th Street Grants Administration Branch, Kansas City, KS 66101 913-551-7346

Region VIII
Wayne Anthofer | Grants Administration Branch, 8PM-GFM 999 18th Street, Suite 500, Denver, CO 80202-2466

Region X
Michael Gearhead, Director | Office of Environmental Cleanup 1200 6th Avenue, Seattle, WA 98101 206-553-7151

AIR POLLUTION CONTROL PROGRAM SUPPORT

Award: Project Grants

Purpose: To assist State, Tribal, Municipal, Intermunicipal, and Interstate agencies in planning, developing, establishing, improving, and maintaining adequate programs for the continuing prevention and control of air pollution and/or in the implementation of national primary and secondary air quality standards.

Applicant Eligibility: Municipal, Intermunicipal, State, Federally Recognized Indian Tribe, or Interstate or Intertribal with legal responsibility for appropriate air pollution planning, development, establishment, implementation, and maintenance of Clean Air Act air pollution control activities, including management of grant support for those activities, provided such organization furnishes funds for the current year that are equal to or in excess of its recurrent expenditures for the previous year for its approved section 105 air pollution program. The determination of expenditures is subject to decisions based on provisions of the Clean Air Act and applicable grant regulations.

Beneficiary Eligibility: Municipalities (local governments), Intermunicipalities, States, Federally Recognized Indian Tribes, and Interstate and Intertribal agencies.

Award Range/Average: From approximately $70,000 to $7,000,000 per recipient; average approximately $1,545,000.

Funding: FY 17 $228,219,000; FY 18 est $228,219,000; FY 19 est $159,450,000; FY 16 $228,219,000.

HQ: Office of Air and Radiation Office of Air Quality Planning and Standards 109 TW Alexander Drive, P.O. Box C404-02

Research Triangle Park, NC 27709

Phone: 919-541-5523

Email: whitlow.jeff@epa.gov

http://www.epa.gov/aboutepa/about-office-air-and-radiation-oar

EPA 66.032 STATE INDOOR RADON GRANTS "SIRG"

Award: Project Grants

Purpose: To assist States and Federally Recognized Indian Tribes to provide radon risk reduction through activities that will result in increased radon testing, mitigation and radon resistant new construction.

Applicant Eligibility: Eligible entities include States (including District of Columbia (DC)), Puerto Rico, the Virgin Islands, Guam, the Canal Zone, American Samoa, the Northern Mariana Islands, Federally recognized Indian Tribes and Tribal consortia, or any other U.S. Territory or possession.

Beneficiary Eligibility: State agencies: local, municipal, district, or area wide governments and organizations; U.S. territories or possessions, Federally Recognized Indian Tribes, colleges, universities, multi-state agencies, nonprofit organizations, low-income individuals, homeowners, and the general public.

Award Range/Average: Federal funding in FY 2018 may range from $15,000 to a maximum of $805,100 (by law 10% of the annual appropriation amount) per State/Tribal applicant. Regional allotments for FY 2018 are proportionally identical to the FY 2017 allotments (see https://www.epa.gov/radon/state-indoor-radon-grant-sirg-program).

Funding: (Project Grants) FY 17 $7,911,000; FY 18 est $7,867,000; FY 19 est $0; FY 16 $7,978,000; - SIRG funds are not requested in the FY 19 President's Budget

HQ: 1200 Pennsylvania Avenue NW, P.O. Box 6202A

Washington, DC 20460

Phone: 202-564-2984

Email: hesla.kirsten@epa.gov

http://www.epa.gov/radon/state-indoor-radon-grant-sirg-program

EPA 66.033 OZONE TRANSPORT COMMISSION "OTC"

Award: Project Grants

Purpose: To develop or recommend air quality implementation plans for air quality control regions designated pursuant to Section 106 (interstate pollution) or Section 111 (interstate ozone pollution) of the Clean Air Act of 1990.

Applicant Eligibility: An agency or commission designated by the Governors of the affected States, which is capable of recommending to those Governors' plans for implementation of national primary and secondary ambient air quality standards and which includes representation from the States and the appropriate political subdivisions within the affected air quality control region. For certain competitive funding opportunities under this CFDA description, the Agency may limit eligibility to compete to a number or subset of eligible applicants consistent with the Agency's Assistance Agreement Competition Policy.

Beneficiary Eligibility: Municipalities, intermunicipalities, States, interstate agencies or commissions, and Federally recognized Indian tribes.

Award Range/Average: $600,000 to $650,000/fiscal year with an average award of $639,000.

Funding: (Project Grants (Cooperative Agreements)) FY 17 $639,000; FY 18 est $639,000; FY 19 est $639,000; FY 16 $639,000

HQ: 1200 Pennsylvania Avenue NW
Washington, DC 20460
Phone: 202-564-1668
Email: jefferson.catrice@epa.gov
http://otcair.org

SURVEYS, STUDIES, RESEARCH, INVESTIGATIONS, DEMONSTRATIONS, AND SPECIAL PURPOSE ACTIVITIES RELATING TO THE CLEAN AIR ACT

Award: Project Grants

Purpose: To support Surveys, Studies, Research, Investigations, Demonstrations and Special Purpose assistance relating to the causes, effects (including health and welfare effects), extent, prevention, and control of air pollution.

Applicant Eligibility: Assistance under this program is generally available to States, local governments, territories, Indian Tribes, and possessions of the U.S., including the District of Columbia, international organizations, public and private universities and colleges, hospitals, laboratories, other public or private nonprofit institutions, which submit applications proposing projects with significant technical merit and relevance to EPA's Office of Air and Radiation's mission. Eligibility for projects awarded or competed exclusively with State and Tribal Assistance Grant (STAG) funds is limited to air pollution control agencies, as defined in section 302(b) of the Clean Air Act that are also eligible to receive grants under section 105 of the Clean Air Act, and/or federally recognized tribes and inter-tribal consortia, consisting of federally recognized tribe members.

Beneficiary Eligibility: State and local governments, U.S. territories and possessions, Indian Tribes, universities and colleges, hospitals, laboratories, and other public and private nonprofit institutions.

Award Range/Average: EPA generally award grants ranging in value from $5,000 to $750,000 per fiscal year. The average value of each grant is $150,000 per fiscal year.

Funding: (Cooperative Agreements (Discretionary Grants)) FY 17 $53,809,688; FY 18 est $52,014,743; FY 19 est $46,455,000; FY 16 $4,661,355

HQ: 1200 Pennsylvania Avenue NW
Washington, DC 20460
Phone: 202-564-0890
Email: geer.eric@epa.gov
http://www.epa.gov/grants/air-grants-and-funding

INTERNSHIPS, TRAINING AND WORKSHOPS FOR THE OFFICE OF AIR AND RADIATION

Award: Project Grants

Purpose: To provide, Internships, Training, Workshops, and Technical Monitoring in support of the Clean Air Act.

Applicant Eligibility: Assistance under this program is generally available to States, local governments, territories, Indian Tribes, and possessions of the U.S., including the Federally Recognized Indian Tribal

Government, District of Columbia and possessions of the U.S., international organizations, public and private universities and colleges, hospitals, laboratories, other public or private nonprofit institutions, which submit applications proposing projects with significant technical merit and relevance to EPA's Office of Air and Radiation's mission.

Beneficiary Eligibility: State and local governments, U.S. territories and possessions, universities and colleges, hospitals, laboratories, other public and private nonprofit institutions, and Federally Recognized Indian Tribal Governments.

Award Range/Average: EPA generally awards grants ranging in value from $100,000 to $300,000 per fiscal year. The average amount is $250,000.

Funding: FY 17 $2,000,000; FY 18 est $1,860,000; FY 19 est $1,900,000

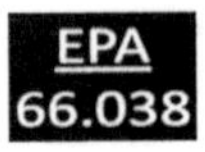

HQ: 1200 Pennsylvania Avenue NW, P.O. Box 6102A

Washington, DC 20460

Phone: 202-564-1082

Email: geer.eric@epa.gov

http://www.epa.gov

EPA 66.038 TRAINING, INVESTIGATIONS, AND SPECIAL PURPOSE ACTIVITIES OF FEDERALLY-RECOGNIZED INDIAN TRIBES CONSISTENT WITH THE CLEAN AIR ACT (CAA), TRIBAL SOVEREIGNTY AND THE PROTECTION AND MANAGEMENT OF AIR QUALITY

"Tribal CAA 103 Project Grants"

Award: Project Grants

Purpose: To support Federally-recognized Indian Tribes' efforts to understand, assess and characterize air quality; design methods and plans to protect and improve air quality on tribal lands through surveys, studies, research, training, investigations, and special purpose activities.

Applicant Eligibility: Assistance under this program is generally available to Federally-recognized Indian Tribes and Intertribal Consortia, which submit applications proposing projects with significant technical merit and relevance to EPA's Office of Air and Radiation's mission.

Beneficiary Eligibility: Federally-recognized Indian Tribes and Intertribal Consortia.

Award Range/Average: The general range is $25,000 to $500,000. The average is $75,000.

Funding: (Cooperative Agreements (Discretionary Grants)) FY 17 $11,545,000; FY 18 est $12,000,000; FY 19 est $11,545,000; FY 16 $12,712,000

HQ: Ariel Rios Building 1200 Pennsylvania Avenue NW, P.O. Box 6103A

Washington, DC 20460

Phone: 202-564-1082

Email: childers.pat@epa.gov

http://www.epa.gov/tribal-air

EPA 66.039 NATIONAL CLEAN DIESEL EMISSIONS REDUCTION PROGRAM "DERA Clean Diesel Funding Assistance Program"

Award: Project Grants

Purpose: To award grants, rebates and low-cost revolving loans to eligible entities to fund the costs of a retrofit technology that significantly reduces emissions.

Applicant Eligibility: Eligible applicants are: A regional, State, local or tribal agency or port authority with jurisdiction over transportation or air quality; and a nonprofit organization or institution that represents or provides pollution reduction or educational services to persons or organizations that own or operate diesel fleets; or has, as its principal purpose, the promotion of transportation or air quality are eligible for assistance under this program. City, county, or municipal agencies, school districts, and metropolitan planning organizations (MPOs) that have jurisdiction over transportation or air quality are all eligible entities under this program to the extent that they fall within the definition above.

Beneficiary Eligibility: Owners of eligible diesel powered vehicles and equipment. Both public owned fleets and privately owned fleets may benefit.

Award Range/Average: Smaller grants typically range from $100,000 - $300,000 with an average award of $125,000. Larger grants typically range from $500,000 - $2 million with an average award of $650,000. Recovery Act Funding awarded under the National Clean Diesel Emissions Reduction Program totaled $205,800,000.

Funding: (Project Grants) FY 17 $34,000,000; FY 18 est $42,000,000; FY 19 est $7,000,000; FY 16 $35,000,000

HQ: 1200 Pennsylvania Avenue NW
Washington, DC 20460
Phone: 202-343-9541
Email: keller.jennifer@epa.gov
http://www.epa.gov/cleandiesel

EPA 66.040 STATE CLEAN DIESEL GRANT PROGRAM "DERA State Program"

Award: Formula Grants

Purpose: To award assistance agreements to States to develop and implement such grant, rebates, and low-cost revolving loan programs in the State as are appropriate to meet State needs and goals relating to the reduction of diesel emissions.

Applicant Eligibility: Assistance under this program is available to the 50 states and the District of Columbia, Puerto Rico, the Virgin Islands, American Samoa, Guam, and the Northern Mariana Islands.

Beneficiary Eligibility: Owners of eligible diesel powered vehicles and equipment. Both public owned fleets and privately owned fleets may benefit.

Award Range/Average: For FY 2018, the range is estimated from $68,000 (Territory Base Amount) to $273,000 (State Base Amount, including Puerto Rico and the District of Columbia). In addition, a bonus of 50% of the Base Amount is available to states and territories that match the Base Amount dollar for dollar. The average funding amount for FY 2018, including Base Amount and Bonus, is approximately $372,000.

Funding: (Formula Grants) FY 17 $15,300,000; FY 18 est $20,100,000; FY 19 est $3,000,000; FY 16 $9,000,000.

HQ: 1200 Pennsylvania Avenue NW, P.O. Box 6405J
Washington, DC 20460
Phone: 202-343-9541
Email: keller.jennifer@epa.gov
http://www.epa.gov/cleandiesel

CLIMATE SHOWCASE COMMUNITIES GRANT PROGRAM

Award: Project Grants

Purpose: To award competitive grants to communities to develop plans and demonstrate and implement projects which reduce greenhouse gas emissions.

Applicant Eligibility: Local governments - a county, municipality, city, town, township, local public authority (including any public and Indian housing agency) school district, special district, intrastate district, council of governments, any other regional or interstate government entity, or any agency or instrumentality of a local government. Federally recognized Indian tribal governments - the governing body or a governmental agency of any Indian tribe, band, nation, or other organized group or community (including Native villages) certified by the Secretary of the Interior as eligible for the special programs and services provided by him through the Bureau of Indian Affairs.

Beneficiary Eligibility: Local Governments and Federally-recognized Indian Tribes, Intertribal Consortia, General Public.

Award Range/Average: There is no minimum amount of assistance. $500,000 is the maximum.

Funding: (Project Grants) N/A

HQ: 1200 Pennsylvania Avenue NW, P.O. Box 6102A
Washington, DC 20460
Phone: 202-564-0890
Email: geer.eric@epa.gov
http://www.epa.gov/statelocalenergy

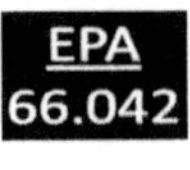

TEMPORALLY INTEGRATED MONITORING OF ECOSYSTEMS (TIME) AND LONG-TERM MONITORING (LTM) PROGRAM "TIME/LTM"

Award: Project Grants

Purpose: To conduct and promote the coordination and acceleration of research, investigations, experiments, demonstrations, surveys, and studies relating to the causes, effects, extent, prevention and control of air pollution.

Applicant Eligibility: Assistance under this program is generally available to States, local governments, territories, Indian Tribes, and possessions of the U.S. (including the District of Columbia); public and private universities and colleges; hospitals; laboratories; public or private nonprofit institutions; intertribal consortia; and individuals. Nonprofit organizations described in Section 501(c)(4) of the Internal Revenue

Code that engage in lobbying activities as defined in Section 3 of the Lobbying Disclosure Act of 1995 are not eligible to apply.

Beneficiary Eligibility: State and local governments in acid-sensitive regions of the U.S., institutions of higher education, scientific research community, general public.

Award Range/Average: There is no minimum amount of assistance. EPA anticipates annual awards ranging in value of $100,000 to $205,000, with an average award of $150,000.

Funding: (Project Grants (Cooperative Agreements)) FY 17 $130,000; FY 18 est $130,000; FY 19 est $130,000; FY 16 $3,775,411

HQ: 1200 Pennsylvania Avenue NW

Washington, DC 20460

Phone: 202-343-9257

Email: lynch.jason@epa.gov

http://www.epa.gov/airmarkets/clean-air-markets-monitoring-surface-water-chemistry

EPA 66.110 HEALTHY COMMUNITIES GRANT PROGRAM "Healthy Communities"

Award: Project Grants

Purpose: Grants are awarded to support projects that meet two criterias: 1) They must be located in and directly benefit one or more Target Investment Areas and 2) They must achieve measurable environmental and public health results in one or more of the Target Program Areas.

Applicant Eligibility: Assistance under this program is available to State, Local, public nonprofit institutions/organizations, private nonprofit institutions/organizations, quasi-public nonprofit institutions/ organizations, Federally Recognized Indian Tribal Governments, K-12 schools or school districts; and non-profit organizations (e.g.

Beneficiary Eligibility: State, Local, Federally Recognized Indian Tribal Governments, public nonprofit institutions/organizations, private nonprofit institutions/organizations, quasi-public nonprofit institutions/ organizations, anyone/general public.

Award Range/Average: $15,000 to $25,000/fiscal year; $22,754/fiscal year.

Funding: (Project Grants (Discretionary)) FY 17 $299,643; FY 18 est $0; FY 19 est $0; FY 16 $270,566

HQ:

Boston, MA 2114

Phone: 617-918-1797

Email: brownell.sandra@epa.gov

http://www3.epa.gov/region1/eco/uep

EPA 66.121 PUGET SOUND PROTECTION AND RESTORATION: TRIBAL IMPLEMENTATION ASSISTANCE PROGRAM

Award: Cooperative Agreements

Purpose: To attain and maintain water quality in designated estuaries that would assure protection of public water supplies and the protection and propagation of a balanced, indigenous population of shellfish, fish and wildlife and allows recreational activities in and on the water.

Applicant Eligibility: All federally recognized Indian Tribes located within the greater Puget Sound basin, and any consortium of these eligible Tribes, may apply for funding under the program. The greater Puget Sound basin is defined as all watersheds draining to the U.S. waters of Puget Sound, southern Georgia Basin, and the Strait of Juan de Fuca.

Beneficiary Eligibility: The beneficiary of this assistance under this program would be the Federally recognized Indian Tribes or the consortia of these Tribes that receive the assistance. Ultimate beneficiaries would include the tribal members and the general public (due to the general public's interest in restoring and protecting the resources of Puget Sound).

Award Range/Average: In past years, the average capacity award for individual tribes and consortia has been approximately $150,000. For the Tribal Lead Organization grant, the funding has ranged from $2.490M to $5.48M.

Funding: (Cooperative Agreements (Discretionary Grants)) FY 17 $7,750,000; FY 18 est $7,700,000; FY 19 est $7,700,000; FY 16 $4,000,000

HQ: Region 10 Office of Water and Watersheds 1200 Sixth Avenue, Suite 900 OWW-193

Seattle, WA 98101

Phone: 206-553-0332

Email: adams.angela@epa.gov

http://www.epa.gov/puget-sound

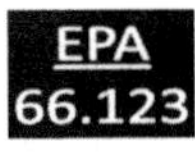

EPA 66.123 PUGET SOUND ACTION AGENDA: TECHNICAL INVESTIGATIONS AND IMPLEMENTATION ASSISTANCE PROGRAM

Award: Cooperative Agreements

Purpose: To attain and maintain water quality in designated estuaries that would assure protection of public water supplies and the protection and propagation of a balanced, indigenous population of shellfish, fish and wildlife and allows recreational activities in and on the water.

Applicant Eligibility: Federal government agencies and Washington State government agencies are eligible to apply under this program. Public and private institutions of higher education located in the United States are eligible to apply under this program.

Beneficiary Eligibility: The direct beneficiaries would be the entities receiving the assistance. Due to the fact that the program is designed and intended to assist in the restoration and protection of the Puget Sound estuary, the ultimate beneficiaries will be the residents of the greater Puget Sound region.

Award Range/Average: The EPA made awards for scientific and technical studies in the range of $200,000 - $700,000. Awards for implementation assistance and for managing and monitoring the implementation of the CCMP ranged from $200,000 to $6,000,000 each. Funding for the Strategic Initiative leads and the Management Conference Support for Implementation Lead will range from $2.490M to $5.500M.

Funding: (Project Grants (Cooperative Agreements)) FY 17 $17,500,000; FY 18 est $18,000,000; FY 19 est $18,000,000; FY 16 N/A FY 15 est $15,671,520

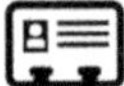

HQ: Region 10 Office of Water and Watersheds 1200 Sixth Avenue, Suite 900 OWW-193

Seattle, WA 98101

Phone: 206-553-0332

Email: adams.angela@epa.gov

http://www.epa.gov/puget-sound

EPA 66.124

COASTAL WETLANDS PLANNING PROTECTION AND RESTORATION ACT

"CWPPRA also known as The Breaux Act"

Award: Cooperative Agreements

Purpose: To assist the State, local government, college or university in planning and implementing projects that create, protect, restore and enhance wetlands in coastal Louisiana.

Applicant Eligibility: Eligible applicants for assistance include State and local governments, including their universities and colleges. For certain competitive funding opportunities under this CFDA description, the Agency may limit eligibility to compete to a number or subset of eligible applicants consistent with the Agency's Assistance Agreement Competition Policy.

Beneficiary Eligibility: State and local governments, including their universities and colleges involved in administering coastal wetlands protection, restoration and/or management programs or programs related to or that complement coastal wetlands protection programs.

Award Range/Average: $100,000 to $30,000,000. If a Phase I (E&D) project is selected for funding, the estimated amount could be from $1- $6 million. If it is a Phase II (construction) project, the estimate could be up to $30 million.

Funding: (Cooperative Agreements (Discretionary Grants)) FY 17 $0; FY 18 est $34,200,000; FY 19 est $0; FY 16 $1,997,636

HQ: USEPA Region 6 6WQ-AT 1445 Ross Avenue

Dallas, TX 75202

Phone: 214-665-7187

http://www.epa.gov/wetlands/coastal-wetlands

EPA 66.125

LAKE PONTCHARTRAIN BASIN RESTORATION PROGRAM (PRP)

"Lake Pontchartrain Restoration Program"

Award: Cooperative Agreements

Purpose: To restore the ecological health of the Basin by developing and funding restoration projects and related scientific and public education projects.

Applicant Eligibility: The grants for this program are awarded to the Management Conference, also know as the PRP, for restoration projects, studies and public education projects. Eligible sub-grantees for this program include the Parishes and Cities within the 16 parish area of the Lake Pontchartrain Basin Watershed and the Lake Pontchartrain Basin Foundation.

Beneficiary Eligibility: Eligible applicants for assistance include the Parishes and Cities within the Lake Pontchartrain Basin Watershed and the Lake Pontchartrain Basin Foundation.

Award Range/Average: The range of funding for the projects for FY 2017 for fifteen (15) projects was $20,000 to $300,000. The average including all sixteen (15) projects was $62,698. The range for FY 2016, for fourteen (14) projects was $25,000 to $327,680. The average including all fourteen (14) projects was $47,500.

Funding: (Cooperative Agreements (Discretionary Grants)) FY 17 $947,000; FY 18 N/A FY 19 N/A FY 16 $948,000

HQ: 1445 Ross Avenue (6WQ AT) Dallas
Dallas, TX 75202
Phone: 214-665-2773
Email: rauscher.leslie@epa.gov
http://www.epa.gov

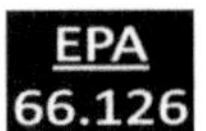

THE SAN FRANCISCO BAY WATER QUALITY IMPROVEMENT FUND "SF Bay Grant Program"

Award: Project Grants

Purpose: To improve water quality and restore aquatic habitat (i.e. wetlands) in the San Francisco Bay and its watersheds. Funded projects will reduce polluted run-off, restore impaired waters and enhance aquatic habitat.

Applicant Eligibility: State, local government agencies, districts, and councils; regional water pollution control agencies and entities; State coastal zone management agencies; and public and private universities and colleges, public or private non-governmental, non-profit institutions are eligible to apply, unless restricted by the authorizing statutes. For certain competitive funding opportunities under this CFDA description, the Agency may limit eligibility to compete to a number or subset of eligible applicants consistent with the Agency's Assistance Agreement Competition Policy.

Beneficiary Eligibility: The outcomes from the SF Bay grant program will ultimately benefit the urban resident and business populations of the nine county San Francisco Bay Area, as well as the State of California in general.

Award Range/Average: $800,000 to $2mil. Average award is $1mil each.

Funding: (Project Grants (Discretionary)) FY 17 $4,331,000; FY 18 est $4,407,000; FY 19 FY 15 $4,481,000.

HQ: 75 Hawthorne Street
San Francisco, CA 94105
Phone: 415-972-3400
Email: valiela.luisa@epa.gov
http://www.epa.gov/sfbay-delta/san-francisco-bay-water-quality-improvement-fund

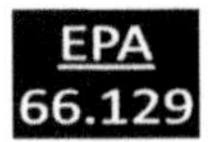

SOUTHEAST NEW ENGLAND COASTAL WATERSHED RESTORATION "SNEP"

Award: Cooperative Agreements

Purpose: To develop and support the Southeast New England Program (SNEP) for coastal watershed restoration. SNEP is a geographically-based program intended to serve as a collaborative framework for advancing ecosystem resiliency, protecting and restoring water quality, habitat, and ecosystem function, and developing and applying innovative policy, science, and technology to environmental management in southeast coastal New England.

Applicant Eligibility: Assistance under SNEP is available to state, local, territorial, and Tribal governments; institutions of higher education; nonprofit institutions and organizations; intertribal consortia; and interstate agencies. Private businesses, federal agencies, and individuals are not eligible to be grant recipients; however, they are encouraged to work in partnership with eligible applicants on projects.

Beneficiary Eligibility: Same as Applicant Eligibility.

Award Range/Average: Range: $2,000,000 - $5,000,000/fiscal year Average: $3,500,000/year (estimated).

Funding: (Cooperative Agreements (Discretionary Grants)) FY 17 $4,510,000; FY 18 est $4,200,000; FY 19 N/A FY 16 $4,637,000

HQ: 5 Post Office Square, Suite 100
Boston, MA 2109
Phone: 617-918-1672
Email: simpson.karen@epa.gov
http://www.epa.gov/snecwrp

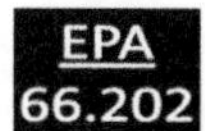

CONGRESSIONALLY MANDATED PROJECTS "CONGRESSIONAL EARMARKS"

Award: Cooperative Agreements; Project Grants

Purpose: To implement special Congressionally directed projects or programs identified in EPA's annual appropriations act, committee reports incorporated by reference into the annual appropriation act, and other statutes mandating that EPA provide financial assistance agreements to designated recipients for projects or programs.

Applicant Eligibility: Eligible applicants are specified in the statute authorizing the earmark. Examples of recipients that may receive assistance under this program include local, state, intrastate, interstate, U.S. territories or possessions, public or nonprofit institutions/organizations, public/private nonprofit institutions/organizations, quasi-public nonprofit institutions/organizations, institutions of higher education, Federally Recognized Indian Tribal Governments, Native American Organizations, and international organizations.

Beneficiary Eligibility: Beneficiaries vary with the project Congress has directed EPA to fund. For example, an earmark for a wastewater treatment plant or sewer system would benefit the community in which the project is constructed.

Award Range/Average: No range; no appropriated funds were enacted in FY 2017 and FY 2018.

Funding: (Cooperative Agreements) FY 17 $0; FY 18 est $0; FY 19 est $0; FY 16 $20,000,000; - EPA did not receive earmark funding in FY 2017 or FY 2018.

HQ: USEPA Headquarters 1200 Pennsylvania Avenue NW
Washington, DC 20460
Phone: 202-564-2835
Email: humes.hamilton@epa.gov
http://www.epa.gov/aboutepa/about-office-chief-financial-officer-ocfo

ENVIRONMENTAL FINANCE CENTER GRANTS "EFC Grant Program"

Award: Cooperative Agreements; Project Grants

Purpose: To support Environmental Finance Centers (EFCs) that provide multi-media environmental finance expertise and outreach to the regulated communities.

Applicant Eligibility: Assistance under this program is available to public and private non-profit universities and colleges and to nonprofit organizations. For certain competitive funding opportunities under this CFDA description, the Agency may limit eligibility to compete to a number or subset of eligible applicants consistent with the Agency's Assistance Agreement Competition Policy.

Beneficiary Eligibility: States, tribes, local governments, businesses and community organizations and the general public are the beneficiaries of this program.

Award Range/Average: Range: $60,000 to $190,000 per fiscal year Average: $138,000 per fiscal year.

Funding: (Cooperative Agreements (Discretionary Grants)) FY 17 $2,162,417; FY 18 est $600,000; FY 19 est $1,000,000; FY 16 $1,825,000

HQ: 1200 Pennsylvania Avenue NW, P.O. Box 4201T

Washington, DC 20460

Phone: 202-564-4996

Email: mcprouty.timothy@epa.gov

http://www.epa.gov/waterfinancecente

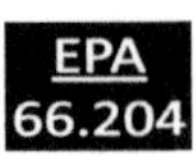

EPA 66.204 MULTIPURPOSE GRANTS TO STATES AND TRIBES "Multipurpose Grants to States and Tribes"

Award: Formula Grants

Purpose: To implement high priority activities, including the processing of permits, which complement programs under established environmental statutes.

Applicant Eligibility: Assistance under this program is generally available to states, the District of Columbia, the Commonwealth of Puerto Rico, the Virgin Islands, Guam, American Samoa, the Commonwealth of the Northern Marianas, and tribes qualified under Clean Water Act Section 518(e) that have received authorization (TAS) for WQS. Applicable grant guidance may further limit applicant eligibility.

Beneficiary Eligibility: States, the District of Columbia, the Commonwealth of Puerto Rico, the Virgin Islands, Guam, American Samoa, the Commonwealth of the Northern Marianas, and tribes qualified under Clean Water Act Section 518(e) with TAS for WQS.

Award Range/Average: Range: $15,000 to $900,000 per fiscal year. Average: $275,000 (estimated)

Funding: (Project Grants) FY 17 $162,900; FY 18 est $9,800,000; FY 19 N/A FY 16 $20,809,000

HQ: 1200 Pennsylvania Avenue

Washington, DC 20460

Phone: 202-564-2835

Email: humes.hamilton@epa.gov

http://www.epa.gov/grants/specific-epa-grant-programs

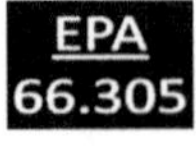

EPA 66.305 COMPLIANCE ASSISTANCE SUPPORT FOR SERVICES TO THE REGULATED COMMUNITY AND OTHER ASSISTANCE PROVIDERS "Compliance Assistance Centers"

Award: Project Grants

Purpose: The EPA has sponsored partnerships with industry, academic institutions, environmental groups, and other agencies to launch sector-specific Compliance Assistance Centers. The Compliance Assistance Center addresses real world issues in language that is used by the regulated entities.

Applicant Eligibility: Applicants must be nonprofit organizations as that term is defined in Section 4(6) of the Federal Financial Assistance Management Improvement Act of 1999.

Beneficiary Eligibility: The primary beneficiaries are small businesses, local governments and colleges/ universities that are being serviced by the grantees. Other beneficiaries include state, local, general public, and the regulated business community.

Award Range/Average: $5,000/year - $110,000/year. Generally, individual Centers will receive between $5,000 - $10,000 this fiscal year to continue maintenance and operation of the Web site. An average is $27,000.

Funding: (Project Grants (Discretionary)) FY 17 $220,000; FY 18 est $350,000; FY 19 N/A FY 16 $220,000

HQ: Office of Enforcement and Compliance Assurance 1200 Pennsylvania Avenue NW, P.O. Box 2227A

Washington, DC 20460

Phone: 202-564-7076

Email: back.tracy@epa.gov

http://www.epa.gov/compliance/compliance-assistance-centers

EPA 66.306 ENVIRONMENTAL JUSTICE COLLABORATIVE PROBLEM-SOLVING COOPERATIVE AGREEMENT PROGRAM "EJCPS"

Award: Cooperative Agreements

Purpose: The Environmental Justice Collaborative Problem-Solving Cooperative Agreement Program provides funding to support community-based organizations in their efforts to collaborate and partner with local stakeholder groups as they develop and implement solutions that address environmental and/or public health issues for underserved communities.

Applicant Eligibility: An eligible applicant must be one of the following: incorporated non-profit organizations —including, but not limited to, environmental justice networks, faith based organizations and those affiliated with religious institutions; federally recognized tribal governments—including Alaska Native Villages; OR tribal organizations. Applicant organizations claiming non-profit status must include documentation that shows the organization is either a 501(c) (3) non-profit organization as designated by the Internal Revenue Service; OR a non-profit organization recognized by the state, territory, commonwealth or tribe in which it is located.

Beneficiary Eligibility: Eligible beneficiaries are the Non-Profit Community Groups as described under "Applicant Eligibility", and the residents of the communities they serve.

Award Range/Average: $100,000 to $300,000; average awards is $120,000. The total funding is $1,200,000. 10 awards will be issued one per each of the 10 EPA regions.

Funding: (Cooperative Agreements (Discretionary Grants)) FY 16 $20,809,000.

HQ: Office of Environmental Justice 1200 Pennsylvania Avenue NW, P.O. Box 2202A

Washington, DC 20460

Phone: 202-564-0152

Email: burney.jacob@epa.gov

http://www.epa.gov/environmentaljustice

SURVEYS, STUDIES, INVESTIGATIONS, TRAINING AND SPECIAL PURPOSE ACTIVITIES RELATING TO ENVIRONMENTAL JUSTICE "EJSS"

Award: Cooperative Agreements

Purpose: The program provides funding in support of surveys, studies and investigations, and special purpose assistance programs as they relate to environmental and/or public health issues, with a particular emphasis on environmental justice.

Applicant Eligibility: Assistance under this program is generally available to States, territories, Indian Tribes, intertribal consortia, and possessions of the U.S., including the District of Columbia, public and private universities and colleges, hospitals, laboratories, and other public or private nonprofit institutions which submit applications proposing projects concerning environmental justice issues with significant technical merit and relevance to EPA's mission. Some of EPA's statutes may limit assistance to specific types of interested applications.

Beneficiary Eligibility: States, territories, Indian Tribes, and possessions of the U.S., including the District of Columbia, public and private universities and colleges, hospitals, laboratories, and other public or private nonprofit institutions and the communities they serve.

Award Range/Average: $15,000 to $35,000/fiscal year; $20,000. This program was not funded in 2017 or in 2018.

Funding: (Cooperative Agreements (Discretionary Grants)) FY 17 $0; FY 18 est $0; FY 19 est $0; FY 16 $30,000.

HQ: 1200 Pennsylvania Avenue NW
Washington, DC 20460
Phone: 202-564-2907
Email: burney.jacob@epa.gov
http://www.epa.gov/environmentaljustice

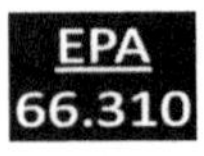

CAPACITY BUILDING GRANTS AND COOPERATIVE AGREEMENTS FOR COMPLIANCE ASSURANCE AND ENFORCEMENT ACTIVITIES IN INDIAN COUNTRY AND OTHER TRIBAL AREAS

Award: Project Grants

Purpose: The funds provide financial resources to build and improve the compliance assurance and enforcement capacity of federally-recognized Indian tribes, inter-tribal consortia, or tribal organizations.

Applicant Eligibility: Tribal Organizations, Inter-tribal Consortia, and Federal Organizations, Colleges and Universities, and non-for-profit organizations; eligible applicants must also have enforcement and compliance assurance responsibilities in Indian country and/or other tribal areas or provide support for enforcement and compliance assurance projects in Indian country and/or other tribal areas. EPA may also limit eligibility for certain competitive funding opportunities under this CFDA assistance listing to: (1) tribes and intertribal consortia located in the Region where a project is going to be performed; and/or (2) applicants that have access to Indian country or other tribal areas.

Beneficiary Eligibility: Federally Recognized Indian Tribal Governments; Inter-tribal Consortia and Tribal Organizations; Federal, State, and Multi-jurisdictional State Organizations; colleges and universities; and non-for-profit organizations.

Award Range/Average: $3000 to $30,000/fiscal year

Funding: (Project Grants (Discretionary)) FY 17 $140,000; FY 18 est $60,000; FY 19 est $0; FY 16 $129,000; - FY 2016 $129,000; FY 2017 $140,000; FY 2018 Estimate: $60,000.

HQ: Office of Enforcement and Compliance Assurance 1200 Pennsylvania Avenue NW, P.O. Box 2221A

Washington, DC 20460

Phone: 202-564-2516

Email: binder.jonathan@epa.gov

http://www.epa.gov/compliance

CONSTRUCTION GRANTS FOR WASTEWATER TREATMENT WORKS

Award: Project Grants

Purpose: Assists and serves as an incentive in construction of municipal wastewater treatment works which are required to meet State and/or Federal water quality standards and improve the water quality in the waters of the United States.

Applicant Eligibility: Funding for this construction grants program is for American Samoa, Commonwealth of Northern Mariana Islands, Guam, Virgin Islands, and the District of Columbia because they are exempt by the U.S. Congress from establishing a State Revolving Fund (SRF). Grants are awarded to only these territories and the District of Columbia from the SRF funds (Title VI grants), which are awarded as Title II grants.

Beneficiary Eligibility: General Public. Anyone to be served by a wastewater treatment works assisted by this program.

Award Range/Average: CWA Title II grants Range: $100,000 to $10,000,000/fiscal year; Average: $5,000,000/fiscal year.

Funding: (Project Grants) FY 17 $26,170,000; FY 18 est $31,791,000; FY 19 est $28,000,000; FY 16 $26,848,000.

HQ: Sustainable Communities Branch (4204M) Municipal Support Division Office of Wastewater Management

Washington, DC 20460

Phone: 202-564-6186

Email: johnson.tara@epa.gov

http://www.epa.gov/environmental-topics/water-topics

WATER POLLUTION CONTROL STATE, INTERSTATE, AND TRIBAL PROGRAM SUPPORT "Section 106 Grants"

Award: Formula Grants

Purpose: Assists States and interstate agencies in establishing and maintaining adequate measures for prevention and control of surface and ground water pollution from both point and nonpoint sources.

Applicant Eligibility: Eligible entities include States (including the District of Columbia and territories), interstate water pollution control agencies as defined in the Federal Water Pollution Control Act, and Indian tribes qualified under CWA Section 518(e). Agencies making application for funds must annually submit their pollution-control program to the appropriate EPA Regional Administrator for approval.

Beneficiary Eligibility: States (including the District of Columbia), Territories, interstate water pollution control agencies and Indian tribes qualified under Section 518(e) of the Clean Water Act (CWA).

Award Range/Average: Range: $30,000 to $11,700,000/fiscal year; Average: $4,000,000/fiscal year.

Funding: (Formula Grants) FY 17 $227,150,000; FY 18 est $225,525,000; FY 19 est $153,683,000;

HQ: 1200 Pennsylvania Avenue NW
Washington, DC 20460
Phone: 202-564-3880
Email: delehanty.robyn@epa.gov
http://www.epa.gov

SURVEYS, STUDIES, INVESTIGATIONS, DEMONSTRATIONS, AND TRAINING GRANTS - SECTION 1442 OF THE SAFE DRINKING WATER ACT

Award: Project Grants

Purpose: Supports surveys, studies, investigations, demonstrations, and training associated with source water and drinking water; to develop and expand capabilities of programs to carry out the purposes of the Safe Drinking Water Act.

Applicant Eligibility: Assistance under this program is generally available to States, local governments, territories, Indian Tribes, and possessions of the U.S. (including the District of Columbia); public and private universities and colleges; hospitals; laboratories; public or private nonprofit institutions; and individuals. Nonprofit organizations described in Section 501(c)(4) of the Internal Revenue Code that engage in lobbying activities as defined in Section 3 of the Lobbying Disclosure Act of 1995 are not eligible to apply.

Beneficiary Eligibility: State and local governments, U.S. territories and possessions, Indian Tribes, universities and colleges, hospitals, laboratories, and other public and private nonprofit institutions and individuals.

Award Range/Average: Range: $10,000 to $6,900,000/fiscal year; Average: $1,150,000/fiscal year.

Funding: (Cooperative Agreements (Discretionary Grants)) FY 17 $11,610,000; FY 18 est $22,769,235; FY 19 est $1,050,000

HQ: 1200 Pennsylvania Avenue
Washington, DC 20460
Phone: 202-564-3817
Email: jackson.joe-a@epa.gov
http://www.epa.gov

STATE PUBLIC WATER SYSTEM SUPERVISION

Award: Formula Grants

Purpose: The objective of the grant is to provide financial assistance to eligible States and Tribes for the Public Water System Supervision Program, for implementation and enforcement of the requirements of the Safe Drinking Water Act that apply to public water systems.

Applicant Eligibility: Eligibility is limited to the governments of the fifty States; the District of Columbia; the Commonwealth of Puerto Rico; the Northern Mariana Islands; the Virgin Islands; Guam; American Samoa; and federally recognized Tribes, that have either assumed primary enforcement responsibility for the PWSS Program or that want to develop a program that will allow them to seek delegation for a PWSS Program. EPA may also use funds allotted for a State or Tribal program, if the State or Tribe does not have, or is not developing, primary enforcement responsibility, or EPA may use all or part of the funds to support the PWSS Program in absence of an acceptable State program.

Beneficiary Eligibility: The beneficiaries are the agencies within the fifty States; the District of Columbia; the Commonwealth of Puerto Rico; the Northern Mariana Islands; the Virgin Islands; Guam; American Samoa; and federally recognized Tribes, that have been designated by the jurisdiction's Governor or Chief Executive Officer as being responsible for the supervision of water supplies within the State, Territory, or Tribe.

Award Range/Average: Range of $116,000 to $6,570,000/fiscal year; Average of $1,509,606/fiscal year.

Funding: (Formula Grants) FY 17 $100,194,000; FY 18 est $99,634,000; FY 19 est $67,892,000.

HQ: Office of Ground Water and Drinking Water 1200 Pennsylvania Avenue NW, P.O. Box 4606M
Washington, DC 20460
Phone: 202-564-4588
Email: roland.kevin@epa.gov
http://www.epa.gov/ground-water-and-drinking-water

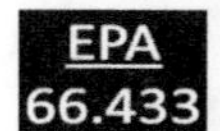

STATE UNDERGROUND WATER SOURCE PROTECTION "UIC"

Award: Formula Grants

Purpose: Fosters development and implementation of underground injection control programs under the Safe Drinking Water Act. The objective of the grant program is to provide financial assistance, to eligible States and Tribes, for the implementation of their UIC Program.

Applicant Eligibility: States, U.S. Territories and possessions, and Indian Tribes that qualify as Programs that have delegated primary Enforcement Authority pursuant to SDWA amendments of 1986

Beneficiary Eligibility: States, U.S. Territories, and Indian Tribes.

Award Range/Average: $5,000 to $939,000/fiscal year; $180,000/fiscal year.

Funding: (Formula Grants) FY 17 $10,109,000; FY 18 est $7,188,000; FY 19 FY 16 $8,859,300

HQ: Office of Ground Water and Drinking Water Office of Water 1200 Pennsylvania Avenue
Washington, DC 20460
Phone: 202-564-3879
Email: cruz.denny@epa.gov
http://www.epa.gov/uic

SURVEYS, STUDIES, INVESTIGATIONS, DEMONSTRATIONS, AND TRAINING GRANTS AND COOPERATIVE AGREEMENTS - SECTION 104(B)(3) OF THE CLEAN WATER ACT

Award: Project Grants

Purpose: Supports the coordination and acceleration of research, investigations, experiments, training, demonstrations, surveys, and studies relating to the causes, effects, extent, prevention, reduction, and elimination of water pollution.

Applicant Eligibility: Assistance under this program is generally available to States, local governments, territories, Indian Tribes, and possessions of the U.S. (including the District of Columbia); public and private universities and colleges; hospitals; laboratories; public or private nonprofit institutions; intertribal consortia; and individuals. Nonprofit organizations described in Section 501(c)(4) of the Internal Revenue Code that engage in lobbying activities as defined in Section 3 of the Lobbying Disclosure Act of 1995 are not eligible to apply.

Beneficiary Eligibility: State and local governments, U.S. territories and possessions, Indian Tribes, universities and colleges, hospitals, laboratories, other public and private nonprofit institutions, and individuals.

Award Range/Average: Range: $10,000 to $580,000/fiscal year; Average: $295,000/fiscal year.

Funding: (Project Grants (Discretionary)) FY 17 $5,036,000; FY 18 est $6,400,000; FY 19 est $2,000,000.

HQ: 1200 Pennsylvania Avenue NW
Washington, DC 20460
Phone: 202-564-0783
Email: miller.tracey@epa.gov
http://www.epa.gov/environmental-topics/water-topics

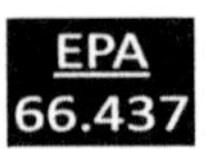

LONG ISLAND SOUND PROGRAM
"Long Island Sound Study (LISS)"

Award: Project Grants

Purpose: Implements the Long Island Sound Study Comprehensive Conservation and Management Plan and assists the states of Connecticut and New York and other public or nonprofit entities in implementation, research, planning, and citizen involvement and education related to reducing pollution and improving the quality of the environment to sustain living resources in the Long Island Sound.

Applicant Eligibility: State, interstate, and regional water pollution control agencies, and other public or nonprofit private agencies, institutions, and organizations are eligible. Private profit-making entities, and individuals, are not eligible.

Beneficiary Eligibility: Assistance under this program generally benefits state, interstate, and regional water pollution control agencies and other public or nonprofit private agencies, institutions, and organizations. The general public and Long Island Sound user groups such as swimmers, beach goers, sport and commercial fishermen, boaters, and shellfishes, benefit from the results of the program through cleaner water, restored and protected habitat, and preserved and enhanced ecosystems.

Award Range/Average: Range: $20,000 to $2,000,000/fiscal year; Average: $438,611/fiscal year

Funding: (Project Grants (Discretionary)) FY 17 $8,000,000; FY 18 est $12,000,000; FY 19 N/A FY 16 $3,893,000

HQ: Division 1200 Pennsylvania Avenue NW
Washington, DC 20460
Phone: 202-564-3833
Email: shah.surabhi@epa.gov
http://longislandsoundstudy.net

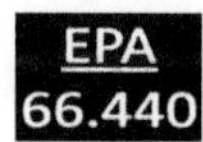

URBAN WATERS SMALL GRANTS

Award: Project Grants

Purpose: The objective of the Urban Waters Program is to protect and restore America's urban waterways. The funding priority is to achieve the goals and commitments established in the Agency's Urban Waters Strategic Framework.

Applicant Eligibility: Assistance under the Urban Waters Small Grants is generally available to States, local governments, Indian Tribes, public and private universities and colleges, public or private nonprofit institutions/organizations, intertribal consortia, and interstate agencies. Nonprofit organizations described in Section 501(c)(4) of the Internal Revenue Code that engage in lobbying activities as defined in Section 3 of the Lobbying Disclosure Act of 1995 are not eligible to apply.

Beneficiary Eligibility: Residents of urban areas adversely impacted by water pollution, State and local governments, Indian Tribes, other public and private nonprofit institutions, intertribal consortia, and interstate agencies.

Award Range/Average: Range: $40,000 to $60,000/fiscal year; Average: $50,000/fiscal year

Funding: (Project Grants) FY 18 est $0; FY 17 est $0; FY 16 $1,600,000; - FY 16 $1,600,000; FY 17 est. $0; and FY 18 est. $0.

HQ: 1200 Pennsylvania Avenue NW, P.O. Box 4601M
Washington, DC 20460
Phone: 202-564-3868
Email: simon.roy@epa.gov
http://www.epa.gov/urbanwaters

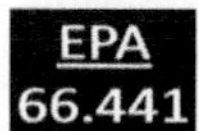

HEALTHY WATERSHEDS CONSORTIUM GRANT PROGRAM

Award: Cooperative Agreements

Purpose: Supports strategically protecting healthy watersheds across the country. The program's focus is to protect freshwater ecosystems and their watersheds.

Applicant Eligibility: Universities, colleges and institutions of higher education and hospitals are not eligible under this announcement. Non-profit, non-governmental organizations, interstate agencies, and intertribal consortia which are capable of undertaking activities that advance watershed protection programs are eligible to compete in this program.

Beneficiary Eligibility: Public and private nonprofit institutions/ organizations, federally recognized Indian tribal governments, states, local governments, U.S. territories and interstate agencies.

Award Range/Average: $3,750,000 every six years. Average: $625,000/fiscal year.

Funding: (Project Grants (Discretionary)) FY 17 $1,017,000; FY 18 est $655,000; FY 19 est $183,000; FY 16 $1,270,000; - Projects Grants and Cooperative Agreements

HQ: Nonpoint Source Management Branch Office of Oceans Wetlands and Watersheds
Washington, DC 20460
Phone: 202-566-1202
Email: solloway.chris@epa.gov
http://www.epa.gov/hwp

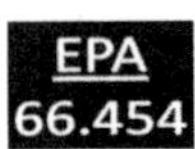

WATER QUALITY MANAGEMENT PLANNING "205(j)(2)) or 604(b)"

Award: Formula Grants

Purpose: To assist States, Regional Public Comprehensive Planning Organizations, and Interstate Organizations in carrying out water quality management planning.

Applicant Eligibility: State Water Quality Management Agencies.

Beneficiary Eligibility: Same as Applicant Eligibility.

Award Range/Average: Range: $100,000 to $1,478,000/fiscal year; Average: $251,000/fiscal year.

Funding: (Formula Grants) FY 17 $14,047,000; FY 18 est $16,608,000; FY 19 est $16,608,000;

HQ: 1200 Pennsylvania Avenue NW
Washington, DC 20460
Phone: 202-566-1202
Email: solloway.chris@epa.gov
http://www.epa.gov

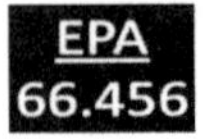

NATIONAL ESTUARY PROGRAM "NEP"

Award: Project Grants

Purpose: The National Estuary Program's goal is to protect and restore the water quality and estuarine resources of estuaries and associated watersheds designated by the EPA Administrator as estuaries of national significance.

Applicant Eligibility: Assistance agreements are issued only to those estuaries designated by the Administrator. The Administrator is authorized to make grants to State, interstate, and regional water pollution control agencies and entities; State coastal zone management agencies; interstate agencies; and other public and private nonprofit agencies, institutions, organizations, and individuals (Section 320(g)(l)).

Beneficiary Eligibility: Anyone/General Public.

Award Range/Average: The NEPs generally receive base funding in the amount of $600,000. For FY 18, each of the NEPs received base funding in the amount of $600,000.

Funding: (Project Grants (Discretionary)) FY 17 $17,763,900; FY 18 est $16,800,000; FY 19 N/A FY 16 $17,915,300

HQ: 1200 Pennsylvania Avenue
Washington, DC 20460

Phone: 202-566-2954

Email: benson.robert@epa.gov

http://www.epa.gov/nep

CAPITALIZATION GRANTS FOR CLEAN WATER STATE REVOLVING FUNDS "CW State Revolving Fund"

Award: Formula Grants

Purpose: Creates State Revolving Funds through a program of capitalization grants to States which will provide a long term source of State financing for construction of wastewater treatment facilities and implementation of other water quality management activities.

Applicant Eligibility: States and Puerto Rico are eligible to receive capitalization grants under Title VI. Indian tribes are eligible to receive grants from Title VI for the construction of municipal wastewater facilities.

Beneficiary Eligibility: For loans and other financial assistance (but not grants) for wastewater treatment facilities: local communities, intermunicipal, State, interstate agencies, and Indian tribes. For nonpoint source management programs and estuary activities in approved State Nonpoint Source Management Programs and Comprehensive Conservation and Management Plans: the public agencies listed above, individuals, and programs.

Award Range/Average: $6,500,000 to $147,000,000/fiscal year; $26,000,000;/fiscal year.

Funding: FY 16 $1,319,293,600; FY 17 est $1,369,202,000; FY 18 est $1,393,387,000; - FY 16 $1,319,293,600; FY 17 est. $1,369,202,000; and FY 18 est. $1,393,387,000.

HQ: Office of Wastewater Management State Revolving Fund Branch 1200 Pennsylvania Avenue NW, P.O. Box 4204M

Washington, DC 20460

Phone: 202-564-0686

Email: platt.sheila@epa.gov

http://www.epa.gov/cwsrf

NONPOINT SOURCE IMPLEMENTATION GRANTS "319 Program"

Award: Formula Grants

Purpose: Assists States, the District of Columbia, American Samoa, Guam, Northern Marianas, Puerto Rico, Virgin Islands, and qualified Indian Tribes and intertribal consortia in implementing EPA-approved Section 319 nonpoint source management programs. EPA's funding priority is to award grants that implement a grant recipient's nonpoint source management program plan, particularly the development and implementation of watershed-based plans, focusing on watersheds with water quality impairments caused by nonpoint sources, which result in improved water quality in impaired waters.

Applicant Eligibility: Eligible entities include States and qualified Indian Tribes and intertribal consortia who have approved nonpoint source assessment reports and management plans. To be qualified, Tribes must have treatment in a manner similar to a state (TAS) status for the 319 Program.

Beneficiary Eligibility: State and local governments; interstate and intrastate agencies; federally recognized Indian tribal governments; intertribal consortia; the following US territory or possessions: the District of Columbia, American Samoa, Guam, Northern Marianas, Puerto Rico, Virgin Islands; public and private nonprofit organizations and institutions. The lead nonpoint source agency may distribute grant funds to other organizations in accordance with a work program which is approved by EPA.

Award Range/Average: States/Territories: $443,000 to $8,603,800; $2,867,600. Indian Tribes: base grants $30,000 to $50,000; competitive grants up to $100,000. Ranges vary year-to-year based on size of appropriation (and also varies depending on number of applicants for grants to Indian Tribes or intertribal consortia).

Funding: (Formula Grants) FY 17 $167,900,000; FY 18 est $167,011,000; FY 19 est $0; FY 16 $166,177,000

HQ: 1200 Pennsylvania Avenue NW

Washington, DC 20460

Phone: 202-566-0340

Email: curtis.cynthia@epa.gov

http://www.epa.gov/nps

EPA 66.461 REGIONAL WETLAND PROGRAM DEVELOPMENT GRANTS

Award: Cooperative Agreements

Purpose: Assists state, tribal, local government agencies, and interstate/intertribal entities in building programs which protect, manage, and restore wetlands. The primary focus of the grants is to build state and tribal wetland programs. A secondary focus is to build local e.g. county or municipal programs.

Applicant Eligibility: States, Tribes, local government agencies, interstate agencies, and intertribal consortia are eligible to apply to the Regions. Past recipients include, but are not limited to, wetland regulatory agencies, water quality agencies (Section 401 water quality certification), planning offices, wild and scenic rivers agencies, departments of transportation, fish and wildlife or natural resources agencies, agriculture departments, forestry agencies, coastal zone management agencies, park and recreation agencies, non-point source or storm water agencies, and city or county and other S/T/LG governmental agencies that conduct wetland-related activities.

Beneficiary Eligibility: State, Tribal, and local governments involved in administering wetlands protection, restoration and/or management programs, or programs related to or that complement wetlands protection programs.

Award Range/Average: Range: $20,000 to $600,000/fiscal year; Average: $220,000/fiscal year.

Funding: (Cooperative Agreements (Discretionary Grants)) FY 17 $14,277,576; FY 18 est $13,594,000; FY 19 est $9,515,000; FY 16 $14,028,000

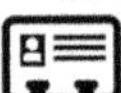

HQ: Office of Oceans Wetlands and Watersheds Office of Water 1200 Pennsylvania Avenue NW, P.O. Box 4502T

Washington, DC 20460

Phone: 202-566-1225

Email: price.myra@epa.gov

http://www.epa.gov/wetlands/wetland-program-development-grants

EPA 66.462 NATIONAL WETLAND PROGRAM DEVELOPMENT GRANTS AND FIVE-STAR RESTORATION TRAINING GRANT

Award: Cooperative Agreements

Purpose: Assists state, tribal, and local government agencies, and interstate/intertribal entities in building programs which protect, manage, and restore wetlands.

Applicant Eligibility: Non-profit, non-governmental organizations, Interstate agencies, and Intertribal consortia which are capable of undertaking activities that advance wetland programs on a national basis are eligible to compete in this program. The term "interstate agency" is defined in CWA Section 502 as "an agency of two or more States established by or pursuant to an agreement or compact approved by the Congress, or any other agency of two or more States, having substantial powers or duties pertaining to the control of pollution as determined and approved by the Administrator.

Beneficiary Eligibility: State, Tribal, and local governments involved in administering wetlands protection, restoration, and/or management programs or programs related to or complement wetlands protection programs.

Award Range/Average: National Wetlands Program Development Grants: $75,000 to $200,000/every two years; $160,500/every two years; Five-Star Restoration Training Grant: $1,000,000 every four years

Funding: (Cooperative Agreements (Discretionary Grants)) FY 17 $1,437,424; FY 18 est $732,000; FY 19 est $512,000; FY 16 $650,000

HQ: 1200 Pennsylvania Avenue NW
Washington, DC 20460
Phone: 202-566-1225
Email: price.myra@epa.gov
http://www.epa.gov/wetlands/wetland-program-development-grants

CHESAPEAKE BAY PROGRAM
"Chesapeake Bay Program"

Award: Project Grants

Purpose: The EPA's Chesapeake Bay Program awards annual grants to states, local governments, and non-governmental organizations to reduce and prevent pollution and to improve the living resources in the Chesapeake Bay. Grants are awarded for implementation projects, as well as for research, monitoring, environmental education, and other related activities.

Applicant Eligibility: Under section 117(d), funds are available for technical and general assistance grants to nonprofit organizations, State and local governments, colleges, universities, and interstate agencies; under section 117(e)(1)(A) and 117e(1)(B), respectively, funds are available for implementation, regulatory and accountability, and monitoring grants to signatory jurisdictions; and under section 117(g)(2), funds are available for technical assistance and assistance grants under the Small Watershed Grants Program to local governments and nonprofit organizations and individuals in the Chesapeake Bay region.

Beneficiary Eligibility: Same as Applicant Eligibility.

Award Range/Average: $50,000 to $6,000,000 per fiscal year; $350,000 per fiscal year average.

Funding: (Project Grants (Discretionary)) FY 17 $53,652,760; FY 18 est $54,223,000; FY 19 est $7,300,000; FY 16 $64,744,800

HQ: 410 Severn Avenue, Suite 109
Annapolis, MD 21403
Phone: 800-968-7229
Email: dietrich.julie@epa.gov
http://www.epa.gov/restoration-chesapeake-bay/chesapeake-bay-program-grant-guidance

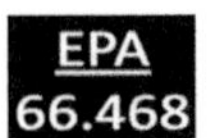

CAPITALIZATION GRANTS FOR DRINKING WATER STATE REVOLVING FUNDS
"Drinking Water State Revolving Fund"

Award: Formula Grants

Purpose: Grants are made to States to capitalize their Drinking Water State Revolving Funds which will provide a long-term source of financing for the costs of drinking water infrastructure.

Applicant Eligibility: States, the District of Columbia, U.S. Territories or Possessions (the Commonwealth of Puerto Rico, Virgin Islands, Mariana Islands American Samoa, and Guam), and Federally Recognized Indian Tribal Governments are eligible for grants from the program.

Beneficiary Eligibility: States, U.S. Territories or Possessions (the Commonwealth of Puerto Rico, Virgin Islands, Mariana Islands American Samoa, and Guam), and Federally Recognized Indian Tribal Governments are eligible for grants from the program.

Award Range/Average: States: $8,787,000 to $97,000,000/fiscal year; $16,318,800/fiscal year. Tribes: $6,000 to $2,400,000/fiscal year; $480,000/fiscal year. Territories: $1,532,000 to $8,787,000/fiscal year; $4,189,000/fiscal year. Recovery Act funds - States: $19,500,000 to $160,000,000/fiscal year. Territories: $500,000 to $2,100,000/fiscal year. Tribes: $15,600 to $3,200,000/fiscal year.

Funding: FY 17 $844,255,000; FY 18 est $1,136,657,000; FY 19 est $863,000,000; FY 16 $833,218,900.

HQ: Drinking Water Protection Division Office of Ground Water and Drinking Water Office of Water
1200 Pennsylvania Avenue NW, P.O. Box 4606M
Washington, DC 20460
Phone: 202-564-6239
Email: fort.felecia@epa.gov
http://www.epa.gov/drinkingwatersrf

GREAT LAKES PROGRAM
"Great Lakes Restoration Initiative (GLRI)"

Award: Project Grants; Use of Property, Facilities, and Equipment; Dissemination of Technical Information

Purpose: Helps to restore and maintain the chemical, physical, and biological integrity of the Great Lakes Basin Ecosystem.

Applicant Eligibility: Qualified non-federal entities eligible to apply for grants include non-federal governmental entities, nonprofit organizations, and institutions. This includes state agencies; any agency or instrumentality of local government; interstate agencies; federally-recognized tribes and tribal organizations; colleges and universities; non-profit organizations; and other public or non-profit private agencies, institutions, and organizations.

Beneficiary Eligibility: Beneficiaries include non-federal governmental entities, nonprofit organizations, and institutions. This includes state agencies; any agency or instrumentality of local government; interstate agencies; federally-recognized tribes and tribal organizations; colleges and universities; non-profit organizations; and other public or non-profit private agencies, institutions, and organizations.

Award Range/Average: Some awards are fully funded at award and others are funded incrementally over several years. Representative Award Range: $30,000/fiscal year to $5,000,000/fiscal year.

Funding: (Project Grants (Discretionary)) FY 17 $88,840,023; FY 18 est $65,000,000; FY 19 N/A FY 16 $690,351,000

HQ: USEPA Great Lakes National Program Office (G-17J) 77 W Jackson Boulevard
Chicago, IL 60604
Phone: 312-353-4513
Email: mosier.bart@epa.gov
http://www.epa.gov/greatlakes

BEACH MONITORING AND NOTIFICATION PROGRAM IMPLEMENTATION GRANTS
"BEACH Act Program"

Award: Formula Grants

Purpose: To assist Coastal and Great Lakes States and Tribes in developing and implementing programs for monitoring and notification for coastal recreation waters adjacent to beaches or similar points of access that are used by the public.

Applicant Eligibility: Coastal and Great Lakes States, territories (Puerto Rico, the U.S. Virgin Islands, Guam, American Samoa, and the Commonwealth of the Northern Mariana Islands), and Tribes eligible under Section 518(e) of the Clean Water Act, as amended. The Administrator may make a grant to a local government under this subsection for implementation of a monitoring and notification program only if, after the one-year period beginning on the date of publication of performance criteria under Section 406 (a)(1), the Administrator determines that the State is not implementing a program that meets the requirements of Section 406(a)(1), regardless of whether the State has received a grant under Section 406(a)(1).

Beneficiary Eligibility: States, U.S. territories, Federally recognized Indian Tribal Governments, environmental and public health agencies, and local governments involved in implementing monitoring and notification programs.

Award Range/Average: $150,000 to $432,000/fiscal year for states and territories; average award was $239,300. Tribes typically receive $50,000 each.

Funding: FY 17 $9,540,300; FY 18 est $9,331,000; FY 19 est $0; FY 16 $9,487,000.

HQ: USEPA Office of Water Standards and Health Protection Division 1200 Pennsylvania Avenue NW, P.O. Box 4305T
Washington, DC 20460
Phone: 202-566-1017
Email: larimer.lisa@epa.gov
http://www.epa.gov/waterscience/beaches

EPA 66.473 DIRECT IMPLEMENTATION TRIBAL COOPERATIVE AGREEMENTS "DITCA"

Award: Project Grants

Purpose: Direct Implementation Tribal Cooperative Agreements enables EPA to award cooperative agreements to federally recognized Indian tribes and eligible intertribal consortia to help carry out the Agency's function to directly implement Federal environmental programs required or authorized by law in the absence of an authorized or delegated tribal program, notwithstanding the Federal Grant and Cooperative Agreement Act.

Applicant Eligibility: DITCAs may be awarded to: (1) Federally Recognized Indian Tribal Government, and (2) intertribal consortia consistent with applicable provisions. In order for an intertribal consortium to be eligible to receive cooperative agreements under this authority, an intertribal consortium should be consistent with the provisions in 40 C.

Beneficiary Eligibility: Federally Recognized Indian Tribal Government and intertribal consortia consistent with applicable provisions.

Award Range/Average: Cooperative agreement amounts range between $10,000 and $100,000/fiscal year; Average: $55,000/fiscal year.

Funding: (Project Grants) FY 17 $350,000; FY 18 est $350,000; FY 19 est $350,000; FY 16 $350,000; - FY 2017 $350,000; and FY 2018 est. $350,000 and FY 2019 est. $350,000 in active cooperative agreements.

HQ: Indian Environmental Office (2690M) 1200 Pennsylvania Avenue NW

Washington, DC 20460

Phone: 202-564-4368

http://www.epa.gov/tribal

EPA 66.474 WATER PROTECTION GRANTS TO THE STATES

Award: Formula Grants

Purpose: Assists states, territories, and possessions of the United States with critical water infrastructure protection.

Applicant Eligibility: Assistance under this program is available to States, Tribes, Territories, and possessions of the United States.

Beneficiary Eligibility: Water programs of States, Territories, and possessions of the United States.

Award Range/Average: Funds are awarded by each Regional Office. The range of financial assistance available to States varies according to program and fiscal year. $16,700 to $380,300/fiscal year; $198,500/fiscal year.

Funding: (Formula Grants) FY 17 $0; FY 18 est $0; FY 19 est $0; FY 16 $0

HQ: 1200 Pennsylvania Avenue NW

Washington, DC 20460

Phone: 202-564-2106

Email: goldbloom-helzner.david@epa.gov

http://www.epa.gov

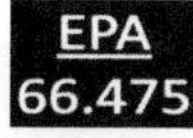

GULF OF MEXICO PROGRAM

Award: Cooperative Agreements

Purpose: Assists States, Indian Tribes, interstate agencies, and other public or nonprofit organizations in developing, implementing, and demonstrating innovative approaches relating to the causes, effects, extent, prevention, reduction, and elimination of water pollution.

Applicant Eligibility: Funds are available to State and local governments, interstate agencies, Tribes, colleges and universities, and other public or nonprofit organizations. For certain competitive funding opportunities under this CFDA assistance listing, the Agency may limit eligibility to compete to a number or subset of eligible applicants consistent with the Agency's Assistance Agreement Competition Policy.

Beneficiary Eligibility: State and local governments, interstate agencies, Tribes, colleges and universities, and other public or nonprofit organizations.

Award Range/Average: FY 17: $25,000 - $1,000,000, Average $330,000 FY 18 (est.): $25,000 - $1,000,000, Average $430,000

Funding: (Cooperative Agreements (Discretionary Grants)) FY 17 $6,401,500; FY 18 est $9,500,000; FY 19 est $9,500,000; FY 16 $459,000

HQ: EPA/Gulf of Mexico Program Office 2510 14th Street, Suite 1212
Gulfport, MS 39501
Phone: 228-304-7441
Email: houge.rachel@epa.gov
http://www.epa.gov/gulfofmexico

LAKE CHAMPLAIN BASIN PROGRAM
"Lake Champlain Program"

Award: Project Grants

Purpose: To implement the Lake Champlain Basin Management Plan, Opportunities for Action: An Evolving Plan for the Future of the Lake Champlain Basin 2017, and to assist the states of New York and Vermont in protecting, restoring and preserving the Lake Champlain ecosystem.

Applicant Eligibility: In accordance with Section 120 of the Clean Water Act, EPA may provide funding to the states of Vermont and New York and the New England Interstate Water Pollution Control Commission for the implementation of the Lake Champlain Basin Program. In addition, EPA may choose to solicit applications from other state, interstate, and regional water pollution control agencies, and public or nonprofit agencies, institutions, and organizations that are eligible to receive grants from EPA through this program.

Beneficiary Eligibility: Assistance under this program generally benefits State environmental, health, and agriculture agencies; interstate water pollution control agencies; public nonprofit institutions and organizations; sponsored organizations; Federal agencies; local agencies; intrastate agencies; public and private nonprofit institutions and organizations; private organizations; small businesses; and quasi-public nonprofit institutions.

Award Range/Average: $365,000 to $3,504,022/fiscal year; Average $1,465,000/fiscal year

Funding: Project Grants (Discretionary) FY 17 $4,395,000; FY 18 N/A FY 19 N/A FY 16 $4,395,000

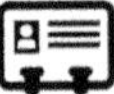

HQ: 5 Post Office Square, Suite 100 P.O. Box OEP 6 1
Boston, MA 2109
Phone: 617-918-1211
Email: dore.bryan@epa.gov
http://www.epa.gov

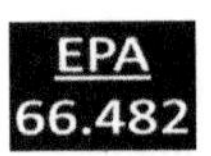

DISASTER RELIEF APPROPRIATIONS ACT (DRAA) HURRICANE SANDY CAPITALIZATION GRANTS FOR CLEAN WATER STATE REVOLVING FUNDS

"Clean Water State Revolving Fund Hurricane Sandy Supplemental Appropriation"

Award: Formula Grants

Purpose: The funding priority established by the Hurricane Sandy Supplemental Appropriation is to fund projects at wastewater facilities that will improve the resiliency of those facilities against future disasters. Only facilities that were impacted by Hurricane Sandy in the States of New York and New Jersey are eligible.

Applicant Eligibility: The States of New York and New Jersey.

Beneficiary Eligibility: The States of New York and New Jersey, and wastewater treatment facilities funding resiliency projects that were impacted by Hurricane Sandy.

Award Range/Average: $191,136,855 to $283,148,135/fiscal year; $237,142,500/fiscal year.

Funding: (Formula Grants) FY 17 $0; FY 18 est $0; FY 19 est $0; FY 16 $0

HQ: State Revolving Fund Branch Municipal Support Division Office of Water 1200 Pennsylvania Avenue NW, P.O. Box 4204M
Washington, DC 20460
Phone: 202-564-0686
http://www.epa.gov/cwsrf

DISASTER RELIEF APPROPRIATIONS ACT (DRAA) HURRICANE SANDY CAPITALIZATION GRANTS FOR DRINKING WATER STATE REVOLVING FUNDS

"Drinking Water State Revolving Fund Hurricane Sandy Supplemental Appropriation"

Award: Formula Grants

Purpose: The funding priority established by the Hurricane Sandy Supplemental Appropriation is to fund projects at drinking water facilities that will improve the resiliency of those facilities against future disasters. Only facilities that were impacted by Hurricane Sandy in the States of New York and New Jersey are eligible. No additional awards are anticipated in FY 2019.

Applicant Eligibility: The States of New York and New Jersey.

Beneficiary Eligibility: The States of New York and New Jersey, and drinking water facilities funding resiliency projects that were impacted by Hurricane Sandy.

Award Range/Average: $38,189,000 to $56,572,000/fiscal year; $47,381,000/fiscal year.

Funding: (Formula Grants) FY 17 $0; FY 18 est $0; FY 19 est $0; FY 16 $0

HQ: Drinking Water Protection Division Office of Ground Water and Drinking Water Office of Water 1200 Pennsylvania Avenue NW, P.O. Box 4606M

Washington, DC 20460

Phone: 202-564-6239

Email: fort.felecia@epa.gov

http://www.epa.gov/drinkingwatersrf

SENIOR ENVIRONMENTAL EMPLOYMENT PROGRAM "SEE"

Award: Cooperative Agreements

Purpose: Uses the talents of Americans 55 years of age or older to provide technical assistance to Federal, State, and local environmental agencies for projects of pollution prevention, abatement, and control to achieve the Agency's goals of clean air; clean and safe water; land preservation and restoration; healthy communities and ecosystems; and compliance and environmental stewardship.

Applicant Eligibility: Private, nonprofit organizations designated by the Secretary of Labor under Title V of the Older Americans Act of 1965.

Beneficiary Eligibility: Federal, State, and local environmental agencies and individuals 55 years old or older.

Award Range/Average: New awards and amendments: $1,000 to $750,000/FY 2017; Average $69,276/FY 2017; $332 to $837,500/FY 2018; Average $30,635/FY 2018. Estimates of $1,000 to $750,000/FY 2019; Average $60,000/FY 2019.

Funding: (Cooperative Agreements (Discretionary Grants)) FY 17 $50,000,000; FY 18 est $50,000,000; FY 19 est $50,000,000; FY 16 $38,346,358.

HQ: Office of Administration and Resources Management Office of Human Resources, 1200 Pennsylvania Avenue NW

Washington, DC 20460

Phone: 202-564-4390

Email: hughes.angela@epa.gov

http://www.epa.gov/careers/senior-environmental-employment-see-program

SCIENCE TO ACHIEVE RESULTS (STAR) RESEARCH PROGRAM

Award: Project Grants

Purpose: The Science to Achieve Results Program's goal is to stimulate and support scientific and engineering research that advances EPA's mission to protect human health and the environment.

Applicant Eligibility: Public and private nonprofit institutions/organizations, public and private institutions of higher education, and hospitals located in the U.S., state and local governments, Federally Recognized

Indian Tribal Governments, and U.S. territories or possessions are eligible to apply. Profit-making firms and individuals are not eligible to apply.

Beneficiary Eligibility: Public nonprofit institutions/organizations and private nonprofit institutions/ organizations located in the U.S.; state and local governments; Federally Recognized Indian Tribal Governments; U.S. territories or possessions; Anyone/General Public, Education Professional, Student/ Trainee, Graduate Student, Scientists/Researchers.

Award Range/Average: \$399,000 to \$2,996,426 total per grant. Average total \$500,000.

Funding: (Project Grants (Discretionary)) FY 17 \$28,180,686; FY 18 est \$28,500,000; FY 19 est \$0.

HQ: 1200 Pennsylvania Avenue NW, P.O. Box 8725R
Washington, DC 20460
Phone: 202-564-7823
Email: josephson.ron@epa.gov
http://www.epa.gov/research-grants

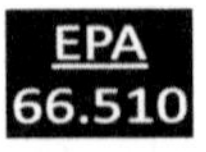

EPA 66.510 SURVEYS, STUDIES, INVESTIGATIONS AND SPECIAL PURPOSE GRANTS WITHIN THE OFFICE OF RESEARCH AND DEVELOPMENT

Award: Project Grants

Purpose: Supports surveys, studies and investigations and special purpose assistance to determine the environmental effects of air quality, drinking water, water quality, hazardous waste, toxic substances, and pesticides.

Applicant Eligibility: These programs are available to each State, territory and possession, and Tribal nation of the U.S., including the District of Columbia, for public and private State universities and colleges, hospitals, laboratories, State and local government departments, other public or private nonprofit institutions, and in some cases, individuals or foreign entities. Profit-making firms are not eligible to receive assistance agreements from the EPA under this program.

Beneficiary Eligibility: Public nonprofit institutions/organizations and private nonprofit institutions/ organizations; state and local governments; Federally Recognized Indian Tribal Governments; U.S. territories or possessions; anyone/general public; education professionals; students/trainees; graduate students; scientists/researchers; hospitals; foreign entities; and individuals.

Award Range/Average: \$10,000 to \$170,000 and average \$55,000.

Funding: (Project Grants (Discretionary)) FY 17 \$800,000; FY 18 est \$1,700,000; FY 19 est \$800,000.

HQ: 1200 Pennsylvania Avenue NW
Washington, DC 20460
Phone: 202-564-4756
Email: nanartowicz.john@epa.gov
http://www.epa.gov/research

EPA 66.511 OFFICE OF RESEARCH AND DEVELOPMENT CONSOLIDATED RESEARCH/TRAINING/FELLOWSHIPS

Award: Project Grants

Purpose: The Office of Research and Development supports research and development to determine the environmental effects of air quality, drinking water, water quality, hazardous waste, toxic substances, and pesticides, and identify, develop, and demonstrate effective pollution control techniques.

Applicant Eligibility: These programs are available to each State, territory and possession, and Tribal nation of the U.S., including the District of Columbia, public and private universities and colleges, hospitals, laboratories, State and local government departments, other public or private nonprofit institutions, and foreign entities. Profit-making firms are not eligible to receive assistance agreements from the EPA under this program.

Beneficiary Eligibility: Public nonprofit institutions/organizations and private nonprofit institutions/ organizations; state and local governments; Federally Recognized Indian Tribal Governments; U.S. territories or possessions; education professionals; students/trainees; graduate students; scientists/ researchers; hospitals; and foreign entities.

Award Range/Average: Awards can range for new grants/cooperative agreements from $75,000 to $1,000,000; and average $250,000.

Funding: (Cooperative Agreements (Discretionary Grants)) FY 17 $17,500,000; FY 18 est $18,200,000; FY 19 est $8,700,000; FY 16 $22,000,000

HQ: 1200 Pennsylvania Avenue
Washington, DC 20410
Phone: 202-564-4756
Email: nanartowicz.john@epa.gov
http://www.epa.gov/research-grants

GREATER RESEARCH OPPORTUNITIES (GRO) FELLOWSHIPS FOR UNDERGRADUATE ENVIRONMENTAL STUDY

Award: Project Grants

Purpose: The National Center for Environmental Research offers undergraduate fellowships to students in environmentally related fields of study. This program is intended to strengthen the environmental research capacity of institutions of higher education that receive limited funding to build such capacity.

Applicant Eligibility: Applicants must attend a fully accredited four-year U.S. college or university (located in the U.S. or its territories) for the fellowship period. Individuals must be citizens of the U.S. or its territories or possessions, or be lawfully admitted to the U.S. for permanent residence.

Beneficiary Eligibility: Individual/Family; Student/Trainee

Award Range/Average: The undergraduate fellowship provides up to $20,700 per year of academic support and $8,600 for internship support for a combined total of up to $50,000 over the life of the fellowship. Awards average $50,000.

Funding: (Project Grants (Discretionary)) FY 17 $0; FY 18 est $0; FY 19 FY 16 $0

HQ: Office of Research and Development/NCER 1200 Pennsylvania Avenue NW, P.O. Box 8725R
Washington, DC 20460
Phone: 202-564-7823
Email: josephson.ron@epa.gov
http://www.epa.gov/research-grants

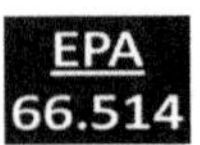

SCIENCE TO ACHIEVE RESULTS (STAR) FELLOWSHIP PROGRAM

Award: Project Grants

Purpose: The National Center for Environmental Research, as part of its Science to Achieve Results program, offers graduate fellowships for master's and doctoral level students in environmentally related fields of study.

Applicant Eligibility: Applicants must attend a fully accredited U.S. college or university (located in the U.S. or its territories) for their graduate studies. Individuals must be citizens of the U.S. or its territories or possessions, or be lawfully admitted to the U.S. for permanent residence.

Beneficiary Eligibility: Individual/Family; Student/Trainee and Graduate Student.

Award Range/Average: A maximum of $88,000 ($44,000/year) will be provided for master's fellows (two years) and up to $132,000 (three years) for doctoral fellows. Awards range from $88,000 to $132,000 total per fellowship and average $120,000.

Funding: (Project Grants (Discretionary)) FY 17 $0; FY 18 est $0; FY 19 est $0; FY 16 $6,700,000

HQ: Office of Research and Development/NCER 1200 Pennsylvania Avenue NW, P.O. Box 8725R
Washington, DC 20460
Phone: 202-564-7823
Email: josephson.ron@epa.gov
http://www.epa.gov/research-grants

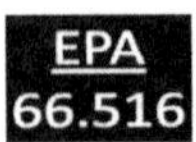

P3 AWARD: NATIONAL STUDENT DESIGN COMPETITION FOR SUSTAINABILITY

"People, Prosperity and the Planet (P3) Student Design Competition"

Award: Project Grants

Purpose: The U.S. Environmental Protection Agency – as part of its People, Prosperity and the Planet Award Program – is seeking applications proposing to research, develop, design, and demonstrate solutions to real world challenges.

Applicant Eligibility: Public and private institutions of higher education (limited to degree-granting institutions of higher education) located in the U.S. (includes eligible institutions of higher education located in U.S. territories and possessions) are eligible to apply to be the recipient of a grant to support teams of undergraduate and/or graduate students. Profit-making firms are not eligible to receive assistance agreements from the EPA under this program.

Beneficiary Eligibility: Public Nonprofit Institutions/Organizations, Private Nonprofit Institutions/ Organizations, Anyone/General Public, Education Professional, Student/Trainee, Graduate Student, Scientists/Researchers.

Award Range/Average: Phase I Awards range from $13,939 to $15,000 total per grant. Average awards total $14,750. Phase II Awards range from $40,240 to $75,000 total per grant. Average awards total $72,000.

Funding: (Project Grants (Discretionary)) FY 17 $992,076; FY 18 est $1,041,037; FY 19 est $0; FY 16 $0

HQ: 1200 Pennsylvania Avenue NW
Washington, DC 20460
Phone: 202-564-7823

Email: josephson.ron@epa.gov

http://www.epa.gov/p3

REGIONAL APPLIED RESEARCH EFFORTS (RARE) "RARE"

Award: Project Grants

Purpose: Support surveys, studies and investigations and special purpose assistance to determine the environmental effects of air quality, drinking water, water quality, hazardous waste, toxic substances, and pesticides.

Applicant Eligibility: NOTE: Only Regions are eligible to send applications or proposals. Federal Agencies may not apply.

Beneficiary Eligibility: NOTE: Only Regions are eligible to submit proposals or applications

Award Range/Average: New cooperative agreements shall not exceed $60,000 per Year/per Region.

Funding: (Cooperative Agreements (Discretionary Grants)) FY 17 $200,000; FY 18 est $200,000; FY 19 est $0; FY 16 est $135,000

HQ: Office of Research and Development/OSP 1200 Pennsylvania Avenue NW, P.O. Box 8104R

Washington, DC 20460

Phone: 202-564-1720

Email: blank.valerie@epa.gov

http://www.epa.gov/aboutepa/about-office-science-policy-osp

STATE SENIOR ENVIRONMENTAL EMPLOYMENT PROGRAM "SEE"

Award: Cooperative Agreements

Purpose: Provides technical assistance to State environmental agencies for projects of pollution prevention, abatement, and control to achieve the Agency's goals of Clean Air, Clean and Safe Water, Land Preservation and Restoration, Healthy Communities and Ecosystems, and Compliance and Environmental Stewardship.

Applicant Eligibility: Private, nonprofit organizations designated by the Secretary of Labor under Title V of the Older Americans Act of 1965.

Beneficiary Eligibility: State environmental agencies and individuals 55 years old or older.

Award Range/Average: New awards and amendments: $1,000 to $750,000/FY 2017; Average $69,276/FY 2017; $100,000/FY 2018; Average $100,000/FY 2018.

Funding: (Cooperative Agreements) FY 17 $500,000; FY 18 est $500,000; FY 19 est $500,000.

HQ: Office of Administration and Resources Management Office of Human Resources 1200 Pennsylvania Avenue NW, P.O. Box 3102A

Washington, DC 20460

Phone: 202-564-4390

Email: hughes.angela@epa.gov

http://www.epa.gov/careers/senior-environmental-employment-see-program

EPA 66.600 ENVIRONMENTAL PROTECTION CONSOLIDATED GRANTS FOR THE INSULAR AREAS - PROGRAM SUPPORT "Consolidated Program Support Grants"

Award: Formula Grants

Purpose: The program support grant is an alternative assistance delivery mechanism which allows an Insular Territory responsible for continuing pollution control programs to develop an integrated approach to pollution control.

Applicant Eligibility: The Territories of Guam, American Samoa, and the Virgin Islands, and the Commonwealth of the Northern Mariana Islands are eligible to receive and administer funds for more than one environmental program.

Beneficiary Eligibility: Same as Applicant Eligibility.

Award Range/Average: $2,000,000 to $3,300,000/territory/fiscal year for environmental program assistance. The total estimated average is $8,000,000/fiscal year.

Funding: (Formula Grants (Cooperative Agreements)) FY 17 $7,800,000; FY 18 est $7,800,000; FY 19 est $7,800,000; FY 16 est $26,000,000.

HQ: Grants Management Office (PMD-7) EPA Region 9 75 Hawthorne St
San Francisco, CA 94105
Phone: 415-972-3667
Email: espitia.alba@epa.gov
http://www2.epa.gov/aboutepa/epa-region-9-pacific-southwest

EPA 66.604 ENVIRONMENTAL JUSTICE SMALL GRANT PROGRAM "EJSG"

Award: Project Grants

Purpose: Develops a comprehensive understanding of environmental and public health issues, identify ways to address these issues at the local level, and educate and support the community.

Applicant Eligibility: For certain competitive funding opportunities under this CFDA description, the Agency may limit eligibility to compete to a number or subset of eligible applicants consistent with the Agency's Assistance Agreement Competition Policy. An eligible applicant MUST BE: an incorporated non-profit organization; OR a Native American tribal government (Federally recognized) (AND) located within the same, territory, commonwealth, or tribe that the proposed project will be located.

Beneficiary Eligibility: Eligible beneficiaries are the Non-Profit Community Groups as described in 081 above and the residents of the communities they serve. List selected may not be all inclusive.

Award Range/Average: $20,000 to $50,000/fiscal year; average $30,000.

Funding: (Project Grants (Discretionary)) FY 17 $1,080,000; FY 18 est $0; FY 19 est $1,200,000.

HQ: Office of Environmental Justice 1200 Pennsylvania Avenue NW, P.O. Box 2202A
Washington, DC 20460
Phone: 202-564-2907
Email: burney.jacob@epa.gov
http://www.epa.gov/environmentaljustice

EPA 66.605 PERFORMANCE PARTNERSHIP GRANTS "PPGs"

Award: Formula Grants; Project Grants

Purpose: Performance Partnership Grants are the cornerstone of the National Environmental Performance Partnership System -- EPA's strategy to strengthen partnerships and build a results-based management system.

Applicant Eligibility: All States, interstate agencies, U.S. territories, the District of Columbia, and federally recognized Indian Tribes eligible to receive more than one of the 20 categorical grant programs referred to in "Uses and Use Restrictions" above are eligible to apply for PPGs. Any duly authorized State or tribal entity that currently receives or is eligible to receive EPA categorical program grants may request a PPG for the funds it administers.

Beneficiary Eligibility: States, U.S. territories, federally recognized Indian tribal governments, and interstate agencies.

Award Range/Average: There is no low-end limit for PPG awards, which may be as small as combining two programs and thousands of dollars to Tribes, or as large as combining up to 20 categorical grants to States. PPG totals for larger States can exceed $10 million.

Funding: (Formula Grants) FY 17 $445,000,000; FY 18 est $445,000,000; FY 19 N/A FY 16 $445,000,000

HQ: 1200 Pennsylvania Avenue NW, P.O. Box 3903R
Washington, DC 20460
Phone: 202-564-3792
Email: osinski.michael@epa.gov
http://www.epa.gov/ocir/nepps

EPA 66.608 ENVIRONMENTAL INFORMATION EXCHANGE NETWORK GRANT PROGRAM AND RELATED ASSISTANCE "Exchange Network Grant Program"

Award: Project Grants

Purpose: Objectives of the grant program is to facilitate sharing environmental data, especially through shared and reusable services.

Applicant Eligibility: Eligible applicants for the Exchange Network Grant program include states, U.S. Territories (i.e., American Samoa, the Commonwealth of the Northern Mariana Islands, the District of Columbia, Guam, Palau, Puerto Rico, the U.S. Virgin Islands), federally recognized Indian tribes and native Alaska villages, and inter-tribal consortia of federally recognized tribes (e.g., the Northwest Indian Fisheries Commission). Other entities, such as regional air pollution control districts and some public universities may apply for assistance if they are agencies or instrumentalities of a state under applicable state laws. These entities, as well as other entities that submit applications asserting they are agencies or instrumentalities of a state, must provide with the application a letter from the appropriate state Attorney General certifying that the applicant is an agency or instrumentality of the state. EPA will not consider an application that does not contain the required documentation. EPA recognizes that the delegation for some programs extends to local governments, which are responsible for reporting data to EPA. Local governments that can demonstrate that they are instrumentalities of the state by providing the documentation described in the preceding paragraph are eligible to apply for Exchange Network Grants. Most local governments that implement EPA programs, however, are not agencies or instrumentalities of the state (i.e., a true agency or instrumentality is under the direct control of the state and the management of a state agency or instrumentality may generally be changed by the state executive or other state officials) and, therefore, are not eligible to apply. EPA encourages such entities to partner with a state applicant to allow for their data to be reported and shared through the Exchange Network. Interstate commissions and other interstate entities, likewise, are not eligible to apply and are encouraged to partner with a state applicant.

Beneficiary Eligibility: Eligible applicants for the EN Grant Program include states, the District of Columbia, U.S. territories (American Samoa, Guam, the Commonwealth of the Northern Mariana Islands, Puerto Rico, and the U.S. Virgin Islands), federally recognized Indian tribes, and intertribal consortia of federally recognized tribes.

Award Range/Average: Average grant award $50,000/fiscal year.

Funding: (Project Grants (Discretionary)) FY 17 $8,609,000; FY 18 est $9,646,000; FY 19 est $6,422,000.

HQ: Office of Information Collection Office of Environmental Information 1200 Pennsylvania Avenue NW, P.O. Box 2823-T

Washington, DC 20460

Phone: 202-566-1709

Email: blake-coleman.wendy@epa.gov

http://www.epa.gov/exchangenetwork/exchange-network-grant-program

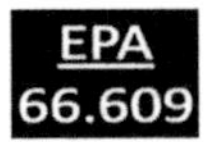

PROTECTION OF CHILDREN FROM ENVIRONMENTAL HEALTH RISKS
"Children's Environmental Health"

Award: Cooperative Agreements

Purpose: Supports efforts by organizations, educational institutions, and/or State, local, and tribal governmental agencies to establish or enhance their ability to take actions that will reduce environmental risks to the health of children.

Applicant Eligibility: Assistance under this program is generally available to States or state agencies, territories, the District of Columbia, American Indian Tribes (federally recognized), and possessions of the U.S. It is also available to public and private universities and colleges, hospitals, laboratories, other public or private nonprofit institutions, and 501(c)(3) organizations. Nonprofit organizations described in Section 501(c)(4) of the Internal Revenue Code that engage in lobbying activities as defined in Section 3 of the Lobbying Disclosure Act of 1995 are not eligible to apply.

Beneficiary Eligibility: State agencies and local governments, U.S. territories and possessions, American Indian Tribes, universities and colleges, hospitals, laboratories, and other public and private nonprofit institutions and organizations.

Award Range/Average: Range: $10,000 to $100,000 per grant. Average: $100,000 per grant (2 year grants).

Funding: (Project Grants (Cooperative Agreements)) FY 17 $25,000; FY 18 est $50,000; FY 19 est $0

HQ: Office of Childrens Health Protection 200 Pennsylvania Avenue NW

Washington, DC 20460

Phone: 202-564-2711

Email: switzer.lavonne@epa.gov

http://www.epa.gov/children

SURVEYS, STUDIES, INVESTIGATIONS AND SPECIAL PURPOSE GRANTS WITHIN THE OFFICE OF THE ADMINISTRATOR

Award: Project Grants

Purpose: Supports surveys, studies, investigations, and special purpose assistance associated with air quality, acid deposition, drinking water, water quality, hazardous waste, toxic substances and/or pesticides.

Applicant Eligibility: Assistance under this program is generally available to State agencies, territories, the District of Columbia, Indian Tribes, and possessions of the U.S. Assistance is also available to public and private universities and colleges, hospitals, laboratories, and other public or private nonprofit institutions. Nonprofit organizations described in Section 501(c)(4) of the Internal Revenue Code that engage in lobbying activities as defined in Section 3 of the Lobbying Disclosure Act of 1995 are not eligible to apply.

Beneficiary Eligibility: State agencies and local governments, U.S. territories and possessions, Indian Tribes, universities and colleges, hospitals, laboratories, and other public and private nonprofit institutions.

Award Range/Average: Range $40,000 to $520,000 per amendment. Average amount approximately $341,000 per amendment.

Funding: (Project Grants (Discretionary)) FY 17 $1,024,035; FY 18 N/A FY 19 N/A FY 16 $340,000

HQ: 1200 Pennsylvania Avenue NW
Washington, DC 20460
Phone: 202-564-3227
Email: murphy.dan@epa.gov
http://www.epa.gov/aboutepa/about-office-policy-op

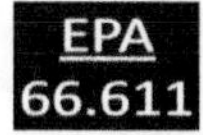

ENVIRONMENTAL POLICY AND INNOVATION GRANTS

Award: Project Grants

Purpose: The program supports analyses, studies, evaluations, workshops, conferences, and demonstration projects that lead to reduced pollutants generated and conservation of natural resources.

Applicant Eligibility: Assistance under this program is generally available to States and local governments, territories and possessions, foreign governments, international organizations, Indian Tribes, interstate organizations, intrastate organizations, and possessions of the U.S., including the District of Columbia, public and private universities and colleges, hospitals, laboratories, other public or private nonprofit institutions, and individuals. Nonprofit organizations described in Section 501(c)(4) of the Internal Revenue Code that engage in lobbying activities as defined in Section 3 of the Lobbying Disclosure Act of 1995 are not eligible to apply.

Beneficiary Eligibility: State and local governments, U.S. territories and possessions, Indian Tribes, universities and colleges, hospitals, laboratories, other public and private nonprofit institutions, individuals, and international organizations.

Award Range/Average: Environmental Economic Workshops: range is $35,000 - $95,000, with an average award of ~ $70,000. Environmental Economics Dissertations and Early Career Research: range is $35,000 - $75,000, with an average of ~ $60,000. Environmental Economic Research: range is $75,000- $300,000, with an average of ~ $250,000. For recent awards related to community driven environmental protection strategies, the range is from $25,000 to $200,000, with an average around $100,000.

Funding: (Project Grants (Discretionary)) FY 17 $0; FY 18 est $0; FY 19 est $0; FY 16 $450,000

HQ: Office of Policy Office of the Administrator 1200 Pennsylvania Avenue NW, P.O. Box 1809T
Washington, DC 20460
Phone: 202-566-2261
Email: snyder.brett@epa.gov
http://www.epa.gov/aboutepa/about-office-policy-op

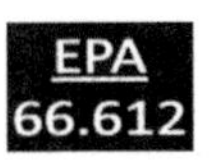

SURVEYS, STUDIES, INVESTIGATIONS, TRAINING DEMONSTRATIONS AND EDUCATIONAL OUTREACH RELATED TO ENVIRONMENTAL INFORMATION AND THE RELEASE OF TOXIC CHEMICALS

Award: Cooperative Agreements

Purpose: The program provides funding in support of surveys, studies, investigations, training/demonstrations, educational outreach and special purpose assistance as they relate to environmental information and the release of toxic chemicals. This program educates the public on how to obtain access to and effectively use environmental information, including information about toxic chemical releases and other waste management activities.

Applicant Eligibility: Assistance under this program is generally available to states, the District of Columbia, U.S. territories (for example, American Samoa, Guam, the Commonwealth of the Northern Mariana Islands, Puerto Rico, and the U.S. Virgin Islands), federally recognized Indian tribes, intertribal consortia of federally recognized tribes, public and private colleges and universities, and other public or private nonprofit organizations. Nonprofit organizations exempt from taxation under Section 501(c)(4) of the Internal Revenue Code that lobby are not eligible for financial assistance.

Beneficiary Eligibility: State, territory, city, town, county, and regional governments; federally recognized Indian tribes and intertribal consortia of federally recognized tribes; public institutions and industries subject to EPA regulatory reporting requirements; and the public.

Award Range/Average: Estimated $175,000 to $225,000 with an average of $200,000 annually.

Funding: (Cooperative Agreements (Discretionary Grants)) FY 17 $175,000; FY 18 est $175,000; FY 19 est $0; FY 16 $200,000.

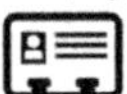

HQ: 1200 Pennsylvania Avenue NW
Washington, DC 20460
Phone: 202-566-0612
Email: kaalund.dnise@epa.gov
http://www.epa.gov/toxics-release-inventory-tri-program

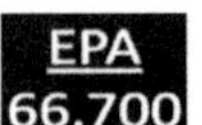

CONSOLIDATED PESTICIDE ENFORCEMENT COOPERATIVE AGREEMENTS

Award: Cooperative Agreements

Purpose: The Cooperative agreement program receives funds to support and strengthen their pesticide compliance programs, including pesticide compliance monitoring, inspection and enforcement activities.

Applicant Eligibility: State agencies having pesticide compliance program responsibilities in each state, territory and possession of the United States, including the District of Columbia and Indian Tribes.

Beneficiary Eligibility: States, Federally Recognized Indian Tribal Governments, U.S. Territories and the District of Columbia

Award Range/Average: 32,000 (territory) to 701,000; average 245,000.

Funding: (Formula Grants (Cooperative Agreements)) FY 17 $17,737,000; FY 18 est $11,050,000; FY 19 FY 16 $17,886,000.

HQ: Office of Enforcement and Compliance Assurance 1200 Pennsylvania Avenue NW, P.O. Box 2227A

Washington, DC 20460

Phone: 202-564-4153

Email: yaras.michelle@epa.gov

http://www.epa.gov/compliance/federal-insecticide-fungicide-and-rodenticide-act-compliance-monitoring

EPA 66.701 TOXIC SUBSTANCES COMPLIANCE MONITORING COOPERATIVE AGREEMENTS

Award: Cooperative Agreements

Purpose: Develops and maintains compliance monitoring programs to prevent or eliminate unreasonable risks to health or the environment associated with chemical substances or mixtures in their communities, specifically with lead-based paint, asbestos, and PCB.

Applicant Eligibility: For the Lead-based paint program, state agencies, Indian tribes, and tribal consortiums that have toxic substance compliance responsibilities, who have the authority to enter into these cooperative agreements, and who have their own lead laws in place are eligible to apply for assistance under the TSCA Compliance Monitoring Grant. For the PCB and Asbestos programs, Grantees should have toxic substance compliance responsibilities and be designated as the lead agency with the authority to enter into these cooperative agreements.

Beneficiary Eligibility: For the Lead-based paint, PCB, and Asbestos programs: States, including the District of Columbia, the Commonwealth of Puerto Rico, Guam, America Samoa, the Northern Marianas, the Trust Territories of the Pacific Islands, the Virgin Islands, and Indian Tribes.

Award Range/Average: Lead: $15,000 to $23,000/year per authorized lead-based paint program and PCB and Asbestos: $52,000 to $68,000/year.

Funding: (Formula Grants (Cooperative Agreements)) FY 17 $4,834,000; FY 18 est $4,807,000; FY 19 est $3,276,000; FY 16 $4,874,000.

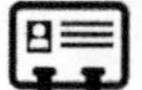

HQ: 1200 Pennsylvania Avenue NW

Washington, DC 20460

Phone: 202-564-2059

Email: engle.kelly@epa.gov

http://www.epa.gov/compliance/toxic-substances-control-act-tsca-compliance-monitoring

EPA 66.707 TSCA TITLE IV STATE LEAD GRANTS CERTIFICATION OF LEAD-BASED PAINT PROFESSIONALS

"State Lead Certification Grants"

Award: Formula Grants

Purpose: The goal of the program is to eliminate childhood lead poisoning.

Applicant Eligibility: Eligible applicants for purposes of funding under these grant programs include any state of the United States, the District of Columbia, the Commonwealth of Puerto Rico, U.S. Virgin Islands, Guam, American Samoa, the Commonwealth of the Northern Mariana Islands, and any agency or instrumentally thereof exclusive of local governments (includes public institutions of higher education and hospitals).

Beneficiary Eligibility: State any state of the United States, the District of Columbia, the Commonwealth of Puerto Rico, U.S. Virgin Islands, Guam, American Samoa, the Commonwealth of the Northern Mariana Islands, and any agency or instrumentally thereof exclusive of local governments may receive assistance under Section 404(g) of TSCA.

Award Range/Average: $16,000 to $350,000; average of $200,000.

Funding: (Formula Grants) FY 17 $14,049,000; FY 18 est $14,049,000; FY 19 N/A FY 16 $13,921,000

HQ: 1200 Pennsylvania Avenue NW
Washington, DC 20460
Phone: 202-566-0744
Email: price.michelle@epa.gov
http://www.epa.gov/lead

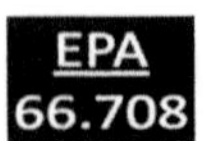

POLLUTION PREVENTION GRANTS PROGRAM
"P2 Grant Program"

Award: Project Grants

Purpose: The P2 grant program was enacted under the Pollution Prevention Act of 1990 to provide technical assistance and/or training to businesses/facilities about source reduction techniques to help them adopt and implement source reduction approaches, and to increase the development, adoption, and market penetration of greener products and sustainable manufacturing practices.

Applicant Eligibility: Eligible applicants include the 50 states, the District of Columbia, the U.S. Virgin Islands, the Commonwealth of Puerto Rico, any territory or possession of the United States, any agency or instrumentality of a state, including state colleges and universities, and federally-recognized Indian tribes that meet the requirements for treatment in a manner similar to a state as described in 40 CFR 35.663, and Intertribal Consortia that meet the requirements in 40 CFR 35.

Beneficiary Eligibility: State agencies, State colleges and universities that are instrumentalities of the State and federally-recognized Tribes are encouraged to establish partnerships with businesses and environmental assistance providers to deliver seamless P2 assistance. The most successful applicants will be those that make the most efficient use of government funding.

Award Range/Average: During the FY 2018 - FY 2019 grant competition cycle, P2 grant awards may potentially be in the range of $40,000- $500,000 issued over a two-year funding period.

Funding: (Project Grants (Discretionary)) FY 17 $3,942,000; FY 18 est $4,690,000; FY 19 est $4,690,000

HQ: 1200 Pennsylvania Avenue NW, P.O. Box 7409M
Washington, DC 20460
Phone: 202-564-8857
Email: amhaz.michele@epa.gov
http://www.epa.gov/p2/grant-programs-pollution-prevention

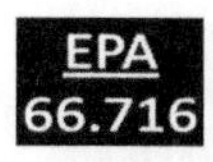

RESEARCH, DEVELOPMENT, MONITORING, PUBLIC EDUCATION, OUTREACH, TRAINING, DEMONSTRATIONS, AND STUDIES

Award: Project Grants

Purpose: Grants are awarded to support Research, Development, Outreach, Demonstration, and Studies relating to the protection of public health and the environment from pesticides, and potential risk from toxic substances.

Applicant Eligibility: Eligible applicants for purposes of funding under these grant programs include any state of the United States, the District of Columbia, Native American Organizations, the Commonwealth of Puerto Rico, U.S. Virgin Islands, Guam, American Samoa, the Commonwealth of the Northern Mariana Islands, and any agency or instrumentally thereof exclusive of local governments (includes public institutions of higher education and hospitals). For certain competitive funding opportunities under this CFDA description, the Agency may limit eligibility to compete to a number or subset of eligible applicants consistent with the Agency's Assistance Agreement Competition Policy.

Beneficiary Eligibility: State and local governments, U.S. territories and possessions, federally recognized Indian tribal governments and Native American Organizations, universities and colleges, hospitals, laboratories, other public and private nonprofit institutions, general public, and other Non-Governmental Organizations.

Award Range/Average: $1,000 to $1,500,000. Average: $500,000 For OPPT: $80,000 to $250,000. Average: $165,000

Funding: (Project Grants (Discretionary)) FY 17 $3,150,000; FY 18 est $3,150,000; FY 19 N/A.

HQ: 1200 Pennsylvania Avenue, P.O. Box 7401M
Washington, DC 20460
Phone: 202-564-8818
Email: kapust.edna@epa.gov
http://www.epa.gov/aboutepa/about-office-chemical-safety-and-pollution-prevention-ocspp

SOURCE REDUCTION ASSISTANCE "SRA Grants"

Award: Project Grants

Purpose: The SRA program's goal is to provide grants to support pollution prevention, source reduction and/ or resource conservation activities.

Applicant Eligibility: Eligible applicants for purposes of funding under these grant programs include any state of the United States, the District of Columbia, the Commonwealth of Puerto Rico, U.S. Virgin Islands, Guam, American Samoa, the Commonwealth of the Northern Mariana Islands, and any agency or instrumentally thereof exclusive of local governments (includes public institutions of higher education and hospitals), city or township governments, independent school district governments, state controlled institutions of higher education, non-profit organizations (other than institutions of higher education), private institutions of higher education, community-based grassroots organizations, and federally-recognized tribes and intertribal consortia.

Beneficiary Eligibility: Any state, federally-recognized tribal government, intertribal consortia, college/ university, non-profit organization, local government or independent school district.

Award Range/Average: Federal funding amounts for individual grant awards may potentially be in the range of $20,000- $260,000 in total issued; over a two-year funding period Average award total: $110,000.

Funding: (Project Grants (Discretionary)) FY 17 $1,294,000; FY 18 est $1,000,000; FY 19 est $1,000,000.

HQ: Office of Pollution Prevention and Toxics Pollution Prevention Division 1200 Pennsylvania Avenue NW, P.O. Box 7409-M

Washington, DC 20460

Phone: 202-564-8857

Email: amhaz.michele@epa.gov

http://www.epa.gov/p2/grant-programs-pollution-prevention

HAZARDOUS WASTE MANAGEMENT STATE PROGRAM SUPPORT

Award: Formula Grants

Purpose: Assists State governments in the development and implementation of authorized hazardous waste management program for the purpose of controlling the generation, transportation, treatment, storage and disposal of hazardous wastes.

Applicant Eligibility: State agencies responsible for hazardous waste management within the 50 States, the District of Columbia, the Commonwealth of Puerto Rico, the Virgin Islands, Guam, American Samoa, the Commonwealth of the Northern Mariana Islands, and interstate agencies established by the appropriate states and approved by the EPA Administrator under Section 1005 of the Solid Waste Disposal Act are eligible.

Beneficiary Eligibility: Same as Applicant Eligibility.

Award Range/Average: Most fiscal years range $350,000 to $8,500,000; average: $2,000,000.

Funding: (Formula Grants (Cooperative Agreements)) FY 17 $99,503,000; FY 18 est $3,050,000; FY 19 est $3,000,000; FY 16 $98,994,000

HQ: Office of Land and Emergency Management US EPA Headquarters, P.O. Box 5303P

Washington, DC 20460

Phone: 703-308-8630

Email: roepe.wayne@epa.gov

http://www.epa.gov/epawaste

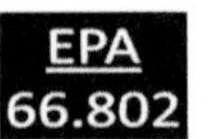

SUPERFUND STATE, POLITICAL SUBDIVISION, AND INDIAN TRIBE SITE-SPECIFIC COOPERATIVE AGREEMENTS

Award: Cooperative Agreements

Purpose: Conducts site characterization activities at potential or confirmed hazardous waste sites; and also undertakes response planning and implementation actions at sites on the National Priorities List to clean up the hazardous waste sites that are found to pose hazards to human health.

Applicant Eligibility: States (and political subdivisions thereof), Commonwealths, U.S. Territories and Possessions, and Federally Recognized Indian Tribal Governments, including intertribal consortia.

Beneficiary Eligibility: Same as Applicant Eligibility.

Award Range/Average: Range: $812 to $9 million; Average: $312,746

Funding: (Cooperative Agreements) FY 18 N/A FY 16 $81,500,000; FY 17 est $81,500,000.

HQ: 1200 Pennsylvania Avenue NW
Washington, DC 20460
Phone: 202-566-2775
Email: fine.ellyn@epa.gov
http://www.epa.gov/superfund

UNDERGROUND STORAGE TANK PREVENTION, DETECTION AND COMPLIANCE PROGRAM

"UST Prevention, Detection and Compliance Program"

Award: Formula Grants

Purpose: To assist States, Territories, Tribes and/or Intertribal Consortia that meet the requirements at 40 CFR 35.504 in the development and implementation of underground storage tank (UST) programs and for leak prevention, compliance and other activities authorized by the Energy Policy Act (EPAct) of 2005, Public Law 105-276, and EPA's annual appropriations acts.

Applicant Eligibility: Prevention, detection and compliance assistance agreements are only available to States and Territories and to Federally-recognized Tribes and Intertribal Consortia that must meet the requirements, as described in the Federal Register Notice, Vol. 67, No.

Beneficiary Eligibility: States, Territories, Tribes and Intertribal Consortia.

Award Range/Average: Range for States and Territories: The STAG and LUST prevention financial assistance is based on states' needs. There is no STAG distribution for Tribes. In FY 2018, estimated STAG funding - Range for States and Territories: $30,000 to $280,000 Average for States and Territories = $97,600. LUST PREVENTION Funding: In FY 2018, estimated LUST Prevention funding - Range for States and Territories: $86,377 to $1,327,934. Average for States and Territories = $427,348. Range for Tribes: $20,000 to $250,000; Average for Tribes = $75,658.

Funding: (Formula Grants) FY 17 $26,867,000; FY 18 est $0; FY 19 - STAG Obligations - Grants to States FY 17 estimate: $1,498,000, FY 18 estimate: $0. LUST Prevention Obligations - Assistance Agreements to State and Tribes (for state staff oversight and inspection activities related to the UST program; for Tribal staff to build capacity and provide training for prevention activities identified in Section :50): FY 17 estimate: $25,369,000, FY 18 estimate: $0. (Formula Grants) FY 17 $26,867,000; FY 18 est $26,833,000; FY 19 est $0; - FY 17: STAG Obligations - Grants to States: FY 17 Actual $1,498,000. LUST Prevention Obligations - Assistance Agreements to States and Tribes: FY 17 Actual $25,369,000. FY 18: STAG Obligations - Grants to States: FY 18 Estimate $1,464,000. LUST Prevention Obligations - Assistance Agreements to States and Tribes: FY 18 Estimate $25,369,000.

HQ: 1200 Pennsylvania Avenue NW
Washington, DC 20460
Phone: 202-564-2182
Email: edwards.christine@epa.gov
http://www.epa.gov/ust

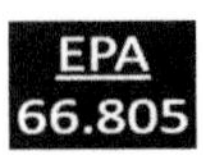

LEAKING UNDERGROUND STORAGE TANK TRUST FUND CORRECTIVE ACTION PROGRAM "Leaking UST Corrective Action Program"

Award: Formula Grants

Purpose: To support State and Tribal corrective action programs that address releases from underground storage tanks.

Applicant Eligibility: Cooperative agreements are only available to States and Territories that have UST programs. Additionally, these cooperative agreements are only available to Federally-recognized Tribes and Intertribal Consortia that must meet the requirements, as described in the Federal Register Notice, Vol.

Beneficiary Eligibility: States, Territories, Tribes and Intertribal Consortia and the communities and industries affected by leaks from underground storage tanks.

Award Range/Average: For FY 2018, the Range for Territories and States: $40,868 - $3,149,070; Territory Average: $120,139; State Average: $1,059,331. It is anticipated that there will be approximately 4 Tribal cooperative agreements in FY 2018 for a total of $395,000.

Funding: (Formula Grants) FY 17 $55,430,000; FY 18 est $39,040,000; FY 19 FY 16 $55,424,775; - LUST Obligations - Assistance Agreements to States and Tribes (for state and tribal staff oversight of initiating and cleaning up contamination from leaking underground storage tanks): For LUST State Cooperative Agreements: FY 2016 actual: $55,049,775; FY 2017 estimate: $55,040,000; FY 2018 estimate:$38,840,000. For LUST Tribal Cooperative Agreements: FY 2016 actual: $375,000, FY 2017 estimate: 390,000; FY 2018 estimate: $200,000. (Formula Grants) FY 17 $56,980,000; FY 18 est $64,028,000; FY 19 est $39,743,000; - 2018 Estimate: Includes supplemental hurricane appropriation of $7,000,000.

HQ: 1200 Pennsylvania Avenue NW
Washington, DC 20460
Phone: 202-564-2182
Email: edwards.christine@epa.gov
http://www.epa.gov/ust

SUPERFUND TECHNICAL ASSISTANCE GRANTS (TAG) FOR COMMUNITY GROUPS AT NATIONAL PRIORITY LIST (NPL) SITES

Award: Project Grants

Purpose: To authorizes Technical Assistance Grants to be awarded to groups of individuals affected by or threatened by a release at a Superfund site.

Applicant Eligibility: A technical assistance grant (TAG) is available to any qualified group of individuals which: may be "affected" by a release or threatened release at any facility listed on the NPL or proposed for listing under the NCP where a "response action" under CERCLA has begun; meets minimum administrative and management capability requirements found in 2 CFR 200 by demonstrating they have or will have reliable procedures for record keeping and financial accountability related to TAG management; and incorporates as a nonprofit for the specific purpose of representing "affected" individuals at the site. "Affected" means subject to an actual or potential health, economic or environmental threat.

Beneficiary Eligibility: This program benefits groups of individuals affected by Superfund hazardous waste sites. Groups should be representative of the community affected by the Superfund site, which may include homeowners, land/property owners, local businesses, as well as any other individuals in the general public who live near a site.

Award Range/Average: Initial awards for assistance agreements awarded under this CFDA number will not exceed $50,000. After the initial award, additional funding may be awarded based on the criteria detailed under 40 CFR 35.4065, and subject to the availability of funds. The average additional award is $40,000 (per agreement).

Funding: (Project Grants) FY 18 est $200,000; FY 17 est $300,000; FY 16 $305,000; - (Includes initial awards and additional funds) In FY 2016, $305,000 was awarded. It is estimated that $300,000 will be awarded in FY 2017 and $200,000 in FY 2018.

HQ: Ariel Rios Building 1200 Pennsylvania Avenue NW
Washington, DC 20460
Phone: 703-603-8889
Email: margand.freya@epa.gov
http://www.epa.gov/superfund

SOLID WASTE MANAGEMENT ASSISTANCE GRANTS

Award: Cooperative Agreements

Purpose: To promote use of integrated solid waste management systems to solve solid waste generation and management problems at the local, regional and national levels.

Applicant Eligibility: State (including the District of Columbia, Puerto Rico, Virgin Islands, Guam, American Samoa, and Northern Mariana Islands), local, Tribal, interstate, and intrastate government agencies and instrumentalities, and non-profit organizations that are not 501(c)(4) organizations that lobby, including non-profit educational institutions and non-profit hospitals. Individuals and for-profit organizations are not eligible.

Beneficiary Eligibility: State and local governments, U.S. territories and possessions, the public, and interstate agencies.

Award Range/Average: $10,000 to $460,000/FY 18; $50,000/FY 19

Funding: (Cooperative Agreements) FY 17 est $500,000; FY 16 $463,500; FY 18 est $500,000.

HQ: USEPA Headquarters Ariel Rios Building 1200 Pennsylvania Avenue NW, P.O. Box 5305P
Washington, DC 20460
Phone: 703-308-8460
Email: vizzone.nick@epa.gov
http://www.epa.gov/epawaste/index.htm

EPA 66.809 SUPERFUND STATE AND INDIAN TRIBE CORE PROGRAM COOPERATIVE AGREEMENTS

Award: Cooperative Agreements

Purpose: To provide funds to conduct CERCLA activities which are not assignable to specific sites.

Applicant Eligibility: States (and political subdivisions thereof), Commonwealths, U.S. Territories and Possessions, and Federally Recognized Indian Tribal Governments, including intertribal consortia.

Beneficiary Eligibility: Same as Applicant Eligibility.

Award Range/Average: $15,000 to $207,514; with an average award of $88,128.

Funding: (Cooperative Agreements) FY 17 est $4,600,000; FY 18 N/A FY 16 $4,600,000; - FY 15 $5.6 million; FY 16 $4.6 million; FY 17 $4.6 million (estimate)

HQ: Assessment and Remediation Division, P.O. Box 5204P EPA

Washington, DC 20460

Phone: 703-603-8714

Email: singer.yolanda@epa.gov

http://www.epa.gov/superfund

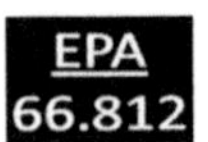

HAZARDOUS WASTE MANAGEMENT GRANT PROGRAM FOR TRIBES

"Hazardous Waste Grants"

Award: Cooperative Agreements

Purpose: To provide assistance for the development and implementation of hazardous waste management programs; to improve and maintain regulatory compliance; and for developing solutions to address hazardous waste management issues in Indian country.

Applicant Eligibility: The following are eligible to receive financial assistance: (a) an Indian tribal government, and (b) an intertribal consortium or consortia. An Indian tribal government is any tribe, band, nation, or other organized group or community, including any Alaska Native village or regional or village corporation (as defined in or established pursuant to the Alaska Native Claims Settlement Act, 43 U.S.C.

Beneficiary Eligibility: Federally Recognized Indian Tribal Governments.

Award Range/Average: Range = $18,000 to $100,000; Average = $56,000.

Funding: (Cooperative Agreements (Discretionary Grants)) FY 17 $300,000; FY 18 est $305,000; FY 19 est $305,000; FY 16 $297,000

HQ: Office of Resource Conservation and Recovery 1200 Pennsylvania Avenue NW, P.O. Box 5303P

Washington, DC 20460

Phone: 703-308-8458

Email: roy.denise@epa.gov

http://www.epa.gov/tribal-lands

ALTERNATIVE OR INNOVATIVE TREATMENT TECHNOLOGY RESEARCH, DEMONSTRATION, TRAINING, AND HAZARDOUS SUBSTANCE RESEARCH GRANTS

Award: Project Grants

Purpose: To support grants for alternative treatment programs that refers to new technologies and techniques for treating solid waste and sites.

Applicant Eligibility: Assistance under this program is generally available to States, territories, Indian Tribes, and possessions of the U.S., including the District of Columbia, public and private universities and colleges, hospitals, laboratories, other public or private nonprofit institutions, and individuals. In some instances, EPA will consider applications from profit makers, proposing projects with significant technical merit and relevance to EPA's Office of Solid Waste and Emergency Response.

Beneficiary Eligibility: State and local governments, U.S. territories and possessions, Indian Tribes, universities and colleges, hospitals, laboratories, industry, and other public and private institutions and individuals.

Award Range/Average: For each fiscal year it is $50,000 - $1,000,000 Average $500,000

Funding: (Project Grants (Discretionary)) FY 17 $500,000; FY 18 est $0; FY 19 N/A FY 16 est $200,000

HQ: Office of Superfund Remediation and Technology Innovation USEPA (5202-P), 1200 Pennsylvania Avenue NW

Washington, DC 20460

Phone: 703-603-9042

http://www.epa.gov/superfund/index.htm

BROWNFIELDS TRAINING, RESEARCH, AND TECHNICAL ASSISTANCE GRANTS AND COOPERATIVE AGREEMENTS "Brownfields 104(k)(7) Grants"

Award: Cooperative Agreements

Purpose: To assist the individuals and organizations to facilitate the inventory of brownfields properties, assessments, cleanup of brownfields properties, community involvement, or site preparation.

Applicant Eligibility: A general purpose unit of local government; a land clearance authority or other quasi-governmental entity that operates under the supervision and control of, or as an agent of, a general purpose unit of local government; a government entity created by a State legislature; a regional council or group of general purpose units of local government; a redevelopment agency that is chartered or otherwise sanctioned by a State; a State (note CERCLA 107(27) defines term "State" to include territories or possessions over which the United States has jurisdiction); an Indian Tribe other than in Alaska; an Alaska Native Regional Corporation, Alaska Native Village Corporation and the Metlakatla Indian Community. Nonprofit organizations are also eligible for training, research, and technical assistance grants.

Beneficiary Eligibility: Cooperative agreement-funded activities will benefit the community members and local stakeholders who are proximate to brownfield sites (whether in an urban, suburban or rural setting) including local governments, non-profit organizations, quasi public nonprofits, residents, local business owners, community groups, universities and colleges, industry, other public and private institutions, individuals, states and tribes.

Award Range/Average: $200,000,000 to $2,000,000 over the entire cooperative agreement, depending on the specific focus area of solicitation and the project period of the award (typical project period is 5 years) New awards made for other research, training and technical assistance grants usually range between $200,000 and $2 million and usually incrementally funded over the project period if the award is above $200,000.

Funding: (Cooperative Agreements (Discretionary Grants)) FY 17 $8,500,000; FY 18 est $5,000,000; FY 19 N/A FY 16 $4,400,000; - For FY 2017, EPA awarded up to $8.5 million in new and incremental funding for cooperative agreements awarded under this CFDA assistance listing. This included approximately $3.8 million for new awards made under the FY 2017 Brownfields Area-Wide Planning (BF AWP) Grant Program, approximately $2.9 million for new awards made under the FY 2017 Technical Assistance to Brownfields (TAB) Program and approximately $1.8 million in incremental funding for other Research, Training and Technical Assistance (k6) grants awarded in previous years. At this time the total funding estimated for FY 2018 is approximately $5 million. This amount is based on the following anticipated funding opportunities: -Based on their satisfactory progress, EPA intends to incrementally fund cooperative agreements that the Agency already awarded in previous years under CFDA 66.814 with approximately $3.5 million of those funds ($2 million of these funds expected for incremental funding to TAB grantees; approximately $600,000 for incremental funding to other research, training and technical assistance grantees) -EPA expects the remaining funds to support initial funding of a multi purpose grant anticipated to be approximately $2 million over a three year project period.

HQ: Office of Brownfields and Land Revitalization Office of Land and Emergency Management US EPA 1200 Pennsylvania Avenue NW, P.O. Box 5105T

Washington, DC 20460

Phone: 202-566-2745

Email: lentz.rachel@epa.gov

http://www.epa.gov/brownfields

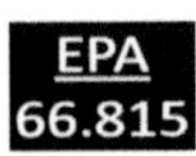

ENVIRONMENTAL WORKFORCE DEVELOPMENT AND JOB TRAINING COOPERATIVE AGREEMENTS

Award: Cooperative Agreements

Purpose: To recruit, train, and place unemployed and under-employed, including low-income, residents of solid and hazardous waste-impacted communities with the skills needed to obtain full-time, sustainable employment in solid and hazardous waste cleanup, wastewater treatment, chemical safety, and the environmental field at large.

Applicant Eligibility: Proposals will be accepted from either eligible governmental entities as defined in CERCLA Section 104(k)(1) or eligible nonprofit organizations as defined in Public Law 106-107, the Federal Financial Assistance Management Improvement Act. Eligible governmental entities include a general purpose local unit of government; a land clearance authority or other quasi-governmental entity that operates under the supervision and control of, or as an agent of, a general purpose unit of government; a governmental entity created by a state legislature; a regional council or group of general purpose units of local government; a redevelopment agency that is chartered or otherwise sanctioned by a state; a state; an Indian Tribe (other than in Alaska), or an Alaskan Native Regional Corporation and an Alaska Native Village Corporation as those terms are defined in the Alaska Native Claims Settlement Act (43 U.S.C.

Beneficiary Eligibility: Environmental Workforce Development and Job Training grants will provide environmental job training unemployed and underemployed residents of solid and hazardous waste-impacted neighborhoods and help them take advantage of job opportunities created as a result of the management, assessment, and cleanup of contaminated properties, as well as employment in wastewater, alternative energy, and chemical safety related positions.

Award Range/Average: Up to $200,000.

Funding: (Cooperative Agreements (Discretionary Grants)) FY 17 $2,700,000; FY 18 est $3,300,000; FY 19 N/A FY 16 est $3,000,000

HQ: Office of Brownfields and Land Revitalization OSWER 200 Pennsylvania Avenue NW, P.O. Box 5105T

Washington, DC 20460

Phone: 202-566-1564

Email: congdon.rachel@epa.gov

http://www.epa.gov/brownfields

EPA 66.816 HEADQUARTERS AND REGIONAL UNDERGROUND STORAGE TANKS PROGRAM

Award: Project Grants

Purpose: To support activities that promote the prevention, compliance, and identification of underground storage tanks, and to support activities that promote corrective action, enforcement and management of releases from underground storage tank systems.

Applicant Eligibility: These assistance agreements are only available to public authorities (State, interstate, intrastate, agencies designated by States or Territorial Governors to receive UST notifications, federally-recognized Tribes and Intertribal Consortia, and local), public agencies and institutions; private non-profit organizations and agencies that meet the requirements of Section 8001(a) and (b) of the Solid Waste Disposal Act. Profit-making organizations and the general public are not eligible.

Beneficiary Eligibility: State and local governments, territories and possessions, interstate agencies, Tribes, Intertribal Consortia, members of the regulated community and residents in areas impacted by federally regulated underground storage tanks.

Award Range/Average: FY 2018 Range: $85,000 - $203,143; Average: $165,322.

Funding: (Project Grants (Discretionary)) FY 17 $164,242; FY 18 est $661,286; FY 19 N/A FY 16 $1,182,503

HQ: 1200 Pennsylvania Avenue NW, P.O. Box 3803R

Washington, DC 20460

Phone: 202-564-2182

Email: edwards.christine@epa.gov

http://www.epa.gov/ust

EPA 66.817 STATE AND TRIBAL RESPONSE PROGRAM GRANTS

Award: Formula Grants

Purpose: To provide financial support to establish and enhance the four elements of an effective state or tribal response program as specified in CERCLA Section 128.

Applicant Eligibility: States (as defined in CERCLA Section 101(27) and tribes (as defined in CERCLA Section 101(36) are eligible for funding under Section 128(a). To be eligible to receive funding under CERCLA Section 128(a), a state or tribe must demonstrate that its response program includes, or is taking reasonable steps to include, the four elements of a response program.

Beneficiary Eligibility: Beneficiaries include individuals living in recipient states', territories', and tribes' jurisdiction.

Award Range/Average: Most fiscal years range from $50,000 to $1,000,000; average approximately $450,000.

Funding: (Formula Grants) FY 17 $46,917,000; FY 18 est $33,600,000; FY 19 N/A FY 16 $47,311,000.

HQ: Office of Brownfields and Land Revitalization 1200 Pennsylvania Avenue NW, P.O. Box 5105T
Washington, DC 20460
Phone: 202-566-2745
Email: lentz.rachel@epa.gov
http://www.epa.gov/brownfields

BROWNFIELDS ASSESSMENT AND CLEANUP COOPERATIVE AGREEMENTS

Award: Cooperative Agreements

Purpose: To provide real property, the expansion, redevelopment, or reuse of which may be complicated by the presence or potential presence of a hazardous substance, pollutant, or contaminant.

Applicant Eligibility: Eligibility for Multipurpose, Assessment, Revolving Loan Fund, and Cleanup Grants: a general purpose unit of local government; a land clearance authority or other quasi-governmental entity that operates under the supervision and control of, or as an agent of, a general purpose unit of local government; a government entity created by a State legislature; a regional council or group of general purpose units of local government; a redevelopment agency that is chartered or otherwise sanctioned by a State; a State; an Indian Tribe other than in Alaska; an Alaska Native Regional Corporation, Alaska Native Village Corporation and the Metlakatla Indian Community.

Beneficiary Eligibility: Generally, those eligible entities identified above will benefit from the brownfields grant actions. Specifically, individuals and commercial organizations in brownfields grant communities will benefit from brownfields assessment, cleanup, and revitalization funding.

Award Range/Average: (1) For community-wide assessment grants, an eligible entity may apply for up to $300,000 to address sites contaminated by hazardous substances, pollutants, or contaminants (including hazardous substances co-mingled with petroleum), and sites contaminated by petroleum. For site-specific assessment grants, an eligible entity may apply for up to $200,000 to address one site contaminated by hazardous substances, pollutants, or contaminants (including hazardous substances co-mingled with petroleum) and sites contaminated by petroleum. An entity may request a waiver of the $200,000 limit up to $350,000 based on the anticipated level of contamination, size, or ownership status of the site. These limits are mandatory under CERCLA 104(k)(5)(A). An assessment coalition of eligible entities may apply for up to $600,000 to address sites contaminated by hazardous substances or petroleum on a community-wide basis. (2) For revolving loan fund grants, an eligible entity may apply for up to $1,000,000 for an initial RLF grant. This limit is mandatory under CERCLA 104(k)(5)(A). In addition, an RLF coalition of eligible entities may apply together under one recipient for up to $1,000,000 per grant. (3) For cleanup grants, an eligible entity may apply for up to $500,000 per site. The $500,000 per site limit is mandatory under CERCLA 104(k)(3)(A) as amended by the BUILD ACT of 2018. (4) For Multipurpose grants, an eligible entity may apply for up to $800,000 to address one or more brownfield sites contaminated by hazardous substances, pollutants, or contaminants (including hazardous substances co-mingled with petroleum), and sites contaminated by petroleum.

Funding: (Cooperative Agreements (Discretionary Grants)) FY 17 $0; FY 18 est $54,300,000; FY 19 N/A FY 16 est $66,000,000.

HQ: Office of Brownfields and Land Revitalization OSWER US EPA 1200 Pennsylvania Avenue NW, P.O. Box 5105T
Washington, DC 20460
Phone: 202-566-2777
Email: lloyd.davidr@epa.gov
http://www.epa.gov/brownfields

INDIAN ENVIRONMENTAL GENERAL ASSISTANCE PROGRAM (GAP) "GAP Grants"

Award: Project Grants

Purpose: To provide financial and technical assistance to tribal governments and intertribal consortia to assist tribes in planning, developing, and establishing the capacity to implement federal environmental programs administered by the EPA and to assist in implementation of tribal solid and hazardous waste programs.

Applicant Eligibility: The following are eligible to receive financial assistance: Indian tribal governments (tribes) and intertribal consortia are eligible to receive funds under this program. These terms are defined in 40 CFR 35.

Beneficiary Eligibility: Federally Recognized Indian Tribal Governments and eligible Intertribal Consortia.

Award Range/Average: The minimum for the first year is $75,000; avg. $110,000

Funding: (Project Grants (Discretionary)) FY 17 $64,880,000; FY 18 est $64,340,000; FY 19 est $45,746,000; FY 16 $64,880,000;

HQ: 1200 Pennsylvania Avenue NW
Washington, DC 20260
Phone: 202-566-1387
Email: roose.rebecca@epa.gov
http://www.epa.gov

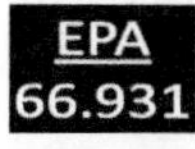

INTERNATIONAL FINANCIAL ASSISTANCE PROJECTS SPONSORED BY THE OFFICE OF INTERNATIONAL AND TRIBAL AFFAIRS

Award: Project Grants

Purpose: To protect human health and the environment while advancing U.S. national interests through international environmental collaboration.

Applicant Eligibility: Assistance under this program is generally available to States and local governments, territories and possessions, foreign governments, international organizations, Indian Tribes, and possessions of the U.S., including the District of Columbia, public and private universities and colleges, hospitals, laboratories, other public or private nonprofit institutions, which submit applications proposing projects with significant technical merit and relevance to EPA's Office of International Affairs' mission. For certain competitive funding opportunities under this CFDA description, the Agency may limit eligibility to compete to a number or subset of eligible applicants consistent with the Agency's Assistance Agreement Competition Policy.

Beneficiary Eligibility: States and local governments, territories and possessions, foreign governments, international organizations, Indian Tribes, and possessions of the U.S., including the District of Columbia, public and private universities and colleges, hospitals, laboratories, other public or private nonprofit institutions.

Award Range/Average: $15,000 - $300,000; Average is $150,000.

Funding: (Cooperative Agreements (Discretionary Grants)) FY 17 $4,000,000; FY 18 est $3,500,000; FY 19 est $1,500,000

HQ: 1200 Pennsylvania Avenue NW
Washington, DC 20460
Phone: 202-564-5343
Email: connell.lenore@epa.gov
http://www.epa.gov

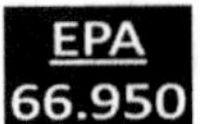

NATIONAL ENVIRONMENTAL EDUCATION TRAINING PROGRAM
"Teacher Training Program"

Award: Cooperative Agreements

Purpose: To train education professionals in the development and delivery of environmental education and training programs and studies.

Applicant Eligibility: Assistance under this program is available to universities, non-profit organizations, or a consortia of such institutions to deliver environmental education training and support for education professionals.

Beneficiary Eligibility: Education (0-8), education (9-12), education (13+), nonprofit institutions.

Award Range/Average: This is a 5-year program; one recipient is selected every 5 years. The project is funded on an annual basis and the amount of the annual funding depends on Congressional appropriation. In this case, per the National Environmental Education Act, 25% of the annual appropriation and average financial assistance for the full 5-year project period is approximately $10,877,500.

Funding: (Cooperative Agreements (Discretionary Grants)) FY 17 $2,157,500; FY 18 est $3,000,000; FY 19 N/A FY 16 $2,157,500

HQ: 1200 Pennsylvania Avenue NW
Washington, DC 20460
Phone: 202-564-0453
Email: potter.ginger@epa.gov
http://www.epa.gov/education

ENVIRONMENTAL EDUCATION GRANTS

Award: Project Grants

Purpose: To supports projects to design, demonstrate, and/or disseminate practices, methods, or techniques related to environmental education and teacher training.

Applicant Eligibility: Assistance under this program is generally available to local education agencies, colleges and universities, state education and environmental agencies, nonprofit organizations described in Section 501(c)(3) of the Internal Revenue Service, and noncommercial educational broadcasting entities as defined and licensed by the Federal Communications Commission. Applicant organizations must be located in the United States or territories and the majority of the educational activities must take place in the United States, Canada, or Mexico.

Beneficiary Eligibility: Education (0-8), education (9-12), education (13+), nonprofit institutions and organizations, state and local government agencies.

Award Range/Average: The FY 2018 solicitation notice listed a range of $50,000 - $100,000.

Funding: (Project Grants (Discretionary)) FY 17 $3,306,600; FY 18 est $3,000,000; FY 19 N/A FY 16 $3,306,600

HQ: 1200 Pennsylvania Avenue NW, P.O. Box 1704A
Washington, DC 20460
Phone: 202-564-2194
Email: scott.karen@epa.gov
http://www.epa.gov/education

TARGETED AIR SHEDS GRANT PROGRAM "Targeted Air Sheds"

Award: N/A

Purpose: To reduce air pollution in the nation's nonattainment areas with the highest levels of ozone and fine particulate matter (PM2.5) ambient air concentrations.

Applicant Eligibility: Entities eligible to receive targeted airshed grants are those air pollution control agencies, as defined by Section 302(b) of the Clean Air Act (CAA), that: (a) have responsibilities for development and/or implementation of a State Implementation Plan or Tribal Implementation Plan to attain and maintain national ambient air quality standards for either ozone or PM2.5 within one or more of the top five most polluted areas relative to ozone (O3), annual average fine particulate matter (PM2.

Beneficiary Eligibility: Certain state, local, and tribal air pollution control agencies, as defined by Section 302(b) of the Clean Air Act (CAA).

Award Range/Average: In FY 17 EPA awarded 9 targeted airshed grants. The funding amount range was $3,184,875 to $4,000,000 and the average value of each grant was $3,275,444. In FY 19, EPA plans to award 6-12 grants, valued at $3,000,000 to $7,000,000 each (total $39,086,491), subject to the quality of applications received.

Funding: (Project Grants) FY 17 $29,479,000; FY 18 est $39,086,491; FY 19 est $40,000,000

HQ: 109 TW Alexander Drive
Research Triangle Park, NC 27709
Phone: 919-541-3223
Email: blais.gary@epa.gov
http://www.epa.gov/grants/air-grants-and-funding

Programs Administered by Regional - State - Local Offices

EQUAL EMPLOYMENT OPPORTUNITY COMMISSION

Alabama

Delner Franklin-Thomas, Director | 1130 22nd Street, South, Suite 200, Birmingham, AL 35205 205-212-2089

Arizona

Elizabeth T. Cadle, Acting Director Norwest Tower | 3300 N. Central Avenue, Suite 690, Phoenix, AZ 85012-2504 602-640-5015

Arkansas

William A. Cash, Director | 820 Louisiana Street, Suite 200, Little Rock, AR 72201 501-324-5539

California

Christopher Green, Director | 555 West Beech Street, Suite 504, San Diego, CA 92101 619-557-7235

Dana C. Johnson, Director | 1301 Clay Street, Suite 1170-N, Oakland, CA 94612-5217 510-637-3242

Melissa Barrios, Director | 2300 Tulare Street, Fresno, CA 93721 559-487-5793, 559-487-5787

Rosa M. Viramontes, Director | 255 E. Temple Avenue, 4th Floor, Los Angeles, CA 90012 213-894-1000

Terrie B. Brodie, Acting Director | 96 North 3rd Street, Suite 200, San Jose, CA 95112 408-291-7447

William R. Tamayo, Director | Phillip Burton Federal Building, Suite 5000 450 Golden Gate Avenue, San Francisco, CA 94102-3661 415-625-5611

Colorado

Amy Burkholder, Acting Director | 303 East 17th Avenue, Suite 510, Denver, CO 80203-9634 303-866-1311

District of Columbia

Mindy Weinstein, Acting Director | 131 M Street, N.E., Washington, DC 20507 202-419-0711

Florida

Evangeline Hawthorne, Director | 501 East Polk Street, Room 1000, Tampa, FL 33602 813-228-7953, 813-228-7928

Michael J. Farrell, Director | 100 SE 2nd Street, Ste. 1500, Miami, FL 33131 305-808-1740

Georgia

Bernice Williams-Kimbrough, Director | 100 Alabama Street, Suite 4R30, Atlanta, GA 30303 404-562-6930

Omayra Padilla, Director | 7391 Hodgson, Suite 200, Savannah, GA 31406-2579 912-652-4077

Hawaii

Glory A. Gervacio-Saure, Director | 300 Ala Moana Boulevard, Room 7-127 P.O. Box 50082, Honolulu, HI 96850-0051 808-541-3118

Illinois

Julianne Bowman, Director | 500 West Madison Street, Suite 2000, Chicago, IL 60661 312-869-8000

Indiana

Lloyd J. Vasquez, Acting Director | 101 West Ohio Street, Suite 1900, Indianapolis, IN 46204-4203 317-226-7212

Kansas

Natascha DeGuire, Director | Gateway Tower II 400 State Avenue, Suite 905, Kansas City, KS 66101 913-551-5692

Kentucky

Richard T. Burgamy, Director | U.S. Post Office and Courthouse 600 Martin Luther King Jr. Place, Suite 268, Louisville, KY 40202 502-582-6082

Las Vegas

333 Las Vegas Blvd., South, Suite 8112, Las Vegas, NV 89101 702-388-5013

Louisiana

Keith T. Hill, Director | Hale Boggs Federal 500 Poydras Street, Room 809, New Orleans, LA 70112 504-595-2826, 504-595-2837

Maryland

Rosemarie Rhodes, Director | City Crescent Building 10 South Howard Street, 3rd Floor, Baltimore, MD 21201 410-209-2624

Massachusetts

Feng K. An, Director | John F. Kennedy Federal Building Government Center 4th Floor 1 Congress Street, Room 475, Boston, MA 02203-0506 617-565-4805

Michigan

Gail Cober, Director | McNamara Federal Building 477 Michigan Avenue, Suite 865, Detroit, MI 48226-9704 313-226-4600

Minnesota

Julie Schmid, Acting Director | 330 South Second Avenue, Suite 720, Minneapolis, MN 55401-2224 612-335-4040

Mississippi

Wilma Scott, Director | Dr. A. H. McCoy Federal Building 100 West Capitol Street, Suite 207, Jackson, MS 39269 601-948-8400

Missouri

James R. Neely, Director | Robert A. Young Building 1222 Spruce Street, Room 8100, St. Louis, MO 63103 314-539-7831

Mobile

Erika E. La'Cour, Director | 63 South Royal Street, Suite 504, Mobile, AL 36602 251-690-3001

New Jersey

John Waldinger, Director | One Newark Center, 21st Floor, Newark, NJ 07102-5233 973-645-4689

New Mexico

Derrick Newton, Director | 505 Marquette Avenue, N.W., Suite 900, Albuquerque, NM 87102-2189 505-248-5201

New York

John E. Thompson, Director | 6 Fountain Plaza, Suite 350, Buffalo, NY 14202 716-551-4442

Kevin J. Berry, Director | 33 Whitehall Street, 5th Floor, New York, NY 10004-2112 212-336-3705

North Carolina

Arlene M. Glover, Acting Director | 2303 West Meadowview Road, Suite 201, Greensboro, NC 27407 336-547-4188

Rueben Daniels, Director | 129 West Trade Street, Suite 400, Charlotte, NC 28202 704-954-6422

Thomas Colclough, Acting Director | 434 Fayetteville Street, Ste. 700, Raleigh, NC 27601-1701 919-856-4085

Ohio

Cheryl Mabry-Thomas, Director | Anthony J Celebrezze Federal Bldg. 1240 E. 9th Street, Ste. 3001, Cleveland, OH 44199 216-522-7447

Melanie L. Breen, Director | John W. Peck Federal Office Building 550 Main Street, Suite 10-019, Cincinnati, OH 45202-5202 513-684-3967

Oklahoma

Holly J. Cole, Director | 215 Dean A. McGee Avenue, Suite 524, Oklahoma City, OK 73102-2265 405-231-4356

Pennsylvania

Roosevelt L. Bryant, Acting Director | William S. Moorhead Federal Building 1000 Liberty Avenue, Suite 1112, Pittsburgh, PA 15222-4187 412-395-5902

Spencer H. Lewis, Director | 801 Market Street, 13th Floor, Philadelphia, PA 19103 215-440-2624

Puerto Rico

William Sanchez, Director | Plaza Las Americas 525 F.D. Rooseveldt Avenue, Suite 1202, San Juan, PR 00918-8001 787-771-1464, 787-771-1432

South Carolina

Patricia Bynum-Fuller, Director | 301 N. Main Street, Suite 1402, Greenville, SC 29601 864-241-4407

Tennessee

Katharine Kores, Director | 1407 Union Avenue, 9th Floor, Memphis, TN 38104 901-544-1051

Sarah Smith, Director | 220 Anthens Way, Suite 350, Nashville, TN 37228 615-736-5820

Texas

Lucy V. Orta, Director | 300 East Main Street, Suite 500, El Paso, TX 79901 915-534-4192

Pedro Esquivel, Director | Travis G. Hicks, Director 5410 Fredericksburg Road, Suite 200, San Antonio, TX 78229-3555 210-281-2550

Rayford O. Irvin, Director | Mickey Leland Federal Building 1919 Smith Street, 7th Floor, Houston, TX 77002 713-651-4951

Shirley Richardson, Director | Belinda F. McCallister, Deputy Director 207 South Houston Street, 3rd Floor, Dallas, TX 75202-4726 214-253-4726

Virginia

Daron L. Calhoun, Director | 400 North 8th Street, Ste 350, Richmond, VA 23219 804-771-2200

Norberto Rosa-Ramos, Director | Federal Building 200 Granby Street, Suite 739, Norfolk, VA 23510 757-441-6678

Washington

Nancy A. Sienko, Director | Federal Office Building 909 First Avenue, Suite 400, Seattle, WA 98104-1061 206-220-6870

Wisconsin

Rosemary J. Fox, Director | Henry S. Reuss Federal Plaza 310 West Wisconsin Avenue, Suite 500, Milwaukee, WI 53203-2292 414-297-1112

EEOC 30.001 EMPLOYMENT DISCRIMINATION TITLE VII OF THE CIVIL RIGHTS ACT OF 1964

Award: Advisory Services and Counseling; Investigation of Complaints; Federal Employment

Purpose: To prohibit employment discrimination against applicants or employees based on race, color, religion, sex (including pregnancy, gender and sexual orientation), and national origin.

Applicant Eligibility: Any aggrieved individual, or any individual, organization, or agency filing on behalf of an aggrieved individual, who has reason to believe that an unlawful employment practice within the meaning of Title VII, as amended, has been committed by an employer with 15 or more employees, a state or local government entity, an employment agency, labor organization, or joint labor-management committee controlling apprenticeship or other training or retraining, including on-the-job training programs. Any aggrieved individual who believes he or she has been retaliated against for opposing employment practices that discriminate, or who testifies, or participates in any way in an investigation, proceeding, or litigation under Title VII.

Beneficiary Eligibility: Applicants, current employees, or former employees of the named respondent(s) who have been subjected to employment practices based on race, color, religion, sex, or national origin by the named respondent(s), and/or who have been subjected to retaliation for opposing discrimination or participating in a Title VII investigation, proceeding, or litigation.

Award Range/Average: N/A

Funding: (Salaries and Expenses) FY 17 $364,500,000; FY 18 est $379,500,000; FY 19 est $363,807,000

HQ: Office of Communications and Legislative Affairs 131 M Street NE
Washington, DC 20507
Phone: 202-663-4191
http://www.eeoc.gov/laws/statutes/titlevii.cfm

EMPLOYMENT DISCRIMINATION PRIVATE BAR PROGRAM

Award: Provision of Specialized Services

Purpose: To assist individuals who have filed a charge with the Commission, or on whose behalf a charge has been filed, in contacting members of the private bar.

Applicant Eligibility: Any individual who has filed a charge with the Commission, or on whose behalf a charge has been filed.

Beneficiary Eligibility: Same as Applicant Eligibility.

Award Range/Average: N/A

Funding: FY 17 $364,500,000; FY 18 est $379,500,000; FY 19 est $363,807,000.

HQ: Office of General Counsel 131 M Street NE
Washington, DC 20507
Phone: 202-663-4719
http://www.eeoc.gov

EEOC 30.008

EMPLOYMENT DISCRIMINATION AGE DISCRIMINATION IN EMPLOYMENT

Award: Advisory Services and Counseling; Investigation of Complaints; Federal Employment

Purpose: Prohibits discrimination based on age (40 or older) with respect to any term, condition, or privilege of employment, including hiring, firing, promotion, layoff, compensation, benefits, job assignments, training and harassment.

Applicant Eligibility: Any aggrieved individuals age 40 and over, or any individual, organization, or agency filing on behalf of an aggrieved individual who has reason to believe that a covered employer has committed an unlawful employment practice within the meaning of the ADEA, as amended.

Beneficiary Eligibility: Applicants, current employees, or former employees of the named respondent(s) who are age 40 or older and who have been subjected to unlawful employment practices based on age by the named respondent(s), and/or who have been subjected to retaliation for opposing age discrimination, filing a charge of discrimination, or participating in an ADEA investigation, proceeding, or litigation.

Award Range/Average: N/A

Funding: (Investigation of Complaints) FY 17 $364,500,000; FY 18 est $379,500,000; FY 19 est $363,807,000

HQ: Office of Communications and Legislative Affairs 131 M Street NE
Washington, DC 20507
Phone: 202-663-4191
http://www.eeoc.gov/laws/types/age.cfm

EMPLOYMENT DISCRIMINATION EQUAL PAY ACT

Award: Advisory Services and Counseling; Investigation of Complaints; Federal Employment

Purpose: Prohibits sex discrimination in the payment of wages to men and women performing jobs that require substantially equal skill, effort and responsibility, under similar working conditions within the same establishment.

Applicant Eligibility: Any aggrieved individual, or any individual, organization, or agency filing on behalf of an aggrieved individual, who has reason to believe that a covered employer has committed an unlawful employment practice within the meaning of the EPA. An employee who believes he or she has been retaliated against for opposing compensation practices that discriminate based on sex or who files a discrimination charge, testifies, or participates in any way in an investigation, proceeding, or litigation under the EPA.

Beneficiary Eligibility: Applicants, current employees, or former employees of the named respondent (s) who have been subjected to unlawful compensation practices based on gender by the named respondent (s), and/or who have been subjected to retaliation for filing a charge of discrimination, for opposing gender-based compensation discrimination or participating in an EPA investigation, proceeding, or for litigation.

Award Range/Average: N/A

Funding: (Investigation of Complaints) FY 17 $364,500,000; FY 18 est $379,500,000; FY 19 est $363,807,000

HQ: 131 M Street NE
Washington, DC 20507
Phone: 202-663-4191
http://www.eeoc.gov/laws/types/equalcompensation.cfm

EEOC 30.011

EMPLOYMENT DISCRIMINATION TITLE I OF THE AMERICANS WITH DISABILITIES ACT

Award: Advisory Services and Counseling; Investigation of Complaints; Federal Employment

Purpose: Prohibits employment discrimination against applicants or employees based on disability.

Applicant Eligibility: Any aggrieved individual, or any individual, or any organization, or agency filing on behalf of an aggrieved individual, who has reason to believe that an unlawful employment practice within the meaning of Title I of the ADA has been committed by an employer with 15 or more employees, including state or local governments, an employment agency, labor organization, or joint labor-management committee controlling apprenticeship or other training or retraining, including on-the-job training programs. Any aggrieved individual who believes he or she has been retaliated against for opposing employment practices that discriminate based on disability or who files an ADA charge, testifies, or participates in any way in an investigation, proceeding, or litigation under the ADA.

Beneficiary Eligibility: Applicants, for employment, current employees, and former employees of the named respondent(s) in a charge who have been subjected to unlawful employment practices based on disability by the named respondent (s), and/or who have been subjected to retaliation for filing a charge of discrimination, for opposing disability discrimination or for participating in an ADA or Rehabilitation Act investigation, proceeding, or litigation.

Award Range/Average: N/A

Funding: (Investigation of Complaints) FY 17 $364,500,000; FY 18 est $379,500,000; FY 19 est $363,807,000

HQ: Office of Communications and Legislative Affairs 131 M Street NE
Washington, DC 20507
Phone: 202-663-4191
http://www.eeoc.gov/laws/statutes/ada.cfm

EEOC 30.013 EMPLOYMENT DISCRIMINATION-TITLE II OF THE GENETIC INFORMATION NONDISCRIMINATION ACT OF 2008 "GINA Title II"

Award: Advisory Services and Counseling; Investigation of Complaints; Federal Employment

Purpose: Prohibits the use of genetic information in making employment decisions, restricts employers and other entities covered by Title II from requesting, requiring or purchasing genetic information, and strictly limits the disclosure of genetic information.

Applicant Eligibility: Any aggrieved individual, or any individual, labor union, association, legal representative, or organization filing on behalf of an aggrieved individual, who has reason to believe that an unlawful employment practice within the meaning of Title II of GINA has been committed by an employer, federal agency, an employment agency, labor organization, or joint labor-management committee controlling apprenticeship or other training or retraining, or on-the-job training programs. Any aggrieved individual who believes that he or she has been retaliated against for opposing employment practices that discriminate on the basis of genetic information or who files a charge of discrimination, testifies, or participates in any way in an investigation, proceeding, or litigation under Title II of GINA.

Beneficiary Eligibility: Applicants, current employees, or former employees of the named respondent(s) who have been subjected to employment practices based on genetic information by the named respondent(s), and/or who have been subjected to retaliation for filing a charge of discrimination, opposing discrimination or participating in a Title II of GINA investigation, proceeding, or litigation.

Award Range/Average: N/A

Funding: (Salaries and Expenses) FY 17 est $364,500,000; FY 18 est $363,807,086; FY 16 $364,500,000

HQ: Office of Communications and Legislative Affairs 131 M Street NE
Washington, DC 20507
Phone: 202-663-4191
http://www.eeoc.gov

FARM SERVICE AGENCY

SERVICE CENTER

Alabama
Daniel Robinson | Alabama State FSA Office For letter mail: P.O. Box 235013 4121 Carmichael Road, Suite 600, Montgomery, AL 36106-5013 334-279-3500

Alaska
Karen Olson | Alaska State FSA Office 800 West Evergreen, Suite 216, Palmer, AK 99645-6389 907-745-7982

Arizona
George Arrendondo | Arizona State FSA Office 77 East Thomas Road, Suite 240, Phoenix, AZ 85012-3318 602-640-5200

Arkansas
Mike Dunaway | Arkansas State FSA Office Federal Building, Room 5416 700 West Capitol Avenue, Little Rock, AR 72201-3225 501-301-3000

California
Valente Dolcini, Acting | California State FSA Office 430 G Street, Suite 4161, Davis, CA 95616-4161 530-792-5538

Colorado
Robert Eisenach | Colorado State FSA Office 655 Parfet Street Suite E 305, Lakewood, CO 80215-5517 303-236-2866

Connecticut
Harvey Polinsky | Connecticut State FSA Office 88 Day Hill Road, Windsor, CT 06095 860-285-8483

Delaware
William Donald Clifton II | Delaware State FSA Office 1201 College Park Drive, Suite 101, Dover, DE 19904-8713 302-678-2547

Florida
Kevin L. Kelley | Florida State FSA Office 440 N.W. 25th Place, Suite 1, Gainesville, FL 32606 352-379-4500

Georgia
Hanson Carter | Georgia State FSA Office For letter mail: P.O. Box 1907 Federal Building, Room 102 355 East Hancock Avenue, Athens, GA 30603-1907 706-546-2266

Hawaii
Jo-Anna Nakata | Hawaii State FSA Office 300 Ala Moana Boulevard, Room 5106 For letter mail: P.O. Box 50008, Honolulu, HI 96850 808-541-2644

Idaho
Richard R. Rush | Idaho State FSA Office 9173 W. Barners, Suite B, Boise, ID 83705-1511 208-378-5650

Illinois
Stephen Scates | Illinois State FSA Office For letter mail: P.O. Box 19273 3500 W Avenue, Springfield, IL 62794-9273 217-241-6600

Indiana
Robert D. Peacock | Indiana State FSA Office 5981 Lakeside Boulevard, Indianapolis, IN 46278 317-290-3030, Ext. 317

Iowa
Robert Soukup | Iowa State FSA Office 10500 Buena Vista Court, Des Moines, IA 50322 515-254-1540, Ext. 600

Kansas
Adrian J. Polansky | Kansas State FSA Office 3600 Anderson Avenue, Manhattan, KS 66502-2511 785-539-3531

Kentucky
Hampton (Hoppy) Henton | Kentucky State FSA Office 771 Corporate Drive, Suite 100, Lexington, KY 40503-5478 606-224-7601

Louisiana
Willie F. Cooper | Louisiana State FSA Office 3737 Government Street, Alexandria, LA 71302-3395 318-473-7721

Maine
G.Arnold Roach | Maine State FSA Office 444 Stillwater Avenue, Suite 1 P.O. Box 406, Bangor, ME 04402-0406 207-990-9140

Maryland
James M. Voss | Maryland State FSA Office River Center 8335 Guilford Road, Suite E, Columbia, MD 21046 410-381-4550

Massachusetts
Charles A. Costa | Massachusetts State FSA Office 445 West Street, Amherst, MA 01002-2957 413-256-0232

Michigan
Chris White | Michigan State FSA Office 3001 Coolidge Road, Suite 100, East Lansing, MI 48823-6321 517-337-6659, Ext. 1201

Programs Administered by Regional - State - Local Offices

Minnesota
Linda Hennen, Acting | Minnesota State FSA Office 400 Farm Credit Service Building 375 Jackson Street, St. Paul, MN 55101-1852 612-602-7700

Mississippi
David Warrington | Mississippi State FSA Office P.O. Box 14995 6310 I-55 North, Jackson, MS 39211 601-965-4300

Missouri
Brad Epperson | Missouri State FSA Office 601 Business Loop 70 West Suite 225, Parkade Plaza, Columbia, MO 65203 573-876-0925

Montana
Bruce E. Nelson | Montana State FSA Office For letter mail: P.O. Box 670 10 East Babcock Street, Room 557, Bozeman, MT 59715 406-587-6872

Nebraska
Mark Bowen | Nebraska State FSA Office For letter mail: P.O. Box 57975 7131 A Street, Lincoln, NE 68510-7975 402-437-5581

Nevada
Wendell K. Newman | Nevada State FSA Office 1755 East Plumb Lane, Suite 202, Reno, NV 89502-3207 775-784-5411

New Hampshire
James McConaha | USDA-New Hampshire State FSA Office 22 Bridge Street, 4th Floor P.O. Box 1388, Concord, NH 03302-1338 603-224-7941

New Jersey
Debbie Borie Holtz | New Jersey State FSA Office Mastoris Professional Plaza 163 Route 130 Building 2, Suite E, Bordentown, NJ 08505-2249 609-298-3446

New Mexico
Larry Burnett | New Mexico State FSA Office 6200 Jefferson Street, N.E., Albuquerque, NM 87109 505-761-4900

New York
Marc A. Smith | New York State FSA Office 441 South Salina Street, Suite 356, 5th Floor, Syracuse, NY 13202-2455 315-477-6303

North Carolina
Phillip Farland | North Carolina State FSA Office 4407 Bland Road, Suite 175, Raleigh, NC 27609-6296 919-875-4800

North Dakota
Scott Stofferahn | North Dakota State FSA Office 1025 28th Street, SW For letter mail: P.O. Box 3046, Fargo, ND 58108 701-239-5205

Ohio
Steve Maurer | Ohio State FSA Office Federal Building, Room 540 200 North High Street, Columbus, OH 43215 614-469-6735

Oklahoma
Terry L. Peach | Oklahoma State FSA Office 100 USDA, Suite 102 Farm Road & McFarland Street, Stillwater, OK 74074-2653 405-742-1130

Oregon
Jack L. Sainsbury | Oregon State FSA Office 7620 SW Mohawk For Letter Mail: P.O. Box 1300, Tualatin, OR 97062-8121 503-692-6830

Pennsylvania
William H. Baumgartner | Pennsylvania State FSA Office One Credit Union Place, Suite 320, Harrisburg, PA 17110-2994 717-237-2113

Puerto Rico
Heriberto J. Martinez | P.O. Box 11188 Fernandez Junzos Station Suite 309, Cobian's Plaza 1607 Ponce DeLeon Avenue, Santurce, PR 00909-0001 809-729-6872

Rhode Island
Paul E. Brule | Rhode Island State FSA Office 60 Quaker Lane West Bay Office Complex, Room 40, Warwick, RI 02886-0111 401-828-8232

South Carolina
Laurie C. Lawson | South Carolina State FSA Office 1927 Thurmond Mall, Suite 100, Columbia, SC 29201-2375 803-806-3830

South Dakota
Michael O'Connor | South Dakota State FSA Office 200 Fourth Street, S.W., Room 308 Federal Building, Huron, SD 57350-2478 605-352-1160

Tennessee
David McDole | Tennessee State FSA Office 579 U.S. Courthouse 801 Broadway, Nashville, TN 37203-3816 615-736-5555

Texas
Wayland Shurley, Acting | Texas State FSA Office Commerce National Bank Building, 2nd Floor 2405 Texas Avenue South, 77840 For letter mail: P.O. Box 2900, College Station, TX 77841-0001 409-260-9207

Utah
James L. Humlicek | Utah State FSA Office 125 South State Street, Room 4239 For letter mail: P.O. Box 11350, Salt Lake City, UT 84147-0350 801-524-5013

Vermont
Ronald Allbee, Acting | Vermont State FSA Office Executive Square Office Building 346 Shelburne Street, Burlington, VT 05401-4995 802-658-2803

Virginia
Donald Davis | Virginia State FSA Office Culpeper Building, Suite 138 1606 Santa Rosa Road, Richmond, VA 23229 804-287-1500

Washington
Larry R. Albin | Washington State FSA Office Rock Pointe Tower, Suite 568 316 West Boone Avenue, Spokane, WA 99201-2350 509-323-3000

West Virginia
Billy B. Burke | West Virginia State FSA Office New Federal Building 75 High Street, Room 239 For letter mail: P. O. Box 1049, Morgantown, WV 26507-1049 304-291-4351

Wisconsin
Douglas J. Caruso | Wisconsin State FSA Office 6515 Watts Road, Room 100, Madison, WI 53719-2797 608-276-8732, Ext. 100

Wyoming
Carl Jensen | Wyoming State FSA Office 951 Werner Court, Suite 130, Casper, WY 82601-1307 307-261-5231

DAIRY INDEMNITY PROGRAM "DIPP"

Award: Direct Payments with Unrestricted Use

Purpose: To assist the dairy farmers and manufacturers through compensation because of contamination and other toxic substances.

Applicant Eligibility: Dairy farmers whose milk has been removed from the market by a public agency because of residue of any violating substance in such milk. Manufacturers of dairy products whose product has been removed from the market by a public agency because of pesticide residue in such product.

Beneficiary Eligibility: Same as Applicant Eligibility.

Award Range/Average: No Data Available.

Funding: FY 17 $224,334; FY 18 est $467,000; FY 19 est $500,000; FY 16 $161,410.

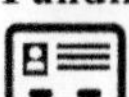

HQ: 1400 Independence Avenue SW
Washington, DC 20250-0512
Phone: 202-720-1919
Email: danielle.cooke@wdc.usda.gov
http://www.fsa.usda.gov/programs-and-services/price-support/index

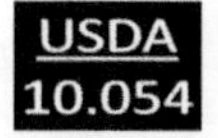

EMERGENCY CONSERVATION PROGRAM "ECP"

Award: Direct Payments for Specified Use

Purpose: To help out farmers to incorporate the habit of water conservation to face drought and other natural calamities.

Applicant Eligibility: Any agricultural producer who as owner, landlord, tenant, or sharecropper on a farm or ranch, including associated groups, and bears a part of the cost of an approved conservation practice in a disaster area, is eligible to apply for cost-share conservation assistance. This program is also available in American Samoa, Guam, Commonwealth of the Northern Mariana Islands, Puerto Rico, and the Virgin Islands.

Beneficiary Eligibility: Same as Applicant Eligibility.

Award Range/Average: No Data Available.

Funding: (Direct Payments with Unrestricted Use) FY 17 $104,312,000; FY 18 est $200,000,000; FY 19 est $70,000,000; FY 16 $71,000,000

HQ: 1400 Independence Avenue SW
Washington, DC 20250
Phone: 202-205-4537
Email: martin.bomar@wdc.usda.gov
http://www.fsa.usda.gov/programs-and-services/conservation-programs/emergency-conservation/index

USDA 10.055 DIRECT AND COUNTER-CYCLICAL PAYMENTS PROGRAM "DCP"

Award: Direct Payments for Specified Use

Purpose: To provide a stable income for covered commodity producers.

Applicant Eligibility: To be eligible for payments under DCP, owners, operators, landlords, tenants, or sharecroppers must (1) share in the risk of producing a crop on base acres on a farm enrolled in DCP, and be entitled to share in the crop available for marketing from the base acres, or would have shared had a crop been produced; (2) annually report the use of the farm's cropland acreage; (3) comply with conservation and wetland protection requirements on all of their land; (4) comply with planting flexibility requirements; (5) use the base acres for agricultural or related activities; and (5) protect all base acres from erosion, including providing sufficient cover as determined necessary by the county FSA committee, and control weeds.

Beneficiary Eligibility: DCP provides payments to eligible producers on farms enrolled for the 2008 through 2013 crop years.

Award Range/Average: No Data Available.

Funding: (Direct Payments with Unrestricted Use) FY 17 $0; FY 18 est $0; FY 19 est $0; FY 15 $23,588,000; FY 16 est $0; - Direct Payments repealed by 2014 Farm Bill(Direct Payments with Unrestricted Use) FY 17 $0; FY 18 est $0; FY 19 est $0; FY 15 $0; FY 16 est $0.

HQ: 1400 Independence Avenue SW, P.O. Box 0517
Washington, DC 20250
Phone: 202-720-7641
Email: dan.mcglynn@wdc.usda.gov
http://www.fsa.usda.gov/programs-and-services/dccp-acre/index

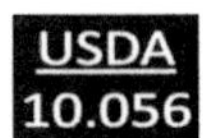

FARM STORAGE FACILITY LOANS "FSFL and SSFL"

Award: Direct Loans

Purpose: The Farm Storage Facility Loan program provides loan for farm products and cattle rearing based on the environmental evaluation and also provides loan for producers of sugarcane and raw sugar.

Applicant Eligibility: A FSFL eligible borrower is any person who, as landowner, landlord, operator, producer, tenant, leaseholder, or sharecropper: (1) Has a satisfactory credit history and demonstrates an ability to repay the debt arising under this program using a financial statement acceptable to CCC prepared within 90 days of the date of application; (2) has no delinquent Federal debt defined by the Debt Collection Improvement Act of 1996 at the time of loan disbursement; (3) is a producer of a facility loan commodity as defined by CCC; (4) demonstrates a need for storage capacity as defined by CCC; (5) provides proof of crop insurance offered under the Federal Crop Insurance Program for crops of economic significance on all farms operated by the borrower in the county where the storage facility is located; (6) is in compliance with USDA provisions for highly erodible land and wetlands provisions according to 7 CFR Part 12; (7) demonstrates compliance with any applicable local zoning, land use, and building codes for the applicable farm storage facility structures; (8) provides proof of flood insurance if CCC determines such insurance is necessary to protect the interests of CCC, and proof of all peril structural insurance, to CCC annually; (9) demonstrates compliance with the National Environmental Policy Act regulations at 40 CFR, Parts 1500- 1508; and (10) has not been convicted under Federal or State law of a controlled substance violation under 7 CFR Part 718.

Beneficiary Eligibility: Applicants/borrowers are the direct beneficiaries when they meet all eligibility criteria. Landowners, landlords, operators, producers, tenants, leaseholders, or sharecroppers are the beneficiaries.

Award Range/Average: No Data Available.

Funding: FY 17 $308,500,000; FY 18 est $308,500,000; FY 19 est $308,500,000; FY 16 est $180,000,000

HQ: USDA-FSA-PSD 1400 Independence Avenue SW, P.O. Box 0512
Washington, DC 20250-0512
Phone: 202-720-2270
Email: toni.williams@wdc.usda.gov
http://www.fsa.usda.gov/fsa/webapp?area=home&subject=prsu&topic=flp

CONSERVATION RESERVE PROGRAM "CRP"

Award: Direct Payments for Specified Use

Purpose: To safeguard natural food, water, and improve wildlife.

Applicant Eligibility: An individual, partnership, association, Indian Tribal ventures corporation, estate, trust, other business enterprises or other legal entities and, whenever applicable, a State, a political subdivision of a State, or any agency thereof may submit an offer to enroll acreage.

Beneficiary Eligibility: If their offer is accepted for enrollment, an individual, partnership, association, Indian Tribal ventures, corporation, estate, trust, other business enterprises or other legal entities and, whenever applicable, a State, political subdivision of State, or any agency thereof may earn benefits.

Award Range/Average: No Data Available.

Funding: FY 17 $1,881,845,000; FY 18 est $2,127,813,000; FY 19 est $2,219,797,000; FY 16 $2,120,000,000.

HQ: 1400 Independence Avenue SW
Washington, DC 20250
Phone: 202-720-9563

Email: beverly.preston@wdc.usda.gov

http://www.fsa.usda.gov/programs-and-services/conservation-programs/conservation-reserve-program/index

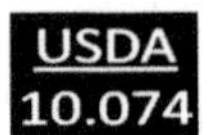

COMMODITY CREDIT CORPORATION AUDIT OF FINANCIAL STATEMENTS "CCC Audit of Financial Statements"

Award: Direct Payments with Unrestricted Use

Purpose: The program provides a contract to a private Audit Firm to conduct an audit of CCC's financial statement.

Applicant Eligibility: CCC is a government owned cooperation that will use funds to solicit the most qualified and cost effective contract within a reasonable range.

Beneficiary Eligibility: The audit firm will perform the required audit services using a firm fixed price contract. This has resulted in a reduction of total costs in the requested funding.

Award Range/Average: N/A

Funding: (Salaries and Expenses) FY 17 $1,483,931,000; FY 18 est $1,525,248,000; FY 19 est $1,187,403,000; FY 13 est $2,000,000; FY 11 $1,248,978; FY 12 est $2,000,000

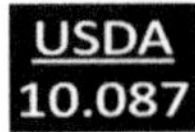

BIOMASS CROP ASSISTANCE PROGRAM "BCAP"

Award: Direct Payments with Unrestricted Use

Purpose: To promote biofuels and funds for the producers of renewable biomass products.

Applicant Eligibility: To be eligible to enter into a BCAP contract for the purposes of receiving an annual payment or establishment payments, a person or legal entity must be an owner, operator, or tenant of eligible land within a project area. Eligible land must be agricultural land or nonindustrial private forest land.

Beneficiary Eligibility: Owners and operators of agricultural and non-industrial private forest land will receive the ultimate benefits because it will provide financial assistance to establish, produce, and deliver biomass feedstocks. Eligible material owners who are the person or entity having the right to collect or harvest eligible material, who has the risk of loss in the material that is delivered to an eligible facility and who has directly or by agent delivered or intends to deliver the eligible material to a qualified biomass conversion facility.

Award Range/Average: No Data Available.

Funding: (Direct Payments for Specified Use) FY 17 $3,000,000; FY 18 est $0; FY 19 est $0; FY 16 $3,000,000

HQ: USDA FSA Conservation and Environmental Programs (CEPD)Independence Avenue SW, Room 4975

Washington, DC 20250

Phone: 202-720-4053

Email: kelly.novak@wdc.usda.gov

CONSERVATION LOANS

Award: Guaranteed/insured Loans

Purpose: To provide loan for the less financially established farmers for implementing conservation measures.

Applicant Eligibility: An applicant must (1) Not have caused a loss to the Agency after April 4, 1996, or received debt forgiveness on more than three occasions prior to April 4, 1996 to receive a guaranteed loan, and for a direct loan, must not have received debt forgiveness from the Agency on any direct or guaranteed loan; (2) be a U.S. citizen, non-citizen national or qualified alien; (3) posses the legal capacity to incur the obligations of the loan; (4) for a direct loan, have the necessary education and/or experience, training, and managerial ability to operate a farm; and (5) for a direct loan, fulfill the Agency's borrower training requirements. If the applicant is an entity, it must be controlled by farmers engaged primarily and directly in farming in the U.S., after the loan is made.

Beneficiary Eligibility: Applicants are the direct beneficiaries and must meet the applicant eligibility requirements. Families, individual, and entities who are farmers are the beneficiaries.

Award Range/Average: Maximum indebtedness for direct loans, combined; farm ownership, conservation, soil and water, and recreation $300,000. Maximum indebtedness for guaranteed loans combined: farm ownership, conservation, and soil and water loan indebtedness of $1,399,000 (for FY 2017, amount adjusted annually for inflation).

Funding: (Direct Loans) FY 17 $150,000,000; FY 18 FY 19 FY 15 $1,355,000; FY 16 est $150,000,000; - (Guaranteed/Insured Loans) FY 17 $0; FY 18 est $150,000,000; FY 19 est $150,000,000; FY 15 $1,355,000; FY 16 est $150,000,000.

HQ: 1400 Independence Avenue SW
Washington, DC 20250
Phone: 202-690-0756
Email: connie.holman@wdc.usda.gov
http://www.fsa.usda.gov/programs-and-services/farm-loan-programs/index

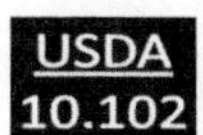

EMERGENCY FOREST RESTORATION PROGRAM "EFRP"

Award: Direct Payments with Unrestricted Use

Purpose: This program assists an EFRP participant with financial assistance for the disasters caused by natural calamities.

Applicant Eligibility: To be eligible to participate in EFRP, a person or legal entity must be an owner of nonindustrial private forest land affected by a natural disaster, and must be liable for or have the expense that is the subject of the financial assistance. The owner must be a person or legal entity (including Indian tribes) with full decision-making authority over the land, as determined by FSA, or with such waivers as may be needed from lenders or others as may be required, to undertake program commitments.

Beneficiary Eligibility: The owners of nonindustrial private forest land will receive the ultimate benefit.

Award Range/Average: N/A

Funding: FY 17 $5,382,000; FY 18 est $15,000,000; FY 19 est $15,000,000; FY 16 $3,000,000.

HQ: 1400 Independence Avenue SW
Washington, DC 20250
Phone: 202-690-0794
Email: james.michaels@wdc.usda.gov

http://www.fsa.usda.gov/programs-and-services/disaster-assistance-program/emergency-forest-restoration/index

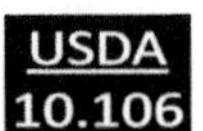

DISASTER RELIEF APPROPRIATIONS ACT, EMERGENCY FOREST RESTORATION PROGRAM
"Disaster Relief Appropriations Act, EFRP"

Award: Direct Payments for Specified Use; Direct Payments With Unrestricted Use

Purpose: This program assists an EFRP participant with financial assistance for the disasters caused by natural calamities.

Applicant Eligibility: To be eligible to participate in EFRP, a person or legal entity must be an owner of nonindustrial private forest land affected by a natural disaster, and must be liable for or have the expense that is the subject of the financial assistance. The owner must be a person or legal entity (including Indian tribes) with full decision-making authority over the land, as determined by FSA, or with such waivers as may be needed from lenders or others as may be required, to undertake program commitments.

Beneficiary Eligibility: The owners of industrial private forest land will receive the ultimate benefit.

Award Range/Average: No Data Available.

Funding: (Direct Payments with Unrestricted Use) FY 17 $15,000,000; FY 18 est $5,751,000; FY 19 est $0; FY 16 est $0; FY 15 $2,254,000

HQ: 1400 Independence Avenue SW

Washington, DC 20250

Phone: 202-205-4537

Email: martin.bomar@wdc.usda.gov

http://www.fsa.usda.gov/programs-and-services/disaster-assistance-program/emergency-forest-restoration/index

LIVESTOCK INDEMNITY PROGRAM-2014 FARM BILL
"LIP"

Award: Direct Payments with Unrestricted Use

Purpose: To compensate those who have lost their livestock due to natural disasters.

Applicant Eligibility: To be eligible for benefits, an individual or legal entity must be a citizen of the United States (U.S.); Resident alien; Partnership of citizens of the U.S; or Corporation, limited liability corporation, or other farm organizational structure organized under State law.

Beneficiary Eligibility: The eligible livestock or contract owner will receive the ultimate benefit from LIP.

Award Range/Average: No Data Available.

Funding: (Direct Payments with Unrestricted Use) FY 17 $25,066,000; FY 18 est $30,671,000; FY 19 est $31,350,000; FY 16 $43,000,000

HQ: 1400 Independence Avenue SW, P.O. Box 0517

Washington, DC 20250

Phone: 202-720-8954

Email: amy.mitchell1@wdc.usda.gov

http://www.fsa.usda.gov

USDA 10.109 LIVESTOCK FORAGE PROGRAM-2014 FARM BILL "LFP"

Award: Direct Payments with Unrestricted Use

Purpose: The LFP compensates those who lost their livestock due to fire or natural calamities.

Applicant Eligibility: To be eligible for benefits, an individual or legal entity must be a citizen of the United States (U.S.); Resident alien; Partnership of citizens of the U.S.; or Corporation, limited liability corporation, or other farm organization structure organized under State law. An eligible livestock producer must own, cash or share lease, or be a contract grower of covered livestock during the 60 calendar days before the beginning date of a qualifying drought or fire; provide pastureland or grazing land for covered livestock, including cash-rented pastureland or grazing land that is either physically located in a country affected by a qualifying drought during the normal grazing period for the county, or rangeland managed by a federal agency and the eligible livestock producer is prohibited from grazing the normally permitted livestock because of a qualifying fire.

Beneficiary Eligibility: The eligible livestock or contract owner will receive the ultimate benefit from LFP.

Award Range/Average: No Data Available.

Funding: (Direct Payments with Unrestricted Use) FY 17 $350,709,000; FY 18 est $393,550,000; FY 19 est $416,125,000; FY 16 $430,000,000

HQ: 14th and Independence Avenue SW, P.O. Box 0517
Washington, DC 20250
Phone: 202-720-7997
Email: scotty.abbott@wdc.usda.gov
http://www.fsa.usda.gov/programs-and-services/disaster-assistance-program/livestock-forage/index

EMERGENCY ASSISTANCE FOR LIVESTOCK, HONEYBEES AND FARM-RAISED FISH PROGRAM-2014 FARM BILL "ELAP"

Award: Direct Payments for Specified Use

Purpose: The ELAP assists producers who have lost their livestock due to disease or other natural calamities.

Applicant Eligibility: To be eligible for benefits, an individual or legal entity must be a citizen of the United States (U.S.); Resident alien; Partnership of citizens of the U.S.; or Corporation, limited liability corporation, or other farm organizational structure organized under State law. The eligible applicant must have legal ownership of the livestock on the day the livestock died and must be a producer or contract grower of livestock, honeybee, or farm-raised fish that assumes the production and market risks associated with the agricultural production of crops or livestock on a farm and that meet the requirements to receive ELAP payments.

Beneficiary Eligibility: Eligible producers of livestock, honeybees, and farm-raised fish will receive the ultimate benefits from ELAP. An eligible livestock producer, honeybee producer.

Award Range/Average: No Data Available.

Funding: FY 17 $18,223,000; FY 18 est $19,500,000; FY 19 est $19,500,000; FY 16 $17,000,000

HQ: USDA FSA Production Emergencies and Compliance Division 1400 Independence Avenue SW, P.O. Box 0517

Washington, DC 20250

Phone: 202-720-8954

Email: amy.mitchell1@wdc.usda.gov

http://www.fsa.usda.gov/programs-and-services/disaster-assistance-program/emergency-assist-for-livestock-honey-bees-fish/index

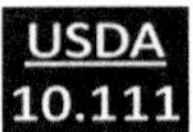

TREE ASSISTANCE PROGRAM-2014 FARM BILL "TAP"

Award: Direct Payments with Unrestricted Use

Purpose: TAP compensate orchardists and nursery growers for the damage caused by natural calamities.

Applicant Eligibility: To be eligible for benefits, an individual or legal entity must be a citizen of the United States (U.S.); Resident alien; Partnership of citizens of the U.S; or Corporation, limited liability corporation, or other farm organizational structure organized under State law.

Beneficiary Eligibility: The eligible orchardists and nursery tree grower receives the TAP benefit.

Award Range/Average: No Data Available.

Funding: (Direct Payments with Unrestricted Use) FY 17 $6,912,000; FY 18 est $20,000,000; FY 19 est $20,000,000; FY 16 $30,000,000

HQ: 14th and Independence Avenue SW, P.O. Box 0517

Washington, DC 20250

Phone: 202-720-5172

Email: steve.peterson@wdc.usda.gov

http://www.fsa.usda.gov/programs-and-services/disaster-assistance-program/tree-assistance-program/index

COTTON TRANSITION ASSISTANCE PROGRAM "CTAP"

Award: Direct Payments with Unrestricted Use

Purpose: The CTAP provides benefits for the cotton producers.

Applicant Eligibility: An eligible producer for CTAP is required to be a person or legal entity who is actively engaged in farming and otherwise eligible to receive payment. CTAP payments in each of the 2014 and 2015 program years are limited to $40,000 per person or legal entity, similar to the $40,000 per person or legal entity limitation to applied to DCP under The Food, Conservation, and Energy Act of 2008, P.

Beneficiary Eligibility: The Farm Service Agency (FSA) will provide adequate notice to producer about the new CTAP regulations so they will be ready to begin sign-up for CTAP.

Award Range/Average: No Data Available.

Funding: FY 17 $956,933; FY 18 est $112,080; FY 19 est $0; FY 16 $1,000,000.

HQ: 1400 Independence Avenue SW, Room 4759-S

Washington, DC 20024

Phone: 202-720-7641

Email: brent.orr@wdc.usda.gov

http://www.fsa.usda.gov/fsa/newsreleases?area=newsroom&subject=landing&topic=pfs&newstype=prfactsheet&type=detail&item=pf_20150706_insup_en_ctap.html

USDA 10.116 THE MARGIN PROTECTION PROGRAM "MPP-Dairy"

Award: Direct Payments for Specified Use

Purpose: To provide compensation for the dairy producers when there is a cost reduction in the dairy products.

Applicant Eligibility: All dairy operations in the U.S. shall be eligible to participate in the MPP-Dairy program to receive margin protection payments. A dairy operation must produce milk from cows in the U.S. and must be commercially marketing milk produced at the time of enrollment and continue to market milk for the duration of the program.

Beneficiary Eligibility: The ultimate benefit of the MPP-Dairy program will help protect farm equity and reduce financial losses that occur during times of low margins.

Award Range/Average: No Data Available.

Funding: (Direct Payments for Specified Use) FY 17 $357,000; FY 18 est $30,998,000; FY 19 est $57,344,000; FY 16 $10,678,513.

HQ: 1400 Independence Avenue SW
Washington, DC 20250
Phone: 202-720-1919
Email: danielle.cooke@wdc.usda.gov
http://www.fsa.usda.gov/programs-and-services/dairy-mpp/index

USDA 10.119 DAIRY ASSISTANCE PROGRAM FOR PUERTO RICO "DAP-PR"

Award: Direct Payments with Unrestricted Use

Purpose: To compensate for the dairy producers for marketing dairy products.

Applicant Eligibility: The eligible applicants are the licensed dairy operations in Puerto Rico for acquiring feed from feed dealers in Puerto Rico.

Beneficiary Eligibility: Same as Applicant Eligibility.

Award Range/Average: No Data Available.

Funding: FY 18 est $0; FY 16 $0; FY 17 est $0.

HQ: 355 E Street SW Patriot Plaza III, 11th Floor
Washington, DC 20024
Phone: 202-772-6029
Email: veronica.richardson@wdc.usda.gov
http://www.fsa.gov

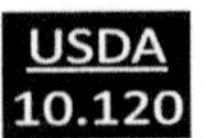

2017 WILDFIRES AND HURRICANES INDEMNITY PROGRAM "2017 WHIP"

Award: Direct Payments with Unrestricted Use

Purpose: To compensate the citrus producers to repair the damages and for replanting citrus trees.

Applicant Eligibility: Agriculture producers are eligible to apply.

Beneficiary Eligibility: N/A

Award Range/Average: Producers are subject to a $125,000 payment limitation, meaning a producer can't receive more than $125,000 for losses. But a producer can receive a higher payment if three-fourths or more of their income is derived from farming or another agricultural-based business. Producers who derived 75 percent of their income in tax years 2013, 2014 and 2015 will be subject to a $900,000 payment limitation.

Funding: FY 17 N/A FY 18 N/A FY 19 N/A - This is a new program.

HQ: 1400 Independence Avenue SW
Washington, DC 20250
Phone: 202-720-9882
Email: jennifer.fiser@wdc.usda.gov
http://www.fsa.usda.gov

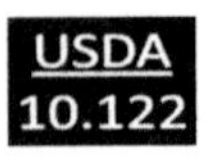

CONSERVATION RESERVE PROGRAM FOREST INVENTORY ANALYSIS PILOT PROGRAM "CRPFIA"

Award: N/A

Purpose: To provide grants for the bottomland hardwood tree species through the Farm Service Agency.

Applicant Eligibility: Non-profit organizations dedicated to conservation, forestry, and wildlife habitats, that have experience in conducting forest inventory analysis through the use of remote sensing data and technology are eligible to apply. The term "non-profit organization" means any corporation, trust, association, cooperative, or other organization that is operated primarily for scientific educational, service, charitable, or similar purposes in the public interest.

Beneficiary Eligibility: N/A

Award Range/Average: New program.

Funding: (Project Grants (Cooperative Agreements)) FY 17 N/A FY 18 est $1,000,000; FY 19 N/A

HQ: 1400 Independence Avenue SW
Washington, DC 20024
Phone: 202-720-5291
Email: richard.iovanna@wdc.usda.gov
http://www.fsa.usda.gov

USDA 10.404

EMERGENCY LOANS

Award: Direct Loans

Purpose: To compensate farmers and aquaculture operators with essential needs to recover from natural disasters.

Applicant Eligibility: Requires that an applicant: (a) Not have caused a loss to the Agency after April 4, 1996, or received debt forgiveness on no more than 1 occasion prior to April 4, 1996. (b) be an established family farmer, rancher, or aquaculture operator (either tenant-operator or owner-operator), who was conducting a farming operation at the time of occurrence of the disaster either as an individual proprietorship, a partnership, a cooperative, a corporation, or a joint operation; (c) have suffered qualifying crop loss and/or physical property damage caused by a designated natural disaster; (d) be a citizen of the United States or legal resident alien, or be operated by citizens and/or resident aliens owning over a 50 percent interest of the farming entity; (e) be unable to obtain suitable credit from any other source(s) to qualify for subsidized loss loans; (f) have sufficient training or farming experience in managing and operating a farm or ranch (1 year's complete production and marketing cycle within the last 3 years immediately preceding the application); (g) be able to project a feasible and sound plan of operation; (h) be a capable manager of the farming, ranching, or aquaculture operations (in the case of a cooperative, corporation, partnership or joint operation, if members, stockholders, partners or joint operators own a majority interest and are related by blood or marriage, at least one member, stockholder, partner or joint operator must operate the family farm; if not related, the majority interest holder(s) must operate the family farm); (I) have legal capacity to contract for the loan; (j) obtain eligibility certification; (k) provide adequate collateral to secure the loan request; (l) have not been convicted of crop insurance fraud (in certain situations); (m) have crop insurance if available for affected crops comply with the highly erodible land and wetland conservation provisions of Public Law 99-198.

Beneficiary Eligibility: Applicants/borrowers are the direct beneficiaries when they meet all eligibility criteria. Families, individuals and entities who are farmers, ranchers or aquaculture operators are the beneficiaries.

Award Range/Average: The maximum emergency loan amount may not exceed $500,000.

Funding: FY 17 $15,131,000; FY 18 est $54,616,000; FY 19 est $72,132,000; FY 16 est $74,554,000.

HQ: 1400 Independence Avenue SW
Washington, DC 20250
Phone: 202-690-0756
Email: connie.holman@wdc.usda.gov
http://www.fsa.usda.gov/programs-and-services/farm-loan-programs/index

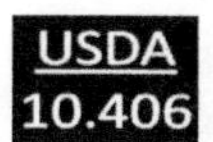

FARM OPERATING LOANS
"Farm Operating Loans (Direct & Guaranteed)"

Award: Direct Loans; Guaranteed/Insured Loans

Purpose: To assist farmers in making productive use of their land and maintain operations such as farming and ranching.

Applicant Eligibility: Except for youth loans, individual applicants must: (1) Be a citizen of the Untied States, United States non-citizen national, or a qualified alien under applicable Federal immigration laws; (2) have the legal capacity to incur the obligations of the loan; (3) be unable to obtain credit elsewhere or unable to obtain the loan without a guarantee; (4) not have had a previous loan which resulted in a loss to the Agency (with certain conditions); (5) not be delinquent on any federal debt; (6) after the loan is closed, be an owner/tenant operator of a family farm. For an operating loan (OL), the producer must be the operator of a family farm; (7) not have been convicted of crop insurance fraud (in certain circumstances); and (8) not have any controlled substance convictions.

Beneficiary Eligibility: Applicants/borrowers are the direct beneficiaries and must meet the applicant eligibility requirements Families, individuals, and entities who are or plan to become farmers, ranchers or aquaculture operators are the beneficiaries.

Award Range/Average: Direct Farm Operating Loans up to $300,000. ($50,000 total or less is considered a microloan); Guaranteed Farm Operating Loans up to $1,399,000.

Funding: (Guaranteed/Insured Loans) FY 17 $1,366,897,000; FY 18 est $1,876,541,000; FY 19 est $1,600,000,000; - (Direct Loans) FY 17 $1,284,035,000; FY 18 est $1,602,482,000; FY 19 est $1,500,000,000.

HQ: 1400 Independence Avenue SW
Washington, DC 20250
Phone: 202-690-0756
Email: connie.holman@wdc.usda.gov
http://www.fsa.usda.gov/programs-and-services/farm-loan-programs/index

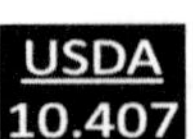

FARM OWNERSHIP LOANS
"Farm Onwership Loans (Direct and Guaranteed)"

Award: Direct Loans; Guaranteed/Insured Loans

Purpose: The Farm Service Agency provides loan for farmers in making productive use of their land to make a standard of living.

Applicant Eligibility: An applicant must: (1) Be a citizen of the Untied States, United States non-citizen national, or a qualified alien under applicable Federal immigration laws; (2) have the legal capacity to incur the obligations of the loan; (3) be unable to obtain credit elsewhere or unable to obtain the loan without a guarantee; (4) not have had a previous loan which resulted in a loss to the Agency (with certain conditions); (5) not be delinquent on any federal debt; (6) after the loan is closed, be an owner/tenant operator of a family farm. For an operating loan (OL), the producer must be the operator of a family farm; (7) have participated in the business operations of a farm for at least 3 out of the 10 years prior to the application (for direct loans only); (8) not have been convicted of crop insurance fraud (in certain circumstances); and (9) not have any controlled substance convictions.

Beneficiary Eligibility: Applicants/borrowers are the direct beneficiaries and must meet the applicant eligibility requirements. Families, individuals, and entities who are or plan to become farmers, ranchers or aquaculture operators are the beneficiaries.

Award Range/Average: Direct Farm Ownership Loans up to $300,000; Guaranteed Farm Ownership Loans up to $1,399,000. (amount adjusted annually) FY 2015: Direct Farm Ownership Loan average loan size $180,000. FY 2015: Guaranteed Farm Ownership Loan average loan size $465,000.

Funding: (Guaranteed/Insured Loans) FY 17 $2,278,602,000; FY 18 est $2,750,000,000; FY 19 est $2,750,000,000; FY 15 $2,041,130,000; FY 16 est $2,000,000,000; - (Direct Loans) FY 17 $1,044,115,000; FY 18 est $1,500,000,000; FY 19 est $1,500,000,000; FY 15 $1,007,898,000; FY 16 est $1,500,000,000

HQ: 1400 Independence Avenue SW
Washington, DC 20250
Phone: 202-690-0756
Email: connie.holman@wdc.usda.gov
http://www.fsa.usda.gov/programs-and-services/farm-loan-programs/index

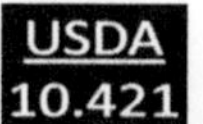

INDIAN TRIBES AND TRIBAL CORPORATION LOANS

Award: Direct Loans

Purpose: To support Indian tribes and corporations with land situated within the tribal reservations.

Applicant Eligibility: Limited to any Indian tribe recognized by the Secretary of the Interior or tribal corporation established pursuant to the Indian Reorganization Act or community in Alaska incorporated by the Secretary of Interior pursuant to the Indian Reorganization Act which does not have adequate uncommitted funds to acquire lands within the tribe's reservation or in a community in Alaska. The tribe must be unable to obtain sufficient credit elsewhere at reasonable rates and terms and must be able to show reasonable prospects of repaying the loan as determined by an acceptable repayment plan and a satisfactory management plan for the land being acquired.

Beneficiary Eligibility: American Indian Tribe or tribal corporation recognized by the Secretary of the Interior, or a community in Alaska incorporated by the Secretary of the Interior.

Award Range/Average: No Current Data Available.

Funding: (Direct Loans) FY 17 $0; FY 18 est $20,000,000; FY 19 est $20,000,000; FY 15 $0; FY 16 est $2,000,000. The agency estimates 20 loans being made in FY 2018 for total obligations of $20,000,000.

HQ: 1400 Independence Avenue SW
Washington, DC 20250
Phone: 202-690-0756
Email: connie.holman@wdc.usda.gov
http://fsa.usda.gov/fsa/webapp?area=home&subject=fmlp&topic=landing

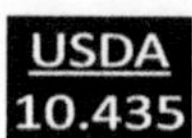

STATE MEDIATION GRANTS

Award: Project Grants

Purpose: To assist the agricultural producers and creditors of producers affected by the intervention of the Department of Agriculture.

Applicant Eligibility: State governments.

Beneficiary Eligibility: Agricultural producers, creditors of producers (as applicable) and persons directly affected by actions of the Department of Agriculture.

Award Range/Average: No Data Available.

Funding: (Project Grants) FY 17 $3,904,000; FY 18 est $3,904,000; FY 19 est $3,228,000.

HQ: 1400 Independence Avenue SW, P.O. Box 0523
Washington, DC 20250-0523
Phone: 202-720-1360
Email: courtney.dixon@wdc.usda.gov
http://www.fsa.usda.gov/fsa/newsreleases?area=newsroom&subject=landing&topic=pfs&newstype=prfactsheet&type=detail&item=pf_20130820_admin_en_agmed.html

USDA 10.449 BOLL WEEVIL ERADICATION LOAN PROGRAM

Award: Direct Loans

Purpose: To support the U.S. government to eradicate boll weevils.

Applicant Eligibility: Applicants may be determined eligible if the organization: (a) Meets the Animal and Plant Health Inspection Service (APHIS) cost-sharing requirements; (b) possesses a legal nonprofit corporate authority; (c) possesses the legal authority to enter into a contract; (d) operates in an area approved by a majority of cotton producers via referendum; (e) is unable to obtain funds elsewhere; and (f) may pledge producer assets as loan collateral.

Beneficiary Eligibility: The beneficiaries of this program include the local boll weevil organization and agricultural community as well as local, State, and national governments.

Award Range/Average: N/A

Funding: FY 17 $0; FY 18 est $60,000,000; FY 19 est $60,000,000; FY 16 $0.

HQ: USDA FSA DAFLP LMD 1400 Independence Avenue SW

Washington, DC 20250-0522

Phone: 202-690-0756

Email: connie.holman@wdc.usda.gov

http://fsa.usda.gov/fsa/webapp?area=home&subject=fmlp&topic=landing

FEDERAL AVIATION ADMINISTRATION

NATIONAL MINE HEALTH AND SAFETY ACADEMY

Alaska

Byron K. Huffman, Division Manager | 222 W. 8th Ave, Rm A36, Anchorage, AK 99513 907-271-5438

Tom Vanderwest | AHT-200 202-267-3436

Alaska Region

Byron K. Huffman, Division Manager | 222 W. 7th Ave., M/S #14, Anchorage, AK 99513 907-271-5438 (Southern Region) 1701 Columbia Avenue For letter mail: P.O. Box 20636, Atlanta, GA 30320-0631 404-305-6701

Atlanta District Office

ScottSeritt-- ASO | Federal Aviation Administration, Southern Region, Atlanta ADO, 1701 Columbia Ave., Campus Bldg. 2-260, College Park, GA 30337-2747

California

Mark McClardy - AWP -600 | 310-725-3600

P.O. Box 92007 Worldway Postal Center, Los Angeles, CA 90009-2007 310-725-3608

Region Airports Division 15000 Aviation Boulevard, Room 3012, Lawndale, CA 90261 310-725-3600

Georgia

Federal Aviation Administration, Southern Region, Airports Division, Suite 540, College Park, GA 30337 404-305-6700

Illinois

Federal Aviation Administration, Airports Division, OHare Lake Office Center, 2300 East Devon Avenue, Des Plaines, IL 60018 847-294-7272

Jim Keefer -- AGL | 847-294-7335

O'Hare Lake Office Center 2300 East Devon Avenue, Des Plaines, IL 60018 847-294-7272

Massachusetts

12 New England Executive Park, Burlington, MA 01803 617-238-7600

Sheila Bauer, ANE-40 | 12 New England Executive Park, Burlington, MA 01803-5299 781-238-7378

Missouri

601 East 12th Street, Kansas City, MO 64106-2808 816-329-2600

Jim A. Johnson - ACE-600 | 816-329-2600

Rm 335, 901 Locust, Kansas City, MO 64106-2325 816-329-2600

New Jersey
Atlantic City International Airport, Atlantic City, NJ 08405 516-227-3800

New York
600 Old Country Road, Suite 446, Garden City, NY 11530 516-227-3800

Debbie Roth -- AEA -600 | 718-553-3330

Eastern Region, 159-30 Rockaway Blvd., Jamaica, NY 11434 718-553-3330

Oklahoma
P.O. Box 25082, Oklahoma City, OK 73135 817-222-5600

(Southwestern Region) 2601 Meacham Boulevard, Fort Worth, TX 76137-4298 817-222-5600

Texas
2601 Meacham Boulevard, Fort Worth, TX 76137-4298 817-222-5600

Kelvin Solco -- ASW-600 | 817-222-5600

Washington
1601 Lind Avenue, S.W., Suite 315, Renton, WA 98057-3356 206-227-2600

Sarah Dalton -- ANM-600 | 425-227-2600

DOT 20.106 AIRPORT IMPROVEMENT PROGRAM "AIP"

Award: Project Grants; Advisory Services and Counseling

Purpose: To assist sponsors, owners, or operators of public-use airports in the development of a nationwide system of airports adequate to meet the needs of civil aeronautics.

Applicant Eligibility: States, counties, municipalities, U.S. Territories and possessions, and other public agencies including an Indian tribe or pueblo, the Republics of the Marshall Islands and Palau, and the Federated States of Micronesia are eligible for airport development grants if the airport on which the development is required is listed in the National Plan of Integrated Airport Systems (NPIAS). Certain local government organizations may be eligible for grants to implement noise planning and compatibility projects.

Beneficiary Eligibility: States, counties, municipalities, U.S. Territories and possessions, and other public agencies including an Indian tribe or pueblo, the Republics of the Marshall Islands and Palau, the Federated States of Micronesia, and private owners of reliever airports or airports having at least 2,500 passenger boarding annually and receiving scheduled passenger aircraft service.

Award Range/Average: FY 2017 AIP grant awards ranged from $25,110 to $49,541,344 with an average award of $1,903,369.

Funding: (Project Grants) FY 17 $3,332,799,409; FY 18 est $3,179,927,000; FY 19 est $3,451,289,997

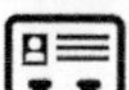

HQ: 800 Independence Avenue
Washington, DC 20591
Phone: 202-267-8744
Email: jonathan.dimartino@faa.gov
http://www.faa.gov/airports/aip

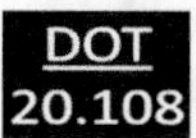

DOT 20.108 AVIATION RESEARCH GRANTS

Award: Project Grants; Use of Property, Facilities, and Equipment

Purpose: To encourage and support innovative, advanced, and applied research and development in areas of potential benefit to the growth of civil aviation.

Applicant Eligibility: The eligibility of applicants for the award of a research grant varies depending upon the nature of the proposer's organization as well as the character of work one proposes to perform. In general, colleges, universities, and other non-profit research institutions are eligible to qualify for research grants.

Beneficiary Eligibility: Colleges, Universities, and Non-profit research institutions are eligible to benefit from assistance.

Award Range/Average: Proposals received range from $15,000 to $5,000,0000; the average range is between $50,000 and $250,000, while larger proposals received are for multi-year research.

Funding: (Salaries and Expenses) FY 17 $36,961,441; FY 18 est $9,000,000; FY 19 FY 16 $8,500,000

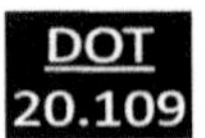

HQ: William J Hughes Technical Center Atlantic City International Airport
Atlantic City, NJ 8405
Phone: 609-485-7483

DOT 20.109 AIR TRANSPORTATION CENTERS OF EXCELLENCE "FAA Centers of Excellence"

Award: Project Grants; Use of Property, Facilities, and Equipment; Provision of Specialized Services

Purpose: To conduct long term research in critical and specific areas of aviation related technology.

Applicant Eligibility: FAA COE applicants are limited to colleges and universities with the financial resources to meet statutory requirements for matching Federal funds and maintenance of effort. Academic institutions may partner with industry affiliates, other public and private entities, government laboratories and other interested parties.

Beneficiary Eligibility: Recipients are limited to colleges and universities with the financial resources to meet statutory requirements for matching Federal grants and maintenance of effort. In conducting research, a Center of Excellence may contract with nonprofit research organizations and other appropriate persons.

Award Range/Average: Program started in fiscal year 1992. Grant assistance is expected to be a minimum of $500,000 per year for each Center, and may be augmented by tasks funded through IDIQ contract awards.

Funding: (Salaries and Expenses) FY 18 est $16,400,000; FY 17 est $24,600,000; FY 16 $22,500,000

HQ: Centers of Excellence Program Office FAA William J Hughes Technical Center Building 300 L28
Atlantic City International Airport, NJ 8405
Phone: 609-485-5043
Email: patricia.watts@faa.gov
http://www.faa.gov/go/coe

FEDERAL HIGHWAY ADMINISTRATION

Alabama
Joe D. Wilkerson | 500 Eastern Boulevard, Suite 200, Montgomery, AL 36117-2018 334-223-7370

Alaska
David Miller | 709 West 9th Street, Room 851 P.O. Box 21648, Juneau, AK 99802-1648 907-586-7180

Arizona
Robert E. Hollis | 234 North Central Avenue, Suite 330, Phoenix, AZ 85004-2220 602-379-3646

Arkansas
Sandra L. Otto | 700 West Capitol Avenue, Room 3130, Little Rock, AR 72201-3298 501-324-5625

California
Michael G. Ritchie | 980 9th Street, Suite 400, Sacramento, CA 95814-2724 916-498-5001

Central
Larry C. Smith | 555 Zang Street, Lakewood, CO 80228-1010 303-716-2000

Colorado
William C. Jones | 555 Zang Street, Room 250, Lakewood, CO 80228-1097 303-969-6730, Ext. 3

Connecticut
Donald J. West | 628-2 Hebron Avenue, Suite 303, Glastonbury, CT 06033-5007 860-659-6703, Ext. 3009

Delaware
Tommy D. Myers | 300 South New Street, Room 2101, Dover, DE 19904-0726 302-734-5323

District of Columbia
Gary L. Henderson | Union Center Plaza 820 First Street, N.E., Suite 750, Washington, DC 20002-4205 202-523-0163

Eastern
Melisa L. Ridenour | 21400 Ridgetop Circle Loudoun Technical Center, Sterling, VA 20166-6511 703-404-6201

Florida
James E. St. James | 227 North Bronough Street Room 2015, Tallahassee, FL 32301-1330 850-942-9650

Georgia
Larry Dreihaup | 61 Forsyth Street, S.W., Suite 17T100, Atlanta, GA 30303-3104 404-562-3630

Hawaii
Abraham Y. Wong | Prince Jonah Kuhio Kalanianaole Federal Building 300 Ala Moana Boulevard P.O. Box 50206, Room 3-306, Honolulu, HI 96850-5000 808-541-2700, Ext. 312

Idaho
Stephen Moreno | 3050 Lakeharbor Lane, Suite 126, Boise, ID 83703-6243 208-334-9180

Illinois
Norman R. Stoner | 3250 Executive Park Drive, Springfield, IL 62703-4514 217-492-4640

Indiana
Robert F. Talley | 575 North Pennsylvania Street, Room 254, Indianapolis, IN 46204-1576 317-226-7475

Iowa
Phil Barnes | 105 6th Street, Ames, IA 50010-6337 515-233-7300

Kansas
J. Michael Bowen | 3300 South Topeka Boulevard, Suite 1, Topeka, KS 66611-2237 785-267-7281

Kentucky
John C. Watts | Federal Building 330 West Broadway, Frankfort, KY 40601-1922 502-223-6720

Louisiana
William A. Sussmann | 5304 Flanders Drive, Suite A, Baton Rouge, LA 70808-4348 225-757-7600

Maine
Jonathan McDade | Edmund S. Muskie Federal Building 40 Western Avenue, Room 614, Augusta, ME 04330-6394 207-622-8487, Ext. 19

Maryland
Nelson Castellanos | 711 West 40th Street, Suite 220, Baltimore, MD 21211-2108 410-962-4440

Massachusetts
Stanley Gee | 55 Broadway, 10th Floor, Cambridge, MA 02142-1093 617-494-3657

Michigan
James J. Steele | Federal Building, Room 207 315 West Allegan Street, Room 207, Lansing, MI 48933-1528 517-377-1844

Minnesota
Alan R. Steger | Galtier Plaza, Box 75 380 Jackson Street, Suite 500, St. Paul, MN 55101-2904 651-291-6100

Mississippi
Andrew H. Hughes | 666 North Street, Suite 105, Jackson, MS 39202-3199 601-965-4215

Missouri
Allen Masuda | 209 Adams Street, Jefferson City, MO 65101-3203 573-636-7104

Montana
Janice W. Brown | 2880 Skyway Drive, Helena, MT 59602-1230 406-449-5303, Ext. 235

Nebraska
William Brownell | Federal Building, Room 220 100 Centennial Mall North, Lincoln, NE 68508-3851 402-437-5765

Nevada
Susan Kelepar | 705 North Plaza Street, Suite 220, Carson City, NV 89701-0602 775-687-1204

New Hampshire
Kathleen O. Laffey | 279 Pleasant Street, Suite 204, Concord, NH 03301-7502 603-228-0417

New Jersey
Dennis L. Merida | 840 Bear Tavern Road, Suite 310, West Trenton, NJ 08628-1019 609-637-4200

New Mexico
J. Don Martinez | 604 West San Mateo Road, Santa Fe, NM 87505-3920 505-820-2021

New York
Robert E. Arnold | Leo W. O'Brien Federal Building, Room 719 Clinton Avenue and N. Pearl Street, Albany, NY 12207 518-431-4125

North Carolina
John Sullivan | 310 New Bern Avenue, Suite 410, Raleigh, NC 27601-1441 919-856-4346

North Dakota
Al Radliff | 1471 Interstate Loop, Bismarck, ND 58503-0567 701-250-4204

Ohio
Dennis Decker | 200 North High Street, Room 328, Columbus, OH 43215 614-280-6896

Oklahoma
Walter J. Kudzia | 300 N. Meridlan, Suite 105S, Oklahoma City, OK 73107-6560 405-605-6011

Oregon
David O. Cox | The Equitable Center 530 Center Street, N.E., Suite 100, Salem, OR 97301-3740 503-399-5749

Pennsylvania
James A. Cheatham | 228 Walnut Street, Room 558, Harrisburg, PA 17101-1720 717-221-3461

Puerto Rico
Lubin M. Quipones | Frederico Degetau Federal Building 330 Carlos Chardon Ave., Room 210, San Juan, PR 00916 787-766-5600, Ext. 223

Rhode Island
Lucy Garliauskos | 380 Westminster Mall, 5th Floor, Providence, RI 02903-3246 401-528-4560

South Carolina
Robert L. Lee | Strom Thurmond Federal Building 1835 Assembly Street, Suite 1270, Columbia, SC 29201-2483 803-765-5411

South Dakota
John Rohlf | 116 East Dakota Avenue, Pierre, SD 57501-3110 605-224-8033

Tennessee
Bobby Blackmon | 640 Grassmere Park Road, Suite 112, Nashville, TN 37211-3658 615-781-5770

Texas
Curtis Dan Reagan | Federal Office Building 300 East 8th Street, Room 826, Austin, TX 78701-3233 512-536-5900

Utah
David Gibbs | 2520 West 4700 South, Suite 9A, Salt Lake City, UT 84118-1847 801-963-0182

Vermont
Charles E. Basner | Federal Building 87 State Street PO Box 568, Montpelier, VT 05601-0568 802-828-4423

Virginia
Roberto Fonseca Martinez | 400 North 8th Street, Room 750 P.O. Box 10249, Richmond, VA 23240-0249 804-775-3320

Washington
Daniel M. Mathis | Evergreen Plaza 711 South Capitol Way, Suite 501, Olympia, WA 98501-1284 360-753-9480

West Virginia
Thomas J. Smith | Geary Plaza 700 Washington Street East, Suite 200, Charleston, WV 25301-1604 304-347-5928

Western
Ronald W. Carmichael | 610 East Fifth Street, Vancouver, WA 98661-3801 360-619-7700

Wisconsin
Bruce E. Matzke | Highpoint Office Park 567 D'Onofrio Drive, Madison, WI 53719-2814 608-829-7500

Wyoming
Philip E. Miller | 2617 E. Lincolnway, Suite D, Cheyenne, WY 82001-5662 307-772-2101, Ext.40

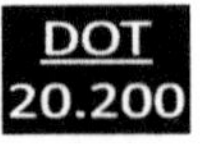

HIGHWAY RESEARCH AND DEVELOPMENT PROGRAM
"Highway Research and Development Program Surface Transportation Research, Development, and Technology"

Award: Project Grants

Purpose: To carry out the highway research and development program as authorized by the FAST Act and conduct research needed to maintain and improve our vital transportation infrastructure.

Applicant Eligibility: Varies by project.

Beneficiary Eligibility: State Departments of Transportation, Local Governments, General Public

Award Range/Average: Varies by project.

Funding: (Cooperative Agreements) FY 17 $104,187,924; FY 18 est $104,187,924; FY 19 est $104,665,850; FY 16 $98,168,571

HQ: 1200 New Jersey Avenue SE
Washington, DC 20590
Phone: 202-366-4211
Email: aimee.drewry@dot.gov
http://www.fhwa.dot.gov

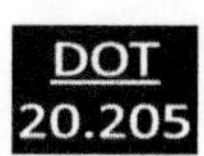

DOT 20.205 HIGHWAY PLANNING AND CONSTRUCTION "Federal-Aid Highway Program, Federal Lands Highway Program)"

Award: Formula Grants; Project Grants

Purpose: This Assistance Listing encompasses several transportation programs such as the Federal-aid Highway Program, The Federal Lands Highway Program, The FAST Act established two new freight programs, The Highway Infrastructure Programs in the Department of Transportation Appropriations Act, 2018.

Applicant Eligibility: By law, the Federal-aid highway program is a federally assisted State administered program that requires each State to have a suitably equipped and organized transportation department. Therefore, most projects are administered by or through State transportation departments (State DOTs).

Beneficiary Eligibility: State transportation departments, and in some instances, Federal agencies, other State agencies, local agencies, and private, community-based organizations.

Award Range/Average: Federal-aid highway funds are provided to States on an annual basis, by a combination of statutory formula and discretionary allocation. The most recent authorization act is the Fixing America's Surface Transportation Act (FAST Act).

Funding: (Salaries and Expenses) FY 17 $42,108,275,885; FY 18 est $43,090,835,692; FY 19 est $45,633,101,183; FY 16 $41,666,093,741; - Part of this funding is used for salaries and expenses, but these obligation totals are not just for salaries.

HQ: 1200 New Jersey Avenue SE
Washington, DC 20590
Phone: 202-366-4211
Email: aimee.drewry@dot.gov
http://www.fhwa.dot.gov

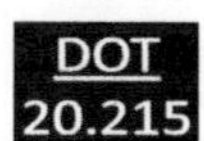

DOT 20.215 HIGHWAY TRAINING AND EDUCATION

Award: Cooperative Agreements; Training

Purpose: Encompasses several transportation training and education programs.

Applicant Eligibility: Depends on the program: 1) NHI Training Program: Employees of State and local transportation agencies, private sector transportation company employees are eligible to participate in NHI courses. 2) DDETFP: Undergraduate (juniors and seniors at Minority Institutes of Higher Education (MIHE)) and graduate students matriculating full-time at a U.S. university or college in a transportation-related discipline participate.

Beneficiary Eligibility: N/A

Award Range/Average: N/A

Funding: Project Grants (Cooperative Agreements) FY 17 $15,233,879; FY 18 est $15,233,879; FY 19 est $15,303,760; FY 16 $23,410,493

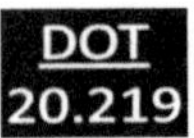

HQ: 1310 N Courthouse Road, Suite 300
Arlington, VA 22201
Phone: 703-235-1263
Email: virginia.tsu@dot.gov
http://www.fhwa.dot.gov/innovativeprograms/centers/workforce_dev/professionals.aspx

DOT 20.219

RECREATIONAL TRAILS PROGRAM

Award: Formula Grants

Purpose: The purpose of this program is to provide funds to the States to develop and maintain recreational trails and trail-related facilities for both nonmotorized and motorized recreational trail uses.

Applicant Eligibility: The FHWA may enter into contracts with for-profit organizations or contracts, partnerships, or cooperative agreements with other government agencies, institutions of higher learning, or nonprofit organizations using its administrative funds. For funds available to the States: the Governor of each State must designate the State agency or agencies responsible for administering this program.

Beneficiary Eligibility: Same as Applicant Eligibility.

Award Range/Average: Awards ranged from $816,847 to $5,698,627; the average was $1,647,316.

Funding: (Formula Grants (Apportionments)) FY 17 $83,165,826; FY 18 est $80,000,000; FY 19 est $80,000,000; FY 16 $69,579,184

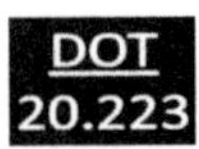

HQ: 1200 New Jersey Avenue SE
Washington, DC 20590
Phone: 202-366-5013
Email: christopher.douwes@dot.gov
http://www.fhwa.dot.gov/environment/recreational_trails

DOT 20.223

TRANSPORTATION INFRASTRUCTURE FINANCE AND INNOVATION ACT (TIFIA) PROGRAM "TIFIA Credit Program"

Award: Direct Loans; Guaranteed/Insured Loans

Purpose: To finance projects of national or regional significance by filling market gaps and leveraging substantial non-Federal and private co-investment.

Applicant Eligibility: Public or private entities seeking to finance, design, construct, own, or operate an eligible surface transportation project may apply for TIFIA assistance. Examples of such entities include state departments of transportation; local governments; transit agencies; special authorities; special districts; railroad companies; and private firms or consortia that may include companies specializing in engineering, construction, materials, and/or the operation of transportation facilities.

Beneficiary Eligibility: Same as Applicant Eligibility.

Award Range/Average: No Data Available.

Funding: (Salaries and Expenses) FY 17 est $3,982,000,000; FY 18 est $3,736,000,000.

HQ: 1200 New Jersey Avenue SE, Room E
Washington, DC 20590
Phone: 202-366-1059
Email: dimitri.kombolias@dot.gov
http://www.transportation.gov/buildamerica/programs-services/tifia

DOT 20.224 FEDERAL LANDS ACCESS PROGRAM "Access Program or FLAP"

Award: Formula Grants; Project Grants

Purpose: The goal of the Federal Lands Access Program is to improve transportation facilities that provide access to, are adjacent to, or are located within Federal lands.

Applicant Eligibility: Only the owner of the affected transportation asset or assets may submit an application.

Beneficiary Eligibility: State transportation departments, other State agencies, local agencies, and Federal agencies.

Award Range/Average: No Data Available.

Funding: (Formula Grants) FY 17 $241,067,936; FY 18 est $241,099,883; FY 19 est $251,750,000; FY 16 $232,009,953.

HQ: 1200 New Jersey Avenue SE
Washington, DC 20590
Phone: 202-493-0271
Email: frances.ramirez@dot.gov
http://flh.fhwa.dot.gov/programs/flap/reports

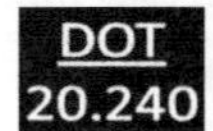

DOT 20.240 FUEL TAX EVASION-INTERGOVERNMENTAL ENFORCEMENT EFFORT "Fuel Tax Evasion"

Award: Project Grants

Purpose: The purpose of this program is to increase intergovernmental activities and enforcement efforts among public agencies to reduce Federal and State fuel tax evasion.

Applicant Eligibility: States, and the District of Columbia,

Beneficiary Eligibility: States, and the District of Columbia.

Award Range/Average: Minimum: $10,000; Maximum $250,000

Funding: (Project Grants) FY 17 $7,626,160; FY 18 est $4,000,000; FY 19 est $4,000,000; FY 16 $738,057

HQ: Office of Highway Policy Information (HPPI) 1200 New Jersey Avenue SE
Washington, DC 20590
Phone: 202-366-9234
Email: michael.dougherty@dot.gov
http://www.fhwa.dot.gov/policy/otps/fueltax.htm

FEDERAL MOTOR CARRIER SAFETY ADMINISTRATION

Alabama
Judy VanLuchene | 500 Eastern Boulevard, Suite 200, Montgomery, AL 36117-2018 334-223-7244

Alaska
John Quartuccio | 605 W. 4th Avenue, Room 249 Historic Federal Building, Anchorage, AK 99501 907-271-4068

Arizona
Eric Ice | 234 North Central Avenue, Suite 305, Phoenix, AZ 85004-2002 602-379-6851

Arkansas
J. Mark Westmoreland | 700 West Capitol Avenue, Room 3130, Little Rock, AR 72201-3298 501-324-5050

California
Richard Brennan | 980 9th Street, Sacramento, CA 95814-2724 916-498-5050

Colorado
William Copley | 555 Zang Street, Room 264, Lakewood, CO 80228-1097 303-969-6748

Connecticut
Jeffrey Cimahosky | 628-2 Hebron Avenue, Suite 303, Glastonbury, CT 06033-5007 860-659-6700

Delaware
Veron Kirkendoll | 300 South New Street, Room 2101, Dover, DE 19904-0726 302-734-8173

District of Columbia
Taft Kelly | Union Center Plaza 820 First Street, N.E., Suite 750, Washington, DC 20002-4205 202-523-0178

Florida
James Gregg | 227 North Bronough Street Room 2060, Tallahassee, FL 32301-1330 850-942-9338

Georgia
Tom Marlow | 61 Forsyth Street, S.W., Suite 17T85, Atlanta, GA 30303-3104 404-562-3620

Hawaii
Wendy Burke | Prince Jonah Kuhio Kalanianaole Federal Building 300 Ala Moana Boulevard, Room 3-243 P.O. Box 50206, Honolulu, HI 96850-5000 808-541-2700

Idaho
John Francis | 3050 Lakeharbor Lane, Suite 126, Boise, ID 83703-6243 208-334-1842

Illinois
John Mulcare | 3250 Executive Park Drive, Springfield, IL 62703-4514 217-492-4608

Indiana
Kenneth Stickland | 575 North Pennsylvania Street, Room 261, Indianapolis, IN 46204-1570 317-226-7474

Iowa
Kent Fleming | 105 6th Street, Ames, IA 50010-6337 515-233-7400

Kansas
Teri Graham | 3300 South Topeka Boulevard, Suite 1, Topeka, KS 66611-2237 785-267-7288

Kentucky
Buddy Yount | 330 West Broadway, Frankfort, KY 40601-1922 502-223-6779

Louisiana
Sterlin Williams | 5304 Flanders Drive, Suite A, Baton Rouge, LA 70808-4348 225-757-7640

Maine
Gerald Amato, Acting | Edmund S. Muskie Federal Building 40 Western Avenue, Room 601, Augusta, ME 04330-6394 207-622-8358

Maryland
Terry Runge-Erle | 711 West 40th Street, Suite 220, Baltimore, MD 21211-2100 410-962-2889

Massachusetts
Richard Bates | 55 Broadway, Room I-35, Cambridge, MA 02142-1093 617-494-2770

Michigan
Patrick Muinich | 315 West Allegan Street, Room 205, Lansing, MI 48933-1528 517-377-1866

Minnesota
Daniel Drexler | Galtier Plaza, Box 75 175 E. 5th Street, Suite 500, St. Paul, MN 55101-2904 651-291-6150

Mississippi
Benny Wood | 666 North Street, Suite 103, Jackson, MS 39202-3199 601-965-4219

Missouri
Joseph Boyd | 209 Adams Street, Jefferson City, MO 65101-3203 573-636-3246

Montana
Kristin Phillipps | 2880 Skyway Drive, Helena, MT 59602-1230 406-449-5304

Nebraska
Elyse Mueller | 100 Centennial Mall North, Room 220, Lincoln, NE 68508-3851 402-437-5986

Nevada
Bill Bensmiller | 705 North Plaza Street, Suite 220, Carson City, NV 89701-0602 775-687-5335

New Hampshire
Timothy Cotter | 279 Pleasant Street, Room 202 Federal Building, Concord, NH 03301-7502 603-228-3112

New Jersey
Christopher Rotondo | 840 Bear Tavern Road, Suite 310, West Trenton, NJ 08628-1019 609-637-4222

New Mexico
Martha Brooks | 2400 Louisiana Boulevard N.E. AFC-5, Suite 520, Albuquerque, NM 87110 505-346-7858

New York
Brian Temperine | Leo W. O'Brien Federal Building, Room 719 Clinton Avenue and N. Pearl Street, Albany, NY 12207 518-431-4145

North Carolina
Christopher Harley | 310 New Bern Avenue, Suite 468, Raleigh, NC 27601-1441 919-856-4378

North Dakota
Jeffrey Jensen | 1471 Interstate Loop, Bismarck, ND 58503-0567 701-250-4346

Ohio
Steven Mattioli | 200 North High Street, Room 328, Columbus, OH 43215 614-280-5657

Oklahoma
Mac Kirk | 300 N. Meridan, Suite 106-S, Oklahoma City, OK 73107-6560 405-605-6047

Oregon
Andrew Eno | 530 Center Street, N.E., Suite 100, Salem, OR 97301-3740 503-399-5775

Pennsylvania
Patrick Quigley | 228 Walnut Street, Room 536, Harrisburg, PA 17101-1720 717-221-4443

Puerto Rico
Enid Martinez | US Courthouse & Federal Building Carlos Chardon Street, Room 329, Hato Rey, PR 00918 787-766-5985

Rhode Island
Robert Molla | 380 Westminster Mall, Room 547, Providence, RI 02903-3246 401-528-4578

South Carolina
Curtis Thomas | 1835 Assembly Street, Suite 1253, Columbia, SC 29201-2430 803-765-5414

South Dakota
Mark Gilmore | 116 East Dakota Street, Pierre, SD 57501-3110 605-224-8202

Tennessee
Richard Gobbell | 640 Grassmere Park Road, Suite 111, Nashville, TN 37211 615-781-5781

Texas
David Martin | Federal Office Building 300 East 8th Street, Room 826, Austin, TX 78701-3233 512-536-5980

Utah
Robert Kelleher | 2520 West 4700 South, Suite 9B, Salt Lake City, UT 84118-1847 801-963-0096

Vermont
Gerard Amato | 87 State Street, Room 216, Montpelier, VT 05602-2954 802-828-4480

Virginia
Craig Feister | 400 North 8th Street, Room 750, Richmond, VA 23240 804-775-3322

Washington
Roger Kraft | Evergreen Plaza 711 South Capitol Way, Suite 501, Olympia, WA 98501-1284 360-753-9875

West Virginia
Michael Myers | 700 Washington Street East, Suite 205, Charleston, WV 25301-1604 304-347-5935

Wisconsin
William Vickery | 567 D'Onofrio Drive, Suite 101, Madison, WI 53719-2814 608-829-7534

Wyoming
Gary Lowe | 1916 Evans Avenue, Cheyenne, WY 82001-3764 307-772-2305

DOT 20.218 MOTOR CARRIER SAFETY ASSISTANCE "MCSAP "

Award: Formula Grants

Purpose: Provides financial assistance to States to reduce the number and severity of crashes and hazardous materials incidents involving commercial motor vehicles (CMV).

Applicant Eligibility: All States, the District of Columbia, the Commonwealth of Puerto Rico, the Commonwealth of the Northern Mariana Islands, American Samoa, Guam, and the U.S. Virgin Islands, are eligible for MCSAP. The MCSAP grants are provided annually to the State's MCSAP lead agency.

Beneficiary Eligibility: Under the Basic and Incentive grant programs, a State lead MCSAP agency, as designated by its Governor, is eligible to apply for Basic and Incentive grant funding by submitting a commercial vehicle safety plan (CVSP), in accordance with the provisions of Title 49 of the Code of Federal Regulations (CFR) Part 350.201 and 205.

Award Range/Average: No Data Available.

Funding: (Salaries and Expenses) FY 17 $288,211,000; FY 18 est $294,416,500; FY 19 est $299,735,500; FY 16 $168,275,000

HQ: 1200 New Jersey Avenue SE
Washington, DC 20590
Phone: 202-366-0621
http://www.fmcsa.dot.gov/mission/grants

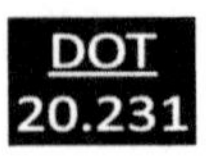

DOT 20.231 PERFORMANCE AND REGISTRATION INFORMATION SYSTEMS MANAGEMENT "PRISM"

Award: Project Grants

Purpose: To determine the safety fitness of a motor carrier or registrant when applying for registration or while the registration is in effect.

Applicant Eligibility: The FMCSA may award these grants to the agencies of States, the District of Columbia, the Commonwealth of Puerto Rico, the Commonwealth of the Northern Mariana Islands, American Samoa, Guam, and the U.S. Virgin Islands. According to 49 U.S.C.

Beneficiary Eligibility: Eligible applicants include State agencies located in one of the fifty States, the District of Columbia, Puerto Rico, Northern Mariana Islands, American Samoa, Guam, and the U.S. Virgin Islands. Applicants must work on highway traffic safety activities and must demonstrate a capacity to work with highway traffic safety stakeholders.

Award Range/Average: Awards can range from $100,000 to $750,000

Funding: (Project Grants) FY 18 est $0; FY 16 $5,000,000; FY 17 est $0; - Awards are no longer being made under this CFDA; however, pre-existing grants will remain active until project completion and/or period of performance on the individual grant agreements expires.

HQ: 1200 New Jersey Avenue SE W66-443
Washington, DC 20590
Phone: 202-366-1736

Email: lisa.ensley@dot.gov

http://www.fmcsa.dot.gov/safety-security/prism/prism.htm

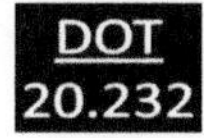

COMMERCIAL DRIVER'S LICENSE PROGRAM IMPLEMENTATION GRANT "CDLPI"

Award: Cooperative Agreements; Project Grants

Purpose: To assist States in complying with CDL requirements and dedicate funding to priority activities for research, development and testing, demonstration projects, public education, and other special activities and projects relating to commercial drivers licensing.

Applicant Eligibility: States may receive grant funds to comply with the requirements of section 31311 of SAFETEA-LU or if making good faith efforts toward substantial compliance with the requirements of section 31311 and 31313 receive grant funds to improve implementation of the commercial driver's license program. States, local governments, and other persons for projects involving research, development, demonstration projects, public education, and other special activities and projects relating to commercial driver licensing and motor vehicle safety that are of benefit to all jurisdictions of the United States or are designed to address national safety concerns and circumstances.

Beneficiary Eligibility: State (includes District of Columbia, public institutions of higher education and hospitals). Local (includes State-designated Indian Tribes, excludes institutions of higher education and hospitals). Public nonprofit institution/organization, other private institutions/organizations, anyone/general public.

Award Range/Average: $20,000 - $1,500,000

Funding: (Project Grants) FY 17 $31,200,000; FY 18 est $31,800,000; FY 19 est $0; FY 16 $30,673,509; - Salary and Expenses -- In part or in full; applications may include other eligible costs such as travel, supplies, contractual expenses, and indirect costs.

HQ: FMCSA Grants Management Office 1200 New Jersey Avenue SE

Washington, DC 20590

Phone: 202-366-0621

Email: cim.weiss@dot.gov

http://www.fmcsa.dot.gov/grants/cdl-program-implementation-grant/commercial-drivers-license-program-implementation-grant

BORDER ENFORCEMENT GRANTS

Award: Project Grants

Purpose: To ensure motor carriers operating commercial vehicles entering the United States from a foreign country are in compliance with commercial vehicle safety standards and regulations, financial responsibility regulations and registration requirements of the United States, and to ensure drivers of those vehicles are qualified and properly licenses to operate the commercial vehicle.

Applicant Eligibility: Entities and States that share a land border with a foreign country.

Beneficiary Eligibility: States that share a land border with a foreign country (Entities and Accredited public institutions of higher education). The States of Alaska, Arizona, California, Idaho, Maine, Michigan, Minnesota, Montana, New Hampshire, New Mexico, New York, North Dakota, Texas, Vermont and

Washington, and entities and local governments within these enumerated States are eligible to receive funding.

Award Range/Average: For Border Enforcement awards ranged from $22,000 to $18,000,000.

Funding: (Project Grants (Discretionary)) FY 17 est $0; FY 18 est $0; FY 16 $32,000,000; - Awards are no longer being made under this CFDA; however, pre-existing grants will remain active until project completion and/or period of performance on the individual grant agreements expires.

HQ: 1200 New Jersey Avenue SE W66-443
Washington, DC 20590
Phone: 202-366-1736
Email: lisa.ensley@dot.gov
http://www.fmcsa.dot.gov

SAFETY DATA IMPROVEMENT PROGRAM "SaDIP"

Award: Project Grants

Purpose: To fund State programs designed to improve the overall quality of commercial motor vehicle (CMV) data in accordance with the FMCSA State Safety Data Quality (SSDQ) measures, specifically to increase the timeliness, efficiency, accuracy and completeness of processes and systems related to the collection and analysis of large truck and bus crash and inspection data.

Applicant Eligibility: A State shall be eligible for a grant under this section in a fiscal year if the Secretary determines that the State has (1) conducted a comprehensive audit of its commercial motor vehicle safety data system within the preceding 2 years; (2) developed a plan that identifies and prioritizes its commercial motor vehicle safety data needs and goals; and (3) identified performance-based measures to determine progress toward those goals. Eligible applicants include State Departments of Public Safety, Departments of Transportation, or State Law Enforcement Agencies in any of the several States of the United States, the District of Columbia, and the Commonwealth of Puerto Rico, any territory or possession of the United States, or any agency or instrumentality of a State exclusive of local governments.

Beneficiary Eligibility: Any of the several States of the United States, the District of Columbia, the Commonwealth of Puerto Rico, any territory or possession of the United States, or any agency or instrumentality of a State exclusive of local governments. The term does not include any public and Indian housing agency under United States Housing Act of 1937.

Award Range/Average: Range $5,000 - $500,000; Average award $250,000

Funding: (Project Grants) FY 17 $0; FY 18 est $0; FY 19 est $0; FY 16 $0; - Awards are no longer being made.

HQ: 1200 New Jersey Avenue SE W66-443
Washington, DC 20590
Phone: 202-366-1736
Email: lisa.ensley@dot.gov
http://www.fmcsa.dot.gov/mission/policy/safety-data-improvement-program-2015-2016-biennial-report-congress

COMMERCIAL MOTOR VEHICLE OPERATOR SAFETY TRAINING GRANTS "CMVOST"

Award: Project Grants

Purpose: To help reduce the severity and number of crashes on U.S. roads involving commercial motor vehicles, as defined in 49 U.S.C. 31301, and to assist current or former members of the U.S. Armed Forces, including National Guard and Reservists to obtain a CDL.

Applicant Eligibility: Eligible applicants must be accredited by a government organization such as the Department of Education.

Beneficiary Eligibility: Same as Applicant Eligibility.

Award Range/Average: Fiscal Year 2017: The average award was $110,000 Fiscal Year 2018: N/A. Applications are still under review.

Funding: (Project Grants (Discretionary)) FY 17 $1,000,000; FY 18 est $1,000,000; FY 19 est $0; FY 16 $996,947

HQ: FMCSA Grants Management Office 1200 New Jersey Avenue SE

Washington, DC 20590

Phone: 202-366-0621

Email: rikita.jarrett@dot.gov

http://www.fmcsa.dot.gov/mission/grants/fy2018-cmvost-nofo

MOTOR CARRIER SAFETY ASSISTANCE HIGH PRIORITY ACTIVITIES GRANTS AND COOPERATIVE AGREEMENTS "High Priority (HP) Grant"

Award: Project Grants

Purpose: To support, enrich, and augment Commercial Motor Vehicle (CMV) safety programs through partnerships with States, local governments, Federally recognized Indian tribes, other political jurisdictions, and other persons to carry out high priority activities and projects.

Applicant Eligibility: HP grants are eligible to any State agency, local government (including county, city, township, special district, and Federally-recognized Native American tribal governments), institutions of higher education (public, private, and State-controlled), non-profit organizations with or without having a 501(c)(3) status with the Internal Revenue Service, for-profit entities (including small businesses), and other persons. Other persons is defined as an entity not included above and may not be an individual, foreign entity, hospital, public/Indian housing authority, or Federal institution.

Beneficiary Eligibility: FMCSA may award these grants to the agencies of States, the District of Columbia, the Commonwealth of Puerto Rico, the Commonwealth of the Northern Mariana Islands, American Samoa, Guam, and the U.S. Virgin Islands.

Award Range/Average: Awards range from $50,000 to $1,000,000.

Funding: (Project Grants) FY 17 $41,557,857; FY 18 est $42,452,500; FY 19 est $43,340,000; FY 16 $15,000,000

HQ: 1200 New Jersey Avenue SE
Washington, DC 20590
Phone: 202-366-0621
http://www.fmcsa.dot.gov/mission/grants

FEDERAL RAILROAD ADMINISTRATION

Region I (Northeastern)
Mark H. McKeon, Regional Administrator | 55 Broadway, Room 1077, Cambridge, MA 02142 617-494-2302

Region II (Eastern)
David R. Myers, Regional Administrator | 2 International Plaza, Suite 550, Philadelphia, PA 19113 610-521-8200

Region III (Southern)
L.F. Dennin, Regional Administrator | Atlanta Federal Center, Suite 16T20 61 Forsyth Street, S.W., Atlanta, GA 30303-3104 404-562-3800

Region IV (Central)
Hiram J. Walker, Regional Administrator | 111 North Canal Street, Suite 655, Chicago, IL 60606 312-353-6203

Region V (Southwestern)
John F. Megary, Regional Administrator | 8701 Bedford Euless Road, Suite 425, Hurst, TX 76053 817-284-8142

Region VI (Midwestern)
Darrell J. Tisor, Regional Administrator | 901 Locust Street, Suite 464, Kansas City, MO 64106-2095 816-329-3840

Region VII (Western)
Alvin Settje, Regional Administrator | 801 I Street, Suite 466, Sacramento, CA 95814-2559 916-498-6540

Region VIII (Northwestern)
Dick Clairmont, Regional Administrator | Murdock Executive Plaza, Suite 650 703 Broadway, Vancouver, WA 98660 360-696-7536

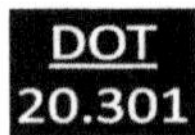

RAILROAD SAFETY

Award: Project Grants
Purpose: Reduces railroad-related casualties and accidents.
Applicant Eligibility: Anyone concerned with railroad safety.
Beneficiary Eligibility: General public.
Award Range/Average: The range was between 986 to 1,910,785, and the average was 440,764.
Funding: (Project Grants) FY 17 $18,170,000; FY 18 est $13,200,000; FY 19 est $1,360,000; FY 16 $1,105,000

HQ: 1200 New Jersey Avenue SE
Washington, DC 20590
Phone: 202-493-6377
Email: michael.longley@dot.gov
http://www.fra.dot.gov

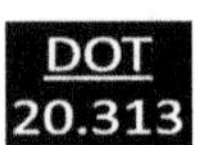

RAILROAD RESEARCH AND DEVELOPMENT

Award: Project Grants

Purpose: To foster long-range enhancement of the Federal Railroad Administration's program of research in support of rail safety by developing cooperative research relationships.

Applicant Eligibility: Applicants can be major academic and industry research institutions with backgrounds in the rail transportation arena. A minimum of 5 years of railroad or railroad related research experience is typically required.

Beneficiary Eligibility: No restrictions.

Award Range/Average: Range for FY 2017 was $100,073 to $1,900,000, with an average of $675,018.

Funding: (Cooperative Agreements) FY 17 $2,700,073; FY 18 est $2,000,000; FY 19 est $1,000,000

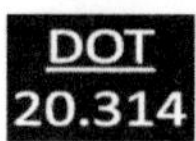

HQ: 1200 New Jersey Avenue SE
Washington, DC 20590
Phone: 202-493-6377
Email: michael.longley@dot.gov
http://www.fra.dot.gov

DOT 20.314 RAILROAD DEVELOPMENT

Award: Project Grants

Purpose: To provide financial assistance for: planning and developing railroad corridors (including environmental studies), purchasing rail equipment, rail line relocation and improvement projects, construction projects that improve rail lines, enhance service, and add capacity to the national rail system.

Applicant Eligibility: State governments, Regional and local governments, For-profit organizations, such as railroads.

Beneficiary Eligibility: Same as Applicant Eligibility.

Award Range/Average: Grants within these programs ranged from $190,000 to $40,200,000 in FY 2017, with an average of $7,727,689.

Funding: (Cooperative Agreements) FY 17 $25,904,800; FY 18 est $44,049,200; FY 19 est $3,000,000

HQ: 1200 New Jersey Avenue SE
Washington, DC 20590
Phone: 202-493-6377
Email: michael.longley@dot.gov
http://www.fra.dot.gov

DOT 20.315 NATIONAL RAILROAD PASSENGER CORPORATION GRANTS "Amtrak Grants"

Award: Project Grants

Purpose: To provide financial assistance to support the operation of and capital investment in intercity passenger rail service.

Applicant Eligibility: As directed by authorizing and appropriating statute, assistance is available only to the National Railroad Passenger Corporation.

Beneficiary Eligibility: Same as Applicant Eligibility.

Award Range/Average: Awards under this program ranged from $1,250,000 to $1,159,165,000 in FY 2018 and depend on the amount and break down of assistance made available through specific appropriation laws.

Funding: (Project Grants (Cooperative Agreements)) FY 17 $1,489,652,000; FY 18 est $1,946,892,000; FY 19 est $727,207,513; FY 16 $1,390,892,500

HQ: 1200 New Jersey Avenue SE
Washington, DC 20590
Phone: 202-493-6377
Email: michael.longley@dot.gov
http://www.fra.dot.gov

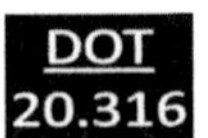

RAILROAD REHABILITATION AND IMPROVEMENT FINANCING PROGRAM "RRIF Loan Program"

Award: Direct Loans; Guaranteed/Insured Loans

Purpose: Provides direct loans and loan guarantees to State and local governments, interstate compacts consented to by Congress under section 410(a) of the Amtrak Reform and Accountability Act of 1997 (49 U.S.C. 24101).

Applicant Eligibility: Eligible borrowers include railroads, state and local governments, government-sponsored authorities and corporations, joint ventures that include at least one railroad, and limited option freight shippers who intend to construct a new rail connection.

Beneficiary Eligibility: The beneficiaries of the Program will be the State or local government organizations, railroad, joint ventures that include a railroad, and limited option freight shippers that will receive the financial assistance to permit them to complete the specified projects.

Award Range/Average: No new loans were made in FY 2017. One new loan was issued in FY 2018 for 220,000,000.

Funding: (Direct Loans) FY 17 $0; FY 18 est $220,000,000; FY 19 est $600,000,000

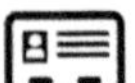

HQ: 1200 New Jersey Avenue SE W12-426
Washington, DC 20590
Phone: 202-366-1059
Email: duane.callendar@dot.gov
http://www.transportation.gov/buildamerica/programs-services/rrif

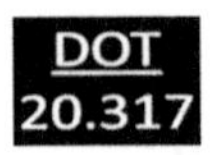

CAPITAL ASSISTANCE TO STATES - INTERCITY PASSENGER RAIL SERVICE "IPR Program"

Award: Project Grants

Purpose: To provide financial assistance to fund capital improvements necessary to support improved or new intercity passenger rail service.

Applicant Eligibility: Profit organization, Other private institutions/organizations, State & Transportation

Beneficiary Eligibility: The general public, both users and non-users of intercity passenger rail service. State departments of transportation and other public agencies, although private transportation companies may participate through contractual arrangements with a State department of transportation.

Award Range/Average: The range was $80,875 to $80,875, and the average was $80,875.

Funding: (Project Grants (Cooperative Agreements)) FY 17 $80,875; FY 18 est $0; FY 19 est $0; FY 16 $7,189,643.

HQ: Management Division 1200 New Jersey Avenue SE
Washington, DC 20590
Phone: 202-493-6377
Email: michael.longley@dot.gov
http://www.fra.dot.gov

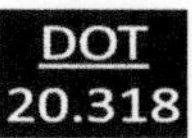

MAGLEV PROJECT SELECTION PROGRAM - SAFETEA-LU

Award: Cooperative Agreements

Purpose: Provides financial assistance for a demonstration magnetic levitation transportation project.

Applicant Eligibility: Only for existing Maglev projects.

Beneficiary Eligibility: State governments.

Award Range/Average: One obligation beyond FY 2019 is planned for $13,800,000.

Funding: (Cooperative Agreements) FY 17 $0; FY 18 est $0; FY 19 est $0; FY 16 $27,800,000

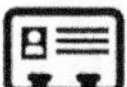

HQ: Office of Program Delivery 1200 New Jersey Avenue SE
Washington, DC 20590
Phone: 202-493-6377
Email: michael.longley@dot.gov
http://www.fra.dot.gov

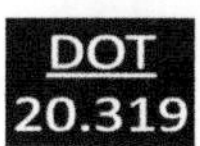

HIGH-SPEED RAIL CORRIDORS AND INTERCITY PASSENGER RAIL SERVICE – CAPITAL ASSISTANCE GRANTS "HSR/IPR Program"

Award: Cooperative Agreements; Project Grants

Purpose: To assist in financing the capital costs of facilities, infrastructure, and equipment necessary to provide or improve high-speed rail and intercity passenger rail service.

Applicant Eligibility: Profit organization, Other private institutions/organizations, State & Transportation

Beneficiary Eligibility: The general public, both users and non-users of intercity passenger rail service. State departments of transportation and other public agencies, although private transportation companies may participate through contractual arrangements with a State department of transportation.

Award Range/Average: There was one award in FY 2017 for $2,000,000.

Funding: (Project Grants) FY 17 $2,000,000; FY 18 est $0; FY 19 est $3,000,000; FY 16 $5,218,600

HQ: Office of Program Delivery 1200 New Jersey Avenue SE
Washington, DC 20590
Phone: 202-493-6377
Email: michael.longley@dot.gov
http://www.fra.dot.gov

DOT 20.320 RAIL LINE RELOCATION AND IMPROVEMENT "Rail Line Relocation"

Award: Project Grants

Purpose: Provides financial assistance for rail line relocation and improvement projects.

Applicant Eligibility: Government - General and Transportation

Beneficiary Eligibility: States, Political Subdivisions of States, and the District of Columbia

Award Range/Average: No awards were made in FY 2017.

Funding: (Project Grants (Cooperative Agreements)) FY 17 $0; FY 18 est $0; FY 19 est $0; FY 16 $3,000,000

HQ: 1200 New Jersey Avenue SE
Washington, DC 20590
Phone: 202-493-6377
Email: michael.longley@dot.gov
http://www.fra.dot.gov

RAILROAD SAFETY TECHNOLOGY GRANTS

Award: Project Grants

Purpose: To facilitate the deployment of train control technologies, train control component technologies, processor-based technologies, electronically controlled pneumatic brakes, rail integrity inspection systems, rail integrity warning systems, switch position indicators and monitors.

Applicant Eligibility: There is no additional information.

Beneficiary Eligibility: Passenger and freight railroad carriers; Railroad suppliers; and State and local governments for projects that have a public benefit of improved safety and network efficiency. To be eligible for assistance, the above entities subject to 49 U.S.C.

Award Range/Average: The range was $771,070 to $3,000,000, and the average was $2,254,202

Funding: (Project Grants) FY 17 $13,005,150; FY 18 est $22,160,000; FY 19 est $0; FY 16 $1,275,000

HQ: New Jersey Avenue SE, P.O. Box 25 1200
Washington, DC 20590
Phone: 202-493-1332
Email: mark.hartong@dot.gov
http://www.fra.dot.gov

DOT 20.323 FISCAL YEAR 2013 HURRICANE SANDY DISASTER RELIEF GRANTS TO THE NATIONAL RAILROAD PASSENGER CORPORATION

Award: Project Grants

Purpose: Provides supplemental assistance to the National Passenger Railroad Corporation for disaster assistance related to Hurricane Sandy.

Applicant Eligibility: As directed by authorizing and appropriating statute, assistance is available only to the National Railroad Passenger Corporation.

Beneficiary Eligibility: Same as Applicant Eligibility.

Award Range/Average: $13,479,978 to $21,300,000 with an average of $14,926,659.

Funding: (Project Grants) FY 17 $0; FY 18 est $45,000,000; FY 19 est $0; FY 16 $32,000,000

HQ: Office of Program Delivery
Washington, DC 20590
Phone: 202-493-6377
Email: michael.longley@dot.gov
http://www.fra.dot.gov

DOT 20.324 RESTORATION AND ENHANCEMENT

Award: Project Grants

Purpose: Provides operating assistance grants for the purpose of initiating, restoring, or enhancing intercity rail passenger transportation.

Applicant Eligibility: (1) a State, including the District of Columbia; (2) a group of States; (3) an Interstate Compact; (4) a public agency or publicly chartered authority established by 1 or more States; (5) a political subdivision of a State; (6) Amtrak or another rail carrier that provides intercity rail passenger transportation; (7) Any rail carrier in partnership with at least 1 of the entities described in (1) through (5); and (8) any combination of the entities described in paragraphs (1) through (7).

Beneficiary Eligibility: Same as Applicant Eligibility

Award Range/Average: N/A – new program

Funding: (Project Grants) FY 17 $0; FY 18 est $0; FY 19 est $3,000,000.

HQ: Office of Program Delivery 1200 New Jersey Avenue SE
Washington, DC 20590
Phone: 202-493-6377
Email: michael.longley@dot.gov
http://www.fra.dot.gov

DOT 20.325 CONSOLIDATED RAIL INFRASTRUCTURE AND SAFETY IMPROVEMENTS "CRISI"

Award: Project Grants

Purpose: Assists in financing the cost of improving passenger and freight rail transportation systems in terms of safety, efficiency, or reliability.

Applicant Eligibility: (1) A State. (2) A group of States.

Beneficiary Eligibility: Same as Applicant Eligibility.

Award Range/Average: N/A – new program

Funding: (Project Grants) FY 17 $0; FY 18 est $0; FY 19 est $109,000,000; FY 16 $0

HQ: Office of Program Delivery 1200 New Jersey Avenue
Washington, DC 20590
Phone: 202-493-6377
Email: michael.longley@dot.gov
http://www.fra.dot.gov

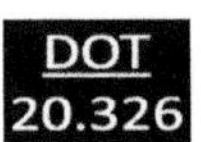

FEDERAL-STATE PARTNERSHIP FOR STATE OF GOOD REPAIR

Award: Project Grants

Purpose: Funds capital projects that reduce the state of good repair backlog with respect to qualified railroad assets.

Applicant Eligibility: (A) a State (including the District of Columbia); (B) a group of States; (C) an Interstate Compact; (D) a public agency or publicly chartered authority established by 1 or more States; (E) a political subdivision of a State; (F) Amtrak, acting on its own behalf or under a cooperative agreement with 1 or more States; or (G) any combination of the entities described in (A) through (F).

Beneficiary Eligibility: Same as Applicant Eligibility.

Award Range/Average: N/A – new program

Funding: (Project Grants) FY 19 est $13,000,000

HQ: Office of Program Delivery 1200 New Jersey Avenue SE
Washington, DC 20590
Phone: 202-493-6377
http://www.fra.dot.gov

FEDERAL TRANSIT ADMINISTRATION

Region I
Mary Beth Mello, Regional Administrator Region I | Transportation Systems Center, Kendall Square 55 Broadway, Suite 921, Cambridge, MA 02142-1093 617-494-2055

Region II
Marilyn Shazor, Region II - New York, NY One | Bowling Green, Suite 429, New York, NY 10004-1415 212-668-2170

Region III
Brigid Hynes-Cherin, Regional Administrator for | Region III, 1760 Market Street, Suite 500, Philadelphia, PA 19103-4124 215-656-7100

Region IV
Yvette G. Taylor, Regional Administrator for | Region IV 230 Peachtree St., N.W., Suite 800, Atlanta, GA 30303-8917 404-865-5600

Region IX
Leslie Rogers, Regional Administrator | 201 Mission Street, Suite 2210, San Francisco, CA 94105-1926 415-744-3133

Region V
Marisol Simon, Regional Administrator Region V | 200 West Adams Street Suite 320, Chicago, IL 60606-5232 312-353-2789

Region VI
Robert C. Patrick, Regional Administrator | Fritz Lanham Federal Building 819 Taylor Street, Suite 8A36, Fort Worth, TX 76102 817-978-0550

Region VII
Mokhtee Ahmad, Regional Administrator | 901 Locust Street, Room 404, Kansas City, MO 64106 816-329-3920

Region VIII
Linda Gehrke, Regional Administrator for Region 8 | 12300 West Dakota Avenue Suite 310, Lakewood, CO 80228-2583 720-963-3300

Region X
Rick Krochalis, Regional Administrator for | Region X. Jackson Federal Building, 915 Second Avenue, Suite 3142, Seattle, WA 98174-1002 206-220-7954

DOT 20.500 FEDERAL TRANSIT CAPITAL INVESTMENT GRANTS "New Starts, Small Starts, and Core Capacity"

Award: Formula Grants; Project Grants

Purpose: Provides funding for fixed guideway investments such as new and expanded heavy rail, commuter rail, light rail, streetcar, bus rapid transit, and ferries as well as corridor-based bus rapid transit investments that emulate the features of rail.

Applicant Eligibility: Public agencies, including States; municipalities and other subdivisions of States; public agencies and instrumentalities of one or more States; and public corporations, boards, and commissions established under State law. Applicant must have legal, financial, and technical capacity to carry out proposed project, including safety and security aspects, and maintain facilities and equipment purchased with Federal assistance.

Beneficiary Eligibility: Same as Applicant Eligibility.

Award Range/Average: No Data Available.

Funding: (Project Grants) FY 17 $1,744,368,363; FY 18 est $2,381,000,000; FY 19 est $99,000,000; FY 16 $2,177,000,000

HQ: 1200 New Jersey Avenue SE
Washington, DC 20590
Phone: 202-366-5159
Email: elizabeth.day@dot.gov
http://www.fta.dot.gov

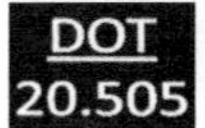

METROPOLITAN TRANSPORTATION PLANNING AND STATE AND NON-METROPOLITAN PLANNING AND RESEARCH

Award: Formula Grants

Purpose: To assist in development of metropolitan and state transportation improvement programs, long-range transportation plans, and other technical studies in a program for a unified and officially coordinated Statewide Transportation system and Metropolitan Transportation system(s) within the state.

Applicant Eligibility: Apportionments are made to the States for 1) statewide planning and 2) formula distribution to the Metropolitan Planning Organizations designated for the urbanized areas within each State for planning within urbanized areas.

Beneficiary Eligibility: Apportionments for metropolitan planning and for state planning and research are made to the States. Funds for metropolitan planning are distributed by formula to the Metropolitan Planning Organizations (MPOs) designated for the urbanized areas within each State.

Award Range/Average: Range and Average of Financial Assistance $20,000 to $5,000,000.

Funding: FY 17 $105,761,566; FY 18 est $121,000,000; FY 19 est $119,000,000

HQ: 1200 New Jersey Avenue SE
Washington, DC 20590
Phone: 202-366-2996
Email: victor.austin@dot.gov
http://www.fta.dot.gov

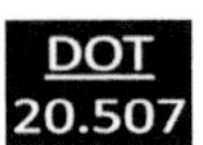

FEDERAL TRANSIT FORMULA GRANTS "Urbanized Area Formula Program; Section 5307"

Award: Formula Grants

Purpose: To support public transportation services in urbanized areas.

Applicant Eligibility: Funds will be made available to urbanized areas (as defined by the U.S. Census Bureau) through designated recipients, which must be public entities and have the legal capacity to receive and dispense federal funds. The Governor, responsible local officials, and publicly owned operators of mass transportation services must jointly select the designated recipient(s) for an urbanized area with a population of 200,000 or more.

Beneficiary Eligibility: The general public, both users and non-users, and publicly owned operators of public transportation services.

Award Range/Average: Varies according to local programming of available formula funds and the level of operating expenses incurred.

Funding: (Formula Grants) FY 17 $5,568,835,693; FY 18 est $6,422,365,464; FY 19 est $6,297,864,412; FY 16 $4,538,905,700

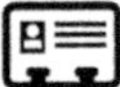

HQ: 1200 New Jersey Avenue SE
Washington, DC 20590
Phone: 202-366-2623
Email: tara.clark@dot.gov
http://www.transit.dot.gov

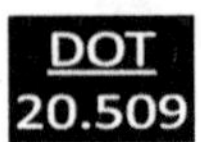

FORMULA GRANTS FOR RURAL AREAS "Rural Area Program"

Award: Formula Grants

Purpose: To improve, initiate, or continue public transportation service in nonurbanized areas and to provide technical assistance for rural transportation providers.

Applicant Eligibility: Only designated State agencies and Indian Tribes may apply directly to FTA for grants. Eligible sub-recipients may include State agencies, local public bodies and agencies thereof, nonprofit organizations, Indian tribes, and operators of public transportation services, including intercity bus service, in rural and small urban areas.

Beneficiary Eligibility: The general public, both users and nonusers, and private and public providers of public transportation in nonurbanized areas.

Award Range/Average: No Data Available.

Funding: (Formula Grants) FY 17 $754,361,641; FY 18 est $870,000,000; FY 19 est $852,000,000; FY 16 $619,956,000

HQ: 1200 New Jersey Avenue SE
Washington, DC 20590
Phone: 202-366-3800
Email: elan.flippin@dot.gov
http://www.fta.dot.gov

DOT 20.513 ENHANCED MOBILITY OF SENIORS AND INDIVIDUALS WITH DISABILITIES

Award: Formula Grants; Project Grants

Purpose: To provide financial assistance in meeting the transportation needs of seniors and individuals with disabilities where public transportation services are unavailable, insufficient or inappropriate.

Applicant Eligibility: Eligible sub-recipients include private nonprofit organizations, public bodies approved by the State to coordinate services for elderly persons and individuals with disabilities and public bodies which certify that no nonprofit organizations or associations are readily available in an area to provide the service.

Beneficiary Eligibility: Seniors and persons with disabilities.

Award Range/Average: No Data Available.

Funding: (Formula Grants (Apportionments)) FY 17 $391,637,862; FY 18 est $452,000,000; FY 19 est $443,000,000; FY 16 $262,949,400

HQ: 1200 New Jersey Avenue SE
Washington, DC 20590
Phone: 202-366-3102
Email: kelly.tyler@dot.gov
http://www.fta.dot.gov

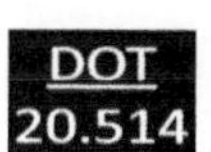

DOT 20.514 PUBLIC TRANSPORTATION RESEARCH, TECHNICAL ASSISTANCE, AND TRAINING "National Research Programs"

Award: Project Grants; Direct Payments for Specified Use; Dissemination of Technical Information; Training

Purpose: To seek to develop solutions that improve public transportation. Its primary goals are to increase transit ridership, improve safety and emergency preparedness, improve operating efficiencies, protect the environment, promote energy independence, and provide transit research leadership.

Applicant Eligibility: Applicants may include State and local DOT's, nonprofit institutions, universities, and legally constituted public agencies and operators of public transportation services, and private for-profit organizations. Also, urban and rural transit agencies, Indian Tribes, public 4-year degree-granting institutions of higher education as defined in section 101(a) of the Higher Education Act of 1965 (20 U.S.C.

Beneficiary Eligibility: N/A

Award Range/Average: None established.

Funding: (Project Grants (Contracts)) FY 17 $33,825,912; FY 18 est $6,000,000; FY 19 est $0; FY 16 $42,000,000

HQ: 1200 New Jersey Avenue SE
Washington, DC 20590
Phone: 202-366-0671
Email: edwin.rodriguez@dot.gov
http://www.transit.dot.gov/research

DOT 20.516 JOB ACCESS AND REVERSE COMMUTE PROGRAM "JARC"

Award: Project Grants

Purpose: Offers grants to local governments, nonprofit organizations, and designated recipients of Federal transit funding to develop transportation services to connect welfare recipients and low- income persons to employment and support services.

Applicant Eligibility: State and local government agencies, nonprofit agencies, and transit providers.

Beneficiary Eligibility: Low income individuals; individuals traveling to suburban work places.

Award Range/Average: $10,890 to $1,293,611. Average: $180,588

Funding: (Project Grants) FY 17 $0; FY 18 est $0; FY 19 est $0; FY 16 $0

HQ: 1200 New Jersey Avenue SE E Building, 4th Floor
Washington, DC 20590
Phone: 202-366-3800
Email: elan.flippin@dot.gov
http://www.fta.dot.gov/funding/grants/grants_financing_3550.html

DOT 20.518 CAPITAL AND TRAINING ASSISTANCE PROGRAM FOR OVER-THE-ROAD BUS ACCESSIBILITY

Award: Project Grants

Purpose: To make funds available to private operators of over-the-road buses to finance the incremental capital and training costs of complying with requirements of the Department of Transportation's Over-the-Road Bus Accessibility regulation, "Transportation for Individuals with Disabilities" (49 CFR Part 37, Subpart H).

Applicant Eligibility: Private operators of over-the-road buses that provide intercity fixed route bus service and other providers, including operators of over-the-road buses of local fixed-route service, commuter service and charter or tour service.

Beneficiary Eligibility: Persons with disabilities.

Award Range/Average: $25,000 to $ 180,000. Average: $25,000.

Funding: FY 17 $195,330; FY 18 est $0; FY 19 est $0; FY 16 $0; - This program was repealed under the MAP-21 Act.

HQ: Office of Program Management 1200 New Jersey Avenue SE
Washington, DC 20590
Phone: 202-366-3800
Email: elan.flippin@dot.gov
http://www.fta.dot.gov

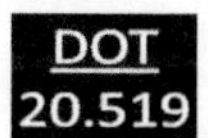

CLEAN FUELS

Award: Project Grants

Purpose: To assist in financing the acquisition of clean fuel vehicles and related facilities for agencies providing public transportation and operating in an urbanized and non-urbanized area designated as a non-attainment or maintenance area for ozone or carbon monoxide.

Applicant Eligibility: Public agencies, including States; municipalities and other subdivisions of States; public agencies and instrumentalities of one or more States; and public corporations, boards, and commissions established under State law. Applicant had legal, financial, and technical capacity to carry out proposed project and maintain facilities and equipment purchased with Federal assistance.

Beneficiary Eligibility: The general public, both users and non-users of public transportation.

Award Range/Average: $69,720 - $5,000,000. Average $2,165,596.

Funding: FY 17 $0; FY 18 est $0; FY 19 est $0; FY 16 $0; - The Clean Fuels Grant program was repealed in 2013, and funds are no longer available.

HQ: Department of Transportation 1200 New Jersey Avenue SE
Washington, DC 20590
Phone: 202-366-4818
Email: vanessa.williams@dot.gov
http://www.fta.dot.gov

PAUL S. SARBANES TRANSIT IN THE PARKS "Transit in the Parks"

Award: Cooperative Agreements; Project Grants

Purpose: It addresses the challenge of increasing vehicle congestion in and around our national parks and other federal lands.

Applicant Eligibility: Eligible applicants are:(1) The following Federal land management agencies: The National Park Service, the Fish and Wildlife Service, the Bureau of Land management, the Forest Service, and the Bureau of Reclamation; and (2) State, tribal and local governments with jurisdiction over land in the vicinity of an eligible area acting with the consent of a Federal land management agency, alone or in partnership with a Federal land management agency or other governmental or non-governmental participant.

Beneficiary Eligibility: N/A

Award Range/Average: No one project could receive more than 25 percent of funds.

Funding: (Project Grants (Cooperative Agreements)) FY 16 $0; FY 17 est $0; FY 18 est $0; - The Transit in Parks Program was repealed under MAP-21, and funds are no longer available.

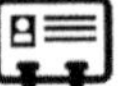

HQ: 1200 New Jersey Avenue SE
Washington, DC 20590
Phone: 202-366-4818
Email: vanessa.williams@dot.gov
http://www.fta.dot.gov

NEW FREEDOM PROGRAM

Award: Formula Grants

Purpose: The New Freedom program provided grants for new capital and operating projects aimed at reducing, beyond the requirements of the Americans with Disabilities Act of 1990, transportation barriers faced by individuals with disabilities to expand mobility through transportation, including transportation to and from jobs and employment support services.

Applicant Eligibility: The chief executive officer of each State or an official designee must designate a public entity to be the recipient for New Freedom funds. In urbanized areas with populations less than 200,000 and in non-urbanized areas, the State is the designated recipient.

Beneficiary Eligibility: Individuals with Disabilities.

Award Range/Average: Project funding varied based on competitive selection process at State or urbanized area level. Urbanized area apportionments range from $111 to $2.2 M. for an average of $150K. State apportionments for small urbanized areas range from $644 to $1.5 M for an average of $115K, and for rural areas from $459 to $701K for an average of 160K.

Funding: (Formula Grants) FY 17 $0; FY 18 est $0; FY 19 FY 16 $0; - The program has been repealed.

HQ: 1200 New Jersey Avenue SE
Washington, DC 20590
Phone: 202-366-2160
Email: kelly.tyler@dot.gov
http://www.fta.dot.gov/funding/grants/grants_financing_3549.html

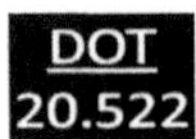

ALTERNATIVES ANALYSIS

Award: Project Grants

Purpose: Assisted in financing the evaluation of all reasonable modal and multimodal alternatives and general alignment options for identified transportation needs.

Applicant Eligibility: Public agencies, including States; municipalities and other subdivisions of States; public agencies and instrumentalities of one or more States; and public corporations, boards, and commissions established under State law. Applicant must have legal, financial, and technical capacity to carry out proposed project and maintain facilities and equipment purchased with Federal assistance.

Beneficiary Eligibility: The general public, both users and non-users of public transportation and public agencies. Private consultants may participate through contractual arrangements with a public agency grantee.

Award Range/Average: In FY 2006 Congressional designations ranged from $300,000 to $2,500,000.

Funding: (Project Grants (for specified projects)) FY 17 $0; FY 18 est $0; FY 19 est $0; FY 16 $0

HQ: FTA Office of Planning and Environment 1200 New Jersey Avenue SE
Washington, DC 20590
Phone: 202-366-1636
Email: maurice.foushee@dot.gov
http://www.fta.dot.gov

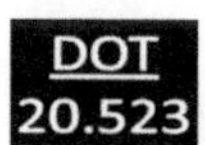

DOT 20.523 CAPITAL ASSISTANCE PROGRAM FOR REDUCING ENERGY CONSUMPTION AND GREENHOUSE GAS EMISSIONS "Transit Investments for Greenhouse Gas and Energy Reduction or "TIGGER" Grants"

Award: Project Grants

Purpose: Assists public agencies that provide transit service in financing the acquisition of capital assets to reduce energy consumption or greenhouse gas emissions.

Applicant Eligibility: Only public transportation agencies are eligible recipients.

Beneficiary Eligibility: Same as Applicant Eligibility.

Award Range/Average: N/A.

Funding: (Project Grants) FY 17 $0; FY 18 est $0; FY 19 est $0; FY 16 $17,000

HQ: Department of Transportation 1200 New Jersey Avenue SE
Washington, DC 20590
Phone: 202-366-0725
Email: marcel.belanger@dot.gov
http://www.transit.dot.gov/research

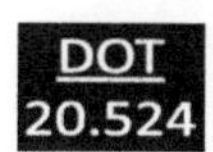

DOT 20.524 PASSENGER RAIL INVESTMENT AND IMPROVEMENT (PRIIA) PROJECTS FOR WASHINGTON METROPOLITAN AREA TRANSIT AUTHORITY (WMATA) "PRIIA -- WMATA"

Award: Project Grants

Purpose: To assist in financing part of the capital and preventive maintenance projects included in the Capital Improvement Program approved by the Board of Directors of the Washington Metropolitan Area Transit Authority.

Applicant Eligibility: This program is only for the Washington Metropolitan Area Transit Authority (Public Law 110-432, Section 601 of the Passenger Rail Investment and Improvement Act of 2008) for construction, renewal, and rehabilitation.

Beneficiary Eligibility: WMATA, transit riders, and general public.

Award Range/Average: No Data Available.

Funding: (Project Grants) FY 17 $164,160,637; FY 18 est $149,000,000; FY 19 est $120,000,000; FY 16 $150,000,000

HQ: 1200 New Jersey Avenue SE
Washington, DC 20590
Phone: 202-366-0870

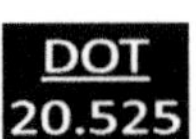

STATE OF GOOD REPAIR GRANTS PROGRAM

Award: Formula Grants

Purpose: To assist in financing capital projects to maintain public transportation systems in a state of good repair and to ensure public transit operates safely, efficiently, reliably, and sustainably.

Applicant Eligibility: Eligible applicants are state and local governmental authorities in urbanized areas. FTA will apportion funds to designated recipients in the urbanized areas with fixed guideway and high intensity motorbus transportation systems operating at least 7 years.

Beneficiary Eligibility: The general public, both users and non-users of public transportation. Public agencies, although private transportation companies may participate through contractual arrangements with public agency grantee.

Award Range/Average: No Data Available.

Funding: (Formula Grants) FY 17 $2,343,939,637; FY 18 est $2,700,000,000; FY 19 est $2,648,000,000.

HQ: 1200 New Jersey Avenue SE
Washington, DC 20590
Phone: 202-366-0870
Email: eric.hu@dot.gov

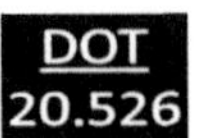

BUS AND BUS FACILITIES FORMULA PROGRAM
"Bus Program"

Award: Formula Grants; Project Grants

Purpose: Provides capital funding to replace, rehabilitate, purchase, or lease buses and bus related equipment and to rehabilitate, purchase, construct, or lease bus-related facilities.

Applicant Eligibility: Beneficiaries of funding include states and direct recipients. After allocation of funds, fixed-route bus operators, the general public, both users and non-users of public transportation, public agencies, and private transportation companies may benefit.

Beneficiary Eligibility: Same as Applicant Eligibility.

Award Range/Average: Current year: $165,000 - $40,000,000.

Funding: (Formula Grants) FY 17 $302,272,050; FY 18 est $348,000,000; FY 19 est $341,000,000; FY 16 $427,800,000.

HQ: 1200 New Jersey Avenue SE
Washington, DC 20590
Phone: 202-366-9955
Email: mark.bathrick@dot.gov
http://www.transit.dot.gov

DOT 20.527 PUBLIC TRANSPORTATION EMERGENCY RELIEF PROGRAM "Transit Emergency Relief Program (ER Program)"

Award: Project Grants

Purpose: To provide operating assistance and capital funding to aid recipients and sub-recipients in restoring public transportation service, and in repairing and reconstructing public transportation assets to a state of good repair, as expeditiously as possible following an emergency or major disaster.

Applicant Eligibility: An entity that operates public transportation service in an area impacted by an emergency or major disaster, as defined by a gubernatorial or presidential declaration of such an emergency or disaster, and that receives federal transit funds directly from FTA.

Beneficiary Eligibility: Beneficiaries of funding include public transportation operators and the general public in areas for which an emergency or major disaster has been declared as defined under section 5324.

Award Range/Average: Future obligations will be made in response to assessed needs and subject to the availability of program funds.

Funding: (Project Grants) FY 17 $2,093,010,830; FY 18 est $2,185,000,000; FY 19 est $801,000,000; FY 16 $487,049,008

HQ: 1200 New Jersey Avenue SE
Washington, DC 20590
Phone: 202-366-9091
Email: john.bodnar@dot.gov
http://www.transit.dot.gov/funding/grant-programs/emergency-relief-program/emergency-relief-program

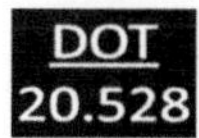

RAIL FIXED GUIDEWAY PUBLIC TRANSPORTATION SYSTEM STATE SAFETY OVERSIGHT FORMULA GRANT PROGRAM "State Safety Oversight Formula Grant Program"

Award: Formula Grants

Purpose: To improve public transportation safety by assisting States with the financing of safety oversight of rail fixed guideway public transportation systems in the jurisdiction of the state not regulated by the Federal Railroad Administration.

Applicant Eligibility: Eligible States are those with a rail fixed guideway public transportation system within the jurisdiction of the State that is not subject to regulation by the Federal Railroad Administration; or a rail fixed guideway public transportation system in the engineering or construction phase of development within the jurisdiction of the State that will not be subject to regulation by the Federal Railroad Administration. Subrecipients must be public agencies that are eligible to become Federal Transit Administration recipients.

Beneficiary Eligibility: Same as Applicant Eligibility.

Award Range/Average: No Data Available.

Funding: (Project Grants (Contracts)) FY 17 $28,273,294; FY 18 est $23,634,536; FY 19 est $24,135,588

HQ: 1200 New Jersey Avenue SE
Washington, DC 20590
Phone: 202-366-5922
Email: maria1.wright@dot.gov

DOT 20.529 BUS TESTING FACILITY "FTA Bus Testing Program"

Award: Project Grants

Purpose: To provide assistance for the operation and maintenance of one facility capable of testing new transit bus models and reporting on their maintainability, reliability, safety, performance (including braking performance), structural integrity, fuel economy, emissions, and noise performance characteristics.

Applicant Eligibility: Applicants may include: local, anyone/general public

Beneficiary Eligibility: N/A

Award Range/Average: $3,000,000

Funding: FY 17 $4,721,158; FY 18 est $6,000,000; FY 19 est $6,000,000; FY 16 $3,000,000; - This program is authorized at $3,000,000 annually. The amount awarded for fiscal year 2017 is a combination of full funding for FY 2016 and partial FY 2017 funds due to a continuing resolution, this included full funding of Fiscal year 2016 funds in the amount of $3,000,000 and a partial award of FY 2017 funding in the amount of $1,721,158. FY 2018: Authorized at $3M annually, in FY 2018 program was appropriated an additional $2M supplemental in the Fiscal Year 2018 omnibus appropriations, and awarded the remaining $1,278,842 of fiscal year 2017 funds.

HQ: Office of Mobility Innovation TRI-12, Room E43-465 1200 New Jersey Avenue SE E Building 4th Floor

Washington, DC 20590

Phone: 202-366-0725

Email: marcel.belanger@dot.gov

http://www.transit.dot.gov/about/12351_4584.html

DOT 20.530 PUBLIC TRANSPORTATION INNOVATION "5312 Research Program"

Award: Project Grants; Direct Payments for Specified Use; Dissemination of Technical Information; Training

Purpose: The objectives of Public Transportation Innovation Projects is to provide various transportation services such as services to seniors, low-income individuals, performance management and operating efficiencies, advancement in vehicle technology, and safety measures. It also supports other innovative projects that improve public transportation. It also assists in the evaluation of low or no emission vehicles.

Applicant Eligibility: Federal Government departments, agencies, and instrumentalities of the Government, including Federal laboratories; State and local governmental entities; providers of public transportation; private or non-profit organizations; institutions of higher education; and technical and community colleges.

Beneficiary Eligibility: State, Local, Public nonprofit institution/organization, Private nonprofit institution/ organization.

Award Range/Average: None established.

Funding: (Project Grants) FY 17 $28,676,560; FY 18 est $33,000,000; FY 19 est $31,000,000; FY 16 $28,000,000

HQ: 1200 New Jersey Avenue SE

Washington, DC 20590

Phone: 202-366-2204

Email: mary.leary@dot.gov

http://www.transit.dot.gov/research

DOT 20.531 TECHNICAL ASSISTANCE AND WORKFORCE DEVELOPMENT

Award: Project Grants; Direct Payments for Specified Use; Dissemination of Technical Information; Training

Purpose: The program encourage States to adopt effective programs to reduce highway deaths and injuries resulting from individuals riding unrestrained or improperly restrained in motor vehicles.

Applicant Eligibility: Federal Government departments, agencies, and instrumentalities of the Government; Metropolitan Planning Organizations; State and local governmental entities; providers of public transportation; and national non-profit organizations (that have the appropriate demonstrated capacity to provide public transportation-related technical assistance); public four-year degree-granting institutions of higher education, as defined in section 101(a) of the Higher Education Act of 1965 to carry-out the duties of the institute.

Beneficiary Eligibility: State, Local, Public nonprofit institution/organization and Private nonprofit institution/organization. Specific applicant eligibility may vary with different program areas within this section.

Award Range/Average: None established.

Funding: (Project Grants) FY 17 $9,071,693; FY 18 est $9,000,000; FY 19 est $9,000,000.

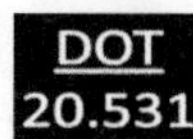

HQ: 1200 New Jersey Avenue SE

Washington, DC 20590

Phone: 202-366-2204

Email: mary.leary@dot.gov

http://www.transit.dot.gov/research

FOOD AND NUTRITION SERVICE

REGIONAL OFFICES

California
Dick Montoya | 550 Kearny Street, Room 400, San Francisco, CA 94108 415-705-1310

Colorado
Craig Forman | 1244 Speer Boulevard, Suite 903, Denver, CO 80204 303-844-0300

Georgia
Jerry Redding | First Floor, Martin Luther King, Jr. Federal Annex 77 Forsythe Street, S.W., Suite 112, Atlanta, GA 30303 404-730-2565

Illinois
Lawrence Rudmann | 77 West Jackson Boulevard, 20th Floor, Chicago, IL 60604-3507 312-353-6664

Massachusetts
Charles DeJulius | 10 Causeway Street, Room 501, Boston, MA 02222-1068 617-565-6370

New Jersey
Walt Haake | Mercer Corporate Park Corporate Boulevard CN 02150, Trenton, NJ 08650 609-259-5025

Texas
Judy Snow | 1100 Commerce Street, Room 5-C-30, Dallas, TX 75242 214-767-0222

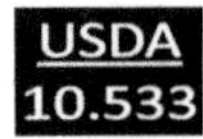

SNAP-ED TOOLKIT

Award: N/A

Purpose: The Supplemental Nutrition Education Toolkit provides educators with evaluation tools such as evaluation framework, training the guides implementation, evidence-based nutrition programs. These programs are apt for low-income audiences.

Applicant Eligibility: N/A

Beneficiary Eligibility: N/A

Award Range/Average: One award was made to the University of North Carolina at Chapel Hill in the amount of $140,836.

Funding: (Cooperative Agreements) FY 17 FY 18 FY 19 est $140,836

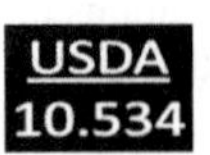

CACFP MEAL SERVICE TRAINING GRANTS "Child and Adult Care Food Program (CACFP) Meal Service Training Grants"

Award: Formula Grants

Purpose: The CACFP program provides training for technical assistance in child care centers, group homes, afterschool programs, day care centers, etc., to ensure that the meals are in based on the standards of CACFP patterns.

Applicant Eligibility: State Agencies that administer the CACFP

Beneficiary Eligibility: These are noncompetitive grants for State agencies to provide Child and Adult Care Food Program (CACFP) meal service training to CACFP operators.

Award Range/Average: N/A

Funding: (Formula Grants (Apportionments)) FY 17 $0; FY 18 est $3,715,609; FY 19 est $0

HQ: 3101 Park Center Drive
Alexandria, VA 22302
Phone: 703-457-7768
Email: franciel.ikeji@fns.usda.gov
http://www.fsa.usda.gov

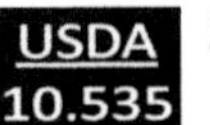

SNAP RECIPIENT INTEGRITY EDUCATION GRANT

Award: Project Grants

Purpose: To support SNAP that provides awareness programs on fraud prevention, trafficking, and other technical assistance.

Applicant Eligibility: This grant opportunity is open to the 53 State agencies that administer SNAP. FNS will consider only one application per State agency.

Beneficiary Eligibility: Agreements are established between State agencies and FNS. Grants funds can be used for projects educating recipients on eligibility fraud as well as trafficking and misuse of benefits.

Award Range/Average: No Data Available.

Funding: (Project Grants) FY 17 $2,772,731; FY 18 est $0; FY 19 est $0; FY 16 $0

HQ: 3101 Park Center Drive, Room 818
Alexandria, VA 22302
Phone: 703-605-4385
Email: jane.duffield@fns.usda.gov

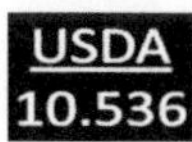

CACFP TRAINING GRANTS
"Child and Adult Care Food Program Competitive Grants and Cooperative Agreements"

Award: Cooperative Agreements; Project Grants

Purpose: To develop and promote training program that provides knowledge and skills to CACFP operators to effectively operate their institutions such as child care centers, day care homes, and other facilities of CACFP.

Applicant Eligibility: This is an announcement of the availability of funds for one new cooperative agreement for a 2-year time-frame (September 2017 – August 2019) with an accredited public or private Academic Institute of Higher Learning, a Research, or Training Institution (i.e.

Beneficiary Eligibility: Selected applicant is to plan, develop, design, promote, and ultimately execute and evaluate a training program that uses a tiered approach to equip State agencies with the knowledge and skills necessary to train their CACFP program operators (including CACFP institutions such as sponsoring organizations and/or independent centers as well as CACFP facilities including child care centers and day care homes) to effectively operate the CACFP at the local-level.

Award Range/Average: No Data Available.

Funding: (Project Grants (Cooperative Agreements)) FY 17 $3,000,000; FY 18 est $0; FY 19 est $0

HQ: 3101 Park Center Drive
Alexandria, VA 22302
Phone: 703-605-0784
Email: barbara.smith@fns.usda.gov
http://www.fns.usda.gov/cacfp/child-and-adult-care-food-program

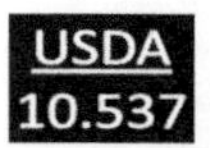

SUPPLEMENTAL NUTRITION ASSISTANCE PROGRAM (SNAP) EMPLOYMENT AND TRAINING (E&T) DATA AND TECHNICAL ASSISTANCE GRANTS
"SNAP E&T DATA Grants"

Award: Project Grants

Purpose: To provide support through the Food and Nutrition Act for agencies like SNAP and E and T with funds and technical assistance to become effective in their services.

Applicant Eligibility: This grant opportunity is open to the 53 State agencies that administer SNAP. There is no State matching requirement for this grant program.

Beneficiary Eligibility: Agreements are established between State agencies and FNS. State agencies will use funds to develop and analyze outcome reporting systems.

Award Range/Average: The range is from $371,736 to $1,000,000. The average grant award is $714,799.

Funding: (Salaries and Expenses) FY 17 $5,718,393; FY 18 est $0; FY 19 est $0.

HQ: 3101 Park Center Drive, 8th Floor
Alexandria, VA 22302
Phone: 703-305-2515
Email: moira.johnston@fns.usda.gov
http://www.fns.usda.gov/snap

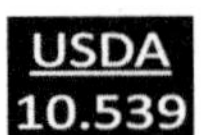

CNMI NUTRITION ASSISTANCE "Commonwealth of the Northern Mariana Islands Nutrition Assistance Program"

Award: Direct Payments for Specified Use

Purpose: The Nutrition Assistance Program provides an allowance for certain foods to eligible residents of the CNMI.

Applicant Eligibility: Eligibility criteria are determined by the Commonwealth of the Northern Mariana Islands

Beneficiary Eligibility: Low-income individuals and households are eligible for benefits as determined by the Commonwealth of the Northern Mariana Islands.

Award Range/Average: No Data Available.

Funding: (Salaries and Expenses) FY 17 $20,648,000; FY 18 est $12,148,000; FY 19 est $12,148,000; FY 16.

HQ: 3101 Park Center Drive
Alexandria, VA 22302
Phone: 703-305-4397
Email: sarah.goldberg@fns.usda.gov
http://www.fns.usda.gov/snap/supplemental-nutrition-assistance-program-snap

USDA 10.540

PARTICIPANT RESEARCH INNOVATION LABORATORY FOR ENHANCING WIC SERVICES

Award: Cooperative Agreements; Project Grants

Purpose: To support PRIL that develops interactive tools, technical resources, and innovative solutions to improve the services in WIC clinics and to improve retention for eligible children in WIC. It also supports the projects that are promoted for those eligible for WIC services.

Applicant Eligibility: The grant is to be used to establish a cooperative agreement to identify, develop and undertake projects to meet Food and Nutrition Service (FNS) program needs and the food, nutrition, and health needs of WIC eligible participants.

Beneficiary Eligibility: All Accredited Colleges/Universities, and Private or Public Research Institutions are eligible to apply to this opportunity. This is a requirement for the selected recipient of the grants and cooperative agreements, not the sub-grantees.

Award Range/Average: No Data Available.

Funding: (Salaries and Expenses) FY 17 FY 18 FY 19 est $2,000,000; FY 16 N/A

HQ: 3101 Park Center Drive, Room 1014
Alexandria, VA 22302
Phone: 703-305-2309
Email: anthony.panzera@fns.usda.gov

USDA 10.541 CHILD NUTRITION-TECHNOLOGY INNOVATION GRANT "TIG"

Award: Project Grants

Purpose: To promote funds for Child Nutrition Programs that promote innovative technology for performance measurement and to identify error-prone areas in the State and local educational agencies.

Applicant Eligibility: Grants are only available to State agencies administering the Child Nutrition Programs. The grants must relate to technology solutions for planning and implementation.

Beneficiary Eligibility: State agencies (and the local organizations that have agreements with the State agencies) administering the Child Nutrition Programs benefit from funded technology solutions.

Award Range/Average: For FY 2017: Nine (9) grants were awarded with a range of $93,222 - $1,942,547 The average grant was $745,694.

Funding: FY 17 $6,711,245; FY 18 est $0; FY 19 est $7,000,000; FY 16 $0.

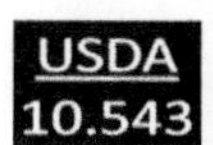

HQ: 3101 Park Center Drive, Room 628
Alexandria, VA 22302
Phone: 703-305-2590
Email: cindy.long@fns.usda.gov
http://www.grants.gov/search-grants.html?cfda=10.541

USDA 10.543 HEALTHIER US SCHOOL CHALLENGE: SMARTER LUNCHROOMS "HUSSC"

Award: Direct Payments for Specified Use

Purpose: The HUSSC is a voluntary certification that recognizes schools that participate in the National School Lunch Program and School Breakfast Program and provides healthier surroundings, smart lunchrooms, nutrition education, and physical activity.

Applicant Eligibility: N/A

Beneficiary Eligibility: School decision makers, school food service staff, teachers, children, parents, other educators.

Award Range/Average: Schools are awarded monetary incentive based on the applied award level: Bronze - $500 Silver - $1000 Gold - $1500 Gold Award of Distinction - $2000

Funding: FY 17 $1,500,000; FY 18 est $1,500,000; FY 19 est $0

HQ: 3101 Park Center Drive
Alexandria, VA 22302

Phone: 703-305-2893

Email: sheldon.gordon@fns.usda.gov

http://www.fns.usda.gov/hussc/healthierus-school-challenge-smarter-lunchrooms

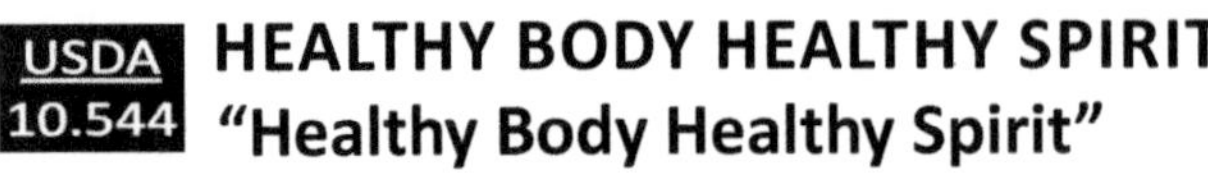

USDA 10.544 HEALTHY BODY HEALTHY SPIRIT
"Healthy Body Healthy Spirit"

Award: Cooperative Agreements

Purpose: The SNAP compensates to improve nutrition and to avoid obesity.

Applicant Eligibility: N/A

Beneficiary Eligibility: N/A

Award Range/Average: No Data Available.

Funding: Cooperative Agreements (Discretionary Grants) FY 17 $0; FY 18 est $0; FY 19 est $0

HQ: 3101 Park Center Drive
Alexandria, VA 22302
Phone: 703-305-2397
Email: usha.kalro@fns.usda.gov
http://www.fns.usda.gov/snap/supplemental-nutrition-assistance-program-snap

USDA 10.547 PROFESSIONAL STANDARDS FOR SCHOOL NUTRITION EMPLOYEES

Award: Project Grants

Purpose: The Healthy Hunger-Free Kids Act of 2010 provides standards for nutrition employees managing National School Lunch and School Breakfast programs to ensure nutritious and enjoyable meals are provided in the school premises.

Applicant Eligibility: The State agency applies for and signs an agreement to receive Federal fund for disbursement. The State agency enters into an agreement with each sponsor that has been approved for participation.

Beneficiary Eligibility: Agreements are between USDA-FNS and State agencies.

Award Range/Average: Each State can apply for up to 150,000 for this grant

Funding: N/A

HQ: 3101 Park Center Drive
Alexandria, VA 22302
Phone: 703-605-4437
Email: julie.maxwell@fns.usda.gov
http://www.fns.usda.gov/school-meals/child-nutrition-programs

USDA 10.549 RURAL CHILD POVERTY NUTRITION CENTER "Child Nutrition Program Coordination in Rural Counties"

Award: Cooperative Agreements

Purpose: The USDA Rural Child Poverty Nutrition Center develops and administers sub-grants, supports researchers, implementing strategies and evaluation findings, reduces food insecurity, and focuses the services for rural areas.

Applicant Eligibility: The grant is to be used to establish grants and cooperative agreements to identify, develop and undertake projects to meet Food and Nutrition Service (FNS) program needs and the food, nutrition, and health needs of program eligible participants.

Beneficiary Eligibility: Cooperative agreements are awarded to State and local governments, hospitals, non-profit organizations and accredited colleges/universities. This is a requirement for the selected recipient of the grants and cooperative agreements, not the sub-grantees.

Award Range/Average: Grant and sub-grant funds will be made available on a competitive basis, subject to availability of federal funds. This grant was funded at approximately $2.5 million; $1,275,500 of which will be distributed as sub-grants with a maximum award amount of $100,000 per sub-grantee.

Funding: (Salaries and Expenses) FY 17 $529,306; FY 18 est $580,000; FY 19 est $550,000; FY 16 est $456,507; FY 15 $56,457

HQ: 3101 Park Center Drive

Alexandria, VA 22302

Phone: 703-305-2698

Email: danielle.berman@fns.usda.gov

SUPPLEMENTAL NUTRITION ASSISTANCE PROGRAM "SNAP"

Award: Direct Payments for Specified Use

Purpose: SNAP improves nutrition and provides nutrition assistance for low-income people and also provides monthly benefits to increase the purchase of healthy foods.

Applicant Eligibility: SNAP Benefits: SNAP is a Federal program administered by the States. The State or U.S. Territory agency responsible for Federally aided public assistance programs submits requests for funding to USDA's Food and Nutrition Service.

Beneficiary Eligibility: Applications for SNAP are made through a local social services agency which determines eligibility and benefit amount. Eligibility is based on household size, income, and expenses.

Award Range/Average: Varies by income and household size. The average benefit for a household of 4 in FY 15 was $257.73

Funding: (Salaries and Expenses) FY 17 $5,000,000,000; FY 18 est $3,000,000,000; FY 19 est $0; FY 16 est $3,000,000,000; - Contingency Fund: Placed in reserve for use only in such amounts and at such times as may be necessary to carry out program operations. Enables the program to react to shifts in program need that we not anticipated at the time of a budget request. (Formula Grants) FY 17 $67,754,435,000; FY 18 est $62,638,952,000; FY 19 est $62,065,748,000; FY 16 est $70,124,319,000.

HQ: 3101 Park Center Drive
Alexandria, VA 22302
Phone: 703-305-2022
Email: jessica.shahin@fns.usda.gov
http://www.fns.usda.gov/snap

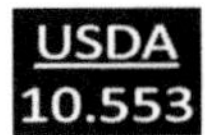

SCHOOL BREAKFAST PROGRAM "SBP"

Award: Formula Grants

Purpose: To compensate States through food donations for providing nutritious meals to school children.

Applicant Eligibility: States, including the District of Columbia and U.S. Territories, as applicable, may apply to administer the SBP and work in collaboration with public and nonprofit private schools and other institutions for children, such as public and nonprofit private residential child care institutions. All participating schools and institutions must agree to serve free and reduced price meals to eligible children, and operate a nonprofit meal service that is available to all children regardless of race, sex, color, national origin, age, or disability.

Beneficiary Eligibility: All children attending schools where this program is operating may receive nutrition benefits, which are determined based on the household income and size. Breakfast is served free to children who are determined by the local education agency to have household income levels at or below 130 percent, and at a reduced price to children from households with incomes higher than 130 but at or below 185 percent of the Federal poverty line.

Award Range/Average: State grants vary according to participation in this program.

Funding: (Formula Grants) FY 17 $4,385,502,000; FY 18 est $4,789,418,000; FY 19 est $5,081,770,000.

HQ: 3101 Park Center Drive
Alexandria, VA 22302
Phone: 703-305-2590
Email: cndinternet@fns.usda.gov
http://www.fns.usda.gov

NATIONAL SCHOOL LUNCH PROGRAM "School Lunch"

Award: Formula Grants

Purpose: To compensate States through food donations for providing nutritious agricultural commodities to school children.

Applicant Eligibility: States, including the District of Columbia and U.S. Territories, as applicable, may apply to administer the National School Lunch Program and work in collaboration with public and nonprofit private schools and other institutions, such as residential child care institutions, to provide nutritious lunches for children. All participating schools and institutions must agree to operate a nonprofit food service that is available to all children regardless of race, sex, color, national origin, age, or disability.

Beneficiary Eligibility: All children enrolled in schools where this program is operating may receive a lunch daily. Eligibility for free, reduced-price, or paid lunches is determined based on the household income and size.

Award Range/Average: State grants vary according to participation in this program.

Funding: (Formula Grants) FY 17 $12,302,521,000; FY 18 est $12,916,680,000; FY 19 est $13,303,240,000; FY 16 $12,259,688,000

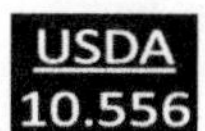

HQ: 3101 Park Center Drive
Alexandria, VA 22302
Phone: 703-305-2590
http://www.fns.usda.gov

USDA 10.556 SPECIAL MILK PROGRAM FOR CHILDREN "SMP"

Award: Formula Grants

Purpose: To assist school children with subsidies and promote milk consumption.

Applicant Eligibility: The State, including the District of Columbia, or U.S. Territory as applicable, administers this program. Public and nonprofit private school of high school grade or under, and public and private nonprofit residential and nonresidential child care institutions, except Job Corps centers, may participate in this program upon request if they do not participate in a meal service program authorized under the Richard B.

Beneficiary Eligibility: All children enrolled in participating schools and institutions who do not have access to other Child Nutrition Programs, may participate in this program.

Award Range/Average: State grants vary according to participation in this program.

Funding: (Formula Grants) FY 17 $8,491,000; FY 18 est $8,431,000; FY 19 est $8,777,000.

HQ: 3101 Park Center Drive
Alexandria, VA 22302
Phone: 703-305-2590
Email: cndinternet@fns.usda.gov
http://www.fns.usda.gov

USDA 10.557 WIC SPECIAL SUPPLEMENTAL NUTRITION PROGRAM FOR WOMEN, INFANTS, AND CHILDREN "WIC Program"

Award: Formula Grants; Project Grants

Purpose: To assist breastfeeding, postpartum women, infants, and children below five with nutritious food and provide free health services. WIC also supports this cause and it provides awareness on substance abuse and healthy living habits. WIC also encourages and supports breastfeeding mothers and provides essential health and nutrition services.

Applicant Eligibility: A local agency is eligible to apply to deliver locally the services of the WIC Program, provided that: (1) it serves a population of low-income women, infants, and children at nutritional risk; and (2) it is a public or private nonprofit health or human service agency. All local agencies must apply through the responsible State, Indian Tribal Organization or U.S. Territory agency.

Beneficiary Eligibility: Pregnant, breastfeeding and postpartum women, infants, and children up to 5 years of age are eligible if: (1) they are individually determined by a competent professional to be in need of the special supplemental foods supplied by the program because of nutritional risk; and (2) meet an income standard, or receive or have certain family members that receive benefits under the Supplemental Nutrition Assistance, Medicaid or Temporary Assistance for Needy Families Programs. They must also reside in the State in which benefits are received.

Award Range/Average: For fiscal year 2017, FNS approved the operation of the WIC Program in 90 State agencies. This figure includes 50 States, 34 Indian agencies, Puerto Rico, the Virgin Islands, Guam, American Samoa, the Commonwealth of the Northern Marianas and the District of Columbia. During fiscal year 2017, an average of approximately 7,286,161 women, infants and children received WIC benefits every month.

Funding: (Formula Grants) FY 17 $6,512,698,000; FY 18 est $6,501,000,000; FY 19 est $5,660,000,000; - FY 17 Administrative costs -$2,084,063,000; Food costs - $4,428,635,000 FY 18 Administrative costs - $2,080,320,000; Food costs - $4,420,680,000 (estimated) FY 19 Administrative costs - $1,811,200,000; Food costs - $3,848,800,000

HQ: Supplemental Food Programs Division 3101 Park Center Drive 1200 Pennsylvania Avenue NW

Alexandria, VA 22302

Phone: 703-305-2746

Email: sarah.widor@fns.usda.gov

http://www.fns.usda.gov/wic

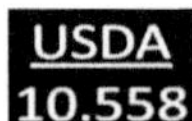

CHILD AND ADULT CARE FOOD PROGRAM "CACFP"

Award: Formula Grants

Purpose: To support nonprofit food service programs that assist children, elderly, or impaired at daycare centers, low-income areas, shelters by providing nutritious foods and all kinds of assistance for the differently abled.

Applicant Eligibility: The State or U.S. Territory agency applies for and signs an agreement to receive Federal funds for disbursement. The State agency enters into an agreement with each institution that has been approved for participation.

Beneficiary Eligibility: Approved institutions providing nonresidential day care services may participate in CACFP. Eligible public and nonprofit private organizations may include day care centers, outside-school-hours care centers, family day care homes, and Head Start programs.

Award Range/Average: No Data Available.

Funding: FY 17 $3,647,052,000; FY 18 est $3,637,916,000; FY 19 est $3,933,393,000; FY 16 $3,451,559,000.

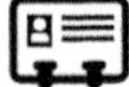

HQ: 3101 Park Center Drive, Room 628

Alexandria, VA 22302

Phone: 703-305-2590

Email: cindy.long@fns.usda.gov

http://fns.usda.gov

SUMMER FOOD SERVICE PROGRAM FOR CHILDREN "SFSP"

Award: Formula Grants

Purpose: To support nonprofit food service programs that assist children and USDA and other local organizations that initiate to provide meals to eligible children at apt times.

Applicant Eligibility: The State or U.S. Territory agency applies for and signs an agreement to receive Federal funds for disbursement. The State agency enters into an agreement with each sponsor that has been approved for participation.

Beneficiary Eligibility: A service institution that conducts a regularly scheduled program for children from areas in which poor economic conditions exist is eligible to participate as a sponsor in this program. Sponsors include public or private nonprofit school food authorities; public or private nonprofit colleges or universities operating the National Youth Sports Program during the months of May to September; units of local, municipal, county, or State governments; and other faith or community-based private nonprofit organizations.

Award Range/Average: No Data Available.

Funding: (Formula Grants) FY 17 $505,695,000; FY 18 est $501,823,000; FY 19 est $519,461,000.

HQ: 3101 Park Center Drive, Room 628
Alexandria, VA 22302
Phone: 703-305-2590
Email: cindy.long@fns.usda.gov
http://fns.usda.gov

STATE ADMINISTRATIVE EXPENSES FOR CHILD NUTRITION "State Administrative Expense (SAE) Funds"

Award: Formula Grants

Purpose: To compensate State agencies for providing technical assistance and nutrition programs for schools and adult care centers.

Applicant Eligibility: State agencies responsible for the administration of the Child Nutrition Programs and agencies responsible for the distribution of USDA Foods to schools and child or adult care institutions, including agencies in the U.S. Territories, may apply.

Beneficiary Eligibility: N/A

Award Range/Average: FY 2018: Range is $375,533 - $35,742,589 Average is $5,533,912 (50 States, DC, PR, GU, VI) FY 2017: Range is $371,295 - $33,655,506 Average is $5,230,874 (50 States, DC, PR, GU, VI)

Funding: (Formula Grants) FY 17 $282,486,399; FY 18 est $298,847,210; FY 19 est $300,000,000.

HQ: 3101 Park Center Drive, Room 628
Alexandria, VA 22302
Phone: 703-305-2590
Email: cindy.long@fns.usda.gov
http://www.fns.usda.gov

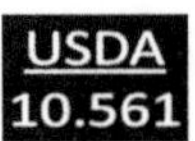

STATE ADMINISTRATIVE MATCHING GRANTS FOR THE SUPPLEMENTAL NUTRITION ASSISTANCE PROGRAM "Supplemental Nutrition Assistance Program (State Administrative Match)"

Award: Formula Grants

Purpose: SNAP assists State agencies and E and T programs to provide employment oriented activities. USDA also provides reimbursement for transportation for those who participate in E and T programs. The Nutrition Education and Obesity Prevention education program assists low-income people.

Applicant Eligibility: SNAP SAE, E&T, and SNAP Ed: Agreements are between USDA-FNS and State cooperators. (U.S. Territories qualify as States for grant purposes.

Beneficiary Eligibility: Same as Applicant Eligibility.

Award Range/Average: Unavailable

Funding: (Salaries and Expenses) FY 17 $3,796,002,000; FY 18 est $4,483,411,000; FY 19 est $4,604,463,000; FY 16 est $5,106,107,000; - (Salaries and Expenses) FY 17 $318,932,000; FY 18 est $366,706,000; FY 19 est $376,607,000; FY 16 est $346,669,000; (Salaries and Expenses) FY 17 $411,096,000; FY 18 est $421,000,000; FY 19 est $428,000,000; FY 16 est $411,000,000; (Salaries and Expenses) FY 17 $118,813,000; FY 18 est $110,000,000; FY 19 est $110,000,000; FY 16 est $110,000,000.

HQ: 3101 Park Center Drive
Alexandria, VA 22302
Phone: 703-305-2026
Email: jessica.shahin@fns.usda.gov
http://www.fns.usda.gov/fsp

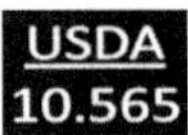

COMMODITY SUPPLEMENTAL FOOD PROGRAM

Award: Formula Grants; Sale, Exchange, or Donation of Property and Goods

Purpose: To maximize the supply of nutritious USDA foods for low-income and elderly persons and assist children with CSFP benefits as long as they are eligible.

Applicant Eligibility: Agreements are made between USDA and the State agency or an ITO recognized by the Department of the Interior or the appropriate area office of the Indian Health Service of the Department of Health and Human Services.

Beneficiary Eligibility: To be certified as eligible to receive USDA Foods through the program, individuals must be at least 60 years of age. As required by the Agricultural Act of 2014 (P.

Award Range/Average: On average, $1,016,169 in appropriated administrative funding was allocated to each State for FY 18. Funding ranged from $6,395 to $7,442,023 per State. For FY 18, States received $76.12 in administrative funding per assigned caseload slot.

Funding: (Salaries and Expenses) FY 17 $50,739,000; FY 18 est $54,873,125; FY 19 est $54,873,125; FY 16 $45,854,000; - These funds are provided to State agencies for administrative expenses. States receive an administrative grant per assigned caseload slot.(Formula Grants) FY 17 $155,279,000; FY 18 est $183,246,875; FY 19 est $168,017,875; FY 16 $173,152,000; - These funds are used for the purchase of USDA Foods to be used in CSFP.

HQ: 3101 Park Center Drive
Alexandria, VA 22302
Phone: 703-305-2680
Email: erica.antonson@fns.usda.gov
http://www.fns.usda.gov/csfp/commodity-supplemental-food-program-csfp

NUTRITION ASSISTANCE FOR PUERTO RICO "NAP"

Award: Direct Payments for Specified Use

Purpose: To support needy people with healthy food residing in the Commonwealth of Puerto Rico.

Applicant Eligibility: The Commonwealth of Puerto Rico alone is eligible.

Beneficiary Eligibility: Low-income individuals and households are eligible for benefits as determined by the Commonwealth.

Award Range/Average: No Data Available.

Funding: (Salaries and Expenses) FY 17 $1,949,001,000; FY 18 est $1,929,646,000; FY 19 est $1,961,927,000; FY 16 est $1,959,136,000; FY 15 $1,951,397,000

HQ: 300 Corporate Boulevard
Robbinsville, NJ 8691
Phone: 609-259-5025
Email: patricia.dombroski@fns.usda.gov
http://www.fns.usda.gov

FOOD DISTRIBUTION PROGRAM ON INDIAN RESERVATIONS "FDPIR"

Award: Project Grants; Sale, Exchange, or Donation of Property and Goods

Purpose: The Food Distribution Program on Indian Reservations provides nutrition assistance and nutrition education to the Indian Tribal and funds are provided for these activities.

Applicant Eligibility: The administration of FDPIR is limited to ITOs or to SAs that assume administration on behalf of/at the request of a Tribe(s).

Beneficiary Eligibility: FDPIR eligibility is limited to income-eligible households residing on participating reservations or income-eligible Indian Tribal Households (see definition at 7 CFR 253.2) residing in approved areas near a reservation or in approved service areas in Oklahoma.

Award Range/Average: Monthly per person food package was approximately $71.96.

Funding: (Project Grants) FY 17 $103,310,000; FY 18 est $104,976,000; FY 19 est $103,238,000; FY 16 $103,664,000; - USDA Foods in-lieu of SNAP(Direct Payments for Specified Use) FY 17 $47,690,000; FY 18 est $48,024,000; FY 19 est $49,762,000; FY 16 $41,527,000; - Administrative Expenses

HQ: 3101 Park Center Drive, 5th Floor
Alexandria, VA 22302
Phone: 703-305-2680
Email: erica.antonson@fns.usda.gov
http://www.fns.usda.gov/fdpir/food-distribution-program-indian-reservations-fdpir

USDA 10.568 EMERGENCY FOOD ASSISTANCE PROGRAM (ADMINISTRATIVE COSTS) "TEFAP"

Award: Formula Grants

Purpose: To provide assistance to needy people through State agencies and organizations such as food pantries, food banks, and other food providing organizations.

Applicant Eligibility: State agencies that are designated as distributing agencies by the Governor or other appropriate State executive authority may receive these administrative funds to support the distribution of USDA Foods to low-income persons.

Beneficiary Eligibility: Public or private non-profit organizations, such as food banks, food pantries, and soup kitchens, which provide food assistance to low-income persons.

Award Range/Average: In Fiscal Year 2017, the range for assistance to State agencies was from $30,585 to $11,442,518, after conversions and recoveries; the average amount of assistance was $1,509,276.

Funding: (Formula Grants) FY 17 $77,930,804; FY 18 est $59,401,000; FY 19 est $54,401,000; FY 16 $77,930,804

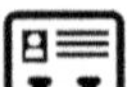

HQ: 3101 Park Center Drive

Alexandria, VA 22302

Phone: 703-305-2680

Email: erica.antonson@fns.usda.gov

http://www.fns.usda.gov/tefap/emergency-food-assistance-program-tefap

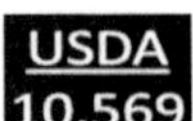

EMERGENCY FOOD ASSISTANCE PROGRAM (FOOD COMMODITIES) "TEFAP, USDA Foods, Commodities"

Award: Formula Grants

Purpose: To supply USDA foods through food agencies for low-income persons.

Applicant Eligibility: State agencies that are designated as distributing agencies by the Governor or other appropriate State executive authority may receive and distribute USDA Foods. States can distribute these foods to eligible recipient agencies, such as food banks, food pantries, soup kitchens, and other eligible agencies, including faith-based organizations.

Beneficiary Eligibility: Low-income and needy individuals, including persons that are homeless, unemployed, underemployed, or receiving public assistance. The State agency must establish income-based eligibility criteria to ensure USDA Foods are provided to the needy.

Award Range/Average: In Fiscal Year 2017, the range of awards was from $156,693 to $35,848,511, after conversions; the average award was $5,297,088.

Funding: (Formula Grants) FY 17 $291,339,820; FY 18 est $287,500,000; FY 19 est $294,000,000; FY 16 $292,068,571; - In FY 2016 and 2017, appropriations legislation provided State agencies with the opportunity to convert up to 10% of their TEFAP food funds to administrative funds. In FY 2016, States elected to convert $23,374,343 to administrative funds. In FY 2017, States elected to convert $22,871,278 to administrative funds.

HQ: 3101 Park Center Drive
Alexandria, VA 22302
Phone: 703-305-2680
Email: erica.antonson@fns.usda.gov
http://www.fns.usda.gov/tefap/emergency-food-assistance-program-tefap

USDA 10.572 WIC FARMERS' MARKET NUTRITION PROGRAM (FMNP)

Award: Formula Grants

Purpose: The WIC Farmers' Market Nutrition Program provides nutritious foods for women, infants, and children and it also expands income at farmer's markets.

Applicant Eligibility: Each State agency desiring to administer the FMNP shall annually submit a State Plan of Operations and enter into a written agreement with FNS for administration of the Program in the jurisdiction of the State agency. New State agencies are selected based on the availability of funds, after base grants for currently participating State agencies.

Beneficiary Eligibility: Women, infants (over 4 months old) and children (ages 1 year up to age 5) who have been certified to receive WIC program benefits, or who are on a waiting list for WIC certification, are eligible to participate in the FMNP. State agencies may serve some or all of these categories.

Award Range/Average: From $6,337 to $3,985,456. (estimated)

Funding: (Formula Grants) FY 17 $18,548,000; FY 18 est $18,548,000; FY 19 N/A FY 16 $18,548,000

HQ: 3101 Park Center Drive
Alexandria, VA 22302
Phone: 703-305-2746
Email: sarah.widor@fns.usda.gov
http://www.fns.usda.gov/fmnp/wic-farmers-market-nutrition-program-fmnp

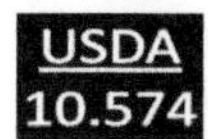

TEAM NUTRITION GRANTS "Team Nutrition Training Grants"

Award: Project Grants

Purpose: Team Nutrition support child nutrition programs. It compensates for the school meals implemented by USDA nutrition program. It promotes a fat-free diet. It implements the most recent Dietary Guidelines. Provides technical assistance to maintain childcare environment. The FY 2016 Team Nutrition Training Grant Objectives are to assist students in participating School Breakfast Program, improve nutritional content, administer schools in providing nutritious meals, and promotes healthy eating.

Applicant Eligibility: State agencies that administer the Child Nutrition Programs (e.g.

Beneficiary Eligibility: School decision makers, school food service staff, students, parents, teachers, childcare professionals, and educators.

Award Range/Average: FY 2015 (Competitive) Team Nutrition Training Grants In FY 2015, State agencies could apply for up to $350,000 in competitive grants, and competitive awards ranged from $141,054 to $349,984. Average award per State agency was $297,017.05.

Funding: (Salaries and Expenses) FY 17 $5,311,436; FY 18 est $0; FY 19 N/A; FY 15 $5,643,324; - FY 2015 (Competitive) Team Nutrition Training Grants: $5,643,324.

HQ: Division Food and Nutrition Service 3101 Park Center Drive, Room 6th Floor
Alexandria, VA 22302
Phone: 703-305-2590
Email: cindy.long@fns.usda.gov
http://www.fns.usda.gov/tn/team-nutrition-training-grants

USDA 10.575 FARM TO SCHOOL GRANT PROGRAM
"USDA Farm to School Grant Program"

Award: Cooperative Agreements; Project Grants; Dissemination of Technical Information; Training

Purpose: To support Farm to School program to provide local foods in eligible schools.

Applicant Eligibility: State Agencies, local agencies, Indian Tribal Organizations, small- and medium-sized agricultural/groups of agricultural producers, schools/school districts, and non-profit entities.

Beneficiary Eligibility: Eligible entities, and therefore beneficiaries, include schools/school districts, Indian Tribal Organizations, non profit organizations, schools, producer and producer groups and State and local agencies.

Award Range/Average: Planning grants range from $20,000 - $50,000 while Implementation grants range from $50,000 - $100,000. Training grants range $20,000 - $50,000.

Funding: (Cooperative Agreements) FY 2018: Planning - $1.5 million; Implementation - $3.0 million; Training - $.5 million FY 2019: Planning - $2 million; Implementation - $4.5 million; Training - $1 million

HQ: 3101 Park Center Drive
Alexandria, VA 22302
Phone: 703-305-2163
Email: mieka.sanderson@fns.usda.gov
http://www.fns.usda.gov/farmtoschool/farm-school

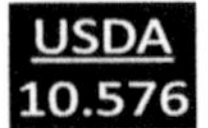

SENIOR FARMERS, MARKET NUTRITION PROGRAM
"Senior Farmers' Market Nutrition Program (SFMNP)"

Award: Formula Grants

Purpose: The Senior Farmer's Market Nutrition Program promotes fresh agricultural commodities, expands domestic farmer's market, aides and supports community supported agriculture.

Applicant Eligibility: State means any of the 50 States, the District of Columbia, and U.S. Territories. State agencies include State Agriculture Department, Agency on Aging, or Health Department, and Indian Tribal Organizations (ITOs).

Beneficiary Eligibility: Persons eligible for the program are low-income seniors, generally defined as individuals who are at least 60 years old and who have household incomes of not more than 185 percent of the federal poverty income guidelines published each year by the Department of Health and Human Services. Some State agencies accept proof of participation or enrollment in another means-tested program, such as the Commodity Supplemental Food Program (CSFP) or Supplemental Nutrition Assistance Program (SNAP), for SFMNP eligibility.

Award Range/Average: FY 2017 grants ranged from $9,925 to $1,770,555 (actual). FY 2018 grants range from $9,925 to $1,788,983 (estimate).

Funding: (Formula Grants) FY 17 $20,600,000; FY 18 est $20,600,000; FY 19 est $20,600,000.

HQ: 3101 Park Center Drive
Alexandria, VA 22302
Phone: 703-305-2746
Email: sarah.widor@fns.usda.gov
http://www.fns.usda.gov/sfmnp/senior-farmers-market-nutrition-program-sfmnp

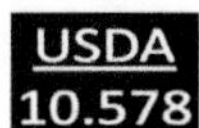

WIC GRANTS TO STATES (WGS)

Award: Cooperative Agreements; Project Grants

Purpose: To assist WIC State agencies to support the implementation of projects, develops MIS system for management plans, compensates for State Agency Model amendments, encounters challenges of EBT implementation, supports Breastfeeding Peer Counseling program, and assists Maternal Nutrition Intensive Course.

Applicant Eligibility: State agencies that administer the WIC Program are eligible to apply for WIC Grant to States funds. States may apply individually or as a coalition of States for WIC technology funds.

Beneficiary Eligibility: WIC participants will be the ultimate beneficiary in that improved technology will allow for more efficient and effective clinic operations. Additionally, the WIC Program is moving towards the issuance of benefits through electronic benefit transfer.

Award Range/Average: In FY 2017, 79 Breastfeeding Peer Counseling grants totaling $59,900,000 were awarded. Grants ranged from $21,000 to $8,731,149 The remaining $100,000 in Breastfeeding Peer Counseling funds were awarded as Breastfeeding Performance Bonus awards to 3 large (>1000 participants) and 3 small (<1000 participants) State agencies shown to have greatest percentage increase of the number of fully breastfed infants than in the previous fiscal year. Awards ranged from $1,217 to $60,195. 18 General Infrastructure grants ranging from $18,000 to $750,000 and four Special Project Grants focusing on improving the delivery of WIC services; the grant amounts totaled $1,128,749

Funding: (Project Grants (Cooperative Agreements)) FY 17 $0; FY 18 est $20,000,000; FY 19 N/A. The following Technology grants were awarded for FY 2017: 1. WIC EBT Amendments (non-competitive), no grants awarded. 2. WIC EBT Implementation (non-competitive) 9 awards totaling $ 19,956,987 3. WIC SAM Amendments (non-competitive) no grants awarded. 4. WIC EBT Planning Grants (non-competitive) 4 awards totaling $910,549 5. WIC Technical Innovation Grants (competitive) no grants awarded 6. WIC SAM Transfer Grants (non-competitive), 1 award totaling $1,888,569 7. WIC MIS Amendments (non-competitive), no grants awarded. 8. WIC MIS Implementation (non-competitive); 5 awards totaling $31,468,209 9. WIC MIS Planning (non-competitive), 1 award totaling $244,000. 10. WIC SAM Product Management Office Grants (non-competitive) 3 awards totaling $3,900,788. There was no funding estimated for FY 2017. Grants were funded using FY 2016 funding.(Project Grants (Discretionary)) FY 17 $60,000,000; FY 18 est $60,000,000; FY 19 est $60,000,000; FY 16 $60,000,000; - Breastfeeding Peer Counseling funds are awarded to States under this grant. In FY 2017, an States/ITOs allocated $59,900,000 in Breastfeeding Peer Counseling grants and $100,000 in Breastfeeding Bonus Awards.(Cooperative Agreements) FY 17 $35,700; FY 18 est $35,700; FY 19 N/A FY 16 $35,700; - Maternal Nutrition Intensive Course is awarded under this grant. (Project Grants (Discretionary)) FY 17 $13,600,000; FY 18 est $13,600,000; FY 19 est $13,600,000; FY 16 $13,600,000; - General Infrastructure and Special Project Grants are awarded under this grant.(Project Grants (Discretionary)) FY 17 $0; FY 18 N/A FY 19 N/A - WIC Disaster Infrastructure Grants are granted under these funds.

HQ: Supplemental Food Programs Division 3101 Park Center Drive
Alexandria, VA 22302
Phone: 703-305-2746
Email: sarah.widor@fns.usda.gov
http://www.fns.usda.gov/wic/women-infants-and-children-wic

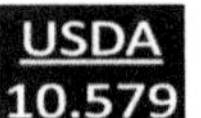

CHILD NUTRITION DISCRETIONARY GRANTS LIMITED AVAILABILITY

Award: Project Grants

Purpose: The National School Lunch Program assists food authorities with grants and provides certification and evaluates meal counting. The State agencies conduct administrative reviews receive grants. The Electronic Benefits Transfer develop methods for addressing the nutritional status of children. Grants are provided to the State agencies that look into the health and wellness of children.

Applicant Eligibility: Determined by the legislation authorizing the grants.

Beneficiary Eligibility: Same as Applicant Eligibility.

Award Range/Average: For FY 2018, the National School Lunch Program (NSLP) Equipment Assistance Grants ranged from $37,410 to $3,662,051. Grant average was $555,556.

Funding: (Project Grants (Discretionary)) FY 17 $30,000,000; FY 18 est $30,000,000; FY 19 N/A FY 16 $30,000,000; - School Lunch (NSLP) Equipment Grants(Project Grants (Discretionary)) FY 17 $0; FY 18 est $2,011,426; FY 19 est $0; FY 16 $1,550,000; - Direct Certification Grants (Project Grants (Discretionary)) FY 17 $4,000,000; FY 18 est $4,000,000; FY 19 est $4,000,000; FY 16 $4,000,000; - Administrative Review and Training Grants(Project Grants (Discretionary)) FY 17 $0; FY 18 est $0; FY 19 est $0; FY 16 $0; - Improve Health and Nutrition - no grants were awarded for 2015, 2016, 2017 or expected for 2018.(Project Grants (Discretionary)) FY 17 $0; FY 18 est $0; FY 19 est $0; FY 16 $0; - School Breakfast Expansion, no grants were awarded for 2017. The last time grants were awarded was 2013.(Project Grants (Discretionary)) FY 17 $25,181,000; FY 18 est $22,844,000; FY 19 est $22,957,000; - Summer EBT for Children (SEBTC)

HQ: 3101 Park Center Drive, Room 628
Alexandria, VA 22302
Phone: 703-305-2590
Email: cindy.long@fns.usda.gov
http://www.fns.usda.gov

SUPPLEMENTAL NUTRITION ASSISTANCE PROGRAM, PROCESS AND TECHNOLOGY IMPROVEMENT GRANTS "Process and Technology Improvement Grants (PTIG)"

Award: Project Grants

Purpose: The process and Technology Improvement Grants support State agencies to implement SNAP and capable systems and improves the processes in the SNAP office.

Applicant Eligibility: State agencies that administer the SNAP, State or local governments; agencies that provide health or welfare services; public health or educational entities and private nonprofit entities such as community-based or faith-based organizations, food banks, or other emergency feeding organizations.

Beneficiary Eligibility: The entities eligible to receive grants under this competition are: The 53 State agencies that administer the SNAP; State or local governments; Agencies providing health or welfare services; Public health or educational entities; and Private non-profit entities such as community-based or faith-based organizations, food banks, or other emergency feeding organizations. (1) State agencies and State and local governments should have the necessary approvals of state officials (such as councils or legislatures) of funding prior to submitting the application.

Award Range/Average: FNS anticipates awarding between 6 and 11 awards annually.

Funding: (Salaries and Expenses) FY 17 $5,000,000; FY 18 est $5,000,000; FY 19 est $5,000,000; FY 16 est $5,000,000.

HQ: 3101 Park Center Drive, 8th Floor
Alexandria, VA 22302
Phone: 703-305-2803
Email: maryrose.conroy@fns.usda.gov
http://www.fns.usda.gov/grant-opportunities

FRESH FRUIT AND VEGETABLE PROGRAM "FFVP"

Award: Project Grants

Purpose: To support States in supplying agricultural commodities to elementary schools and deduct meal price.

Applicant Eligibility: In order to be eligible to participate in the FFVP, the school must be a low-income public or nonprofit private elementary school, and must participate in the National School Lunch Program.

Beneficiary Eligibility: All elementary school children enrolled in schools participating in the Fresh Fruit and Vegetable Program receive free fresh fruits and vegetables outside of the National School Lunch and School Breakfast Programs.

Award Range/Average: FFVP funds are allocated at a level of $50 to $75 per student per school year. Funding is allocated among States based on a funding formula, which is adjusted every July 1 to reflect changes in the Consumer Price Index. The minimum grant to each of the 50 States and the District of Columbia will equal one percent of the funds made available to carry out this program for the school year. Additional funding will be allocated to all States, the District of Columbia, Guam, Puerto Rico and the Virgin Islands, on the basis of population.

Funding: (Project Grants) FY 17 $184,213,000; FY 18 est $171,000,000; FY 19 est $174,000,000; FY 16 $166,565,000; - A steady source of funding is provided through an annual transfer from the Agricultural Marketing Service.

HQ: 3101 Park Center Drive
Alexandria, VA 22302
Phone: 703-305-2590
Email: cndinternet@fns.usda.gov
http://www.fns.usda.gov

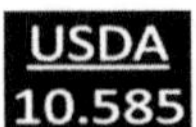

USDA 10.585 FNS FOOD SAFETY GRANTS

Award: Cooperative Agreements; Project Grants

Purpose: The Food and Nutrition Service's provide funds to the U.S. Department of Agriculture, Food and Nutrition Service. The FNS promotes child nutrition programs, food safety education programs, and supports the National Academies of Sciences Food Forum that works in the various disciplines of food aspects.

Applicant Eligibility: Assistance may be used to conduct research or perform other tasks to benefit FNS nutrition assistance programs in the area of food safety.

Beneficiary Eligibility: FNS nutrition assistance program decision makers, FNS nutrition assistance program providers, and FNS nutrition assistance program recipients

Award Range/Average: $15,000 - $1.8 million

Funding: (Cooperative Agreements (Discretionary Grants)) FY 17 $800,000; FY 18 est $600,000; FY 19 est $600,000; FY 16 $800,000; - (Project Grants (Discretionary)) FY 17 $15,000; FY 18 est $15,000; FY 19 est $0; FY 16 $15,000; - National Academy of Sciences Food Forum (Cooperative Agreements) FY 17 $168,000; FY 18 est $300,000; FY 19 est $300,000; FY 16 $300,000; - Institute of Child Nutrition (ICN).

HQ: 3101 Park Center Drive, Room 628
Alexandria, VA 22302
Phone: 703-305-2590
Email: cindy.long@fns.usda.gov
http://www.fns.usda.gov

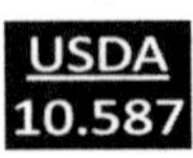

USDA 10.587 NATIONAL FOOD SERVICE MANAGEMENT INSTITUTE ADMINISTRATION AND STAFFING GRANT "ICN"

Award: Cooperative Agreements; Project Grants

Purpose: The National Institute of Child Nutrition Programs provides education, research, educational resources, training and technical assistance for child nutritional professionals.

Applicant Eligibility: Non-competitive. Appropriated by Congress to provide financial and other assistance to the University of Mississippi, in cooperation with the University of Southern Mississippi, to establish and maintain a food service management institute.

Beneficiary Eligibility: FNS nutrition assistance program decision makers, FNS nutrition assistance program providers, and children and teachers.

Award Range/Average: Available Administration and Staffing Grant (non-competitive) - $5,000,000. Available General Education Cooperative Agreement (non-competitive) - $800,000 - $2,000,000

Funding: (Cooperative Agreements) FY 17 $1,170,045; FY 18 est $2,183,000; FY 19 est $800,000; FY 14 $800,000; N/A FY 15 est $800,000; FY 16 est $800,000; - General Education Cooperative Agreement(Salaries and Expenses) FY 17 $5,000,000; FY 18 est $5,000,000; FY 19 est $5,000,000; FY 14 $5,000,000; N/A FY 15 est $5,000,000; FY 16 est $5,000,000; - Administration and Staffing Grant(Cooperative Agreements) FY 17 FY 18 est $2,000,000; FY 19 FY 14 est $500,000; FY 15 est $500,000; FY 16 N/A - School Nutrition Culinary Institute (SNCI)

HQ: 3101 Park Center Drive, Room 628
Alexandria, VA 22302
Phone: 703-305-2590
Email: cindy.long@fns.usda.gov
http://www.fns.usda.gov

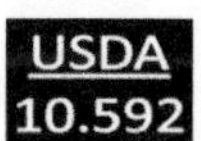

HEALTHY, HUNGER-FREE KIDS ACT OF 2010 CHILDHOOD HUNGER RESEARCH AND DEMONSTRATION PROJECTS
"Demonstration Projects to End Childhood Hunger Healthy, Hunger-Free Kids Act (HHFKA) of 2010"

Award: Cooperative Agreements

Purpose: To provide strategies to end childhood hunger and promote food security. The Healthy Hunger-Free Kids Act provides $ 40 million to conduct and evaluate projects to End Childhood Hunger.

Applicant Eligibility: N/A

Beneficiary Eligibility: N/A

Award Range/Average: Chickasaw: 9.7 million Kentucky: 3.6 million Navajo Nation: 2.4 million Nevada: 3.1 million Virginia: 8.8 million Total: 27.6 million Average: 5.52 million

Funding: (Cooperative Agreements) FY 17 $0; FY 18 est $0; FY 19 est $0; FY 16 est $30,000,000; - $30 million for the grants will be obligated in FY 2015. This money is FY 13-17 funds.

HQ: 3101 Park Center Drive, Room 1014
Alexandria, VA 22302
Phone: 703-305-4369
Email: michael.burke@fns.usda.gov
http://www.fns.usda.gov/school-meals/healthy-hunger-free-kids-act

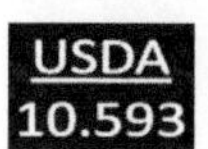

BILL EMERSON NATIONAL HUNGER FELLOWS AND MICKEY LELAND INTERNATIONAL HUNGER FELLOWS PROGRAMS
"Bill Emerson and Mickey Leland Fellows Programs"

Award: Project Grants

Purpose: The Bill Emerson Hunger Fellowship Program addresses hunger and poverty in the United States. It encourages leaders in public service, understands the needs of low-income people, supports people in need, and increases awareness on humanitarian services.

Applicant Eligibility: N/A

Beneficiary Eligibility: N/A

Award Range/Average: Congressional Hunger Center (CHC) $2,000,000 (non-competitive)

Funding: (Project Grants (Fellowships)) FY 17 $2,000,000; FY 18 est $2,000,000; FY 19 est $2,000,000; FY 16 $2,000,000.

HQ: 3101 Park Center Drive, Room 732
Alexandria, VA 22302
Phone: 703-305-2048
Email: lael.lubing@fns.usda.gov

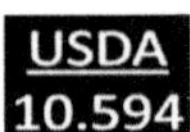

FOOD DISTRIBUTION PROGRAM ON INDIAN RESERVATIONS NUTRITION EDUCATION GRANTS
"Food Distribution Program Nutrition Education Grants"

Award: Project Grants

Purpose: The Food Distribution Program Nutrition Education compensates $1 million to Indian Tribal Organizations for nutrition assistance and provides nutrition knowledge.

Applicant Eligibility: A current FDPIR allowance holder must submit the application. Applicants must propose projects that result in the delivery of nutrition education activities to FDPIR participants.

Beneficiary Eligibility: Applicant ITO/SDA administrators must provide services to FDPIR participants or FDPIR-eligible participants only.

Award Range/Average: Awards range from $2,000 to $214,000.

Funding: FY 17 $972,504; FY 18 est $991,950; FY 19 est $0; FY 16 $981,935

HQ: 3101 Park Center Drive
Alexandria, VA 22302
Phone: 703-305-2833
Email: lindsay.williams@fns.usda.gov
http://www.fns.usda.gov/fdpir/fdpir-nutrition-education-grant-awards

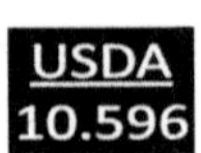

PILOT PROJECTS TO REDUCE DEPENDENCY AND INCREASE WORK REQUIREMENTS AND WORK EFFORT UNDER SNAP
"SNAP Employment and Training Pilots"

Award: Cooperative Agreements

Purpose: Pilot projects increase work and efforts under SNAP. It develops methods to increase workforce and maximizes the income of the workforce and provide public assistance.

Applicant Eligibility: Only State agencies that currently administer the Supplemental Nutrition Assistance Program (SNAP) Employment and Training (E&T) program are eligible for these grants.

Beneficiary Eligibility: Same as Applicant Eligibility.

Award Range/Average: $8,959,379 to $22,329,952. Average is $17,509,239.

Funding: (Cooperative Agreements) FY 17 $0; FY 18 est $0; FY 19 est $0

HQ: 3101 Park Center Drive, 8th Floor
Alexandria, VA 22303
Phone: 703-305-2022
Email: moira.johnston@fns.usda.gov
http://www.fns.usda.gov/snap

USDA 10.597 SCHOOL WELLNESS POLICY COOPERATIVE AGREEMENT "Local Wellness Policy Grant"

Award: Cooperative Agreements

Purpose: The Local Wellness Policy Surveillance System monitors State law and policy data and their effects on student health outcomes. The major national surveillance systems provide School Nutrition Dietary Assessment to analyze data on school meals and environment, meal cost, wastage of meals, the nutritional quality of school meals. The National Cancer Institute's Classification of Laws is a policy to evaluate nutrition and physical education in schools, information about obesity and other cancer-related behaviors. School Health Policies and Practices Study is a national, comprehensive survey conducted to assess school wellness in all areas. Surveys cover health education, physical education, and health services.

Applicant Eligibility: Education, Primary (0-8); Education, Secondary (9-12)

Beneficiary Eligibility: N/A

Award Range/Average: Award amount = $1,699,985

Funding: (Cooperative Agreements) FY 17 $549,318; FY 18 est $305,878; FY 19 est $300,750.

HQ: 3101 Park Center Drive
Alexandria, VA 22302
Phone: 703-305-2105
Email: holly.figueroa@fns.usda.gov

FOOD SAFETY AND INSPECTION SERVICE

REGIONAL OFFICES

Arkansas
Mr. Paul Kiecker, District Manager | Country Club Center 4700 South Thompson, Building B, Suite 201, Springdale, AR 72764 479-751-8412

California
Dr. Yudhbir Sharma, District Manager | 620 Central Avenue, Building 2C, Alameda, CA 94501 510-337-5000

Colorado
Dr. Ron Nelson, District Manager | Denver Federal Center P.O. Box 25387, Building 45, Denver, CO 80225 303-236-9800

Georgia
Dr. Phyllis Adams, District Manager | 100 Alabama Street, S.W., Building 1924, Suite 3R90, Atlanta, GA 30303 404-562-5900

Illinois
Mr. Paul Wolseley, District Manager | 1919 South Highland Avenue, Suite 115C, Lombard, IL 60148 630-620-7474

Iowa
Dr. Dawn Sprouts, District Manager | Room 985, Federal Building 210 Walnut Street, Des Moines, IA 50309 515-727-8960

Mississippi
Dr. Paul Resweber, District Manager | 713 South Pear Orchard Road, Suite 402, Ridgeland, MS 39157 601-965-4312

North Carolina
Dr. Steve Lalicker, District Manager | 6020 Six Forks Road, Raleigh, NC 27609 919-844-8400

Pennsylvania
Mr. Jan Behney, District Manager | U.S. Department of Agriculture Mellon Independence Center 701 Market Street, Suite 4100A, Philadelphia, PA 19106 215-597-4219

Texas
Dr. Jennifer Beasley-McKean, District Manager | 1100 Commerce, Room 516, Dallas, TX 75242 214-767-9116

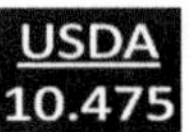

COOPERATIVE AGREEMENTS WITH STATES FOR INTRASTATE MEAT AND POULTRY INSPECTION
"Meat and Poultry Inspection State Programs"

Award: Project Grants

Purpose: To assist Federal agencies to inspect meat and poultry producers to ensure that the products are qualified and properly labeled.

Applicant Eligibility: An appropriate State or U.S. Territory agency administering State or Territorial meat or poultry inspection programs under laws equal to the Federal Meat and Poultry Products Inspection Acts.

Beneficiary Eligibility: General Public.

Award Range/Average: No Data Available.

Funding: (Salaries and Expenses) FY 17 $51,000,000; FY 18 est $51,000,000; FY 19 est $51,000,000; FY 16 $51,000,000

HQ: Outreach and Partnership Division Office of Outreach Employee Education and Training, 355 E Street Patriot Plaza III Building Room 9-256
Washington, DC 20024
Phone: 202-418-8897
Email: dean.norman@fsis.usda.gov
http://www.fsis.usda.gov

MEAT, POULTRY, AND EGG PRODUCTS INSPECTION

Award: Provision of Specialized Services

Purpose: To ensure that meat, poultry, and egg products are inspected by the federal for safety, proper labeling, and shipped carefully.

Applicant Eligibility: Any meat or poultry plant planning to engage in slaughtering or processing meat and poultry products, and all egg products processing plants for shipment in commerce. This program is available in the U.S. and its Territories.

Beneficiary Eligibility: General public (meat, poultry, and egg products.).

Award Range/Average: N/A

Funding: (Salaries and Expenses) FY 17 $1,040,000,000; FY 18 est $1,033,000,000; FY 19 est $1,032,000,000; FY 16 $1,023,000,000

HQ: 344 E Jamie Whitten Building
Washington, DC 20250
Phone: 202-720-8803
Email: william.smith@fsis.usda.gov
http://www.fsis.usda.gov

USDA 10.479 FOOD SAFETY COOPERATIVE AGREEMENTS

Award: Project Grants

Purpose: To minimize illnesses associated with meat, poultry, and egg products. The FSIS conducts educational programs to ensure the safety of these products and directs the Food Emergency Response Network to carry out qualified food supply.

Applicant Eligibility: State, local and tribal government agencies; academic institutions and non-profit organizations.

Beneficiary Eligibility: General public.

Award Range/Average: No Data Available.

Funding: (Cooperative Agreements) FY 17 $3,000,000; FY 18 est $3,000,000; FY 19 est $3,000,000; FY 16 $3,000,000

HQ: US Department of Agriculture FERN Staff 950 College Station Road

Athens, GA 30605

Phone: 706-546-2349

Email: robert.phillips@fsis.usda.gov

http://www.fsis.usda.gov

FOREST SERVICE

REGIONAL OFFICES

Alaska

709 W. 9th Street, Juneau, AK 99801-1807 907-586-8806

Colorado

740 Simms Street P.O. Box 25127, Golden, CO 80401-4720 303-275-5741

Georgia

1720 Peachtree Road, N.W., Atlanta, GA 30309 404-347-7486

Montana

Federal Building 200 East Broadway P.O. Box 7669, Missoula, MT 59807-7669 406-329-3511

New Mexico

333 Broadway Blvd., SE, Santa Fe, NM 87102-3407 505-842-3292

Oregon

333 S.W. First Street, P.O. Box 3623, Portland, OR 97208-3623 503-808-2204

Pennsylvania

11 Campus Blvd., Suite 200, Newtown Square, PA 19073-3200 610-557-4103

Puerto Rico

Jardin Botanico Sur, 1201 Calle Ceiba, San Juan, PR 00926-1119 787-766-5335

Utah

Federal Office Building, 324 25th Street, Ogden, UT 84401-2300 801-625-5239

Wisconsin

626 East Wisconsin Ave., Suite 800, Milwaukee, WI 53202-4616

RESEARCH HEADQUARTERS

California

1323 Club Drive, Vallejo, CA 95492-1110 707-562-8737

800 Buchanan Street, West Annex Building, Albany, CA 94701-0245 510-559-6300

Colorado

2150 Centre Ave, Building A, Fort Collins, CO 80526-1891 303-275-5350

North Carolina

200 W. T. Weaver Boulevard, Asheville, NC 28804-3454 704-257-4301

Oregon

333 SW First Ave, Portland, OR 97204 503-808-2592

Pennsylvania
11 Campus Blvd., Suite 200, Newtown Square, PA 19073-3200 610-557-4023

Wisconsin
One Gifford Pinchot Drive, Madison, WI 53726-2398 608-231-9200

Utah
Denver P. Burns | 324 25th Street, Ogden, UT 84401 801-625-5421

USDA 10.652 FORESTRY RESEARCH "Research Grants & Cooperative Agreements"

Award: Cooperative Agreements; Project Grants

Purpose: To promote research activities of the Forest Service and award grants to the educational institutions and organizations engaged in renewable resources research.

Applicant Eligibility: Grants and cooperative agreements for basic or applied research may be made to State Agricultural Experiment Stations, universities and colleges, State and local governments, U.S. Territories, nonprofit research institutions or organizations, international organizations, individuals, and for-profit organizations.

Beneficiary Eligibility: Organizations and scientists involved in basic and applied research activities related to forest and rangeland renewable resources.

Award Range/Average: $2,000 to $300,000. Average: $35,000.

Funding: (Project Grants) FY 17 $2,384,910; FY 18 est $1,357,076; FY 19 FY 16 $6,502,028

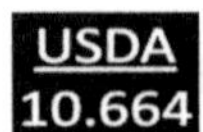

HQ: 201 14th Street SW 2 NW
Washington, DC 20024
Phone: 202-205-1665
Email: crodriguezfranco@fs.fed.us
http://www.fs.fed.us/links/research.html

USDA 10.664 COOPERATIVE FORESTRY ASSISTANCE

Award: Formula Grants; Project Grants

Purpose: To promote forest resources management and conservation, control insects and diseases affecting trees and forests, avoid accidental fires, recycle biomass, maintenance of fish and wildlife habitat, and to encourage educational, technical, and financial assistance programs to assist owners of non-Federal forest lands.

Applicant Eligibility: State Forestry or equivalent State agencies, Tribes, non-profits, and municipalities are eligible. All States, the District of Columbia, the Commonwealth of Puerto Rico, the Virgin Islands of the United States, the Commonwealth of the Northern Mariana Islands, the Federated States of Micronesia, the Republic of the Marshall Islands, the Republic of Palau, and the territories and possessions of the United States are eligible.

Beneficiary Eligibility: Landowners of nonfederal lands; rural community fire fighting forces; urban and municipal governments, non-profit organizations, Tribes and other State, local, and private agencies acting through State Foresters, equivalent State officials, or other official representatives.

Award Range/Average: $25,000 to $6,000,000. Average $1,000,000

Funding: (Project Grants) FY 17 $21,515,695; FY 18 FY 19

HQ: 1400 Independence Avenue SW, P.O. Box 1109
Washington, DC 20250
Phone: 202-205-1657
Email: phirami@fs.fed.us
http://www.fs.fed.us/spf

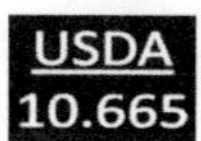

SCHOOLS AND ROADS – GRANTS TO STATES "Payments to States"

Award: Formula Grants

Purpose: To assist the National Forests and supplemental mandatory appropriations.

Applicant Eligibility: Title I payments are made to States or territories of the United States to be allocated to counties in which national forests are situated. Title II project funds are reserved in special account in the U.S. Treasury and may be used by the Secretary of Agriculture for the purpose of entering into and implementing cooperative agreements with willing Federal agencies, State and local governments, private and nonprofit entities, and landowners.

Beneficiary Eligibility: A beneficiary of title II special project funds is a person or entity that receives a grant or enters into a cooperative agreement with the Secretary of Agriculture to carry out a project for protection, restoration, and enhancement of fish and wildlife habitat, and other resource objectives consistent with the purposes of the Secure Rural Schools Act on national forests and on non-national forest land where projects would benefit the resources on national forests.

Award Range/Average: 25% 7 yr. average: $2 to $1,397,323 – average: $151,756 (19 states) Title I: $1 to $9,587,418 - average $366,907: (42 states) Title II: $1,922 to $1,294,931 – average: $98,145 (31 states) Title III: $1,682 to $789,552 – average: $54,134 (31 states)

Funding: (Cooperative Agreements) FY 17 $10,279,660; FY 18 est $5,199,200; FY 19 FY 16 $2,059,485.

HQ: 201 14th Street SW, Suite 4 NW
Washington, DC 20024
Phone: 202-649-1177
Email: lveldhuis@fs.fed.us
http://www.fs.usda.gov/main/pts/home

SCHOOLS AND ROADS – GRANTS TO COUNTIES "Direct payments to States"

Award: Direct Payments for Specified Use

Purpose: To assist the National Grasslands and Land Utilization Projects with the Counties.

Applicant Eligibility: Eligible applicants are counties of the United States containing National Grassland or a LUP.

Beneficiary Eligibility: Counties within the United States

Award Range/Average: No Data Available.

Funding: (Direct Payments for Specified Use) FY 17 FY 18 FY 19 FY 16.

HQ: 201 14th Street SW, Suite 4 NW
Washington, DC 20024
Phone: 202-649-1177
Email: lveldhuis@fs.fed.us
http://www.fs.fed.us/srs

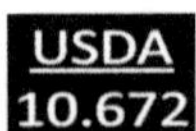

RURAL DEVELOPMENT, FORESTRY, AND COMMUNITIES
"Rural Development Through Forestry"

Award: Project Grants

Purpose: To assist rural areas in assessing forest resource opportunities to develop and expand the diversify communities' economic base.

Applicant Eligibility: Tribal nations, State and Federal agencies, State Foresters, local governments, not-for-profit organizations, and others working in support of community identified goals.

Beneficiary Eligibility: Tribal nations, State and Federal agencies, State Foresters, local governments, not-for-profit organizations, and others. Forest Service Regions/Areas/Institutes are encouraged to further define program policies that focus resources to meet the regional, State and local needs of communities.

Award Range/Average: No Data Available.

Funding: (Project Grants (Special)) FY 17 $0; FY 18 est $0; FY 19 est $0; FY 16 $0

HQ: 201 14th Street SW
Washington, DC 20024
Phone: 202-205-1380
Email: smarshall@fs.fed.us

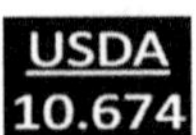

WOOD UTILIZATION ASSISTANCE
"State and Private Forestry Technology, Marketing Assistance Program"

Award: Cooperative Agreements; Project Grants

Purpose: To provide technical assistance to Forest Service, tribes, and private organizations with technologies to effectively manage forests. The State & Private Forestry staff provides awareness of forest products utilization and biofuels conservation.

Applicant Eligibility: Entities eligible include: Non-profits, local, state, and Tribal governments, business, companies, corporations (for Profit), institutions of higher education, and special purpose districts, (public utilities districts, fire districts, conservation districts, or ports).

Beneficiary Eligibility: N/A

Award Range/Average: Typical awards are $250,000 per award. Exceptions may be made for special circumstances.

Funding: (Project Grants) FY 17 $10,280,943; FY 18 est $9,000,000.

HQ: 201 14th Street SW
Washington, DC 20250

Phone: 703-605-5346

Email: melissaljenkins@fs.fed.us

http://www.na.fs.fed.us/werc

USDA 10.675 URBAN AND COMMUNITY FORESTRY PROGRAM

Award: Project Grants

Purpose: To protect forests and related natural resources in cities and towns. The urban and community forestry program promotes ecosystem services.

Applicant Eligibility: State Foresters or equivalent State agencies, Tribal nations, interested members of the public, private non-profit organizations and others. All States, as well as the District of Columbia, Puerto Rico, the United States Virgin Islands, the Commonwealth of the Northern Mariana Islands, American Samoa and Guam, and other territories and possessions of the United States are eligible.

Beneficiary Eligibility: Same as Applicant Eligibility.

Award Range/Average: No Data Available.

Funding: (Project Grants) FY 17 $6,960,009; FY 18 FY 19 FY 16 $900,000

HQ: 1400 Independence Avenue SW, P.O. Box 1151

Washington, DC 20250

Phone: 202-401-4416

Email: jkdavis@fs.fed.us

http://www.fs.fed.us/ucf/contact_regional.shtml

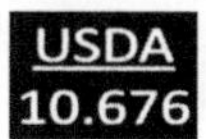

USDA 10.676 FOREST LEGACY PROGRAM "FLP"

Award: Project Grants

Purpose: The Forest Legacy Program promotes conservation of forests and forest services that includes utilization of forest products in a positive manner.

Applicant Eligibility: Projects are evaluated and prioritized by State lead agencies, in consultation with the State Forest Stewardship Coordinating Committees. All States and territories participate except North Dakota, the Commonwealth of the Northern Mariana Islands, and Guam.

Beneficiary Eligibility: State agency, landowners of private forest lands, and land trust organizations.

Award Range/Average: N/A

Funding: (Project Grants) FY 17 $63,909,167; FY 18 est $67,025,000; FY 19 est $0; FY 16 $55,947,000

HQ: 1400 Independence Avenue SW, P.O. Box 1123

Washington, DC 20850

Phone: 202-205-1618

Email: sstewart@fs.fed.us

http://www.fs.fed.us/spf/coop/programs/loa/flp.shtml

USDA 10.678 FOREST STEWARDSHIP PROGRAM "FSP"

Award: Project Grants

Purpose: To encourage the long-term active management of non-industrial private and non-federal forest land to preserve the multiple values and uses.

Applicant Eligibility: State forestry or equivalent State agencies, tribes, non-profits, and municipalities are eligible. All States, the District of Columbia, Puerto Rico, the United States Virgin Islands, the Commonwealth of the Northern Mariana Islands, American Samoa, Guam, the Trust Territory of the Pacific Islands, and territories and possessions of the United States may be eligible.

Beneficiary Eligibility: Landowners of non-federal lands, non-profit organizations, tribes and other State, local, and private agencies acting through State Foresters, equivalent State officials, or other official representatives are eligible. Landowners seeking assistance through the Forest Stewardship Program should contact their state forest agency directly.

Award Range/Average: $50,000 to $400,000

Funding: (Project Grants) FY 17 $8,000,000; FY 18 N/A FY 19 FY 16 $7,774,163

HQ: 1400 Independence Avenue SW
Washington, DC 20250
Phone: 202-205-0929
Email: lschoonhoven@fs.fed.us
http://www.fs.fed.us/managing-land/private-land/forest-stewardship

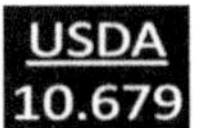

COLLABORATIVE FOREST RESTORATION "CFRP"

Award: Project Grants

Purpose: To promote watersheds to control high-intensity wildfires, insect infestation, protect wildlife biodiversity, improve communication in restoring the diversity and productivity of forested watersheds, and encourage forest restoration techniques in New Mexico.

Applicant Eligibility: Local and tribal governments, educational institutions, landowners, conservation organizations, and other interested public and private entities. Grant proponents must include a diverse and balanced group of stakeholders as well as appropriate Federal, Tribal, State, County, and Municipal government representatives in the design and implementation of the project.

Beneficiary Eligibility: See Applicant Eligibility.

Award Range/Average: $66,361- $360,000

Funding: (Project Grants) FY 17 $3,000,000; FY 18 est $2,999,993; FY 19 FY 16 $3,525,157

HQ: 333 Broadway Boulevard SE
Albuquerque, NM 87102
Phone: 505-842-3425
Email: wdunn@fs.fed.us
http://www.fs.usda.gov/goto/r3/cfrp

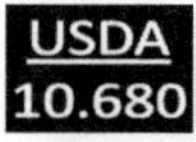

FOREST HEALTH PROTECTION

Award: Formula Grants; Project Grants

Purpose: To protect non-Federal forest and tree resources from insects, diseases, and invasive plants and to improve forest health protection technologies to safeguard forests.

Applicant Eligibility: State Forestry, State Agriculture or equivalent State agencies, subdivisions of states, Alaska native corporations and tribal governments (for lands not held in trust), institutions (public and private), organizations (profit and non-profit), and municipalities are eligible. All States, the District of Columbia, Puerto Rico, the Virgin Islands, the Northern Mariana Islands, the Trust Territory of the Pacific Islands, and the territories and possessions of the United States are eligible.

Beneficiary Eligibility: State Foresters, State Plant Regulatory Officials, equivalent State officials or other official representatives, tribes, subdivisions of states, agencies, institutions (public and private), organizations (profit or nonprofit), and individuals on non-Federal lands.

Award Range/Average: No Data Available.

Funding: (Project Grants) FY 17 $21,515,698; FY 18 FY 19 FY 16 $33,424,000

HQ: 1400 Independence Avenue SW, P.O. Box 1110
Washington, DC 20250
Phone: 703-605-5340
Email: rcooksey@fs.fed.us
http://www.fs.fed.us/spf/foresthealth

WOOD EDUCATION AND RESOURCE CENTER (WERC) "WERC"

Award: Cooperative Agreements; Project Grants

Purpose: To compensate with technical assistance for projects to sustain forest products, maintain the health of forests, technologies to improve profitability and promote green buildings, knowledge on sanitizing wood packaging materials, and promoting the use of woody biomass to reduce hazardous fuels.

Applicant Eligibility: Nonfederal agencies; public and private agencies including State, local and tribal governments; institutions of higher education; non-profit organizations; for-profit organizations; corporations; businesses; and others.

Beneficiary Eligibility: Same as Applicant Eligibility

Award Range/Average: $10,000 to $80,000. Average is approximately $50,000.

Funding: (Project Grants (Discretionary)) FY 17 $0; FY 18 est $0; FY 19 est $0; FY 16 $0; - No available funding for annual competitive grant program.

HQ: 1400 Independence Avenue SW
Washington, DC 20250
Phone: 202-205-1380
Email: smarshall@fs.fed.us
http://www.na.fs.fed.us/werc

USDA 10.682 NATIONAL FOREST FOUNDATION "NFF"

Award: Direct Payments for Specified Use

Purpose: The National Forest Foundation encourages the activities and services of the Forest Service of the Department of Agriculture. It promotes educational, technical, and other assistance that support the programs conducted by the Forest Service.

Applicant Eligibility: Program is authorized for the National Forest Foundation under National Forest Foundation Act, Public Law 101-593 as amended by Public Law 103-106.

Beneficiary Eligibility: Potential beneficiaries include non-governmental, nonprofit 501(c)(3) and for profit organizations, state and local governments and Native American tribes working on or adjacent to National Forests and Grasslands throughout the United States.

Award Range/Average: N/A

Funding: (Direct Payments for Specified Use) FY 17 $3,000,000; FY 18 est $3,000,000; FY 19 est $3,000,000; FY 16 est $3,000,000; - 1:1 matching requirement

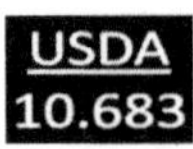

HQ: 201 14th Street SW, Suite 4NW
Washington, DC 20250
Phone: 202-649-1177
Email: lveldhuis@fs.fed.us
http://www.nationalforests.org

USDA 10.683 NATIONAL FISH AND WILDLIFE FOUNDATION "National Fish and Wildlife Foundation (NFWF)"

Award: Direct Payments for Specified Use

Purpose: National Fish and Wildlife Foundation directs public conservation dollars to the environmental needs. The Foundation's method is simple and effective to work for conservation challenges.

Applicant Eligibility: Program authorized for the National Fish and Wildlife Foundation (NFWF) only.

Beneficiary Eligibility: No additional information

Award Range/Average: N/A

Funding: (Direct Payments for Specified Use) FY 17 $3,000,000; FY 18 est $3,000,000; FY 19 FY 16 $3,671,633

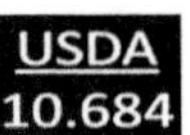

HQ: 201 14th Street NW 3SE
Washington, DC 20024
Phone: 202-205-1671
Email: rharper@fs.fed.us
http://www.nfwf.org

USDA 10.684 INTERNATIONAL FORESTRY PROGRAMS

Award: Cooperative Agreements; Project Grants

Purpose: Forest Service efforts improve forest policies and practices and assists forest-dependent peoples by compensating into cooperative agreements with nonprofit organizations and governments engaged in forest conservation and management.

Applicant Eligibility: Potential applicants include U.S. and international organizations, educational institutions, government entities, and individuals. International applicants must be from countries sanctioned by the State Department.

Beneficiary Eligibility: Potential beneficiaries include host-country forest management agencies, non-profit organizations, forest landowners in the target countries, forest-dependent communities and peoples in the targeted countries, and U.S. landowners and organizations involved in or concerned with invasive species mitigation, migratory species conservation, legal trade in forest products, and the impact of climate change on forests.

Award Range/Average: N/A

Funding: (Project Grants) FY 17 $12,803,332; FY 18 est $3,557,236; FY 19 FY 16 $4,535,457

HQ: 1 Thomas Circle NW, Suite 400
Washington, DC 20005
Phone: 202-644-4613
Email: vanessapinkney@fs.fed.us
http://www.fs.fed.us

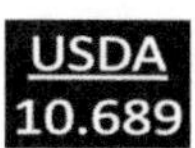

COMMUNITY FOREST AND OPEN SPACE CONSERVATION PROGRAM (CFP)
"Community Forest Program (CFP)"

Award: Project Grants

Purpose: The purpose of CFP is to provide financial assistance to local governments, Indian tribes, and nonprofit organizations; to encourage economic benefits through forest management; to promote natural resource conservation; to provide public access to the forests to enhance health, and to provide technical assistance for implementing forest projects.

Applicant Eligibility: Project grants are awarded to local governments, Indian tribes, or nonprofit organizations qualified to acquire land and with the authority to manage land.

Beneficiary Eligibility: No additional information

Award Range/Average: Range is from $86,150 to $400,000, with an average of $304,283.

Funding: (Project Grants (Discretionary)) FY 17 $2,000,000; FY 18 N/A FY 19 FY 16 $2,000,000; - Annual funding levels to be determined per Presidential budget request.

HQ: 1400 Independence Avenue SW, P.O. Box 1123
Washington, DC 20850
Phone: 202-205-1618
Email: sstewart@fs.fed.us
http://www.fs.fed.us/managing-land/private-land/community-forest/program

USDA 10.690 LAKE TAHOE EROSION CONTROL GRANT PROGRAM

Award: Cooperative Agreements; Project Grants

Purpose: To fund for research projects for land management in the Tahoe Basin. To promote relevant research to address natural resource management needs, to protect the natural environment and maintain public health, to safeguard water quality and wildlife, and to maintain soil conservation and vegetation.

Applicant Eligibility: Eligible applicants for National Forest System awards includes State Forestry or equivalent agencies, tribes, non-profits, and municipalities in the local governing bodies of political subdivisions in the Lake Tahoe basin. Eligible applicants for competitive research awards includes State Agricultural Experiment Stations, universities and colleges, State and local governments, U.S. Territories, nonprofit research institutions or organizations, international organizations, individuals, and for-profit organizations.

Beneficiary Eligibility: Beneficiary eligibility for National Forest System awards include governing bodies of each of the political subdivisions (including public utilities) located in the Lake Tahoe Basin. Beneficiary eligibility for competitive research awards include organizations and scientists involved in basic and applied research activities related to forest and rangeland renewable resources.

Award Range/Average: No Data Available.

Funding: (Project Grants (Discretionary)) FY 17 $263,000; FY 18 est $611,350; FY 19 FY 16 $700,622

GOOD NEIGHBOR AUTHORITY
"Good Neighbor"

Award: Cooperative Agreements

Purpose: To promote restoration and protection services on Federal land.

Applicant Eligibility: State includes state agencies that are part of a State university system. State universities are not eligible.

Beneficiary Eligibility: Program authorized for states containing or affected by National Forest System Land, including the Commonwealth of Puerto Rico.

Award Range/Average: Variable. Projects may range from $5,000 - $1,000,000

Funding: (Cooperative Agreements) FY 17 $11,799,404; FY 18 est $16,319,125; FY 19 FY 16 $37,720,435

HQ: 201 14th Street SW
Washington, DC 20250
Phone: 202-205-1495
Email: jwcrockett@fs.fed.us
http://www.fs.fed.us/managing-land/farm-bill/gna

USDA 10.693 WATERSHED RESTORATION AND ENHANCEMENT AGREEMENT AUTHORITY
"Wyden Amendment"

Award: Cooperative Agreements

Purpose: To promote cooperative agreements for the protection, restoration, and enhancement of wildlife habitat and reduction of risk from natural disaster where public safety is threatened.

Applicant Eligibility: Private landowners, State, local or Tribal governments or other public entities, educational institutions or private nonprofit entities.

Beneficiary Eligibility: Projects must be located in the same watershed where the public resource benefits will occur.

Award Range/Average: Varies by type of project and funding available.

Funding: (Cooperative Agreements (Discretionary Grants)) FY 17 $4,590,515; FY 18 est $1,098,493; FY 19 FY 16 $3,968,460; -

HQ: 201 14th Street NW, Room 3SE
Washington, DC 20024
Phone: 202-205-1671
Email: rharper@fs.fed.us

SOUTHWEST FOREST HEALTH AND WILDFIRE PREVENTION

Award: Direct Payments for Specified Use

Purpose: To enhance restoration treatments that will reduce the risk of wildfires, to improve the health of the dry forest, to implement forest and woodland restoration, to use ecological restoration and wildfire treatments, to assist land managers in new management technologies, and to assist Federal and non-Federal land managers in the role of fire management.

Applicant Eligibility: N/A

Beneficiary Eligibility: One (1) Institute each of (A) the State of Arizona, to be located at Northern Arizona University; (B) the State of New Mexico, to be located at New Mexico Highlands University, while engaging the full resources of the consortium of universities represented in the Institute of Natural Resource Analysis and Management (INRAM); and (C) the State of Colorado, to be located at Colorado State University

Award Range/Average: Range of assistance is $150,000 - $1,500,000

Funding: (Direct Payments for Specified Use) FY 17 $1,500,000; FY 18 est $1,500,000; FY 19 FY 16 $1,500,000

HQ: 333 Broadway Boulevard SE
Albuquerque, NM 87102
Phone: 505-842-3425
Email: wdunn@fs.fed.us
http://www.fs.usda.gov/goto/r3/sweri

STATE & PRIVATE FORESTRY HAZARDOUS FUEL REDUCTION PROGRAM

"S&PF Hazardous Fuels Program"

Award: Cooperative Agreements; Project Grants

Purpose: To reduce wildfires, minimize the use of hazardous fuels, and to safeguard communities from wildfires.

Applicant Eligibility: Hazardous fuel reduction projects on non-Federal land

Beneficiary Eligibility: Program supports activities on non-Federal land.

Award Range/Average: No Data Available.

Funding: (Project Grants (Discretionary)) FY 17 $15,000,000; FY 19 N/A FY 18 est $15,000,000

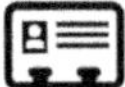

HQ: 201 14th Street SW
Washington, DC 20250
Phone: 202-205-1129
Email: ffay@fs.fed.us

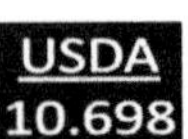

STATE & PRIVATE FORESTRY COOPERATIVE FIRE ASSISTANCE "Cooperative Fire Assistance"

Award: N/A

Purpose: To assist in the control of rural fires, to develop new and improved fire prevention and fire technologies, to promote efficient fire mitigation and protection, to assist local rural firefighting forces.

Applicant Eligibility: Primary recipients are State Forestry agencies. Other non-profit organizations, tribal organizations, and educational institutions.

Beneficiary Eligibility: N/A

Award Range/Average: No Data Available.

Funding: (Project Grants) FY 17 N/A FY 18 est $15,000,000; FY 19 N/A.

HQ: 201 14th Street SW
Washington, DC 20250
Phone: 202-205-1504
Email: jfortner@fs.fed.us

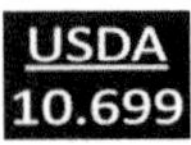

PARTNERSHIP AGREEMENTS

Award: Direct Payments for Specified Use

Purpose: To increase participation in forest service related programs and activities.

Applicant Eligibility: The Forest Service partners with non-profits; for-profit; institutions of higher education; federal, state, local, and Native American tribe governments; individuals; foreign governments and organizations.

Beneficiary Eligibility: The Forest Service has partnership authorities to enter into agreements and cooperative arrangements with willing members of the public, which include but are not limited to, for profit; non-profits; institutions of higher education; federal, state, local, and Native American tribe governments; foreign governments and organizations.

Award Range/Average: No Data Available.

Funding: (Direct Payments for Specified Use) FY 17 $139,956,169; FY 18 est $74,769,656; FY 19 FY 16 $74,792,047

HQ: 1400 Independence Avenue SW, P.O. Box 1138
Washington, DC 20228
Phone: 202-205-2254

Email: jemanuel@fs.fed.us

http://www.fs.fed.us/working-with-us/partnerships

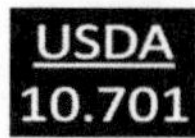

STEWARDSHIP AGREEMENTS
"Stewardship End Result Contracting"

Award: Cooperative Agreements

Purpose: To assist in achieving land management goals and rural community needs, including contributing to the sustainability of rural communities and providing a continuing source of local income and employment.

Applicant Eligibility: The Forest Service may enter into stewardship agreements with any entity that has the ability to either perform the work or contract it out. This can include, state and local governments, Federally recognized tribes and non-profit organizations.

Beneficiary Eligibility: Stewardship Agreements should not be used for: Forest Service overhead costs; Forest Service salaries for contract/agreement development, preparation, or administration; Project planning or environmental analysis; Construction of administrative facilities or major developed facilities; Utilization of forage within an allotment that could be authorized through a grazing permit; Protection, operation, or maintenance of improvements resulting from stewardship projects; Research; Preparation and planning of administrative studies; Land Acquisition.

Award Range/Average: No Data Available.

Funding: (Cooperative Agreements) FY 17 $13,372,179; FY 18 est $5,625,052; FY 19 FY 16 $1,586,637.

HQ: 1400 Independence Avenue SW, P.O. Box 1138

Washington, DC 20250

Phone: 202-205-1495

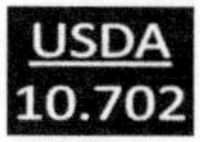

ALASKA NATIONAL INTEREST LANDS CONSERVATION ACT (ANILCA) AGREEMENTS
"ANILCA Agreements"

Award: Direct Payments for Specified Use

Purpose: This multidisciplinary collaborative program sustains fisheries and wildlife management on public lands, conservation of healthy populations of fish and wildlife and other renewable resources to rural Alaskans.

Applicant Eligibility: The U.S. Forest Service's mission is to sustain the health, diversity, and productivity of the nation's forests and grasslands to meet the needs of present and future generations. The agency manages 193 million acres of public land, provides assistance to state and private landowners, and maintains the largest forestry research organization in the world.

Beneficiary Eligibility: An individual/Family, profit organization, other private institution/organization, public nonprofit institution/organization; an officer, employee, agent, department, or instrumentality of the Federal government, of the State of Alaska, municipality or political subdivision of the State of Alaska.

Award Range/Average: No Data Available.

Funding: N/A

HQ: 161 E 1st Street Avenue Door 8

Anchorage, AK 99501

Phone: 907-743-9500
Email: twhitford@fs.fed.us
http://www.fs.usda.gov/r10

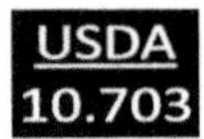

COOPERATIVE FIRE PROTECTION AGREEMENT

Award: Direct Payments for Specified Use

Purpose: To provide reciprocal furnishing for fire protection and compensate for sustaining wildland fire management activities, including suppression and post-fire restoration.

Applicant Eligibility: The Forest Service may enter into Cooperative Fire Protection Agreements with a "fire organization." The term "fire organization" means any governmental entity or public or private corporation or association maintaining fire protection facilities within the United States, its Territories and possessions, and any governmental entity or public or private corporation or association which maintains fire protection facilities in any foreign country in the vicinity of any installation of the United States.

Beneficiary Eligibility: Forest Service enters into non-assistance cooperative agreements with willing fire organizations for the purpose of cooperation in the performance of wildland fire protection projects and during wildfires, emergencies and/or disasters.

Award Range/Average: No Data Available.

Funding: (Cooperative Agreements (Discretionary Grants)) FY 17 $1,671,485; FY 18 est $1,100,910; FY 19.

HQ: 1400 Independence Avenue SW, P.O. Box 1138
Washington, DC 20250
Phone: 208-387-5100
http://www.fs.fed.us/managing-land/fire/master-agreement-template

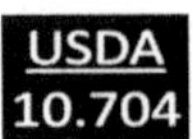

LAW ENFORCEMENT AGREEMENTS

Award: Cooperative Agreements

Purpose: To implement the enforcement of laws on lands within the unit of the National Forest System and to increase the protection of persons and their property to carry out specific responsibilities related to the National Forest System.

Applicant Eligibility: Cooperators include any State or political subdivision (that is, local governments). Cooperative Law Enforcement Agreements are most commonly entered into with county governments.

Beneficiary Eligibility: Agreements must comply with requirements in FSM 5360, Law Enforcement.

Award Range/Average: No Data Available.

Funding: FY 17 $2,289,179; FY 18 est $1,024,448; FY 19 FY 16 $3,446,563

HQ: 201 14th Street SW
Washington, DC 20024
Phone: 202-205-1664
Email: tracielwilkinson@fs.fed.us

COOPERATIVE FOREST ROAD AGREEMENTS

Award: Cooperative Agreements

Purpose: To encourage Forest Service to cooperate with State, county, or road authorities for the construction, improvement, and maintenance of certain forest roads.

Applicant Eligibility: State, county or local public road authorities

Beneficiary Eligibility: Other Requirements.

Award Range/Average: No Data Available.

Funding: (Cooperative Agreements) FY 17 $7,260,141; FY 18 est $4,579,586; FY 19 FY 16 $616,950

HQ: 201 14th Street SW, Suite 3C
Washington, DC 20024
Phone: 202-205-0963
Email: davidpayne@fs.fed.us

RESEARCH JOINT VENTURE AND COST REIMBURSABLE AGREEMENTS

Award: N/A

Purpose: To increase participation in Agricultural and forestry research activities.

Applicant Eligibility: Joint Venture Agreements: State cooperative institution, State department of agriculture, college, university, other research or educational institution or organization, Federal or private agency or organization, individual, or any other party Cost Reimbursable Agreements: State cooperative institutions or other colleges and universities Forestry and Rangeland Research Institutions.

Beneficiary Eligibility: The Forest Service has partnership authorities to enter into agreements and cooperative arrangements with willing members of the public, which include but are not limited to, for profit; non-profits; institutions of higher education; federal, state, local, and Native American tribe governments; foreign governments and organizations.

Award Range/Average: No Data Available.

Funding: (Direct Payments for Specified Use) FY 17 $70,997,322; FY 18 est $51,653,417.

HQ: 1400 Independence Avenue SW
Washington, DC 20250
Phone: 703-605-4776
Email: jacquelinehenry@fs.fed.us
http://www.fs.fed.us

Programs Administered by Regional - State - Local Offices

INTERNATIONAL TRADE ADMINISTRATION

RESEARCH HEADQUARTERS

Alabama
George Norton, Director | Medical Forum Building, Room 707 950 22nd Street, North, Birmingham, AL 35203 205-731-1331

Alaska
Charles Becker, Director | 550 West 7th Avenue, Suite 1770, Anchorage, AK 99501 907-271-6237

Arizona
Eric Nielsen, Manager | 166 West Alameda, Tucson, AZ 85701 520-670-5540

Frank Woods, Director | 2901 N. Central Avenue, Suite 970, Phoenix, AZ 85012 602-640-2513

Arkansas
Lon J. Hardin, Director | 425 West Capitol Avenue, Suite 700, Little Rock, AR 72201 501-324-5794

California
530 Water Street, Suite 740, Oakland, CA 94607 510-273-7350

Dale Wright, Manager | 917 7th Street, 2nd Floor, Sacramento, CA 95814 916-498-5155

Eduardo Torres, Manager | 390-B Fir Avenue, Clovis, CA 93611 559-325-1619

Elizabeth Krauth, Manager | 330 Ignacio Boulevard, Suite 102, Novato, CA 94949 415-883-1966

Fred Latuperissa, Manager | Inland Empire Export Assistance Center 2940 Inland Empire Boulevard, Suite 121, Ontario, CA 91764 909-466-4134

Greg Mignano, Director | 101 Park Center Plaza, Suite 1001, San Jose, CA 95113 408-271-7300

Julie Anne Hennesey, Manager | 11150 Olympic Boulevard, Suite 975, Los Angeles, CA 90064 310-235-7104

Julie Anne Hennessey, Acting Manager | 350 S. Figueroa Street, Suite 509, Los Angeles, CA 90071 213-894-4022

Mark A. Weaver, Manager | c/o Monterey Institute of International Studies 411 Pacific Street, Suite 320, Monterey, CA 93940 831-641-9850

Mary Boscia, Director | One World Trade Center, Suite 1670, Long Beach, CA 90831 562-980-4550

Matt Andersen, Director | 6363 Greenwich Drive, Suite 230, San Diego, CA 92122

Paul Tambakis, Director | Orange County Export Assistance Center 3300 Irvine Avenue, Suite 305, Newport Beach, CA 92660 949-660-1688

R.J. Donovan, Manager | 5201 Great America Parkway, Suite 456, Santa Clara, CA 95054 408-970-4610

Stephen Crawford, Manager | 250 Montgomery Street, 14th Floor, San Francisco, CA 94104 415-705-2300

Colorado
Isabella Cascarano, Acting Director | 1625 Broadway, Suite 680, Denver, CO 80202 303-844-6623

Connecticut
Carl Jacobsen, Director | 213 Court Street, Suite 903, Middletown, CT 06457-3346 860-638-6950
(see Philadelphia Export Assistance Center)

Delaware

Florida
George L. Martinez, Manager | 1130 Cleveland Street, Clearwater, FL 33755

John McCartney, Director Miami, USEAC | 777 North West 72nd Avenue P.O. Box: 3L2, Miami, FL 33126-3009 305-526-7425

John McCartney, Manager | 200 E. Las Olas Boulevard, Suite 1600, Ft. Lauderdale, FL 33301 954-356-6640

Michael E. Higgins, Manager | 325 John Knox Road, Suite 201, Tallahassee, FL 32303 850-942-9635

Philip A. Ouzts, Manager | Eola Park Centre 200 East Robinson Street, Suite 1270, Orlando, FL 32801 407-648-6235

Georgia
Barbara Myrick, Manager | 6001 Chatham Center Drive, Suite 100, Savannah, GA 31405 912-652-4204

Samuel P. Troy, Director | 285 Peachtree Center Avenue NE, Suite 200, Atlanta, GA 30303-1229 404-657-1900

Hawaii
1001 Bishop Street, Bishop Square, Pacific Tower P.O. Box 50026, Suite 1140, Honolulu, HI 96813 808-522-8040

Idaho (Portland, Oregon District)
James Hellwig, Manager | 700 West State Street, 2nd Floor, Boise, ID 83720 208-334-3857

Illinois
James Mied, Manager | 515 North Court Street P.O. Box 1747, Rockford, IL 61103 815-987-8123

Mary N. Joyce, Director | Chicago USEAC Xerox Center 55 West Monroe Street, Room 2440, Chicago, IL 60603 312-353-8045

Robin F. Mugford, Manager | 610 Central Avenue, Suite 150, Highland Park, IL 60035 847-681-8010

Indiana
Dan Swart, Manager | Indianapolis Export Assistance Center Pennwood One, Suite 106 11405 North Pennsylvania Street, Carmel, IN 46032 317-582-2300

Iowa
Allen Patch, Director | 700 Locust Street, Suite 100, Des Moines, IA 50309-3739 515-288-8614

Kansas (Kansas City, Missouri District)
George D. Lavid, Manager | 209 East William, Suite 300, Wichita, KS 67202-4012 316-263-4067

Kentucky
2292 S. Highway 27, Suite 240, Somerset, KY 42501 606-677-6160

John Autin, Director | 601 West Broadway, Room 634B, Louisville, KY 40202

Louisiana
Donald Van de Werken, Director | Delta Export Assistance Center 365 Canal Street, Suite 1170, New Orleans, LA 70130 504-589-6546

Patricia Holt, Manager | 7100 West Park Drive, Shreveport, LA 71129 318-676-3064

Maine (Boston, Massachusetts District)
Jeffrey Porter, Manager | 511 Congress Street, Portland, ME 04101 207-541-7400

Maryland
Thomas Cox, Director | Baltimore USEAC World Trade Center, Suite 2432 401 E. Pratt Street, Baltimore, MD 21202

Massachusetts
Frank J. O'Connor, Director | 164 Northern Avenue, Suite 307 World Trade Center, Boston, MA 02210-2071 617-424-5990

Michigan
Neil Hesse, Director | 211 W. Fort Street, Suite 2220, Detroit, MI 48226 313-226-3650

Paul Litton, Manager | 425 S. Main Street, Suite 103, Ann Arbor, MI 48104

Richard Corson, Manager | Oakland Pointe Office Building, Suite 1300 West 250 Elizabeth Lake Road, Pontiac, MI 48341 248-975-9600

Thomas J. Maquire, Manager | 301 West Fulton Street, Suite 718-S, Grand Rapids, MI 49504 616-458-3564

Minnesota
Ronald E. Kramer, Director | 45 South 7th Street, Suite 2240, Minneapolis, MN 55402 612-348-1638

Mississippi
Harrison Ford, Director | 704 East Main Street, Raymond, MS 39154 601-857-0128

Missouri
Frank Spector, Acting Director | 2345 Grand, Suite 650, Kansas City, MO 64108 816-410-9201

Randall J. LaBounty, Director | 8182 Maryland Avenue, Suite 303, St. Louis, MO 63105

Montana
Mark Peters, Manager | c/o Montana World Trade Center Gallagher Business Building Suite 257, Missoula, MT 59812

Nebraska
Meredith Bond, Manager | 11135 "O" Street, Omaha, NE 68137 402-221-3664

Nevada
Jere Dabbs, Manager | 1755 East Plumb Lane, Suite 152, Reno, NV 89502 775-784-5203

New Hampshire (Boston, Massachusetts District)
Susan Berry, Manager | 17 New Hampshire Avenue, Portsmouth, NH 03801-2838 603-334-6074

New Jersey
Rod Stuart, Director | 3131 Princeton Pike Building #4, Suite 105, Trenton, NJ 08648 609-989-2100

William Spitler, Director | One Gateway Center, 9th Floor, Newark, NJ 07102 973-645-4682

New Mexico (Dallas, Texas District)
Sandy Necessary, Manager | c/o New Mexico Department of Economic Development 1100 St. Francis Drive, Santa Fe, NM 87503 505-827-0350

New York
George Soteros, Manager | Long Island Export Assistance Center 1550 Franklin Avenue, Room 207, Mineola, NY 11501 516-739-1765

James Mariano, Director | 111 West Huron Street, Room 1304, Buffalo, NY 14202 716-551-4191

Joan Kanlian, Manager | Westchester Export Assistance Center 707 Westchester Avenue, Suite 209, White Plains, NY 10604 914-682-6712

John Lavelle, Acting Director | 6 World Trade Center, Room 635, New York, NY 10048 212-466-5222

K.L. Fredericks, Manager | Harlem Export Assistance Center 163 West 125th Street, Suite 904, New York, NY 10027 212-860-6200

North Carolina

Roger Fortner, Acting Manager | 400 West Market Street, Suite 102, Greensboro, NC 27401 336-333-5345

Roger Fortner, Director | 521 E. Morehead Street, Suite 435, Charlotte, NC 28202 704-333-4886

North Dakota

Northern Virginia

Ellen Moore, Acting Manager | 1911 N. Ft. Myer Drive, Suite 601, Arlington, VA 22209 703-524-2885

Ohio

Dao Le, Director | 36 E. 7th Street, Suite 2650, Cincinnati, OH 45202 513-684-2944

Mary Beth Double, Manager | Two Nationwide Plaza, Suite 1400, Columbus, OH 43215

Michael Miller, Director | Bank One Center 600 Superior Avenue, East, Suite 700, Cleveland, OH 44114 216-522-4750

Robert Abrahams, Manager | 300 Madison Avenue, Toledo, OH 43604 419-241-0683

Oklahoma

Jimmy Williams, Manager | 700 N. Greenwood Avenue, Suite 1400, Tulsa, OK 74106 918-581-7650

Ronald L. Wilson, Director | 301 N.W. 63rd Street, Suite 330, Oklahoma City, OK 73116 405-608-5302

Oregon

John O'Connell, Manager | 1401 Willamette Street, Eugene, OR 97401-4003 541-465-6575

Scott Goddin, Director | One World Trade Center, Suite 242 121 S.W. Salmon Street, Portland, OR 97204 503-326-3001

Pennsylvania

Deborah Doherty, Manager | One Commerce Square 228 Walnut Street, Suite 850 P.O. Box 11698, Harrisburg, PA 17108-1698 717-221-4510

Edward Burton, Director | The Curtis Center, Suite 580 West Independence Square West, Philadelphia, PA 19106 215-597-6101

Ted Arnn, Manager | Federal Building, Room 2002 1000 Liberty Avenue, Pittsburgh, PA 15222

Puerto Rico (Hato Rey)

525 F.D. Roosevelt Avenue, Suite 905, San Juan, PR 00918 787-766-5555

Keith Yatsuhashi, Manager One West Exchange Street, Providence, RI 02903 401-528-5104

South Carolina

5300 International Boulevard, Suite 201-C, North Charleston, SC 29418 843-760-3794

Ann Watts, Director | Strom Thurmond Federal Building, Suite 172 1835 Assembly Street, Columbia, SC 29201 803-765-5345

Denis Csizmedia, Manager | Upstate Export Assistance Center Park Central Office Park, Building 1, Suite 109 555 N. Pleasantburg Drive, Greenville, SC 29607

South Dakota

Cinnamon King, Manager | Siouxland Export Assistance Center Augustana College 2001 S. Summit Avenue, Room 122, Sioux Falls, SD 57197 605-330-4264

Tennessee

George Frank, Manager | Old Historic City Hall 601 West Summit Hill Drive, Suite 300, Knoxville, TN 37902-2011 865-545-4637

Michael Speck, Director | 211 Commerce Street 3rd Floor, Suite 100, Nashville, TN 37201 615-736-5161

Ree Russell, Manager | c/o Centre For Enterprise, Buckman Hall 3rd Floor 650 E. Parkway South, Suite 348, Memphis, TN 38104 901-323-1543

Texas

Daniel G. Rodriguez, Manager | 203 South St. Mary Street, Suite 360, San Antonio, TX 78205 210-228-9878

James D. Cook, Director | 500 Dallas, Suite 1160, Houston, TX 77002 713-718-3062

Karen Parker, Manager | 1700 Congress, 2nd Floor P.O. Box 12728, Zip 78711, Austin, TX 78701 512-916-5939

Loree Silloway, Director | P.O. Box 420069, Zip: 75342-0069 2050 North Stemmons Freeway, Suite 170, Dallas, TX 75207 214-767-0542

Vavie Sellschopp, Manager | 711 Houston Street, Fort Worth, TX 76102 817-212-2673

Utah

Stanley Rees, Director | 324 South State Street, Suite 221, Salt Lake City, UT 84111 801-524-5116

Vermont

Susan Murray, Manager | National Life Building, Drawer 20, 6th Floor, Montpelier, VT 05620-0501 802-828-4508

Virginia

Helen D. Lee Hwang, Director | 400 N. 8th Street, Suite 540 P.O. Box 10026, Richmond, VA 23240 804-771-2246

Washington

950 Pacific Avenue, Suite 410, Tacoma, WA 98402 253-593-6736

David Spann, Director | 2001 6th Avenue, Suite 650, Seattle, WA 98121 206-553-5615

Janet Dauble | 801 West Riverside Avenue, Suite 400, Spokane, WA 99201 509-353-2625

West Virginia

David Kotler, Manager | Wheeling Jesuit University/ NTTC 316 Washington Avenue, Wheeling, WV 26003

Harvey Timberlake, Director | 405 Capitol Street, Suite 807, Charleston, WV 25301 304-347-5123

Wisconsin

Paul D. Churchill, Director | 517 East Wisconsin Avenue, Room 596, Milwaukee, WI 53202 414-297-3473

Wyoming

JoAllyn Scott | 101 Park Center Plaza, Suite 1001, San Jose, CA 95113

Michael Hoffman | 3300 Irvine Avenue, Suite 345, Newport Beach, CA 92660-3198 714-660-0144

DOC 11.112 MARKET DEVELOPMENT COOPERATOR PROGRAM "MDCP"

Award: Project Grants

Purpose: The Market Development Cooperator Program develops and expands foreign markets for nonagricultural goods and services produced in the United States.

Applicant Eligibility: Applicants are found to be eligible in one of three categories.

Beneficiary Eligibility: U.S. firms that sell non-agricultural goods or services. While private firms benefit from MDCP project activity, as noted above, they are generally not eligible to apply for MDCP funds.

Award Range/Average: Individual awards may not exceed $300,000.

Funding: Cooperative Agreements (Discretionary Grants) FY 17 $0; FY 18 est $0; FY 19 N/A; FY 16 $1,328,246

HQ: 14th Street and Constitution Avenue NW, Room 20023
Washington, DC 20230
Phone: 202-482-2969
Email: brad.hess@trade.gov
http://www.export.gov/mdcp

MARITIME ADMINISTRATION

(NORTH ATLANTIC GATEWAY (New York):Maine, New Hampshire, Vermont, Massachusetts, Rhode Island, and Connecticut, New York, New Jersey, and Pennsylvania)

One Bowling Green, Room 418, New York, NY 10004-1415 212-668-3330

California

JOHN HUMMER | US Department of Transportation Maritime Administration Northern California Gateway Office 201 Mission Street, Suite 1800, San Francisco, CA 94105 415-744-2924

Florida

LAUREN BRAND, Director | US Department of Transportation Maritime Administration 51 SW 1st Avenue, Suite 1305, Miami, FL 33130 305-530-6420

Illinois

Floyd Miras | US Department of Transportation Maritime Administration Great Lakes Gateway Office 1701 E. Woodfield Rd. Suite 203, Schaumburg, IL 60173

Louisiana
James Murphy | US Department of Transportation Maritime Administration Eastern Gulf/Lower Mississippi Gateway Office 500 Poydras Street, Room 1223, New Orleans, LA 70130-3394 504-589-2000, Ext. 229

Missouri
ROBERT GOODWIN, US Department of Transportation Maritime Administration | Upper Mississippi Office 1222 Spruce St. Suite 2.202F, St Louis, MO 63103-2818 314-539-6783

New York
Shashi N. Kumar | United States Merchant Marine Academy, Kings Point, NY 11024-1699 516-773-5000

Southern California
ALAN HICKS | US Department of Transportation Maritime Administration Southern California Gateway Office, Glenn M. Anderson Federal Bldg 501 West Ocean Blvd, Room 5190, Long Beach, CA 90802 562-628-0246

Virginia
FRANK MACH | US Department of Transportation Maritime Administration Mid Atlantic Gateway Office 7737 Hampton Blvd Bldg 19 Suite 300, Norfolk, VA 23505-1204 757-322-5800

Washington
RANDY ROGERS | US Department of Transportation Maritime Administration Pacific Northwest Gateway Office Henry M. Jackson Federal Building. 915 2nd Avenue 31st Floor, Room 3196, Seattle, WA 98174

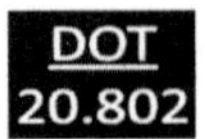

FEDERAL SHIP FINANCING GUARANTEES "Title XI"

Award: Guaranteed/insured Loans

Purpose: To provide competitive financing through the issuance of guarantees of debt issued for the purpose of financing or refinancing the construction, reconstruction or reconditioning of vessels built in United States shipyards.

Applicant Eligibility: An individual with the ability, experience, financial resources, and other qualifications necessary for the adequate operation and maintenance of a vessel or an eligible shipyard.

Beneficiary Eligibility: U.S. and foreign shipowners, or eligible U.S. shipyards.

Award Range/Average: Less than $1 million to several hundred million.

Funding: (Guaranteed/Insured Loans) FY 17 $394,501,000; FY 18 est $413,000,000; FY 19 est $0; FY 16 $3,135,000; - (Salaries) FY 17 $3,94,501,000; and FY 18 413,000,000, FY 19 $0(Guaranteed/Insured Loans) FY 17 $373,748,000; FY 18 est $0; FY 19 est $0; FY 16 $0; - (Guaranteed/Insured Loans) FY 17 $373,748,000; FY 18 est. $0 and FY 19 est. $0

HQ: 1200 New Jersey Avenue SE
Washington, DC 20590
Phone: 202-366-2118
Email: david.gilmore@dot.gov
http://www.marad.dot.gov

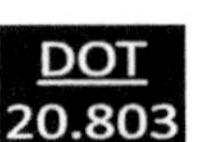

MARITIME WAR RISK INSURANCE "Title XII, MMA, 1936"

Award: Insurance

Purpose: Provides war risk insurance to U.S.-flag and foreign vessels whenever it appears to the Secretary of Transportation that adequate insurance for waterborne commerce cannot be obtained on reasonable terms and conditions from commercial companies.

Applicant Eligibility: All U.S. flag vessels, and certain foreign flag vessels meeting specific criteria as determined by the Maritime Administrator.

Beneficiary Eligibility: Covered beneficiaries include vessel owners, third party liabilities, merchant mariners, and certain designated beneficiaries of deceased mariners.

Award Range/Average: Applicable only in designated combat areas, subject to terms of the binder.

Funding: (Insurance) FY 17 $100,000; FY 18 est $100,000; FY 19 est $100,000

HQ: 1200 New Jersey Avenue SE
Washington, DC 20590
Phone: 202-366-1915
Email: michael.yarrington@dot.gov
http://www.dot.gov

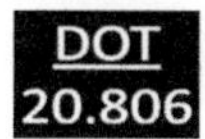

STATE MARITIME SCHOOLS
"State Maritime Schools or Academies (SMA)"

Award: Cooperative Agreements; Direct Payments for Specified Use; Use of Property, Facilities, and Equipment; Training

Purpose: To educate and train future merchant marine officers at the State Maritime Academies (SMA).

Applicant Eligibility: State institutions of higher education. Assistance is limited to one maritime academy in any one State.

Beneficiary Eligibility: Students, meeting eligibility requirements.

Award Range/Average: Annual assistance payment of $500,000 to each regional school provided State matches funds and admits eligible out-of-state student. A subsistence of $8,000 per academic year, not to exceed 4 years, paid to selected students in good standing in the Student Incentive Payment (SIP) Program, NTE a total of 300 students.

Funding: (Direct Payments for Specified Use) FY 17 $3,000,000; FY 18 est $6,000,000; FY 19 N/A.

HQ: Office of Maritime Labor and Training (MAR-650) 1200 New Jersey Avenue SE
Washington, DC 20590
Phone: 202-366-0284
Email: rita.jackson@dot.gov
http://www.dot.gov

U.S. MERCHANT MARINE ACADEMY
"Kings Point"

Award: Training

Purpose: Educates and trains merchant marine officers.

Applicant Eligibility: High school graduates who are U.S. citizens and international students in accordance with legislation. In general, criteria are similar to those generally used for college admission.

Beneficiary Eligibility: High school graduates who are U.S. citizens and eligible international students.

Award Range/Average: Annual assistance payment of $400,000 to each regional school provided State matches funds and admits eligible out-of-state student. An allowance of $48,000 per academic year, not to exceed 5 years, payment to selected students in good standing in the student incentive payment program.

Funding: (Training) FY 17 $140,000; FY 18 est $112,073; FY 19 est $158,023; FY 16 $140,000

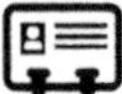

HQ: 300 Steamboat Road
Kings Point, NY 11024
Phone: 516-726-5641
Email: michael.bedryk@usmma.edu
http://www.dot.gov

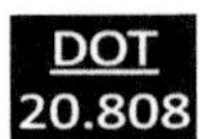

CAPITAL CONSTRUCTION FUND (CCF)

Award: Direct Payments for Specified Use

Purpose: Provides for replacement vessels, additional vessels or reconstructed vessels, built and documented under the laws of the United States for operation in the United States foreign, Great Lakes, Marine Highways or noncontiguous domestic trades.

Applicant Eligibility: An applicant must be a U.S. citizen, own or lease one or more eligible vessels, have a program for the acquisition, construction or reconstruction of a qualified vessel and demonstrate the financial capabilities to accomplish the program.

Beneficiary Eligibility: N/A

Award Range/Average: Applicant receives tax benefits for depositing assets in accordance with the program.

Funding: (Direct Payments for Specified Use) FY 17 $0; Company's own funds are used for the program.

HQ: Office of Financial Approvals 1200 New Jersey Avenue SE
Washington, DC 20590
Phone: 202-366-1859
Email: daniel.ladd@dot.gov
http://www.dot.gov

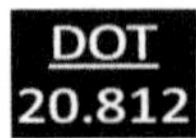

CONSTRUCTION RESERVE FUND (CRF)

Award: Direct Payments for Specified Use

Purpose: To promote the construction, reconstruction, reconditioning, or acquisition of merchant vessels built and documented under the laws of the United States for purposes of national defense.

Applicant Eligibility: A Construction Reserve Fund (CRF) may be established by any citizen of the United States who owns, in whole or in part, a vessel or vessels operating in the foreign or domestic commerce of the U.S., or in the fisheries. Additionally, any citizen who is operating such vessel or vessels owned by another individual may establish a CRF.

Beneficiary Eligibility: Any citizen of the United States who owns, in whole or in part, a vessel or vessels operating in the foreign or domestic commerce of the U.S. or in the fisheries. Additionally, any citizen who is operating such vessel or vessels owned by another individual.

Award Range/Average: Defer tax on gains by depositing the gains attributable to the sale of or indemnification for loss of vessels in accordance with the program.

Funding: FY 17 $0; FY 18 est $0; FY 19 est $0; FY 16 $0; - Company's own funds are used for the program.

HQ: Office of Financial Approvals 1200 New Jersey Avenue SE
Washington, DC 20590
Phone: 202-366-1859
Email: daniel.ladd@dot.gov
http://www.marad.dot.gov

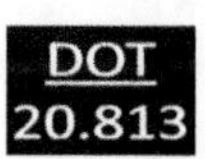

MARITIME SECURITY FLEET PROGRAM OR SHIP OPERATIONS COOPERATION PROGRAM "Maritime Security Program"

Award: Direct Payments for Specified Use

Purpose: The MSP helps sustain a fleet of 60 active, commercially viable, militarily useful, privately-owned vessels operating under U.S. registry to meet national defense and other security requirements.

Applicant Eligibility: U.S. citizens and operators of U.S. flag vessels.

Beneficiary Eligibility: Ownership and operation of vessels and facilities useful to the United States in time of war or national emergency.

Award Range/Average: Authorized $3.1 million per vessel per year (FY 2012-2015); $3.5 million (FY 2016); $4.999 (FY 2017); $5.0 million (FY 2018-20); $5.23 million (FY 2021); and $3.7 million (FY2022-2025)

Funding: (Direct Payments for Specified Use) FY 17 $299,997,000; FY 18 est $300,000,000; FY 19 est $300,000,000; FY 16 $210,000,000; - (Direct payments) FY 16 $3.5mil per ship/annually = $210,000 annual; FY 17 $ $4,999,950 per ship/annually = $299,997mil annual; FY 2018 $5,000,000 per ship/annually = $300,000 mil annual; FY 19 $5,000,000 per ship/annually = $300,000 mil annual

HQ: 1200 New Jersey Avenue SE
Washington, DC 20590
Phone: 202-366-5076
Email: william.mcdonald@dot.gov
http://www.marad.dot.gov

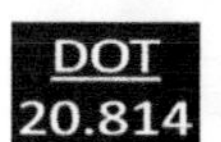

ASSISTANCE TO SMALL SHIPYARDS "Small Shipyard Grants"

Award: Direct Payments for Specified Use

Purpose: Awards grants for capital improvements and related infrastructure improvements at qualified shipyards that will facilitate the efficiency, cost effectiveness, and quality of domestic ship construction for commercial and Federal Government use.

Applicant Eligibility: Either a shipyard or a State or local government on behalf of a shipyard can apply. The shipyard must be one in a single geographical location, located in or near a maritime community, that (1) is a small business concern within the meaning of section 3 of the Small Business Act (15 U.S.C.

Beneficiary Eligibility: Shipyard.

Award Range/Average: Awards can be in any amount up to $19,600,000.

Funding: (Project Grants) FY 17 $9,800,000; FY 18 est $19,600,000; FY 19 est $0; FY 16 $10,000,000; - Either a shipyard or a State or local government on behalf of a shipyard can apply. The shipyard must be one in a single geographical location, located in or near a maritime community, that (1) is a small business concern within the meaning of section 3 of the Small Business Act (15 U.S.C. 632); and (2) does not have more than 600 production employees. Other factors taken into account when grants are awarded will be (a) the economic circumstances and conditions of the maritime community near to which a shipyard is located; and (B) the local, State and regional economy in which such community is located.

HQ: Office of Shipyards and Marine Engineering 1200 New Jersey Avenue, Room W21-318
Washington, DC 20590
Phone: 202-366-5737
Email: david.heller@dot.gov
http://www.marad.dot.gov

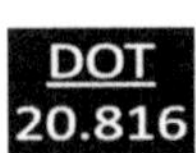

AMERICA'S MARINE HIGHWAY GRANTS
"Marine Highway Program"

Award: Cooperative Agreements; Project Grants

Purpose: Mitigates landside congestion, expand transportation options, and realize public benefit and external cost savings by awarding Marine Highway grants to qualified applicants to implement designated Marine Highway projects.

Applicant Eligibility: Grant applicants must be public agencies at the state, regional or local level including, but not limited to, Metropolitan Planning Organizations, State governments (including State Departments of Transportation) and port authorities. They must also have had their projects for which they are requesting funds be designated as "Marine Highway Projects" by the Secretary of Transportation under America's Marine Highway Program (110th Congress, Public Law 110-140).

Beneficiary Eligibility: Eligible beneficiaries include those entities defined in OMB 2CFR 200.

Award Range/Average: No Data Available.

Funding: (Project Grants (Cooperative Agreements)) FY 17 $5,000,000; FY 18 est $4,500,000; FY 19 est $0; FY 16 $5,000,000

HQ: Office of Marine Highways and Passenger Services 1200 Pennsylvania Avenue NW, P.O. Box 201
Washington, DC 20590
Phone: 202-366-0951
Email: scott.davies@dot.gov
http://marad.dot.gov/ships

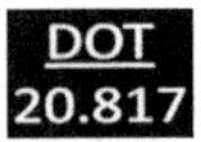

AIR EMISSIONS AND ENERGY INITIATIVE

Award: Cooperative Agreements

Purpose: MARAD will use projects results and data for a variety of purposes including further support of air emissions reduction research, demonstration, and pilot projects.

Applicant Eligibility: Eligible applicants include vessel owners, operators, or public sponsors. Shore side equipment upgrade or shore power projects are not eligible for funding.

Beneficiary Eligibility: The benefit of this project will be for the federal government as well as anyone in the general public and research organizations.

Award Range/Average: No Data Available.

Funding: FY 17 $0; FY 18 est $0; FY 19 est $0; FY 16 $0; - Funding was available in 2015 in the amount of $1,230,000 total; $730,000 for LNG conversion project and $500,000 for exhaust gas cleaning system project.

HQ: Department of Transportation/Maritime Administration 1200 New Jersey Avenue SE
Washington, DC 20590
Phone: 202-366-1913

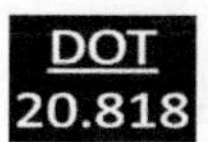

GREAT SHIPS INITIATIVE "Great Waters Research Collaberative (GWRC)"

Award: Cooperative Agreements

Purpose: The Great Waters Research Collaborative (GWRC) is a collaboration whose objective is to end the problem of ship-mediated invasive species in the Great Lakes-St. Lawrence Seaway System.

Applicant Eligibility: Applicants must have the following capabilities and resources: A current EPA-approved Quality Management Plan (QMP). The facilities and equipment for conducting biological analyses to determine concentrations of living organisms in three size-classes (less than 10 microns, between 10 and 50 microns, greater than 50 microns) at the levels of the proposed USCG discharge standard.

Beneficiary Eligibility: Eligible beneficiaries include those entities defined in OMB A-102 and OMB Circular A-122.

Award Range/Average: N/A

Funding: (Salaries and Expenses) FY 18 est $0; FY 16 $0; FY 17 est $0

HQ: Maritime Administration 1200 New Jersey Avenue SE
Washington, DC 20590
Phone: 202-366-1920
Email: carolyn.junneman@dot.gov

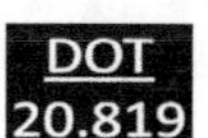

BALLAST WATER TREATMENT TECHNOLOGIES

Award: Cooperative Agreements

Purpose: MARAD will use the projects results and data for a variety of purposes.

Applicant Eligibility: The assistance will be used to support the Evaluation and Verification of Ballast Water Treatment Technologies and other Green Shipping Initiatives. Applicants must be able to provide technical services, equipment and to support the testing, evaluation, and demonstration of treatment methods, practices, systems and equipment.

Beneficiary Eligibility: Beneficiary eligibility include State, Public nonprofit institution/organization, other public institution/organization, Private nonprofit institution/organization, and Education Professional.

Award Range/Average: Past Fiscal Year: 2017 -- $1,000,000 Projection: Current Fiscal Year: 2018 -- $0 Budget Fiscal Year: 2019 -- $0

Funding: (Salaries and Expenses) FY 17 $1,000,000; FY 18 est $0; FY 19 est $0; FY 16 $1,128,840; - Future funding is subject to availability of funds.

HQ: Office of Environmental 1200 New Jersey Avenue SE, Room W26-418
Washington, DC 20590
Phone: 202-366-1920
Email: carolyn.junemann@dot.gov

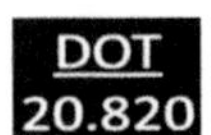

MARITIME STUDIES AND INNOVATIONS

Award: Cooperative Agreements

Purpose: The purpose of this program is to provide assistance for projects involving studies and innovations related to shipping, vessel operations, shipyards, maritime financing and insurance.

Applicant Eligibility: The assistance must be used for projects involving studies and innovations related to shipping, vessel operations, shipyards, maritime financing and insurance, and all other maritime activities in support of the policy of the United States Government to encourage and aid the development and maintenance of a merchant marine. Limitations on applicant eligibility for a specific project, if any, will be explained and included in any Notice of Funding Opportunity posted on grants.

Beneficiary Eligibility: The ultimate beneficiaries will be the United States Government and the general public.

Award Range/Average: The range of funding depends on funds available during the fiscal year.

Funding: (Cooperative Agreements) FY 17 est $200,000; FY 16 $5,000; FY 18 est $5,000

HQ: 1200 New Jersey Avenue SE
Washington, DC 20590
Phone: 202-366-2526
Email: todd.ripley@dot.gov

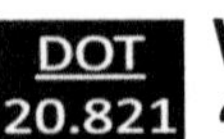

WOMEN ON THE WATER (WOW)
"WOW Conference"

Award: Cooperative Agreements

Purpose: The purpose of the WOW program is to promote diversity in the maritime industry.

Applicant Eligibility: Eligible applicants for financial assistance for WOW program activities are the six State Maritime Academies, regional maritime academies, and the U.S. Merchant Marine Academy.

Beneficiary Eligibility: Beneficiaries are individuals attending the State Maritime Academies and the U.S. Merchant Marine Academy.

Award Range/Average: FY -2017 -- $15,000

Funding: (Cooperative Agreements) FY 17 $15,000; FY 18 est $15,000; FY 19 est $0

HQ: 1200 New Jersey Avenue SE
Washington, DC 20590
Phone: 202-366-0284
Email: rita.jackson@dot.gov
http://www.marad.dot.gov

DOT 20.822

PORT OF GUAM IMPROVEMENT ENTERPRISE PROGRAM

Award: Cooperative Agreements

Purpose: The purpose of this program is to provide financial assistance for the planning, design, and construction of projects for the Port of Guam.

Applicant Eligibility: Port of Guam or any subdivision, instrumentality, or agent thereof.

Beneficiary Eligibility: Same as Applicant Eligibility.

Award Range/Average: No financial assistance awards made in any prior years.

Funding: (Cooperative Agreements) FY 17 $2,268,367; FY 18 est $0; FY 19 est $0; FY 16 $0

HQ: 1200 New Jersey Avenue SE
Washington, DC 20590
Phone: 202-366-5076
Email: robert.bouchard@dot.gov
http://www.portofguam.com

MINE SAFETY AND HEALTH ADMINISTRATION

COAL MINE SAFETY AND HEALTH

Alabama
Richard Gates | 135 Gemini Circle, Suite 213, Birmingham, AL 35209 205-290-7300

Colorado
P.O. Box 25367, DFC, Denver, CO 80225-0367 303-231-5458

District No. 10 (Counties of Kentucky west of and including Gallatin, Owen, Franklin, Anderson, Mercer, Boyle, Casey, Russell And Cumberland).
Jim W. Langley | 100 YMCA Drive, Madisonville, KY 42431-9019 270-821-4180

District No. 7 (North Carolina, South Carolina, Tennessee, counties of Kentucky east of and including Boone, Grant, Scott, Woodford, Jessamine, Garrard, Lincols, Pulaski, and Cinton, up to the District 6 Boundary).
Irvin T. hooker | 3837 S. U.S. Highway 25 E., Barbourville, KY 40906 606-546-5123

Indiana
A. Simms | 2300 Willow Street, Suite 200, Vincennes, IN 47591 812-882-7617

Kentucky
G. Page | 100 Fae Ramsey Lane, Pikeville, KY 41501-3211 606-432-0943

Pennsylvania
The Stegmaier Building, Suite 034 7 North Wilkes-Barre Boulevard, Wilkes-Barre, PA 18702 570-826-6321

Thomas Light | Paladin Professional Center 631 Excel Drive, Suite 100, Mt. Pleasant, PA 15666 724-925-5150

Virginia
Gregory Meikle | P.O. Box 560, Norton, VA 24273 540-679-0230

Wes Virginia
Timothy Watkins | 1301 Airport Road, Beaver, WV 25813 304-253-5237

West Virginia
Bob Cornett | 604 Cheat Road, Morgantown, WV 26508 304-225-6800

David S. Mandeville | 100 Bluestone Road, Mt. Hope, WV 25880 304-877-3900

METAL AND NONMETAL MINE SAFETY AND HEALTH

Alabama
Doniece Schlick | 135 Gemini Circle, Suite 212, Birmingham, AL 35209 205-290-7294

California
Steve Cain | 2060 Peabody Rd, Suite 610, Vacaville, CA 95687-6696 707-447-8425

Colorado
Richard Laufenberg | P.O. Box 25367, Denver, CO 80225-0367 303-231-5511

Minnesota
Steve Richetta | 515 West First Street, #333, Duluth, MN 55802-1302 218-720-5448

Pennsylvania
Donald Foster | 230 Executive Drive, Suite 2, Cranberry Township, PA 16066-6415 724-772-2333

Texas
Michael Davis | 1100 Commerce Street, Room 4C50, Dallas, TX 75242-0499 214-767-8401

NATIONAL MINE HEALTH AND SAFETY ACADEMY

West Virginia
Janet Bertinuson | 1301 Airport Road, Beaver, WV 25813-9426 304-256-3200

TECHNICAL SUPPORT

Pennsylvania
William J. Francart | Cochrans Mill Road P.O. Box 18233, Pittsburgh, PA 15236 412-386-6902

West Virginia
John P. Faini | R.R. 1, Box 251 Industrial Park Road, Triadelphia, WV 26059 304-547-2029

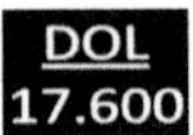

MINE HEALTH AND SAFETY GRANTS

Award: Project Grants

Purpose: Assists States in providing safety and health training and develop programs to improve mine health and safety conditions.

Applicant Eligibility: Any mining State of the United States.

Beneficiary Eligibility: States.

Award Range/Average: From $31,493 to $689,756. Average: $233,912.

Funding: (Project Grants) FY 17 $10,537,000; FY 18 est $10,537,000; FY 19 est $10,537,000; FY 15 $8,440,875; FY 16 $8,441,000

HQ: 201 12th Street S
Arlington, VA 22202
Phone: 202-693-9570
Email: duncan.jeffrey@dol.gov
http://www.msha.gov

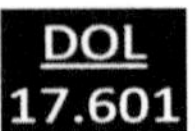

MINE HEALTH AND SAFETY COUNSELING AND TECHNICAL ASSISTANCE

Award: Advisory Services and Counseling; Dissemination of Technical Information

Purpose: Improves conditions of health and safety in and around coal, metal and nonmetallic mines and mineral processing facilities through technical advice, special studies, investigations, and development of mine health and safety programs.

Applicant Eligibility: Applicants should be authorized by their individual organization to request assistance, and should work cooperatively with mine management to facilitate communications with MSHA representatives.

Beneficiary Eligibility: Representatives of state and local government agencies, professional and labor organizations, and mine operators.

Award Range/Average: No Data Available.

Funding: (Salaries and Expenses) FY 17 $24,150,000; FY 18 est $24,859,000; FY 19 est $24,859,000; FY 16 $17,281,000

HQ: William Francart 201 12th Street S 4W210
Arlington, VA 22202
Phone: 202-693-9470
Email: francart.william@dol.gov
http://www.msha.gov

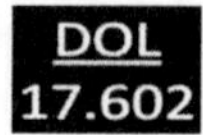

MINE HEALTH AND SAFETY EDUCATION AND TRAINING

DOL 17.602

Award: Training

Purpose: Provides technical training for Federal Mine Inspectors and representatives of the mining industry.

Applicant Eligibility: Any mine operator, miner or their agent can request training or training materials.

Beneficiary Eligibility: Mine operators, miners or their agent, organizations and individuals.

Award Range/Average: N/A

Funding: (Salaries and Expenses) FY 17 $16,869,000; FY 18 est $16,011,000; FY 19 est $16,011,000; FY 16 $13,100,000

HQ: 201 12th Street S
Arlington, VA 22202
Phone: 202-693-9570
Email: duncan.jeffrey@dol.gov
http://www.msha.gov

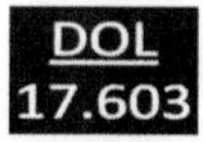

BROOKWOOD-SAGO GRANT

DOL 17.603

Award: Project Grants

Purpose: To provide mine safety and health training and education programs for workers and mine operators, to better identify, avoid, and prevent unsafe working conditions in and around mines.

Applicant Eligibility: Any mining State of the United States, nonprofit public and private organizations.

Beneficiary Eligibility: Mine operators and any organization employing miners or creating training materials.

Award Range/Average: At a minimum, $50,000, depending on the project needs as detailed in the solicitation for grant application and availability of funds.

Funding: FY 17 $250,000; FY 18 est $250,000; FY 19 N/A FY 15 $1,000,000; FY 16 $100,000.

HQ: 201 12th Street S
Arlington, VA 22202
Phone: 202-693-9570
Email: oates.janice@dol.gov
http://www.msha.gov

SAFETY AND HEALTH GRANTS

Award: Project Grants

Purpose: To provide mine safety and health training and education to miners, mine operators, and other individuals who may work at a mine; and to develop training and other programs to improve health and safety conditions at mines.

Applicant Eligibility: Any mining State of the United States, non-profit public and private organizations, commercial entity, or the legislatively mandated entity.

Beneficiary Eligibility: Individuals employed in workplaces covered by the Mine Act, as amended by Miner Act that receive training and/or educational services and owners and employers covered by the Mine Act receiving the benefits of the health and safety project under these grants.

Award Range/Average: No Data Available.

Funding: (Cooperative Agreements) FY 17 $125,000; FY 18 N/A FY 19 N/A FY 16 $125,000

HQ: 201 12th Street S

Arlington, VA 22202

Phone: 202-693-9570

Email: duncan.jeffrey@dol.gov

http://www.msha.gov

MINORITY BUSINESS DEVELOPMENT AGENCY

California

Melda Cabrera, Director | 221 Main Street, Room 1280, San Francisco, CA 94105 415-744-3001

Rudy Guerra, District Officer | 9660 Flair Drive, Suite 455, El Monte, CA 91731 818-453-8636

Florida

Federal Building, Room 1314 51 S.W. First Avenue Box 25, Miami, FL 33130 305-536-5054

Georgia

Robert M. Henderson, Director | 401 West Peachtree Street, N.W., Room 1715, Atlanta, GA 30308-3516 404-730-3300

Illinois

Carlos Guzman, Director | 55 East Monroe Street, Suite 1406, Chicago, IL 60603 312-353-0182

Massachusetts

R. K. Schwartz, District Officer | 10 Causeway Street, Room 418, Boston, MA 02222-1041 617-565-6850

New York

Heyward Davenport, Director | 26 Federal Plaza, Room 3720, New York, NY 10278 212-264-3262

Pennsylvania

Alfonso Jackson, District Officer | Federal Office Building 600 Arch Street, Room 10128, Philadelphia, PA 19106 215-597-9236

Texas

John F. Iglehart, Director | 1100 Commerce Street, Room 7B23, Dallas, TX 75242 214-767-8001

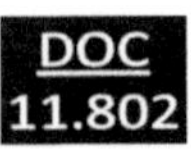

MINORITY BUSINESS RESOURCE DEVELOPMENT

Award: Cooperative Agreements; Project Grants

Purpose: To provide financial assistance for minority business enterprises and assist in the development of competitiveness of MBEs through the administration and demonstration projects.

Applicant Eligibility: Applicants eligible to provide services under pilot or demonstration projects are nonprofit organizations, for-profit firms, State and local governments, Native American Tribal entities, and educational institutions. Applicants for congressionally mandated projects are those specifically identified in applicable legislation.

Beneficiary Eligibility: Congressionally mandated award beneficiaries are members of the minority business community. Pilot or demonstration project beneficiaries are minority business enterprises.

Award Range/Average: N/A

Funding: (Cooperative Agreements) FY 17 $407,668; FY 18 est $13,291,873; FY 19 est $12,000,000

HQ: 1401 Constitution Avenue NW
Washington, DC 20230
Phone: 202-482-0065
Email: nchambers@mbda.gov
http://www.mbda.gov

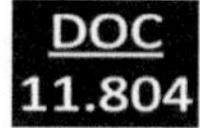

MBDA BUSINESS CENTER – AMERICAN INDIAN AND ALASKA NATIVE

Award: Cooperative Agreements

Purpose: The MBDA Business Center - American Indian and Alaska Native program provides a strategic deal for business consulting services to eligible American Indian and Alaska Native Minority Business Enterprises. It also supports the competitiveness of U.S. businesses that are minority-owned and secures private sectors.

Applicant Eligibility: Applicants eligible to operate an MBDA Business Center are nonprofit organizations, for-profit firms, State and local governments, Native American Tribal entities, and educational institutions.

Beneficiary Eligibility: The MBDA Business Center program serves all eligible minority business enterprises through direct services or through strategic partner referral. Eligible beneficiaries of this program are: Native Americans and Alaska Natives (including Alaska Natives, Alaska Native Corporations and Tribal entities), African Americans, Hispanic Americans, Asian and Pacific Islander Americans, Asian Indians and Hasidic Jews.

Award Range/Average: $255,000 to $300,000.

Funding: (Cooperative Agreements) FY 18 est $1,320,000; FY 16 $1,320,000; FY 17 est $1,320,000

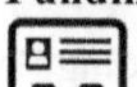

HQ: 1401 Constitution Avenue NW
Washington, DC 20230
Phone: 202-482-0065
Email: nchambers@mbda.gov
http://www.mbda.gov

MBDA BUSINESS CENTER "Business Center Program"

Award: Cooperative Agreements

Purpose: The MBDA Business Center program provides strategies for business. It supports the Agency that supports the growth of U.S. businesses. It assists in minority business development, private contracts, job creation, and retention.

Applicant Eligibility: Applicants eligible to operate MBC projects are nonprofit organizations, for-profit firms, State and local governments, Native American Tribal entities, and educational institutions.

Beneficiary Eligibility: The Minority Business Center program serves all eligible minority business enterprises through direct services or through strategic partner referral. Eligible beneficiaries of this program are: African Americans, Hispanic Americans, Asian and Pacific Islander Americans, Native Americans (including Alaska Natives, Alaska Native Corporations and Tribal entities), Asian Indians and Hasidic Jews.

Award Range/Average: $225,000 to $500,000.

Funding: (Cooperative Agreements) FY 17 $7,846,955; FY 18 est $9,115,294; FY 19 est $12,000,000; FY 16 $8,157,505

HQ: 1401 Constitution Avenue NW
Washington, DC 20230
Phone: 202-482-0065
Email: nchambers@mbda.gov
http://www.mbda.gov

NATIONAL AGRICULTURAL STATISTICS SERVICE

REGIONAL OFFICES

Arkansas/ Delta Region
10800 Financial Centre Parkway, Suite 110, Little Rock, AR 72211 501-228-9926

California/ Pacific Region
650 Capitol Mall, Suite 6-100, P.O. Box 1258 Zip: 95812, Sacramento, CA 95814 916-498-5161

Colorado/ Mountain Region
One Denver Federal Ctr, Building 67, Room 630, P.O. Box 150969 Zip: 80215-0969, Denver, CO 80225 720-787-3150

Georgia/Southern Region
Ste 100, 355 E Hancock Ave, Stephens Federal Bldg, Athens, GA 30601 706-546-2236

Iowa/ Upper Midwest Region
Federal Building, 210 Walnut Street, Suite 833, Des Moines, IA 50309 515-284-4340

Kentucky/ Eastern Mountain Region
Gene Snyder and Courthouse Building 601 W. Broadway, Room 645 For letter mail: P.O. Box 1120 Zip: 40201, Louisville, KY 40202 502-582-5293

Michigan/ Great Lakes Region
3001 Coolidge Road, Suite 400, P.O. Box 30239 Lansing, Zip:48909-7739, East Lansing, MI 48823 517-324-5300

Missouri/ Heartland Region
601 Business Loop, 70 West, Suite 213E, Columbia, MO 65203 573-876-0950

Nebraska/ Northern Plains Region
Rm 263 Federal Bldg, 100 Centennial Mall North, P.O. Box 81069 Zip 68501, Lincoln, NE 68508 402-437-5541

Pennsylvania/ Northeastern Region
4050 Crums Mill Road, Suite 203, P.O. Box 60607 Zip: 17106-0607, Harrisburg, PA 17112-2875 717-787-3904

Texas/Southern Plains Region
300 East 8th Street Room 500, Federal Building For letter mail: P.O. Box 70, Zip: 78676, Austin, TX 78701 512-916-5581

Washington/ Northwest Region
112 Henry St, NE, Suite 202, P.O. Box 609 Zip: 98507, Olympia, WA 98506 360-709-2400

AGRICULTURAL STATISTICS REPORTS "Agricultural Estimates"

Award: Dissemination of Technical Information

Purpose: The National Agricultural Statistics Agency is to provide timely, accurate, and useful statistics in service to the U.S. agriculture economy and makes marketing decisions on a wide range of agricultural commodities. It also develops and administers programs for collecting statistics related to agriculture, resources, and rural communities. It assists rural communities and ensures national forests and private working lands are conserved and restored so that all of America's children have access to safe and nutritious meals.

Applicant Eligibility: Farmers and agricultural producers, marketing and processing groups, transportation and handler groups, consumers, state and local governments, educational institutions, and the general public including those located in the U.S. Territories. The type of assistance NASS provides is: Dissemination of Technical Information: specifically Agricultural Statistics.

Beneficiary Eligibility: Same as Applicant Eligibility.

Award Range/Average: USDA National Agricultural Statistics Service (NASS) does not award grants. The federal domestic assistance type NASS provides is: Dissemination of Technical Information: Agricultural Statistics and the Census of Agriculture.

Funding: (Dissemination of Technical Information) FY 17 $182,790,867; FY 18 est $191,717,000; FY 19 est $165,000,000; FY 16 $179,472,000; - FY 2017 Actual funds include recovery over the estimated funds. FY 2018 Enacted funds were more than the FY 2018 President's Budget.

HQ: 1400 Independence Avenue SW Room 5803 S, P.O. Box 3201
Washington, DC 20250
Phone: 202-690-0919
Email: ann.johnson@nass.usda.gov
http://www.nass.usda.gov

NATIONAL GUARD BUREAU

ANG ENVIRONMENTAL
ANG/A7AN Ms. Elaine Magdivec | 3500 Fetcher Avenue, Andrews AFB, MD 20331-5157 301-836-8904

ANG FACILITIES O&M
ANG/A7RP Mr. Tony Latuff | 3500 Fetcher Avenue, Andrews AFB, MD 20331-5157 301-836-8194

ANG FIRE PROTECTION
ANG/A7CXF Mr. Steve Waldelich | 3500 Fetcher Avenue, Andrews AFB, MD 20331-5157 301-278-8170

ANG LOGISTICS FACILITIES
ANG/A4P Mr. Robert Sinclair | 3500 Fetchet Ave., Andrews AFB, MD 20762-5157 301-836-8338

ANG NATURAL & CULTURAL RESOURCES MGT
ANG/A7AN Ms. Melissa Mettz | 3500 Fetchel Ave, Andrews AFB, MD 20762-5157 301-836-8427

ANG SECURITY GUARD
ANG/A7SX Mr. Kevin Leavy | 3500 Fetcher Avenue, Andrews AFB, MD 20331-5157 301-836-7809

ANG SERVICES RESOURCES MGT
ANG/A7V Maj Gerald Cullens | 3500 Fetchet Ave., Andrews AFB, MD 20762-5157 301-836-8162

ARNG ADMIN SERVICES
ARNG-ZX Ms. Cindy Kadin | ARNG Readiness Center 111 S. George Mason Drive, Arlington, VA 22204 703-607-7056

ARNG ANTI-TERRORISM PROGRAM
ARNG-ODP Mr. Dean Connors | ARNG Readiness Center 111 S. George Mason Drive, Arlington, VA 22204-1302 703-607-9198

ARNG AVIATION OPERATIONS
NGB-AVS-O CW5 Bob Fleming | ARNG Readiness Center 111 S. George Mason Drive, Arlington, VA 22204-1382 703-607-7752

ARNG DISTRIBUTIVE LEARNING PROGRAM
ARNG-ILL MAJ Leslie Myers | ARNG Readiness Center 111 S. George Mason Drive, Arlington, VA 22204 703-601-9869

ARNG ELECTRONIC SECURITY SYSTEM
ARNG-ILI-E Mr. Mark Brown | ARNG Readiness Center 111 S. George Mason Drive, Arlington, VA 22204-1382 703-607-7956

ARNG ENVIRONMENTAL RESOURCES MANAGEMENT

ARNG-ILE MAJ Anthony Bryant | ARNG Readiness Center 111 S. George Mason Drive, Arlington, VA 22204-1382 703-607-7340

ARNG FULL TIME DINING FACILITY OPERATIONS
ARNG-ILL-E CW4 Stanley Jung | ARNG Readiness Center 111 S. George Mason Drive, Arlington, VA 22204-1382 703-607-7344

ARNG REAL PROPERTY
ARNG-IILI-F MAJ Paul Crigler | ARNG Readiness Center 111 S. George Mason Drive, Arlington, VA 22204-1382 703-607-7916

ARNG REIMBURSABLE MAINTENANCE OPERATIONS
ARNG-AVL MAJ David Cooper | ARNG Readiness Center 111 S. George Mason Drive, Arlington, VA 22204 703-607-7721

ARNG SECURITY GUARD ACTIVITIES
ARNG-ODP Ms. Deidra Wallace | ARNG Readiness Center 111 S. George Mason Drive, Arlington, VA 22204-1382 703-607-7353

ARNG SUSTAINABLE RANGE PROGRAM
ARNG-TRS Mr. Nick Long | ARNG Readiness Center 111 S. George Mason Drive, Arlington, VA 22204-1382 703-607-7884

ARNG TELECOMMUNICATIONS
ARNG-IMS Ms Freida Parks | ARNG Readiness Center 111 S. George Mason Drive, Arlington, VA 22204-1382 703-607-7654

STATE FAMILY PROGRAM ACTIVITIES
NGB-FP Ms Joyce Wallace | 1411 Jefferson Davis Highway, Alexandria, VA 22202-3231 703-607-0882

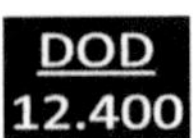

MILITARY CONSTRUCTION, NATIONAL GUARD

Award: Cooperative Agreements

Purpose: For the acquisition of facilities essential for the training and administration of Army National Guard (ARNG) units in the 50 states, the District of Columbia, the Commonwealth of Puerto Rico, the Virgin Islands and Guam, by purchase, transfer, construction, expansion, rehabilitation or conversion.

Applicant Eligibility: The 50 States, the District of Columbia, the Commonwealth of Puerto Rico, Guam, and the territories. The State National Guard unit must be federally recognized.

Beneficiary Eligibility: Same as Applicant Eligibility.

Award Range/Average: $300,000 and up.

Funding: (Cooperative Agreements) FY 17 FY 18 FY 19 est $77,213,142; FY 14 $150,012,360; FY 15 est $60,000,000; FY 16 est $60,000,000

HQ: LTC 111 S George Mason Drive
Arlington, VA 22204
Email: elver.crow@us.army.mil
http://www.ngb.dtic.mil/indexshtm

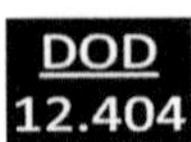

NATIONAL GUARD CHALLENGE PROGRAM

Award: Formula Grants

Purpose: To conduct a National Guard civilian youth opportunities program to use the National Guard to provide military-based training, including supervised work experience in community service and conservation projects, to civilian youth who cease to attend secondary school after graduating so as to improve the life skills and employment potential of such youth.

Applicant Eligibility: The Secretary of Defense shall provide for the conduct of the National Guard Challenge Program in such States and U.S. territories and possession as the Secretary considers to be appropriate, except that Federal expenditures under the program may not exceed $62.5M for fiscal year 01.

Beneficiary Eligibility: Same as Applicant Eligibility.

Award Range/Average: No Data Available.

Funding: (Formula Grants) FY 17 FY 18 FY 19 est $98,015,310

HQ: 4800 Mark Center Drive
Alexandria, VA 22311
Phone: 571-372-8415
Email: barbara.j.orlando.civ@mail.mil
http://www.ngb.dtic.mil/indexstm

NATIONAL HIGHWAY TRAFFIC SAFETY ADMINISTRATION

Region I
George A. Luciano, Regional Administrator Transportation System Center | Kendall Square-Code 903, Cambridge, MA 02142 617-494-3427

Region II
Thomas M. Louizou, Regional Administrator | 222 Mamaroneck Avenue, Suite 204, White Plains, NY 10605 914-682-6162

Region III
Elizabeth A. Baker, Regional Administrator | The Cresent Building 10 South Howard Street, Suite 4000, Baltimore, MD 21201 410-962-0077

Region IV
Troy Ayers, Regional Administrator | 61 Forsyth Street, S.W., Suite 17T30, Atlanta, GA 30303-3104 404-562-3739

Region IX
David Manning, Acting Regional Administrator | 201 Mission Street, Suite 2230, San Francisco, CA 94105 415-744-3089

Region V
Donald J. McNamara, Regional Administrator | 19900 Governors Drive, Suite 201, Olympia Fields, IL 60461 708-503-8822

Region VI
Georgia S. Chakiris, Regional Administrator | 819 Taylor Street, Room 8A38, Fort Worth, TX 76102-6177 817-978-3653

Region VII
Romell W. Cook, Regional Administrator | P.O. Box 412515, Kansas City, MO 64141 816-822-7233

Region VIII
Louis R. DeCarolis, Regional Administrator | 555 Zang Street, Room 430, Lakewood, CO 80228 303-969-6917

Region X
Curtis A. Winston, Regional Administrator | 3140Jackson Federal Building 915 Second Avenue, Seattle, WA 98174 206-220-7640

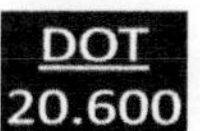

STATE AND COMMUNITY HIGHWAY SAFETY

Award: Formula Grants

Purpose: Provides a coordinated national highway safety program to reduce traffic crashes, deaths, injuries, and property damage.

Applicant Eligibility: States, federally recognized Indian tribes, the District of Columbia, Puerto Rico, American Samoa, Guam, Northern Marianas, and the Virgin Islands.

Beneficiary Eligibility: Political subdivisions, through the State Highway Safety Agencies.

Award Range/Average: FY 2018 $646,425 - $23,687,928

Funding: Formula Grants (Apportionments) FY 17 $252,300,000; FY 18 est $261,200,000; FY 19 est $270,400,000; FY 16 $243,500,000

HQ: Regional Operations and Program Delivery 1200 New Jersey Avenue SE NRO-010
Washington, DC 20590
Phone: 202-366-2121
Email: maggi.gunnels@dot.gov

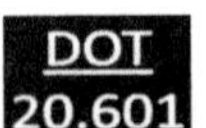

ALCOHOL IMPAIRED DRIVING COUNTERMEASURES INCENTIVE GRANTS I

Award: Project Grants

Purpose: Encourages States to adopt programs to reduce crashes resulting from persons driving while under the influence of alcohol.

Applicant Eligibility: States, Puerto Rico, the Virgin Islands, Guam, American Samoa, and the Commonwealth of the Northern Mariana Islands. States are provided with two alternative means to qualify for a Section 410 grant.

Beneficiary Eligibility: State Highway Safety Agency.

Award Range/Average: $972,388 to $17,973,219

Funding: Project Grants (with Formula Distribution) FY 17 $0; FY 18 est $0; FY 19 est $0; FY 16 $143,717,499; - $ 4,933,409.21 of SAFETEA-LU funds.

HQ: Regional Operations and Program Delivery 1200 New Jersey Avenue SE NRO-010
Washington, DC 20590
Phone: 202-366-2121
Email: maggi.gunnels@dot.gov
http://www.nhtsa.gov/impaired

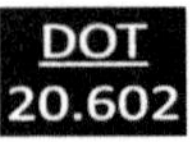

OCCUPANT PROTECTION INCENTIVE GRANTS

Award: Project Grants

Purpose: Encourages States to adopt effective programs to reduce highway deaths and injuries resulting from individuals riding unrestrained or improperly restrained in motor vehicles.

Applicant Eligibility: States, the District of Columbia, Puerto Rico, American Samoa, Guam, Northern Marianas, Virgin Islands, and the Bureau of Indian Affairs.

Beneficiary Eligibility: State Highway Safety agencies.

Award Range/Average: $ 74,843 – 3,109,419.

Funding: (Formula Grants) FY 17 $135,748; FY 18 est $0; FY 19 est $0; FY 16 $77,862

HQ: NRO 010
Washington, DC 20590
Phone: 202-366-2121
Email: maggi.gunnels@dot.gov
http://www.nhtsa.gov

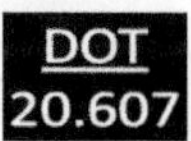

ALCOHOL OPEN CONTAINER REQUIREMENTS

Award: Project Grants

Purpose: public transportation.

Applicant Eligibility: States, the District of Columbia, and Puerto Rico.

Beneficiary Eligibility: State Highway Safety agencies.

Award Range/Average: Varies.

Funding: Formula Grants (Apportionments) FY 17 $43,071,086; FY 18 est $42,058,790; FY 19 est $0; FY 16 $0

HQ: Regional Operations and Program Delivery 1200 New Jersey Avenue SE NRO-010
Washington, DC 20590
Phone: 202-366-2121
Email: maggi.gunnels@dot.gov
http://www.nhtsa/whatsup/fedassist/index.html

MINIMUM PENALTIES FOR REPEAT OFFENDERS FOR DRIVING WHILE INTOXICATED

Award: Project Grants

Purpose: Encourages States to enact and enforce Repeat Intoxicated Offender laws.

Applicant Eligibility: States, the District of Columbia, and Puerto Rico.

Beneficiary Eligibility: State Highway Safety agencies.

Award Range/Average: The grants range were from $2,489,000 - $54,546,000.

Funding: (Project Grants) FY 17 $60,293,336; FY 18 est $62,207,643; FY 19 est $0; FY 16 $0; - (Project Grants) FY 17 $60,293,336; FY 18 est $62,207,643; FY 19 est $62,207,643

HQ: 1200 New Jersey Avenue SE NTI 200
Washington, DC 20590
Phone: 202-366-2121
Email: maggi.gunnels@dot.gov
http://www.nhtsa/whatsup/fedassist/index.html

SAFETY BELT PERFORMANCE GRANTS

Award: Project Grants

Purpose: Successful research ideas can result in innovation and development projects that improve public transportation systems nationwide to provide more efficient and effective delivery of public transportation services.

Applicant Eligibility: The 50 States, District of Columbia, Puerto Rico, American Samoa, the Commonwealth of the Northern Mariana Islands, Guam and the Virgin Islands are eligible to apply for a grant.

Beneficiary Eligibility: State Highway Safety Agencies.

Award Range/Average: States are spending down their SAFETEA-LU grant awards.

Funding: (Formula Grants (Apportionments)) FY 17 $0; FY 18 est $0; FY 19 est $0; FY 16 $0; - No new money authorized. States are spending down their SAFETEA-LU grant awards. (Formula Grants) FY 17 $0; FY 18 est $0; FY 19 est $0.

HQ: Regional Operations and Program Delivery 1200 New Jersey Avenue SE NRO-010
Washington, DC 20590
Phone: 202-366-2121
Email: maggi.gunnels@dot.gov
http://www.nhtsa.gov

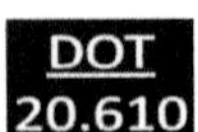

STATE TRAFFIC SAFETY INFORMATION SYSTEM IMPROVEMENT GRANTS

Award: Project Grants

Purpose: Encourages States to adopt and implement effective programs to improve the timeliness, accuracy, completeness, uniformity, integration and accessibility of State data.

Applicant Eligibility: To qualify for a first-year grant, a State demonstrated that it has an established multi-disciplinary highway safety data and traffic records coordinating committee; a developed multi-year safety data and traffic records strategic plan, approved by the coordinating committee and containing performance-based measures; certify that the State has adopted and is using the model data elements determined by the Secretary to be useful, or certify that grant funds will be used toward adopting and using the most elements practicable. To qualify for a subsequent-year grant, a State must certify that an assessment or audit of the State traffic records system has been conducted or updated within the preceding 5 years; certify that the coordinating committee continues to operate and supports the multi-year plan; specify how the grant funds and any other funds of the State will support the multi-year strategic plan; demonstrate measurable progress toward achieving the goals and objectives identified in the multi-year plan; and submit a report, showing measurable progress in the implementation of the multi-year plan.

Beneficiary Eligibility: State Highway Safety Agencies.

Award Range/Average: The ranges were $500- $2,344,000

Funding: (Project Grants) FY 17 $0; FY 18 est $0; FY 19 est $0; FY 16 $0.

HQ: Regional Operations and Program Delivery 1200 New Jersey Avenue SE NRO-010
Washington, DC 20590

Phone: 202-366-2121

Email: maggi.gunnels@dot.gov

http://www.nhtsa.gov

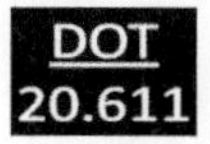

INCENTIVE GRANT PROGRAM TO PROHIBIT RACIAL PROFILING "Section 1906"

Award: Formula Grants

Purpose: Encourages States to enact and enforce laws that prohibit the use of racial profiling in the enforcement of traffic laws on Federal-aid highways, and to maintain and allow public inspection of statistics on motor vehicle stops.

Applicant Eligibility: This Grant is available to the 50 states, the District of Columbia, Puerto Rico, the Virgin Islands, Guam American Samoa, and the Commonwealth of the Northern Mariana Islands.

Beneficiary Eligibility: State Highway Safety agencies.

Award Range/Average: $885,460- $454,170. Average $668,544

Funding: (Formula Grants) FY 17 $0; FY 18 est $0; FY 19 est $0; FY 16 $0

HQ: 1200 New Jersey Avenue SE NRO-100

Washington, DC 20590

Phone: 202-366-2121

Email: maggi.gunnels@dot.gov

http://www.nhtsa.gov

INCENTIVE GRANT PROGRAM TO INCREASE MOTORCYCLIST SAFETY "Section 2010"

Award: Formula Grants

Purpose: Encourages States to adopt and implement effective programs to reduce the number of single and multi-vehicle crashes involving motorcyclists.

Applicant Eligibility: This Grant was available to the 50 states, the District of Columbia, and Puerto Rico.

Beneficiary Eligibility: State Highway Safety Agencies.

Award Range/Average: $100,000 - $482,959

Funding: (Formula Grants) FY 17 $0; FY 18 est $0; FY 19 est $0; FY 16 $0

HQ: 1200 New Jersey Avenue SE NRO-100

Washington, DC 20590

Phone: 202-366-2121

Email: maggi.gunnels@dot.gov

http://www.nhtsa.gov

DOT 20.613 CHILD SAFETY AND CHILD BOOSTER SEATS INCENTIVE GRANTS
"Section 2011"

Award: Project Grants

Purpose: Encourages States to enact and enforce a child restraint law that requires children up to 65 pounds and under 8 years of age to be properly restrained in a child restraint, unless they are 4' 9' tall.

Applicant Eligibility: The grant program was available to the 50 States, the District of Columbia and Puerto Rico.

Beneficiary Eligibility: State Highway Safety Agencies.

Award Range/Average: The range was normally $100,000 - $700,000.

Funding: FY 17 $0; FY 18 est $0; FY 19 est $0; FY 16 $0; - No new funds will be authorized. States are in the process of spending down these funds.

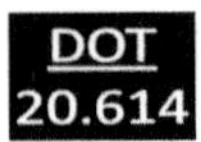

HQ: 1200 New Jersey Avenue SE NRO-100
Washington, DC 20590
Phone: 202-366-2121
Email: maggi.gunnels@dot.gov
http://nhtsa.dot.gov

DOT 20.614 NATIONAL HIGHWAY TRAFFIC SAFETY ADMINISTRATION (NHTSA) DISCRETIONARY SAFETY GRANTS AND COOPERATIVE AGREEMENTS
"NHTSA Section 403 Discretionary Grants and Cooperative Agreements"

Award: Cooperative Agreements; Project Grants

Purpose: To provide technical and financial assistance to State and local government agencies, for-profit and non-profit organizations, educational institutions, hospitals, and other persons (as defined in Title 1 USC Chapter (1)) in support of highway safety research and development, special studies, educational and public awareness projects.

Applicant Eligibility: Eligibility requirements will be specified on a project-by-project basis. Generally speaking, and historically, projects have been made available to the following types of organizations: Intrastate, Local, Sponsored Organization, Public nonprofit institution/organization, Other public institution/organization, Federally Recognized Indian Tribal Government, U.S. territory or possession, Specialized Group, Small Business, Profit Organization, Private nonprofit institution/organization, Quasi-public nonprofit institution/organization, Other private institution/organization, and Native American Organization.

Beneficiary Eligibility: Intrastate, State, Local, Sponsored Organization, Public Nonprofit Institution/Organization, Other Public Institution/organization, Federally Recognized Indian Tribal Government, U.S. territory or possession, Specialized Group, Small Business, Profit Organization, Private nonprofit institution/organization, Quasi-public nonprofit institution/organization, Other private institution/organization, Native American Organization, Anyone/General Public, Health Professional, Scientist/Researcher, Consumer, Minority Group, Handicapped, Youth, Senior Citizen,

Award Range/Average: $100,000 - $482,959.

Funding: (Project Grants) FY 17 $27,606,000; FY 18 est $0; FY 19 est $0; FY 16 $31,058,580

HQ: 1200 New Jersey Avenue
Washington, DC 20590
Phone: 202-366-9561
Email: pete.shultz@dot.gov
http://dot.gov

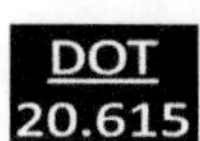

E-911 GRANT PROGRAM
"911 Grant Program"

Award: Formula Grants

Purpose: To provide federal financial assistance for the implementation and operation of 911 services, E-911 services, migration to an IP-enabled emergency network, and adoption and operation of NG911 services and applications.

Applicant Eligibility: States, U.S. Territories, and Tribal 911 agencies

Beneficiary Eligibility: States, U. S.

Award Range/Average: $250,000 to $8,539,610. Average: $1,950,892.85

Funding: (Formula Grants) FY 17 $0; FY 18 est $0; FY 19 est $109,250.

HQ: National 911 Implementation Coordination Office 1200 New Jersey Avenue SE NPD-400
Washington, DC 20590
Phone: 202-366-2705
http://www.911.gov/project_911grantprogram.html

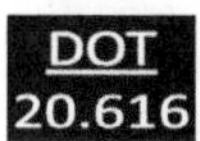

NATIONAL PRIORITY SAFETY PROGRAMS

Award: Formula Grants

Purpose: To encourage States to address national priorities for reducing highway deaths and injuries through occupant protection programs.

Applicant Eligibility: With the exception of the Motorcyclist Safety Program, the 50 States, District of Columbia, Puerto Rico, U.S. territories (American Samoa, Guam, Northern Marianas, and Virgin Islands) are eligible for funding. Under the Motorcyclist Safety Program, the 50 States, District of Columbia, and Puerto Rico are eligible for grant awards.

Beneficiary Eligibility: Funding is provided to State Highway Safety agencies.

Award Range/Average: $33,125 - $8,046,147.33

Funding: (Formula Grants) FY 17 $277,500,000; FY 18 N/A FY 19 N/A FY 16 $270,230,987; - In FY 2016, States spent a total of $270,230,987.01 in Section 402 funds authorized by MAP-21.

HQ: 1200 New Jersey Avenue SE
Washington, DC 20590
Phone: 202-366-2121
Email: maggi.gunnels@dot.gov
http://nhtsa.dot.gov

NATIONAL OCEANIC AND ATMOSPHERIC ADMINISTRATION

Alaska Region
Steven Pennoyer, Regional Administrator | P.O. Box 21668, Juneau, AK 99802-1668 907-586-7221

Northeast Region
Patricia Kurkul, Acting Regional Administrator | One Blackburn Drive, Gloucester, MA 01930 978-281-9250

Northwest Region
William Stelle, Regional Administrator | 7600 Sand Point Way N.E., Seattle, WA 98115 206-526-6150

Southeast Region
William T. Hogarth, Regional Administrator | 9721 Executive Center Drive, North Suite 201, St. Petersburg, FL 33702 727-570-5301

Southwest Fisheries Science Center
Dr. Michael F. Tillman, Science Director | P.O. Box 271, LaJolla, CA 92038-0271 619-546-7081

Southwest Region
Rodney R. McInnis, Acting Regional Administrator | 501 West Ocean Boulevard, Suite 4200, Long Beach, CA 90802-4213 562-980-4001

Virginia
Nicholas A. Prahl, Director |

Nicholas A. Prahl, Director | 439 West York Street, Norfolk, VA 23510-1114 757-441-6776

Washington
RADM Nicholas A. Prahl | 1801 Fairview Avenue East, Seattle, WA 98102 206-553-7656

DOC 11.015 BROAD AGENCY ANNOUNCEMENT "BAA"

Award: Cooperative Agreements; Project Grants

Purpose: The BAA is a mechanism to encourage educational research and innovative projects.

Applicant Eligibility: N/A

Beneficiary Eligibility: N/A

Award Range/Average: $5,000 - $4.2 million

Funding: (Project Grants) FY 17 FY 18 FY 19 - The BAA is simply a vehicle to enable receipt of applications for innovative projects. Projects selected for funding carry the CFDA number of the program to which the work outlined in the project is most closely aligned.

HQ: 1315 E W Highway 9th floor Building 2, Room 9328
Silver Spring, MD 20910
Phone: 301-628-1308
Email: lamar.revis@noaa.gov
http://www.noaa.gov/index.html

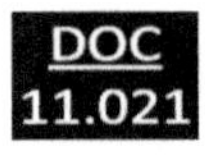

DOC 11.021 NOAA SMALL BUSINESS INNOVATION RESEARCH (SBIR) PROGRAM "NOAA SBIR Program"

Award: Project Grants

Purpose: The Small Business Innovation Research stimulates technological innovation in the private sector, strengthens the role of small businesses, and encourages participation by women-owned and socially disadvantaged small business firms in technological innovation.

Applicant Eligibility: Applicant Eligibility (1) is organized for profit, with a place of business located in the United States, which operates primarily within the United States, or which makes a significant contribution to the United States economy through the payment of taxes or use of American products, materials or labor; (2) is in the legal form of an individual proprietorship, partnership, limited liability company, corporation, joint venture, association, trust or cooperative, except that where the form is a joint venture, there can be no more than 49 percent participation by foreign business entities in the joint venture; (3) is at least 51 percent owned and controlled by one or more individuals who are citizens of, or permanent resident aliens in, the United States, except in the case of a joint venture, where each entity in the venture must be 51 percent owned and controlled by one or more individuals who are citizens of, or permanent resident aliens in the United States; and (4) has, including its affiliates, not more than 500 employees. The term "affiliates" is defined in greater detail in 13 CFR 121.

Beneficiary Eligibility: Each year, NOAA sets aside a portion of its extramural R&D budget to fund research from small science and technology-based firms. The NOAA SBIR Program supports innovative research projects that fall within NOAA's core mission of science, service, and stewardship.

Award Range/Average: Maximum allowable amounts are as follows: Phase I grants: $120,000 each Phase II grants: $400,000 each

Funding: (Project Grants) FY 18 est $0; FY 19 est $9,000,000; FY 17 $0

HQ: 1315 E W Highway 11th Floor, Room 11460
Silver Spring, MD 20910
Phone: 301-734-1174
Email: brenda.alford@noaa.gov
http://techpartnerships.noaa.gov/sbir.aspx

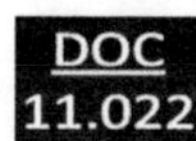

BIPARTISAN BUDGET ACT OF 2018

Award: Cooperative Agreements; Project Grants

Purpose: To identify risks related to disasters, issuing payments for disaster relief, and ensuring the funds are expended.

Applicant Eligibility: N/A

Beneficiary Eligibility: Entities affected by hurricanes, wildfires, and other disasters.

Award Range/Average: No Data Available.

Funding: (Cooperative Agreements) FY 17 $0; FY 19 N/A FY 18 N/A - N/A

HQ: 1315 E W Highway Building 2 9th Floor, Room 9314
Silver Spring, MD 20910
Phone: 301-628-1310
Email: alan.p.conway@noaa.gov
http://www.noaa.gov

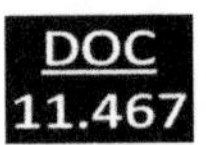

METEOROLOGIC AND HYDROLOGIC MODERNIZATION DEVELOPMENT "Hydrometeorological Development"

Award: Project Grants; Direct Payments With Unrestricted Use; Dissemination of Technical Information; Training

Purpose: To foster Federal partnerships and provide training, education, and professional development to minimize tsunamis through hazard assessment, warning guidance, and mitigation.

Applicant Eligibility: Eligible applicants are accredited Federally recognized institutions of higher learning, consortia of these institutions, agencies of State or local governments including school systems, quasi-public institutions, consultants, and companies involved in using and developing meteorological or hydrologic forecasts or forecast methodology. In addition, the National Tsunami Hazard Mitigation Program (NTHMP) funding provides resources to reduce the impact of tsunamis through hazard assessment, warning guidance, and mitigation.

Beneficiary Eligibility: The benefits of the overall program are for reduction in loss of life and damage which the general public can realize from improvement in weather forecasts, watches, and warnings of hazardous weather and resultant flooding. For the improvements from the modernization of the Nation's weather and hydrologic services to be realized, there must be significant involvement of the entire hydrometeorological community.

Award Range/Average: $6,000 to $5,814,360 Average: $400,000

Funding: (Project Grants) FY 18 est $6,184,257; FY 19 N/A FY 17 $6,011,612

HQ: 1315 E W Highway
Silver Spring, MD 20910
Phone: 301-427-9322
Email: leroy.spayd@noaa.gov
http://www.noaa.gov

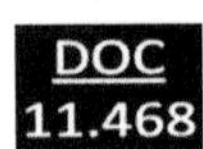

APPLIED METEOROLOGICAL RESEARCH

Award: Project Grants

Purpose: The Collaborative Science, Technology, and Applied Research program compensate for highly collaborative research for the transition from basic and applied research. The Hurricane Forecast Improvement funds to the university to provide guidance for hurricane track and forecasts. The Next Generation Global Prediction System program funds to the university for developing a unified global modeling system to improve weather forecasting.

Applicant Eligibility: Institutions of higher education, federally funded educational institutions, and in some cases private organizations (profit and non-profit)

Beneficiary Eligibility: Same as Applicant Eligibility.

Award Range/Average: $75,000 to $250,000 Average: $180,000

Funding: (Cooperative Agreements) FY 18 est $5,200,000; FY 17 est $6,250,112; FY 19 est $5,200,000

HQ: 1315 E W Highway SSMC2 Room 3348, P.O. Box W/OPS17
Silver Spring, MD 20910
Phone: 301-427-9242

Email: craig.hodan@noaa.gov
http://www.noaa.nws.gov

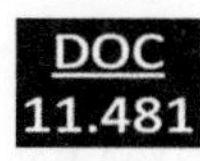

EDUCATIONAL PARTNERSHIP PROGRAM
"Educational Partnership Program (EPP) with Minority Serving Institutions (MSI)"

Award: Cooperative Agreements

Purpose: To continue the development of education and natural resource management programs aimed at increasing education and graduation rates in NOAA mission.

Applicant Eligibility: Applicants are designated as minority serving institutions by the United States Department of Education list of minority serving institutions. Non-minority institutions may also participate in this program when partnered with a minority serving institution.

Beneficiary Eligibility: The benefits to the Nation are an increased number of academic institutions capable of providing services and products in support of the agency's mission to describe and predict changes in the environment, and to conserve and manage the nation's coastal and marine resources to ensure sustainable economic opportunities. Collaboration among NOAA and academic institutions will increase the number of trained professionals in NOAA-related sciences and will also lead to a larger number of institutions participating in collaborative research and co-management of the nation's natural resources with State, local and tribal governments.

Award Range/Average: $45 K - Undergraduate Scholarship award $3.0 - $3.2M annually to Cooperative Science Centers

Funding: (Formula Grants (Cooperative Agreements)) FY 18 est $13,200,000; FY 19 est $12,000,000; FY 17 $12,000,000

HQ: Office of Education 1315 E-W Highway SSMC 3, 10th Floor
Silver Spring, MD 20910
Phone: 301-628-2905
Email: jacqueline.j.rousseau@noaa.gov
http://www.epp.noaa.gov

NATIONAL PARK SERVICE

NATIONAL PARK SERVICE

Terrel Emmons | Professional Services 1849 C Street N.W., Washington, DC 20240 202-208-3264

REGIONAL OFFICES

Alaska Support Office

Robert D. Barbee, Regional Director | 2525 Gambell Street, Anchorage, AK 99503-2892 907-257-2690

Intermountain Region

Karen Wade, Intermountain Region | 12795 West Alameda Parkway P.O. Box 25287, Denver, CO 80225-0287 303-969-2503

Midwest Region

Alan M. Hutchings, Associate Regional Director, Professional Services and Legislation | National Park Service 1709 Jackson Street, Omaha, NE 68102 402-221-3084

National Capital Region

David Linderman, Chief, Finance Management Officer | 1100 Ohio Drive, SW, Washington, DC 20242 202-619-7160

Northeast Region

Marie Rust, Director | National Park Service U.S. Custom House 200 Chestnut Street, 3rd Floor, Philadelphia, PA 19106 215-597-7013

Pacific West Region
Resources, Stewardship and Partnership 111 Jackson Street, Suite 700, Oakland, CA 94607 415-427-1321

Southeast Region
Jerry Belson, Director | National Park Service Atlanta Federal Center, 1924 Building 100 Alabama Street, S.W., Atlanta, GA 30303 404-562-3100

SERVICE CENTER

Alabama
Dr. Lee M. Warner, State Historical Preservation, Office | 468 South Perry Street, Montgomery, AL 36130-0900 334-242-3184

Alaska
Ms. Judith E. Bittner, Chief, History and Archeology | Department of Natural Resources Division of Parks and Outdoor Recreation 550 W. 7th Avenue, Suite 1310, Anchorage, AK 99501-3565 907-269-8908

American Samoa
Mr. John Enright, Territorial Historic Preservation, Officer | American Samoa Historic Preservation Office American Samoa Government, Pago Pago, AS 96799 684-633-2384

Arizona
Mr. James Garrison, State Historic Preservation, Officer | Office of Historic Preservation Arizona State Parks 1300 W. Washington, Phoenix, AZ 85007 602-542-4174

Arkansas
Arkansas Historic Preservation Program 1500 Tower Building 323 Center Street, Little Rock, AR 72201 501-324-9880

California
Dr. W. Knox Mellon Jr., State Historic, Preservation Officer | Office of Historic Preservation Department of Parks and Recreation P.O. Box 942896, Sacramento, CA 94296-0001 916-653-6624

Colorado
Ms. Geogianna Contiguglia, State Historic, Preservation Officer, Colorado Historical | Colorado History Museum 1300 Broadway, Denver, CO 80203-2137 303-866-3355

Commonwealth of Puerto Rico
Ms. Lilliane D. Lopez, State Historic Preservation Officer | La Fortaleza P.O. Box 82, San Juan, PR 00901 787-721-3737

Commonwealth of the Northern Mariana Islands
Mr. Joseph P. Deleon Guerrero, Historic, Preservation Officer | Department of Community and Cultural Affairs Commonwealth of the Northern Mariana Islands, Saipan, MP 96950 670-664-2120

Connecticut
Mr. John W. Shannahan, State Historic, Preservation Officer and Director, Connecticut | Historical Commission 59 South Prospect Street, Hartford, CT 06106 860-566-3005

Delaware
Mr. Daniel R. Griffith, Director | Division of Historical and Cultural Affairs Halls of Records The Green, Dover, DE 19901 302-739-5685

Denver Service Center
Manager, National Park Service | P.O. Box 25287, Denver, CO 80225 303-969-2100

District of Columbia
Mr. Gregory McCarthy, State Historic, Preservation Officer | Office of Policy & Program Evaluation 441 4th Street, N.W., Suite 920-S, Washington, DC 20002 202-727-6979

Federated States of Micronesia (FSM)
Dr. Rufino Mauricio, State Historic Preservation Officer | Department of Health, Education & Social Affairs FSM National Government P.O. Box PS 70, Palikir Pohnpei State, FM 96941 691-320-2343

Florida
Dr. Janet Snyder Matthews, State Historic, Preservation Officer and Director | Division of Historical Resources Department of State R.A. Gray Building 500 S. Bronough Street, Tallahassee, FL 32399-0250 850-488-1480

Georgia
Mr. Lonice Barrett, Commissioner and State, Historic Preservation Officer | Department of Natural Resources 156 Trinity Avenue S.W., Suite 101, Atlanta, GA 30333 404-656-3500

Guam
Ms. Lynda B. Aguon, State Historic Preservation Officer | Department of Parks and Recreation Division of Historic Resources P.O. Box 2950, Agana Heights, GU 96910 011-671-475-6290

Harpers Ferry Center, National Park Service
Gary Cummins, Manager | P.O. Box 50, Harpers Ferry, WV 25425-0050 304-535-6211

Hawaii
Mr. Gilbert Coloma-Agaran, State Preservation Officer | Department of Land and Natural Resources 601

Komokila Boulevard, Room 555, Honolulu, HI 96813 808-587-0401

Idaho
Mr. Steve Guerber, Interim State Historic Preservation Officer | 210 Main Street, Boise, ID 83702-7264 208-334-3890

Illinois
Mr. William L. Wheeler, Associate Director | Illinois Historic Preservation Agency Preservation Services Division One Old State Capitol, Springfield, IL 62701 217-785-9045

Indiana
Mr. Larry D. Macklin, State Historic Preservation Officer and Director | Department of Natural Resources 402 West Washington Street, Room W274, Indianapolis, IN 46204 317-232-4020

Iowa
Ms. Anita Walker, Acting State Historic Preservation Officer | State Historical Society of Iowa 600 East Locust Street, Des Moines, IA 50319-0290 515-281-8837

Kansas
Mr. Ramon S. Powers, Executive Director | Cultural Resources Division 6425 Southwest 6th Avenue, Topeka, KS 66615-1099 785-272-8681, Ext. 205

Kentucky
Mr. David Morgan, State Historic Preservation, Officer and Director | Kentucky Heritage Council 300 Washington Street, Frankfort, KY 40601 502-564-7005, Ext. 11

Louisiana
Ms. Laurel Wyckoff, Assistant Secretary | Office of Cultural Development P.O. Box 44247, Baton Rouge, LA 70804 225-342-8160

Maine
Mr. Earle G. Shettleworth, Director | Maine Historic Preservation Commission 55 Capitol Street, Station 65, Augusta, ME 04333-0065 207-287-2132

Maryland
Mr. J. Rodney Little, Executive Director Historical and Cultural Programs | Department of Housing and Community Development Peoples Resource Center 100 Community Place, 3rd Floor, Crownsville, MD 21032-2023 410-514-7600

Massachusetts
Ms. Brona Simon, Acting State Historic, Preservation Officer | Executive Director, Massachusetts Historical Commission 220 Morrissey Boulevard, Boston, MA 02125 617-727-8470

Michigan
Mr. Brian D. Conway, State Historic Preservation Officer | Bureau of Michigan History Department of State 717 W. Allegan, Lansing, MI 48918-0001 517-373-0511

Minnesota
Dr. Nina M. Archabal, Director | Minnesota Historical Society State Historic Preservation Office 345 Kellogg Boulevard West, St. Paul, MN 55102 612-296-2747

Mississippi
Mr. Elbert Hilliard, Director | Mississippi Department of Archives and History P.O. Box 571, Jackson, MS 39205 601-359-6850

Missouri
Mr. Stephan Mahfood, Director | Department of Natural Resources P.O. Box 176, Jefferson City, MO 65102 573-751-4732

Montana
Dr. Mark Baumler, State Historic Preservation, Officer | Montana Historical Society 1410 8th Avenue, P.O. Box 201202, Helena, MT 59620-1202 406-444-7715

Nebraska
Mr. Lawrence J. Sommer, Director | Nebraska State Historical Society 1500 R Street P.O. Box 82554, Lincoln, NE 68501 402-471-4746

Nevada
Mr. Ronald M. James, State Historic Preservation, Officer | Department of Museums, Library and Arts 100 North Stewart Street Capitol Complex, Carson City, NV 89710-4285 775-684-3440

New Hampshire
Mrs. Nancy C. Dutton, Director | Division of Historical Resources P.O. Box 2043, Concord, NH 03302-2043 603-271-6435

New Jersey
Mr. Robert C. Shinn, Commissioner | Department of Environmental Protection 401 East State Street P.O. Box 304, Trenton, NJ 08625 609-292-2885

New Mexico
Mr. Elmo Baca, State Historic Preservation, Division | Office of Cultural Affairs Villa Rivera Building, 3rd Floor 228 E. Palace Avenue, Santa Fe, NM 87503 505-827-6320

New York
Mrs. Bernadette Castro, Commissioner | Office of Parks, Recreation and Historic Preservation Empire State Plaza Agency Building 1, 20th Floor, Albany, NY 12238 518-474-0443

North Carolina
Dr. Jeffrey J. Crow, Director | Department of Cultural Resources Division of Archives and History 4617 Mail Service Center, Raleigh, NC 27699-4617 919-733-7305

North Dakota
Mr. Merl Paaverud, Interim Superintendent | State Historical Society of North Dakota ND Heritage Center 612 East Boulevard Avenue, Bismarck, ND 58505-0830 701-328-2666

Ohio
Dr. Amos J. Loveday, State Historic, Preservation Officer | Ohio Historic Preservation Office Ohio Historical Society 567 E. Hudson Street, Columbus, OH 43211-1030 614-298-2000

Oklahoma
Dr. Bob L. Blackburn, State Historic Preservation Officer | 2100 N. Lincoln Boulevard, Oklahoma City, OK 73105 405-521-2491

Oregon
Mr. Mike Carrier, Director | Oregon Parks and Recreation Department 1115 Commercial Street NE, Salem, OR 97310-1001 503-378-5019

Pennsylvania
Dr. Brent D. Glass, State Historic Preservation, Officer | Pennsylvania Historical and Museum Commission 400 North Street, Harrisburg, PA 17108-1026 717-787-2891

Republic of Palau
Ms. Victoria N. Kanai, Historic Preservation, Officer | Ministry of Social Services Division of Cultural Affairs P.O. Box 100, Government of Palau, Koror, PW 96940 680-488-2489

Republic of the Marshall Islands
Mr. Frederick deBrum, Secretary of Interior Affairs and Historic Preservation Officer | Republic of the Marshall Islands P.O. Box 1454, Majuro, MH 96960 692-625-4642

Rhode Island
Mr. Frederick C. Williamson, State Historic, Preservation Officer | Historical Preservation and Heritage Commission Old State House 150 Benefit Street, Providence, RI 02903 401-222-2678

South Carolina
Dr. Rodger E. Stroup, Director | Department of Archives and History 8301 Parkland Road, Columbia, SC 29223-4905 803-896-6100

South Dakota
Mr. Jay D. Vogt, State Historic Preservation, Officer | South Dakota State Historical Society 900 Governors Drive, Pierre, SD 57501-2217 605-773-3458

Tennessee
Mr. Milton H. Hamilton Jr., Commissioner and, State Historic Preservation Officer | Department of Environment and Conservation 2941 Lebanon Road, Nashville, TN 37243-0442 615-532-0109

Texas
Mr. Lawerence Oaks, Executive Director | Texas Historical Commission P.O. Box 12276, Capitol Station, Austin, TX 78711-2276 512-463-6100

Utah
Mr. Max J. Evans, State Historic Preservation, Officer and Director | Utah State Historical Society 300 Rio Grande, Salt Lake City, UT 84101 801-533-3551

Vermont
Ms. Emily Wadhams, State Historic Preservation Officer and Director | Agency of Commerce and Community Development Vermont Division for Historic Preservation National Life Building, Drawer 20, Montpelier, VT 05620-0501 802-828-3056

Virgin Islands
Mr. Dean C. Plaskett, Commissioner | Department of Planning and Natural Resources Preservation Niskey Center, Suite 231 Number 45A, Estate Nisky, St. Thomas, VI 00802 340-776-8605

Virginia
Ms. Kathleen S. Kilpatrick, Director | Department of Historic Resources 2801 Kensington Avenue, Richmond, VA 23221 340-367-2323

Washington
Dr. Allyson Brooks, State Historic Preservation, Officer | Office of Archaeology and Historic Preservation, Washington State Department of Community, Trade, and Economic P.O. Box 48343, Olympia, WA 98504-8343 360-407-0765

West Virginia
Ms. Nancy Herholdt, State Historic Preservation, Officer & Commissioner | Division of Culture and History 1900 Kanawha Boulevard East Capitol Complex, Charleston, WV 25305-0300 304-558-0220

Wisconsin
Dr. George L. Vogt, Director and State Historic, Preservation Officer | State Historical Society 816 State Street, Madison, WI 53706 608-264-6500

Wyoming
Mr. Richard Curritt, Director | Wyoming State Historic Preservation Office 2301 Central Avenue, 3rd Floor, Cheyenne, WY 82002 307-777-7697

NATIONAL PARK SERVICE CENTENNIAL CHALLENGE

Award: Cooperative Agreements

Purpose: An effort to prepare national parks for another century of conservation, preservation, and public enjoyment. Project efforts will improve parks and serve all Americans.

Applicant Eligibility: Non-federal partners may include state agencies, Tribes, local governments, non-governmental organizations, private companies, and private individuals. Non-federal partners are expected to match NPS Centennial Challenge Cost Share funds at or above 1:1 for their respective projects.

Beneficiary Eligibility: State and local governments, private, public, profit, nonprofit organizations and institutions who are positioned to contribute at least 50 percent of the value of projects included in the list of approved Centennial Challenge projects.

Award Range/Average: Range: $20,090 Average: $20,090

Funding: Project Grants (Cooperative Agreements) FY 17 $40,719; FY 19 est $995,272; FY 18 est $995,272; - PROJECT GRANTS (Discretionary) FY 17 $40,719 FY 18 $995,272 FY 19 $995,272

HQ: 1849 C Street NW
Washington, DC 20240
Phone: 202-513-7218
http://www.nps.gov/subjects/centennial/nps-centennial-challenge-projects.htm

KEWEENAW NATIONAL HISTORICAL PARK (NHP) PRESERVATION GRANTS
"Keweenaw Heritage Grants"

Award: Cooperative Agreements

Purpose: Program intends to offer annual ONPS base funding to the Keweenaw NHP Advisory Commission to aid in the fulfillment of their legislated duties: to carry out historical, educational, or cultural programs which enhance understanding and preservation of the historic and cultural resources in the park and surrounding area on Michigan's Keweenaw Peninsula.

Applicant Eligibility: Eligibility for these funds include the Keweenaw NHP Advisory Commission and owners or operators of nationally significant, or potentially significant, properties on the Keweenaw Peninsula located: within the boundaries of Keweenaw NHP; affiliated with an existing Keweenaw Heritage Site; at the Cliff Mine in Keweenaw County, along Torch Lake in Houghton County, or within the community of Painesdale in Houghton County.

Beneficiary Eligibility: Beneficiaries may include: Public Nonprofit Institution / Organization: Keweenaw NHP Advisory Commission; Keweenaw NHP Heritage Sites; local or regional units of government; academic institutions, or federally recognized Indian tribes.

Award Range/Average: $115,000 to $300,000, Average is $250,000

Funding: Project Grants (Discretionary) FY 17 $206,909; FY 18 est $252,000; FY 19 est $25,200; - PROJECT GRANTS (Discretionary):FY 17 $206,909; FY 18 $252,000; FY 19 $252,000

HQ: 25970 Red Jacket Road
Calumet, MI 49913
http://www.nps.gov/kewe/index.htm

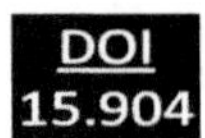

HISTORIC PRESERVATION FUND GRANTS-IN-AID "HPF"

Award: Formula Grants; Project Grants

Purpose: To provide FORMULA grants eligible grantees to assist in the identification, evaluation, and protection of historic properties by such means as education, survey, planning, technical assistance, preservation, documentation, and financial incentives like grants and tax credits available for historic properties. And, to provide PROJECT grants to eligible grantees to provide for the identification, evaluation, and protection of historic properties as defined by Congress.

Applicant Eligibility: FORMULA grants: States, Territories and Tribes (commonly known as the National Historic Preservation Act), operate programs administered by a State Historic Preservation Officer or Tribal Historic Preservation Officer appointed by the Governor, Tribal government or according to State or Tribal law, and which are otherwise in compliance with the requirements of the Act. PROJECT grants: Eligible tribal applicants include Federally recognized Indian Tribes, Alaska Native Corporations, and Native Hawaiian organizations.

Beneficiary Eligibility: FORMULA grants: State, Tribal and local governments, public and private nonprofit organizations, and individuals. According to their own priorities and plans, States and Tribes select their own projects and may sub-grant to public and private parties, including local governments, nonprofit and for-profit organizations, and/or individuals to accomplish program objectives.

Award Range/Average: Range $50,000 - $1,4000,000 Average $290,0000

Funding: (Project Grants) FY 18 est $20,500,000; FY 19 est $70,500,000; FY 17 $13,500,000; - Project Grants (Mandatory): FY 17 $13,500,000; FY 18 $20,500,000; FY 19 $70,500,000(Formula Grants) FY 19 est $58,000,000; FY 18 est $58,410,000; FY 17 $56,309,039; - Formula Grants (Mandatory): FY 17 $56,309,039; FY 18 $58,410,000; FY 19 $58,000,000

HQ: Department of Interior 1849 C Street NW, P.O. Box 7360
Washington, DC 20005
Phone: 202-354-2020
http://www.nps.gov/stlpg

NATIONAL HISTORIC LANDMARK

Award: Advisory Services and Counseling

Purpose: To preserve for public use historic sites, buildings, and objects of national significance, to make a survey of historic and archaeologic sites, buildings, and objects, to make necessary investigations and researches in the United States relating to particular sites, buildings, or objects, and to erect and maintain tablets to mark or commemorate historic or prehistoric places and events of national historical or archaeological significance.

Applicant Eligibility: Property owners and general public.

Beneficiary Eligibility: Anyone may suggest that a property be considered for inclusion in an appropriate National Historic Landmark theme study, provided the property has a high degree of historic integrity and potential national significance with relation to some broad facet of American history. The owner of the property may be an individual, government, or corporate body.

Award Range/Average: Range $20,000 to $100,000 in nonmonetary support. Average $50,000 on non-monetary support.

Funding: (Advisory Services and Counseling) FY 17 $0; FY 19 est $0; FY 18 est $0; - (Advisory Services and Counseling) FY 17 $0; FY 18 est. $0; and FY 19 est. $0

HQ: 1849 C Street NW
Washington, DC 20240
Phone: 202-354-2246
Email: christopher_hetzel@nps.gov
http://www.nps.gov/nhl

NATIONAL REGISTER OF HISTORIC PLACES "The National Register"

Award: Advisory Services and Counseling

Purpose: To expand and maintain the National Register of Historic Places, to make the information on districts, sites, buildings, structures and objects of historical, architectural, archeological, engineering and cultural significance more accessible to the public, and to promote greater appreciation of America's heritage.

Applicant Eligibility: Eligible applicants are the States and territories as defined in the National Historic Preservation Act, operating under programs administered by State Historic Preservation Officers appointed by the Governors (listed in Appendix IV of the Catalog); or the Tribal Preservation Officers; Federal agencies required to nominate and consider historic properties within their jurisdiction or as a result of the National Environmental Policy Act of 1969 and Executive Order 11593, and the National Historic Preservation Act operating under programs administered by representatives (listed in Appendix IV of the Catalog) appointed by the heads of the agencies; and, in States without approved State Historic Preservation Programs, persons and local governments. Applicants eligible for Federal Tax benefits include owners of individually listed properties and properties certified by the Secretary of Interior as being historic and in a district certified as historic.

Beneficiary Eligibility: Public and private owners of historic properties listed in the National Register of Historic Places or of properties certified by the Secretary of Interior as being historic and in a district certified as historic.

Award Range/Average: Range $20,000 - $111,000 Non-monetary assistance through consultation with NPS staff Average $71,000.

Funding: (Advisory Services and Counseling) FY 18 est $0; FY 19 est $0; FY 17 $0; N/A - FY 17 (Estimated) Non-monetary assistance through consultation with NPS staff; FY 18 (Estimated) Non-monetary assistance through consultation with NPS staff; FY 19 (Estimated) Non-monetary assistance through consultation with NPS staff.

HQ: 1849 C Street NW
Washington, DC 20240
Phone: 202-345-2003
Email: paul_loether@nps.gov
http://www.nps.gov/nr

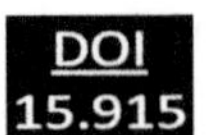

TECHNICAL PRESERVATION SERVICES

Award: Dissemination of Technical Information

Purpose: The Technical Preservation Services office provides standards and technical preservation assistance on rehabilitating historic buildings that are used by federal, state, and local government agencies, and other general property owners.

Applicant Eligibility: Anyone/general public can use this program.

Beneficiary Eligibility: Same as Applicant Eligibility.

Award Range/Average: Range: NA Average: N/A

Funding: (Advisory Services and Counseling) FY 17 $0; FY 19 est $0; FY 18 est $0; - N/A

HQ: 1849 C Street NW, P.O. Box 7243

Washington, DC 20240

Phone: 202-354-2033

http://www.nps.gov

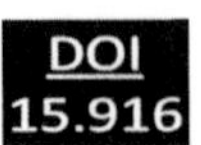

OUTDOOR RECREATION ACQUISITION, DEVELOPMENT AND PLANNING

"Land and Water Conservation Fund Grants"

Award: Formula Grants; Project Grants

Purpose: To give financial assistance to the States and their political subdivisions project that are included in Statewide Comprehensive Outdoor Recreation Plans (SCORPs) to meet current and future needs.

Applicant Eligibility: For planning grants, only the State agency formally designated by the Governor or State law as responsible for the preparation and maintenance of the SCORP is eligible to apply. (Treated as "States" for this purpose are the District of Columbia, Puerto Rico, the Virgin Islands, American Samoa, the Northern Mariana Islands, and Guam.

Beneficiary Eligibility: Same as Applicant Eligibility.

Award Range/Average: Range: $5,000 - $2,000,000 Average: $200,000

Funding: (Project Grants) FY 19 est $65,000,000; FY 18 est $65,000,000; FY 17 $75,932,422; FY 17: $75,932,422; FY 18 est: $65,000,000; FY 19 est: $65,000,000

HQ: 1849 C Street NW, P.O. Box 1353

Washington, DC 20240

Phone: 202-354-6905

Email: joel_lynch@nps.gov

http://http/www.nps.gov/ncrc/programs/lwcf/contact_list.html

DISPOSAL OF FEDERAL SURPLUS REAL PROPERTY FOR PARKS, RECREATION, AND HISTORIC MONUMENTS "Federal Lands to Parks Program (FLP); Historic Surplus Property Program (HSPP)"

Award: Sale, Exchange, or Donation of Property and Goods

Purpose: FLP: To transfer surplus Federal real property for state and local public park and recreation use. HSPP: To transfer Federal historic real property to state and local governments for historic preservation purposes.

Applicant Eligibility: FLP: Only State or local units of government and territories are eligible to apply for surplus real property for public parks and recreation. Recipients must agree to manage the property in the public interest and for public recreational use.

Beneficiary Eligibility: General public.

Award Range/Average: N/A. Value varies by the value of the available real property.

Funding: (Sale, Exchange, or Donation of Property and Goods) FY 18 est $589,000; FY 19 est $0; FY 17 $0.

HQ: 1849 C Street NW, P.O. Box 1353

Washington, DC 20005

Phone: 202-354-6905

Email: joel_lynch@nps.gov

http://http:/www.nps.gov/ncrc/programs/lwcf/contact_list.html

RIVERS, TRAILS AND CONSERVATION ASSISTANCE "Rivers and Trails; RTCA"

Award: Cooperative Agreements; Advisory Services and Counseling

Purpose: To implement the natural resource conservation and outdoor recreation mission of the National Park Service in communities across America.

Applicant Eligibility: Private nonprofit organizations and Federal, State and local government agencies.

Beneficiary Eligibility: Same as Applicant Eligibility.

Award Range/Average: Range: $3,000 - $330,000 Average: $150,000

Funding: (Advisory Services and Counseling) FY 19 est $2,000,000; FY 17 $1,448,588; FY 18 est $2,000,000; - FY 17: $1,448,588, FY 18 est: $2,000,000, FY 19 est: $ 2,000,000.

HQ: 1849 C Street NW ORG CODE 2240

Washington, DC 20240

Phone: 202-354-6922

Email: stephan_nofield@nps.gov

http://www.nps.gov/rtca

DOI 15.922 NATIVE AMERICAN GRAVES PROTECTION AND REPATRIATION ACT "NAGPRA"

Award: Project Grants

Purpose: Providing grants to museums to assist in the consultation on and documentation of Native American human remains and cultural items, to Indian tribes and Native Hawaiian organizations to assist in identifying human remains and cultural items, and to museums, Indian tribes and Native Hawaiian organizations to assist in the repatriation of human remains and cultural items.

Applicant Eligibility: An eligible applicant is: A museum that has control of Native American human remains, funerary objects, sacred objects, or objects of cultural patrimony and has received Federal funds. The term "Museum" includes state or local government agencies, private institutions, and institutions of higher learning that have received Federal funds.

Beneficiary Eligibility: State, local, public nonprofit institution/organization, other public institution/ organization, Federally Recognized Indian Tribal Government, Native American organization, American Indian.

Award Range/Average: Range: $5,000 - $90,000 Average: $25,000

Funding: (Project Grants (Discretionary)) FY 19 est $1,657,000; FY 17 $1,497,143; FY 18 est $1,657,000; - Project Grants (Discretionary): FY 17 $1,497,143; FY 18 $1,657,000; FY 19 $1,657,000. FY 18 and FY 19 totals are an estimate based on prior year funding levels only.

HQ: 1849 C Street NW, P.O. Box 7360
Washington, DC 20240
Phone: 202-354-2201
http://www.nps.gov/nagpra

DOI 15.923 NATIONAL CENTER FOR PRESERVATION TECHNOLOGY AND TRAINING "NCPTT"

Award: Project Grants

Purpose: To develop and distribute preservation and conservation skills and technologies; to develop and facilitate training for Federal, State, and local resource preservation professionals, cultural resource managers, maintenance personnel, and others working in the preservation field; to take steps to apply preservation technology benefits from ongoing research by other agencies and institutions; to facilitate the transfer of preservation technology among Federal agencies, State and local governments, universities, international organizations, and the private sector; and to cooperate with related international organizations.

Applicant Eligibility: U.S. universities and two and four year colleges; U.S. private nonprofit institution/ organizations and quasi-public nonprofit institution/organizations that are directly associated with educational or research activity; Federal, State, local government agencies, Federally recognized Indian Tribal governments and their Tribal Historic Preservation Offices; For-profit organizations and private individuals may submit proposals only in partnership with an eligible U.S. organization.

Beneficiary Eligibility: Anyone/General Public.

Award Range/Average: $15,000 to $500,000; The average funding for a grant or cooperative agreement is $40,000.

Funding: (Project Grants (Discretionary)) FY 18 est $764,600; FY 17 $1,112,247; FY 19 est $695,600; - PROJECT GRANTS (Discretionary): FY 17 $1,112,247; FY 18 $764,600; FY 19 est $695,600.

HQ: 645 University Parkway
Natchitoches, LA 71457
Phone: 318-356-7444
Email: mary_striegel@nps.gov
http://www.ncptt.nps.gov

NATIONAL MARITIME HERITAGE GRANTS
"Maritime Heritage Grants"

Award: Project Grants

Purpose: To provide matching grants for preservation or education projects and to help State, Tribal, and local governments and private nonprofit organizations preserve and interpret their maritime heritage.

Applicant Eligibility: State, local, tribal governments and private nonprofit institutions/organizations are eligible to apply. Individuals are not eligible applicants.

Beneficiary Eligibility: Any State or local government or private non-profit institution/organization will benefit directly from grant funds. It is intended that the general public will ultimately benefit from the information conveyed by the funded projects.

Award Range/Average: Range: $15,000 to $200,000 Average: $66,000

Funding: (Project Grants) FY 17 $2,293,929; FY 18 est $2,535,826; FY 19 est $0; FY 16 $2,058,164

HQ: 1849 C Street NW, P.O. Box 7508
Washington, DC 20240
Phone: 202-354-2266
Email: kelly_spradley-kurowski@nps.gov
http://www.nps.gov/maritime/grants/intro.htm

AMERICAN BATTLEFIELD PROTECTION
"Planning Grants"

Award: Cooperative Agreements

Purpose: To fund non-acquisition preservation methods such as planning, education, survey, and inventory to promote the protection and preservation of battlefield lands on American soil.

Applicant Eligibility: Applicant may be Federal, intrastate, interstate, State and local agencies, public or private nonprofit institutions/organizations, federally recognized Indian tribal governments, U.S. territory and possessions, Native American organizations, State colleges and universities, public and private colleges and universities. Multi-organizational applications are encouraged.

Beneficiary Eligibility: Federal, intrastate, interstate, State and local agencies, public and private nonprofit institutions/organizations, Federally recognized Indian tribal governments, U.S. territories and possessions, Native American organizations, State college or universities, public and private colleges and universities.

Award Range/Average: Range: $5,000 to $122,000 Average: $40,000

Funding: (Project Grants (Discretionary)) FY 17 $1,139,010; FY 18 est $1,198,000; FY 19 est $1,198,000; FY 16 $1,095,306; - FY 18 and FY 19 totals are an estimate based on prior year funding levels only.

HQ: American Battlefield Protection Program 1849 C Street NW, Room 7228
Washington, DC 20240
Phone: 202-354-2037
Email: kristen_mcmasters@nps.gov
http://www.nps.gov/abpp/grants/planninggrants.htm

DOI 15.927 HYDROPOWER RECREATION ASSISTANCE "FERC Hydropower Licensing"

Award: Advisory Services and Counseling

Purpose: To support government, industry, and nonprofit partnerships in ongoing consultations and negotiations about applications for hydropower licensing; to meet present and future outdoor recreation and river conservation needs; and to maintain and improve a project's riparian areas.

Applicant Eligibility: Private nonprofit organizations, Federal, State, and Local government agencies and hydropower licensing applicants.

Beneficiary Eligibility: Private nonprofit organizations, Federal, State, and Local government agencies and hydropower licensing applicants, as well as the general public.

Award Range/Average: N/A

Funding: (Advisory Services and Counseling) FY 17 $0; FY 18 est $0; FY 19 FY 16 $0; - Advisory Services and Counseling (Mandatory)

HQ: 1849 C Street NW
Washington, DC 20240
Phone: 202-354-6929
Email: joan_harn@nps.gov
http://www.nps.gov/hydro

DOI 15.928 BATTLEFIELD LAND ACQUISITION GRANTS "BLAGs"

Award: Project Grants

Purpose: To aid States and local communities acquire and preserve threatened battlefield lands from the Revolutionary War, War of 1812, and Civil War.

Applicant Eligibility: State and local governments. Private nonprofit organizations seeking to acquire battlefield land or easements must apply in partnership with the State or local government agency that has jurisdiction over the proposed parcel.

Beneficiary Eligibility: State and local governments (local communities, nonprofits, and battlefield landowners) benefit.

Award Range/Average: Range: $1,000 to $2,000,000 Average: $250,000.

Funding: (Project Grants (Discretionary)) FY 17 $9,516,237; FY 18 est $10,000,000; FY 19 est $10,000,000; - Project Grants (Discretionary): FY 17 $9,516,237; FY 18 est $10,000,000; and FY 19 est $10,000,000. FY 18 and FY 19 totals are an estimate based on prior year funding levels only.

HQ: 1849 C Street NW, Room 7228
Washington, DC 20240
Phone: 202-354-2034
Email: kelley_smith@nps.gov
http://www.nps.gov/abpp/grants/cwblaggrants.htm

SAVE AMERICA's TREASURES

Award: Project Grants

Purpose: To provide matching grants for preservation or conservation work on nationally-significant: intellectual and cultural artifacts and historic structures and sites.

Applicant Eligibility: State and Local agencies, Public or Private nonprofit institutions/organizations, State Colleges and Universities, Public and Private Colleges and Universities, and Federally Recognized Indian Tribes. Individuals are not eligible applicants.

Beneficiary Eligibility: Any Federal, Intrastate, Interstate, State and local agencies, Public or Private nonprofit institution/organization, State Colleges or University, Public and Private College or University, or Federally recognized Indian tribes.

Award Range/Average: FY 17: $125,000 to $500,000 (for preservation), $25,000 to $500,000 (for collections).

Funding: (Project Grants) FY 17 $0; FY 18 est $13,000,000; FY 19 N/A FY 16 $0; - PROJECT GRANTS (Discretionary): FY 17 $0; FY 18 $13,000,000; FY 19 No appropriation at this time.

HQ: State Tribal Local Plans and Grants Division 1849 C Street NW, P.O. Box 7360
Washington, DC 20240
Phone: 202-354-2020
http://www.nps.gov/stlpg

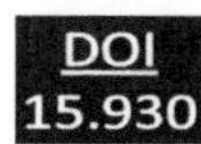

CHESAPEAKE BAY GATEWAYS NETWORK "Chesapeake Bay Gateways and Trails"

Award: Cooperative Agreements

Purpose: To increase access to the Chesapeake and rivers, to preserve important landscapes and resources, to promote tourism and local economies, to engage youth in meaningful work and placed-based education, to improve recreational opportunities, and to interpret the natural and cultural resources of the Chesapeake region.

Applicant Eligibility: Recipients must either be a non-profit organization qualified as such under section 501(c) of the Internal Revenue Code or a state or local government. NPS Chesapeake technical and financial assistance strategically supports projects and programs that meet DOI's key responsibilities in the Chesapeake Bay watershed.

Beneficiary Eligibility: General Public.

Award Range/Average: Range: $25,000 - $125,000. Average: $70,000

Funding: (Cooperative Agreements (Discretionary Grants)) FY 17 $206,313; FY 18 N/A FY 19 N/A FY 16 $253,000; - FY 17 $206,313; FY 18 TBD (subject to appropriation); FY 19 TBD (subject to appropriation)

HQ: Department of the Interior US Custom House 200 Chestnut Street, 3rd Floor
Philadelphia, PA 19106
Phone: 215-597-9153
Email: jamie_cupples@nps.gov
http://www.nps.gov/chba/learn/management/financial-assistance-for-partners.htm

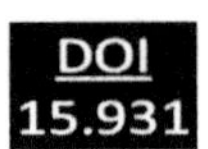

CONSERVATION ACTIVITIES BY YOUTH SERVICE ORGANIZATIONS
"21st Century Conservation Service Corps Program"

Award: Cooperative Agreements

Purpose: To employ qualified nonprofit youth and young adult serving organizations to carry out natural and cultural resource conservation, education, volunteer service, and education projects on Department of the Interior lands through authorized NPS programs.

Applicant Eligibility: Private non-profit institutions and organizations; public and private non-profit academic institutions; state and local government agencies; quasi-public non-profit institutions and organizations that support youth and young adult career training and development, and education in the areas of natural and/or cultural resource conservation and management.

Beneficiary Eligibility: Individuals/families; students; and the general public will receive a benefit from the development and execution of these programs and projects.

Award Range/Average: Range: $5,000 - $900,000

Funding: (Cooperative Agreements (Discretionary Grants)) FY 17 $37,078,851; FY 18 FY 19 N/A FY 16 $36,580,234.

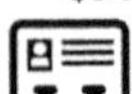

HQ: 1849 C Street NW
Washington, DC 20240
Phone: 202-513-7146
Email: george_mcdonald@nps.gov
http://www.nps.gov/subjects/youthprograms/index.htm

PRESERVATION OF JAPANESE AMERICAN CONFINEMENT SITES
"Japanese American Confinement Sites Grant Program"

Award: Project Grants

Purpose: To encourage projects that identify, research, evaluate, interpret, protect, restore, repair, and acquire historic confinement sites so that the present and future generations may learn and gain inspiration from these sites since they demonstrate the Nation's commitment to equal justice under the law.

Applicant Eligibility: Applicant may be State and local agencies, public or private nonprofit institutions/ organizations, Federally recognized Indian tribal governments, State colleges and universities, public and private colleges and universities.

Beneficiary Eligibility: Providing present and future generations of Americans learning opportunities about the nation's commitment to equal justice under the law.

Award Range/Average: Range: $16,000 - $250,000 Average: $150,000

Funding: (Project Grants (Discretionary)) FY 17 $2,687,513; FY 18 est $1,000,000; FY 19 est $1,000,000; FY 16 $2,913,275; - FY 19 total is an estimate based on prior year funding levels only.

HQ: 12795 W Alameda Parkway
Lakewood, CO 80228
Phone: 303-969-2885
Email: kara_miyagishima@nps.gov
http://www.nps.gov/jacs

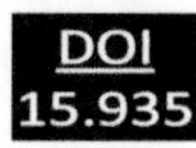

NATIONAL TRAILS SYSTEM PROJECTS

Award: Cooperative Agreements

Purpose: To preserve, protect, and develop the elements of the National Trails System.

Applicant Eligibility: States or their political subdivisions, landowners, private organizations, or individuals.

Beneficiary Eligibility: General public, and States or their political subdivisions, landowners, private organizations, or individuals.

Award Range/Average: Range: $7,000 - $821,000 Average: $100,000

Funding: (Project Grants) FY 17 $38,928,877; FY 18 est $4,000,000; FY 19 est $4,000,000; FY 16 $5,092,435

HQ: 1849 C Street NW
Washington, DC 20240
Phone: 202-354-6900
Email: stephan_nofield@nps.gov
http://www.nps.gov.nts

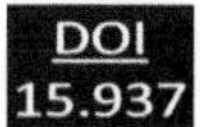

REDWOOD NATIONAL PARK COOPERATIVE MANAGEMENT WITH THE STATE OF CALIFORNIA

Award: Cooperative Agreements; Sale, Exchange, or Donation of Property and Goods; Use of Property, Facilities, and Equipment; Advisory Services and Counseling; Dissemination of Technical Information; Training

Purpose: To develop joint operating procedures and standards to assure effective accomplishment of park activities.

Applicant Eligibility: Agencies within the State of California Government

Beneficiary Eligibility: General Public and the State of California.

Award Range/Average: Range: $15,000 - $35,000 Average: $18,000

Funding: (Cooperative Agreements (Discretionary Grants)) FY 17 $78,620; FY 18 est $65,000; FY 19 est $75,000; FY 16 $59,516

HQ: 1849 C Street NW
Washington, DC 20240
Phone: 202-208-3100
Email: steven_mietz@nps.gov
http://www.nps.gov/redw

DOI 15.938 BOSTON AFRICAN-AMERICAN NATIONAL HISTORIC SITE "Rehab African Meetinghouse"

Award: Cooperative Agreements

Purpose: To rehabilitate the African Meetinghouse in Boston, MA.

Applicant Eligibility: Museum of African-American History.

Beneficiary Eligibility: Museum of African-American History and the General public.

Award Range/Average: Range: $37,000 - $225,000 Average: $40,000

Funding: (Project Grants) FY 17 $82,685; FY 18 est $70,000; FY 19 est $60,000

HQ: 1849 C Street NW
Washington, DC 20240
Phone: 202-208-3100
Email: michael_creasey@nps.gov
http://www.nps.gov.boaf

NATIONAL HERITAGE AREA FEDERAL FINANCIAL ASSISTANCE

Award: Cooperative Agreements

Purpose: To preserve and interpret for the educational and inspirational benefit of present and future generations, to encourage a broad range of economic opportunities, and to provide a management framework to help state/local government entities, non profits, and others in developing policies and programs.

Applicant Eligibility: State, local, or tribal government or other public entity, an educational institution, or a private nonprofit organization.

Beneficiary Eligibility: General public, states, their political subdivisions, non-profits, private entities, the heritage area management/coordinating entity.

Award Range/Average: Range: $4,000- $650,000 Average: $215,000

Funding: (Direct Payments for Specified Use (Cooperative Agreements)) FY 17 $19,064,765; FY 18 est $17,000,000; FY 19 est $17,000,000; FY 16 $20,000,000

HQ: 1201 Eye Street NW, 6th Floor
Washington, DC 20005
Phone: 202-354-2222
Email: martha_raymond@nps.gov
http://www.nps.gov/history/heritageareas

NEW BEDFORD WHALING NATIONAL HISTORIC PARK COOPERATIVE MANAGEMENT

Award: Cooperative Agreements

Purpose: To provide for visitor understanding, appreciation, and enjoyment by collaborating with the interested entities and individuals.

Applicant Eligibility: State, local and tribal governments, other public entities, education institutions, and private nonprofit organizations.

Beneficiary Eligibility: General Public

Award Range/Average: Range: $2,500 - $122,500 Average: $7,500

Funding: (Cooperative Agreements) FY 17 $0; FY 18 est $15,000; FY 19 est $15,000; FY 16 $60,933

HQ: 33 William Street
New Bedford, MA 2740
Email: meghan_kish@nps.gov
http://www.nps.gov/nebe

DOI 15.941 MISSISSIPPI NATIONAL RIVER AND RECREATION AREA STATE AND LOCAL ASSISTANCE

Award: Cooperative Agreements; Advisory Services and Counseling

Purpose: To assist or fund to improve partner planning for and interpretation of non-Federal publicly owned lands within the area.

Applicant Eligibility: The State of Minnesota or its political subdivisions, counties, cities, non-profits

Beneficiary Eligibility: Same as Applicant Eligibility.

Award Range/Average: Range: $18,000 - $170,000 Average: $25,000

Funding: (Project Grants (Cooperative Agreements)) FY 17 $761,898; FY 18 N/A FY 19 N/A FY 16 $312,253

HQ: 111 E Kellogg Boulevard, Suite 105
St. Paul, MN 55101
Phone: 651-290-3030
Email: denise_st_marie@nps.gov
http://www.nps.gov/miss

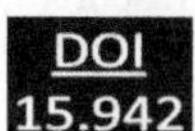

ENVIRONMENTAL EDUCATION AND CONSERVATION - NORTH CASCADES

Award: Cooperative Agreements

Purpose: To provide programs of public education, youth engagement, involvement in conservation, natural science, history and related fields of study, and conduct interpretive activities about the Skagit River and the North Cascades bioregion.

Applicant Eligibility: State, local, or tribal government or other public entity, an educational institution, or a private nonprofit organization.

Beneficiary Eligibility: General public

Award Range/Average: Range: $0 Average: $0

Funding: (Cooperative Agreements (Discretionary Grants)) FY 17 $0; FY 18 est $0; FY 19 est $0

HQ: North Cascades National Park Service Complex Denise Shultz 810 State Route 20
Sedro Woolley, WA 98284

Phone: 360-854-7302

Email: denise_m_shultz@nps.gov

http://nps.gov/noca

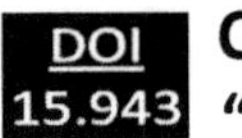

CHALLENGE COST SHARE
"National Park Service Challenge Cost Share"

Award: Cooperative Agreements; Direct Payments for Specified Use

Purpose: To increase participation by qualified partners in the preservation and improvement of NPS natural, cultural, and recreational resources in all authorized programs and activities.

Applicant Eligibility: State, local, or tribal government or other public entity, an educational institution, or a private nonprofit organization.

Beneficiary Eligibility: General public, trail system users, and organizations with conservation missions.

Award Range/Average: Range: $1,0000 - $25,000 (subawards) Average: $20,000

Funding: (Direct Payments for Specified Use) FY 17 $409,399; FY 18 est $300,000; FY 19 est $300,000; FY 16 $377,199.

HQ: 1201 Eye Street NW, 9th Floor

Washington, DC 20005

Phone: 202-354-6907

Email: charlie_stockman@nps.gov

http://www.nps.gov/ccsp

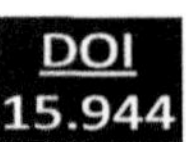

NATURAL RESOURCE STEWARDSHIP

Award: Cooperative Agreements

Purpose: To evaluate and improve the health of watersheds, landscapes, and marine and coastal resources; to sustain biological communities on the lands and waters in parks; and to improve the resiliency of these natural resources and adapt them to the effects of climate change.

Applicant Eligibility: State, local, or tribal governments, other Federal agencies, other public entities, educational institutions, private nonprofit organizations.

Beneficiary Eligibility: General public

Award Range/Average: Range: $4,000 - $185,000 Average: $55,000

Funding: (Cooperative Agreements) FY 17 $13,645,377; FY 18 est $8,000,000; FY 19 est $8,000,000; FY 16 $13,314,435

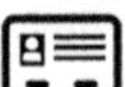

HQ: 1201 Eye Street NW

Washington, DC 20024

Phone: 202-513-7204

Email: karel_morales@nps.gov

http://www.nature.nps.gov

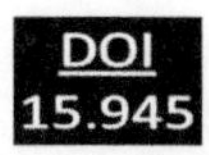

COOPERATIVE RESEARCH AND TRAINING PROGRAMS – RESOURCES OF THE NATIONAL PARK SYSTEM "Cooperative Ecosystem Studies Units (CESU) Network"

Award: Cooperative Agreements

Purpose: To support coordinated cooperative research, technical assistance, education and training, and usable knowledge development to inform science-based management of the National Park System and to establish and maintain cooperative study units.

Applicant Eligibility: State and local governments, federally recognized Indian tribal governments, public/private nonprofit organizations, nonprofit institutions of higher education, and individuals.

Beneficiary Eligibility: Same as Applicant Eligibility.

Award Range/Average: Range: $5,000 - $970,000 Average: $48,500

Funding: (Cooperative Agreements (Discretionary Grants)) FY 17 $52,778,345; FY 18 est $40,000,000; FY 19 est $40,000,000; FY 16 $45,304,275.

HQ: Network National Program Office 1849 C Street NW, Room #2649
Washington, DC 20240
Phone: 202-354-1825
Email: tom_fish@nps.gov
http://www.cesu.org

CULTURAL RESOURCES MANAGEMENT

Award: Cooperative Agreements

Purpose: To conduct cultural resource stewardship largely at the park level. To carry out and further this stewardship responsibility, the Service implements programs that cover a broad range of research, operational, and educational activities.

Applicant Eligibility: State, local, or tribal government or other public entity, an educational institution, or a private nonprofit organization.

Beneficiary Eligibility: State and local governments, Federally recognized Indian Tribal governments, nonprofit organizations, educational or scientific institutions, associations, individuals.

Award Range/Average: Range: $1,000 - $5,500,000 Average: $192,000

Funding: (Cooperative Agreements) FY 17 $7,951,735; FY 18 est $15,000,000; FY 19 est $15,000,000; FY 16 $16,260,471

HQ: US Department of the Interior1849 C Street NW, Room #2737
Washington, DC 20240
Phone: 202-208-7625
Email: joy_beasley@nps.gov
http://www.nps.gov/history

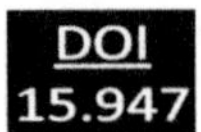

BOSTON HARBOR ISLANDS PARTNERSHIP

Award: Cooperative Agreements; Direct Payments for Specified Use

Purpose: To acquire from and provide to the partners goods and services for cooperative management of lands within the Park and to provide for safe visitor access, public information, youth programs, resource management, and citizen science and scholarly research.

Applicant Eligibility: The Commonwealth of Massachusetts, members of the Boston Harbor Islands Partnership, and other public entities, education institutions, and private nonprofit organizations.

Beneficiary Eligibility: General Public

Award Range/Average: Range: In FY 17, the range was $10,978 - $691,154 supporting projects under cooperative management agreements therefore direct funding is through task agreements with management partners. Average: The average of $140, 767 is based on individual financial assistance task agreements with the management partners.

Funding: (Cooperative Agreements (Discretionary Grants)) FY 17 $1,353,507; FY 18 est $550,000; FY 19 est $450,000; FY 16 $546,694

HQ: Boston Harbor Islands National Recreation Area 15 Stark Street, Suite 1100

Boston, MA 2109

Email: michael_creasey@nps.gov

http://www.nps.gov/boha

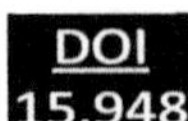

NATIONAL FIRE PLAN-WILDLAND URBAN INTERFACE COMMUNITY FIRE ASSISTANCE

Award: Cooperative Agreements; Use of Property, Facilities, and Equipment; Provision of Specialized Services; Advisory Services and Counseling; Dissemination of Technical Information

Purpose: To enforce the National Fire Plan and assist communities at risk from catastrophic wildland fires.

Applicant Eligibility: States and local governments at risk as published in the Federal Register or as determined by the state, Indian Tribes, public and private education institutions, nonprofit organizations.

Beneficiary Eligibility: Same as Applicant Eligibility.

Award Range/Average: Range: $7,000 - $20,000 Average: $20,000

Funding: (Cooperative Agreements (Discretionary Grants)) FY 17 $102,987; FY 18 est $50,000; FY 19 est $50,000; FY 15 $27,512; FY 16 est $100,000

HQ: 3833 S Development Avenue

Boise, ID 83705

Phone: 208-387-5090

Email: mark_koontz@nps.gov

http://www.forestsandrangelands.gov

DOI 15.954 NATIONAL PARK SERVICE CONSERVATION, PROTECTION, OUTREACH, AND EDUCATION

Award: Cooperative Agreements

Purpose: To assist projects complementary to National Park Service (NPS) program endeavors in resource conservation and protection, historical preservation, and environmental sustainability.

Applicant Eligibility: State, local and tribal governments, educational institutions, and nonprofit organizations.

Beneficiary Eligibility: Profit organizations, public nonprofit institutions/organizations, private nonprofit institutions/organizations, and State, local and tribal governments, industry and public decision makers, research scientists, engineers, and the general public.

Award Range/Average: Range: $2,000 - $925,000 Average: $67,000

Funding: (Cooperative Agreements) FY 17 $23,656,912; FY 18 est $20,000,000; FY 19 est $20,000,000

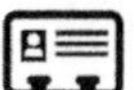

HQ: 12795 W Alameda Parkway
Lakewood, CO 80228
Phone: 303-969-2065
Email: heidi_sage@nps.gov
http://www.nps.gov

DOI 15.955 MARTIN LUTHER KING JUNIOR NATIONAL HISTORIC SITE AND PRESERVATION DISTRICT

Award: Cooperative Agreements

Purpose: To protect and interpret for the benefit, inspiration, and education of present and future generations the places where Martin Luther King, Junior, was born, where he lived, worked, and worshipped, and where he is buried.

Applicant Eligibility: Owners of properties of historical or cultural significance within the District, State, local, or tribal government or other public entity, an educational institution, or a private nonprofit organizations.

Beneficiary Eligibility: State, local and tribal governments, public nonprofit institutions/organizations, private nonprofit institutions/organizations, general public, institutions of higher education will ultimately benefit from knowledge gained under this program.

Award Range/Average: Range: $100,000 to $800,000 Average: $600,000

Funding: (Cooperative Agreements) FY 17 $971,000; FY 18 est $800,000; FY 19 est $800,000; FY 16 $809,168

HQ: MLK NHS 450 Auburn Avenue NE
Atlanta, GA 30303
Phone: 404-331-2022
Email: judy_forte@nps.gov
http://www.nps.gov

DOI 15.956 EBEY'S LANDING NATIONAL HISTORICAL RESERVE TRUST BOARD

Award: Direct Payments for Specified Use; Provision of Specialized Services

Purpose: To manage the Reserve; administer and protect sites acquired by the NPS; administer programs within the scope of the Reserve purposes; participate in the land use review process; cooperate with Town and County departments and staff to assure awareness and protection of resources of the Reserve; and enter into contracts with individuals, private organizations and local community and governmental bodies to protect, research enhance document, and interpret the resources of the Reserve.

Applicant Eligibility: The authorizing legislation for Ebey's Landing National Historical Reserve states that the Secretary of Interior is authorized to transfer management and administration of the Reserve to an appropriate unit of local government. A joint administrative board called the Ebey's Landing National Historical Reserve Trust Board (Trust Board), was created in accordance with the provision of RCW 39.

Beneficiary Eligibility: Other Public Institution/organization

Award Range/Average: Range: $1,000 - $200,000 Average: $200,000

Funding: (Direct Payments for Specified Use (Cooperative Agreements)) FY 17 $46,554; FY 18 N/A FY 19 N/A

HQ: Pacific W Regional Office 909 First Avenue #500
Seattle, WA 98104
Phone: 206-220-4000
Email: roy_zipp@nps.gov
http://www.nps.gov/ebla/learn/management/staffandoffices.htm

EMERGENCY SUPPLEMENTAL HISTORIC PRESERVATION FUND
"HPF Hurricane Sandy Relief Grant Program"

Award: Formula Grants; Project Grants

Purpose: To assist the historic resources within a major disaster declaration area that are listed in or determined eligible for the National Register.

Applicant Eligibility: Eligible applicants are State and Tribal Historic Preservation Offices located within areas receiving major disaster declarations from FEMA.

Beneficiary Eligibility: States and Tribes

Award Range/Average: Range: $500,0000 to $10,000,000 Average: $5,000,000.

Funding: (Formula Grants) FY 17 $0; FY 18 est $47,500,000; FY 19 N/A - (Project Grants) FY 17 $0; FY 18 est $1,000,000; FY 19 N/A

HQ: 1849 C Street NW, P.O. Box 7360
Washington, DC 20240
Phone: 202-354-2062
Email: megan_brown@nps.gov
http://www.nps.gov/stlpg

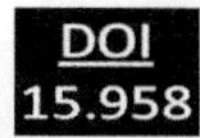

ROUTE 66 CORRIDOR PRESERVATION
"Route 66 Corridor Preservation Program"

Award: Cooperative Agreements

Purpose: To preserve the cultural resources of the Route 66 corridor and to authorize the Secretary of the Interior to give assistance.

Applicant Eligibility: Interstate, intrastate, state, local, sponsored organizations, public nonprofit institution/organizations, other public institution/organizations, Federally recognized tribal governments, individual/family, minority groups, specialized groups, small businesses, profit organizations, private nonprofit institution/organizations, quasi-public nonprofit institution/organization, other private institution/organizations, anyone/general public, native American organizations.

Beneficiary Eligibility: Interstate, Intrastate, State, Local, Sponsored Organization, Public Nonprofit Institution/Organization, Other Public Institution/organization, Federally Recognized Indian Tribal Government, Individual/Family, Minority Group, Specialized Group, Small Business, Profit Organization, Private Organization, Quasi-Public Nonprofit Organization, Other Private Institution/organization, Anyone/General Public, Native American Organization, Health Professional, Education Professional, Student/Trainee. Graduate Student, Scientists/Researcher, Artist/Humanist, Engineer/Architect.

Award Range/Average: Range: $5,000- $30,000

Funding: (Project Grants (Discretionary)) FY 17 $174,551; FY 18 est $90,000; FY 19 est $90,000.

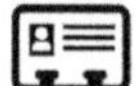

HQ: 1100 Old Santa Fe Trail, P.O. Box 728
Santa Fe, NM 87505
Phone: 505-988-6701
Email: kaisa_barthuli@nps.gov
http://www.nps.gov/rt66/grnts

FEDERAL HISTORIC PRESERVATION TAX INCENTIVE
"Historic Tax Credit"

Award: Advisory Services and Counseling

Purpose: To promote historic preservation and community improvement through the private investment in the rehabilitation of historic buildings.

Applicant Eligibility: For the rehabilitation tax credit: private owners of commercial and other income-producing historic buildings held for investment purposes. For the conservation easement deduction; private owners of historic buildings proposed as the subject of charitable easement donations.

Beneficiary Eligibility: For the rehabilitation tax credit: private owners of historic buildings held for investment purposes. For the income tax deduction for the donation of conservation easements: private owners of buildings.

Award Range/Average: N/A

Funding: (Provision of Specialized Services) FY 17 $0; FY 18 est $0; FY 19 est $0; FY 16 $0.

HQ: Technical Preservation Services 1849 C Street NW, P.O. Box 7243
Washington, DC 20240
Phone: 202-354-2033
http://www.nps.gov/tps/tax-incentives.htm

DOI 15.962 NATIONAL WILD AND SCENIC RIVERS SYSTEM "Partnership Wild and Scenic Rivers"

Award: Cooperative Agreements

Purpose: To plan, protect, and manage river resources associated with those rivers designated into the National Wild and Scenic River system whereas the Department of Interior will act as the federal administrator.

Applicant Eligibility: States or their political subdivisions, landowners, private non-profit organizations, other federal agencies or duly authorized by a river's enabling legislation wild and scenic river management councils or committees.

Beneficiary Eligibility: Same as Applicant Eligibility.

Award Range/Average: Range: $20,000 - $350,000 Average: $85,000

Funding: (Project Grants (Cooperative Agreements)) FY 17 $1,202,500; FY 18 est $974,000; FY 19 est $974,000; FY 16 $0

HQ: 1849 C Street
Washington, DC 20240
Phone: 202-354-6929
Email: joan_harn@nps.gov
http://www.nps.gov/pwsr

NATURAL RESOURCES CONSERVATION SERVICE

LONGSHORE AND HARBOR WORKERS' COMPENSATION

Billy Teels, Director | Wetlands Science Institute Snowden Hall 11400 American Holy Drive, Laurel, MD 20708-4014 301-497-5911

Carolyn Adams, Director | Watershed Sciences Institute 101 SW Main Street, Suite 1700, Portland, OR 97204-3225 502-414-3001

Dean M. Thompson, Director | NRI&A Institute Statistical Laboratory 202 Snedecor Hall Iowa State University, Ames, IA 50011 515-294-8177

Dennis Lytle, Chair | National Soil Survey Center Federal Building, Room 152 100 Centennial Mall North, Lincoln, NE 68508-3866 402-437-5499

Frank Clearfield, Director | Social Sciences Institute North Carolina A&T State University Applied Survey Research Laboratory Beech & Lindsay Streets, Greensboro, NC 27411 202-720-1511

John Werner, Co-Director | National Water & Climate Center 101 SW Main Street, Portland, OR 97204-3225 503-414-3107

Maurice Mausbach, Director | Soil Quality Institute 14th & Independence Avenue, N.W., Washington, DC 20250 202-720-4525

National Employee Development Center 501 Felix Street, Building 23, Ft. Worth, TX 76115

Phillip Jones, Head | National Soil Mechanics Center Federal Building, Room 152 100 Centennial Mall North, Lincoln, NE 68508-3866 402-437-5318

Rhett Johnson, Director | Grazing Lands Institute 501 Felix Street, Building 23 P.O. Box 6567, Ft. Worth, TX 76115

Richard Folsche, Director | National Carto & Geospatial Database Center 501 Felix street, Building 23, Ft. Worth, TX 76115 817-334-5292, Ext. 3031

Scott Peterson, Director | National Plant Data Center P.O. Box 74490, Baton Rouge, LA 70874 504-775-6280

Wildon Fontenot, Co-Director | P.O. Box 2890, Washington, DC 20013-2890 202-720-4909

REGIONAL OFFICES

Charles Whitmore | Midwest Regional Office One Gifford Pinchot Drive, Room 204, Madison, WI 53705-3210 608-264-5281

Diane Gelburd | East Regional Office 1400 Wilson Boulevard, Suite 1100, Arlington, VA 22209 703-312-7282

Jeffery Vonk | Northern Plains Regional Office 100 Centennial Mall North, Room 152, Lincoln, NE 68508 402-437-5315

Judy Johnson | South Central Regional Office 501 W. Felix Street, Building 23 P.O. Box 6459, Ft. Worth, TX 76115

Rosendo Trevino III, Acting | West Regional Office 650 Capitol Mall, Room 6072, Sacramento, CA 95814 916-498-5284

SERVICE CENTER

Alabama
Ronnie D. Murphy | 3381 Skyway Drive, Auburn, AL 36830 334-887-4500

Alaska
Robert N. Jones | 800 W. Evergreen Avenue Suite 100, Palmer, AK 99645 907-761-7760

Arizona
Michael Somerville | 3003 North Central Avenue, Suite 800, Phoenix, AZ 85012-2945 602-280-8808

Arkansas
Kalvin L. Trice | 700 W. Capitol Avenue Federal Building, Room 5404 P.O. Box 2323, Little Rock, AR 72201-3228 501-324-5445

California
Henry Wyman, Acting | 2121-C 2nd Street, Suite 102, Davis, CA 95616-5475 916-757-8215

Colorado
Leroy Stokes, Acting | 655 Parfet Street, Room E200C, Lakewood, CO 80215-5517 303-236-2886, Ext. 202

Connecticut
Margo L. Wallace | 16 Professional Park Road, Storrs, CT 06268-1299 203-487-4014

Delaware
Elesa K. Cottrell | 1203 College Park Drive, Suite 101, Dover, DE 19904-8713 302-678-4160

Florida
T. Niles Glasgow | 2614 Northwest 43rd Street Box 141510, Gainesville, FL 32606-6611 904-338-9500

Georgia
Earl Cosby | Federal Building P.O. Box 13 355 East Hancock Avenue, Athens, GA 30601-2769 706-546-2272

Hawaii
Kenneth M. Kaneshiro | 300 Ala Moana Boulevard, Room 4316 P.O. Box 50004, Honolulu, HI 96850-0002 808-541-2601

Idaho
Luana E. Kiger | 3244 Elder Street, Room 124, Boise, ID 83705-4711 208-378-5700

Illinois
William J. Gradle | 1902 Fox Drive, Champaign, IL 61820-7335 217-398-5267

Indiana
Robert L. Eddleman | 6013 Lakeside Boulevard, Indianapolis, IN 46278-2933 317-290-3200

Iowa
LeRoy Brown | 210 Walnut Street, Suite 693 Federal Building, Des Moines, IA 50309-2180 515-284-6655

Kansas
Tomas M. Dominguez | 760 South Broadway, Salina, KS 67401 913-823-4565

Kentucky
David G. Sawyer | 771 Corporate Drive, Suite 110, Lexington, KY 40503-5479 606-224-7350

Louisiana
Kevin Norton | 3737 Government Street, Alexandria, LA 71302-3727 318-473-7751

Maine
Darrel Dominick | 5 Godfrey Drive, Orono, ME 04473 207-866-7241

Maryland
David P. Doss | John Hansen Business Center, Suite 301 339 Busch's Frontage Road, Annapolis, MD 21401-5534 410-757-0861

Massachusetts
Chris Clarke | 451 West Street, Amherst, MA 01002-2995 413-253-4351

Michigan
Jane E. Hardisty | 1405 South Harrison Road, Room 101, East Lansing, MI 48823-5243 517-337-6701, Ext. 1201

Minnesota
William Hunt | 600 Farm Credit Building 375 Jackson Street, St. Paul, MN 55101-1854 612-290-3675

Mississippi
Homer L. Wilkes | Suite 1321, Federal Building 100 West Capital Street, Jackson, MS 39269-1399 601-965-5205

Missouri
Roger A. Hansen | Parkade Center, Suite 250 601 Business Loop, 70 West, Columbia, MO 65203-2546 573-876-0901

Montana
Shirley Gammon, Acting | Federal Building, Room 443 10 East Babcock Street, Bozeman, MT 59715-4704 406-587-6813

Nebraska
Stephen K. Chick | Federal Building, Room 152 100 Centennial Mall North, Lincoln, NE 68508-3866 402-437-5327

Nevada
William D. Goddard | 5301 Longley Lane Building F, Suite 201, Reno, NV 89511-1805 702-784-5863

New Hampshire
Dawn W. Genes | Federal Building, 2 Madbury Road, Durham, NH 03824-1499 603-433-0505

New Jersey
Wayne Maresch | 1370 Hamilton Street, Somerset, NJ 08873-3157 908-246-1205

New Mexico
Dennis Alexander | 6200 Jefferson Northeast, Room 305, Albuquerque, NM 87109-3734 505-761-4400

New York
Richard D. Swenson | 441 South Salina Street, Suite 354, Room 520, Syracuse, NY 13202-2450 315-477-6504

North Carolina
Mary T. Kollstedt | 4405 Bland Road, Suite 205, Raleigh, NC 27609-6293 919-873-2102

North Dakota
Scott Hoag | Federal Building P.O. Box 1458 220 East Rosser Avenue & 3rd Street, Room 270, Bismarck, ND 58502-1458 701-250-4421

Ohio
Terry J. Cosby | Federal Building 200 N. High St., Rm 522, Columbus, OH 43215-2478 614-255-2472

Oklahoma
Ronnie L. Clarke | 100 USDA, Suite 203, Stillwater, OK 74074-2624 405-742-1204

Oregon
Robert J. Graham | Federal Building, 16th Floor 101 S.W. Main Street, Suite 1300, Portland, OR 97204-3221 503-414-3201

Pacific Basin Area
Joan B. Perry | Suite 301, FHB Building 400 Route 9, Guam, GU 96927 9-011-671-472-7490

Pennsylvania
Janet L. Oertly | One Credit Union Place, Suite 340, Harrisburg, PA 17110-2993 717-782-2202

Puerto Rico
Juan Martinez, Director | IBM Building, Suite 604 654 Munoz Rivera Avenue, Hato Rey, PR 00918-4123

Rhode Island
Denis G. Nickel | 60 Quaker Lane, Suite 46, Warwick, RI 02886-0111 401-828-1300

South Carolina
Mark W. Berkland | Strom Thurmond Federal Building 1835 Assembly Street, Room 950, Columbia, SC 29201-2489 803-765-5681

South Dakota
Dean F. Fisher | Federal Building 200 4th Street, S.W., Huron, SD 57350-2475 605-352-1200

Tennessee
James W. Ford | 801 Broadway 675 U.S. Courthouse, Nashville, TN 37203-3878 615-736-5471

Texas
John P. Burt | W. R. Poage Federal Building 101 South Main Street, Temple, TX 76501-7682 817-774-1214

Utah
Phillip J. Nelson | Wallace F. Bennett Federal Building 125 South State Street, Room 4402, Salt Lake City, UT 84147 801-524-5050

Vermont
John C. Titchner | 69 Union Street, Winooski, VT 05404-1999 802-951-6795

Virginia
M. Denise Doetzer | Culpeper Building 1606 Santa Rosa Road, Suite 209, Richmond, VA 23229-5014 804-287-1691

Washington
Lynn A. Brown | USDA, Natural Resources Conservation Service W. 316 Boone Avenue, Suite 450, Spokane, WA 99201-2348 509-323-2900

West Virginia
William J. Hartman | 75 High Street Room 301, Morgantown, WV 26505 304-291-4153

Wisconsin
Patricia S. Leavenworth | 6515 Watts Road, Suite 200, Madison, WI 53719-2726 608-264-5577

Wyoming
Lincoln E. Burton | Federal Office Building 100 East B Street, Room 3124, Casper, WY 82601 307-261-5201, 1911

USDA 10.072

WETLANDS RESERVE PROGRAM "WRP"

Award: Cooperative Agreements

Purpose: To safeguard wetlands and to understand the advantages of wildlife.

Applicant Eligibility: An individual landowner, partnership, association, corporation, estate, trust, other business or other legal entities and Indian Tribe. This program was repealed by the Agricultural Act of 2014 (2014 Farm Bill), effective February 7, 2014.

Beneficiary Eligibility: An individual landowner, partnership, association, corporation, estate, trust, other business enterprises or other legal entities and Indian Tribe. This program was repealed by the Agricultural Act of 2014 (2014 Farm Bill), effective February 7, 2014.

Award Range/Average: N/A

Funding: (Cooperative Agreements) FY 17 $88,663,000; FY 18 est $136,568,000; FY 19 est $0; (Salaries and Expenses) FY 17 $38,616,000; FY 18 est $39,876,000; FY 19 est $0;

HQ: 1400 Independence Avenue SW
Washington, DC 20250
Phone: 202-690-1905
Email: jerome.faulkner@wdcusda.gov
http://www.nrcs.usda.gov/wps/portal/nrcs/main/national/programs/easements/wetlands

USDA 10.093

VOLUNTARY PUBLIC ACCESS AND HABITAT INCENTIVE PROGRAM "VPA-HIP"

Award: Formula Grants

Purpose: The VPA-HIP program provides access to the public on private farms and lands for recreational purposes.

Applicant Eligibility: Only States and Tribal governments are eligible for VPA-HIP. An eligible State government means any State or local government, including State, city, town, or county government.

Beneficiary Eligibility: The beneficiary eligibility is extended to the public for the purposes of expanding existing public access programs or create new public access programs or provide incentives to improve habitat on enrolled program lands. Proposals for grant money should be submitted to the local State or Tribal governments by owners and operators of privately-held farm, ranch, and forest land.

Award Range/Average: No Data Available.

Funding: (Project Grants) FY 17 $0; FY 18 est $18,000; FY 19 est $0; - (Formula Grants) FY 17 $0; FY 18 est $3,000; FY 19 est $0;

HQ: 1400 Independence Avenue, Room 5237-S
Washington, DC 20250
Phone: 202-720-1844
Email: maggie.rhodes@wdc.usda.gov
http://www.nrcs.usda.gov

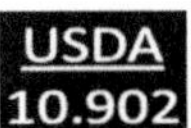

SOIL AND WATER CONSERVATION

Award: Advisory Services and Counseling

Purpose: To provide technical assistance in conserving, improving and sustaining natural resources and environment to local landowners.

Applicant Eligibility: The CTA Program is delivered to private individuals, groups of decision makers, tribes, units of governments, and non-governmental organizations in all 50 States, the District of Columbia, Puerto Rico, U.S. Virgin Islands, Guam, American Samoa, the Commonwealth of the Northern Mariana Islands, the Federated States of Micronesia, the Republic of Palau, and the Marshall Islands.

Beneficiary Eligibility: General public, State governments, and local governments.

Award Range/Average: N/A

Funding: (Salaries and Expenses) FY 17 $754,457,000; FY 18 est $839,314,000; FY 19 est $575,862,000.

HQ: 1400 Independence Avenue SW
Washington, DC 20250
Phone: 202-720-5322
Email: dan.lawson@wdc.usda.gov
http://www.nrcs.usda.gov/wps/portal/nrcs/site/national/home

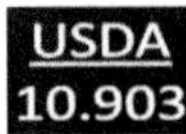

SOIL SURVEY

Award: Dissemination of Technical Information

Purpose: To provide soil survey information of the United States to assist interested agencies, organizations, and individuals to make use of this information.

Applicant Eligibility: All individuals and groups that have a need for soil survey information can access it on the Web Soil Survey at websoilsurvey.nrcs.

Beneficiary Eligibility: All individuals and groups that have a need for soil survey information are eligible to receive assistance.

Award Range/Average: N/A

Funding: (Salaries and Expenses) FY 17 $76,723,000; FY 18 est $85,210,000; FY 19 est $74,438,000.

HQ: 1400 Independence Avenue SW
Washington, DC 20250
Phone: 202-205-4211
Email: pam.thomas@wdc.usda.gov
http://www.nrcs.usda.gov/wps/portal/nrcs/site/national/home

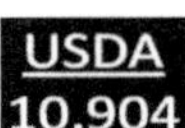

WATERSHED PROTECTION AND FLOOD PREVENTION
"Watershed Program; Public Law 566 Operations Phase"

Award: Project Grants; Advisory Services and Counseling

Purpose: To assist in technical and financial assistance in the development and utilization of land and water resources.

Applicant Eligibility: Any State agency, county or groups of counties, municipality, town or township, soil and water conservation district, flood prevention or flood control district, Indian tribe or tribal organization, or any other nonprofit agency with authority under State law to levy taxes, condemnation authority, and to carry out maintenance, and operate watershed works of improvement may apply for assistance. This program is available in Puerto Rico, the Virgin Islands, Guam, American Samoa, the Mariana Islands and the Trust Territories of the Pacific Islands.

Beneficiary Eligibility: N/A

Award Range/Average: (per State) $0 to $2,164,000; $650,000.

Funding: (Salaries and Expenses) FY 17 $13,524,000; FY 18 est $35,223,000; FY 19 est $0; (Project Grants (Cooperative Agreements)) FY 17 $52,115,000; FY 18 est $212,379,000; FY 19 est $0

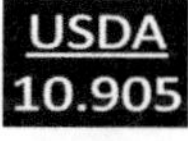

HQ: 1400 Independence Avenue SW
Washington, DC 20113
Phone: 202-720-3413
Email: kevin.farmer@wdc.usda.gov
http://www.nrcs.usda.gov

USDA 10.905 PLANT MATERIALS FOR CONSERVATION

Award: Provision of Specialized Services

Purpose: To promote the use of soil, water, and related resource conservation and to develop technology for land management and restoration with plant materials.

Applicant Eligibility: Cooperating State and Federal agencies and cooperators of conservation districts where structured evaluations are conducted and commercial seed growers and nurserymen interested in the commercial production of selected plant materials. Applicants are also eligible in Puerto Rico and the Virgin Islands.

Beneficiary Eligibility: Cooperating State and Federal agencies and cooperators of conservation districts and commercial seed growers and nurserymen interested in the production of selected plant materials. Applicants are also eligible in Puerto Rico and the Virgin Islands.

Award Range/Average: N/A

Funding: (Salaries and Expenses) FY 17 $11,857,000; FY 18 est $10,158,000; FY 19 est $9,417,000

HQ: 1400 Independence Avenue SW, P.O. Box 2890
Washington, DC 20013
Phone: 202-720-0536
Email: john.englert@wdc.usda.gov
http://www.nrcs.usda.gov/wps/portal/nrcs/site/national/home

USDA 10.907 SNOW SURVEY AND WATER SUPPLY FORECASTING "Snow Surveys"

Award: Dissemination of Technical Information

Purpose: To support NRCS conservation by providing timely and accurate forecasts of surface water supply to water managers and information on snow, water, climate, and hydrologic conditions.

Applicant Eligibility: General public, including those located in the U.S. Territories.

Beneficiary Eligibility: Same as Applicant Eligibility.

Award Range/Average: N/A

Funding: (Salaries and Expenses) FY 17 $8,523,000; FY 18 est $10,142,000; FY 19 est $9,316,000.

HQ: National Water and Climate Center Natural Resources Conservation Service Department of Agriculture, P.O. Box 2890

Washington, DC 20013

Phone: 503-414-3055

Email: michael.strobel@por.usda.gov

http://www.nrcs.usda.gov

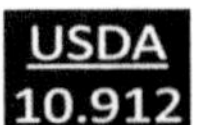

ENVIRONMENTAL QUALITY INCENTIVES PROGRAM "EQIP"

Award: Direct Payments for Specified Use

Purpose: To promote agricultural production, forest management, environmental benefits, and implementation of structural vegetative land management practices on eligible lands through Commodity Credit Corporation.

Applicant Eligibility: Agricultural producers who face serious threats to soil, water, and related natural resources, or who need assistance with complying with Federal and State environment laws. A participant may be an owner, landlord, operator, or tenant of eligible agricultural lands or non-industrial forestlands.

Beneficiary Eligibility: Same as Applicant Eligibility.

Award Range/Average: Total EQIP conservation payments are limited to $450,000 in financial assistance per person or legal entity. Average to be $23,000.

Funding: (Salaries and Expenses) FY 17 $404,716,000; FY 18 est $505,937,000; FY 19 est $381,226,000; FY 16 $358,186,000; - (Direct Payments for Specified Use) FY 17 $1,253,638,000; FY 18 est $1,396,608,000; FY 19 est $1,354,041,000; FY 16 $1,083,250,000

HQ: Financial Assistance Programs Division Department of Agriculture, P.O. Box 2890

Washington, DC 20113

Phone: 202-690-2621

Email: jeff.white@wdc.usda.gov

http://www.nrcs.usda.gov

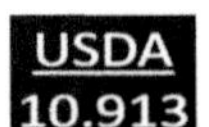

FARM AND RANCH LANDS PROTECTION PROGRAM "FRPP"

Award: Direct Payments for Specified Use

Purpose: To compensate for eligible agricultural lands that possess important soils and archaeological resources from converting into non-agricultural farms and preserve them using conservation methods.

Applicant Eligibility: An eligible entity was any local or State agency, county or groups of counties, municipality, town or township, soil and water conservation district, or Indian tribe or tribal organization, that has a farmland protection program that purchases conservation easements for the purpose of protecting agricultural use and related conservation values by limiting conversion to non- agricultural uses of land, and that has pending offers. This program was available in all 50 States, Puerto Rico, the Virgin Islands, Guam, American Samoa, the Mariana Islands, and the Trust Territories of the Pacific Islands.

Beneficiary Eligibility: Landowners must be in compliance with the Wetland Compliance (WC) and Highly Erodible Land (HEL) provisions of the Farm Bill and met the Adjusted Gross Income (AGI) limitations in the Farm Bill.

Award Range/Average: $2,700 to $1,000,000 per landowner. Average: $97,000.

Funding: (Direct Payments for Specified Use) FY 17 $917,000; FY 18 est $92,448,000; FY 19 est $0; FY 16 $770,000; - (Salaries and Expenses) FY 17 $6,738,000; FY 18 est $55,137,000; FY 19 FY 16 $2,057,000

HQ: 1400 and Independence Avenue SW
Washington, DC 20250
Phone: 202-690-1905
Email: jerome.faulkner@wdc.usda.gov
http://www.nrcs.usda.gov

WILDLIFE HABITAT INCENTIVE PROGRAM "WHIP"

Award: Direct Payments for Specified Use

Purpose: To assist those protecting wildlife, wetland, endangered species, and fisheries.

Applicant Eligibility: Applicant must meet Highly Erodible Land and Wetland Conservation (HEL/WC) requirements, Adjusted Gross Income (AGI) requirements, verification that applicant will be in control of land for the duration of a contract.

Beneficiary Eligibility: A participant may be an owner, landlord, operator, or tenant of eligible lands. Limited resource producers, small-scale producers, producers of minority groups, Federally Recognized Indian Tribal Governments, Alaska natives, and Pacific Islanders are encouraged to apply.

Award Range/Average: Average contract payments are estimated to be $4,500.

Funding: (Direct Payments for Specified Use) FY 17 $172,000; FY 18 est $3,214,000; FY 19 est $0; - FY 16 $8,401,000

HQ: 1400 Independence Avenue SW, Room 5237 S
Washington, DC 20250
Phone: 202-720-1844
Email: jeffery.white@wdc.usda.gov
http://www.nrcs.usda.gov

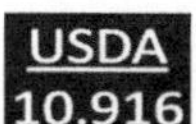

WATERSHED REHABILITATION PROGRAM "Watershed Rehabilitation; PL-566 Watershed Program"

Award: Advisory Services and Counseling

Purpose: To provide technical and financial assistance to dams that are in bad condition and which are constructed with the assistance of USDA Watershed Programs.

Applicant Eligibility: Sponsoring local organizations for existing watershed projects that include dams that were originally constructed with assistance from one of the following water resource programs:

Public Law 78-534, Section 13 of the Flood Control Act of 1944; Public Law 156-67, the pilot watershed program authorized under the heading Flood Prevention of the Department of Agriculture Appropriation Act of 1954; Public Law 83-566, the Watershed Protection and Flood Prevention Act of 1954; and Subtitle H of Title XV of the Agriculture and Flood Act of 1981, commonly known as the Resource Conservation and Development Program.

Beneficiary Eligibility: Any State agency, county or groups of counties, municipality, town or township, soil and water conservation district, flood prevention or flood control district, Indian tribe or tribal organization, or any other nonprofit agency with authority under State law to carry out, maintain, and operate watershed works of improvement may become a sponsoring local organization for a watershed rehabilitation project.

Award Range/Average: $0 to $6,451,000; $770,000 average per state.

Funding: (Salaries and Expenses) FY 17 $359,000; FY 18 est $5,078,000; FY 19 est $0; (Cooperative Agreements (Discretionary Grants)) FY 17 $12,300,000; FY 18 est $8,655,000; FY 19 est $0; (Salaries and Expenses) FY 17 $225,000; FY 18 est $0; FY 19 est $0; (Direct Payments for Specified Use) FY 17 $15,497,000; FY 18 est $8,485,000; FY 19

HQ: 14th and Independence Avenue, P.O. Box 2890

Washington, DC 20113

Phone: 202-720-3414

Email: kevin.farmer@wdc.usda.gov

http://www.nrcs.usda.gov

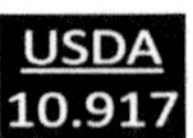

AGRICULTURAL MANAGEMENT ASSISTANCE

Award: Direct Payments for Specified Use

Purpose: To assist producers in private lands to improve water management structures to improve water quality, maximize conservation practices, soil erosion control, pest management, etc.

Applicant Eligibility: The land must be in one of the 16 following eligible states: Connecticut, Delaware, Hawaii, Maine, Maryland, Massachusetts, Nevada, New Hampshire, New Jersey, New York, Pennsylvania, Rhode Island, Utah, Vermont, West Virginia, and Wyoming.

Beneficiary Eligibility: Applicants must have control of the land for the length of the contract which may not be more than 10 years.

Award Range/Average: The total financial assistance payments paid per participant must not exceed $50,000 for any fiscal year.

Funding: (Salaries and Expenses) FY 17 $527,000; FY 18 est $656,000; FY 19 est $0; FY 16 $842,000; - (Direct Payments for Specified Use) FY 17 $2,512,000; FY 18 est $2,677,000; FY 19 est $0; FY 16 $3,662,000.

HQ: 1400 Independence Avenue SW, Room 5231-S

Washington, DC 20250

Phone: 202-690-2621

Email: jeffrey.white@wdc.usda.gov

http://www.nrcs.usda.gov

USDA 10.920 GRASSLAND RESERVE PROGRAM "GRP"

Award: Direct Payments for Specified Use

Purpose: To assist landowners in protecting eligible grazing lands and other lands through rental contracts and easements.

Applicant Eligibility: GRP is available on privately owned lands. Eligible land includes grassland, land that contains forbs, or shrubs, including rangeland and pasture land; or land that is located in an area that has historically been dominated by grassland, forbs, and shrubs; and has potential to provide habitat for animal or plant populations of significant ecological value.

Beneficiary Eligibility: Only landowners may submit applications for easements; landowners and others who have general control of the acreage may submit applications for rental contracts. Easements may also be acquired by eligible entities based on a 50 percent cost-share with the Federal government.

Award Range/Average: The 5 year average estimated cost per acre for easement acquisition was approximately $400, ranging from $65 per acre to over $30,000 per acre. The average estimated cost per acre for rental contracts was $134 per acre over the life of the rental contract. Over 250 GRP easements were acquired on over 117,000 acres.

Funding: (Direct Payments for Specified Use) FY 17 $255,000; FY 18 est $11,536,000; FY 19 est $0; FY 16 $138,000; - (Salaries and Expenses) FY 17 $4,700,000; FY 18 est $21,903,000; FY 19 est $0; FY 16 $1,621,000

HQ: 1400 and Independence Avenue SW, Room 5234-S
Washington, DC 20250
Phone: 202-690-1905
Email: jerome.faulkner@wdc.usda.gov
http://www.nrcs.usda.gov

CONSERVATION SECURITY PROGRAM "CSP"

Award: Direct Payments for Specified Use

Purpose: The CSP assists for conservation and improvement of soil, water, air, energy, plant and animal life, on Tribal and private lands. It rewards those farmers and ranchers for maintaining and enhancing natural resources.

Applicant Eligibility: Applicants must have applied prior to Oct. 1, 2008.

Beneficiary Eligibility: An individual producer, partnership, association, corporation, estate, trust, other business or other legal entities controlling eligible lands. The term producer means and owner, operator, landlord, tenant or sharecropper that shares in the risk of producing any crop or livestock; and must be entitled to share in the crop or livestock available for marketing from an agricultural operation.

Award Range/Average: N/A

Funding: (Direct Payments for Specified Use) FY 17 $1,339,000; FY 18 est $5,450,000; FY 19 est $0; FY 16 $1,464,000; - (Salaries and Expenses) FY 17 $429,000; FY 18 est $1,600,000; FY 19 est $0; FY 16 $561,000

HQ: 1400 Independence Avenue SW, Room 5247-S
Washington, DC 20250

Phone: 202-690-2267
Email: michael.whitt@wdc.usda.gov
http://www.nrcs.usda.gov

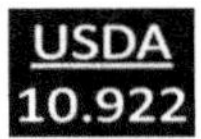

HEALTHY FORESTS RESERVE PROGRAM (HFRP)

Award: Direct Payments for Specified Use

Purpose: To assist landowners in enhancing forest ecosystems, safeguard endangered species, improve biodiversity, etc.

Applicant Eligibility: To be eligible to enroll an easement or restoration agreement in the HFRP, a person must: be the landowner of eligible private land for which enrollment is sought; agree to provide such information to the Natural Resources Conservation Service (NRCS) as the Agency deems necessary or desirable to assist in its determination of eligibility for program benefits and for other program implementation purposes.

Beneficiary Eligibility: Only landowners.

Award Range/Average: The average estimated cost per acre for easement acquisition was approximately $1,048.

Funding: (Salaries and Expenses) FY 17 $18,000; FY 18 est $1,000,000; FY 19 est $0; FY 16 $33,000; - (Direct Payments for Specified Use) FY 17 $135,000; FY 18 est $6,572,000; FY 19 est $0; FY 16 $671,000

HQ: 1400 and Independence Avenue SW
Washington, DC 20250
Phone: 202-690-1905
Email: jerome.faulkner@wdcusda.gov
http://www.nrcs.usda.gov

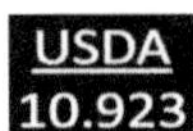

EMERGENCY WATERSHED PROTECTION PROGRAM "EWP"

Award: Project Grants

Purpose: The EWP Program assists landowners and operators in implementing emergency recovery measures to prevent erosion and safeguard methods from natural disaster.

Applicant Eligibility: Public and private landowners are eligible for assistance but must be represented by a project sponsor. Project sponsor means a State government or a State agency or a legal subdivision thereof, local unit of government, or any Native American tribe or tribal organization as defined in section 4 of the Indian Self-Determination and Education Assistance Act (25 U.S.C.

Beneficiary Eligibility: N/A

Award Range/Average: No Data Available.

Funding: (Salaries and Expenses) FY 17 $14,480,000; FY 18 est $108,200,000; FY 19 est $0; FY 16 $16,384,000; - (Cooperative Agreements (Discretionary Grants)) FY 17 $122,334,000; FY 18 est $432,800,000; FY 19 est $0; FY 16 $98,779,000

HQ: Division 14th and Independence Avenue SW, P.O. Box 2890
Washington, DC 20250

Phone: 202-720-3413

Email: kevin.farmer@wdc.usda.gov

http://www.nrcs.usda.gov/programs/ewp

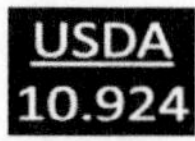

CONSERVATION STEWARDSHIP PROGRAM (CSP)

Award: Cooperative Agreements

Purpose: The CSP and NRCS provide financial and technical assistance to conserve soil, water, air, and related natural resources on their land. CSP encourages to improve conservation performance on agricultural lands and nonindustrial private forest lands.

Applicant Eligibility: The program provides equitable access to all producers, regardless of operation size, crops produced, or geographic location. Individual producers, legal entities, corporations, and Indian Tribes may be eligible for the program.

Beneficiary Eligibility: Same as Applicant Eligibility.

Award Range/Average: CSP payments to a person or legal entity may not exceed $40,000 in any year and $200,000 during any 5-year period. Each CSP contract will be limited to $200,000 over the term of the initial contract period. The above limitations exclude funding arrangements with federally recognized Indian tribes or Alaska Native corporations as described in §1470.24. The program shall have a national average rate of $18 per acre.

Funding: (Cooperative Agreements) FY 17 $895,359,000; FY 18 est $1,257,721,000; FY 19 est $1,221,465,000; FY 16 $891,786,000; - (Salaries and Expenses) FY 17 $239,175,000; FY 18 est $320,192,000; FY 19 est $290,180,000; FY 16 $237,509,000.

HQ: 1400 Independence Avenue SW, Room 5241-S

Washington, DC 20250

Phone: 202-690-2267

Email: michael.whitt@wdc.usda.gov

http://www.nrcs.usda.gov/wps/portal/nrcs/main/national/programs/financial/csp

AGRICULTURAL WATER ENHANCEMENT PROGRAM "AWEP"

Award: Direct Payments for Specified Use

Purpose: AWEP promotes ground and surface water conservation on agricultural lands and to improve water quality on eligible agricultural lands.

Applicant Eligibility: Partners representing agricultural producers who face serious threats to soil, water, and related natural resources, or who need assistance with complying with Federal and State environment laws. A participant may be an owner, landlord, operator, or tenant of eligible agricultural lands or non-industrial forestlands.

Beneficiary Eligibility: To be eligible the agricultural producers must be in compliance with highly erodible land and wetland conservation provisions and in compliance with the Adjusted Gross Income (AGI) payment limitations.

Award Range/Average: Conservation payments are limited to a maximum payment limitation per producer of $300,000 for the life of the 2008 Farm Bill. Average contracts are estimated to be $40,841.

Funding: (Salaries and Expenses) FY 17 $6,375,000; FY 18 est $6,360,000; FY 19 est $0; FY 16 $3,707,000; - (Direct Payments for Specified Use) FY 17 $87,000; FY 18 est $1,122,000; FY 19 est $0; FY 16 $175,000.

HQ: 1400 Independence Avenue SW, Room 5231-S
Washington, DC 20250
Phone: 202-690-2621
Email: jeffrey.white@wdc.usda.gov
http://www.nrcs.usda.gov/wps/portal/nrcs/main/national/programs/financial/awep

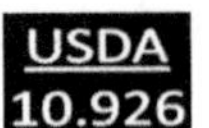

CHESAPEAKE BAY WATERSHED PROGRAM "CBWP"

Award: Direct Payments for Specified Use

Purpose: The Chesapeake Bay Watershed Program assists producers in improving water quality and quantity, preserve soil, air, and related resources through the implementation of conservation practices.

Applicant Eligibility: Only agricultural producers owning or operating within the Chesapeake Bay Watershed are eligible to participate in CBWP. In addition, NRCS applies the eligibility requirements of the particular natural resource program used to implement CBWP (e.

Beneficiary Eligibility: To be eligible, the agricultural producers must be in compliance with highly erodible land and wetland conservation provisions at 7 CFR part 12, and in compliance with the Adjusted Gross Income (AGI) payment limitations at 7 CFR part 1400.

Award Range/Average: Conservation payments are limited to the rules for the particular natural resource program used to implement CBWP (e.g., EQIP, WHIP).

Funding: (Direct Payments for Specified Use) FY 17 $126,000; FY 18 est $6,082,000; FY 19 est $0; FY 16 $503,000; - (Salaries and Expenses) FY 17 $4,950,000; FY 18 est $4,759,000; FY 19 est $0; FY 16 $1,114,000

HQ: 1400 Independence Avenue SW, Room 5231-S
Washington, DC 20250
Phone: 202-690-2621
Email: jeffery.white@wdc.usda.gov
http://www.nrcs.usda.gov/wps/portal/nrcs/detailfull/national/programs/initiatives/?cid=stelprdb1047323

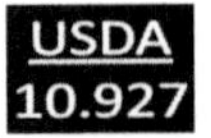

EMERGENCY WATERSHED PROTECTION PROGRAM - DISASTER RELIEF APPROPRIATIONS ACT "EWP - Disaster Relief (Hurricane Sandy)"

Award: Project Grants

Purpose: The EWP Program is to assist sponsors, landowners, and operators in implementing emergency recovery measures to prevent erosion and safeguard methods from a natural disaster that causes a sudden watershed.

Applicant Eligibility: For this appropriation, only applicants affected by Hurricane Sandy and only in those areas declared as a major disaster are eligible for assistance through the EWP program. Public and private landowners are eligible for assistance but must be represented by a project sponsor.

Beneficiary Eligibility: N/A

Award Range/Average: N/A

Funding: (Salaries and Expenses) FY 17 $2,013,000; FY 18 est $0; FY 19 est $0; FY 16 $283,000; - (Project Grants (Cooperative Agreements or Contracts)) FY 17 $18,064,000; FY 18 est $0; FY 19 est $0; FY 16 $0

HQ: Division 14th and Independence Avenue SW, P.O. Box 2890
Washington, DC 20250
Phone: 202-720-3413
Email: kevin.farmer@wdc.usda.gov

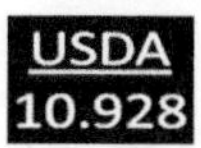

EMERGENCY WATERSHED PROTECTION PROGRAM - FLOODPLAIN EASEMENTS – DISASTER RELIEF APPROPRIATIONS ACT "EWP-FPE Hurricane Sandy"

Award: Direct Payments for Specified Use

Purpose: The Emergency Watershed Protection-Floodplain Easement Program provides an alternative measure to restore the flood storage, erosion control, and improve the practical management of the easement.

Applicant Eligibility: For this appropriation, only applicants affected by Hurricane Sandy and only in those areas declared as a major disaster are eligible for assistance through the EWP-FPE program. Pursuant to 7 CFR § 624.

Beneficiary Eligibility: Private and non-federal landowners are eligible for EWP-FPE. To be eligible for FPE, the NRCS will require participating landowners to— 1) Comply with the terms of the easement.

Award Range/Average: N/A

Funding: (Direct Payments for Specified Use) FY 17 $13,699,000; FY 18 est $0; FY 19 est $0; FY 16 $3,427,000; - (Salaries and Expenses) FY 17 $906,000; FY 18 est $0; FY 19 est $0; FY 16 $457,000

HQ: 1400 and Independence Avenue SW, Room 5234-S
Washington, DC 20250
Phone: 202-690-1905
Email: jerome.faulkner@wdcusda.gov
http://www.nrcs.usda.gov/programs/ewp

WATER BANK PROGRAM

Award: Direct Payments for Specified Use

Purpose: To preserve wetlands habitat, wildlife, conserve waters, reduce soil and wind erosion, flood control, improve water quality, etc.

Applicant Eligibility: N/A

Beneficiary Eligibility: Landowners and operators of specified types of wetlands in designated important migratory waterfowl nesting, breeding and feeding areas.

Award Range/Average: $20 to $50 per acre. Average: $35.

Funding: (Project Grants (Cooperative Agreements or Contracts)) FY 17 $4,369,000; FY 18 est $3,788,000; FY 19 est $0 - (Salaries and Expenses) FY 17 $91,000; FY 18 est $705,000; FY 19 est $0;

HQ: 1400 Independence Avenue SW, Room 5237-S
Washington, DC 20250
Phone: 202-690-2621
Email: jeffery.white@wdc.usda.gov
http://www.nrcs.usda.gov

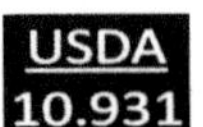

AGRICULTURAL CONSERVATION EASEMENT PROGRAM "ACEP"

Award: Cooperative Agreements

Purpose: The Agricultural Conservation Easement Program compensates to eligible entities to purchase conservation easements to protect the agricultural lands and to reduce nonagricultural uses of the land and to enhance wetlands.

Applicant Eligibility: For ACEP-ALE an eligible entity that is an Indian Tribe, State government, local government, or a nongovernmental organization which has a farmland or grassland protection program that purchases agricultural land easements for the purpose of protecting agriculture use and related conservation values, including grazing uses and related conservation values, by limiting conversion to nonagricultural uses of the land, and that has pending offers may apply for funds. This program is available in all 50 States, Puerto Rico, the Virgin Islands, Guam, American Samoa, the Mariana Islands, and the Trust Territories of the Pacific Islands.

Beneficiary Eligibility: All landowners applying for ACEP must be in compliance with the Wetland Compliance (WC) and Highly Erodible Land (HEL) provisions of the Farm Bill and, within the exception of FY2014, meet the Adjusted Gross Income (AGI) limitations in the Farm Bill. For ACEP-ALE, applications are submitted by an eligible entity who will be the participant in the program.

Award Range/Average: Under ACEP-ALE, cost-share provided by NRCS for the purchase of an agricultural land easement ranges from $216 per acre for grassland easements to $13,670 per acre for cropland easements. The average per acre cost-share amount provided by NRCS is $2,790 per acre. Under ACEP-WRE, easement compensation amounts provided directly to eligible landowners ranges from $1,200 per acre to $13,000 per acre, with an average cost of $2,600 per acre.

Funding: (Cooperative Agreements) FY 17 $431,547,000; FY 18 est $328,931,000; FY 19 est $155,577,000; FY 16 $242,844,000; - (Salaries and Expenses) FY 17 $104,484,000; FY 18 est $122,770,000; FY 19 est $70,616,000; FY 16 $102,833,000

HQ: 1400 and Independence Avenue SW
Washington, DC 20250
Phone: 202-690-1905
Email: jerome.faulkner@wdcusda.gov
http://www.nrcs.usda.gov/wps/portal/nrcs/main/national/programs/easements/acep

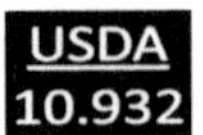

REGIONAL CONSERVATION PARTNERSHIP PROGRAM "RCPP"

Award: Cooperative Agreements

Purpose: To further the conservation of soil, water, wildlife, related natural resources on eligible land; avoid local natural resource regulatory requirements; and encourage the four former conservation programs partners to understand the conservation needs.

Applicant Eligibility: Eligible partners include advocate groups for conservation and those interested in assisting agricultural producers who face serious threats to soil, water, and related natural resources, or who need assistance with complying with Federal and State environment laws. Eligible partnering organizations include: An agricultural or silvicultural producer association or other group of producers; A State or unit of local government; An Indian Tribe; A farmer cooperative; A water district, irrigation district, rural water district or association, or other organization with specific water delivery authority to producers on agricultural land; A municipal water or wastewater treatment entity; An institution of higher education; An organization or entity with an established history of working cooperatively with producers on agricultural land; Conservation driven nongovernmental organizations.

Beneficiary Eligibility: To be eligible the agricultural producers participating within an approved project area must be in compliance with highly erodible land and wetland conservation provisions and in compliance with the Adjusted Gross Income (AGI) payment limitations. Conservation payments for the Conservation Stewardship Program are limited to a maximum payment limitation per producer of $200,000 for the life of the 2014 Farm Bill.

Award Range/Average: There is no minimum amount and the maximum amount for any fiscal year.

Funding: (Salaries and Expenses) FY 17 $25,778,000; FY 18 est $27,455,000; FY 19 est $18,960,000; - (Cooperative Agreements) FY 17 $26,574,000; FY 18 est $69,884,000; FY 19 est $74,840,000.

HQ: 1400 Independence Avenue SW, Room 5237-S
Washington, DC 20250
Phone: 202-720-1844
Email: maggie.rhodes@wdc.usda.gov
http://www.nrcs.usda.gov/wps/portal/nrcs/main/national/programs/farmbill/rcpp

WETLANDS MITIGATION BANKING PROGRAM

Award: Cooperative Agreements; Project Grants

Purpose: The Wetlands Mitigation Banking Program helps producers with wetland conservation to maintain eligibility for the Federal crop insurance premium subsidy.

Applicant Eligibility: Eligible entities that may submit applications include Tribal Nations, State, and local units of government, and nongovernmental organizations (NGOs), including for profit NGOs. NRCS will accept proposals for the development and establishment of mitigation banks submitted under this notice by eligible applicants from all 50 States, the District of Columbia, the Caribbean Area (Puerto Rico and the U.S. Virgin Islands), and the Pacific Islands Area (Guam, American Samoa, and the Commonwealth of the Northern Mariana Islands).

Beneficiary Eligibility: Mitigation banks established through this program are for the explicit and sole purpose of assisting agricultural producers with wetland conservation compliance, also known as Swampbuster compliance.

Award Range/Average: This is a one-time direct appropriation provided in FY 2014, and the funds are available until expended. Up to $9 million will be available for awards.

Funding: (Cooperative Agreements) FY 17 $7,325,000; FY 18 est $1,081,000; FY 19 est $0; - (Salaries and Expenses) FY 17 $281,000; FY 18 est $1,080,000; FY 19 est $0.

Programs Administered by Regional - State - Local Offices

HQ: USDA NRCS 8000 S 15th Street
Lincoln, NE 68508
Phone: 402-560-1309
Email: shaun.vickers@wdc.usda.gov
http://www.nrcs.usda.gov/wps/portal/nrcs/detail/national/programs/farmbill/?cid=nrcseprd362686

OCCUPATIONAL SAFETY AND HEALTH ADMINISTRATION

Alabama

3737 Government Boulevard, Suite 100, Mobile, AL 36693-4309 251-441-6131

Todd Mall, 2047 Canyon Road, Birmingham, AL 35216-1981 205-731-1534, Ext. 133

Alaska

301 West Northern Lights Boulevard, Room 407, Anchorage, AK 99503-7571 907-271-5152

Arizona

3221 North 16th Street, Suite 100, Phoenix, AZ 85016 602-640-2007

Arkansas

TCBY Building, Suite 450 425 West Capitol Avenue, Little Rock, AR 72201 501-324-6291

TCBY Building, Suite 450 425 West Capitol Avenue, Little Rock, AR 72201 501-324-6291

California

101 El Camino Boulevard, Suite 105, Sacramento, CA 95815 916-566-7470

5675 Ruffin Road, Suite 330, San Diego, CA 92123 619-557-5904

71 Stevenson Street, Suite 420, San Francisco, CA 94105 415-975-4316

Colorado

1391 Speer Boulevard, Suite 210, Denver, CO 80204-2552 303-844-5285

7935 E. Prentice Avenue, Suite 209, Englewood, CO 80111-2714 303-843-4500

Connecticut

Clark Building 1057 Broad Street, 4th Floor, Bridgeport, CT 06604 203-579-5581

Clark Building 1057 Broad Street, 4th Floor, Bridgeport, CT 06604 203-579-5581

Federal Office Building 450 Main Street, Room 613, Hartford, CT 06103 860-240-3152

Federal Office Building 450 Main Street, Room 613, Hartford, CT 06103 860-240-3152

Delaware

Caleb Boggs Federal Building 844 King Street, Room 2209, Wilmington, DE 19801 302-573-6518

Caleb Boggs Federal Building 844 King Street, Room 2209, Wilmington, DE 19801 302-573-6518

Florida

5807 Breckenridge Parkway, Suite A, Tampa, FL 33610 813-626-1177

Building H100 8040 Peters Road, Fort Lauderdale, FL 33324 954-424-0242

Building H100 8040 Peters Road, Fort Lauderdale, FL 33324 954-424-0242

Ribault Building, Suite 227 1851 Executive Center Drive, Jacksonville, FL 32207 904-232-2895

Ribault Building, Suite 227 1851 Executive Center Drive, Jacksonville, FL 32207 904-232-2895

Georgia

2400 Herodian Way, Suite 250, Smyrna, GA 30080-2968 770-984-8700

450 Mall Boulevard, Suite J., Savannah, GA 31406-1418 912-652-4393

Building 7, Suite 110 2183 N. Lake Parkway La Vista Perimeter Office Park, Tucker, GA 30084-4154 770-493-6644

Hawaii

300 Ala Moana Boulevard, Suite 5-146, Honolulu, HI 96850 808-541-2685

Idaho

1150 North Curtis Road, Suite 201, Boise, ID 83703 208-321-2960

Illinois

11 Executive Drive, Suite 11, Fairview Heights, IL 62208 618-632-8612

1600 167th Street, Suite 12, Calumet City, IL 60409 708-891-3800

2918 West Willow Knolls Road, Peoria, IL 61614 309-671-7033

365 Smoke Tree Plaza, North Aurora, IL 60542 630-896-8700

701 Lee Street Suite 950, Des Plains, IL 60016 847-803-4800

701 Lee Street Suite 950, Des Plains, IL 60016 847-803-4800

Indiana

U.S. Post Office and Courthouse 46 East Ohio Street, Room 423, Indianapolis, IN 46204 317-226-7290

Iowa

210 Walnut Street, Room 815, Des Moines, IA 50309 515-284-4794

Kansas

271 W. 3rd Street, Room 400, Wichita, KS 67202 316-269-6644

8600 Farley, Suite 105, Overland Park, KS 66212-4677 913-385-7380

Kentucky

U.S. Department of Labor-OSHA John C. Watts Federal Building 330 West Broadway, Room 108, Frankfort, KY 40601-1922 502-227-7024

U.S. Department of Labor-OSHA John C. Watts Federal Building 330 West Broadway, Room 108, Frankfort, KY 40601-1922 502-227-7024

Louisiana

202 Harlow Street, Room 211, Bangor, ME 04401-4906 207-941-8177

9100 Bluebonnet Centre Boulevard, Suite 201, Baton Rouge, LA 70809 225-389-0474

Maine

Edmund S. Muskie Federal Bldg. 40 Western Ave., RM G26, Augusta, ME 04330 207-626-9160

Maryland

1099 Winterson Road, Suite 140, Linthicum, MD 21090 410-865-2055, 2056

Massachusetts

1441 Main Street, Room 550, Springfield, MA 01103-1493 413-785-0123

639 Granite Street, 4th Floor, Braintree, MA 02184 617-565-6924

Valley Office Park 13 Branch Street, First Floor, Methuen, MA 01844 617-565-8110

Valley Office Park 13 Branch Street, First Floor, Methuen, MA 01844 617-565-8110

Michigan

801 South Waverly Road, Suite 306, Lansing, MI 48917-4200 517-327-0904

Minnesota

300 S. 4th Street, Suite 1205, Minneapolis, MN 55415 612-664-5460

Mississippi

3780 I-55 North, Suite 210, Jackson, MS 39211-6323 601-965-4606

Missouri

6200 Connecticut Avenue, Suite 100, Kansas City, MO 64120 816-483-9531

U.S. Department of Labor-OSHA 911 Washington Avenue, Room 420, St. Louis, MO 63101 314-425-4249

U.S. Department of Labor-OSHA 911 Washington Avenue, Room 420, St. Louis, MO 63101 314-425-4249

Montana

2900 4th Avenue, North, Suite 303, Billings, MT 59101 406-247-7494

Nebraska

Overland-Wolf Building, Room 100 6910 Pacific Street, Omaha, NE 68106 402-221-3182

Overland-Wolf Building, Room 100 6910 Pacific Street, Omaha, NE 68106 402-221-3182

Nevada

Federal Building, Room 204 705 North Plaza, Carson City, NV 89701 775-885-6963

Federal Building, Room 204 705 North Plaza, Carson City, NV 89701 775-885-6963

New Hampshire

55 Pleasant Street, Room 3901, Concord, NH 03301 603-225-1629

New Jersey

299 Cherry Hill Road, Suite 304, Parsippany, NJ 07054 973-263-1003

500 Route 17 South, 2nd Floor, Hasbrouck Heights, NJ 07604 201-288-1700

Marlton Executive Park 701 Route 73 South, Building 2, Suite 120, Marlton, NJ 08053 856-757-5181

Marlton Executive Park 701 Route 73 South, Building 2, Suite 120, Marlton, NJ 08053 856-757-5181

Plaza 35, Suite 205 1030 St. Georges Avenue, Avenel, NJ 07001 732-750-3270

Plaza 35, Suite 205 1030 St. Georges Avenue, Avenel, NJ 07001 732-750-3270

New Mexico

Western Bank Building 505 Marquette Avenue, N.W., Suite 820, Albuquerque, NM 87102 505-248-5302

Western Bank Building 505 Marquette Avenue, N.W., Suite 820, Albuquerque, NM 87102 505-248-5302

New York

1400 Old Country Road, Suite 208, Westbury, NY 11590 516-334-3344

201 Varick Street, Room 905, New York, NY 10014 212-620-3200

3300 Vickery Road, North Syracuse, NY 13212 315-451-0808

42-40 Bell Boulevard, Bayside, NY 11361 718-279-9060

5360 Genesee Street, Bowmansville, NY 14026 716-684-3891

660 White Plains Road, 4th Floor, Tarrytown, NY 10591-5107 914-524-7510

John Tomich Federal Building 401 New Karner Road, Suite 300, Albany, NY 12205-3809 518-464-4338

John Tomich Federal Building 401 New Karner Road, Suite 300, Albany, NY 12205-3809 518-464-4338

North Carolina

Century Station, Federal Building, Room 438 300 Fayetteville Mall, Raleigh, NC 27601-9998 919-856-4770

Century Station, Federal Building, Room 438 300 Fayetteville Mall, Raleigh, NC 27601-9998 919-856-4770

North Dakota

Federal Office Building 1640 East Capitol Avenue, Bismarck, ND 58501 701-250-4521

Federal Office Building 1640 East Capitol Avenue, Bismarck, ND 58501 701-250-4521

Ohio

420 Madison Avenue, Suite 600, Toledo, OH 43604 419-259-7542

Federal Office Building 200 North High Street, Room 620, Columbus, OH 43215 614-469-5582

Federal Office Building 200 North High Street, Room 620, Columbus, OH 43215 614-469-5582

Federal Office Building, Room 4028 36 Triangle Park Drive, Cincinnati, OH 45246 513-841-4132

Federal Office Building, Room 4028 36 Triangle Park Drive, Cincinnati, OH 45246 513-841-4132

Federal Office Building, Room 899 1240 East Ninth Street, Cleveland, OH 44199 216-522-3818

Federal Office Building, Room 899 1240 East Ninth Street, Cleveland, OH 44199 216-522-3818

Oklahoma

55 N. Robinson, Suite 315, Oklahoma City, OK 73102 405-278-9560

Oregon

1220 Southwest Third Avenue, Room 640, Portland, OR 97204 503-326-2251

Pennsylvania

3939 West Ridge Road, Suite B-12, Erie, PA 16506 814-833-5758

49 North Progress Avenue Progress Plaza, Harrisburg, PA 17109 717-782-3902

49 North Progress Avenue Progress Plaza, Harrisburg, PA 17109 717-782-3902

7 North Wilkes-Barre Boulevard Suite 410, Wilkes-Barre, PA 18702 570-826-6538

7 North Wilkes-Barre Boulevard Suite 410, Wilkes-Barre, PA 18702 570-826-6538

850 North 5th Street, Allentown, PA 18102 610-776-0592

Federal Building, Room 1428 1000 Liberty Avenue, Pittsburgh, PA 15522-4101 412-395-4903

Federal Building, Room 1428 1000 Liberty Avenue, Pittsburgh, PA 15522-4101 412-395-4903

U.S. Customs House, Room 242 Second and Chestnut Streets, Philadelphia, PA 19106 215-597-4955

Puerto Rico

BBV Plaza Building 1510 F.D. Roosevelt Avenue, Suite 5B, Guaynabo, PR 00968 787-277-1560

BBV Plaza Building 1510 F.D. Roosevelt Avenue, Suite 5B, Guaynabo, PR 00968 787-277-1560

Region I

Marthe Kent, Regional Administrator | Department of Labor, OSHA JFK Federal Building, Low Rise Building, Room E-340, Boston, MA 02114 617-565-9860

Region II

Robert Kulick, Regional Administrator | Department of Labor, OSHA 201 Varick Street, Room 670, New York, NY 10014 212-337-2378

Robert Kulick, Regional Administrator | Department of Labor, OSHA 201 Varick Street, Room 670, New York, NY 10014 212-337-2378

Region III

John Hermanson, Regional Administrator | The Curtis Center - Suite 740 West 170 Independence Mall West, Philadelphia, PA 19106-3309 215-861-4900

John Hermanson, Regional Administrator | The Curtis Center - Suite 740 West 170 Independence Mall West, Philadelphia, PA 19106-3309 215-861-4900

Region IV

Cindy Coe, Regional Administrator | 61 Forsyth Street S.W., Room 6T50, Atlanta, GA 30303 404-562-2300

Region IX

Ken Atha, Regional Administrator | Department of Labor, OSHA 71 Stevenson Street, Room 420, San Francisco, CA 94105 415-975-4310

Ken Atha, Regional Administrator | Department of Labor, OSHA 71 Stevenson Street, Room 420, San Francisco, CA 94105 415-975-4310

Region V

Michael Connors, Regional Administrator | Department of Labor, OSHA 230 South Dearborn Street 32nd Floor, Room 3244, Chicago, IL 60604 312-353-2220

Region VI

Dean McDaniel, Regional Administrator | Department of Labor, OSHA 525 Griffin Street, Room 602, Dallas, TX 75202 214-767-4731

Dean McDaniel, Regional Administrator | Department of Labor, OSHA 525 Griffin Street, Room 602, Dallas, TX 75202 214-767-4731

Region VII

Charles E. Adkins, Regional Administrator | Department of Labor, OSHA City Center Square 1100 Main Street, Suite 800, Kansas City, MO 64105 816-426-5861

Region VIII

Greg Baxter, Regional Administrator | Department of Labor, OSHA 1999 Broadway Street, Room 1690, Denver, CO 80202-5716 303-844-1600

Greg Baxter, Regional Administrator | Department of Labor, OSHA 1999 Broadway Street, Room 1690, Denver, CO 80202-5716 303-844-1600

Region X

Richard Terrill, Regional Administrator | Department of Labor, OSHA 1111 Third Avenue, Suite 715, Seattle, WA 98101-3212 206-553-5930

Richard Terrill, Regional Administrator | Department of Labor, OSHA 1111 Third Avenue, Suite 715, Seattle, WA 98101-3212 206-553-5930

Rhode Island

380 Westminster Mall, Room 243, Providence, RI 02903 401-528-4669

South Carolina

1835 Assembly Street, Room 1468, Columbia, SC 29201 803-765-5904

Tennessee

2002 Richard Jones Road, Suite C-205, Nashville, TN 37215-2809 615-781-5423

Texas

17625 El Camino Real, Suite 400, Houston, TX 77058 281-286-0583

507 North Sam Houston Parkway East, Suite 400, Houston, TX 77060 281-591-2438

700 E. San Antonio Street, Room C-408, EL Paso, TX 79901 915-534-6251

8344 East R.L. Thornton Freeway, Suite 420, Dallas, TX 75228 214-320-2400

903 San Jacinto Boulevard, Suite 319, Austin, TX 78701 512-916-5783

Corpus Christi Area Office U.S. Department of Labor, OSHA Wilson Plaza West 606 N. Carancahua, Suite 700, Corpus Christi, TX 78476 361-888-3420

Federal Building, Room 806 1205 Texas Avenue, Lubbock, TX 79401 806-472-7681

North Star II, Suite 302 8713 Airport Freeway, Ft. Worth, TX 76180-7610 817-428-2470

North Star II, Suite 302 8713 Airport Freeway, Ft. Worth, TX 76180-7610 817-428-2470

Utah

1781 South 300 West P.O. Box 65200, Salt Lake City, UT 84165-0200 801-487-0521

1781 South 300 West P.O. Box 65200, Salt Lake City, UT 84165-0200 801-487-0521

Virginia

200 Granby Street, Room 614, Norfolk, VA 23510 757-441-3820

Washington

505 106th Avenue N.E., Suite 302, Bellevue, WA 98004 206-553-7520

West Virginia
405 Capitol Street, Suite 407, Charleston, WV 25301 304-347-5937

Wisconsin
1310 West Clairmont Ave., Eau Claire, WI 54701 715-832-9019

1648 Tri Park Way, Appleton, WI 54914 920-734-4521

4802 E. Broadway, Madison, WI 53716 608-441-5388

Henry S. Reuss Building 310 Wisconsin Avenue, Suite 1180, Milwaukee, WI 53203 414-297-3315

Henry S. Reuss Building 310 Wisconsin Avenue, Suite 1180, Milwaukee, WI 53203 414-297-3315

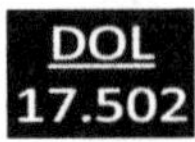

OCCUPATIONAL SAFETY AND HEALTH SUSAN HARWOOD TRAINING GRANTS
"Susan Harwood Training Grants"

Award: Project Grants

Purpose: To provide occupational safety and health training and education to employees and employers, particularly in the recognition, avoidance and abatement of workplace hazards.

Applicant Eligibility: Non-profit organizations including qualifying labor unions, community-based and faith-based organizations, employer associations that are not an agency of a state or local government, state or local government-supported institutions of higher education, Indian tribes, tribal organizations, Alaska Native entities, Indian-controlled organizations serving Indians, and Native Hawaiian organizations may apply.

Beneficiary Eligibility: Individuals employed in workplaces that receive training and/or educational services under grants

Award Range/Average: Fiscal Year 2017 grants ranged from $47,000 to $155,000.

Funding: (Training) FY 17 $10,461,000; FY 18 est $10,537,000; FY 19 est $0

HQ: 200 Constitution Avenue NW
Washington, DC 20210
Phone: 847-759-7769
Email: robertson.donna@dol.gov
http://www.osha.gov

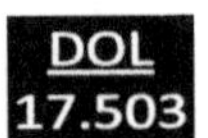

OCCUPATIONAL SAFETY AND HEALTH STATE PROGRAM
"State Plan Grant Awards"

Award: Project Grants

Purpose: Funds federally approved comprehensive State occupational safety and health programs that are "at least as effective" as the Federal program.

Applicant Eligibility: Designated State agencies which have federally approved occupational safety and health plans.

Beneficiary Eligibility: Any employer, worker or their representative from a business engaged in interstate commerce except those under jurisdiction of other Federal agencies.

Award Range/Average: Fiscal year 2017 grants ranged from $196,000 to $26,544,000.

Funding: (Salaries and Expenses) FY 17 $100,100,000; FY 18 est $100,850,000; FY 19 est $100,165,000; FY 16 $100,850,000

HQ: 200 Constitution Avenue NW
Washington, DC 20210
Phone: 202-693-2423
Email: krivitskiy.aleks@dol.gov
http://www.osha.gov

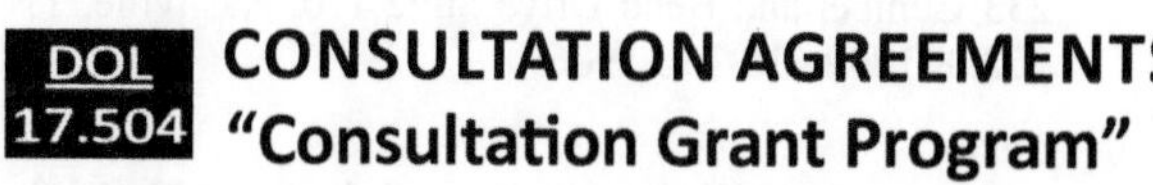

DOL 17.504 CONSULTATION AGREEMENTS "Consultation Grant Program"

Award: Cooperative Agreements

Purpose: Funds consultative workplace safety and health services, targeting smaller employers with more hazardous operations.

Applicant Eligibility: Designated State agencies which have been authorized by the Governor to enter into a Cooperative Agreement with full power to perform the obligations funded therein and to expend Federal funds as well as State funds as required.

Beneficiary Eligibility: Any private employer operating within a State, with priority given to smaller employers with the more hazardous operations.

Award Range/Average: Fiscal year 2017 grants ranged from $196,000 to $5,453,000. These awards represent approximately 90 percent of total program costs.

Funding: (Salaries and Expenses) FY 17 $57,769,000; FY 18 est $59,500,000; FY 19 est $59,096,000; FY 16 $57,775,000.

HQ: DOL OSHA CFDA Rep 200 Constitution Avenue NW N-3419
Washington, DC 20210
Phone: 202-693-2423
Email: krivitskiy.aleks@dol.gov
http://www.osha.gov

OFFICE OF LABOR-MANAGEMENT STANDARDS

REGIONAL OFFICES

California

90 7th Street Room 2825, San Francisco, CA 94103-6701 415-625-2661

915 Wilshire Boulevard Suite 910, Los Angeles, CA 90017 213-534-6405

Colorado

1244 Speer Boulevard Room 415, Denver, CO 80204 720-264-3232

District of Columbia

375 E Street SW, Washington, DC 20024 202-513-7300

375 E Street SW, Washington, DC 20024 202-513-7300

Georgia

Atlanta Federal Building | Room 8B85 61 Forsyth Street, S.W., Atlanta, GA 30303-2219 404-562-2083

Illinois

Suite 774 230 S. Dearborn Street, Chicago, IL 60604-1505 312-596-7160

Louisiana

600 South Maestri Place Room 604, New Orleans, LA 70130 504-589-6174

Massachusetts

JFK Federal Building Room E-365, Boston, MA 02203-0002 617-624-6690

Programs Administered by Regional - State - Local Offices

Michigan
211 West Fort Street Suite 1313, Detroit, MI 48226-3237 313-226-6200

Missouri
1222 Spruce Street Suite 9.109E, St. Louis, MO 63103-2830 314-539-2667

New York
130 South Elmwood Street Room 510, Buffalo, NY 14202-2465 716-842-2900

201 Varick Street Suite 878, New York, NY 10014 646-264-3190

Ohio
36 East Seventh Street Room 2550, Cincinnati, OH 45202-3168 513-684-6840

Suite 831 1240 East Ninth Street, Cleveland, OH 44199-2053 216-357-5455

Pennsylvania
Room 1411 1000 Liberty Avenue, Pittsburgh, PA 15222-4004 412-395-6925

The Curtis Center 170 S. Independence Mall West Room 760W, Philadelphia, PA 19106-3310 215-861-4818

Tennessee
233 Cumberland Bend Drive Suite 110, Nashville, TN 37228-1809 615-736-5906

Texas
A. Maceo Smith Federal Building Suite 300 525 Griffin Street, Dallas, TX 75202-5007 972-850-2500

Washington
300 5th Avenue Room 1290, Seattle, WA 98104-3308 206-398-8099

Wisconsin
310 West Wisconsin Avenue Room 1160W, Milwaukee, WI 53203-2213 414-297-1504

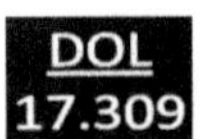

LABOR ORGANIZATION REPORTS
"Labor-Management Reporting and Disclosure Act (LMRDA)"

Award: Advisory Services and Counseling; Dissemination of Technical Information; Investigation of Complaints

Purpose: To provide for the reporting and disclosure of financial transactions and administrative practices of labor organizations, employers, labor consultants and others required to report under the Labor-Management Reporting and Disclosure Act (LMRDA).

Applicant Eligibility: Officers of unions may obtain assistance in preparing reports or otherwise complying with the Act. Union members or union organizations may request assistance in investigating alleged violations.

Beneficiary Eligibility: Union officers, union members, union organizations. All reports required to be filed are available for inspection and disclosure to the general public.

Award Range/Average: N/A

Funding: (Salaries and Expenses) FY 17 $39,332; FY 18 est $41,392; FY 19 est $46,634; FY 16 $40,593

HQ: OLMS, Room N 5119 200 Constitution Avenue NW
Washington, DC 20011
Phone: 202-693-1182
Email: willertz.stephen@dol.gov
http://www.dol.gov/olms

OFFICE OF SURFACE MINING, RECLAMATION AND ENFORCEMENT

OFFICE OF SURFACE MINING

U.S. Department of the Interior

1027 Virginia Street, East, Charleston, WV 25301 304-347-7162

135 Gemini Circle, Suite 215, Homewood, AL 35209 205-290-7282

1951 Constitution Avenue N.W., Washington, DC 20240 202-208-4006

1999 Broadway, Suite 3320, Denver, CO 80202-5733 303-844-1401

2675 Regency Road, Lexington, KY 40503-2922 859-233-2494

505 Marquette Avenue N.W., Suite 1200, Albuquerque, NM 87102 505-248-5070

5100 East Skelly Drive, Suite 470, Tulsa, OK 74135 918-581-6431

530 Gay Street, S.W., Suite 500, Knoxville, TN 37902

575 North Pennsylvania Street, Room 301, Indianapolis, IN 46204 317-226-6700

Alton Federal Building 501 Belle Street, Room 216, Alton, IL 62002 618-463-6460

Federal Building 100 East "B" Street, Room 2128, Casper, WY 82601-1918 307-261-6555

Harrisburg Transportation Center, Harrisburg, PA 17101 717-782-4036

Powell Valley Square Shopping Center 1941 Neeley Road, Suite 201 Compartment 116, Big Stone Gap, VA 24219 540-523-4303

Three Parkway Center, Pittsburgh, PA 15220 412-937-2828

REGULATION OF SURFACE COAL MINING AND SURFACE EFFECTS OF UNDERGROUND COAL MINING
"Regulatory Grant Program"

Award: Project Grants; Direct Payments for Specified Use

Purpose: To aid the States and Tribes with active coal mining in administering approved regulatory programs.

Applicant Eligibility: The State must have an approved program to regulate surface coal mining and a designated State agency to receive and administer grants.

Beneficiary Eligibility: State agencies responsible for regulation, reclamation and enforcement of provisions protecting the environment from negative effects of coal mining operations.

Award Range/Average: $38,343 to $3,034,757; $615,988. (FY 2017 final distribution not yet awarded.)

Funding: (Project Grants) FY 18 est $65,500,000; FY 17 $65,500,000; FY 19 est $0

HQ: Department of the Interior 1849 C Street Avenue NW, Room 4545
Washington, DC 20240
Phone: 202-208-2868
http://www.osmre.gov

ABANDONED MINE LAND RECLAMATION (AMLR)
"Abandoned Mine Lands (AML) Program"

Award: Formula Grants; Project Grants

Purpose: The key aspect is to protect the public, health, safety and general welfare, and restore land, water and environmental resources affected by coal and non-coal mining practices.

Applicant Eligibility: The AML program is restricted to states with (1) an approved coal mining regulatory program, (2) lands eligible for reclamation, and (3) active coal mining operations within their borders that are paying coal reclamation fees into the Abandoned Mine Reclamation Fund; and to Federally-recognized Indian tribes with (4) eligible lands, and (5) active mining operations paying fees into the Fund. An eligible state or Indian tribe may submit a reclamation plan to the Office of Surface Mining Reclamation and Enforcement (OSMRE) for approval.

Beneficiary Eligibility: Citizens and the general public are protected from physical hazards and benefit from the reclamation of abandoned mine lands and polluted waters by reducing exposure to safety and health risks.

Award Range/Average: The range of financial assistance is $126,440 to $97,794,527; $11,499,

Funding: (Project Grants) FY 18 est $327,600,000; FY 19 est $0; FY 17 $321,979,595

HQ: 1849 C Street NW
Washington, DC 20240
Phone: 202-208-2868
Email: ynorman@osmre.gov
http://www.osmre.gov/programs/aml.shtm

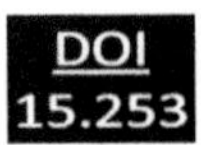

NOT-FOR-PROFIT AMD RECLAMATION "Watershed Cooperative Agreement Program (WCAP)"

Award: Cooperative Agreements

Purpose: It seeks applications from eligible applicants to restore streams affected by Acid Mine Drainage (AMD) to a level that will support a diverse biological community and provide recreational opportunities for the community.

Applicant Eligibility: Recipients must be not-for-profit IRS 501(c) (3) status organizations. Federal, state, local governments, colleges, and universities are not eligible to receive direct funding.

Beneficiary Eligibility: Communities impacted by streams polluted by AMD will benefit from this program.

Award Range/Average: The approximate average amount of the financial assistance is $100,000

Funding: (Cooperative Agreements) FY 19 est $0; FY 17 $1,500,000; FY 18 est $1,500,000

HQ: 1849 C Street NW
Washington, DC 20240
Phone: 202-208-2868
http://www.osmre.gov

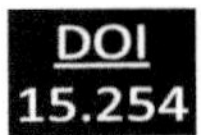

OSM/VISTA AMERICORPS "OSMRE/AmeriCorps Program; OSMRE/VISTA Program; OSMRE Semester Internship Program"

Award: Cooperative Agreements

Purpose: The purpose is to promote and stimulate public purposes such as education, job training, development of responsible citizenship and productive community involvement. The program is designed to further the understanding and appreciation of natural and cultural resources through the involvement of youth and young adults. It is also designed to continue the longstanding efforts of OSMRE to provide opportunities for public service, youth employment, minority youth development, training, and participation of young adults in accomplishing environmental-related work.

Applicant Eligibility: The not-for-profit sponsor organization will be responsible for the daily operation of the OSMRE/VISTA Program, working closely with OSMRE to ensure the program aligns with the mission of the Bureau.

Beneficiary Eligibility: Youth and local communities that benefit from reclamation of abandoned mine lands; Youth interested in gaining experience in a Federal agency

Award Range/Average: $87,000 – $700,000

Funding: (Direct Payments for Specified Use) FY 19 est $0; FY 18 est $357,500; FY 17 $357,500; - OSMRE AmeriCorps Program: (Direct payments for Specified Use) 2017 $357,500 BY 2018 est. $357,500. FY 19 estimate is based on prior year funding levels.(Direct Payments for Specified Use) FY 17 $200,000; FY 19 est $0; FY 18 est $200,000; - OSMRE/VISTA Team: (Direct payments for Specified Use) PY 2017 est. $200,000; and BY 2018 est. $200,000. FY 19 estimate is based on prior year funding levels.(Direct Payments for Specified Use) FY 17 $80,701; FY 19 est $0; FY 18 est $0

HQ: 1849 C Street NW Main Interior Building, Room 4545
Washington, DC 20240
Phone: 202-208-2585
http://www.osmre.gov

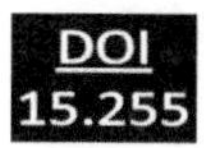

SCIENCE AND TECHNOLOGY PROJECTS RELATED TO COAL MINING AND RECLAMATION
"Technology Development and Transfer Program"

Award: Cooperative Agreements

Purpose: Supports applied Science projects that develop and demonstrate improved technologies to address public safety and environmental issues related to coal mining and reclamation of abandoned mined lands and polluted waters.

Applicant Eligibility: Applied Science Projects: Recipients may be any of the following: public, private, or non-profit entities; Federal, state, local or tribal governments; and colleges and universities located in the United States. Underground Mine Map Projects: Recipients may be any state or Indian tribe where coal mining or reclamation activities authorized under SMCRA are occurring.

Beneficiary Eligibility: Communities impacted by coal mining and reclamation of the land after mining.

Award Range/Average: Award amounts ranges from $116K to $200K.

Funding: (Cooperative Agreements) FY 17 $0; FY 18 est $0; FY 19 est $0.

HQ: 1849 C Street NW, P.O. Box 4550
Washington, DC 20240
Phone: 202-208-2895
Email: hpayne@osmre.gov
http://www.osmre.gov

RISK MANAGEMENT AGENCY

REGIONAL OFFICES

Billings
Doug Hagel, Director | 3490 Gabel Rd, Suite 100, Billings, MT 59102-6440 406-657-6447

Central
Alvin Gilmore, Director | 6501 Beacon Dr, Kansas City, MO 64131 816-926-7963

Davis
Jeff Yasui, Director | 430 G Street, Suite 4168, Davis, CA 95616-4168 530-792-5871

Eastern
Jessica Dedrick, Director | 4405 Bland Road, Suite 165, Raleigh, NC 27609 919-875-4930

Jackson
Rock Davis, Director | 803 Liberty Road, Jackson, MS 39232 601-965-4771

Midwest
Ronie Griffin, Director | 6045 Lakeside Blvd, Indianapolis, IN 46278 317-290-3050

Northern
Scott Tincher, Director | 3440 Federal Drive, Suite 200, Eagan, MN 55122-3500 651-452-1688, 222

Oklahoma City
Debra J. Bouziden, Director | 205 NW 63rd Street, Suite 170, Oklahoma City, OK 73116-8209 405-879-2710

Raleigh
Scott Lucas, Director | 4405 Bland Road, Suite 160, Raleigh, NC 27609 919-875-4880

Southern
Billy M. Pryor, Director | 1111 West Mockingbird Lane, Suite 280, Dallas, TX 75247-5016 214-767-7700

Spokane
Dave Paul, Director | 11707 E. Sprague Avenue, Spokane Valley, WA 99206-6125 509-228-6322

Springfield
Brain Frieden, Director | 3500 Wabash Ave, Springfield, IL 62711 217-241-6600, 113

St. Paul
Duane Voy, Director | 30 Seventh Street, East Suite 1890, St. Paul, MN 55101-4901 651-290-3304, 233

Topeka
Rebecca Davis, Director | 2651 SW Wanamaker Rd. Suite 201, Topeka, KS 66614-4971 785-228-5512

Valdosta
Diane Amera, Director | 106 South Patterson Street, Suite 250, Valdosta, GA 31601-5673 912-242-3044

Western
Susan Choy, Director | 430 G Street, Suite 4167, Davis, CA 95616-4167 530-792-5850

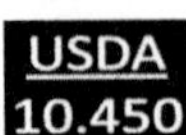

CROP INSURANCE

Award: Insurance

Purpose: The Risk Management Agency provides risk-management strategies to America's agricultural producers and strengthens the economic stability of agricultural producers and rural communities.

Applicant Eligibility: Unless otherwise restricted by the insurance policy, owners or operators of farmland, who have an insurable interest in a crop in a county where insurance is offered on that crop, are eligible for insurance.

Beneficiary Eligibility: This program is excluded from coverage under OMB Circular No. A-87.

Award Range/Average: Level of assistance varies according to policy, crop and indemnities paid.

Funding: (Insurance) FY 17 $4,081,989,205; FY 18 est $4,080,000,000; FY 19 est $2,476,000,000; FY 16 $3,291,101,228; - These amounts represent Delivery Expenses and Underwriting Gains.(Insurance) FY 17 $4,617,361,200; FY 18 est $6,570,000,000; FY 19 est $9,783,000,000; FY 16 $5,282,039,801; - These amounts represent total indemnities.

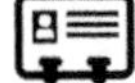
HQ: 2641 SW Wanamaker Road, Suite 201
Topeka, KS 66614

Phone: 785-228-5531
Email: carl.frazier@rma.usda.gov
http://www.rma.usda.gov

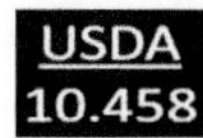

CROP INSURANCE EDUCATION IN TARGETED STATES "Targeted States"

Award: Cooperative Agreements

Purpose: To provide crop insurance education and information to U.S. agricultural producers to the Targeted States of U.S. such as Alaska, Connecticut, Delaware, Hawaii, Vermont, West Virginia, etc.

Applicant Eligibility: Eligible applicants include State departments of agriculture, universities, non-profit agricultural organizations, and other public or private organizations with the capacity to lead a local program of crop insurance education for farmers and ranchers in a Targeted State. Individuals are eligible applicants.

Beneficiary Eligibility: The ultimate beneficiaries of this education program are agricultural producers in the Targeted States. Applicants receiving awards will ensure that such producers receive effective crop insurance education and information either directly or through agribusiness professionals that can impart crop insurance information to producers.

Award Range/Average: $0 to $613,000 per agreement as announced in the Request for Applications. Average $207,716

Funding: (Cooperative Agreements) FY 17 $4,985,191; FY 18 est $5,000,000; FY 19 est $5,000,000; FY 16 $4,332,346.

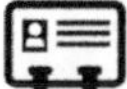

HQ: 1400 Independence Avenue USDA S Building, Room 6717-S
Washington, DC 20250-0808
Phone: 202-720-1416
Email: young.kim@rma.usda.gov
http://www.rma.usda.gov

RISK MANAGEMENT EDUCATION PARTNERSHIPS

Award: Cooperative Agreements

Purpose: To provide training and activities in the management of production, marketing, financial to the U.S. agricultural producers, especially for those not insured with Federal crop insurance.

Applicant Eligibility: Eligible applicants include State departments of agriculture, universities, non-profit agricultural organization and other public or private organizations with the capacity to lead a local program of risk management education for farmers and ranchers in an RMA Region. Individuals are not eligible applicants.

Beneficiary Eligibility: The ultimate beneficiaries of this education program are agricultural producers with a priority of producers of crops not insurable by Federal crop insurance, specialty crops, and undeserved commodities. Applicants receiving awards will ensure that such producers receive effective risk management education, information and outreach activities that can impact the risk management decision making.

Award Range/Average: RMA awarded approximately 52 cooperative agreements with an average of $91,418 (the lowest amount being $12,041 and the highest award at $199,811).

Funding: (Cooperative Agreements) FY 17 $4,753,757; FY 18 est $4,160,000; FY 19 est $4,300,000.

HQ: 1400 Independence Avenue USDA S Building, Room 6717-S
Washington, DC 20250-0808
Phone: 202-720-1416
Email: young.kim@rma.usda.gov
http://www.rma.usda.gov

SOCIAL SECURITY ADMINISTRATION

Region I
Pam Dutcher | John F. Kennedy Federal Building, Rm. 1975, Boston, MA 2203 617-565-2845

Region II
Erica Day | Federal Building, Rm. 40-160 26 Federal Plaza, New York, NY 10278 410-965-9512

Region III
Linda Seidle | Social Security Administration Mid-Atlantic Social Security Center 300 Spring Garden Street, Philadelphia, PA 19123 215-597-9143

Region IV
Rickie Bowens | Sam Nunn Federal Bldg. Suite 22T64 61 Forsyth Street, Atlanta, GA 30303 404-562-1433

Region IX
Renata Terry | Frank Hagel Federal Building 1221 Nevin Avenue, FMT R6 Richmond, California, CA 94801 510- 970-8355

Region V
Babafemi Littlejohn | Social Security Administration Regional Contracting Office 600 West Madison Street, Chicago, IL 60661 312-575-4148

Region VI
Linda Washeck | Suite 550 1301 Young Street, Dallas, TX 75202 214-767-3233

Region VII
Cynthia Ragland | Rm. 409 Richard Bolling Federal Office Building 601 East 12th Street, Kansas City, MO 64106 816-936-5535

Region VIII
Lisa Walker | Rm. 1052 Federal Office Building 1961 Stout Street, Denver, CO 80294 303-844-7344

Region X
Renata Terry | Suite 2900 M/S 3022 701 Fifth Avenue, Seattle, WA 510- 970-8355

SUPPLEMENTAL SECURITY INCOME

Award: Direct Payments for Specified Use; Direct Payments With Unrestricted Use

Purpose: The program ensures that physically-challenged people aged 65 and above receive a better income when it is below the specified level.

Applicant Eligibility: To be found disabled for SSI purposes: an individual age 18 or older must be unable to perform any substantial gainful activity by reason of any medically determinable physical or mental impairment which can be expected to result in death or which has lasted or can be expected to last for a continuous period of at least 12 months; an individual under age 18 must have a medically determinable physical or mental impairment or combination of impairments that causes marked and severe functional limitations, and that can be expected to cause death or that has lasted or can be expected to last for a continuous period of at least 12 months. An individual under age 18 who files a new application for benefits and is engaging in substantial gainful activity will not be considered disabled.

Beneficiary Eligibility: Individuals who have attained age 65 or are blind or disabled, who continue to meet the income and resources tests, citizenship/qualified alien status, U.S. residence, and certain other requirements. Eligibility may continue for beneficiaries who engage in substantial gainful activity despite disabling physical or mental impairments.

Award Range/Average: Monthly Federal cash payments range from $1 to $750 for an aged, blind, or disabled individual who does not have an eligible spouse, and from $1 to $1,125 for an aged, blind, or disabled individual and an eligible spouse. These rates became effective January 2018. The average Federal monthly benefit payment for January 2018 was $536.

Funding: (Direct Payments with Unrestricted Use) FY 17 $54,600,000,000; FY 18 N/A FY 19 N/A FY 16 $54,800,000,000; - FY 2017 $54.6 billion, FY 2016 $54.6 billion.

HQ: 6401 Security Boulevard
Baltimore, MD 21235
Phone: 800-772-1213
http://www.socialsecurity.gov

SOCIAL SECURITY RESEARCH AND DEMONSTRATION "SSA Research and Demonstration"

Award: Project Grants

Purpose: The program's purpose is to conduct research on social, economic and demographic topics related to the Social Security Old Age, Survivors and Disability Insurance and Supplemental Security Income programs while focusing on the current and future well-being of their beneficiaries. It also conducts research on rehabilitating beneficiaries and encouraging them to return to work.

Applicant Eligibility: Applicants applying for grant funds may include research organizations, associations of research organizations, State and local governments, educational institutions, hospitals, public and private organizations, and nonprofit and profit organizations. Private individuals are not eligible to apply.

Beneficiary Eligibility: State agencies, local governments, educational institutions, hospitals, nonprofit organizations, and profit organizations are eligible to apply for grant funding.

Award Range/Average: Range: $275,000 to $2,065,938 and Average $3,300,000.

Funding: (Salaries and Expenses) FY 17 $11,293,230; FY 18 est $11,293,230; FY 19 est $10,695,000.

HQ: Social Security Administration Office of Acquisition and Grants, 1540 Robert M Ball Building
6401 Security Boulevard
Baltimore, MD 21235
Phone: 410-965-9534
Email: dionne.mitchell@ssa.gov
http://www.ssa.gov

SOCIAL SECURITY - WORK INCENTIVES PLANNING AND ASSISTANCE PROGRAM "SSA Work Incentives Planning and Assistance (WIPA) Program) or Work Incentives Outreach Program"

Award: Project Grants

Purpose: The Work Incentives Planning and Assistance Program complies with the Ticket-to-Work and Work Incentives Improvement Act of 1999 and Social Security Protection Act of 2004 to support beneficiaries who want to return to work to make a successful and profitable transition to the workforce. It also acts as a repository for information about benefits counseling and work incentive services.

Applicant Eligibility: Applicants applying for cooperative agreement funds may include State or local governments (excluding any State administering the State Medicaid program), public or private organizations, or nonprofit or for-profit organizations (for-profit organizations may apply with the understanding that no cooperative agreement funds may be paid as profit to any awardee), as well as Native American tribal organizations that the Commissioner determines is qualified to provide work incentives planning and assistance to all SSDI and SSI beneficiaries with disabilities, within the targeted geographic area. These may include Centers for Independent Living established under Title VII of the Rehabilitation Act of 1973, protection and advocacy organizations, Native American tribal entities, client assistance programs established in accordance with Section 112 of the Rehabilitation Act of 1973, State Developmental Disabilities Councils established in accordance with Section 124 of the Developmental Disabilities Assistance and Bill of Rights Act, and State agencies administering the State program funded under Part A of Title IV of the Act.

Beneficiary Eligibility: WIPA projects serve beneficiaries who are age 14 and older, and receive any of the following benefits based on their own disabilities: Social Security Disability Insurance BenefiDisability Benefits; Disabled Widow(er)s Benefits; SSI based on blindness or disability; Medicare under the Extended Period of Medicare Coverage (for former disability beneficiaries performing substantial work); Medicaid under Section 1619(b) of the Social Security Act (for SSI beneficiaries ineligible for payment due to work income); A State supplementary SSI payment (even if the beneficiary is not due a Federal SSI payment); or Medicare coverage based on disability and Medicare qualified government employment.

Award Range/Average: Range $100,000 to $300,000, average $235,940

Funding: (Salaries and Expenses) FY 17 $19,583,013; FY 18 est $19,583,013; FY 19 est $19,583,013.

HQ: Social Security Administration Office of Acquisition and Grants, 1540 Robert M Ball Building 6401 Security Boulevard

Baltimore, MD 21235

Phone: 410-965-9534

Email: dionne.mitchell@ssa.gov

http://www.ssa.gov

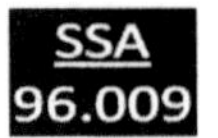

SSA 96.009

SOCIAL SECURITY STATE GRANTS FOR WORK INCENTIVES ASSISTANCE TO DISABLED BENEFICIARIES
"Protection and Advocacy (P&A) Systems: PABSS and SPSSB"

Award: Project Grants

Purpose: The Protection and Advocacy for Beneficiaries of Social Security provide information and legal support to help people resolve their disability employment-related concerns, while the Strengthening Protections of Social Security Beneficiaries program pays for performance reviews and monitoring the representative payees.

Applicant Eligibility: Applicants applying for grant funds are limited to State protection and advocacy systems established pursuant to Part C of Title I of the Developmental Disabilities Assistance and Bill of Rights Act.

Beneficiary Eligibility: All individuals within the State who are entitled to SSDI or eligible for SSI benefits based on disability or blindness.

Award Range/Average: PABSS Range: $50,000 to $319,000 average $107,496. SPSSB Range: $30,000 to $2,200,000 average $431,138.

Funding: (Project Grants) FY 17 $6,725,001; FY 18 est $6,725,001; FY 19 est $6,725,001; FY 16 $6,725,001.

HQ: 1540 Robert M Ball Building 6401 Security Boulevard
Baltimore, MD 21235
Phone: 410-965-9534
Email: dionne.mitchell@ssa.gov
http://www.ssa.gov

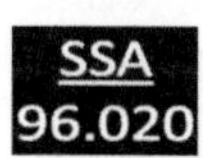

SPECIAL BENEFITS FOR CERTAIN WORLD WAR II VETERANS "Special Veterans Benefits; SVB"

SSA 96.020

Award: Direct Payments with Unrestricted Use

Purpose: The program pays special privileges for World War II veterans who are eligible for Supplemental Security Income benefits while meeting other criteria when residing outside of the United States.

Applicant Eligibility: Be age 65 or older on December 14, 1999, be a World War II veteran (includes Filipino veterans of World War II or organized guerrilla forces under the auspices of the U.S. military); be eligible for SSI benefits for December 1999 and for the month that the application for SVB was filed; and, have other benefit income that is less than 75 percent of the SSI Federal benefit rate. For 2018, 75 percent of the SSI Federal benefit rate is $562.

Beneficiary Eligibility: Benefits are paid to certain World War II veterans meeting the criteria specified under Applicant Eligibility. Credentials/Documentation.

Award Range/Average: The maximum monthly SVB payable for current year 2018 is $562.50 (Per Title VIII of the Act, the benefit amount equals 75 percent of the SSI Federal benefit rate.) This amount will change yearly. The monthly SVB amount payable to an individual is reduced by the amount of that person's other benefit income for the month. Other benefit income includes any recurring payment received as an annuity, pension, retirement or disability benefit. In FY 2017, there were 549 beneficiaries receiving SVB payments totaling $208,888. The average monthly federal payment for January 2017 is $380.49.

Funding: (Direct Payments with Unrestricted Use) FY 16 $2,906,072; FY 17 est $2,388,885; FY 18 N/A

HQ: OISP 6401 Security Boulevard Robert M Ball Building
Baltimore, MD 21235
Phone: 410-965-3549
Email: phyllis.mathers@ssa.gov
http://www.socialsecurity.gov

U.S. CENSUS BUREAU

California

James T. Christy, Regional Director, Census Bureau | 15350 Sherman Way, Suite 300, Van Nuys, CA 91406-4224 818-904-6393

Colorado

Susan A. Lavin, Regional Director, Census Bureau | 6900 West Jefferson Avenue Suite 100, Denver, CO 80235-2032 303-969-6750

Georgia

James F. Holmes, Regional Director, Census Bureau | 101 Marietta Street, N.W., Suite 3200, Atlanta, GA 30303-2700 404-730-3832

Illinois

Stanley D. Moore, Regional Director, Census Bureau | 2255 Enterprise Drive, Suite 5501, Westchester, IL 60154-5800 708-562-1376

Indiana
Jean Ann Banet, Technical Services Supervisor | Bureau of the Census P.O. Box 1545, Jeffersonville, IN 47131 812-218-3046

Kansas
Henry Palacios, Regional Director, Census Bureau | 1211 North 8th Street, Kansas City, KS 66101-2129 913-551-6728

Massachusetts
Arthur G. Dukakis, Regional Director, Census Bureau | 2 Copley Place, Suite 301 P.O. Box 9108, Boston, MA 02117-9108 617-424-0500

Michigan
Dwight P. Dean, Regional Director, Census Bureau | 1395 Brewery Park Boulevard, Detroit, MI 48207-5405 313-259-1158

New York
Lester A. Farthing, Regional Director, Census Bureau | 395 Hudson Street, Suite 800, New York, NY 10014 212-264-3860

North Carolina
Susan B. Hardy, Regional Director, Census Bureau | 901 Center Park Drive, Suite 106, Charlotte, NC 28217-2935 704-344-6142

Pennsylvania
Fernando E. Armstrong, Regional Director, Census Bureau | 1601 Market Street, 21st Floor, Philadelphia, PA 19103-2395 215-656-7550

Texas
Alfonso E. Mirabal, Regional Director, Census Bureau | 8585 North Stemmons Fwy, Suite 800S, Dallas, TX 75247-3841 214-640-4400

Washington
Ralph J. Lee, Regional Director, Census Bureau | Key Tower 700 5th Avenue, Suite 5100, Seattle, WA 98104-5018 206-553-5837

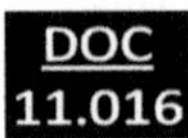

STATISTICAL, RESEARCH, AND METHODOLOGY ASSISTANCE

Award: Cooperative Agreements

Purpose: To make awards to cooperative agreements, Federal, State, or local governmental unit and to analyze information for program and policy considerations for undertaking special research.

Applicant Eligibility: Activities under this program must relate to the Census Bureau's mission to serve as the leading source of quality data about the nation's people and economy that honors privacy, protects confidentiality, and is guided by scientific objectivity, and research-based innovation.

Beneficiary Eligibility: Eligible respondents include any appropriate entities, including but not restricted to Federal, State, or local governmental unit, or institution of higher education.

Award Range/Average: $300,000 - $1,000,000

Funding: (Cooperative Agreements) FY 17 est $5,000,000; FY 16 est $1,000,000

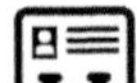

HQ: 4600 Silver Hill Road
Suitland, MD 20746
Phone: 301-763-4628
http://www.census.gov

U.S. FISH AND WILDLIFE SERVICE

(Region VI: Colorado, Kansas, Montana, Nebraska, North Dakota, South Dakota, Utah, Wyoming)
Ralph O. Morgenweck | P.O. Box 25486 Denver Federal Center, Denver, CO 80025 303-236-7920

(Region VII: Alaska)
Rowan Gould | 1011 E. Tudor Road, Anchorage, AK 99503 907-786-3306

California/Nevada
Judy Frye | 2800 Cottage Way, Suite W2606, Sacramento, CA 95825 916-414-6486

Georgia
Sam Hamilton | 1875 Century Boulevard, Atlanta, GA 30345 404-679-4006

Massachusetts
Marvin Moriarty | 300 Westgate Center Drive, Hadley, MA 01035 413-253-8308

Minnesota
Robyn Thorson | Federal Building, 1 Federal Drive, Fort Snelling, MN 55111 612-713-5284

New Mexico
Dale Hall | P.O. Box 1306 500 Gold Avenue, S.W., Room 3018, Albuquerque, NM 87103 505-248-6910

Oregon
Dave Allen | 911 N.E. 11th Avenue, Portland, OR 97232-4181 503-872-2716

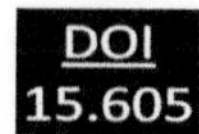

SPORT FISH RESTORATION "Dingell-Johnson Sport Fish Restoration Program"

Award: Formula Grants

Purpose: Supports activities designed to restore, conserve, manage, or enhance sport fish populations; the public use and benefits from these resources; and activities that provide boat access to public waters.

Applicant Eligibility: Agencies from the 50 States, the District of Columbia, the Commonwealths of Puerto Rico and the Northern Mariana Islands, and the territories of Guam, the U.S. Virgin Islands, and American Samoa with primary responsibility for fish and wildlife conservation may submit grant proposals to the U.S. Fish and Wildlife Service. To be eligible, they must pass assent legislation to the provisions of the Act for the conservation of sport fish that includes a prohibition against the diversion of license fees paid by anglers for any purpose other than the administration of the fish and wildlife agency.

Beneficiary Eligibility: General Public (While direct participation is limited to fish and wildlife agencies, the public will ultimately benefit from these fishery conservation measures.)

Award Range/Average: Range is $900,000 to $14,700,000; Average $5,200,000.

Funding: (Formula Grants) FY 18 est $351,917,385; FY 17 $349,442,840; FY 19 est $353,889,852

HQ: Wildlife and Sport Fish Restoration Program Policy and Programs Division 5275 Leesburg Pike, P.O. Box WSFR

Falls Church, VA 22041-3803

Phone: 703-358-2156

http://wsfrprograms.fws.gov

FISH AND WILDLIFE MANAGEMENT ASSISTANCE

Award: Project Grants

Purpose: Provides technical and financial assistance to other federal agencies, states, local governments, native American tribes, non-governmental organizations, citizen groups, and land owners on the conservation and management of fish and wildlife resources.

Applicant Eligibility: Applicants may be other federal agencies, state agencies, local governments, native American organizations, interstate, intrastate, public nonprofit institution/organization, other public institution/organization, nonprofit/organization, private landowners, or any other organization subject to the jurisdiction of the United States with interests that support the mission of the U.S. Fish and Wildlife Service on a cost recoverable basis. Applicants applying for State/Interstate ANS Management Plan funds must be a State or Interstate organization with an ANS Task Force approved plan.

Beneficiary Eligibility: Federal agencies, state agencies, local governments, Native Americans, Interstate, Intrastate, public nonprofit institution/organization, other public institution/organization, private nonprofit/ organization, or any other organization subject to the jurisdiction of the United States with interests that support the mission of the Service on a cost recoverable basis.

Award Range/Average: Range is $1,000 to $750,000; Average $75,000.

Funding: (Project Grants (Discretionary)) FY 19 est $3,176,156; FY 18 est $3,176,156; FY 17 $3,176,156; - NFHAP - (Discretionary): FY 17 $3,176,156; FY 18 $3,176,156; FY 19 $3,176,156. (Project Grants (Discretionary)) FY 17 $13,900,000; FY 18 est $13,900,000; FY 19 est $13,900,000; - NFPP – (Discretionary) National Fish Passage Program: FY 17 $13,900,000 FY 18 $13,900,000; FY 19 est $13,900,000. (Project Grants (Discretionary)) FY 19 est $2,000,000; FY 18 est $2,000,000; FY 17 $2,000,000; - ANS - (Discretionary) State/Interstate ANS Management Plan Grant Program: FY 17: $2,000,000; FY 18: $2,000,000; FY 19 $2,000,000.

HQ: Fish and Aquatic Conservation Department of the Interior 5275 Leesburg Pike, P.O. Box FAC
Falls Church, VA 22041-3803
Phone: 703-358-2373
Email: julie_jackson@fws.gov
http://www.fws.gov/fisheries

WILDLIFE RESTORATION AND BASIC HUNTER EDUCATION "Pittman-Robertson Wildlife Restoration Program"

Award: Formula Grants

Purpose: Provides grants to State, Commonwealth, and territorial fish and wildlife agencies for projects to restore, conserve, manage, and enhance wild birds and mammals and their habitat.

Applicant Eligibility: Agencies from the 50 States, the Commonwealths of Puerto Rico and the Northern Mariana Islands, and the territories of Guam, the U.S. Virgin Islands, and American Samoa with primary responsibility for fish and wildlife conservation may submit grant proposals to the Fish and Wildlife Service. To be eligible, they must pass assent legislation to the provisions of the Act for conservation of wildlife that includes a prohibition against the diversion of license fees paid by hunters for any other purpose than the administration of the fish and wildlife agency.

Beneficiary Eligibility: General Public

Award Range/Average: Range is $268,000 to $7,187,000; Average $2,750,000.

Funding: (Formula Grants) FY 18 est $152,019,384; FY 19 est $159,000,000; FY 17 $142,628,785; - Hunter Education and Safety (Formula Grants): FY 17 $142,628,785; FY 18 $152,019,384 ; FY 19 $159,000,000(Formula Grants) FY 19 est $667,560,000; FY 17 $629,410,911; FY 18 est $637,010,140; - Wildlife Restoration (Formula Grants): FY 17 $629,410,911; FY 18 $637,010,140; FY 19 $667,560,000

HQ: Policy and Programs Division 5275 Leesburg Pike, P.O. Box WSFR
Falls Church, VA 22041-3803
Phone: 703-358-2156
http://wsfrprograms.fws.gov

COASTAL WETLANDS PLANNING, PROTECTION AND RESTORATION "National Coastal Wetlands Grants"

Award: Project Grants

Purpose: Provides competitive matching grants to coastal States for coastal wetlands conservation projects.

Applicant Eligibility: Eligible applicants include any agency or agencies designated by the Governor of a coastal State. It is usually a State natural resource or fish and wildlife agency.

Beneficiary Eligibility: States, Commonwealths, or territories as designated in the applicant eligibility section.

Award Range/Average: Range: $125,000 - $1,000,000; Average: $575,000

Funding: (Project Grants (Discretionary)) FY 19 est $17,000,000; FY 17 $17,000,000; FY 18 est $18,000,000; - PROJECT GRANTS (Discretionary): FY 17 $17,000,000; FY 18 $18,800,000; and FY 19 est. $17,000,000.

HQ: The National Refuge System - Division of Natural Resources and Conservation Planning 5275 Leesburg Pike, P.O. Box NWRS
Falls Church, VA 22041-3803
Phone: 703-358-1849
http://wsfrprograms.fws.gov/subpages/grantprograms/cw/cw.htm

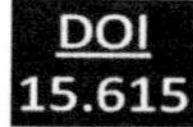

COOPERATIVE ENDANGERED SPECIES CONSERVATION FUND

Award: Project Grants

Purpose: Provides federal financial assistance through its appropriate State or territorial agency, to assist in the development of programs for the conservation of endangered and threatened species.

Applicant Eligibility: Participation limited to State agencies that have a cooperative agreement with the Secretary of the Interior. The annual Notice of Funding Opportunity (NOFO), announced through www.

Beneficiary Eligibility: All States that have entered into a cooperative agreement with the Secretary of the Interior.

Award Range/Average: Varies by program element.

Funding: (Project Grants (Discretionary)) FY 19 est $0; FY 18 est $0; FY 17 $11,141,000; - 5954 Species Recovery Land Acquisition Grants (Discretionary): FY 17 $11,141,000 (est); FY 18 $0 (est); FY 19 $0 (est)(Project Grants (Discretionary)) FY 17 $9,467,000; FY 18 est $6,518,000; FY 19 est $6,518,000; - 5944 Habitat Conservation Planning Assistance Grants (Discretionary): FY 17 $9,467,000 (est); FY 18 $6,518,000 (est); FY 19 $6,518,000 (est) (Project Grants (Discretionary)) FY 19 est $10,487,000; FY 18 est $10,487,000; FY 17 $10,508,000; - 5941 Conservation Grants (Discretionary): FY 17 $10,508,000 (est); FY 18 $10,487,000 (est); FY 19 $10,487,000 (est) (Project Grants (Discretionary)) FY 18 est $0; FY 19 est $0; FY 17 $19,601,000; - 5943 Habitat Conservation Plan Land Acquisition Grants (Discretionary): FY 17 $19,601,000 (est); FY 18 $0 (est); FY 19 $0 (est)

HQ: Department of the Interior 5279 Leesburg Pike, P.O. Box ES
Falls Church, VA 22041-3803
Phone: 703-358-2171
http://www.fws.gov/endangered/grants/index.html

DOI 15.616 CLEAN VESSEL ACT "CVA"

Award: Project Grants

Purpose: Program provides funding to States, the District of Columbia, Commonwealths, and territories for the construction, renovation, operation, and maintenance of sewage pump out stations, waste reception facilities, and pump out boats for recreational boaters.

Applicant Eligibility: Agencies from the 50 States, the District of Columbia, the Commonwealths of Puerto Rico and the Northern Mariana Islands, and the territories of Guam, the U.S. Virgin Islands, and American Samoa may submit grant proposals to the U.S. Fish and Wildlife Service.

Beneficiary Eligibility: General public, recreational boaters, municipalities, and private marinas within eligible States, the District of Columbia, Commonwealths, and territories.

Award Range/Average: Maximum Federal award is $1,500,000. The average award is approximately $350,000.

Funding: (Project Grants (Discretionary)) FY 18 est $14,218,239; FY 17 $15,441,567; FY 19 est $14,000,000; - Project Grants (Discretionary) FY 17 $15,441,567; FY 18 estimated $14,218,239; FY 19 estimated $14,000,000. FY 18 estimates are preliminary and FY 19 estimates are based on prior year funding levels.

HQ: Wildlife and Sport Fish Restoration Program Policy and Programs Division 5275 Leesburg Pike, P.O. Box WSFR
Falls Church, VA 22041-3803
Phone: 703-358-2156
Email: paul_rauch@fws.gov
http://wsfrprograms.fws.gov/subpages/grantprograms/cva/cva.htm

RHINOCEROS AND TIGER CONSERVATION FUND

Award: Project Grants

Purpose: Provides financial assistance for projects for the effective long-term conservation of rhinoceros and tigers. This program supports projects that focuses on enhanced protection of at-risk rhinoceros and tiger populations; protected area/reserve management in important rhinoceros and tiger range.

Applicant Eligibility: Applications may be submitted by any government agency responsible for the conservation and protection of rhinoceroses and/or tigers and any other organization, multi-national secretariat or individual with demonstrated experience in rhinoceros and/or tiger conservation may submit proposals to this Fund. U.S. non-profit, non-governmental organizations must submit documentary evidence of their Section 501(c)(3) non-profit status.

Beneficiary Eligibility: Any government agency responsible for conservation and protection of rhinoceros and/or tigers and any other organization or individual with demonstrated experience in rhinoceros or tiger conservation.

Award Range/Average: Variable amounts. Largely $50,000 or less. Higher amounts may be requested.

Funding: (Project Grants (Discretionary)) FY 17 $4,831,742; FY 19 est $4,800,000; FY 18 est $4,800,000; - Project Grants (Discretionary): FY 17 $4,831,742; FY 18 $4,800,000; FY 19 $4,800,000.

HQ: Department of the Interior 5275 Leesburg Pike, P.O. Box IA
Falls Church, VA 22041-3803

Phone: 703-358-1754

http://www.fws.gov/international/wildlife-without-borders/rhino-and-tiger-conservation-fund.html

AFRICAN ELEPHANT CONSERVATION FUND

Award: Project Grants

Purpose: Provides financial assistance to support projects that will enhance sustainable conservation programs to ensure effective, long-term conservation of African elephants. The African Elephant Conservation fund supports projects that promote conservation through applied research on elephant populations and their habitat, including surveys and monitoring; development and execution of elephant conservation management plans.

Applicant Eligibility: Applications may be submitted by any African government agency responsible for African elephant conservation and protection and any other organization or individual with demonstrated experience in African elephant conservation.

Beneficiary Eligibility: Any African government agency responsible for African elephant conservation and protection and any other organization or individual with demonstrated experience in African elephant conservation.

Award Range/Average: Variable amounts. Generally $50,000 or less. Higher amounts may be requested

Funding: (Project Grants (Discretionary)) FY 17 $3,085,085; FY 18 est $3,000,000; FY 19 est $3,000,000; - Project Grants (Discretionary): FY 17 $3,085,085; FY 18 $3,000,000; FY 19 $3,000,000. FY 18 and FY 19 amounts are estimates based on prior year funding levels.

HQ: Department of the Interior 5275 Leesburg Pike, P.O. Box IA

Falls Church, VA 22041-3803

Phone: 703-358-1754

http://www.fws.gov/international/wildlife-without-borders/african-elephant-conservation-fund.html

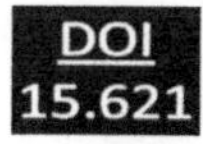

ASIAN ELEPHANT CONSERVATION FUND

Award: Project Grants

Purpose: To support the conservation of Asian elephants, to promote research and monitoring of laws that prohibit trade of Asian elephant, to regulate conservation education and management plans, to reduce human-elephant conflicts, to inspect wildlife and law enforcement.

Applicant Eligibility: Applications may be submitted by any Asian government agency responsible for Asian elephant conservation and protection, and any other organization or individual with demonstrated experience in Asian elephant conservation.

Beneficiary Eligibility: Any Asian government agency responsible for Asian elephant conservation and protection, and any other organization or individual with demonstrated experience in Asian elephant conservation.

Award Range/Average: Variable amounts. Generally $50,000 or less. Higher amounts may be requested.

Funding: (Project Grants (Discretionary)) FY 18 est $1,800,000; FY 17 $1,835,320; FY 19 est $1,800,000; - Project Grants (Discretionary): FY 17 $1,835,320; FY 18 $1,800,000; FY 19 $1,800,000. FY 18 and FY 19 amounts are estimates based on prior year funding levels.

HQ: Department of the Interior 5276 Leesburg Pike, P.O. Box IA
Falls Church, VA 22041-3803
Phone: 703-358-1754
http://www.fws.gov/international/wildlife-without-borders/asian-elephant-conservation-fund.html

SPORTFISHING AND BOATING SAFETY ACT

Award: Project Grants

Purpose: To fund to States of Columbia and territories for renovation and maintenance of docking and other facilities for recreational purposes.

Applicant Eligibility: Agencies from the 50 States, the District of Columbia, the Commonwealths of Puerto Rico and the Northern Mariana Islands, and the territories of Guam, the U.S. Virgin Islands, and American Samoa may submit grant proposals to the U.S. Fish and Wildlife Service.

Beneficiary Eligibility: General Public, specifically owners and/or users of transient, recreational boats 26 feet or greater in length, and municipalities and private marinas within those eligible States, the District of Columbia, Commonwealths, and territories.

Award Range/Average: Tier 1 grants average $179,000; Tier 2 range from $100,000 to $1,500,000; Average $954,000.

Funding: (Project Grants (Discretionary)) FY 18 est $14,218,239; FY 19 est $14,000,000; FY 17 $14,743,095; - Project Grants (Discretionary) FY 17 $14,743,095; FY 18 estimated $14,218,239; and FY 19 estimated $14,000,000.

HQ: Wildlife and Sport Fish Restoration Program Policy and Programs Division 5275 Leesburg Pike, P.O. Box WSFR
Falls Church, VA 22041
Phone: 703-358-2156
http://wsfrprograms.fws.gov

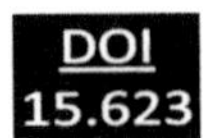

NORTH AMERICAN WETLANDS CONSERVATION FUND "NAWCF"

Award: Project Grants

Purpose: To compensate for conservation projects in the United States, Canada, and Mexico.

Applicant Eligibility: Available to private or public organizations or to individuals who have developed partnerships to carry out wetlands conservation projects in the U.S., Canada, and Mexico.

Beneficiary Eligibility: Available to any private or public organization or individual.

Award Range/Average: Range is $0 to $75,000 for Small Grants; over $75,000 to $1,000,000 for U.S. Standard Grants. Average award is approximately $42,000 and $710,000 for Small Grants and U.S. Standard Grants, respectively.

Funding: (Project Grants (Discretionary)) FY 17 $64,020,000; FY 18 est $65,000,000; FY 19 est $65,000,000; - Project Grants (Discretionary): FY 17 $64,020,000; FY 18 $65,000,000; FY 19 $65,000,000

HQ: Division of Bird Habitat Conservation 5275 Leesburg Pike, P.O. Box MB
Falls Church, VA 22041-3803
Phone: 703-358-1784
http://www.fws.gov/birds/grants/north-american-wetland-conservation-act.php

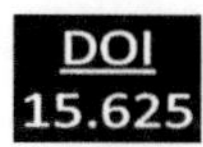

WILDLIFE CONSERVATION AND RESTORATION

Award: Formula Grants

Purpose: To assist States and territories in implementing projects for wildlife and associated habitats, including wildlife education and recreation activities.

Applicant Eligibility: Agencies from the 50 States, the District of Columbia, the Commonwealths of Puerto Rico and the Northern Mariana Islands, and the territories of Guam, the U.S. Virgin Islands, and American Samoa with primary responsibility for fish and wildlife conservation may submit grant proposals to the U.S. Fish and Wildlife Service. To be eligible, they must pass assent legislation to the provisions of the Act for the conservation of wildlife that includes a prohibition against the diversion of license fees paid by hunters for any other purpose than the administration of the fish and wildlife agency.

Beneficiary Eligibility: General Public: While direct participation is limited to fish and wildlife agencies, the public will ultimately benefit from these wildlife conservation measures.

Award Range/Average: No Data Available.

Funding: (Formula Grants) FY 18 est $0; FY 19 est $0; FY 17 $0

HQ: Policy and Programs Division 5275 Leesburg Pike
Falls Church, VA 22041-3803
Phone: 703-358-2231
http://wsfrprograms.fws.gov

ENHANCED HUNTER EDUCATION AND SAFETY

Award: Formula Grants

Purpose: To fund for archery education programs and construction of firearm shooting and archery ranges.

Applicant Eligibility: Agencies from the 50 States, the Commonwealths of Puerto Rico and the Northern Mariana Islands, and the territories of Guam, the U.S. Virgin Islands, and American Samoa with primary responsibility for fish and wildlife conservation may submit grant proposals to the Fish and Wildlife Service. To be eligible, they must pass assent legislation to the provisions of the Act for the conservation of wildlife that include a prohibition against the diversion of license fees paid by hunters for any other purpose than the administration of the fish and wildlife agency.

Beneficiary Eligibility: General Public (While direct participation is limited to fish and wildlife agencies, the general public will ultimately benefit from these wildlife conservation measures).

Award Range/Average: Range is $13,300 to $240,000; Average $145,000.

Funding: (Formula Grants) FY 18 est $8,000,000; FY 17 $8,000,000; FY 19 est $8,000,000; - Formula Grants: FY 17 $8,000,000; FY 18 $8,000,000; FY 19 $8,000,000

HQ: Wildlife and Sport Fish Restoration Program Policy and Programs Division 5275 Leesburg Pike, P.O. Box WSFR

Falls Church, VA 22041-3803

Phone: 703-358-2156

http://wsfrprograms.fws.gov

MULTISTATE CONSERVATION GRANT

Award: Project Grants

Purpose: To fund for fish and wildlife restoration projects.

Applicant Eligibility: Projects must benefit at least 26 States, a majority of States in a Region of the U.S. Fish and Wildlife Service, or a Regional association of State fish and game departments.

Beneficiary Eligibility: Same as Applicant Eligibility.

Award Range/Average: The range based on FY 2017 awards was $50,000 to $560,000; Average $150,000.

Funding: (Project Grants (Discretionary)) FY 19 est $6,000,000; FY 17 $6,000,000; FY 18 est $6,000,000; - Project Grants (Discretionary): FY 17 $6,000,000; FY 18 estimated $6,000,000; FY 19 estimated $6,000,000. Future fiscal years estimated based on previous year funding level.

HQ: 5275 Leesburg Pike

Falls Church, VA 22041-3803

Phone: 703-358-2156

http://wsfrprograms.fws.gov

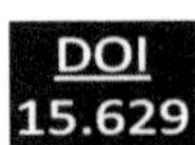

GREAT APES CONSERVATION FUND

Award: Project Grants

Purpose: To assist for the conservation of great apes and their habitats, to promote ape conservation management plans; to implement laws that prohibit trade of ape, to encourage conservation education, to decrease human-ape conflicts, to inspect wildlife and law enforcement for protecting apes.

Applicant Eligibility: Applications may be submitted by any government agency responsible for conservation and protection of apes and any other organization or individual with demonstrated experience in ape conservation.

Beneficiary Eligibility: Any government agency responsible for conservation and protection of apes and any other organization or individual with demonstrated experience in ape conservation.

Award Range/Average: Variable amounts. Generally $50,000 or less. Higher amounts may be requested.

Funding: (Project Grants (Discretionary)) FY 19 est $2,900,000; FY 18 est $2,900,000; FY 17 $2,992,302; - Project Grants (Discretionary): FY 17 $2,992,302; FY 18 $2,900,000; FY 19 $2,900,000 FY 18 and FY 19 amounts are estimates based on prior year funding levels.

HQ: Department of the Interior 5275 Leesburg Pike, P.O. Box IA

Falls Church, VA 22041-3803

Phone: 703-358-1754

http://www.fws.gov/international/wildlife-without-borders/great-ape-conservation-fund.html

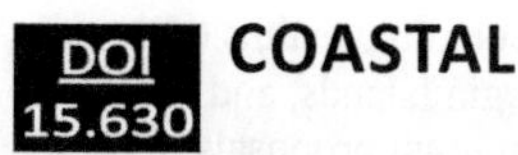

COASTAL

Award: Cooperative Agreements

Purpose: To assist in protecting and improving habitats for fish and wildlife.

Applicant Eligibility: Federal, State, interstate and intrastate agencies; local and tribal governments; public nonprofit institutes and organizations (such as conservation organizations, watershed councils, land trusts, schools and institutions of higher learning); U.S. territories and possessions; private landowners including individuals and businesses.

Beneficiary Eligibility: Same as Applicant Eligibility.

Award Range/Average: Range is $5,000 to $50,000.

Funding: (Cooperative Agreements (Discretionary Grants)) FY 17 $13,000,000; FY 18 est $13,000,000. Cooperative Agreements (Discretionary): FY 17 $13,000,000; FY 18 $13,000,000.

HQ: Department of the Interior 5278 Leesburg Pike, P.O. Box NWRS
Falls Church, VA 22041-3803
Phone: 703-358-2332
http://www.fws.gov/coastal

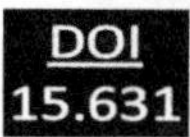

PARTNERS FOR FISH AND WILDLIFE

Award: Project Grants

Purpose: To provide financial assistance to landowners, States, and Tribes in restoring habitats for fish and wildlife on their lands.

Applicant Eligibility: Private landowners, tribal governments, local and state governments, educational and non-profit institutions and organizations are eligible for financial and technical assistance from Partners for Fish and Wildlife Program. Projects must be located on private lands.

Beneficiary Eligibility: Same as Applicant Eligibility.

Award Range/Average: Cost-share range per project is from $200 to $25,000. The average cost per project is $5,400.

Funding: Project Grants (Discretionary) FY 18 est $52,000,000; FY 17 $52,000,000; FY 19 est $52,000,000; - Project Grants (Discretionary): FY 17 $52,000,000; FY 18 $52,000,000

HQ: 5275 Leesburg Pike, P.O. Box NWRS
Falls Church, VA 22041-3803
Phone: 703-358-2011
http://www.fws.gov/partners

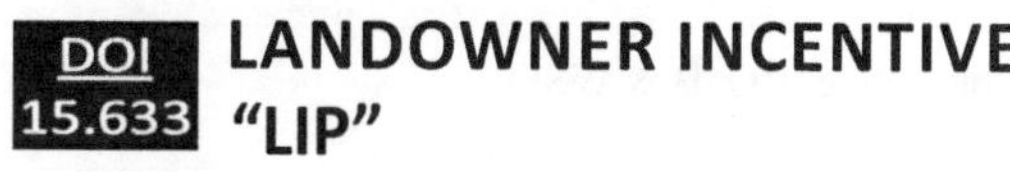

LANDOWNER INCENTIVE "LIP"

Award: Project Grants

Purpose: To provide financial assistance to landowners and States in managing habitats and protecting species and other endangered species.

Applicant Eligibility: Agencies from the 50 States, the District of Columbia, the Commonwealths of Puerto Rico and the Northern Mariana Islands, and the territories of Guam, the U.S. Virgin Islands, and American Samoa with primary responsibility for fish and wildlife conservation may submit grant proposals to the U.S. Fish and Wildlife Service.

Beneficiary Eligibility: Private landowners and the public (While direct participation is limited to State, the District of Columbia, Commonwealth, or territorial fish and wildlife agencies, private landowners will directly benefit from financial and technical assistance and the public will ultimately benefit from these wildlife conservation measures implemented on private lands).

Award Range/Average: Funds are available until expended.

Funding: (Project Grants (Discretionary)) FY 17 $0; FY 19 est $0; FY 18 est $0; - Project Grants (Discretionary): FY 17: $0, FY 18: $0, FY 19: $0 This program did not award any funds in FY 17, and will not be accepting applications during FY 18 and FY 19. CFDA should remain active through FY 19 to allow Bureau to close all currently open awards and report any associated amendments to government-wide systems that require the identification of an active CFDA number as a key reporting element.

HQ: WSFR 5275 Leesburg Pike
Falls Church, VA 22041
Phone: 703-358-2231
http://wsfrprograms.fws.gov

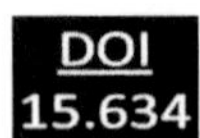

DOI 15.634 STATE WILDLIFE GRANTS "SWG"

Award: Formula Grants; Project Grants

Purpose: To fund for the development and implementation of conservation projects for the benefit of fish and wildlife habitats and other endangered species.

Applicant Eligibility: Agencies from the 50 States, the District of Columbia, the Commonwealths of Puerto Rico and the Northern Mariana Islands, and the territories of Guam, the U.S. Virgin Islands, and American Samoa with primary responsibility for fish and wildlife conservation may submit grant proposals for formula or competitive project grants to the U.S. Fish and Wildlife Service if they maintain a current, Service-approved Comprehensive Wildlife State Wildlife Action Plan. The four regional Associations of Fish and Wildlife Agencies (NEAFWA, SEAFWA, MAFWA, and WAFWA) are eligible for competitive project grants at the discretion of recipient State fish and wildlife agencies.

Beneficiary Eligibility: General Public

Award Range/Average: Range is $30,000 to $3,000,000; Average $500,000.

Funding: (Formula Grants) FY 18 est $51,000,000; FY 17 $51,000,000; FY 19 est $5,100,000; - FORMULA GRANTS (Mandatory): FY 17 $51,000,000; FY 18 $51,000,000 (estimated); FY 19 $51,000,000 (estimated). (Project Grants (Discretionary)) FY 18 est $5,400,000; FY 17 $5,487,000; FY 19 est $5,400,000; - PROJECT GRANTS (Discretionary): FY 17 $5,487,000; FY 18 $5,400,000 (estimated); FY 19 $5,400,000 (estimated).

HQ: Division of Policy and Programs 5275 Leesburg Pike, P.O. Box WSFR
Falls Church, VA 22041-3803
Phone: 703-358-2231
http://wsfrprograms.fws.gov

NEOTROPICAL MIGRATORY BIRD CONSERVATION

Award: Project Grants

Purpose: To fund for the conservation of migrating birds.

Applicant Eligibility: An individual, corporation, partnership, trust, association, or other private entity; an officer, employee, agent, department, or instrumentality of the Federal Government, of any State, municipality, or political subdivision of a State, or of any foreign government; a State municipality, or political subdivision of a State; or any other entity subject to the jurisdiction of the United States or of any foreign country; or international organization with an interest in neotropical migratory bird conservation.

Beneficiary Eligibility: Same as Applicant Eligibility.

Award Range/Average: Ranged from $2,000 to $200,000, with an average of $100,000.

Funding: (Project Grants (Discretionary)) FY 19 est $3,792,700; FY 18 est $3,792,700; FY 17 $3,802,084; - PROJECT GRANTS (Discretionary): FY 17 $3,802,084; FY 18 $3,792,700 and FY 19 $$3,792,700.

HQ: Division of Bird Habitat Conservation 5275 Leesburg Pike

Falls Church, VA 22041-3803

Phone: 703-358-1784

http://www.fws.gov/birds/grants/neotropical-migratory-bird-conservation-act.php

ALASKA SUBSISTENCE MANAGEMENT

Award: Cooperative Agreements

Purpose: To sustain fisheries and wildlife management on Federal public lands. The Fisheries Resource Monitoring Program funds to manage Federal fisheries. The Partners for Fisheries Monitoring Program strengthens Alaska Native and rural areas in fisheries management and research.

Applicant Eligibility: An individual/family, profit organization, other private institution/organization, public nonprofit institution/organization; an officer, employee, agent, department or instrumentality of the Federal government, of the State of Alaska, municipality or political subdivision of the State of Alaska; Federally recognized Indian Tribal Government (including any Native village as defined in the Alaska Native Claims Settlement Act).

Beneficiary Eligibility: An individual/Family, profit organization, other private institution/organization, public nonprofit institution/organization; an officer, employee, agent, department, or instrumentality of the Federal government, of the State of Alaska, municipality or political subdivision of the State of Alaska, or of any foreign government.

Award Range/Average: Variable amounts. Monitoring Program: Awards range from $60,000 to $860,000 for up to a 4-year project period. Partners Program: Awards range from $120,000 to $680,000 over a 4- year period.

Funding: (Cooperative Agreements (Discretionary Grants)) FY 18 est $2,867,223; FY 19 est $2,961,124; FY 17 $3,565,180; - COOPERATIVE AGREEMENTS (Discretionary Grants): FY 17 $3,565,180; FY 18 $2,867,223; FY 19 $2,961,124. FY 18 and FY 19 amount are estimates based on prior year funding levels.

HQ: Office of Subsistence Management 1011 E Tudor Road, P.O. Box 121

Anchorage, AK 99503

Phone: 907-786-3387

Email: karie_crow@fws.gov

http://www.doi.gov/subsistence

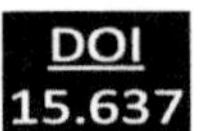

MIGRATORY BIRD JOINT VENTURES

Award: Project Grants

Purpose: To assist in the conservation of migratory birds.

Applicant Eligibility: Federal, State and local government agencies, Federally recognized Indian Tribal governments, private nonprofit institutions/organizations; public nonprofit institutions/organizations; profit organizations, interstate and intrastate entities, and individuals or families who are also private landowners.

Beneficiary Eligibility: General Public.

Award Range/Average: Range is $2,400 to $900,000; Average $225,000.

Funding: (Cooperative Agreements (Discretionary Grants)) FY 19 est $5,000,000; FY 17 $4,933,459; FY 18 est $5,000,000; - Project Grants (Discretionary): FY 17 $4,933,459; FY 18 est $5,000,000; and FY 19 est $5,000,000

HQ: 5275 Leesburg Pike, P.O. Box MBSP

Falls Church, VA 22041-3803

Phone: 703-358-1784

http://www.fws.gov/birdhabitat/jointventures/index.shtm

TRIBAL WILDLIFE GRANTS "TWG"

Award: Project Grants

Purpose: To assist in the protection of wildlife habitat and other endangered species.

Applicant Eligibility: Participation is limited to Federally recognized Indian tribal governments.

Beneficiary Eligibility: Anyone/General Public (While direct participation is limited to Federally recognized Indian tribal governments, the general public will ultimately benefit from these wildlife conservation measures).

Award Range/Average: Range $0 - $200,000; Average $167,000.

Funding: (Project Grants (Discretionary)) FY 19 est $4,084,000; FY 18 est $4,084,000; FY 17 $4,414,427; - Project Grants (Discretionary): FY 17 $4,084,000 (actual = $4,414,427 – Included previous fiscal year carryover and recoveries); FY 18 est. $4,084,000; FY 19 est. $4,084,000 FY 18 and FY 19 estimates are subject to the President's Budget.

HQ: 1211 SE Cardinal Court, Suite 100

Vancouver, WA 98683

Phone: 360-604-2531

http://www.fws.gov/nativeamerican

DOI 15.640 WILDLIFE WITHOUT BORDERS- LATIN AMERICA AND THE CARIBBEAN

Award: Project Grants

Purpose: To assist in innovative training programs in Latin America and the Caribbean that will train future generations to adapt to modern society and the landscapes on which the society depends.

Applicant Eligibility: Participation is limited to Federal, State and local governments, non-profit, non-governmental organizations; public and private institutions of higher education; and any other organization or individual with demonstrated experience deemed necessary to carry out the proposed project.

Beneficiary Eligibility: Federal, State and local government agencies; non-profit, non-governmental organizations; public and private institutions of higher education; and any other organization or individual with demonstrated experience deemed necessary to carry out the proposed project.

Award Range/Average: Variable amounts. Generally $50,000 or less. Higher amounts may be requested

Funding: (Project Grants (Discretionary)) FY 17 $1,100,312; FY 18 est $1,000,000; FY 19 est $1,000,000; - PROJECT GRANTS (Discretionary): FY 17 $1,100,312.34; FY 18 $1,000,000; FY 19 $1,000,000

HQ: Wildlife Service Division of International Conservation 05275 Leesburg Pike, P.O. Box IA
Falls Church, VA 22041
Phone: 703-358-1754
http://www.fws.gov/international/wildlife-without-borders/western-hemisphere

DOI 15.641 WILDLIFE WITHOUT BORDERS-MEXICO

Award: Project Grants

Purpose: To assist in creating innovative nature of training on the conservation of biodiversity management in Mexico.

Applicant Eligibility: Participation is limited to Federal, State and local governments, non-profit, non-governmental organizations; public and private institutions of higher education; and any other organization or individual with demonstrated experience deemed necessary to carry out the proposed project.

Beneficiary Eligibility: Federal, State and local government; public nonprofit institution/organizations; public and private institutions of higher education; and any other organization or individual with demonstrated experience deemed necessary to carry out the proposed project.

Award Range/Average: The average grant amount is $35,000.

Funding: (Project Grants (Discretionary)) FY 17 $612,166; FY 19 est $0; FY 18 est $0; - Project Grants (Discretionary): FY 17 $612,166.50; FY 18 $0; FY 19 $0

HQ: Division of International Conservation 5275 Leesburg Pike, P.O. Box IA
Falls Church, VA 22041-3803
Phone: 703-358-1754
http://www.fws.gov/international/wildlife-without-borders/mexico/index.html

DOI 15.642 CHALLENGE COST SHARE "CCS"

Award: Project Grants

Purpose: To promote partnerships with nonfederal governments, organizations, educational institutions, and businesses to protect fish, wildlife, and plants for the benefit of the U.S. citizens.

Applicant Eligibility: Applicants may be an individual/family, minority group, specialized group, small business, profit organization, private nonprofit/organization, quasi-public nonprofit institution/organization, native American, Federal, Interstate, Intrastate, State, Local, Sponsored organization, public nonprofit institution/organization, other public institution/organization, U.S. territory, or any organization with interests which support the mission of the Service. This program requires the cooperator(s) to provide a minimum of 50 percent of cost share from non-Federal sources, for local programs on National Wildlife Refuges, or benefitting other Service lands.

Beneficiary Eligibility: The Challenge Cost Share program is not a grant program, although they do use cooperative agreements for donations to these field projects. Service field station managers are encouraged to form partnerships and to secure project cost-sharing for projects initiated at that refuge or field station.

Award Range/Average: N/A.

Funding: (Project Grants (Discretionary)) FY 17 $16,000; FY 18 est $0; FY 19 est $0; - Project Grants (Discretionary): FY 17: $16,000

HQ: Department of the Interior 5277 Leesburg Pike, P.O. Box NWRS
Falls Church, VA 22041-3803
Phone: 703-358-2248
http://www.fws.gov

DOI 15.643 ALASKA MIGRATORY BIRD CO-MANAGEMENT COUNCIL "AMBCC"

Award: Project Grants

Purpose: To facilitate and administer regional programs to involve hunters of migratory birds in the management and regulation of migratory birds.

Applicant Eligibility: Native American Organizations, Public nonprofit institutions/organizations, other public institutions/organizations, Federally Recognized Indian Tribal Governments, and Local governments.

Beneficiary Eligibility: Native American Organizations, Public nonprofit institutions/organizations, Federally recognized Indian Tribal Governments, local governments, and Alaska Native American Indians.

Award Range/Average: Range is $14,800 to $129,400.

Funding: (Project Grants (Discretionary)) FY 19 est $430,810; FY 17 $539,434; FY 18 est $430,810; - Project Grants (Discretionary): FY 17 $539,434; FY 18 $ 430, 810; FY 19 $430,810. FY 18 and FY 19 amounts are estimates based on prior funding levels.

HQ: Office of the Alaska Migratory Bird Co-Management Council 1011 E Tudor Road, P.O. Box 201
Anchorage, AK 99503
Phone: 907-786-3499
Email: donna_dewhurst@fws.gov
http://alaska.fws.gov/ambcc/index.htm

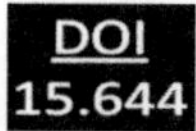

FEDERAL JUNIOR DUCK STAMP CONSERVATION AND DESIGN "Junior Duck Stamp Contest"

Award: Cooperative Agreements

Purpose: To make use of visual arts programs and a nation-wide art contest to teach school students environmental science, wildlife management, wetlands ecology, and the importance of habitat conservation.

Applicant Eligibility: Federal, State and Local Governments, Non-profit organizations both with and without 501(c)(3) IRS status, Private Institutions of Higher Education, Public and State controlled Institutions of Higher Education.

Beneficiary Eligibility: Individual/Family, Student/Trainee, Artist/Humanist, U.S. citizens, resident aliens, or nationals who are in kindergarten through twelfth grades at a public, private, or home school in the United States or U.S. territories.

Award Range/Average: Each award may range from $500 to $2,500.

Funding: (Cooperative Agreements (Discretionary Grants)) FY 17 $48,112; FY 19 est $51,000; FY 18 est $51,000; - Cooperative Agreements (Discretionary): FY 17 $48,112; FY 18 est $51,000; FY 19 est $51,000. Estimated based on prior year funding reported.

HQ: Federal Duck Stamp Office Department of the Interior 5275 Leesburg Pike, P.O. Box MBSP
Falls Church, VA 22041-3803
Phone: 703-358-1784
Email: suzanne_fellows@fws.gov
http://www.fws.gov/juniorduck

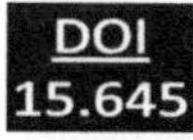

MARINE TURTLE CONSERVATION FUND

Award: Project Grants

Purpose: To help conserve marine turtles and their nesting habitats in foreign countries by supporting and providing financial resources.

Applicant Eligibility: Applications may be submitted by any government agency responsible for conservation and protection of marine turtles and any other organization or individual with demonstrated experience in marine turtle conservation.

Beneficiary Eligibility: Same as Applicant Eligibility.

Award Range/Average: Variable amounts. Generally $50,000 or less. Higher amounts may be requested.

Funding: Project Grants (Discretionary) FY 19 est $2,200,000; FY 18 est $2,200,000; FY 17 $2,203,383; - Project Grants (Discretionary): FY 17 $2,203,383.57; FY 18 $2,200,000; FY 19 $2,200,000

HQ: 5275 Leesburg Pike, P.O. Box IA
Falls Church, VA 22041
Phone: 703-358-1754
Email: mscf_marineturtle@fws.gov
http://www.fws.gov/international/wildlife-without-borders/marine-turtle-conservation-fund.html

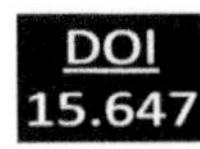

MIGRATORY BIRD CONSERVATION

Award: Project Grants

Purpose: To maintain and enhance populations and habitats of migratory bird species found in the Upper Midwest (IL, IN, IA, MI, MN, MO, OH, and WI).

Applicant Eligibility: Federal, State and local government agencies; Federally-recognized Indian Tribal governments; private nonprofit institutions/organizations; and public nonprofit institutions/organizations.

Beneficiary Eligibility: Federal, State and local government agencies; Federally-recognized Indian Tribal governments; private nonprofit institutions/organizations; public nonprofit institutions/organizations; and general public.

Award Range/Average: Range $15,000 to $79,606; average $43,218 in FY 16.

Funding: (Project Grants (Discretionary)) FY 18 est $250,000; FY 17 $302,528; FY 19 est $220,000; - Project Grants (Discretionary): FY 17 $302,528; FY 18 $250,000; FY 19 $220,000

HQ: 1400 Independence Avenue SW
Washington, DC 20250
Phone: 804-287-1559
Email: myron.wooden@wdc.usda.gov
http://www.rurdev.usda.gov

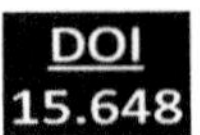

CENTRAL VALLEY PROJECT IMPROVEMENT ACT (CVPIA) "CVPIA"

Award: Project Grants

Purpose: To protect, restore, and enhance fish, wildlife, and associated habitats in the Central Valley and Trinity River basins of California; to address impacts of the Central Valley Project on fish, wildlife, and associated habitats; to improve the operational flexibility of the Central Valley Project; to increase water-related benefits; to achieve a reasonable balance among competing demands for use of Central Valley Project water.

Applicant Eligibility: Applicants may be State, local governments, Native American Organizations, other public nonprofit institutions/organizations, private nonprofit/organizations, or for profit organizations. No other Federal agency may apply.

Beneficiary Eligibility: General public.

Award Range/Average: No Data Available.

Funding: (Project Grants (Discretionary)) FY 18 est $5,000,000; FY 17 $2,000,000; FY 19 est $5,000,000; - Project Grants (Discretionary): FY 17 $2,000,000; FY 18 $5,000,000; FY 19 $5,000,000 Estimates based on prior year funding.

HQ: 2800 Cottage Way, Suite W2606
Sacramento, CA 95825
Phone: 916-414-6464
http://www.fws.gov/lodi/anadromous_fish_restoration/afrp_index.htm

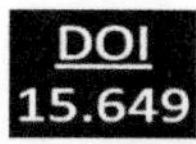

DOI 15.649 SERVICE TRAINING AND TECHNICAL ASSISTANCE (GENERIC TRAINING)

Award: Project Grants

Purpose: To support and provide financial resources for training, meetings, workshops and conferences to promote the public's conservation awareness.

Applicant Eligibility: Federal, State and local government agencies; Federally-recognized Tribal governments; private nonprofit institutions/organizations; public nonprofit institutions/ organizations; for profit organizations.

Beneficiary Eligibility: Federal, State and local government agencies; Federally-recognized Tribal governments; private nonprofit institutions/organizations; public nonprofit institutions/ organizations; general public.

Award Range/Average: Range and average varies by program activity.

Funding: (Project Grants (Discretionary)) FY 19 est $0; FY 18 est $329,499; FY 17 $2,540,119; - Project Grants (Discretionary): FY 17: $2,540,119.18; FY 18: $329,499.98 awarded through March, 2018.

HQ: Policy Branch Financial Assistance Support and Oversight Division Chief Wildlife and Sport Fish Restoration Program 5275 Leesburg Pike, P.O. Box WSFR

Falls Church, VA 22041-3803

Phone: 703-358-2701

http://www.fws.gov

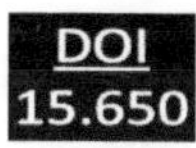

DOI 15.650 RESEARCH GRANTS (GENERIC)

Award: Project Grants

Purpose: To provide financial assistance for land management, research, and data collection/analysis to further the conservation of natural resources.

Applicant Eligibility: Federal, State and local government agencies; Federally-recognized Tribal governments; private nonprofit institutions/organizations; public nonprofit institutions/ organizations; for profit organizations.

Beneficiary Eligibility: Federal, State and local government agencies; Federally-recognized private nonprofit institutions/organizations; public nonprofit institutions/ organizations; general public.

Award Range/Average: Range and average varies by program activity.

Funding: (Project Grants (Discretionary)) FY 17 $5,099,247; FY 18 est $106,998; FY 19 est $0; - Project Grants (Discretionary): FY 17: $5,099,247.35; FY 18: $106,998; FY 19: $0. The program is no longer active.

HQ: 5275 Leesburg Pike, P.O. Box WSFR

Falls Church, VA 22041-3803

Phone: 703-358-2701

http://www.fws.gov

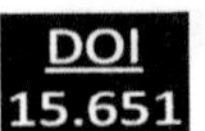

DOI 15.651 WILDLIFE WITHOUT BORDERS-AFRICA

Award: Project Grants

Purpose: Wildlife Without Borders-Africa funds projects that reduce threats to key wildlife populations and undertakes long-term conservation programs.

Applicant Eligibility: Federal, State and local government agencies; non-profit, non-governmental organizations; and public and private institutions of higher education, or any of the stated associate entities on behalf of an eligible individual.

Beneficiary Eligibility: Same as Applicant Eligibility.

Award Range/Average: Generally $50,000 or less. Higher amounts may be requested.

Funding: (Project Grants (Discretionary)) FY 19 est $15,000,000; FY 17 $15,170,086; FY 18 est $15,000,000; - Project Grants (Discretionary): FY 17 $15,170,086; FY 18 $15,000,000; FY 19 $15,000,000

HQ: Division of International Conservation 5275 Leesburg Pike, P.O. Box IA

Falls Church, VA 22041-3803

Phone: 703-358-1754

http://www.fws.gov/international/wildlife-without-borders/africa/index.html

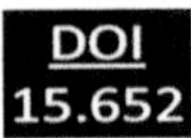

DOI 15.652 INVASIVE SPECIES "Invasive Species Program"

Award: Project Grants

Purpose: To encourage coordination and integration of endeavors between the U.S. Fish and Wildlife Service (USFWS) and interested parties to accomplish successful prevention or management of invasive species.

Applicant Eligibility: Applicants may be State and local governments, educational institutions, private and public nonprofit organizations, and institutions and private individuals which support the mission of the Service.

Beneficiary Eligibility: State and local governments; private and public nonprofit organizations; other private and public organizations; and private individuals who support the mission of the Service.

Award Range/Average: Range: $9,000 - $200,000 Average: $45,000

Funding: Project Grants (Discretionary) FY 17 $495,000; FY 19 est $350,000; FY 18 est $350,000; - Project Grants (Discretionary): FY 17 $495,000; FY 18 $350,000; FY 19 $350,000. FY 18 and FY 19 amounts are estimates based on prior year funding levels only.

HQ: 5275 Leesburg Pike, P.O. Box NWRS

Falls Church, VA 22041

Phone: 703-358-1744

http://www.fws.gov

DOI 15.653 NATIONAL OUTREACH AND COMMUNICATION "NOC "

Award: Cooperative Agreements

Purpose: To improve communications with anglers, boaters, and the public to reduce obstacles to participate in these activities; to advance adoption of fishing and boating practices; to promote conservation and the responsible use of the nation's aquatic resources; and to further safety in fishing and boating.

Applicant Eligibility: N/A

Beneficiary Eligibility: Anyone/General Public.

Award Range/Average: No Data Available.

Funding: (Project Grants) FY 17 $12,150,266; FY 18 est $12,027,892; FY 19 est $12,304,001; - Cooperative Agreements (Discretionary): FY 17 $12,150,266; FY 18 $12,027,892; FY 19 $12,304,001

HQ: 5275 Leesburg Pike, P.O. Box FAC
Falls Church, VA 22041-3803
Phone: 703-358-2435
Email: brian_bohnsack@fws.gov
http://www.fws.gov/fisheries

DOI 15.654 NATIONAL WILDLIFE REFUGE SYSTEM ENHANCEMENTS "Refuges and WIldlife"

Award: Cooperative Agreements

Purpose: To provide technical and financial assistance; deliver public access and high-quality outdoor recreational opportunities; build a volunteer cadre; and inspire the next generation of hunters, anglers. and wildlife enthusiasts.

Applicant Eligibility: Applicants may be State and local governments, private, public, nonprofit organizations, institutions and private individuals, which support the mission of the Service.

Beneficiary Eligibility: State and local governments; private and public nonprofit organizations; other private and public organizations; and private individuals who support the mission of the Service.

Award Range/Average: $1,000 to $1,000,000, or greater.

Funding: (Cooperative Agreements (Discretionary Grants)) FY 19 est $3,900,000; FY 17 $3,914,671; FY 18 est $3,900,000; - Cooperative Agreements (Discretionary): FY 17 $3,914,671; FY 18 $3,900,000; FY 19 $3,900,000

HQ: 5275 Leesburg Pike, P.O. Box NWRS
Falls Church, VA 22041-3803
Phone: 703-358-1744
http://www.fws.gov

DOI 15.655

MIGRATORY BIRD MONITORING, ASSESSMENT AND CONSERVATION
"Migratory Bird"

Award: Project Grants

Purpose: To conserve, enhance, and understand the ecology and habitats of migratory bird species.

Applicant Eligibility: Federal; Interstate; Intrastate; State; Local; including Tribal Government; Public Nonprofit Institution/Organization; Other Public Institution/Organization; Federally Recognized Tribal Government; U.S. Territory or Possession; Institutions of Higher Education including Public Private, State College, University, Junior, and Community College; Individual/Family; Specialized Group; Small Business; Profit Organization; Private Nonprofit Institution/Organization; Quasi-Public Nonprofit Institution/Organization; Other Private Institution/Organization; or Native American Organization.

Beneficiary Eligibility: Federal; Interstate; Intrastate; State; Local; including Tribal Government; Public Nonprofit Institution/Organization; Other Public Institution/Organization; Federally Recognized Tribal Government; U.S. Territory or Possession; Institutions of Higher Education including Public Private, State College, University, Junior, and Community College; Individual/Family; Specialized Group; Small Business; Profit Organization; Private Nonprofit Institution/Organization; Quasi-Public Nonprofit Institution/Organization; Other Private Institution/Organization.

Award Range/Average: N/A

Funding: (Project Grants (Discretionary)) FY 17 $1,635,200; FY 19 est $1,400,000; FY 18 est $1,400,000; - Project Grants (Discretionary): FY 17 $1,635,200; FY 18 $1,400,000; FY 19 $1,400,000

HQ: 5275 Leesburg Pike, P.O. Box MB
Falls Church, VA 22041-3803
Phone: 703-358-1757
http://www.fws.gov/migratorybirds

RECOVERY ACT FUNDS - HABITAT ENHANCEMENT, RESTORATION AND IMPROVEMENT.
"ARRA"

Award: Cooperative Agreements

Purpose: To provide technical and financial assistance to identify, protect, conserve, manage, enhance, or restore habitat or species on both public and private lands.

Applicant Eligibility: N/A

Beneficiary Eligibility: N/A

Award Range/Average: N/A

Funding: (Cooperative Agreements (Discretionary Grants)) FY 19 est $0; FY 17 $0; FY 18 est $0; - Project Grants (Discretionary): FY 17: $0; FY 18: $0; FY 19: $0 This program is no longer active.

HQ: Department of the Interior 1849 C Street NW
Washington, DC 20240
Phone: 202-208-6394
http://www.fws.gov

DOI 15.657 ENDANGERED SPECIES CONSERVATION – RECOVERY IMPLEMENTATION FUNDS

Award: Project Grants

Purpose: To provide federal financial assistance to secure endangered or threatened species information, undertake restoration actions that will lead to delisting of a species, help prevent extinction of a species, or aid in the recovery of species.

Applicant Eligibility: State and local government agencies, institutions of higher education, including public, private, state colleges and universities, nonprofits that have a 501(c)(3) status with the IRS, Native American tribal organizations (other than recognized tribal governments), city, county or township governments, individuals, Native American tribal governments (federally-recognized), for-profit organizations, and small businesses.

Beneficiary Eligibility: N/A

Award Range/Average: Varies by Region

Funding: (Project Grants (Discretionary)) FY 17 $3,976,711; FY 19 est $0; FY 18 est $0; - Project Grants (Discretionary): FY 17 $3,976,711; FY 18 $0 (est); FY 19 $0 (est) This program uses U.S. Fish and Wildlife Service Regional and Field Office discretionary funding, if available.

HQ: Division of Restoration and Recovery 5275 Leesburg Pike, P.O. Box ES

Falls Church, VA 22041-3803

Phone: 703-358-2171

http://www.fws.gov/endangered/recovery/index.html

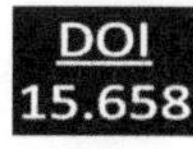

DOI 15.658 NATURAL RESOURCE DAMAGE ASSESSMENT AND RESTORATION "NRDAR"

Award: Project Grants

Purpose: To restore natural resources injured by oil spills or hazardous substance releases. The purpose of the Natural Resource Damage Assessment and Restoration (NRDAR) Program is to restore natural resources and their services that have been injured by an oil spill or hazardous substance release for the benefit of the American people.

Applicant Eligibility: Anyone/general public. Use of assistance is primarily for natural resources but also can be for public education and recreation.

Beneficiary Eligibility: Anyone/general public.

Award Range/Average: Projects may range from $1,000 to $1,000,000 or greater.

Funding: (Project Grants (Discretionary)) FY 17 $4,615,818; FY 19 est $4,000,000; FY 18 est $3,787,318; - Project Grants (Discretionary): FY 17 $4,615,818; FY 18 $3,787,318; FY 19 $4,000,000. FY 19 amount is an estimate based on prior year funding levels. These amounts are for the assessment sub-activity and are based on appropriated dollars for the DOI NRDAR Program to conduct NRDAR cases. Amounts for non-discretionary funds used for the restoration sub-activity cannot be estimated as they are dependent on NRDAR case consent decrees and court-lodged settlements and can vary widely between fiscal years.

HQ: 5275 Leesburg Pike, P.O. Box ES

Falls Church, VA 22041-3803

Phone: 703-358-2171

http://www.fws.gov/ecological-services/habitat-conservation/nrda.html

DOI 15.659 NATIONAL WILDLIFE REFUGE FUND "Refuge Revenue Sharing"

Award: Direct Payments with Unrestricted Use

Purpose: The USFWS makes revenue-sharing payments to counties for the lands that are administered.

Applicant Eligibility: No functional Application/Unlimited Application of any local unit of government where fee owned NWRS lands are located automatically receive payments based on legislated formulas.

Beneficiary Eligibility: Same as Applicant Eligibility.

Award Range/Average: No Data Available.

Funding: (Direct Payments with Unrestricted Use) FY 17 $0; FY 19 est $0; FY 18 est $0; - Direct Payments: FY 17: $0; FY 18: $0; FY 19: $0 This program is no longer active.

HQ: Division of Realty U S Fish and Wildlife Service Department of the Interior MS NWRS, 5275 Leesburg Pike

Falls Church, VA 22041-3803

Phone: 703-358-1713

Email: a_eric_alvarez@fws.gov

http://www.fws.gov/refuges/realty/rrs.html

DOI 15.660 ENDANGERED SPECIES – CANDIDATE CONSERVATION ACTION FUNDS

Award: Project Grants

Purpose: To provide a means by which the ecosystems upon which candidate and at-risk species depend may be conserved.

Applicant Eligibility: Natural Resources

Beneficiary Eligibility: Anyone/general public

Award Range/Average: Varies by Region

Funding: (Cooperative Agreements (Discretionary Grants)) FY 17 $406,000; FY 19 est $0; FY 18 est $0; - Project Grants (Discretionary): FY 17 $406,000; FY 18 $0 (est); FY 19 $0 (est) This funding opportunity uses U.S. Fish and Wildlife Service Regional and Field Office discretionary funding, if available.

HQ: Branch of Communications and Candidate Conservation 5275 Leesburg Pike, P.O. Box ES

Falls Church, VA 22041-3803

Phone: 703-358-2171

DOI 15.661 LOWER SNAKE RIVER COMPENSATION PLAN "LSRCP"

Award: Cooperative Agreements

Purpose: To mitigate for the losses of fish and wildlife caused by the U.S. Army Corps of Engineers while constructing four hydroelectric dams on the lower Snake River.

Applicant Eligibility: Natural Resources (mineral, water, wildlife, land)

Beneficiary Eligibility: Anyone/general public; 49 - Farmer/Rancher/Agriculture Producer

Award Range/Average: Range $274,268 to $5,609,594

Funding: (Cooperative Agreements (Discretionary Grants)) FY 18 est $33,483,000; FY 19 est $33,483,000; FY 17 $32,949,000; - Cooperative Agreements (Discretionary): FY 17 $32,949,000; FY 18 $33,483,000; FY 19 estimate $33,483,000.

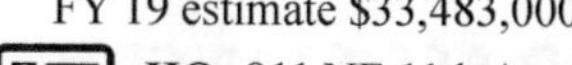

HQ: 911 NE 11th Avenue
Portland, OR 97232
Phone: 503-231-2763
http://www.fws.gov/lsnakecomplan

GREAT LAKES RESTORATION "Great Lakes Restoration Initiative; Great Lakes Restoration Program"

Award: Project Grants

Purpose: To provide technical and financial aid to enforce the highest priority actions in order to protect and restore the Great Lakes.

Applicant Eligibility: Program-specific.

Beneficiary Eligibility: Same as Applicant Eligibility.

Award Range/Average: Projects may range from $1,000 to $1,000,000, or greater.

Funding: (Project Grants (Discretionary)) FY 19 est $42,140,933; FY 17 $41,794,404; FY 18 est $42,140,933; - Project Grants (Discretionary): FY 17 $41,794,404; FY 18 $42,140,933; FY 19 $42,140,933 FY 18 and FY 19 amounts are estimates based on prior year funding levels.

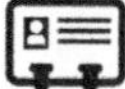

HQ: Department of the Interior 1849 C Street NW
Washington, DC 20240
Phone: 202-208-6394
Email: katie_steiger-meister@fws.gov
http://www.fws.gov/glri

NATIONAL FISH AND WILDLIFE FOUNDATION "NFWF"

Award: Project Grants

Purpose: National Fish and Wildlife Foundation provides grants to recipients who work to conserve and protect fish and wildlife species and their habitats.

Applicant Eligibility: Specified in the National Fish and Wildlife Foundation Establishment Act.

Beneficiary Eligibility: Beneficiaries include fish, wildlife and their habitats, the American people and, where applicable, international partners, wildlife and natural resources.

Award Range/Average: N/A

Funding: (Project Grants) FY 17 $7,022,000; FY 18 est $5,009,000; FY 19 est $0; - Project Grants: FY 17 $7,022,000; FY 18 est $5,009,000; FY 19 est N/A

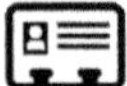

HQ: 5275 Leesburg Pike
Falls Church, VA 22041-3803
Phone: 703-358-2156
http://www.nfwf.org

FISH AND WILDLIFE COORDINATION AND ASSISTANCE "FWCA"

Award: Project Grants

Purpose: To implement legislation mandating specific conservation and/or environmental project activity(ies), including, but not limited to, financial assistance funding for special appropriations projects to a designated recipient(s); and/or unfunded Congressional mandates.

Applicant Eligibility: Eligibility is limited to entity(ies) designated by the authorizing legislation.

Beneficiary Eligibility: The general public benefits from the conservation and environmental efforts as identified by the authorizing legislation.

Award Range/Average: Range and average varies by program activity.

Funding: (Project Grants (Discretionary)) FY 19 est $10,750,000; FY 18 est $10,750,000; FY 17 $3,118,839; - Project Grants (Discretionary): FY 17 $3,118,839.18 awarded; FY 18 est $10,750,000; FY 19 est $10,750,000.

HQ: Policy Branch Financial Assistance Support and Oversight Division 5275 Leesburg Pike, P.O. Box WSFR
Falls Church, VA 22041-3803
Phone: 703-358-2701

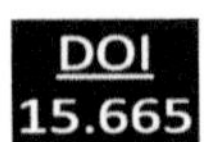

NATIONAL WETLANDS INVENTORY "NWI"

Award: Project Grants

Purpose: For mapping wetlands of the nation, digitizing the maps, archiving and distributing the data, and producing a ten-year national wetlands status and trends report to the Congress.

Applicant Eligibility: Organizations receiving financial assistance must be experienced in image-interpretation for wetlands and for arid western riparian for targeted ecosystems using National standards (Cowardin et al. 1979 and Wetlands Mapping Standard 2009); in wetlands mapping or delivery research or technologies, or in supporting activities (e.

Beneficiary Eligibility: The American public, and Federal, State, Tribal, Territorial, and local agencies, profit and nonprofit corporations or institutions benefit from having wetlands geospatial data to help inform decision making for clean water, fish and wildlife conservation, wetlands conservation, landscape-level planning, green infrastructure, and urban, rural, infrastructure, and energy development.

Award Range/Average: $30,000- $532,000

Funding: (Project Grants (Discretionary)) FY 17 $400,000; FY 18 est $50,000; FY 19 est $50,000; - Project Grants (Discretionary): FY 17 $400,000; FY 18 $50,000; FY 19 $50,000 FY 18 and FY 19 amounts are estimated on prior year average amounts

HQ: 5275 Leesburg Pike
Falls Church, VA 22041-3803
Phone: 703-358-2171
http://www.fws.gov/wetlands

ENDANGERED SPECIES CONSERVATION-WOLF LIVESTOCK LOSS COMPENSATION AND PREVENTION
"Wolf Livestock Demonstration Project Grant Program"

Award: Project Grants

Purpose: To reduce the risk of livestock loss due to wolf attacks, and to compensate livestock manufacturers for the losses due to such predation.

Applicant Eligibility: State governments/agencies Indian tribes as defined in Public Law111-11

Beneficiary Eligibility: Individual/ Family Small Business Profit Organization Private Organization Anyone/ General Public Farmer/ Rancher/ Agricultural Producer Small Business Person Land/ Property Owner

Award Range/Average: $9,000 - $100,000. Average grant award amount is $50,000.

Funding: (Project Grants (Discretionary)) FY 19 est $900,000; FY 18 est $900,000; FY 17 $900,000; - Project Grants (Discretionary): FY 17 $900,000 (est); FY 18 $900,000 (est); FY 19 $900,000 (est).

HQ: Division of Restoration and Recovery 5275 Leesburg Pike, P.O. Box ES
Falls Church, VA 22041-3803
Phone: 703-358-2171
http://www.fws.gov/endangered/grants/index.html

HIGHLANDS CONSERVATION

Award: Project Grants

Purpose: To preserve and protect high-priority conservation land in the Highland regions by conserving priority lands and natural resources and recognizing the importance of the water, forest, agricultural, wildlife, recreational, and cultural resources.

Applicant Eligibility: Any state or state agency with authority to own and manage land located within the Highlands region for conservation purposes may apply by identifying the source of non-Federal funds, describing the management objectives for the project land, identifying the purpose of the use of the land, and providing that the land will not be converted, used or disposed of for a purpose inconsistent with land conservation.

Beneficiary Eligibility: Beneficiaries are states or state agencies with authority to own and manage land within the Highlands region for conservation purposes, including the Palisades Interstate Park Commission.

Award Range/Average: Range : $646,600 to $1,940,000; Average $970,000

Funding: (Project Grants (Discretionary)) FY 17 $4,840,000; FY 18 est $0; FY 19 est $0; - Project Grants (Discretionary): FY 17 $4,840,000; FY 18 Unknown; FY 19 Unknown.

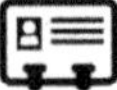

HQ: Wildlife and Sport Fish Restoration 300 West gate Center Drive
Hadley, MA 1035
Phone: 413-253-8501
Email: colleen_sculley@fws.gov
http://www.fws.gov/r5fedaid/index.html

DOI 15.668 COASTAL IMPACT ASSISTANCE "CIAP"

Award: Formula Grants

Purpose: To disburse funding to entitled producing States and coastal political subdivisions for the purpose of conservation, protection, or restoration of coastal areas.

Applicant Eligibility: States eligible to receive funding are Alabama, Alaska, California, Louisiana, Mississippi, and Texas and 67 coastal political subdivisions among the six States.

Beneficiary Eligibility: The producing coastal states, their eligible coastal political subdivisions, and the public will ultimately benefit from the program.

Award Range/Average: $20,000 - $20,000,000; average $1,000,000

Funding: (Formula Grants) FY 17 $7,114,625; FY 18 est $0; FY 19 est $0; - Project Grants (Discretionary): FY 17: $7,114,625.87; FY 18: $0; FY 19: $0 FY 17 was the last active year for this program.

HQ: 5275 Leesburg Pike, P.O. Box WSFR
Falls Church, VA 22041-3803
Phone: 703-358-2156
http://wsfrprograms.fws.gov/subpages/grantprograms/ciap/ciap.htm

DOI 15.669 COOPERATIVE LANDSCAPE CONSERVATION "Landscape Conservation Cooperatives (LCCs)"

Award: Project Grants

Purpose: No awards anticipated.

Applicant Eligibility: N/A

Beneficiary Eligibility: N/A

Award Range/Average: Range is $1,000 - $1,000,000. Average award amount varies by project type and duration.

Funding: (Project Grants (Discretionary)) FY 18 est $0; FY 19 est $0; FY 17 $1,630,963; - Project Grants (Discretionary): FY 17 $1,630,963; FY 18 $0; FY 19 $0 No new funding for this program is expected. CFDA should remain active through FY 19 to allow Bureau to close all currently open awards.

HQ: Science Applications US Fish and Wildlife Service Department of the Interior 5275 Leesburg Pike, P.O. Box SA
Falls Church, VA 22041-3803
Phone: 703-358-1881
Email: anna-marie_york@fws.gov
http://lccnetwork.org

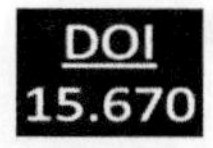

ADAPTIVE SCIENCE

Award: Project Grants

Purpose: Strategic Habitat Conservation is based on the principles of adaptive management and uses population and habitat data, ecological models, and focused monitoring and assessment efforts to develop and utilize strategies that result in measurable fish and wildlife population outcomes. It uses the best available scientific information to predict how fish and wildlife populations will respond to changes in the environment.

Applicant Eligibility: N/A

Beneficiary Eligibility: N/A

Award Range/Average: Range is $1,000 - $1,000,000. Average award amount varies by project type and duration.

Funding: (Project Grants (Discretionary)) FY 17 $744,977; FY 18 est $2,300,000; FY 19 est $2,300,000; - Project Grants (Discretionary): FY 17 $744,977; FY 18 $2,300,000; FY 19 $2,300,0000 FY 18 and FY 19 amounts are estimates based on prior year funding levels.

HQ: Department of the Interior 5275 Leesburg Pike, P.O. Box SA

Falls Church, VA 22041-3803

Phone: 703-358-1881

Email: anna-marie_york@fws.gov

http://www.fws.gov/science

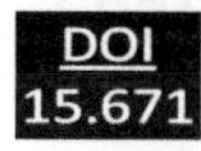

YUKON RIVER SALMON RESEARCH AND MANAGEMENT ASSISTANCE
"R&M Fund"

Award: Project Grants

Purpose: Yukon River Salmon Research and Management Assistance funds projects that increase/improve the understanding of research and management of Yukon River salmon.

Applicant Eligibility: The intended result of this funding is to improve the understanding of the biology and management of Yukon River salmon species.

Beneficiary Eligibility: Projects that are awarded money from this source will ultimately benefit the rural and urban American and Canadian public that subsist off of the salmon resources of the Yukon River.

Award Range/Average: Range: $3,000-220,456; Average: $40,756

Funding: (Project Grants (Discretionary)) FY 17 $260,000; FY 18 est $260,000; FY 16 $260,000; FY 19 est $260,000; - Project Grants (Discretionary): FY 17 $260,000; FY 18 $260,000; FY 19 $260,000. FY 18 and FY 19 funding amounts are estimates based on prior year funding levels.

HQ: 1011 E Street Tudor Road

Anchorage, AK 99503

Phone: 907-786-3523

http://alaska.fws.gov/fisheries/fieldoffice/fairbanks/index.htm

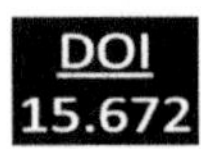

WILDLIFE WITHOUT BORDERS – AMPHIBIANS IN DECLINE

Award: Project Grants

Purpose: To provide funding for specific conservation actions to amphibian species facing imminent threat of extinction.

Applicant Eligibility: Applications may be submitted by any non-domestic (outside of the United States) government agency responsible for amphibian conservation and any other U.S.-based or non-domestic public or private organization or institution or individual with demonstrated experience in amphibian conservation.

Beneficiary Eligibility: Non-domestic (outside of the United States) government agencies responsible for amphibian conservation and any other U.S.-based or non-domestic public or private non-governmental organization or institution or individual with demonstrated experience in amphibian conservation.

Award Range/Average: N/A

Funding: (Project Grants (Discretionary)) FY 19 est $0; FY 18 est $0; FY 17 $4,972; - Project Grants (Discretionary): FY 17 $4,972.50; FY 18 $0; FY 19 $0.

HQ: Division of International Conservation 5275 Leesburg Pike, P.O. Box IA

Falls Church, VA 22041-3803

Phone: 703-358-1754

http://www.fws.gov/international/wildlife-without-borders/amphibians-in-decline.html

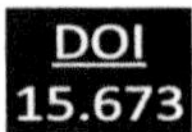

WILDLIFE WITHOUT BORDERS – CRITICALLY ENDANGERED ANIMAL CONSERVATION FUND

Award: Project Grants

Purpose: To reduce threats to highly endangered wildlife in their natural habitat. The proposals should identify specific conservation actions that have a high likelihood of creating durable benefits.

Applicant Eligibility: Applications may be submitted by any non-domestic (outside of the United States) government agency responsible for endangered species conservation and any other U.S.-based or non-domestic public or private organization or institution or individual with demonstrated experience in endangered species conservation.

Beneficiary Eligibility: Non-domestic (outside of the United States) government agencies responsible for endangered species conservation and any other U.S.-based or non-domestic public or private non-governmental organization or institution or individual with demonstrated experience in endangered species conservation.

Award Range/Average: N/A

Funding: (Project Grants (Discretionary)) FY 19 est $0; FY 18 est $0; FY 17 $0; - Project Grants (Discretionary): FY 17: $0; FY 18: $0; FY 19: $0

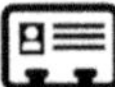

HQ: Division of International Conservation 5275 Leesburg Pike, P.O. Box IA

Falls Church, VA 22041-3803

Phone: 703-358-1754

http://www.fws.gov/international/wildlife-without-borders/critically-endangered-animals-conservation-fund.html

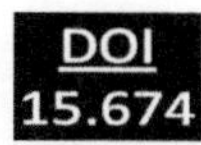

DOI 15.674 NATIONAL FIRE PLAN-WILDLAND URBAN INTERFACE COMMUNITY FIRE ASSISTANCE

Award: Cooperative Agreements; Use of Property, Facilities, and Equipment; Provision of Specialized Services; Advisory Services and Counseling; Dissemination of Technical Information; Training

Purpose: To utilize the National Cohesive Wildland Fire Management Strategy and aid communities at risk from catastrophic wildland fires.

Applicant Eligibility: State and local governments and communities at risk and communities of interest.

Beneficiary Eligibility: State and local governments and communities at risk and communities of interest, as published in the Federal Register or updated Governor-signed list, Indian Tribes, private land owners, public and private education institutions, and nonprofit organizations that manage lands. All selectees must be identified as significant to FWS.

Award Range/Average: No Data Available.

Funding: (Cooperative Agreements (Discretionary Grants)) FY 18 est $200,000; FY 17 $0; FY 19 est $300,000; - Cooperative Agreements (Discretionary Grants): FY 17 $0; FY 18 est $200,000; FY 19 est $300,000

HQ: 3833 S Development Avenue
Boise, ID 83705
Phone: 208-387-5941
http://www.fws.gov/fire

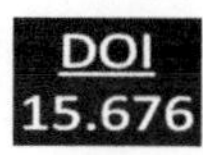

DOI 15.676 YOUTH ENGAGEMENT, EDUCATION, AND EMPLOYMENT "YEEEP"

Award: Project Grants

Purpose: To provide experiential, education, and employment program opportunities for youth to participate in conservation activities conducted by the U.S. Fish and Wildlife Service, and/or in collaboration with other Department of the Interior bureaus, and thereby promoting intra-agency and external partnership and employment opportunities.

Applicant Eligibility: Applicants may be state agencies, local governments, Tribal organizations, interstate, Intrastate, public nonprofit institution/organization, other public institution/organization, private nonprofit/ organization, or any other organization subject to the jurisdiction of the United States with interests that support the mission of the Service.

Beneficiary Eligibility: Same as Applicant Eligibility.

Award Range/Average: $750 - $200,000

Funding: (Project Grants (Discretionary)) FY 18 est $8,900,000; FY 19 est $8,900,000; FY 17 $8,921,113; - Project Grants (Discretionary): FY 17 $8,921,113; FY 18 $8,900,000; FY 19 $8,900,000

HQ: 5275 Leesburg Pike
Falls Church, VA 22041-3803
Phone: 703-358-2386
Email: deborah_moore@fws.gov
http://www.fws.gov

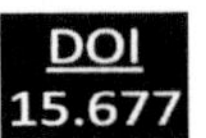

HURRICANE SANDY DISASTER RELIEF ACTIVITIES-FWS

Award: Project Grants

Purpose: To provide technical and financial assistance to identify, protect, conserve, manage, improve, or reconstruct habitat and structures on both public and private lands that have been impacted by Hurricane Sandy.

Applicant Eligibility: Awards may be made to State/Local Governments, Indian Tribal Governments, Non-Profits, Institutes of Higher Education, Hospitals and For-Profit companies.

Beneficiary Eligibility: These projects will directly benefit the public as a whole.

Award Range/Average: Newly established program

Funding: Project Grants (Discretionary) FY 17 $869,857; FY 19 est $0; FY 18 est $5,000,000; Project Grants (Discretionary): FY 17 $832,982 plus $36,875 for Student Conservation Association (SCA); FY 18 $5,000,000, no SCA anticipated in FY 18; FY 19 $0

HQ: 300 West gate Center Drive
Hadley, MA 1035
Phone: 413-253-8243

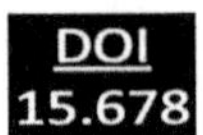

COOPERATIVE ECOSYSTEM STUDIES UNITS "CESU"

Award: Cooperative Agreements

Purpose: To provide scientific research, technical assistance, and education on natural and cultural resource issues to federal land management, environmental, and research agencies.

Applicant Eligibility: Same as Beneficiary Eligibility.

Beneficiary Eligibility: University faculty; federal employees by accessing increased opportunities for interdisciplinary, multi-agency research projects related to federal resource management issues; any entity which may, will, or can benefit from the contemplated activity; students, researchers, experts, and instructors as members of the general public.

Award Range/Average: $20,000 - $150,000 ($85,000)

Funding: (Project Grants (Discretionary)) FY 19 est $4,000,000; FY 17 $4,970,500; FY 18 est $4,000,000; - Project Grants (Discretionary): FY 17 $4,970,500; FY 18 $4,000,000; FY 19 $4,000,000.

HQ: 5275 Leesburg Pike, P.O. Box SA
Falls Church, VA 22041-3803
Phone: 703-358-1881
Email: anna-marie_york@fws.gov
http://www.fws.gov/science/cesu.html

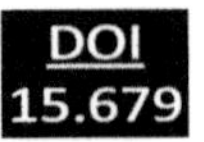

COMBATING WILDLIFE TRAFFICKING

Award: Project Grants

Purpose: Combating Wildlife Trafficking program funds projects that helps to advance counter-wildlife trafficking activities.

Applicant Eligibility: N/A

Beneficiary Eligibility: Non-domestic (outside of the United States) government agencies responsible for combating wildlife trafficking and any other U.S.- based or non-domestic public or private non-governmental organization or institution or individual with demonstrated experience in the activities proposed.

Award Range/Average: 10 awards for $100,000 or less each to be used for projects lasting one year.

Funding: (Project Grants (Discretionary)) FY 18 est $4,850,000; FY 17 $4,866,038; FY 19 est $4,850,000; - Project Grants (Discretionary): FY 17 $4,866,038.17; FY 18 $4,850,000; FY 19 $4,850,000 FY 18 and FY 19 amounts are estimates based on prior year funding levels.

HQ: Headquarters Office Division of International Conservation 5275 Leesburg Pike, P.O. Box IA
Falls Church, VA 22041
Phone: 703-358-2379
http://www.fws.gov/international/grants-and-reporting/how-to-apply.html

MEXICAN WOLF RECOVERY

Award: Project Grants

Purpose: To provide federal financial assistance to secure Mexican Wolf information, initiate actions that will lead to delisting of the Mexican Wolf, and help prevent extinction or aid in the recovery of the Mexican Wolf.

Applicant Eligibility: State and local government agencies; Institutions of higher education, including public, private state colleges and universities; nonprofits that have 501(c)(3) status with the IRS; Native American tribal organizations (other than recognized tribal governments); city, county or township governments; individuals; Native American tribal governments (federally-recognized); for-profit organizations; and small businesses.

Beneficiary Eligibility: Same as Applicant Eligibility.

Award Range/Average: 0 to $250,000; Average $78,571

Funding: (Project Grants (Discretionary)) FY 17 $554,143; FY 18 est $580,000; FY 19 est $0; - Project Grants (Discretionary): FY 17 $554,143; FY 18 est $580,000; FY 19 Data N/A

HQ: 500 Gold Avenue SW
Albuquerque, NM 87102
Phone: 505-248-6477
http://www.fws.gov/southwest/es/mexicanwolf

COOPERATIVE AGRICULTURE

Award: Use of Property, Facilities, and Equipment

Purpose: To produce or modify specific cover types and/or growing methods to meet the life history requirements of species and produce foods for wildlife species.

Applicant Eligibility: Applicants must be private individuals or small business entities.

Beneficiary Eligibility: Selected cooperators who conduct cooperative agriculture on NWRS lands under this program, excluding coordination areas (which are areas managed by the Service in coordination with the States).

Award Range/Average: $0. This is a nonfinancial assistance program.

Funding: N/A

HQ: National Wildlife Refuge System Headquarters
Falls Church, VA 22041-3803
Phone: 703-358-2678
Email: aaron_mize@fws.gov
http://www.fws.gov/refuges

U.S. GEOLOGICAL SURVEY

Menlo Park, CA 94025 415-650-5102

California

Administrative Officer, WR 345 Middlefield Road, MS-919

Alan M. Mikuni | 345 Middlefield Road, MS-531, Menlo Park, CA 94025-3591 415-329-4254

T. John Conomos, Regional Hydrologist | 345 Middlefield Road, MS-470, Menlo Park, CA 94025-3591 415-329-4414

Colorado

Administrative Officer, CR Federal Center, MS 911, Denver, CO 80225 303-236-5435

Dave J. Lystrom, Regional Hydrologist | Mail Stop 406, Box 25046 Denver Federal Center, Building 25, Lakewood, CO 80225-0046 303-236-5950, Ext. 0

Dr. J. Larry Ludke, Regional Chief Biologist | DFC Building, 020, Room A1419 P.O. Box 25046, MS 300, Denver, CO 80225 303-236-2739, 238

Randle W. Olsen | Denver Federal Center, Building 810, Mail Stop 508, P.O. Box 25046, Denver, CO 80225-0046 303-202-4040

Georgia

Wanda C. Meeks, Regional Hydrologist | Spalding Woods Office Park, Suite 160 3850 Holcomb Bridge Road, Norcross, GA 30092-2202 404-409-7701

Missouri

Max Ethridge | 1400 Independence Road, Mail Stop 300, Rolla, MO 65401 573-308-3800

South Dakota

Donald T. Lauer | Mundt Federal Building, Sioux Falls, SD 57198 605-594-6123

Virginia

953 National Center, Reston, VA 20192 703-648-6662

Pat Dunham | National Center, MS-567, Reston, VA 20192 703-648-6002

William Carswell, Regional Hydrologist | 433 National Center, Mail Stop 433, Reston, VA 22092 703-648-5813

Washington

Dr. John D. Buffington, Regional Chief Biologist | 909 First Avenue, Suite 800, Seattle, WA 98104 206-220-4600

West Virginia

Mr. Gregory Smith, Acting Regional Chief | Biologist National Center, Room 4A100 12201 Sunrise Valley Drive, MS 300, Reston, VA 20192 703-648-4060

ASSISTANCE TO STATE WATER RESOURCES RESEARCH INSTITUTES

"Water Research Institute Program"

Award: Formula Grants; Project Grants

Purpose: Providing financial assistance to Water Resources Research Institutes located at designated State universities.

Applicant Eligibility: One University Water Research Institute is authorized in each State and other jurisdictions specified in Section 104. Other colleges and universities within a State are encouraged to participate in the program in cooperation with the designated Institute.

Beneficiary Eligibility: Researchers at qualified universities and colleges in the State through the designated Institute for the State.

Award Range/Average: (Formula Grants) $92,335 to $277,005; average $95,755. (Competitive Grants) $140,162 to $249,949; average $212,950.

Funding: (Cooperative Agreements (Discretionary Grants)) FY 18 est $6,200,000; FY 17 $6,200,000; FY 19 est $6,200,000

HQ: Department of the Interior Office of External Research 5522 Research Park Drive
Baltimore, MD 21228
Phone: 443-498-5505
Email: eagreene@usgs.gov
http://water.usgs.gov/wrri

DOI 15.807 EARTHQUAKE HAZARDS PROGRAM ASSISTANCE "Earthquake Hazards Program Grants"

Award: Project Grants

Purpose: To support earthquake hazards research and monitoring and develop information, knowledge, and methods relevant to the major Earthquake Hazards Program elements.

Applicant Eligibility: Public and private colleges and universities; Non-profit, non-academic organizations; For-profit organizations; State and Local Governments; and unaffiliated scientists.

Beneficiary Eligibility: Research scientists, engineers, and the general public will ultimately benefit from the program.

Award Range/Average: $6,000 to $1,340,000; average $74,000.

Funding: (Cooperative Agreements (Discretionary Grants)) FY 19 est $16,999,000; FY 18 est $16,999,000; FY 17 $16,999,000; - FY 18 and FY 19 amounts are estimates based on prior year funding levels only.

HQ: Department of the Interior National Center 12201 Sunrise Valley Drive, P.O. Box 905
Reston, VA 20192
Phone: 703-648-6716
Email: jfranks@usgs.gov
http://earthquake.usgs.gov/research/external

DOI 15.808 U.S. GEOLOGICAL SURVEY RESEARCH AND DATA COLLECTION

Award: Cooperative Agreements

Purpose: To support research in classification of the public lands and examination of the geological structure, water, mineral, and biological resources, and products of the national domain.

Applicant Eligibility: Profit organizations, public nonprofit institutions/organizations, private nonprofit institutions/organizations, and State and local governments may make application for support by a named principal investigator. Due to limited availability of funds to support new external projects, consultation with USGS is strongly recommended prior to submission of applications.

Beneficiary Eligibility: Profit organizations, public nonprofit institutions/organizations, private nonprofit institutions/organizations, and State and local governments, industry and public decision makers, research scientists, engineers, and the general public will ultimately benefit from knowledge gained under the program.

Award Range/Average: Range: $1,000 to $933,000; average $56,650

Funding: (Cooperative Agreements (Discretionary Grants)) FY 17 $14,681,264; FY 18 est $14,000,000; FY 19 est $14,000,000.

HQ:

Reston, VA 20192

Phone: 703-648-4582

Email: lmahoney@usgs.gov

http://www.usgs.gov/contracts

NATIONAL COOPERATIVE GEOLOGIC MAPPING "StateMap and EdMap"

Award: Cooperative Agreements

Purpose: To create geologic maps of areas where the knowledge of geology is important to the economic, social, or scientific welfare of individual states.

Applicant Eligibility: State Map program is restricted by statue to State geological surveys. Where State surveys are organized under a State university system, an application may be submitted by a State college or university on behalf of the State geological survey.

Beneficiary Eligibility: State geological surveys participating in this program and the general public will ultimately benefit from this program.

Award Range/Average: State Map: $8,000 to $364,442; proposal average $115,064. EdMap: $5,572 to $10,948 per student; average per student $7,971. The maximum award allowed per graduate student is $17,500 and $10,000 per undergraduate student.

Funding: (Cooperative Agreements (Discretionary Grants)) FY 17 $5,982,437; FY 19 est $5,982,437; FY 18 est $5,982,437; - FY 18 and FY 19 amounts are estimates based on prior year funding levels.

HQ: 12201 Sunrise Valley Drive

Reston, VA 20192

Phone: 703-648-6973

Email: dmcphee@usgs.gov

http://www.ncgmp.usgs.gov

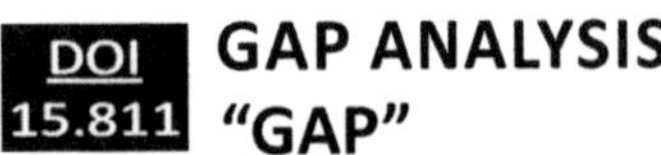

GAP ANALYSIS "GAP"

Award: Cooperative Agreements

Purpose: To document where native animal species and natural plant communities occur and identify gaps in their representation to assist preservation of diverseness.

Applicant Eligibility: Profit organizations, public nonprofit institutions/organizations, private nonprofit institutions/organizations, and State and local governments may make application for support by a named principal investigator.

Beneficiary Eligibility: Same as Applicant Eligibility.

Award Range/Average: Range: $50,000 to $250,000; average $125,000

Funding: (Cooperative Agreements (Discretionary Grants)) FY 18 est $400,000; FY 19 est $400,000; FY 17 $250,000

HQ: Forest and Rangeland Ecosystem Science Center - Snake River Field Station 970 Lusk Avenue
Boise, ID 83706
Phone: 208-426-5219
Email: gergely@usgs.gov
http://gapanalysis.usgs.gov

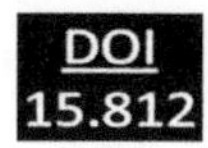

COOPERATIVE RESEARCH UNITS "CRUP"

Award: Cooperative Agreements

Purpose: To work in partnership with States and universities to address the information requirements of local, state, and federal fish, wildlife, and natural resource agencies via research, technical assistance, and education.

Applicant Eligibility: Universities hosting Cooperative Fish and Wildlife Research Units established under authority of the Cooperative Research Units Act of 1960.

Beneficiary Eligibility: Federal, State and local governments, industry and public decision makers, research scientists, State institutions of higher education, and the general public will ultimately benefit from the program.

Award Range/Average: $5,000 to $721,603; average $52,081.

Funding: (Cooperative Agreements (Discretionary Grants)) FY 19 est $12,000,000; FY 17 $11,305,814; FY 18 est $12,000,000.

HQ: Cooperative Research Units 12201 Sunrise Valley Drive, P.O. Box 303
Reston, VA 20192
Email: jthompson@usgs.gov
http://www.coopunits.org

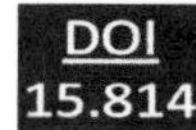

NATIONAL GEOLOGICAL AND GEOPHYSICAL DATA PRESERVATION

Award: Project Grants

Purpose: To preserve and provide access to geological, geophysical, and engineering samples extracted from the earth to inform science and decision-making.

Applicant Eligibility: State geological surveys are eligible to apply. For State geological surveys organized under a State university system, such universities may submit a proposal on behalf of or through the State geological survey.

Beneficiary Eligibility: Research scientists, engineers, and the general public will ultimately benefit from the program.

Award Range/Average: $10,209 to $79,472; average is $37,042.

Funding: Project Grants (Discretionary) FY 19 est $950,000; FY 18 est $1,029,690; FY 17 $968,583

HQ: P.O. Box 25046
Denver, CO 80225
Phone: 302-202-4828
Email: lpowers@usgs.gov
http://datapreservation.usgs.gov/index.shtml

DOI 15.815 NATIONAL LAND REMOTE SENSING EDUCATION OUTREACH AND RESEARCH
"National Cooperative Geographic Information System"

Award: Project Grants

Purpose: To encourage the uses of space-based land remote sensing data and technologies through educational activity and outreach.

Applicant Eligibility: Nonprofit organizations, Public and Private colleges and universities, and State and local governments may make an application for support by a named principal investigator.

Beneficiary Eligibility: States, research scientists, engineers, education (0-13+) and the general public will ultimately benefit from the program.

Award Range/Average: $1,217,400 to $1,217,400; average $1,217,400.

Funding: (Project Grants (Discretionary)) FY 17 $378,100; FY 18 est $1,250,000; FY 19 est $1,250,000; - Grants: Actual FY 17 $378,100; Estimated FY 18 $1,250,000; Estimated FY 19 $1,250,000. Funding amount in FY 17 reflects the conclusion of a 5-year competitive grant capped at $5 million over 5 years. FY 18 estimate reflects the anticipation of a newly awarded 5-year competitive grant. FY 19 funding is subject to the availability of funds.

HQ: 516 National Center
Reston, VA 20192
Phone: 703-648-5551
Email: tcecere@usgs.gov
http://www.usgs.gov

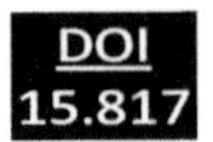

NATIONAL GEOSPATIAL PROGRAM: BUILDING THE NATIONAL MAP
"The National Map"

Award: Cooperative Agreements

Purpose: To encourage the uses of space-based land remote sensing data and technologies through educational activity and outreach.

Applicant Eligibility: Proposals from State, Local, Interstate, Federally or State recognized Indian Tribal Governments, US Territories and Possessions, Institutions of Higher Education, Private Foundations, and Nonprofit Organizations are invited. Due to limited availability of funding to support new external projects, consultation with the U.S. Geological Survey (USGS) is strongly recommended prior to submission of applications.

Beneficiary Eligibility: Interstate, State, intrastate, and local government agencies, educational institutions, private firms, private foundations, nonprofit organizations, Federally-acknowledged or state-recognized Native American tribes or groups, U.S. territories and possessions, public decision makers, research scientists, engineers, graduate students, students/trainees, and the general public will ultimately benefit from knowledge gained under the program.

Award Range/Average: $25,000 to $770,500; average $134,682.

Funding: (Cooperative Agreements (Discretionary Grants)) FY 17 $2,350,000; FY 18 est $3,563,000; FY 19 est $0

HQ: P.O. Box 25046
Reston, VA 20192
Phone: 703-648-5519
Email: lpalmer@usgs.gov
http://www.nationalmap.gov

VOLCANO HAZARDS PROGRAM RESEARCH AND MONITORING
"Volcano Hazards Program"

Award: Cooperative Agreements

Purpose: To improve the scientific understanding of volcanic processes and to decrease the harmful impacts of volcanic activity. The Volcano Hazards Program (VHP) provides domestic assistance to expand the expertise and capabilities applied to fulfilling its mission.

Applicant Eligibility: N/A

Beneficiary Eligibility: N/A

Award Range/Average: $20,000 to $2,000,000; average $250,000.

Funding: (Cooperative Agreements) FY 18 est $3,500,000; FY 19 est $370,000; FY 17 $3,344,444

HQ: 3A204 National Center
Reston, VA 20192
Phone: 703-648-4773
Email: cmandeville@usgs.gov
http://volcanoes.usgs.gov

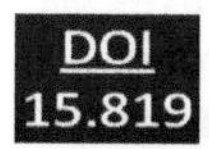

ENERGY COOPERATIVES TO SUPPORT THE NATIONAL ENERGY RESOURCES DATA SYSTEM
"NCRDS"

Award: Cooperative Agreements

Purpose: To collect, interpret, correlate, and assess energy-related data that support USGS Energy Resources Program research initiatives, to build and maintain national energy databases of, to conduct energy-related research and conduct resource assessments within the United States.

Applicant Eligibility: Applicants can be affiliated (but are not required to be affiliated) with State agencies, universities, Tribal governments or organizations. Applications must have the ability to conduct research consistent with the Energy Resources Program goals.

Beneficiary Eligibility: Research scientists, their agencies, and ultimately the general public will benefit from the program.

Award Range/Average: $15,000- $26,000; average $15,190.

Funding: (Cooperative Agreements (Discretionary Grants)) FY 19 est $15,000; FY 18 est $15,000; FY 17 $15,000; - USGS Energy Resources Program (ERP) reduced grant amount from 300,000 to 15,000 for rest of 5 year cycle.

HQ: Department of the Interior National Center 12201 Sunrise Valley Drive

Reston, VA 20192

Phone: 703-648-6450

Email: jeast@usgs.gov

http://energy.er.usgs.gov/coal_quality/state_coops

NATIONAL AND REGIONAL CLIMATE ADAPTATION SCIENCE CENTERS "NRCASC"

Award: Cooperative Agreements

Purpose: To provide national and regional habitat and population modeling and forecasting tools, integrating physical climate models with ecological models, assessing vulnerabilities and forecasting changes, and developing standardized approaches.

Applicant Eligibility: There are eight (8) DOI CSCs; each CSC has a single "Host Institution" that is eligible to apply on behalf of themselves and members of the CSC university consortium: Alaska CSC: University of Alaska, Fairbanks; Southeast CSC: North Carolina State University, Raleigh; Northwest CSC: Oregon State University, Corvallis; Southwest CSC: University of Arizona, Tucson; North Central CSC: Colorado State University, Ft. Collins; South Central CSC: Oklahoma University, Norman; Northeast CSC: University of Massachusetts, Amherst; Pacific Islands CSC: University of Hawaii, Manoa.

Beneficiary Eligibility: Research scientists, policy makers, natural resource managers, educators, and the general public will benefit from the program.

Award Range/Average: The range for individual DOI CSCs financial assistance awards (individual projects) is up to $1,000,000 in FY 2016.

Funding: (Cooperative Agreements (Discretionary Grants)) FY 17 $6,500,000; FY 18 est $6,500,000; FY 19 est $6,500,000; - Recipients request payment as needed throughout the award period. Obligations for the climate change science projects will be made under the NCCWSC and DOI CSC program activity via grants or cooperative agreement awards through the USGS Office of Acquisitions and Grants (OAG).

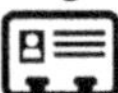

HQ: 12201 Sunrise Valley Drive

Reston, VA 20192

Phone: 703-648-4607

Email: nhartke@usgs.gov

http://nccwsc.usgs.gov

UPPER MISSISSIPPI RIVER RESTORATION LONG TERM RESOURCE MONITORING "LTRM"

Award: Cooperative Agreements

Purpose: To supply decision makers with information needed to maintain the Upper Mississippi River System (UMRS) as a sustainable large-river ecosystem.

Applicant Eligibility: State agencies stipulated in the Water Resources Development Act of 1986 (Public Law 99-662) are eligible to apply.

Beneficiary Eligibility: UMRS State, Federal, and private natural resource managers, users, and the general public.

Award Range/Average: $389,475 to $785,628 average $455,294.

Funding: (Cooperative Agreements (Discretionary Grants)) FY 18 est $3,300,000; FY 19 est $3,300,000; FY 17 $3,214,380;

HQ:

http://www.usgs.gov/ltrmp.html

HURRICANE SANDY

Award: Cooperative Agreements

Purpose: To support research and data collection complementary to continued USGS activities supporting recovery and restoration efforts related to the Hurricane Sandy.

Applicant Eligibility: Proposals from State, Local, Interstate, Federally or State recognized Indian Tribal Governments, US Territories and Possessions, Institutions of Higher Education, Private Foundations, and Nonprofit Organizations are invited. Due to limited availability of funding to support new external projects, consultation with the Geological Survey is strongly recommended prior to submission of applications.

Beneficiary Eligibility: Federal, State and local governments, Federally or State recognized Indian Tribal Governments, industry and public decision makers, research scientists, State institutions of higher education, private firms, private foundations, nonprofit organizations, and the general public will ultimately benefit from the program.

Award Range/Average: N/A

Funding: Cooperative Agreements (Discretionary Grants) FY 19 est $0; FY 17 $0; FY 18 est $0

HQ: 12201 Sunrise Valley Drive

Reston, VA 20192

Phone: 703-715-7020

Email: hsweyers@usgs.gov

http://www.usgs.gov/contracts

NATIONAL GROUND-WATER MONITORING NETWORK

Award: Cooperative Agreements

Purpose: To provide support to multi-state, State, Tribal, or local Water-Resource agencies that collect groundwater data to serve as data providers for the National Ground-Water Monitoring Network.

Applicant Eligibility: Proposals will be accepted from interstate, State, U.S. territory or possession, local, public nonprofit water-resource agencies/organizations which collect and maintain groundwater-level or groundwater-quality data. Various elements of the data which are required for the National Ground-Water Monitoring Network are often available from different agencies within a state.

Beneficiary Eligibility: Federal, State, Federally recognized Indian Tribal, and local governments, public nonprofit institutions/organizations, private nonprofit institutions/organizations, profit organizations, industry and public decision makers, research scientists, engineers, and the general public will ultimately benefit from data made available through the program.

Award Range/Average: $15,000 to $150,000 per year for each of two years; average $55,000 per year.

Funding: (Cooperative Agreements (Discretionary Grants)) FY 18 est $1,800,000; FY 17 $1,150,000; FY 19 est $1,800,000; - FY 18 amount based on expected funding and submissions of proposals totaling more than $2,200,000. FY 19 based on estimated funding.

HQ: 12201 Sunrise Valley Drive
Reston, VA 20192
Phone: 703-648-5005
Email: wcunning@usgs.gov
http://www.usgs.gov/contracts

WATER USE AND DATA RESEARCH

Award: Cooperative Agreements

Purpose: To provide support to State water resource agencies in developing water use and availability datasets maintained by the USGS.

Applicant Eligibility: Proposals will be accepted from state agencies that collect and maintain water use data and databases. Various elements of the data that are required for the Water Use Data and Research (WUDR) program are often available from different agencies within a state; however only one agency is eligible to submit a proposal for the program.

Beneficiary Eligibility: State, Federally recognized Indian Tribal, and local governments, public nonprofit institutions/organizations, private nonprofit institutions/organizations, profit organizations, industry and public decision makers, research scientists, engineers, and the general public will ultimately benefit from data made available through the program.

Award Range/Average: $24,000 to $125,000; average $75,000.

Funding: (Cooperative Agreements (Discretionary Grants)) FY 17 $1,500,000; FY 18 est $1,500,000; FY 19 est $1,500,000;

HQ:
Reston, VA 20192
Phone: 770-283-9728
Email: msdalton@usgs.gov
http://www.usgs.gov

VETERAN'S EMPLOYMENT AND TRAINING SERVICE

REGIONAL ADMINISTRATORS AND STATE DIRECTORS FOR VETERANS' EMPLOYMENT AND TRAINING

Region I

DVET John Dunn | Veterans' Employment and Training Service Department of Labor 57 Spruce Street, Westerly, RI 02891 401-528-5134

DVET Jon Guay | Veterans' Employment and Training Service Department of Labor 5 Mollison Way P.O. Box 3106, Lewiston, ME 04243 207-753-9090

DVET Paul L. Desmond | Veterans' Employment and Training Service Department of Labor 19 Staniford Street C.F. Hurley Building, 2nd Floor, ES Operations Section, Boston, MA 02114 617-626-6699

DVET Richard Ducey | Veterans' Employment and Training Service Department of Labor 143 North Main Street, Room 208, Concord, NH 03301 603-225-1424

DVET Richard Gray | Veterans' Employment and Training Service Department of Labor P.O. Box 603 Post Office Building 87 State Street, Room 303, Montpelier, VT 05602 802-828-4441

DVET William Mason | Veterans' Employment and Training Service Department of Labor CT Department of Labor Building 200 Folly Brook Boulevard, Wethersfield, CT 06109 860-263-6490

RAVET David Houle | Veterans' Employment and Training Service Department of Labor JFK Federal Building, Room E-315 Government Center, Boston, MA 02203 617-565-2080

Region II

DVET Alan E. Grohs | Veterans' Employment and Training Service Department of Labor Labor Building, 11th Floor, CN058, Trenton, NJ 08625 609-292-2930

DVET Angel Mojica | Veterans' Employment and Training Service Department of Labor Puerto Rico Department of Labor and Human Services 198 Calle Guayama, 20th Floor, Hato Rey, PR 00917 787-754-5391

DVET James H. Hartman | Veterans' Employment and Training Service Department of Labor Harriman State Campus Building 12, Room 518, Albany, NY 12240-0099 518-457-7465

Veterans' Employment and Training Service Department of Labor 201 Varick Street, Room 766, New York, NY 10014 212-337-2211

Region III

DVET Charles Stores | Veterans' Employment and Training Service Department of Labor 112 California Avenue Capitol Complex - Room 204, Charleston, WV 25305-0112 304-558-4001

DVET David White | Veterans' Employment and Training Service Department of Labor 4425 N. Market Street, Room 420, Wilmington, DE 19809-0828 302-761-8138

DVET Gary Lobdell | Veterans' Employment and Training Service Department of Labor 1100 North Eutaw Street, Room 210, Baltimore, MD 21201 410-767-2110

DVET Lawrence Babitts | Veterans' Employment and Training Service Department of Labor Labor and Industry Building, Room 1108 Seventh and Forster Streets, Harrisburg, PA 17121 717-787-5834

DVET Roberto Pineda | Veterans' Employment and Training Service Department of Labor 703 E. Main street, Room 118, Richmond, VA 23219 804-786-7269

DVET Stanley Williams | Veterans' Employment and Training Service Department of Labor 500 C Street, N.W., Room 108, Washington, DC 20001 202-724-7005

RAVET Joseph Hortiz | Veterans' Employment and Training Service Department of Labor The Curtis Center, Suite 770 West 170 South Independence Mall West, Philadelphia, PA 19106 215-861-5390

Region IV

Derek W. Taylor | Veterans' Employment and Training Service Department of Labor P.O. Box 1527, Tallahassee, FL 32302-1527 850-942-8800

DVET Angelo Terrell | Veterans' Employment and Training Service Department of Labor 1520 West Capitol Street P.O. Box 1699, Jackson, MS 39215-1699 601-965-4204

DVET Charles R. Netherton | Veterans' Employment and Training Service Department of Labor C/O Department for Employment Services 275 East Main Street, Frankfort, KY 40621-2339 502-564-7062

DVET Richard E. Ritchie | Veterans' Employment and Training Service Department of Labor 915 8th Avenue North, Nashville, TN 37219-3795 615-736-7680

DVET Steven W. Guess | Veterans' Employment and Training Service Department of Labor P.O. Box 27625, Raleigh, NC 27611-7625 919-733-7402, 733-7407

DVET Thomas Karrh | Veterans' Employment and Training Service Department of Labor 649 Monroe Street, Room 543, Montgomery, AL 36131-6300 334-223-7677

DVET William C. Plowden | Veterans' Employment and Training Service Department of Labor P.O. Box 1755, Columbia, SC 29202-1755 803-765-5195

Ed Gresham | Veterans' Employment and Training Service Department of Labor Sussex Place, Suite 504 148 International Boulevard, N.E., Atlanta, GA 30303-1751 404-656-3127

RAVET William Bolls | Veterans' Employment and Training Service Department of Labor Sam Nunn Atlanta Federal Center 61 Forsyth Street, S.W., Room 6-T85, Atlanta, GA 30303 404-562-2305

Region IX

DVET Gilbert N. Hough | Veterans' Employment and Training Service Department of Labor P.O. Box 3680, Honolulu, HI 96811 808-522-8216

DVET Judy A. Carlisle | Veterans' Employment and Training Service Department of Labor 1923 North Carson Street, Room 205, Carson City, NV 89702 702-687-4632

DVET Michael Espinsoa | Veterans' Employment and Training Service Department of Labor P.O. Box 6123-SC760E 1400 West Washington Street, Phoenix, AZ 85005 602-379-4961

DVET Rosendo A. Cuevas | Veterans' Employment and Training Service Department of Labor 800 Capitol Mall, Room W-1142 P.O. Box 826880, Sacramento, CA 94280-0001 916-654-8178

RAVET Rex A. Newell | Veterans' Employment and Training Service Department of Labor 71 Stevenson Street, Suite 705, San Francisco, CA 94105 415-975-4700

Region V

DVET Carl Price | Veterans' Employment and Training Service Department of Labor P.O. Box 1618, Columbus, OH 43216 614-644-3688

DVET D. Bruce Redman | Veterans' Employment and Training Service Department of Labor Richard A. Mock 10 North Senate Avenue, Room SE103, Indianapolis, IN 46204 317-232-6804

DVET James R. Gutowski | Veterans' Employment and Training Service Department of Labor P.O. Box 8310, Madison, WI 53708-8310 608-266-3110

DVET Kim Fulton | Veterans' Employment and Training Service Department of Labor 7310 Woodward Avenue, Suite 407, Detroit, MI 48202 313-876-5613

DVET Michael D. Graham | Veterans' Employment and Training Service Department of Labor 390 Robert Street North, 1st Floor, St. Paul, MN 55101 651-296-3665

DVET Samuel L. Parks | Veterans' Employment and Training Service Department of Labor 401 South State Street, 744 North, Chicago, IL 60605 312-793-3433

RAVET Ronald G. Bachman | Veterans' Employment and Training Service Department of Labor 230 South Dearborn, Room 1064, Chicago, IL 60604 312-353-0970

Region VI

DVET Billy R. Threlkeld | Veterans' Employment and Training Service Department of Labor P.O. Box 128, Little Rock, AK 72203 501-682-3786

DVET Darrell H. Hill | Veterans' Employment and Training Service Department of Labor 201 North Lincoln Boulevard P.O. Box 52003, Oklahoma City, OK 73152-2003 405-231-5088

DVET John D. McKinny | Veterans' Employment and Training Service Department of Labor P.O. Box 1468, Austin, TX 78767 512-463-2814

DVET Lester L. Parmenter | Veterans' Employment and Training Service Department of Labor P.O. Box 94094, Room 184, Baton Rouge, LA 70804-9094 225-389-0339

RAVET Lester L. Williams | Veterans' Employment and Training Service Department of Labor 525 Griffin Street, Room 858, Dallas, TX 75202 214-767-4987

Sharon I. Mitchell | Veterans' Employment and Training Service Department of Labor P.O. Box 25085, Albuquerque, NM 87125-5085 505-346-7502

Region VII

DVET Anthony J. Smithhart | Veterans' Employment and Training Service Department of Labor 150 Des Moines Street, Des Moines, IA 50309-5563 515-281-9061

DVET Gayle Gibson | Veterans' Employment and Training Service Department of Labor 401 Topeka Boulevard, Topeka, KS 66603-3182 913-296-5032

DVET Mickey J. Jones | Veterans' Employment and Training Service Department of Labor P.O. Box 1087 421 East Dunklin Street, Jefferson City, MO 65102-1087 573-751-3921

DVET Richard Nelson | Veterans' Employment and Training Service Department of Labor P.O. Box 94600 550 South 16th Street, Lincoln, NE 68508 402-437-5289

RAVET Lester L. Williams | Veterans' Employment and Training Service Department of Labor City Center Square Building 1100 Main Street, Suite 850, Kansas City, MO 64105-2112 816-426-7151

Region VIII

DVET Dale Brockbank | Veterans' Employment and Training Service Department of Labor 140 East 300 South, Salt Lake City, UT 84111-2333 801-524-5703

DVET David McNulty | Veterans' Employment and Training Department of Labor P.O. Box 2760 100 West Midwest Avenue, Casper, WY 82602-2760 307-261-5454

DVET Earl R. Schultz | Veterans' Employment and Training Service Department of Labor P.O. Box 4730 420 South Roosevelt Street, Aberdeen, SD 57402-4730 605-626-2325

DVET Jerry Meske | Veterans' Employment and Training Service Department of Labor P.O. Box 1632 1000 E. Divide Avenue, Bismarck, ND 58502-1632 701-328-2865

DVET Mark McGinty | Veterans' Employment and Training Service Department of Labor 1515 Arapahoe Street, 2 Park Central, Suite 400, Denver, CO 80202-2117 303-844-2151

DVET Polly Latray-Halmes | Veterans' Employment and Training Department of Labor 1215 8th Avenue, Helena, MT 59601-4144 406-449-5431

RAVET Ronald G. Bachman | Veterans' Employment and Training Service Department of Labor 1999 Broadway, Suite 1730, Denver, CO 80202-2614 303-844-1175

Region X

DVET Daniel Travis | Veterans' Employment and Training Service Department of Labor P.O. Box 25509 1111 West 8th Street, Juneau, AK 99802-5509 907-465-2723

DVET Ron Cannon | Veterans' Employment and Training Service Department of Labor 312 Employment Division Building, Room 108 875 Union Street, N.E., Salem, OR 97311-0100 503-947-1490

RAVET Rex A. Newell | Veterans' Employment and Training Services Department of Labor 1111 Third Avenue, Suite 900, Seattle, WA 98101-3212 206-553-4831

Thomas Pearson | Veterans' Employment and Training Service Department of Labor P.O. Box 165, Olympia, WA 98507-0165 360-438-4600

Veterans' Employment and Training Service Department of Labor P.O. Box 2697, Boise, ID 83701 208-334-6163

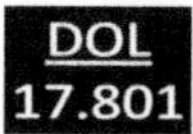

DISABLED VETERANS' OUTREACH PROGRAM (DVOP) "DVOP"

Award: Formula Grants

Purpose: To provide individualized career services to meet the employment needs of disabled and other eligible veterans identified by the Secretary of Labor with maximum emphasis in meeting the employment needs of those who are economically or educationally disadvantaged.

Applicant Eligibility: The state administrative entity designated by each Governor.

Beneficiary Eligibility: Veterans and eligible persons with emphasis on service-connected special disabled veterans, other disabled veterans, economically or educationally disadvantaged veterans, homeless veterans and veterans with other significant barriers to employment.

Award Range/Average: FY 2016, range from $115,000 to $13,524,029 and average $2,055,404. FY 2017, range from $136,620 - $13,376,652 and average $2,156,223.

Funding: FY 17 $116,436,068; FY 18 est $115,078,724; FY 19 est $115,078,724; FY 16 $110,991,836.

HQ: 200 Constitution Avenue NW, Room S-1325
Washington, DC 20210
Phone: 202-693-4706
Email: temiquel.maria@dol.gov
http://www.dol.gov/vets

LOCAL VETERANS' EMPLOYMENT REPRESENTATIVE PROGRAM "LVER Program"

Award: Formula Grants

Purpose: Perform outreach to employers including conducting seminars for employers, job search workshops and establishing job finding clubs; and facilitates employment, training, and placement services furnished to veterans in a state under the applicable State employment service.

Applicant Eligibility: The state administrative entity designated by each Governor.

Beneficiary Eligibility: Veterans, transitioning service members and eligible persons; business associations, businesses and other employers.

Award Range/Average: FY 2016, ranges from $0 to $5,958,324 and the average assistance: $1,071,745 (rounded). FY 2017, ranges from $0 to $4,677,738 and the average assistance: $1,004,468 (rounded)

Funding: (Formula Grants) FY 17 $54,241,316; FY 18 est $54,409,398; FY 19 est $52,409,398; FY 16 $57,874,265; - Estimated obligations by are determined by aggregating requests for funding from States.

HQ: 200 Constitution Avenue NW, Room S 1325
Washington, DC 20210
Phone: 202-693-4706
Email: temiquel.maria@dol.gov
http://www.dol.gov/vets

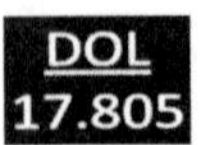

DOL 17.805

HOMELESS VETERANS' REINTEGRATION PROGRAM (HVRP)

Award: Project Grants

Purpose: Provide services to assist in reintegrating homeless veterans into meaningful employment within the labor force; and to stimulate the development of effective service delivery systems that will address the complex problems facing homeless veterans.

Applicant Eligibility: State and Local Workforce Investment Boards, State and State Agencies, local public agencies, Native American tribal governments (federally recognized), Native American tribal organizations, non-profit organizations (including faith-based and community organizations) and for-profit/commercial entities, and for-profit commercial entities. Potential jurisdictions are metropolitan areas of the largest U.S. cities or Non-Urban areas in need, as announced in the latest solicitation for grant applications (SGA).

Beneficiary Eligibility: Individuals who are homeless veterans. The term "homeless" or "homeless individual" includes: (1) An individual who lacks a fixed, regular, and adequate night-time residence; and (2) an individual who has a primary night-time residence that is: (a) a supervised publicly or privately operated shelter designed to provide temporary living accommodations including welfare hotels, congregate shelters, and transitional housing for the mentally ill; (b) an institution that provides a temporary institutionalized; or (c) a public or private place not designed for, or ordinarily used as, a regular sleeping accommodations for human beings.

Award Range/Average: $100,000 to $500,000 for an average of $279,763

Funding: (Project Grants) FY 17 $45,000,000; FY 18 est $50,000,000; FY 19 est $50,000,000; FY 16 $38,109,000

HQ: 200 Constitution Avenue NW, Room S-1325
Washington, DC 20210
Phone: 202-693-4706
Email: temiquel.maria@dol.gov
http://www.dol.gov/dol/vets

AGENCY INDEX

Agency Index

DEPARTMENT OF AGRICULTURE (USDA) 10.001–10.962

The Department of Agriculture is the federal department of U.S. government. It is also a part of U.S. executive department. It is responsible for creating laws with regard to farming, forestry, and food. It works at meeting the needs of the farmers, promotes agricultural trade and production, assures food safety, ensures to protect natural resources, etc.

DEPARTMENT OF COMMERCE (DOC) 11.013–11.805

The Department of Commerce serves at increasing the exports and imports of the country in many other commodities. The main purpose of this department is the development and promotion of international trade. The other services of the Department include promoting commercial relationships with other countries, increasing economic zones, developing trading facilitation, regulation of industries, providing job opportunities, etc.

DEPARTMENT OF DEFENSE (DOD) 12.225–12.910

The Department of Defense is to provide the security of a country. The military defends the homeland and builds security. The defense is prepared to fight against any adversaries. The Department is not only in charge of the military but also employs civilian workforce. The Department of Defense is the backbone for national security. The Department also provides training and programs for joining the Department of Defense.

DEPARTMENT OF HOUSING AND URBAN DEVELOPMENT (HUD) 14.008–14.899

The Department of Housing and Urban Development creates shelter and facilities for the citizens. The Department also builds discrimination-free environment. Creating inclusive communities, affordable homes, protecting people, strengthening housing market, boosting the economy, etc., are some of the services that the Department of Housing and Urban Development is involved in.

DEPARTMENT OF THE INTERIOR (DOI) 15.020–15.981

The Department of the Interior serves at protecting natural resources, heritage, cultures and traditions, tribal communities, etc. The Department also works at building external and internal affairs, land management, energy management, natural resources management, wildlife management, address societal challenges, fights natural hazards, etc.

DEPARTMENT OF JUSTICE (DOJ) 16.015–16.842

The Department of Justice is to enforce the law and defend the public against threats. The Department works at preventing and controlling crime. Right punishment for those found guilty, fair and impartial administration of justice, protecting the civil rights, administering justice for the victims and offenders, instituting law enforcement academies, etc., are some of the areas the Department is involved.

DEPARTMENT OF LABOR (DOL) 17.002–17.805

The Department of Labor provides information on jobs and training and work-related benefits. The DOL works for the welfare of the workforce. The Department of Labor works at resolving issues impacting employees, programs for employers and employees, employment training services, information of labor market information, safety and regulations, the welfare of the wage earners, work-related benefits and rights, etc.

DEPARTMENT OF STATE (DOS) 19.009–19.979

The Department of State promotes democratic values and develops economic prosperity. It implements various operations in and around a state. The state department's services include initiating foreign policy, makes agreements with neighboring countries, promotes the economic welfare of the country, boosts the country's development in various aspects, etc.

DEPARTMENT OF TRANSPORTATION (DOT) 20.106–20.934

The Department of Transportation is a separate entity that plays a major role in the development of a country. It serves at providing safe and secure travel for the citizens. The DOT serves at providing infrastructure for a proper transportation. Its other administrations include aviation, highway, traffic safety, motor carrier safety, railroad, hazardous material safety, etc.

DEPARTMENT OF THE TREASURY (TREAS) 21.006–21.021

The Treasury Department promotes economic growth. The Department takes care of all economic and financial issues. It fosters governance in a critical financial situation. It maintains financial infrastructure, produces currency, works with neighboring governments, promotes economic growth, provides shelter for a living, fights financial crises, provides national security, etc.

Community Development Financial Institutions 21.011–21.021
Department of the Treasury 21.009–21.015
Internal Revenue Service 21.006–21.008

EQUAL EMPLOYMENT OPPORTUNITY COMMISSION (EEOC) 30.001–30.013

The Equal Employment Opportunity Commission enforces federal laws. It investigates into issues of discrimination on the basis of race, color, religion, and gender. The EEOC promotes equal employment opportunity, provides technical assistance, monitors and evaluates federal agencies, ensures affirmative employment programs, conducts training for stakeholders, etc.

Equal Employment Opportunity Commission 30.001–30.013

NATIONAL CREDIT UNION ADMINISTRATION (NCUA) 44.003–44.003

The National Credit Union Administration is a U.S. federal agency. It fosters governance in a critical financial situation. It maintains financial infrastructure, works with neighboring governments, promotes economic growth, provides shelter for a living, fights financial crises, provides national security, etc.

National Credit Union Administration 44.003–44.003

NATIONAL ENDOWMENT FOR THE ARTS (NEA) 45.024–45.025

The Federal Council on the Arts and Humanities helps to minimize the costs of insuring international exhibitions. The organization covers for works of art owned by U.S. entities while on exhibition in the United States. It provides advice and consultation to the National Endowment for the Arts, the National Endowment for the Humanities on major problems and the Institute of Museum and Library Services that includes joint support of activities. Other services include planning and coordinating programs, activities and participation in major and historic national events. Conduct studies and prepare reports that address the state of arts and humanities in the country, especially with their economic problems and needs.

National Endowment for the Arts 45.024–45.025

NATIONAL ENDOWMENT FOR THE HUMANITIES (NEH) 45.129–45.169

The Federal Council on the Arts and Humanities helps to minimize the costs of insuring international exhibitions. The organization covers for works of art owned by U.S. entities while on exhibition in the United States. It provides advice and consultation to the National Endowment for the Arts, the National Endowment for the Humanities on major problems and the Institute of Museum and Library Services that includes joint support of activities. Other services include planning and coordinating programs, activities and participation in major and historic national events. Conduct studies and prepare reports that address the state of arts and humanities in the country, especially with their economic problems and needs.

National Endowment for the Humanities 45.129–45.169

THE FEDERAL COUNCIL ON THE ARTS AND HUMANITIES (NFAH) 45.201–45.201

The Federal Council on the Arts and Humanities helps to minimize the costs of insuring international exhibitions. The organization covers for works of art owned by U.S. entities while on exhibition in the United States. It provides advice and consultation to the National Endowment for the Arts, the National Endowment for the Humanities on major problems and the Institute of Museum and Library Services that includes joint support of activities. Other services include planning and coordinating programs, activities and participation in major and historic national events. Conduct studies and prepare reports that address the state of arts and humanities in the country, especially with their economic problems and needs.

The Federal Council on the Arts and Humanities 45.201–45.201

Agency Index

NATIONAL SCIENCE FOUNDATION (NSF) 47.041–47.083

The National Science Foundation is an agency of the U.S. government. The NSF works for the welfare of national health and national defense. It organizes research and education through various disciplines such as biological sciences, technological information science and engineering, mathematical and physical sciences, behavior and economic sciences, etc.

RAILROAD RETIREMENT BOARD (RRB) 57.001–57.001

The Railroad Retirement Board is an agency that provides retirement benefits. It supports the workers and their families under the railroad retirement plan and administers social insurance for the workers.

SMALL BUSINESS ADMINISTRATION (SBA) 59.007–59.069

The Small Business Administration helps small businesses in the United States. It provides suggestions for business development. The SBA provides practical guidelines for risk management, disaster assistance, promotes equal employment opportunity and civil rights, international trade, increasing performance of the business, effective communication, etc.

ENVIRONMENTAL PROTECTION AGENCY (EPA) 66.001–66.956

The Environmental Protection is an agency of the U.S. government. It has implemented various environmental laws. It serves by protecting endangered species, food quality and protection, water pollution, etc. Its principal implementation of laws includes Clean Air Act, Environmental Response Act, Emergency Planning and Recovery Act, Insecticide and Fungicide Act, Conservation Act, Toxic Substances Control Act, Safe Drinking Water Act, etc.

DEPARTMENT OF ENERGY (DOE) 81.005–81.250

The Department of Energy provides awareness with regard to handling nuclear material. It is responsible for creating awareness of nuclear weapons. The DOE works under the administration of U.S. Secretary of Energy. It serves at supporting research for projects related to physical sciences. It provides programs based on science and innovation, clean energy, energy efficiency, nuclear security, saving natural energies such as electricity and fuel, etc.

DEPARTMENT OF EDUCATION (ED) 84.002–84.938

The Department of Education promotes education and looks into issues that affect education. The Department of Education works under the administration of U.S. Secretary of Education. It provides assistance to education by collecting data on schools that have been established in the United States. It also ensures proper education for all, especially the homeless. It supports the education system through funds and monitors that the funds are accessed for the right purpose and ensures equal education access without discrimination.

INTER-AMERICAN FOUNDATION (IAF) 85.750–85.750

The Inter-American Foundation is a department that funds projects undertaken by non-governmental organizations and other groups. The IAF provides economic opportunities for individual development. The IAF strengthens the relationship with people of the hemisphere by providing business opportunities, develops and encourages partnership with government and various community organizations, assists people who are in the development process, and many other services.

GULF COAST ECOSYSTEM RESTORATION COUNCIL (GCER) 87.051–87.052

The Gulf Coast Ecosystem Restoration Council was established to restore the natural ecosystem and economy of the Gulf Coast. The Gulf Coast Ecosystem Restoration Task Force enacts certain functions for restoration purposes. The functions of the task force are as follows: It implements restoration steps to improve the government efforts, it supports the relevant departments responsible for restoration actions, engages public, communities, and stakeholders to develop restoration strategies, etc.

ELECTION ASSISTANCE COMMISSION (EAC) 90.404–90.404

The U.S. Election Assistance Commission was established to provide guidelines for the voting system. It also provides information on election administration. It also maintains the national mail voter registration form. It certifies voting system, reports the effects of elections, administers funds to State as per requirements, develops innovative election technology, delivers strategies for effective administration, implements election law and procedures, etc.

UNITED STATES INSTITUTE OF PEACE (USIP) 91.005–91.005

The United States Institute of Peace works at resolving conflicts. It promotes national security, supports groups that oppose extremism, and helps countries to resolve conflicts in a peaceful manner. It provides individuals with research, analysis, mediation, and other peace-building measures. It works on peace information services to promote international peace. It operates programs in conflict areas, operates a training academy, conducts conferences and workshops for building peace.

DEPARTMENT OF HEALTH AND HUMAN SERVICES (HHS) 93.007–93.998

The U.S. Department of Health and Human Services protects the health and services for U.S. citizens. It serves at enhancing public health and social services. It strengthens the nation's healthcare system, protects the health of Americans, enhances social well-being, promotes effective management in stewardship, grants healthcare policies, etc.

CORPORATION FOR NATIONAL AND COMMUNITY SERVICE (CNCS) 94.002–94.026

The Corporation for National and Community service help at improving the lives of U.S. citizens. It meets the community needs throughout the localities of America. It provides services related to education, economic development, and disaster recovery services. Other services include building houses for the homeless, provides computer skills to youth, health services, small business development, promotes leadership programs, etc.

EXECUTIVE OFFICE OF THE PRESIDENT (EOP) 95.001–95.008

The Executive Office of the President consists of several agencies and administrations. It supports the works of the president. Some of the agencies are as follows: office of president and vice-president, council of economic advisers, national security council, national drug control policy, science and technology policy. The executive office looks into overall administration works and implementations in the United States.

SOCIAL SECURITY ADMINISTRATION (SSA) 96.006–96.020

The Social Security Administration is a U.S. government agency that serves at providing retirement benefits and Social Security awareness. It provides citizenship eligibility, Medicare programs, provides Social Security numbers, Social Security benefits, death and survivorship benefits, insurance coverage, etc.

DEPARTMENT OF HOMELAND SECURITY (DHS) 97.005–97.134

The Department of Homeland Security works at providing security for the nation. The Department secures the nation from many threats. The DHS enhances security by preventing terrorism, administering laws, securing borders, protecting cyberspace, disaster recovery plans, etc. It also strengthens homeland security enterprises.

FEDERAL HEADQUARTERS INDEX

Federal Headquarters Index

Federal Headquarters Index

Federal Headquarters Index

REGIONAL-STATE-LOCAL OFFICES INDEX

Regional-State-Local Offices Index